BLUE GUIDE

NORTHERN ITALY

FROM THE ALPS TO ROME

Alta Macadam

*Atlas, maps and plans
by John Flower*

A & C Black
London

WW Norton
New York

Ninth edition 1991

Published by A & C Black (Publishers) Limited
35 Bedford Row, London WC1R 4JH

© A & C Black (Publishers) Limited 1991

Published in the United States of America by
W W Norton & Company, Inc.
500 Fifth Avenue, New York, NY 10110

Published simultaneously in Canada by
Penguin Books Canada Limited
2801 John Street, Markham, Ontario L3R 1B4

ISBN   0–7136–3276–3

A CIP catalogue record for this book
is available from the British Library

ISBN   0–393–30727–1 USA

Alta Macadam learnt the craft of writing Blue Guides when she
became assistant in 1970 to Stuart Rossiter, distinguished editor of
many Guides in the series. She has lived in Florence since 1973 and,
as author of the Blue Guides to *Northern Italy*, *Rome*, *Venice*, *Sicily*,
Florence, and the forthcoming *Tuscany and Umbria*, she travels
extensively in Italy every year in order to revise new editions of the
books. Combined with work on writing the guides she also spent four
years updating the well-known Italian photo-library of Alinari, and
now works part-time for Harvard University at the Villa I Tatti in
Florence.

Photographs by kind permission of Susan Benn and Anthony
Kersting.

Printed and bound in Great Britain by
William Clowes Limited, Beccles and London

THE BLUE GUIDES

Countries
Austria
Belgium and Luxembourg
Channel Islands
Corsica
Crete
Cyprus
Egypt
England
France
Germany
Greece
Holland
Hungary
Ireland
Northern Italy
Southern Italy
Malta and Gozo
Morocco
Portugal
Scotland
Sicily
Spain
Switzerland
Turkey: Bursa to Antakya
Wales
Yugoslavia

Cities
Boston and Cambridge
Florence
Istanbul
Jerusalem
London
Moscow and Leningrad
New York
Oxford and Cambridge
Paris and Versailles
Rome and Environs
Venice

Themes
Churches and Chapels of Northern England
Churches and Chapels of Southern England
Literary Britain and Ireland
Museums and Galleries of London
Victorian Architecture in Britain

The Romanesque Cathedral of Lucca

PREFACE

This edition of 'Blue Guide Northern Italy' comes out at a time when there is probably more real concern about the preservation of the natural beauty of Italy and the conservation of her works of art than there ever has been before. Since the last edition numerous spectacular restorations have been completed including the Cappella Brancacci in Florence, the Palazzo Ducale in Urbino, the walls of Ferrara, Palazzo Te in Mantua, and the cathedrals of Milan, Modena, and Lucca. In Arezzo detailed studies are being carried out before restoration can begin on the frescoes in San Francesco by Piero della Francesca, and in Milan painstaking restoration is still underway of Leonardo's Cenacolo. In Florence four of the sculpted reliefs of the Baptistery doors, three of the marble statues of Orsanmichele, and Donatello's Judith have all been restored, but it has been decided that they cannot be returned to their original positions outside.

Attention is now having to be given to the problem of how to protect works of art once restored, not only from the elements, but also from the 'pollution' caused by visitors themselves. Indeed it seems likely that frescoes will now have to be protected by limiting the number of people looking at them at any one time, and some sculptures made for the exteriors of buildings will have to be brought in under cover.

Since the last edition of the guide the historical centre of almost every town and village in Northern Italy has been closed to traffic, at least for certain periods of the day, which is a major step forward in eliminating the damage caused by pollution to monuments and inhabitants alike. It also, of course, renders towns much more pleasant places to visit. However, there is still a long way to go in resolving the problem of car parks for private cars, and providing efficient public transport in the larger cities. Perhaps the most spectacular solution has been found in Perugia where visitors now leave their cars in a huge car park below the town and ascend the hill by a series of (mostly underground) escalators.

Numerous museums have been reopened or rearranged in the last few years, notably the Museo Civico in Bologna, the Museo Nazionale in Ravenna, the Museo Civico in Padua, the Museo dell'Antichità in Turin, the Museo dell'Opera del Duomo in Pisa, the Museo Civico in Piacenza, and the Ca' d'Oro in Venice. Some museums now also have longer opening hours, and even stay open seven days a week, which greatly facilitates a visit to Italy. However, opening times change constantly, and while every effort has been made to give details in the text, this information is bound to be out of date in many cases before many months have passed. It is therefore essential to allow for differences in opening times, and if possible to always ask at the local tourist office on arrival for the latest information about museum opening hours.

The classification of hotels is now by the 'star' system as in the rest of Europe, and the official category of 'Pensione' has been abolished. Local tourist boards are undergoing reorganisation and amalgamation and in most localities are now called 'A.P.T.' ('Azienda di Promozione Turistica'). Some train services between large cities have been greatly improved, and it is now possible to reach Rome from Milan in just four hours.

On the negative side, since 1988 the pollution of the Adriatic coast south of Rimini has reached unacceptable levels, and the beaches have been invaded by seaweed and algae. It is still not clear how this can be resolved. Less than five per cent of the geographical area of Italy is protected as a national park or nature reserve, despite the efforts of the World Wildlife Fund who now administer a number of oases. In 1988 a law was finally passed to protect the land, as in other countries, but serious problems remain, including that of undertaking a geological survey of the terrain which would hopefully prevent natural disasters such as the tragic landslide in the Valtellina in 1987.

The collapse of the Torre Civica in Pavia in 1989, which killed four people, was only one of the more clamorous events signalling the decay of many important monuments in the country. Even Pisa's Leaning Tower had to be closed to the public in 1990 for safety reasons.

The country has been over-supplied with motorways in the last few years; these are now almost invariably built on stilts and ruin the landscape around them. There has also been a proliferation of 'marinas', often to the detriment of the beauty of the coast.

As if these problems were not enough, additional threats to the natural beauty of the peninsula have arisen from the choice of Italy as the venue for the 1990 Football World Cup. Vast sums of public money are being spent with few controls to build new roads and hotels, and enlarge the stadiums in all twelve towns in which matches are to be played. Genoa is planning Columbus celebrations for 1992 including the construction of a tower in the old port some 260 metres high. But in 1989 a last-minute volte face by the Florence local government saved that city from being engulfed on its north-western outskirts by a 'development' by the Fiat and Fondiaria companies of some 4 million cubic metres including tower blocks 50 metres high.

The routes in this guide have been reorganised, and shortened, particularly in Tuscany and Umbria, in an attempt to provide more useful itineraries for the visitor. Many fine new town plans and ground plans have been specially drawn for this edition by John Flower.

In the preparation of this guide the author is indebted in the first instance to Bruce Boucher of University College, London, who made many corrections to the text, and a number of suggestions for its improvement. Dott. Ugo Bazzotti was extremely helpful to the author in the revision of the text for Mantua. Raffaella Trabalza kindly supplied much information about Umbria, including Foligno.

The author is always grateful to correspondents who take the trouble to write and suggest improvements to the guide, and travellers who point out corrections after visits to Italy.

A NOTE ON BLUE GUIDES

The Blue Guides series began in 1918 when Muirhead Guide-Books Limited published 'Blue Guide London and its Environs'. Finlay and James Muirhead already had extensive experience of guide-book publishing: before the First World War they had been the editors of the English editions of the German Baedekers, and by 1915 they had acquired the copyright of most of the famous 'Red' handbooks from John Murray.

An agreement made with the French publishing house Hachette et Cie in 1917 led to the translation of Muirhead's London Guide, which became the first 'Guide Bleu'—Hachette had previously published the blue-covered 'Guides Joanne'. Subsequently, Hachette's 'Guide Bleu Paris et ses Environs' was adapted and published in London by Muirhead. The collaboration between the two publishing houses continued until 1933.

In 1931 Ernest Benn took over the Blue Guides, appointing Russell Muirhead, Finlay Muirhead's son, editor in 1934. The Muirheads' connection with Blue Guides ended in 1963 when Stuart Rossiter, who had been working on the Guides since 1954, became house editor, revising and compiling several of the books himself.

The Blue Guides are now published by A & C Black, who acquired Ernest Benn in 1984, so continuing the tradition of guide-book publishing which began in 1826 with 'Black's Economical Tourist of Scotland'. The Blue Guide series continues to grow: there are now more than 40 titles in print with revised editions appearing regularly and many new Blue Guides in preparation.

'Blue Guides' is a registered trade mark.

EXPLANATIONS

TYPE. The main routes are described in large type. Smaller type is used for branch-routes and excursions, for historical and preliminary paragraphs, and (generally speaking) for descriptions of greater detail or minor importance.

ASTERISKS indicate points of special interest or excellence.

DISTANCES are given cumulatively from the starting-point of the route or sub-route in kilometres. Mountain heights have been given in the text and on the atlas in metres.

MAIN ROADS are designated in the text by their official number. Autostrade (motorways) always carry 'A' before their number.

POPULATIONS (approximated to the nearest hundred) have been given from the latest official figures based on the census of 1971). They refer to the size of the Commune or administrative area, which is often much larger than the central urban area.

PLANS. Double-page town plans are gridded with numbered squares referred to in the text thus: (Pl. 1, 16). On the ground plans of museums figures or letters have been given to correspond with the descriptions which appear in the text.

ABBREVIATIONS. In addition to generally accepted and self-explanatory abbreviations, the following occur in the guide:

AA   Automobile Association
ACI   Automobile Club Italiano
Adm.   admission
A.P.T.   Azienda di Promozione Turistica (official local tourist office)
C   century
c   circa
C.A.I.   Club Alpino Italiano
C.I.T.   Compagnia Italiana Turismo
ENIT   Ente Nazionale per il Turismo
FAI   Fondo per l'Ambiente Italiano (founded in 1975 on the model of the British National Trusts)
fest.   *festa*, or festival (i.e. holiday)
fl.   floruit (flourished)
FS   Ferrovie dello Stato (Italian State Railways)
km   kilometre(s)
m   metre(s)
Pl.   plan
pron.   pronounced
RAC   Royal Automobile Club
Rif.   Rifugio (mountain hut)
Rte   Route
TCI   Touring Club Italiano

CONTENTS

MAPS AND PLANS

MAPS

ROUTE MAPS

TOWN PLANS

14 CONTENTS

GROUND PLANS

ART IN NORTHERN ITALY, TUSCANY, AND UMBRIA

by *Andrew Martindale*

This brief account of Italian art is designed to do three things. First, it will draw the attention of the reader to the main stylistic changes which occurred in the major arts of architecture, sculpture, and painting. Second, mention will be made in passing of important examples of the varying styles and characteristics so that the reader will possess by the end an anthology of significant monuments. Third, some attempt will be made to indicate the relative importance of the different provinces which constitute Italy north of Rome. This last point is important. The traveller in northern Italy will quickly realise that the art has for much of its history a provincial basis. This is especially true of the Middle Ages. Medieval Lombard art is not like Venetian art; and this in turn is not like Roman art. Even so, with the coming of the High Renaissance this provincial character underwent a distinct change, in that Rome became the pre-eminent centre in the world of art. In the provinces, from c 1470 onwards, art tended to reflect events in Rome; and at this point the interested traveller in northern Italy will be at a permanent disadvantage. Italian art of the 16C and 17C cannot be understood without an appreciation of the great works and monuments produced in Rome during this period. In international terms, the acknowledged artistic importance of Italy survived up to the middle of the 18C. Thereafter this importance, already long since rivalled by France and other countries, dwindled sharply and it was not until the 20C that Italy again achieved European importance.

Roman and Byzantine Art. Few large Italian towns lack visible evidence of their antique origins; major Roman remains are scattered through northern Italy—the great amphitheatre and the so-called Porta dei Borsari at Verona or the arch at Fano being among the more impressive examples. However, with the shift of the capital of the Empire from Rome to Constantinople (4C), Italian art in many important aspects became orientated towards the Eastern Mediterranean and remained predominantly so until the 13C. A few notable monuments of Byzantine art survive, especially in the group of churches in Ravenna, decorated with Byzantine mosaics (5C and 6C). In practice, Italian painting remained a provincial offshoot of Byzantine art down to the great pictorial developments in Rome c 1275. Superb late instances of this fascination with Byzantine art are the 12–14C mosaics in San Marco, Venice. Still heavily influenced by Byzantine painting are the long series of 12C and 13C panel painting, especially those of Tuscany.

The Middle Ages. Lombardy produced some of the largest and most impressive Romanesque churches in Europe. The material is invariably brick and certain obvious characteristics (for instance, the small external rows of blind arches known as 'Lombard arcading') had already appeared by the 9C. Thereafter, some particular features may be noted—broad screen-like façades, sometimes decorated with sculpture (Pavia, San Michele 12C); external wall passages set behind arcading (Bergamo, Santa Maria Maggiore and elsewhere); and large internal galleries over the aisles, usually called Tribune galleries (Pavia, San Michele and Milan, Sant'Ambrogio). The largest churches (e.g. Cremona or Parma cathedrals) are enormous and extremely magnificent and are often dominated by vast bell-towers or *campanili*. Cremona campanile has a very elaborate spire. Developments in this type of architecture are hard to define since the buildings are seldom heavily decorated. However, in the late Gothic period (14–15C) a fashion for moulded brick decoration is found (Mantua, Sant'Andrea, campanile and elsewhere). It is perhaps especially as examples of brick engineering on a gigantic scale that the greater churches catch the imagination.

The greatest immediate difference in Tuscany is one of material. Large amounts of marble were easily available and a façade such as that of San Miniato al Monte, Florence (12C) relies almost entirely on coloured marble for its effect. The most influential Tuscan Romanesque building was Pisa cathedral and its façade (12C) with its superimposed rows of arcading and passages, became the model for countless other smaller churches. Romanesque forms survived well into the 13C and it may be some surprise to find that the rounded arcades of the nave of Siena cathedral are roughly contemporary with Amiens cathedral. Those of Orvieto cathedral are even later (begun 1290).

The development of a Gothic style of architecture in Italy was spasmodic and idiosyncratic. The spread of the Cistercian Order introduced a somewhat muted form of Burgundian Gothic architecture (see, for instance, San Galgano near Siena) but this did not lead to the growth of a homogeneous Italian Gothic style. Gothic churches vary, as much as Romanesque ones, according to area. Santa Croce and Santa Maria Novella, Florence (late 13C) were probably influenced in plan by Cistercian precedents. Sant'Andrea, Vercelli (c 1230) is notable for its capitals and attached columns which are obviously French in derivation. Santi Giovanni e Paolo and the Frari church are the most impressive examples of Venetian Gothic. San Petronio, Bologna (begun 1390) would have been one of the largest churches in Europe, had it been completed. In spite of the general aversion to the more elaborate forms of external and internal decoration, such as developed north of the Alps, there is one notable exception to the rule—Milan cathedral (begun c 1386) heavily covered with tracery decoration and topped by innumerable pinnacles. The origins of this fashion were probably German and appear to stem from the Rhineland.

Italy is, of course, rich in medieval secular buildings. The Palazzo Ducale at Mantua (mainly 14–16C) is one of the largest, most rambling medieval palace complexes in Europe. Far more compact is the Doge's Palace, Venice (also mainly 14–16C). The Castello Sforzesco, Milan, and the Castello Estense, Ferrara, represent late and different types of private fortress. Important medieval fortified town-halls survive in the Palazzo Pubblico, Siena, and the Palazzo Vecchio, Florence (later much altered inside). Two small papal palaces are to be seen at Orvieto and Viterbo. Finally, San Gimignano is famous for the survival of its medieval private defensive towers which give it a distinctive and memorable skyline.

SCULPTURE. The main development of Romanesque figure sculpture began in the early 12C. To the beginning of the century belong a series of Old Testament reliefs, placed across the façade of Modena cathedral. According to an inscription, they are by a mason called

Wiligelmo. The quality of these reliefs is extraordinarily good. In spite of the rather stiff and formal conventions, the figures communicate in a convincing way, and it is still not clear where Wiligelmo learnt to carve. He had, however, a number of northern Italian successors, including a mason who signed his name, *Niccolò*, and worked at Ferrara and Verona (c 1130–40). Niccolò also carved reliefs on lintels, and from his circle come the large series of reliefs flanking the main portal of San Zeno, Verona. Niccolò's work contains numerous points of interest, including the early use of carved figures to decorate the jambs of a portal.

Much of this figure sculpture decorated the exterior of churches. In Tuscany, external figure sculpture was generally confined to lintels over doors, and the first important named sculptor in Pisa left his name on a characteristic piece of Tuscan interior sculpture, a pulpit. This pulpit, originally in Pisa cathedral, is now in Cagliari (Sardinia). The sculptor's name was *Guglielmo* and the date 1162. The style is reflected in carving by other masons in and around Pisa (see San Cassiano) and is a little disappointing, being, if anything, over-ornate. However, it formed the basis of a flourishing line of masons, including the more concise work of *Gruamonte* (see Pistoia, Sant'Andrea).

Probably more considerable than any of these was the workshop of *Benedetto Antelami* which flourished at the end of the 12C and the beginning of the 13C. Something of Antelami's background can be deduced from clear stylistic and iconographic links with Provence. He worked chiefly in Parma and Borgo San Donnino and his *chef d'oeuvre* was the baptistery at Parma with its three carved portals. These are important for their iconographic coherence. The programme is carefully worked out—perhaps for the first time in Italy—and includes doors dedicated to the Virgin and to the Last Judgement. Carved tympana are employed, and large standing figures (unusual in Italy) occur higher up on the façade.

Nevertheless, the first unequivocally Gothic sculptor was another Tuscan, **Nicola Pisano**. His work marks an enormous step in the development of a realistic figure style, and it is of interest that in pursuing this aim he borrowed heavily from antique art (see the pulpit, Pisa cathedral baptistery, 1259–60). A second pulpit in Siena cathedral is far less heavily antique and there are indications that he was borrowing more deliberately from the contemporary sculpture of France. These northern tendencies come out far more strongly in his son *Giovanni*, who is one of the most interesting 13C Italian artists. Giovanni's masterpiece should have been the façade of Siena cathedral but it was only completed many years after his death, and in considerably altered form. From Giovanni's time, however, survive a number of large dramatically animated standing figures, which with their grimacing faces and twisting poses are among the most memorable Italian creations of the 13C. Also by Giovanni are two further pulpits—one in Pisa cathedral itself.

It is of some interest that the excellence of Tuscan masons was recognised outside Tuscany. Nicola Pisano's workshop produced the shrine of St Dominic (San Domenico, Bologna c 1260–65, later much altered); and another protégé, *Arnolfo di Cambio*, became the chief sculptor in Rome, and was the author of one of the most splendid 13C tombs (in San Domenico, Orvieto). *Tino da Camaino*, who probably learnt under Giovanni Pisano, eventually ended up in Naples; and another Tuscan, Giovanni di Balduccio, took a workshop north to work on the Shrine of St Peter Martyr in Sant'Eustorgio, Milan (1339).

Thus the formative influence of the Pisano family can hardly be overrated.

Only one sculptor-architect stands apart—*Lorenzo Maitani*, who designed the west front of Orvieto cathedral. This was designed (c 1310) as a most interesting combination of delicate relief and sparkling mosaic, and remains one of the most important medieval façades in Italy.

In fact there were few dramatic stylistic developments in the 14C, but it was a period of considerable formal inventiveness. Especially notable are a series of tombs to the Scaliger Lords of Verona, outside Santa Maria Antica. The most elaborate and latest of these, to Cansignorio della Scala (died 1375), is from the workshop of the leading Lombard mason, *Bonino da Campione*, and is a memorable mass of niches, pinnacles, and crocketted gables.

PAINTING. The 'Byzantine manner' in Italian painting survived up to the end of the 13C. The means by which it changed are now unclear, but the important centre was Rome. It is enough to record here that **Giotto** (c 1267–1337) was probably trained in Rome or by Roman artists, and that the Franciscan church at Assisi, where he may or may not have painted (it was at any rate decorated by Roman artists), remains the best place to see the development of an Italian Gothic style of painting.

Giotto was, of course, by birth a Florentine and some of his major works are in Florence (Santa Croce). But the best preserved paintings are those in the Arena Chapel, Padua (c 1305–10). His importance as a painter can be gauged by his immense influence which includes not merely subsequent 14C Florentine painters but also artists north of the Apennines such as *Altichiero* (Padua and Verona). The only city to provide an effective challenge to Giotto was Siena. The great series of frescoes by *Simone Martini*, and *Ambrogio* and *Pietro Lorenzetti* (San Francesco, Assisi and Palazzo Pubblico, Siena, c 1230) although frequently drawing from Giotto for the figure style, generally contain far more incidental detail and are less serious and forbidding in tone. This predilection is already to be found in the work of *Duccio* (c 1260–1318/19) whose masterpiece, the *Maestà* for Siena cathedral, is still to be seen in the Museo dell'Opera del Duomo there.

The International Style. The art of the period c 1400 is normally termed 'International Gothic'. This derives from the fact that a particular figure style, compounded of flowing drapery and graceful forms, achieved a fashionable status on both sides of the Alps. Alongside this style went a liking for detailed realism and gay décor. It was a style to be found north of the Apennines in Milan and Venice and one of its chief exponents was *Gentile da Fabriano* (c 1370–1427) whose main surviving work is, however, now in Florence (the Uffizi). In spite of subsequent stylistic change, it might be argued that *Pisanello* (c 1395– 1455/56) really belongs to this group of painters. Florence of course had its own exponents of this style, the most famous being the painter *Lorenzo Monaco* (c 1370–c 1425; several works now in the Uffizi, Florence) and *Lorenzo Ghiberti* (1378–1455; see especially his first doors for the Florentine baptistery). With Ghiberti, however, one also reaches the beginning of the Florentine Renaissance.

The Early Renaissance in Florence. The changes which took place in Florentine art c 1400–30 were of fundamental importance for the subsequent history of Western art. They were inspired partly by a reaction against the elegance and refinement of the International Style, partly by reverence for the art of antiquity, and partly by a new scientific interest in realistic portrayal. The three major figures are **Masaccio** the painter (1401–28), **Donatello** the sculptor (1386–1466), and **Brunelleschi** the architect (1377–1446). As yet there was little attempt at archaeological exactitude in the use of antique motifs. Antiquity was seen much more as a source for ideas. With this went experiments in a new system of perspective construction, probably pioneered by Brunelleschi, but codified by a further great Florentine architect *Alberti* (c 1404–72). Major monuments of this early period include the Brancacci chapel of Masaccio (Santa Maria del Carmine), Donatello's statues for Or San Michele, and Brunelleschi's church of San Lorenzo. Many of the ideas of these artists were accepted and developed by subsequent painters and sculptors such as *Paolo Uccello* (1396/97–1475), *Andrea del Castagno* (?1423–57), *Filippo Lippi* (c 1406–69) or *Luca della Robbia* (1400–82). It is, however, to be observed that the severity of Masaccio or the drama of Donatello do not appear to have been especially attractive and much of the subsequent art seems to be pitched in an appreciably lower key.

This is also true of the second half of the century which produced a number of artists of astonishing ability and virtuosity. The chief painters were *Ghirlandaio* (1449–94; see his frescoes in Santa Maria Novella, Florence) and *Botticelli* (c 1445–1510) who both painted for the Medici family or their agents. The chief sculptors were two men of great ability. *Antonio Rossellino* (1427–c 1479) and *Andrea Verrocchio* (c 1435–88; many works in Florence). Of equal importance for the development of figure painting was the sculptor-painter *Antonio Pollaiolo* (c 1432–98) under whose influence two great artists emerged. The first, *Luca Signorelli* (c 1441–1523), was the author of a major series of frescoes in the chapel of San Brizio, Orvieto cathedral (begun 1499). The other far greater artist who had as his immediate master *Andrea Verrocchio*, was **Leonardo da Vinci** (1452–1519).

One further painter should be noted as probably the most distinguished offshoot of the early Florentine Renaissance—*Piero della Francesca* (c 1415–92). He was trained in Florence, but worked most of his life in central Italy and the Marches, being closely connected with the court of Urbino. His most complete surviving work is now the fresco cycle in San Francesco, Arezzo.

Brunelleschi's achievements were partially those of an engineer (the dome of Florence cathedral) and partly those of a designer (see also the church of Santo Spirito, Florence). The classical motifs which he incorporated into his buildings were widely copied throughout the century. Alberti, already mentioned, probably possessed a more profound archaeological appreciation of classical architecture (see the façade of the Rucellai Palace, Florence, or San Francesco, Rimini) which he later carried to Mantua. A third architect, *Michelozzo* (1396–1472) was responsible for one of the most influential palace designs of the 15C, namely the Medici Palace, Florence.

Florentine ideas quickly spread outwards from Tuscany, artists visiting both Rome (*Fra Angelico*) and cities north of the Apennines. (*Masolino* painted at Castiglione d'Olona, near Milan, c 1435; Michelozzo worked in Milan c 1460; Donatello, Uccello, Castagno, and Filippo Lippi all visited the Veneto; Leonardo went to Milan c 1473.) This in turn affected the provincial northern schools.

The Early Renaissance in the North of Italy. The two major political centres in North Italy were Milan and Venice. Both had flourishing local schools and each was influenced in a different way by Renaissance ideals. The stay of Leonardo in Milan (c 1473–99) had in general a destructive effect since Leonardo's interests in tonal effects, complicated figure structure, and the problems of painting emotion ran counter to the tendencies of the local painters (especially *Foppa*, 1427/30–1515/16; see the two panels in the Accademia Carrara, Bergamo) and introduced a fashion which was never effectively assimilated but only imitated (for example, by *Boltraffio* 1467–1516, many of whose works are in Milan).

The Veneto was fortunate in producing two near-contemporary artists, each of whom moulded the ideas from Tuscany into an individual and influential style. The first, *Mantegna* (1431–1506), was trained in Padua; and his early work (see especially the altarpiece in San Zeno, Verona, c 1456–59) demonstrates a firm control of Tuscan ideas coupled with an ardent feeling for antique remains. Mantegna's skill as a painter secured for him the post of court artist to the Gonzagas at Mantua where the *Camera degli Sposi* in the Castello (1474) still ranks as one of the outstanding pieces of European palace decoration. His influence as an observer of antique remains was probably equally important, directing the course of the subsequent Renaissance towards an ever more sensitive appreciation of Antiquity.

The second great artist of the late Quattrocento was *Giovanni Bellini* (c 1435–1516)—brother-in-law of Mantegna and initially much influenced by him. Bellini dominated Venetian painting up to c 1505. His portraits and Madonnas were much in demand and his altarpieces (see especially his San Giobbe altar, Accademia, Venice) provided a canon to which other painters conformed. Not to be missed are his latest works, which are among the most memorable (see the altars in San Zaccaria and San Giovanni Evangelista, Venice). Giovanni's father, *Jacopo*, and brother, *Gentile*, were also eminent painters of large narrative paintings, some of which survive (Accademia, Venice). A more sensitive and attractive painter of the same genre was *Carpaccio* (c 1470–1523/26. See the great cycle of paintings of Sant'Orsola, now in the Accademia, Venice).

The impact of Paduan and Venetian painting can be found in numerous North Italian centres. The most important was probably Ferrara, which had a court 'school' of its own dominated by the curious and mannered styles of *Cosmè Tura* (c 1430–95), *Cossa* (1435/36–77) and *Ercole Roberti* (c 1448/55–96). This current style is well illustrated by the decorations in the Palazzo Schifanoia, Ferrara (completed in 1470). An extension of Paduan-Venetian influence is to be found in the Marches where the Venetian *Carlo Crivelli* spent much of his life (c 1435–93. See especially the early altar at Massa Fermana, 1468).

The sculptors of the period were also much influenced by the archaeological tendencies of Mantegna. One of the most famous, *Piero Buonacolsi*, was nicknamed 'Antico' because much of his time he either made antique-looking bronze figures, or repaired real antiques for Isabella, the Marchesa of Mantua. Padua again produced some notable sculptors (see especially the bronze sculpture of *Riccio* and *Bellano* in the church of the Santo, Padua); and Venice attracted some remarkable marble sculptors (see the many works by the Lombardo family in Venice, and also in the Santo, Padua), one of whom, *Tullio Lombardo*, showed a striking sensitivity for the softer qualities of good classical sculpture.

The clarity which is to be found in much of this Quattrocento art is not so apparent in the architecture, which tended to be elaborate and over-ornate in appearance. The recovery of classical detail went ahead but there was much uncertainty about its effective use. Monuments to this confusion are the façade of the Certosa at Pavia (begun 1473 but never completed) and the Colleoni chapel at Bergamo (1470s). Milanese architecture also tended to elaboration and there was a continuation of the fashion, already mentioned, for moulded terracotta decoration. This is of some interest, since it is in this context that the greatest architect of the High Renaissance, Donato Bramante, first achieved fame. Bramante, before his departure to Rome (1499), had already worked for twenty years in Milan and his works tend to be ornate (see especially the ingenious church of Santa Maria presso San Satiro, Milan, begun c 1483). One of the interesting effects of his later contact with Rome was that he immediately dropped this rather provincial aspect of his work.

The High Renaissance and Mannerism in Florence. The art of the High Renaissance is closely connected with the sustained patronage of three Popes—Julius II, Leo X, and Clement VII. Their reigns saw the establishment in Rome of a nucleus of brilliant artists who came to dominate art for the next half-century or more. Although none of the major figures was a Roman by birth, they all found Rome a congenial place in which to live and work. Their names are now household words—**Michelangelo,** from Florence (1475–1564), **Raphael**, originally from Urbino (1483–1520), and **Bramante** (1444–1514), from Urbino, although immediately from Milan (see above). But the first monuments of High Renaissance art are (or were) to be found in Florence. For between c 1500 and c 1507 Michelangelo, Raphael, and Leonardo (lately returned from Milan, see above) all lived here. It was largely the success of Julius II in forcing or persuading artists to work for him which caused what in retrospect can be seen as one of the major 'population shifts' in the history of art.

The concerns of the High Renaissance were many, and it is misleading to see it as a monolithic 'movement'. Michelangelo's interests lay particularly in the recreation of an heroic figure style akin to the more grandiose monuments of Hellenistic art. This is already clear in the famous David and the unfinished St Matthew (both in the Accademia, Florence). But Leonardo's interests were still especially bound up in complex figure-patterns and in the problems of portraying human emotion. And although none of his late work may now be seen in Italy, it made a deep impression on the young Raphael, who arrived in Florence from Perugia in 1504. Northern Italy is also somewhat denuded of the early work of Raphael, but some examples are to be found in Florence.

The artists who went to Rome, c 1505–07, found Bramante already installed there, supervising the first stages of one of the most gigantic architectural enterprises undertaken since the end of the Roman Empire—the rebuilding of St Peter's. Bramante's outstanding abilities were partly those of an engineer (his training in Lombardy must have stood him in good stead) and partly those of an artist able to manipulate mass and to devise a decoration consistent with the enormous surfaces involved. The result was the rebirth of classical architecture on a new scale.

Evidence of these developments outside Rome is not difficult to find. Michelangelo himself lived in Florence, 1516–30, and from this period dates the Medici chapel in San Lorenzo. At the same time, a considerable body of artists remained working in Florence, assimilating the various interests that went to make up the High Renaissance. Chief among the painters was probably *Andrea del Sarto*, one of the great colourists of this period (1486–1531; see his frescoes in the churches of the Scalzo and Santissima Annunziata, Florence). His followers included *Pontormo* (1494–1556) and *Rosso Fiorentino* (1495–1540), many of whose works are still in Florence.

This process of assimilation is intimately linked with a stage of art usually called Mannerism. This was never an organised movement; it is, rather, a convenient word to describe the wide response to the major works of the great artists already mentioned. These ideas were worked out over a long period occupying a large part of the 16C, the fund of art being constantly enriched by the particular contributions of talented individuals. Florence remained important as the centre of Medici power and the first Grand Duke of Tuscany, Cosimo, numbered among his painters *Bronzino* (1503–72) and the historian *Giorgio Vasari* (1511–74). The decorations done for Cosimo in the Palazzo Vecchio, Florence, are among the best examples of Mannerist court art. Another example of an artist decisively influenced by Roman art is *Parmigianino* (1503–40), whose work in Parma includes frescoes in the church of the Madonna della Steccata (paintings also in the Pitti Palace, Florence).

Harder to place is the painter *Correggio* (?1489–1534) whose main achievements consist of two magnificent dome paintings in the cathedral and the church of San Giovanni Evangelista in Parma. Correggio may not have visited Rome but these enormous undertakings must certainly have been inspired by the great works of Raphael and Michelangelo. On a totally different scale and closer in feeling to Mantegna is his Camera di San Paolo in Parma.

Other provincial centres of importance might be mentioned briefly, reflecting as they did the Mannerist art of central Italy—as for instance Cremona, where a flourishing local school is found in the second half of the century (see especially San Sigismondo, with its especially well-preserved decoration). But most important of all was probably Mantua, where court art from 1524 to 1546 came under the direction of Raphael's pupil, *Giulio Romano* (?1499–1546). Numerous buildings and schemes of decoration survive in Mantua, produced either by him or under his direction. A short distance from Mantua lies the tiny Gonzaga town of Sabbioneta, which is also rich in monuments reflecting the art of Mantua and also Venice.

In central Italy, the position of sculptors was analogous to that of the painters. Rome came to occupy a central position and most important artists spent some of their formative years there. This is true of one of the greatest sculptors of the first part of the century, *Jacopo Sansovino* (1486–1570). He began work in Florence (St Matthew, now in the Museo dell'Opera del Duomo) but soon moved to Rome, ultimately going to Venice (see below). Probably the true central Italian heir to Michelangelo was *Giovanni da Bologna* (1529–1608)—actually a Fleming called Jean de Boulogne (Giambologna) who came to Italy c 1555. He ultimately settled in Florence and worked for Cosimo I.

Works of almost every description, from small bronzes (in the *Studiola*, Palazzo Vecchio) to colossal two- and even three-figure groups and a fountain (Boboli Gardens), survive in Florence to demonstrate his versatility (see also the Neptune Fountain, Bologna), and to provide a link between Mannerist sculpture at its most highly developed stage and the Baroque art of the 17C.

Venice in the 16C. Of all the great 15C centres of artistic production, Venice alone continued to preserve through the 16C some kind of independence of central Italy; so that Venetian art has in a special sense a recognisable character of its own which is not merely a provincial reflection of Rome. Many of the interests of High Renaissance Florence and Rome are apparent in the works of *Giorgione* (c 1476–1510) and the young *Titian* (c 1495–1576); but whereas in central Italy great importance came to be attached to anatomy, figure articulation, and draughtsmanship, in Venice these counted for little beside the manipulation of colour and tone. A number of important works survive in Venice (see the Accademia and many churches, especially the Frari) which demonstrate this moment of transition in Venetian art.

The development of High Renaissance ideas into what might be called a Mannerist style took comparatively long in Venice, since the penetration and absorption of the ideas themselves were slow, and to some extent resisted. Their impact was assisted among other things by the activities of *Giulio Romano* at Mantua, *Parmigianino* at Parma, by the work of *Pordenone* (1483/84–1539) in Venice itself (see the church of San Rocco), and by the coming of *Jacopo Sansovino* from Rome (1527). Even so the greatest changes in Venetian art are apparent, not around 1500, but in 1540. These changes involve the later work of *Titian,* and the painting of *Veronese* (c 1528–88) and *Tintoretto* (1518–94), the later sculpture of *Sansovino* and the work of *Vittoria* (1525–1608).

Evidence of change in Titian's work towards a more complicated and agitated figure style and more sombre colour palette is visible in the ceiling paintings now in Santa Maria della Salute (c 1542). This change of interest and technique is similar to the style developed by Tintoretto with its mighty figures and dramatic tonal contrasts (Venice contains innumerable masterpieces, but see especially the Scuola di San Rocco, 1564–88). Sculptural parallels to this painting are to be found in the giant figures of Mars and Neptune by Jacopo Sansovino (completed 1567, Palazzo Ducale) and in the work of Vittoria (see Santa Maria de'Frari and other churches).

Alongside this strongly characterised style must be set the far more obviously attractive work of Veronese, who is famous for his colourful and decorative narrative painting and ceilings (see the Accademia and especially San Sebastiano, Venice). He continued the tradition of Pisanello, Carpaccio, and Gentile Bellini, and his work was immensely influential later in the 18C.

The restrained and decorative beauty of Veronese's painting finds an architectural parallel in the work of his friend and collaborator, *Palladio* (1508–80). Palladio was famous both for his theoretical treatise on architecture, and also for his many country villas on the Venetian mainland. Among many, the Villa Maser still survives, designed by Palladio and decorated inside by Veronese. But the best centre for seeing Palladio's work is probably Vicenza. Palladio's work grows directly out of the architectural activities of Sansovino (for instance, the Libreria di San Marco and Loggetta, Venice), so that he has direct links with one of the most elegant and restrained artists of High Renaissance Rome.

Baroque Art. Italian art of the 17C is perhaps even more obviously dominated by Rome than that of the 16C. Moreover, since most Baroque art is, in a very obvious sense, something to be experienced, it is difficult for the traveller to do justice to it or to understand it without a visit there. All the greatest artists practised there—some of them almost exclusively. Among these must be mentioned *Gian Lorenzo Bernini* (1598–1680), whose major work is almost entirely in Rome and includes architecture and town planning, and sculptural schemes such as altars, tombs, and fountains; and *Algardi* (1595– 1654) and *Duquesnoy* (1594–1643), his rivals in sculpture, who worked in a more restrained style. Besides Bernini, as architects, were *Borromini* (1599–1667) and *Pietro da Cortona* (1596–1669), the last being also a celebrated decorator. His ceilings and interior paintings form, in fact, an essential element in Roman Baroque art, together with those of *Gaulli* (1639–1709) and *Pozzo* (1642–1709).

PAINTING. Nevertheless, the contribution of the central and northern provinces was considerable. Many of the 'Roman' artists and architects were born in the north; and many of them subsequently maintained links with the towns and areas from which they came. In this respect, Bologna stands out as perhaps the most important centre in North Italian painting. Here, already in the later 16C, the art was dominated by the three **Carracci**, who, together, exercised a most important formative influence on the style of the 17C. Of these, Annibale (1560–1609), who was the most important, went to Rome in 1595, leaving Lodovico (1555–1619) to run the Academy which had been founded in 1585–86. All, however, were much in sympathy with the great artists of the first half of the 16C and with the great works of classical antiquity; and, by reinterpreting these, paved the way for a 'classical' revival which ran counter in some respects to the 'Baroque' tendencies found elsewhere. (Numerous examples of their works are to be found in and around Bologna.) They in turn produced followers who developed this classicism and idealism still further. Of these, *Guido Reni* (1575–1642) worked mainly in Rome and Bologna; and *Andrea Sacchi* (1599– 1661) was in part trained in Bologna although his important work was all done in Rome. Another pupil, *Domenichino* (1581–1641) worked mainly in Rome and also in Naples.

The other great formative influence on 17C painting was **Michelangelo da Caravaggio** (1573–1610), born at Caravaggio near Milan. Although he went to Rome c 1590 and never returned north, his painting, which is full of strong colouring and chiaroscuro, and portrays a dramatic unidealised world, formed a strong contrast to the Bolognese painting. He was much criticised in Rome (but patrons still bought his paintings), and some of the more important effects of his activities are to be seen either in the south of Italy (Naples) or north of the Alps (see, for instance, Rubens and Rembrandt). However, his work exercised a pervasive influence throughout Italy and this can be easily detected in different ways in the paintings of *Guercino* (1591–1666) or *Orazio Gentileschi* (1563–1638; a Pisan by birth).

There are many areas of local activity in North and central Italy during this period, some of them disappointing. Of these the most obvious is Venice, dominated by the imitators of Tintoretto and

Veronese. The brief appearance of two outsiders during the 1620s (*Domenico Feti*, 1589–1623, and *Giovanni Lys*, 1597–1629/30) offers a slight interlude. To the west, however, more considerable achievements are found. In Milan, an Academy was founded in 1621, and a flourishing local school existed, dominated by *Giulio Cesare Procaccini* (1574–1625), *Il Cerano* (c 1575–1632), and *Il Morazzone* (1573–1626). Many works still exist by these artists in Milan cathedral (cycle of paintings of St Charles Borromeo) and in Milanese churches. In Genoa, too, a local Baroque school flourished led by *Bernardo Strozzi* (1581–1644) and *Gioacchino Assereto* (1600–49). Strozzi himself lived in Venice at the end of his life.

In fact, Genoa preserved throughout the century an interesting nucleus of talented painters. *Giovanni Battista Castiglione* (? before 1610–65) displayed an astonishing range of style (works in Genoese churches; he became court painter at Mantua in 1648) while the tradition of great fresco painting was kept alive into the 18C by *Domenico Piola* (1628–1723) and *Gregorio de Ferrari* (1647–1726; many examples in Genoa). Outside Genoa, isolated artists such as *Francesco Maffei* at Vicenza (c 1600–60) displayed an unorthodox style which contrasted strongly with the mid-century Baroque classicism which seems to have developed in the wake of the Carracci. This tendency towards a rather dull academicism was occasionally disrupted by the visits of eminent outsiders from other parts of Italy. Thus Pietro da Cortona worked for a short time in Florence (Palazzo Pitti, 1643–47) and left some direct record of the Roman Grand Manner, to be reflected in the paintings of *Il Volteranno* (1611–89; numerous works in Florence). Important at a later stage was the activity of the Neapolitan *Luca Giordano* (1632–1705) who executed commissions both in Florence and Venice.

In sculpture there was no city outside Rome to play a role equivalent to that of Bologna in painting. Nevertheless, in Florence, the tradition of Giambologna was carried on by his pupil *Pietro Tacca* (1577–1640) whose work includes parts of the monument to the Grand Duke Ferdinand I in Livorno and the tomb-sculpture in the sumptuous Cappella dei Principi, San Lorenzo (Florence, mentioned below). Later examples of Florentine Baroque are to be seen in the work of *Giovanni Battista Foggini* (1652–1725—for instance, in Santa Maria del Carmine). Much 'local' Baroque is disappointing and it is worth noting that a number of first-class works by Roman-based sculptors exist in the north. In Piacenza stand two magnificent equestrian monuments to the Farnese by *Francesco Mochi* (1580–1654) and in San Paolo, Bologna stands an altar group by *Algardi* (1595–1654). Work by Algardi is also to be found in San Carlo, Genoa; but Genoa also produced one first-class Baroque sculptor who, trained in Rome, worked in Genoa: *Filippo Parodi* (1630–1702; various works in and around Genoa).

With a few exceptions the achievements in architecture were less spectacular than in painting. The rich and extravagant effects of some Roman work are well caught in Florence by the Cappella dei Principi (San Lorenzo). *Bartolomeo Bianco* (before 1590–1657) is probably the greatest Baroque architect of Genoa (see especially the University), while Milan is celebrated for *Francesco Maria Ricchino* (1583–1658) whose work is to be seen in San Giuseppe, the Palazzo di Brera and the Collegio Elvetico. In Venice, no visitor can miss the splendid Santa Maria della Salute, the masterpiece of *Baldassarre Longhena* (1598–1682) standing at the entrance to the Grand Canal. But of all the exciting and impressive 17C architecture north of Rome, the greatest concentration is to be found in Turin, which had become the capital of Piedmont in 1563. The great developments in planning and architecture spread across the 17C into the 18C, and the most striking buildings are those of *Guarino Guarini* (1624–83) under whom Turin became one of the most stimulating centres of Baroque architectural design. Guarini was succeeded by two more great architects: *Filippo Juvarra* (1678–1736), of international renown, who designed the great basilica at Superga and the 'Castello' of Stupinigi, and *Bernardo Vittone* (1704/05–70) who successfully combined the contrasting traditions of his two great predecessors and carried them far into the second half of the 18C.

Post-Baroque Art. With the 18C, the international importance of Italian art dwindled. Foreigners indeed came to Italy in unprecedented numbers. But Italy was now regarded particularly as a repository of *antique* art. The great developments in *contemporary* art happened elsewhere—mainly in France.

Nevertheless, one final brilliant flowering of Italian art took place in Venice; for here a group of artists, overthrowing much of the cumbrous tradition of the Baroque 18C, created a distinctive Italian Rococo style. Probably the initiator of the change was *Sebastiano Ricci* (1659–1734), but the greatest representative of this style was **Giambattista Tiepolo** (1696–1770), whose many works are to be found not only in Venice, but also in Milan and elsewhere in northern Italy. Alongside Tiepolo were many lesser masters among whose works the *vedute* of Venice by *Antonio Canaletto* (1697–1768) and *Francesco Guardi* (1712–93) are probably the best known. It is of interest that almost all the chief painters of Venice during that period travelled to foreign courts—such was the popularity of the Venetian style. Thus Venice, in this final phase, produced an art which was truly international.

It is, however, evident that in spite of isolated exceptions Italian art of the late 18C and 19C has not the central importance that it had held since the late 15C. The obvious exceptions would include the great neo-classical sculptor *Canova* (1757–1822), who possessed in his day an unequalled international reputation. But even so, the most interesting developments in Neo-classicism belong to France, Germany, and England. This pattern, in which Italy reflected rather than led Europe, was repeated through the 19C into the era of Art Nouveau where, once again, Italy produced a number of striking reflections of an international movement (see, for instance, the exciting and bizarre but little-known *Camera di Commercio*, Mantua 1914 by Aldo Andreani).

The greatest Italian contributions to European art since the time of Tiepolo undoubtedly came in the 20C. There is indeed one important Italian movement, Futurism, which began with a manifesto in 1909 and had a distinctive effect on the development of Cubism north of the Alps. The Futurists were above all concerned with art and its relevance to the 20C environment. Their impact was to some extent lessened by the death, during the First World War, of the most creative of them, *Umberto Boccioni* (1882–1916).

The attempt to relate art directly to their view of the character of 20C existence can also be seen in the visionary drawings of the Futurist architect, *Antonio Sant'Elia* (1888–1916; who likewise died during the First World War). Thereafter, Italian art has developed in step with northern art, frequently making important contributions. Notable was the work of the so-called *scuola metafisica* founded (c 1917) by *Giorgio de'Chirico* (1888–1978) in which was produced a species of proto-Surrealist painting; and this account of Italian art may be ended by alluding to more recent achievements of Italian architects, especially of Pier Luigi Nervi (see, for instance, the Exhibition Hall, Turin, or the earlier Stadio Comunale at Florence).

Glossary

AEDICULE, small opening framed by two columns and a pediment, originally used in classical architecture

AMBO (pl. *ambones*), pulpit in a Christian basilica; two pulpits on opposite sides of a church from which the gospel and epistle were read

AMPHORA, antique vase, usually of large dimensions, for oil and other liquids

ANCONA, retable or large altarpiece (painted or sculpted) in an architectural frame

ANTEFIX, ornament placed at the lower corners of the tiled roof of a temple to conceal the space between the tiles and the cornice

ANTIPHONAL, choir-book containing a collection of *antiphonae*—verses sung in response by two choirs

ARCA, wooden chest with a lid, for sacred or secular use. Also, monumental sarcophagus in stone, used by Christians and pagans

ARCHITRAVE, lowest part of an entablature, horizontal frame above a door

ARCHIVOLT, moulded architrave carried round an arch

ATLANTES (or *Telamones*), male figures used as supporting columns

ATRIUM, forecourt, usually of a Byzantine church or a classical Roman house

ATTIC, topmost storey of a classical building, hiding the spring of the roof

BADIA, *Abbazia*, abbey

BALDACCHINO, canopy supported by columns, usually over an altar

BASILICA, originally a Roman building used for public administration; in Christian architecture, an aisled church with a clerestory and apse, and no transepts

BORGO, a suburb; street leading away from the centre of a town

BOTTEGA, the studio of an artist: the pupils who worked under his direction

BOZZETTO, sketch, often used to describe a small model for a piece of sculpture

BROCCATELLO, a clouded veined marble from Siena

BROLETTO, name often given to the town halls of North Italy

BUCCHERO, Etruscan black terracotta ware

BUCRANIA, a form of classical decoration—heads of oxen garlanded with flowers

CAMPANILE, bell-tower, often detached from the building to which it belongs

CAMPOSANTO, cemetery

CANEPHORA, figure bearing a basket, often used as a caryatid

CANOPIC VASE, Egyptian or Etruscan vase enclosing the entrails of the dead

CANTORIA, singing-gallery in a church

CARTOON, from *cartone*, meaning large sheet of paper. A full-size preparatory drawing for a painting or fresco

CARYATID, female figure used as a supporting column

CASSONE, a decorated chest, usually a dower chest

CAVEA, the part of a theatre or amphitheatre occupied by the row of seats

CELLA, sanctuary of a temple, usually in the centre of the building

CENACOLO, scene of the Last Supper (often in the refectory of a convent)

CHALICE, wine cup used in the celebration of Mass

CHIAROSCURO, distribution of light and shade, apart from colour in a painting

CIBORIUM, casket or tabernacle containing the Host

CIPOLLINO, onion-marble; a greyish marble with streaks of white or green

CIPPUS, sepulchral monument in the form of an altar

CISTA, casket, usually of bronze and cylindrical in shape, to hold jewels, toilet articles, etc., and decorated with mythological subjects

CLOISONNÉ, type of enamel decoration

COLUMBARIUM, a building (usually subterranean) with niches to hold urns containing the ashes of the dead

CONFESSIO, crypt beneath the high altar and raised choir of a church, usually containing the relics of a saint

CORBEL, a projecting block, usually of stone

CRENELLATIONS, battlements

CUPOLA, dome

CYCLOPEAN, the term applied to walls of unmortared masonry, older than the Etruscan civilisation, and attributed by the ancients to the giant Cyclopes

DIPTYCH, painting or ivory panel in two sections

DUOMO, cathedral

EXEDRA, semicircular recess

EX VOTO, tablet or small painting expressing gratitude to a saint

FRESCO (in Italian, *affresco*), painting executed on wet plaster. On the wall beneath is sketched the *sinopia*, and the *cartone* (see above) is transferred onto the fresh plaster (*intonaco*) before the fresco is begun either by pricking the outline with small holes over which a powder is dusted, or by means of a stylus which leaves an incised line on the wet plaster. In recent years many frescoes have been detached from the walls on which they were executed

GIALLO ANTICO, red-veined yellow marble from Numidia

GONFALON, banner of a medieval guild or commune

GRAFFITI, design on a wall made with iron tool on a prepared surface, the design showing in white. Also used loosely to describe scratched designs or words on walls

GREEK-CROSS, cross with the arms of equal length

GRISAILLE, painting in various tones of grey

GROTESQUE, painted or stucco decoration in the style of the ancient Romans (found during the Renaissance in Nero's Golden House in Rome, then underground, hence the name, from 'grotto'). The delicate ornamental decoration usually includes patterns of flowers, sphynxes, birds, human figures, etc., against a light ground

HERM (pl. *Hermae*), quadrangular pillar decreasing in girth towards the ground surmounted by a bust

HYPOGEUM, subterranean excavation for the interment of the dead (usually Etruscan)

ICONOSTASIS, high balustrade with figures of saints, guarding the sanctuary of a Byzantine church

IMPASTO, early Etruscan ware made of inferior clay

INTARSIA (or *Tarsia*), inlay of wood, marble, or metal

INTRADOS, underside or soffit

of an arch

KRATER, Antique mixing-bowl, conical in shape with rounded base

KYLIX, wide shallow vase with two handles and short stem

LATIN-CROSS, cross with a long vertical arm

LAVABO, hand-basin usually outside a refectory or sacristy

LOGGIA, covered gallery or balcony, usually preceding a larger building

LUNETTE, semicircular space in a vault or ceiling, or above a door or window, often decorated with a painting or relief

MAESTÀ, Madonna and Child enthroned in majesty

MATRONEUM, gallery reserved for women in early Christian churches

MEDALLION, large medal; loosely, a circular ornament

MONOCHROME, painting or drawing in one colour only

MONOLITH, single stone (usually a column)

NARTHEX, vestibule of a Christian basilica

NIELLO, black substance used in an engraved design

NIMBUS, luminous ring surrounding the heads of Saints in paintings; a square nimbus denoted that the person was living at that time

OCULUS, round window

OPERA (DEL DUOMO), the office in charge of the fabric of a building (i.e. the Cathedral)

OPUS TESSELLATUM, mosaic formed entirely of square tesserae

PALA, large altarpiece

PALAZZO, any dignified and important building

PALOMBINO, fine-grained white marble

PAVONAZZETTO, yellow marble blotched with blue

PAX, sacred object used by a priest for the blessing of peace, and offered for the kiss of the faithful. Usually circular,

engraved, enamelled or painted in a rich gold or silver frame

PENDENTIVE, concave spandrel beneath a dome

PERISTYLE, court or garden surrounded by a columned portico

PIETÀ, group of the Virgin mourning the dead Christ

PIETRE DURE, hard or semi-precious stones, often used in the form of mosaics to decorate cabinets, table-tops, etc.

PIEVE, parish church

PISCINA, Roman tank; a basin for an officiating priest to wash his hands before Mass

PLAQUETTE, small metal tablet with relief decoration

PLUTEUS (pl. *plutei*), marble panel, usually decorated; a series of them used to form a parapet to precede the altar of a church

POLYPTYCH, painting or panel in more than three sections

PORTA DEL MORTO, in certain old mansions of Umbria and Tuscany, a narrow raised doorway, said to be for the passage of biers of the dead, but more probably for use in troubled times when the main gate would be barred

PREDELLA, small painting or panel, usually in sections, attached below a large altarpiece, illustrating the story of a Saint, the life of the Virgin, etc.

PRESEPIO, literally, crib or manger. A group of statuary of which the central subject is the Infant Jesus in the manger

PRONAOS, porch in front of the cella of a temple

PUTTO (pl. *putti*), figure of a boy sculpted or painted, usually nude

QUADRATURA, painted architectural perspectives

QUATREFOIL, four-lobed design

REREDOS, decorated screen rising behind an altar

RHYTON, drinking-horn

usually ending in an animal's head

ROOD-SCREEN, a screen below the Rood or Crucifix dividing the nave from the chancel of a church

SCHIACCIATO, term used to describe very low relief in sculpture, where there is an emphasis on the delicate line rather than the depth of the panel

SCHOLA CANTORUM, enclosure for the choristers in the nave of an early Christian church, adjoining the sanctuary

SCUOLA (pl. *scuole*), Venetian lay confraternity, dedicated to charitable works

SINOPIA, large sketch for a fresco made on the rough wall in a red earth pigment called sinopia (because it originally came from Sinope on the Black Sea). By detaching a fresco it is now possible to see the sinopia beneath and detach it also

SITULA, water-bucket

SOFFIT, underside or intrados of an arch

SPANDREL, surface between two arches in an arcade or the triangular space on either side of an arch

STAMNOS, big-bellied vase

with two small handles at the sides, closed by a lid

STELE, upright stone bearing a monumental inscription

STEMMA, coat-of-arms or heraldic device

STEREOBATE, basement of a temple or other building

STOUP, vessel for Holy Water, usually near the W door of a church

STYLOBATE, basement of a columned temple or other building

TELAMONES, see *Atlantes*

TESSERA, a small cube of marble, glass, etc., used in mosaic work

THERMAE, Roman Baths

THOLOS, a circular building

TONDO, round painting or bas-relief

TRANSENNA, open grille or screen, usually of marble, in an early Christian church

TRIPTYCH, painting or panel in three sections

TROMPE L'OEIL, literally, a deception of the eye. Used to describe illusionist decoration, painted architectural perspectives, etc.

VILLA, country house with its garden

The terms QUATTROCENTO, CINQUECENTO (abbreviated in Italy '400, '500), etc., refer not to the 14C and 15C, but to the 'fourteen-hundreds' and 'fifteen-hundreds', i.e. the 15C and 16C, etc.

PRACTICAL INFORMATION

Approaches to Northern Italy

Throughout the year direct air services operate between London and Milan, Turin, Genoa, Venice, Pisa (the nearest international airport to Florence), and Bologna. There are scheduled flights to Rimini in summer, as well as numerous charter flights. Principal Italian towns and tourist resorts are linked with London by direct rail routes from Calais, Ostend, Dunkirk, and Boulogne. Car-sleeper trains run from Calais, Brussels, and Paris to Milan. The easiest approaches by road are the motorways through the Mont Blanc, St Bernard, or Mont Cenis tunnels, or over the Brenner Pass.

Italian Tourist Boards. General information may be obtained in London from the *Italian State Tourist Office* (*ENIT: Ente Nazionale Italiano per il Turismo*, 1 Princes Street, WIR 8AY), who distribute free an excellent 'Traveller's Handbook' (revised c every year). In Italy, the local tourist boards provide invaluable help to travellers on arrival: they supply free hotel lists, maps, and up-to-date information on museum opening times, etc. They are undergoing reorganisation, and the regional offices are now usually called *Aziende di Promozione Turistica* or *APT*. In the larger cities there are also subsidiary information offices at railway stations, etc. Their addresses have been indicated in the text, although because of reorganisation these may not always be accurate.

Travel Agents (most of whom belong to the Association of British Travel Agents) sell travel tickets and book accommodation, and also organise inclusive tours and charter trips to Italy. These include: *Citalia*, 51 Conduit St, London W1 (agents for the Italian State Railways); *Thomas Cook & Son*, 45 Berkeley St, London W1, and other branches; *American Express*, Windsor House, Victoria, London SW1, etc. Other tour operators to Italy include Martin Randall Travel, Fine Art Courses Ltd, Nadfas Tours, Pilgrim Air, Prospect Music and Art, Serenissima and Heritage Travel, Swan Hellenic, and numerous others.

Air Services between London and Italy are operated by British Airways and Alitalia. Charter flights (often much cheaper) are also now run to most of the main cities in Italy throughout the year (several times a week); the fare often includes hotel accommodation. All scheduled services have a monthly excursion fare, and a limited number of special reduced fares (usually only available if booked well in advance). The airline companies offer a 25 per cent reduction of the return fare to full-time students (12–26 yrs old) and young people between the ages of 12 and 21. Car hire schemes in conjunction with flights can also be arranged.

Railway Services. The three most direct routes from Calais via Paris are: Marseille–Ventimiglia–Sanremo–Genoa (c 22 hrs); Modane–Turin (c 16 hrs); Lausanne–Domodossola–Milan (c 16 hrs). All these services have sleeping cars (1st class: single or double compartment; 2nd class: 3-berth compartments) and couchettes (seats converted into couches at night: 1st class: four; 2nd class: six). Return fares for the journey from London are usually double the single fare. The luxury class Orient Express now runs twice a week in summer from

London via Paris to Milan, Venice, and Florence. Information on the Italian State Railways (and tickets and seat reservations) may be obtained in London from Citalia.

A **European Bus Service** now operates in two days between London (Victoria Coach Station) and Rome (Piazza della Repubblica) via Dover, Paris, Mont Blanc, Aosta, Turin, Genoa, Milan, Bologna, and Florence, daily from June to September, and once or twice a week for the rest of the year. Reduction for students. Information in London from the National Express office at Victoria Coach Station, and, in Italy from SITA offices.

Motoring. British drivers taking their own cars by any of the multitudinous routes across France, Belgium, Luxembourg, Switzerland, Germany, and Austria need only the vehicle registration book, a valid national driving licence (accompanied by a translation, issued free by the RAC, AA, and ENIT offices), and an International Insurance Certificate (the 'Green Card'), and a nationality plate (e.g. GB). Motorists who are not owners of the vehicle must possess the owner's permit for its use abroad. A Swiss Motorway Pass is needed for Switzerland, and can be obtained from the RAC, the AA or at the Swiss border.

The continental rule of the road is to drive on the right and overtake on the left. The provisions of the respective highway codes in the countries of transit, though similar, have important variations, especially with regard to priority, speed limits, and pedestrian crossings. Membership of the *Automobile Association* (071 930 9559), or the *Royal Automobile Club* (membership enquiries and insurance 081 686 2314; route information 081 686 2525) entitles motorists to many of the facilities of affiliated societies on the Continent and may save trouble and anxiety. The UK motoring organisations are represented at most of the sea and airports, both at home and on the Continent, to assist their members with customs formalities.

Motorway Routes to Italy from Europe. The main routes from France, Switzerland, and Austria are described below.

A.   The direct motorway route from France, by-passing Geneva, enters Italy through the **Mont Blanc Tunnel** (see Rte 2). The road from Courmayeur to Aosta has not yet been improved. At Aosta the A5 motorway begins; it follows the Val d'Aosta. Just beyond Ivrea is the junction with the A4/5 motorway; the A5 continues S to Turin , while the A4/5 diverges E. At Santhia the A4 motorway from Turin is joined for Milan via Novara, or the A26/4 can be followed S via Alessandria, reaching the coast at Voltri, just outside Genoa. For motorists heading S there is a choice between the 'Autostrada del Sole' (A1) from Milan or the Florence–Pisa motorway from Genoa. The latter route avoids the Apennine pass between Bologna and Florence which carries very heavy traffic and can be subject to delays.

B.   The most direct approach to Turin from France is through the **Mont Cenis Tunnel** (Rte 1A) from Modane in France to Bardonecchia. A road continues to Oulx where a motorway is under construction via Susa to Turin parallel to the old road. From Turin a motorway (A6) descends direct to the coast at Savona, or the motorway (A21, A26) via Asti and Alessandria leads to Genoa; either one joins directly the coastal motorway for Pisa and Florence. Alternatively, the A4 motorway leads from Turin E to Milan for destinations in the Veneto and Emilia Romagna.

C.   The **Coastal route from the South of France** follows the A10 motorway through the foothills with frequent long tunnels to enter Italy just before Ventimiglia (Rte 4). The motorway continues past Alassio, Albenga, and Savona (where the motorway from Turin comes in), to Voltri (where the A26 motorway from Alessandria comes in) and Genoa (with the junction of the A7 motorway from Milan). The coastal motorway continues beyond Rapallo and La Spezia past the resorts of Versilia, and at Viareggio divides. The left branch (A11) continues via Lucca to Florence (and the 'Autostrada del Sole'), while the coastal branch (A12) continues to Pisa and Livorno.

D.   The approach to Italy from Switzerland (Lausanne) is usually through the **Great St Bernard Tunnel** (Rte 2, or by the pass in summer) which only becomes motorway at Aosta (see A. above).

E.   Another motorway route from Switzerland is via the St Gotthard Tunnel (opened in 1980) and Lugano. The motorway (A9) enters Italy at Como (Rte 12) and continues to Milan where the 'Autostrada del Sole' (A1) begins for central Italy, and other motorways lead to Genoa, or E via Brescia and Verona to Venice.

F.   From Germany and Austria (Innsbruck) the direct approach to Northern Italy is by the motorway over the **Brenner Pass** (Rte 27). The motorway (A22) continues down the Isarco valley to Bolzano and the Adige valley via Trento to Verona. Here motorways diverge W for Brescia and Milan, or E for Vicenza and Venice, or continue S via Mantua to join the A1 motorway just W of Modena for Florence and central Italy.

Car Sleeper Train services operate from Boulogne and Paris, Hamburg, Vienna, and Munich to Milan, Bologna, Rome, etc.

Passports or Visitors Cards are necessary for all British travellers entering Italy and must bear the photograph of the holder. American travellers must carry passports. British passports valid for ten years are issued at the Passport Office, Clive House, Petty France, London SW1, or may be obtained for an additional fee through any tourist agent. No visa is required for British or American travellers to Italy. Travellers are strongly advised to carry some means of identity with them at all times while in Italy.

Currency Regulations. Exchange controls have been suspended by the British Government since 1979. There are now no restrictions on the amount of sterling travellers may take out of Great Britain. There are frequent variations on the amount of bank notes which may be taken in or out of Italy. Since there are normally strict limitations, the latest regulations should be checked before departure.

Money. The monetary unit is the Italian lira (plural: lire). The current exchange value is approximately 2100 lire to the £ sterling (1300 lire to the US dollar). There are coins of 5, 10, 20, 50, 100, 200 and 500 lire, and notes of 1000, 2000, 5000, 10,000, 50,000, and 100,000 lire. Travellers' cheques and Eurocheques are the safest way of carrying money while travelling, and certain credit cards are now generally accepted. (The commission on cashing travellers' cheques can be quite high.) For banking hours, see under 'General Information', below. Money can also be changed at exchange offices ('cambio') usually open 7 days a week at airports, and some main railway stations, and (usually at a lower rate) at some hotels, restaurants, and shops.

Customs. As the regulations about the import of articles purchased abroad change frequently, travellers are advised to consult the Italian State Tourist Office, or their travel agent about details.

Police Registration is required within three days of entering Italy. For travellers staying at a hotel the management will attend to the formality. The permit lasts three months, but can be extended on application.

Hotels and Restaurants

Hotels. Hotels in Italy are now classified by 'stars' as in the rest of Europe. Since 1985 the official category of 'Pensione' has been abolished. There are now five official categories of hotels from the luxury 5-star hotels to the most simple 1-star hotel. In this Guide hotels have not been indicated in the text since it can now be taken for granted that almost every small centre in the country will be provided with adequate accommodation. Hotels of every class exist in the larger towns. In Italy, each local Tourist Board (*Azienda di Promozione Turistica*, or *A.P.T.*) issues a free list of hotels giving category, price, and facilities. Local tourist offices help travellers to find accommodation on the spot, and run booking offices at the main railway stations (i.e. Milan, Venice, and Florence). It is, however, essential to book well in advance at Easter and in summer, especially in Florence and Venice. In the larger cities when trade fairs are being held it is virtually impossible to find accommodation. To confirm the booking a deposit should be sent. There are now numerous agencies and hotel representatives in Britain and America who specialise in making hotel reservations (normally for 5-star and 4-star hotels only).

Up-to-date information about hotels and restaurants can be found in the red guide to Italy published by Michelin ('Italia', revised annually). In Italian, the Touring Club Italiano publish useful information about hotels in 'Alberghi in Italia' (published c every year), and in the 'Guida Rapida d'Italia' (four volumes cover the area in this book). The guides published in Italian by 'l'Espresso' to hotels and restaurants in Italy are now issued (in a reduced single volume) in English every year. Other specialised guides include the 'Charming Small Hotel Guide: Italy' (Papermac/Hunter).

Charges vary according to class, season, services available, and locality. Every hotel has its fixed charges agreed with the Regional Tourist Board. In all hotels the service charges are included in the rates. VAT is added in all hotels at a rate of 9 per cent (14 per cent in 5-star hotels). However, the total charge is exhibited on the back of the door of the hotel room. Breakfast (usually disappointing and costly) is by law an optional extra charge, but is often now included in the price of the room. When staying in hotels in the centre of towns it is often advisable to go round the corner to the nearest bar for breakfast. Hotels are now obliged by law (for tax purposes) to issue an official receipt to customers, who should not leave the premises without this document ('ricevuta fiscale').

ALBERGHI DIURNI ('day hotels'), in the larger towns, are provided with bathrooms, hairdressers, cleaning services, rest rooms and other amenities, but no sleeping accommodation. They are usually situated in or near the main railway station, open from 6 am to midnight.

Youth Hostels. The Italian Youth Hostels Association (Associazione Italiana Alberghi per la Gioventù, Palazzo della Civiltà del Lavoro, 00144 EUR, Rome) has 52 hostels situated all over the country. A membership card of the AIG or the International Youth Hostel Federation is required for access to Italian Youth Hostels. Details from the Youth Hostels Association, 14 Southampton Street, London WC2.

Students' Hostels exist in many Italian university towns and are available not only to students taking courses, but also to students visiting the country for holiday purposes. Application should be made to the 'Casa dello Studente' in Bologna, Camerino, Ferrara, Florence, Genoa, Macerata, Modena, Milan, Parma, Pavia, Perugia, Pisa, Siena, Urbino, Padua (Casa Fusinato, Via Marzolo), and Venice (Foresteria dell'Istituto di Ca' Foscari). Meals may be taken at the University Canteens. The 'Guide for Foreign Students' giving detailed information on students' facilities etc. can be obtained from the Italian Ministry of Education, Viale Trastevere, Rome. There are also some hostels run by religious organisations (information from local tourist offices).

Camping is very popular in Italy, where the international camping Carnet is useful. The local Tourist Office of the nearest town will give information and particulars of the most suitable sites. There are over 1600 official camping sites in Italy. Full details of the sites are published annually by the Touring Club Italiano and Federcampeggio in 'Campeggi e Villaggi Turistici in Italia'. The Federazione Italiana del Campeggio have an information office near Florence (Telephone 055/882391), and a booking service (Centro Internazionale Prenotazioni Campeggio-Itcamp travel, Casella Postale 23, 50041 Calenzano, Florence).

Renting accommodation for short periods in Italy has recently become easier and better organised. Villas, farmhouses, etc. can be rented for holidays through specialised agencies (information from ENIT, London) and Agriturist (main office, 101 Corso Vittorio Emanuele, Rome).

Restaurants in Italy are called 'Ristoranti' or 'Trattorie'; there is now no difference between the two. Italian food is usually good and inexpensive. The least pretentious restaurant almost invariably provides the best value. Many Italians eat out at restaurants frequently, sometimes alone (when travelling on business, etc.). Almost every locality has a simple restaurant (often family run) which caters for them; the décor is usually very simple and the food excellent value. This type of restaurant does not always offer a menu and the choice is usually limited to three or four first courses, and three or four second courses, with only fruit as a sweet.

The more sophisticated restaurants are more attractive and comfortable and often larger (with a menu displayed outside). They are also usually considerably more expensive. Information about these restaurants can be obtained from the local tourist boards or by asking at one's hotel. They also appear in the annual guides to Italian restaurants: 'Italia', the red guide published by Michelin; 'La Guida d'Italia', published by L'Espresso (also now in a reduced English version), and 'I Ristoranti di Veronelli'. Not quite so up-to-date, but also extremely useful are: 'Ristoranti in Italia' and the 'Guida Rapida d'Italia' (4 volumes), all published by the Touring Club Italiano. The standard sometimes deteriorates once a restaurant becomes well known. The most famous restaurants in this category offer international cuisine, and cater also for travellers on expense accounts. Fish is always the most expensive item on the menu in any restaurant.

Prices on the menu do not include a cover charge (*coperto*, shown separately on the menu) which is added to the bill. The service charge is now almost always automatically added at the end of the bill. Tipping is therefore not strictly necessary, but a few thousand lire are appreciated. Restaurants are now obliged by law (for tax purposes) to issue an official receipt to customers who should not leave the premises without this document ('ricevuta fiscale').

Pizze (a popular and cheap food throughout Italy) and other excellent snacks are served in a *Pizzeria, Rosticceria* and *Tavola Calda*. Some of these have no seating accommodation and sell food to take away or eat on the spot. A *Vinaio* or *Osteria* (mostly now found only in the Veneto) sells wine by the glass and good simple food for very reasonable prices. For **Picnics** sandwiches ('panini') are made up on request (with ham, salame, cheese, anchovies, tuna fish, etc.) at *Pizzicherie* and *Alimentari* (grocery shops) and *Fornai* (bakeries) often sell delicious individual pizzas, bread with oil and salt ('focaccia' or 'scacciata'), cakes, etc.

Bars (*Cafés*), which are open all day, serve numerous varieties of excellent refreshments which are usually taken standing up. The cashier should be paid first and the receipt given to the barman in order to get served. If the customer sits at a table the charge is considerably higher (at least double) and he will be given waiter service (and should not pay first). However some simple bars have a few tables which can be used with no extra charge (it is always best to ask before sitting down). Black coffee (*caffè* or *espresso*) can be ordered diluted (*alto* or *lungo* or *'americano'*), or with hot milk (*cappuccino*), or with a liquor (*'corretto'*). In summer, cold coffee (*caffè freddo*), or cold coffee and milk (*caffè-latte freddo*) are served.

Food and Wine. Characteristic dishes of the Italian cuisine, to be found all over the country, are included in the MENU given below. Many of the best dishes are regional specialities; these are given in a separate section at the end.

Antipasti, Hors d'oeuvre
Prosciutto crudo o cotto, Ham, raw or cooked
Prosciutto e melone, Ham (raw) and melon
Salame, Salami
Salame con funghi e carciofini sott'olio, Salami with mushrooms and artichokes in oil
Salsicce, Dry sausage
Tonno, Tuna fish
Fagioli e cipolle, Beans with onions
Carciofi o finocchio in pinzimonio, Raw artichokes or fennel with a dressing
Antipasto misto, Mixed cold hors d'œuvre
Antipasto di mare, Seafood hors d'œuvre
Bresaola, Cured beef
Crostini, Fresh liver paste served on bread (sometimes together with other 'homemade' paté)
Frittata, Omelette

Minestre e Pasta (Primi Piatti) Soups and pasta (First Courses)
Minestre, zuppa, Thick soup
Brodo, Clear soup
Minestrone alla toscana, Tuscan vegetable soup
Spaghetti al sugo or *al ragu*, Spaghetti with a meat sauce
Spaghetti al pomodoro, Spaghetti with a tomato sauce
Tagliatelle, Flat spaghetti-like pasta, almost always made with egg
Lasagne, Layers of pasta with meat filling and cheese and tomato sauce
Cannelloni, Rolled pasta with meat filling and cheese and tomato sauce
Ravioli, Pasta filled with spinach and ricotta cheese, or with minced veal
Tortellini, Small coils of pasta, filled with a rich stuffing served either in broth or with a sauce, or with cream
Agnolotti, Ravioli filled with meat
Fettuccine, Ribbon noodles
Spaghetti alla carbonara, Spaghetti with bacon, beaten egg, and black pepper sauce
Spaghetti alle vongole, Spaghetti with clams
Pappardelle alla lepre, Pasta with hare sauce
Gnocchi, A heavy pasta, made from potato, flour, and eggs
Risotto, Rice dish
Risotto alla Milanese, Rice with saffron and white wine
Stracciatella, Broth with beaten egg
Taglierini in brodo, Thin pasta in broth
Ribollita, Thick soup made with bread, white beans, cabbage, etc.
Pasta e fagioli, Pasta and beans
Penne all'arrabbiata (or *'Strascicata'*), Short pasta with a rich spicy sauce
Spaghetti alla matriciana, Spaghetti with salt pork and tomato sauce

Cappelletti, Form of ravioli, often served in broth
Polenta, Yellow maize flour, usually served with a meat or tomato sauce
Pappa di pomodoro, A thick tomato 'soup', with bread, seasoned with basil, etc.

Pesce, Fish (always more expensive than meat)
Zuppa di pesce, Various types of fish (usually in a sauce (or soup)
Fritto misto di mare, Various types of fried fish
Fritto di pesce, Fried fish
Pesce arrosto, Pesce alla griglia, Roast, grilled fish
Pescespada, Sword-fish
Aragosta, Lobster (an expensive delicacy)
Calamari, Squid
Sarde, Sardines
Coda di Rospo, Angler fish (monkfish)
Dentice, Dentex
Orata, Bream
Triglie, Red mullet
Sgombro, Mackerel
Baccalà (alla Livornese), Salt cod (fried and cooked in a tomato sauce)
Anguilla, Eel
Sogliola, Sole
Tonno, Tuna fish
Trota, Trout
Cozze, Mussels
Gamberi, Prawns
Polipi, Octopus
Seppie, Cuttlefish
Acciughe, Anchovies

Secondi Piatti, Main courses
Bistecca alla fiorentina, T-bone steak (usually cooked over charcoal)
Vitello, Veal
Manzo, Beef
Agnello, Lamb
Maiale (arrosto), Pork (roast)
Pollo (bollito), Chicken (boiled)
Costolette Milanese, Veal cutlets, fried in breadcrumbs
Costoletta alla Bolognese, Veal cutlet with ham, covered with melted cheese
Saltimbocca, Rolled veal with ham and sage
Bocconcini, As above, with cheese
Ossobuco, Stewed shin of veal
Spezzatino, Veal stew, usually with red pepper, tomatoes, onions, peas, and wine
Petto di pollo, Chicken breasts
Pollo alla cacciatore, Chicken with herbs and (usually) tomato and pimento sauce
Cotechino e Zampone, Pig's trotter stuffed with pork and sausages
Stracotto, Beef cooked in a sauce, or in red wine
Trippa, Tripe
Fegato, Calf's liver
Tacchino arrosto, Roast turkey
Cervello, Brains (usually served fried)
Bollito, Stew of various boiled meats
Fagiano, Pheasant
Coniglio, Rabbit
Lepre, Hare
Cinghiale, Wild boar
Scaloppine al marsala, Veal escalope cooked in wine
Coda alla vaccinara, Oxtail cooked with herbs and wine
Stufato, Stewed meat served in pieces in a sauce
Polpette, Meat balls (often served in a sauce)
Involtini, Thin rolled slices of meat in a sauce
Fegatini, Chicken livers cooked with sage
Fegatelli, Pork livers
Rosticciana, Grilled spare ribs
Arista, Pork chop
Rognoncini trifolati, Sliced kidneys in a sauce
Animelle, Sweetbreads
Piccione, Pigeon

Contorni, Vegetables
Insalata verde, Green salad
Insalata mista, Mixed salad
Pomodori, Tomatoes
Funghi, Mushrooms
Asparagi, Asparagus
Zucchine, Courgettes
Melanzane alla parmigiana, Aubergines in a cheese sauce
Radicchio rosso, Red chicory (in the Veneto, often served grilled)
Fagioli, Haricot (dried) beans
Peperonata, Stewed red peppers, often with aubergine, onion, tomato, potato, etc.
Spinaci, Spinach
Broccoletti, Tender broccoli
Piselli, Peas
Piselli al prosciutto, Peas cooked with bacon and parsley
Fagiolini, French beans
Carciofi, Artichokes
Peperoni, Red peppers
Finocchi, Fennel
Patatine fritte, Fried potatoes

Dolci, Sweets
Torta, Tart
Monte Bianco, Chestnut flavoured pudding
Zuppa inglese, Trifle
Panettone, Milanese sweet cake
Gelato, Ice cream
Sant Honorè, Rich meringue cake
Crostata, Fruit flan
Zabaione, A hot sweet with beaten eggs and Marsala wine

Frutta, Fruit
Fragole con panna, Strawberries and cream
Fragole al limone, Strawberries with lemon
Fragole al vino, Strawberries with wine
Fragoline di bosco, Wild strawberries
Melone, Melon
Cocomero or *Anguria,* Water melon
Mele, Apples
Pere, Pears
Arance, Oranges
Ciliegie, Cherries
Pesche, Peaches
Albicocche, Apricots
Uva, Grapes
Macedonia di frutta, Fruit salad
Fichi, Figs

Regional Dishes include:
Piedmont—*Fonduta,* a hot dip with fontina cheese, milk, and egg yolks sprinkled with truffles and white pepper
Bagna Cauda, a hot spicy sauce with garlic and anchovies used as a dip for raw vegetables
Bolliti misti (*con salsa verde*), various boiled meats stewed together (with a green sauce made with herbs)
Lombardy—*Risotto alla Milanese,* Rice cooked in broth with saffron
Zuppa Pavese, Clear soup with poached eggs
Veneto—*Fegato alla Veneziana,* Calf's liver thinly sliced fried with onions
Baccalà alla vicentina, Salt cod simmered in milk
Polenta, a maize flour cake served with a sauce as a pasta dish, or with sausages, game, fish etc.
Liguria—*Pesto,* a sauce made of fresh basil, garlic, pine nuts, and cheese and served with pasta
Tuscany—*Cacciucco alla livornese,* a stew of fish in a hot sauce
Tortino di carciofi, Baked artichoke pie
Panzanella, Summer salad made with bread, tomatoes, capers, basil, etc.
Fagioli all'uccelletto, Haricot beans in a tomato sauce
Baccalà alla livornese, Salt cod cooked in tomatoes, black olives and black pepper (an acquired taste)

Castagnaccio, Chestnut cake with pine nuts and sultanas
Umbria—*Porchetta,* Roast suckling pig with herbs, fennel, etc.

Italian Wines are very regional, and travellers will usually find the local carafe wine the best value for money. In Lombardy and Piedmont, the rather heavy red wines include *Barolo* and *Barbera*. Verona is the centre of the wines of the Veneto, somewhat lighter, among the best of which are *Soave, Bardolino,* and *Valpolicella*. The excellent wines of the Friuli region include *Pinot, Merlot, Tocai,* and *Cabernet*. The white wines of the Alto Adige are less well known but are well worth seeking out (particularly good are those from *Tramin, Lake Caldaro,* and *Novacella*). In Emilia, the sparkling red *Lambrusco* and *Sangiovese* are to be recommended and the white *Albana,* as well as the unusual *Fontanina* and *Malvasia di Maiatico*.

The most famous wine of central Italy is *Chianti* (the name is protected by law, and only those wines from a relatively small district which lies between Florence and Siena are entitled to the name 'Chianti Classico'). *Chianti Classico 'Gallo Nero'* (distinguished by a black cock on the bottle) is usually considered the best, but *Chianti 'Putto'* and *Chianti 'Grappolo'* are also very good. Other wines in Tuscany (where the red table wine is usually of better quality than the white) such as *Vino nobile di Montepulciano, Vernaccia* (white, from San Gimignano) *Aleatico* (a dessert wine from Elba), and *Brunello di Montalcino* (not cheap) are particularly good. In Umbria the red *Torgiano* and the white *Orvieto* are very popular. The Marches produce the dry, white *Verdicchio* in its distinctive bottle (excellent with fish).

Transport

Railways. The Italian State Railways (FS—Ferrovie dello Stato) now run five categories of trains. (1) *E.C. (Eurocity),* international express trains (with a special supplement, approximately 30 per cent of the normal single fare) running between the main Italian and European cities (seat reservation is sometimes obligatory). (2) *I.C. (Intercity),* express trains running between the main Italian towns, with a special supplement (on some of these seat reservation is obligatory, and some carry first class only). (3) *Espressi,* long-distance trains (both classes), not as fast as the 'Intercity' trains. (4) *Diretti,* although not stopping at every station, a good deal slower than the 'espressi'. (5) *Locali,* local trains stopping at all stations.

The **Eurocity** train services operating in Italy are as follows: Dortmund–Sestri Levante; Hamburg–Milan; Geneva –Milan; Zurich–Milan; Dortmund–Munich–Milan; Vienna–Rome; Geneva–Venice; Nuremburg–Munich–Rome; (with sleeping accommodation) Paris–Venice; Paris–Florence; Paris–Milan; and Paris–Rome.

In the last few years the Italian railways have been greatly improved, and the service reorganised. With the construction of the new 'direttissima' line between Rome and Florence the time of the journey between these two cities has been reduced to c two hours (on 'Intercity' trains). In 1989 an extra fast service was introduced (ETR.450) which has daily connections between Milan, Turin, Bologna, Florence (Rifredi station), Venice, and Padua (as well as Naples and Salerno). These trains which carry 1st class only, cost considerably more, and advance booking is obligatory (the price of the ticket includes restaurant service). The 'Pendolino' operates non-stop, reaching a maximum speed of 250km an hour, between Milan and Rome in just under 4 hours.

Trains in Italy are usually crowded, especially in summer; seats can be booked in advance from the main cities at the station booking office (or by telephoning 110). The timetable of the train services changes on about 25 September and 28 May every year. Excellent timetables are published twice a year in several volumes ('Nord e centro' covers the area in this book) by Pozzorario, and by the Italian State Railways ('L'Orario Ufficiale'; 1 volume for the whole of Italy). These can be purchased at newstands and railway stations.

Fares and Reductions. In Italy fares are still much lower than in England. Tickets must be bought at the station (or at Agencies for Italian State Railways) before the journey, otherwise a fairly large supplement has to be paid to the ticket-collector on the train. Time should be allowed for this as there are often long queues at the station ticket offices. Some trains carry 1st class only; some charge a special supplement; and on some seats must be booked in advance. It is therefore always advisable to specify which train one is intending to take as well as the destination when buying tickets. In the main stations the better known credit cards are now generally accepted. There are limitations on travelling short distances on some first-class 'Intercity' trains.

Children under the age of 4 travel free, and between the ages of 4 and 12 travel half price, and there are certain reductions for families. For travellers over the age of 60 (with Senior Citizen Railcards), the 'Rail Europ S' card offers a 30 per cent reduction on Italian rail fares. The Inter-rail card (valid 1 month) which can be purchased in Britain by young people up to the age of 26, is valid in Italy. The 'Biglietto Turistico di libera circolazione' ('Travel at Will ticket'), available for visitors, gives freedom of the Italian railways for 8, 15, 21, or 30 days. It is obtainable in Britain or at main stations in Italy. A 'Chilometrico' ticket is valid for two months for 3000 kilometres (and can be used by up to five people at the same time). There is a 15 per cent discount on Day Return tickets (maximum distance, 50km), and on 3-Day Return tickets (maximum distance 250km).

Left Luggage Offices are usually open 24 hrs at the main stations; at smaller stations they often close at night.—**Porters** are entitled to a fixed amount (shown on notice boards at all stations) for each piece of baggage.

RESTAURANT CARS (sometimes self-service) are attached to most international and internal long-distance trains. A lunch tray brought to the compartment (including three courses and wine, and costing slightly less) is a convenient way of having a meal while travelling. Also, on most express trains, snacks, hot coffee and drinks are sold throughout the journey from a trolley wheeled down the train. At every large station good snacks are on sale from trolleys on the platform and can be bought from the train window. Carrier-bags with sandwiches, drink and fruit ('cestini da viaggio') or individual sandwiches ('Panini') are available.

SLEEPING CARS with couchettes or first class cabins are also carried on certain trains, as well as 'Sleeperette' compartments with reclining seats (first class only).

Local Country Buses abound between the main towns, and offer an excellent alternative to the railways. It is difficult to obtain accurate information about these local bus services outside Italy. The principal

Italian coach companies which operate daily long-distance services include: *SITA*, 15 Via Santa Caterina da Siena, Florence; *Lazzi*, 4 Piazza Stazione, Florence; *Sadem*, Piazza Carlo Felice, Turin; and *Autostradale*, Piazza Castello, Milan. Details can be obtained from Citalia, London, or at the local tourist offices (A.P.T.) in Italy. (Some information is given in the text of the main towns, and at the beginning of routes.)

Air Services. Frequent internal flights are operated between most main towns (airports are indicated in the text).

Town Buses. Now that most towns have been partially closed to private traffic, town bus services are usually fast and efficient. In the larger cities, the main bus routes have been indicated in the text. It is now almost always necessary to purchase tickets before boarding (at tobacconists, bars, newspaper kiosks, information offices, etc.) and stamp them on board at automatic machines. Twenty-four hour tickets, monthly tickets, etc, are usually available in the larger cities.

Bicycle Hire. In the main cities, the municipality now sometimes provide bicycles (available at bicycle stands in several parts of the city) for the temporary use of residents and visitors.

Taxis (yellow or white in colour) are provided with taximeters; it is advisable to make sure these are operational before hiring a taxi. They are hired from ranks or by telephone; there are no cruising taxis. A small tip of about a thousand lire is expected. A supplement for night service, and for luggage is charged.

Driving in Italy

Temporary membership of the *Automobile Club d'Italia* (*ACI*) can be taken out on the frontier or in Italy. The headquarters of the ACI is at 8 Via Marsala, Rome (branch offices in all the main towns). Concessions gained from membership include parking facilities, legal assistance, and discounts on tolls and car hire. Also, a breakdown service is provided for foreign motorists by the *Soccorso ACI*.

It is obligatory to carry a red triangle in the car in case of accident or breakdown. This serves as a warning to other traffic when placed on the road at a distance of 50 metres from the stationary car. It can be hired from the ACI for a minimal charge, and returned at the frontier. In case of breakdown, the nearest ACI office can be contacted by telephone number 116. On the Autostrada del Sole (and some other motorways), there is an emergency press button box on the right of the road every two kilometres. It is now compulsory to wear seat-belts in the front seat of cars while driving in Italy.

PETROL COUPONS are at present (1990) available, for foreign motorists in Italy with a vehicle registered outside the country, who are entitled to purchase a certain number of petrol coupons at 15 per cent less than the market price of petrol in Italy. Petrol coupons can be purchased only outside Italy or at the frontier and cannot be paid for in Italian currency. There are four schemes according to the regions to be visited. Some motorway vouchers giving a slight discount on motorway tolls are included with petrol coupons. Information in Italy at ACI offices. Petrol coupons and motorway vouchers are issued with a Fuel card ('Carta Carburante') which can be used for the free breakdown service provided by ACI for foreign motorists. Petrol Coupons are available in England at Citalia, 50 Conduit Street, London WI and Wasteel Travel Ltd, 121 Wilton Road, London SW1 (or AA and RAC offices), or at ACI offices at frontier stations. Purchasers must present passports and car log book. Unused coupons can be refunded at the frontier, or by the issuing office.

Italian law requires drivers to carry a valid driving licence when travelling. Petrol Stations are normally closed between 12 or 12.30 and 14.30 or 15 (but do not close on motorways). British drivers in Italy may find the speed of the traffic much faster than in Britain.

Almost all towns now have part of their historic centre closed to traffic (although access is allowed to hotels, and for the disabled). Visitors are strongly recommended to park their cars on the outskirts (car parks have been indicated in the text) and explore towns by foot (or by public transport). Near the centre of towns car parking is usually extremely difficult (if allowed at all). Valuables should never be left in parked cars. When leaving a car parked on a street, it should be borne in mind that once a week street cleaning takes place at night and so cars have to be removed (or they may be fined and towed away); ask locally for information.

Car Hire. Self-drive hire is available in most Italian cities. Arrangements for the hire of cars in Italy can be made through Alitalia or British Airways (at specially advantageous rates in conjunction with their flights) or through any of the principal car-hire firms (the most well-known include Maggiore, Avis, and Hertz). It should be noted that travellers hiring cars in Italy are not entitled to petrol coupons.

Italian Motorways (Autostrade). Italy probably has the finest motorways in Europe, although in the last ten years or so too many have been constructed to the detriment of the countryside. Tolls are charged according to the rating of the vehicle and the distance covered. There are Service areas on all autostrade, and some of them have SOS points every two kilometres. On motorways cars with foreign number plates can sometimes use coupons which reduce the tolls (see above).

The Autostrada del Sole (Milan–Rome) continues to the S. The E coast of Italy from Trieste to Bari is now served by autostrade. In the north, autostrade connect Milan, Turin, Modena, Padua, Verona, Venice, Bologna, and the other main cities, and there is an autostrada along the coast from Ventimiglia to Livorno. **'Superstrade'** are dual carriageway fast roads which do not charge tolls and which do not have service stations or SOS points. Generally speaking travel by car in Italy is much more pleasant on ordinary roads.

Maps. The Italian Touring Club publishes several sets of excellent maps: these are constantly up-dated and are indispensable to anyone travelling by car in Italy. They include the *Grande Carta stradale d'Italia* on a scale of 1:200,000. This is divided into 15 sheets covering the regions of Italy, of which nine ('Piemonte, Valle d'Aosta'; 'Lombardia'; 'Trentino-Alto Adige'; 'Veneto, Friuli-Venezia Giulia'; 'Liguria'; 'Emilia-Romagna'; 'Toscana'; 'Umbria, Marche'; and 'Lazio') refer to the area dealt with in this guide. These are also published in a handier form as an atlas (with an index), called the 'Atlante stradale d'Italia' (two volumes, 'Nord' and 'Centro' cover the area in this book). They also produce larger scale maps: the 'Carta turistica d'Italia', on a scale of 1:400,000 (3 sheets), and the 'Carta Stradale d'Italia', on a scale of 1:800,000 (1 sheet for this area). Special maps at 1:50,000 are also available for certain popular Alpine areas and national parks. All these maps can be purchased from the Italian Touring Club Offices and at many booksellers; in London they are obtainable at the RAC, Stanford's, 12–14 Long Acre, WC2, and McCarta Ltd, 122 King's Cross Road, WCI.

The *Istituto Geografico Militare* of Italy has for long been famous for its map production (much of it done by aerial photography). Their headquarters are in Florence (10 Via Cesare Battisti). Their maps are now available at numerous bookshops in the main towns of Italy. They publish a map of Italy on a scale of 1:100,000 in 277 sheets, and a field survey partly 1:50,000, partly 1:25,000, which are invaluable for the detailed exploration of the country, especially its more mountainous regions; the coverage is, however, still far from complete at the larger scales.

General Information

Season. The best months for a visit to the greater part of northern Italy are September and October, and May and June, although there is always a risk of rain. The earlier spring months, though often dry and sunny, are sometimes unexpectedly chilly, with strong northerly winds. In Umbria and Tuscany, however, the green countryside is very beautiful in early spring before the main tourist season. The height of the summer is unpleasantly hot, especially in the Po valley and the larger towns, and in the low basin of Florence, which is enclosed by hills. Winter days in Milan or Venice are sometimes as cold and wet as an English winter. The Tuscan autumn is particularly lovely. The upper Alpine valleys of Piedmont, Lombardy, and the Dolomites are cool in summer, while the winter sports season in the high Alpine resorts is becoming more popular every year and is extended even to midsummer in the high Alps. Seaside resorts are crowded from mid-June to early September; before and after this season many hotels are closed and the bathing-beaches are practically deserted.

Churches are normally closed for a considerable period during the middle of the day (12 to 15, 16, or 17), although cathedrals and some of the large churches (indicated in the text) may be open without a break during daylight hours. Smaller churches and oratories are often open only in the early morning, but it is sometimes possible to find the key by inquiring locally. The sacristan will also show closed chapels, crypts, etc., and a small tip should be given. Some churches now ask that sightseers do not enter during a service, but normally visitors may do so, provided they are silent and do not approach the altar(s) in use. An entrance fee is becoming customary for admission to treasuries, cloisters, bell-towers, etc. Lights (operated by 100 lire coins) have now been installed in many churches to illuminate frescoes and altarpieces, but a torch and binoculars are always useful. Sometimes visitors are not allowed to enter important churches wearing shorts or with bare shoulders.

Museums. The opening times of state-owned museums and monuments are in the process of change: they are usually open 9–14, fest. 9–13, but in some cases they are now also open in the afternoon. On Monday, for long the standard closing day, many museums are now staying open (so that they remain open 7 days a week). However, there is not, as yet, a standard timetable, and great care should be taken to allow enough time for variations in the hours shown in the text when planning a visit to a museum or monument. *Opening times vary and often change without warning*: when possible it is always advisable to consult local tourist offices on arrival about the up-to-date times. Some museums etc. are closed on the main public holidays: 1 January, Easter, 1 May, 15 August, and Christmas Day (but there is now a policy to keep at least some of them open on these days in the larger cities; information has to be obtained about these on the spot). Admission charges vary, but are usually between Lire 5000 and Lire 2000. British citizens under the age of 18 and over the age of 60 are entitled to free admission to state-owned museums and monuments in Italy (because of reciprocal arrangements in Britain). The 'Settimana per i Beni Culturali e Ambienti' is usually held early in December when for a week there is free entrance to all state-owned museums and others are specially opened, etc.

Public Holidays. The Italian National Holidays when offices, shops, and schools are closed are as follows: 1 January (New Year), 25 April (Liberation Day), Easter Monday, 1 May (Labour Day), 15 August (Assumption), 1 November (All Saints' Day), 8 December (Conception), Christmas Day and 26 December (St Stephen). Each town keeps its Patron Saint's day as a holiday, e.g. Venice (25 April, St Mark), Florence, Genoa, and Turin (24 June, St John the Baptist), Bologna (4 October, St Petronius), Milan (7 December, St Ambrose).

Concerts and Annual Festivals. The Opera season in Italy usually begins in December and continues until April or May. The principal opera houses in northern Italy are La Scala in Milan, La Fenice in Venice, and the Teatro Comunale in Florence. During the summer operas are performed in the open air in the Arena of Verona.

Annual MUSIC AND DRAMA FESTIVALS take place in many towns; among the most famous international festivals are the Festival of the Two Worlds in Spoleto (June and July), the Maggio Musicale in Florence (May–July), and the Drama Festival in the Roman Theatre at Verona (June–September). Details of their programmes are widely published in advance. Annual festivals are celebrated in most towns and villages in commemoration of a local historical or religious event, and are often very spectacular (the most well known are mentioned in the text). Among the most famous are the Palio in Siena (2 July and 16 August), and the Football Match in 16C costume in Florence (usually on three consecutive Sundays in June).

Telephones and Postal Information. Stamps are sold at tobacconists (displaying a blue 'T' sign), and Post Offices (open 8.15–14, Monday–Saturday). Correspondence can be addressed c/o the Post Office by adding 'Fermo Posta' to the name of the locality. It is always advisable to post letters at Post Offices or Railway Stations; collection from letterboxes may be erratic. There are numerous public telephones all over Italy in bars, restaurants, kiosks, etc. These are operated by coins, or by metal disks (200 lire) known as 'gettone' which are bought from tobacconists, bars, some newspaper stands, and Post Offices.

Newspapers. The most widely read northern Italian newspapers are the *Corriere della Sera* of Milan, the *Stampa* of Turin, *La Nazione* of Florence, *Il Resto del Carlino* of Bologna, and *La Repubblica* of Rome. Foreign newspapers are readily obtainable at central street kiosks and railway stations.

Working Hours. Government offices usually work from 8–13.30 or 14 six days a week. Shops (clothes, hardware, hairdressers, etc.) generally open from 9–13, 16–19.30, including Saturday, and for most of the year are closed on Monday morning. Food shops usually open from 8–13, 17–19.30 or 20, and for most of the year are closed on Wednesday afternoon. From mid-June to mid-September all shops are closed instead on Saturday afternoon. Banks are usually open Monday–Friday 8.20–13.20, and for one hour in the afternoon (usually 14.30 or 15–15.30 or 16). They are closed on Saturday & holidays, and close early (about 11.00) on days preceding national holidays.

Public Conveniences. There is a notable shortage of public conveniences in Italy. All bars (cafés) should have toilets available to the public (generally speaking the larger the bar, the better the facilities). Nearly all museums now have toilets. In larger towns there are 'Alberghi diurni' which have pay toilets.

Health Service. British citizens, as members of the EEC, have the right to claim health services in Italy if they are in possession of the Form E111 (obtainable from the Department of Health and Social Security). There are also a number of private holiday health insurance policies. First Aid services ('Pronto Soccorso') are available at all hospitals, railway stations, and airports. **Chemist Shops** ('Farmacie') are usually open Monday–Friday, 9–13, 15.30–19.30. On Saturdays and Sundays (and holidays) a few are open (listed on the door of every chemist). In every town there is also at least one chemist shop open at night (also shown on the door of every chemist). For emergencies, dial 113.

I PIEDMONT AND LIGURIA

The ancient principality of **Piedmont** (since 1970, a Region), the cradle of the Italian nation, with 4,432,000 inhabitants in an area of 25,399 sq. km, is divided into the provinces of Alessandria, Asti, Cuneo, Novara, Turin, and Vercelli, and the autonomous region of the Val d'Aosta. Physically the region occupies the upper basin of the Po, and, as its name implies, lies mainly 'at the foot of the mountains' which encircle it—the Pennine, Graian, Cottian, and Maritime Alps. The cultural relations of Piedmont with France have always been very close, and the French language was used at the Court and Parliament of Turin down to the days of Cavour, and its influence survives in the Piedmontese dialects.

Historically Piedmont combines the territories of the old marquessates of Ivrea and Monferrato and of the county of Turin; the name Piedmont does not occur until the 13C. In 1045 the territory of Turin

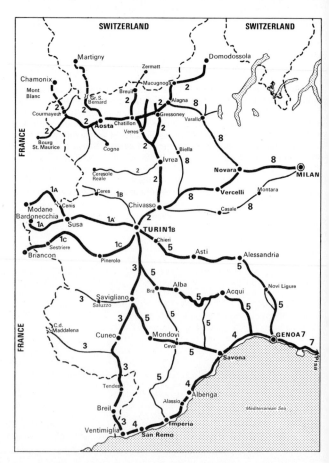

came into the hands of the House of Savoy by the marriage of Adelaide of Susa with Otho (Oddone), son of Humbert the White-Handed, Count of Savoy, and the provincial history from then onwards followed the fortunes of the House of Savoy. These princes, faced with the movement towards civic independence in the 12–13C, did not, like most of the feudal families of Italy, lose hold of their lands, and in the 14C, under the guidance of the Green Count and the Red Count (Amadeus VI and VII), the princely house gained so much power that Amadeus VIII was made Duke of Savoy by the Emperor in 1391. Under him Vercelli was annexed, and the life of the province became orientated more towards Italy. In the 16C another period of activity began, under Emmanuel Philibert and Charles Emmanuel I, and Saluzzo was added to Piedmont. In 1714 Monferrato was included by treaty in the dominions of the Savoy princes, and in 1720 Victor Amadeus II, appointed King of Sicily in 1713, was awarded the Kingdom of Sardinia in exchange for the other island. The Piedmontese kingdom, like all other Italian states, was obliterated by the Napoleonic conquests, but the Treaty of Vienna reinstated the Savoy kings at Turin and gave them suzerainty over Liguria in addition. Victor Emmanuel II, who, thanks to the astuteness of his minister Cavour, had taken part in the Crimean War, and so won the goodwill of France and England, found a powerful though expensive ally in Napoleon III when the second War of Italian Independence, against Austria, broke out in 1859. The Austrian army was crushed in a succession of defeats, and Lombardy was annexed to Piedmont after the final victory of Solferino. The Piedmontese dominions west of the Alps (Savoy and Nice) were handed over to France, and the remaining Italian provinces were added one by one to Victor Emmanuel's kingdom. In 1865 he transferred his capital from Turin to Florence, and the history of Piedmont became merged in the history of Italy. By the peace treaty of 1947 the districts of Tenda and Briga in the Maritime Alps were ceded to France, after a plebiscite; and this, with some minor adjustments of the frontier at the Montgenèvre, Mont Cenis, and Little St Bernard passes, reduced the provincial area by c 140 sq. km. At the same time the Val d'Aosta was granted a special measure of autonomy.

Liguria comprises the strip of land lying between the Mediterranean and the summits of the Maritime Alps and the Apennines from the frontier of France to the borders of Tuscany. It is the smallest in area, though not in population, of the ancient Italian provinces (1,853,000 inhab.; 5413 sq. km) and is made up of the provinces of Genoa, Imperia, La Spezia, and Savona. It was designated a Region in 1970. It includes two of the most fertile stretches of the Italian coastline—the Riviera di Ponente and the Riviera di Levante—respectively W and E of Genoa—where the mild winter climate encourages a luxuriant growth of vegetation, including palms, oranges, and lemons, and the cultivation of flowers in early spring is important.

The Ligurian people, occupying a territory that has always been easier of access by sea than by land, are noted seafarers, and they have been influenced by immigrations from overseas rather than by landward invasions. Traces of Punic and Greek relations are evident, superimposed on the rather primitive civilisation of the native Ligurians (about whom little definite is known), and later Genoa became an important Roman seaport. Less exposed, on the whole, by its inaccessibility, to the incursions of the Gothic invaders of Italy,

Liguria was all the more open to the attacks of the Saracenic corsairs of the later Middle Ages, and the medieval importance of Genoa sprang from the measures of organised defence taken against these pirates. The aristocratic republic of Genoa ruled the destinies of the whole seaboard from the 13C to the days of Napoleon, reaching its apogee as a colonising power after the rival republic of Pisa had been crushed in 1290, but suffering a severe check at the hands of Venice in 1380. In the succeeding centuries Savona and the towns of the Western Riviera, jealous of Genoa, took advantage of the factious spirit of the times, and Liguria fell alternately into the power of Lombard, Piedmontese, and French overlords. The revival of local energy under Andrea Doria in the 16C was short-lived. The Napoleonic campaigns of 1796 and 1799 resulted first in the creation of a 'Ligurian Republic' and then of the absorption of the province into the French Empire; but in 1815 Liguria was attached to the kingdom of Piedmont. Genoa played an important part in the history of the Risorgimento, and Ligurian vessels provided transport for Garibaldi's attack on Sicily in 1860. In the Second World War the coastal area, especially Genoa, suffered severely from air attack.

1   Western Piedmont

A.   Modane to Turin

ROAD, 108·5km, through the Mont Cenis tunnel.—20·5km *Bardonecchia.* N 335.—54km **Susa.** N 25.—85km *Avigliana.*—108·5km **Turin.**

A new motorway from Bardonecchia to Turin is under construction parallel to the crowded old road.

RAILWAY, 106km, via the Mont Cenis Tunnel in 1¼–1¾hrs. This route is followed by through trains from Paris to Rome. The line has recently been improved.

The *Mont Cenis Railway Tunnel* or *Tunnel du Fréjus*, which crosses the Franco-Italian frontier, begun in 1857 and finished in 1871 on the plans of the engineers Sommeiller, Grandis, and Grattoni, was the first great Transalpine tunnel and reaches a summit level of 1295m. It had an immediate effect on world communications, speeding the transmission of mail from the East to northern Europe by several days, with Brindisi replacing Marseille as the transit port. Originally 12·2km long, the tunnel was realigned in 1881 and again after the Second World War and is now 12·8km long. Cars were carried by train through the tunnel from 1935 until the opening of the road tunnel in 1980.

From Modane in France (see 'Blue Guide France') it is a short way to *Freney* with the French and Italian frontier-posts at the mouth of the **Mont Cenis Tunnel** (*Traforo del Frejus*), the second longest road tunnel in Europe (12·8km; the new St Gotthard tunnel is over 16km long). It was begun by France and Italy in 1974–75 and opened to traffic in 1980. The motorway through the tunnel (toll; 12m wide) ascends from 1228m to 1296m at the Italian exit.

An alternative route to Turin (113km) crosses the **Mont Cenis Pass**. From Modane the N6 climbs via (22km) *Lanslebourg* (1399m) to (32km) the Mont Cenis Pass or *Colle del Moncenisio* (2081m). The Mont Cenis Pass is one of the historic passes over the Alps, crossed by Pepin the Short (755), Charlemagne (774), and Charles the Bald (877) and many other sovereigns with their armies. It is probable, however, that Hannibal crossed by the Col du Clapier (but see p 83). Before the carriage road was constructed by Napoleon in 1803–13 the old road from Italy terminated at Novalesa (see below). Here travellers could choose to negotiate the pass either on mule-back or, as was the case with Edward Gibbon on his way from Lausanne to Rome in 1764, in a wicker chair in the hands of the 'dexterous and intrepid Chairmen of the Alps'. The Italians attacked the pass in June 1940 but were unable to storm its defences.—The road descends past the huge lake of Moncenisio (1974m) used for hydroelectricity. The ancient *Hospice du Mont-Cenis* founded by Louis the Debonair c 815 at the instance of St Heldrad, abbot of Novalesa, and enlarged in 1811 was submerged when a dam was built to enlarge the lake. —The former hotel at (39km) *Grand' Croix* is now the French frontier-post. The actual frontier, moved to this point from the pass itself in 1947, is c 2km farther on, and the Italian frontier-post is at (50km) *Molaretto* (1139m) below an abrupt zigzag.— 59km Susa, see below.

20·5km **Bardonecchia** lies in a wide basin at the junction of several valleys. It is visited by the Torinese as a ski-resort in both winter and summer. The old village (3000 inhab.) has good 14C stalls in its church.

A by-road leads to (2·5km) *Mélezet* and, on the French border, *Pian del Colle*, with its 15C frescoed chapel. Beyond lies the Valle Stretta and Vallée Etroite. There are other interesting little mountain churches at *Millaures*, 3km E, and *Rochemolles*, 6·5km N. A chair-lift ascends in two stages to 2026m on *Monte Colomion* (2053m; *View of the Pelvoux range).

Road and railway descend the picturesque glen of the Dora di Bardonecchia via (24km) *Beaulard* (1217m) to 30·5km. **Oulx** (1121m), a scattered village and an important centre for mountain excursions. Here the road joins the N24 coming down the Dora Riparia from the Montgenèvre pass and Cesana Torinese (11km; see Rte 1C).

Sauze d'Oulx (1510m), 5km SE, is one of the most famous skiing resorts in Piedmont. Its old church is surrounded by many huge new residential buildings. It is connected by cableway with Sportinia (2148m) on a pleasant forested plateau below Monte Triplex (2506m).

Road and railway now follow the combined waters of the Dora down the Valle di Susa.—At (36·5km) *Salbertrand* the Waldensians defeated the French in 1689. It is surrounded by woods and has a fine parish church (1506–36).—42km *Exilles*, is dominated by an old fort.—46·5km *Chiomonte* has two Romanesque churches, and an electric power station on the river. The dolphin symbol which appears carved here and there recalls that this valley belonged to Dauphiny until transferred to Turin in 1713. It is a winter sports resort (chairlifts).—On the following steep descent the road twice passes under the railway.

54km **Susa** (502m), an interesting old town (7200 inhab.), stands at the junction of the main roads over the Montgenèvre and Mont Cenis passes on the Dora Riparia.

Susa, the Roman *Segusio*, was the seat of the Gaulish chief Cottius who received the dignity of prefect from Augustus and gave his name to the surrounding *Cottian Alps* (Alpi Cozie). The town was burned in 1173 by Barbarossa in revenge for its rebellion against him in 1168.

SAN GIUSTO, a cathedral since 1772, is a notable 11C church (W front restored), with a fine massive tower. It has 14C stalls, and in the S transept are an incomplete polyptych attributed to Bergognone (with Saints Hugh of Lincoln and Hugh of Grenoble) and a wooden figure of a kneeling lady (16C). In the SE chapel is the *Triptych of Rocciamelone, a Flemish brass of 1358 (shown on

5 August), with the Madonna, Saints George and John the Baptist, and the donor.

The triptych was originally in a chapel on the summit of the *Rocciamelone* (3538m), which rises to the N; it was carried there by Bonifacio Rotario, a Piedmontese nobleman, in fulfilment of a vow made in a Turkish prison in 1358. The mountain is now crowned by a bronze statue of the Virgin (1900; pilgrimage on 4–5 August).

Passing under the 4C *Porta Savoia*, Via Archi ascends past the Parco d'Augusto to the *Arco di Augusto*, an arch erected in 8 BC by Cottius in honour of Augustus, decorated with processional reliefs. Higher up is a double Roman arch, with remains of an aqueduct. Excavations here have revealed remains of Roman baths. Below a tower of the *Castle* of Countess Adelaide (11C; small archaeological museum) is Piazza della Torre, with the best of the medieval mansions of the town (13C). The tall Romanesque tower to the left is that of *Santa Maria Maggiore* (church destroyed), while SW of the town is the 13C church of *San Francesco*, with ruined 15C frescoes. Nearby is a small Roman *Amphitheatre* (2C AD?).

Novalesa, a little over 8km N of Susa, is at the end of the old Mont Cenis road (see above). Here are the remains of the Benedictine *Abbazia di Novalesa*, founded in 726. A famous centre of learning in the Middle Ages (Charlemagne stayed here in 773), it was suppressed under Napoleon, but the Benedictines returned here in 1973. The main church was rebuilt in 1712, but several Romanesque (11C) chapels survive, only one of them (St Eldrado), containing 12C or 13C frescoes, now serving as such.
   The church of (4km) *Giaglione*, to the left of the Mont Cenis road, has remarkable external paintings of the 15C (Cardinal Virtues and Deadly Sins).

The road (alternative route on either bank of the Dora) descends the Valle di Susa, passing (62km) *Bussoleno*, with its 12C campanile, and, on the opposite bank of the river, the ruined castle of *San Giorio*.— The river is crossed at (69km) *Borgone*.—81km *Sant'Ambrogio di Torino*, where the parish church was built by Bernardo Antonio Vittone in 1760–63.—85km *Avigliana*, an ancient little town (8800 inhab.) with many fine old mansions of the 15C, is dominated by a ruined castle of the Counts of Savoy. The church of San Giovanni contains two paintings by Defendente Ferrari, and the Romanesque church of San Pietro is interesting.

A road traverses the isthmus between two small lakes and ascends (right) to (14km) the **Sacra di San Michele** (962m), a famous abbey founded c 1000 and suppressed in 1622. The buildings (open 9–12, 15–19; 9–12, 14–dusk in winter), which stand on the end of the ridge of Monte Pirchiriano overlooking the valley from a height of 610m (*View of the valley and the Alps), were enlarged in the 12C. The 154 rock-hewn steps of the *Scalone dei Morti* pass beneath the *Porta dello Zodiaco*, with Romanesque sculptures (1135) to reach the *Church*, a 12–13C building, with remains of older work and supported by massive substructures. The crypt contains tombs of the House of Savoy-Carignano. On the high altar is a triptych of the Madonna enthroned by Defendente Ferrari (restored in 1986).

89km The *Abbey Church of Sant'Antonio di Ranverso*, to the right of the road, is one of the most interesting buildings in Piedmont. Founded in 1188, it was extended in the 13–14C, while in the 15C the apse and the strange façade, with its sharply-gabled doorways and terracotta decorations, were added. The interior (open 9–12, 15–18; winter 9–12, 14–17; except Friday & Monday; visitors are conducted by a guide) has 15C frescoes and a polyptych of the Nativity by Defendente Ferrari (1531) on the high altar. The presbytery and sacristy contain good frescoes by Giacomo Jaquerio. The tower and the little cloister are Romanesque.—From (94km) *Rivoli* into the centre of (108km) **Turin**, see the end of Rte IB.

B. Turin and environs

TURIN, in Italian **Torino**, the chief town (1,168,000 inhab.) of Piedmont and the capital of the former kingdom of Sardinia, is one of the most important industrial centres of Italy, famous since 1899 as the site of the Fiat motor works. It stands on the Po at the confluence of the Dora Riparia in a plain at the foot of the Alps, whose summits are visible to the west, while to the east the foothills beyond the Po complete the panorama. The town itself is regularly built on a Roman plan consciously developed in the 17–18C, which gives it a European air. The centre of the city presents a remarkably homogeneous nineteenth century aspect, while trams still traverse the long straight streets. Most of the palace façades of the city have been cleaned in recent years. Although one of the least visited large towns in Italy, Turin also has notable artistic and archaeological collections.

Railway Stations. *Porta Nuova* (Pl. 9), the main station, for all services. *Porta Susa* (Pl. 1), a secondary station on the Milan, Domodossola, and Aosta lines, at which all trains call; also for the line to Pont Canavese.—*Torino Céres* (Pl. 3), for Cirié, Lanzo, and Céres, was closed in 1988.

Airport, *Caselle*, 16km N, with services to Milan, Rome, London, Paris, etc.—*Air Terminal* (Pl. 1), Corso Inghilterra (corner of Via Cavalli). Buses to the airport c every hour.

Information Office, *A.P.T.*, 222 Via Roma, and at Porta Nuova Station.—**Post Office** (Pl. 6), 10 Via Alfieri.

Car Parking near the centre of the city is difficult. Via XX Settembre and Via Arsenale are open only to cars with special permits, and Via Garibaldi is a pedestrian precinct. Limited car parking available in Corso Galileo Ferraris (Pl. 5), Piazza Solferino (Pl.6), and near the Station (Piazza Carlo Felice; Pl. 9,10).

Public Transport. Trams. **4**: *Via XX Settembre* (near the main railway station) to the *Duomo*; and **1**: *Stazione Porta Nuova*—Corso Vittorio Emanuele II—*Stazione Porta Susa.*—**15**. *Station* (Corso Vittorio Emanuele)—Via XX Settembre—*Piazza Castello*—Via Po—Piazza Vittorio Veneto—Via Napione—Corso Regina Margherita—Corso Belgio—Corso Casale—*Sassi* (for the Superga cogtramway).—**13**. *Stazione Porta Susa*—Via Cernaia—Via Micca—*Piazza Castello*—Via Po—Piazza Vittorio Veneto—*Piazza Gran Madre di Dio* (at the foot of Monte de Cappuccini). **16**. *Piazza Repubblica*—Corso Regina Margherita—Via Rossini—Corso San Maurizio—Via Bava—Piazza Vittorio Veneto—Corso Cairoli—Corso Vittorio Emanuele II—Corso Massimo d'Azeglio (*Parco del Valentino*).—**Buses. 67**. *Largo Marconi*—Corso Marconi—Corso Massimo d'Azeglio—Piazza Zara—Corso Moncalieri—Via Bogino—Via Cavour—*Moncalieri.*—**35**. *Stazione Porta Nuova*—Lingotto. **Suburban buses. 41**. Corso Vittorio—*Stupinigi*. **36**. Corso Francia—*Rivoli*.

Country Buses from the Bus Station (Pl. 1) to *Sestriere, Milan, Valle d'Aosta*, etc., and from Corso Marconi (corner of Via Nizza; Pl. 9) to *Cuneo, Saluzzo, Alba*, etc.

Guided Tours of the city by tram (with lunch on board) are organised by Franco Rosso Italia, 61 Via Roma, from May–October.

THEATRES. *Regio* (Pl. 7), Piazza Castello, the opera-house; *Stabile di Torino*, 215 Piazza Castello; *Carignano*, Piazza Carignano; *Alfieri*, Piazza Solferino; *Nuovo*, Palazzo Torino Esposizioni.—CONCERTS. *Auditorium della R.A.I.* (Pl. 7), 15 Via Rossini; *Conservatoire Giuseppe Verdi*, 11 Via Mazzini.

History. The marriage of Countess Adelaide (died 1090), heiress of a line of French counts of Savoy, to Oddone (Otho), son of Humbert 'the White-handed', united the Cisalpine and Transalpine possessions of the House of Savoy, and Turin became their capital. After a period of semi-independence in the 12–13C, the city consistently followed the fortunes of the princely house of Savoy. In 1506–62 it was occupied by the French, but it was awarded to Duke Emmanuel

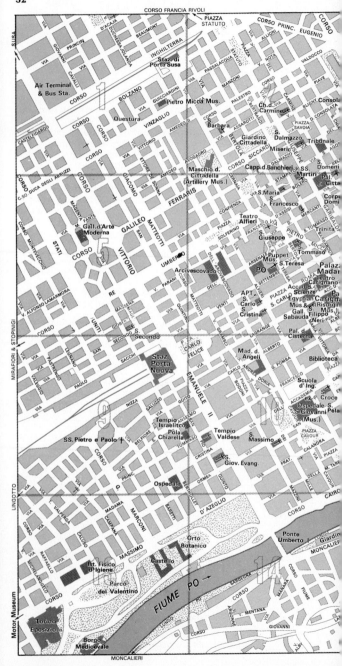

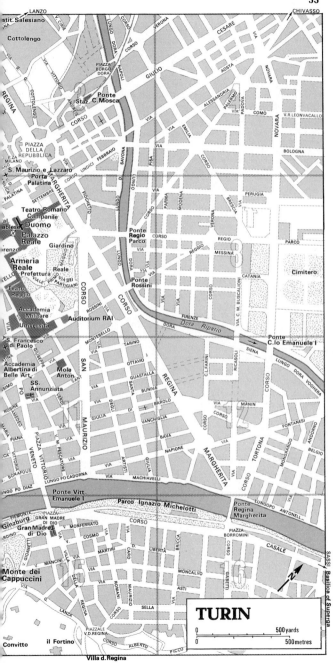

TURIN

0   500 yards
0   500 metres

Philibert 'the Iron-Headed' by the Treaty of Cateau-Cambrésis (1559). In 1639–40 and in 1706 it was besieged, being relieved on the latter occasion by the heroic action of Pietro Micca, a Piedmontese sapper, who exploded a mine and saved the beleaguered citadel at the cost of his life. From 1720 Turin was capital of the kingdom of Sardinia, and after the Napoleonic occupation (1798–1814) it became a centre of Italian nationalism, and the headquarters of Camillo Cavour (1810–61), a native of the town and the prime mover of Italian liberty. Silvio Pellico lived here from 1838 until his death in 1854. In 1861–65 it was the capital of Victor Emmanuel II (1820–78) as King of Italy. During the Second World War, Allied air raids caused heavy and scattered damage. Since the War ugly new suburbs have grown up around the city to accommodate the huge number of immigrants from the S of Italy who have been able to find work here.—Besides Cavour and Victor Emmanuel II (as well as many other distinguished princes of the House of Savoy), Turin's famous natives include the mathematician Joseph Lagrange (1736–1813), the physicist Amedeo Avogadro (1776–1856), the politician, author, and painter Massimo d'Azeglio (1798–1866), and the sculptor Carlo Marochetti (1805–68). The unfortunate Princesse de Lamballe (1749–92), friend of Marie Antoinette, was also born at Turin. The artists known as the 'Gruppo dei Sei' were influential in Turin from about 1928 until 1935; one of the them was Carlo Levi, born here in 1902 (died 1975). The writer Cesare Pavese committed suicide in the Albergo Roma in the city in 1950 (at the age of 42). The writer Primo Levi (1919–87) was born in Turin.

The centre of the civic life of Turin is included in the area lying between Corso Vittorio Emanuele, Corso Galileo Ferraris and its continuations, Corso Regina Margherita and Corso San Maurizio, and the Po. Roughly bisecting this area is the fashionable VIA ROMA (Pl. 6), lined with wide arcades, which connects the main station with Piazza Castello; and on either side of it and parallel with it are streets laid out at right angles.

The main railway station, STAZIONE DI PORTA NUOVA (Pl. 9) was built in 1868 and has a monumental façade in the form of an arch (by Alessandro Mazzucchetti and Carlo Ceppi) which was designed to close the vista from Via Roma. It faces Piazza Carlo Felice (1823–55), with a garden, and half-way along Via Roma is the arcaded PIAZZA SAN CARLO (Pl. 6) a handsome monumental square begun in 1640 (unfortunately now used as a car park). Here are the twin churches of *San Carlo* and *Santa Cristina*, the latter with a façade by Filippo Juvarra (1715–18) and 18C stucco decoration on the vault in the interior. The *Monument to Duke Emmanuel Philibert* (1838), whose equestrian figure ('el caval d'brôns') is shown sheathing his sword after the victory of St Quentin (1557), is considered the masterpiece of the local sculptor Carlo Marochetti. The two long yellow and grey palazzi have wide porticoes, beneath which are several cafés, including, on the corner of Via San Teresa, the well-known *Caffè San Carlo*. On the opposite side of the piazza, *Palazzo Solaro del Borgo* (No. 183), partly reconstructed by Benedetto Alfieri in 1753, is the seat of the Accademia Filarmonica and the Circolo del Whist, an exclusive club with delightful 18C premises.

At the end of the piazza (right; entrance on Via Accademia delle Scienze) is the **Palazzo dell'Accademia delle Scienze** (Pl. 6) with a fine exterior (restored in 1989), built for the Jesuits by Guarino Guarini (1678). The *Accademia delle Scienze*, founded in 1757, has had its seat here since 1783. The building also houses the Egyptian Museum (on the ground floor and first floor), and the Galleria Sabauda (on the second floor and third floor). The famous ***Egyptian Museum** has the third most important collection of Egyptian antiquities in existence, after Cairo and London. Admission 9–14;

Thursday & Saturday also 15–19.30; fest. 9–13; closed Monday. It is undergoing radical restoration and reorganisation.

The real founder of this remarkable museum was Charles Felix, who in 1824 bought the collections of Bernardo Drovetti, the trusted counsellor of Mohammed Ali. Later important acquisitions came from the expeditions of Schiaparelli (1903–20) and Farina (1930–37), notably in the Theban region, at Ghebelein (Aphroditopolis), Qau el-Kebir (Antaepolis, near Assiut), and Heliopolis. The museum played a leading part in the rescue digs in Nubia before the completion of the Aswan high dam, and was rewarded with the **Rock Temple of Ellessya** (15C BC); this was transported by sea in sections via Genoa in 1967 and has been reconstructed complete with its bas-relief frieze showing Thothmes III.

The large sculptures are on the GROUND FLOOR: ROOM I. Colossal Pharaonic head (XVIII Dynasty); black diorite *Statue of Rameses II (1299–33 BC), statues of Amenhotep II (XVIII Dynasty), of Thothmes I (XVIII Dynasty); Horemheb and his wife (end of XVIII Dynasty); figures of Sekhmet, the lion-headed goddess, and of Ptah.—RII. *Seated figure of Thothmes III (1496–1422 BC); sarcophagus of the court official Gemnefharbak (XXVI Dynasty); naos of Sethi I, from Heliopolis (XIX Dynasty); statue of Tutankhamen, with the god Amen-ra (XVIII Dynasty). Another room contains the reconstructed Rock Temple of Ellessya (see above).

FIRST FLOOR. In ROOM I (right), round the walls are tombstones.—In the centre are the most important discoveries from Heliopolis (fragments of reliefs from the time of Zoser: III Dynasty); Qau el-Kebir (objects of the XII Dynasty, including fine limestone heads); and Ghebelein (objects of the II–XII Dynasty). Many pieces are from Deir el Medina (tomb-gateway of the XIX–XX Dynasty, and fine wooden statuettes).—RII contains mummies and mummy-cases, scarabs, amulets, Canopic vases, ushabti figures, and several copies of the funerary papyrus, the 'Book of the Dead'; in the middle window, fragments of a mummy-case inlaid with enamel.—RIII. Egyptian archaeological material arranged chronologically, from the Predynastic to the Coptic periods. It gives an excellent idea of the evolution of Egypt over the centuries. This room contains, on the left, a reconstruction of a frescoed funerary chapel (XVIII Dynasty), and the reconstructed Tomb of Khaiè, director of the works at the Necropolis of Thebes, and his wife Meriè (XVIII Dynasty), with the furniture, food, cooking utensils, etc., found intact. Mummy and contents of the tomb of Princess Ahmose (XVII Dynasty); sarcophagus-cover of Nefertari queen of Rameses II. Cases of pottery, alabaster, and glass.—The small RIV contains the Mensa Isiaca, in bronze with silver inlay, discovered in the Sack of Rome in 1527, and textiles.—RV contains administrative and literary papyri with architectural plans and plans of gold mines; a love-poem; the Royal Papyrus, with a list of the Kings of Egypt from the Sun to the XVII Dynasty; the Papyrus of the Palace Conspiracy (XX Dyn.); writing materials, rolls of papyrus, etc.—RVI. Objects showing the daily life of the Egyptians: clothes, furniture, toilet articles, and some interesting jewels.—RVII. Statuettes of animal deities.—RVIII contains mural paintings from the tomb of Iti at Ghebelein (c 2100 BC), and wooden statues, models of ships, and sarcophagi of the same period.

The ***Galleria Sabauda** (adm. Tuesday, Thursday, Saturday & Sunday 9–14; Wednesday & Friday 14.30–19.30; closed Monday) on the second and third floors, had as a nucleus the collections of paintings made by the princes of the House of Savoy, from the 16C onwards and first opened to the public in 1832 by Carlo Alberto.

Remarkably rich in Flemish and Dutch works (acquired in 1741 through Eugenio di Savoy), it is interesting also for its paintings by Veneto and Piedmontese masters, some of them hardly represented elsewhere. Recent acquisitions include works by Rubens, Defendente Ferrari, and David Teniers. Most of the gallery was reopened in 1985 after rearrangment, but some rooms are still closed. The rooms are un-numbered, but arranged in groups by school, and the works are all labelled.

At the top of the stairs are four rooms (closed in 1988) which contain works by the PIEDMONTESE SCHOOL. A. *Macrino d'Alba*, 26. Madonna with Saints and angel musicians, 31–34. Panels of a polyptych from San Francesco at Alba.—B. *Gaudenzio Ferrari*, 49. Madonna, 51. Deposition, 46. St Peter and a donor, 50. Crucifixion; 65. *Bernardino Lanino*, Madonna; 39. *Girolamo Giovenone*, Madonna and donors.—C. 35. *Defendente Ferrari*, Marriage of St Catherine; 52. *Vercelli Master* (15C), Adoration of the Magi; 29 bis. *Giovanni Martino Spanzotti*, Madonna with Saints Ubaldo and Sebastian (triptych).—D. 30 bis. *Defendente Ferrari*, Donor, with Saints John the Baptist and Jerome; fragments of frescoes from destroyed churches; 21. *Barnaba da Modena*, Madonna and Child.

The rooms to the left at the top of the stairs are devoted to the ITALIAN SCHOOLS generally. ROOM I. 102. *Bernardo Daddi*, Coronation of the Virgin; 108. *Taddeo Gaddi*, Four doctors of the Church; *Fra Angelico*,*105. Madonna (c 1433), 103, 104. Angels; *Desiderio da Settignano*, Bas-relief of Madonna and Child; 186. *Francesco Botticini*, Coronation of the Virgin; 117. *Antonio and Piero Pollaiolo*, *Tobias and the Archangel Raphael (formerly in the church of Orsanmichele in Florence).—RII. 106. *Gherardo Del Fora* (Florentine, c 1446–97), formerly attributed to Cosimo Rosselli, Triumph of Chastity; 113. *Filippino Lippi*,*Tobias, and the three archangels; 115, 116. *Lorenzo di Credi*, Madonnas; *Botticelli*, 173. Madonna and Child, 201. Tondo of the Madonna and Child and St John.—RIII. 141. *Paolo da Brescia*, Polyptych (school of Foppa; from San Lorenzo at Mortara); *Bergognone*, 135. Madonna, 134. Saints Ambrose and Augustine, and other works; 578. *Moretto*, Madonna and Child.—RIV. 164. *Mantegna*, *Madonna and Saints (removed for restoration); *Savoldo*, 573. Holy Family and St Francis, 574. Adoration of the Shepherds; 157.*Giovanni Bellini*, Madonna and Child.—RV. 140. *Giampietrino*, Saints Catherine of Alexandria and Peter Martyr; 136. *Cesare da Sesto*, Madonna.—RVI. *Bronzino*, Portrait of a Lady, once thought to be Eleonora da Toledo, Portrait of Cosimo I; *Daniele da Volterra*, Beheading of St John the Baptist; *Sodoma*, 56. Holy Family, 59. Death of Lucrezia, *63. Madonna and four Saints (removed for restoration).—RVII. 4. *Argenta*, Charles Emmanuel I as a child; 124. *16C Roman Mannerist school*, formerly attributed to Giulio Campi, Adoration of the Magi; 558. *Luca Cambiaso*, Diana and Calixtus.

Beyond several more rooms and the stairs begins the superb FLEMISH AND DUTCH COLLECTION, recently rearranged (and some of the frames restored). Room 1. 362. *Cornelis Engelbrechtsz*, Crucifixion (a triptych); 189. *Roger van der Weyden*, Visitation, with an interesting landscape; 192. *16C Flemish Master*, Crucifixion.—R. 2. *Jan van Eyck*, 187. Stigmata of St Francis; 188. *Petrus Christus*, Madonna and Child; 393. *Rembrandt*, *Old man asleep; *Willem van de Velde the Younger*, Seascape; *Jacob van Ruisdael*, Landscape; 202. *Hans Memling*, *Passion of Christ; 194. *Bernart van Orley*, Scene from a Legend.—R. 3. 406. *Paulus Potter*, Four bulls; portraits by

David Teniers the Younger; still lives by *Jan van Huysum*.—R. 4. Works by *Jan Brueghel, Phillipe Wouwerman, Paul Mignard*, and *Jan de Heem*. —R. 5. More charming works by *Jan Brueghel*; 375. *Gerard Dou*, Portrait of a geographer; 303. *Holbein the Younger*, Portait of Erasmus; 241. *Van Dyck*, *Madonna and Child.

A modern flight of stairs leads up to a room (A) with large VENETIAN WORKS. *Veronese*, 572. The Queen of Sheba, 580. Christ in the house of the Pharisee; 566. *Tintoretto*, Trinity; 575. *Veronese*, Moses saved from the Red Sea (being restored); 560. *Francesco Bassano*, Rape of the Sabines, and other works by the Bassano family.—Room B. *Francesco Albani*, 489, 495, 500, 509. The Elements; works by *Guercino*, including (497.) The Prodigal Son, Madonna and Child; 505. *Guido Reni*, St John the Baptist. Marble bust of Cardinal Maurizio of Savoy, by *Francesco Duquesnoy*.—R. C. Works by *Giulio Cesare Procaccini, Francesco Cairo* (1598–1674), and *Il Cerano*.—R. D. *Orazio Gentileschi*, 469. *Annunciation (painted in 1653 for Carlo Emanuele I), Saints.

On the floor above a large room is being arranged with 17C and 18C works: at present only the equestrian portrait of Tommaso of Savoy Carignano by *Van Dyck* is on show.—Steps lead up to a room overlooking the entrance hall. In the room to the right are works by *Bernardo Strozzi*; *Van Dyck*, 264. *Children of Charles I (1635, presented by Henrietta Maria to her sister Christina of Savoy); 704. *Flemish School* (formerly attributed to Van Dyck), *Young boy; *Rubens*, 1059, 1060. Two mythological scenes; 279. *Van Dyck*, Portrait of the Infanta Isabella, Governess of the Netherlands. —Opposite this room is another gallery with works reflecting the artistic taste of the Sabauda court from 1730 to 1830. These include: two *Views of Turin commissioned by Carlo Emanuele III in 1745 from *Bernardo Bellotto*; two more views of Turin by *Carle André Van Loo*; *Sebastiano Conca*, Prayer in the Garden.—Portaits by *Pompeo Batoni, Anton Raphael Mengs* (also St Peter), and *Elisabeth Vigée-Lebrun* (Margherita Porporati, 1792).—The copies on porcelain of famous works owned by the Tuscan grand-dukes and acquired by Carlo Alberto in 1826 are by *Abrahan Constantin*.

The GUALINO COLLECTION (closed in 1988), donated to the museum in 1928, which occupies the remainder of this floor, contains good Italian and German paintings, ancient sculpture; Byzantine, Roman, and medieval ivories, goldsmiths' work, Chinese works (good 6C head), medieval furniture, and lace.

Opposite the palace, on the corner of Via Accademia delle Scienze, is the large church of SAN FILIPPO NERI (Pl. 6), rebuilt by Filippo Juvarra (c 1714), with a Corinthian pronaos by Giuseppe Talucchi (1823). The fine Baroque interior (with, unexpectedly, a parquet floor) has a high altar by Antonio Bertola (1697), with a Madonna and Child with Saints by Carlo Maratta. The 1st left chapel has a Martyrdom of St Laurence by Francesco Trevisani.

From Piazza San Carlo (see above) Via San Teresa leads to *San Teresa* (Pl. 6), a Baroque church probably by Andrea Costaguta (1642–74), hemmed in between two modern buildings. Inside, in the 4th right chapel, is a Holy Family by Sebastiano Conca.—Next to the church is the *Teatro Gianduja*, the puppet theatre of the Lupi family (performances on Sunday and fest. at 16.00), with a delightful *Puppet Museum (Pl. 6; 9–13; fest. 9–13, 15–18; closed Monday), with puppets, back-cloths, etc. collected by the family since the 18C.

Via San Teresa continues to Piazza Solferino. Here **Via Pietro Micca** (Pl. 6), an elegant street with a portico on one side, leads back to Piazza Castello. It was laid

out in 1894 on a diagonal line, and has a conspicuous neo-Gothic palace by
Carlo Ceppi. Via Cernaia continues the line of Via San Teresa W to the
MASTIO (Pl. 2), or keep of the old citadel (1564–68), the rest of which was
demolished in 1857. It contains an **Artillery Museum** (Pl. 2; adm. Tuesday &
Thursday, 9–13.30; Saturday & Sunday, 9–12), founded by Carlo Emanuele III
in 1731, and here since 1899. It is one of the most important museums of its
kind.—Farther on, on the corner of Via Guicciardini is the *R.A.I.* skyscraper
(1965–68). At No. 7 in Via Guicciardini is the **Museo Pietro Micca** (Pl. 1; adm.
Tuesday & Saturday, 9–12, 15–18; Sunday 9–14; July & August daily except
Monday, 9–14), with material relating to the French siege of 1706. Part of the
remarkable underground defence works (which extend for several kilometres
beneath the city) can be visited.

From the Mastio (see above) Corso Galileo Ferraris leads S across
Corso Vittorio Emanuele II to Via Magenta, in which (right) is the
entrance to the **Galleria d'Arte Moderna** (Pl. 5), opened here in a new
building in 1959, but closed since 1982 for structural repairs. It is one
of the most important collections of 19C and 20C painting in Italy,
with Italian and French artists well represented. It has good works by
Felice Casorati and Giorgio Morandi.—Nearby, at No. 8 Via Bricher-
asio, is the **Museo Civico di Numismatica, Etnografia e Arte Orientale**
(weekdays 13.30–18.30; fest. 9–12.30; closed Monday). It contains Greek,
Roman, and Byzantine coins; ethnographical material collected from 1864 onwards, and a section on Oriental art.

Just beyond Palazzo dell'Accademia delle Scienze (see above), on
Piazza Carignano, is **Palazzo Carignano** (Pl. 6; recently restored), the
residence of the princes of Savoy until 1831. It has an interesting
Baroque front (faced with brick) by Guarino Guarini (1679). It has an
oval vestibule with a pretty double staircase; the courtyard is being
restored in 1988. The E façade on Piazza Carlo Alberto dates from
1864–71. Here is the entrance to the **Museo Nazionale del Risorgimento** (adm. 9–18, Sunday 9–12; closed Monday & fest.), founded in
1878, and one of the most important of its kind.

The palace was the birthplace (1798) of Carlo Alberto and (1820) of Victor
Emmanuel II, and it was used for the meetings of the lower house of the
Subalpine Parliament (1848–59) and of the first Italian Parliament (1861–64). On
the piano nobile the Risorgimento museum has a particularly interesting
collection arranged chronologically in 27 rooms. The fine hall of the Subalpine
Parliament (restored in 1988) is also shown.

Piazza Carlo Alberto has a bronze equestrian statue of Charles Albert by
Marochetti (1861). Here is the *Biblioteca Nazionale*, with over 850,000 vols and c
5000 MSS mainly from religious institutions in Piedmont.—At No. 9 Via Bogino is
the 17C Palazzo Graneri della Roccia, seat of the Circolo degli Artisti, founded in
1855 and closed to women until 1987.

In Piazza Carignano, with a monument by Giovanni Albertoni (1859) to
Vincenzo Gioberti (1801–52), the philosopher, is the *Teatro Carignano*,
reconstructed in 1787 by Giovanni Battista Feroggio. Here Vittorio Alfieri's
'Cleopatra' was given its first performance in 1775. In the square is the
celebrated Ristorante del Cambio, famous as a meeting place during the
Risorgimento.

Via dell'Accademia delle Scienze ends in the huge rectangular **Piazza
Castello** (Pl. 6, 7), the centre of the city, laid out by Ascanio Vittozzi in
1584 around the castle, now called Palazzo Madama. It is surrounded
by uniform monumental buildings with porticoes. Several trams
traverse the piazza which is lit by pretty lamps. Near Via Roma is a skyscraper of 1934. Beneath the porticoes, on the corner nearest Via
Accademia delle Scienze are two elegant cafés (Mulassano and
Baratti, with elaborate decorations by Edoardo Rubino) on either side
of the GALLERIA DELL'INDUSTRIA SUBALPINA (Pl. 6), a delightful
shopping arcade built in 1873–74 by Pietro Carrera. In the centre of
the square, beside Palazzo Madama, is a monument to the Duke of

Aosta (died 1931) by Eugenio Baroni (1937), and war memorials by Vincenzo Vela (1859) and Pietro Canonica (1923). **Palazzo Madama** (Pl. 6,7), the most imposing of the ancient buildings of Turin, is a four-square castle of the 15C, one side of which has been replaced by a characteristic wing and façade of 1718–21, by Filippo Juvarra.

A castle was begun here after 1276 by William VII of Monferrato on the site of the Roman Porta Praetoria, the E gate of the Roman city. The palace takes its present name from the two regents, Maria Cristina, widow of Victor Amadeus I, and Giovanna Battista, widow of Charles Emmanuel II, both of whom were entitled 'Madama Reale', who resided here and 'improved' the old castle. The palazzo was the seat in 1848–60 of the Subalpine Senate and in 1861–65 of the Italian Senate.

Since 1935 the palace has housed the civic *Museum of Ancient Art, which has been closed for several years for restoration. When it reopens the arrangement may have changed. GROUND FLOOR. Romanesque and Gothic sculpture, in wood and stone, both religious and secular, from Piedmont and the Val d'Aosta, notably a fine ceiling from St-Marcel. The ground floor of a 16-sided tower of the Porta Decumana contains stained glass; in a room with a painted ceiling from a house near the cathedral are exhibited the Codice delle Catene, the illuminated 14C statutes of the city of Turin, and stallwork from the abbey of Staffarda (near Saluzzo) and elsewhere. Off the Great Hall, in the medieval NE tower of the main guard-room (unlocked by the custodian) are copies of the celebrated *Book of Hours of the Duc de Berry ('Les très riches Heures de Milan', c 1450), illustrated by *Jan van Eyck*, and a late 15C missal of Cardinal Domenico della Rovere. Although owned by the museum the originals are rarely on display. Also here are paintings by *Defendente Ferrari* (including a fine Madonna and Child, and a night scene of the Nativity).

The GREAT HALL displays the treasures of the collection: *Maestro della Trinità di Torino*, The Holy Trinity; *Barnaba da Modena*, Madonna and Child, a large work; Greek and Roman jewellery; works by *Defendente Ferrari* (notably St Michael); *Nerroccio di Landi*, Bust of St Catherine; tilework from Savona; *Macrino d' Alba*, Triptych; jewellery, including a gold ring (12C); a *Portrait of a man by *Antonello da Messina*, signed and dated 1476, one of his best and last works; various paintings by *Giovanni Martino Spanzotti*. In the centre of the room: *Tino da Camaino*, Madonna and Child; *Antonio Vivarini*, Coronation of the Madonna; *Giovanni Martino Spanzotti*, Madonna and Child with angels; *Pontormo*, St Michael; two books of drawings by *Filippo Juvarra*; the shield of Giovanni Maria della Rovere painted by *Polidoro da Caravaggio* (1512). In the next room is Renaissance sculpture, including high reliefs, by *Bambaia*, for the tomb of Gaston de Foix, and the tombstone of Matteo Sanmicheli, from Calcineri (near Saluzzo); while in the basement of the SW tower of the Porta Decumana (part of an arch of which is visible) is preserved an 11C mosaic from Acqui cathedral.

The lift (or spiral staircase) in the SW tower ascends to the SECOND FLOOR in which is a remarkable collection of gilded and painted glass (verre églomisé; 15–19C including a triptych by *Jacopino Cietario* (1460). Here also are the main collections of applied art, comprising ivories, enamels, glass, majolica (notably from Turin and Savona), textiles, bookbindings. etc.—On the FIRST FLOOR, beyond the Salone Centrale (the seat of the Senate; see above) are the Royal Apartments. Some of the furniture here dates from Charles Emmanuel II (died 1675), but the fittings are mainly in early-18C style, with paintings by *Vittorio*

Amedeo Cignaroli and sculptures by *Simon Troger* (Judgement of Solomon; 1741). The best of this series of rooms is frescoed by *Domenico Guidobono* (1714), with 18C tapestries of local weave, after Cignaroli.

In the NE corner of the square, beneath the arcades, is the *Teatro Regio* (Pl. 7), rebuilt in 1973, with a disappointing interior (closed in 1989). Remnants of the old theatre, burnt down in 1936, survive behind the modern buildings. Farther on, beneath the portico, is the Prefettura (No. 201). At No. 191 is the entrance to the ***Armeria Reale** (Pl. 7; visitors are admitted every 45 minutes; Tuesday & Thursday 14.30–19.30; Wednesday, Friday & Saturday 9–14; closed Sunday & Monday), housed in a wing of the Palazzo Reale (see below). The Royal Armoury is one of the most important in Europe, and includes some remarkable pieces by the great Bavarian and Austrian armourers and gunsmiths.

The armoury was transferred here by Carlo Alberto and opened to the public in 1837. The monumental staircase, designed by Filippo Juvarra and built by Benedetto Alfieri leads up to the three 18–19C galleries which provide a magnificent setting for the collection. The so-called *'Rotonda'* (from 'rondò') was decorated in 1841–45 by Pelagio Pelagi. Here are displayed the collections of the last princes of the House of Savoy, and arms and ensigns of the Risorgimento period.—The splendid *Galleria Beaumont*, designed by Filippo Juvarra in 1733, is named after Claudio Francesco Beaumont who painted the vault in 1738–64. Here is a superb display of about 30 complete suits of armour (12 equestrian), some of which were made for the Martinengo family of Brescia. Also here: etched and gilt armour; small arms, including a pistol of Charles V; sword, with a forged signature of Donatello now thought to be the work of Il Riccio; late-14C 'pig-faced' bascinet; shield with lantern for night service; uniform worn by Prince Eugene at the battle of Turin (1706); small *Shield designed by Étienne Delaune associated with the court of Henri II; ceremonial armour of Emmanuel Philibert; hunting weapons from Munich presented by Maximilian of Bavaria in 1650; sword, with scabbard and cover, said to have belonged to St Maurice, actually a 13C work; Roman and Etruscan armour. Among the swords, one is said to be that of Alfonso d'Este; another is of the time of the Thirty Years' War; a third (two-handed), with contemporary shield, is of the reign of Henri IV; equestrian armour worn by Emmanuel Philibert at St Quentin (1557).—In the *Medagliere* are displayed Oriental arms.

The *Royal Library* (for adm. apply to the director), has 150,000 volumes, 5000 MSS, and many miniatures and drawings, including a self-portrait of Leonardo da Vinci.

The PIAZZETTA REALE, with railings by Pelagio Pelagi of 1842 surmounted by statues of the Dioscuri by Abbondio Sangiorgio, precedes **Palazzo Reale** (Pl. 7), the former royal residence, built for Madama Reale Cristina of France, with a façade on the piazzetta by Amedeo di Castellamonte (1646–60). The Chapel of the Sacra Sindone was built in 1694 to contain the Holy Shroud in the W wing of the place adjoining the apse of the cathedral (described below); its delightful spiral dome by Guarino Guarini is well seen from here.

The State Apartments (being restored and rearranged) on the first floor are shown from 9–13.30 (except Monday) on conducted tours (every 30 minutes). When exhibitions are in progress (or being mounted) not all the rooms are shown. The rooms, lavishly decorated from the mid-17C to the mid-19C, contain some good ceilings and floors, as well as elaborate furnishings, paintings, porcelain and tapestries. Many of the 17C ceilings are by *Carlo Morello*, *Jan Miel*, and *Daniel Seyter*; *Claudio Francesco Beaumont* continued the decoration in the 18C. Some of the 18C furniture is by *Pietro Piffetti*. In the Camera da Letto di Carlo Alberto is a Madonna enthroned with Saints by *Defendente Ferrari* (1523). The Gabinetto Cinese is a delightful work by *Filippo Juvarra*. The Galleria del Daniele is a fine gallery begun in 1684 by *Daniel Seyter*. The charming neo-classical dancing figures in the Sala da Ballo were painted by

Carlo Bellosio and *Francesco Gonin* (1842). The *Scala degli Forbici is an ingenious staircase by *Filippo Juvarra* (1720).

The **Giardino Reale**, approached through the palace, is normally open from May–October, daily 9–dusk. From beneath the portico in Piazza Castello, beside the Teatro Regio (see above) Viale Primo Maggio leads down through the gardens towards Corso San Maurizio. The gardens were enlarged by Le Nôtre in 1697 for Carlo Emanuele II but have since been altered. In the centre is a fountain by Simone Martinez (c 1750).

On the right side of the Piazzetta Reale, at the end of the wing of the palace which houses the Armeria Reale (see above) is the loggia from which Charles Albert proclaimed war against Austria in 1848. Opposite is the sober *Palazzo Chiablese*, which used to house the Museum of the Cinema (in the course of being moved to a new building in Via Po, see below). Beside it, in Piazza Castello, is the church of **San Lorenzo** (Pl. 7), formerly the chapel royal, a superb Baroque work by Guarino Guarini, with a delightful cupola and lantern. The beautifully lit *Interior (1667), on a complicated plan, contains 18C statues of the Annunciation attributed to Ignazio Collino (2nd left altar), and a Nativity by Pierre Dufour (17C; 3rd left altar).

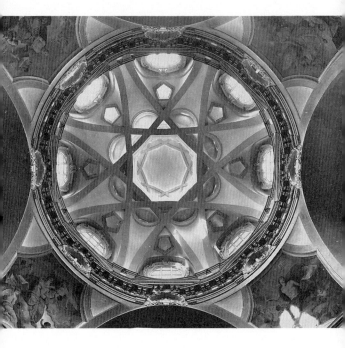

The dome of San Lorenzo in Turin, by Guarini (1667)

Between Palazzo Chiablese and the Palazzo Reale a road across the Piazzetta Reale leads beneath an archway to emerge beside the **Duomo** (Pl. 7; *San Giovanni Battista*), built in 1491–98 for Archbishop Domenico della Rovere by Meo del Caprino and other Tuscans, after three churches had been demolished to make way for it. The handsome plain Renaissance façade has three beautifully carved doorways. The campanile (1468–70; covered for restoration) was completed by Juvarra in 1720. Behind can be seen the delightful Baroque cupola of the chapel of the Sacra Sindone (see above).

INTERIOR. Immediately to the right is the tomb of Jeanne de la Balme (died 1478), with kneeling effigy and female 'weepers'; to the left are two Romagnano effigies: Marquis Antonio (died 1479) and his son Bishop Amedeo (died 1509), the latter by *Antonio Carlone*. In the second S chapel is a *Polyptych, in a fine Gothic frame, formerly attributed to *Defendente Ferrari*, but now thought to be by *Giovanni Martino Spanzotti*, with, on the walls, delightful little pictures of the life of Saints Crispin and Crispinian, with scenes of mercantile life.

Behind the apse is the **Chapel of the Holy Shroud** (*Cappella della Sacra Sindone*; open 8.30–12, 15–17; festivals 9.45–12; closed Monday), by *Guarino Guarini* (1668–94). Its walls, entirely lined with black marble, throw an effective contrast the white monuments erected in 1842 by Charles Albert to the memory of four of his ancestors. On the altar is the urn containing the Holy Shroud in which the body of Christ was traditionally believed to have been wrapped after his descent from the Cross. This sacred relic was said to have been taken from Jerusalem to Cyprus, and from there to France in the 15C, and to have been brought to Turin by Emmanuel Philibert in 1578. When it was exposed for 43 days in 1978 it was seen by some 4 million pilgrims. On the linen shroud (4·36 × 1·10m) is the negative image of a crucified man. In 1988 the Archbishop of Turin announced that scientific research using carbon 14 dating had proved that this icon must have been made between 1260 and 1390, but discussion still continues about its origins. It is kept in a silver casket inside an iron box enclosed in a marble case. The keys are held respectively by the Archbishop of Turin and the Chief of the Palatine Clergy.

Beside the campanile are the pretty railings in front of a wing of Palazzo Reale (see above), built in 1900. Here are the ruins of a *Roman Theatre* (1C AD). On the left, in an unattractive setting, is a stretch of Roman and medieval wall beside the conspicuous ***Porta Palatina** (Pl. 7), an exceptionally well preserved two-arched Roman gate flanked by two 16-sided towers (restored). This was the Porta Principalis Sinistra of the wall of the Roman colony Augusta Taurinorum.

In a garden house of Palazzo Reale (entrance at No. 105 Corso Regina Margherita) is the **Museo di Antichità**, (open Wednesday, Thursday, and Saturday 9–13; Tuesday & Friday 15–19; 1st & 3rd Sunday of the month, 9–13; closed Monday) formerly in the Palazzo dell'Accademia delle Scienze. The archaeological material includes objects discovered mainly in Piedmont and Liguria: Piedmontese material from the Stone Age up to the Barbarian invasions; Paleolithic instruments, Bronze Age swords, Iron Age helmets; Bronze Age implements, forks, compasses, surgical instruments, and statuettes; Vases in terra sigillata.—Roman gold, silver, and bronze work, including two statuettes of a Faun and dancer; and the Marengo treasure discovered in 1928 with a silver bust of Emperor Lucius Verus; Roman glass.—Greek vases (Attic red- and black-figure ware); Roman statues and bas reliefs (copies of Hellenistic works); portrait busts.—Etruscan and Cypriot collections.

Beyond the Porta Palatina is the large PIAZZA DELLA REPUBBLICA (Pl. 3), known locally as Porta Palazzo, the scene of a popular general market (and, on Saturdays and the second Sunday of the month, of the 'Balôn' antique market). From here Via Cottolengo leads to two noted charitable institutions of Piedmontese origin: the *Cottolengo*, founded for the aged infirm in 1828 by St Joseph Benedict Cottolengo (1786–1842), canon of the Corpus Domini (see below); and the *Istituto Salesiano*, established in 1846 by St John Bosco (1815–88) for the education of poor boys, where the basilica of *Maria Santissima Ausiliatrice*, by Antonio Spezia (1865–68), with the founder's tomb, is preceded by a monument to him (by Gaetano Cellini, 1920). The saint's modest apartment, where he died, may be seen at the back of the first courtyard.

Via XX Settembre leads back towards the centre of the city from the Duomo to the handsome long **Via Garibaldi** (Pl. 6, 2), lined with some characteristic 18C balconied palaces, and now a pedestrian precinct. At the beginning on the right is the church of the *Trinità* (1590–1606; closed in 1988), by Ascanio Vittozzi, with a marble interior by Filippo Juvarra (1718). The carved confessionals are notable. In Via Porta Palatina on the right is the church of *Corpus Domini* (1607–71), also by Vittozzi, with a lavishly decorated interior by Benedetto Alfieri. In this church, in 1728, Jean Jacques Rousseau abjured the Protestant faith. From here Via Porta Palatina leads into *Piazza di Palazzo di Città*, laid out in 1756 by Benedetto Alfieri, with a bronze monument to the 'Green Count' Amadeus VI (died 1383), the conqueror of the Turks, by Pelagio Pelagi (1853). Here is the *Palazzo di Città* (Pl. 6), the town hall, begun in 1659 by Francesco Lanfranchi and modified a century later by Benedetto Alfieri. The church of *San Domenico* (Pl. 2), on the corner of Via San Domenico, dates from 1354, and its belfry from 1451. At the E end of the S aisle, Madonna and Saints Catherine and Dominic by *Guercino*. At the E end of the N aisle, the chapel is decorated with 14C frescoes (restored in 1986), the only ones of this date in the city.

Via Milano, a less elegant street, continues from San Domenico past the huge elliptical domed church of *Santi Maurizio e Lazzaro*, begun in 1679 by Carlo Emanuele Lanfranchi, with a neo-classical façade by Carlo Bernardo Mosca.— Beyond lies Piazza della Repubblica (see above).
    From Palazzo di Città (see above) Via San Francesco d'Assisi leads back through an archway to Via Garibaldi. Farther on in Via Garibaldi (left) is the church of the **Santi Martiri** (Pl. 6), begun in 1577 probably by Pellegrino Tibaldi, with another good Baroque interior. The frescoed ceiling is by Luigi Vacca (1836). On the first right altar is St Paul, by Federico Zuccari. The high altar is by Filippo Juvarra.—Next door is the **Cappella dei Banchieri e Mercanti** (No. 25; Pl. 2, 6; adm. Sunday 10–12; Tuesday and Saturday, 14.30–18), a delightful Baroque chapel dating from the late 17C, with paintings by Andrea Pozzo, Stefano Maria Legnani, Carlo Innocenzo Carlone, and others, in huge black frames decorated in gold. The painted wood statues are by Carlo Giuseppe Plura, and the vault is frescoed by Stefano Maria Legnani. On the high altar by Filippo Juvarra is an Adoration of the Magi by Andrea Pozzo. The benches and lanterns survive intact, and it has a good organ of 1748–50. In the Sacristy is an ingenious mechanical calendar constructed by Antonio Plana in 1831.

Farther on in Via Garibaldi Via della Consolata diverges right through Piazza Savoia, with an obelisk, to the church of the **Consolata** (Pl. 2), a popular place of worship made up of the union of two churches by Guarino Guarini (1679), one oval, the other hexagonal, with a group of Baroque cupolas contrasting with the 11C campanile of the demolished church of Sant'Andrea. Against the apse-wall is a tower of the Roman wall. In the hexagonal church is a venerated image of the Virgin; and in a chapel on the left of the altar are kneeling figures of Maria Teresa, wife of Charles Albert, and Maria Adelaïde, wife of Victor Emmanuel II, by Vincenzo Vela (1861). The corridor outside the Sacristy is covered with ex votos.—Via Garibaldi ends in Piazza dello Statuto, with a monument (1879) to the engineers of the Mont Cenis railway tunnel.

From Piazza Castello (see above; Pl. 6,7) the arcaded VIA PO (Pl. 7,11), the main street of the E district of Turin leads towards the river. On the left at No. 17 is the *University* (Pl. 7), with a brick façade facing Via Verdi. The college, which has a chequered history dating back to the early 15C, has occupied its present site since 1720. Erasmus took a degree here in theology in 1506. On the right is the church of *San Francesco di Paola*, containing 17C sculptures by Tommaso Carlone.

Beyond, in Via dell'Accademia Albertina (right) is the *Accademia Albertina di Belle Arti* (Pl. 11), with a small picture gallery (closed in 1990, but normally open daily 10–12 except for Sunday and fest.; apply to the Segreteria), principally interesting for drawings by Guadenzio Ferrari and Lanino and paintings by Piedmontese masters.

Via Accademia dell'Albertina leads through Piazza Carlo Emanuele II, with a monument to Cavour by Giovanni Dupré (1873) to the ex-*Ospedale di San Giovanni* (Pl. 10), where the University museums of Zoology, Anatomy, Mineralogy, and Geology are being arranged.

Off the other side of Via Po, in Via Montebello, rises the *Mole Antonelliana* (Pl. 11), which has become the symbol of Turin. Begun in 1863 as a synagogue, it is the most famous work of the Piedmontese architect Alessandro Antonelli. It is an extraordinary feat of engineering skill. It was finished by the municipality in 1897 and became a monument of Italian Unity, when the Risorgimento museum (now in Palazzo Carignano, see above) was first opened here. It was much admired by Nietzsche. The terrace (86m; view) is reached by a lift (9–19; closed Monday); the granite spire, 167m high, was rebuilt in aluminium after it lost its upper 47m in a gale in 1953. In Via Po the Palazzo degli Stemmi (ex-Ospedale della Carità) is to be restored as the CINEMA MUSEUM, with a particularly interesting collection formerly displayed in Palazzo Chiablese.

Via Po ends in the spacious Piazza Vittorio Veneto (Pl. 11), laid out in 1825–30, beyond which Ponte Vittorio Emanuele I leads across the Po, with the Parco Michelotti on the right bank, to the church of the *Gran Madre di Dio* (Pl. 15), built by Bonsignore in 1818–31, in imitation of the Pantheon at Rome, to celebrate the return from exile of Victor Emmanuel I (1814). The king's monument, by Giuseppe Gaggini, stands in front of the church.

From Piazza di Gran Madre di Dio, Via Villa della Regina leads straight to the Baroque *Villa della Regina* (Pl. 15), built for Cardinal Maurizio of Savoy on a design probably by Ascanio Vittozzi, executed by Amedeo di Castellamonte in 1620. It was altered in the 18C by Filippo Juvarra. It is named after Marie-Anne d'Orléans, queen of Victor Amadeus II, who resided here. It has a beautiful park and garden laid out in terraces on the hillside in the style of a Roman villa. After years of neglect it is being restored and may be opened to the public.

From Corso Moncalieri (right) Via Giardino ascends to the wooded **Monte dei Cappuccini** (283m; Pl. 15), on whose summit are a Capuchin church by Ascanio Vittozzi (1596), and convent, and the *Duke of Abruzzi Mountain Museum* (relief plans, etc.; adm. 9–12, 14.30–18).—Farther upstream, beyond more pleasant gardens and the Ponte Umberto I, is the beautiful **Parco del Valentino** (Pl. 14, 13), laid out on the left bank of the Po and opened in 1856.

It contains a fine *Botanic Garden*, founded in 1729, with a museum and library (containing the famous 'Iconographia Taurinensis', 1752–1868). The *Castello del Valentino* (in urgent need of restoration), built in 1630–60 by Maria Cristina in the style of a French château, is now occupied by the School of Architecture of the University. The reproduction of a *Medieval Village* and *Castle* (open except Monday & festivals 9–16, Sunday, 10–16) was erected for the exhibition of 1884. The village (Borgo) shows types of old Piedmontese houses. The castle is modelled on various strongholds in the Val d'Aosta, etc. In the park, nearby, is the fine equestrian monument of Prince Amadeus, the masterpiece of Davide Calandra (1902). Boats may be hired for rowing on the river.

At the SW end of the park are the buildings of the *Turin Exhibition*, built in 1948 for the first Motor Show (now held at the Lingotto, see below). There are

The eighteenth-century Basilica of Superga by Filippo Juvarra (1717–32)

now five halls (used frequently for exhibitions), one of which is adapted in winter as a skating-rink.

Beyond the park the Corso Massimo d'Azeglio is prolonged as Corso Unità d'Italia, where (No. 40; 2km farther) stands the splendid **Carlo Biscaretti di Ruffia Motor Museum* (adm. 9.30 or 10–12.30 & 15–17.30 or 19; closed Monday, & also Tuesday in winter), founded in 1933 and moved here in 1960. The building, designed by Amedeo Albertini, contains an international collection of vehicles, admirably displayed and technically documented. Farther on still, overlooking the river, is the huge *Palazzo del Lavoro*, designed by Pier Luigi Nervi for the 1961 exhibition, now a study centre of the International Labour Office.

In Via Nizza (see Pl. 9), parallel to Corso Unità to the W, beside the railway, is the huge **Lingotto Fiat Factory**, which started production in 1923, and closed down in 1983. The Turin Motor Show is now appropriately held here (biennially in April–May). The interesting building which has played an important part in the history of the industrialisation of the city has a test circuit on the roof. Heated debate continues in the city about its future: there are plans by Renzo Piano to convert it into an exhibition and congress centre.

Environs of Turin

To SUPERGA, 8km, on the right bank of the Po. Tram No. 15 from Via XX Settembre and Piazza Castello to *Sassi*. The rack-railway from there to Superga (in 16 minutes) is closed for repairs and is at present substituted by a bus service. The **Basilica of Superga** (open 8– 12.30; 14.30–18.30), crowning a hill-top (672m) which commands a splendid *View, was built in 1717–31 by Victor Amadeus II in fulfilment of a thanksgiving vow for the deliverance of Turin in 1706. It is considered the masterpiece of Filippo Juvarra; it is being restored. The exterior, with its columned portico, its dome, and its two campanili, is impressive.

In the *Crypt* (entrance to the left of the church) are the tombs of the Kings of Sardinia from Victor Amadeus II (died 1732) to Charles Albert (died 1849), and of other princes of Savoy. In the garden to the S a monument to Humbert I shows an Allobrogian warrior swearing fealty to the dynasty.—Behind the basilica a plaque records the air disaster of 4 May 1949 in which 31 people, including the whole team of Turin Football Club, were killed.

The COLLE DELLA MADDALENA, 5km, also on the right bank of the Po, is reached by Bus No. 70 from Piazza Vittorio Veneto (Pl. 11). The slopes of the *Colle della Maddalena* (766m) are laid out as a huge *Parco della Rimembranza*, with fine trees, for a War Memorial of the First World War. A colossal bronze torch-bearing Victory, over 18m high, by Edoardo Rubino (1928), stands below the summit. The *View is almost equal to that from Superga.

To MONCALIERI, 8·5km (bus No. 67, from Porta Nuova Station), on the right bank of the Po (beyond Pl. 13). **Moncalieri** (56,100 inhab.) lies just beyond the SE suburban limits of Turin across the Po. Its hill-top centre has industrial surroundings that almost double its population. The *Castle* reconstructed in the 15C, and much enlarged in the 17–18C, was the favourite residence of Victor Emmanuel II; and Victor Amadeus II (1732) and Victor Emmanuel I (1824) died here. In the principal square is the 14C church of *Santa Maria della Scala*, containing good stalls (1748) and Pietro Canonica's monument to Princess Clotilde (died 1911).

To STUPINIGI, 10km (beyond Pl.9), Bus No. 41 from Corso Vittorio Emanuele II and Via Sacchi (beside the Porta Nuova Station). The Pinerolo road (N23) runs from Porta Nuova station (Via Sacchi and Corso Turati), to the Corso Unione Sovietica which continues past the huge Fiat works of *Mirafiori*, opened in 1939, to (10km) **Stupinigi**. Here is the magnificent *Palazzina di Caccia*, a royal hunting-lodge built for Victor Amadeus II in 1729–30 by Filippo Juvarra on an ingenious and complicated plan, the property of the Mauritian Order. The roof of the elliptical Salone Centrale is crowned with an 18C bronze stag by Francesco Ladetto. The palace is undergoing a lengthy restoration. It is open 9.30–18.30; fest. 10–13, 14–18.30; closed Monday, and contains a *Museum of Furniture* in some 40 rooms. The Appartamento della Regina is decorated with ceiling-paintings by Carle Van Loo and Giovanni Battista Crosato, and the splendid Salone Centrale is frescoed with the Triumph of Diana by Giuseppe and Domenico Valeriani (1732). It is surrounded by a fine park.—The parish church contains the relics of St Hubert, patron of huntsmen (procession on 3 November).

To RIVOLI, 13km (Bus No. 36 from Piazza Statuto). From Piazza Statuto (Pl. 2) Corso Francia leads W. Beyond Piazza Rivoli it passes (right) *Villa La Tesoriera*, built in 1714 by Jacopo Maggi. The garden is open to the public. The Corso continues through industrial suburbs to **Rivoli**, once a favoured residence of the Counts of Savoy. The Casa del Conte Verde (so called) is a typical early 15C patrician house. The huge *Castello di Rivoli* was left unfinished by Filippo Juvarra in 1715. It was restored and modernised in 1984 to house an international collection of contemporary art, and as an exhibition centre (open 9–19, except Monday).—The Abbey of Sant'Antonio di Ranverso (described in Rte 1A) is 5km farther on.

The Valli di Lanzo

These Alpine valleys NW of Turin, are less visited than they deserve by visitors from beyond Piedmont, for their scenery is as fine as any in the western Alps. They are the heart of the *Graian Alps*, which lie between the valleys of the Dora Riparia and Dora Baltea. Railway from Turin c every hour to *Lanzo* in 35–55 minutes, and *Céres* in 1–1½hrs. The road leaves by Piazza Repubblica (Pl. 3), Corso Giulio Cesare, and Corso Emilia (left). To the left (9km) is *Venaria*, with the Venaria Reale, a royal hunting lodge built c 1660 by Amedeo di Castellamonte, and destroyed by French troops in 1693. It was reconstructed by Juvarra in 1714–28. Part of the buildings are used as a barracks. The Galleria di Diana has been restored and is open on request; the rest of the building is being restored and may be used as a museum.—13km *Caselle*, with the airport on the right.—Beyond (21km) *Ciriè*, where the Gothic Duomo has a good campanile and portal, the industrial area is left behind as the road ascends the Stura valley.—33km **Lanzo Torinese** (5670 inhab.) is a picturesque little place, with houses huddled round the 14C *Torre del Comune*. The old Turin road crosses the Stura below the town by the *Ponte del Diavolo* (1378), a daring, single-arched bridge.—35km *Germagnano* (488m).

The VALLE DI VIÙ, which starts at Germagnano (bus to Margone), is watered by the S branch of the Stura.— 13km **Viù** (774m) is a good centre for climbing. A hill-road runs S over the *Colle del Lis* (1311m: two ski-lifts) to Rubiana and (34km) Avigliana.— **Usseglio**, the highest commune in the valley, is strung out for 5km in a series of hamlets. It has many ski-lifts. The chief hotels are at (28km) *Cortevicio* (1265m), beneath the *Rifugio Cibrario* (2615m), the base for the ascent of the *Croce Rossa* (3517m) and other frontier peaks.—Beyond (33km) *Margone* (1410m) the road continues to (38km) *Lago Malciaussia*, visited by climbers, beneath *Founs d'Rumour* (2649m; Rifugio Tazzetti), and *Rocciamelone* (3537m).

The main road goes on to (46km) **Céres** (689m), the railway terminus, at the junction of the Val Grande and the Valle d'Ala. It is a summer resort.

The VALLE D'ALA, the central one of the three Lanzo valleys, is visited by skiers and climbers. It is ascended by a bus from Céres to Balme, going on (in July and August) to Piano della Mussa.—8km **Ala di Stura** (1079m) is the chief village. A chair lift ascends to (1415m) Pian Belfé. Other centres are (12km) *Mondrone* (1230m), near a fine gorge and waterfall of the Stura; and (15km) **Balme** (1431m) with ski-lifts, beneath the rocky *Via di Mondrone* (2964m).—20km *Piano della Mussa* (1720m) is a lovely little basin at the head of the valley. The *Rifugio Gastaldi* (2659m), farther on, is a base for the ascent of the *Bessanese* (3604m), on the French frontier.

The VAL GRANDE (bus from Céres to Forno), to the N, is the least visited of the Lanzo valleys. The chief villages are (9·5km) *Chialamberto* (876m), (13km) *Bonzo*, and (16km) *Groscavallo-Pialpetta* (1069m). The *Colle della Crocetta* (2636m) provides a fine mountain walk N from Pialpetta to Ceresole Reale.—21km *Forno Alpi Graie* (1226m), the uppermost village lies in a magnificent cirque of mountains. The *Rifugio Paolo Daviso* (2375m), to the W, serves as an approach to the *Monte Levanna* (central peak, 3503m) via the *Colle Girard* (3078m).

From Turin to *Aosta*, see Rte 2; to *Genoa*, see Rte 5; to *Milan*, see Rte 8; to *Ventimiglia and Nice*, see Rte 3.

C. Turin to Briançon

ROAD, 123km.—N23. 10km. *Stupinigi*.—36km **Pinerolo**.—53km *Perosa Argentina*.—69km *Fenestrelle*.—91km **Sestriere**.—102·5km *Cesana Torinese*.—N24. 109km *Claviere* (frontier).—N94. 111km *Col du Montgenèvre*.—123km **Briançon**.

BUS daily from Turin (Corso Inghilterra) to *Briançon* in 4¼hrs; more
frequently to *Pinerolo* (¾hr), *Perosa* (1¼hrs) and *Sestriere* (2½hrs).

RAILWAY, via (25km) *Airasca* (junction for Saluzzo and Cuneo), to
Pinerolo, 38km in 35–60 minutes (going on to Torre Pellice).

From the centre of Turin to (10km) *Stupinigi*, see the end of Rte
1B.—23km *Airasca*.—36km **Pinerolo** (37,800 inhab.), the historic
capital of the Princes of Acaia, ancestors of the House of Savoy, is
beautifully situated at the foot of the hills where the Chisone and
Lemina valleys merge into the Piedmontese plain. It is a commercial
and industrial centre. In the centre of the old town is the restored
Gothic *Cathedral*. Via Trento and Via Principi d'Acaia (right), with
ancient houses, ascend to the early 14C *Palace of the Princes of Acaia*,
and the church of *San Maurizio*, reconstructed in 1470, with a fine
campanile of 1336. It is the burial place of eight princes of Acaia
(1334–1490). Via Ortensia di Piossasco descends from here to the
Public Garden in which stands the *Waldensian Church* (1860).

The fortress of *Pignerol* (as it is called in French) was under French control in
1630–1706, and, thanks to its remoteness from Paris, was found convenient as a
State prison. The 'Man in the Iron Mask' was held here from 1668 to 1678, and
the Duc de Lauzun in 1671–81; while the chancellor Nicolas Fouquet died here
in 1681 after 19 years' incarceration.

The **Vaudois Valleys** (*Valli Valdesi*). The valleys of the Chisone and the
Pellice (described below) are inhabited mainly by the Protestant Waldenses or
Vaudois. This sect originated in the S of France about 1170, under the inspiration
of Peter Waldo, a Lyons merchant who sold his goods and started preaching the
gospel. His adherents were formally condemned by the Lateran Council in 1184
and persecution drove them to take refuge in these remote valleys of the
Piedmontese Alps. About 1532 the Vaudois became absorbed in the Swiss
Reformation. When renewed persecution broke out in 1655 under Charles
Emmanuel II, assisted by the troops of Louis XIV, a strong protest was raised by
Cromwell in England, and Milton wrote his famous sonnet. Still further
persecution followed the Revocation of the Edict of Nantes (1685), but the
remnant of the Vaudois, about 2600 in number, were allowed to retreat to
Geneva. In 1698 Henri Arnaud led a band of 800 to the reconquest of their
valleys, and a rupture between Louis XIV and Victor Amadeus of Savoy was
followed by their recognition as subjects of Savoy, in a spirit of religious
tolerance. Since the beginning of the 19C much interest has been taken in
Protestant countries on their behalf, and an Englishman, General Beckwith,
helped them personally and built their church in Turin (1849). Since 1848 they
have been allowed complete religious liberty. Towards the close of the 19C large
colonies emigrated to Sicily, Uruguay, and the Argentine Republic.

The road running S from Pinerolo to (31km) *Saluzzo* (see Rte 3) passes
(12·5km) *Cavour*, the ancestral home of the great statesman's family. Here
Giovanni Giolitti died in 1928. **Staffarda** (20km) has a fine Cistercian *Abbey,
founded in 1135 and well restored.

Another interesting road from Pinerolo (railway as far as Torre Pellice) ascends
the Pellice valley.—15·5km **Torre Pellice** (518m), the headquarters of the
Waldensians (4700 inhab.), is a pleasant little town with some good 19C
buildings, including a Waldensian church and college, and a museum illustrating their history. It also has ski facilities (chair-lift). To the N extends the pleasant
valley of *Angrogna*.—Further up the main valley are (22km) *Villar Pellice*
(664m), and (25km) *Bobbio Pellice* (732m), two little summer resorts.—The road
runs as far as (32km) *Villanova*, skirting a long flood-embankment built with the
aid of a grant from Cromwell.—The long upland valley of *Pra* beneath *Monte
Granero* (3171m) can be reached from Bobbio.

Beyond Pinerolo the Briançon road ascends the Chisone valley.—
53km *Perosa Argentina*, a silk-working town, lies at the foot of the *Val
Germanasca*, a Waldensian stronghold with talc deposits.

A road ascends the valley via (8km) *Perrero* to (17km) *Prali* and (19km) *Ghigo*
(1759m), beyond which a chair-lift ascends to Cappello d'Envie (2556m). A

rough road continues to (21km) *Ribba*, from where a bridle-path (open in summer) crosses the *Colle Nuovo d'Abriès* (2635m) to *Abriès* in France.

63km *Villaretto* is the chief hamlet of Roreto, at the S foot of the *Orsiera* (2878m). Just beyond is a dramatic view of the remarkable fortifications built in 1727 by Charles Emmanuel III to defend (69km) **Fenestrelle** (1154m), a little town visited as a summer resort, with a small local museum. The tall sombre houses are surrounded by forests and dominated from the S by the *Albergian* (3043m).

The plateau of *Pra Catinat* (1829–1981m) is reached by a winding road from the Dépôt di Fenestrelle, a little downstream; while a cableway leads up to the Agnelli Sanatoria, 152m below. The road, often difficult, goes on over the *Colle delle Finestre* (2176m) to Meana and (37km) *Susa* (Rte 1A).

80km *Pragelato* is noted for its Alpine flowers and for the honey they produce. It has become an important ski resort. The road now ascends more steeply, soon leaving the Chisone valley, and passes on the left the old village of Sestriere.

91km **Sestriere**, on the Colle di Sestriere (2030m), is the most fashionable summer and winter alpine resort in Piedmont, with unusual 'tower-hotels'. The ski slopes in the neighbourhood are excellent.

Buses. Daily express service to *Turin* and *Milan*; service to Cesana and *Oulx* (for the railway).—**Cable Railways**, hourly or oftener to *Monte Banchetta*; via *Alpette* to *Monte Sixes*; to *Fraitève*. There are also 21 ski-lifts and 2 chair- lifts for winter sports.—18-hole golf course.

The principal ski-runs are on the slopes of *Monte Banchetta* (2830m) to the E, and the *Monte Sises* (2658m) to the SE, both spurs of the *Rognosa* (3280m).

The descent from Sestriere passes (95km) *Champlas du Col*, and reaches the Dora Riparia valley at (102·5km) **Cesana Torinese** (1361m), a large red-roofed village with an old church, at the junction of the road to Oulx (Rte 1A). Paul Cézanne's family came from Cesana, and the painter spent much time here. As another ski resort, it has numerous chair-lifts and ski-lifts. *Sansicario*, nearby, has also recently been developed as a ski-resort.

A chair-lift rises to the *Colle La Bercia* (2236m); while an interesting road ascends the valley running S to (3km) *Bousson* (1489m), with an old church. There are numerous mountain walks in the area, and a winding upland road leads from Cesana to *Sauze* in the long and beautiful Ripa valley.

A zigzag ascent of the Piccola Dora valley leads to the frontier, with the Italian customs, at (109km) **Claviere** (1768m), another winter and summer resort, with fine easy ski-slopes.—Beyond the new frontier an easy slope leads up to (111km) the **Col du Montgenèvre** or **Monginevro** (1860m), the frontier before 1947, where an obelisk commemorates the construction of the road by Napoleon. The French mountain-resort of *Montgenèvre*, with custom-house, is only 2km from Claviere (see 'Blue Guide France').

A little to the S, and almost from a common source, rise the Dora, which flows through the Po into the Adriatic, and the Durance, flowing through the Rhone into the Mediterranean.

The Mont-Genèvre (*Mons Janus*) is one of the oldest, as well as one of the lowest passes over the main chain of the Alps. It was crossed by the armies of Marius, Augustus, Theodosius, and Charlemagne; and again in 1494 by Charles VIII and his army, dragging with them 600 cannon. The present road was

constructed under Napoleon in 1802–07. French armies entered Italy by it in
1818 and 1859; and in 1917–18 French reinforcements were sent to the Italian
armies over the pass.

The descent leads by *La Vachette* to (123km) **Briançon** in France (see 'Blue
Guide France').

2   Turin to the Valle d'Aosta, Courmayeur, and Chamonix. The Great St Bernard

MOTORWAY, A5, to **Aosta** (c 10km shorter; see below).—The old
ROAD (N26) diverges 1eft from N 11 at (23km) *Chivasso* (see Rte 10)
and strikes N.—36km *Caluso*.—46km *Strambino*, with a castle (11–
14C).—56km **Ivrea**. Beyond Ivrea road and motorway are both
confined in the valley. There is access from the motorway only to the
main places; the old road has many sharp corners and traverses
narrow village streets.—73km *Pont-St-Martin*.—87km *Verrès*.—
98km **St-Vincent**.—10km *Châtillon*. The motorway ends just before
(125km) **Aosta**, where N27 branches (right) to the Great St Bernard
Tunnel.—N26 (the road is to be improved as far as the Mont Blanc
Tunnel). 156km **Pré-St-Didier**.—161km **Courmayeur**.—166km
Entrèves (custom-house at the tunnel mouth).—181km **Chamonix-
Mont Blanc.**— BUS services from Turin to Aosta in 3hrs, with some
international services through the tunnels.

RAILWAY to *Prè-St-Didier*, 161km in 3¼–5hrs, usually with a change
at (129km) *Aosta* (2–3hrs).

The **Val d'Aosta**, the district which includes the main valley of the Dora Baltea
and its numerous tributary valleys, is one of the most beautiful parts of Italy. The
mountains which surround its head (Gran Paradiso, Mont Blanc, Matterhorn,
and Monte Rosa), its glaciers, its forests, and its pastures, combine with its
Roman remains and many feudal castles (only four of which, Verrès, Fénis,
Issogne, and Sarre, are open to the public) to make it an area of great beauty and
interest. It is divided into three parts by 'narrows' at Bard and Montjovet.
Although Italian is now the main language, French is still an important second
language, and in the villages 'patois', a French/Italian dialect is spoken. An
interesting relic of the colonisation of the valley from the Swiss Valais remains in
the German dialect which still survives at Gressoney. Under the Italian
Constitution of 1945 the valley was granted a statute of administrative and
cultural autonomy, with a Regional Council of 35 members, sitting in Aosta.

The most important tourist centres are Gressoney, Cogne, Champoluc,
Brusson, Breuil, Courmayeur, and St-Vincent, all of which have good hotels. The
guides of Valtournenche and Courmayeur are world-famous and many have
accomplished first ascents not only in Switzerland, but also in America and
Africa and among the Himalayas. The roads are apt to be crowded in summer,
including the two great arteries which offer an additional exit from the upper
valley—the Mont Blanc and Great St Bernard tunnels.

For climbing and skiing in the Val d'Aosta the Assessorato Turismo in Aosta
supplies a number of publications with maps. Detailed maps and specialised
guides of the area are published by the TCI and the CAI.

From Turin the old road and the motorway (10km shorter) both cross
the low moraine ridge through which the Dora Baltea, farther E, cuts
its way into the Po valley.—After (36km) *Caluso*, the Lago di Candia is
visible on the right. Beyond a stretch of heavily wooded country the
mountains come into view.—56km **Ivrea**, a pleasant old town (29,100
inhab.), was the Roman *Eporedia*, a bulwark in the 1C BC against the
Salassian Gauls of the Upper Dora. In the Middle Ages its marquesses
rose to power, and Arduin of Ivrea was crowned King of Italy in 1002.
Ivrea is well known for its carnival, culminating in a battle of oranges.

The Olivetti typewriter factories were founded here in 1908, and it has expanded as an industrial centre.

On the approach from the S, *Ponte Nuovo* crosses the Dora Baltea. On the left is the *Ponte Vecchio*, a bridge of 1716 on older foundations. In the upper part of the town, approached by steep lanes, is the CATHEDRAL, of which two apsidal towers and the crypt date from the 11C. In the raised ambulatory is a row of columns taken from older buildings. On the left of the façade (1854) is a Roman sarcophagus of the 1C BC. The sacristy contains two paintings by Defendente Ferrari. Behind the cathedral is the *CASTLE (no adm., but being restored), built by Aymon de Challant (1358) for Amadeus VI, the 'Green Count', with four tall angle towers, one of which was partially destroyed by an explosion in 1676. The *Bishop's Palace*, also opening on the untidy old Piazza Castello, has Roman and medieval fragments in its loggia. A *Diocesan Museum* has been arranged in San Nicola da Tolentino. In Piazza Ottinetti (neo-classical, 1843), the *Museo Civico* has oriental and archaeological collections.

In the public park by the river, below the Dora bridges, is the Romanesque campanile (1041) of *Santo Stefano*.—Beyond the Station are the extensive *Olivetti* works (open to the public) built between 1898 and 1971. They incorporate the late-Gothic convent of San Bernardino with an interesting fresco cycle of the life of Christ by Giovanni Martino Spanzotti (late 15C).

13km S of Ivrea is the castle of *Masino*, one of the best preserved in Piedmont; purchased by the F.A.I. in 1989 it is open to the public.

Ivrea is the capital of the **Canavese**, the subalpine district extending from the level moraine ridge of the *Serra d'Ivrea*, to the E, up to the foot of the Gran Paradiso. The VALLE DELL'ORCO, the chief valley of this district, is reached direct from Turin (Porta Susa) by railway or rail bus to (52km) *Pont Canavese* (see below). The railway serves (21km) *San Benigno*, which preserves the 11C campanile and other remains of the abbey of *Fruttuaria*, where Arduin of Ivrea died, a monk, in 1013.

The road from Ivrea (bus) joins the road from Turin opposite (23km) *Cuorgnè*, an ancient little town on the Orco, with many medieval houses, now somewhat suffocated by new industrial buildings. Beneath the portico of the Municipio the so-called 'Masso di Navetta' is exhibited, an incised rock dating from the middle Neolithic age. *Valperga*, 3km S, has a restored castle, near which is a charming little 15C church (frescoes). Above rises the *Santuario di Belmonte*, founded by Arduin, but rebuilt in the 14C.—29km *Pont Canavese*, the railway terminus, stands at the foot of the flowery Val Soana, which is served by a bus from Pont to *Ronco Canavese* (13km) and *Valprato* (16km).—Beyond Pont the road (bus to Noasca daily, to Ceresole in June–October) keeps close to the Orco, passing (33km) *Sparone*.—40km *Locana* (613m) is the last big village. The ascent becomes steeper and the outliers of the Gran Paradiso loom up on the right. The road now skirts the S limits of the Gran Paradiso National Park (see below).—At (42km) *Rosone*, a by-road leads up the Valle di Piantonetto to the artificial lake of Talessio (14km) with the Rifugio Pontese (2217m).—Above (54km) *Noasca* (1035m), with its charming waterfall (above the houses to the right), the road enters a narrow gorge through which the Orco foams in a sequence of cascades, and after a tunnel the road emerges suddenly into the pastoral plain of Ceresole.—62km **Ceresole Reale** (1495m), stands in a long upland basin, dominated by the peaks of the Levanna, whose natural beauty has been somewhat marred by the dam and reservoir of the Turin electric-power works. Ceresole was the scene in 1544 of a victory of the troops of Francis I over those of Charles V, when the young Coligny was knighted on the field. It is a good centre for climbing and has skiing facilities. The road continues through the National Park to (78km) the *Col du Nivolet* (2841m), with the Rifugio Città di Chivasso (2604m). Here the road becomes a bridle-path (although there are plans to open it to cars) to (94km) Pont Valsavarenche (see below). Near the artificial lake of Serrù is the Rifugio Pian Ballotta (2400m).

Beyond (59km) *Montalto Dora*, with its well-restored 15C castle prominent on the right, begins the Val d'Aosta proper, whose slopes are covered with trellised vineyards.—73km **Pont-St-Martin** (343m), an attractive town, second in importance in the Val d'Aosta, with a fine *Roman bridge (1C BC) on the Lys, and the ruins of a 12C castle.

FROM PONT-ST-MARTIN TO GRESSONEY-LA-TRINITÉ, 34km. Bus 2–3 times daily (oftener in summer), in 1hr; through coaches from Genoa and Turin and Milan.—The **Val de Lys** or **Val di Gressoney** contains the largest and oldest of the German-speaking colonies which crossed over from Valais in the Middle Ages. The people of this valley, who are mentioned as early as 1218, were subjects of the Bishop of Sion; they have kept their language and customs even more distinct from their Italian neighbours than have the people of Alagna or Macugnaga, and both the attractive chalets ('rascards'), and the costume of the women, which is brightly coloured and adorned with hand-made gold lace, suggest a northern origin.

7km *Lillianes* (655m) and (10km) *Fontainemore* (760m) are surrounded by luxuriant chestnut groves.—12km *Pont de Guillemore* is an old bridge spanning the Lys where it plunges into a deep chasm.—14km *Issime* (939m) and (18km) *Gaby* (1032m) are summer resorts. At Issime the church, rebuilt after 1567, has a repainted Last Judgement by the brothers De Henricis on its façade. The *Bec de Frudière* (3075m) can be ascended via *Col de Chasten* (2552m) from Issime. The *Colle della Vecchia* (2185m) can be climbed from Gaby.

The road ascends the beautiful Val de Lys, of which (28km) **Gressoney-St-Jean** (1385m) is the principal village. It is a summer and winter resort, with a chair-lift on the W side to *Weissmatten* (or Pra' Bianco; 2019m).—The sister-village of (34km) **Gressoney-la-Trinité** (1628), is a pleasant mountaineering and skiing resort. On the E side of the valley a chair-lift rises to *Punta Iolanda* (2350m), and a cableway mounts to the Alpe Gabiet (2362m), with two refuges. Above is the *Corno del Camoscio**, or *Gemshorn* (3026m), with a view of the grand line of snow peaks from Monte Rosa to the Gran Paradiso. For Punta Indren and the Funivia di Monte Rosa, and Alagna, see Rte 8.

Ski-lifts also ascend from the end of the road to *Colle de la Bettaforca* (2672m). From Gressoney-St-Jean there is a cross-country climbing route to *Colle di Pinter* (2780m) and Champoluc, also reached by the Passo di Mascognaz (2947m). The *Testa Grigia** or *Grauhaupt* (3315m; guide essential) can be climbed from Colle di Pinter.—To the S is the *Corno Vitello* or *Kalberhorn* (3057m).—Higher climbs to the N can be made via the *Gnifetti Refuge* (3647m) and the *Quintino Sella Refuge* (3601m).

Beyond (76km) *Donnas* station, before the level-crossing, a row of old houses ends by a stretch of Roman road with a remarkable rock-hewn arch.—The road enters the narrow Gorge de Bard, through which in 1800 Napoleon passed unnoticed with an army during the night. At the other end are the villages of *Hône* (left) and *Bard* (right), with its forbidding fortress (the train tunnels beneath its promontory), an 11C foundation largely reconstructed in the 19C, (no adm.). As an over-Liberal young officer, Cavour was despatched to this remote garrison by Charles Felix (1830–31).

To the left is the steep Ayasse valley, up which a road runs to (15km) *Champorcher* (1315m), a small resort. From here a bridle-path crosses the *Finestra di Champorcher* (2838m) to Cogne (see below).

On the right (83km) is the church of *Arnad*, revealed since its restoration in 1950–52 as the oldest in the region (c 1000) with mural paintings (?15C); here also are a ruined castle and many tower-houses.—87km **Verrès** (395m) stands at the mouth of the Val d'Ayas. Its four-square *Castle* commands this valley (right of road and railway), at the head of which can be glimpsed snow-capped mountains. A road leads up to the castle (open 9.30–11.30 or 12, 14–16 or 16.30; closed Wednesday) or a path ascends in 15 minutes from Piazza Chanoux. It was founded by the Challant family in 1380 and strengthened in 1536, and has sheer walls 30m high. The *Castle of Issogne*, rebuilt by Georges de Challant in 1497–98, 10 minutes SW of the station beyond the Dora, is a splendid example of a late-medieval residence (adm. as for Verrès, except closed Monday), with a notable series of frescoes, including scenes of everyday life (in the loggia), and fitted up with local furniture.

FROM VERRÈS TO CHAMPOLUC, 27km. Bus twice daily to St-Jacques in 1¾hrs (oftener in July & August); through coaches from Turin and Genoa in summer. This route traverses the Evançon valley, known in its lower reaches as the **Val de Challand**, above Brusson as the **Val d'Ayas**. The latter has always been noted for its pine forests and for its massive wooden chalets.

The first steep ascent ends at (4km) *Targnod* (724m).—5km *Ville* (765m) is the centre of the commune of *Challant-St-Victor*. The ruined castle was the original home of the Challant family (12–14C).—7km *Corliod* (1006m) and (9km) *Quinçod* (1050m) are two hamlets of *Challant-St-Anselme*. Farther on, through a defile, can be seen on the left the *Tête de Comagna* (2098m).—13km *Arcesaz* is dominated by the ruined castle of *Graines* (13C). The road now ascends in zigzags to (16km) **Brusson** (1330m), a village made up of several hamlets well situated on the Evançon.The road ascends the Val d'Ayas. On the left at (19km) *Extrepieraz* (1378m) diverges the old bridle-road to Antagnod, above which rises the crest of Mont Zerbion.—At (24km) *Periasc* (1500m) the road emerges in the basin of Ayas, whose slopes are dotted with numerous villages. High up on the left are the hamlets of *Lignod* (1638m) and *Antagnod* (1710m), charmingly grouped round its conspicuous old campanile.

27km **Champoluc** (1570m), an important winter and summer resort amid splendid forests, enjoying a fine view of Castor and Pollux and the other peaks at the head of the valley. A cableway leads up to Crest (2000m), and from there a chair lift rises between Monte Sarezza (2828m) and Testa Grigia (3315m; see above). It is connected by ski-lift and chair lift to Gressoney, and is a base for skiing on Monte Rosa. Above Champoluc the road becomes rougher, and, beyond (3km) *Fracney* and (4km) **St-Jacques-d'Ayas** (1676m), it degenerates into a bridle-path. A tablet commemorates the Abbé Gorret, a famous alpinist, for 21 years parish priest of St-Jacques.—5km *Fiéry* (1878m) is a peaceful hamlet at the upper end of the Val d'Ayas, where it divides into the *Val de Verra* (NE) and Val de Cortot (NW). —Above the Verra Glacier rises the *Breithorn* (4171m), more easily climbed from Breuil and farther E are *Castor* and *Pollux* (4230m and 4094m). These may be climbed via the *Mezzalama Refuge* (3036m) beside the Verra Glacier. To the W of Fiéry rises the *Grand Tournalin* (3379m), usually ascended from Valtournenche.

Beyond (94km) *Montjovet* the road traverses another ravine.—98km **St-Vincent** (434m), situated amid groves of chestnuts, has been famous since 1770 as a health resort. It is well served by buses, and is a good centre for walking holidays. A new congress hall was built in 1983, and it is notorious for its casino. The old church has a 13C fresco in a niche outside the apse. Recent restorations have revealed its foundations on the baths of a Roman villa (adm. to excavations 16–18, Monday, Wednesday & Friday, June–August). The Romanesque interior has 13–16C frescoes. A funicular rises in 3 minutes to the *Palazzo delle Fonti* (1960), the source of the mineral spring (*Fons Salutis*).

By-roads lead to the castle of *Montjovet* and *Emarese*, a village with a fine view below an ice grotto. A road (22km) ascends the *Col de Joux* (1638m) a grass-grown plateau on the SE shoulder of Mont Zerbion. *Moron* has an old church, and *Arnay* a wonderful view of the upper Val d'Aosta. The road descends through magnificent forests to *Brusson.*

101km **Châtillon** (549m; 4340 inhab.) preserves a number of 16–17C houses. In the district are quarries of green marble. The Marmore torrent (a waterfall is well seen on the left side of the valley), flowing down from the Valtournenche is here crossed by three bridges: the uppermost dates from 1766, while farther down is the Roman bridge, with another bridge immediately above it. The feudal castle of the

Challant family was twice renovated in the 18C after damage by French troops (1706) and earthquake (1755).

A by-road ascends from Chambave to *St-Denis*, a village overhung by the ruined castle of *Cly* (1351m). Across the Dora another road leads to *Ussel* with another ruined 14C castle. Mont Zerbion (2721m) and Mont Barbeston (2483m) are climbed from Châtillon.

FROM CHÂTILLON TO VALTOURNENCHE AND BREUIL-CERVINIA, 27km (bus twice daily in 1½hrs; in summer innumerable coaches from Northern Italian towns). The **Valtournenche**, just over 27km long, extending from the base of the Matterhorn to the Val d'Aosta, is noteworthy especially for the fine perspective of the great peak at its head, and for its broad pastoral plateaux which offer fine ski-slopes.

2km *Champlong*, with remains of 14–15C aqueducts which formerly conveyed water to St-Vincent.—At (7km) *Antey-St-André* (1081m), with the mother-church of the valley (12C campanile), the road crosses to the left bank of the Marmore.

On the high plateau, 9km W by road (bus from Châtillon on weekdays in summer), lie the scattered hamlets of *Torgnon* (1478m–1634m), a quiet resort visited by climbers among the little-known peaks overlooking the Val St-Barthélemy (see below).—A road leads E from Antey-St-Andre to (8km) *La Magdeleine* (1644m), a summer and winter-sports resort.

Beyond (9km) *Fiernaz* the valley begins to narrow.—From (11km) *Buisson* a cable-car ascends to *Chamois* (1815m; no road), a summer and winter resort with a ski lift up to Punta Fontana Fredda (2513m).—At (14km) *Ussin* (1259m) the valley widens again.—Beyond the Cignana, with a cascade on the left, at *Moulin-Dessous*, is (18km) **Valtournenche** (1528m), the chief village of the valley, visited by skiers and walkers. The village square is charming; and outside the church is a tablet to the memory of Canon Georges Carrel of Aosta (died 1870), one of the first to attract attention to the interest of the neighbouring peaks; others commemorate guides who perished on the High Alps. A cableway ascends to *Salette* (2245m) from where ski-lifts continue to the *Cime Bianche* (2982m) and Plateau Rosa to connect with the Breuil–Cervinia cableway (see below).

PASSES. Fiéry (see above) may be reached on foot via the beautiful upland basin of *Cheneil* and the *Col de Nana* (2805m).—ASCENTS. The *Grand Tournalin* (3379m) is ascended via *Cheneil* and the *Col Sud du Tournalin* (3100m) between the Grand and Petit Tournalin. *Mont Roisetta* (3349m) rises farther N.

A pleasant path follows the hills above the left bank of the river via *Chamois* (see above) and *Antey-la-Magdeleine* (1640m) to *Châtillon*.—Another path leads W to *Falegnon* (1914m), the *Lago Cignana* (2108m), and up the Vallone Cignana, to the foot of the *Becca Sale* (3091m). From the lake a path leads S via *Torgnon* (see above) to Châtillon.

Higher up in the valley beyond the hamlet of *Crépin* is the entrance (right) of the narrow Gouffre des Buserailles, made accessible by wooden galleries. After the chapel of *Notre Dame de la Garde* (1829m) comes a narrow defile, from which the road emerges in the pastoral basin of (27km) *Breuil*, walled in on the N and W by the Matterhorn, the Dent d'Hérens, and the Château des Dames.

Breuil-Cervinia (2004m) has become one of the most popular skiing resorts in Italy. Thanks to the great extension of its cable-railways affording access to the splendid ski-slopes on the Italian side of the main ridge of the Alps, 'winter' sports can be enjoyed in summer also. The surname 'Cervinia' is an addition of the 1920s. Its inhabitants are famous as mountain guides.

Ski-School all the year round. *Ski Lifts* on the slopes to the N and SW of the village; another from Plan Maison (see below). *Bob Sleigh Run.—Cable Railway* to Furggen and Plateau Rosà, see below.—Golf course, Swimming Pool, Tennis courts, and skating rink in the village.

Breuil is the starting-point of the cable ascending to the main frontier ridge on either side of the Theodule Pass. The first section ascends to *Plan Maison* (2600m). From here are two branches: the left-hand branch leads to the crest of the *Furggen* ridge (3499m); the right-hand branch ascends to *Cime Bianche* (2899m), from where another car goes on up to the *Plateau Rosà* (3499m), with ski-lifts in summer. A remarkable new cableway on the Plateau Rosà in Swiss territory was opened in 1980. It is the highest in Europe and ascends from

Trockener Steg (2939m) to a height of 3820m. A lift continues to the summit of the Piccolo Cervino. Splendid ski-slopes descend from here to Zermatt and to Cervinia and Valtournenche.The *Breithorn (4171m) has a magnificent view extending from the Bernese Alps to the Gran Paradiso.

From Breuil were started most of the earliest attempts to scale the **Matterhorn** (4478m: *Mont Cervin* or *Monte Cervino*), but the summit was not reached from this side by a direct route until 1867. The ascent may now be made by practised mountaineers in c 12hrs. A path leads to *L'Oriondé* (2885m), with the Duca degli Abruzzi refuge, from where the ascent follows the SW arête passing the Rifugio J.A. Carrel (3830m), the *Pic Tyndall* (4241m; named after Professor Tyndall), and the precipitous rock walls beneath the summit, now fitted with ropes.—Other ascents are those of the *Gran Sometta* or Cemetta (3167m), reached either via the *Motta di Plête* (2889m; by bridle-path) or via the upper Col des Cimes-Blanches; the *Château des Dames* (3488m) via the Col de Valcornère, and the difficult *Pointe Sella* (3860m) and *Pointe Giordano* (3876m), peaks of the *Jumeaux*, via the *Jumeaux Refuge* (2803m).—From Plateau Rosà a good route leads over the *Col Supérieur des Cimes-Blanches* (2980m) to *Fiéry*.

FROM BREUIL TO ZERMATT a rough track leads over pastures and rock and rubble to *Les Fornets* (3077m; Rifugio Bontadini), at the foot of the Lower Theodule Glacier, where traces remain of the fort erected in 1688 by Victor Amadeus II to prevent the return of the exiled Waldenses. The track ascends the glacier and reaches the **Theodule Pass** (3292m; numerous ski-lifts), on the Swiss frontier. On the pass is the *Rifugio Teodulo*. The awkward descent of the Upper Theodule Glacier leads to *Zermatt*.

106km *Chambave* (475m), beneath the castle of Cly (see above), once noted for its wine (moscato). To the S extends the *Val Clavalité*, with the snowy *Pyramid of the Tersiva visible at its head. Just beyond, on the left, appears the *Castle of Fénis (adm. as for Verrés, above, except closed Tuesday), one of the finest in the Valle d'Aosta, rebuilt c 1340 by Aymon de Challant. The courtyard and the loggias have frescoes of saints and sages, with proverbs in Old French; the chapel is equally well decorated.—113km *Nus* (474m), with the ruins of its castle, lies at the mouth of the Val St-Barthélemy.

The wooded VAL ST-BARTHÉLEMY, 25km long (bus daily in July & August for the first 13km), leads to (16km) *Lignan* (1628m), its principal village.

To the right is the 12C castle of *Quart* (725m).—The valley expands into the fertile basin of Aosta, with a small airfield. A large steelworks S of the town is very prominent.

125km **AOSTA** (579m), surrounded by lofty snow-capped mountains at the junction of the Buthier and the Dora Baltea, is a town (36,900 inhab.) of ancient foundation. The old centre, less than two kilometres square, is still enclosed by its Roman walls and contains many Roman and medieval survivals. Industrial expansion outside the walls detracts from the beautiful position and fine monuments of the town.

Hotels, mostly outside the walls.—**Buses** run all year to centres of the Val d'Aosta, also to *Turin*, and to *Milan*; and via the Great St Bernard tunnel to *Martigny*, and to *Courmayeur* and *Chamonix* (via the Mt Blanc tunnel).—**Tourist Offices**. *Assessorato Turismo*, Piazza Narbonne; *Information Office*, Piazza E. Chanoux.

History. Once the chief town of the Gallic Salassi, Aosta was captured by Terentius Varro in 24 BC and renamed *Augusta Praetoria*; and its centre still retains a Roman plan almost intact. The character of the later city, however, is Southern French rather than Italian, the architecture is essentially Burgundian, and the people speak a French dialect. Throughout the later Middle Ages town and valley owed allegiance to the great house of Challant, viscounts of Aosta, and later the dukedom was a prized appanage of the house of Savoy. The most famous native of Aosta is St Anselm (1033–1109), Archbishop of Canterbury from 1093. St Bernard of Menthon (died c 1081), founder of the famous Hospice, was Archdeacon of Aosta.

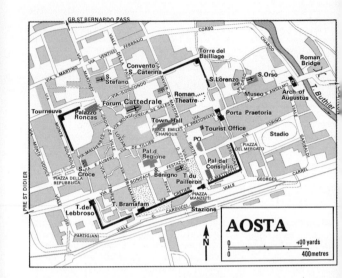

PIAZZA EMILE CHANOUX is the centre of the town, with the *Town Hall* (1837). From here Via Porte Pretoriane leads E to the **Porta Praetoria**, a massive double gateway of three arches. On the left is the tall rear wall of the *Roman Theatre* (adm. 9.30–12, 14 or 14.30–16.30 or 18.30), comparable with that of Orange, with remains of the cavea and scena. Excavations are being carried out to the S and W. Via Sant'Anselmo continues E to the *Arch of Augustus*, a triumphal arch erected in 24 BC to commemorate the defeat of the Salassi. This is decorated with ten Corinthian columns, and is fairly well preserved though rather disfigured by a roof of 1716. The Crucifixion below was added in 1540. Farther on, beyond the modern bridge over the Buthier, is a remarkable single-arched *Roman Bridge* (still in use) over a dried-up channel.

To the right, on the return, Via Sant'Orso leads to the priory and collegiate church of **Sant'Orso**, or *St-Ours*, founded by St Anselm, with a campanile finished in 1131 and an outré Gothic façade. It contains 16C stalls. Ottonian frescoes (early 11C) in the roof vaulting have been restored. They are shown by the sacristan (adm. 9–12, 14.30–17.30; closed Monday). By means of platforms and walkways in the roof they can be seen at close range (some of the scenes show the miracles on Lake Gennesaret and at the Marriage at Cana; they were damaged in the 15C by the construction of the vault). In the crypt are 12 plain Roman columns. The treasury is shown on request. The venerable CLOISTER (adm. as for the frescoes in the church) has fascinating *Capitals carved in white marble covered with a dark patina. At the top of unusually low columns, they can be examined with ease. The *Priory* (1494–1506), with an octagonal tower, has fine terracotta decoration. Opposite Sant'Orso excavations in 1972–79 beneath the church of *San Lorenzo* revealed an unusual palaeochristian church of the 5C. It has a Latin-cross plan with four apses, and was the burial place of the first bishops of Aosta (sarcophagus of Bishop Agnello, died 528). The church was destroyed in the Carolingian era. Adm. to the excavations as for the frescoes in Sant'Orso.—In the lane behind the priory the *Archaeological Museum* has been closed since 1973 awaiting transfer to a new building.

Via Sant'Orso continues beyond the church to meet Via Guido Rey which leads left to the *Torre del Baillage*, a 12C addition to the Roman walls. Nearby, in the Convent of St Catherine (ring for adm.), are eight arches of the Roman *Amphitheatre*, a building once capable of holding 15,000 spectators. Some of the arches have been built into the wall of the convent; the others traverse the orchard.

The **Cathedral** (*San Giovanni Battista*), an ancient foundation preserving Romanesque campanili at the E end, was rebuilt in the Gothic style, and given a sculptured W portal in 1526, now framed within a neo-classical façade of 1848. In the choir are good mosaic pavements (12C and 14C), one with the Labours of the Months, the other with lively animals and the Tigris and Euphrates. Here also are good stalls (c 1469).

The *Museo del Tesoro* was opened in 1984 in the deambulatory and in the Chapel of Reliquaries (adm. 10–12, 15–17; winter & fest. 15–17.45; closed Monday). It contains an ivory diptych of 406, and reliquaries of Saints Gratus and Jucundus, local patron saints, and of St John the Baptist. The tombs include those of Thomas II of Savoy (died 1259), and two bishops (c 1375 and 1431), of local workmanship.—The Romanesque *Crypt* has antique columns. The cloister to the N of the church dates from 1460.

In a sunken garden on the NW side of the cathedral are some remains of the *Roman Forum* with the base of a temple. From here there is access (daily 10–12, 14.30–16.30 or 18) to a splendid underground *Cryptoporticus* (perhaps used as a horreum). The double north walk, over 92m long, is particularly remarkable.

The **Roman Walls*, forming a rectangle c 732m long and 572m broad, are in best preservation on the S and W sides. Standing across the W wall is the medieval *Torre del Lebbroso*, celebrated in Xavier de Maistre's tale, 'Le Lépreux de la Cité d'Aoste'. Recently restored, it is now used for exhibitions. Near the *Torre Bramafam*, a relic (11C) of the lords of Challant, remains of the Porta Principalis Dextera have been unearthed; while the *Torre del Pailleron* stands in a garden near the station.

The road (bus) crossing the Dora Báltea by the Pont Suaz, S of Aosta, ascends in rapid zigzags through the hamlets of Charvensod to (12km) *Péroulaz* (1364m), and (18km) *Pila* (1814m) with numerous ski-slopes, connected by chair-lift with *Chamolé* (2310m) on the N slope of the ridge separating the main valley from the Val de Cogne.—The **Becca di Nona** (3142m) is reached from Péroulaz by a track leading past the hermitage of *St-Grat* and over the *Col de Plan-Fenêtre* (2225m) to *Comboé* (2121m). The **View of the Alps extends from Mont Blanc to the Mischabelhörner.—The ascent of **Mont Emilius** (3559m) is made via Comboé (see above), the *Lac d'Arbolé* (2961m), and the S arête.—*Mont Fallère* (3061m), to the N, is reached by an easy track via *Sarre* and the *Val Clusetta*, or via *St-Pierre* and *Verrogne* (see below).

FROM AOSTA TO THE GREAT ST BERNARD, 34km by the old road to the pass (usually closed in November–May); 29km to the tunnel mouth. A railway is projected from Aosta to Martigny with a tunnel under the

Great St Bernard. The road (N27) has striking views, including that of Aosta itself. Amidst a country of trellised vines and fields of maize is (4·5km) *Variney* (785m), where a road diverges to Valpelline. On the other side of the valley, 152m below, lies Roisan.—8km *Gignod* (994m) has a 15C church tower on the ruins of an ancient castle.— From (11km) *Condemine* (1128m) there is a magnificent view of the whole length of the Valpelline.—At (16km) **Étroubles** (1280m), a quiet summer resort, the road crosses the stream and there is an impressive view up the valley, closed by the Grand Golliaz and the Aiguille d'Artanavaz.—18km *St-Oyen* (1376m) lies at the foot of *Mont Fallère* (3061m). A little farther on the road divides.

The left branch, following the infant Artavanaz through *St-Léonard*, becomes motorway, making a long loop to the W before turning E, then N beneath long snow galleries. The Italian custom-house is just below the tunnel mouth. The **Great St Bernard Tunnel**, built in 1958–64 (toll), is 5·8km long and rises slightly from the Italian side (1875m) to the Swiss (1918m).

The old road (right), narrow and sometimes slippery, climbs through (22km) *St-Rhémy* (1632m), a dreary village. From 1658 until 1915 the young men of Étroubles and St-Rhémy exercised the right to act as guides and snow-sweepers on the St Bernard road instead of serving in the army. To the NW is a view of the striking *Pain de Sucre* (2793m). An old bridle-path keeps to the right side of the valley, and is more direct than the road. The Italian customs post is on the Swiss border by a small lake. Just beyond the frontier is (34km) the **Great St Bernard Hospice** (2469m), one of the highest habitations in Europe, a massive stone building on the summit of the pass, exposed to storms from the NE and SW. On the NW it is sheltered by the *Chenalette* (2889m), on the SE by *Mont Mort* (2867m).

The Hospice was supposedly founded in the 11C by St Bernard of Menthon, archdeacon of Aosta, a native of Savoy, though the earliest known documents (1125) called it then after St Nicolas; by 1215 it was regularly manned by Austin canons from their mother-house at Martigny, and its riches, both in lands and money, increased steadily until the Reformation. The resources of the monks were severely taxed by Napoleon, who, though he made numerous donations to the Hospice, quartered a garrison of 40 men there for some months. Since 1925 the Hospice has been managed by 10 or 12 canons assisted by a number of lay brothers or 'aumoniers'. In their rescue of snow-bound travellers the canons are assisted by the famous St Bernard dogs, a breed said to be a cross between the Pyrenean sheepdog and the Newfoundland, although modern conditions have made their services much less important.

The pass of the *Great St Bernard (2472m) is more remarkable for its historical and religious associations than for its scenery, which is less impressive than that on most of the other great passes. Known and used by Celts and Romans, its ancient name was *Mons Jovis* (Mont Joux), from a temple of Jupiter Paeninus which once stood on the Plan de Jupiter, and it was only in the 12C that it acquired its present name. The pass was much used by pilgrims and clerics bound to or from Rome, and between 774 and 1414 it was crossed twenty times by the medieval emperors, including Frederick Barbarossa in 1162. In the campaigns of 1798–1800 many French and Austrian soldiers crossed the pass. The most famous passage was made by Napoleon, who on 14–20 May 1800 led 40,000 troops by this route into Italy and a month later defeated the Austrians at the battle of Marengo. Each regiment took three days on the crossing, halting the first night at Bourg-St-Pierre, the second at St-Rhémy or Étroubles, the third at Aosta.

The road, now Swiss No. 21, descends via (41km) *Bourg St Pierre* and (55km) *Orsières* to (61km) *Sembrancher* and (73km) **Martigny** (all described in 'Blue Guide Switzerland').

The VALPELLINE, NE of Aosta, leads to the foot of the Pennine Alps and is ascended by buses from Aosta. From (4·5km) *Variney*, on the St Bernard road (see above), the road descends to cross the Buthier.—13km **Valpelline** (951m) stands at the junction of the Val d'Ollomont with the main valley. In the former, 3km N, lies *Ollomont* (1336m), with disused copper mines, and now a climbing centre. It lies at the foot of the *Col de Fenêtre* (2786m). Calvin escaped into Switzerland by this pass after an unsuccessful attempt at reforming the Aostans. Above the beautiful alpine basin of *By* (2042m) is the *Rifugio d'Amiante* (2964m) beneath *Mont Vélan* (3709m). The narrow Valpelline road now ascends NE past a power station to (20km) *Oyace* (1367m), high above the Buthier, with an old tower of the lords of the valley. To the S towers the imposing *Monte Faroma* (3073m).—The road continues beyond (26km) *Bionaz* (1600m) to end at a dam beneath the *Col de Luseney* (3265m).— *Prarayé* (1993m), the uppermost hamlet in the valley, lies at the foot of two frontier passes into Switzerland, the *Col de Collon* (Refuge; 3130m), and the *Col de Valpelline* (3562m). On the way to the latter is the *Rifugio Aosta* (2850m), on the Za-de-Zan Glacier, above which rises the *Dent d'Hérens* (4180m).

The winding road from Aosta to Courmayeur is always crowded with heavy international traffic. There are long-term plans to improve the road as far as the Mont Blanc tunnel, although this will damage the landscape. Beyond *Sarre* with its 13C Castle rebuilt in 1710 (decorated with hunting trophies; adm. in summer 10–11, 14.30–16.30 except Tuesday; open only Saturday & Sunday in June), it reaches (133km) *St-Pierre* (661m), with its restored castle on an isolated rock, affording a good view S. The castle contains a Natural History Museum (open May–September 9–12, 15–19; closed Tuesday). On the S side is the castle (mainly 14C) of *Sarriod de la Tour* (open May–September 9–12, 15–19; closed Monday). An archaeological exhibition has been set up here with material from the Museum in Aosta. The road on the right ascends in 8km to *St-Nicolas* (1126m), a little summer resort.

To the S extends the Val di Cogne, traversed by a road (N 507; bus from Aosta) through (1km) *Aymavilles*, with its turreted castle (mostly 18C),—5km *Pondel* has a Roman aqueduct of 3 BC over the Grand'Eyvia.—21·5km **Cogne** (1533m) stands in a wide basin at the junction of the main valley with the Valnontey, which runs due S to the Gran Paradiso. It is a summer and winter resort (particularly known for cross-country skiing), and a climbing centre. The magnetite mines, once some of the most productive in the country, have been closed down. The craft of lace-making survives here.

A by-road leads S to *Valnontey*, with the 'Paradisia' alpine garden (1700m) founded in 1955 (open July–September). The whole of the **Gran Paradiso** (4061m) massif, extending from the E ridge of the Valle Rhêmes (W) to the upper Val Soana (E), including the upper Valsavarenche, the Valnontey and the Valeille, and bounded on the S by the N side of the Locana valley, an area of some 70,000 hectares, is dedicated as the **National Park of the Gran Paradiso**, the oldest national park in Italy. Hunting, shooting, and digging up plants are rigorously prohibited, even though the natural beauty of the park has been threatened by attempts to open up part of the Valsavarenche as a resort for skiiers. The park was started as a hunting preserve for Victor Emmanuel II in 1856; presented to the State by Victor Emmanuel III in 1919, it was established as a nature reserve in 1922. Many of the bridle-paths constructed by the king are still in use. This is the only part of the Alps in which the ibex (stambecco) has survived in its natural state, and the chamois and Alpine marmot are common. The flowers are at their best in May–June. For information about climbs and walks, see the TCI map of the park and leaflets available locally from the visitors' centres in Rhêmes-Notre-Dame and Degioz-Valsavarenche. The main offices of the Park are in Turin (47 Via della Rocca) and Aosta (5 Via Losanna). Ordinary visitors can find accommodation on the borders of the park and climbers are allowed to use the Alpine refuges on the Col du Nivolet, the Gran Paradiso (Rifugio Vittorio Emanuele II), and the Grivola (Rifugio Vittorio Sella). Permission to use the 'case' and 'casotti' of the park organisation may be obtained by naturalists for research purposes from the main offices of the park in Turin.

136km **Villeneuve** (671m), a village beneath the ruined 12C Châtel d'Argent, is the best starting-point for exploring the Valsavarenche and Vale de Rhêmes in the Gran Paradiso National Park.

The **Valsavarenche**, to the E, is ascended by bus in summer via (4km) *Introd*, with its castle and medieval tithe barn and ancient stone and wood houses. The bus terminates at (17km) *Dégioz* (1541m), except in July & August when it goes on to (20km) *Eau-Rousse* (1666m) and to (25km)*Pont Valsavarenche* (1946m). Dégioz is connected with Rhemes-Notre-Dame and with Cogne by several easy passes. A royal hunting road built by Victor Emmanuel II leads from Dégioz, over the Nivolet plateau and pass, to the Gran Piano di Noasca (2222m) and, beyond several other passes, descends to Noasca (see above). Dégioz and Colle Loson (3296m) are on the mountaineering route (known as the 'alta via No. 2') which connects Champorcher and Courmayeur (via the valleys to the S of Aosta). Pont is a base for the ascent of the *Gran Paradiso*, reached via the *Rifugio Vittorio Emanuele II* (2775m).—From the head of the valley the Col du Nivolet leads via the Rifugio Città di Chivasso (2604m) to Ceresole Reale (see above; road in construction).

The delightful **Val de Rhêmes**, farther W, is ascended by bus in summer from Villeneuve to (9km) Rhêmes-St-Georges (1170m) and (19km)*Rhêmes-Notre-Dame* (1676m), another climbing centre in a charming upland basin. A private road continues to the *Rifugio Benevolo* (2285m) beneath the *Granta Parey* (3474m), the striking peak at the head of the vale. To the SE is *Mont Tout-Blanc* (3439m).

141km *Arvier* (774m), with the 13C Chateau de la Mothe, grows good wine and stands at the foot of the Valgrisenche.

The **Valgrisenche**, narrow and rocky in its lower reaches, and almost blocked by the castle-crowned rock of Montmajeur, is ascended by a bus in summer.— 10km *Planaval* (1554m), with a distant view of the Matterhorn, and (16km)*Valgrisenche* (1664m), the bus terminus, with a fine campanile, are the principal centres. To the W rises the *Rutor* (3486m). A huge dam holds the waters of the *Lago di Beauregard*, a long power-reservoir, along which the road continues to end at *Surier*, a climbing centre.

Passing *Avise* (right), a pleasant village with three castles (10C, 12C, and 15C), the road threads the fine gorge of the Pierre-Taillée and, crossing the Dora (785m), comes into view of Mont Blanc. On the opposite side of the river can be seen the village of *Derby*, notable for its medieval houses.—149km *La Salle*.—Beyond the 13C tower of Châtelard (right) is (152km) **Morgex** (920m), the principal village in the Valdigne, the upper valley of the Dora. The church has 6C elements.

156km **Pré-St-Didier** (1010m) is a little holiday resort once famous for its chalybeate springs. With an 11C church tower, it stands at the junction of the Dora de la Thuile and the Dora Baltea. It is the terminus of the railway from Aosta and stands at the foot of the little St Bernard Pass beneath the *Tête de Crammont** (2737m).

FROM PRÉ-ST-DIDIER TO BOURG-ST MAURICE, 54km. N26 branches left and ascends in zigzags high above the gorge of the Dora de la Thuile, passing through two tunnels.—10km **La Thuile** (1440m), a summer and winter resort in a pastoral basin amid wooded mountain-slopes. It has good skiing facilities (it is joined by ski-lift to La Rosiene), and is a climbing centre.

From Grande Golette, at the foot of the Val des Chavannes (right), a chair-lift ascends in two stages, on the left, to *Les Suches* (2149m) and *Chaz Dura* (2560m), giving access to remarkably fine ski-slopes. *Mont Bério Blanc* (3258m) lies to the N, and to the S is the *Lac du Rutor*, and three fine waterfalls.

Beyond the *Pont Serrand* (1650m), high above the torrent, *Lac Verney* (2085m; fine view of Mont Blanc from the shore; good fishing) can be seen on the right. At (22km) is the frontier, near which remains of a Roman posting-station and an old hospice have been found. Here is the Italian customs post. Just over the frontier is (23km) the **Little St Bernard Pass** (2188m), on the watershed between the Dora Baltea and the Isère.

Nearby is the *Colonne de Joux* (Jupiter's Column) a Celtic or Roman monument of cipollino marble, with a statue of St Bernard added in 1886, and a little below it is an Iron Age stone burial circle just over 73m in diameter, in which Gaulish and Roman coins have been discovered. The best view is from the *Belvedere* (2641m; path to the left).

A gentle descent leads past the ruined *Hospice du Petit-St-Bernard* (2152m), the medieval Hospitale Columnae Jovis, founded c 1000, which used to offer free hospitality to poor travellers. After war damage, it was ceded to France in 1947 and is now derelict. The monks, who depended for food on an estate near Paris, have mostly moved to Econe, near Martigny (Switzerland). The Botanical Garden founded here in 1897 by Abbot Pierre Chanoux is being reconstituted and is open to the public. The descent goes on, through forest, to (51km) *Séez* (904m), with the French customhouses, and (54km) **Bourg-St-Maurice** (see 'Blue Guide France').

The road (N26dir) ascends past the hamlets of *Pallusieux* (1108m) and *Verrand* (1250m), served by the old steep and winding road.

161km **Courmayeur** (1228m), situated in a deep vale at the S foot of the Mont Blanc range, is the Chamonix of the Val d'Aosta, but has a much milder climate than its rival of Savoy. It is visited in summer by both alpinists and lovers of mountain scenery, and it is a famous winter sports resort. The winter season lasts from mid-December to mid-April.

Hotels, some seasonal, here, and many others in the near environs; and at Entrèves, La Palud, and Dolonne.—**Winter sports**. In 1985 Courmayeur, Cervinia-Breuil, La Thuile, and La Rosiene were all joined by ski-lift. The main ski-slopes are on the *Colle Checrouit* (ski-lifts, cableways, chair-lifts, etc.). *Ski School* in winter in the village, and in summer at the Rifugio Torino. Cableways from the village and from La Palud (see below).—**Golf course** (9 holes; July–August) at Planpincieux in the Val Ferret.—**Buses to** *Planpincieux, Pré-St-Didier, Petit-St-Bernard, Chamonix, Cogne, Aosta, Morgex, St-Vincent, Turin* and *Milan.*

A cableway, passing above *Dolonne* to the W, ascends via *Plan Chécrouit* (1696m) to the *Col de Chécrouit* (1899m). The cable cars go on to *Creta d'Arp* (2755m), with another marvellous view of the chain of Mont Blanc.—A bridle-path leads up the *Mont de la Saxe* (2358m), NE of Courmayeur.

FROM COURMAYEUR TO THE COL FERRET (Orsières). The road leads N and reaches the long VAL FERRET at (3km) *Entrèves* (1300m), a hamlet with a castle between the old and new roads.—3·5km *La Palud* (1370m), with the lower station of the Mont-Blanc cable railway (see below).—The road goes on via the chalets of (6km)*Planpincieux* (1448m), between which and (10km) *La Vachey*, but beyond the stream, lies the golf course.—At (15km) the foot of the Triolet Glacier the road ends. A bridle-path continues to the *Pré-de-Bar* chalets (2060m).—The **Col Ferret** (2533m) lies on the Swiss frontier, between the Italian Val Ferret and the Swiss Val Ferret (see 'Blue Guide Switzerland').

FROM COURMAYEUR TO THE COL DE LA SEIGNE (Les Chapieux). The road crosses the Dora beyond Le Larzey and ascends the right bank, rounding Mont Chétif.—4km *Notre-Dame de la Guérison* commands a view of the Grandes Jorasses above Entrèves and the Val Ferret, and of the Brenva Glacier. The road ascends the VAL VENY, leaving on the right (6km) *Purtud* (1490m), and traverses the forest of St-Nicolas. The road deteriorates at (9km) the inn of La Visaille (1658m), above which towers the Aiguille Noire de Peuterey, with the Aiguille Blanche and the Dames Anglaises behind, but continues to *Lac Combal*, the starting pint of the most usual ascent from the Italian side of **Mont Blanc** (4810m), the highest mountain in western Europe (the highest summit is in France and it is fully described in 'Blue Guide France'). It was first climbed from Chamonix by Michel Gabriel Paccard and Jacques Balmat in 1786. Many climbs can be taken beneath the **Col de la Seigne** (2512m), on the French frontier, the water-shed between the basins of the Po and the Rhône.

FROM COURMAYEUR TO CHAMONIX BY CABLE RAILWAY, c 1½hrs. This *Traverse of the Mont Blanc massif is the most sensational excursion from Courmayeur. Its working depends, naturally enough, on the weather, but normally a car starts every hour from La Palud. Passengers going the whole way should take French money as well as a passport. The last car for the return leaves Chamonix at 16.45. From La Palud (see above) the route ascends (all the year), with a break at the *Pavillon du Mont-Fréty* (2131m; *View) to (15 minutes) the **Rifugio Torino** (3322m). There are ski-lifts serving the adjoining slopes (Colle del Gigante), and a summer ski-school. A little higher is the **Col du Géant** (3369m). It provides a magnificent panorama of the Graian Alps, to the S, and the S side of the Pennine Alps, to the W. The next stage of the railway leads to the *Punta Helbronner* (3462m), which marks the frontier; from there the line goes on, across the magnificent expanse of the Vallée Blanche, to the Gros Rognon and (40 minutes) the *Aiguille du Midi* station. The descent to *Chamonix* (55 minutes) leads via the Plan des Aiguilles.

The new fast road by-passes Entrèves and La Palud (see above) and, beyond a short tunnel, reaches the Italian customs-post (1381m) by the mouth of (166km) the **Mont Blanc Tunnel** (*Traforo del Monte Bianco*) a road tunnel (11·6km) opened through the mountains in 1958–65. At the far end (1274m) a brief zigzag descends to (181km) **Chamonix-Mont Blanc** (see 'Blue Guide France').

3   Turin to Ventimiglia

ROAD, N20, 177km, open all the year.—20km *Carignano.*—28km *Carmagnola.*—53km *Savigliano.*—86km **Cúneo**.—94km *Borgo San Dalmazzo.*—112km *Limone Piemonte.*—118km Tunnel (Italian customs).—131km *Tende* (French customs).—150km *La Giandola.*—177km **Ventimiglia**.—The A6 MOTORWAY from Turin to Savona follows this route fairly closely up to (50km) *Fossano*, 14km S of Savigliano.—BUSES several times daily from Turin to Cúneo via Saluzzo in 2¼–2½hrs; also from Cúneo to Limone.

RAILWAY, 187km in c 4hrs. To *Cúneo*, 89km in 1–1½hrs, where a change is necessary to a diesel train. The spectacular line between Cúneo and Ventimiglia through the mountains is a remarkable feat of engineering skill with numerous tunnels and viaducts. Inaugurated in 1928 it was finally reopened in 1979, having been put out of action in the Second World War. Between Limone Piemonte and Ventimiglia it traverses 46km of French territory (passports necessary). From *Breil-sur-Roya* (164km) a secondary line diverges for *Nice* (6 trains a day; 43km in c 1hr).—There is a longer alternative route to Cúneo via Airasca and Saluzzo in 2–3hrs (94km).

The initial tract of N20 is now a minor road, the main road (N393; c 1km shorter) running to the E near the right bank of the Po to rejoin N20 just before Carmagnola (see below).—19·5km *Carignano*, on the old road, is an ancient lordship long associated with the royal house of Savoy. The Cathedral (1757–67) is the masterpiece of Benedetto Alfieri. In the ex Villa Bona is a Museo Civico with archaeological finds, etc. *Pancalieri*, 13km SW off the Saluzzo road, was the birthplace in c 1533 of David Rizzio, the favourite of Mary Queen of Scots, murdered in 1566.—28km *Carmagnola*, beyond the Po, was the birthplace of the condottiere Francesco Bussone (c 1380–1432), called 'Il Carmagnola'. The 'Carmagnole', a popular song in Paris during the

French Revolution, was originally sung by strolling minstrels from Piedmont. The road bears right in the town.—At (39km) *Racconigi* is the royal palace of the House of Savoy, built in 1676–1842, with a fine park. Here Umberto of Savoy was born in 1904 (the ex-King died in exile in 1983). Not at present open to the public, there are plans to restore the palace.—46km *Cavallermaggiore.*—53km **Savigliano** (19,100 inhab.) was the birthplace of Giovanni Schiaparelli (1835–1910), the astronomer. It has several interesting churches and a local museum.

Saluzzo (17,900 inhab.), the historic seat of a famous line of marquesses, 13km W of Savigliano, is connected with it by railway, and with Cúneo by frequent buses. It was the birthplace of Giambattista Bodoni (1740–1813), the famous printer, and of Silvio Pellico (1789–1854), the patriot author. The large *Cathedral* was built in 1481–1511. The ancient streets of the upper town lead up to the *Castle* (turned into a prison in 1821). Just below it is the church of *SAN GIOVANNI, erected in 1281 with a choir extension of 1472 containing good stalls and the tomb of Marquess Ludovic II (died 1503), by Benedetto Briosco. On the N side are the cloister and chapter house, the latter with a monument of 1528. Farther along Via San Giovanni, the charming 15C *Casa Cavassa*, with a portal by Sanmicheli, houses the small town museum (with a Madonna della Misericordia between Margherita di Foix and the Marquess Ludovic II, dated 1499).—On the Cúneo road is the imposing 14C castle of *Manta* which contains good frescoes (1418–30; restored in 1989) by Giacomo Jaquerio in the International Gothic style. They show 18 historical heroes and heroines in contemporary costume. Donated to the FAI in 1984, there are plans to open it to the public. Nearby is the 14C castle of *Verzuolo.* To *Pinerolo,* see Rte 1C.

The road continuing W from Saluzzo ascends the upper valley of the Po; bus (coming from Cúneo) 5 times daily to Paesana, in connection with the Pinerolo-Crissolo bus.—At (34km) *Paesana* the hills close in. The road goes on past a by-road (left) which mounts in steep curves to *Serre* and (45km) **Crissolo** (1333m), a summer and winter resort (chair-lift), and climbing centre, standing at the base of the graceful pyramid of the **Monviso** (3841m; the Rifugio Quintino Sella at 2640m, first built in 1905, was modernised in 1980). The road ends at (52km) *Pian del Re* (2050m), at the source of the Po. From above Pian del Re the remarkable *Pertuis de la Traversette,* a tunnel pierced beneath the Col de la Traversette (2950m), leads into the French valley of the Guil and Abriès (see 'Blue Guide France'). Originally dug by Marquess Ludovic II in 1478–80 for the use of merchants trading into Dauphiny, the tunnel has been many times blocked up. It was completely restored in 1907, but is now not usually traversable. The pass is considered by some authorities to have been Hannibal's route over the Alps.

From Savigliano to *Mondovì,* see Rte 5C.

86km **Cúneo** (533m), approached by a monumental viaduct over the Stura, is a regularly built provincial capital (54,500 inhab.) deriving its name from the 'wedge' of land at the confluence of the Gesso and the Stura. The huge arcaded piazza, the cathedral, and the public buildings were mostly rebuilt after the destructive but unsuccessful siege by Conti in 1744. On Tuesdays the square is the scene of a lively market. Via Roma, with heavy arcades, is the main street of the old town. A tall square tower surmounts the former town hall. *San Francesco,* a secularised church of 1227, with a good portal (1481), houses a Museo Civico. Magnificent boulevards have replaced the former ramparts.

The Stura viaduct also carries the railway to the new station; from the old station (*Cúneo-Gesso*), below the town to the E, electric trains run to Borgo San Dalmazzo.—BUSES to Turin, the Western valleys, to Mondovì and Savona, and to Garessio and Imperia, start from the Largo Audifredi (Via Roma).

Cúneo is the gateway to the southern Cottian Alps approached by the Val Maira (or Macra) and the Val Varaita, to the NW; they are served by buses several times daily to Acceglio, Pradlèves, and Pontechianale.—The road (N22) up the VAL MAIRA leaves on the left at (12km) *Caraglio* the Valle Grana (see below).—At (20km) *Dronero* (622m), with a 15C bridge and market-hall, the road enters hill country.—The church of *San Costanza al Monte*, 4km N, preserves a notable 12C apse.—From (55km) **Acceglio** (1219m) a poor road goes on to (6km) *Chiappera* (1591m), the highest hamlet in the valley, beneath the *Brec de Chambeyron* (3389m), on the frontier.

A road from (12km) Caraglio leads up the VALLE GRANA. Beyond (21km) *Monterosso Grana* with a local ethnographic museum, is the summer resort of *Pradléves* (510m). The road ends at the top of the valley at (31km) *Castelmagno*, with the sanctuary of San Magno (1761m; 15C chapel and church of 1710).

The road up the VAL VARAITA begins at (23km) *Costigliole*, on the Saluzzo road. From there it runs via (50km) *Sampeyre* (980m) to (61km) **Casteldelfino** (1295m), a village taking its name from a castle founded in 1336, once the centre of the Dauphins' Cisalpine territory.—To the N of (68km) *Pontechianale* (1614m), a winter resort with a chairlift to Chiosis (2340m) beside a power reservoir, rises the Monviso (see above). Above the village a rough road goes on to the *Col Agnel* (2699m) on the frontier, and descends to Fontgillarde in France. This was a route favoured by invading troops, and was crossed by Bayard in 1515 and by Philip, Duke of Parma, in 1743.

The *Certosa di Pesio* (1000m), 26km SE of Cúneo (bus), is a 12C foundation greatly altered, in the VALLE DEL PESIO, an attractive upland vale, a protected area since 1978 destined to become part of the Alpi Marittime National Park.

94km **Borgo San Dalmazzo** (631m) is named after St Dalmatius, the apostle of Piedmont, martyred here in 304. Above it is the picturesque church of the Madonna di Monserrato.

A road (bus from Cúneo) runs SW up the valley of the Gesso via (10km) *Valdieri* (774m) and from there by a side valley on the S to (16km) *Entracque* (904m), a hill resort. In summer other buses ascend the main valley via (18km) *Sant'Anna* (975m) to (25km) the **Terme di Valdieri** (975m), rebuilt in 1952–53, with hot sulphur springs, rather similar in their properties to those of Aix-les-Bains. A curiosity of the neighbourhood is a cryptogamic plant (*Ulva labyrinthiformis*) which grows in gelatinous masses over the rock down which the sulphur water flows; this substance ('muffa') is applied to wounds and inflammations. The *Monte Matto* (3087m) to the NW, and the *Punta dell'Argentera* (3300m) to the SE, the highest peak of the Maritime Alps, lie within the Argentera Park, once part of the royal hunting reserve of Valdieri-Entracque, and declared a protected area in 1980. It adjoins the Parc National du Mercantour in France, and both areas are destined to become part of the Alpi Marittime International Park.   There are long term plans to tunnel under Monte Argentera to join the road from Terme di Valdieri with that to Le Boréon and St-Martin-Vésubie in France (see 'Blue Guide France').

FROM BORGO SAN DALMAZZO TO THE COLLE DELLA MADDALENA, 60km, on N21, ascending the wooded VALLE STURA. Bus daily from Cúneo to Pietraporzio, oftener to Vinadio; twice daily in summer to the Colle; also in June–September from Cúneo to the Terme di Vinadio.—17km *Demonte* (774m) is the ancient capital of the valley.—27km *Vinadio* (899m) has imposing fortifications.—From (33km) *Pianche* (980m) a road leads S to (5km) the *Terme di Vinadio* (1274m), with hot sulphur springs.—Beyond (42km) *Pietraporzio* (1247m), with the Italian customs, the road traverses the striking defile of *Le Barricate* (stormed by Francis I in 1515), and reaches (49km) *Bersezio* (1625m).—53km *Argentera* (1695m) is the highest village, and beyond the *Lago della Maddalena* (1974m), the summit is reached at (60km) the **Colle della Maddalena** (1995m), or *Col de Larche*, an easy pass amid pastures noted for their varied flowers, and free from snow between mid-May and mid-October. Francis I passed this way on his invasion of Italy in 1515 and Napoleon decreed that 'the imperial road from Spain to Italy' should be carried over it. The descent leads via (7km) *Larche*, with the French custom-house, to (32km) *Barcelonnette* (see 'Blue Guide France').

A road leads E via *Bóves* (where the Santuario della Madonna dei Boschi has 16C frescoes) and *Peveragno* to the Valle del Pesio (see above).

Across the Gesso the road ascends the Val Vermenagna with the railway traversing a series of short tunnels and viaducts higher up.—106km *Vernante* (797m) faces a ruined castle across the valley. A by-road leads right for the Palanfrè park in the upper Val

Vermenagna, with remarkable beechwoods and interesting wild life.—112km **Limone Piemonte** (998m) is a large village among open pastures, one of the oldest ski resorts in Italy, with a 12–14C church. There are chair-lifts to the *Capanna Chiara* (1500m; refuge) and to *Maire Buffe* for high-level climbs.—Above Limone the road ascends, passing a by-road (right) for *Limonetto* (1294m), another ski resort. At 1321m it enters a tunnel 3km long (customs-post at tunnel mouth), emerging at 1280m. The old road over the *Colle di Tenda* (1909m) above it (walkers only) marks the present frontier with France.

The districts of Tende and La Brigue, although parts of the County of Nice, were expressly reserved to Italy in the Franco-Italian treaty of 1860, by courtesy of Napoleon III, because a great part of the territory was a favourite hunting-ground of Victor Emmanuel II. In 1947 they were rejoined to the rest of the county by treaty, an act which was confirmed a month later by a local plebiscite resulting in a large majority in favour of France.

From the tunnel exit there is a striking view of the 20 hairpin bends below; the descent traverses two rocky gorges, between which is the lofty railway viaduct of Vievola.—131km **Tende**, or *Tenda* (815m), with the French custom-house, described, with the places below in the 'Blue Guide France'. The road (now Route Nationale 204) follows the Roia, threading magnificent gorges. On the right, at San Dalmazzo di Tende, a by-road leads towards *Monte Bego* (2873m) where the Vallée des Marveilles (reached by walkers) has 40,000 graffiti on a glazed wall from a Ligurian cult that survived from Palaeolithic times to the Iron Age.—150km *La Giandola*, just above *Breil* (or Breglio), where its more important branch leaves the valley for Nice.—The road continues to descend the Roia past Breil, 11km beyond which it passes again into Italy (more customs-posts).—177km **Ventimiglia**.

4   Ventimiglia to Genoa

ROAD, N1, 163km.—5km **Bordighera**.—17km **Sanremo**.—40km *Imperia (Porto Maurizio)*.—43km *Imperia (Oneglia)*.—65km **Alassio**.—72km **Albenga**.—82km *Loana*.—93km *Finale Ligure*.—103km *Sportorno*.—117km **Savona**.—127km *Varazze*.—152km **Pegli**.—163km **Genoa**.—BUSES at frequent intervals for the whole distance or parts of it.

MOTORWAY (AUTOSTRADA DEI FIORI; A10) runs 'en corniche' farther inland among the foothills, with frequent long tunnels, and exits at all the main towns.

RAILWAY, 151km in 2¼–3hrs; all trains stop at *Sanremo* and *Savona*. Through sleeping-cars run on this route from Calais to Sanremo; through carriages from Marseille to Vienna, Spain to Rome, Ventimiglia to Amsterdam, etc.

The *Riviera di Ponente, that part of the Italian Riviera lying W of Genoa, is less rugged than the Riviera di Levante, but equally charming and luxuriant, with many coast resorts, planted with palms, bougainvillaea, and exotic plants.

VENTIMIGLIA (25,200 inhab.), is divided by the Roia into an old medieval town on a hill to the W and a new town on the coastal plain between the railway and the Via Aurelia, at the E end of which is the site of the Roman *Albintimilium* where Agricola spent his boyhood. Since its decline in the 13C Ventimiglia has had all the characteristics of a frontier town. In the old town the restored 11–12C *Cathedral* has a portal of 1222, and a Madonna by Barnaba da Modena (3rd N altar; removed since 1982 for safety). The apse of the cathedral adjoins the 11C *Baptistery. San Michele* was rebuilt c 1100 on the site of an 8–10C church, and later restored. The stoups are made up from Roman milestones and the Romanesque crypt is interesting.—The lower town expanded after 1872 when it became an important station on the railway line to France. The excavations of the Roman town which include a theatre of 2C AD are now isolated by modern buildings and the railway; they can be seen from a viaduct on the Aurelia. Finds from the Roman settlement and the earlier Ligurian Albium Intemelium, exhibited in the Archaeological Museum until 1977, have not yet been rehoused.

An attractive coastal drive leads W to (5km) *Mortola Inferiore*, where the road divides; the upper road (right) passes the famous **Giardino Hanbury*, a remarkable botanic garden founded in 1867 by Sir Thomas Hanbury and his brother Daniel. It was acquired by the Italian State from the Hanbury family in 1960, and is now run by Genoa University, but has been in a grave state of abandon for many years. It includes exotic plants from Asia and Africa. Here is exposed a section of Roman road; a tablet recalls famous travellers by this route (including Dante, Machiavelli, and Pius VII). Beyond the cape on which the garden is laid out is the frontier village of *Grimaldi*. A lift descends to the beach at the *Balzi Rossi* ('red rocks'), in which are several caves where relics of Palaeolithic man were discovered in 1892 (small museum on the site). The international customs-post is at (8km) *Ponte San Luigi*.—The main road, by the sea, passes in tunnels beneath the Hanbury Gardens and enters France by the *Ponte San Ludovico*.

The flowery valleys of the Vallecrosia and the Nervia are ascended by buses from Ventimiglia. In the former is (16km) *Perinaldo*, birthplace of G.D. Cassini (1625–1712), the astronomer. In the Nervia valley is (9km) the pretty village of *Dolceacqua*, with a ruined 15C castle of the Doria and a medieval bridge, and (24km) *Pigna*, a delightful little spa, picturesquely situated opposite the fortified village of *Castel Vittoria*.

5km **BORDIGHERA** (11,600 inhab.) is a famous winter resort. It became known to the English after 1855 when 'Doctor Antonio' by Giovanni Ruffini, set in the town, was translated, and a large English colony was established here by the end of the 19C. It is also a centre for the cultivation of flowers.

Post Office in the Station square.—*Tourist Office*, Palazzo del Parco.—**Buses** to *Bordighera, Ventimiglia,* and *Nice*; to *Alassio* and *Genoa*; to *Cúneo*.—**Tennis Club**, Via Stoppani.—*International Library*, 30 Via Romana.

The new town consists of two parallel thoroughfares, Via Vittorio Emanuele, near the shore, and Via Romana (on the line of the Roman road), higher up, with their connecting streets. In Via Romana the villa in which Margherita di Savoia died (1926) faces the *Museo Bicknell* (9–13, 15–18; Monday and fest. closed), founded by the Englishman Clarence Bicknell in 1888, with a good local natural history collection. Here, too, is the *Istituto Internazionale di Studi Liguri*. At No. 30 Via Romana is the *International Library*, also founded by Bicknell. The road ends on the E in the *Spianata del Capo*, with the old town above (gates restored in 1960), and the Capo Sant'Ampelio below. Here the church was stripped inside in 1964 to reveal its Romanesque structure. Delightful walks may be taken along the Lungomare W to the Kursaal and to the E to the palm-gardens known as the *Giardino Winter* and *Giardino Madonna della Ruota*. Several buildings in the town were built in the 1870s by the Frenchman Charles Garnier.

Via dei Colli provides splendid coastal views. In the Communal Cemetery in Valle di Sasso, NE of the town, is a *British Military Cemetery*, with 72 graves.

11km **Ospedaletti**, on a sheltered bay, is particularly popular as a winter resort. It is also a horticultural centre, and has fine palms and eucalyptus trees. The streets form the circuit for an annual motorcycle race (April). The town supposedly takes its name from a 14C hospice of the Knights of Rhodes, who were established at Porto Maurizio. They are unlikely to be commemorated in the name of *Coldirodi*, a village 6km inland (bus; panoramic road) where there is a Pinacoteca.—The road rounds the Capo Nero.

17km **SANREMO** is the largest summer and winter resort (62,200 inhab.) on the Italian Riviera. It has been famous since the mid-19C and has a superb climate. Its villas and gardens lie in an amphitheatre between Capo Nero and Capo Verde, in a wide bay 8km across.

Post Office, 132 Via Roma.—**Tourist Office**, 1 Via Nuvoloni.—**English Church**. *All Saints*, Corso Matuzia at the W end of the town.—**Buses** to *Bordighera*, *Ventimiglia*, and *Nice*; to *Alassio* and *Genoa*; to *Cúneo* and *Turin*; to *Poggio*; to *Ceriana* and *Baiardo*; to *Coldirodi*; etc.—**Golf Course** (18 holes) on the San Romolo road (4km N); cable railway (at present out of action) from the Corso degli Inglesi for Monte Bignone. *Tennis Club*, 18 Corso Matuzia; *Swimming Pool* on Capo Nero. *Harbour* for small boats.

Edward Lear (1812–88) spent his last years at Sanremo, and built the Villa Emily (now Villa Verde) and Villa Tennyson (both named after Tennyson's wife). He died at the latter and was buried in Sanremo. Alfred Nobel (1833–96) also died here, and here in 1878 Tchaikovsky finished his 4th Symphony and 'Eugen Onegin'. His empress, Maria Alexandrovna, consort of Alexander II, was here surrounded after 1874 by a large Russian colony.—Amongst the annual festivals for which the town is famous is the International Song Contest.

Via Roma and the parallel Via Matteotti, are the main streets of the modern town. In the latter, at No. 143 is *Palazzo Borea d'Olmo* (early 16C), seat of the Archaeological Museum. To the SW, surrounded by gardens, is the **Casinò Municipale** (always open), with celebrated gaming rooms. It is an Art Nouveau building by Eugenio Ferret (1904–06). On the other side of Piazza Colombo is the rococo church of Santa Maria degli Angeli beside the Flower Market. From the Casinò the *CORSO DELL'IMPERATRICE, lined with magnificent palm-trees, leads past the delightful Russian church to the *Parco Marsaglia*, in which is a monument to Garibaldi by Leonardo Bistolfi (1908). Along the shore in the other direction Via Nino Bixio leads to the Genoese fort of *Santa Tecla* (1755) and the mole of the *Harbour*. Corso Trento e Trieste (pedestrians only) continues along the waterfront past the huge new harbour for small boats, to the public gardens. At No. 112 Corso Cavallotti is the house where Alfred Nobel died in 1896.

High up on the left is LA PIGNA, the old town, with quaint narrow streets, steep flights of steps, tunnels, and arches. The *Duomo* (San Siro) is a 13C building enlarged in the 17C. Fine views of the town and the coast are obtained from the *Madonna della Costa*, a church of 1630 with a dome of 1775, and from the Corso degli Inglesi which passes the *Castello Devachan*, scene of an international conference of 1920.

A road (or cable railway from Corso degli Inglesi; not at present working) via San Romolo leads to (7km) *Monte Bignone* (1309m), the highest of the horseshoe of hills surrounding Sanremo. Another road leads to (4km E) the *Madonna della Guardia*, a viewpoint overlooking Capo Verde. In the Armea valley, via Poggio and Ceriana, is (24km) the picturesque village of *Baiardo* (899m), partly ruined by an earthquake in 1887 but now a mountain resort.

Beyond Sanremo the coast road rounds Capo Verde and passes (left) *Bussana Nuova*, above which stands ruined *Bussana Vecchia*, deserted after the earthquake of 1887, but since the 1960s repopulated by a colony of artists.—25km *Arma di Taggia* is a bathing resort.

Taggia, the old village 3km up the pretty Argentina valley (bus from Sanremo), has a 15C Gothic church with a polyptych and other works by Lodovico Brea, and a cloister incorporating older columns. The Dominican Convent (adm. 9–12, 15–18, except Thursday) preserves numerous works of art. A Romanesque and medieval bridge of 16 arches crosses the Argentina. At Castellaro is the Santuario della Madonna di Lampedusa.

The road passes the small resorts of *Cipressa* and *San Lorenzo al Mare* and approaches the double town of **Imperia** (40,600 inhab.) created in 1923 by the fusion of Porto Maurizio, Oneglia, and adjoining villages to form a provincial capital.—40km **Porto Maurizio** is dominated by a large church (San Maurizio; 1781–1832) and has an old district of stepped streets.—43km **Oneglia**, important centre of the olive-oil trade, is at the mouth of the Impero torrent from which the province takes its name. Between the two towns are the Municipio and post office.

Oneglia was the birthplace of Andrea Doria (1466–1560), the Genoese admiral, of Edmondo De Amicis (1846–1909), the author, and of Jean Vieusseux (1779–1863), the bibliophile; and here in 1959 died Grock (Adrien Wettach), the great Swiss clown.
    From Imperia (Oneglia) to *Ormea* and *Ceva*, see Rte 5C.

An ascent over Capo Berta leads to (48km) **Diano Marina**, another olive-growing town, with a sandy beach, a summer and winter resort.—50km *San Bartolomeo al Mare* is a modern resort with many hotels.—53km *Cervo* retains its medieval structure, and has a rich Baroque church, by G.B. Marvaldi (1686).—Beyond (56km) *Marina di Andora* the road rounds the prominent Capo Mele (view N to Alassio).—62km **Laigueglia** is a resort preserving old streets and an imposing 18C church, by Gian Domenico Baguti.

A by-road leads inland to the *Castello di Andora* (94m), a ruined castle with a late-13C church, the finest late-Romanesque building on the Riviera. A medieval bridge crosses the Merula.

65km **ALASSIO** (13,700 inhab.), standing at the head of a wide and beautiful bay, facing nearly E, is famed for the luxuriance of its gardens, and is one of the most visited Ligurian coast resorts. It was well known to the English by the end of the 19C. It has an exceptionally mild winter climate and an excellent sandy beach.

English Church, St John's.—**Buses** frequently from Piazza Libertà to *Albenga* and *Laigueglia*; hourly to *Nice* and to *Genoa*.—**Motor-Boat** trips in summer to the *Isola Gallinaria*, etc.
    Olive Schreiner spent c 6 months here in 1887–88, her longest sojourn in any one place during her stay in Europe (1882–89); and while wintering here in 1904 Elgar composed his overture 'In the South (Alassio)'. Carlo Levi, the writer and painter spent much time in Alassio, and a collection of his paintings are to be exhibited in the town.

Alassio preserves its old main street, a campanile of 1507, and the 16C *Torrione*, built for defence against Barbary pirates.

Pleasant hill walks may be taken inland to the *Madonna della Guardia* (586m) or *Monte Pisciavino* (600m); or NE along the old Roman road (beyond the railway) to the ruined medieval arch and the little chapel; *View above *Capo Santa Croce*.

The road ascends over Capo Santa Croce; out at sea is the *Isola Gallinaria* (now usually called *Gallinara*), to the N of which were dredged up the Roman amphorae now in Albenga.

Little remains of the once powerful Benedictine monastery founded here in the 8C, and which at one time owned most of the Riviera. St Martin of Tours took refuge here in 356–360 from his Arian persecutors. The island is now privately owned but it can be seen by motorboat from Loano or Alassio.

72km **Albenga**, a fascinating old town (21,500 inhab.), was the Roman port *Albium Ingaunum*, but is now 1km from the sea thanks to the shifting of the course of the Centa in the 13C. It preserves most of its medieval wall (on foundations of the 1C BC) and three 17C gates; also about a dozen 12–14C brick tower-houses, mostly well-restored. Since the 19C the town has expanded towards the sea.

In the centre of the town the elegant campanile (1391) of the cathedral forms a striking group with two other towers. The interior of the *Cathedral*, was reconstructed in its medieval form during a radical (and controversial) restoration in 1964–67. During excavations its paleochristian predecessor was discovered (late 4C, or early 5C) with the same dimensions, and there is evidence of numerous later rebuildings. *Palazzo Vecchio del Comune* (1387 and 1421), incorporating a tall tower of c 1300, houses the Civico Museo Ingauno (9–12, 15–18 except Monday) with Roman and medieval remains including a fine Roman mosaic. Steps descend to the level of the 5C *BAPTISTERY (open 9–12, 15–18), ten-sided without and octagonal within, preserving a fine Byzantine mosaic (5C or 6C) in its principal apse and 8C transennae; the original roof was destroyed in 1900. Beyond the N flank of the cathedral is the charming Piazzetta dei Leoni, with three Renaissance lions brought from Rome in 1608 by the Costa, and the *Torre Costa del Carretto*. Behind the Bishop's Palace (16C) is the old *Palazzo Vescovile* with external frescoes (15C). In 1981 a Diocesan Museum was arranged here, which contains finds from the Cathedral, church silver, and a Martyrdom of St Catherine by Guido Reni. The evocative Via Bernardo Ricci (the Roman decumanus) crosses Via delle Medaglie (cardo maximus) at the 13C *Loggia dei Quattro Canti*.

To the W of the cathedral in Piazza San Michele rises the 13C tower of the Palazzo Peloso-Cepolla, the rooms of which form the *Museo Navale Romano* (9–12, 15–18; except Monday), containing more than 1000 wine amphorae and marine fittings salved since 1950 from a Roman vessel sunk offshore in 100–90 BC. This is the largest Roman transport ship yet found in the Mediterranean; it was carrying more than 10,000 amphorae of wine from Campania to southern France and Spain. Attached to the museum is an important centre for underwater archaeology. In a fine 18C hall a collection of Albisola pharmacy jars has been provisionally arranged, while other rooms are in the course of rearrangement. The church of *Santa Maria in Fontibus*, S of the cathedral, has a Gothic doorway.

Along the river Centa are scanty remains of the Roman city. At Monte, the hill SW of the town, is a funerary monument of the 2C known as 'Il Pilone', damaged in 1944. Nearby the form of the Roman amphitheatre is marked by pine trees. N of the town (reached by Viale Pontelungo), beyond remains of the palaeochristian basilica of San Vittore, is *Pontelungo* a 13C bridge of 10 arches which crossed the Centa before its course was changed. Its sunken remains now survive alongside the old road.

BUSES run frequently along the coast road; also to *Villanova d'Albenga*, a fortified outpost of Albenga, 6·5km W; and to *Campochiesa*, 4km N beyond the Ponte Lungo, where in the 12–14C church are wall-paintings of the 13–16C including a Last Judgement (1446) inspired by the 'Divina Commedia'.

77km *Ceriale* and (79km) *Borghetto Santo Spirito* are modest seaside resorts.—82km **Loano**, an old seaside town (12,600 inhab.) with palm-groves, recently disfigured by new buildings. It has a town hall (1578), formerly the Palazzo Doria, containing a 3C mosaic pavement; and to the N a Carmelite convent with a dignified church (1603–08) commanding a good view. No. 32 Via Cavour was the birthplace of Rosa Raimondi, Garibaldi's mother.

Inland, via Borghetto (see above), are the old hill-villages of *Toirano* (6km) and *Balestrino* (9km), the latter with a Del Carretto castle. The *Grotta della Basura*, 1·5km N of Toirano off the Bardineto road, is a remarkable stalactite cavern (guided tours of c 1½hrs at 9.30–11.30, 14.30–17 or 18), with the only footprints of Mousterian man so far discovered. The Museo Preistorico della Val Varatella has been opened here.—A road runs via Toirano to (22km) *Calizzano*, a summer resort with a ruined castle of the Del Carretto.

85km **Pietra Ligure** is another old town (8200 inhab.) with a ruined Genoese fort and a church (San Nicola) by Fantone (1791). The fine modern seaside district is succeeded on the W by shipyards, with the large Istituto Santa Corona behind.—91km *Borgio* is a bathing resort with the little Romanesque cemetery church of San Pietro to the W. Inland, at Valdemino, are the *Grotte di Borgio* (9–11.30, 15–17; closed Tuesday), more stalactite caverns.—93km *Finale Marina*, with a large Baroque church, is the chief section of the town of **Finale Ligure** (14,000 inhab.). The Capuchin church stands on an earlier Pieve (6–8C). Adjoining is *Finale Pia* where the church has a 13C campanile. Both are popular seaside resorts.

The old village of *Finalborgo*, 2km inland from Finale Marina (bus every ½hr), has a church with a fine octagonal campanile (13C). It contains a 16C tomb of the Del Carretto family, whose ruined castle commands the place from the NW. In the cloister of Santa Caterina a museum has been arranged with finds from the many local limestone caves in which prehistoric remains have been found (adm. 9–12, 14.30–16.30; fest. 9–12).—None of the 50 or so prehistoric caverns in the district are at present open to the public; they include the Grotta delle Arene Candide, one of the most important in Europe. On the old Roman road which (to avoid the coastal cliffs) ascended the Valle di Ponci N of Finale Pia and then descended the Val Quazzola to Vado are about a dozen Roman bridges (1C AD), five of them intact.

From (96km) *Varigotti* the road ascends the 'Malpasso' over the Capo di Noli, with fine views in both directions between tunnels and cuttings.—100km **Noli**, an important port in the Middle Ages, preserves its walls and three tall towers of brick, as well as many old houses, despite the fact that the environs have been spoilt in recent years by much new building. The 11C church of *San Paragorio* (W end), with a 15C porch, preserves its crypt, a 13C bishop's throne in wood, and a 'Volto Santo' Crucifix (12C) like that at Lucca. Remains of an earlier palaeochristian church have also been revealed. Dominating the town from the E is the *Castello di Monte Ursino*.—103km *Spotorno* has a fine sandy beach, but much ugly new building has taken place here since D.H. Lawrence's sojourn in 1926 when he wrote 'Lady Chatterley's Lover'.—Beyond the headland of *Bergeggi*, with its islet offshore, and another cape, is (113km) *Vado Ligure*, once a Roman port, now an industrial suburb of Savona with oil-discharging docks connected by pipeline with a refinery at Trecate.

117km **SAVONA**, an important port and provincial capital (79,800 inhab.), consists of an old district, overlooking the inner harbour, surrounded by the regular and rather banal streets of the new town.

Ironfounding and shipbreaking are the chief industries and crystallized fruit is a local speciality.

History. The Gallo-Roman *Savo*, used as a Carthaginian depot during the Second Punic War, was dependent on the port of Vada Sabatia (Vado) and was of little importance until the Crusades. Later, under the Alerami and the Del Carretto, it waged naval war against the Barbary pirates; but in 1528 its harbour was blocked by the jealous Genoese. In 1809–12 and in 1814 Pius VII was interned at Savona by order of Napoleon; and in the Second World War the town was shelled from the sea.

The main arcaded Via Paleocapa runs from Piazza del Popolo to the harbour. On its N side is the 16C church of *San Giovanni Battista*, containing an early Flemish triptych (behind the high altar) and, in the NE chapel, an Adoration of the Shepherds by Antonio Semino, and 18C works by the local painters Carlo Giuseppe and Giovanni Agostino Ratti. Behind the church are the *Post Office* and the *Theatre* (1850–53) called after the native lyric poet Gabriello Chiabrera (1553–1638), the 'Italian Ronsard'. At the seaward end, which has a terrace of pretty Art Nouveau houses with tiled façades, commanding the harbour, is the *Torre Pancaldo*, a 14C tower recalling Leon Pancaldo of Savona, Magellan's 'Genoese' pilot.

The port may be visited by motor-boat excursion on Sundays and holidays. From the quay an aerial ropeway transports carbon to factories at San Giuseppe di Cairo (21km).

Opposite San Giovanni the VIA PIA, with many fine stone doorways in the Genoese style, leads into the old town. A right turn, through the colonnade of the Town Library, leads to the *Cathedral*, built in 1589–1605 (façade of 1886) to replace its medieval forerunner demolished to make way for the Genoese fort (see below). The font (?12C) and choir-stalls (1495) are from the old building. A diocesan Museum contains a triptych by Lodovico Brea, the church treasury, etc. Nearby is the 17C oratory of *Santa Maria di Castello* (adm. fest. 8.30–10) which contains a polyptych by Vincenzo Foppa and Lodovico Brea (1490). Facing the cathedral is the *Palazzo Della Rovere*, begun by Giuliano da Sangallo for Julius II but never finished; it now contains law courts. On the right of the cathedral is the *Sistine Chapel* (if closed, apply at the cathedral), erected by Sixtus IV (see below) in memory of his parents, and given a harmonious Baroque interior in 1764. It contains a fine marble tomb, by Michele and Giovanni De Aria, with figures of the two Della Rovere Popes, Sixtus IV and Julius II. Via Pia (right) threads an archway to Piazza del Mercato, where are the two *Torri del Brandale* (12C; restored) and the *Archivolto del Brandale*, on the old quay. Most of the quayside buildings were destroyed in the bombardment of 1941, and on the left appear two medieval tower-houses. Farther on is the portal of the house of Ansaldo Grimaldi (1552), brought from Genoa in 1957 and erected in the front of the house of Lamba Doria. In Via Quarda Superiore (the first street parallel with the quay) a small *Civic Art Gallery* (adm. 10–12, 15–18 except Mondays and in September), on the fourth floor of the Palazzo Pozzobonello, contains a Calvary by Donato de'Bardi and a polyptych by Vincenzo Foppa.—The *Fortezza del Priamar*, on a hill on the southern seafront by the public gardens, was erected by the Genoese in 1542 (later altered). Here Mazzini was imprisoned in 1830–31. An Archaeological Museum has been opened here.

In the cemetery of *Zinola*, half-way to Vado, is a *British Military Plot*, with 104 graves, mostly from the wreck of the 'Transylvania', torpedoed off Savona in 1917.—About 6km NW, with a station on the Turin railway, is the *Santuario di Nostra Signora della Misericordia*, with a 16C church (festival on 18 March) and a museum (reopened in 1988) in the Palazzetto del Duca.

BUSES run frequently from the station to the harbour and to *Vado* or *Varazze*: to the *Santuario* (see above); and along the coast in both directions; and to *Cairo Montenotte*; twice daily to *Millesimo* and *Calizzano*, and to *Sassello*; daily to *Acqui*, *Alessandria*, and *Milan*; to *Alba*; and to *Turin* (see Rte 5C).

East of Savona the beaches are less attractive.—121km *Albisola Marina* and *Albisola Superiore* are resorts. The latter was the birthplace of Julius II (Giuliano della Rovere; 1443–1513), and has been famous since the 16C for its ceramics (a Museum of Ceramics was opened in Viale Matteotti in 1987). Sporadic excavations have revealed remains of a Roman villa in the vicinity.

A road climbs inland to (16km) the *Colle del Giovo* (516m), and from there descends, past (23km) the summer resort of *Sassello*, to (59km) *Acqui* (Rte 5B).

124km *Celle Ligure*, another resort, was the birthplace of Sixtus IV (Francesco della Rovere; 1414–84), uncle of Julius II.—127km **Varazze**, a popular seaside resort (14,800 inhab.), is an old town retaining much of its rampart, at the N corner of which is preserved the 10C façade of the original church of *Sant'Ambrogio*. The present church (1535) has a 13C campanile and contains Baroque altar-paintings; 4th chapel, polyptych by Giovanni Barbagelata (1500). Jacopo da Voragine (1230–98), author of the 'Golden Legend', was born here.—134km *Cogoleto* is a small industrial town connected with the family of Columbus; and Tennyson stopped here to pledge the explorer's memory.—137km *Arenzano* is another popular resort with fine gardens.—At (147km) *Voltri*, an industrial suburb, the road reaches the boundary of 'Greater Genoa', and from here onwards is built up almost uninterruptedly.

At the *Santuario dell'Acquasanta* (1683–1710), c 5km inland (station on the Genoa-Acqui railway), Maria Cristina of Savoy was married to Ferdinand II of the Two Sicilies in 1832.—To *Turin* via Acqui, see Rte 5B.

Beyond *Palmaro*, the road traverses *Pra*, with foundries.—From (152km) **Pegli** to the centre of Genoa, see Rte 6D.

5   Turin to Genoa

A.   Via Asti and Alessandria

ROAD, 175km. N10. 18km **Chieri** (by-pass, left).—30km *Villanova*.— 55km **Asti**.—91km **Alessandria**.—98km N35 bis.—112km Novi Ligure (2km right).—120km N35 comes in on the left.—122km *Serravalle Scrivia*.—147km *Busalla*.—149km *Passo dei Giovi* (472m).—175km **Genoa**.

MOTORWAY, A21, to (94km) *Tortona*, where the A7 motorway continues S, joining this route at Serravalle and following it closely into Genoa.

RAILWAY, 169km in 1¾hrs–2½hrs; to *Asti*, 56km in 30–60 minutes; to *Alessandria*, 91km in 1–1½hrs. Through trains from Calais, Paris, and Rome run on this line.

N10 leaves Turin by the Ponte Regina Margherita and the Corso Casale and turns SE into the hills. A tunnel takes the road under *Pino Torinese*, served by a hillier road (17km, via Superga, Rte 1B), which this road joins in 15km.—19km **Chieri**, served by bus and local train from Turin, is a pleasant little industrial town (30,500 inhab.), the old streets of which contain many fine old houses. The *CATHEDRAL, built in 1405–36, has one of the tallest of the pointed porches characteristic of Piedmontese Gothic. Its 13C baptistery has a fresco cycle of the Passion, restored in 1988 and attributed to the 15C painter Guglielmo Fantini. The polyptych is after Spanzotti. During restoration work, the original walls and Roman remains beneath the floor were found. The church contains a marble altarpiece attributed to Matteo Sanmicheli (S transept); 15C choir stalls; and a small 9–10C crypt incorporating Roman work. The sacristy has good 16C woodwork.—Beyond a *Triumphal Arch*, in the main street, much altered since its erection in 1580 in honour of Emmanuel Philibert, is the 14C church of *San Domenico*, which has a graceful campanile and fine capitals and mouldings. Farther on, in the Istituto Don Bosco (at the corner of Via Roma; adm. freely granted) are remains of a *Commandery of the Templars*, including part of the church, rebuilt in the 15C, with columns of reticulated brickwork.

An alternative road to Asti leads past (12km) the hill-village of *Castelnuovo Don Bosco*, the home of St John Bosco. He was born at *Becchi*, 5km S, where a large Salesian pilgrimage church has been erected.—Vezzolano (Rte 8) is 5·5km N of Castelnuovo.

At (30km) *Villanova d'Asti* begin the famous Asti vineyards as the road enters the Monferrato.

55km **ASTI**, a famous old Piedmontese city (76,100 inhab.) reached the zenith of its importance in the 13C, and was a possession of the house of Savoy from 1532. It is now the capital of a province. The district is noted for its wines, including Barbera, Grignolino, and Asti Spumante.

The ancient Palio of Asti, a costume pageant and horse race similar to that of Siena, was revived in 1967. It takes place in early September in the Campo del Palio near the station. It provides an added attraction to the annual wine fair.

The W approach from Piazza Torino leads into the long CORSO VITTORIO ALFIERI, the main street extending the whole length of the town. The *Torre San Secondo*, a Romanesque tower on a Roman base, serves as campanile for the church of Santa Caterina (1773). On the corner of Piazza Cairoli the *Palazzo Alfieri*, birthplace of the poet Vittorio Alfieri (1749–1803), has collections and study rooms devoted to his work (adm. 10–12, 15.30–17.30; closed Sunday & Monday). The early 18C mansion was built by his cousin Benedetto Alfieri. Beneath the adjoining Liceo is the 8C crypt of the destroyed church of *Sant'Anastasio* (adm. 9–12, 16–18; Sunday 10–12; closed Monday) with fine capitals, and an interesting lapidary collection. A turning to the left leads to the CATHEDRAL, a dignified Gothic building of 1309–54, with a campanile of 1266, and a florid S porch of c 1470; the E end was extended in 1764–69. At the W end are two holy-water stoups made from Romanesque capitals supported by inverted Roman capitals, and a font also constructed of Roman material in the 15C. On the W piers of the crossing are two 12–13C reliefs. The Baroque frescoes are by *Carlo Carlone* (c 1760) and *Francesco Fabbrica* (nave; 1696–1700), and the inlaid stalls (1768) are good.

To the NE, is a cloister (?11C), while to the left of that is the small church of *San Giovanni*, covering a 7C or 8C crypt, perhaps the original baptistery.—Farther to the N Via Natta, in a district containing many 13–14C houses, leads to Via Gioberti, which ends (left) at the surviving portion of the town walls.

The road leading back from the cathedral to the Corso Alfieri crosses Via Carducci, No. 35 in which is the 15C *Palazzo Zoia*. At the corner of Via Gioberti and the Corso the 18C *Palazzo Mazzetti* (formerly Di Bellino) houses the small PINACOTECA CIVICA and Museo del Risorgimento (adm. 9–12, 16–18; Sunday 10–12; closed Monday). The gallery of 15–18C paintings includes works by Valerio Castello (1624–59), and carved stalls of 1477.—Palazzo Ottolenghi, on the opposite side of the Corso, is to house the Museo Archeologico.

The streets descending S from the Corso still retain a number of crumbling tower-houses of the old Astigiano nobility (Alfieri, Malabayla, Rocro, Solari, etc.); the *Palazzo Malabayla*, in Via Mazzini, is a fine though dilapidated Renaissance mansion.

Farther on in the Corso is Piazza Roma, with the 13C *Torre Comentina*, beyond which Via Morelli leads (left) to Piazza Medici, with the *Torre Troyana*, the finest medieval tower in the city.

To the right, opposite Via Morelli, a short street leads to Piazza San Secondo, with the large Gothic church of *San Secondo*, containing a fine polyptych by Gaudenzio Ferrari (just within the SW door), and covering a 6C crypt. From here Via Cavour leads on past the *Torre dei Guttuari* to the station. On the right (26 Via Venti Settembre) is the late-14C *Palazzo Catena*, with terracotta decoration.

The Corso skirts the triangular Piazza Alfieri (right), with a statue of the poet, separated by a block of public offices (including the Prefettura and the Tourist office), from the public garden and Piazza del Campo del Palio. At the E end of the Corso, 550m farther, is the church of *San Pietro in Consavia* (1467), now, with its cloister, containing a small local geological and archaeological collection. This with the adjoining circular 10C *Baptistery (earlier the church of the Order of St John of Jerusalem) are open daily except Monday, 9–12, 16–18, Sunday 10–12.

There is a charming little Romanesque church (12–14C) at *Viatosto*, 4km N of Asti; while from *Montechiaro* (16km NW by the road or railway to Chivasso) may be visited San Nazario (early 11C), 5km NW of the station, and San Secondo (11C) above *Cortazzone*, 8km SW.

Road and railway follow the Tanaro valley to (91km) **Alessandria**, a cheerful but uninteresting provincial capital (102,000 inhab.) that takes importance from a position almost equidistant from Turin, Milan, and Genoa. A rail centre, with felt-hat factories, it is mainly of 18–19C appearance.

It was founded by seven castellans of the Monferrato who rebelled against Frederick Barbarossa in 1168, and named their new city after Pope Alexander III. An old carved figure at the corner of the 18–19C *Cathedral* is said to depict the peasant Gagliaudo who by an ancient trick induced the Emperor to raise the siege of 1175. Nearby is the Pinacoteca and Museo Civico.—The *Palazzo della Prefettura* (1733), by Benedetto Alfieri, in the central Piazza della Libertà, is the best of the city's mansions, but there are others here and in Via Guasco which leads N to the 14–15C church of *Santa Maria di Castello*. During restoration work, parts of the 6C church and medieval building came to light.

Alessandria has direct rail communication with Alba, Acqui, Ovada, Novara, Vercelli, Milan, Pavia, Piacenza, Genoa, and Turin.

The Genoa road crosses (101km) the battlefield of *Marengo*, where Napoleon defeated the Austrians on 14 June 1800, in a battle which he regarded as the most brilliant of his career, though General Desaix fell on the field. The commemorative column was removed by the Austrians in 1814 and not brought back until 1922. A small Museum has been arranged in the Villa di Marengo (16–19; fest. also 9.30–12; winter: 14.30–17.30; fest. also 10–12; closed Monday).

At *Boscomarengo*, 9km S, is the remarkable church of Santa Croce, erected in 1567 by Pius V (died 1572), a native of the village, as his mausoleum. His splendid tomb remains empty, however, as he is buried in Santa Maria Maggiore in Rome. The paintings include works by Giorgio Vasari.

Diverging from N10 (which continues E to Tortona; see Rte 15) N35 bis (right) crosses a plain to pass just E of (112km) **Novi Ligure** (2km right) a modern-looking town (30,000 inhab.) with a 12C castle-tower. The battle of Novi (15 August 1799), where the Austrians and Russians defeated the French, was avenged at Marengo (see above).

FROM NOVI TO GENOA VIA GAVI, 56km, a pleasant alternative, shorter but hillier than the main road.—The road ascends S to give a fine view of the 16C castle of (10km) *Gavi*, an ancient little town with a good 13C church.—20km *Voltaggio* (341m) is a summer resort in the upper Lemme valley. It has a Pinacoteca and local ethnographical Museum. The road continues through the Capanne di Marcarolo nature reserve and rises to 773m, then descends rapidly on the Ligurian side, with fine views seaward.—41km *Pontedecimo*, and from there to Genoa, see below.

Beyond Novi this route joins N35 from Milan (Rte 15) and ascends the narrowing valley of the Scrivia.—122km *Serravalle Scrivia* lies 2km N of the excavations (open daily), of the Roman town of *Libarna*, of which the decumanus maximus, the amphitheatre, and theatre have been exposed (flanking the railway).

From Serravalle the old 'camionale', one of Italy's earliest motorways, has doubled as part of the A7, the 'Autostrada dei Fiori' (see Rte 15); it provides the most direct route into (173km) **Genoa**.

From (125km) *Arquata Scrivia*, on the old road, there are two railway lines to Genoa, running more or less parallel. The communal cemetery contains 94 graves of British soldiers.—The valley becomes more attractive on the approach to (141km) *Ronco Scrivia* (325m), the first Ligurian village. The newer railway line plunges into the Giovi Tunnel, over 8km long. The road, beyond (147km) *Busalla* (359m), ascends to (149km) the *Passo dei Giovi* (472m), then descends in zigzags into the industrial Polcevera valley.—160km *Pontedecimo* (91m) is within the territory of the city of Genoa; the road traverses an almost continuous series of industrial suburbs—*San Quirico, Bolzaneto*, and *Rivarolo* (with a view of the great viaduct that takes the coastal motorway over the railway)—to join the coast road at *Sampierdarena*.—175km **Genoa**, see Rte 6.

B.   Via Alba and Acqui Terme

ROAD, 202km: To (27km) *Carmagnola*, see Rte 3.—47km *Bra*.—64km **Alba**.—87km *Castino*.—115km *Bistagno*.—125km **Acqui Terme**.—148km *Ovada*.—186km *Voltri*.—202km **Genoa**. This is a roundabout route, traversing the characteristic Piedmontese hill country of *Le Langhe*, with many ruined castles. The partisans were active here in 1944–45.

MOTORWAY, A26, from Ovada to Genoa.

RAILWAY to *Acqui Terme* via Asti (change), 102km in 2–2½hrs. *Alba* is reached (not very frequently) in 1hr direct from Turin via Bra. From Acqui to *Genoa*, 58km in 1¾hrs.

From Turin to (27km) *Carmagnola*, see Rte 3. N393 diverges left across the railway for (37km) *Sommariva del Bosco*, with a picturesque castle and (47km) **Bra**, a town of 23,500 inhabitants, important for its tanneries in the last century. It was the birthplace of St Joseph Cottolengo (1786–1842). It preserves a few old houses. A museum contains finds from Roman Pollentia, and, near the rococo church of Santa Chiara (1742–48) is a Natural History Museum, founded in 1860.

At *Pollenzo*, 5km SE, the church contains fine 15C stalls, brought from Staffarda. The Castello Reale dates partly from the 14C.—The road running S from Bra, following the railway to Savona, passes (7km) *Cherasco*, an ancient little town with a 13C church, a castle of 1348, and the Museo Adriani (good coins and medals).—25km *Dogliani* a wine producing centre in the Langhe hills, has medieval origins. *Carrù* 8km SW of Dogliani, is the birthplace of Luigi Einaudi (1874–1961), President of Italy in 1948–55.—33km *Murazzano*.—52km *Ceva*, see Rte 5C.

The road (N231) turns E to descend the valley of the Tanaro, on whose N bank, opposite Alba, come in a road from Asti and alternative routes, shorter but hillier, from Carmagnola via Corneliano d'Alba and from Turin direct via Poirino and Canale (N29).—64km **Alba**, with 28,600 inhabitants, one of the most important vine-growing centres of Piedmont. Famous wines produced on the neighbouring Langhe hills include Barolo, Dolcetto, Nebbiolo, and Barbera. It is noted also as the birthplace of the Emperor Pertinax (126–193) and of Macrino d'Alba, the early 16C painter. The ancient town with an interesting polygonal plan preserves some tall medieval brick tower-houses, and decorated house fronts. The *Duomo*, over-restored in the 19C, contains fine carved and inlaid stalls by Bernardino da Fossato (1512). In *Palazzo Comunale* is one of Macrino's best paintings (Madonna and Child enthroned with Saints and two donors), and a Concert attributed to Mattia Preti. The deconsecrated church of the *Maddalena* (rebuilt in 1749) contains the *Museo Federico Eusebio* with local neolithic finds, Roman material, and natural history and ethnographic sections. *San Giovanni* contains a Madonna by Barnaba da Modena (1377) and two more paintings by Macrino. *San Domenico*, being restored, preserves 14C and 15C frescoes.

The road leaves the Tanaro and begins to climb. Beyond (87km) *Castino* it enters the valley of the Bormida di Millesimo, where the Acqui road turns left.—97km *Vesime*.

N29 goes on up the valley from Castino to (2·5km) *Cortemilia*, and from there either to Millesimo or on to the Acqui-Savona road. From Vesime a hill-road ascends in 11km to *Roccaverano*, a typical cheese-making townlet of the Langhe, with a church (1509–16) in a Bramantesque style and the tall round tower (1204) of its ruined castle.—-From Vesime a by-road leads N to *Santo Stefano Belbo* (15km), birthplace of Cesare Pavese (1908–50), the writer.

At (115km) *Bistagno* the two branches of the Bormida join, and the road descends their united stream.—125km **Acqui Terme** (165m), the Roman *Aquae Statiellae*, is famous for its sulphurous waters and mud baths. In the middle of the town (21,800 inhab.) the sulphurous waters

(75°C) bubble up beneath a little pavilion, known as *La Bollente* (1870; by Giovanni Ceruti). The Romanesque *Cathedral* has a fine portal beneath a 17C loggia, and preserves its triple apse of the 11C, a campanile completed in the 13C, and a spacious crypt. In the sacristy is a triptych by Bermejo (15C Catalan). Behind the cathedral, in the public garden, are remains of the *Castle* of the Paleologhi (with an archaeological museum); while in the other direction the church of *San Pietro* has a fine 11C apse and octagonal campanile. On the other side of the Bormida, near the Antiche Terme, are four arches of a *Roman Aqueduct* and an open-air swimming-pool.

Acqui is also on the road and railway from Alessandria to Savona. The road to (74·5km) Savona (N30) ascends the valley of the Bormida di Spigno, passing (25km) *Spigno* and (40km) *Dego.*—47km *Cairo Montenotte* recalls Napoleon's first victory in Italy (April 1796), won over the Austrians and Piedmontese at Montenotte, c 15km E. *San Giuseppe di Cairo*, beyond, has large carbon works.—52km *Carcare*, and from there by N29 to Savona, see Rte 5C.

At (148km) *Ovada*, the A26 motorway from Alessandria to Genoa joins the route. Ovada, birthplace of St Paul of the Cross (Paolo Danei; 1694–1775), founder of the Passionist Order, stands at the foot of the last ascent, the summit of which (532m) is reached in a short tunnel beneath the *Passo del Turchino*. The road descends rapidly to the coast at (186km) *Voltri*, now part of (202km) **Genoa**, see Rte 4.

C.   Via Mondovì and Savona

ROAD, 207km. To (52km) *Savigliano*, see Rte 3.—N28, 66km *Fossano.*—88km *Mondovì.*—111km *Ceva.*—N28 bis. 133km *Millesimo.*—At (141km) *Carcare* N29 is joined.—161km **Savona**. From there to **Genoa**, see Rte 4.

MOTORWAY, A6, 127km, takes much the same route to Savona, where it joins A10 (45km) for Genoa (172km, by-passing Savona).

RAILWAY to Savona, 149km in 2–3hrs; to *Mondovì*, 83km in 1–1¾hrs. Another route to Savona, via Bra, joining the above route at Ceva, is 3km shorter (stopping trains only). From Savona to *Genoa*, see Rte 4.

From Turin to (52km) *Savigliano*, 6km beyond which N28 branches left from the Cúneo road, see Rte 3.—66km *Fossano* is noteworthy for its massive 14C castle and its Baroque churches.—88km **Mondovì** is a pleasant town (21,600 inhab.), lying partly in the Ellero valley (Mondovì Breo, the modern town; 381m) and partly on a hill (Mondovì Piazza; 558m). The town grew up in the Middle Ages and by the 16C it probably had more inhabitants than any other city in Piedmont. The architect Francesco Gallo (1672–1750), a native, designed numerous buildings in the town. In the upper town are the *Cathedral* built by Gallo in 1743–63 to replace the Renaissance cathedral destroyed by Emmanuel Philibert in the 16C, and the *Belvedere*, a garden with a superb view, laid out round the old Torre dei Bressani. In Piazza Maggiore is the elaborate *Chiesa della Missione* (1678), with a 'trompe-l'oeil' vault-painting by Andrea Pozzo. Mondovì was the scene of a victory of Napoleon in 1796, and was the birthplace of

Giovanni Giolitti (1842–1928). Five times prime minister from 1892 to 1921, he introduced universal suffrage into Italy.

Lurisia, a spa with radioactive springs, developed since 1928, lies 15km SW of Mondovì beyond Villanova, and is reached by bus from Mondovì or from Cúneo, 22km NW.

Frabosa Soprana (892m), 16km S of Mondovì (bus), is locally famed as a summer and winter resort. The road continues to *Artesina* (1315m) and *Prato Nevoso* (1474m), and ski-lifts and chair-lifts ascend to Monte Moro (1760m), Monte Malanotte (1740m), Sella Pogliola (1590m), and Monte Mondolè in the E group of the Maritime Alps. A fairly hilly road runs SE to (10km) *Bossea* in the Val Corsaglia (bus daily or oftener from Mondovì, 24km), with stalacite *Caves, among the most interesting in Italy (guided tours 10–12, 14–18). A skeleton of the Ursus Spelaeus found here is on display.—*Roburent* (788m) and *Pamparato* (817m) are smaller hill resorts on a road leading S of Vicoforte (bus from Mondovì).

95km *Vicoforte*, by-passed by the main road, has a huge domed pilgrimage church, begun in 1596 by Ascanio Vittozzi, continued after 1728 by Francesco Gallo, and completed in 1890.—111km **Ceva** (370m) is an important road and railway junction.

FROM CEVA TO IMPERIA, N28, 87km. Railway to Ormea, infrequently in 1hr; bus from there in 2hrs. The road follows the railway up the Tanaro valley.—11km *Bagnasco* (485m), dominated by a ruined castle. From here a road leads to (20·5km) *Viola* (827m), a small resort with a chair-lift to Monte Nej (1725m), and ski-lifts and a ski school.—23km **Garessio** (579m), a popular summer resort and small spa, lies in a delightful situation among the hills, mainly along the side-road (bus) which here diverges for Albenga (37km) via the *Colle San Bernardo* (957m). Another road leads W from Garessio to the winter sports centre on *Colle di Casotto*.—35km **Ormea** (732m), another pleasant hill-resort, with a ruined castle, and Gothic frescoes of 1397 in the parish church.—42km *Ponte di Nava* (818m). The road enters Liguria, passing (44km) *Case di Nava*, and crosses the watershed at (46km) the *Colle di Nava* (934m). *Monesi*, 16km W, is a small winter-sports centre on Monte Saccarello (2201m).—After a descent to (56km) *Pieve di Teco* (244m), this route crosses the inland road from Bordighera to Albenga. After another ascent to (64km) the *Colle San Bartolomeo* (621m), the road descends the Impero valley, passing (79km) *Pontedassio*, with a spaghetti museum, to (87km) *Imperia* (Oneglia, see Rte 4).

The Savona road next reaches (133km) *Millesimo*, an old-walled village with a castle and quaint fortified bridge. A hilly road leading S to Albenga (56km) passes (25km) *Calizzano* (Rte 4).—At (141km) *Carcare* the road from Acqui and Cairo comes in (Rte 5B).—Just beyond (148km) *Altare*, a small glass-making town, the road tunnels beneath the *Bocchetta di Cadibona* (435m), a pass usually regarded as marking the division between Alps and Apennines. The descent leads down the Letimbro valley, amid chestnut woods.—161km **Savona**, and from there to (207km) **Genoa**, see Rte 4.

6   Genoa

GENOA, in Italian **Genova** (816,800 inhab.), is now one of the main cities of Italy and its most important port. It is built on an unusually awkward site, on the irregular seaward slopes of an amphitheatre of hills, and preserves many relics of an ancient and honourable history, including the numerous palaces and magnificent art collections of its great maritime families (many of which are still in private hands). It was the birthplace of Christopher Columbus. The old city, with its steep and narrow alleys of tall houses clustered round the port, contrasts with the newer town laid out at the beginning of this century in the hinterland. Suburbs of tower blocks sprawl across the hills behind and the city limits now extend along the coast in both directions for some 30 kilometres between Nervi and Voltri.

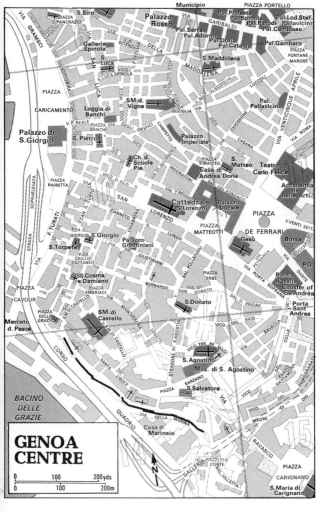

Railway Stations. *Porta Principe* (Pl. 1), usually the most convenient for visitors, and **Brignole** (Pl. 12).

The main **Quay** for passenger and car ferries is *Ponte Colombo* next to the *Stazione Marittima* at Ponte Andrea Doria and Ponte dei Mille (Pl. 5). Regular car ferries to Sardinia, Sicily, and Tunis.

Airport. *Cristoforo Colombo*, at Sestri Ponente (6km W), built into the sea (and modernised in 1986). Flights to London, Paris, Frankfurt, and Zurich (and internal services). Airport bus ('Volabus') regularly from Brignole Station, with stops in Piazza de'Ferrari (Pl. 11) and at Porta Principe Station (Piazza Acquaverde).

Hotels in the vicinity of the old city: near Porta Principe station, Via Balbi, and near Piazza Fontane Marose; in the modern city: in Via XX Settembre and Piazza Corvetto.

Tourist Office, *E.P.T.* 114 Via Roma (Pl. 11); information offices at Porta Principe Station and at the Airport.—**Post Office.** 1 Via Boccardo (Piazza De Ferrari; Pl.11).—**British Consulate,** 2 Via XII Ottobre (Pl.11).—*Associazione Italo-Britannico*, Piazza della Vittoria.

Theatres. *Teatro Margherita*, 16A Via Venti Settembre (used by the opera company of the Teatro Carlo Felice, which is being rebuilt). For prose: *Sala Duse*, 6 Via Bacigalupo (Piazza Corvetto), *Politeama Genovese*, 2 Via Bacigalupo.

City Transport. A Tourist Ticket (1000 lire) valid for one day on any line can be purchased at the A.M.T. office at Brignole Station. The buses most useful to the visitor are: **1.** *Piazza Caricamento*—Sampierdarena—Pegli—*Voltri*; **3.** *Piazza Caricamento*—Stazione Principe—Sampierdarena—*Pegli Lido*; **4.** *Stazione Brignole*—Corso Saffi—Piazza Cavour—Piazza Caricamento—Piazza Principe—Via Cornigliano—*Sestri*; **15.** *Piazza Caricamento*—Piazza Tommaseo—Sturla—Quarto—Quinto—*Nervi*; **33.** *Piazza Principe*—Circonvallazione a Monte—Piazza Manin—Piazza Corvetto—Piazza De Ferrari—*Stazione Brignole*; **34.** *Piazza Dinegro*—Piazza Principe—Piazza Nunziata—Piazza Corvetto—Piazza Manin—*Cimetero di Staglieno*; **36.** *Via Piave*—Corso Buenos Aires—Piazza De Ferrari—*Piazza Corvetto*—*Piazza Manin*; **42.** *Piazza De Ferrari*—Piazza Vittoria—Galleria Mameli—*Boccadasse*.

Country Buses in all directions from the Bus Station in Piazza della Vittoria (Pl. 16); frequent service along the coast in both directions.

Motor Boats. Organised trips round the harbour (c 1hr), from the Stazione Marittima (Ponte dei Mille, Calata Zingari; Pl. 5). Groups of 10 or more, 8–12, 13–17.

Funicular Railways. F. Largo della Zecca (Pl. 6) to *Castellaccio* (Righi) via San Nicolò (Pl. 2), out of operation in 1988; **H.** Piazza Portello (Pl. 7) to *Corso Magenta*.—Rack Railway (**G**) from Via del Lagaccio, near Piazza Principe (Pl. 1) to *Granarolo*.—Lifts. **I.** Via XX Settembre to *Corso Podestà* (Ponte Monumentale; Pl. 11); **M.** Corso Magenta to *Via Crocco*; **N.** Piazza Portello to the *Castelletto*.

International Exhibitions, at the Fiera Internazionale, off Corso Aurelio Saffi (beyond Pl. 14). *Salone Nautico*, a boat show held annually in October. *Mostra internazionale dei Fiori*, a flower show held in the Spring every five years (next in 1991).

History. The position of Genoa at the northernmost point of the Tyrrhenian Sea and protected by mountains, has given it a lasting maritime importance; and the original Ligurian inhabitants of the site established early contact with the first known navigators of the Mediterranean—the Phoenicians and the Greeks—and objects excavated have proved the existence of a trading-post here in the 6C BC. In the 3C BC Genoa took up alliance with Rome against the invading Carthaginians and the town, destroyed by the latter in 205 BC, was soon rebuilt under the Roman praetor Sp. Cassius. Roman connections were not entirely severed until the arrival of the Lombards in 641. In the succeeding centuries the raids of Saracen pirates spurred the Genoese to retaliation and the sailors of Genoa not only withstood the pirates' attacks, but also captured their strongholds of Corsica and Sardinia. The latter island was taken with the aid of Pisa, and its occupation led to two centuries of war, which ended in the final defeat of the Pisans at the Meloria (1284) and at Porto Pisano (1290). With this success began the acquisition of Genoa's great colonial empire, which extended as far as the Crimea, Syria, and North Africa; and important Genoese colonies were established in the Morea. These advances, and the large profits made during the Crusades, led to a collision with the ambitions of Venice; and the subsequent war ended in the defeat of the Genoese at Chioggia (1380). After the fall of the consuls in 1191, power passed to the podestà or mayors and the 'Capitani del Popolo' (1258–1340), with intervals of submission to the Emperor Henry VII (1311–13) and to Robert of Anjou, King of Naples (1318–35). In 1340 came the election of the first Doge, Simone Boccanegra. Petrarch, on a vist in 1358, described the city as 'la superba', a name used by numerous subsequent travellers to Genoa. The continual strife between the great families—the Doria, the Spinola, and the Fieschi—made Genoa an easy victim to the rising military powers in the 15C and a succession of foreign masters followed. Charles VI of France (1396–1409) was followed by the Marquess of Monferrato (1409–13) and Filippo Maria Visconti (1421–35), under whom the Genoese inflicted a crushing defeat on the fleet of Aragon at Ponza (1435). The domination of the Sforza (1466–99) was followed by a further French conquest under Louis XII (1499–1512). In 1528, however, Andrea Doria (1466–1560), the greatest of the Genoese naval leaders, formulated a constitution for Genoa which freed the city from foreign rule, though it established despotic government at home, and was followed (1547–48) by the insurrections of Fieschi and Cibo. The conquests of the Turks in their oriental regions, the transfer of overseas trade with America to Atlantic ports, and the domination of Spain, brought about the rapid decline of Genoa in the 17C, and in 1684 Louis XIV entered the town after a bombardment. The Austrian occupation of 50 years later was ended by a popular insurrection (5–10 December, 1746), which was started by the action of a boy, Battista Perasso. In 1768 Genoa's last remaining colony, Corsica, revolted under Paoli, and the Genoese sold their rights in the island to France. In 1796 Napoleon entered Genoa, and four years later the city was attacked by the Austrians on land and the English at sea; but Massena's stubborn defence was relieved by the victory of Marengo. The Ligurian Republic, formed in 1802, soon became a French province, but in 1815 Genoa was joined to Piedmont by the treaty of Vienna, and fast developed into a stronghold of the Risorgimento, with Mazzini as the leading spirit, abetted by Garibaldi, the brothers Ruffini and their heroic mother, the soldier patriot Nino Bixio (1821–73), and Goffredo Mameli (1827–49) the warrior poet. The ill-fated expedition of Pisacane and Nicotera (June 1857) started out from Genoa, and it was in Genoa that Garibaldi planned his expedition with the 'Thousand' in 1860. Genoa, especially the old town, was damaged by Allied air and sea bombardment in the Second World War. The city has expanded rapidly since the last War, and the raised motorway running between the old town and the port symbolizes the chaotic town planning to which Genoa has been subjected in the last few decades. The hinterland is now covered with tower blocks, and it is one of the most polluted cities in Italy. The economic outlook for the port has become more optimistic in the last few years. Preparations are being made to celebrate the 500th anniversary of the discovery of America by Columbus in 1992 in the city, and it is hoped that a number of important restorations will be completed by that date.

Among the most famous natives of Genoa besides Christopher Columbus (1447–1506), the navigator, are Nicolò Paganini (1784–1840), the violinist and composer; and Giuseppe Mazzini (1805–72), the ideologist of the Risorgimento. Popes Innocent IV (Sinibaldo Fiesco; died 1254) and Innocent VIII (Giovanni Battista Cibo; 1432–92) were Genoese. Eugenio Montale (1896–1981), the poet, was born in Genoa.

Chaucer was sent to Genoa in 1372–3 by Edward II to arrange a commercial treaty with the maritime Republic. Alessandro Stradella (1642–82), the composer, was murdered in Genoa by assassins hired by the former lover of his Venetian wife. Charles Dickens and his family visited Italy in 1844. He spent much time in Genoa (see Rte 6C), and came 'to have an attachment for the very stones in the streets of Genoa, and to look back upon the city with affection as connected with many hours of happiness and quiet!' He left an interesting description of his stay in 'Pictures from Italy'.

Art. The architecture of medieval Genoa is characterised by the black-and-white striped façades of the older churches and other buildings; and the earliest sculpture came from the workshops of the Pisano family and the Comacini. The Renaissance brought the work of Galeazzo Alessi, the Perugian architect, while the 16C sculpture of the Gaggini was followed by the work of the Carlone and the disciples of Bernini. The Genoese school of painting is said to derive from the Florentine Perin del Vaga, who was commissioned to decorate the Palazzo Doria in 1527. Through its close commercial links with the Netherlands, the city came in possession of many Dutch and Flemish paintings. In 1607 Rubens visited Genoa, and in 1621 Van Dyck arrived and stayed on and off in the city for six years. Luca Cambiaso, Lazzaro Calvi, and Giovanni Battista Castello are the most illustrious names of the 16C, but the most productive period of Genoese painting is the 17C, with such masters as Bernardo Strozzi ('il Prete Genovese'), Bernardo and Valerio Castello, Giovanni Battista Castiglione, Domenico

Fiasella, and the Piola brothers. Painters of the 18C include Alessandro Magnasco and Carlo Alberto Baratta.

A. Central Genoa

The main thoroughfare leading, under various names, from *Porta Principe Station* (Pl. 1) to the central Piazza De Ferrari skirts the brow of the group of hills on which Genoa is built. To the right, below, is the labyrinth of the old town; to the left are the newer districts on the hillside.

From Piazza Acquaverde, with its subways, bus-stations and Columbus monument (1862), VIA BALBI (Pl. 1,6), now one-way towards the station and busy with traffic, leads downhill towards the centre. This street and its continuations contain many dignified old mansions, though the narrowness of the roadway detracts from the full effect of their external façades. On the right (No. 10) is the former **Palazzo Reale** (Pl. 6), designed c 1650 for the Balbi family by Michele Moncino and Pier Francesco Cantone and remodelled in 1705 for the Durazzo by Carlo Fontana. The exterior was covered for restoration in 1988.

It is now occupied by the various 'Soprintendenze' of Liguria, and is officially known as Palazzo Balbi-Durazzo. From 1842 to 1922 it was the royal seat in Genoa and it contains several suites of sumptuously decorated 18C rooms (open daily 9–13). On the upper floor the Gallery of Mirrors and the Ballroom are magnificent; and among the paintings are some charming portraits of royal ladies, a 16C Dutch series of Scenes from the life of St Agnes, and a Crucifixion by *Van Dyck. Luca Giordano* is represented by two large paintings, and there are characteristic works by *Domenico Parodi, Bartolomeo Guidobono,* and *Bernardo Strozzi.*

Opposite, at No. 5, is a palace (1634–36) built as a Jesuit college by Bartolomeo Bianco, occupied by the *University* since 1803. A flight of steps flanked by lions (1704) leads to an imposing court from where another staircase ascends to the Aula Magna, in which are statues and reliefs by Giambologna (1579). The library is in a former Jesuit church next door. The Botanical Garden (Pl. 2; entrance from Corso Dogali by appointment) was founded in 1803. No. 1, the *Palazzo Durazzo-Pallavicini* (now Giustiniani Adorno), also by Bartolomeo Bianco, has a later double loggia. It contains a remarkable private collection (no adm.) including the best works by Van Dyck in the city. The *Palazzo Balbi-Senarega*, opposite (No. 4; also used by the University), is also by Bianco. On Piazza della Nunziata, beyond, stands the **Santissima Annunziata** (Pl. 6), a church rebuilt in 1591–1620, and badly damaged in 1942, with a 19C portico. The domed interior is richly adorned with coloured marble and good altarpieces by the 17C Genoese school (numerous works by Giovanni Battista Carlone). Via Bensa leads on to Largo della Zecca, in which is the entrance to the *Galleria Garibaldi*, a road-tunnel of 1927 leading to Piazza Portello and continued from there by the *Galleria Nino Bixio* to Piazza Corvetto.

To the right is the quieter VIA CAIROLI (Pl. 6), in which at the beginning on the right, *Palazzo Balbi* (No. 18) has an ingenious staircase by Gregorio Petondi (1780). This street ends in Piazza della Meridiana with the *Palazzo della Meridiana*, a good plain 16C building.

*Via Garibaldi (Pl. 6, 7) leads out of this piazza: it has been
totally closed to traffic. Formerly known as the Strada Nuova it was
laid out in 1558 by Bernardino Cantone, pupil of Galeazzo Alessi.
In the following decade the leading Genoese patrician families built
their magnificent mansions here making it one of the most handsome streets in Europe. Narrow lanes lead down from the street
into the old city (see Rte 6B). *Palazzo Bianco (No. 11; adm. 9–19;
Sunday & Monday 10–12, 15.30–17.30) was so named because of its
colour, although it has now darkened considerably. It was built for
the Grimaldi c 1565 and enlarged after 1711 by *Giacomo Viano* for
Maria Durazzo, widow of Giovanni Francesco Brignole Sale. It was
presented to the State by Maria Brignole Sale, the Duchess of
Galliera in 1884. It contains part of her collection of paintings,
together with later acquisitions, with some particularly beautiful
Flemish and Dutch paintings. The gallery was excellently
rearranged and modernised in 1950 by *Franco Albini*. Only the
outstanding pieces are on view; the remainder is accessible to
students on application. Many of the paintings which have been restored recently are exhibited on iron stands in various rooms.

ROOM 1 (beyond Room 2). *Byzantine (13C) School*, Madonna
and Child (restored); *Tomaso Busaccio*, Madonna and Child;
Barnaba da Modena, *Madonna of the Goldfinch (restored); works
by the *Brea* family (late 15–16C), including a Crucifixion by
Ludovico; Byzantine embroidered altarcloth of the 13C (from the
Cathedral).—R. 2. *Giovanni Mazone*, Crucifixion (restored); works
by *Luca Cambiaso* (including the 'Madonna della candela').—
SECOND FLOOR. R. 3 (South Loggia). *Filippino Lippi*, Madonna and
Child with Saints; *Pontormo*, Portrait of a Florentine gentleman.—R.
4. *Master of St John the Evangelist* (Flemish, late 15C), *Four
scenes from the life of the Saint, with Saints Mark and Luke in
monochrome on the back; *Hugo van der Goes*, *Christ blessing;
Joos van Cleve, Madonna and Child; *Gerard David*, *Madonna and
Child with two Saints, Madonna 'della pappa', Crucifixion
(removed for restoration); *Jan Provost*, *St Peter, *Annunciation, *St
Elisabeth; *Filippino Lippi*, St Sebastian between Saints John the
Baptist and Francis.—R. 5. *Jan Matsys*, Portrait of Andrea Doria,
Madonna and Child; works by *Jan van Scorel* (including Holy
Family, recently restored).—R. 6. *Ludovico Brea*, Crucifixion and St
Peter (restored); *Palma Vecchio*, *Madonna and Child with St John
the Baptist and Mary Magdalene; *Moretto da Brescia*, *Madonna
and Child; *Veronese*, *Crucifixion.—R. 7. *Van Dyck*, Christ and the
Tribute Money, Vertumnus and Pomona, Genoese patrician lady,
and Andrea Spinola (the last two attributed). *Rubens*, Venus and
Mars (restored).—R. 8. Flemish and Dutch 17C genre paintings.
David Teniers the younger, Watchmen; *Jan Steen*, Hostelry party;
Jacob Ruysdael, Landscape; *Jan van Goyen*, Landscape with
rabbits.—R. 9. *Simone Vouet*, David with the head of Goliath.—R.
10 (North Loggia), *Guercino*, God the father. R. 11. Works of the
Spanish school, including *Murillo* (Flight into Egypt), and *Francesco Zurbaran*, Saints Eufemia and Ursula.

RR. 12–15 contain interesting paintings of the 17–18C Genoese school. R. 12.
Works by *Bernardo Strozzi*. R. 13. *Pisanello*, *Portrait of a man in profile
(restored), and works by *Anton Maria Vassallo*. R. 14 contains works by
Sarzana. R. 15. *Gioacchino Assereto, Lorenzo De Ferrari, Pellegro Piola*. The
local collection is continued on the ground floor (across the courtyard) in RR.
16–20 (*Domenico Piola, Gregorio De Ferrari, Bartolomeo Guidobono, Il*

Baciccio, Valerio Castello, Giovanni Benedetto Castiglione, and *Alessandro Magnasco*).

Almost opposite Palazzo Bianco is **Palazzo Rosso (Pl. 6; adm. as for Palazzo Bianco, see above), also named from its colour, a magnificent building of 1671–77 erected for Ridolfo and Gio Francesco Sale Brignole, probably by *Pier Antonio Corradi* (or by *Matteo Lagomaggiore*), and decorated in 1687 by *Gregorio De Ferrari, Domenico Piola, Antonio Haffner*, and *Nicolò Viviano*. Like Palazzo Bianco it was bequeathed to the city (in 1874) by the Duchess of Galliera, together with her magnificent art collection, which includes fine portraits of the Brignole family by *Van Dyck*, and it, too, was well restored after damage in the War, in 1953–61 by *Franco Albini*.

FIRST FLOOR. R. 2. *Pisanello*, Portrait of a man; *Paris Bordone*, Portrait of a young man, Portrait of a man holding a letter; *Bonifazio Veronese*, Adoration of the Magi; *Paolo Veronese*, Judith.—R. 3. *Veronese*, Nativity (a small work).—R. 4. Works by *Mattia Preti* and *Caravaggio* (Ecce Homo).—R. 5. *Guercino*, Cleopatra; *Guido Reni*, St Sebastian.—RR. 6–10 contain works by the local Ligurian school. R. 6. *Luca Cambiaso*.—R. 7. *Bernardo Strozzi*.—R. 10. *Bartolomeo Guidobono*.— SECOND FLOOR. There is a good view of the striped campanile of the Duomo, the campanile of Santa Maria della Vigna, and the Torre degli Embriachi. R. 12, the Salone, has frescoes by *Antonio* and *Enrico Haffner*. RR. 13 & 14 have vault frescoes by *Gregorio De Ferrari*. R. 13. *Van Dyck*, Portraits of Geronima Brignole Sale with her daughter Raggia, of Frederick, Prince of Orange, of a Genoese patrician, and of **Puccio, the goldsmith and his son. R. 14. *Dürer*, Portrait of a young boy; *Van Dyck*, equestrian portrait of Anton Giulio Brignole Sale, and of his wife Paolina; *Frans Pourbus the Elder*, Viglius Von Aytta; *Rubens*, Christ carrying the Cross.—RR. 15–16 have vaults decorated by *Domenico Piola*. R. 15. *Murillo*, St Francis; *Giacinto Rigaud*, Portrait of Gio Francesco Brignole Sale who built the palace.

The collection of decorative arts (not part of the Brignole donation) is arranged on three floors in a wing of the palace. On the Second Floor RR. 23–28 display Genoese 17C & 18C dolls and crêche figures (some by Giovanni Battista Gaggini and Maragliano); on the First Floor, RR. 29–34 contains the numismatic collection, and medals; and on the ground floor RR. 35–39 contain Ligurian ceramics. There is also a Prints and Drawings collection.

Immediately beyond Palazzo Rosso, on the left, is **Palazzo Doria Tursi (the *Municipio*), flanked by raised gardens. Begun in 1568 for Nicolò Grimaldi by the Ponzello brothers, the loggie were added in 1597 around the magnificent courtyard.

Visitors (admitted 9–12, 14–17) are shown the ex *Sala del Consiglio Generale* and the adjoining *Sala della Giunta* with Paganini's Guarnerius violin (1742). In the *Sala del Sindaco* (shown only when not in use) is preserved a bronze tablet inscribed with a decree (117 BC) delimiting the boundary between the Genuates and the Veturii, and three letters from Columbus.

Most of the other mansions in this street can be admired only from the outside, though the courtyards are usually accessible; notable among them are the late-16C *Palazzo Serra* or *Campanella* (No. 12) and *Palazzo Cattaneo-Adorno* (Nos 8–10); the *Palazzo Podestà* (No. 7), begun by Giovanni Battista Castello in 1563, with a good stucco vestibule and a rococo grotto and fountain in the courtyard; *Palazzo Spinola* (No. 5), now a bank, with frescoes in the atrium and vestibule (the fine courtyard has been enclosed for use as a banking hall); *Palazzo Doria* (No. 6) of 1563, remodelled in 1684, with a charming little courtyard; *Palazzo Carrega Cataldi* (No. 4) by Giovanni Battista Castello (1558–60), now the Chamber of Commerce. *Palazzo Parodi* (No. 3) is by Galeazzo Alessi (1567), with a portal with two atlantes by Taddeo Carlone (1581); No. 2, the *Palazzo Gambaro*, now a bank, is by Ponzello (1565); No. 1, the *Palazzo Cambiaso*, also a bank, is by Bernardino Cantone (1565).—The irregular Piazza Fontane Marose (Pl. 11) has several fine mansions: *Palazzi Pallavicini*, No. 2, begun 1575; *Negrone*, No. 4, rather later, altered c 1750; and *Spinola dei Marmi*, No. 6, of the 15C, with a particoloured marble façade and statues of the family (being restored in 1988).

Via Venticinque Aprile leads south to PIAZZA DE FERRARI (Pl. 11), the most traffic-ridden square in Genoa, where numerous main roads converge. It has an abundant fountain. Here the *Teatro Carlo Felice*, with a neo-classical pronaos, was gutted by fire in 1944. Work was finally begun on its reconstruction in 1987 on a much criticised design by Aldo Rossi. Behind Augusto Rivalta's Garibaldi monument (1893), is the *Accademia Ligustica di Belle Arti*, built by Carlo Barabino in 1827–31 (restored after war damage). A Pinacoteca (adm. 9–13 except Sunday & fest.) here, arranged in four rooms contains paintings by Ligurian artists (14–19C), including Bernardo Strozzi and the De Ferrari, and a polyptych by Perin del Vaga. Here also is the civic *Biblioteca Berio*. Between Via XX Settembre and Via Dante which lead to the newer districts of the city (see Rte 6C) is the elaborate curved façade of the *Borsa* (1907–12). Opposite is the side of Palazzo Ducale (described below; covered for restoration), and on the last side is the Palazzo della Società di Navigazione Italia (1923, by Cesare Gamba). Behind this, just out of the square, in Piazza Matteotti (Pl. 10), is the Baroque church of the **Gesù** (Pl. 11; also called Santi Ambrogio e Andrea), built in 1589–1606 by Giuseppe Valeriani; the façade (covered for restoration) was completed in 1892 to the original design. The sumptuous polychrome interior provides a fit setting for the good 17C paintings. The frescoes in the vaults and cupola are by Giovanni Carlone, and his younger brother Giovanni Battista. The altarpieces include an Assumption, by *Guido Reni* (3rd chapel on the right); a Circumcision (1608; high altar), and St Ignatius curing the sick (1620; 3rd chapel on the left), both by *Rubens*.—Surrounding Piazza Matteotti is **Palazzo Ducale** (Pl. 10, 11), a huge building of different periods which since 1975 has been undergoing a lengthy restoration (expected to be completed in 1990) as a cultural centre.

The left wing, the earliest part of the building, was the seat of the Capitano del Popolo in 1274. In 1291 it was united with the adjacent Palazzo del Comune (see Rte 6B). After numerous additions during the following centuries, when it became the residence of the doges (from 1340 onwards), Il Vannone (c 1591–1620) carried out radical modifications in order to unify the various parts of the building. After a fire, the palace was reconstructed by Simone Cantoni in 1778–83 and given a neo-classical façade. The attractive vestibule with a cortile at either end (one with a 17C fountain) has remains of statues of the Doria family by Montorsoli and Taddeo Carlone. Excavations in the piazza in 1975 revealed an Imperial Roman house.

In Via San Lorenzo is the flank of the **Cathedral* (*San Lorenzo*; Pl. 10), a Romanesque building consecrated (unfinished) in 1118 and modified in the 13–14C and during the Renaissance. The façade was restored in 1934. On the S side of the church are Hellenistic sarcophagi, a 15C Grimaldi tomb, and the portal of *San Gottardo*, with Romanesque sculpture. The façade, approached by a flight of steps between two lions (1840), is decorated with bands of particoloured marble: the three W doorways have good carvings in the French Gothic style. The column-bearing lions on the extreme right and left of the façade are early-13C works, one bears a statue known as the 'Arrotino'. The *Campanile* (restored) was completed in 1522. On the N side are more sarcophagi and the 12C portal of *San Giovanni.

The INTERIOR has dark Corinthian columns. The proportions were altered when the nave roof was raised in 1550, and the cupola, by Galeazzo Alessi, added in 1567. The pulpit (1526) is by *Pier Angelo Scala* of Carona. The lunette over the W door has early-14C frescoes (being restored) of Christ and the Apostles. In the South Aisle, beside a British naval shell that damaged the chapel without exploding in 1941, is a marble Crucifixion of 1443. In the chapel to the right of the high altar (on the right wall), *Federico Barocci*, Vision of St Sebastian of the Crucifixion. The stalls in the apse date from 1514–64. In the Lercari Chapel, to the left of the high altar, are wall and ceiling paintings by *Luca Cambiaso* and *Giovanni Battista Castello*. The great *CHAPEL OF ST JOHN THE BAPTIST, on the N side, has a richly decorated front by Domenico Gagini and other 15C sculptors from Bissone (Lugano). The interior was designed in 1492 by *Giovanni D'Aria*: the statues of Old Testament characters are by *Matteo Civitali*, and those of John the Baptist and the Virgin are by *Andrea Sansovino* (1504). Above the altar (1950, by Guido Galletti) is a baldacchino (1532) by *Nicolò da Corte* and *Gian Giacomo* and *Guglielmo Della Porta*. The 13C sarcophagus, of French workmanship, on the left, formerly held relics of the saint.—In the adjoining chapel is the tomb of Giorgio Fieschi (died 1461) by *Giovanni Gagini*; beyond the N door are fragments of the tomb of Luca Fieschi (c 1336), by the school of *Giovanni Pisano*.

The sacristy, on the N side of the church, leads to the ***Treasury** (adm. 9.30–11.30, 15–17; closed Sunday, Monday, & fest.), beautifully displayed in a series of round vaults built in 1956 by Franco Albini. Here are a 1C Roman green glass dish, said to have been used at the Last Supper; two copes, one of the mid-15C (but popularly assigned to Pope Gelasius), another of the mid-16C; the *Zaccaria Cross, a Byzantine work of the 10C refashioned in the 13C; the 11–12C reliquary of the Arm of St Anne, brought from Pera (Istanbul) in 1461; a 12C casket, perhaps given by Frederick Barbarossa in 1178; a silver-gilt casket for the ashes of St John the Baptist, by Teramo Danieli and Simone Caldera (c 1440); a chalcedony dish (?1C) with the head of John the Baptist (a French 15C addition); the consecration Bull of Pope Gelasius II (1118); and many reliquaries, chalices, etc.

B.   The Old Town and the Harbour

The Old Town, lying between the port, Via Garibaldi, and Via Venticinque Aprile, with its narrow lanes or 'carugi', some less than 3m wide, and its tall houses, is, although damaged by war and flood, still a most interesting district of Genoa. A walk through its narrow alleys, some of them, however, greatly deteriorated in recent years, gives an excellent insight into Genoese life. Many of the houses have charming portals in white marble or black stone, often bearing reliefs of St George, patron of the city, who gave his name to the famous Genoese bank (see below). The two itineraries given below, although at times traversing unsalubrious areas, include most of the points of interest.

From Piazza San Lorenzo beside the cathedral the narrow Via Chiabrera (Pl. 10) leads SW. Busts and reliefs decorate the portico (usually closed) of the 17C *Palazzo Giustiniani* (No. 6). From Via San Bernardo, on the right, Vico dei Giustiniani leads left to Piazza Embriaci (Pl. 10), in which steps lead up to the Doric portal (by

Giovanni Battista Orsolino) of the *Casa Brignole Sale* (No. 5; formerly
Embriaci; 1580) On the right the steep stepped Salita, passing the 12C
Torre degli Embriaci, embattled in 1923, ascends to ***Santa Maria di
Castello** (Pl. 10), a Romanesque church with 15C Gothic additions,
well restored. It occupies the site of the Roman castrum and preserves
some Roman columns.

INTERIOR (closed 12–15.30). On the W wall, fresco of the Madonna and Child with
two Dominican Saints by *Lorenzo Fasolo* (c 1498). South Aisle. 2nd chapel,
Aurelio Lomi, Martyrdom of San Biagio; 3rd chapel, *Pier Francesco Sacchi*, Saints
John the Baptist, Anthony, and Thomas Aquinas, and 16C Genoese majolica on
the walls; 4th chapel, *Bernardo Castello*, Martyrdom of St Peter of Verona; 5th
chapel, *Aurelio Lomi*, Assumption of the Virgin. In the chapel to the right of the
Sanctuary, *Aurelio Lomi*, St Giacinto. In the Sanctuary, marble group of the
Assunta by *Antonio Domenico Parodi*. In the chapel to the left of the Sanctuary,
Domenico Piola, St Rosa of Lima. The Baptistery in the North Aisle (1st chapel),
contains a polyptych by the *Ligurian School* (1480–90), some ruined 15C frescoes,
and a Roman sarcophagus.
    From the end of the South Aisle, a beautifully carved portal (inner face) by
Giovanni Gagini and *Leonardo Riccomanno* (1452) gives acess to the SACRISTY.
From here is reached the **Dominican Convent** of 1442 with a second cloister, well
restored in 1966. In the ATRIUM are vault frescoes attributed to *Giacomo Serfolio*
(late 15C). Beyond is the LOGGIA OF THE SECOND CLOISTER (1452–55) with pretty
frescoes in the vault of the Mystery of the Incarnation of uncertain attribution,
possibly by *'Iustus de Alemania'* (Giusto di Ravensburg), the Flemish painter who
signed and dated (1451) the *Annunciation on the wall. Above the two portals are
frescoes of St Dominic and Peter Martyr.—Stairs lead up to the UPPER LOGGIA
(view of the port), with Roman and medieval capitals, and three doors in black
stone with carved architraves. In the left walk, marble statue of St Catherine of
Alexandria attributed to *Leonardo Riccomanno*, and a *Tabernacle of the Trinity
by *Domenico Gagini*. In the right walk, detached *Fresco in monochrome of St
Dominic with Dominicans in Paradise, attributed to *Braccesco*.—From here there
is access to the 15C OLD LIBRARY, with sculptures attributed to *Domenico Gagini*,
a wood Crucifix (c 1100), and a Polyptych of the Annunciation, by *Giovanni
Mazone* (1470; one of only two works known by this local artist).—The **Museum** in
another room (opened on request) contains the *Coronation of the Virgin (or
Paradise), a painting with an unusually large number of figures (showing Flemish
influence), signed and dated 1513 by *Ludovico Brea*. Also here: *Barnaba da
Modena*, Madonna and Child (a fragment); *Maestro di Santa Maria di Castello*
(mid 14C), Madonna and Child; *Ludovico Brea*, Conversion of St Paul.

The Salita Santa Maria di Castello descends to Via Santa Croce which
ascends left under an archway to the large *Piazza Sarzano* (Pl. 14),
once a centre of the old city, but now sadly deteriorated and of no
distinction. The area was badly damaged in the war and is still in a
partly derelict state. On the site of the bombed convent of *San Silvestro*
(left) excavations revealed the remains of the medieval Castello built
above the pre-Roman walls of the ancient city, and part of a necropolis.
Here is the pink building of the **Museo di Sant'Agostino** (Pl. 14; adm.
9–19; Sunday & Monday 10–12, 15.30–17), built in 1984 on the site of
the Convent of Sant'Agostino to display the city's collection of architectural fragments, sculptures, and detached frescoes. The Gothic
church of **Sant'Agostino**, begun in 1260, and now deconsecrated,
which preserves a fine campanile with graceful windows and spire, is
still being restored for use as an auditorium. It will be approached off
the triangular Cloister, used for exhibitions (or from the Stradone di
Sant'Agostino, see below).

The **Museum** interior is built in a pretentious modern style with much of the
structure in black. GROUND FLOOR. A small display illustrating how Roman
fragments were reused in the city; old plans and views of Genoa; late medieval
sculpture (good 10–11C capitals). The lower ground floor has extensive
deposits.—A long stair ramp leads up to the FIRST FLOOR, with galleries around a
modern white marble cloister displaying 11–12C capitals (notably from the

destroyed church of San Tomaso), and 13–14C carved panels from Sant'Agostino.—In the large hall: two detached frescoes by *Manfredino d'Alberto di Pistoia* (active 1280–93); (on the steps) three angels holding inscriptions by *Giovanni di Balduccio*, and fragments of the *Funerary monument of Margherita di Brabante (died 1311), by *Giovanni Pisano*, recomposed after restoration in 1987. Beyond are rooms still being arranged, (and sometimes used for exhibitions), with a 14C carved Crucifix, and a painted *Crucifix by *Barnaba da Modena* (restored in 1979).—Another long stair ramp leads up to the SECOND FLOOR. At the top are 14C fresco fragments and four 15C English alabaster reliefs. The chronological arrangement continues in the galleries around the cloister: to the left are a series of 15C black stone *Architraves with reliefs of St John the Baptist and St George; 15–16C Genoese busts, and carved masques by *Taddeo Carlone*; detached frescoes by *Luca Cambiaso*, including a Battle of Tritons; 16C sculptures (*Gian Giacomo Della Porta, Silvio Cosini*), and 17C statues of Madonnas. In the large hall: two fine column-bearing lions (12C, Campionese, from Montesano); paintings by *Domenico Piola*; two marble kneeling angels by *Filippo Parodi*; a marble group of the Rape of Helena by *Pierre Puget* (1683).—In another large room beyond, Penitent Magdalene signed and dated 1790 by *Antonio Canova*.

The Stradone di Sant'Agostino leads down past a building under construction for the University and (right) a road in front of the church of Sant'Agostino (see above). It ends beside a pretty 18C tabernacle on the side of **San Donato** (Pl. 10), a fine church probably founded in the early 12C with a splendid polygonal campanile and a good doorway. In the beautiful basilican interior a Madonna and Child by *Nicolò da Voltri* (late-14C) has been placed in an incongruous modern frame (chapel to the right of the high altar). The *Adoration of the Magi by *Joos van Cleve* stolen from the church in 1974 has been displayed in Palazzo Spinola (see below) since its recovery. From the church the Salita Pollaiuoli, crossing Via Canneto il Lungo, a typical long street of the old town, with food shops, and some good doorways (at No. 23, remains of Palazzo Fieschi, covered for restoration) leads back up to Piazza Matteotti.

From San Donato the decaying Via San Bernardo leads left, with several fine doorways and a good courtyard at No. 20 (Palazzo Schiaffino), to Piazza Grillo Cattaneo, where a splendid portal by Tamagnino survives at No. 6 surrounded by delapidated buildings. Vico dietro il Coro leads past the E end of the church of *Santi Cosma e Damiano* (Pl. 10; reached by a lane on the right), an 11C church with traces of an earlier building. Just to the NE of Piazza Cattaneo is the untidy *Piazza San Giorgio* (Pl. 10), an important market square in the Middle Ages. Here are the two attractive domed centrally planned churches of San Giorgio and San Torpete (both closed, and the former covered with scaffolding). *San Giorgio*, documented as early as 964, was reconstructed in 1695 by Giacomo Lagomaggiore. The curved façade was altered in 1859. *San Torpete*, consecrated in 1180, was rebuilt with an eliptical cupola after 1730 on a design by Antonio Maria Ricca. From here Via Canneto il Corto, another typical street of the old town, leads past the Piazzetta Stella (black stone doorway at No. 3) back up to Via San Lorenzo and the Cathedral.

A SECOND ITINERARY THROUGH THE OLD TOWN starts between the Palazzo Ducale and the cathedral, following Via Reggio. In this street is (right) the old *Palazzo del Comune* (1291) with the *Torre del Popolo* (1307), now incorporated in the Ducal Palace, and covered for restoration (see Rte 6A). On the other side of the street are the 16C *Palazzetto Criminale* (now the City and Republic Archives) and (No. 12) the *Cloister of San Lorenzo* (being restored). The Salita Arcivescovato (a few metres back) descends to the square PIAZZA SAN MATTEO, created in 1278 when it was surrounded by the mansions and church of the Doria family with striped black and white façades. *San Matteo** (Pl. 11), founded in 1125 but rebuilt by the Doria in 1278, has a striped black and white Gothic façade with inscriptions recounting the glorious deeds of the Dorias.

The INTERIOR was transformed in 1543 for Andrea Doria by *Giovanni Angelo Montorsoli (1543) and Giovanni Battista Castello (Bergamasco)* (1559). The Sanctuary is an interesting sculptural work by *Montorsoli* (with the help of *Silvio Cosini*). The nave was decorated with stuccoes and frescoes by *Bergamasco* and *Luca Cambiaso*. In a niche in the left aisle is a wood group of the Deposition by *Anton Maria Maragliano* (being restored). The *Crypt (apply to the sacristan) and staircase, decorated with marbles and stuccoes were designed by *Montorsoli* for the tomb of Andrea Doria.—An archway on the left of the church leads to the cloister (1308–10) by *Magister Marcus Venetus*, with coupled columns, and notable capitals at the two W corners.

Opposite the church is the *Casa di Lamba Doria* (No. 15), built in the 13C with a portico (restored after War damage). On the corner of the Salita Arcivescovato is the *Casa di Andrea Doria* (No. 17), built for Lazzaro Doria in 1468 and presented to the famous admiral by his native city in 1528 (inscription; restored in 1930). On the left of the church is the *Casa di Branca Doria* (No.14), with a charming relief over the portal. Off Via Chiossone, in which No. 1 is another Doria house with a blackened portal by Pace Gaggini, the ancient Vico della Casana, a busy lane, leads to the left. The animated Via Luccoli (left again), with many good shops, and pretty street lighting, crosses Piazza Soziglia (with a café founded in 1828) to reach the Campetto (Pl. 10). *Palazzo Imperiale* (1560) here (No. 8) is a sumptuous building by Giovanni Battista Castello. The upper part of the curved façade is decorated with paintings and stucchi by Ottavio Semino. On the other side of Via degli Orefici a short road leads to **Santa Maria delle Vigne** (Pl. 10), a church redesigned after 1598 (good Baroque interior) with a façade of 1842. Parts of its Romanesque predecessors (10C and 12C) can be seen from the lane on the left side, including the cloister, the nave wall, and, beneath an arch supporting the five-spired campanile, an interesting 14C tomb incorporating the front of a 2C sarcophagus. Inside, in the left aisle, is the tomb slab of the goldsmiths' corporation, with a fine relief of St Eligius (1459).

From the piazza in front Vico dei Greci leads W to the unsalubrious Vico Mele with some interesting houses: No. 16 (red) has a black stone relief of St John the Baptist (15C); No. 6, the *Palazzo Serra*, has an imposing portal and a Gothic outside stair; No. 8 is also noteworthy.

In the crooked and busy Via degli Orefici (see above), No. 9 (47 red) has a charming 15C marble relief of the Adoration of the Magi, and No. 7 a portal carved with the Labours of Hercules by the Della Porta. At the end of the street is PIAZZA BANCHI, which, until the end of the 18C, was the commercial centre of the city where the money-changers had their 'banchi'. Here is the *Loggia dei Mercanti*, designed in 1589–95 by Vannone, restored in the 19C, when it became an exchange, the first of its kind in Italy, and rebuilt after War damage. It is now used for exhibitions. The restored centrally-planned church of *San Pietro in Banchi*, approached by steps, was designed by Bernardino Cantone, and built by Giovanni Ponzello and Vannone (1581; covered with scaffolding). The 16C Palazzo Serra, seat of the Banca Commerciale since 1894, has recently been restored. Via Ponte Reale leads down to the quays, past the house where Daniel O'Connell, 'the Liberator', died in 1847 (plaque). Here is *Piazza Caricamento* (Pl. 10), with a statue of Raffaello Rubattino (1809–72), the shipowner who, against his will, supplied two vessels for Garibaldi's expedition, and the Gothic ***Palazzo di San Giorgio** (Pl. 10; being extensively restored in 1989), begun c 1260 and extended in 1571. The façade facing the port was frescoed by Lazzaro

Tavarone in 1606–08. Once the palace of the Capitani del Popolo, it became in 1408 the seat of the famous Banco di San Giorgio, which was largely responsible for the prosperity of the city from the mid-15C onwards. Here citizens could lend money for compound interest, and the idea of cheques was introduced. It is now occupied by the Harbour Board. Inside is a typical courtyard with staircases restored in the 13C style and a two-storeyed portico. The Salone dei Capitani del Popolo and the Salone delle Compere are interesting (for adm. apply to the keeper).

From Piazza Banchi VIA SAN LUCA (Pl. 6,10) leads N. It was the main street of the city in the Middle Ages, when it was the principle place of residence of the great Genoese families; it no longer pretends to elegance. The church of *San Luca*, to the right, has an interior (closed since 1984), decorated by Domenico Piola. Beyond Vico Pellicceria leads right to Piazza Pellicceria with palaces of the Spinola (No. 3 has a 15C portal). No. 1 is now the **Galleria Nazionale di Palazzo Spinola** (Pl. 6; adm. 9–19, Sunday and Monday 9–13).

This 16C mansion became the property of the Spinola in the early 18C when the collection of paintings was formed. It was left by the family, with the contents, to the Italian State in 1958. It is a particularly interesting example of a patrician Genoese residence, which preserves more or less intact its 17–18C decorations, as well as its furniture and paintings. The first two floors are to be restored as far as possible to their original state under the Spinola, while the two upper floors are to be opened as the *Galleria Nazionale della Liguria*, with restored works from churches, etc.

The **First Floor** was decorated in 1614–24 by *Lazzaro Tavarone*. Room I. *Pietro Muttoni*, Portrait of a man sheathing his sword; 16C Flemish Triptych from the church of San Pancrazio (to be restored).—R. 2. Works by *Giovanni Battista Carlone*; *Antonio Van Dyck*, Madonna in Prayer.—R. 3. *Van Dyck*, *Portrait of a young boy (a fragment).—The two masterpieces of the collection in R. 4 have been removed for restoration: *Antonello da Messina*, *Ecce Homo, and the statue of Justice by *Giovanni Pisano* from the funerary monument of Margherita di Brabante (other fragments are in the Museo di Sant'Agostino, see above). Also here: *Simon Vouet*, Madonna and Child, and *Joos van Cleve*, *Polyptych of the Adoration of the Magi, from the church of San Donato (restored).—R. 5. *Stefano Magnasco*, Holy Family with the young St John.

On the **Second Floor** are rooms decorated in 1736 by *Giovanni Battista Natali* as a setting for the paintings by *Gregorio De Ferarri*, *Luca Giordano*, *Bernardo Strozzi*, and *Domenico Piola*. In R. 3, *Van Dyck*, Four Evangelists.—R. 4. *Joos van Cleve*, Virgin in Prayer; two small female portraits by the school of *Ferdinando Voet* in exquisite 17C frames, one by *Filippo Parodi*; a 16C oval painting of the Madonna and Child with the young St John; *Carlo Maratta*, Virgin Annunciate and Annunciatory Angel; *School of Alessandro Allori*, Portrait of a lady.—The Galleria degli Specchi (R. 5) was decorated in 1734 by *Lorenzo de'Ferrari*.—In the last room is displayed a huge painted Crucifix by the *Master of Santa Maria di Castello*, from the church of Santa Maria di Castello.

Vico della Scienza leads E from the piazza into Via della Posta Vecchia, with many noble portals, especially at No. 16 (1531).

Via San Luca (see above) continues to **San Siro** (Pl. 6), a large church rebuilt by Andrea Ceresola and Daniele Casella (1586–1613), with a façade of 1821. Its predecessor was the first cathedral of Genoa before the 9C. The nave and apse are frescoed by Giovanni Battista Carlone and in the 5th chapel on the N side is a Nativity by Pomarancio.

Opposite the side door of the church a palace (No. 2) has a good black stone doorway, and a relief of San Giorgio, and a series of Gothic windows (blocked up).—From the other side of Via San Luca Vico dell'Agnello leads to Piazza dell'Agnello in which No. 6 is Palazzo Cicala of 1542 by Bernardo Cantone.

From Via San Luca the pretty Via della Maddalena (Pl. 6, 10) leads E past a tabernacle at No. 34, a courtyard at No. 29, and a good portal at

No. 39 (red), to the church of **Santa Maria Maddalena** (Pl. 11), rebuilt in 1588 by *Andrea Ceresola*. The richly decorated interior contains paintings by *Bernardo Castello*, *Giovanni Battista Parodi*, and other Genoese masters. In a chapel off the right side, four beautiful *Statuettes of the Virtues, formerly on the façade, have been attributed to *Giovanni Pisano* since their restoration. A fifth statue is still in restoration. From here numerous alley-ways lead back up to Via Garibaldi.

N of San Siro (see above) is Via Lomellini (Pl. 6), wide enough for cars. At No. 2 is a delapidated courtyard. The **Casa Mazzini** (No. 13; adm. 9–13, 15–18, Sunday 9–12; closed Monday), where Giuseppe Mazzini (1805–72) was born, contains an excellent **Museum of the Risorgimento** reopened and enlarged in 1982. The library of the Istituto Mazziniano is on the third floor.—On the left is the church of **San Filippo Neri**, with a fine 18C interior decorated by Antonio Maria Haffner, and a polychrome Deposition group (at the beginning of the left aisle) by Anton Maria Maragliano. The ORATORY, next door (No. 10; if closed ask for the key at the Casa Mazzini) has an *Interior of 1749 (used for concerts), with a statue of the Immacolata by Pierre Puget.

From Via San Luca and Piazza Fossatello Via del Campo (Pl. 6; portals at Nos 1, 9, and 35 red), leads to the Gothic arch of *Porta dei Vacca* (1155). From here the long and disreputable Via di Pré (Pl. 5) leads past the circular neo-classical church of *San Sisto* (1827), behind Palazzo Reale, to the church of **San Giovanni di Pré** (Pl. 5), founded in 1180, with a severe interior (often restored) with an apse at each end. There is an upper and lower church which adjoin the COMMENDA (Pl. 1,5), the *Commandery of the Knights of St John*, built at the same time as a convent and hospice for crusaders. On Piazza Commenda is the fine five-spired campanile and flank of the church (with Gothic arches), next to the beautiful triple loggia of the Commenda, altered in the Renaissance (being restored in 1988, but normally used for exhibitions).—From the piazza there is access to the **Port**, along the great length of which runs the 'Sopraelevata' an ugly raised motorway (1965) which has isolated the old town from the harbour, and which distributes the motorway traffic to the city. A wall separates the main quay from the wharves and landing stages, and visitors are not admitted without a pass from the Ufficio dei Permessi at the Stazione Marittima (boat trips, see the beginning of Rte 6).

The old mole (Molo Vecchio, Pl. 9) was begun in 1257 by the Cistercian friars Oliverio and Filippo, and new works were undertaken in 1553 and 1642. An important extension of the harbour (1876–88) was due to the generous donation of 20 million lire by De Ferrari, Duke of Galliera. The Bacino della Lanterna and Bacino Sampierdarena unite Genoa with Sampierdarena. The harbour now occupies c 1300 acres, of which two-thirds are water. It is principally important for its import trade in oil, coal, grain, and cotton. At the end of the Second World War it was full of mines and sunken ships, and most of the docks were badly damaged, but the efficiency of the port was re-established by 1950, since when new petrol quays have been constructed and the Cristoforo Colombo Airport built out over the water (and modernised in 1986). After a decade of economic crisis, the port appears to have recovered its importance as one of the chief ports in the Mediterranean.

Via Gramsci ascends to Piazza Principe, with a monument to Galliera (1897), and the main approach to the **Stazione Marittima** (Pl. 5), beyond which is **Palazzo Doria Pamphilj** (Pl. 1; no adm.), or *Palazzo del Principe*, composed of two buildings acquired by Andrea Doria in 1521 which were thrown into one by *Domenico Caranca* (1529); *Montorsoli* may have added the loggia (1543–47), towards the garden. Charles V and Napoleon were entertained here, and the

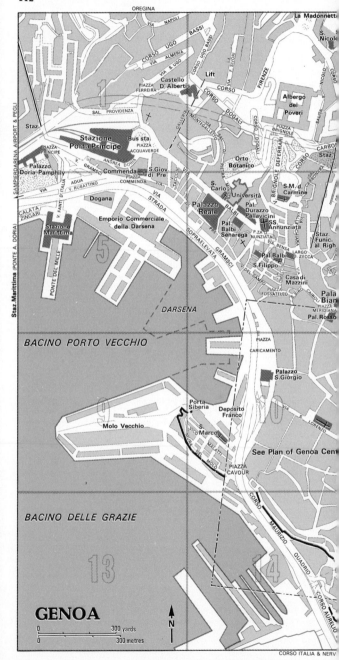

OREGINA

La Madonnett

S. Nicole

VIA NAPOLI

CORSO UGO BASSI

VIA ALMERIA

VIA S. UGO

CORSO UGO BASSI

BASSI

VIA S. SILOH

FIRENZE

S. NICOLO

Lift

CORSO

CORSO

DOGALI

Castello D'Albertis

PIAZZA FERREIRA

Albergo dei Poveri

SAL PROVIDENZA

VIA MONTEGALLETTO

PIAZZA BRIGNOLE

CORSO DOGALI

SALITA

Staz.

Stazione Porta Principe

Bus sta.

PIAZZA ACQUAVERDE

VIA PIETRA

Orto Botanico

CARBO

Staz

PIAZZA PRINCIPE

ANDREA DORIA

V. GRAMSCI

Commenda

S.Giov. di Pre

PIAZZA COMMENDA

S. Carlo

Università

BRIGNOLE DEFERRARI

S.M.d. Carmine

Palazzo Doria Pamphily

VIA

V. RUBATTINO

VIA STRADA

Pal. Durazzo Pallavicini

VALLE CHIARA

VIA

ADUA

Dogana

Palazzo Reale

SS. Annunziata

CALATA ZINGARI

V. FANTI D'ITALIA

Emporio Commerciale della Darsena

VIA BALBI

Pal. Balbi Senarega

P.ZA NUNZIATA

VIA BENSA

Staz. Funic. al Righ

Stazione Marittima

PONTE DEL MILLE

SOPRAELEVATA

GRAMSCI

Pal.Balbi

D. ZECCA

LARGO

S.Filippo

V. DEL CAMPO

Casa di Mazzini

PIAZZA FOSSATELLO

CAIROLI

Pala Bian

DARSENA

PIAZZA MERIDIANA

Pal. Rosso

BACINO PORTO VECCHIO

PIAZZA CARICAMENTO

Palazzo S.Giorgio

Molo Vecchio

Porta Siberia

Deposito Franco

VIA S. LORENZO

S.Marco

MALATTI

See Plan of Genoa Cent

PIAZZA CAVOUR

BACINO DELLE GRAZIE

CORSO MAURIZIO

QUADRIO

CORSO AURELIO

13

14

GENOA

0   300 yards
0   300 metres

N

Staz. Marittima (PONTE A. DORIA)

SAMPIERDARENA AIRPORT & PEGLI

CORSO ITALIA & NERV

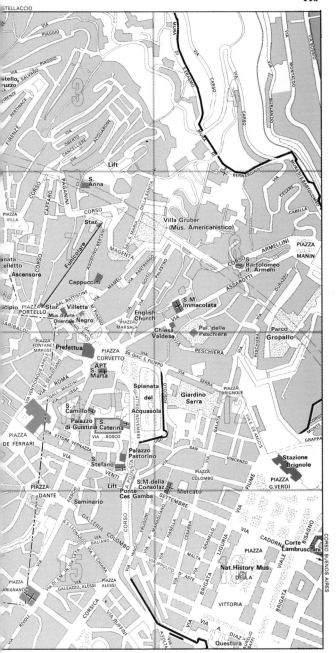

composer Verdi after 1877. It contains frescoes by *Perin del Vaga* and stuccoes by *Luzio Romano* and *Guglielmo della Porta* in the vestibule and on the stairs.—Conspicuous above the E side of the harbour is the **Lanterna**, a medieval lighthouse restored in 1543, which is the characteristic feature of the seaboard of Genoa, and much beloved by the Genoese.

In the other direction Via Gramsci passes the Custom House, the Harbourmaster's Office, and many warehouses, and Piazza Caricamento with Palazzo di San Giorgo (see above). From behind the Palazzo the long Piazza Raibetta and Via Filippo Turati lead to Piazza Cavour (Pl. 10), at the foot of the *Old Mole* (see above), on which is the imposing *Porta del Molo* or *Porta Siberia* designed by Galeazzo Alessi and built by Antonio Roderio (1553). On the right in Piazza Cavour is the *Pescheria*, a modern building by Mario Braccialini. From here Corso Maurizio Quadrio, continued by Corso Aurelio Saffi, gradually ascends to Via Rivoli (Pl. 15), commanding a view of the harbour. For the new districts of the town, see below.

C.   The Modern Town

From Piazza De Ferrari (see Rte 6A) the wide and lively VIA VENTI SETTEMBRE and the short but broad VIA DANTE run SE, the latter prolonged by a tunnel. Between them are the large Borsa and Post Office buildings. On the right, in Via Dante, beside a little house reconstructed in the 18C, and supposed to be that of Columbus, is a little garden with the reconstructed 12C *Cloister of Sant'Andrea*, brought from a demolished convent. Above rises **Porta Soprana** (Pl. 11), a tall gateway of 1155 (restored).

Piazza Dante, with skyscrapers built in the 1930s, leads into Via Fieschi, which ascends above a rebuilt part of the city to the high-lying classical church of **Santa Maria Assunta di Carignano** (Pl. 15), one of the best works of Galeazzo Alessi (begun in 1552). The sculptures on the façade are by *Claude David*, and inside on the dome-piers are four great Baroque statues of saints (1662–90), two by *Pierre Puget*, one by *Filippo Parodi*, and one by *Claude David*. Via Rivoli goes on to Corso Saffi and the harbour (see above).

The arcaded Via Venti Settembre leads SE to the *Ponte Monumentale* (Pl. 11), officially *Ponte Cesare Gamba*, which carries Corso Andrea Podestà (lift). The area to the N has been rebuilt on a completely new plan.

Via Venti Settembre beyond the bridge passes the fashionable church of **Santa Maria della Consolazione** (Pl. 11, 12), by *Pier Antonio Corradi* (1681–1706) with a dome by *Simone Cantone* (1769) and a front of 1864. In the choir is a Descent from the Cross, in monochrome, attributed to *Perin del Vaga*. Farther on is a large open space with the gardens of Piazza Verdi (Pl. 12) on the left (leading to Brignole station) and Piazza della Vittoria (Pl. 16) on the right. In the centre of the latter is the *War Memorial* (1931), a triumphal arch by Marcello Piacentini; on the right of the square, in Via Brigata Liguria, in a building of 1905–12, is the *Natural History Museum* (Pl. 16; open 9–12. 15–17.30, except Monday & Friday), founded in 1867 with the zoological collections of Giacomo Doria.

Corso Buenos Aires, the continuation of Via Venti Settembre, leads past the new skyscrapers of Corte Lambruschini by Renzo Piano, to Piazza Tommaseo, in which is a monument to General Manuel Belgrano (1770–1820), liberator of the Argentine Republic, by Arnaldo Zocchi (1927). The interesting 19C district of *Foce* extends to the S as far as the sea-front. Via Montevideo and Corso Gastaldi lead NE towards Viale Benedetto XV, where the *Museo degli Ospedali Civili* (open Monday, Wednesday, and Friday, 9–13) contains a huge collection of ceramics (17–19C), and Genoese paintings. From Piazza Tommaseo steps mount to the Via Pozzo, rising below the *Villa Saluzzo Bombrini*, known as *Villa Paradiso*, with its beautiful garden. Built by Andrea Vannone in the 16C, it is one of the best preserved of the many villas in the district of Albaro. Via Pozzo ends at Via Albaro, with *Palazzo Saluzzo Parodi* (No. 1), where Byron lived in 1822. Farther on to the left the Faculty of Engineering of the University occupies the splendid *Villa Giustiniani Cambiaso* (1548, on a design by Galeazzo Alessi), with another garden. Opposite stands the church of *San Francesco d'Albaro* (1324–87, but altered later), beyond the E end of which in Piazza Leopardi is *Santa Maria del Prato*, a church restored in this century to its original appearance of 1172. Beyond Piazza Leonardo da Vinci, centre of the district of ALBARO, is the huge municipal swimming-pool above **Lido d'Albaro**. In Via San Nazzaro at the Villa Bagnerello (plaque) Dickens lived in 1844 before moving into Genoa (see below): 'I was set down in a rank, dull, weedy courtyard, attached to a kind of pink jail; and was told I lived there' (but see the beginning of Rte 6).—A short way E is the tiny old fishing port of *Boccadasse*, well preserved, with gas street lighting. It has good fish restaurants and a popular ice-cream shop. Above it is a mock medieval castle by Gino Coppedè. The return may be made along the sea front (Corso Italia) past the little church of *San Giuliano d'Albaro* (1240, enlarged in the 15C) and the buildings of the *Fiera Internazionale*, where big international exhibitions are held. On the corner of Via Ruffini (beyond Pl. 15) is *Villa Croce*, with a contemporary art museum (open 9–13, 15–18, Sunday 9–12.30; closed Monday), and a library.

Just before the Ponte Monumentale a ramp ascends to Piazza Santo Stefano, where the church of **Santo Stefano** (Pl. 11) has a particoloured front of the 13–14C and a 10C crypt. The choir-gallery of 1499 is the work of *Donato Benti* and *Benedetto da Rovezzano*. On the S wall is a Martyrdom of St Stephen by *Giulio Romano*. Viale Quattro Novembre ascends between the *Acquasola Gardens* (Pl. 11, 12) with fine trees and (left) *Santa Caterina* (or Santissima Annunziata di Portorio; Pl. 11), a church largely rebuilt in 1566, with a portal of 1521 by Pier Antonio Piuma, and good 16C Genoese paintings, including works by Giovanni Battista Castello.

Beyond, the road descends to PIAZZA CORVETTO (Pl. 11), an important centre, connected by tunnel with Piazza Portello. The Victor Emmanuel monument is by Francesco Barzaghi (1886). In front *Palazzo della Prefettura* occupies the 16C Palazzo Doria Spinola. To the left Via Roma (with a well-known confectioners shop), and the parallel Galleria Mazzini, leads back to Piazza De Ferrari; the Salita Santa Caterina, with several 16C palazzi, leads down to Piazza delle Fontane Marose.

Behind the Mazzini monument (by Pietro Costa, 1882), with its flight of steps, is the charming hillside garden of the Villetta Di Negro (Pl. 7), with busts of famous citizens. At the top of the hill in a beautiful quiet position, a fine building (1971, by Mario Labò) houses the *Museo d'Arte Orientale Edoardo Chiossone** (adm. 9–13, 15–18 or 14–17; Sunday 9–12.30; closed Monday). This splendid collection of Japanese, Chinese, and Thai art was left to the Accademia Ligustica di Belle Arti by the painter Edoardo Chiossone (1832–98), and has been augmented during this century.

The objects are displayed to great advantage and are well catalogued and labelled. Interesting exhibitions from the collection are held every six months. The collection is especially notable for its Japanese works, and includes: large Chinese, Thai, and Japanese sculptures (12–18C); Japanese arms and armour; Kakemono paintings; a prehistoric section; ceramics and porcelain; theatrical masks; small bronzes, etc.

From Piazza Corvetto the long straight Via Assarotti leads NE to Piazza Manin passing (left; Pl. 8) the sumptuous church of the *Immacolata* (1864–73).

The turning nearly opposite leads up to Via San Bartolomeo, No. 5 in which is the beautiful *Villa Pallavicino delle Peschiere* (by Galeazzo Alessi), where Dickens stayed in 1845.

Piazza Manin (Pl. 8) is the starting place for a tour of the avenues known as the *CIRCONVALLAZIONE A MONTE (Pl. 8, 7, 3, & 2), described below. This thoroughfare, over 4 km long (bus 33) provides an interesting view of the city. The lifts and funicular railways mentioned at the beginning of Rte 6 serve as intermediate approaches. Corso Carlo Armellini leads left out of the piazza, passing the church of *San Bartolomeo degli Armeni*, founded by refugee monks from Armenia in 1308, but completely rebuilt and incorporated into a secular structure. The altarpiece is a triptych by Turino Vanni (1415). On the right of the Corso Solferino is the 17C *Villa Gruber* (Pl. 8), incorporating a 15C tower. It is now the seat of the *Museo Americanistico Federico Lunardi*, with archaeological and ethnographical material from N and S America. At the end of the Corso Paganini is the *Spianata Castelletto* (Pl. 7) with, just to the S, the Belvedere Montalto (view).

The Corso Carbonara (left) leads down to the huge **Albergo dei Poveri** (Pl. 2), founded by the Brignole in 1655 as one of the first poorhouses of its kind, and built to a functional design by Stefano Scaniglia and Giovanni Battista Ghiso. Restored in the 18C and 19C, it still serves as a hospice.—*Santa Maria del Carmine* (Pl. 6), below the hospice, preserves some remains of the original 14C church on this site.

From the Spianata the long Corso Firenze bends round the neo-Gothic *Castello Bruzzo* (Pl. 3), by Gino Coppedè, and reaches the church of *San Nicola da Tolentino* (Pl. 2), with a good interior (1597; restored), and statues of the Madonna by Tommaso Orsolino (?) and Taddeo Carlone.

The funicular railway (out of action in 1988) goes on up to *Castellaccio* or *Righi* (302m) where terraces afford panoramic views of the city and its fortifications; the view is even better from a point c 7 minutes up the road towards the fort of Castellaccio and the Parco del Peralto.

Corso Firenze is continued by Corso Ugo Bassi, which passes (left) the magnificent *Castello D'Albertis* (Pl. 1), a reconstruction of 1886 of a medieval Ligurian castle on the old bastion of *Monte Galletto*. The interior, with an Ethnographical Museum (pre-Columbian art), is closed for restoration. From here Corso Ugo Bassi and its continuations wind down to the Salita della Provvidenza and Porta Principe station.

Via Spinola ascends from Corso Ugo Bassi to Via Napoli, above which is the *Santuario d'Oregina* (1653), dedicated to Our Lady of Loreto, (bus 40 from Brignole station). The church, which commands a fine view, is the object of a partriotic pilgrimage on 10 Dec in memory of the defeat of the Austrians on that date in 1746.—Farther W Via Napoli (see above), crossing the Granarolo rack-railway, leads to the 14C church of *San Rocco*, rebuilt in the 16–17C, with stucco work by Marcello Sparzo (1574), and the basilica of *Gesù e Maria* (rebuilt in 1628), both containing 16–17C paintings. The San Rocco station of the rack-railway is about midway between the upper terminus at *Granarolo* (236m; view) and Piazza Principe (Pl. 1).

From Piazza Manin (see above) are reached the *Mura Nuove*, the 17C walls (see Pl. 4) which extend as far as Forte Sperone. On Via Cesare Cabella, just above Piazza Manin, is the *Castello Mackenzie*, built at the end of the last century by Gino Coppedè (being restored).

D.   The outskirts of the city

In the Bisagno valley, 3 km NW of the city (bus No. 34 from Piazza Principe) is the *****Staglieno Cemetery**, or *Camposanto di Staglieno*. The cemetery (open daily 8–17), covering nearly 400 acres with its galleries and gardens, was laid out in

1844–51 and gives an interesting idea of Genoese funerary sculpture during the last century. The conspicuous colossal statue of Faith is by Santo Varni; and near the upper gallery, in a clump of trees known as the Boschetto dei Mille, is the simple tomb of Mazzini, surrounded by memorials of members of Garibaldi's 'Thousand'. To the left of the Pantheon and the main enclosure is the *Protestant Temple and Cemetery*, on the third terrace, planted with oak trees. Here the wife of Oscar Wilde, Constance Mary Lloyd, is buried. From the Viale a long staircase ascends to the *English Cemetery*, designed by Gino Coppedè (1902). This includes the British Military Cemetery from the First and Second World Wars.

PEGLI is now at the W limit of the city (bus Nos 1 & 3 from Piazza Caricamento). W of Porta Principe Station and the harbour is the newer port of *Sampierdarena*, known for its old established engineering and metallurgical works. At the Ansaldo works in 1854 was built the first Italian locomotive. Beyond the mouth of the Polcevera are the industrial suburbs of *Cornigliano*, just beyond which, at *Sestri Ponente*, a petroleum port, is the airport of Genoa built out into the sea on reclaimed land (and modernised in 1986).— 11km **Pegli**, once a popular weekend resort of the Genoese, retains a few fine villas backed by pine-woods. Inland from the station is the *Villa Doria*, a pleasant public park with a 16C mansion (with frescoes by Nicoloso Granello and Lazzaro Tavarone) housing the *Naval and Maritime Museum*, illustrating the history of the great Genoese maritime republic (adm. 9–13, 14–17; closed Sunday, Monday, & fest.). The good collection includes 16–17C maps and globes; ship-models; and maritime prints and paintings including a portrait of Columbus ascribed to Ridolfo Ghirlandaio.—Much finer is the *Villa Durazzo-Pallavicini* (adm. as for Villa Doria, above), just to the E, a luxuriant garden with good views, and containing many scenic and architectural conceits of the 1840s, such as a partly underground lake, a 'Chinese' temple, etc. The mansion of 1837 houses in 23 rooms the *Museum of Ligurian Archaeology*, notable for prehistoric finds from Ligurian cave-dwellings, and pre-Roman necropolis finds from the city of Genoa.

NERVI is at the E limit of the city (Bus No. 15 from Piazza Caricamento). The old coastal road leaves the centre of Genoa by the Corso Italia, which traverses *Albaro* and ends at *Boccadasse* (both described above, in Rte 6C). Beyond *Sturla* is (6·5km) *Quarto dei Mille*, where a monument marks the starting-point of Garibaldi and the Thousand ('i Mille') on their expedition to Sicily (5 May 1860), which ended in the liberation of Italy. In Villa Spinola where Garibaldi stayed while planning the expedition with his friend Candido Augusto Vecchi, is a small Garibaldi Museum (adm. 9–13 except Thursday).—Beyond (9·5km) *Quinto al Mare* the Corso Europa, the main road from the centre of Genoa via Brignole station comes in on the left.—11km **Nervi** is now included in the city of Genoa. The town was bombarded by William Bentinck in 1814 and became the earliest winter resort of the Riviera di Levante in 1863. The principal attractions of Nervi are the *Passeggiata Anita Garibaldi*, a pleasant walk between the railway and the rock-bound shore; and the *Parco Municipale*, formed by the junction of the gardens of the Villa Gropallo and the Villa Serra. In the latter is the *Galleria d'Arte Moderna* (9–13, 14–17; closed Sunday, Monday, & fest.), a large collection of modern Italian art. Farther E is the charming park of the *Villa Luxoro* (adm. as for the Modern Art

Gallery, above),with a small museum of furniture, lace, paintings, etc.—The village of *Sant'Ilario*, 3km inland, has fine views.

From Genoa to *Milan*, see Rte 16; to *Piacenza*, see Rte 38; to *Pisa*, see Rte 8; to *Turin*, see Rte 6; to *Ventimiglia*, see Rte 5.

7 Genoa to Pisa

ROAD, N1, 190km. To (11km) *Nervi*, see above.—20km *Recco* (for *Camogli*, 2km).—28km *San Lorenzo della Costa* (for **Santa Margherita**, 3km, and **Portofino**, 8km).—32km *Rapallo*.—43km *Chiavari*.—53km. **Sestri Levante**.—71km *La Baranca* (for *Levanto*, 15km).—113km **La Spezia**.—129km *Sarzana*.—140km *Avenza* (for *Carrara*, 4km).—147km *Massa*.—159km *Pietrasanta*.—167km *Viareggio*.—190km **Pisa**.—BUSES; frequent and fast services on all sections between Genoa and Spezia.

MOTORWAY, A12, 149km. The section up to La Spezia has a succession of long tunnels with breathtaking glimpses of the coast in between.

RAILWAY, from *Genova-Brignole*, 162km in 2–3½hrs; to *Rapallo*, 27km in c ½hr; to *La Spezia*, 87km in 1–1½hrs. From *Piazza Principe* station the journey is c 10 minutes longer. Through-trains on this route between Paris, Turin, and Rome or Florence.

The first part of this route traverses the **Riviera di Levante**, a delightful strip of coast now threatened by indiscriminate new building. The landscape is diversified by olive-groves and villas amid bright gardens. By far the best views are gained from the road, as on the railway numerous tunnels cause frequent interruptions; the railway, however, follows the coast between Sestri and La Spezia, where the main road runs well inland. In the isolated **Cinque Terre** a coastal road is still under construction, the subject of much controversy since it is opening up this area also to speculative new building. All along this coast pollution is an increasing problem, and the fishing is deteriorating.

From the centre of Genoa to (11km) **Nervi**, see Rte 6D. The little seaside resorts which follow have good views of the Portofino peninsula.—13km *Bogliasco* is separated by a tunnel and viaduct from (15km) *Pieve Ligure*.—16km *Sori*.—20km *Recco* is a little port noted for its hardy seamen in the Middle Ages and for clockmaking today. Rebuilt since its railway viaducts attracted air attacks in 1944, it has an interesting church (1951–60). The main road begins to climb inland across the base of the Portofino peninsula, but a coast road descends to the right for 1·5km to Camogli, rejoining the main road by a steep hill 4km farther on.

Camogli, a picturesque little fishing port (7200 inhab.) descending steeply to a rocky shore, was famous for its merchant ships in the days of sail, its fleet having played a prominent part in the naval wars of Napoleon, of Louis-Philippe, and in the Crimea. The Blessing of the Fish (2nd Sunday in May) and the 'Stella Maris' procession of boats to the Punta della Chiappa (1st Sunday in August) are popular festivals. The Dragonara castle has an aquarium. The Museo Marinaro (open Wednesday, Saturday, & fest. 9–12, 15 or 16–18 or 19) has models of ships, ex votos, navigational instruments, etc. Hourly service in summer to Punta Chiappa and San Fruttuoso (see below).

A pleasant path leads S from Camogli to (25 minutes) *San Rocco*, 14 minutes beyond which the path forks, the level left branch leading to the Semaforo Nuovo (see below), the right branch descending to (50 minutes) the old church of *San Nicolò*, beyond which is (1¼hrs) the *Punta della Chiappa*, where the view is remarkable for the ever-changing colours of the sea. A rough-hewn altar on the point reproduces in mosaic a graffito found at San Nicolò.

24km *Ruta* is a good centre for visiting the W part of the Portofino peninsula, with buses to Camogli, Portofino Vetta, and on the main road.

A road (bus) leads S in 1·5km to *Portofino Vetta* in a large park beneath the *Monte di Portofino (610m). This is a protected area because of its natural beauty, although long-term plans to designate the area a national park have still not been settled. From the summit there is a wonderful view of the Riviera from Alassio to La Spezia, the Apuan (SE) and Cottian Alps (W), and, out at sea, Elba and (in exceptionally clear weather) Corsica. The bridlepath from Ruta to the Monte (1hr) leads off beside a tunnel on the Rapallo road, rises to 427m, then descends to a cross-roads.—The right-hand path leads to (1hr) the *Semaforo Nuovo* (470m) on a cliff overlooking the sea.—The left path bears to the right at (10 minutes) the *Pietre Strette* and descends steeply to (1¾hrs) *San Fruttuoso*, a picturesque little village with the Gothic church and cloister of an abbey founded before the 10C, and the grey *Torre dei Doria*. It was donated by the Doria Pamphilj family to the FAI and was restored in 1989. A boat runs hourly from Camogli or Portofino, and twice daily from Santa Margherita and Rapallo (in summer only). A bronze statue of Christ, by Galletti (1954), stands offshore, eight fathoms down, as protector of all those who work beneath the sea.—The left-hand path at Pietre Strette leads to (2hrs from Ruta) Portofino.

The road to the right at Ruta descends to (½hr) San Rocco (see above).

The main road penetrates a short tunnel.—Beyond (28km) *San Lorenzo della Costa*, where the church has a triptych by Quentin Matsys (1499), the road to Santa Margherita descends to the right (3km; short cut by path).

Santa Margherita Ligure (12,700 inhab.), on the W side of the Bay of Rapallo or Golfo Tigullio, is one of the most popular resorts of the Riviera. It is the point of departure for the boat trip to Portofino.

Post Office, Via Gramsci, behind Lido hotel.—**Buses** to *Portofino* and *Rapallo* every 15 minutes: to *Ruta* and to *Genoa* many times daily.—*Boat Trips* to Portofino, the Cinque Terre, and in the gulf.

The pleasant road along the shore of Santa Margherita leads on S to Portofino. At 3km it passes (right) the former monastery of *La Cervara*, where Francis I of France was held prisoner after Pavia (1525), and where Gregory XI rested on the return of the papacy from Avignon to Rome (1377). Then, passing a modern castle on a point, it reaches (3·5km) the tiny bay of *Paraggi*, at the mouth of its wooded glen.—5·5km **Portofino** is a romantic fishing village, situated partly on a small headland, partly in a little bay much visited by the English in the 19C, and now the haunt of rich yachtsmen. A foreground of sea and a background of trees combine charmingly with the gay little houses. High above the village, towards the Capo, is the little church of *San Giorgio*, which is reputed to contain the relics of St George, brought by Crusaders from the Holy Land. In front of the church is the *Castle* (adm. 10–19 except Monday; closed in January).

The classic walks are to the *Capo, a walk of ¼hr over the hill of San Giorgio; to San Fruttuoso by bridle-path via Case del Prato; or to Portofino Vetta (see above; 1½–2hrs on foot). Boat trips (20 minutes) to San Fruttuoso (see above).

The pretty road from Santa Margherita to Rapallo (3km) passes *San Michele di Pagana*, where the church contains a fine Crucifixion by Van Dyck. Nearby, in a large garden, is the *Villa Spinola*, where the Italo-Yugoslav Treaty of Rapallo was signed in 1920.

32km **RAPALLO** (26,700 inhab.), in a sheltered position at the head
of its gulf, is the best known holiday resort on the Riviera di Levante,
and is popular both in summer and in winter. The mole of the new
port still under construction has blocked the view out to sea.

Post Office, Via Boccoleri.— **Buses** frequently to *Genoa*, to *Santa Margherita*,
to *Ruta*, to *San Maurizio*, to *Santa Maria del Campo*, and to *Chiavari*; daily to
La Spezia, Pisa, and beyond; also to *Portofino*.—**Golf Course** (18 holes) and
Tennis at Sant'Anna, N of the town (bus). *Boat Trips* in the gulf.—*Procession*
at Montallegro on 1–3 July.

The lovely surroundings, which used to be the main attraction of
Rapallo, have been spoilt in the 1960s and 1970s by new buildings.
In the town are the *Collegiate Church* (1606), with its 20C
adornments, and the restored *Castello* in the harbour (open for
exhibitions). The *Museo Civico* (9–12) contains material of local
interest. The *Villino Chiaro*, on the coast road, was the home of
Max Beerbohm (1872–1956) from 1910. Ezra Pound also spent
much time in Rapallo after 1959.

A winding road (the funivia is out of action) via *San Maurizio* (11km; bus
twice daily) ascends inland through woods to the sanctuary of *Montallegro*,
where the 16C church contains frescoes by Nicolò Barabino, and, over the
high altar, the Byzantine painting of the Dormition of the Virgin, which
according to legend was miraculously transported from Dalmatia.—The
ruined convent of *Valle Christi* (13–16C) lies above the S side of the Bogo
valley, 2km NW of Rapallo; farther up the main valley is the ruined church of
San Tomaso (1160).—Some 20km inland, on Monte Caucaso, is *Monteghirfo*,
an isolated hamlet amid chestnut woods with a local anthropological museum
('Casa-Museo Contadino') opened on request.

Beyond Rapallo the road zigzags across a series of small valleys,
one of the longest bends now avoided by a tunnel.—37km *Zoagli*,
another resort, stands at the mouth of a narrow glen. The road now
passes *Sant'Andrea di Rovereto*.—43km **Chiavari** is a shipbuilding
town (30,800 inhab.) with an arcaded old main street, and a sandy
beach and port for small boats at the mouth of the Entella. A large
necropolis dating from the 8–7C BC has been excavated here; the
interesting finds are exhibited in the *Civico Museo Archeologico*
(open Tuesday, Thursday, Saturday & Sunday), in the 17–18C
Palazzo Rocca. The second floor of the palace has been opened as a
gallery (16–17C paintings, particularly of the Genoese school). The
Galleria di Palazzo Torriglia (9–12, 15–18 except Saturday &
Sunday) also contains 16C and 17C paintings.

Here Garibaldi, arriving in exile from the S, was arrested 'in the most polite
and friendly manner possible' on 6 September 1849, since his forbears were
native to the town. It was also the family home of Nino Bixio and Giuseppe
Mazzini.
  A road runs inland via *Carasco*, there diverging right from an alternative
route to Genoa (67km; via the Valle Fontanabuona) to run N up the Sturla
valley past *Terrarossa*, popularly thought to be the home of Columbus'
grandparents, to (12·5km) *Borgonovo* (keep left) and (16km) *Borzonasca*, and
from there over a pass into the Aveto valley. A road leads right to the pretty
Abbey of Borzone, with a church of c 1244.—43km *Rezzoaglio* and (58km)
Santo Stefano d' Aveto (1017m) are quiet little summer resorts.
  The right fork at Borgonovo (see above) takes the main road by corkscrew
turns over (28km) the *Passo del Bocco* (956m) into the *Val di Taro*. Here
Monte Penna and Monte Chiodo are the centre of a beautiful nature

reserve.—61km *Bedonia*, beyond which at 69km the road joins that from Sestri (see below).—75km *Borgo Val di Taro*.

46km *Lavagna*, separated from Chiavari by the Entella bridge, has a long sandy beach, and is famous for its slate quarries. It was the birthplace of Innocent IV (Sinibaldo Fieschi; died 1254). A pretty road leads up the valley to Varese Ligure (42km; see below) past the fine early-Gothic *Basilica dei Fieschi* (San Salvatore), founded by Innocent IV.—50km *Cavi*.—53km **Sestri Levante** (21,200 inhab.), delightfully situated at the base of a peninsula known as L'Isola, is a summer resort, spoilt since the 1950s by new buildings. From Piazza Matteotti, with the 17C parish church, a street ascends past the restored Romanesque church of San Nicolò to the *Albergo dei Castelli*, rebuilt with antique materials (1925) on Genoese foundations, with a magnificent park (adm. May–September 9–12, 16–19), at the end of the peninsula. From the Torretta here Marconi carried out his first experiments in short wave transmission. The *Galleria Rizzi* (10 Via Cappucchini) is open from May to September (Thursday & Saturday 14.30–17.30; Sunday 9.30–12).

Monte Castellaro (255m), c 1hr SE, above the Punta Manara, commands a good view of the coast.

The road (N523) from Sestri to (62km) Borgo Val di Taro (bus) is a tortuous and steeply undulating link between Liguria and the Emilian plain. It runs E at first, then N. The road has been improved by a tunnel over 2km long beneath (17km) Colle di Velva.—31km *Varese Ligure*, on the Vara, has a 15C castle of the Fieschi, well restored in 1965.—At (43km) the *Passo di Cento Croci* (1053m; *View) the road enters Emilia and begins the descent into the Taro valley.—62km *Borgo Val di Taro*, and from there to Berceto and the Spezia-Parma road, see Rte 39.

FROM SESTRI LEVANTE TO LA SPEZIA BY THE COAST ROAD (N370), under construction for many years and still not complete. It is much discussed in relation to the new building which is taking place in its train which threatens the beauty of the coast. It is now open as far as Deiva Marina; the towns beyond, as far as Monterosso al Mare, are accessible only by winding and steep inland roads. There is no road yet between Monterosso and Manarola. The road route closely follows the railway (many tunnels). 3km beyond Sestri this route branches right to pass above *Riva Trigoso*, with naval shipyards. A by-road serves (10km) *Moneglia*, a little seaside town (recently expanded) with two old castles, the birthplace of Luca Cambiaso (1527–85), the painter, and (14km) *Deiva Marina*, both by-passed by N370.—24km *Bonassola* is a village in beautiful surroundings.—27km **Levanto**, once a secluded bathing resort in a little bay, but now also developed for tourism. It has lovely gardens, a fine swimming-pool, and a good sandy beach. It preserves remains of its old walls and a 13–15C church.—The road avoids,and the railway tunnels through,Monte Vé (487m).—39km *Monterosso al Mare*, which has a good church of 1300, is the first of the five attractive seagirt villages called the **Cinque Terre**, noted for their wine. The vines are trained on wires across gorges and up the cliffs. The terrain is subject to landslides and while methods are being studied to prevent them, the villages are suffering from depopulation. Eugenio Montale spent much of his youth at Monterosso. The road (1988) ends here. The others are *Vernazza, Corniglia, Manarola*, and *Riomaggiore*, and all have interesting old churches. The villages were previously linked from Levanto to Portovenere only by a network of *Footpaths (map published by CAI available in La Spezia) on the edge of the cliffs, and before the advent of the railway had for centuries been accessible only by sea. A railway tunnel 7km long connects Riomaggiore with La Spezia, while the road threads two shorter tunnels.—66km *La Spezia*, see below.

Beyond Sestri the main road winds steeply up the *Passo del Bracco*. The road passes to landward of the motorway. The Vetta del Petronio rises prominently on the left.—From (63km) *Bracco* a road of 6km descends vertiginously to Moneglia (see above). After the summit-level of 620m the road begins the descent to (71km) *La Baracca* at the junction of the road through pine-woods to Levanto (15km).—In the

Vara valley this road recrosses the motorway just before (88km) *Borghetto di Vara*, then ascends a side-valley to the low pass of (105km) *La Foce* (241m), with a good view of La Spezia and its gulf.

113km **LA SPEZIA**, at the head of its fine gulf, is one of the chief naval ports of Italy. A provincial capital (124,500 inhab.) and (since 1929) the seat of a bishop, the town forms a rectilinear L round a prominent hill.

Post Office, Piazza Verdi.—**Tourist Office**, 47 Viale Mazzini.—**Buses** from below the Station (steps) to Via Chiodo and the quayside.—From Piazza Chiodo: every ¼hr to *Portovenere*, and to *Lerici*, going on less frequently to *Tellaro*; to *Sarzana* and *Carrara*; to *Sestri Levante*; to *Reggio Emilia*; from Via Rosselli, every 2hrs to *Viareggio* and *Florence*.—**Boat trips** run by Navigazione Golfo dei Poeti from the Public Gardens (Passeggiata Morin) to Portovenere and to Lerici and Fiascherino.—*Teatro Civico*, Piazza Mentana.—**Swimming Pool**, Viale Fieschi.

The main Corso Cavour runs NW to SE through the town, passing the *Musei Civici* (9–12, 14–17 or 19 except Monday) with the *Museo Archeologico Lunense*. This contains the interesting Ligurian statue-stelae of the Lunigiana cult found on the bed of the river Magra (Bronze and Iron Age), and Roman remains from Luni. On the left is *Santa Maria Assunta*, founded in 1271 but rebuilt, the cathedral until 1975 (see below). It contains a large polychrome terracotta by Andrea della Robbia. At the seaward end an equestrian statue of Garibaldi stands in the fine *Public Gardens* that extend between the busy Via Chiodo and the Viale Italia bordering the gulf. To the right, the Piazza Chiodo commemorates the architect of the *Naval Arsenal*, the most important in Italy (1861–69; open day 19 March; weekdays by permit, apply at guardroom, passport), by the entrance to which is the *NAVAL MUSEUM (adm. Tuesday 9–12; Thursday & Saturday 15–18; contribution expected to orphans' fund), where models and relics collected since 1571 illustrate the marine history of Savoy and Italy. From here Via Chiodo runs NE to the Post Office, behind which rises the 13C *Castello di San Giorgio* (undergoing lengthy restoration); farther on opens the huge PIAZZA EUROPA, enclosed by modern administrative buildings, and the new Cathedral (1975).

The old village of *Biassa* (8·5km) is reached by a panoramic road from La Spezia.—For the Cinque Terre, see above.

The *Gulf of Spezia* is nearly everywhere accessible by car, but is better seen by boat. PORTOVENERE, at the extremity of the S arm of the gulf, is reached either by boat from the Public Gardens (¾hr), or by road (bus in 35 minutes), passing the arsenal. A by-road (right) leads up to the little medieval village of *Campiglia*, in a fine position. Beyond *Cadimare* the views improve, and the dyke protecting the harbour is prominent. Beyond the N coast of the gulf rise the Apuan Alps. Beyond the Punta di Pezzino opens the charming bay called the Seno delle Grazie, now spoilt by holiday houses. On the opposite horn of the bay is the ex-Lazzaretto, an isolation hospital begun by the Genoese in 1724, and now the property of the Navy (no adm.). After many zigzags through olive groves around numerous little capes and bays the island of Palmaria comes into sight, opposite Portovenere.—12km **Portovenere**, the ancient *Portus Veneris*, a dependency of Genoa since 1113, is a charming fortified village built on the sloping shore of the *Bocchetta*, the narrow strait (114m wide) separating the *Isola Palmaria* from the mainland. On a rocky promontory at the S end of the village the restored 6C and 13C church of *San Pietro* commands a splendid view of Palmaria and the lofty cliffs of the Cinque Terre. The church has had to be closed since the structure was found to be unstable. *Byron's Cave*, or the *Grotto Arpaia*, formerly beneath it, collapsed in 1932. It was from here that the poet started his swim across the gulf to San Terenzo to visit Shelley at Lerici (1822). In the upper part of the village is the beautiful 12C church of *San Lorenzo*, above which (steep climb) towers the 16C *Castello* (*View). Below the church steps descend to the characteristic '*Calata Doria*', where tall houses rise from the sea. An excursion may be made by boat round the rugged island of *Palmaria*, visiting its caves. The island has recently been purchased by a company which may turn it into a tourist resort. On the N point is the old *Torre della Scuola*, built by the Genoese in 1606 and blown up by the English fleet in 1800. The island is noted for the gold-veined black 'portoro' marble. Farther out is the *Isola del Tino*, with remains of an 8C monastery.

LERICI, on the N shore of the gulf, is reached from La Spezia either by boat in ½–¾hr, or by car (bus in 35 minutes). The road passes the shipyards of *San Bartolomeo* and *Muggiano* (bus terminus), and the foundry of *Pertusola*, and, piercing the *Punta di Calandrello*, reaches the beautiful bay of Lerici. The fishing village of (8km) *San Terenzo*, with its castle, is on the nearer shore of the bay; here died Paolo Mantegazza (1831–1910), founder of the first pathological laboratory in Europe. A little farther along, on a small cape, is the *Casa Magni*, the 'white house with arches', the last home of Shelley (1822). From here he set out on the fatal sail to Leghorn (see below); Mary Shelley wrote: 'I am convinced that the few months we passed there were the happiest he had ever known. He was never better than when I last saw him, full of spirits and joy, embark for Leghorn, that he might there welcome Leigh Hunt to Italy'. The Casa Magni Shelley Museum was created here in 1972, but when the house was sold in 1979 the contents had to be moved back to England to Boscombe Manor, the home of Shelley's son.—10km **Lerici**, is a resort (14,600 inhab.), on the point beyond which is the splendid *Castle* of the 13–16C which was taken by the Genoese from the Pisans. Before the modern Via Aurelia existed Tuscan coaches were embarked here by felucca for Genoa. A bus connects Lerici with Sarzana (7·5km; see below) on the main road into Tuscany.—The coast road goes on above the charming little bays of *Fiascherino*, where D.H. Lawrence lived in 1913–14, to (14km) *Tellaro*, a medieval village rising sheer from the sea.

Another pretty by-road from Lerici continues around the wooded peninsula up to *Montemarcello*, a pretty little village of red and pink houses surrounded by olives, with fine views of Tellaro and of the gulf of Spezia. A path leads to 'Punto Corvo' with a bird's eye view of the coast.—The road descends through lovely woods to Ameglia (see below). From La Spezia to *Parma* and to *Reggio Emilia*, see Rte 39.

From La Spezia the Pisa road traverses the N suburb of Migliarina and then skirts the wide Magra valley, beyond which rise the Apuan Alps. It joins the road from Lerici, and crosses the river.

An alternative road (N432) continues to (4km) *Ameglia*, dominated by a 10C castle. Here the port of Luni and a necropolis have been excavated (see below). The road then crosses the river lower down, with picturesque houses and fishing boats, and hugs the shore all the way to Viareggio.

129km **SARZANA**, an ancient fortified town (18,700 inhab.), once of great strategic importance. It was the SE outpost of the Genoese Republic. The *Cittadella*, a rectangular fort with six circular bastions was rebuilt for Lorenzo il Magnifico in 1487 by Francesco di Giovanni (Il Francione). For years used as a prison, it is now empty and awaiting restoration. On the main Via Mazzini is the *Cathedral* (the see of the Bishop of Luni was transferred here in 1204). It contains a panel painting of the *Crucifix, signed and dated 1138 by Guglielmus, a Tuscan master, and good 15C marble reliefs by Leonardo Riccomanni of Pietrasanta (1432–33). Some of the paintings are by Domenico Fiasella who was born here in 1589. Nearby is *Sant'Andrea*, the oldest monument in the town probably dating from the 11C. The 16C portal has pagan caryatids. The church of *San Francesco*, N of the town, is also interesting: it contains the tomb of Guarnerio degli Antelminelli, son of Castruccio Castracani, who died as a child in 1322, by Giovanni di Balduccio. A market is held on Thursdays in Piazza Matteotti.—On a hill to the E reached by road (2km) is the *Fortezza di Sarzanello* (closed for restoration; there are plans to open a museum here), known as the Fortezza of Castruccio Castracani, restored by the Florentines in 1493 (Il Francione and Luca Caprina). Tommaso

Parentucelli (Nicholas V, Pope 1447–55), was a native of Sarzana.—
11km NE is the medieval fortified borgo of *Fosdinovo*, on the border
between Tuscany and Liguria. In the restored 13C Malaspina castle
here, Dante was a guest in 1306. Still the property of the Malaspina,
visitors are admitted (9–12, 15–18 except Monday); in 1981 much of
the furniture was stolen.—133km A by-road leads inland to the pretty,
old village of *Castelnuovo Magra*. In the church is a painting of the
Crucifixion attributed to Van Dyck. A large Calvary by Brueghel the
Younger was stolen from the church in 1979, but was later recovered.
The old 13C castle here also has associations with Dante.—135km
Luni station.

About 2km right are the excavations (still in progress) of the important Roman
colony of **Luni** founded in 177 BC beside the sea on the site of a prehistoric
settlement (famous for its statue-stelae, displayed in the museum of Pontremoli,
see Rte 39). Of great commercial and strategic importance, it was famous for its
marble. The city was still thriving in the Middle Ages, and it was well known for
its bishopric, and was important enough to lend its name to the whole district
(*Lunigiana*). Its fame was recorded by Dante ('Paradise', XVI, 73–78). By the
13C, partly because of the flooding of the river Magra, and malaria, it had
disappeared. The walled city has a typical Roman plan; remains of the forum, a
temple, and (later) amphitheatre have come to light, as well as two large houses.
The MUSEUM (9–12, 14–17 or 19 except Monday), in the centre of the excavated
area, contains interesting finds from here and the surrounding territory (Orto-
novo, Ameglia, etc.) including marble sculptures, bronzes, mosaics, etc. An
honorific inscription is dedicated to M. Acilius Glabrio, who defeated Antiochus
III at Thermopylae in 191 BC.

High up among the Apuan Alps (left) appear the first of the white
marble quarries of Carrara as the road enters Tuscany.—140km
Avenza is important as the road and railway junction for Carrara, 4km
NE. Near the bridge is a tower built by Castracani, tyrant of Lucca.

Carrara (67,700 inhab.), world-famous for its white marble, is a flourishing town
with a good Romanesque *Duomo* altered in the 13C, when the attractive Gothic
storey was added to its façade (in need of restoration). In the square are a house
believed to have sheltered Michelangelo on his visits to buy marble, and a
monument to Andrea Doria left unfinished by Baccio Bandinelli. The *Accademia
di Belle Arti* occupies the old Malaspina castle and 16C palace.—The famous
Marble Quarries in the Apuan Alps, which have been worked for over 2000
years, are well worth a visit. They produce 500,000 tons of marble a year, and
over 300 quarries are now in use. They are best reached by bus from Carrara to
Colonnata (6 times a day; 3 times on fest.) or to Fantiscritti (Ponte di Vara;
weekdays only). It is interesting to follow up this visit by an inspection of the
marble-sawing mills and sculpture workshops in the town. In Viale XX
Settembre a modern building houses a permanent exhibition of marble quarrying and craftsmanship.—Carrara has been well known in Italy since the 19C as a
centre of the Anarchist movement. In 1986 the local government voted in favour
of erecting a monument in the town to Gaetano Bresci who assassinated King
Umberto I in 1900 and died a year later in prison.

Marina di Carrara, 3km SW of Avenza, is interesting as a marble port. It is the
first of a series of more or less exclusive resorts which stretch all the way along
the coast to Viareggio and are extremely crowded (mostly with Florentines) in
summer. Called *Marina di Massa, I Ronchi, Forte dei Marmi*, etc., they consist of
elegant villas and hotels surrounded by gardens; the only high building is the
round Torre Fiat, a skyscraper built as an industrial holiday colony. The sea and
wide beaches, separated from the road by colourful beach huts, are not as clean
as they once were. All the resorts have spectacular views inland to the Apuan
Alps (often snow-capped) and white marble quarries.

The main road turns inland to (147km) **Massa**, a small provincial
capital (62,900 inhab.) with marble quarries, pleasantly situated
below the Apuan foothills. Massa was from 1442 to 1790 the capital of
the Malaspina duchy of Massa-Carrara, and in the Piazza Aranci is

the large *Palazzo Cybo Malaspina*, a 17C building given a charming courtyard by Gian Francesco Bergamini. High above it is the 14–16C *Rocca* (adm. 9–12, 16–19 except Monday; in need of restoration), where earlier Malaspina dukes entertained many distinguished guests. The *Duomo*, founded in the 15C, contains beautiful 16C Malaspina tombs and an interesting Museum.—155km *Querceta* is the junction for the roads to Seravezza (3km left) and Forte dei Marmi (3km right), both served by bus.

From *Seravezza*, a small town with a 16C cathedral and a palace, on the river, built by Duke Cosimo I of Tuscany (recently restored), a road goes up the valley, past numerous small marble quarries, to (10km) *Levigliani*, a centre for climbing in the Apuan Alps. Another road leads N from Seravezza for Azzano passing the 13C pieve of La Cappella in a fine position with a view of Monte Altissimo and its marble quarries. This is one of numerous Romanesque churches to be found in Versiglia.

Forte dei Marmi and *I Ronchi* are the most elegant bathing resorts along this stretch of coast, with numerous villas and small hotels set in thick vegetation. The pine-woods were severely damaged in a tornado in 1977. The beaches are mostly private and have splendid views of the mountains. In Forte dei Marmi Aldous Huxley wrote 'Crome Yellow' in 1921, and, two years later, 'Antic Hay'. The Molo, a low pier, is the scene of the evening 'passeggiata'.

159km **Pietrasanta** a town (25,300 inhab.) in the district of *Versilia*, is also famous for its marble. The attractive old piazza is surrounded by fine buildings. The *Cathedral* (1330), has a good façade and an unfinished campanile of 1380 by Donato Benti. It contains a pulpit, candalabra, and marble choir made in the early 16C by the local sculptors Lorenzo and Stagio Stagi, and two angels and a Crucifix by Ferdinando Tacca. The paintings include works by Matteo Rosselli and Pietro Dandini and a late Gothic Madonna and Saints. In the Oratory next door is a font by Donato Benti (1509). The 14C church of *Sant'Agostino*, with a handsome façade, is being restored; opposite is the imposing doorway (1515) of the *Pretura*. In Palazzo Moroni is the *Museo Civico Archeologico Versiliese* (open 16–19 except Monday) with an interesting display of local finds from the Neolithic to Roman periods. Another section has medieval and Renaissance ceramics found in Sant'Agostino.—On the hillside above can be seen the 12C *Rocca*.

Valdicastello, 3km E, was the birthplace of the poet Giosuè Carducci (1835–1907). Buses connect Pietrasanta with its Marina and with Seravezza and Pontestazzemese (see above).

167km **VIAREGGIO** is the main town (55,700 inhab.) of *Versilia*, the bathing beaches of which stretch N for some 30km as far as Marina di Carrara, making it the most popular seaside resort on the W coast of Italy. In summer this stretch of coast is crowded with holiday-makers, many of them from Florence. Viareggio first became fashionable for its bathing beaches in the early 19C, and it retains an old-fashioned air with an esplanade planted with palm trees, Art Nouveau houses, and huge old Grand Hotels and cafés.

Post Office, Piazza Shelley.—*Information Office*, 5 Viale Carducci.—**Buses** from the station (circular service) along the sea-front (Viale Carducci) to *Lido di Camaiore* and *Forte dei Marmi*; also inland to *Camaiore*; from Piazza Mazzini to *Pisa*; to *Lucca* and *Florence*; to *Spezia*; and to *Torre del Lago*.—The CARNIVAL held in February is one of the most famous in Italy. The parade of typical allegorical floats takes place on 4 consecutive Sundays.

A splendid double promenade, with a roadway and a footway, leads along the shore from the Giardini d'Azeglio to Piazza Puccini. Some

old 'Bagni' (bathing establishments) survive here. At the inner corner
of the Giardini d'Azeglio is the Piazza Shelley, with a bust of the poet
by Urbano Lucchesi (1894). Beautiful pine-woods extend along the
shore in either direction from the town, and there is a distant view of
the Apuan Alps. The outer harbour is busy with boat-yards and a 16C
tower guards the inner basins where there is a port.

Shelley and his friend, Lieutenent Williams, drowned on 8 July, 1822, when their
little schooner 'Ariel' sank off Viareggio on a voyage from Leghorn to La Spezia.
Their bodies, washed ashore on the beach of II Gombo (see Rte 45), N of the
mouth of the Arno, were there cremated in the presence of Trelawny, Byron, and
Leigh Hunt. Shelley's ashes were collected and buried in the Protestant
cemetery at Rome.
    The fine road along the coast to Forte dei Marmi and Marina di Carrara (see
above) passes (5km) the *Lido di Camaiore*, another extended bathing-resort.—
Inland from Viareggio (11km N) is the little town of *Camaiore*, with a pleasant
Romanesque church (1278) and, in the little museum, a Flemish tapestry of 1516.

174km *Torre del Lago Puccini* has adopted the name of Giacomo
Puccini (1858–1924), who made his bohemian home on the *Lago di
Massaciuccoli*, 1km E where he enjoyed shooting waterfowl. The lake
is now part of the Parco Naturale Migliarino-San Rossore (see Rte 46);
there is a boat service to visit the marshes from Torre del Lago.
Puccini's house (9–12, 15–19; winter 14–17) on the lakeside preserves
mementoes and his tomb is in the chapel. All his operas except his
last, 'Turandot', were to a great extent written here. An opera festival
is held here in summer.—At 181km the motorway to Florence
diverges left, while this route crosses the Serchio.—190km **Pisa**, see
Rte 46.

8   Turin to Milan

ROAD. (*a*) MOTORWAY (A4), 139km, leaving the old road beyond the
Stura bridge and keeping for the most part N of the old road.—(*b*)
VIA VERCELLI AND NOVARA, N11, 144km.—23km *Chivasso.*—41km
Cigliano—74km **Vercelli.**—96km **Novara.**—117km *Magenta.*—
144km **Milan**. (*c*) VIA MORTARA, 148km—23km *Chivasso*. N31
bis.—71km **Casale**—N596 dir, N494. **Mortara.**—113km *Vigevano*—
125km *Abbiategrasso.*—148km **Milan.**

RAILWAY, 153km in 1½–2hrs; to *Vercelli*, 79km in 50–60 minutes; to
Novara. 101km in 1–1½hrs.

The N11 leaves Turin as the Corso Giulio Cesare, crossing the Stura
and branching right at the entrance to the motorway to traverse the
long town of (11km) *Settimo Torinese*.—23km **Chivasso** is an important railway junction (25,800 inhab.). The 15C church, with a fine
doorway, contains a Descent from the Cross, by *Defendente Ferrari*
(1470–1535), a native of the town. In 3km more N11 diverges left from
N31 bis (see below).—41km *Cigliano*, N of the motorway and beyond
the Dora Baltea, is at the junction of the road to Biella.

FROM CIGLIANO TO BIELLA, N593, N143, 31km. At (12km) *Cavaglià* this route
crosses the Vercelli-Ivrea road, just N of the A5 motorway spur. The Lago di
Viverone, 5km W, is locally popular for swimming and water-sports.—At (17km)
Salussola the church contains good 18C woodwork.—27km *Gaglianico* has a
splendid castle, mainly 16C, with a well-decorated cortile.—31km **Biella**, on the
Cervo, is a busy textile-making town (54,000 inhab.) divided into two portions,
Biella Piano (410m) and *Biella Piazzo* (475m), connected by funicular railway. In
the lower town are the ill-restored Gothic *Cathedral* of 1402, with a neo-Gothic

narthex of 1825; the interesting 10C *Baptistery; and the 11C Romanesque campanile of the demolished church of Santo Stefano. The *Museo Civico* (15–18 except Wednesday; in summer opened on request) contains local archaeological material, frescoes, paintings (works by Fattori, De Chirico, Chagall, etc.), and ceramics (Sèvres, etc.). The elegant Renaissance church of *San Sebastiano* (1504, with a 19C façade), contains paintings by Lanino and notable stalls incorporating panels of an 11C reliquary. In the upper town are many 15–16C mansions, including the austere *Palazzo Cisterna* (late 16C), and the 13–16C church of *San Giacomo*.—Across the Cervo, in the park of San Gerolamo, is the *Villa Sella* with a fine 15C cloister. This was the home of the photographer, alpinist, and explorer Vittorio Sella (1859–1943; nephew of Quintino Sella). The *Istituto Nazionale di fotografia alpina Vittorio Sella* here (adm. by written request) conserves his remarkable collection of negatives made during mountain expeditions in Europe, Asia, Africa, and Alaska, as well as his photographic equipment.

A direct railway service via Santhià connects Biella with Turin or Vercelli; and buses run to Vercelli and Ivrea. N144 leads NW to Oropa, via the *Parco della Burcina* (7km; left on the Pollone road), created in 1849 by Giovanni Piacenza, with fine trees and flowers (open daily).—12km *Santuario d'Oropa* (1181m), a large hospice of three quadrangles, with a modest church by Juvarra, the most popular pilgrimage resort in Piedmont, said to have been founded by St Eusebius in 369. A new church (completed in 1960), with a large dome, begun in 1885 to a design by Ignazio Galletti (1774), rises beyond the farthest quadrangle. Below the sanctuary a cable railway ascends from the valley in 10 minutes to the Rifugio Mucrone; from here a walk of 20 minutes leads to the *Lago del Mucrone* (1902m), on the slope of *Monte Mucrone* (2335m; good ski slopes; a cable railway ascends to the summit). A chair-lift goes up from the lake to *Monte Camino* (2391m), on the watershed E of the Val de Lys.

From Biella a road (bus) ascends the Cervo valley via (7km) *Andorno Micca* and (15km) *Campiglia Cervo*, a holiday resort, to (20km) **Piedicavallo** (1036m), the highest village in the Cervo valley, connected by mountain passes with Gaby in the Val de Lys (see Rte 2) and with Rassa in the Valsesia (see below).

Other places of interest near Biella are *Candelo* (5km SE), with a remarkable Ricetto, or communal fortress and storehouse, built in the 14C as a refuge for the townsfolk; *Graglia* (9km W), above which rises the *Santuario di Graglia* (247m), a fine viewpoint, where mineral water springs have been utilised; and *Mosso Santa Maria* (19km NE) and *Trivero* (26km) made up of hamlets.

From Trivero the STRADA PANORAMICA ZEGNA (N232; named after its originator) winds upwards to the W.—Beyond (4km) *Caulera* are splendid woods of rhododendrons. The views N to Monte Rosa are very fine.—13km *Bielmonte* (1517m) is a winter sports centre (chair-lift to Monte Marca, 1625m).—24km *Rosazza*, in the Cervo valley (see above).

The Milan road soon recrosses the motorway and bypasses (54km) *Tronzano*, where a road on the left leads in 3km to *Santhià*, an important railway junction, whose name is a corruption of Sant'Agata. Here is a rice-growing district, in summer covered with water. Just to the NW the Valle d'Aosta motorway (A5) joins the A4.

74km **VERCELLI**, the largest rice-producing centre in Europe, is an interesting old town (56,500 inhab.). It was noted in the 16C for its school of painters, including Giovanni Martino Spanzotti, Sodoma, Gaudenzio Ferrari, and Bernardino Lanino. The wide Corso Garibaldi, on the W, skirts the old town from S to N. To the left, in front of the station, is the basilica of *Sant'Andrea** (1219–27), Romanesque but showing Cistercian Gothic elements very early for Italy. It was founded by Cardinal Guala Bicchieri with the revenues of the abbey of St Andrew, Chesterton (Cambridgeshire) bestowed on him by his young ward, Henry III. The fine façade is flanked by two tall towers connected by a double arcade, and the cupola is topped by a third tower. In the lunettes are sculptures attributed to Antelami. The detached campanile (1407), to the SE, is in the same style. The interior has pointed arcades carried on slender clustered piers, with shafts carried up unbroken to the springing of the vaults. To the N the remains of the Cistercian abbey include a fine cloister with clustered columns and a chapter-house with a 16C vault on four columns.—Via Bicchieri leads to the **Cathedral**, with three cupolas, begun in 1572 to a design of Pellegrino Tibaldi, but preserving the Romanesque campanile of an older church.

In the S transept, the octagonal chapel of the Blessed Amadeus IX of Savoy (died in the castle 1472) contains his tomb and that of his successor Charles I (died 1490); also an 11C or 12C Byzantine crucifix of hammered bronze.—The CHAPTER LIBRARY (adm. on application) includes the 4C Evangelistary of St Eusebius (in a 12C binding); some Anglo-Saxon poems (11C); the Laws of the Lombards (8C); and other early MSS, perhaps relics of the Studium, or early university which flourished here from 1228 for about a century.

Via del Duomo runs S past the 18C church of Santa Maria Maggiore, behind which is the restored 13C *Castle*, to Via Gioberti. This leads (left) to *San Francesco*, a restored church of 1292 containing a good St Ambrose, by Girolamo Giovenone (1535); behind its apse is the CIVICO MUSEO BORGOGNA (Tuesday & Thursday 14.30–16.30 or 15–17, Sunday 10.30–12.30; other days on request), with an important collection of works by Piedmontese and Vercelli painters including Sodoma, Defendente and Gaudenzio Ferrari, Bernardino Lanino, Girolamo Giovenone, and Boniforte Oldoni. The upper floor with foreign and modern paintings was opened in 1985.

Via Borgogna ends in the Corso Libertà, the main street of the old town. On the left is seen the Gothic *Torre dei Tizzoni*; on the right is *San Giuliano* with its Romanesque campanile. Nearly opposite, the *Palazzo Centori* (No. 87) has a delightful interior court arcaded in the Tuscan style (1496). Via Cagna leads left to the church of **San Cristoforo**, notable for the fine series of *Frescoes by Gaudenzio Ferrari* (1529–34), and for the *Madonna* (1529), on the high altar, considered his masterpiece. The first street on the left, on the return, opens into Piazza del Municipio, in which are the *Town Hall* and the church of *San Paolo* (begun c 1260), containing a Madonna and Saints by Bernardino Lanino. Across the Corso is Piazza Cavour, the old market square, with the machicolated *Torre degli Angeli* rising above the houses. To the right, in Via Gioberti, is the tall square *Torre di Città*; while in Via Verdi, to the N, the *Museo Leone* (April–November, Tuesday & Thursday 15–17.30, Sunday 10–12; other days in request) is a good archaeological and historical collection in a building incorporating 15C and 18C palazzi.

Farther along the Corso, to the right opposite the Post Office, is Piazza Zumaglini, the modern business centre of the town, with the banks.—Vercelli is connected by direct railways with Alessandria via Casale Monferrato; and with Pavia, via Mortara.

The road crosses the Sesia and Monte Rosa is seen to the N.—80km *Borgo Vercelli*. A road runs N to *San Nazzaro Sesia* (10km), on the river Sesia, with remains of a fortified Benedictine abbey.

96km **NOVARA**, a provincial capital (100,700 inhab.) and one of the oldest towns in Piedmont, is celebrated for its four battles, most important of which were the first (1500) when Lodovico il Moro was taken prisoner by the French, and the fourth (1849), when the Piedmontese were defeated by Radetzky's Austrians.

Post Office, Corso XX Settembre.—**Tourist Office**, 8 Via Ravizza.—**Theatre**, Piazza Martiri della Libertà.—*Swimming Pools*: W of the station (open-air), Palazzo dello Sport (covered).

The most striking building is the church of **San Gaudenzio** (1577–1690), in part to a design of Pellegrino Tibaldi, on to which a tall slender cupola, with a spire 121m high, was built by Alessandro Antonelli (1840–88). The attractive campanile (1763–96) is by Benedetto Alfieri. Inside (N side) is a good polyptych by Gaudenzio Ferrari (1514) and (S transept) the Baroque chapel of the patron saint. Nearby, in Palazzo Faraggiana, is an Ethnographical Museum, a Natural History Museum, and a Music Museum (9 or 10–12, 15–17.30 or 18.30; fest. 9–12; closed Monday). To the S, across the main Corso Italia, is the *Broletto*, a group of well-restored buildings of the 13C, 15C, and 18C; here is installed the *Museo Civico* (10–12, 15 or 15,30–17.30 or 18.30; fest. 10–12; closed Monday) with an archaeological section, and a pinacoteca (paintings by Cerano, etc.) and modern art gallery (19C paintings, including works by the Macchiaioli). Across Piazza della Repubblica rises the **Duomo**, rebuilt by Alessandro Antonelli in 1863–65 with a remarkable vault. It contains an altarpiece of the Marriage of St Catherine by Gaudenzio Ferrari, and, in the lower sacristy, detached frescoes by Bernardino Lanino and Raffaele Giovenone. The Chapel of San Siro, which survives from the earlier church, contains interesting Romanesque frescoes (12–13C). The church also owns a series of 16C Flemish tapestries, and in the 15C cloister is a small lapidary collection. The BAPTISTERY is a palaeochristian building heightened in the Romanesque era; the remarkable frescoes of the Apocalypse found during restoration work are thought to date from the end of the 10C.—Piazza Martiri, just to the W, is ringed by the neo-classical buildings of the *Palazzo del Mercato* (1817–44) and the *Teatro Coccia* (1886), and the remains of a *Castle* of the Sforza (which may be used as a new seat for the Museo Civico), with a park to the S and W.

Novara is connected by road and direct railway with *Alessandria*; with *Arona*, on Lago Maggiore (Rte 10); with *Orta* (Rte 9B), via Borgomanero; and with *Varallo* (see below).

The Milan road by-passes *Trecate*, with its oil refinery, and crosses the Ticino to enter Lombardy.—117km *Magenta*, by-passed to the N, is famous for the victory of the French and Italians over the Austrians in 1859, which is commemorated by an ossuary and a monument to Marshal MacMahon.—144km **Milan**, see Rte 13.

FROM NOVARA TO VARALLO AND ALAGNA, 92km; bus or railway to *Varallo* in 1½–1¾hrs; bus to *Alagna* in 1½hrs.—This route, leading NW, reaches the Sesia at (30km) *Romagnano Sesia*, a papermaking and cotton-spinning town, also on the Santhià-Arona railway. At *Gattinara*, 2·5km S beyond the river, known for its red wine, the parish church contains paintings by Lanino.—The road now enters the VALSESIA, a winding valley which provides an attractive approach to the high Alps from the S. It is famous for its lace, an important feature in the gala costumes of the villages in the upper valley. The lower valley is industrial, with manufacturers of paper, furniture, etc.—44km *Borgosesia* is the largest of several small cotton-spinning towns. It has a folklore museum (open at weekends). A pretty road (18km) runs E via *Valduggia*, the birthplace of Gaudenzio Ferrari (1471–1546). In the church of San Giorgio is a Nativity by him, and a Madonna and Child by Bernardino Luini. Beyond *Cremosina* it continues to Lake Orta (Rte 9B).—57km **Varallo** (450m; formerly *Verallo Sesia*), the capital of the upper Valsesia, is a pleasant little town (7600 inhab.). The church of *San Gaudenzio*, picturesquely placed at the head of a stairway, contains a polyptych by Gaudenzio Ferrari. The *Pinacoteca* (May–September, 10–12, 15–18 except Friday; other days on request at the Tourist office) contains paintings by Valsesian artists including Gaudenzio Ferrari and Tanzio da Verallo. There is also a *Natural History Museum* here. The chief sight of Varallo is the *SACRO MONTE, the ascent to which begins at the church of *Madonna delle Grazie*, which has a *Fresco of the Life of Christ, by Gaudenzio Ferrari (1513) in 21 scenes.

The *Santuario* (608m; reached on foot in 20 minutes or by cable railway or road), or *Nuova Gerusalemme del Sacro Monte*, was founded c 1486 by the Blessed Bernardino Caimi, a Friar Minor. The building was started in 1493 but not completed until the late 17C. It is surrounded by 45 chapels intended to recall the various holy sites in Jerusalem, and these were decorated by contemporary artists of the Valsesia (Gaudenzio Ferrari, Giovanni Tabacchetti, Giovanni D'Errico, Morazzone). Tabacchetti's best chapels are the Temptation (No. 38; with a Crucifixion by Ferrari) and Adam and Eve (No. 1). D'Errico's is the Vision of St Joseph (No. 5). The *Basilica dell'Assunta* dates from 1641–49, with a façade of 1896.

A by-road (23·5km) leads from Varallo to *Pella* on the Lake of Orta via the *Madonna di Loreto* (frescoes by Gaudenzio Ferrari and Andrea Solario), *Civiasco*, and *La Colma* (942m).—In the great bend of the Sesia rises the *Becco d'Ovaga* (1630m; marked path from Varallo via Crevola and the *Rifugio Spanni*, near the summit).

The picturesque VAL MASTALLONE, leading N from Varallo, is ascended by road (bus) to (18km) *Fobello* (881m), above which lies (20 minutes) *Cervatto* (1021m), two small summer resorts. From Ponte delle Due Acque, 2km below Fobello, a road diverges right for (20km from Varallo; bus) *Rimella* (1180m), a scattered village retaining many traces in its dialect of the German-speaking colony from the Valais that migrated here in the 14C. Both Rimella and Fobello are connected by mountain passes with the Val Anzasca (Rte 9A).

Above Varallo the Valsesia is known as VALGRANDE, and at (67km) *Balmuccia* the Val Sermenza leads N to Rimasco, for Rima and Carcoforo.—From (74km) *Scopello* (658m) a chair-lift ascends to *Alpe di Mera* (1600m), a winter-sports resort. The road turns N, passing the mouth of the *Val Rassa*, out of which passes lead to Piedicavallo (see above).—Beyond (81km) *Campertogno* (815m) the ascent becomes steeper, and from (83km) *Mollia* (881m) there is a fine view of the Alagna basin backed by Monte Rosa.—90km *Riva Valdobbia* (1143m) stands at the foot of the Colle Valdobbia, an important pass into the Gressoney valley.—92km **Alagna Valsesia** (1183m), a fashionable summer and winter resort. In a characteristic wooden house here (1628) is the Museo Walser. Alagna is the starting point of the Funivia di Monte Rosa, a cableway in three stages (via Bocchetta delle Pisse, with ski-lifts) to Punta Indren (3260m), a summer and winter ski-resort. The Regina Margherita CAI Refuge observatory (4559m) was reconstructed in 1980 on the sight of a hut built here in 1893 and inaugurated by Queen Margherita. It is the highest refuge in Europe.

An alternative ROAD FROM TURIN TO MILAN (148km; bus to Casale, and from there to Milan) diverges from the main road beyond (23km) *Chivasso* (see above) and follows the Po, with the Monferrato hills rising above the S bank.—57km *Trino* has been noted for its printers and binders since the 15C. Roman remains have been excavated here, and NE of the town is the ancient Basilica of San Michele in Insula.—71km **Casale Monferrato** (43,600 inhab.), just off the main road, on the S bank of the Po, is the chief town of the old duchy of Monferrato, whose princes of the Paleologhi family held a famous court in 1319–1533. In 1873 the first Italian Portland cement was made here, and it was noted for its production of cement and artificial stone up until the Second World War. The *Duomo*, consecrated in 1107, was over-restored in the 19C, but it preserves a remarkable narthex. Inside is a Romanesque sculpted Crucifix. *San Domenico* is a late-Gothic church to which a fine Renaissance portal of 1505 has been added. Via Mameli has a number of fine buildings including *Palazzo Treville* by Giovanni Battista Scapitta (1725; fine rococo atrium and courtyard), *Palazzo Sannazzaro* and the *Municipio*, both also 18C, and the church of *San Paolo* (1586). In Via Cavour the cloister of Santa Croce is to be used to house the *Museo Civico*, with sculpture by Leonardo Bistolfi (1859–1933) and late-16C paintings by Matteo da Verona, Moncalvo, etc. The *Synagogue* (1595) contains a *Jewish Museum*. The huge Piazza Castello to the W, on the Po, surrounds the 14C *Castle* (transformed in the 19C); the church of *Santa Caterina* here is by Giovanni Battista Scapitta (c 1725).—Direct railways connect Casale with Turin, Mortara, Vercelli, Asti, and Alessandria.

The Monferrato hills are traversed by the roads from Casale and from Chivasso to Asti (42km and 52km). Just W of the latter road (21km from Chivasso) is *Albugnano*, with the Benedictine ***Abbey of Vezzolano** (1095–1189; open 9–12.30, 15–18; winter 9–12, 14–16; closed Monday & Friday afternoons), the finest group of Romanesque buildings in Piedmont, with remarkable sculptures, especially on the façade and the unusual rood-screen, and a cloister the W side of which appears to be older than the church, while the S side dates from 1600.

From the Casale-Asti road at *Serralunga* station (14km from Casale) a by-road diverges right (W) for the **Santuario di Crea** (4·5km), founded in 1590 on the site of the refuge of St Eusebius, Bishop of Vercelli in 340–70. In the church (13C, altered 1608–12) are a Madonna and Saints, in fresco, by *Macrino d' Alba* (1503), and a triptych of 1474 with the donors, William VIII of Monferrato and his wife. The 23 main chapels of the sanctuary contain characteristic late-15C sculptures by *Tabacchetti* and paintings by *Moncalvo*. The highest chapel (del Paradiso) has a good view over the Monferrato.—*Moncalvo*, 22km from Asti on the Casale road, has a good and typical Gothic church of the 14C (with paintings by the local artist, Guglielmo Caccia, called Moncalvo), some houses of similar date, and a fragment of an old castle. The local vines are renowned.

Beyond Casale the road crosses the Sesia and enters Lombardy.—101km **Mortara** (15,400 inhab.), an important railway junction retains the churches of Santa Croce, with paintings by Bernardino Lanino, and San Lorenzo (Romanesque and Gothic) with pictures by Bernardino Lanino and Giulio Cesare Procaccini. It is the chief town of the cultivated plain of *Lomellina*, which has been provided with irrigation canals since the 14C.

111km **Vigévano** is an ancient town which grew to prominence in the 14C under the Visconti. Lodovico il Moro and Francesco Il Sforza were born here. It has been famous for the manufacture of shoes since the end of the 19C and the modern city expanded rapidly in the 1950s. *Piazza Ducale (138 x 48m) was built by order of Ludovico il Moro in 1492–94 when buildings were demolished to create the space for this beautiful rectangular Renaissance piazza. It is surrounded on three sides by uniform graceful arcades and its classical design may have been projected with the help of Bramante (or even Leonardo da Vinci). The other end was closed in 1680 when the strange eliptical façade of the *Duomo* was added to give the cathedral prominence (1532–1612) is interesting for its paintings by 16C Lombards. A Museum (opened by the sacristan) houses its rich treasury, which includes Flemish and local tapestries, illuminated codexes, and goldsmiths' work. A tall Lombard tower (probably redesigned by Bramante) belongs to the huge *Castle* begun by Lucchino Visconti in the mid-14C. On a raised site, this was connected to the Piazza by a monumental entrance (destroyed) beneath the tower. The castle was transformed by Ludovico il Moro (with the help of Bramante and possibly also Leonardo) into a very grand ducal palace. For long used for military purposes, it is at last being restored, but is meanwhile closed. It has remarkable stables and a beautiful loggia. The raised covered way built by Lucchino Visconti to connect the Castle with the Rocca Vecchia survives (no adm.). The *Museo Civico*, on Corso Cavour on the outskirts of the old town, contains an archaeological collection and a picture gallery. —About 4km SE is the large *Sforzésca*, a model farm designed by Guglielmo da Camino for Il Moro in 1486.—Vigevano is in the centre of the large **Parco della Valle del Ticino** instituted in 1974 as a protected area on either side of the Ticino river from Sesto Calende to Pavia (90,000 hectares). Where cars are banned the paths can be followed on foot or by bicycle to see the wildlife in an interesting landscape.

Beyond the Ticino the road by-passes the big agricultural town of (125km) **Abbiategrasso** (26,900 inhab.). Here the church of Santa Maria Nuova is preceded by a quadriporticus and a pronaos of 1497 by Bramante. The late-13C

Castle is being restored as the seat of the archaeological and natural history museums. A road (N526) leads S to *Morimondo* (6km), with a 12C abbey with a fine church (good choir of 1522). Abbiategrasso is on the canal known as the *Naviglio Grande* which extends N for some 30km and continues E into Milan. It was cut in the 12C and 13C when it first became navigable. It was used to carry commodities to and from Milan and to irrigate the surrounding fields. There was a regular passenger navigation service along the canal from the beginning of the 19C. The Milanese nobility built their country villas here in the 17C and 18C. Places of interest on the canal N of Abbiategrasso include *Cassinetta di Lugagnano* and *Robecco sul Naviglio*, both with fine villas (some of them recently restored).

The main road now follows the canal towards Milan. At 133km the road becomes dual carriageway, by-passing *Gaggiano*. A by-road (5km) follows a secondary canal cut by Filippo Maria Visconti N to *Cusago* with a castle in the main piazza, the 14C country residence of Bernabò Visconti. The woods of Cusago are a bird sanctuary.—The main road continues N of *Trezzano*, on the outskirts of the city, where much new building has taken place in the last few decades, then passes under the motorway into the centre of (148km) *Milan*, see Rte 13.

II   THE LAKES AND LOMBARDY

Lombardy, with Milan, the largest city in northern Italy, as its capital, has played an important part in the making of Italy. The region includes areas of remarkable diversity within its boundaries, extending as it does from the summits of the central Alps to the low-lying fertile plain of the Po. Some of the loveliest scenery in the country surrounds the great Italian Lakes (all of which, except Orta, are wholly or partly in Lombardy), while the southern part of the province is either industrialised or given over to intensive agriculture. The population of 543,300 is included within an area of 23,850 sq. km and varies remarkably in density; the modern Lombard provinces are Bergamo, Brescia, Como, Cremona, Mantua, Milan, Pavia, Sondrio, and Varese.

In Roman times the centre of Cisalpine Gaul, Lombardy takes its present name from the Lombards or Longobards, one of the so-called barbarian tribes that invaded Italy in the 6C. They settled in various

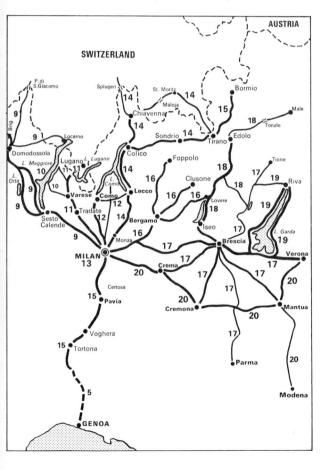

parts of the peninsula and founded several states, but for some reason that which centred roughly round Milan achieved a more than ephemeral duration, and retained the founders' name. The association of Lombardy with transalpine powers dates from the time of Charlemagne, and Lombardy, though actually under the control of the Bishops of Milan, remained nominally a part of the Germanic Empire until the 12C. Then the people of the great Lombard cities, having overthrown the temporal power of the bishops, formed themselves into the Lombard League, and defeated the Emperor, Frederick Barbarossa, at Legnano in 1176. Out of the citizens' organisations, however, individual families soon rose to despotic power, and for two centuries or more local dynasties held sway and were able, incidentally, by virtue of their control of finance, to encourage the arts within their dominions. Notable among them were the Torriani, Visconti, and Sforza at Milan, Pavia, Cremona, and Bergamo; the Suardi and Colleoni at Bergamo; the Pallavicini, Torriani, Scaligeri, and Visconti at Brescia; and the Bonacolsi and Gonzaga at Mantua. With the fall of the powerful Visconti at the beginning of the 15C the power of Venice encroached from the E, and in the 16C Lombard territory was invaded by the kings of France; in the outcome the Duchy of Milan in 1535 became a dependency of the Spanish Habsburgs, though Ticino and the Valtellina in the N attached themselves to the Swiss Confederation. The extinction of the Habsburg line in Spain transferred Lombardy to the Austrian dominion, and, with the brief intervention of the Napoleonic Cisalpine Republic and the French kingdoms of Lombardy and of Italy (1797–1814), it remained a subject-province of Austria, the Valtellina being detached from Switzerland in 1797. National aspirations were savagely repressed by the Austrian military governors of the 19C until the victory of the allied French and Piedmontese brought Lombardy beneath the Italian flag in 1859.

9   (Brig) Domodossola to Milan

FROM BRIG TO DOMODOSSOLA, 65km. The **Simplon Pass** (2009m; *Passo del Sempione*) and the steep parts of its approaches are wholly on Swiss soil (see 'Blue Guide Switzerland'). The pass was only intermittently of importance until Napoleon chose it as the passage for his road connecting the Rhône Valley with the Northern Italian plain. The work, decided upon immediately after the passage of the St Bernard and the battle of Marengo, was begun on the Italian side in 1800, on the Swiss side a year later, and was completed in 1805, this mountain section being the final achievement in the construction of the great highway extending 182km from Geneva to Sesto Calende.—About 1km below the summit on the S side stands the *Simplon Hospice* (2001m), built by Napoleon as barracks in 1811 and acquired by the monks of St Bernard in 1825.

The Italian custom-house is at *Paglino*, just within (43km) the frontier. N33 descends the **Val Divedro**, past the mouth of the railway tunnel, to (52km) *Varzo* (568m), a climbing centre beneath Monte Cistella (2880m). A road (continued by a mule path) ascends the Val Cairasca to *Alpe Veglia* (1753m), a summer resort below *Monte Leone* (3552m).—65km *Domodossola* (see below).

The RAILWAY from Brig (40km) passes through the *Simplon Tunnel*, the longest rail tunnel in the world (19·8km), the first gallery of which was pierced in 1898–1905. Although a subsidiary gallery, connected by cross-shafts, formed part of the original construction, this was not enlarged to take a second track until 1912–21. The maximum elevation is only 705m and the Simplon is thus the lowest of the great Alpine tunnels; but there are 2134m of mountain overhead where the main ridge is pierced.—CAR CARRIER trains frequently between Iselle and Brig.

A. Via Stresa

FROM DOMODOSSOLA, N33. 125km—6·5km *Villadossola*.—20km *Cuzzago*.—30·5km *Gravellona*. From there along the shore of Lago Maggiore, via (42km) *Stresa*.—58km **Arona**.—67km *Sesto Calende*.—84km *Gallarate*.—125km **Milan**. From just beyond Sesto Calende the MOTORWAY (A8) offers a faster approach (3km shorter) to Milan.

RAILWAY 125km in 1¼–2¼hrs; to *Stresa* (39km) in 30–50 minutes; to *Arona* (56km) in 40–70 minutes. Through carriages on this route from Calais to Milan and Venice.

Domodossola (271m), the chief place of the Valle d'Ossola, at the foot of the Simplon Pass, is a characteristic little Italian town (19,700 inhab.), of Roman origin, with an old arcaded market-place. In the *Palazzo Silva* (with a frieze of 1519), near the market-place, is a *Museum of Antiquities*. The church of *Santi Gervaso e Protasio*, nearby, has an old porch (15C frescoes) and bronze doors of 1955. In *Palazzo San Francesco*, which incorporates remains of a church, the 19C Fondazione Galletti is now owned by the Comune. The *Museum* here includes a room which illustrates the construction of the Simplon tunnel, and there is material relating to the flight of Georges Chavez (see below), a small pinacoteca, and a natural history collection. Via Mattarella leads to an interesting 17C *Via Crucis* (view from the top). A monument in Piazza Liberazione (No. 9) commemorates Georges Chavez, the Peruvian airman, who was killed in his fall near Domodossola, after having made the first flight over the Alps (29 September 1910).

In the pretty wooded VALLE BOGNANCO, W of Domodossola, a road leads to (8km) **Bognanco Fonti** (663m), a popular little spa. The road ends at *Bognanco San Lorenzo* (980m).

FROM DOMODOSSOLA TO THE SAN GIACOMO PASS, 55km, bus twice daily in 2¼hrs to Ponte di Formazza, 40km. The scenery on the route is very spectacular. At (5km) the foot of the Val Divedro this route leaves the road and railway to the Simplon.—Near (13·5km) *Crodo* (356m) is a little spa, with iron springs.—The gorge of the Devero is crossed to reach (19km) **Baceno** (685m), where the interesting double-aisled *Church* (14–16C) has frescoes by Antonio Zanetti. At the head of the Devero valley (left) is *Alpe Devero* (1640m), a pleasant fishing and winter-sports resort.—21km *Premia*.—26km *San Rocco* (754m) has an ancient church.—The road traverses the most typical stretch of the VAL ANTIGORIO, with its vineyards, fig-trees, and chestnuts, and comes to (32km) *Foppiano* or *Unter Stalden* (933m) the first German-speaking village. After twice crossing the Toce in the grand *Gola delle Casse*, the route enters the beautiful **Val Formazza**, an interesting region colonised in the Middle Ages by German-speaking families from the Valais.—35km *Chiesa*, or *Andermatten* (1235m), like Foppiano, is in the commune of **Formazza**, a series of picturesque hamlets extending through (39km) *Ponte*, the municipal centre for the frontier. It is now a winter and summer ski resort (chair-lift from Ponte).—45km *Cascata del Toce* (1661m). The ***Falls of the Toce**, or *Cascata della Frua*, are among the grandest in the Alps, though they now function only on days when their source is not being tapped for hydroelectric power (June–September, Sunday only, 9–17; 10–20 August every day). The stream spreads out like a fan in its descent and, gliding down a series of steps, forms an uninterrupted mass of white foam for over 300m, while the perpendicular descent is about 143m. The best viewpoints are a little footbridge close to the hotel, and a bend in the track leading to Domodossola, 10 minutes lower down.

The road deteriorates as it approaches (48km) *Riale* (1720m) which lies at the junction of the routes to the Gries (footpath) and San Giacomo passes. The right-hand route passes (right) a power-reservoir to reach (56km) the *Passo di San Giacomo* (2315m) where at present the road ends. A bridle-path (road under construction) goes on across the Swiss frontier to All'Acqua in the Val Bedretto (on the road for Airolo at the S entrance to the St Gotthard tunnel; see 'Blue Guide Switzerland').

FROM DOMODOSSOLA TO LOCARNO. Road, 48·5km. Railway, 51km in 40–70 minutes, closely following the road. This spectacular line was first opened in 1923, and has been repaired since flood damage put it out of action in 1978. The road crosses the Toce to reach (4·5km) *Masera* (306m) where there is an old church tower. Here is the entrance to the VAL VIGEZZO, much visited by artists since the 19C and known as the 'Valle dei Pittori', which rises near (13km) *Druogno* to an indefinite watershed separating the W and E branches of the Melezzo.—17km **Santa Maria Maggiore** (815m), the chief village of the valley, is finely situated in an upland basin. It has a little Museum illustrating the work of chimney-sweeps. It is connected by bus with *Toceno*, *Vocogno*, and *Craveggia*, three pleasant villages across the torrent. The area has been opened up for skiers (cable railway to Piana di Vigezzo, 1724m).—20km *Malesco* (760m) stands at the divergence of a road to Cannobio (see Rte 10C).—23km *Re* (710m) has a shrine (1922) of the Madonna, which attracts many pilgrims.—At (29km) the bold *Ponte della Ribellasca* (552m; custom house) the road enters Switzerland (see 'Blue Guide Switzerland').—Below (30km) *Camedo* the valley is joined by innumerable side streams which give the district its name (Centovalli, the 'Hundred Valleys').—41km *Intragna* (369m) is conspicuous by its lofty church tower. The village was the original home of the Gambetta family, from where the grandfather of Léon Gambetta emigrated to Genoa.—48·5km *Locarno.*

6·5km **Villadossola**, with a 12C campanile, lies at the SE foot of *Moncucco* (1899m), at the mouth of the Valle d'Antrona, which ascends on the right.

The VALLE D'ANTRONA. Bus daily from Domodossola to Antronapiana in 1½hrs.—Beyond (8km) *Viganella* (582m), with its graceful waterfall, the road crosses the Ovesca and, as the valley widens, there is a view of the Punta di Saas rising at its head. From (12km) *San Pietro di Schieranco* (652m), the Passo dei Salarioli leads S to the Val Anzasca.—16km **Antronapiana** (902m), charmingly situated among larch and fir woods, is the chief village of the valley noted for trout-fishing.In the neighbourhood are some delightful walks, best of which is that to (¾hr) the beautiful little *Lago d'Antrona* (1083m) formed in 1642 by a landslip from the *Cima di Pozzoli* (2546m) to the N.

9km *Pallanzeno.* Beyond the village a road diverges right for (12km) *Piedimulera* (248m). Here N549 diverges right up the Valle Anzasca for Macugnaga.

The VALLE ANZASCA, follows the Anza river through scenery which combines the loveliness of Italy with the grandeur of Switzerland. After two short rock-tunnels, a distant view of Monte Rosa towers at the head of the valley.—5km *Castiglione d'Ossola* (514m) lies near the foot of the *Valle della Segnara* (2km farther on).—The road descends to the level of the Anza, crossing the torrent of the Val Bianca, with its waterfalls, just before reaching (13km)*Pontegrande* (510m).

Here a road on the left diverges for **Bannio-Anzino** (669m), the chief village and climbing centre of the Valle Anzasca, with a picturesque campanile and a fine bronze figure of Christ (probably 16C Flemish). A chair-lift ascends to the winter-sports resort of Alpi Provaccio-Val Baranca (1355m).

20km *Ceppo Morelli* (753m) has a remarkably steep bridge crossing the Anza. Above *Prequartera* the valley appears blocked by an enormous rock called the *Morghen*, which in fact divides the Valle Anzasca proper from the Macugnaga basin. The road runs through a narrow gorge and emerges at (25km) *Pestarena* (1154m), the first hamlet of the commune of Macugnaga, where gold-bearing ore is worked.—At (27km) *Borca* (1202m) begins the Colle del Turlo (see below), but it is preferable to go on to (29km) *Staffa*, the chief centre of the scattered commune of **Macugnaga** (1326m). The valley is inhabited largely by the descendants of an Alemannic colony transplanted from the Valais in 1262–90. It is now a popular summer resort and climbing centre, famed for its wonderful view of Monte Rosa, of which the Macugnaga face is the most stupendous 'wall' in the Alps. With the construction of ski-lifts it has also developed into an important winter-sports centre. The *Old Church* (late 13C; restored in 1580), above Staffa, preserves German characteristics in its S door and chancel windows. The road ends at (41km) *Pecetto* (1399m), the highest of the commune's hamlets. From here a chair-lift ascends in two stages to the **Belvedere* (1932m), or *Wengwald*, a fine viewpoint, as its name implies, above the wooded medial moraine of the Macugnaga Glacier. There are ski-lifts above and below Pecetto, and a cableway from Staffa to the *Passo Monte Moro* (2868m; Refuge), a winter and summer ski resort. **Monte Rosa** (*Dufourspitze*, 4638m) has been ascended from Macugnaga, but this route, though not unduly difficult for the expert, is one of the most dangerous in the Alps on account of its frequent avalanches.

The main road for Stresa now crosses the Toce to (14km) *Vogogna* with a 14C castle of the Visconti.—Beyond (20km) *Cuzzago* the road bears right to recross the railway and the Toce.

The road on the left bank of the river leads to (18km) Pallanza (Rte 10A) via (8km) *Mergozzo*, on its pretty little lake (swimming and water-skiing). A walk may be taken to *Montorfano*, with the Romanesque church of San Giovanni.

25km *Ornavasso*, near the marble quarries of Candoglia, was colonised in the 13C by a Germanic immigration from the Valais.—30·5km **Gravellona Toce**, near the junction of the Strona and the Toce, has a small *Antiquarium* (closed for rearrangement) of Iron Age and Roman finds.—35km *Feriolo* is the junction with the road along the shore of Lago Maggiore.—38km *Baveno*, and from there to (42km) **Stresa**, see Rte 10A.

Beyond Stresa the road continues along the southern reach of the lake, where the scenery is less impressive. On the E bank is the picturesque old church of *Arolo*.—47km *Belgirate*, standing on a conspicuous headland, was the home of the five heroic brothers Cairoli, only one of whom, the statesman Benedetto (1825–89), survived the wars of Italian independence.—49km *Lesa* is famous for its vineyards and orchards. It has sports facilities, including a swimming pool. The Palazzo Stampa here was a residence of Manzoni. At *Ispra*, on the opposite shore, was the first centre in Italy for nuclear studies (Euratom).—54km *Meina*.

On the right above appears the colossal statue called San Carlone (see below).—58km **Arona**, an ancient town (15,700 inhab.) and an important railway junction, is the S terminus of the boat service (hydrofoil to Locarno). The lakeside promenade provides a good view of Angera. The palace of the Podestà dates from the 15C. In the upper town in the church of *Santa Maria* the Borromeo chapel contains an **Altarpiece* (1511) of six panels by Gaudenzio Ferrari. The lunette over the main door has a charming 15C relief of the Holy Family. The neighbouring church of the *Santi Martiri* has a Madonna by Bergognone over the high altar.

To the N, above the Simplon road, stands the *San Carlone*, a colossal copper statue of San Carlo Borromeo (1538–84), archbishop of Milan, who was born in the castle that now lies in ruins above the town. The statue, 23m high, standing on a 12m pedestal, was erected in 1697 by a relative of the saint. The pedestal may be ascended by outside steps, and the statue itself by an internal stair.

The boat to Stresa calls first at *Angera* (5 minutes) beneath the chapel-crowned hill of San Quirico (412m) on the Lombard side of the lake. Anciently a place of some importance, the town possesses a fine old castle of the Visconti, the *Rocca di Angera* (April–October, 9.30–12, 14–17), which passed to the Borromei in 1449, and was extensively restored in the 16–17C. The Sala di Giustizia has interesting 14C Gothic frescoes commissioned by Giovanni Visconti, Bishop of Milan, with signs of the zodiac and episodes from the battles of Ottone Visconti.

In other rooms are displayed paintings, a small lapidary collection, and detached frescoes from Palazzo Borromeo in Milan.—A large Roman necropolis is being excavated at Angera (still not open to the public), and there is a small archaeological museum. Angera and other places on the E bank are served by the Luino-Novara railway and connected by bus with Varese.

Beyond Arona the route curves round the S end of the lake, leaving the Novara road on the right. This passes Borgo Ticino where a by-road leads W to *Agrate Conturbia* with a nature reserve and an interesting baptistery in the church. Farther S the Novara road by-passes *Oleggio* where the Romanesque church of San Michele has frescoes of the 11C and 13C.—The main road and railway for Milan cross the Ticino by a two-storeyed bridge near its outflow from the lake.—67km **Sesto Calende**, on the left bank, is said to derive its name from its market day in Roman times–the sixth day before the Kalends. Here the little *Museo Civico* (Wednesday & Saturday 20–22; fest. 17–19.30; winter: Saturday 16–18; fest. 15–18) houses archaeological finds from tombs of the local 'Golasecca' culture (800–450 BC). Sesto Calende is at the N end of the Parco del Ticino (see Rte 8). The Milan motorway begins 4km farther on, running slightly to the NE of this road, while to the S is (76km) *Somma Lombardo* with its Visconti castle. Nearby at *Arsago Seprio* is the ancient basilica of San Vittore and its Baptistery (12C), and an archaeological museum. Another road leads from Somma Lombardo to *Golasecca* with its Iron Age necropolis (see above). Farther S lies *Malpensa*, the intercontinental airport of Milan, connected by a motorway spur with the A8 motorway for Milan. —84km **Gallarate** is the first of three large industrial towns along this road NW of Milan, noted in the 19C for their cotton-spinning works, and now important manufacturing towns inhabited mainly by immigrant workers from the S. Situated near the Olona river (now polluted) the other towns are Busto Arsizio and Legnano. In Gallarate (46,600 inhab.), the cathedral dates from 1856–60, and the church of San Pietro from the 12C. There is a small archaeological museum at No.4 Borgo Antico. **Busto Arsizio** (78,500 inhab.) has a church (Santa Maria di Piazza, 1515–23), with paintings by Gaudenzio Ferrari and Bernardino Luini. **Legnano** (48,700 inhab.) is famous for the battle in which Barbarossa was defeated by the Lombard League in 1176 (monument). The battle is also celebrated in a traditional festival in the town in May (the 'Palio del Carroccio'). *San Magno* (1504) houses a polyptych by Bernardino Luini and frescoes by Bernardino Lanino. The *Museum* (10–12, 15–17; closed Monday) contains local Roman finds. In the locality of *Castellanza* is the Fondazione Enzo Pagani, with a museum of open-air sculpture by contemporary artists.—The road becomes dual carriageway as it by-passes (110km) *Rho*, with a large oil-refinery and chemical works. Here the railway from Novara and Turin comes in, and the road passes under the A1 and A4 motorways into the centre of (125km) **Milan**, see Rte 13.

B. Via Orta

ROAD, 132km.—30·5km *Gravellona*.—37km *Omegna*.—48km **Orta**.—60km *Borgomanero*.—75km *Sesto Calende*.—132km **Milan**.

RAILWAY, to *Borgomanero*, 60km in 1¼–2hrs, continuing to Novara; to *Orta*, 47km in 60–80 minutes.

From Domodossola to (30·5km) *Gravellona Toce*, see above.—37km *Omegna*, a small manufacturing town (16,300 inhab.) at the N end of the Lake of Orta, retains a few old houses, a medieval bridge, and the ancient town gate leading to the Valle Strona. A bus runs via Gravellona to Pallanza and Intra.

The upper VALSTRONA, which descends from the hills to the NW, is a narrow winding glen, c 20km long, ending at the *Laghetto di Capezzone* (2104m), a lovely tarn beneath the *Cima di Capezzone* (2420m).

On the right beyond (45km) *Pettenasco* is a view of the Sacro Monte, behind which Orta lies concealed.—48km **Orta San Giulio** is pleasantly situated on the lakeward side of a little peninsula. From the Piazza Principale, which enjoys a good view of the Isola San Giulio and the lake, a road passing the *Church of the Assumption*, with an 11C doorway, and Baroque decorations inside, leads to the gateway of the SACRO MONTE, a low hill ascended on foot in 20 minutes, or by road (1·5km).

The *Sacro Monte (396m), dedicated to St Francis of Assisi, has a single path flanked by 20 chapels in early-Renaissance style built between 1596 and 1670 (two are 18C and a 21st chapel has only recently been finished). In them frescoes and groups of life-size terracotta figures illustrate scenes in the life of the saint. The most interesting chapels are the 10th, 11th, 13th, 16th, and 20th, while the terrace of the 15th, and the campanile at the top, have fine views. The frescoes are by Giulio Cesare Procaccini, Antonio Maria Crespi, and Giovanni Battista and Giovanni Mauro delle Rovere; the sculptures by Dionigi Bussola, Cristoforo Prestinari, and Carlo Beretta.

The **Lake of Orta** (290m), 12·8km long and about 1·2km wide, a quiet sheet of water surrounded by mountains, is less visited by tourists than the larger lakes.

BOATS run to (5 minutes) the *Isola San Giulio* and (20 minutes) *Pella*; to (1hr) *Oira* and (1¼hrs) *Omegna*.

The *Isola San Giulio, opposite Orta, once thought to be the haunt of serpents and other dangerous beasts, was purged of the pest in 390 by St Julius, the founder of the original island church. In 962 the island was defended by Willa, wife of Berengar II of Lombardy, against the incursions of the Emperor Otho the Great. Today the pretty island contains villas belonging to the Milanese aristocracy. Inside the interesting *Basilica* is a remarkable *Pulpit* of black Oira marble (11–12C), with interesting carvings. The white marble sarcophagus with Roman carvings, near the door, is said to be that of the traitor Duke Meinulphus, and now serves as an alms-box. Some of the chapels are decorated with 15C Lombard frescoes, one of which (Virgin and Child enthroned, with four saints), is attributed to Gaudenzio Ferrari. In the sacristy is a charter of Otho the Great giving thanks for his eventual capture of the island, and a whale's vertebra passing for a bone of one of the serpents destroyed by St Julius.

Between Orta San Giulio and Gozzano is *Vacciago* where, in the studio of the painter Antonio Calderara (1903–78) a large collection of modern art is open in summer. Just before the S end of the lake, the road skirts a hill crowned by the *Buccione*, a restored Lombard tower (24m).—Beyond (55km) *Gozzano* (linked by bus with Arona) is (60km) **Borgomanero**. The road straight ahead continues to (82km) *Novara* (Rte 8). This route turns left for (75km) *Sesto Calende*, from where to (132km) **Milan**, see Rte 9A.

10 Lago Maggiore

LAGO MAGGIORE (193m) the *Lacus Verbanus* of the Romans, is the second largest lake in Italy (212 sq. km; Lago di Garda, 370 sq. km). Its total length, from Magadino to Sesto Calende, is 64·3km, and its greatest breadth 4·8km between Baveno and Laveno; its greatest depth, off Ghiffa, is 372 metres. About one-fifth of the lake, at the N end, belongs to Switzerland. The chief affluent is the Ticino, which flows in at Magadino and out at Sesto Calende. Other important feeders are the Maggia, which enters the lake at Locarno; the Toce or Tosa, which flows into the gulf of Pallanza, and is joined just before its inflow by the Strona, fed by the waters of the Lake of Orta; and on the E side the Tresa, which drains the Lake of Lugano and enters Lago Maggiore at Luino. These numerous tributaries, fed mostly by mountain snows, subject the lake to sudden floods. The *tramontana* blows regularly from the N in the early morning, followed after 10 by the *inverna* from the S. The *mergozzo* blows from the W in the gulf of Pallanza, and the usually placid waters can be made unexpectedly rough by the *maggiora*.

Though the W Italian bank has belonged to Piedmont since 1743, the history of the lake is bound up with its Lombard E shore. Since the 15C the greatest power around the lake has been the Italian family of Borromeo, who still own the islands that bear their name and the fishery rights all over the lake.

BOAT SERVICES. Frequent services ply up and down the lake, though only a few boats pass the frontier between Cannobio and Brissago. The central ports, Laveno, Verbania, Pallanza, Baveno and Stresa, are linked by additional services which also serve the Isola Madre and Isola Bella. In summer hydrofoils and a Swiss boat maintain direct services between Arona and Locarno (passports necessary). Between Brissago and Locarno more frequent service in 50–60 minutes. Information about timetables, etc. from Navigazione Lago Maggiore, 1 Viale Baracca, Arona.

Approaches by Rail. FROM MILAN TO ARONA VIA SESTO CALENDE, 69km in c 1hr, see Rte 9A.

FROM MILAN (Porta Garibaldi) TO LUINO VIA GALLARATE, 91km in 1½hrs (irregularly), via Busto Arsizio and Besozzo.

FROM MILAN TO LAVENO VIA VARESE, 73km, Nord-Milano railway in 1¼–1¾hrs; road parallel. *Milan*, see Rte 13.—22km **Saronno** is an industrial town (32,600 inhab.), noted for its macaroons. The sanctuary of the *Madonna dei Miracoli* (1498) by Giovanni Antonio Amadeo and Vincenzo Seregni contains frescoes by Gaudenzio Ferrari, Luini, and others. From Saronno branch lines diverge for *Como* and for *Novara* and buses run to *Seregno*.—46km *Malnate*. About 8km SW of Malnate is **Castiglione Olona**, which was practically rebuilt by Cardinal Branda Castiglioni (1350–1443) when he returned from a stay in Florence, bringing with him Masolino da Panicale. The works of art he commissioned to adorn the little town take their inspiration from the Florentine Renaissance. In the piazza are the *Chiesa di Villa*, built and decorated by local masons and sculptors in the style of Brunelleschi; and the *Casa dei Castiglioni* (adm. 9–12, 14.30–17; Sunday 15–18; closed Monday), with an interesting interior (restored in 1988), where the cardinal was born and died. Among the frescoes is a view, by Masolino, of the Hungarian city of Veszprem, where the cardinal served as bishop in 1412–24. At the top of the hill is the *Collegiata* (adm. as for the Casa dei Castiglioni), replacing the family's feudal castle (c 1428). It is decorated with *Frescoes by Florentine artists, notably the Life of the Virgin, in the semidome, by Masolino (detached and restored); here too is the tomb of the cardinal; while in the Baptistery, a little to the left (in a former tower of the castle; shown by the sacristan) are further *Frescoes by Masolino (life of St John the Baptist, his masterpiece executed on his return to the town in 1435), and a font, with putti recalling those at San Giovanni in Bragora in Venice. There is a small museum attached to the Collegiata, with two paintings attributed to Masolino and Fra' Angelico. On the first Sunday of the month an antique and bric-a-brac market is held in the streets of the town.—4km farther S, at **Castelseprio**, is an extensive archaeological area (adm. 9–17 except Monday) with ruins of a Roman Longobard castrum on the site of a late-Bronze Age settlement. A fortified borgo grew up around the camp, but this was destroyed in 1287. The most interesting building is *Santa Maria Foris Portas*, of uncertain date (5–6C or 7–8C) which contains some extraordinary mural paintings in an Oriental (Alexandrian) style thought to date from the 8C (restored in 1988). They were discovered by a partisan in the Second World War. Part of the camp extended across the Olona to *Torba* where monastic buildings survive, probably from the 8C (with frescoes in the tower). These were restored in 1986 by the FAI.—51km **Varese**, see Rte 11.

62km *Gavirate* on the N shore of the **Lago di Varese**, 8·5km long, a sheet of water once famous for its quantity of fish, but now threatened with pollution. *Voltorre*, 2km SE, on the shore of the lake, has an old monastery with an interesting Romanesque brick cloister (restored in 1988). Concerts and exhibitions are now held here. There is a boat service from Gavirate to the little island known as *Isolino Virginia* where the Museo Preistorico di Villa Ponti (open June–September) contains objects found in prehistoric lake dwellings here (Neolithic to Bronze Age).—69km *Cittiglio* is the terminus of a bus running N through the Valcuvia to Luino.—73km *Laveno*, see below.

Approaches by road. The main road from the Simplon Pass to Milan (Rte 9) touches the lake at Baveno and follows the W bank to Sesto Calende. The upper half of the W bank is followed by a good road from Bellinzona to Baveno via Locarno, while another road follows the E bank from Magadino to Laveno. These two are connected by a car-ferry between Intra and Laveno.

A.   Stresa and the Centre of the Lake

Boat service approximately hourly to Laveno, in c 80 minutes.

Stresa (5100 inhab.) has the most charming position on the lake, on the S shore of the gulf of Pallanza. It has been an elegant holiday place of international renown since the 19C with pleasant villas and luxuriant gardens, and is now also an important conference centre.

Post Office and *Information Office* near Palazzo dei Congressi, Piazzale Europa.—*Boat Services*, see above (frequent services to the Isole Boromee). *Rowing Boats* and *Motor-boats* for hire.—*Cableway* for the Mottarone.—*Buses* to Domodossola, to Milan, to Novara, to Turin, to Locarno.—Coach tours of the lakes in summer.— *Golf Course* (9 holes) at Vezzo.—INTERNATIONAL MUSIC FESTIVAL in late August and September ('Le Settimane Musicali').

By the landing-stage and just N of the 18C church is the *Villa Ducale*, which belonged to Antonio Rosmini (1797–1855), who died there in 1855, and later to the Duchess of Genoa (died 1912), mother of Queen Margherita. It is now a study centre devoted to the philosopher. On the other side of the pier are *Villa Pallavicino* with fine botanical and zoological gardens (open March–October, 9–18), and *Villa Vignola* (no adm.). On the Lungolago with its pleasant gardens, villas, and hotels overlooking the lake is the large Grand Hotel et des Iles Borromees opened in 1863 which has had many famous guests. Frederick Henry in Hemingway's 'Farewell to Arms' also stayed here. Above the town to the SE is the *Collegio Rosmini*, which occupies the buildings of a convent of Rosminians, an order of charity founded by Rosmini. In the adjoining church is his monument, by Vincenzo Vela (1859).—Pleasant walks may be taken among the woods on the hillside to the W between Stresa and Levo.

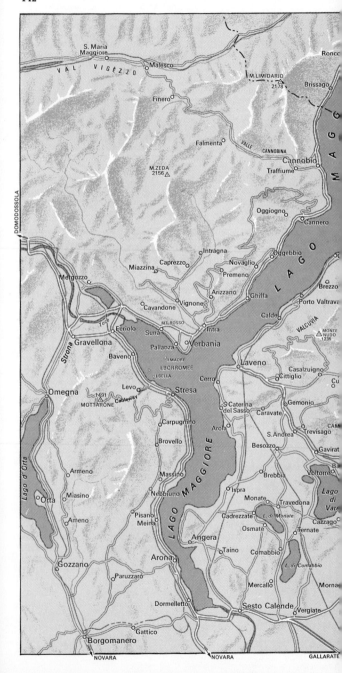

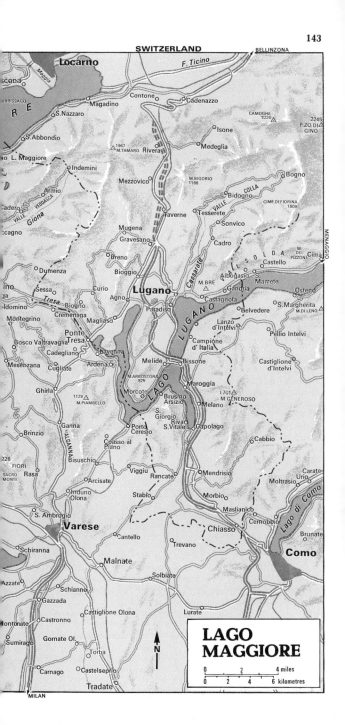

LAGO MAGGIORE

FROM STRESA TO MONTE MOTTARONE. Cableway (which replaces a funicular inaugurated in 1911) from Stresa Lido (in connection with trains on the Milano Nord line to Laveno Monbello and the boat to Stresa). ROAD, 21km (bus as far as Gignese, going on to Alpino in summer only). The road climbs in turns, touching (5km) *Vezzo* (483m) and *Panorama* (view), near the golf course. Just before *Gignese*, which has an Umbrella Museum (open April–September; at other times enquire at the Comune), the road branches right to (10km) *Alpino* (777m) where the Giardino Alpinia (open May–October) has some 2000 species of plants. A toll-road continues through a wood and after a steep climb it joins a road from Orta (see below).—20km *Mottarone* (1379m), an old Lombard ski resort, is 20 minutes from the summit of *Monte Mottarone (1491m). The *View includes the whole chain of the Alps from Monte Viso in the W to the Ortler and Adamello in the E, with the Monte Rosa group especially conspicuous to the NW. Seven lakes are seen close at hand, and in clear weather Milan Cathedral can be distinguished standing out in the Lombard plain.

On leaving Stresa all boats touch at the *Isola Bella* and the *Isola dei Pescatori*, and the majority also at the *Isola Madre* (beyond Baveno; see below).

The *Borromean Islands, so named from the noble Italian family of Borromeo, to which all but the Isola dei Pescatori belong, are four islets at the mouth of the bay of Pallanza, noted for their wealth of vegetation and for the beauty of their surroundings. Stresa is perhaps the best centre for a visit to the group, though the *Isola Madre* lies nearer Pallanza and the *Isola dei Pescatori* nearer Baveno, both of which also have boat trips to the islands. The small *Isola San Giovanni* or *Isolino* (no adm.; see below), lies close to Pallanza. There is a combined ticket for the visit to the Isola Bella and Isola Madre.— ROWING-BOATS from *Stresa*, see above; from *Pallanza*, see below. Circuits of the islands at fixed tariffs.

Nearest to Stresa is the **Isola Bella**, the most famous of the islands. It was a barren rock, with a small church and a few cottages, until, with the architect Angelo Crivelli (died 1630), Count Charles III Borromeo conceived its transformation in honour of his wife Isabella, from whom it takes its name. Renato II and his brother, Vitaliano II (died 1690), brought it to its present appearance by constructing a palace, surrounded with terraced gardens, the soil for which had to be brought from the mainland. Edward Gibbon stayed here in 1764 as a guest of the Borromeo. The palace was only finished in 1958.

The *Garden consists of ten terraces, the lowest built on piles thrown out into the lake, and all decorated with statues, vases, and fountains, in an ornate style, and enhanced by the luxuriance of the rare exotic plants. The view of the lake and its surroundings is famous, as are also the white peacocks.

The *Palace* (adm. March–October, 9–12, 13.30–17.30) is decorated with fine furniture, tapestries, ancient weapons, etc. The paintings include works by Annibale Carracci, Giovanni Battista Tiepolo, and Luca Giordano. The chapel contains family tombs by Giovanni Antonio Amadeo and Bambaia, brought from demolished churches in Milan. In the basement are artificial grottoes and an 18C collection of puppets.

Nearer Baveno lies the **Isola dei Pescatori** or *Isola Superiore*, occupied almost entirely by a pretty little fishing village.

4·8km **BAVENO** (4200 inhab.) is beautifully situated on the S shore of the gulf of Pallanza opposite the Borromean Islands. Quieter than Stresa, it preserves a pleasant little square with a Renaissance baptistery (frescoes) and a church with an early façade and bell-tower. The famous shore-road to Stresa, with a charming view of the Borromean Islands, is flanked by villas, among which is the Castello Branca (formerly Villa Clara), occupied by Queen Victoria in the spring of 1879.

To the NW of Baveno rises *Monte Camoscio* (890m), reached by a road ascending through the village of *Oltrefiume* and climbing the S side of a large granite quarry.—A shady road mounting the hillside S of Baveno leads to *Levo* (see above).

The **Isola Madre**, nearer to Pallanza, is the largest of the Borromean Islands, and, like the Isola Bella, has a splendid *Botanic Garden* (March–October, 9–12, 13.30–17.30) planted with exotic trees of even greater luxuriance; the rhododendrons, the camellias (in April), and the azaleas (in May) are especially striking. The garden is inhabited by peacocks and pheasants. The 16C *Villa* of the Borromeo in the centre is also now open to the public; it has 17C and 18C furnishings. It is surrounded by avenues which provide delightful glimpses of the mainland, especially towards Pallanza in the afternoon.

After leaving the island a few of the boats call at (8·8km) *Suna* (swimming pools).

10·8km **PALLANZA**, charmingly situated in full view of the Borromean Islands, is sun-baked in summer, but delightful in spring and autumn, and enjoys a mild winter climate. The flora of the neighbourhood is luxuriantly beautiful. In 1939 Pallanza and Suna were united with Intra to form the commune of **Verbania** (34,700 inhab.), a name derived, like the Latin name of the lake (Lacus Verbanus), from the vervain (verbena) which grows abundantly on its shores.

Post Office, Piazza Gramsci.—*Information Office* on the lake shore.— **Bus** to *Intra* and to the station of *Verbania-Pallanza*, going on to *Omegna*; also to *Arona*; to *Locarno*; to *Milan*; to *Novara*.—**Tennis Courts and Swimming** on the shore between Pallanza and Suna.—**Boats** for hire.

The pleasant lake-front is planted with magnolias. Near the pier is the mausoleum, by Marcello Piacentini, of Marshal Cadorna (1850–1928), a native of Pallanza; and just inland is the market-place, with the *Municipio* and the church of *San Leonardo* (16C; modernised in the 19C), the tall tower of which was completed by Pellegrino Tibaldi in 1589. In the Baroque Palazzo Dugnani is a small local *Museum* (9–12, 15–18 except Monday). The narrow Via Cavour leading N from the market-place, is continued to (1km) the fine domed church of the *Madonna di Campagna*, which was begun in 1519 and contains contemporary decorations including works attributed to Carlo Urbino, Aurelio Luini, and Gerolamo Lanino.

Intra may be reached by the pleasant lake-side road or (shorter) by the road passing behind the Punta della Castagnola. Between the two roads are the *Villa San Remigio* (now the seat of the administrative offices of the Regional government), with fine gardens and, farther on, the **Villa Taranto**, with remarkable *Botanical Gardens* (open in April–October, 8.30–19.30). They were created in 1931 by Captain Neil McEacharn and donated by him to the Italian State in 1939. They contain exotic plants from all over the world, as well as superb camellias (in April) and azaleas and rhododendrons (in May and June). The villa is now used for official receptions by the Italian Prime Minister. A Roman cippus is built into the wall of the church of *Santo Stefano*, just N of the upper road.

A serpentine road diverging on the left just beyond Madonna di Campagna ascends to (9km from Pallanza) the top of *Monte Rosso* (693m). The road goes on to (13km) *Cavandone*, from where a road returns to Pallanza via Suna.

The boat passes the little *Isola San Giovanni* (with a villa that was once the summer home of Toscanini), then rounds the Punta della Castagnola.—14·5km **Intra**, a busy industrial town, lies between the mouths of the San Giovanni and San Bernardino torrents. To the N, close to the lake, are the beautiful private gardens of the *Villa Poss* and *Villa Ada*. A car-ferry (½-hourly) connects Intra with Laveno.

A road runs to (10km) *Miazzina* (719m), at the foot of *Monte Zeda* (2188m). Another road ascends N from Intra, via (6km) *Arizzano* and (9km) *Bée*, to (13km; 30 minutes) **Premeno** (802m), a popular summer resort (with winter sports facilities also). Above is *Pian di Sole* (949m), with a 9-hole golf course.

As the boat crosses towards Laveno the prominent Rocca di Caldè, backed by Monte Tamaro, comes into view. Behind Intra, with Monte Rosso to the E of it, is Monte Orfano, and the snows of the Mischabelhörner and the Weissmies on the horizon. To the right Monte Mottarone rises above Stresa, with Monte Rosa in the distance on its right hand.

19km **Laveno Mombello**, an important port (8600 inhab.), was strongly fortified by the Austrians in 1849–59. It is noted for its ceramics, and is visited for its good climate. Of its two stations that of the State Railways is c 1km from the lake; the main Nord-Milano station for Varese and Milan adjoins the pier. A monument in the piazza by the waterside commemorates the Garibaldini who fell in an attempt to capture the town in 1859. The *Villa Pullè*, on the site of an Austrian fort, on the Punta di San Michele to the NW, contains a small Garibaldian museum.

The *View from Laveno, which extends as far N as Monte Rosa, the Mischabel group, and the Fletschhorn group, is best from the cableway to Poggio Sant'Elsa, from where it is 30 minutes on foot to the *Sasso del Ferro* (1062m), the beautiful hill to the E. Still wider is the panorama from *Monte Nudo* (1235m).—The road which follows the shore of the lake S passes *Cerro* (with a local ceramics museum) and *Leggiuno* where the Oratory of Santi Primo e Feliciano (9C) has Roman foundations.—5·5km *Santa Caterina del Sasso* (reached by a path in 10 minutes), a convent founded in the 13C, and restored since 1970. It was reinhabited by Dominicans in 1986 and is again open (daily 8.30–12, 14 or 15–17 or 18). It stands in a commanding position above the lake and provides a good view of the gulf of Pallanza and the Borromean Isles.

FROM LAVENTO TO LUINO, by road (16·5km), bus; also railway in 20 minutes.—At (5km) the road skirts a conical hill (380m) crowned by the *Rocca di Caldè*, the 10C castle of the Marquesses of Ivrea, which was destroyed by the Swiss in 1518.—8·5km *Porto Valtravaglia*.—16·5km *Luino*, see below. The road continues via (22km) *Maccagno* (see below) and (30km) *Pino sulla sponda del Lago Maggiore* which boasts the longest Italian place-name. Beyond the frontier (custom-house) it joins at 49km the main road from Locarno to Bellinzona (see 'Blue Guide Switzerland').

B.   Intra to Locarno by road

ROAD, 40km. N34 to the frontier, N21 beyond; bus.

Intra, see above. The road follows the lakeside.—4·5km *Ghiffa*, a scattered village, centres on the fine Castello di Frino. The little 13C church of *Novaglio*, above the road, is a curious mixture of Lombard and Gothic architecture.—Above (8km) *Oggebbio*, another scattered village among chestnut groves, is the little oratory of *Cadessino*, with 15–16C frescoes. Ahead, across the lake, Luino comes into view, as, beneath *Oggiogno* high up on its rock, the road passes the favourite villa of the statesman Massimo d'Azeglio (1798–1866), where he wrote most of his memoirs.

11km **Cannero Riviera**, a holiday resort lying in a sheltered and sunny position at the foot of *Monte Carza* (1118m). Off the coast are two rocky islets (accessible by rowing-boat) on which stood the castles of *Malpaga* or Cannero (12–14C), once the refuge of the five robber brothers Mazzarditi. The existing ruins date partly from a villa built by Ludovico Borromeo after 1414.

On the hill above the town is the church (14–15C) of *Carmine Superiore*, built on the summit of a precipice, and containing some good ceiling-paintings and a triptych of the 14C Lombard school.—Higher up is *Monte Zeda* (2188m).

The road rounds Punta d'Amore opposite Maccagno.—20km *Cannobio*, see below. About 5km farther on is the frontier into Switzerland. The road goes on via (30km) Brissago and (36km) Ascona to (40km) **Locarno** (see 'Blue Guide Switzerland').

C.   Luino to Cannobio (Locarno) by boat

Boats in summer make the journey from Arona via Luino to Locarno; others, including slower boats from the S part of the lake (see above), connect Luino to Cannobio (in 25 minutes).

Luino is the most important tourist centre on the Lombard side of the lake. A small industrial town (15,400 inhab.), it lies a little N of the junction of the Tresa and Margorabbia, which unite to flow into the lake at Germignaga. Near the landing stage is a statue of Garibaldi, commemorating his attempt, on 14 August 1848, to renew the struggle against Austria with only 1500 men, after the armistice which followed the defeat of Custozza. The *Town Hall* occupies an 18C palazzo by Felice Soave. Luino is the probable birthplace of the painter, Bernardino Luini (c 1490). An Adoration of the Magi attributed to him decorates the cemetery church of *San Pietro*, and the *Madonna del Carmine* has frescoes by his pupils (1540).

On the landward side of the town is the railway station (with custom-house), where the Swiss line from Bellinzona meets the Italian line from Novara and Milan.

A road runs via *Cremenaga* and from there along the Italian side of the frontier to (12km) *Ponte Tresa* on Lake Lugano.—From Luino to *Laveno*, and to *Varese*, see above.

About 5km N of Luino *Maccagno Superiore* and *Maccagno Inferiore*, two little holiday resorts, at the narrowest point of the lake, lie on either side of the mouth of the Giona, which waters the Valle Veddasca. Above the second village can be seen (right) the picturesque Santuario della Madonnina, supported by two lofty arches, while higher still is an old watch-tower.—A by-road leads up to (9km) *Lago Delio* (922m; used for hydroelectric power), separated from the main lake by *Monte Borgna* (1158m).

Fifteen minutes to the NW across the lake **Cannobio**, a busy place (5400 inhab.) of considerable antiquity, is the principal station of the 'torpediniere' or anti-smuggling launches. Near the pier is the *Santuario della Pietà* (reconstructed in 1583–1601), with a fine altar-painting by Gaudenzio Ferrari. The *Town Hall*, called Il Parrasio, is a 13C building with 17C alterations.

A road, running inland from Cannobio, ascends the *Val Cannobina* to *Traffiume*, above the *Orrido di Sant'Anna*, a romantic gorge with a waterfall. From there it goes on via *Finero* and over the watershed (945m) to *Malesco* in the Val Vigezzo, where it hits the road and railway from Locarno to Domodossola (Rte 9A).

11 The Lake of Lugano

Approaches. The most interesting approach from the south is the route via Varese and Ponte Tresa or Porto Ceresio (preferably the latter) going on to Porlezza and Menaggio; in this way it is only necessary to set foot on Swiss soil at Lugano to change boats. The road from Ponte Tresa through Lugano to Gandria traverses Swiss territory.

ROAD, 69km. Motorway (A8) direct to (56km) Varese, bearing right from the Sesto Calende branch on the outskirts of Gallarate (37km).—From Varese Via René Vanetti joins the minor road (N344) to (69km) *Porto Ceresio*.

RAILWAY FROM MILAN (*Porta Garibaldi*) to Porto Ceresio via Gallarate, 77km, in 1½–2hrs.
An alternative approach by rail may be made direct FROM MILAN (*Centrale*) TO LUGANO VIA COMO, 77km in 1–1½hrs, part of the main St Gotthard route. *Milan*, see Rte 13; from there via Monza to 46km *Como*, see Rte 12. The railway tunnels beneath Monte Olimpino and enters Switzerland from Lombardy.—51km **Chiasso** (241m), with the Swiss and Italian custom-house is important only as an international station. From here to (77km) **Lugano** the line skirts the lake, crossing it half-way up on a causeway.

From Milan to (37km) *Gallarate*, see the end of Rte 9A.—The Lago di Varese soon comes into view on the left.

56km **VARESE** is a flourishing town of 90,900 inhabitants, with footwear factories. In the pleasant surroundings many Milanese have their summer homes.

Railway Stations. *State Railway*, E of the town, for Milan via Gallarate.—*Nord-Milano*, a few metres farther N, for Laveno and Milan via Saronno.—**Post Office** opposite Nord-Milano station.—**Tourist Office**, Piazza Monte Grappa.— **Buses** from the State station to the *Sacro Monte*; from between the stations to *Gavirate*, etc., on the Lake of Varese; to *Luino* and *Angera*, on Lago Maggiore; to *Porto Ceresio* and *Ponte Tresa*, on the Lake of Lugano; to *Como*, etc.—**Golf Course** (18 holes) at Luvinate, 5km along the Laveno road.—*Indoor Swimming Pool*, SW of Public Gardens.—*Ice Skating* rink (open all year), swimming-pools and tennis courts, near the Bettole Hippodrome.

The principal street extends from Piazza XX Settembre, near the stations, to Piazza Monte Grappa (1927–35). A little to the N an archway (right) leads to the *Basilica of San Vittore*, built in 1580–1615 from the designs of Pellegrino Tibaldi, with a façade of 1795 by Leopold Pollack. It contains large altarpieces by Carlo Francesco Nuvolone, Morazzone, Il Cerano, and Luca Giordano, and highly elaborate woodcarving. The *Baptistery* behind dates from the 12C and contains 14C Lombard frescoes and a 13C font (for adm. apply to the sacristan). The detached campanile (72m) dates from the 17C. From Piazza Monte Grappa Via Marcobi leads to Via Luigi Sacco, in which is the *Palazzo Estense* (now the Municipio) built by Francis III of Modena in 1766–72. The fine *Public Gardens*, formerly the duke's private grounds, have a good distant view of the Alps. Here Villa Mirabello houses the *Musei Civici* (9.30–12, 15–18; closed Monday) with interesting prehistoric finds from Lombardy, a Pinacoteca (Lombard 17–18C school, and detached frescoes from the chapel at Castelseprio), etc.—To the N, on a hill, is the residential district of Biumo Superiore. In the 18C Villa Litta is the Giuseppe Panza collection of 20C art purchased in 1990 by the Guggenheim Museum of New York.

A by-road leads via (4km) *Sant'Ambrogio Olona*, with an interesting church and (5km) *Prima Cappella* to the foot of the pilgrims' ascent to the Sacro Monte. Higher up the road divides. On the right the road winds up high above the valley to (8km) the *Sacro Monte* (880m), a small village huddled on the hill-top round the Rococo pilgrimage church of *Santa Maria del Monte*, rebuilt in 16–17C. Flanking the broad cobbled path leading down to Prima Cappella are a statue of Moses and 14 shrines by Giuseppe Bernascone, with frescoes (Morazzone, Carlo Francesco Nuvolone, etc.) and terracotta groups by Dionigi Bussola representing the Mysteries of the Rosary. In 1983 the 3rd chapel was 'restored' and a fresco of the Flight into Egypt by Renato Guttuso replaced one by Carlo Francesco Nuvolone. There is a small Museum attached to the sanctuary. The *Museo Pogliaghi* (open April–September) is arranged in the villa which belonged to the sculptor Lodovico Pogliaghi (1857–1950). It contains his eclectic collection of works of art, archaeological material, and some of his own sculptures including the model for the bronze doors of the Duomo of Milan.—The longer left branch above Prima Cappella ascends to (9.5km) the *Monte delle Tre Croci* (1033m) which has a wonderful view, and the road deteriorates into a track to cross the *Campo dei Fiori* (1226m; observatory), with an even wider panorama.

Castiglione Olona and Castelseprio are 13km S; see the beginning of Rte 10. The road passes close to the locality of *Bizzozero* (3km), on the outskirts of Varese. Here the Romanesque cemetery church on 7–8C foundations contains interesting frescoes (14–16C) including some by Galdino da Varese (1498) and an 11C frescoed altar.

FROM VARESE TO PONTE TRESA (Lugano), 21km. The road ascends the Valganna, the narrow valley of the Olona, passing the little *Laghetto di Ganna*. From (11km) *Ganna*, a by-road leads to the *Abbey of San Gemolo* founded in 1095, and Benedictine until 1556. There is a 12C church and a small museum. Farther on along the main road is the *Lago di Ghirla* (1·2km long). To the right rises *Monte Piambello* (1129m), a fine view-point for the Lake of Lugano.—At (14km) *Ghirla* the Lugano road keeps to the right, descending sharply to (21km) **Ponte Tresa**, which consists of an Italian village and a Swiss village separated by the river Tresa, which here marks the frontier, entering a little land-locked bay of the lake. *Lavena*, 1·5km E is at the narrow entrance to the lake itself.—On the Swiss side of the Tresa the road continues to (32km) *Lugano* (see 'Blue Guide Switzerland').

FROM VARESE TO LUINO, 29km. This route follows the Lugano road (see above) to (14km) *Ghirla*, then turns left to follow the Margorabbia in its descent of the *Valtravaglia*. Below (19km) *Bosco Valtravaglia* the Valcuvia road from Cittiglio comes in from the left. It reaches the lake at *Germignaga* just SW of (29km) *Luino*.—From Varese to *Laveno*, and to *Milan* via Saronno, see Rte 10.

From Varese this route follows the Ponte Tresa road (see above) and immediately turns right beneath the railway to reach (60km) *Induno Olona*, at the foot of *Monte Monarco* (857m).—Near (62km) *Arcisate*, in 1848, a handful of Garibaldini withstood for four hours an Austrian force of 5000. A road goes off to (right 6km E) *Viggiù*, a small holiday resort.—At (64km) *Bisuschio*, the 16C Villa Cicogna Mozzoni, frescoed by the school of the Campi brothers, is open to the public (15 April–October, 9–12, 14–18). A classical Renaissance garden and fine park surround the villa.—69km **Porto Ceresio** stands on a wide bend in the lake at the foot of *Monte Pravello*. The railway terminates by the lakeside.

The **Lake of Lugano** (270m; *Lago di Lugano* or *Lago Ceresio*) is a very irregularly shaped sheet of water made up of three main reaches and the deep narrow bay of Capolago. Of its area (52 sq. km) rather more than half is politically Swiss; only the NE arm, the SW shore between Ponte Tresa and Porto Ceresio, and the enclave of Campione, nearly opposite Lugano, belong to Italy. The scenery of the shores, except for the bay of Lugano, is far wilder and more desolate than on the greater lakes. There are regular boat services between all the main places on its shore. For a full description of the lake, see 'Blue Guide Switzerland'.

Lugano, the main place on the lake, and the largest town of the Swiss Canton Ticino (see 'Blue Guide Switzerland') is Italian in character. In the Villa Favorita here is the famous collection of *Paintings made by Baron Heinrich Thyssen-Bornemisza (which, however, it was decided in 1988 to transfer to Spain for a period of at least 10 years), and Santa Maria degli Angeli contains frescoes by Bernardino Luini.

In the centre of the lake is the small Italian enclave of **Campione d'Italia**, which uses Swiss money and postal services. It has long been noted for its sculptors and architects; the chapel of St Peter (1327) is a good example of their work. In the parish church are some 15C reliefs and here is kept the key to the cemetery chapel of *Santa Maria dei Ghirli* with frescoes outside (Last Judgement; 1400) and in the interior (14C). The village is visited for its Casinò, with gaming-room and dancing (boats from Lugano).

At the head of the NE arm of the lake, in Italian territory, is **Porlezza**, where the church of San Vittorio contains notable 18C stucco work. A road runs from here to (17·5km) Lugano along the shore past *Castello* at the mouth of the Val Solda, and the picturesque village of *San Mamette*, with a 12C campanile.—In the other direction, N340 leads from Porlezza across the Cuccio and past the lovely Lago del Piano (279m) to Grandola (377m). It then descends to (12·5km) Maneggio on Lake Como (see Rte 12).

12 Como and its Lake

The **LAKE OF COMO** (199m) is Virgil's *Lacus Larius*, from which is derived the alternative name of *Lago Lario*. The lake is formed of three long, narrow arms which meet at Bellagio, one stretching SW to Como, another SE to Lecco, the third N to Colico. Its total length is 50km from Como to Gera, its greatest breadth 4·4km just N of Bellagio, its greatest depth 410m off Argegno, and its area 145 sq. km. The chief feeder is the *Adda*, which flows in at Colico and out at Lecco. The lake is subject to frequent floods (last in 1980 when Como was inundated), and is swept regularly by two winds, the *tivano* (N to S), and the *breva* (S to N) in the afternoon. It was for long a holiday retreat of the English: Wordsworth lived here in 1790, Shelley and Byron visited the lake, and D.H. Lawrence made it his home from 1925–27. Many Milanese now live here. The characteristic *lucie* fishing boats can still be seen, particularly around Lecco.

BOAT AND HYDROFOIL SERVICES. A frequent service of boats and hydrofoils is maintained between Varenna, Menaggio, Bellagio, Tremezzo, Como and Colico. The service from Bellagio to Lecco runs once daily (more frequently on holidays). In the central part of the lake a service runs between Bellano (or Varenna) and Lenno. A car ferry runs frequently between Bellagio and Varenna (in 15 minutes), Bellagio and Cadenabbia (in 10 minutes), and Cadenabbia and Varenna (in 30 minutes). Fewer services in winter. Information from Navigazione Lago di Como, 44 Piazza Volta, Como. Tourist tickets are available.

Approaches by Rail. FROM MILAN TO COMO BY THE MAIN ST-GOTTHARD LINE, 46km in 35–55 minutes. Trains depart from Centrale and (slower trains) from Porta Garibaldi stations.—To (10·5km) *Monza*, see Rte 13.—21km *Seregno* is a furniture-making town on the direct road from Milan to Erba.—34km *Cantù-Cermenate* is 4km W of Cantù. Beyond Como the Express trains go on to the frontier at (51km) *Chiasso*, for Lugano and the north.—FROM MILAN TO COMO VIA SARONNO, 46km. Nord-Milano railway in ¾–1¼hrs to *Como-Lago*.—FROM MILAN TO LECCO AND COLICO, 90km, see Rte 14.—FROM MILAN TO CANZO-ASSO, 52km, Nord-Milano railway in 60–80 minutes.—22km *Seveso* became notorious in 1976 as the centre of one of the worst incidents of industrial pollution. After a chemical leakage from a Swiss factory (Hoffman La Roche) contaminated a large area, the district had to be evacuated. After legal proceedings against those responsible, and the payment of compensation to the victims, the plant was finally demolished in 1985.—In the wood of *Barlassina*, to the right, St Peter Martyr was murdered in 1252. In the fertile *Brianza*, a region with many imposing country houses is (35km) *Inverigo*, with a fine villa (La Rotonda) built by Luigi Cagnola (1813–33), now a children's home.—*Cassago Brianza*, about 5km, is thought to be the place where St Augustine stayed in 387.—44km *Erba* on the Como-Lecco road, is a scattered community with an open-air theatre (1926). In the Villa Comunale at *Crevenna* an Archaeological Museum is open on Saturday & Sunday, 14–16, and on Thursday 10–12. The *Buco del Piombo*, a limestone cavern, lies 1½hrs uphill to the NW. It is open and illuminated on request at the Comune di Erba.

    Approaches by Road. FROM MILAN there is a MOTORWAY (A9) direct to (49km) *Como*, bearing right from the Lago Maggiore motorway at 19km; the old main road (N35), 43·5km, runs via Seveso, leaving Milan by the Via Carlo Farini and the suburb of Affori. At *Bregnano*, 3km W of the road, there is a museum of bee-keeping (open on the last Sunday of the month, 9–12).

COMO (213m), beautifully situated at the SW extremity of the Lake of Como, is a manufacturing town (97,900 inhab.), the capital of the province which bears its name, and the seat of a bishop. Conspicuous to the N is Monte Bisbino, while to the S rises the tower of Baradello. The industry is the weaving of silk, long a domestic occupation, but nowadays mainly concentrated in large factories. The centre, nevertheless, preserves to a marked degree its Roman street plan.

Railway Stations. *San Giovanni* for State Railway trains to Milan, Lecco, and to Lugano and the rest of Switzerland. *Como-Lago* (on the lakeside; the most convenient station for visitors) and *Como-Borghi* for Nord-Milano trains to Milan via Saronno.—**Hotels**, near the water front.—**Parking**. The centre of the town is closed to traffic. Parking in Piazza Volta, around the walls, and on the lakeside.—-**Post Office**, Via Gallio. **Tourist Office**, 17 Piazza Cavour; *Information Office*, Stazione Centrale (San Giovanni).—**Buses and trolleybuses** from Piazza Matteotti for towns on the lake; and for *Bergamo*.—Country buses from Piazza Cavour to *Cernobbio*; *Ponte Chiasso* (via Maslianico); *Cantù*; *Erba*; *Lanzo d'Intelvi* via Argegno; *Bellagio* via Nesso; *Colico* via Menaggio; *Porlezza*; *Lecco*; etc.—**Boat and hydrofoil services** on the lake, see above. *Rowing-Boats* and *Motor-Boats* for hire at Piazza Cavour.—**Swimming** in summer at Villa Geno, on the E shore, beyond the funicular station; and at Villa Olmo, on the W shore.—*Golf Course* (18 holes) at Montofrano, 4km SE (Villa d'Este).—*Tennis* at Villa Olmo, Muggio, and Lipomo.

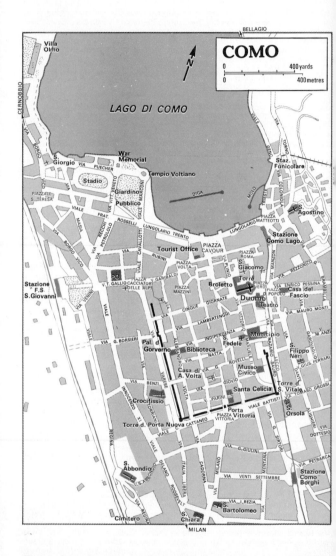

History. Originally a town of the Insubrian Gauls, Como was captured and colonised by the Romans in the 2C BC. The town was a republic in the 11C, but in 1127 it was destroyed by the Milanese. Frederick Barbarossa, however, rebuilt it in 1155, and it secured its future independence by the Peace of Constance (1183). In the struggles between the Torriani and the Visconti Como fell to the latter in 1335, and became a fief of Milan. From on it followed the vicissitudes of the Lombard capital. In March 1848 a popular rising compelled the surrender of the Austrian garrison, and the city was finally liberated by Garibaldi on 27 May 1859. Among the most famous natives ('Comaschi') are the

Elder and the Younger Pliny (AD 23–79 and AD 62–120), uncle and nephew. The Younger Pliny often mentions Como and its surroundings in his *Letters*, and he endowed a library and school here. Paulus Jovius (1483–1552), the historian, and Alessandro Volta (1745–1827), the physicist, were also born here. Walter Savage Landor lived in Como in 1815–18, where he was unjustly suspected of spying on Queen Caroline who was staying at Cernobbio (see below).

The centre of the life of Como is PIAZZA CAVOUR, a pleasant square with cafés and hotels, open to the lake and adjoining the quay. In the delightful Giardini Pubblici, overlooking the lake, are the *Tempio Voltiano* (open 10–12, 14 or 15–16 or 18), erected as a memorial to Volta in 1927, a neo-classical rotonda containing his scientific instruments, charmingly displayed in old-fashioned show cases. The *War Memorial* was designed by Antonio Sant'Elia, a native of Como, himself killed in 1916.

A pleasant path continues round the shore to *Villa Olmo*, built for the Odescalchi by Simone Cantoni (1782–95; altered in 1883) and set in a formal park; it is used as a congress hall, and for exhibitions and concerts. It also houses an exhibition relating to the work of the architect Antonio Sant'Elia.—In the other direction a drive leads along the shore to *Villa Geno*, with another park.

The short Via Plinio leads away from the lake to Piazza del Duomo, in which are the cathedral (see below), the *Broletto* (1215; the old town hall), built in alternate courses of black and white marble, with a few red patches, and the *Torre del Commune* of the same period, used as a campanile since the addition of the top storey in 1435 (partly rebuilt in 1927).

The **Cathedral* (*Santa Maria Maggiore*), built entirely of marble, dates mainly from the late 14C, when it replaced an 11C basilica. The union of the Renaissance with Gothic architecture has here produced a remarkably homogeneous style.

The rebuilding, financed mainly by public subscription, was entrusted first to *Lorenzo degli Spazzi*, who, like his many successors, worked under the patronage of the Milanese court. The West Front (1460–90; recently restored), designed by *Fiorino da Bontá*, and executed by *Luchino Scarabota* of Milan, is in a Gothic style, with a fine rose window, though the three doorways are unexpectedly round-arched. It is decorated with reliefs and statues (c 1500) by *Tommaso* and *Jacopo Rodari* of Maroggia, and others. The delightful seated figures of the two Plinys on either side of the main doorway are probably by *Amuzio da Lurago*. The two lateral doorways, also decorated by the *Rodari*, are wonderful examples of detailed carving. The work of rebuilding continued through the 16C (choir) and 17C (transepts), and ended with completion of the dome in 1770 by *Filippo Juvarra*.

Interior. The cathedral is 87m long, 58m wide across the transepts, and 75m high under the dome.—The aisled NAVE of five bays is covered with a groined vault and hung with 16C tapestries. On the W wall is a relief of the Madonna (1317) from the old cathedral. Two lions at the W end, now supporting stoups, are also survivals from the ancient basilica. A graceful little rotunda (16C) serves as baptistery. In the SOUTH AISLE are figures of saints and six reliefs of the Passion by *Tommaso Rodari* (1492). Beyond the S door (also well carved) is the tomb of Bishop Bonifacio da Modena (1347). The Altar of Sant'Abbondio, finely decorated with gilded woodcarving (early 16C), is flanked by a **Flight into Egypt* by *Gaudenzio Ferrari*, and an **Adoration of the Magi* by *Bernardino Luini*. Farther on is a **Virgin and Child with four saints*, with a celebrated angel-musician in front, also by *Luini*. Between the nave and aisle hangs a painted and embroidered standard of the Confraternity of Sant'Abbondio (1608–10). NORTH

The Broletto and the Cathedral, Como

AISLE. 4th Altar, Deposition, finely carved by *Tommaso Rodari* (1498); hanging in the nave, standard of Giovanni Malacrida (1499). 3rd Altar. *Gaudenzio Ferrari*, *Marriage of the Virgin; *Luini*, Nativity. Just before the N door is the sarcophagus of Giovanni degli Avogadri (died 1293). At the second altar, between busts of Innocent XI and Bishop Rovelli, is a carving of the Madonna between St Louis and St Stephen, by *Tommaso Rodari*.

In Piazza Grimoldi, to the N, are the *Bishop's Palace* and *San Giacomo*. The church has Romanesque elements (columns, brickwork in aisles, apse and dome).—South-east of the cathedral are the *Teatro Sociale* built in 1811 by Giuseppe Cusi with a neo-classical façade, and the *Casa del Fascio* built in 1932–36, by Giuseppe Terragni.

Via Vittorio Emanuele leads S from the cathedral to the 17C *Municipio*; opposite is the five-sided apse of the church of *San Fedele* (12C), which at one time served as cathedral. The angular NE doorway, with remarkable bas-reliefs, shows Byzantine influences. The interior, and the pretty Piazza to the W should not be missed. Farther along the street on the left two good palazzi serve as *Museo Civico* (adm. 9–12, 15–17 except Monday; Sunday 9–12). The collection includes: Neolithic finds; a reconstructed ceremonial carriage of the Iron Age; recent archaeological finds from Mandana; Assyrian and Egyptian antiquities; Roman urns and sarcophagi; Medieval fragments from churches (and casts of the statues of the two Plinys from the Cathedral); and material relating to the Risorgimento and the two World Wars; and a local ethnographic collection. There is a pretty garden.

The second turning on the left off Via Giovio leads to the church of *Santa Cecilia*, the front of which incorporates some Roman columns. Next door was the Liceo where Volta once taught. A fragment of the Roman wall may be seen in the courtyard of the school here. The *Porta Vittoria* is surmounted by a many-windowed tower of 1192.

Two other old towers remain on this section of the wall; that on the E (right) is the *Torre di San Vitale*, that on the SW the *Torre di Porta Nuova*. The Porta Vittoria is named in memory of the surrender of the Austrian garrison (1848), in the barracks immediately opposite. The *Garibaldi Monument*, by Vincenzo Vela, in Piazza Vittoria, was erected in 1889.

Outside the gate, beyond an unattractive traffic-ridden area (see Plan) is the Basilica of **Sant'Abbondio**, isolated amidst industrial buildings near the railway. An 11C building, it has two graceful campanili and a finely decorated apse, well restored. It is dedicated to St Abondius, bishop of Como.

The oldest church on this site was probably founded by St Felix in the 4C and received its present name on the death of Abondius in 469. The existing building consists of five aisles, despite its comparatively small size. In the apse are frescoes of the mid-14C by Lombard artists. The organ is also decorated with frescoes of this period by local artists.

Viale Varese (with the *Crocefisso*, a 16C sanctuary), or Via Alessandro Volta, in which is the house where the scientist lived and died (tablet) lead back towards the lake.

From Viale Geno a funicular railway ascends to (7 minutes) **Brunate** (713m), 5km from Como by road (also reached by path from Via Grossi). The village has a fine view of Como and its lake. Above Brunate a road continues to (½hr) *San Maurizio* (871m).

About 3km S of Como (buses) is *Camerlata*, a suburb dominated by the 11–12C church of *San Carpoforo*, which may occupy the site of a 4C foundation of St Felix. In the sacristy is preserved St Felix's crozier, and a chapel in the crypt may locate his burial place. The *Monte Baradello* (432m), above the church, is crowned by the conspicuous tower of **Castello Baradello** (adm. Monday, Thursday, & fest. 9–12, 14–18), the solitary remnant of a stronghold reconstructed by Barbarossa c 1158 and destroyed by Charles V's Spaniards in 1527. In 1277 Napo Torriani and other members of his family were exposed here in cages after their defeat by the Visconti. From here there is a fine view of the lake. The road goes on to (10·5km) **Cantù**, a pleasant town (32,400 inhab.) with lace and furniture industries. The *Parish Church* has a remarkably slender Romanesque campanile, and *San Teodoro* has a fine apse in the same style. At *Galliano*, 1km E, are the 10–11C basilica and baptistery of San Vincenzo. The church has a **Fresco cycle* of 1007. Cantù has a station on the Lecco railway, but is 4km from Cantù-Cermenate station on the main line to Milan.

FROM COMO TO CERNOBBIO AND MASLIANICO, 8km, trolley-bus every 15 minutes.—The line passes the Villa Olmo and at (4km) *Cernobbio* (see below) the route turns inland to ascend the valley of the Breggia to *Maslianico*. A short walk S along the frontier leads to *Ponte Chiasso*, from where trolley-buses return to Como every 10 minutes.

FROM COMO TO LECCO, 30km by road (bus). An alternative prettier (but longer) road skirts the lakeside (N583; 53km). The State Railway, 42km, takes a more devious southerly route through Cantù, Oggiono, and Civate.—Via Dottesio leaves Como and traverses the Brianza, passing just N of Montorfano.—13km **Erba**, see the beginning of this Rte. On the right (15km) is the *Lago di Pusiano* with its poplar-grown islet. *Bosisio*, on its E shore, was the birthplace of Giuseppe Parini (1729–99), the poet.—Farther on (20km) is the smaller Lago d'Annone. A road on the right leads to Annone (2·5km) where the church has a magnificent carved-wood altarpiece of the 16C (removed), and to *Oggiono* (5km), which has a polyptych by Marco d'Oggiono, Leonardo's pupil, in its church, and a Romanesque Baptistery.—25km *Civate*. In the hills to the N is (1hr; steep climb) **San Pietro al Monte**, where the *Santuario* (keys at Civate church) consists of the partly ruined church of *San Pietro* and the triapsidal oratory of *San Benedetto*, both of the 10C. The former, with lateral apses, has 11–12C mural paintings and a remarkable baldacchino above the main altar. At *Garlate*, 8km SE the old Abegg factory contains a silk museum.—30km *Lecco*, see the end of this Rte.

FROM COMO TO COLICO (88·5km), by the lake, boat once or twice daily on holidays in 3–4hrs; to *Bellagio*, (46km), 6 times daily in 1½–2hrs; to *Menaggio*, (50·25km), 6 times daily in 2–2½hrs (frequent service between Como and Carate, and between Tremezzo, Bellagio, and Varenna). The hydrofoil provides a much quicker service (with fewer stops) but is not recommended to the visitor who has time to enjoy the fine scenery. It traverses the Lake from Como to Colico c 4 times daily in 1¼hrs; to Bellagio frequent service in 35 minutes; to Menaggio frequent service in 40 minutes.

The boat keeps at first to the E bank, rounding the Punta di Geno.—3·25km (W) **Cernobbio**, part holiday-resort, part lakeside village (8000 inhab.), lies at the foot of *Monte Bisbino* (1325m). The Hotel Villa d'Este (well seen from the lake as the boat leaves the dock) occupies a villa built in 1568 by the beneficent Cardinal Tolomeo Gallio (1527–1607), a native of Cernobbio. In 1816–17 it was the home of the future Queen Caroline of England.—On the opposite bank is the scattered village of *Blevio*, with a villa that belonged to Paul Taglioni (1804–84), brother of Maria, both of them famous ballet dancers. At *Perlasca*, the northernmost hamlet of this village, was born Benedetto Odescalchi (1611–89), afterwards Innocent XI.— 6·5km (W) **Moltrasio**, with a 'lido', has a Romanesque church. Here at the Villa Salterio in 1831 Bellini composed the opera 'Norma'.—7·5km (E) *Torno* is a medieval village with two old churches. In the bay to the E is the *Villa Pliniana* (1570), reached only by a footpath or by water. In the garden is the famous intermittent spring described in detail by the Younger Pliny in his Letters, and also studied by Leonardo da Vinci. The abundant flow of water is channelled from a grotto down the cliff into the lake. Ugo Foscolo, Percy Bysshe Shelley, Stendhal, and Rossini (who here composed 'Tancredi' in 1813) were amongst the illustrious visitors to the villa in the 19C. The 18C *Villa Passalacqua* (Thursday 9–12, 15–18) was built by Felice Soave and has an Italianate garden. Bellini composed 'La Sonnambula' here.—Almost continuous with Moltrasio are the villages of (8·8km) *Urio*, with a tall Lombard campanile, and (9·25km) *Carate*, with attractive villas and gardens.

On the opposite bank, above *Riva*, with the pier of (11·75km) *Faggeto Lario*, stand the villages of *Molina*, *Lemma*, and *Palanzo*, high up on the slopes of *Monte Palanzone* (1436m), and farther on are (12·8km) *Pognana* and *Quarzano*. On the W bank, at the narrowest reach of the lake, is (15·25km) *Torriggia-Laglio*. Opposite lies the three-cornered village of (16km) *Careno*, with another tall campanile,

A grotto in the gardens of the Villa d'Este at Cernobbio

and farther on is (18km) *Nesso*, at the mouth of the Orrido, a deep ravine with a waterfall.—20km (W) *Brienno* lies among chestnut groves.—24km (W) **Argegno**, where the high mountain ranges NE of the lake come into view. It lies at the foot of the fertile Val d'Intelvi.

A road runs from Argegno to Lanzo d'Intelvi above Lake Lugano. Beyond (6km) *Castiglione d'Intelvi* and (9km) *San Fedele* a scenic road branches right climbing through *Laino* and *Ponna* before descending to Porlezza on Lake Lugano.—The Lanzo d'Intelvi road continues to (11km) *Pellio*, beyond which *Scaria* has a Museo Diocesano with works by Ercole Ferrata and other local sculptors.—15km **Lanzo d'Intelvi** (907m), a summer resort, and walking centre.

The road goes on to (17km) *Belvedere di Lanzo* (919m), overlooking the Lake of Lugano.

Beyond *Colonno* is (29km; W) *Sala Comacina*, with a good Gothic campanile partly concealed by *Isola Comacina*, used as a hiding place by political refugees during the disturbed medieval history of Lombardy. The island was captured and raided by the men of Como in 1169, but the ruins of some of its nine churches still survive (San Giovanni has an early medieval floor mosaic). In 1917 it passed by inheritance to Albert, King of the Belgians, but was later handed over to the Accademia delle Belle Arti of Milan. It can be visited by ferry from Sala Comacina.—33km (E) *Lezzeno* is near the Grotta dei Bulberi, artificially darkened to resemble the Blue Grotto at Capri (accessible by boat).—36·5km *Ossuccio*, where a Romanesque tower supports an elaborate Gothic belfry, lies between Comacina and the *Punta di Balbianello*, a headland on which stands the *Villa Arconati* (late 16C but enlarged in 1790), once the home of Silvio Pellico (1788–1854), author of 'Le Mie Prigioni'. It was left to the F.A.I. in 1989 and is to be restored and opened to the public. The garden is open from Easter to mid-October on Tuesday, 10–12, 16–18. It can only be visited by water (a 'lucia' can be hired at the harbour of Sala Comacina). The views extend to Bellagio and Argegno.

38·5km (W) **Lenno** lies at the mouth of the Acquafredda, at the S end of the Tremezzina. The parish church has an 11–12C crypt and an 11C octagonal baptistery adjoining. Here on the shore was the site of Pliny's villa 'Comedia', so-called from its lowly position as compared with the 'Tragedia' at Bellagio. Near here, in the locality of *Giulino*, Mussolini was shot by partisans in 1945.—Beyond Lenno the boat coasts the attractive *Tremezzina*, the fertile green shore dotted with villas and gardens, which extends along the foot of Monte di Tremezzo as far as La Maiolica, N of Cadenabbia.—40km *Azzano*.

41km **Tremezzo** and (41·5km) **Cadenabbia**, now almost continuous, are two very popular holiday resorts, consisting almost entirely of hotels and villas. Cadenabbia lies in a sheltered position beneath the Sasso di San Marino (851m).

English Church (*The Ascension*) at Cadenabbia; services in the season.— **Tennis Courts** and **Lido** at Cadenabbia.—**Car Ferry**, in summer, as required, from Cadenabbia to *Bellagio* (10 minutes) and to *Varenna* (15 minutes).

On the shady road between Tremezzo and Cadenabbia is the *Villa Carlotta* (open April–September, 9–18; March–October, 9.30–12.30, 14–16.30), built in 1747 by the Marchese Giorgio Clerici and surrounded by a magnificent park laid out in 1850 by Princess Carlotta, noted for camellias, rhododendrons, and azaleas in Spring.

The collection of sculpture inside includes Thorvaldsen's frieze of the Triumphal Entry of Alexander into Babylon, cast in plaster for Napoleon in 1811–12 and intended for the throne-room at the Quirinal. After the Emperor's downfall the work was continued at the expense of Count Sommariva, who is represented, along with the artist, at the end of the frieze. The opening scenes of 'La Chartreuse de Parme' (1839) recall Stendhal's stay here as Sommariva's guest in 1818. Among works by Canova are Cupid and Psyche (a copy), the Repentant Magdalen, Palamedes, and other sculptures.—Near the water's edge is a little memorial chapel with a Pietà by Benedetto Cacciatori.

At the *Villa Margherita*, on the shore just N of Cadenabbia, staying with his publisher Ricordi, Verdi composed Act II of 'La Traviata' in 1853.

Leaving Cadenabbia the boat crosses the 'Centro Lago', the most beautiful part of the lake, to (43·5km; E) *San Giovanni di Bellagio*, where the church contains an altarpiece by Gaudenzio Ferrari. To the N is *Loppia*, with a half-ruined church romantically placed beside a great grove of cypresses.

45·8km (E) **BELLAGIO** (3400 inhab.), in a lovely position on a headland at the division of the lake, is also a very popular, though quieter, resort; and at the same time retains much of the picturesque aspect of an old Lombard town. There are local industries of silk-weaving and olive-wood carving.

Post Office, 10 Piazza Manzoni.—**Buses** to *Como, Lecco* and *Asso*.—**Car Ferry** to *Cadenabbia* or *Varenna* (10 minutes).

In the upper part of the town stands the church of *San Giacomo*, at the top of Via Garibaldi, to the left of the pier. It has a 12C apse and capitals, and a Deposition by the school of Perugino. The symbols of the Evangelists, on the reconstructed pulpit, were discovered during a restoration in 1907. Behind San Giacomo is the entrance gate of *Villa Serbelloni* standing in a fine park (open in summer except Monday, at 11 and 16 with guided tours of c 1½hrs). It is reputed to occupy the site of the younger Pliny's villa 'Tragedia', so-called by its owner in contrast with the low-lying 'Comedia' at Lenno, being raised above the lake as if on a cothurnus, the high buskin worn by tragic actors. It is now a study centre run by the Rockefeller Foundation of New York. At *Casa Lillia* in 1837 was born Cosima, daughter of the composer and pianist Franz Liszt.—On the road to Loppia is the *Villa Melzi-d'Eryl* (adm. 9–12.30, 14.30–18.30; June–October, 9–18.30) standing in a fine park with an interesting garden. The villa, chapel, and greenhouse were built in 1800–10 by Giocondo Albertolli; the latter contains Egyptian, Greek, Roman and neo-classical sculpture. In front of the Villa are 16C statues of Meleager and Apollo by Guglielmo della Porta.

Farther on are the *Villa Balzaretti*, with a mausoleum of the Gonzagas, and the fine gardens of the *Villa Trotti*, while on the crest of the ridge is the *Villa Giulia*, where Leopold I, king of the Belgians often stayed. At present, however, visitors are not admitted to any of these lovely gardens.

FROM BELLAGIO TO ASSO VIA CIVENNA, 19km; bus in 1¼hrs.—The road ascends S, passing the cemetery and (left) the Villa Giulia. At (6km) *Guello* a road on the right ascends in 8km to the *Parco Monte San Primo*, beneath *Monte San Primo* (1686m).—8·5km *Civenna*. At the edge of the town by the cemetery is a small park with spectacular views of the lake from Gravedona (N) to Lecco (S). The road continues with a fine panorama of the lake.—From (10·5km) the small church of *Madonna del Ghisallo* (754m; with votive offerings from champion cyclists), the highest point of the road, is a *View of the Lake of Lecco (left) with the two Grigne beyond, and of Bellagio behind.—11km *Magreglio* is also beneath Monte San Primo. The road descends the steep Valassina to (19km) *Asso* with remains of a medieval castle. Here the graceful 17C church of San Giovanni Battista has an elaborate gilded wood Baroque altar and an Annunciation by Giulio Cesare Campi. Almost continuous with Asso is *Canzo*, the most important place in the valley.—Another road, with magnificent views, goes along the W bank of the Lake of Lecco, via Limonta, Vassena, and Onno, and ascends the Valbrona to *Asso* (see above).

From Bellagio to *Lecco* by boat, see below.

50·5km **Menaggio** is a cheerful little town (3300 inhab.) on the W shore, a popular resort, with a golf course (18 holes) at Grandola, 3·5km along the Porlezza road. It has two piers; the principal one is near the Grand Hotel; the other, to the N, is seldom used.

Beyond the Sangra river is *Loveno* (317m), near the church of which is the *Villa Vigoni* (now owned by the German State; adm. on application), with a garden pavilion containing sculptures by Thorvaldsen. The *Villa Calabi* was the home of Massimo d'Azeglio (1798–1865), patriot and writer. A by-road goes on to *Plesio* (600m) and *Madonna di Breglia* (785m), above which is the *Belvedere di San Domenico* (820m).—There are several fine walks in the area beneath *Monte **Bregagno (2107m).**

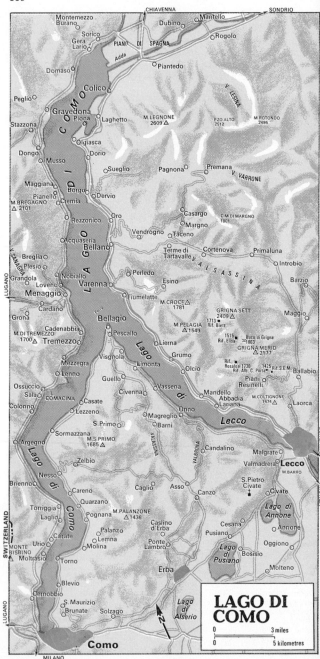

LAGO DI COMO

Pleasant drives may be taken along the shore from Menaggio to *Acquaseria* via *Nobiallo*, with its leaning tower, and the tunnels in the *Sasso Rancio*, the 'orange rock' coloured by a ferruginous spring, or along the Tremezzina to *Cadenabbia*.

From Menaggio to *Porlezza* and *Lugano*, see Rte 11.

Opposite Menaggio is (54km) **Varenna**, picturesquely situated at the mouth of the Esino, which descends from Monte Grigna. An attractive lakeside footpath leads from the ferry landing-stage along the harbour of the village and up to the upper town. In the main square is the 14C church of *San Giorgio* with remains of 15C frescoes and a polyptych by Giovanni Pietro de Brentanis (1467). The *Villa Cipressi* has attractive views across to Menaggio and Griante. The *Villa Monaster*, on the site of a monastery founded in 1208, is now a centre for scientific conventions. The grounds extend along the lower slopes of Monte Foppe and skirt the lake. Both villas have magnificent gardens (open daily, May–September, 10–12, 15–18). An Ornithological Museum, also in the upper town, is open on Thursday (15–17). The neighbouring quarries yield black marble and green lumachella or shell-marble. Above Varenna to the S is the old castle of *Vezio*, said to have been founded by Queen Theodolinda, which has a splendid *View. Car-ferry to Bellagio and Cadenabbia.

From Varenna a road follows the right bank of the Esino via *Perledo* (409m), with the medieval Vezio castle to (12·5km) *Esino* (907m), with the Museo della Grigna (apply at Comune for the key). The road ends at *Cainallo* (1245m) beneath **Monte Grigna Settentrionale** (2410m), a dolomitic peak.

58·5km (E) **Bellano**, a town (3700 inhab.) with silk and cotton mills, lies at the mouth of the Pioverna, which, in its lower course, runs through a deep gorge (visible from stairs and walkways, Easter– September 9.30–12.30, 13.30–17.30 except Wednesday). The restored church of *Santi Nazaro e Celso* is a good example of the 14C Lombard style. Tommaso Grossi (1790–1853) the poet, born here, is commemorated by a monument on the shore.

From Bellano a road runs to (20km) *Premana* (with a local ethnographical museum), via (8·5km) *Taceno*, which adjoins the small spa of *Tartavalle*.—From Taceno a secondary road diverges for (26km) Lecco. It traverses the VALSASSINA, the valley of the Pioverna, which has skiing facilities (chairlift from Margno to 1456m). Its principal village, *Introbio* (18km from Bellano) has cheese-factories. **Barzio**, see below.

62·5km (W) *Acquaseria* lies at the foot of the Cima la Grona, while to the S rises the Sasso Rancio. Farther N on the same side is (64·5km) *Rezzonico*, with a castle, the home of the powerful family which bore its name and numbered Clement XIII among its famous members.— 66·5km (E) *Dervio*, with a ruined castle and an old campanile, at the foot of *Monte Legnone* (2601m).—69km (W) *Cremia*. Beside the pier is the old church of *San Vito*, with a fine Madonna and Angels attributed to Bergognone.—70·8km *Pianello del Lario* has a 12C church, and marble quarries. At *Calozzo*, on the lake, is a museum of boats (adm. Easter–November; guided tours 14.30–17.30) with an interesting collection of boats used on the lake. 72km (W) *Musso* is overlooked by the almost impregnable *Rocca di Musso*, the stronghold in 1525–32 of the piratical Gian Giacomo Medici, surnamed 'Il Medeghino', who levied tribute from the traders of the lake and the neighbouring valleys.—On the same (W) bank is (73·2km) *Dongo*, which, with Gravedona and Sorico, formed the independent *Republic of the Three*

Parishes (Tre Pievi), that survived until the Spanish occupation of Lombardy. Mussolini was captured by partisans at Dongo in the spring of 1945 and was executed at Giulino di Mezzegra above Azzano (see above). The 12C church of Santa Maria in the adjacent hamlet of *Martinico* preserves an interesting doorway.

78km (W) **Gravedona** is the principal village (2700 inhab.) of the upper lake. The great square *Palazzo Gallio* or *del Pero* (adm. on request), with its four corner towers, was built c 1586 by Pellegrino Tibaldi for Cardinal Tolomeo Gallio. To the S is the church of *San Vincenzo*, with a very ancient crypt. Nearby is the little 12C church of *Santa Maria del Tiglio*, with one eastern and two transverse apses. The W tower, square in its lower storeys, becomes octagonal higher up.—80·5km (W) *Domaso*, at the mouth of the Livo, is overlooked by the chapel of Madonna di Livo. At the extreme N end of the lake where the Mera flows in, are the villages of *Gera* and *Sorico*.—84·5km (E) *Piona* is the mouth of the land-locked bay called the *Laghetto di Piona*. The key of the little 12C cloister here is kept by the priest of *Olgiasca*, 1·6km SW.—88·5km (E) **Colico** stands in a plain near the mouth of the Adda and is important mainly as the meeting-place of the routes over the Splügen and Stelvio passes.

From Colico to *Lecco*, and to *Chiavenna* and *Tirano*, see Rte 14.

FROM BELLAGIO TO LECCO BY BOAT, 23km in 80 minutes (once daily, twice on Saturday, three times on Sunday). Leaving Bellagio the boat crosses to the E bank; on the left is the waterfall of Fiumelatte. It enters the lesser (SE) branch of the Lake of Como, usually called the *Lago di Lecco*.—4km (E) *Lierna* lies at the foot of *Monte Palagia* (1549m). Opposite, on the peaceful W bank, is (6·5km) *Limonta*, to the S of which is (10km) *Vassena*. On the same bank is (12km) *Onno*, connected by road through the Valbrona with Asso (see above).—14km (E) **Mandello del Lario**, on the projecting delta of the Meria.

16·5km (E) *Abbadia Lariana* lies at the foot of the Grigna Meridionale (2184m). The W bank of the lake, opposite, is uninhabited; at the foot of the steep *Monte Moregallo* (1276m) are a few limekilns. On the approach to Lecco, *Monte Coltignone* (1474m) rises on the left. On the right is *Malgrate*, beyond the mouth of the Ritorto, which drains the Lago d'Annone.

23km **Lecco** is a manufacturing town (53,200 inhab.) standing at the SE end of the Lake of Como, at the outflow of the Adda. The *Ponte Azzone Visconti*, which spans the Adda, was built in 1336–38, but has lost most of its original character owing to subsequent enlargement. A monument by Francesco Confalonieri commemorates Alessandro Manzoni (1785–1873), the novelist, the scene of whose famous novel 'I Promessi Sposi' is laid partly around Lecco and Monte Resegone. *Villa Manzoni* ('Il Caleotto') in Via Amendola, built in 1710, where Manzoni lived as a boy, contains a small museum of memorabilia on the ground floor, and the Galleria Comunale d'Arte on the first floor (adm. 10–12.30, 14.30–17.30; Saturday & fest. 9–13; closed Monday). In the 18C *Palazzo Belgioioso* (32 Corso Matteotti) is a natural history and archaeological museum (adm. as above), and in the *Torre Viscontea* (Piazza XX Settembre) a museum of the Risorgimento (adm. as above).

To the S of the town the Adda expands to form successively the *Lago di Garlate* and the smaller *Laghetto di Olginate*. On the W is the detached *Monte Barro* (922m), a fine view-point. From the end of the road to Malnago a cableway leads part way up the saw-shaped *Monte Resegone* (1875m) which dominates Lecco from the E. *Ballabio*, 8km N of Lecco on the Valsassina road is a rock-climbing centre. A road leads from here to the little climbing and skiing resort of *Piani Resinelli* (1257m). Here is the wooded Parco Valentino overlooking the lake. Beyond Ballabio the road crosses (11km) the *Colle di Balisio* (722m) to enter the Valsassina.—17·5km *Introbio*, see above.

At the pass the road on the right leads to the holiday resorts of (12km) *Maggio* (770m) and (5km) **Barzio** (768m). From Barzio a chair-lift mounts to *Piani di Bobbio* (1676–1768m), a skiing centre; and from *Cremeno* between Moggio and Barzio, a road leads up to *Moggio* (890m), with a chair lift to the *Rifugio Castelli* (1649m), another popular winter-sports centre.

13 Milan

MILAN, in Italian *Milano*, the famous capital of Lombardy, is the second largest town in Italy (1,580,000 inhab.) and is the principal commercial and industrial centre of the country. It has the appearance and characteristics of a busy modern city with a N skyline punctuated by skyscrapers (*grattacieli*). At the same time it is a place of great historical and artistic interest, with magnificent art collections, a famous cathedral, and many ancient churches. Trams are still a feature of the city, and Milan is a good place to study 19C and 20C Italian architecture.

Information Offices. *Official Tourist Office (A.P.T.),* 1 Via Marconi (Piazza Duomo; Pl. II,11), with an information office at the Central Station. These offices distribute an excellent handbook ('Tutta Milano'), available in English, giving detailed information on the city, as well as a handsheet of Museums giving up-to-date opening times, an annual list of Hotels, etc.

Main Railway Stations. *Centrale* (Pl. I,4), Piazzale Duca d'Aosta, for all main services (NE of the centre).—*Nord* (Pl. II,5) for services of the Nord-Milano railway (Como, Novara, and Laveno via Saronno, etc).—*Porta Genova* (Pl. I,13) for Mortara and Alessandria (connections on to Genoa).—*Porta Vittoria* (beyond Pl. I,12) or *Porta Garibaldi* (Pl. I,3) for car-sleeper expresses to Boulogne, Ostend, Brindisi, etc.—*Lambrate* (beyond Pl. I,4) for Domodossola (Simplon express), Treviglio, Pavia, Bergamo, etc.

Airports at *Malpensa*, 45km NW and at *Linate*, 7km E, both for international and national flights.—For *Linate*, buses from Porta Garibaldi Station (E side) every 20 minutes via the Central Station or Bus No. 73 from Piazza San Babila.—For *Malpensa*, bus from the Central Station (E side) via Porta Garibaldi Station, 2½hrs before flight departures.

Hotels, between the Central Station and Piazza della Repubblica, and S of the Duomo, etc. (free list of all Hotels with prices from Tourist Offices). *Youth Hostel*, 2 Via Salmoiraghi. *Post Office* (Pl. II,10), Via Cordusio. 'Poste Restante', 4 Piazza Edison. *Touring Club Italiano*, 10 Corso Italia; *ACI*, 43 Corso Venezia.

Parking. The centre of the city (see Plan II) is at present closed to traffic from 7.30–18.00 (except for those with permits), and parking is restricted at all times. Visitors are advised to park on the outskirts and make use of public transport.

Public Transport in the city is run by ATM who distribute a map of the system. *Information Office* in the Underground Station in Piazza Duomo. Tickets (which can be used on buses, trams, or the underground) are valid for 1hr 15 minutes (flat rate fare). They are purchased at automatic machines at bus stops or at tobacconists and must be stamped on board. Day tickets for unlimited travel are also available from the A.T.M. Information Office, or the Tourist Offices in Piazza Duomo and the Central Station.

TRAMWAYS. The services most useful to the visitor are the following: **1**. *Central Station*—Piazza Cavour—*Piazza Scala*—Largo Cairoli—*Nord Station*—Corso Sempione; **4**. *Piazza Repubblica*—Via Manzoni— Piazza Scala—Via Legnano—Via Farini (for *Cimitero Monumentale*); **24**. Via Mazzini—Corso Magenta (Santa Maria delle Grazie, for the *Cenacolo*); **19**. *Corso Sempione*—Nord Station—Via Broletto—Via Orefici (for *Duomo*)—Via Torino.—BUSES. **50, 54.** Largo

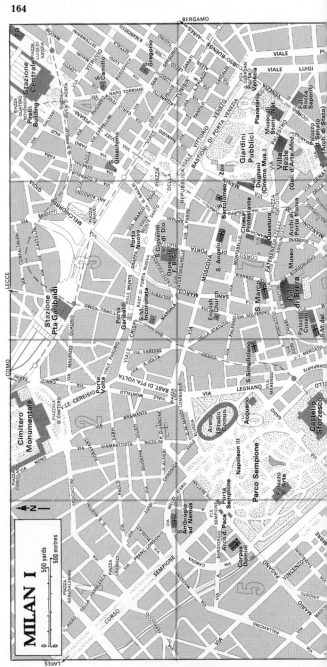

Linate Airport

Augusto (Duomo)—Corso Magenta—Via Carducci (for *Sant'Ambrogio*)—Via San Vittore; **60**. *Central Station*—Largo Cairoli—Piazza Duomo—*Castello Sforzesco*; **61**. Corso Matteotti—Piazza Scala—*Via Brera*—Via Solferino (for *San Marco*); **65**. *Central Station*—Via San Gregorio—Corso Buenos Aires—Corso Venezia—Piazza Fontana—Via Larga—*Corso Italia*—Porta Lodovico.

UNDERGROUND (**MM**: METROPOLITANA MILANESE). Two lines. The most useful section to the tourist is (Line **1**; red) Loreto—Lima—Porta Venezia—Palestro—San Babila—Duomo—Cordusio—Cairoli (for *Castello Sforzesco*)—Cadorna (for *Nord Station*)—Conciliazione. Line **2** (green) links Lambrate, Central, Porta Garibaldi, Milano Nord, and (via Sant'Ambrogio) Porta Genova stations.—A third line is under construction (scheduled to open in 1990) from the Central Station via Piazza della Repubblica, Via Manzoni and the Duomo to southern Milan (Corso di Porta Romano, etc.).

COUNTRY BUSES from Piazzale Cadorna to *Certosa di Pavia*; from Piazzale Medaglie d'Oro (Porta Romana) to *Melegnano* and *Lodi*, from Piazza Castello for most other destinations in Northern Italy.

Plan of Visit. Visitors with only a short time at their disposal should see the Duomo, Museo Poldi-Pezzoli, the Brera, the Castello Sforzesca, Sant'Ambrogio, the Cenacolo of Leonardo, the Pinacoteca Ambrosiana, and San Satiro.

British Consul General, 7 Via San Paolo (off Corso Vittorio Emanuele).—**U.S. Consulate,** 1 Largo Donegani.—**English Church**. *All Saints*, Via Solferino.

Theatres. *La Scala*, Piazza della Scala, the opera house, season in winter and spring; *Piccolo Scala*, Via Filodrammatici (at the side of the main theatre); *Piccolo Teatro*, 2 Via Rovello (Via Dante); *Teatro di Via Manzoni 'Renato Simoni'*, Via Manzoni; *Lirico*, Via Larga; *Nuovo*, Largo San Babila; *Nazionale*, Piazzale Piemonte (for ballet); *Carcano*, Corso Romana.

Sport. GOLF COURSE (27 holes) in the park at Monza (see Rte 13J), and (18 holes) at Barlassina, Birago di Camnago.—TENNIS at Centro Polisportivo, Via Valvassori Peroni, Lido di Milano, Piazzale Lotto, etc.—SWIMMING POOLS (covered), 35 Viale Tunisia; Via Corelli (Parco Forlanini); 12 Via Sant'Abbondio and many others; (open air) *Romano*, 35 Via Ponzio; Lido di Milano, Piazzale Lotto, etc.—HORSE RACING at the Ippodromo San Siro, NW of the centre, with trotting course adjoining; also at Monza.—MOTOR RACING at Monza.

History. *Mediolanum*, a Celtic settlement which first came under Roman power in 222 BC, was of little importance until the later days of the Empire when with a population approaching 100,000 it rivalled Rome for primacy of the West. By the famous Edict of Milan in AD 313 Constantine the Great officially recognised the Christian religion, and the influence of the great bishop St Ambrose (340–397) was so profound that the adjective 'ambrosiano' has become synonymous with 'Milanese'. The Emperor Valentinian II died here in 392. Despite the slaughter of most of the male population by the Goths in 539, Milan rose to prominence again under its archbishops, and by the mid-11C it had developed into a *Comune*, a typical early Italian city-state. It was constantly at war with its neighbours—Pavia, Como, and Lodi. The Emperor Barbarossa took advantage of the troubles to extend his power over Lombardy, and sacked Milan in 1158 and 1162, but his tyranny induced the Lombard cities to join together in the Lombard League, which beat Barbarossa at Legnano (1176) and, by the treaty of Constance (1183), won recognition of its independence. Powerful families now came into prominence and c 1260 the Torriani rose to absolute power in Milan. They were overthrown in 1277 by the Visconti, who ruled Milan until 1447. Under them, especially under Gian Galeazzo (1385–1402), the city increased in wealth and splendour, but the Visconti line died out in 1447, and after three republican years Francesco Sforza (the famous condottiere and defender of Milan against Venice), who had married Bianca, daughter of the last Visconti, proclaimed himself Duke. He was succeeded by his son Galeazzo Maria, and then by his infant grandson Gian Galeazzo, under the regency of his mother Bona di Savoia. But the power was usurped by the child's uncle Lodovico 'il Moro', who brought wealth to Milan and was a great patron of the arts. The expedition in 1494 of Charles VIII of France began a succession of foreign invasions. Between 1499 and 1535 Milan saw her dukes fall three times from power, and passed alternately into the hands of the French and the Spaniards, finally becoming, under Charles V, capital of a province of the Empire. In 1713 it became Austrian, but in 1796 Napoleon entered its gates, proclaiming it three years later capital of the Cisalpine Republic, and again, after a brief occupation by the Austrians and

Russians, capital of the Italian Republic (1802) and of the Kingdom of Italy (1805). The fall of Napoleon brought back the Austrians, who ruled the city with a tyranny against which the Milanese rebelled during the glorious 'Cinque Giornate' (18–22 March 1848). Milan was at last liberated by Victor Emmanuel II and Napoleon III after the battle of Magenta in 1859. Since the end of the 19C Milan has expanded into the most important industrial town in Italy, and has absorbed a huge influx of immigrant workers from all over Italy. The city was bombed fifteen times in the Second World War; the worst air-raids were in August 1943, after which a great part of the city centre burned for several days. The years of reconstruction were followed by a period of economic boom when sprawling new suburbs were built. Since 1974 the population has been in decline.

Among famous natives of Milan are Cesare Beccaria (1738–94), philosopher and jurist, Alessandro Manzoni (1785–1873), Italy's classic novelist, Carlo Cattaneo (1801–69), patriot and scientific writer, and Felice Cavallotti (1842–98), radical dramatist and poet. Giuseppe Parini (1729–99), of Bosisio, the poet, and Cesare Cantù (1804–95), of Brivio, the historian, though born just outside the city, identified themselves with its literary life. The composers Verdi, Boito, and Giordano all died in Milan (1901, 1918, 1948).

Art. The most important relics of the Romanesque age of architecture are Sant'Ambrogio and San Lorenzo. The Cathedral is practically the only building of the Gothic age. But the wealthy and cultured court of the Sforzas attracted many great artists of the Renaissance, among them Filarete, Michelozzo, and Bramante, the architects, Amadeo the sculptor, and Bergognone and Foppa the painters. Milanese art, however, was completely transformed by the arrival in 1483 of the Tuscan, Leonardo; this great artist and the city he adopted were the centre of the new artistic and humanistic impulse that ended with the fall of Lodovico il Moro in 1499; but a host of pupils and disciples carried on his tradition of painting: Boltraffio, Cesare da Sesto, Marco d'Oggiono, Giampietrino, Salaino, Andrea Solario; and Luini and Gaudenzio Ferrari who formed schools of their own. Bambaia and Cristoforo Solari felt his influence in the world of sculpture. The inspiration died out in the 16C, and towards the end of the century Camillo and Giulio Procaccini introduced a new style of painting from Bologna, and Galeazzo Alessi imported into architecture something of the dignity of Rome. The neo-classic buildings of Cagnola and Canonica are a noteworthy feature of the Napoleonic period, and a number of entire districts of the city were built at the turn of the century in a distinctive Art Nouveau style. Some modern buildings continue the tradition of originality.

A.   Piazza del Duomo

Piazza del Duomo (Pl. II,11) is the centre of the life of Milan. It is now closed to traffic (except for the W end). The crowded Portici Settentrionali (1873), along the N side, are characteristic of the bustling atmosphere of the city. The equestrian statue of Victor Emmanuel II is by Ercole Rosa (1896).

The *Duomo* (Pl.II,11), is a magnificent late Gothic building, the only one in Italy. Its elaborate decoration conforms to the Northern Gothic style despite a long and complicated building history and numerous restorations. It was greatly admired in the Romantic Age. The vast dimensions of the church are superseded only by those of St Peter's in Rome. The conservation of the remarkable exterior (described below) with its forest of sculptures and pinnacles has involved a lengthy process of cleaning, and, where necessary, replacing the stone.

It was begun c 1386, on the site of an older church of Santa Maria Maggiore (revealed through excavations, see below), under Gian Galeazzo Visconti, who presented it with a marble quarry at Candoglia which still belongs to the Chapter. The design is attributed to the 'maestri comacini'—Simone da Orsenigo and Giovanni Grassi—who were assisted by French, German, and Flemish craftsmen. In 1400 Filippino degli Organi was appointed master mason, and he

was succeeded by Giovanni Solari and his son Guiniforte, Giovanni Antonio
Amadeo, and (from 1567) Pellegrino Tibaldi, under whom the church was
dedicated by St Charles Borromeo. The topmost spires were added in 1765–69,
but the façade was not completed until 1813.

Buttresses on the north side of the nave roof of Milan Cathedral

Exterior. The best view of the cathedral is from the courtyard of the Palazzo
Reale, on the S side; but the most striking single feature is the apse, with its three
huge windows.—The WEST FRONT (56m high, 61m wide), originally designed
in the Baroque style by Tibaldi (c 1567), was considerably altered by Carlo
Buzzi (1645), who adopted a more Gothic plan, though preserving much of
Tibaldi's work. It was only half finished when Napoleon crowned himself
'king of Italy' with the Iron Crown in 1805. He decreed that it should be
completed at once, but rigidly restricted the cost, with the result that the upper
half is a mock-Gothic creation. The bronze door, with scenes from the Life of

the Virgin, is by Lodovico Pogliaghi (1906), and flanking this are doors (1950) by Franco Lombardi (S) and Giannino Castiglioni (N), dedicated to St Galdino and St Ambrose. The northernmost door is by Arrigo Minerbi (1948), with scenes relating to Constantine's edict establishing Christianity in the Roman Empire; the southernmost, by Luciano Minguzzi (1960), depicts the cathedral's history.

The huge cruciform *INTERIOR (open all day), with double-aisled nave (48m high), single-aisled transepts, and a pentagonal apse, has a forest of 52 tall columns, of which the majority bear circles of figures in canopied niches instead of capitals. The splendid effect is heightened by the stained glass of the windows. The pavement (renewed) is by *Tibaldi*.—SOUTH AISLE. Plain granite Sarcophagus of Archbishop Aribert (died 1045); the copper Crucifix above is a copy of the original now in the Museo del Duomo. The stained glass window, with Stories of the Life of St John the Evangelist, is by *Cristoforo de'Mottis* (1473–77). The sarcophagus in red marble, on pillars, is of Archbishop Ottone Visconti (died 1295). The next three windows have 16C stained glass. The tomb of Marco Carelli, by *Filippino degli Organi* (1406), has six statues in canopied niches. Beyond a plaque with a design for the façade by Giuseppe Brentano (1886) is the small monument of Canon Giovanni Vimercati (died 1548), with two fine portraits and a damaged Pietà by *Bambaia*. The stained glass (1470–75) shows the influence of *Vincenzo Foppa*. The glass above the 6th altar is by *Nicolò da Varallo* (1480–89).

SOUTH TRANSEPT. *Monument of Gian Giacomo Medici, with bronze statues, by *Leone Leoni* (1560–63). The stained glass in the two transept windows is by *Corrado de'Mocchis* (1554–64). In the transept apse is the monumental altar of San Giovanni Bono (1763). On the altar with a marble relief of the Presentation of the Virgin by *Bambaia*, is a statue (right) of St Catherine, by *Cristoforo Lombardo*. The statue of St Bartholomew flayed and carrying his skin is by *Marco d'Agrate* (1562).

On the impressive DOME are medallions (on the pendentives) with 15C busts of the Doctors of the Church and some 60 statues (on the arches). The four piers were reinforced in 1984 in order to consolidate the structure of the building. The *Presbytery (usually open to worshippers only) was designed by *Pellegrino Tibaldi* (1567). It contains two pulpits (with bronze figures by *Francesco Brambilla*), two huge organs, carved choir stalls, and a marble screen between the choir and ambulatory. The large bronze ciborium is also by *Tibaldi*. High above the altar hangs a paschal candlestick by *Lorenzo da Civate* (1447).—A small door right of the main altar leads down to the CRYPT and TREASURY (closed 12.30—14.30).

Here are displayed some 5C ivory carvings; the evangelistary cover of Archbishop Aribert; a small ivory bucket of the 10C; a golden pax ascribed to Caradosso (praised by Cellini as the greatest artist of his kind); a 13C Lombard processional Cross from Chiaravalle (with 16C and 18C additions); a silver reliquary box of the late 4C; and a 13C dove with Limoges enamels. Also, croziers, pastoral crosses, etc.—The CRYPT has stucco reliefs by *Galeazzo Alessi* and *Tibaldi*, and contains the richly-robed body of St Charles Borromeo (pilgrimage on 4–11 November).

In the AMBULATORY is the fine doorway, with sculptural decoration by Hans von Fernach and Porrino and Giovannino De Grassi (1393), of the South Sacristy (which contains a statue of Christ at the column by Cristoforo Solari). Beyond (high up) is a statue of Martin V, the Pope who consecrated the high altar in 1418, by *Jacopino da Tradate*

(1424), and the tomb of Cardinal Caracciolo (died 1538), by *Bambaia*.
Opposite is the doorway of the North Sacristy, by Giacomo da
Campione (1389). The large embroidered standard of the Virgin of the
Rosary dates from the late 16C.—In the middle of the NORTH TRANS-
EPT is the Trivulzio *Candelabrum, a seven-branched bronze candlestick nearly 5m high, of French or German workmanship (13C or
14C). The stained glass window above the sculptured altarpiece of
the Crucifix(1605) is by *Nicolò da Varallo* (1479). The altar in the
transept apse dates from 1768. The Gothic altar of St Catherine has
two statues of Saints attributed to *Cristoforo Solari*.

NORTH AISLE. At the easternmost (8th) altar, The Penance of
Theodosius, by *Barocci*. The next four stained glass windows date
from the 16C. 6th altar, Crucifix carried by St Charles during the
plague of 1576; 3rd altar, Tomb of three archbishops of the Arcimboldi
family, attributed to *Galeazzo Alessi*; 2nd bay, Eight Apostles, marble
reliefs (late 12C) from the former church of Santa Maria Maggiore;
opposite is the Font, a Roman (?) porphyry urn, covered with a canopy
by *Tibaldi*.

Inside the W front of the Cathedral is the entrance (open 10–12, 16–17, except
Monday) to the excavations beneath the church carried out in the 1960s. Here
can be seen a 4C octagonal Baptistery where St Ambrose baptised St Augustine
in 387, and remains of the Basilica of Santa Tecla (begun in the 4C).
Material from the various periods (including Roman baths of 1C BC) is well
labelled.

The entrance (9–17.30, winter 9–16.30; also lift, entered from outside
the N or S transept) to the ROOF is a small door in the corner of the S
transept, near the Medici tomb. The *Ascent provides a superb view
of the sculptural detail of the exterior, and is highly recommended.

158 steps ascend to the roof of the transept from which can be seen a forest of
pinnacles and flying buttresses. From the walkways across the roof the details of
the carving can be seen, and beyond are magnificient views of the city. At the
angle facing the Corso is the Carelli Spire, the oldest pinnacle. From above the W
front it is possible to walk along the spine of the nave roof to the base of the
Dome, by *Amadeo* (1490–1500), who planned also the four turrets but finished
only that at the NE angle. From the SW turret stairs lead up to the platform of the
dome. From here another staircase, in the NE turret, ascends to the topmost
gallery at the base of the central spire, surmounted by the Madonnina (108m
from the ground), a statue of gilded copper, nearly 4m high. From this height
there is a magnificent *View of the city, the Lombard plain, the Alps from Monte
Viso to the Ortler (the outstanding peaks being the Matterhorn, Monte Rosa, the
two Grigne, and Monte Resegone), and the Apennines.

To the S of the cathedral is the former **Palazzo Reale** (Pl. II;11), on the
site of the 13C town hall. It was rebuilt in 1772–78 for the Austrian
grand-dukes by *Giuseppe Piermarini* (and altered again in the 19C).
It now belongs to the municipality. Opposite the S transept of the
cathedral, in a wing of the palace, is the entrance to the **Museo del
Duomo** (Pl. II;11; adm. 9.30–12.30, 15–18 except Monday). The
collection is well labelled.

The first rooms contain a splendid collection of 14–15C sculpture from the
exterior of the cathedral, including a statue of St George (or Gian Galeazzo
Visconti) by *Giorgio Solari*; and a statue in wood of the Madonna and Child, by
Bernardo da Venezia (1392); also stained glass of the 14C–mid 15C.—In R. 4 is
material in facsimile relating to the famous choir school of the cathedral founded
in the 10–11C and directed by Franchino Gaffurio from 1484 to 1522.—In R. 6 is a
statue of a warrior (thought to be Galeazzo Maria Sforza) of the late 15C.—R. 7.
Crucifix in beaten copper (c 1040), from Archbishop Aribert's tomb in the
Duomo.—R. 8. *Benedetto Briosco* (attributed), St Agnes; *Cristoforo Solari*, Job;

*The Galleria Vittorio Emanuele II in Milan, designed by
Giuseppe Mengoni in 1865*

Unknown Master of the 15C, St Paul the Hermit (c 1465); and other works by
Cristoforo Solari.—R. 9 contains sculptures attributed to *Giovanni Antonio
Amadeo* and *Andrea Fusina*, and a 15C Flemish tapestry of the Passion.—R. 10.
Altar frontal of St Charles Borromeo (1610); drawings by *Il Cerano* (Giovanni
Battista Crespi).—R. 11. Tapestries made in Ferrara c 1540 probably on cartoons
by Giulio Romano, and the *Infant Christ among the Doctors, an early work by
Jaeopo Tintoretto.—R. 12 displays numerous sculptures from the Duomo of the
end of 16C and beginning of the 17C, including works by *Francesco
Brambilla.*—R. 13. Models by *Giuseppe Perego* for the Madonnina which crowns
the central spire of the Duomo, and the original armature.—R. 14 contains 19C

sculptures from the façade (*Camillo Pacetti, Pompeo Marchesi*, etc.).—The Gallery (R. 15) displays plans illustrating the history of the Duomo.—R.16 contains a splendid wooden *Model of the Duomo constructed by *Bernardino Zenale da Treviglio* in 1519, and later models.—R.17 is dedicated to the five 20C doors of the Duomo (bozzetti, etc.).—It is now necessary to return through R.12 to reach R.20 with a fine display of church vestments (and statuettes by *Francesco Messina*).

In another part of Palazzo Reale (entered through the main courtyard) the **Civico Museo di Arte Contemporanea** (Pl. II;11) was opened in 1984. It is still in the course of arrangement (open 9.30–12.30, 14.30–17.20, except Monday). The large collection of modern Italian art (well labelled) is particularly interesting for its paintings by *Umberto Boccioni, Giacomo Balla, Gino Severini, Giorgio De Chirico, Alberto Savinio, Pietro Marussig, Carlo Carrà, Virgilio Guidi, Mario Sironi, Giorgio Morandi, Filippo de Pisis*, and sculptures by *Arturo Martini* and *Lucio Fontana*.—In another wing of the palace important exhibitions are held.

Behind Palazzo Reale is the church of *San Gottardo* (Pl. II;11; formerly the palace chapel), entered in Via Pecorari. It is attributed to Francesco Pecorari (1330–36) and there is a fine view of the apse and *Campanile from Via del Palazzo Reale. It contains a fragment of a 14C fresco of the Crucifixion (restored in 1986), showing the influence of Giotto, who is known to have been in the city in 1335. The monument of Azzone Visconti is by Giovanni di Balduccio.—The *Archbishops' Palace* is mainly the work of Tibaldi (1570 et seq), with a façade by Giuseppe Piermarini (1784–1801) on *Piazza Fontana* (where a terrorist bomb killed 16 people in 1969). This adjoins Piazza Beccaria, with a monument to Cesare Beccaria (bronze copy of an original marble of 1871 by Giuseppe Grandi now in the Palazzo di Giustizia). Here is the former *Tribunale* (originally Palazzo del Capitano di Giustizia) of 1578, restored as Police headquarters.

The N side of Piazza del Duomo is connected with Piazza della Scala (see Rte 13B) by the colossal GALLERIA VITTORIO EMANUELE II (Pl. II;7). This huge glass-roofed shopping arcade, with cafés and restaurants, was designed (1865) by Giuseppe Mengoni, who fell from the top and was killed a few days before the inauguration ceremony in 1878. It was built by the City of Milan Improvement Company Ltd, and is being restored.

On the W side of Piazza del Duomo Via Mercanti leads past (right) *Palazzo dei Giureconsulti* (1560–64) and the fine **Palazzo della Ragione** (Pl. II;11; right), erected in 1228–33 with an upper storey added in 1771. During restoration work here in 1988 13C frescoes were discovered. On its rear wall, in the peaceful Piazza Mercanti, is a remarkable equestrian relief of 1233. In this old piazza are also the Gothic *Loggia degli Osii* (1316) and the Baroque *Palazzo delle Scuole Palatine* (1645).

B.   The Scala and Museo Poldi-Pezzoli

PIAZZA DELLA SCALA has a monument to Leonardo da Vinci (by Pietro Magni, 1872) surrounded by figures of his pupils, Boltraffio, Salaino, Cesare da Sesto, and Marco d'Oggiono. Here is the **Teatro alla Scala** (Pl. II;7), famous in operatic art.

The theatre was begun in 1776 by Giuseppe Piermarini on the site of the church of Santa Maria della Scala, after the destruction by fire of the Regio Ducale Teatro. It opened in 1778 with 'Europa Riconosciuta' by Antonio Salieri and Mattia Verazi. Works by Rossini, Donizetti, Bellini, Verdi, and Puccini were first acclaimed here. From the beginning of this century its reputation was upheld by the legendary figure of Toscanini (who led the orchestra again in 1946 when the building was reopened after serious war damage).—The *Piccola Scala* was opened here in 1955 for the performance of opera on a smaller scale, and chamber music concerts.—Under the portico, to the left of the theatre is the *Museo Teatrale* (9–12, 14–18; closed fest.), with a valuable collection relating to theatrical and operatic history. From the museum the theatre may be visited.

Opposite is *PALAZZO MARINO (Pl. II;7; the *Palazzo Municipale*; being restored), with a fine façade on Piazza San Fedele by Galeazzo Alessi (1553–58), who also designed the splendid Mannerist courtyard. The building on Piazza Scala was completed by Luca Beltrami (1886–92). Behind is Piazza San Fedele, in which are a statue of Manzoni and the church of *San Fedele*, begun by Tibaldi (1569) for St Charles Borromeo, and completed by Martino Bassi and Francesco Maria Richini, with an elaborate pulpit.

From the Scala the busy and fashionable VIA MANZONI (Pl. II;7) leads NE towards Piazza Cavour; at No. 29, the Grand Hotel et de Milan (founded in 1865), Giuseppe Verdi died in 1901. At No. 12 is the entrance to the ***Museo Poldi-Pezzoli** (Pl. II;7), the former private house of Gian Giacomo Poldi-Pezzoli, bequeathed by him, with his art collection, to the city in 1879, and opened to the public in 1881.

ADMISSION daily except Monday 9.30–12.30, 14.30–18.00; on Saturday open until 19.30; April–September closed Sunday afternoon.

The portrait of Poldi-Pezzoli in the entrance is by *Francesco Hayez*. On the ground floor the SALONE DELL'AFFRESCO (used for exhibitions), with Tiepolese frescoes by *Carlo Innocenzo Carloni*, displays a Delft tapestry of 1602. The ARMOURY has fine examples of antique and 14–17C arms and armour. Beyond, in the SALA DELL'ARCHEOLOGIA E DEI TAPPETI, are a fragment of Isfahan carpet (16C), a Tabriz carpet (c 1560), antique vases, bronzes, silverware, and gold objects, an Ushak carpet (16C), and a prayer mat (Asia Minor; 18C). Some of these have been removed for restoration.

An elliptical staircase, with a Baroque fountain and landscapes by *Alessandro Magnasco*, ascends to the main picture gallery on the FIRST FLOOR. To the left are the SALETTE DEI LOMBARDI. In the first, *Vincenzo Foppa*, Madonna; *Ambrogio Bergognone*, Madonna; *Lombard painter* (c 1460), Saints. In the second, *Vincenzo Foppa* (?), Portrait; *Andrea Solario*, Rest on the Flight (with charming landscape); *Boltraffio*, Madonna; *Bernardino Luini*, Madonna. The third is devoted to *Luini* and the Lombard school. Beyond the vestibule is the ANTECHAMBER (or Sala degli Stranieri) with paintings by *Cranach* (Portraits of Luther and his wife).—The SALETTA DEGLI STUCCHI contains porcelain from Saxony, Sèvres, and Capodimonte, etc.— SALONE DORATO. In the centre is a wonderful Persian carpet of 1522. *Mantegna*, *Madonna; *Giovanni Bellini*, Pietà; *Botticelli*, Pietà, and *Madonna; *Piero della Francesca*, *St Nicholas of Tolentino; *Antonio Pollaiolo*, *Lady of the Bardi family, one of the best-known portraits in Italy (also attributed to his brother *Piero); *Guardi*, *Venetian lagoon.

The three rooms beyond contain the collection of Emilio Visconti Venosta (including a portrait of Cardinal Ascanio Sforza by the *Lombard School* (c 1490); the Bruno Falck donation of antique clocks and scientific instruments; and a series of portraits (mostly by *Vittore Ghislandi* of Bergamo, 1655–1743).

Beyond the Salone Dorato and the Salette dei Stucchi (right) is the SALA NERA, so called from the decoration (partly preserved) in ivory and ebony: *Mariotto Albertinelli*, Triptych (a tiny portable altar); *Flemish 16C School*, Annunciation, and Saints; Florentine table in

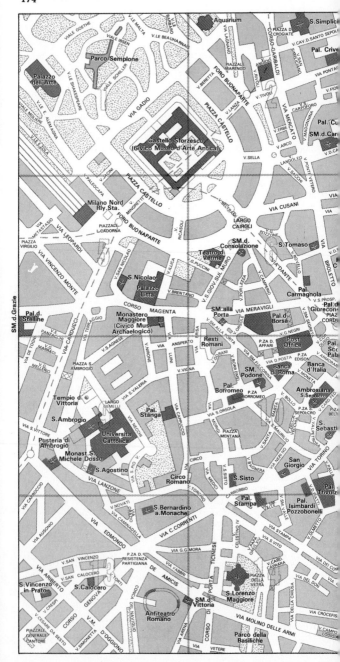

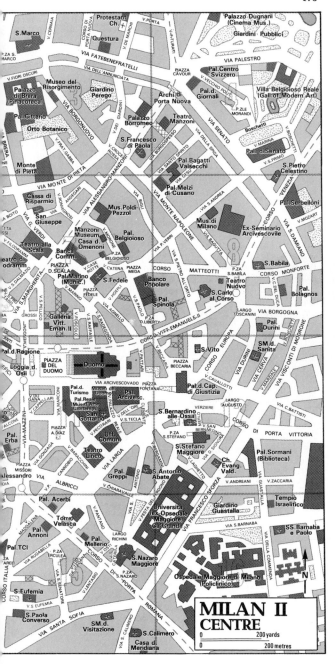

MILAN II
CENTRE

0 ——— 200 yards
0 ——— 200 metres

pietre dure.—The SALA DEI VETRI ANTICHI DI MURANO, as well as examples of glass (15–19C) from Murano, contains miniatures by Venetian and Florentine masters. The two doors at the end lead in to the SALETTA DI DANTE (restored) decorated in the Art Nouveau style at the end of the 19C. The marble bust of Rosa Poldi-Pezzoli is by *Lorenzo Bartolini*.—From the Sala Nera is the entrance to the SALA DEL PALMA, with a portrait of a lady by *Palma il Vecchio*, and a small painting of the Archangel Gabriel by *Giovanni Battista Moroni*.— Beyond are the two SALE TRIVULZIO. The first has paintings by *Bernardino Strozzi, Alessandro Magnasco, Giuseppe Ribera*, etc., and Islamic and Venetian metal work (15–18C) and arms and armour. The second, the SALA DEI BRONZETTI, has a collection of bronzes including small Renaissance bronzes, a bust of Bishop Ulpiano Volpi by *Alessandro Algardi*, and a Hellenistic (2C BC) head of Young Bacchus. Also here is exhibited a small Crucifix painted on both sides by *Raphael*, amd two tapestries.

Beyond the Sala di Palma is the GABINETTO DEGLI ORI, which contains a precious collection of ancient jewellery and goldsmiths' work, and medieval religious bronzes and Limoges enamels. In the SALA DEL SETTECENTO VENETO are works by *Guardi, Rosalba Carriera*, and *Gian Battista Tiepolo*.— The SALA DEL PERUGINO contains a small Madonna and Child with Saints by *Perugino*. Also here: *Francesco Morone*, Samson and Delila; *Francesco Bonsignori*, Head of a female Saint; cassone painted by *Bartolomeo Montagna* (1490); *Cima da Conegliano*, Head of a female Saint; *Biagio di Antonio da Firenze*, Madonna and Child and an angel; *Filippo Lippi*, Pietà; *Cosmè Tura*, St Maurelius. The small paintings in the centre include works by *Pietro Lorenzetti, Lippo Memmi, Vitale degli Equi da Bologna*, and *Carlo Crivelli*.—In the last room, the SALA DEI VENETI are Venetian works including: *Lazzaro Bastiani*, Madonna and Child; *Jacopo Bellini*, Madonna of Humility (very ruined); (in centre) *Bernardo Daddi*, small painted Crucifix; *Lorenzo Lotto*, Madonna and Child; *Andrea Mantegna*, Portrait of a Man.

Recent donations to the museum include the Collezione Portaluppi of some 200 sundials of the 16–19C and a collection of antique lace.

Via Morone (Pl. II;7), a characteristic 19C street, in which Manzoni met Balzac in 1837 and (at No. 1) he died in 1873 (now the **Museo Manzoniano**, open 9–12, 14–16; closed Saturday, Sunday, Monday, & fest.) opens into Piazza Belgioioso, with the huge *Palazzo Belgioioso*, by Giuseppe Piermarini (1772). Via Omenoni (right) is named from the caryatids (recently restored) decorating the house of the sculptor Leone Leoni.

Farther along Via Manzoni, Via Monte Napoleone, another interesting 19C street, diverges right. In Via Santo Spirito (left) *Palazzo Bagatti Valsecchi* (Pl. II;4) was built in 1882 when the family began an eclectic collection of paintings, sculpture, applied arts, and various curiosities. The palace has been acquired by the Regional government and is to be opened to the public.

C. The Brera Gallery

Via Verdi and Via Brera lead N from the Scala to **Palazzo di Brera** (Pl. II;3), famous for its picture gallery. The building was begun by Francesco Maria Richini in 1651. The main portal is by Giuseppe Piermarini (1780).

In the monumental Courtyard (by Richini) is a heroic statue of Napoleon I, by Antonio Canova (1809), a copy in bronze of the colossal marble in Apsley House,

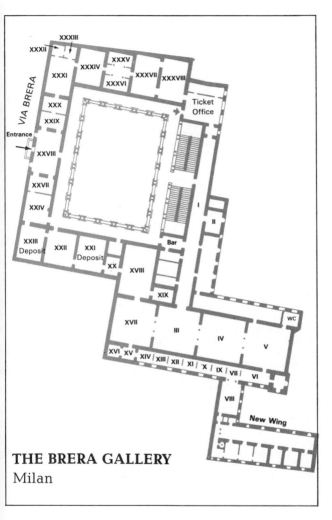

VIA BRERA

Entrance

XXXIII
XXXII
XXXI
XXXIV
XXXV
XXXVI
XXXVII
XXXVIII
XXX
XXIX
XXVIII
XXVII
XXIV
XXIII
Deposit
XXII
XXI
Deposit
XX
XVIII
XIX
XVII
XVI XV
XIV XIII XII XI X IX VII
VI
III
IV
V
VIII
I
II
Ticket Office
Bar
WC
New Wing

THE BRERA GALLERY
Milan

London. Between the columns of the arcades and on the landings of the main staircase are statues and busts of famous artists and authors. The Brera is a centre of the arts and sciences in Lombardy: in addition to the picture gallery, it contains the *Accademia di Belle Arti*, the *Biblioteca Nazionale*, with c 1,000,000 vols, including 2357 incunabula and 2000 MSS, the *Astronomical Observatory*, and the *Institute of Science and Letters*.

The ****Pinacoteca** (adm. daily except Monday 9–13.30; fest. 9–12.30; it has sometimes also been open all day until 19.00; latest information from the tourist office), the famous picture gallery on the first floor, is the finest existing collection of Northern Italian painting. The gallery is in the course of expansion, and the adjacent Palazzo Citterio on Via Brera (see below) is being restored as an extension ('Brera 2') for the modern collections, and as an exhibition centre.

The Pinacoteca was founded in the 18C by the Accademia di Belle Arti, and was enlarged through acquisitions and paintings from Lombard churches before it was officially inaugurated in 1809. The collection has continued to grow in this century with numerous donations, and a large part of the paintings are now well displayed in 38 rooms: the New Wing was not open in 1990 and the arrangement is still not definitive. By no means all the collection is permanently on view. Some rooms are closed when there is a shortage of custodians: scholars can sometimes ask for special permission to see them.

All the rooms are clearly numbered in Roman numerals as on the Plan on p 177, and the pictures are well labelled. The standard of the paintings is exceptionally high, and only some have been mentioned in the description below.

The long Entrance Gallery (Room I) used to display the early 20C works (particularly the Futurists) from the Jucker and Jesi collections. These were withdrawn from the Gallery in 1990. Among the painters represented were *Lucio Fontana, Umberto Boccioni, Mario Sironi, Giorgio De Chirico, Giacome Balla, Gino Severini, Carlo Carrà, Giorgio Morandi* and *Filippo De Pisis*, and the sculptors *Medardo Rosso* and *Arturo Martini*.—RII (temporarily closed). The frescoed Cappella di Sant'Ambrogio and Santa Caterina from Mocchirolo (near Lentate in Brianza) has been reconstructed here. The frescoes are by a close follower of Giovanni da Milano. The collection of portraits at the end of the hall includes works by *Palma Giovane, Daniele Crespi, Francesco Hayez,* and *Sir Thomas Laurence*.—RIII. *Paolo Veronese*, Last Supper, Agony in the Garden; *Gerolamo Savoldo*, Madonna in glory with Saints; *Lorenzo Lotto*, Pietà (1545); *Paris Bordone*, Baptism of Christ; *Veronese*, *Baptism and Temptation of Christ*.—RIV. *Tintoretto*, St Helena with Saints and donors; *Giovanni Cariani*, Resurrection of Christ with Saints Jerome and John the Baptist, signed and dated 1520; *Veronese*, Supper in the house of Simon; *Tintoretto*, Pietà, *Discovery of the body of St Mark at Alexandria; *Bonifazio Veronese*, Finding of Moses.—RV. *Bartolomeo Montagna*, *Madonna and Child with Saints; *Liberale da Verona*, St Sebastian; *Martino da Udine*, St Ursula and her maidens; *Marco Basaiti*, Deposition; *Giovanni Mansueti*, *St Mark baptising St Aniano; *Cima da Conegliano*, Madonna and Child with Saints; *Gentile* and *Giovanni Bellini*, *St Mark preaching in Alexandria, a splendid large painting commissioned by the Scuola Grande di San Marco in Venice (removed for restoration); *Il Padovanino* *Battle Scene (recently restored); *Cima da Conegliano*, *St Peter Martyr and Saints; *Michele da Verona*, Crucifixion; *Giovanni Battista Martini da Udine* (attributed), *Madonna and Child.

RVI. Detached *Frescoes by *Donato Bramante* from the Casa Panigarola, and a painting by him of *Christ at the Column (from Chiaravalle), his only known panel painting.—RVII. *Bonifacio Bembo* (attributed), Portraits of Bianca Maria and Francesco Sforza, and Saints; *Bernardino Butinone*, Madonna and Child.—RVIII (left) contains the earliest works in the collection. 'Maestro di Santa Colomba' (14C Riminese School), Three panels with the Story of St Colomba; *Giovanni da Milano*, The Redeemer; *Barnaba da Modena*, Adoration of the Child; *Jacopo Bellini*, *Madonna and Child (signed and dated 1448); *Gentile da Fabriano*, *Polyptych; *Stefano da Zevio*, Adoration of the Magi (1435); *Ambrogio Lorenzetti*, *Madonna and Child;

Lorenzo Veneziano, Polyptych; *Bernardo Daddi*, St Lawrence.—From RVIII there will be accesss to the New Wing, still in the course of arrangement.—RIX, the first of a series of small rooms, contains works by *Bergognone* (Madonna and Child with St Clare and the Blessed Stefano Marconi, in its original frame), *Bernardo Zenale*, and *Vincenzo Civerchio*.—RX. *Giovanni Antonio Boltraffio*, Portrait of Gerolamo Casio; *'Master of the Pala Sforzesca'* (Lombard School, 1494), *Madonna and Child with Doctors of the Church and the family of Ludovico il Moro (the 'Pala Sforzesca'); *Ambrogio de Predis*, Portrait of a young man.—RXI contains works by *Andrea Solario*.—RXII. *Giovanni Francesco Bembo*, Devout couple kneeling; *Giovanni Agostino da Lodi*, Madonna and Child.—RXIII. *Bernardino Luini*, *Madonna del Roseto; *Sodoma*, Madonna and Child; works by *Cesare da Sesto*; *Giampietrino*, Madonna and Child (unfinished).—RXIV. Works by *Martino Spanzotti*. RRXV & XVI contain paintings and frescoes from the Cappella di San Giuseppe in the church of Santa Maria della Pace in Milan by *Bernardino Luini*.

RXVII. *Andrea Salaino* (attributed), Madonna and Child with Saints; *Marco d'Oggiono*, Archangels casting out Satan; *Calisto Piazza*, Baptism of Christ; *Gaudenzio Ferrari*, Martyrdom of St Catherine of Alexandria; *Bartolomeo Suardi (Bramantino)*, Crucifixion; *Vincenzo Foppa*, *Polyptych with the Madonna and Child and Saints; *Bergognone*, Saints Ambrose, Jerome, and Catherine, Christ in Pietà.—RXVIII (in course of arrangement). *Antonio Vivarini* and *Giovanni d'Alemagna*, Polyptych; *Girolamo da Treviso il Vecchio*, Pietà; *Andrea Mantegna*,*The Dead Christ, a famous painting with remarkable foreshortening, *Polyptych with St Luke the Evangelist and Saints (1453; restored in 1989); *Girolamo di Giovanni*, Polyptych with the Madonna enthroned, Crucifixion and Saints; *Carlo Crivelli*, Crucifixion, *Coronation of the Virgin (1483), and Pietà, *Madonna 'della Candeletta' (removed for restoration), *Triptych from the Duomo of Camerina, a delightful group of paintings.—RXIX. *Alvise Vivarini*, *Christ blessing; *Vittore Carpaccio*, Scenes from the life of the Virgin, two works from the Scuola degli Albanesi in Venice; *Giovanni Bellini*, *Madonna and Child, one of his most beautiful Madonnas (restored in 1986), *Pietà, *Madonna and Child in a landscape (1510; restored in 1986); *Carpaccio*, St Stephen disputing with the Doctors (1514); *Antonello da Messina*, Madonna and Child (very ruined).

RXX contains works by *Gian Francesco Maineri* (Head of St John the Baptist); *Cima*, St Jerome in the desert; *Mantegna*, *Madonna and Cherubims, St Jerome; *Francesco del Cossa*, *St John the Baptist, *St Peter; *Correggio*, Adoration of the Magi, Nativity (a much earlier work); *Filippo Mazzola*, Portrait of a man.—RXXI is partly used as a deposit for paintings (opened on request). *Francesco and Bernardo Zaganelli*, Madonna and Child and Saints, Christ carrying the Cross; *Marco Palmezzano*, Adoration of the Child, Head of St John the Baptist, Madonna and Child.—RXXII. *Flagellation and Madonna and Child, a processional standard painted on both sides, an early work by *Luca Signorelli* (restored in 1986); *Lorenzo Lotto*, Assumption of the Virgin (predella); *Francesco Francia*, Annunciation; *Perin del Vaga*, Scenes from the Passion; *Ercole de'Roberti*, Madonna enthroned with Saints (the 'Pala Portuense', restored in 1988); *Giovanni Luteri*, Saints Sebastian, George, and John the Baptist.—RXXIII is at present used as a deposit.—RXXIV has recently been modernised to display the two masterpieces of the collection: *Raphael's* *Marriage of the Virgin ('lo Sposalizio', 1504), the masterpiece of his Umbrian period, with a remarkable circular temple in the background; and *Piero della Francesca*'s *Madonna with angels and Saints, and Federigo, Duke of Montefeltro, in a highly refined architectural setting. This is Piero's last known work.—RXXXVII. *Girolamo Genga*, Madonna and Child with Saints and Doctors of the Church; works by *Timoteo Viti; Luca Signorelli*, Madonna and Child with Saints; *Girolamo Genga*, Battle of the Ignudi.—RXXVIII. *Federico Barocci*, *Martyrdom of San Vitale; Ludovico Carracci*, Adoration of the Magi; *Annibale Carracci*, *Samaritan at the well; Agostino Carracci*, The Adulteress; *Guido Reni*, *Saints Peter and Paul.—RXXIX. Works by the School of Caravaggio: *Giovanni Battista Caracciolo*, The Samaritan at the well; *Orazio Lomi Gentileschi*, *Three Martyrs; Lo Spagnoletto*, Derision of Christ; *Caravaggio*, *Supper at Emaus; and works by *Bernardo Cavallino*.—RXXX. *Giuseppe de Ribera*, St Jerome; works by *Mattia Preti* (St Peter paying the Tribute Money); *Francesco Albani*, Dance of Cupids; *Carlo Dolci*, *David with the head of Goliath.—RXXXI. *Van Dyck*, *Portrait of the Princess of Orange (restored in 1986), Madonna and Child with St Francis; *Rubens*, Last Supper (recently restored); *Sebastiano Ricci*, St Gaetano comforting a dying man; *Paulus Potter*, Head of a Cow.—RXXXII. *Master of Anversa, 1518*, Adoration of the Magi; *16C School of Anversa*, St Luke painting the Madonna and Child; *Jan de Beer(?)*, Triptych; *El Greco*, *St Francis.—RXXXIII. *Rembrandt*, *Portrait of his sister, and other Dutch works.

RXXXIV. *Pierre Subleyras*, Crucifixion and Saints; works by *Luca Giordano; Francesco Goya*, Procession; *Gian Battista Tiepolo*, Madonna del Carmelo; *Giuseppe Maria Crespi*, Crucifixion.— RXXXV. *Gian Battista Tiepolo*, Sketch for a battle scene; *Pietro Longhi*, The Dentist; works by *Rosalba Carriera, Bernardo Bellotto, Canaletto, Giovanni Battista Piazzetta* (Rebecca at the well), *Francesco Guardi*, and *Sir Joshua Reynolds* (Lord Donoughmore).— RXXXVI. Works by *Giovanni Battista Pittoni, Giovanni Battista Piazzetta* (Old man in prayer); genre scenes by *Giacomo Ceruti; Anton Raphael Mengs*, Portrait of the singer Annibali.—RXXXVII. 15C frescoes by *Gaudenzio Ferrari* detached in 1805 from the church of Santa Maria della Pace (and restored in 1989). RXXXVIII is at present used for exhibitions.

Awaiting arrangement in rooms at present closed are other important works, including: *Titian*, Portrait of Antonio Porcia, St Jerome; *Benozzo Gozzoli*, Miracle of St Dominic; two frescoes by *Vincenzo Foppa* from Santa Maria di Brera; landscapes by *Alessandro Magnasco; Marco d'Oggiono*, Assumption of the Virgin; and works by the Macchiaioli *Giovanni Fattori* and *Silvestro Lega* (*The Pergola). Also fine paintings by *Francesco Hayez* (portraits of Manzoni and his wife, Romantic historical scenes, etc.), and works by *Andrea Appiani, Prud'hon*, and *Girolamo Induno*.

In Via Brera, in the little piazza beside the palace is a monument to the painter Hayez, by Francesco Barzaghi (1898). The 18C *Palazzo Citterio*, which overlooks the *Botanical Gardens*, founded in 1781, is undergoing a lengthy restoration as part of a plan to extend the Brera gallery ('Brera 2'). Opposite is *Palazzo Cusani* (No. 15; by Giovanni Ruggeri, 1719), now a local military headquarters. Via del Carmine leads to the 15C church of *Santa Maria del Carmine* (Pl. II;2) with a façade completed in 1879, and a fine Baroque chapel S of the choir (with decorations by Camillo Procaccini).

Just behind the Brera in Via Borgonuovo is the **Museo del Risorgimento** (Pl. II;3; No. 23; adm. 9.30–12.15, 14.30–17.30 except Monday), in 14 rooms. The exhibits arranged chronologically include material dating from the arrival of Napoleon in Lombardy in 1796 up to the taking of Rome in 1870. There is also a good library.

The church of **San Marco** (Pl. II;3), N of the Brera, dates from 1254, but the interior was wholly altered in the Baroque period. On the mock-Gothic façade (1873) the doorway and three statuettes date from the 14C. Verdi's 'Requiem' received its first performance here.

In the INTERIOR the nave is exceptionally long. SOUTH SIDE. 1st chapel, frescoes and altarpiece by *Gian Paolo Lomazzo* (1571). At the end of the nave, Nativity by *Legnanino*. In the S transept is the tomb of the Blessed Lanfranco da Settala (died 1264), ascribed to *Giovanni di Balduccio*, with six sarcophagi in the same manner. Beneath a later fresco, fresco of the Crucifixion and Assumption of the mid-14C. In the presbytery are four huge paintings by *Camillo Procaccini* and *Cerano.*—NORTH TRANSEPT. *Legnanino*, St Augustine washing Christ's feet and the Apparition of the Holy Girdle (restored in 1986). NORTH SIDE. 9th chapel, *Legnanino*, St Jerome; 7th chapel, *Camillo Procaccini*, Madonna and Saints; 5th chapel, 16C Lombard fresco of the Baptism of Christ; 4th chapel, *Giulio Cesare Procaccini*, Transfiguration; 3rd chapel, Madonna and Child with the young St John, a grisaille fresco discovered in 1975 and attributed by some scholars to *Bernardino Luini.*—A small MUSEUM contains frescoes of the late 13C Lombard school detached from the Campanile.
    To the N, in Via Mosca, is the 16C church of *Sant'Angelo* (Pl. I;7), with paintings and frescoes by Camillo Procaccini (in poor condition).
    The church of **San Simpliciano** (Pl. II;2), to the W, dedicated to the successor of St Ambrose in the episcopal chair, was probably founded by St Ambrose himself in the 4C and, despite the alterations of the 12C, stands, save for the façade and the apse, largely in its original form. Eighteen huge window embrasures have been revealed since 1945. The interior contains, in the restored Romanesque apse, the *Coronation of the Virgin, a fine fresco by Bergognone, masked by the towering altar. At the entrance to the presbytery beneath the organs are frescoes of Saints by *Aurelio Luini.*—In the area farther N (tram 4) is the *Cimitero Monumentale* (Pl. I;2), designed by Carlo Maciachini in 1863–66. It has a central pantheon, or 'famedio', containing the tombs of Manzoni and Cattaneo. Some of the monumental tomb sculpture is to be displayed in a museum here.

D.   The Castello Sforzesco

The spacious Foro Buonaparte, Largo Cairoli (with a monument to Garibaldi by Ettore Ximenes, 1895), and Piazza Castello with its trees, were all designed in a huge hemicycle in 1884 in front of the *Castello Sforzesco (Pl. II;1,2). This was the stronghold built by Francesco Sforza in 1451–66, on the site of a 14C castle of the Visconti destroyed under the 'Ambrosian Republic'. It now contains important art collections.

The designer of the castle was Giovanni da Milano, but the decoration of the principal tower was entrusted to Filarete, the Florentine architect. The Castello was later enriched with works by Bramante and Leonardo; after a long period of use as barracks, it was restored by Luca Beltrami (1893–1904). Badly bombed in 1943, when two-thirds of the archives and many other treasures were lost, it was again carefully restored. It is square in plan; on the façade are three towers, the central one is the *Filarete Tower*, rebuilt by Beltrami in accordance with the supposed design of the original, destroyed by an explosion of powder in 1521. The picturesque Piazza d'Armi, the main courtyard, contains fragments of old buildings from various parts of the city. Concerts are held here in summer. At the back on the left is the *Rocchetta*, which served as a keep, on the right is the *Corte Ducale*, the residential part, and in the centre is the *Torre di Bona di Savoia.*

From the charming courtyard of the Corte Ducale is the entrance to the **Civico Museo d'Arte Antica** (adm. 9.30–12.15, 14.30–17.30, except Monday). The collections of sculpture, paintings and applied arts are beautifully arranged and well labelled. **Ground Floor.** Beyond the monumental 14C *Pusterla dei Fabbri*, ROOM I contains fragments from ancient churches and other Byzantine and Romanesque remains; late Roman sarcophagus, from Lambrate; marble portrait head (6C) supposedly of the Empress Theodora.—RII. Tombs of Barnabò Visconti, by *Bonino da Campione* (1363), with a colossal

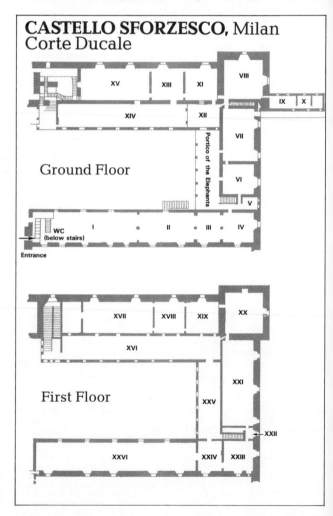

CASTELLO SFORZESCO, Milan
Corte Ducale

equestrian figure, and of Regina della Scala, his wife.—In RIII, beneath a Lombard frescoed ceiling (mid 15C), are remains of the façade of Santa Maria di Brera, by *Giovanni di Balduccio* of Pisa; statues from the E gate of the city by the same artist; tomb assigned to Bona di Savoia (14C).—RIV, where the vault bears the arms of Philip II of Spain and Mary Tudor, contains further fragments of Santa Maria di Brera; *Sepulchral monument of the Rusca family, by a Lombard master (late 14C), from the church of San Francesco in Como.

EAST WING. Beyond a small chapel (RV) with 14C Venetian sculpture, and a fragment of an English alabaster (removed for

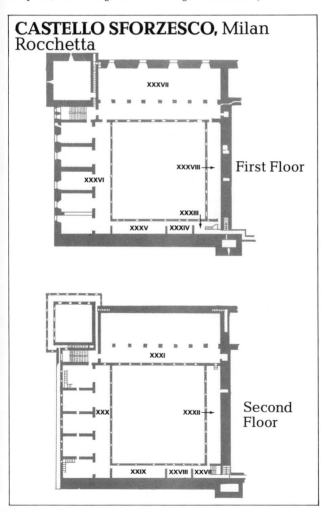

CASTELLO SFORZESCO, Milan
Rocchetta

First Floor

XXXVII

XXXVIII →

XXXVI

XXXIII

XXXV   XXXIV

Second Floor

XXXI

XXXII →

XXX

XXIX   XXVIII XXVII

restoration), RVI contains reliefs from the old Porta Romana, showing the triumph of the Milanese over Barbarossa (1171); bell from the Broletto of Milan.—RVII, with frescoed escutcheons of the Dukes of Milan, is hung with tapestries. In the centre, the Gonfalon of Milan, designed by *Giuseppe Meda* (1566); *Stoldo Lorenzi* (1534–83), Statue of Adam.—The *SALA DELLE ASSE (RVIII), at the NE corner of the castle, has remarkable frescoed decoration, designed in 1498 by *Leonardo da Vinci*, but much altered and restored. The ilex branches and leaves are used in a complicated architectural structure in which the form of the octagon recurs. Two fragments of monochrome frescoes on the wall have recently been discovered.

A little doorway (right; adm. only with special permission) leads to two small rooms (IX, X) over the moat containing Sforza portraits by *Bernardino Luini* and panels in high relief by *Bambaia*; in the first room Lodovico il Moro is said to have mourned the death of his wife, Beatrice d'Este.

RXI (SALA DEI DUCALI), in the N wing, is decorated with coats-of-arms showing the ancestry of Galeazzo Maria Sforza; it contains a relief by *Agostino di Duccio* from the Tempio Malatestiano at Rimini, and good 15C sculptures.—The former CHAPEL (RXII) has restored frescoes attributed to *Bonifacio Bembo* and *Stefano de'Fedeli* and assistants (1466–76). The Madonna and Child is a Lombard work of the late 15C and the statue of the Madonna 'del Coazzone' is by *Pietro Solari*. Outside is the Renaissance Portico of the Elephant, so called from a faded fresco. The SALA DELLE COLOMBINE (right; RXIII) has fresco decorations with the arms of Bona di Savoia, and sculpture by *Amadeo* and *Cristoforo Mantegazza*, including a marble tabernacle. The long SALA VERDE (RXIV) is divided by Renaissance doorways salvaged from Milanese palaces; that from the Banco Mediceo (1455) is by *Michelozzo*; the room contains tombs, armorial sculptures, and a fine collection of armour.—The SALA DEGLI SCARLIONI (RXV) is on two levels. In the higher part are sculptures by *Andrea Fusina* (bishop's tomb of 1519) and *Bambaia*, *Effigy of Gaston de Foix, with fragments of his tomb (1525). Below, uncomfortably placed on a Roman altar, is the RONDANINI PIETÀ, the moving but pathetic unfinished last work of *Michelangelo*, named from the palace in Rome where it used to be displayed. The sculptor worked at intervals on this statue during the last nine years of his life, and up to six days before his death. According to Vasari, he re-used a block of marble in which he had already roughed out a Pietà on a different design and on a smaller scale. A head of Christ, attributed to Michelangelo, but probably intended for the earlier Pietà, has recently been discovered (and is exhibited in the Galleria Borghese in Rome).—On the left is a fine bronze head of Michelangelo, by *Daniele da Volterra* (1564).

From the corner a wooden bridge leads out into the Corte Ducale across a subterranean court with a 16C fountain. On the left stairs lead up to the **First Floor** which contains part of the Museum of Applied Arts (RRXXVI–XIX), and the Pinacoteca (RRXX–XXVI). ROOM XVI is a long room divided into four sections with a splendid collection of *Furniture arranged to give a progressive chronological impression of Lombard interiors of the 15–18C, and hung with tapestries and detached frescoes. RXVII (left) is decorated with 15C frescoes of the Story of Griselda from the Castle of Roccabianca, and contains more furniture of the 15–18C; the display is continued in RRXVIII & XIX.—Steps lead up from RXIX to the vaulted tower room (XX), the first room of the **Pinacoteca**. *Benedetto Bembo*,

Polyptych (signed and dated 1462); *Mantegna*, *Madonna in Glory (the 'Pala Trivulzio', 1497; restored in 1988); *Giovanni Bellini*, *Madonna and Child, a superb work; *Filippo Lippi*, Madonna dell'Umiltà.—RXXI contains works of the Lombard Renaissance: *Vincenzo Foppa*, Martyrdom of St Sebastian; *Bergognone*, Pietà; *Bramantino*, Noli me tangere; works by followers of Leonardo: *Boltraffio, Cesare da Sesto, Sodoma* (St Michael Archangel); 16C Venetian works and *Correggio*, Madonna and Child and the young St John.—The little RXXII has a small Crucifixion by *Daniele da Volterra*.—RXXIII. Lombard works (*Cerano, Morazzone*, etc.).—RXXIV. Late 16C and early 17C North Italian schools, including Spring in the manner of *Giuseppe Arcimboldi*.—RXXV, at present contains a magnificent display of portraits. *Baldassarre d'Este*, Borso d'Este; *Giovanni Antonio Boltraffio*, *Lady in red; *Giovanni Bellini*, Portrait of a Humanist; *Correggio*, Giulio Zandemaria; *Lorenzo Lotto*, *Portrait of a boy holding a book; *Titian*, Monseigneur d'Aramont; *Giovanni Battista Moroni*, Count Giorgio Tasso; *Tintoretto*, Jacopo Soranzo; *Van Dyck*, *Henrietta Maria of France; *Carlo Ceresa*, Portrait of a boy of eight with a hat.—The long RXXVI contains 17C and 18C Lombard, Neapolitan, and Venetian works (*Daniele Crespi, Cerano, Morazzone, Giacomo Ceruti, Bernardino Strozzi, Giuseppe Ribera, Alessandro Magnasco, Sebastiano Ricci, Giovanni Battista Tiepolo*, and *Francesco Guardi*.

A doorway leads out onto a loggia from which a walkway continues into the SECOND FLOOR of the **Rocchetta**, where the collection of APPLIED ARTS is displayed. Beyond the hall, RXXVIII contains wrought ironwork.—RRXXIX–XXX. *Ceramics, Italian and foreign.—Stairs lead up to a display (usually closed) of 17–19C Lombard and Venetain costumes. RXXXI has a fine collection of porcelain. This overlooks the Ball Court (RXXXVII) with tapestries of the Months from designs by *Bramantino* (c 1503; restored in 1989).—RXXXII. Goldsmiths' work, enamels, *Ivories, and small bronzes.—Stairs descend to the FIRST FLOOR. RRXXXIV-XXXV. Textiles (Hellenistic, Coptic, vestments, etc.).—RRXXXVI–XXXVIII contain the MUSEUM OF MUSICAL INSTRUMENTS. This is a charming collection, with lutes, an outstanding group of wind instruments, a clavichord of 1503, a spinet played on by the 14 year old Mozart, and a fortepiano by Muzio Clementi; there is also a rich collection of musical MSS and autographs. RXXXVII, the Ball Court is usually kept closed (see above).

In the arcaded *COURTYARD OF THE ROCCHETTA, in which both *Filarete* and *Bramante* had a hand, are the entrances to the Archaeological Collection, and the Egyptian Museum. The **Egyptian Museum**, arranged in the basement of the Rocchetta, contains an interesting and well displayed collection of objects dating from the Old Kingdom to the age of Ptolemy. It is divided in two sections: the first illustrates the funerary cult of ancient Egypt, with sarcophagi, mummies, and Books of the Dead (papyri). The second room exhibits household and personal objects, canopic vases, jewellery, funerary masks, stelae, etc.—The **Archaeological Collection** contains a didactic display and a recently arranged room with material from Lombardy dating from the late Bronze Age to the Roman period. The Greek, Etruscan and Roman material is displayed at the Monastero Maggiore; see Rte 13E.—The corner tower, with the SALA DI LUCA BELTRAMI (frescoes, including one by Bramante) has been closed for years.—In this courtyard, also, are the **Archivio Storico Civico** and the **Biblioteca Trivulziana** (with an oriental art centre); they are open to students from 9–12, 14–17, except on Saturday. Elsewhere in the Castello are a medal collection, the Bertarelli Collection of prints and maps, and the Belgioioso Collection of architectural fragments, etc.

Beyond the Castello is the PARCO SEMPIONE (Pl. II;1; 47 hectares), laid out by Emilio Alemagna in 1893 on the site of a 15C Ducal park. It contains modern sculpture by Giorgio De Chirico, and others. Also the *Stadio Civico* (Pl. I;6), a sports arena originally built by Luigi Canonica in 1806–07; a high view tower (110m; no adm.) made of aluminium erected in 1933 by Giò Ponti and Cesare Chiodi; a fine equestrian *Monument to Napoleon III*, by Francesco Barzaghi (1881), transferred from the Palazzo del Senato in 1927; and the *Palazzo dell'Arte* (Pl. I;6), a hall for exhibitions (1931–33 by Giovanni Muzio). The *Aquarium* (Pl. I;6) which dates from 1906, has recently been reopened (9–12, 14–17 except Monday), with important study collections. At the farther end is the *Arco della Pace* (Pl. I;5), by Luigi Cagnola (1807–38), a triumphal arch on the model of that of Severus at Rome, with statues and bas-reliefs. It was begun in honour of Napoleon I, but was dedicated to Peace by Ferdinand I of Austria on its completion. It marks the beginning of the *Corso Sempione* (Pl. I;1), the historic Simplon Road, constructed by order of Napoleon (see Rte 9).

E.   Sant'Ambrogio and the Cenacolo

Sant'Ambrogio and the *Museum of Science and Technology* can be reached from Piazza Duomo (Via Marconi) by Bus Nos 50 or 54.—The *Civico Museo Archeologico* and the *Cenacolo* (Santa Maria delle Grazie) can be reached by Tram 24 from near Piazza Duomo (Via Orefici).

The basilica of *Sant'Ambrogio* (Pl. II;9; closed 12 –14.30), the most interesting church in Milan, was the prototype of the Lombard basilica. Founded by St Ambrose, Bishop of Milan, it was built in 379–86 beside a Christian cemetery, and enlarged in the 9C and again after 1080. The present building is the result of numerous careful restorations, and the dating of the various parts of the building is still uncertain. After a radical restoration in the 19C, it had to be repaired again after serious War damage in 1943.

EXTERIOR. The splendid ATRIUM in front of the church, on a palaeochristian plan, was probably built in 1088–99, but was reconstructed in 1150. Beneath its arcades (covered for restoration) are lapidary fragments. The austere FAÇADE consists of a five-bayed narthex below, with five arches above, graduated to fit the gable with decorative arcading. The S or Monks' campanile dates from the 9C, the higher Canons' campanile on the N is a fine Lombard tower of 1128–44, crowned with a loggia of 1889. The great *Doorway* has wood imposts made up of fragments from the 8C and 10C (heavily restored in the 18C); the bronze doors date from the 11–12C.

The beautiful INTERIOR has a low rib-vaulted nave divided from the side aisles by wide arcades supported by massive pillars beneath a matroneum. There are no transepts, and beyond the tower over the crossing, with its magnificent Ciborium, are three deep apses, the centre one raised above the crypt.—On the right is a statue of Pius IX (1880). On the left, beyond a bronze serpent of the 10C, is the *PULPIT reconstituted from fragments of the 11C and early 12C, saved after the vault collapsed in 1196 and one of the most remarkable Romanesque monuments known. Beneath it is a Roman paleochristian *Sarcophagus (4C).—In the SOUTH AISLE: 1st chapel, Descent from the Cross by *Gaudenzio Ferrari* and *Giovanni Battista Della Cerva*; 2nd chapel, altarpiece by *Gaudenzio Ferrari*, and two detached frescoes by

Giovanni Battista Tiepolo; 6th chapel, Legend of St George, by *Bernardino Lanino*. At the end of this aisle is the SACELLO DI SAN VITTORE IN CIEL D'ORO which has been closed for restoration since 1979. This sepulchral chapel was built in a Christian cemetery in the 4C and altered later. Its name refers to the splendid 5C *Mosaics covering the dome representing Saints Ambrose, Gervase, Protasius, etc. —In the NORTH AISLE (1st chapel) is a fresco of the Redeemer by *Bergognone*, and (3rd chapel), Tondo of the Madonna attributed to *Bernardino Luini*.

In the SANCTUARY (light in N aisle; fee), under the dome (which was rebuilt in the 13C and restored in the 19C), is the great *Ciborium*, thought to date from the 9C. The shafts of the columns, however, are probably of the time of St Ambrose. The four sides of the baldacchino are decorated with reliefs in coloured stucco in the Byzantine style (mid 10C; restored in 1979). The *Altar has a magnificent and justly celebrated casing presented in 835 by Archbishop Angilberto II, made of gold and silver plates sculptured in relief, with enamel and gems, the work of Volvinius, and representing scenes from the Lives of Christ and St Ambrose. In the apse are mosaics of the 4C or 8C reset in the 18C and restored after the War, and the 9C marble Bishop's throne.

The CRYPT contains the bodies of Saints Ambrose, Gervase, and Protasius in a shrine of 1897. From the E end of the N aisle a door admits to the *Portico della Canonica*, with columns carved in imitation of tree trunks, which was left unfinished by Bramante in 1499 (and reconstructed after the War). A second side was added in 1955. The upper part houses the **Museo di Sant'Ambrogio** (adm. 10–12, 15–17; fest. & Saturday 15–17; closed Tuesday and in August). This contains the 'Dalmatic of St Ambrose'; Paleochristian mosaic fragments; wood fragments (4C and 9C) from the old doors of the basilica; Medieval capitals; a Triptych by *Bernardino Zenale*; frescoes by *Bergognone* and *Bernardino Luini*; and a 15C embroidered altar frontal. Two 17C Flemish tapestries are being restored, and illuminated MSS (10–18C), including a missal of Gian Galeazzo Visconti (1395) have been removed for conservation purposes. The Treasury contains a 12C cross and the Reliquary of the Innocents (early 15C).—The 15C *Oratorio della Passione* was reopened in 1987 for exhibitions, etc. Most of the frescoes by the school of Bernardino Luini were detached in 1869 and sold to the Victoria and Albert Museum in London.

To the N of the church is the *Monumento ai Caduti*, a war memorial erected in 1928 by Giovanni Muzio. In the piazza is the *Università Cattolica*, founded in 1921, in the ex monastery of Sant'Ambrogio. It incorporates two fine cloisters designed by Bramante: the Ionic cloister was finished by Cristoforo Solari in 1513, and the Doric cloister in 1620–30.

At the beginning of Via San Vittore the *Pusterla di Sant'Ambrogio*, a gate in the medieval city walls, was reconstructed in 1939. Farther on is *San Vittore al Corpo* (Pl. I;9), in part by Galeazzo Alessi (also attributed to Vincenzo Seregni). It contains good 16C choir-stalls and frescoes. The old Olivetan convent (1507), which still contains a collection of frescoes by Bernardino Luini, was rebuilt in 1949–53, after war damage, to house the huge ***Leonardo da Vinci Museum of Science and Technology** (Pl. I;9). Admission daily, except Monday, 9–17. The material is beautifully displayed and well labelled, and the museum is much enjoyed by children.

The vestibule contains frescoes of the 15C Lombard School. To the right in the FIRST CLOISTER are displayed ancient carriages and velocipedes. To the left is the *Library* (entered from No. 19 Via San Vittore; weekdays except Monday, 9.30–12.30, 15–18.30), with the cinema beyond. Staircases mount to the FIRST FLOOR. At the top (left) is a room devoted to temporary exhibitions. On the right in the SALA DELLA BIFORA (closed in 1990) is the Mauro Collection of goldsmiths' work and precious stones; ahead the gallery is devoted to Cinematography. Rooms to the right demonstrate the evolution of the graphic arts (printing, typewriters, etc.). At the end of the gallery, to the right, is the long *GALLERIA LEONARDESCA, with models of machines and apparatus invented by Leonardo.

The rooms (right) that border the first cloister are devoted to Time Measurement and Sound, including musical instruments with a reproduction of a lute-maker's shop. Off the middle of the Leonardo Gallery (right) is the SALA DELLE COLONNE, formerly the conventual library. Three galleries round the second cloister illustrate the science of Physics, including electricity, acoustics, and nuclear reaction. Beyond the Astronomy gallery are rooms devoted to Optics and Radio and Telecommunications (with memorials of Marconi).

The lower floor is devoted to Metallurgy, Petro-Chemical Industries, and Transport with a fine gallery of early motor-cars. An external pavilion, in the form of a 19C railway station, contains Railway Locomotives (from 'Bayard', one of Stephenson's engines supplied from Newcastle for the Naples-Portici line in 1843) and Rolling Stock; beyond is another huge pavilion with aeroplanes and relics of aeronautical history, as well as sea transport (including a naval training ship). On the GROUND FLOOR is the **Civico Museo Navale Didattico**(open 9.30–12.15, 14.30–17.30 except Monday), founded in 1922, with navigational instruments and models of ships.—Two more buildings contain an exhibition of wood and trees, the *Civica Siloteca Cormio* (temporarily closed, this may be transferred to the Natural History Museum).—The Guido Rossi donation of modern art, including works by Giuseppe De Nittis, Giovanni Fattori, Vincenzo Gemito, Silvestro Lega, and Antonio Mancini, has been closed indefinitely.

From Via San Vittore, Via Zenale (right) leads to **Santa Maria delle Grazie** (Pl. I;9; closed 12–15), a church of brick and terracotta, with a very beautiful *Exterior (recently restored). It was erected in 1466–90 to the design of *Guiniforte Solari*. In 1492 Ludovico il Moro ordered the striking new choir and unusual domed crossing, and this has for long been attributed to *Bramante*, although it is now uncertain how much he was directly involved. The fine W portal is also usually attributed to Bramante.

Interior. In the 1st S chapel is a fine tomb of the Della Torre family; in the 4th are frescoes by *Gaudenzio Ferrari* (1542); in the 5th are stucco bas-reliefs (late 16C) of angels. The apse has fine stalls of carved and inlaid wood (being restored in situ). The funerary monument of Ludovico il Moro and Beatrice d'Este by Cristoforo Solari is to be placed here. At the end of the N aisle is the venerated Chapel of the Madonna delle Grazie.

From the N aisle is the entrance to the *CHIOSTRINO, also traditionally attributed to Bramante. The OLD SACRISTY (open for concerts etc.) marks a significant step in the development of Renaissance architecture.

In the *Refectory* of the adjoining Dominican convent (entrance on the left of the façade: usually open 9–13.30, 14–18.30; fest. 9–13.30; closed Monday, although it has been closed for certain periods in the past few years during restoration work) is Leonardo da Vinci's world-famous *Cenacolo** or **Last Supper**, painted in 1495–97. This is a tempera painting, not a true fresco, and the inferior durability of this technique, together with the dampness of the wall, has caused great damage to the picture, which had, in fact, considerably deteriorated by the middle of the 16C. It has been restored repeatedly over the centuries, and since 1979 careful work is being carried out to eliminate the false restorations of the past and to protect the wall from humidity, and to expose as far as possible the original work of Leonardo. Results so far (on the right-hand figures) have been spectacular. Studies are being carried out to find the best way of protecting the fresco after restoration and meanwhile only 15–20 people are allowed into the refectory at one time. On the opposite wall is a large Crucifixion by *Donato da Montorfano* (1495), the fine preservation of which is a vindication of the lasting quality of true fresco-painting. At the bottom of the fresco, at either side, are the kneeling figures, now nearly effaced, of Lodovico il Moro and his wife Beatrice d'Este and their two children, added in 1497 by *Leonardo*.

Corso Magenta (Pl. I;9) leads back towards the centre of the city. At No. 24 *Palazzo Litta*, built by Francesco Maria Ricchino (1648), has a rococo façade added in 1752–63. Opposite is the ex **Monastero Maggiore** to which belonged the church of **San Maurizio** (Pl. II;5; open Wednesday 9.30–12. 15.30–18.30) begun in 1503, perhaps by Gian Giacomo Dolcebuono, with a façade of 1574–81.

The harmonious **Interior* is divided by a wall into two parts. The W portion, originally for lay-worshippers, has small chapels below and a graceful loggia above and contains **Frescoes by Bernardino Luini* and his school (1522–29; recently restored). 3rd S chapel, frescoes by Luini himself (the life of St Catherine) on the dividing wall, Saints Cecilia, Ursula, Apollonia, and Lucia; and two lunettes. In the E portion, formerly the nuns' choir (entered from the 4th N chapel), are five more frescoes by Luini, and a huge organ (1554). A staircase (no adm.) behind the choir leads to the loggia, where are 26 fresco medallions containing half-length figures of holy virgins by *Giovanni Antonio Boltraffio* (1505–10).

The cloisters of the Monastero Maggiore now form the entrance to the **Civico Museo Archeologico** (Pl. II;5; No. 5 Corso Magenta; 9.30–12.15, 14.30–17.30; closed Tuesday), with Greek, Etruscan, and Roman material relating to the history of Milan. In the cloisters are displayed Roman sculpture (sarcophagus of 4C AD), and a large incised stone from Valle Camonica dating from the Late Bronze Age. In the garden is a restored octagonal tower of Roman origin, and a Roman sarcophagus (3C AD) acquired in 1980. On the GROUND FLOOR is a good display of antique vases; Roman sculpture (including a colossal torso of Heracles), and mosaics found in the city. The portrait busts (1C BC–4C AD) include a female head (1C AD), and the portrait of a man (3C AD). The colossal head of Jove, found near Castello Sforzesco, dates from the late 1C AD. Also displayed here are finds from Caesarea in the Holy Land and 6C–7C jewellery from Nocera Umbra and Milan.—In the BASEMENT is Etruscan material from tombs (bucchero vases, etc.); Greek ceramics (including Attic red- and black-figure vases; and Roman glass and mosaic pavements. At the end of the room can be seen the basement of a stretch of Roman wall, part of the city walls. Also displayed here is the silver Parabiago patera with fine reliefs, a Roman work of the 4C AD, and the glass 'Coppa Trivulzio' (4C–5C AD). A small room here displays Indian Gandhara sculpture (2C–3C AD).

Via Santa Maria alla Porta, on the right farther on, and Via Borromei (right) lead to *Palazzo Borromeo* (Pl. II;10), a reconstructed 15C building. In an office (adm. on request), off the second courtyard, are interesting frescoes depicting card games, etc. by a painter of the early 15C, in the International Gothic style.

The *Pinacoteca Ambrosiana* (see below) is a short way to the E.

F.   The Pinacoteca Ambrosiana and San Satiro

The PALAZZO DELL'AMBROSIANA (Pl. II;10) contains the famous library and pinacoteca founded by Cardinal Federico Borromeo at the beginning of the 17C. The palace was begun for the Cardinal by Lelio Buzzi in 1603–09 and later enlarged. It is undergoing a radical restoration. The **Pinacoteca Ambrosiana*, entered from the left side of the courtyard (adm. 9.30–17 except Saturday) contains a superb collection of paintings.

Room I. *Botticelli*, **Tondo of the Madonna and Child with angels; *Ghirlandaio*, Tondo of the Nativity; *Pinturicchio*, Madonna and Child with donor; *Bartolomeo Vivarini*, Madonna and Child with Saints; *Timoteo Viti*, Eternal Father; *Bergognone*, Four Saints, **Madonna enthroned with Saints; *Marco Basaiti*, The Risen Christ; *Bernardino Zenale*, Two Saints, Madonna and Child; *Baldassarre Estense*, Transition of the Virgin (1502; acquired in 1981).—RII. Lombard sculpture of the 8–11C.—RIII. *Bambaia*, *Fragments of the tomb of Gaston de Foix; Lombard frescoes (16C).—RIV. *'Maestro del Santo Sangue'* (also attributed to *Joos van Cleve*), Adoration of the Magi (triptych); *Bernart van Orley*, Madonna 'della Fontana'; 16C German portraits including works by *Hans Muhlich*; case of clocks and astrolabes.—RV. Huge window by *Giuseppe Bertini* (1865) showing Dante with the MS of the 'Divine Comedy'; still lifes by *Jan Soreau* and *Jan Brueghel*; case of glass, ivory, and jewellery.—RVI. *Jan Brueghel the Younger*, Fire, and Water, part of a series of the Four Elements painted for Cardinal Borromeo; all four were taken to France in 1796, when the other two still remain. Also attributed to *Brueghel*: Still life, small landscapes, Paradise, and Original Sin. *Hendrik Averkamp*, Games on the ice.

RVII. *Giorgione* (attributed), Page; *Antonio Solario*, two paintings of the head of the Baptist; *Bramantino*, Adoration of the Child; *Bernardino Luini*, Young St John, Madonna 'del Latte', and Salvator Mundi; *Giampietrino*, Madonna and Child.—RVIII. *Bernardino Luini*, *Holy Family with St Anne and the young St John, from a cartoon by Leonardo; *Bramantino*, Madonna with Saints Michael and Ambrose; *Antonio Salaino*, St John the Baptist; *Leonardo da Vinci* (attributed), *Portrait of a musician (Franchino Gaffurio?); *Ambrogio De Predis*, (attributed), *Profile of a young lady, often identified as Beatrice d'Este; *Marco d'Oggiono*, Madonna and Child with Saints.—RIX. *Sodoma*, Tondo of the Holy Family; *Bachiacca*, Holy Family.

RX, a fine 17C chamber, provides a fit setting for *Raphael*'s *Cartoon for the 'School of Athens', the only remaining cartoon of the fresco cycle in the Vatican. It was purchased by Cardinal Borromeo in 1626, carried off to the Louvre in 1796, and returned to Milan in 1816. Also here: *Gerolamo Mazzola Bedoli*, Annunciation; (above the door) *Andrea Bianchi*(Il Vespino), Copy of Leonardo's Cenacolo made in 1612–16 by order of Cardinal Borromeo (restored in 1978); *Giulio Romano*, Battle of Constantine (fragment of a cartoon for a fresco in the Vatican); *Pellegrino Tibaldi*, Emperor Diocletian (cartoon for a stained glass window in the Duomo of Milan).—RXI *Barocci*, Nativity; *Caravaggio*, *Basket of Fruit; *Gian Domenico Tiepolo*, Presentation in the Temple, Canonised bishop (two small works).—RXII. Empire-period objects; portraits (sculpted) by *Thorvaldsen* and *Canova*, and (painted) by *Andrea Appiani*.—RXIII. Facsimiles of Leonardo's drawings from the 'Codice Atlantico' (see below) are exhibited here. Venetian painters: *Giovanni Battista Moroni*, Cavalier (1554); *Titian*, Deposition, Sacred Conversation, *Adoration of the Magi, painted (with assistants) for Henri II and Diane de Poitiers (1560; in its original frame), Portrait of an old man in armour; *Bonifacio Veronese*, Holy Family; *Jacopo Bassano*, *Rest on the Flight into Egypt.—RXIV, at the bottom of the staircase (right) contains 17C Baroque paintings, including works by *Daniele Crespi*.

The Library (open 9–12, 14.30–16.30; Saturday 9–12) contains about 750,000 vols, including 3000 incunabula, and 35,000 MSS. Among the most precious objects (of which copies only are normally shown) are Arabic and Syriac MSS; a Divine Comedy (1353); Petrarch's Virgil illuminated by *Simone Martini*; the 'Codice Atlantico', a collection of Leonardo's drawings on scientific and artistic subjects; a printed Virgil (Venice, 1470) and Boccaccio (1471). In the SALA DEL LUINI are a fresco of the Crown of Thorns, and portraits of the confraternity of Santa Corona (1521) by *Bernardino Luini*.

To the N, centering on *Piazza Edison* (Pl. II;10) and *Piazza degli Affari* is the main business district of Milan with the *Borsa* (exchange), central *Post Office*, *Banca d'Italia* and other banks, most of them built at the beginning of the century. *Piazza Cordusio* (Pl. II;6) was laid out in 1889–1901 as the financial centre of the city.—Beyond Piazza Cordusio is *Palazzo Clerici* (Pl. II;6,7), in the hall of which is a magnificent ceiling-painting by Gian Battista Tiepolo (1740; adm. sometimes granted on request).

From the Ambrosiana Via Spadari (with superb food shops) leads to the busy Via Torino, across which is the church of *San Satiro* (Pl. II;10; being restored). The beautiful exterior, with a campanile of the mid-11C and the Cappella della Pietà can be seen from Via Falcone. The church was rebuilt by Bramante from 1478, with the exception of the façade, which though begun by Giovanni Antonio Amadeo in 1486 to Bramante's design was finished by Giuseppe Vandoni

(1871). The T-shaped interior, by a clever perspective device and the skilful use of stucco, is given the appearance of a Greek cross; the rear wall (restored in 1987) is actually almost flat. On the high altar is a 13C votive fresco of the Madonna and Child. At the end of the left transept is the *Cappella della Pietà* (restored in 1990), dating from the time of Archbishop Ansperto (868–881), altered at the Renaissance, with charming decoration and a terracotta Pietà, by Agostino De Fondutis. The eight-sided baptistery, off the right aisle, is a gem of Renaissance art, with terracottas by Fondutis from Bramante's design.

In Via Unione, off Via Torino, No. 5 is a fine 16C palazzo (Palazzo Erba Odescalchi; Pl. II;11; now a police headquarters, adm. on request), with a good courtyard, and a remarkable elliptical spiral staircase (restored; sometimes attributed to Bramante).

Via Unione ends in Piazza Missori. Amongst modern buildings to the left, the ruined apse and crypt of the long-lost church of *San Giovanni in Conca* have been revealed (Via Albricci). On the other side of Piazza Missori is *Sant'Alessandro* (Pl. II;10), the best Baroque church in the city. It contains elaborate marquetry and inlaid confessionals, as well as a striking rococo high altar of pietra dura, inlaid gems, and gilt bronze. *Palazzo Trivulzio* (1707–13), which also stands here, is attributed to Giovanni Ruggeri and contains in its courtyard a doorway from a destroyed mansion attributed to Bramante.

Via Torino continues towards the Carrobbio past the round church of *San Sebastiano* (Pl. II; 10; 1577), and *San Giorgio al Palazzo*, a church with a chapel decorated by Bernardino Luini.

G.   Southern Milan

South East of the Duomo is the ex-church of *Santo Stefano Maggiore* (Pl. II;12), a Baroque building (1584–95), with a later campanile, outside the predecessor of which Galeazzo Maria Sforza was murdered in 1476. In the same piazza is the church of *San Bernardino alle Osse*, with an ossuary chapel frescoed by Sebastiano Ricci (restored in 1987). The huge building of the ex-**Ospedale Maggiore** or **Ca' Grande** (Pl. II;16), beyond, has been the headquarters of the **University** since 1958. The hospital was founded by Francesco Sforza in 1456 and the remarkable building was begun by Filarete who was responsible for the fine terracotta decoration on the right wing. The façade and the decorative part of the cloister (right) survived the war; the rest has been beautifully restored. The huge collection of paintings which belonged to the hospital, including portraits of benefactors from 1602 onwards by the best known artists of the day, is to be moved to the Abbazia di Mirasole (see Rte 13J).

The Natural Science schools of the University (founded in 1924) and other important educational institutions are in the Città degli Studi laid out in 1927, which lies c 2km E of Porta Venezia (Pl. I;8).—Opposite the Ospedale can be seen the 12C campanile of *Sant'Antonio Abate* (Pl. II;11,12), a church of 1582 with good 17C stalls. Adjoining (No. 5 Via Sant'Antonio) is a charming cloister of the early 16C.

In Largo Richini, at the SW end, is a colossal bust of Dr Andrea Verga (died 1895), by Giulio Branca, and just beyond is **San Nazaro Maggiore** (Pl. II;15), a basilica consecrated in 386, rebuilt after a fire of 1075 and altered c 1578, but preserving much of its original wall and fragments of the dedication stone. Elegantly placed in front of the (SW) façade is the hexagonal *Trivulzio Chapel* (begun in 1512 by

Bramantino and continued by Cristoforo Lombardo), with family tombs. In the *Chapel of St Catherine* (entered from the N transept) is a large fresco representing the saint's martyrdom, by Bernardino Lanino (1546; covered for restoration in 1990). In the N transept is a 16C gilded wood Adoration of the Magi, and a 15C detached fresco fragment.

Via Lentasio and Via Sant'Eufemia connect the busy Corso di Porta Romana (Pl. II;15; off which rises the Torre Velasca, 1959), with Corso Italia, another traffic-ridden thoroughfare. Here are the churches of *Sant'Eufemia*, rebuilt in a Lombard Gothic style in 1870, and *San Paolo Converso* (Pl. II;15; 1549–80), the latter an attractive building (now used by a cultural society) containing frescoes by Giulio and Antonio Campi.

In Corso Italia, to the right, is the building of the *Touring Club Italiano*, with a statue of the founder, L.V. Bertarelli (1927).

Farther S in Corso Italia stands *Santa Maria dei Miracoli** or **Santa Maria presso San Celso** (Pl. I;15), a church begun by Gian Giacomo Dolcebuono in 1490 with a façade by Galeazzo Alessi and Martino Bassi (1572). The fine atrium is by Cesare Cesariano.

In the dark Interior the pictures are difficult to see. At the end of the S aisle is a *Holy Family, by *Paris Bordone* (light on left); on the dome-piers are statues of the Virgin and St John the Evangelist, by *Annibale Fontana*, and of Elijah and St John the Baptist, by *Stoldo Lorenzi*. The inlaid choir-stalls by *Galeazzo Alessi*, are beautiful. In the ambulatory are a Baptism of Christ (5th chapel), by *Gaudenzio Ferrari*, and the Conversion of St Paul (9th chapel), by *Moretto*. In the W chapel of the N aisle is Christ in the Manger, by *Bergognone*, and (next chapel), a fresco of the Madonna and Saints dating from the early 15C. In the S aisle is the entrance to the Romanesque church of **San Celso** (10C), with a façade reconstructed in 1851–54 and a graceful campanile. In the well-restored interior are fine capitals and a 14C fresco of the Madonna.

From Porta Lodovica, at the end of Corso Italia, Viale Gian Galeazzo leads W to *Porta Ticinese* (Pl. I;14), an Ionic gateway by Luigi Cagnola (1815), to the NE of which is the church of *Sant'Eustorgio** (Pl. I;14), as interesting as Sant'Ambrogio and more attractive in its variety. It was well restored in 1958–59.

The 11C church was rebuilt except for the apse in the 12–13C, and the façade reconstructed in 1863–65. The three 15C chapels on the S side, the apse, the slender campanile (1297–1309), and the graceful Portinari chapel are well seen from the outside. To the left of the façade is a 16C open-air pulpit.

The long and low INTERIOR, with aisles and apse, is typical of the Lombard basilicas, but an important series of chapels was added on the S side in the 15C. The 1st chapel (1484, with good sculptural detail) contains the tomb of Giovanni Brivio, by *Tommaso Cazzaniga* and *Benedetto Briosco* (1486), and an altarpiece by *Bergognone*; in the 2nd is the tomb of Pietro Torelli (died 1412); 4th chapel, Tomb of Stefano Visconti (died 1327), probably by *Giovanni di Balduccio*, fresco fragments, and a 14C painted Crucifix; 6th chapel, Tomb of Uberto Visconti (14C). In the S transept is the CHAPEL OF THE MAGI, where the relics of the Magi were preserved until their transfer to Cologne in 1164 (some were returned to Milan in 1903). It contains a huge Roman sarcophagus that held the relics, and on the altar are reliefs of 1347. On the high altar is a finely carved 14C Dossal.— Entered from the Confessio, with nine slender monolithic columns (above palaeochristian foundations), beneath the raised apse is the

*CAPPELLA PORTINARI (1462–68; to be restored), a gem of the Renaissance, built for Pigello Portinari and dedicated to St Peter Martyr (unlocked by the sacristan; fee). In the drum of the dome is a graceful choir of angels with festoons, in coloured stucco. The frescoed scenes of the life of St Peter Martyr are by *Vincenzo Foppa* (1466–68). In the centre is the *Tomb, borne by eight Virtues, of St Peter Martyr (Pietro da Verona, the inquisitor, murdered in 1252), by *Giovanni di Balduccio* (1339). There is also a small Museum in the church.

Corso di Porta Ticinese leads N past the arches of the ancient *Porta Ticinese* (Pl. I;14; c 1330; with a tabernacle by the workshop of Balduccio), and 16 Corinthian columns (*Colonne di San Lorenzo*), the remains of a porticus erected in the 4C, restored in the Middle Ages and again in 1954–55. On the right is *San Lorenzo Maggiore** (Pl. I;14), a church founded in the 4C. It was rebuilt after the collapse of the vault in 1103 and again in 1574–88 by Martino Bassi (who, however, preserved the original octagonal form and much of the original masonry) and has four heavy square towers. The façade dates from 1894.

The spacious domed INTERIOR is surrounded by an ambulatory beneath a gallery. The octagonal *Chapel of Sant'Aquilino** (opening off the S side; apply to the sacristan; fee) was built in the 4C as an Imperial mausoleum. The door-jambs were brought from a Roman building. It contains an early Christian sarcophagus and remarkable survivals of 5C mosaics, and covers an undercroft which was probably part of a Roman amphitheatre. Architectural fragments from the 2–3C AD onwards are preserved in the matroneum (adm. only with special permission).

Corso di Porta Ticinese ends at the *Carrobbio* (Pl. II;10,14), the Roman and early medieval centre of Milan.

In Via San Sisto is the Studio of Francesco Messina now a museum (open Tuesday, Thursday, Saturday & Sunday 9.30–12.30, 14.30–17.30) of his sculptures, drawings, etc.

H. The Giardini Pubblici and districts to the East

At the end of Via Manzoni (see Rte 13B) are the *Archi di Porta Nuova* (Pl. II;4), a gate reconstructed in 1171, with sculptures by a follower of Giovanni di Balduccio (14C). From Piazza Cavour, outside the gate, with a monument to Cavour by Odoardo Tabacchi (1865) and *Palazzo dei Giornali* by Giovanni Muzio (1937–42) with reliefs by Mario Sironi, is the entrance to the GIARDINI PUBBLICI (Pl. II;4), notable for their fine trees.

The gardens contain monuments to distinguished citizens, a small *Zoo*, and, on Via Manin, *Palazzo Dugnani* (Pl. I;7,8; being restored), with *Frescoes by Giovanni Battista Tiepolo (1731) in the Salone. The *Cinema Museum* has recently been opened here (Tuesday–Friday 15–18). On the farther side is the neo-classical building by Piero Portalupi of the *Planetarium*. Nearby, facing Corso Venezia, is the **Natural History Museum** (Pl. I;8; adm. 9.30–12.30, 14.30–17 except Monday), founded in 1838 and the most important collection of its kind in Italy. The museum building was erected in 1893, but was badly damaged in the War. The mineral collection includes the largest sulphur crystal in the world, and a topaz weighing 40 kilogrammes. The extensive zoological section contains reptiles, giant dinosaurs, etc. There is also a good library, and study collections.

In Via Palestro, S of the Park, is the VILLA BELGIOIOSO or VILLA REALE (Pl. II;4), built by Leopold Pollack in 1790. It was once occupied by the regent Eugène Beauharnais and by Marshal Radetzky, who died there in 1858. It has an attractive garden 'all'inglese' laid out in 1790. It now contains a **Gallery of Modern Art** (open 9.30–12, 14.30–17.30 except Tuesday). The 20C works have been transferred to Palazzo Reale (see Rte 13A); the arrangement may be altered when the gallery reopens. On the FIRST FLOOR are 19C Lombard paintings including the large painting called the 'Quarto Stato', a well-known work by *Giuseppe Pellizza da Volpeda*. Other artists represented include: *Andrea Appiani, Giovanni Carnovali, Francesco Hayez* (good portraits), and the sculptors *Medardo Rosso* and *Enrico Butti*. There is also a section with works by *Marino Marini*.—On the SECOND FLOOR is displayed the large Carlo Grassi bequest of 19C French and Italian works. The first room contains works by *Corot* and *Millet*.—Beyond are 19C Italian paintings by *Domenico Morelli, Guglielmo Ciardi, Vincenzo Cabianca, Giovanni Fattori, Silvestro Lega, Telemaco Signorini, Giuseppe de Nittis*, and *Giovanni Boldini*.—The section dedicated to the French Impressionists is represented by *Eugène Boudin, Sisley, Gauguin, Manet, Van Gogh*, and *Cézanne*.—Beyond more paintings by *Vincenzo Cabianca* are displayed graphic works by *Corot* and *Toulouse-Lautrec*.—In the last group of rooms are Italian paintings of the late 19C and early 20C by *Armando Spadini, Giovanni Segantini, Antonio Mancini, Umberto Boccioni, Giacomo Balla, Giorgio Morandi, Renato Guttuso, Filippo De Pisis, Giorgio de Chirico*, etc. Some of the masterpieces were twice stolen in 1975–76, but were later recovered, except for two paintings by Corot and Renoir.—A PAVILION (built in 1955) displays contemporary works, as well as temporary exhibitions.

From Piazza Cavour Via Filippo Turati and Via Vittor Pisani lead towards the station. In Via Turati the *Palazzi della Montecatini*, office buildings built in 1926–36 by Giò Ponti and others, face the houses known as *Ca' Brutta* (1923) by Giovanni Muzio. The huge Piazza della Repubblica (Pl. I;3,7) has skyscrapers including the first to be built in the city (1936, by Mario Baciocchi) at No. 27, and more houses (Nos 7–9) by Giovanni Muzio. The regularly built Via Pisani leads up to the monumental **Railway Station** (Pl. I;4), the largest in Italy, designed by Ulisse Stacchini and built in 1925–31. In the piazza is the *Pirelli Building* built in reinforced concrete in 1955–59 by Giò Ponti and others (127m high), one of the best modern buildings in the city. On the site of the first Pirelli factory, it is now the seat of the Lombard Regional government. The area to the W around Via Galvani, known as the *Centro Direzionale*, has numerous skyscrapers built in the 1960s.

From the Giardini Via Marina leads SW to *Palazzo del Senato*, now the *State Archives* (Pl.II;4), a fine Baroque building by Fabio Mangone and Francesco Maria Ricchino, originally occupied by the Collegio Elvetico, for Italian-speaking Swiss seminarists.—Opposite, Via Sant'Andrea leads back towards the centre. At No. 6 in this street the 18C *Palazzo Morando* (Pl. II;8) houses two interesting collections (both open daily except Monday, 9.30–12.15, 14.30–17.30).

On the upper floor is the **Museo di Milano**, with a sequence of paintings, drawings, prints, etc., depicting the changing face of Milan from the mid-16C onwards. On the ground floor is the **Museo di Storia Contemporanea**, a collection regarding especially the two World Wars.

Via Sant'Andrea ends in Via Monte Napoleone, with its fashionable shops, which leads (right) to Via Manzoni.

CORSO VITTORIO EMANUELE (Pl. II;8), with hotels, theatres, and shopping arcades, leads NE from behind the Duomo through a newly built area. On the left is the classic portico of the round church of *San Carlo* (1839–47), modelled on the Pantheon, and on the right, at the beginning of CORSO VENEZIA (Pl. II;8), is *San Babila* (Pl. II;8), a 12C church over-restored at the end of the 19C. The 17C column (with the Lion of St Mark) outside is covered for restoration. At No. 11 Corso Venezia is the monumental gateway of the former *Seminary* (1564),

The Pirelli Building in Milan (1955–59)

with huge caryatids; opposite is *Casa Fontana*, now *Silvestri* (No. 10), with interesting terracotta work of c 1475. The Corso, with fine mansions of the 18–19C, including the neo-classical *Palazzo Serbelloni* (No. 16) by Simone Cantoni (1793), *Palazzo Castiglioni* (No. 47; 1900–04), a famous Art Nouveau palace, and *Palazzo Saporiti* (No. 40), built in 1812, goes on to the Giardini Pubblici, the Piazzale Oberdan, and the modern area E of the station.

From San Babila (see above) Corso Monforte continues E to the *Prefettura*, and *Palazzo Isimbardi*, seat of the provincial administration, which has a fresco by Giovanni Battista Tiepolo. Via Conservatorio leads right to reach the huge church of **Santa Maria delle Passione** (Pl. I;12), founded c 1485, with an octagonal dome now attributed to Cristoforo Lombardi (1511–30), and a Baroque front by Giuseppe Rusnati (1692–1729).

It contains paintings by *Daniele Crespi* (nave and dome). In the S transept is a Descent from the Cross, by *Bernardino Luini*; just to the E is the monument of Archbishop Daniele Birago, founder of the church, by *Andrea Fusina* (1495). The N transept contains a Last Supper by *Gaudenzio Ferrari*. The MUSEUM contains frescoes in the Chapter House by *Bergognone* (c 1505), and a gallery of 17C Lombard paintings.

Entered from Via Chiossetto, a turning off Via Corridoni, farther S, is **San Pietro in Gessate** (Pl. I;12), a Gothic church built c 1475. In the S aisle is a detached fresco of the funeral of St Martin, by *Bergognone*. The CAPPELLA GRIFI (N transept; being restored) has remains of frescoes of the Story of St Ambrose, by *Bernardino Butinone* and *Bernardino Zenale* (1490). The N aisle also has fragments of 15C frescoes.

Opposite San Pietro, in the Corso di Porta Vittoria, is the huge *Palazzo di Giustizia* (1932–40, by Marcello Piacentini).—At the E end of the Corso is the *Monument of the Cinque Giornate*, by Giuseppe Grandi (1883–91), commemorating those who died during the 'Five Days' of March 1848, and a little to the S of that is the *Rotonda* (Pl. I;16), the old mortuary of the Ospedale Maggiore locally known as *Foppone*, now a children's garden and exhibition centre. The church was built by Attilio Arrigoni in 1713, and the portico by Francesco Raffagno (1725).

I.   Environs of Milan

The following places are within easy reach of the city; other places of interest include the *Naviglio Grande*, and *Abbiategrasso*, described at the end of Rte 8; *Vigevano* (Rte 8), *Pavia* (Rte 15), and *Lodi* (Rte 39).

The *British Cemetery* for the Second World War is reached by following Via Novara (beyond Pl. I;9) for 7km then turning right (Via Cascina Bellaria) for the suburban village of *Trenno* (Metropolitana 1 to Piazza De Angeli, then bus 72 towards Trenno; 25 minutes in all).

Also reached by Via Novara (bus 72) or (more directly) by Via Monte Rosa (Metropolitana 1 to Piazzale Lotto) is the sports area of SAN SIRO. Here is the football stadium (1926; enlarged 1950), the hippodrome, and the controversial *Palasport* Stadium opened in 1976 and capable of holding 14,500 spectators.

I. The Abbeys of Chiaravalle, Viboldone, and Mirasole

The Abbey of Chiaravalle is rather unattractively situated c 7km S of Milan (tram to Piazzale Corvetto, then bus to within 3 minutes walk of the abbey; or from Rigoredo Station on the Pavia or Lodi railway (20 minutes walk alongside the Pavia line). The third underground railway line from the central station will have a station at Rigoredo.

The Cistercian **Abbazia di Chiaravalle** was founded by St Bernard in 1135 and named after his own abbey of Clairvaux. The brick church (now a parish church), consecrated in 1221, has an imposing tower, of which the lower portion is original, while the upper tiers were added in the 14C. The interior was extensively altered in the 17C, but preserves inside the lantern some 13–14C frescoes; the other frescoes are the work of the *Fiamminghini* (1614), except that at the top of the night-stairs (S transept), which is by *Bernardino Luini* (1512). The carved stalls in the nave are by *Carlo Garavaglia* (1645). The sacristan shows the *Cemetery*, which contains tombs of the 13C; the remains of the *Chapter House*, with interesting graffiti; and two walks of the 13C *Cloister*. In the Chapel of St Bernard fragments of interesting frescoes have come to light, attributed by some scholars to Hieronymous Bosch (c 1499).

The **Abbazia di Viboldone**, c 12km from Milan, is reached by a secondary road from Chiaravalle which crosses over the motorway. The abbey was founded in the 13C and the church contains a Madonna enthroned by a Florentine master (1349), and a 14C Last Judgment by Giusto de'Menabuoi.

The **Abbazia di Mirasole**, c 9km S of Milan, is reached by N412 (for Pavia) and, beyond the motorway, by a road to the right. Founded in the 13C, it has been the property of the Ospedale Maggiore of Milan since 1797. It is being restored to house the pictures and library of the Ospedale Maggiore (see Rte 13G). The paintings include portraits of benefactors from 1602 onwards by the best known artists of the day, including Francesco Hayez, Giovanni Segantini, Mosè Bianchi, Felice Casorati, etc.

II. The Certosa di Pavia

The CERTOSA DI PAVIA stands just off the Milan–Pavia road at the limit of the park that, in the Middle Ages, extended N from the Castello Visconteo (see Rte 15). It is most easily visited from Pavia (8km; bus or train in 10 minutes), but is conveniently reached from Milan by coach excursion (leaving from Piazza Castello at 14.30 on Saturday & fest., January–March, and October–December, fest. only) in 45 minutes (return fare includes guide and entrance fee); or by road to (25km) *Torre del Mangano*, from where a turning on the left leads in 1km to the Certosa. On Sunday it tends to be crowded.

The ***Certosa di Pavia**, one of the famous buildings of Italy, is a Carthusian monastery founded by Gian Galeazzo Visconti in 1396 as a family mausoleum. The building was entrusted to the Campionese masons of Milan cathedral and the builders of the castle of Pavia. The monastery proper was finished in 1452, the church in 1472, under the Sforzas, with the exception of the façade which dates from the 16C. The Certosa is open from 9–11.30, 14.30–17 or 18 (closed on Monday & major national holidays); visitors are conducted in parties.

From the entrance, facing W, a vestibule, with frescoed saints by *Bernardino Luini*, leads through to the great garden-court in front of the church. On the left are the old pharmacy and food and wine stores; on the right the prior's quarters and the so-called *Palazzo Ducale*, rebuilt in the Baroque style by Francesco Maria Richini to house distinguished visitors.

The sculptural and polychrome marble decoration of the ***West Front** of the church, of almost superabundant richness, marks the height of the artistic achievement of the Quattrocento in Lombardy; it was begun in 1473 and worked upon up to 1499 by *Cristoforo* and *Antonio Mantegazza* and *Giovanni Antonio Amadeo*, then in the 16C *Cristoforo Lombardo* continued the upper part in simplified form, though it was never completed. The attribution of the various parts is still under discussion. On the lowest order of the façade are medallions of Roman emperors; above, statues and reliefs of Prophets, Apostles, and Saints, by the *Mantegazza*; and Scenes from the Life of Christ by *Amadeo*. The *GREAT PORTAL was probably designed by *Gian Cristoforo Romano* (also attributed to Gian Giacomo Dolcebuono and Amadeo) and executed by *Benedetto Briosco*, the sculptor also of the bas-reliefs representing the Life of the Virgin and of four large reliefs; the Foundation of the Carthusian Order, 1084; Laying the First Stone of the Certosa, 27 Aug, 1396; Translation to the Certosa of the body of Gian Galeazzo, 1 March, 1474; Consecration of the Church, 3 May, 1497. On each side are two very rich *Windows, by Amadeo. The upper part, by *Cristoforo Lombardo* (1540–60), is decorated with 70 statues of the 16C by Lombard masters. The rest of the exterior is best seen from the NE.

The ***Interior** is purely Gothic in plan, but Renaissance decorative motives appear towards the E end; the chapels opening off the aisle were expensively redecorated and provided with notable Baroque grilles in the 17–18C, and only traces remain of the original frescoes and glass.

NORTH AISLE. 1st chapel: Lavabo by the *Mantegazza* (c 1470).—2nd chapel: Altarpiece by *Perugino* (1499) of which only the panel representing God the Father (restored in 1986) is original; the others are 17C copies of the originals now in the National Gallery, London. —4th chapel: Massacre of the Innocents, by *Dionigi Bussola*, the best of the Baroque altar-reliefs.—6th chapel. *St Ambrose and four saints by *Bergognone* (1492).—NORTH TRANSEPT. In the centre, *Tomb statues of Lodovico il Moro and Beatrice d'Este, by *Cristoforo Solari* (1497), brought from Santa Maria delle Grazie in Milan in 1564. The frescoes include Ecce Homo (over the small W door) and Coronation of the Virgin (N apse), by *Bergognone*; and two *Angels attributed to *Bramante*, on either side of the window, above. The two *Candelabra are by *Annibale Fontana*.—The OLD SACRISTY is entered through a doorway (by *Amadeo*) with medallion-portraits of the Dukes of Milan: it has a good vault. It contains fine 17C presses. A remarkable ivory *Altarpiece, with nearly 100 statuettes, after *Baldassarre degli Embriachi* (early 15C), was formerly exhibited here. The statuettes and plaques were stolen in 1984, but most of them were refound a year later; it will probably be kept in the Museum (see below) after its restoration.

The CHOIR contains carved and inlaid *Stalls (1498), frescoes by *Daniele Crespi* (1629), and a sumptuous late 16C altar.—Another door by *Amadeo*, with medallions of the Duchesses of Milan, admits to the LAVATORIUM. Within is a finely-carved lavabo by *Alberto Maffiolo* of Carrara; on the left, *Madonna, a charming fresco by *Bernardino Luini*.—SOUTH TRANSEPT: *Tomb of Gian Galeazzo Visconti, by *Gian Cristoforo Romano* (1493–97; the Madonna is by *Benedetto Briosco*, the sarcophagus by *Galeazzo Alessi*, the figures of Fame and Victory by *Bernardino da Novate*). The fresco by *Bergognone*, above, depicts Gian Galeazzo, with his children, presenting a model of the chuch to the Virgin; higher up, two Angels attributed to *Bramante*. Over the altar, a Virgin with St Charles and St Bruno, by *Cerano*. The doorway into the little cloister is by the *Mantegazza*.—NEW SACRISTY (adm. only with special permission): Altarpiece, the Assumption, by *Andrea Solari*, completed by *Bernardino Campi*; the 16C illuminated choir-books are notable. The CHAPTER HOUSE is entered through a charming little court, perhaps the work of *Bramante*. Its rooms contain reliefs by the *Mantegazza* and after *Amadeo*.—The pretty *LITTLE CLOISTER, with its garden, has terracotta decorations in the Cremonese manner, by *Rinaldo De Stauris* (1465).—The GREAT CLOISTER, with 122 arches, also has terracotta decoration by *De Stauris* (1478). On three sides are 24 cells, each with a decorative doorway, two rooms, and a little garden below, and a bedroom and loggia above.—The REFECTORY has ceiling frescoes by *Ambrogio* and *Bernardo Bergognone*, a reader's pulpit, and a little fresco of the Madonna by the *Zavattari* or *Bergognone* (1450). From the little cloister the church can be re-entered by a beautiful little *Door adorned with a Madonna by *Amadeo* (1466).—SOUTH AISLE: over the door from the transept, Madonna, by *Bergognone*.—3rd chapel: *Bergognone*, *St Syrus, first bishop of Pavia, and other saints; unrestored ceiling-frescoes by *Jacopo de'Mottis* (1491).—4th chapel: *Bergognone*, Crucifixion.—6th chapel: Risen Christ and saints, by *Macrino d'Alba* (signed; 1496), and Evangelists, by *Bergognone*.— 7th chapel: good Baroque work by *Camillo Procaccini*; lavabo by the *Mantegazza*.—The *Museum* can only be visited with special permission.

III. Monza

MONZA, 15·5km NE of Milan, is best reached by BUS from Via Jacini near Nord station or Piazza Quattro Novembre, beside the Central station, in 20 minutes; the road (leaving Milan by Viale Sarca), entirely built up, traverses the industrial suburb of *Sesto San Giovanni* (92,000 inhab.). Railway inaugurated in 1840 (the second line to be opened in Italy), from Porta Garibaldi station, frequent services in 10–15 minutes.

Monza, nowadays a busy but pleasant industrial community (114,300 inhab.), manufacturing felt hats and cheap carpets, and internationally known to motor-racing enthusiasts, is a Lombard city of great age with a cathedral many centuries older than that of Milan.

The approach from Milan reaches Largo Mazzini just beyond the station. Via Italia leads past the church of *Santa Maria in Strada* (1357), with a terracotta front. On the left are a huge war memorial and the *Municipio*. In Piazza Roma at the end is the *Arengario*, the brick town hall of 1293, with a tall battlemented tower and a balcony for public announcements. An *Archaeological Museum* in the Salone (used also for exhibitions) is open weekdays 15–20 (festivals 10–13, 15–20; closed Monday). Via Napoleone leads back (right) to the CATHEDRAL a 13–14C building on the site of a church founded by Theodolinda, queen of Lombardy, c 595. The fine parti-coloured marble *Façade (in poor repair) by *Matteo da Campione* (1370–96; restored), has a bold doorway and rose-window, and is flanked by a brick campanile (1606, by Pellegrino Tibaldi). The interior also contains work by *Matteo*, including the organ gallery in the nave and the relief of an imperial coronation in the S transept. The chapel on the left of the high-altar contains the plain tomb of Theodolinda and is decorated with frescoes (suffering from humidity) by the *Zavattari* (1444) depicting the story of her life. Enclosed in the altar is the famous *Iron Crown of Lombardy (shown with the contents of the Treasury, see below) used at the coronation of the Holy Roman Emperors since 1311, and containing a strip of iron said to have been hammered from one of the nails used at the Crucifixion. The last emperors crowned with it were Charles V (at Bologna), Napoleon and Ferdinand I (at Milan).

The **Museo Serpero** (9–11.30, 15–17 except Monday; fest. 10–11.30, 15–16.30) houses the rich *Treasury*. Here are the personal relics of Theodolinda, including her silver-gilt *Hen and Chickens*, supposed to represent Lombardy and its seven provinces (possibly dating from the 4C and 7C), her votive cross and crown, and a book-cover with a dedicatory inscription; also 6–7C silk embroideries; a 9C ivory diptych with St Gregory and David; and a processional cross given to Theodolinda by St Gregory (altered in the 15C and 17C)—Below the cathedral to the left is a brick gate-tower of its precinct.

Beyond the Arengario Via Carlo Alberto leads to Piazza Citterio, beyond which Viale Regina Margherita leads to the decayed neo-classical *Villa Reale* (by Giuseppe Piermarini, 1777–80), a residence built for the Archduke Ferdinand of Austria, son of the Empress Maria Teresa, and presented by the King to the State in 1919, and now housing a small Civic Art Gallery of 19C paintings (open April–October, 9–17.30 except Monday). The palace is being restored, and the state rooms and royal apartments are to be opened to the public. In 1985 the Rotonda with frescoes by Andrea Appiani (1789) was restored. Its huge *Park* (7 sq. km) was created in 1805–10 by Luigi Canonica and Luigi Villoresi. It now contains the famous *Autodromo* (adm. 8–19), the motor race-track of Milan (10km), the hippodrome of Mirabello, and an 18-hole golf course. From behind the Villa an avenue leads to the *Cappella Espiatoria* (Expiatory Chapel, by Giuseppe Sacconi), erected by Victor Emmanuel III on the spot where his father Umberto I was assassinated on 29 July, 1900 by the anarchist Gaetano

Bresci.—*Desio*, 7km NW of Monza, was the birthplace of Achille Ratti (1857–1939), afterwards Pope Pius XI.

14 Milan to Tirano and Bormio

ROAD, 203km. Superstrada to (56km) **Lecco**, where it joins N36 (see below). 78km **Varenna**.—97km **Colico**. N38.—138km **Sondrio**.—155km *Tresenda*.—165km *Tirano*.—179km *Grosio*. The road was interrupted after a disastrous landslide at Morignone in 1987, but a new tunnel was opened in 1988.—203km **Bormio**.

RAILWAY TO SONDRIO (From Centrale or Porta Garibaldi station), 130km in 2¼–4hrs. Connecting light railway or bus in ½hr to *Tirano* and bus only (1¼hrs) to *Bormio*.
    The old road from Milan (N36; 3km shorter) passes through (15km) *Monza* (see above) and (26km) *Usmate*, descending into the Adda Valley to skirt *Lago di Garlate*.

The superstrada crosses over the A4 motorway and passes to the W of Monza, through the low hills of the Brianza (see Rte 12), avoiding the small towns with which the region is dotted.—27km *Carate Brianza* (2km E), a textile town visited for the remarkable *Church and baptistery at *Agliate*, on the opposite bank of the Lambro. Traditionally thought to have been founded in 881 by Ansperto, Bishop of Milan, it probably dates from the 10–11C; it was restored by Luca Beltrami in 1895. The remains of 10C frescoes here are being restored. The road passes between Lago di Pusiano and Lago di Annone to join the road from Como (see Rte 12).—56km **Lecco** (described at the end of Rte 12).—N36 now skirts the whole E side of Lake Como; the first 6km, as far as Abbadia, have been made into dual carriageway, part of a controversial and extremely costly scheme to make the road into a superstrada as far as Colico. The work, begun in 1962, has encountered serious difficulties (including several landslides with fatal accidents) as well as local opposition, and has still not been completed. The places along the lakeside are described in detail in Rte 12.—The *Views of the lake on the left are very fine.—66km *Mandello del Lario* has a view of the Grigne up the Meria valley on the right.—76km *Fiumelatte*, with an intermittant waterfall (on the right).—The landscape becomes less austere on the approach to (78km) *Varenna*. The road traverses several tunnels.—82km *Bellano*.—Beyond (90km) *Dorio* the road skirts the small bay of Piona, and at (97km) **Colico** (Rte 12) touches the shore of the Lake of Como for the last time.

FROM COLICO TO CHIAVENNA (Splügen and Maloja Passes) N36, 27km; railway in ½hr following a similar course to the road. This route diverges to the left after 3·5km from the Tirano road to cross the Adda and the partly marshy *Piano di Spagna*. Just before the river on the left can be seen the extensive ruins of the *Forte di Fuentes*, on the hill of Montecchio, now overgrown by thick vegetation. It was built by the Spaniards in 1603 and destroyed in 1798 by the French. The road now skirts the *Lago di Mezzola*, separated from the Lake of Como by the silt brought down by the Adda.—13km *Novate Mezzola*. On the left is the little *Pozzo di Riva*, an expansion of the Mera, beyond which the road enters the *Piano di Chiavenna*. *Samolaco* to the left indicates by its name ('summus lacus') the point to which the Lake of Como extended in Roman times. The valley becomes wilder and is hemmed in by black and tawny rocks. Ahead on the right appears the *Pizzo Stella* (3162m).—27km **Chiavenna** (326m), the Roman *Clavenna*, perhaps so named because it was the key (clavis) of the Splügen, Septimber, and Julier passes, is a charmingly situated town (7100 inhab.) in the fertile valley of the Mera. Above the turreted 15C *Palazzo Balbiani* rises the *Paradiso* (view), a rock on the slopes of which are botanic gardens, and an archaeological collection (to be removed to a new building). The church of *San Lorenzo* dates from the 16C, and has a massive detached campanile. The octagonal baptistery contains a font with reliefs of 1156, and in the treasury is a gold Pax of 12C German work.

The MALOJA ROAD (bus to St Moritz) leads E, ascending the VAL BREGAGLIA, the fertile upper valley of the Mera, to cross the frontier well before the pass. Many traces of a Roman road can be seen from the parallel mule-track. The hamlets form part of the commune of *Piuro*, a once thriving town that was overwhelmed by a landslide in 1618. To the left at (5km) *Santa Croce* can be seen its old campanile.—7·5km *Villa di Chiavenna* is the last Italian village. The Italian and Swiss custom-houses are passed before (10km) *Castasegna* (681m), the first Swiss village. From there the road (N3) continues by a series of zigzags over (32km) the **Maloja Pass** (1817m) into the Upper Engadine and (49km) St Moritz, all described in 'Blue Guide Switzerland'.

The SPLÜGEN ROAD from Chiavenna (N36) is remarkable for its numerous hairpin bends and long snow-galleries.—At (4km) *San Giacomo* (571m) a bridge crosses over an effluent of the Liro.—Beyond (7·5km) *Gallivaggio*, with its tall white campanile (1731) against a background of chestnut woods and precipices, the barren valley is strewn with fallen reddish rocks. The first tunnel emerges at (13km) **Campodolcino** (1103m), a summer and winter resort in a small grassy plain. A cableway mounts to the snow-fields of *Motta* (1725m).—Surmounting ten steep bends and a tunnel the road passes a grand waterfall (best view from a projecting terrace) and crosses the *Val Scalcoggia* into (17·5km) *Pianazzo* (1401m). In this sunless valley (2km right) lies **Madesimo** (1533m), a climbing centre and ski resort beneath the frontier peaks of *Pizzo d' Emet* (3211m) and *Pizzo Spàdolazzo* (2948m). There are extensive snow-fields on the *Pizzo Groppera* (2948m; cable railway) in winter (ski and sledge lifts; ski-school; skating rink). The famous ski slopes were enjoyed by Dino Buzzati. The *Val di Lei* is the only portion of Italian territory of which the waters flow into the Rhine.
    The old road diverges left in the Gola del Cardinello, abandoned in 1834 because of its dangerous position, and climbs through long snow galleries.—21km The *Cantoniera di Teggiate* provides a good sight of the Liro ravine, while from (24km) *Stuetta* there is a grand view (left) of the Pizzo Ferrè (with its fine glacier) and the Cima di Baldiscio.—28km *Montespluga* (1905m) is situated in a desolate basin filled by a hydro-electric storage reservoir.—30km The **Splügen Pass** *(Passo Spluga; 2118m)* lies on the narrow frontier-ridge (customs posts) between the mighty Pizzo Tambò (W; 3274m) and the Surettahorn (E). The pass was known to the Romans, and the route from Clavenna (Chiavenna) to Curia (Coire) is mentioned in the Antonine itinerary. The most famous crossing of the pass, however, was that of Marshal Macdonald in 1800, when despite stormy weather and bad snow conditions he succeeded in conveying an army of infantry, cavalry, and artillery from Splügen to Chiavenna between 26 November and 6 December to guard the left flank of Napoleon's Army of Italy, losing 100 men and over 100 horses in the snow. The pass is usually obstructed in November–May.— A series of steep zigzags leads down to (39km) *Splügen*, see 'Blue Guide Switzerland'.

The Tirano road from Colico keeps close to the railway, ascending the Valtellina (see below), the upper vale of the Adda.—104km *Delebio* at the foot of *Monte Legnone* (2610m) to the S.—113km **Morbegno** (255m) is a pleasant little town (8800 inhab.) at the lower end of the Bitto forge, just S of the Adda. The church of San Lorenzo (the Santuario dell'Assunta), E of the town, was begun in 1418. There is also a small natural history museum here.

A by-road climbs the *Valle del Bitto* via *Pedesina* to (17km) *Gerola Alta*, with skiing facilities. At the end of the road (22km) a chair lift ascends to Monte Ponteranica (1824m). At the head of the W arm of the valley rises the *Pizzo dei Tre Signori* (2554m) so called from its position on the boundaries of the old lordships of Milan, Venice, and the Grisons.—The *Passo di San Marco* (1986m; reached by a rough road (26·5km) from Morbegno) leads from the head of the left branch of the valley to *Mezzoldo* in the Valle Brembana (see the end of Rte 16).

The road crosses the Adda to reach the station of (120km) *Ardenno-Masino*.

N 404 ascends the VAL MASINO, diverging N, to (17km) the Bagni del Masino.—9km *Cataeggio* (791m), a climbing centre. The road winds upwards amid colossal boulders, one of which, the Sasso Remenno, is said to be the biggest in Europe. Another road (13km, right) climbs the lower slopes of *Monte Disgrazia* (3678m).—13km *San Martino* (926m) lies at the junction of the Valle di Mello (right) with the main Valle dei Bagni.—14km **Bagni del Masino** (1171m), is a quiet therapeutic spa in a sheltered site with baths and hotel, and another climbing centre.

138km **Sondrio** the capital (23,400 inhab.) of the Valtellina, stands at the mouth of the Mallero, here canalised to control its floods. The province abounds in ski resorts in the Valtellina and Valchiavenna. The *Museo Valtellinese di Storia e Arte* in Palazzo Quadrio is open 8.30–12.30, 14.30–17 except Saturday & Sunday.

The **Valtellina** or *Veltlin*, the upper valley of the Adda, is famous for the production of wines (Grumello, Sassella, etc.). The vines on the steep hillsides are trained to grow on frames. The valley has had a chequered history, but has a high cultural tradition. In the 14C it passed into the power of Milan, but in 1512 it was united to the Grisons. The Reformation took a firm hold here, and in 1620, at the instigation of the Spanish governor of Milan, the Catholic inhabitants of the valley ruthlessly massacred the Protestants on the day of the Holy Butchery (Il Sacro Macello; 19 July). Twenty years of warfare followed, but in 1639 the valley was regained by the Grisons, who held it until Napoleon's partition of 1797. The area has for long been subject to landslides and flooding, particularly in the last twenty years as a result of uncontrolled new building, deforestation, and changes in the traditional methods of cultivation. Landslides in 1983 killed 17 people, and left over 5000 homeless. In 1987 a large area was flooded and then a disastrous landslide at Morignone, which killed 30 people, isolated the entire upper valley between Sondrio and Bormio.

FROM SONDRIO TO THE VAL MALENCO.—The road ascends the Mallero.—10km *Torre Santa Maria* (796m), at the mouth of the picturesque Torreggio torrent.—14km **Chiesa** (1000m) lies at the junction of the Val Malenco and the Val Lanterna, dominated on the W by Monte Disgrazia and on the N by the snowy mass of the Bernina. Above to the NW is *Primolo*; high up on the other side of the valley is *Caspoggio* (1150m), now nearly as important as a skiing resort.—26km *Chiareggio* is a climbing centre at the head of the Val Malenco. The central massif of the Bernina, rising to 4068m, marks the frontier.—The *Lago del Palù* (1925m) at the foot of *Monte Nero* (2912m) is easily reached by cable-car from Chiesa. Another cableway ascends Monte Motta (2336m). From Caspoggio a chair-lift climbs part way (1720m) up Monte Palino (2686m).—To the S of Sondrio rises the *Corno Stella* (2620m) a famous view-point.

144km *Tresivio.*—146km *Ponte in Valtellina*. The town, 2·5km N, at the foot of the Val Fontana, has a 14–16C church, with a fresco by Bernardino Luini and a bronze ciborium of 1578. A monument commemorates the astronomer Giuseppe Piazzi (1746–1826), a native of the town and discoverer of the first asteroid.—At (154km) *Tresenda* the important road over the Passo dell'Aprica ascends on the right. The village was severely damaged by landslides in 1983.

On the left is **Teglio** (776m), once the principal place in the valley to which it gave its name (Vallis Tellina). The *Palazzo Besta* (1539) and the church of *Santa Eufemia* (late 15C) are interesting. The chapel of *San Pietro* has an 11C campanile.

FROM TRESENDA TO EDOLO, 29km. The steep ascent makes a long loop to the NE, with fine views of the Valtellina.—Just beyond (12km) the *Passo dell'Aprica* (1181m) is the centre of **Aprica**, a scattered summer and winter resort (chair-lifts, cableways, ski-lifts, skating, covered swimming pool). The road descends via (21km) *Corteno Golgito* to (29km) *Edolo*, see Rte 18.

165km **Tirano** (430m), with 8500 inhabitants, is the terminus of the Bernina and Valtellina railways, and a starting-point for the ascent of the Stelvio Pass. The old town, on the left bank of the Adda, contains historic mansions of the Visconti, Pallavicini, and Salis families. Tirano was one of the chief sufferers in the massacre in the Valtellina in 1620.—About 1km N is the pilgrimage church of *Madonna di Tirano*, begun in 1505, in the style of Bramante, with a fine doorway by Alessandro della Scala. The richly stuccoed interior has a large organ of 1617. Outside is a painted fountain of 1780. In the convent buildings is a local ethnographical musuem.

The BERNINA ROAD AND RAILWAY from Tirano to St Moritz via the Bernina Pass enter Switzerland 3km N of Tirano, although Italian is spoken all the way up to the pass. For a description of the road and railway, see 'Blue Guide Switzerland'.

Between Tirano and Bormio the Stelvio road crosses the Adda four times, but it was interrupted in 1987 because of a huge landslide at Morignone (see below). Near (168km) *Sernio* a landslip from Monte Masuccio (2816m) in 1807 fell into the Adda and formed a lake extending to (172km) *Tovo di Sant'Agata*.—174km *Mazzo di Valtellina* (560m). The church of Santo Stefano, with a portal carved by Bernardino Torigi (1508), and the Casa Lavizzari contain frescoes by Cipriano Valorsa (see below).—At (176km) *Grosotto* (615m), with its 15C houses, is the Santuario della Madonna, erected in the 17C as a thank-offering for the defeat of the Swiss Protestants in 1620, with a noteworthy choir.—179km **Grosio** (660m), a large village (4600 inhab.), with 15–16C houses including a Venosta mansion (restored as the seat of the Museo Civico). It was the birthplace of Cipriano Valorsa (1514/17–1604), 'the Raphael of the Valtellina', whose paintings adorn nearly every church in the valley. In the chestnut woods above the road are the ruins of two Venosta castles, one dating from the 12C with the Romanesque campanile of the chuch of Santi Faustino e Giovita, and the other from the 14C, with fine battlements. Here in 1966 were discoverd thousands of rock carvings (including human figures) dating from the Neolithic period to the Iron Age, the most interesting of which are on the Rupe Magna. The park is open April–October, 10–18, otherwise on request at the Municipal Library. Yellow signs indicate the paths through the park from near the huge electric power station (1917–22) beside the main road. To the left opens the Val Grosina.—At (184km) *Bolladore* (850m), cut off from sunlight for two months in winter, can be seen above, on the left, the village of *Sondalo*, with its numerous clinics amid pine woods.— Beyond (189km) *Le Prese Nuove* the road enters the defile named the Serra di Morignone.—194km *Sant'Antonio Morignone* was destroyed by a huge landslide in 1987 which covered the course of the Adda and changed the geological formation of the valley here.—At (197km) *Ponte di Cepina* (1122m) the valley expands again and in front can be seen the windings of the road over the Stelvio. *Cepina* (1139m), on the other side of the Adda, has a curious ossuary, closed by a wrought-iron grille of local workmanship (1737).—On the approach to the plain of Bormio, the town, with its old houses and steeples, backed by a magnificent circle of mountain peaks, makes a striking picture.

203km **Bormio** (920m), once the seat of a count, is an ancient town (3900 inhab.), whose many ruined towers and picturesque old houses with carved doorways and painted façades recall its once prosperous transit trade between Venice and the Grisons. It is now a well-known ski resort. Of the numerous churches, *San Vitale*, near the entrance to the town, was founded in the 12C, but the most interesting is the *Crocifisso*, on the S side of the Frodolfo, which is decorated with 15C and 16C frescoes. The painting of the Crucifixion by Agostino Ferrari dates from 1376. The *Castello de Simoni* contains a small museum. Bormio is the administrative centre of the *Stelvio National Park*, described in Rte 24.

Bormio is an attractive centre for mountain walks and well equipped for a long season of winter sports, with a ski-school and jumps, a cableway and many lifts to the main ski-fields, and a skating-rink. There is also a large covered swimming pool. In 1985 much new building took place for the world ski championships held here, and new ski slopes were created, to the detriment of the natural beauty of the area.

About 3km above Bormio on the Stelvio road are the **Bagni di Bormio**, a well-known spa with warm springs (tennis-courts, thermal swimming pool, mud baths, etc.). The 19C Baths were demolished in 1977. Some remains of the Roman baths are visible.

To the E of Bormio extend the *Val Zebrù* and *Valfurva*. In the latter is (12km) **Santa Caterina** (1718m), a resort equipped for summer climbing and winter skiing. A fine road runs S from Santa Caterina over (13km) the bleak *Passo Gavia* (2621m) to (30km) *Ponte di Legno* in the Val Camonica (see the end of Rte 18); while to the E is the Valle del Forno, with a track leading to (3¾hrs) the *Pizzini Refuge* (2705m) beneath the Ortler-Cevedale group, including *Monte Cevedale* (3780m) and the *Gran Zebrù* (3859m).

A remarkable road ascends the Valdidentro, W of Bormio, and the Valle Viola Bormina with *Arnoga*, to (25km) the *Passo di Foscagno* (2291m; Italian custom-house) beyond which lies the duty-free zone of the VALLE DI LIVIGNO. Watered by the Spöl (good trout fishing) and one of the few portions of Italian territory N of the Alpine watershed, it has recently been developed as a winter sports centre (cableways, chairlifts, and ski school).—39km **Livigno** is a long straggling village (1816m). The characteristic wood houses were built at a distance one from the other to lessen the risk of fire. The church contains good 18C wood carving. Since the 1950s the village has been developed into an important ski resort. It is connected by road with the Bernina Hospice, and with Zernez, see 'Blue Guide Switzerland'.—The *Alpisella Pass* (2285m), is the source of the Adda.—For the road to the *Stelvio Pass* and *Merano*, see Rte 25.

15 Milan to Genoa

ROAD N35, 157km leaving Milan by the Porta Ticinese. 26km *Torre del Mangano.*—34km **Pavia**, entered by the Viale Brambilla and left by the Ponte Libertà.—55km *Casteggio*, from where to Tortona N35 is coincident with N10.—66km **Voghera**.—82km **Tortona**.—102km *Serravalle Scrivia*. From there to (157km) **Genoa**, see Rte 5.

The MOTORWAY (Autostrada dei Fiori) (A7), 143km, leaves Milan just outside the Porta Ticinese and passes well W of Pavia.—Beyond (71km) *Tortona*, it follows the Scrivia running roughly parallel to N35 all the way.

RAILWAY, 150km; expresses in 1½–2¼hrs; to *Pavia*, 39km in 25 minutes; to *Tortona*, 82km in 1–1¼hrs. This route is followed by international expresses from Austria and Germany to the Italian and French rivieras.

From Milan (Porta Ticinese) the road follows the Naviglio di Pavia, an irrigation canal begun by Galeazzo Visconti, through suburbs. Near the intersection of the Genoa motorway and the ring-road, is *Milanofiori*, a commercial district begun in 1976 with a World Trade

Centre by Renzo Piano.—16km *Binasco*, with its castle.—26km *Torre del Mangano*. To the left is the road to the **Certosa di Pavia** (1·25km; described in Rte 13J).

34km **PAVIA** is an old provincial capital (86,800 inhab.) on the Ticino, noted for its university and fine medieval churches. It still preserves a number of feudal tower houses. Its development as an important industrial and agricultural centre has led to indiscriminate new building outside the limits of the historical centre.

History. Originating in the Roman *Ticinum* about 220 BC, Pavia became capital of the Lombards in the 6C, and appears under the name *Papia* in the 7C. In the church of San Michele were crowned Charlemagne (774), Berengar, the first king of Italy (888), Berengar II (950), and Frederick Barbarossa (1155). The commune took the Ghibelline side against Milan and Lodi, and afterwards passed to the Counts of Monferrato and, from 1359 onwards, to the Visconti. On 24 February 1525, in the adjacent commune of Mirabello, was fought the *Battle of Pavia*, in which Francis I was defeated and made prisoner by Charles V. It was of this battle that Francis wrote to his mother 'Madame, tout est perdu fors l'honneur'. The ramparts which still surround the city are of 17C Spanish work. Pavia is the birthplace of Lanfranc (1005–89), the first archbishop of Canterbury under the Normans, of Pope John XIV (died 984), and of Girolamo Cardano (1501–76), the physician and mathematician. The name of the Piazza Petrarca recalls Petrarch's visits to his son-in-law here.

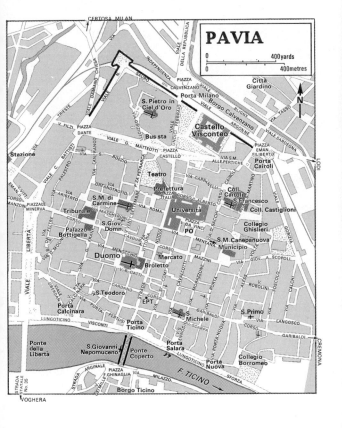

The interior of Pavia Cathedral

The STRADA NUOVA, the main street of Pavia, prolongs the old Milan road straight through the town to the Ticino bridge, and is crossed at right angles by the second main thoroughfare (Corso Cavour, Corso Mazzini) in true Roman style.

Off Corso Cavour opens the huge arcaded Piazza Vittoria (left), its market now relegated below ground to make room for parked cars. Here the *Broletto* (12C; restored in the 19C) has a façade of 1563. To the right is the **Cathedral**, begun in 1488 from designs by Cristoforo Rocchi, Giovanni Antonio Amadeo, and afterwards modified by Bramante, and probably also Leonardo da Vinci. The immense cupola was not added until 1884–85 and the façade was completed in 1933. The rest of the exterior remains unfinished. The centrally-planned interior contains a Madonna and Saints by *Carlo Sacchi* (N transept), a Madonna of the Rosary, by *Bernardino Gatti* (S transept) and a painting by Daniele Crespi on the W wall.—To the left of the church was the *Torre Civica* (78m), the campanile of two demolished Romanesque churches, with a bell-chamber by Pellegrino Tibaldi (1583). This collapsed without warning in 1989, killing four people, and wounding 15. Via dei Liguri leads S to the 12C church of *San Teodoro* with its octagonal cupola-tower. Inside, the remarkable 15–16C frescoes include a View of Pavia (W wall) in 1522, by Bernardino Lanzani, showing the many towers to which it owed its name 'the city of a hundred towers', and the Life of St Theodore (Sanctuary) attributed to Lanzani. The crypt runs crossways beneath the Sanctuary and extends beyond the walls.—From here Via Porta Pertusi descends past modern buildings to the picturesque covered *Bridge*, across the Ticino.

The original bridge built in 1351–54 on Roman foundations and roofed in 1583, collapsed in 1947 as a result of bomb-damage. The present one, a few metres farther E, is on a different design, as is the chapel replacing the 18C bridge-chapel.

The 12C church of *Santa Maria in Betlem*, in the transpontine suburb, has a façade with faience plaques; the plain Romanesque interior was well restored in 1953.

Via Capsoni leads E from the Strada to *San Michele, the finest church in Pavia, consecrated in 1155, with an octagonal cupola. The elaborately ornamented front has profusely decorated triple portals and sculptured friezes (the sandstone in which they are carved has been sadly consumed; but they were restored in 1963–67). The portals of the transept and the galleried apse are also interesting. The interior is similar to that of San Pietro in Ciel d'Oro (see below), while the gallery above the nave recalls that of Sant'Ambrogio in Milan. There is fine sculptural detail in many parts of the interior, particularly on the *Capitals. In the crypt is the tomb of Martino Salimbeni (died 1463), by the school of *Amadeo*.

Corso Garibaldi leads E to the much altered Lombard church of *San Primo*; while to the S (via Via San Giovanni) is the *Collegio Borromeo*, founded by St Charles Borromeo in 1561 and built in 1564–92 largely by Pellegrino Tibaldi; the river façade was added in 1808–20, on a design by Leopold Pollack.

Farther N in the Strada Nuova is the **University**, the successor of a famous school of law, the ancient 'Studio' at which Lanfranc is said to have studied. The school was made a university in 1361 by Galeazzo II Visconti, and is now particularly renowned for its faculties of law and medicine. The buildings were extended by Giuseppe Piermarini in 1771–79 to incorporate existing work of 1533. In the left-hand court is a statue of Volta, the most distinguished alumnus. An interesting *Museum* is open here, with historical collections relating to the university. The Teatro Fisico, and the anatomical theatre (named after Antonio Scarpa) both date from the end of the 18C. The adjoining courts of the former Ospedale di San Matteo (1499), to the E, now form the Collegio Fraccaro; the chapel houses the *Archaeological Museum*.

In the corner of Piazza Leonardo are the *Torri*, three ancient tower-houses of the noble families of Pavia, and beneath the square a 12C crypt with restored frescoes (roofed over; for the key, apply at Commune) thought to belong to the destroyed church of *Sant'Eusebio*. To the NE in Corso Cairoli rises the late-Romanesque church of *San Francesco d'Assisi* (1238–98) with a restored Gothic façade. The Renaissance building to the E was readapted to its original purpose when the *Collegio Cairoli* was founded in 1948. Farther on in Via San Martino (No. 18), the *Collegio Castiglione-Brugnatelli* (for women) occupies a 15C college building. The college Chapel (shown on request) has restored 15C frescoes attributed to Bonifacio Bembo and others. A bronze statue of Pope Pius V, by Francesco Nuvolone (1692) faces the **Collegio Ghislieri**, his foundation. The square is closed by the façade of *San Francesco di Paola*, by Giovanni Antonio Veneroni, beyond which lie the *Botanic Gardens* (roses, aquatic plants, conifers, etc). Via Scopoli returns W, past *Santa Maria delle Cacce* (16C cloister in adjacent school), to the *Palazzo Mezzabarba*, a lively Baroque building (by Giovanni Veneroni, 1730) now the Municipio. The church of *Santa Maria Canepanova*, at the corner of Via Sacchi and Via Mentana, is a graceful octagonal building begun by Giovanni Antonio Amadeo in 1507, probably to a design by Bramante; it has a pretty little cloister.

At the N end of the Strada Nuova a wide esplanade precedes the **Castello Visconteo**, the grim square fortress built by Galeazzo II Visconti in 1360–65. Of the corner turrets, in which the founder housed his great collections of literature and art, two alone remain. Freed in 1921 from four centuries of military occupation, the restored interior (adm. 10–12, 15–17; in winter, 10–12, 14–16; closed Monday), with a splendid arcaded courtyard, houses the collections of the Museo Civico. The *Archaeological Museum*, contains well-arranged fragments from Roman Pavia (including a rich collection of Roman glass), as well as sculptures and inscriptions from Lombard royal tombs. In the medieval section are mosaic pavements, good sculptures, capitals, and reconstructed portals from destroyed 11–12C churches. A damascened saddle of 9C or 10C workmanship found in the Ticino during the reconstruction of the bridge, recovered after its theft, is no longer displayed. Here also are a huge wooden model of the cathedral made by Gian Pietro Fugazza in 1497–1519, and a Museo del Risorgimento with relics of the Pavese Cairoli brothers. The *Pinacoteca Civica Malaspina* (formerly in Piazza Petrarca) has recently been arranged in restored rooms on the first floor. The most precious works include: *Giovanni Bellini*, *Madonna and Child; *Correggio*, Madonna and Child with the young St John; *Antonello da Messina*, Portrait of a Condottiere (stolen in 1970); *Ambrogio Bevilacqua*, Madonna and Child; *Giovanni Antonio Boltraffio*, Portrait of Dr Cesare de'Milio, *Portrait of a lady; *Vincenzo Foppa*, Madonna and Child with Saints; *Bergognone*, Christ carrying the Cross; *Lorenzo Veneziano*, St Augustine; *Hugo van der Goes*, Madonna and Child; *Lucas van Leyden*, Madonna in prayer; *Giovanni Battista Tiepolo*, Head of an oriental. Also, detached frescoes from local churches, and a small collection of ivories, ceramics, enamels, bronzes, and miniatures, and a fine collection of prints and engravings. *Via Griziotti leads NW to the Lombard church of ***San Pietro in Ciel d'Oro**, consecrated in 1132, and named from its former gilded vault, mentioned by Dante in his Paradiso (X, 128; quoted on the façade). The single portal in the handsome façade is asymmetrically placed, and the buttress on the right is made broader than that on the left in order to contain a stairway. The fine Romanesque interior, restored in 1875–99, has good 'bestiary' capitals. The altarpiece is the **Arca di Sant'Agostino*, one of the great sculptured shrines of Italy, executed c 1362 by Campionese masters influenced by the Pisan Giovanni di Balduccio, with a galaxy of statuettes, and bas-reliefs illustrating the story of the saint. It is supposed to contain the relics of St Augustine (died 430), removed from Carthage during the Arian persecutions. The large crypt contains the remains of the Roman poet and statesman Boëthius (476–524), executed by Theodoric on a charge of treason.

To the S, beyond Piazza Petrarca, is the large red brick church of **Santa Maria del Carmine**, begun in 1390, which has an attractive façade adorned with terracotta statues and an elaborate rose-window. The harsh colour of the glass does not enhance the interior. On some of the nave pillars are frescoes by local 15C painters. The charming lavabo in the sacristy (S transept) is by *Giovanni Antonio Amadeo*. Via Venti Settembre returns to Corso Cavour, crossing Via Mascheroni in which (right) is the little Lombard campanile of *San Giovanni Domnarum*. In Corso Cavour is a 15C tower (at No. 17) and the Bramantesque *Palazzo Bottigella* (No. 30), with fine brick ornament.

The Corso Manzoni prolongs the Corso Cavour to the railway, beyond which are (5 minutes) the church of *San Salvatore*, reconstructed in 1467–1511, with good frescoes by Bernardino Lanzani, and (10 minutes farther) *San Lanfranco*, formerly *San Sepolcro*, a 13C building containing the fine cenotaph (by Amadeo; 1498) of the beatified Lanfranc, who is buried at Canterbury, and traces of 13C frescoes (right wall of nave) including one showing the murder of St Thomas Becket at Canterbury. One of the cloisters retains some terracotta decoration also by Amadeo.

On the road (and railway) from Pavia to (42km) *Casalpusterlengo* (Rte 39) is (14km) *Belgioioso*, with the well-preserved medieval castle (open April–September, 14–sunset), where Francis I was imprisoned immediately after the battle of Pavia.

Other branch railways (slow trains) connect Pavia with *Alessandria*, via (31km) *Lomello*, the ancient capital of the Lomellina, interesting for its medieval monuments, including Santa Maria Maggiore (11C) and its Baptistery (5C; upper part rebuilt in the 8C); with *Mortara* (fine churches), and *Vercelli*; and with (32km) *Stradella* (where the museum contains fossils found near the Po, and archaeological material), for Piacenza.

Beyond Pavia the road crosses the Ticino and farther on the Po. It diverges from the railway to join the Piacenza-Alessandria road (N10) at (55km) *Casteggio*. In the 18C Palazzo della Certosa here the *Museo Storico archeologico dell'Oltrepò Pavese* (adm. Sunday 15–17) has recently been opened. It contains material from the Roman Clastidium (222 BC).—58km *Montebello*. On the left a monument marks the site of two battles: the victory of the French over the Austrians in 1800; and the Franco-Italian success of 1859, the first battle of that campaign.—66km **Voghera**, an important industrial centre (43,100 inhab.) and railway junction, has a 12C church (*Santi Flavio e Giorgio*; now the Cavalry memorial chapel) on the E side, and a *Castle* of the Visconti on the S, and a museum of fossils.

A road ascends the Staffora valley to the SE.—9km **Salice** is a little spa with iodine-impregnated waters (season May–October).—Just beyond (21km) Ponte Nizza, a by-road (left) leads to the *Abbazia di Sant'Alberto di Butrio*, founded in the 11C. Three Romanesque churches have here 15C frescoes.—29km *Varzi* is noted for its salami. The road goes on over the *Passo del Penice* (1149m; with skiing facilities) to (56km) **Bobbio** (see Rte 39) on the road from Piacenza to Genoa.

The road crosses into Piedmont just before (82km) **Tortona**, another industrial town (29,800 inhab.), with a church, *Santa Maria Canale*, perhaps dating from the 9C or 10C, and altered in the 13C and 14C, and a *Castle* dismantled by Napoleon. The *Museo Civico* in the 15C Palazzo Guidobono contains relics of ancient Dertona, including the sarcophagus of Elio Sabino (3C AD), medieval works of art, and a terracotta Pietà of 1570–80.—Direct roads and railways run from here to Alessandria and to Novi Ligure (the latter offering an alternative route to Genoa), but this route goes straight through the town, keeping to the left bank of the river Scrivia.—90km *Villalvernia*.

Farther on the road crosses the river to join the road from Novi short of (102km) *Serravalle Scrivia*. From there to (157km) **Genoa**, see Rte 5.

16 Milan to Bergamo

MOTORWAY, A4, 52km, leaving Milan by the Viale Zara to join the motorway NE of the city (it is c 10km farther by the main motorway entrance NW of the centre). This is the busiest section of the Milan–Venice motorway. The views of the Alps on the left and later of the Valley of the Adda are fine. Bergamo is entered by Via San Giorgio.—BUS every ½hr from Piazza Castello.

DIRECT ROAD, N11, 525, 49km via Gorgonzola.

RAILWAY, 54km in 1hr via Treviglio Ovest. Another route runs via Monza and Carnate-Usmate, where a change is usually necessary (51km in 1¼hrs).

The direct road (N11) leaves Milan as Corso Buenos Aires and Via Palmanova, traversing a level plain.—19km *Gorgonzola* and its district are noted for the manufacture of 'Bel Paese' as well as for the creamier veined cheese named from the town.—At (23km) *Villa Fornaci*, N525 keeps straight on to cross the Adda at (31km) *Vaprio*, while 8km farther on the motorway crosses overhead. The towers of the village churches are crowned by statues of saints: *San Colombano*, just S of Vaprio, is a charming little 11–12C church.

49km **BERGAMO**, a beautiful and interesting old city (124,000 inhab.), stands just below the first foothills of the Alps, between the valleys of the Brembo and the Serio. It is divided into two sharply distinguished parts: BERGAMO BASSA, with the station and nearly all the hotels and the principal shops; and BERGAMO ALTA (366m), the old town with its varied and attractive skyline crowning a steep hill. The economy of Bergamo is booming (clothes manufactures, metal works, etc.), and much new building has taken place on the outskirts in recent years. The hotels are often full in the autumn.

Post Office, Via Locatelli.—**Tourist Offices**, Viale Vittorio Emanuele, and 3 Via Tasso.—**Theatre**. *Donizetti* (International Piano Festival, held jointly with Brescia, in April and June).—**Bus** No. 1 from the Station to the Funicular and to Bergamo Alta, etc.—**Funicular Railway** from the end of Viale Vittorio Emanuele to the Upper Town.—**Bus Station** in Piazzale Marconi: country services to *Brescia*; to *Como*; to *Edolo*; to *Iseo*; to *Milan*; to the Bergamesque valleys (see below).

History. Bergamo emerges as a free commune in the 12C, but like other North Italian towns it soon became involved in the quarrels of the noble families. In the 14C the Visconti and the Torriani disputed possession of the city and in 1408–19 Pandolfo Malatesta was its overlord. Another period of Visconti rule ended in 1428, when Venice took the town. Bergamo remained a Venetian possession until the fall of the Republic in 1797, and until 1859 it was part of the Austrian dominion. The Bergamasques played a prominent part in the Risorgimento and furnished the largest contingent to Garibaldi's 'Thousand'. Its most famous citizens were Bartolomeo Colleoni, the 15C condottiere, and Gaetano Donizetti (1797–1848), the composer. Giovanni Battista Moroni (c 1525–78), Palma Vecchio (c 1480–1528), and probably Lorenzo Lotto (1480–1556), painters of the Venetian School, were born in the neighbourhood.

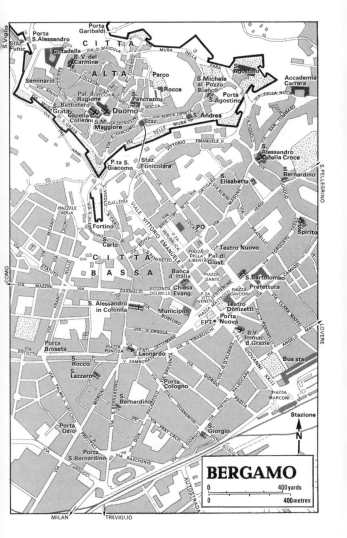

Another native, the explorer Costantino Beltrami (1779–1855), found the source of the Mississippi in 1823.

The broad avenues and pleasant squares of the **LOWER TOWN** were laid out by Marcello Piacentini in the first decades of this century; they give it a remarkable air of spaciousness. The principal thoroughfare consists of Viale Giovanni XXIII and its continuation, Viale Vittorio Emanuele. Beyond Porta Nuova with its two little Doric 'temples' Viale Giovanni XXIII crosses the monumental **Piazza**

Matteotti, which is made up of Piazza Cavour, with gardens (and a monument to Donizetti by Francesco Jerace, 1898), and PIAZZA VITTORIO VENETO, designed by Piacentini (1929), with arcades and the *Torre dei Caduti* as a war memorial. On the right the wide promenade known as the 'SENTIERONE' leads past (right) the 18C *Teatro Donizetti* (façade of 1898), to the church of *San Bartolomeo,* whose large *Altarpiece by Lorenzo Lotto (1516) has been restored. On the other side of Piazza Matteotti, Via XX Settembre, a shopping street, leads to Piazza Pontida, commercial centre of the city. Higher up Viale Vittorio Emanuele is the lower station of the funicular (built in 1886–87) to the UPPER TOWN. Above to the left stands the marble *Porta San Giacomo.* The well-preserved Upper Town is no less prosperous than the lower town. Its peaceful narrow streets have many large mansions and attractive shop fronts.

From the upper station the narrow old Via Gombito climbs past the 12C *Torre di Gombito* (52m) to PIAZZA VECCHIA, with a pretty fountain, the centre of the old town. On the right is *Palazzo Nuovo* (1611, by Vincenzo Scamozzi), opposite which rises *Palazzo della Ragione,* rebuilt in 1538–43, bearing a modern Lion of St Mark, with, to the right, the massive *Torre del Comune* (12C; ascent by lift, 10–12.30, 15–18.30 except Monday). Beyond the arcades of Palazzo della Ragione lies the small PIAZZA DEL DUOMO, crowded with fine buildings.

The CATHEDRAL, altered in 1689, has a 19C west front. Its interesting history is summarised in an inscription on the SW pier of the crossing (covered with scaffolding in 1990). The Baroque transeptal altars have statues by *Andrea Fantoni;* the St Benedict altarpiece on the 1st S altar is by Andrea Previtali (1524), and that on the 1st N altar is by Giovanni Battista Moroni.—The charming little BAPTISTERY, opposite, by Giovanni da Campione (1340), stood originally inside Santa Maria Maggiore. Between them rises the church of Santa Maria Maggiore (see below), against the S wall of which (behind a railing of 1912) is the colourful *Colleoni Chapel.* The famous condottiere Bartolomeo Colleoni, having ordered the demolition of a chapel, commisioned Giovanni Antonio Amadeo in 1472 to erect his funerary chapel on this site. It is one of the most important High Renaissance works in Lombardy, although the overlavish decorations are unconnected with the architectural forms. The elaborate carving celebrates the brilliant 'capitano generale' (who served both the Visconti and the Venetian Republic), by means of complicated allegories combining classical and biblical allusions. The charming exterior details include copies of cannon shafts (which Colleoni used for the first time in pitched battle) in the eccentric windows.

The INTERIOR (9–12, 14–17.30 or 18.30) contains the tomb of Colleoni (died 1476) and the *Tomb of his young daughter Medea (died 1470), both by *Giovanni Antonio Amadeo.* The equestrian statue in gilded wood is by *Leon* and *Sisto Siry* (c 1493). The tomb of Medea was transferred in 1842 from the country church of Basella, on the Crema road. The three altar statues are by *Pietro Lombardo* (1490). The remaining decoration of the chapel is 18C work, including some excellent marquetry seats, ceiling-frescoes by *Giovanni Battista Tiepolo,* and a Holy Family by *Angelica Kauffmann* (left side of the apse).

*Santa Maria Maggiore,** a Romanesque church begun by a certain Maestro Fredo in 1137 has a beautiful exterior. Next to the Colleoni Chapel is the *North Porch* of 1353 by Giovanni da Campione. Above the delightful arch is a tabernacle with three statues of Saints, including an equestrian statue of St Alexander. Above is another tabernacle with the Madonna and Child and Saints sculpted by Andreolo de'Bianchi (1398). Farther on can be seen the exterior of the apses, the Gothic Sacristry door (NE), also Campionese, and the exterior of the polygonal New Sacristry (1485–91). A flight of steps leads up past the fine apse and campanile (1436) to the *South Porch*, also by Giovanni da Campione (1360) above which is a little tabernacle with statues by Hans von Fernach (1401). The Baroque interior, which is hung with 16C Florentine tapestries (on a design by Alessandro Allori), contains, in the S aisle, the tomb of Cardinal Longo (1319); in the N aisle, a Baroque confessional, by *Andrea Fantoni*. Against the W wall is a monument to Donizetti (see above) by *Vincenzo Vela*; and, at the entrance to the choir, are two 16C pulpits with fine bronze rails and six bronze candelabra. The splendid intarsia choir-stalls (1522–55) are by various artists, including *Lorenzo Lotto* and *Andrea Previtali*. In the N transept are interesting 14C frescoes (including a scene in a smithy, and the Last Supper).

Between the Colleoni Chapel and the Baptistery a passageway leads through the *Curia Vescovile* (with frescoes of the 13–14C), out past the *Tempietta di Santa Croce* (probably dating from the 11C, but altered in the 16C) into Via Arena. This leads past the interesting monastery wall of Santa Grata to the *Istituto Musicale Donizetti* (No. 9). Here is a **Donizetti Museum** (open 9–12, 15–18 except Saturday and Sunday; ring for the custodian), founded in 1903. In a large room, decorated at the beginning of the 19C, are MSS., documents, wind instruments, portraits, mementoes, etc. Also here is the piano at which the composer worked.—Farther on Via San Salvatore (right) leads to *Piazza della Cittadella*, with a fine 14C portico. Here is the **Natural History Museum** (open 9–12, 14–17 except Monday), which includes a section devoted to the explorer Costantino Beltrami (see above), and the **Archaeological Museum** (9–12, 15–17.30 except Monday; Saturday and Sunday, '15–18). This well arranged local collection has material from prehistoric times to the paleochristian and Lombard era. The Roman section includes epigraphs, funerary monuments, statues, mosaics, and frescoes from a house in Via Arena.—Beyond the courtyard is the *Porta Sant'Alessandro*. From outside the gateway a bus (the funicular railway has been out of action for years) ascends in 10 minutes to *San Vigilio* (461m). Higher still is the *Castello*, with remains of a Venetian fortress, or the *Bastia* (511m). The *Botanic Garden* (open in summer) on Colle Aperto is reached by Via Beltrami. On the hillside at No. 14 Via Borgo Canale, is Donizetti's birthplace (adm. June–September on Saturday & Sunday only).

From the Cittadella Via Colleoni leads back through the town, past the ancient church of the *Carmine* (rebuilt in the 15C and in 1730), and the *House of Colleoni* (Nos 9–11), beside a little garden, bequeathed by the condottiere to a charitable institution. It has an interesting interior (usually open Tuesday and Friday 9.30–11.30, by appointment) with 15C frescoes, including a Crucifix with St Francis and Bartolomeo Colleoni. The paintings include a portrait of the condottiere by Giovanni Battista Moroni.— Via Gòmbito continues to a pretty piazza called the Mercato delle Scarpe (with the 19C funicular station to the lower town). Just off the piazza in Via Donizetti (No. 3) is the *Casa dell'Arciprete*, a Renaissance mansion of 1520 with an elegant marble façade. It contains a small *Diocesan Museum* (adm. by appointment). Another road leads out of the piazza up to the *Rocca* (no adm.), the ruins of a Visconti and Venetian castle (14C). It is surrounded by a park with fine views. On the esplanade is an important *Museo del Risorgimento* (closed for restoration).

The most pleasant (and easiest) way of reaching the Galleria dell'Accademia Carrara from the upper town is by foot (c 15 minutes). Via Porta Dipinta (for centuries the main approach to the town) descends from the Mercato delle Scarpe past the neo-classical church of *Sant'Andrea* (often closed) with a Madonna enthroned by Moretto (right chapel). Farther on is *San Michele al Pozzo Bianco* (usually open on Saturday) with a fine interior with 12–14C frescoes, and a

fresco cycle of the Life of Mary by Lorenzo Lotto. The ex-church of
Sant'Agostino (being restored as a study centre), with a good Gothic
façade, faces a green with an attractive row of houses. Outside the
Porta Sant'Agostino there is a good view of the Venetian *Walls* (begun
in 1561) which still encircle the upper town. From here Via della Noca
(left; pedestrians only) lead downhill to the *Galleria dell'Accademia
Carrara* (adm. 9.30–12.30, 14.30–17.30 except Tuesday). The Academy and Gallery were founded in 1780 by Count Giacomo Carrara,
and the splendid collection of paintings has since been augmented.
The Venetian school is particularly well represented.

Second Floor. Room I. *Bonifacio Bembo*, illuminated Tarot cards made for Filippo
Maria Visconti; *Ceneda Master*, Madonna and Child with stories of the Passion;
Antonio Vivarini, Martyrdom of St Apollonia, and of St Lucy; *Jacopo Bellini*,
*Madonna and Child.—R. 2. *Alesso Baldovinetti*, *Self-portrait (fresco); *Sandro
Botticelli*, Stories from the life of Virginia Romana, The Redeemer, *Portrait of
Giuliano de'Medici (one of several versions of this subject); *Francesco Botticini*,
Tobias and the angel; *Francesco Pesellino*, Story of Griselda; *Benedetto da
Maiano*, terracotta Angel; *Fra' Angelico* (and his School), Madonna of Humility;
Pisanello, *Portrait of Lionello d'Este; *Lorenzo Monaco*, Pietà.—R. 3. *Jacobello di
Antonello*, Madonna and Child (copy of 1480 of a lost painting by the father of
Antonello da Messina); *Bartolomeo Vivarini*, Triptych (1491); *Pietro de Saliba*, St
Sebastian; *Giovanni Bellini*, Pietà, and *Madonna Lochis; *Marco Basaiti*, The
Redeemer; *Andrea Mantegna*, *Madonna and Child; *Vittore Carpaccio* (attrib-
uted), Portrait of Doge Leonardo Loredan; *Bartolomeo Veneto*, Portrait of
Francesco Maria Della Rovere; *Marco Basaiti*, Madonna and Saints Clare and
Francis (removed for restoration), Portrait of a man; *Giovanni Bellini*, *Madonna
di Alzano; *Gentile Bellini* (attributed), Portrait of Gian Francesco Gonzaga;
Lorenzo Lotto, Portrait of a young boy; *Antonello da Messina* (attributed), St
Sebastian; *Giovanni Bellini*, Portrait of a young man; *Carlo Crivelli*, *Madonna
and Child; *Gentile Bellini*, Portrait of a Man; *Bottega di Giovanni Bellini*, Portrait
of a young man; *Lazzaro Bastiani*, Portrait of Lucio Crasso, the philosopher.
R. 4. *Lorenzo Costa*, St John the Evangelist; *Gian Francesco Bembo*, Portrait of
Giovanni Battista Santini; *Bergognone*, St Ambrose and the Emperor Theodo-
sius, Madonna, Three Saints, Madonna and Child.—R. 5. *Andrea Previtali*,
Madonna between Saints Thomas and Sebastian (1506), Polyptych of Berbenno,
Madonna and Child (1514), Madonna and Child with Saints and Paolo and
Agnese Cassotti, Madonna Baglioni; *Vincenzo Catena*, Supper at Emmaus;
Marco Basaiti, Resurrection of Christ.—R. 6. *Lorenzo Lotto*, Portrait of Lucina
Brembati; *Giovanni Cariani*, *Portrait of Giovanni Benedetto Caravaggi; *Lorenzo
Lotto*, *Mystic Marriage of St Catherine (the landscape was cut out in 1527),
*Holy Family with St Catherine (1533); *Palma Vecchio*, Madonna with Saints
John the Baptist and Mary Magdalene; *Titian*, Orpheus and Euridice, Madonna
and Child.—R. 7. *El Greco*, St Francis receiving the Stigmata; *Jacopo Bassano*,
Pietà; *Raphael*, St Sebastian, a very early work; *Jacopo Bassano*, Madonna and
Child with the young St John; *Guadenzio Ferrari*, Madonna and Child.—R. 8.
Bronzino (attributed), Portrait of Alessandro de'Medici; *Marco Basaiti*, Portrait of
a man; *Pier Francesco Foschi*, Portrait of a young man, once thought to be Baccio
Bandinelli.—R. 9 contains a fine series of portraits by *Giovanni Battista Moroni*,
including an *Old man with a book.—R. 10. *Dürer*, Calvary; *Frankfurt Master*,
Madonna 'del latte'; *Master of the St Ursula Legend*, Portrait of a man; *Jean
Clouet*, *Portrait of Louis of Clèves; *Holbein the Elder*, Christ carrying the Cross
(a standard).
It is now necessary to return to the entrance. The collection continues (left) in
Room 11, with portraits by the local painter *Carlo Ceresa*, including a Friar, and
Diana by *Guercino*.—Room 12. Portraits by *Fra' Galgario*.—R. 13. Flemish and
Dutch paintings. *Rubens*, St Domitilla; *Velasquez*, Portrait of a little girl.—R. 14.
Francesco Zuccarelli, Portrait of Margherita Tassi as a child; *Pietro Longhi*,
Venetian scene.—R. 15. Venetian school, including works by *Francesco Guardi*.
The fine collection of **Prints and Drawings**, especially important for the
Lombard and Venetian schools, is open to scholars by special request.
The seven rooms on the **First Floor** (usually closed, but opened with special
permission) contain more 15–17C paintings (Lombard and Veneto masters), and
a collection of 18C and 19C works.
There are long-term plans to restore the huge Camozzi Barracks (in an ex-14C
monastery), across the road from the Accademia, and transform them into a

Gallery of Modern and Contemporary Art with the 19C and later works belonging to the Accademia.

The centre of the town may be reached by Via San Tomaso and Via Pignolo (beware of fast traffic) which descends steeply, passing many fine 16–18C palazzi (No. 80 was once the house of Tasso's family) and the church of *Sant'Alessandro della Croce*, with many small paintings in the Sacristy including: Lorenzo Lotto, Trinity, with a landscape; Lorenzo Costa, Christ carrying the Cross, and (above) Andrea Previtali, Crucifix (with a donor). Farther on is *San Bernardino*, where the *Altarpiece is a good work by Lorenzo Lotto (Madonna and Saints; 1521). The church of *Santo Spirito*, whose dignified interior (1521) contains a Madonna and Saints by Lorenzo Lotto (4th S altar), St John the Baptist and other saints by Andrea Previtali (1st N altar), and a polyptych by Bergognone (2nd N altar), stands on the corner of Via Torquato Tasso, which leads back to the Sentierone.

To the W of the Sentierone, reached via Via Crispi and Via Garibaldi, is the church of *Sant'Alessandro in Colonna*. Outside is a column made up of antique fragments, said to mark the site of the martyrdom of St Alexander (297). The paintings in the interior include works by Leandro Bassano, Lorenzo Lotto (Deposition in the Sacristy), and Francesco Zucco.

The environs of Bergamo and the Bergamasque Valleys

The *Castle of Malpaga*, 13km SE of Bergamo (bus, going on to Cremona), is surrounded by picturesque farm buildings in the centre of an agricultural estate. It dates from the 13C and 1470, and was the country home of Bartolomeo Fogolino (c 1520; adm. by appointment on Sunday afternoon).
The road and railway from Bergamo to *Lecco* (33km in 45–60 minutes) pass (14km) *Pontida*, where the Benedictine abbey is famous as it was traditionally held to be the meeting-place of the cities that first formed the Lombard League (Milan, Bergamo, Brescia, Cremona, Mantua) in 1167. The upper cloister is a fine work probably by Pietro Isabello (c 1510). There is a small museum here. *Sotto il Monte Giovanni XXIII*, S of Pontida (on the S side of Monte Canto), has taken the name of Angelo Roncalli, born here in 1881 and pope from 1958–63. Nearby at *Carvico*, excavations since 1981 on a fortified hillock, have uncovered the foundations of a single-aisled church incorporating a narthex and semi-circular apse on the site of a wooden structure (7C–9C). —27km *Somasca* gave name to the Somascan order, whose founder, St Jerome Emiliani (1481–1537), died here.

FROM BERGAMO TO PIAZZA BREMBANA (Valle Brembana), N470, 38km; bus hourly in 70 minutes. The valley suffered from severe flooding in 1987. On the outskirts of the city the road traverses part of the *Parco Regionale dei Colli di Bergamo*, an area of some 8500 hectares protected since 1977. A by-road diverges right for *Ponteranica* with a fine parish church containing a polyptych by Lorenzo Lotto.—The main road continues through industrial and residential areas which have grown up since the 1960s.—9km *Villa d'Almè*, an expanding town on the Brembo.
A road leads across the river to *Almenno San Bartolomeo*, with interesting churches, including, outside the town, the circular Romanesque church of *San Tomé* (open 10–12, 15–17 except Friday), in pretty countryside. *Almenno San Salvatore* also has good churches. The interesting *Valle Imagna* extends N to Sant'Omobono.
The main road follows the Brembo valley. —18km *Zogno* is the chief place in the lower Valle Brembana and it has a local museum which records the life of the inhabitants of the valley (the Museo della Valle Brembana; adm. 9–12, 14–17 except Monday). The Grotta delle Meraviglie can also be visited.—From (20km) *Ambria* a road on the right ascends to *Serina* (skiing facilities), the birthplace of

Palma il Vecchio (polyptych in the sacristy of the church), and ends at *Oltre il Colle* (16km; bus from Bergamo), a summer resort, with a mineral museum.—24km **San Pellegrino Terme** (355m), with famous mineral water spings. The elegant spa town was laid out at the beginning of this century: the grand Art Nouveau buildings include the Palazzo della Fonte, the ex-Casinò Municipale, and the Grand Hotel. A funicular railway ascends to *San Pellegrino-Vetta*, a fine view-point. The Grotta del Sogno (June–September, 8–12, 14–18) here is so far the only cave open to the public in the Val Brembana which has many interesting grottoes.—29km *San Giovanni Bianco* (599m) stands at the mouth of the Val Taleggio (noted for its cheese), the fine gorge of the Enna, at the head of which (bus) are the little resorts of *Sottochiesa* and *Olda* (11km).—32km A path leads up to the remarkable medieval village of *Cornello*. This was the 14C home of the Tasso family, who are traditionally thought to have run a European postal service from here.—38km **Piazza Brembana** (510m) is a summer resort and a base for climbs in the mountains.

Above Piazza the valley divides, both branches giving access to numerous little climbing and winter-sports resorts, all served by buses in the season. To the N, on the Brembo Occidentale, is (10km) *Mezzoldo* (835m), from where the road has been improved up to the *Passo di San Marco* (1896m). A rough road continues over the pass to *Morbegno* (Rte 14); this is being repaired so that there will be a direct road between Bergamo and Sondrio in the Valtellina.—To the right of the Mezzoldo road is (9km) *Piazzatorre* at 850m, a ski resort, with a chair-lift to Monte Torcola (1789m).

Another fine road runs NE up the *Val Fondra*, the valley of the Brembo Orientale. From (3·5km) *Ponte di Bordogna* a zigzag road ascends (right) in 5·5km to *Roncobello* (1090m), a well situated resort.—11km *Branzi*, in a pleasant basin, is noted for its cheese.—15km *Carona* (1300m), lies below the *Corno Stella* (2620m), which has a magnificent view of the Alps from the Bernese Oberland to the Ortler.

From Branzi another road climbs N to (9km) **Foppolo** (1545m), the most developed of the Bergamasque mountain resorts, with chair-lifts up to the ski-fields. *San Simone* (2000m), W of Foppolo, is also visited by skiers.

FROM BERGAMO TO CLUSONE, 34km, bus in 55 minutes. The VALLE SERIANA, the principal valley in the Bergamasque Alps, is mainly industrial, with many silk and cotton mills and cement works. The upper reaches, however, are unspoilt.—The road reaches the Serio at (6·5km) *Alzano Lombardo*.—10km *Nembro* and (12·5km) *Albino* are industrial villages. In the latter is a painting of the Crucifixion by Giovanni Battista Moroni in the church of San Giuliano. **Selvino**, a pleasant hill resort has become an important skiing centre. 11km N of Nembro, it is connected by funicular railway with Albino. *Bondo Petello*, a hamlet above Albino, was the birthplace of Giovanni Battista Moroni, the painter.

From (18km) *Gazzaniga* a side-valley (right) may be ascended for **Gandino** (5·5km), an ancient little town, the birthplace of Bartolomeo Bon the elder, sculptor, and Giovanni Battista Castello, painter. It preserves a medieval rampart gate and the *Basilica (1423), with a Baroque interior, including a notable bronze balustrade of 1590. A Museum displays the treasury and ancient textiles. There is also a chair-lift ascending to the Formico plateau (skiing; see below).—20km *Vertova* has a prominent 17C parish church surrounded by a portico.—34km **Clusone** (720m) is a small resort. The town hall has a 16C clock; and on the small *Oratorio del Disciplini* is a frescoed 'Dance of Death' (1485). A road goes on up the valley (left) via (12km) *Gromo*, a summer and winter-sports resort (road up to Spiazzi, 1200m) to (23km) *Valbondione* (890m), a scattered village in a barren mountain-basin. A path to the Rifugio Curò (1915m) passes the Serio waterfall (315m), considered to be the highest in Italy. Now controlled by a hydro-electric plant, it is only opened once a year in July. A road continues to *Lizzola* (chair-lift to Rambasi, 1599m).

From Clusone a good road leads NE via (8km) *Castione della Presolana* to (14·5km) the *Passo della Presolana* (1286m), a popular holiday resort (skiing), below the *Pizzo della Presolana* (2521m). A by-road from Bratto leads in 8km part way up *Monte Pora* (1879m), now developed as a ski resort.—The road descends into the Valle di Scalve and at (22·5km) *Dezzo* joins the road from the Val Camonica (Rte 18).—31km *Schilpario* (1125m), is another summer and winter resort among pine trees in the Valle di Scalve.—The road beyond crosses (43km) the *Passo del Vivione* (1798m) and descends into the Val Camonica. 75km *Edolo*, see Rte 18.

FROM BERGAMO TO LOVERE (VALLE CAVALLINA), 41km, bus in 1¾hrs. Following the Tonale road (N42), this route crosses the Serio at (4·5km) *Seriate*, and bears left.—14km *Trescore Balneario* is a small spa with sulphur and mud baths. A chapel in the Suardi villa at Novale (shown on application) contains frescoes by

Lorenzo Lotto (1524).—From (24km) *Casazza* a road ascends (W) to the small spa of *Gaverina*. Just beyond is the *Lago di Endine*, 6km long.—26km *Spinone*. At (39km) the mouth of the Valle Borlezza the road reaches the Lago d'Iseo.—41km *Lovere*, see Rte 18.—The return may be made by the Val Borlezza and (17km) *Clusone*.

FROM BERGAMO TO BRESCIA, 50km, railway in 1hr. The uninteresting route passes (22km) *Palazzolo sull'Oglio*, and joins the main line from Milan at (32km) *Rovato*. The motorway and the ordinary road run more or less parallel with the railway.

From Bergamo the LAGO D'ISEO (Rte 18) is reached by road, via Seriate, to (27km) *Sarnico*, the starting-point of the boats, at the foot of the lake.

17 Milan to Brescia and Verona

MOTORWAY, 162km; to *Brescia* (98km), passing near Bergamo (see Rte 18).

ROAD, N11, 158km. 23km *Villa Fornaci*; keep right.—35·5km *Treviglio*.—41km *Caravaggio*.—67km *Chiari*.—72km *Coccaglio*.—93km **Brescia**, beyond which the route is almost identical with that of the railway.—121km *Desenzano*.—134km *Peschiera*.—158km **Verona**, entered by the Porta San Zeno.

RAILWAY, 148km in 1¼–1¾hrs; to *Brescia*, 83km in ¾–1¼hrs; to *Desenzano*, 111km in c 1¼hrs.

From Milan to (23km) *Villa Fornaci*, where the Bergamo road continues straight on, see Rte 16. This road branches right to (29·5km) *Cassano d'Adda*, the scene of many battles, on the Adda. Ezzelino da Romano was killed in battle here in 1259. *Rivolta d'Adda*, 6km S beyond the river, has a good church of 1088–99. Here the *Parco Zoo di Preistoria* (open daily except Tuesday) has life-size models of prehistoric animals in a park.—35·5km *Treviglio*, an agricultural and industrial centre (25,900 inhab.), is an important railway junction. The Gothic church of *San Martino* contains a fine polyptych by Bernardino Zenale and Bernardino Butinone (1485). *Santa Maria delle Lacrime* is a Renaissance building with another triptych by Butinone. Here in 1915, while in hospital with jaundice, Mussolini was married (probably bigamously) to Donna Rachele.

41km *Caravaggio*, with a sanctuary of the Blessed Virgin (church of 1575; by Pellegrino Tibaldi), was the probable birthplace of the painter Michelangelo Merisi, known as Caravaggio (c 1573–1610).—At (46km) *Mozzanica* the road crosses the Serio and, beyond (59km) Calcio, the Oglio.—67km *Chiari* has a small Pinacoteca founded in 1854 by Pietro Repossi (adm. 9–12.30, 14-30–18 except Monday and Sunday), and a library founded by Antonio Morcelli in 1817.—At (72km) *Coccaglio* the Bergamo road comes in on the left.—74km *Rovato* is connected by railway-bus with Iseo and with Soncino and Cremona.

93km **BRESCIA**, a lively town (210,000 inhab.) of great historical and artistic importance, is situated at the mouth of the Val Trompia (149m) and commanded by its old castle. Necessary reconstruction in the centre both before and since the war has been pleasantly accomplished. It is the centre of an exceptionally comprehensive network of bus services.

Hotels, near Piazza della Vittoria and the station.—**Town Bus** C from the Station to the centre (via Via Mazzini).—**Country Buses** from the Bus Station, near the railway station (some services also stop again in the town at Via Vittorio Emanuele and Porta Venezia). Frequent services to most towns in the province;

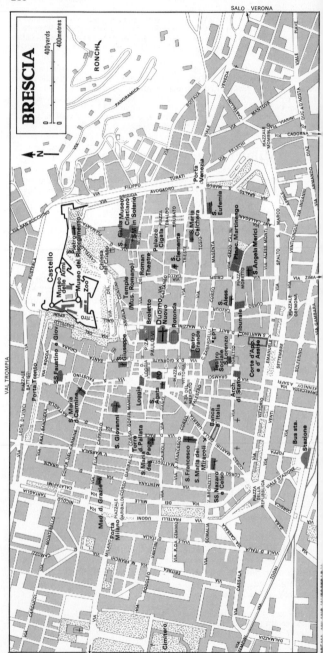

to *Toscolano*, and *Gargnano*; also to *Gardone Val Trompia*, every ½hr; frequently to *Bergamo* and *Lecco*; to *Parma*; to *Cremona*; to *Iseo* and *Edolo*; to *Desenzano*, *Sirmione*, and *Verona*; to *Milan*; to *Piacenza* and *Genoa*, etc.—
Theatre. *Teatro Grande*, with seasons of opera, plays and concerts (and an International Piano Festival, held jointly with Bergamo, in April & June).—
Swimming Pools N of the town, and at the Stadio Comunale, Viale Piave.

History. The Roman colony of *Brixia* emerges again into prominence under the 8C Lombard king Desiderius, who was born in the neighbourhood. The city was a member of the Lombard League, but in 1258 it was captured by the tyrant Ezzelino da Romano. The usual family overlordships followed, with the Lombard Torriani and Visconti, the Veronese Scaligeri, and Pandolfo Malatesta playing prominent parts. From 1426 to 1797 Brescia enjoyed prosperity under Venetian suzerainty. Between 1509 and 1516 it was twice captured by the French under Gaston de Foix. The merciless pillage after its second fall was mitigated by the generosity of Bayard, who was wounded and remained in the town for some days. The bravery of its citizens was again demonstrated in March 1849, when the town held out for ten days against the Austrian general, Haynau (nicknamed the 'hyena of Brescia'). The town suffered a great deal from bombing in the Second World War.—Among famous natives are the painters Vincenzo Foppa (? 1427–1515), Romanino (c 1485–after 1562), and Moretto (1498–1554); the Benedictine monk Arnold of Brescia (died 1155), who preached against the worldliness of the church and was hanged at Rome; the mathematician Tartaglia (Nicolò Fontana; 1506–59); and Tito Speri (1825–50), leader of the 1849 revolution and most famous of the martyrs of Belfiore.

From Milan the main road continues into the town as Corso Garibaldi; from the motorway or the station the entrance to the city is by Corso Martiri della Libertà. The central PIAZZA DELLA VITTORIA, by Marcello Piacentini (finished in 1932), built in grey marble and white stone, is an interesting example of Fascist architecture. The red marble Arengario, a rostrum for public speaking has bas-reliefs of notable events in Brescian history, by Antonio Maraini. At the N end is the striped *Post Office*.

Just to the W (hidden by a War Memorial) is the church of *Sant'Agata*, built c 1438–72. In the attractive interior is an apse fresco of the Crucifixion (1475; attributed to Andrea Bembo). The nave frescoes (1683) are by Pietro Antonio Sorisene and Pompeo Ghitti. In the 18C Chapel of the Sacrament (right) are two oval paintings by Giovanni Antonio Pellegrini.

An archway under the *Monte di Pietà* (with a loggia of 1484, and an addition of 1597), behind the Post Office, leads to the harmonious PIAZZA DELLA LOGGIA. On the left rises the *****Loggia**, a beautiful Renaissance building with exquisite sculptural detail.

The ground floor was built between 1492 and 1508, the upper storey between 1554 and 1574; architects who directed the building included Lodovico Beretta, Jacopo Sansovino, Galeazzo Alessi, and Andrea Palladio. It was restored in 1914.—On the right of the Loggia is a fine 16C portal.

Above the NE corner of the square rises the *Porta Bruciata*, a fragment of the oldest city wall. The arcade at the E end was the scene in 1974 of one of the most brutal political murders in modern Italian history when eight people lost their lives and over 100 were injured (memorial stele by Carlo Scarpa). Beneath the *Torre dell'Orologio* (c 1547) a passageway leads to Piazza del Duomo (now Piazza Paolo VI), with a delightful row of buildings lining its E side. The **Duomo**, begun in 1604 by *Giovanni Battista Lantana* on the site of the old 'summer cathedral' of San Pietro de Dom, has a cupola (1825) 82m high. The bust of Cardinal Querini over the main entrance is by *Antonio Calegari*. It has an elaborate white marble interior. In the middle of the N aisle, above a monument to Pope Paul VI, are four

panels by *Romanino*. By the 3rd S altar is the fine tomb (1510) of Saints
Apollonius and Philastrius, bishops of Brescia. The Romanesque
*Rotonda or *Duomo Vecchio* (sometimes closed in winter; apply at
the Duomo), is a circular building of the early 12C with a central
rotunda supported on eight pillars. The choir is a 15C addition. Over
the high altar is an *Assumption by *Moretto*. In front of the choir, glass
in the pavement shows remains of the walls and mosaic pavement of
Roman Baths of the Republican era excavated in 1975. Also here is a
mosaic fragment of the apse of the 8C *Basilica di San Filastrio*, burned
in 1097 with the exception of the crypt which preserves many
miscellaneous columns and traces of frescoes. Other fragments of the
mosaic pavement can be seen beneath the floor on the W side of the
rotonda. At the W end of the upper gallery is the red marble
*Sarcophagus of Bishop Berardo Maggi (died 1308), by a Campionese
sculptor.

On the right, tomb of Bishop Lambertino Baldovino (died 1349), also Campionese, while on the left is that of Bishop De Dominicis (died 1478). The S
transept altarpiece is a curious fresco of the Flagellation (15C); facing it,
Translation of the patron saints from the castle to the cathedral, an elaborate
work by *Francesco Maffei*. The ancient stairs which led up to the bell tower
(destroyed in 1708) survive.—The contents of the TREASURY are displayed only
on the last Friday in March. They include a Byzantine cross-reliquary and the
'Croce del Campo', both late 11C.
    At No. 3 Via Mazzini, behind the new cathedral, is the *Biblioteca Queriniana*,
founded by Cardinal Querini in 1750 (adm. Tuesday–Saturday 8.30–12, 14.30–
18 or 19). Among the treasures exhibited are a 6C evangelistary, with silver
letters on purple vellum, and a Concordance of the Gospels, by Eusebius (11C).

On the left of the Duomo Nuovo is the **Broletto**, a fine Lombard town
hall of 1187–1230, now serving as the Prefettura. The exterior
preserves the original appearance; in the courtyard one loggia is a
Baroque addition. Frescoes attributed to Gentile da Fabriano were
found in the Cappella Ducale here in 1986: it is known that Pandolfo
III Malatesta commissioned work for the palace from Gentile da
Fabriano in 1414.—Beyond the sturdy battlemented *Torre del Popolo*
(11C), the N part of the Broletto incorporates the little church of
Sant'Agostino, the W front of which has early-15C terracotta
ornamentation, with two lion gargoyles.
    Via dei Musei leads to Piazza del Foro with remains on the E of
porticoes of the *Forum*. On the N side are the imposing remains of the
*Capitoline Temple erected by Vespasian (AD 73), now housing a
Museum of Roman Antiquities (adm. 9–12 and 14–16.30 or 17; closed
Monday and Wednesday; Saturday 9–12, Sunday 14–17). The temple
stands on a high stylobate approached by steps, fifteen of which are
original, and has a hexastyle pronaos of Corinthian columns with a
colonnade of three columns on each side, behind. The three cellae
were probably dedicated to the Capitoline Trinity (Jupiter, Juno, and
Minerva). Beneath it is a Capitolium (unlocked by the custodian) of
the Republican era (after 89 BC) with mosaics of small uncoloured
tesserae. On the right is the Roman *Theatre*, still being cleared and
restored.
    In the cellae are inscriptions and mosaics; the bronzes, ceramics,
and glass are in a modern building behind. Most notable is the famous
*Winged Victory, a bronze statue nearly 2m high, probably the chief
figure of a chariot group from the roof of the Capitol. With it are six
bronze heads, portions of a chariot and horse, the captive Regulus,
etc., from the same group, discovered along with the statue in 1826.

The statue appears to be a Venus of the Augustan age (type of the Venus of Capua) remodelled as a Victory under Vespasian. Also outstanding are an Italic bronze helm and pottery (7–5C BC); a fine Greek amphora (c 510 BC); Gaulish silver horse-trappings (3C BC); and a fine marble head of an athlete (5C BC).

Farther on in Via dei Musei (No. 81) and on Via Piamarta is a huge group of buildings including the ex-church of **Santa Giulia**, with its convent, the church of *San Salvatore*, and *Santa Maria in Solario*, and three cloisters. These have been closed for many years for restoration, and when work is completed the ***Museum of Christian Antiquities** will be reopened here, together with the *Museo Civico d'Arte e Storia*. Excavations in one of the courtyards have brought to light Roman and Lombard buildings.

The most famous pieces in the Museum are temporarily exhibited in the Pinacoteca Tosio-Martinengo (see below). These include: the *Cross of Desiderius (mid-8C), presented to the convent of Santa Giulia by Desiderius, king of the Lombards. It is of wood overlaid with silvergilt and set with over 200 gems and cameos; on the lower arm are three portraits on gold-leaf glass, probably of the 3C. The early *Ivories include: an Ivory Coffer, with scriptural scenes in relief dating from the 4C (being restored in 1986); the Querini Diptych (5C), with Paris and Helen (?) on each leaf; the consular Diptych of Manlius Boethius (5C); and a leaf of the Diptych of the Lampadii, with circus scenes (late 5C).

Other precious possessions belonging to the Museum include: Lombardic gold jewellery; 13–14C ivories; Renaissance medals and plaquettes, including examples by Benedetto Briosco, Moderno, Andrea Riccio, Alessandro Vittoria, Pisanello, and Caradosso; Murano glass, Limoges enamels, and Deruta and other maiolica.

The former church of *Santa Giulia* (still closed) contains 16C frescoes. In the choir, Tomb of Count Marcantonio Martinengo (died 1526) from the Chiesa del Cristo (see below), with bronze and marble reliefs by Maffeo Olivieri; and a marble group by Alessandro Vittoria; on the right, intarsia lectern, by Raffaello da Marone (1520). From the apse can be seen (through a glass window) the Byzantine basilica of **San Salvatore**, a 9C rebuilding of the original Benedictine nunnery, founded by Desiderius, in which Ermengarde, daughter of Lothair I, and many other royal and noble ladies were sisters. Thirteen columns from Roman buildings support the nave, and the SW chapel contains frescoes by *Romanino*. In the crypt are 42 columns of varying origin.

A *Galleria d'Arte Moderna* here (with works by Antonio Canova, Francesco Hayez, Telemaco Signorini, Silvestro Lega, etc.) has been closed since 1975. Off the cloister is the 12C chapel of *Santa Maria in Solario* (also closed). Its square undercroft, of Roman material, has a cippus for a central column.
Via Piamarta ascends to the castle: on the left is the *Chiesa del Cristo* (being restored), with good terracotta decoration (15C) and a marble doorway of the 16C. The **Castello**, on the Cydnean hill (mentioned in Catullus, and now pierced by a road-tunnel), was rebuilt by the Visconti in the 14C and contains a *Museum of the Risorgimento* (adm. 9–12, 14–17; closed Monday & Tuesday; Saturday, 14–17; Sunday, 9–12), surrounded by a pleasant garden (small *Zoo*). The cylindrical *Torre della Mirabella* commands a fine view. A *Museum of Arms and Armour* was opened here in 1988. The interesting collection, left to the city by Luigi Marzoli in 1966, contains material from the 15C to the 18C.

In the other direction Via Gallo leads S past the site (No. 3 Piazza Labus) of the Roman *Curia* (fragments of which can be seen below ground level and on the façade of the house), to the church of **San Clemente** (if closed ring at No. 6 Vicolo San Clemente) which contains the grave of Moretto (modern bust).

Interior. *Moretto*, 2nd S altar, Saints Lucy, Cecilia, Agnes, Barbara, and Agatha; high altar, Madonna in glory; N altars: Abraham and Melchizedek, Marriage of St Catherine, St Ursula and her maidens; *Romanino*. 1st S altar, The risen Christ.

In Via Trieste, a few metres to the left, is *Santa Maria Calchera* (open for services only) containing a painting by Romanino, the Communion of St Apollonius (2nd S altar), and more works by Moretto. In the square is a monument to Tartaglia (see above), by Luigi Contratti (1918).

Via Crispi leads across Corso Magenta to Piazza Moretto, in which is a statue of Moretto. On the left is the **Pinacoteca Tosio-Martinengo** (adm. 9–12, 14–17; closed Monday & Friday; Saturday 9–12, Sunday 14–17), a large collection of paintings and frescoes in which the local schools are well represented.

In Room 1 the most precious possessions from the Museum of Christian Antiquities are displayed, including the famous Cross of Desiderius (described above). RR. 2 & 3. Detached frescoes.—R. 4. *Vincenzo Civerchio*, Saints Nicholas of Tolentino, Sebastian, and Roch (being restored); *Vincenzo Foppa*, Two Saints (being restored), *Standard of Orzinuovi, painted on both sides, Madonna and Child with Saints. The delightful painting of St George and the Dragon, with gilded armour in relief may be a copy of a work by Gentile da Fabriano in the Broletto: it is attributed to the 15C Brescian school.—R. 5. *Andrea Solario*, Christ carrying the Cross and a Cistercian monk; *Marco Palmezzano*, Christ carrying the Cross; and works by *Floriano Ferramola*.—R. 6. Works by *Giovanni Cariani*; *Zenon Veronese*, Pietà; *Venetian School* (1520), Portrait of a young man; *Francesco Bissolo* (attributed), Portrait of a young man. A case contains bronze plaques by *Riccio*, etc.—R. 7. *Raphael*, Christ blessing, *Angel (two fragments of the Coronation of St Nicholas of Tolentino, painted for Città di Castello); and works by *Francesco Francia*.—R. 8. Works by *Gian Gerolamo Savoldo*, *Callisto Piazza*, *Romanino*, *Lorenzo Lotto* (*Adoration of the Shepherds), and *Moretto*.— R. 9. *Romanino* (attributed), Portraits of Gattamelata and Nicolò Orsini da Pitigliano; *Moretto*, Portrait of a Nobleman, Salome (a portrait of Tullia d'Aragona; being restored), *Giovanni Battista Moroni*, *Portrait of a Magistrate.—R. 10. *Moretto*, Madonna in glory with Saints, Adoration of the Child, Supper at Emmaus, *St Nicholas of Bari (with a delightful Madonna and Child).—R. 11. *Moretto*, Ecce Homo with an angel; *Lattanzio Gambara*, Self-portrait (fresco fragment).—R. 13. *Sofonisba Anguissola*, Portrait of a Venetian, Portrait of a Dominican monk; and works by *Antonio Campi*, *Francesco da Bassano*, and *Jacopo Tintoretto*.—R. 16. Genre scenes by *Giacomo Ceruti*.—R. 17. *Clouet*, Henri III.— Outstanding in the fine array of drawings (which are shown only with special permission) is a *Deposition by *Giovanni Bellini*. On the ground floor is an exhibition of 15C illuminated MSS from San Francesco and the Duomo (also shown only with special permission) and the Print room with works by *Jacopo Filippo d'Argento* and others.

Sant'Angela Merici (formerly *Sant'Afra*), just to the S, rebuilt since the war, has a Transfiguration by Jacopo Tintoretto in the apse, and works by Francesco Bassano, and Giulio Cesare Procaccini, etc.

Via Moretto leads back towards the centre of the town passing (right) the church of *Sant'Alessandro*, with an Annunciation, perhaps by Jacopo Bellini, and a Deposition, by Vincenzo Civerchio (1st and 2nd S altars), and (left) the 17C *Palazzo Martinengo-Colleoni*, now the Criminal Courts. Via San Martino della Battaglia leads right to CORSO ZANARDELLI, a pleasant wide promenade (closed to traffic), with the *Teatro Grande* (entered from Via Paganora), founded in 1709, rebuilt in 1863, but with a façade of 1782.

Corso Palestro, its continuation, continues to the church of **San Francesco**, built in 1254–65, with a good façade. The plain and solemn interior has many interesting frescoes. SOUTH AISLE 1st Altar. *Moretto*, St Margaret of Cortona, St Francis, and St Jerome; between the 2nd and 3rd altars: Giottesque *Fresco of the Entombment (with a scene of monks above, dating from mid-14C); between the 3rd and 4th altars: 14C frescoes including a charming frieze of angels. Over the main altar, Madonna and Saints by *Romanino*, in a frame of rich workmanship by *Stefano Lamberti* (1502). The choir contains good stalls. In the middle of the N aisle is an elaborately decorated chapel (15–18C). The fine Cloister (1394) is reached through the Sacristy (good view of the Campanile; upper storey rebuilt).—Just to the S, in Corso Martiri is *Santa Maria dei Miracoli*, rebuilt since the war but preserving intact an elaborate Renaissance façade of 1488–1560. On the other side of the Corso is the 17C *Palazzo Martinengo Villagana* (No. 13), attributed to Stefano Carra. In Via Fratelli Bronzetti, on the right, is the 16C side doorway of the church of **Santi Nazaro e Celso**, an 18C building, noteworthy for its paintings. Over the high altar is a *Polyptych (the Risen Christ, Annunciation, and Saints), by *Titian* (1522), while *Moretto* is represented by a Transfiguration (3rd S altar) and a Coronation of the Virgin (2nd N altar). Over the N side door is an Epiphany by *Giovanni Battista Pittoni*.

From San Francesco Via della Pace leads N to the massive 13C *Torre della Pallata*. Nearby is **San Giovanni Evangelista** which has a good Renaissance doorway, also (3rd S altar) a Massacre of the Innocents (1530) and (in the apse) a *Madonna and Saints, by Moretto. In the Corpus Domini chapel (N side) are a Descent from the Cross by Civerchio, and good paintings of the Evangelists by Moretto and Romanino. In the Baptistery (NW), *Holy Trinity and four saints by Francesco Francia.—To the E, across Via Faustino is the church of *San Giuseppe*, where there is a Diocesan Museum (open 10–12, 15–17) in the two cloisters. Farther N *Santa Maria del Carmine*, a 15C building with a fine façade and portal, contains paintings by Vincenzo Foppa and his school; while, at the W end of Via Capriolo, is the *Madonna delle Grazie* by Lodovico Barcella (1522); the 15C doorway comes from another church. The delightful rococo *Interior (1617) has an exuberance of stucco reliefs and frescoes covering its barrel vault and the domes in the side aisles, in contrast with the plain columns of the nave. A 16C courtyard affords access to a venerated sanctuary rebuilt in the 19C, and covered with charming ex votos.

From Via Turati the Strada Panoramica (see plan; stiff climb) leads up to *Monte Maddalena* (875m), a noted view-point.—N of the *Castello* (see above) at No. 4 Via Ozanam the *Natural History Museum* has recently been reopened.

Environs of Brescia

To the *Lake of Iseo*, and *Edolo*, see Rte 18.

FROM BRESCIA TO THE LAKE OF IDRO AND TIONE; road, N11, & N45bis, 98km (bus).—27·5km *Tormini*. The road ascends the VAL SABBIA, watered by the Chiese.—33km. *Vobarno* has old-established iron-foundries.—At (43km) *Barghe* this route joins a shorter road from Brescia via Caino.—48km *Vestone*, a large village, has vestiges of three old castles.—At (53km) *Pieve Vecchia* a road diverges right to *Idro* village and this road continues to the **Lake of Idro** (*Lacus Eridius*), 9·5km long and 2km wide, surrounded by steep and rugged mountains. Its waters are utilised for hydroelectric power, and it is renowned for its trout. The road follows the W bank. Beyond (59km) *Anfo* it traverses the old castle of that name, founded by the Venetians in 1486 but largely rebuilt.—63km *Sant'Antonio*, where the church has a 15C fresco cycle, is connected by road with *Bagolino* (9km), a mountain village (718m) finely situated on the Caffaro (visited by skiiers, and famous for its carnival), and from there by minor road via the *Passo di Croce Domini* (29km; 1895m) with Breno (46km; Rte 18).—68km *Ponte Caffaro*, beyond the head of the lake, marks the old international frontier. High up on the left is the castle of *Lodrone*.—At (72km) *Ca' Rosso* a road on the right leads to the Val di Ledro and Riva (Rte 19). The left branch ascends the VALLI GIUDICARIE, watered by the Chiese.—77km *Condino*, the principal place in this valley, has a 15C church, with a polychromed wooden altarpiece by Maffeo Olivieri, finished by his brother Andrea (1544–45). —84km *Creto* lies at the foot of the wild *Val Daone* (left), which penetrates into the heart of the Adamello group. Near (89km) *Roncone* the road crosses the watershed (838m) and descends (98km) *Tione*, on the road from Malè to Trento (Rte 23).

Another road from Brescia ascends the VAL TROMPIA to (19km) *Gardone Val Trompia*, where the production of light arms and sporting guns continues the once flourishing firearms industry begun in this valley in the 15C.—34km *Bovegno* and (40km) *Collio* (838m), are both summer resorts, with facilites for winter sports on Monte Pezzeda (1653m; cableway and chair-lift).—43km *San Colombano* (923m) is similarly equipped. A fine new road continues to (52·5km) the *Passo del Maniva* (1670m), beyond which it deteriorates as it negotiates the Passo di Croce Domini (see above).

FROM BRESCIA TO MANTUA, road 67km, N236. At (20km) *Montichiari* this route bears left from the Parma road.—28km *Castiglione delle Stiviere* was once a fief of the Gonzagas, and the birthplace of St Louis Gonzaga (1568–91). The Museo Storico Aloisiano in the Collegio delle Nobili Vergini (adm. 9–11, 15 or 16–17 or 19) has paintings by Francesco Bassano, Federico Barocci, Giulio Carpioni, and Giambettino Cignaroli, as well as collections of glass, ironwork, and furniture. The Museo Internazionale della Croce Rossa commemorates the Red Cross founded after the battle of Solferino (see below).—50km *Goito*, where the road crosses the Mincio and the Via Postumia, was the scene of a victory of the Piedmontese over the Austrians (1848) and the birthplace of the troubadour Sordello (? 1200–1266), mentioned by Dante.—67km *Mantua*, see Rte 20.

FROM BRESCIA TO PARMA, road 98km; railway in 2¼hrs, following a parallel route.—To (20km) *Montichiari*, see above.—26km *Carpenedolo*. On the right, between this village and the station of *Calvisano*, R.S. Conway located the site of Virgil's birthplace, the ancient village of Andes.—42km *Asola* preserves its old walls, and (55km) *Canneto sull'Oglio* has a massive tower of its former castle. At (57·5km) *Piadena* the road crosses the Cremona–Mantua railway (Rte 20).—67km *San Giovanni in Croce*. Here the Villa Medici dei Vascello is a castle of 1407 remodelled with a graceful loggia in the 16C. It is surrounded by a Romantic park.—75km *Casalmaggiore* is notable for its embankments along the Po, which is crossed on a long bridge after the main Mantua-Parma road is joined. From here to (98km) *Parma*, see Rte 39.

FROM BRESCIA TO CREMONA, road 49km; parallel motorway (A21); railway in 1hr. The left fork at 10km leads in 3km to *Montirone* (2km from its station), where the beautiful *Palazzo Lechi* (1738–46), by Antonio Turbino, is completely unspoilt and has magnificent *Stables of c 1754. It contains paintings by Carlo Carloni, and was visited by Mozart in 1773 and Napoleon in 1805.—The chief intermediate town is (27km) *Verolanuova* (3·5km W of the main road), where the church contains two large paintings by Giovanni Battista Tiepolo, in excellent condition.—*Gottolengo*, 18km E of Verolanuova and 34km S of Brescia, was the main residence in 1746–56 of Lady Mary Wortley Montagu.

FROM BRESCIA TO CREMA (50km) the road passes the suburban church of *Chiesanuova*, notable for its charming *Nativity by Foppa, runs beneath the motorway, and crosses the plain.—29km *Orzinuovi* has imposing remains of the Venetian ramparts designed by Michele Sanmicheli.—Beyond the Oglio bridge is (33km) *Soncino*, where the *Castle (adm. Saturday & Sunday 9–12, 15–18, or on request at the town hall), built by Galeazzo Maria Sforza (1473), is among the best preserved in Lombardy.—50km *Crema*, see Rte 20.

Beyond Brescia the mountains gradually recede. At (101km) *Rezzato* is the 18C Villa Avogadro-Fenaroli. On the left a road leads to Salò.—115km *Lonato*, with a castle (reconstructed in its 15C form by Antonio Tagliaferri at the beginning of this century), built by the Visconti, was the scene of French victories over the Austrians in 1509, 1706, and 1796, the last an early success of Napoleon's. The castle houses a small museum (adm. by appointment) and fine library. Farther on road and railway have good views of Lake Garda and the Sirmione peninsula.—121km **Desenzano del Garda**. The main road passes close to the station above the town and to the pier (Rte 19).—124km *Rivoltella*.

A road on the right just beyond leads in 4km to the tower (74m high) of *San Martino della Battaglia*, which commemorates Victor Emmanuel's victory over the Austrian right wing on 24 June 1859. The interior (open 8–12, 14–18 or 19; winter 9–12, 13.30–17.30; closed Tuesday) contains sculptures and paintings relating to the campaign, and there are good views from the summit. At *Solferino*, 8km S, Napoleon III, in alliance with Victor Emmanuel, crushed the rest of the Austrian army on the same day. A memorial was unveiled in 1959 in honour of Jean Henri Dunant, who, horrified by the sufferings of the wounded, took the first steps to found the Red Cross. The tower of Solferino was erected probably by the Scaligers. The low moraine-hills S of the Lake of Garda, thrown up by the ancient glacier of the Adige, have been the theatre of many battles;

during Prince Eugene's campaign in the War of the Spanish Succession (1701–06), during Napoleon's enterprises (1796–1814), and during the Wars of Italian Independence (1848–49, 1859, and 1866).—At *Cavriana*, 4km SE of Solferino, is a local archaeological museum, and a romanesque church (Santa Maria della Pieve).

Beyond the junction with a road left for Sirmione, this road enters the Veneto.—134km **Peschiera del Garda**, an ancient fortress, one of the four corners of the Austrian 'quadrilateral', stands at the outflow of the Mincio from the Lake of Garda. The impressive fortifications (well seen from the road and railway), begun by the Venetians in 1553, were strengthened by Napoleon and again by the Austrians. They fell to the Piedmontese after a prolonged siege in 1848.—The hills to the S of (140km) *Castelnuovo del Garda* were the scene of the two Italian defeats of *Custoza* (1848 and 1866).—The road descends to the plain before reaching (158km) **Verona** (Rte 21).

18   Brescia to Edolo

RAILWAY, 103km in 2–3½hrs, closely following the ROAD (101km; bus in c 3hrs), which leaves Brescia by the Porta Milano and diverges from the Bergamo road at (6km) *Mandolossa*.

After traversing the fertile foothills of the Brescian Alps, planted with vineyards and gardens, called 'Ronchi', the road reaches the *Torbiere*, a large peat-moss at the S end of the Lake of Iseo, where traces of pile-dwellings have been found.—23km **Iseo** (197m), stands on the S bank of the lake which bears its name. It is a pleasant small resort. Pretty country walks may be taken in the neighbourhood. The church tower was built by Count Giacomo Oldofredi (1325), whose tomb is built into the façade alongside. Inside is a painting of St Michael by Francesco Hayez.

The pretty **Lake of Iseo**, an expansion of the Oglio, 24km long and 4·8km wide, was the *Lacus Sebinus* of the Romans. The wooded island of *Monte Isola* which it contains is 3·2km long, and the largest island in any Italian lake. Lovere, Iseo, and Pisogne are the chief holiday resorts on its banks, which have suffered less from modern development than those of the more famous lakes.

BOATS, 5 times daily between Sarnico and Lovere, call at piers on both sides of the lake (more frequent service between Sarnico and Tavernola); some additional services link interim ports; also local service Castro-Lovere-Pisogne.

Sarnico, where the steamer starts, stands at the outflow of the Oglio. It is well-known to motor-boat racing enthusiasts. To the N rise the barren slopes of *Monte Brenzone* (1333m), beneath which the W bank is lined with villas. The boat calls at *Clusane* on the E bank before re-crossing to the W bank for *Predore*, which is noted for its vines. A ruined tower of the old castle is conspicuous.—The next call is made at (½hr) *Iseo* (see above).—The boat now turns N, with Monte Isola in front, and the Punta del Corno on the left. A call is made at the island pier of *Sensole* before *Sulzano* (see below) on the E bank, and at *Peschiera Maraglio*, on the island, before touching at *Sale Marasino* (see below). It returns to the N shore of the island at *Carzano* and *Siviano*, from where a pleasant walk of an hour skirts the W shore of the island to the *Rocca Martinengo*, a half-ruined castle.—1½hr, *Tavernola Bergamasca*, on the W bank, has its campanile built on to an old castle-tower. The slower boats now return to Siviano before continuing via Marone (see below). On the approach to (2½hrs) *Riva di Solto* there is a fine view up the Valle Camonica northwards to the Adamello mountains. The black marble quarries here furnished marble for the columns of St Mark's in Venice. On the left are seen two little bays called the Bogn di Zorzino and Bogn di Castro, with curiously distorted rock-strata.—*Castro* has quarries and an old-established iron foundry.—2¾hrs, *Pisogne* (see below).

3hrs, **Lovere**, at the N extremity of the lake, is the principal tourist resort on its shores. It is reached most conveniently by boat, or by bus from Pisogne (see below) or from Bergamo or Clusone (Rte 16). To the N of the town is the church of *Santa Maria in Valvendra* (1473–83) which contains frescoed decoration and stalls (16C) and organ-shutters decorated outside by Ferramola and inside by Moretto (1518).

To the S on the lake-shore is the GALLERIA DELL'ACCADEMIA TADINI (adm. May–September, 15–18; Sunday 10–12, 15–18), which contains a few interesting paintings (Madonna, by *Jacopo Bellini*; Monks in a cave, by *Magnasco*; Madonna enthroned and Baptism of Christ by *Vincenzo Civerchio*), and in the garden the cenotaph of Faustino Tadini (died 1799), by *Antonio Canova*.

A pleasant walk ascends above the town to the *Altipiano di Lovere* (990m), with some attractive country villas, and to (2½hrs) *Bossico*, among meadows and pinewoods. From there a zigzag road descends to (6·5km) *Sovere* on the Clusone road, 6·5km from Lovere.

The railway and road beyond Iseo skirt the E bank of the lake.—26km *Pilzone* lies beneath the Pizzo dell'Orso (1001m).—28km *Sulzano* is a starting-point for visiting Monte Isola. On the right is Monte Rodondone (1143m).—31·5km *Sale Marasino* has a conspicuous church by Giovanni Battista Caniana (1737–54).—34·5km *Marone*, a large village, lies beneath *Monte Guglielmo* (1949m), the culminating point of the range between the lake and the Val Trompia.

The view is interrupted by tunnels as the road rounds the Corna dei Trenta Passi (1248m).—44·5km **Pisogne** is a large timber-growing and weaving village, principally notable as being the nearest station to Lovere (bus in connection with the trains). Noteworthy are the church of *Santa Maria della Neve*, with frescoes by Girolamo Romanino, and the 14C *Torre del Vescovo*. A winding road leads up to *Faine* (9km; 825m) and *Palot* (1031m; ski-lift). From Pian Camuno a road ascends in 18km to the chair-lift for *Monte Campione* (1762m), another ski resort.—The road now leaves the lake to enter the lovely VAL CAMONICA, the upper course of the Oglio.

Taking its name from the Camuni, a Rhaetian tribe, the valley has always been noted for its pastoral and agricultural riches; chestnut woods are an important source of wealth, both nuts and timber being exported. Wine and cheese are extensively produced, but the ironworks that were established here in the Middle Ages have dwindled in importance and the principal works nowadays are the generating stations for hydro-electric power. The extreme upper end, below the Tonale Pass, suffered severely in the First World War. Remarkable prehistoric rock carvings can be seen throughout the valley, especially in the area around Capo di Ponte (see below).

The first village of importance is (55km) **Darfo** (216m) where a bridge crosses the Oglio. On the other bank is *Corna*, now the most important part of the township, with the railway station and an ironworks at the junction of the road from Bergamo via Lovere (Rte 16). In the parish church of Darfo is a fine Entombment, attributed to Palma Giovane. At Montecchio the little church of the Oratorio contains good 15C frescoes.—56·5km **Boario Terme**, a mineral spa, stands at the junction of the Valle d'Angolo road. Good local wines are made at Erbanno, 1km N. Rock carvings (2200–1800 BC) may be seen at Corni Freschi and Crape.

FROM BOARIO TO DEZZO AND SCHILPARIO (Valle di Scalve), road, 24km, ascending the Valle d'Angolo.—3km *Angolo* has a very fine view of the triple-peaked Pizzo della Presolana. Farther on the road enters the *Gorge of the Dezzo*, a narrow chasm with overhanging cliffs.—The torrent and its falls have been almost dried up by hydro-electric works.—15km *Dezzo*, on the road from Bergamo to Edolo, and (24km) *Schilpario*, see Rte 16.

62km *Esine* (1·5km right) has churches with good frescoes.—66km *Cividate Camuno* (right) is the site of the ancient Roman capital of the valley; it preserves a few antique remains and a much more conspicuous medieval tower. Above it rises the tower of a former convent. Local finds are displayed in the Museo Archeologico della Valcamonica (adm. 9–14, fest. 9–13; closed Monday).

A winding road ascends W via Malegno to (10km) *Borno* (899m), a summer resort among pine woods in the Trobiolo valley, beneath the *Corna di San Fermo* (2326m). Between Borno and *Cogno* is the convent of the Annunziata, with two 15C cloisters.

Road and railway cross the Oglio and reach (70km) **Breno**, the chief town in the valley (5200 inhab.), an excellent centre for climbing. It is dominated by the ruins of its medieval *Castle* (9C and later). The *Parish Church* has a fine granite campanile and frescoes by Giovanni Pietro da Cemmo and Girolamo Romanino. The *Museo Camuno* merits a visit.

FROM BRENO TO THE LAKE OF IDRO, 46km, mountain road.—5km *Bienno* (445m) has two churches with frescoes (those in Santa Maria degli Orti are by Girolamo Romanino) . The road ascends to the E, passing Campolaro and the ski slopes of *Bazena* (1972m). From there (at 18km) by the Passo di Croce Domini to the head of the *Lake of Idro*, the *Passo Maniva* and *Collio*, see Rte 17.

Above Breno the dolomitic peaks of the Concarena (2549m) rise on the left and the Pizzo Badile (2435m) on the right. The villages are mostly high up on the slopes of the foothills on either side.—80km **Capo di Ponte** in the Valcamonica came to prominence with the discovery here in the Permian sandstone of tens of thousands of rock engravings dating from Neolithic to Roman times (16 BC), a span of some 8000 years. These are now the feature of the *Parco Nazionale delle Incisioni Rupestri*, one of the most important prehistoric sites in Europe. So far some 180,000 engravings depicting hunting scenes, everyday life, religious symbols, etc. have been catalogued. The Naquane rock has 900 figures carved in the Iron Age; other rocks have been found in the localities of Cemmo and Seradina. The *Centro camuno di studi preistorici* at Capo di Ponte continues research into this remarkable Alpine civilisation known as the Camuni.

Capo di Ponte is the nearest station to *Cimbergo-Paspardo* (838–945m), a scattered commune with fine views of the Concarena. The road passes *San Salvatore*, a Lombard church of the early 12C. An easier road leaves the valley-road 6·5km downstream.—In Capo di Ponte, overlooking the river, is the church of *San Siro*, dating from the 11C with earlier portions.

86km *Cedegolo*, with a church entirely frescoed by Antonio Cappello (17C), stands at the foot of the lovely Val Saviore, leading up to the Adamello mountain group, including *Cevo* (1024m) and *Saviore dell'Adamello* (1210m), 10km and 13km up the valley, both climbing centres in the *Parco Naturale Regionale dell'Adamello*, an area of 5000 sq. km, protected since 1983. Monte Adamello reaches a height of 3555m.

The road from Schilpario comes in on the right as the valley opens out again and commands fine views of Monte Aviolo and other peaks of the Baitone group to the NE.—98km *Sonico*, on the hill to the right among chestnut woods, has a large hydro-electric station.—101km **Edolo** (690m), chief place (4200 inhab.) in the upper Val Camonica, is the terminus of the railway and stands on the Aprica-Tonale road connecting the Valtellina with the Tyrol. The surroundings are beautiful. Edolo is connected by the **Aprica Pass** to Tirano.

FROM EDOLO TO THE TONALE PASS AND MALÈ, N42 (61km), bus twice daily, in winter once (weather permitting); more frequently to Ponte di Legno. The road follows the right bank of the Oglio nearly all the way, but crosses momentarily to the left bank at (5km) *Incudine*.—9·5km *Vezza d'Oglio* (1080m), stands in a magnificent position at the confluence of two tributary valleys–the Val Grande on the N, the Val Paghera on the S. At the head of the latter rises the Corno Baitone; a rough road ascends the valley to (4km) the *Cascata di Paghera*.

15km *Temù* (1149m) is a resort for winter sports on Monte Calvo (chair-lift to 1958m, and then ski-lifts), and a mountain climbing centre. The Val d'Avio is noted for its lake and its waterfalls. The valley becomes more and more attractive; above the road to the left is *Villa d'Allegno*, dominated by the scanty ruins of a castle; on the right above the pretty hamlet of Poia is seen the modern castle of Belpoggio.—19km **Ponte di Legno** (1260m), the chief resort of the region with summer and winter seasons, stands in a wide open basin with excellent ski-slopes and a chair-lift ascending S to an old fort (1847m) on the Corno d'Aola. To the N the Val di Pezzo is followed by the road to Bormio (Rte 14), while to the S and SE the Adamello and Presanella groups are conspicuous, notably the *Cima Salimmo* (3130m) in the former, and the *Castellaccio* (3028m), the NW spur of the latter.

The road now zigzags through woods up the flank of *Monte Tonale* (2694m).—29km The **Tonale Pass** (1884m), on the former Austro-Italian frontier, separating Lombardy from the Trentino, is a wide opening between the Presanella foothills, or Monticelli, and the lower peaks to the left. To the W of the pass a cable-car gives access to the snowfields of Presena, to the S, where skiing is possible in summer; and beyond the pass, numerous lifts operate on the slopes of Monte Tonale, to the N. A winged Victory marks the War Cemetery adjoining the road.—The road descends the Val Vermiglio, the upper reach of the Val di Sole.—39km *Pizzano* (1218m).—44km **Fucine** (978m) stands at the junction of the Val Vermiglio and Val di Peio, with the ruined castle of *Ossana* rising to the S.

In the latter valley, to the N, are the little summer resorts of *Cogolo* (6km) and **Peio Terme** (9km). Peio Terme is magnificently situated at a height of 1379m in a pastoral valley and is the centre for important ascents among the mountains to the NW. A cable-car and chair-lift rise to 2350m below the *Rifugio Vioz* (3536m) to the NNW on *Monte Vioz* (3644m), below *Monte Cevedale* (3764m), the highest of this group. Another road ascends the Val della Mare from Cogolo.

The main road descends the Val di Sole, which now widens, with many villages and hamlets scattered along the slopes.—46km *Pellizzano* lies on the opposite side of the river Noce.—49km *Mezzana* is a ski resort (chair-lift and cable-car from Marilleva).—52km *Mastellina* (811m), the home of the family of the painter Guardi (tablet on his father's house), lies opposite *Almazzago*, with its Romanesque belfry. The road from Tione and Trento soon comes in on the right.—61km *Malè*, see Rte 23.

19 Lake Garda

*LAKE GARDA (**Lago di Garda**; 65m), the Roman *Lacus Benacus*, is the largest and one of the most beautiful of the Italian lakes (53km long, 3·2–17·75m wide; 370·3 sq. km in area). The narrow N part, between towering cliffs, offers wild and romantic scenery; the broad basin to which the lake widens in the S is encircled by pleasant hills. The only important stream flowing into the lake is the Sarca, descending from the Trentino; the outlet is the Mincio. A purifying plant near Peschiera has been set up in an attempt to recycle the polluted waters of the lake. The natural beauty of the shore is threatened by the construction of new roads, tourist 'villages' and lakeside ports for private boats. The predominant winds (which can swell into violent storms) are the *sover*, from the N in the morning, and the *ora*, from the S in the afternoon.

Wildfowl abound, and fish (though depleted by netting) are fairly numerous. The winter climate is mild, and the summer heat tempered by refreshing breezes. The olive is much cultivated, and plantations of oranges and lemons as well as vineyards flourish on the shores. The W bank belongs to Lombardy, the E bank to Venetia, and the N extremity to the Trentino. The lake is much visited by German holiday-makers, especially since the opening of the autostrada from the Brennero.

Approaches. The 'Serenissima' Motorway (A4; Turin–Milan–Venice) skirts the S end of the lake, with exits at *Desenzano*, *Sirmione*, and *Peschiera*. The Motorway (A22) from the Brennero via Bolzano and Trento runs close to the E side of the lake, with exits at *Lago di Garda Nord* and *Lago di Garda Sud*. Desenzano and Peschiera are both stations on the main railway line from Milan to Verona (Rte 17) and are connected by boat and bus with ports on both banks. *Gargnano* and *Salò* have bus connections with Brescia; *Bardolino* and *Garda* with Verona; *Riva* with Trento (connecting with the main railway from Trento to Verona at Rovereto), Brescia, and Desenzano.

Road round the Lake, 143km. The magnificent road encircling the lake is known as *La Gardesana* (*Occidentale* on the W bank, *Orientale* on the E). This remarkable engineering feat entailed the blasting of a passage for the roadway through many kilometres of solid rock, and the construction of c 80 tunnels. The views are necessarily interrupted, but they are perhaps all the more striking for that, and the expedition by car or bus, at least from Gardone to Riva, is one that should not be missed.

Intermediate distances: Desenzano-Salo, 20km; Salo-Riva, 44km; Riva-Peschiera, 65km; Peschiera-Desenzano, 14km.

Bus Services: by the Gardesana Occidentale from *Peschiera* via *Desenzano* (20 minutes) to *Riva* several times daily; by the Gardesana Orientale from *Peschiera* to *Riva* in 95 minutes; more frequently from Lazise and Garda (c hourly; all services originating in Verona).

Navigational Services (including a paddle-steamer built in 1901). In summer two services daily between Desenzano and Riva in 4½hrs, calling only at ports on the W bank as far as Gargano; hydrofoil service 4 times daily in 2hrs (with fewer stops); reduced services in winter. More frequent boat services between Desenzano and Maderno (in 1hr 50 minutes). Car ferry between Maderno and Torridi Benaco in ½hr. A service runs between Sirmione, Peschiera, and Garda (and a boat or hydrofoil runs c every hour between Desenzano and Sirmione). Tickets allowing free circulation on the lake services for specific periods may be purchased. Tours of the lake in the afternoons in summer are also organised. All information from the offices of the 'Navigazione sul Lago di Garda', 2 Piazza Matteotti, Desenzano sul Garda.

A. Desenzano to Riva by the West Bank

(The kilometre distances are by road.)

Desenzano del Garda (69m), the usual starting-point for excursions on the Lago di Garda, is a lively little town (17,900 inhab.) connected with its station (Rte 17) by bus. From the quay a bridge crosses an inlet used as a harbour for small boats, behind which is the main Piazza Giuseppe Malvezzi, with pretty arcades, and a monument to St Angela Merici (1474–1540), foundress of the Ursuline order. A road leads right out of the piazza to the parish church with a *Last Supper by Giovanni Battista Tiepolo. Just to the W, reached by Via Crocifisso, is an excavated area with a *Roman Villa* (adm. 9–sunset; closed Monday) with polychrome 4C mosaics, and an Antiquarium. Close by, traces of a Basilica have been found.

The ROAD FROM DESENZANO TO SALÒ, N572, 20km, at first skirts the lake.—4km *Lonato Lido*. On the by-road (left) to Lonato (1km; Rte 17) is the Abbey of *Maguzzano*, founded for Benedictines in the 10C and occupied by Trappists in 1903–38.—The road leaves the lake and its many camping sites and crosses the hilly district of *Valtenesi*; on the right is a view of the lake and the castle of Moniga.—20km *Salò*, see below.

The thirteenth-century Rocca Scaligera, Sirmione

On the right as the boat leaves the pier (following the route taken by Tennyson in 1880) can be seen the curious promontory of Sirmione, 3·5km long and in places only 119m wide.

    Sirmione, near the end of the promontory, is a spa, with warm sulphur springs (La Boiola) that rise in the lake. Wealthy Romans favoured Sirmione as a summer residence, and Catullus, who had a villa here, speaks of 'Peninsularum, Sirmio, insularumque ocelle'. It is now virtually given over to tourism with numerous large hotels.

Buses hourly to Brescia and Verona; to Desenzano, Peschiera, etc.

Boats for hire on the lake (with guide), and for water-skiing.—*Bathing Lido* on the E side of the peninsula; swimming off rocks on the W side.

The 15C church of *Santa Maria Maggiore* preserves some antique columns. The picturesque 13C *Rocca Scaligera* (adm. 9–13, 15.30–18.30; winter 9–14; festivals 9–13; closed Monday), where Dante is said to have stayed, was a stronghold of the Scaliger family, lords of Verona. The massive central tower, 29m high commands a good view. A road leads N from Via della Repubblica to *San Pietro in Mavino*, a Romanesque church of 8C foundation, retaining early frescoes. At the end of the headland are the so-called GROTTE DI CATULLO (9–dusk), really the romantic ruins of a large Roman villa set amidst olive groves with a splendid view out over the lake. In the small Antiquarium are fragments of frescoes dating from the 1C BC.

The boat provides a striking view of the promontory as it leaves Sirmione; it then steers NW skirting the *Rocca di Manerba*, a headland once crowned by a castle. Then it passes through the narrow channel between the romantic headland of Punta San Fermo and the *Isola di Garda* on which is the Villa Borghese (no adm.) with a 19C palazzo in the Venetian Gothic manner. The boat turns SW to enter the Gulf of Salò, and passes *Porto Portese*, the landfall for *San Felice del Benaco* (3·5km).

20km **Salò** (10,200 inhab.), the Roman *Salodium*, and the birthplace of Gaspare Bertolotti, or da Salò (1540–1609), generally considered to be the first maker of violins, is perhaps the most beautiful spot on the lake. It gave name to Mussolini's short-lived puppet republic of 1944. The Gothic cathedral (*Annunziata*) has a good Renaissance portal (1509). In the interior are paintings by Romanino (Madonna and Child, in the Baptistery), a polyptych by Paolo Veneziano (W end of N aisle), and a carved wooden tabernacle with ten statues in niches (15C). The *Palazzo Fantoni* is the seat of the Biblioteca Ateneo, which has its origins in the Accademia degli Unanimi founded by Giovanni Maione in 1560. The fine library has over 25,000 vols many of great historical interest.

Between Salò and Gargnano extends the ***Riviera Bresciana**, a succession of villages linked by villas and hotels, and set in cedar and olive groves. The boat passes close to *Barbarano* with the *Palazzo Martinengo* (adm. on written application), built in 1577 by the Marchese Sforza Pallavicino, the Venetian general.

24km **Gardone Riviera** and (25km) **Fasano Riviera**, now practically continuous, make up a popular winter resort in the most sheltered position on the lake. They have an unusually mild winter climate, and the parks and gardens are planted with rare trees. Gardone is a good centre for walks in the hilly hinterland of the Riviera, which soon becomes mountainous.

At Gardone di Sopra (above the Grand Hotel), which has an old campanile, is **Il Vittoriale** (adm. 9–12.30, 14–18.30; villa closed on Monday) built for Gabriele d'Annunzio (1863–1938) in the last years of his life, by Gian Carlo Maroni. The martial poet had a great influence on Italian poetry in this century. He named his home after the Italian victory over Austria in 1918 and died here. The villa, with its elaborate and gloomy décor, has been preserved as a museum. An inscription that d'Annunzio made Mussolini read on his visit to the poet is pointed out: 'Remember that you are made of glass and I of steel'. The garden contains further memorials and his mausoleum, as well as an open-air theatre and concert hall administered by the Fondazione del Vittoriale which promotes the study of his works.

28km **Toscolano-Maderno** (another resort) situated on the delta of the Toscolano, which is more fertile than it is picturesque, and backed by rocky hills, was the chief Roman settlement (*Benacum*) of the Riviera Bresciana. A frequent car-ferry crosses the lake to Torri (see Rte 19B). In Maderno, on the S side, the 12C Romanesque church of *Sant'Andrea* shows remains of Roman and Byzantine architecture, especially in the decoration of the pillar capitals, doors and windows; an older church seems to have been incorporated in the building. In Toscolano, behind the church of Santi Pietro e Paolo (good 16C wood-carvings), are the *Santuario della Madonna del Benaco*, with 15C frescoes and remains of a Roman villa.

A winding road ascends from Toscolano to *Gaino* (301m), a finely situated village, from where steep paths lead down (left) into the Toscolano valley and (right) to Cecina on the coast road.

33km *Bogliaco*, the next boat stop, has a 9-hole golf course. The 18C *Villa Bettoni* (adm. on application) contains a collection of 17–18C works of art.—36km **Gargnano** is notable for the 13C church and cloister of San Francesco.

The Valle Toscolana, a centre of paper-making from 15C–early 20C, is best visited by road from Gargnano or on foot from Gaino (see above). The road passes (12km) the hydro-electric *Lago di Valvestino* and descends to the remote villages of the Valvestino, ending at (25km) *Magasa*.

FROM GARGNANO TO LIMONE by the inland road, 33km. This road soon diverges uphill (left) from the 'Gardesana' and gradually winds its way up to the shelf which carries the scattered commune of *Tignale* (10km).—*Oldesio* (465m) is connected with the pier of Tignale by a steep footpath. Beyond it is a curious view of the lake shore almost vertically beneath, and of Monte Baldo opposite.—12km **Gardola** (555m) is the chief village of Tignale. The *Madonna di Monte Castello* (691m; 20 minutes) has the finest *View of the whole lake. The road leads to the right, just before Gardola, with Monte Castello on the right, and then gradually recedes from the lake.—From (14km) *Prabione* a track descends to the Porto di Campione.—After crossing (20km) the Torrente di San Michele this route leaves on the right a road back to the 'Gardesana' and reaches (25km) *Vesio* (625m), the highest village in the commune of Tremosine (see below). Turning again towards the lake the road descends via (27km) *Voltino* to (33km) *Limone* on the lake shore (see below).

Beyond Gargnano the lake narrows considerably and the W shore becomes a rocky wall through which the Gardesana road tunnels.—Beyond (42km) *Porto di Tignale*, connected by footpath with Tignale (see above), the mighty cliff of the Monte di Castello is conspicuous, with the chapel on its S peak.—46km *Campione* stands on the delta of a torrent and has a large cotton mill.

A very fine *Road ascends, with many tunnels, viaducts, and sharp curves to (5km) **Pieve di Tremosine** (413m) a village on a steep cliff descending into the lake, commanding a fine *View. Two roads go on to the upper village of Vesio (see above), that via Villa being preferable (6km).

The terraced lemon and lime gardens become more noticeable on the approach to (54km) **Limone sul Garda**, which takes its name from its lemon plantations, said to be the first in Europe.

Beyond the next point, the characteristic outline of the Sperone comes into view and the lower end of the lake is lost to sight. The mountains on the left, rising abruptly from the lake, are separated by the gorge of the Ponale, with waterfalls and a power station. The windings of the road up the gorge are conspicuous, and the N end of the lake, with the isolated Monte Brione, offers a splendid panorama.

65km **Riva**, the Roman *Ripa*, a lively pleasant little town (12,100 inhab.), and the most important place on the lake, is sheltered by Monte Rochetta to the W. It became a fashionable winter resort at the turn of the century, and remained in Austrian territory until 1918. The centre of the old town is Piazza 3 Novembre overlooking the little port. Here are the 13C *Torre Apponale*, *Palazzo Pretorio* (1370), *Palazzo Comunale* (1475), and some medieval porticoes. The *Rocca*, a 14C castle encircled by water, has been heavily restored over the centuries. The *Museo Civico* is being rearranged here. The archaeological section includes interesting material from the lake dwellings of the Lago di Ledro. There is also a collection of armour, and locally printed works, including a Talmud of 1558. On the road to Arco, is the church of the *Inviolata*, begun in 1603 by an unknown Portuguese architect, with a graceful Baroque interior.

A chair-lift (or path) ascends to the *Bastione* (view) a round tower built by the Venetians in 1506, and dominated by the craggy Monte Rocchetta (1521m).

About 4km NE of Riva, in the valley of the Sarca (91m) is the little health resort of **Arco** (10,800 inhab.), particularly fashionable before the First World War. The *Collegiata (Assunta)* is a handsome 17C church by Giovanni Maria Filippi. The former palace of the Counts, to the left, is a good 16C building. In the *Giardino Pubblico* is a monument by Bistolfi to the painter Giovanni Segantini (1858–99) who was born here. To the W is the *Parco Arciducale* with remains of the villa of archduke Albert of Austria. Near Via dei Capitelli are a number of large 19C buildings including the former *Casinò* (now a public library). The *Castle* of the counts of Arco, on a rocky eminence (30 minutes) provides a fine *View of the valley of the Sarca and the lake.

The *Cascata del Varone* is approached by road from Riva via (3km N) *Varone*, from where the waterfall, in its gorge, is 1km NW. From Varone a road continues to (8km) *Tenno*, with its castle, and (12km) the turquoise-blue *Lago di Tenno*. From the lake the road goes on to (26km) *Ponte delle Arche* (Rte 23).

It is 4km from Riva by road along the shore, skirting the crescent-shaped *Monte Brione* (376m), to **Torbole**, a summer resort near the mouth of the Sarca. Torbole played a part in the war of 1439 between the Visconti and the Venetians, when fleets of warships were dragged overland by teams of oxen and launched into the lake. Goethe stayed here in 1786. To the S rise the steep spurs of Monte Baldo.

FROM RIVA TO THE LAGO DI LEDRO AND THE LAGO D'IDRO, 40km. This route follows the road on the W bank of the lake for a short distance, then diverges uphill to the right by the *PONALE ROAD, which also tunnels through the cliffs of the Rocchetta and the Sperone. It soon reaches the mouth of the Val di Ledro near the not very impressive falls of the *Cascata del Ponale*, reached also by boat or by the Gardesana road. The road turns inland up the Ledro valley (of great botanical interest) for (10km) the LAGO DI LEDRO (2·8km long), at the further end of which is *Pieve di Ledro* (660m), a little resort. On the E side of the lake near *Molina*, when the water is low, can be seen some of the c 15,000 wood stakes from lake dwellings of the early Bronze Age found here in 1929. There is a small museum (9–12, 13–18) and a hut has been reconstructed on the lakeside.—17km *Bezzecca*.—At (20km) *Tiarno di Sopra* the road crosses the watershed (745m) and descends the Valle d'Ampola, a steep gorge with numerous waterfalls. Just beyond (25km) the little lago d'Ampola, an unmade road (left) leads in 12km to the Passo di Tremalzo (1894m) with a chair-lift and refuges. A tortuous road descends from there to Vesio (see above).—33km *Storo* and *Casa Rossa* in the Valli Giudicarie, 5km above Ponte Caffaro on the Lago d'Idro (see Rte 17).

From Riva to *Molveno*, see Rte 23; to *Rovereto*, see Rte 22.

B. Riva to Peschiera by the East Bank

(Distances are by road; for buses etc. see the beginning of the route.)

Beyond (4km) *Torbole* (see above) the E side of the lake is bounded by the almost inaccessible cliff of *Monte Altissimo di Nago* (2079m), the N peak of the *Baldo* range, which provides a dignified background for the Venetian shore of Lake Garda. An area of great interest for its flora and fauna, there is a long-term project to turn it into a protected area.—13km *Navene* (no pier), a poor hamlet on this inhospitable shore, gives name to the *Bocca di Navene* (1430m; mule track), the only pass of importance across the Monte Baldo chain.—17km **Malcesine**, the seat of the Veronese Captains of the Lake in the 16–17C, preserves their old palazzo as a town hall. More conspicuous is the 13–14C castle of the Scaligers, restored by Venice in the 17C and housing a small Museum (adm. 9–20; in winter open only Saturday & Sunday). The tower has a fine *View.

A cableway mounts to the ski-slopes of Monte Baldo (1748m). The *Punta del Telegrafo* (2201m) is the chief peak of the range. A pleasant walk of c 2hrs among the olive-grown slopes above the town ascends from the Navene road, 15 minutes N of Malcesine, to *Palazzina*, and then turns S to the *Altipiano delle Vigne*, re-entering Malcesine from the S.

The coast becomes less wild farther S past the islets of Olivo and Sogno, the village of *Cassone* (no pier), and the island of *Trimelone*, which bears the remains of a castle.—24km *Assenza* with the small 14C church of San Nicolò di Bari (13–14C frescoes), is in the commune of **Brenzone**.—25km *Porto di Brenzone*.—27km *Magugnano* is the seat of the commune.—Beyond the Romanesque church of San Zeno (early 12C) and (33km) *Pai* there is a magnificent view of the opposite shore of the lake.

39km **Torri del Benaco**, the Roman *Castrum Turrium* and the chief town of the Gardesana after the 13C, preserves a fine castle of the Scaligers dating from 1383 and a church with 15C frescoes. Its red and yellow marbles are locally famous. A car ferry (frequent service) crosses to Maderno (see Rte 19A).

Torri is the landing point for (9km) *San Zeno di Montagna* a mountain resort high above the lake (582m) reached by a zigzag road.

The boat rounds (44km) the *Punta di San Vigilio*, the loveliest headland on the E shore, on which are the little church of *San Vigilio* among cypress groves, and the *Villa Guarienti* (1540), possibly by Sanmicheli.

46km **Garda**, once a fortified town and still retaining some interesting old houses, lies at the head of a deep bay. Famous under both Romans and Longobards, it had origins yet more ancient, as testified by an early necropolis on the outskirts. In the *Castle*, now gone, on Monte Garda, to the SE, Queen Adelaide was held prisoner by

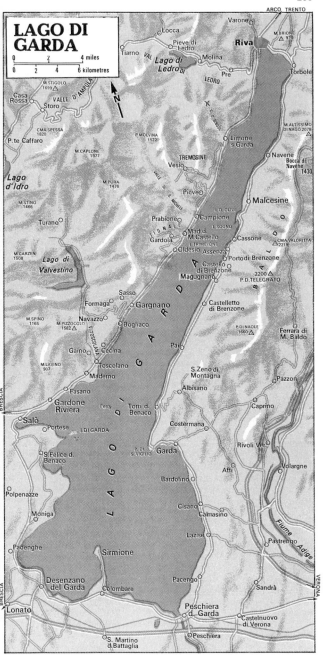

LAGO DI GARDA

0 — 2 — 4 miles
0 — 2 — 4 — 6 kilometres

ARCO, TRENTO

Varone
Locca
Pieve di Ledro
Riva
M.BRIONE 978
Tiarno
VAL Lago di Ledro DI
Molina
Pre
LEDRO
Torbole

Casa Rossa
M.STIGOLO 1699
VALLE D'AMPOLA
Storo
V.D'URSIA
M.ALTISSIMO DI NAGO 2078

CMA.SPESSA 1820
P.te Caffaro
M.CAPLONE 1977
P.MOLVINA 1522
Limone s.Garda
Navene Bocca di Navene 1430

Lago d'Idro
M.STINO 1466
TREMOSINE
Vesio
M.PURA 1476
Pieve
Malcesine

Turano
VALLE D.S.MICHELE
Prabione
Campione
I.D. OLIVE
I.SOGNO

M.CARZEN 1508
Lago di Valvestino
TIGNALE
Gardola
Mad.d M.Castello
I.TRIMELONE
Cassone
CMA.VALORITTA 2218

Oldesio
Assenza
Portodi Brenzone
2200

M.SPINO 1165
Sasso
Formaga
Castello di Brenzone
Magugnano
P.D.TELEGRATO

M.PIZZOCOLO 1582
Navazzo
Gargnano
Castelletto di Brenzone

Gaino
Bogliaco
V.TOSCOLANA
P.DI NAOLE 1660
Ferrara di M. Baldo

M.LAVINO 907
Cecina
Pai

Toscolano
Maderno
S.Zeno di Montagna
Pazzon

Fasano
Gardone Riviera
Ferry
Torri d. Benaco
Albisano
Caprino

Salò
Portese
I.DI GARDA
Costermana

S.Felice d. Benaco
P.DI S.VIGILIO
Garda
Rivoli Ver.

Polpenazze
Affi
Volargne

Moniga
Bardolino

Padenghe
Cisano
Calmasino
Fiume Adige

Sirmione
Lazise
Pastrengo

Desenzano del Garda
Colombare
Pacengo
Sandrà

Lonato
Peschiera d. Garda
Castelnuovo di Verona

S. Martino d.Battaglia
Peschiera

BRESCIA

VERONA

LAGO DI GARDA

Berenger II (c 960), and Julius Caesar Scaliger (1484–1558) was born. The altar chapel of *Santa Maria Maggiore* preserves porch columns of its predecessor. In the *Eremo dei Camaldolesi* (309m) the church houses a painting by Palma Giovane.

The hills become lower and the view less romantic as the broad basin at the foot of the lake opens out.—51km **Bardolino**, another ancient place retaining some commercial importance, gives name to a well-known wine. A tower and two gates remain from an old castle of the Scaligers. The tiny Carolingian church of San Zeno retains its 9C form and, beyond, *San Severo* is 12C with contemporary frescoes. The shore becomes uninteresting on the approach to (53km) *Cisano*, a small village whose church retains a Romanesque façade and campanile.—56km *Lazise*, retaining part of its medieval wall, has been succeeded by Bardolino as the chief port on this shore. A castle of the Scaligers (with Venetian additions) and the 16C Venetian custom house attest to its former importance, and form a charming group on the lake front. San Nicolò is a 12C church with 16C additions (14C frescoes).—66km **Peschiera** is on the main road and railway from Milan to Verona (Rte 17).

20   Milan to Cremona and Mantua

ROAD, 151km, leaving Milan by the Porta Vittoria and the Corso Ventidue Marzo; immediately beyond the railway turn right on N415.—44km **Crema**.—83km **Cremona**, entered by Porta Milano and left by Porta Venezia.—N10, 113km *Piadena*.—151km **Mantua**, entered by the Corso Vittorio Emanuele.

RAILWAY, 149km in 2¼–3hrs; to *Cremona*, 86km, in 1½hr. The line follows the Via Emilia (Rte 37) via Lodi to Casalpusterlengo, then branches at *Codogno*, where a change is sometimes necessary (three through trains daily).—Another line via *Treviglio* (see Rte 17) to *Cremona* (99km; through trains) takes longer but serves *Crema* (56km) in 1¼–2hrs; Crema to Cremona in 1hr.

This route leaves Milan by the Linate airport road, from which, immediately beyond the railway, the Crema road, N415, diverges right.—At (25km) *Bisnate* the Adda is crossed.—At 34km a by road (1km) leads to *Palazzo Pignano* where excavations in 1963–71 beneath the 12C Pieve di San Martino revealed remains of a paleochristian basilica. The Pieve contains 15C frescoes and a terracotta Pietà.—44km **Crema**, a town of 32,700 inhabitants on the W bank of the Serio, was in the Venetian dominion from 1454 to 1797. It was the birthplace of the composer Francesco Cavalli (1600–76). The *Cathedral*, in the Campionese style (1284–1341), has a fine tower, and the piazza in front of it is surrounded by Renaissance buildings, including the 16C *Palazzo Pretorio* with an archway leading to the main street. The pleasant ex-convent of SANT'AGOSTINO houses the library and *Museo Civico* (adm. 15–18; Saturday 10–12, 15–18; Sunday 10–12), where is displayed burial armour from Lombard tombs discovered in 1963 at Offanengo, NE of the town. The *Refectory*, restored as a concert hall, has frescoes attributed to Giovanni Pietro da Cemmo (1498–1505). —*Santa Maria della Croce*, 2km N, is a handsome church (1493–1500), after Bramante, by Giovanni Battagio.

55km *Castelleone* has a 10C tower and the interesting 15C church of Santa Maria di Bressanoro (2km N), with terracotta decorations.

The direct road by-passes the centre and runs straight across the plain to Cremona, while the old road (5km longer) passes through *Soresina*, now more industrial than agricultural, and *Casalbuttano*.

83km **CREMONA** is a busy and cheerful city (82,000 inhab.) notable for its many ancient brick buildings, survivals of the age of the Lombard city-states. It is an important agricultural market. The port of Cremona has recently been connected via the Po with the Adriatic ports of Venice and Chioggia.

Hotels near the Duomo and Piazza Roma.—**Post Office**, Via Verdi.—**Tourist Office**, 5 Piazza del Comune.—**Theatre**, *Ponchielli*, Corso Vittorio Emanuele.— A Festival of stringed instruments is held in October every 3 years (next in 1991).

Trolley-Buses from the Station to Piazza Roma.—*Local Buses* from Piazza Marconi to *Casalmaggiore* and most places in the province.—**Country Buses** from the same to *Milan*; to *Mantua*; to *Brescia*; to *Bergamo*; to *Piacenza*; and to *Soncino*. Also less frequently to *Fidenza* and *Salsomaggiore Terme*; and to *Genoa*. Once daily to *Padua*, *Venice* and *Trieste*.

History. Founded by the Romans as a colony in 218 BC, *Cremona* became an important fortress and road junction on the Via Postumia. Its decline after a siege and sack in AD 69 ended in destruction by the Lombards in 603. Cremona re-emerged as a city-state in 1098, warring as usual with its neighbours–Milan, Brescia, and Piacenza. In 1334 it was taken by Azzone Visconti of Milan, and remained from then on under Milanese domination; being given in dowry to Bianca Maria Visconti on the occasion of her marriage to Francesco Sforza in 1441, it enjoyed a century of patronage and prosperity.—Among Cremonese painters may be mentioned Boccaccio Boccaccino and his son Camillo, the Campi family, and Giovanni Battista Trotti; but Cremona is more celebrated for its terracotta sculpture work, and above all for the manufacture of violins; the most renowned makers being Andrea Amati (fl. 1550–80), Nicolò Amati (1596–1684), Antonio Stradivari (Stradivarius; 1644–1737), and Giuseppe Guarneri (Joseph Guarnerius; 1683–1745). The composer Claudio Monteverdi (1567–1643) is another famous native. Here in 1878 was born Alceo Dossena, famous producer of fake works of art.

Corso Garibaldi descends to the centre of the town from the station. On the left is the church of *San Luca* with a 15C façade in poor repair adorned with the terracotta ornament typical of Cremona: adjoining is the little octagonal Renaissance chapel of Cristo Risorto (1503), attributed to Bernardino De Lera. On the right (No. 178) is the fine *Palazzo Raimondi* (1496; also by Bernardino De Lera) with damaged frescoes on its curved cornice. It is the seat of the International Scuola di Liuteria, and the centre of musical activity in Cremona. The school for violin makers continues a tradition for which the city has been famous since the 16C. Farther on stands *Palazzo del Popolo* or *Cittanova* (1256), with a ground floor portico, the headquarters of the popular, or Guelf party in the days of the free commune of Cremona; it is adjoined by *Palazzo Trecchi* with a neo-Gothic façade of 1843–44. Nearby, in Via Grandi, is the little church of *Santa Margherita*, decorated inside by Giulio Campi, his best work.—Across the Corso rises **Sant'Agata**, with a neo-classical façade of 1848 by Luigi Voghera and a Romanesque campanile. Inside, on the right, is the Trecchi tomb by Giovanni Cristoforo Romano (1502–5), with beautifully carved bas reliefs. In the 3rd chapel in the S aisle is a panel (behind a grille) illustrating the life of St Agatha (painted on both sides) by a North Italian master of the 13C, known from this painting as the 'Maestro della Tavola di Sant'Agata'. The good frescoes of the Life of St Agatha, on the sanctuary walls, are by Giulio Campi (1536).— Farther on along the Corso a detour may be made to the right by Via Milazzo and Via Plasio, to visit ***Sant'Agostino**, a 14C church with a good tower and notable terracotta ornamentation. In the interior are

238

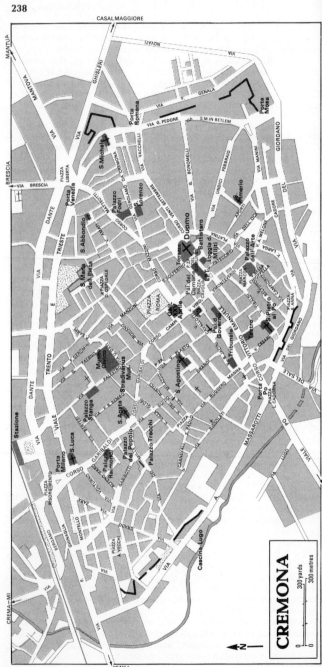

CREMONA

some good sculptures and paintings. S side, 3rd chapel (Cavalcabò), frescoes in the vault by Bonifacio Bembo and two detached fresco portraits of Francesco and Bianca Sforza; on the 4th pilaster, stoup with reliefs by Bonino da Campione (1357); 5th altar, Annunciation by one of the Campi brothers; 6th altar, *Madonna and Saints by Perugino.—Via Cavallotti, to the left beyond Sant'Agostino, leads back to the main street.

At the opposite corner is the monumental *National Insurance Building* (1935), traversed by the Galleria Venticinque Aprile, and beyond that is *Piazza Roma*, a pleasant little park. Here is a statue of the native composer Amilcare Ponchielli (1834–86), and the tombstone of Stradivarius salvaged from the church of San Domenico (demolished 1878).

*PIAZZA DEL COMUNE is the centre of the life of Cremona. The Romanesque *Torrazzo* claims to be the highest medieval tower in Italy (110m; adm. 10–12, 15–18.30; view). It was built in 1250–67 and crowned with a Gothic lantern in 1287–1300 probably by the local sculptor Francesco Pecorari. The *Bertazzola*, a double loggia of the Renaissance (1497–1525), stretches across the front of the cathedral. Beneath its arcades some sculptures are immured, including the sarcophagus of Folchino Schizzi (died 1357), by Bonino da Campione, and that of Andrea Ala (1513), by Giovanni Gaspare Pedoni (beyond the main doorway).

The *Duomo is a splendid Romanesque basilica of 1107, conse-crated in 1190 and finished considerably later. It has a particularly fine exterior. The W front (1274–1606; being restored), has a rose window of 1274 and a tabernacle above the main door with three statues of the Madonna and Child and the patron Saints, Imerio and Omobono, attributed to *Gano da Siena* or *Marco Romano* (c 1310). The main door is flanked by four statues of prophets. The later transepts, which altered the basilican plan of the church to a Latin cross, have splendid brick façades; the N transept, with a fine porch, dates from 1288, and the S transept from 1332. The interior is remarkable especially for the *Frescoes (1514–29; extremely difficult to see without strong light) on the walls of the nave and apse, by *Boccaccino*, *Gian Francesco Bembo*, *Altobello Melone*, *Gerolamo Romanino*, *Pordenone*, and *Bernardino Gatti*. The twelve Brussels tapestries which illustrate the story of Samson (1629, by Jas Raes) are being restored. On the W wall, Crucifixion and Deposition by *Pordenone*. The two pulpits have good reliefs by *Giovanni Antonio Piatti* or *Giovanni Amadeo* (c 1482). In the first S chapel: *Pordenone*, Saints Philip and James presenting a member of the Schizzi family to the Virgin. At the entrance to the N transept, tomb of Monsignor Bonomelli, by *Domenico Trentacoste* (1931), and in the middle E chapel of the transept, Pietà, an original composition by *Antonio Campi*; at the end, reliefs by *Amadeo* (1481). On the right of the Sanctuary steps, high relief by *Amadeo* of the Charity of St Imerio. The choir has inlaid stalls by *Giovanni Maria Platina* (1490), and on the E wall is a huge Assumption, by *Bernardino Gatti* (1575).

In the crypt (closed) is the tomb of Saints Peter and Marcellinus, by *Benedetto Briosco* (1506), while the Treasury (kept locked) contains two fine processional crosses. Some 12C mosaics in the old *Camposanto*, S of the Duomo, are shown by the cathedral sacristan on request.

The octagonal **Baptistery** (at present closed for restoration; apply for the key at the sacristy of the Duomo), a plain Lombard building, with a dark interior, was probably planned by Teodosio Orlandino (1167).

The **Loggia dei Militi** is a fine Gothic Lombard building of 1292 (good three-light windows). It has been restored as a War memorial. *Palazzo del Comune** was rebuilt in 1206–45 but preserves an older tower (the windows have been spoiled by alterations). Adm. 9–12, 15–17 except Saturday; Sunday 9–12. On the first floor landing is a fine Renaissance doorway. In the Sala della Giunta is a marble chimneypiece by Gaspare Pedoni (16C). Another room contains four violins made by Stradivarius, Andrea and Niccolò Amati, and Guarneri del Gesù.

Corso Venti Settembre and Via Gerolamo da Cremona lead to the church of *San Michele*, founded perhaps in the 7C, and rebuilt after a fire in 1113. The exterior of the Romanesque apse is interesting. In the interior are 12C columns in the nave. At the end of the S aisle, the two paintings of the Annunciation from the organ doors, have recently been attributed to Alessandro Pampurino. Here steps lead down to the crypt (usually locked) with rough hewn capitals (now a War sanctuary).—On the other side of Via Matteotti is the little church of *Sant'Abbondio*, with an interesting interior of 1579. The vault frescoes (being restored) are by Orazio Sammacchini. In the Sanctuary, Madonna in Glory by Malosso on a design by Giulio Campi, and, in the apse, Madonna and Child with Saints, also by Giulio Campi. The Loreto chapel dates from 1624. The Renaissance cloister is attributed to Bernardino de Lera.—The dignified Corso Matteotti leads back to the centre past *Palazzo Fodri* (c 1500), the finest of many old mansions in this street, decorated with a terracotta frieze, and with a lovely courtyard.

Corso Vittorio Emanuele leads from Piazza Cavour towards the river past the *Teatro Ponchielli* by Luigi Canonica (1808). Off the S side of the Corso is the monastic church of **San Pietro al Po**, sumptuously decorated with 16C paintings and stuccoes by Malosso, Antonio Campi, Gian Francesco Bembo (Madonna and Child with Saints and a donor, 1524), Bernardino Gatti (Nativity), and others. The cloister at No. 14 Via Cesari is by Cristoforo Solari (1509).

In Via Ugolani Dati, a turning on the right off Via Palestro, which leads back to the station, is the **Museo Civico** (adm. 9.30–12, 15–17.30; Sunday 9.30–12; closed Monday), housed in the huge *Palazzo Affaitati* (by Francesco Dattaro, 1561), with a good staircase by Antonio Arrighi (1769). The vast collection, undergoing partial rearrangement, is divided into numerous sections. The PINACOTECA includes frescoes from demolished churches, and paintings by *Bonifacio Bembo*, the *Campi*, *Giulio Cesare Procaccini*, *Giuseppe Arcimboldi* (a surrealist portrait: 'Scherzo con Ortaggi'), *Alessandro Magnasco*, *Luigi Miradori (Il Genovesino)*, and *Il Piccio (Giovanni Carnevali*; 1804–73). A painting of St Francis in meditation by *Caravaggio* has recently been restored.—Wooden carvings include panels in high relief by *Giacomo Bertesi* (1642–1710), and panels by *Bonifacio Bembo*.—The CATHEDRAL TREASURY includes 28 illuminated antiphonals (1476–96) and a sacristy cupboard with 29 intarsia doors by *Giovanni Maria Platina* (1477).—The ARCHAEOLOGICAL SECTION includes an excellent map of Roman Cremona, good geometric pavements, helmets, Roman coins, and the front of a legionary's strong-box.—Other sections include: the history of the Risorgimento, contemporary art, medieval ivories, ceramics and porcelain, furniture, terracotta friezes, and wrought-iron work.

The *Stradivarius Museum* is now housed at No. 17 Via Palestro (adm. as for the Museo Civico). Here a well arranged gallery contains a fine collection of violins, models made by Stradivarius in wood and paper, his tools, drawings, etc. *Palazzo Stanga*, at No. 36 Via Palestro, has a rococo front rebuilt in the 19C and a handsome courtyard (not usually visible), probably by Pietro da Rho.

About 20 minutes' walk E of Cremona along the bus route to Casalmaggiore is the church of *San Sigismondo, where Francesco Sforza was married to Bianca

Visconti (1441). The present building was started in 1463 in celebration of the event; it is a fine Lombard Renaissance work. It contains splendid painted decorations by local artists including *Camillo Boccaccino*, *Bernardino Gatti*, and the *Campi* family.

Cremona is connected by railway with *Treviglio*, and with *Brescia* (see Rte 17), and also with *Piacenza* and *Fidenza* (Rte 40).

Beyond Cremona the Mantua road, leaving the railway on the right, runs straight for 18km, then turns abruptly SE. Leaving on the right *Torre de'Picenardi* with its 16–18C villa, it crosses the road and railway from Brescia to Parma at (113km) *Piadena*. Here a small museum includes finds from the supposed site of *Bedriacum*, scene of a battle in AD 69 in which the generals of Vitellius defeated Otho.—The road passes N of (123km) *Bozzolo*, with its 14C tower and palace of the Gonzagas, and crosses the Oligo near (128km) *Marcaria*.—143km Santa Maria delle Grazie (see below).

151km **MANTUA**, in Italian *Mantova*, is an ancient and rather sombre city (58,700 inhab.) of the highest historical and artistic importance. It is surrounded on three sides by the Mincio ('smooth-sliding Mincius'), which widens out to form a sluggish lake of three reaches, Lago Superiore, Lago di Mezzo, and Lago Inferiore; the river itself, however, is not a special feature of the city. Mantua is interesting especially for its memorials of the great days of the Gonzagas. Many of the roads of the old town are still cobbled.

Post Office, Piazza Martiri.—**Tourist Office (A.P.T.)**, Piazza Mantegna.—**Buses** from Porta Belfiore for towns in the province, and for *Milan*.

History. Virgil was born on Mantuan territory about 70 BC and some of the town's earliest recorded history is due to the poet's interest in his native place. Mantua became a free community about 1126, and was afterwards dominated by the Bonacolsi and Gonzaga families. Under Gonzaga rule from 1328 the city flourished as a brilliant centre of art and civilisation ('Mantova la Gloriosa'), especially in the reigns of Ludovico II (1444–78), Francesco II (1484–1519), husband of Isabella d'Este, the greatest patron of her time (died at Mantua, 1539), and their son Federico II (1519–40). Giovanni delle Bande Nere, mortally wounded in a skirmish outside Mantua in 1526, is believed to have been buried in San Domenico (demolished). The sack of the city by Imperial troops in 1630 hastened its decline and the duchy came to a miserable end in 1708, when Mantua passed to the Austrians, who fortified it as the SW corner of their 'quadrilateral'. It held out against Napoleon for eight months in 1796–97, and was retaken by the French in 1799. It was in this period that many of the best Gonzaga paintings were taken to France. The town was again Austrian from 1814–66. It was damaged by bombs in 1944. Among the artists who flourished at the court of the Gonzagas were Leon Battista Alberti, Luca Fancelli, and Pisanello. Andrea Mantegna was court artist from 1460 until his death in 1506. Giulio Romano, architect and painter under the patronage of Federico II left numerous monuments in the city where he worked until his death in 1546. Titian often visited Mantua and it was here he first saw the works of Giulio Romano. Bonacolsi, nicknamed 'L'Antico' was born in Mantua, and he was commissioned by the Gonzaga to make bronze copies of Antique statues. Rubens worked at the Court from 1600 to 1606. Sordello (?1200–66) and Baldassare Castiglione (1478–1529) were born on Mantuan territory, and Giovanni Battista Spagnolo (1448–1516), or Mantuanus, the poet, the 'good old Mantuan' of 'Love's Labour's Lost', was a native of the city. The success of Monteverdi's 'Orfeo' at court in 1607 was the first landmark in the history of opera. The popularity of Verdi's 'Rigoletto' has endowed several Mantuan localities with spurious associations.

In recent years naturalists have taken an interest in the birdlife and flora of the marshlands surrounding the lakes of Mantua. Lotus flowers, introduced from China in 1921, grow here in abundance. Boat excursions can be made at *Rivalta*, 12km W of the city.

The approach from the W (or the railway station) follows Corso Vittorio Emanuele through Piazza Cavallotti, with the handsome *Teatro Sociale* (1822, designed by Luigi Canonica) into Corso

Umberto I (closed to traffic). Typical of the old city, with its dark and heavy porticoes, it narrows as it enters Piazza Marconi. Just beyond, in Piazza Mantegna, is the basilica of *Sant'Andrea, a beautiful Renaissance building designed by *Leon Battista Alberti* and executed after his death by the Florentine *Luca Fancelli* (1472–94). Although it has additions from later periods, it remains the most important architectural work by Alberti. The dome was added by *Filippo Juvarra* in 1732 and the brick campanile (covered for restoration) of 1413 is a survival from an earlier church. A notable marble frieze (much blackened) surrounds the W door. The finely proportioned *Interior has paired pilasters raised on pedestals and a coffered barrel vault. It contains frescoes, in the S chapels (1534–70), by *Benedetto Pagni* and *Rinaldo Mantovano*, pupils of Giulio Romano. The first chapel on the N side (closed for restoration) contains the tomb of *Andrea Mantegna* (1431–1506), with his bust in bronze, thought to be a self portrait. The painting of the Holy Family is also attributed to him, while the Baptism of Christ is probably by his son Francesco. The wall paintings, designed by Mantegna, were executed by his pupils, including *Correggio*. In the next chapel is a Madonna, by *Lorenzo Costa*. In the N transept are the Andreasi-Gonzaga tomb, and that of Pietro Strozzi, an ingenious work of 1529 (the design is attributed to *Giulio Romano*), while the S transept contains the Tomb of Giorgio Andreasi, by *Prospero Clementi* (1549).

The neighbouring Piazza delle Erbe, crowded on market-days, contains a 15C house (No. 26), and the *Rotonda di San Lorenzo*, a small round church founded in 1082 and restored in 1908. The domed interior (open 9–12, 14–18) has two orders of columns. Stairs lead up to the matroneum. The PALAZZO DELLA RAGIONE is a building partly of the early 13C with 14–15C additions including a conspicuous clock-tower. The four-square *Broletto* (1227), with its corner-towers, separates this square from Piazza del Broletto. On the farther side of the building and contemporary with it is a quaint figure of Virgil sculpted in the 13C, portraying the poet at the rostrum wearing his doctors' hat. A small *Museum* (No. 9; open 9–12, 15–18 except Monday) is dedicated to Tazio Nuvolari (1892–1953), the famous motor-racing champion who was born in Mantua. Connected to the Broletto by an archway is the *Arengario*, a little 13C building with a loggia. A Café beneath the archway occupies a Gonzaga office with an early-14C fresco of the city (recently restored), and the arms of Gianfrancesco, first Marquis.

Another archway admits to the huge, cobbled PIAZZA SORDELLO, on the left of which rise two grim battlemented palaces of the Bonacolsi family, who ruled Mantua before the Gonzagas. Above the first rises the *Torre della Gabbia*, from which (seen from Via Cavour) protrudes an iron cage where condemned prisoners were exposed. The next (*Palazzo Castiglioni*) dates from the 13C. Beyond that is the Baroque *Bishop's Palace*. The **Duomo**, at the end, has a Baroque façade of 1756, a dismal failure designed to add apparent height to the building. It has a broad brick campanile. Part of the S side remains of the late-Gothic church. The *Interior was designed by *Giulio Romano* (1545) in imitation of a simple palaeochristian basilica. It is covered with exquisite stucco decoration. In the S aisle is a 6C Christian sarcophagus. The *Cappella dell'Incoronata, a charming work in the style of *Alberti*, is reached by a corridor off the N aisle. The octagonal Cappella del Sacramento at the end of the N aisle, has altarpieces by Domenico Brusasorci and Paolo Farinati.

The whole of the opposite side of the piazza is occupied by the plain front of the ***Palazzo Ducale**, or *Reggia dei Gonzaga*, the most interesting building in Mantua, a huge fortress-palace which remains a fitting emblem of the hospitality of the Gonzaga princes, who were especially famous as patrons of the arts. The palace is now chiefly remarkable for its decorations, including the famous Camera degli Sposi, since the great Gonzaga art collections begun by Isabella d'Este, wife of Francesco II, and enriched in the 16C, have been largely dispersed: Charles I acquired a large part of them in 1627–30.

Many of the rooms of the palace now contain excellent classical sculpture, collected in the 18C by the Austrians.

Visitors are conducted in parties c every half hour; March–September, 9–13, 14.30–17; Sunday and Monday 9–13; October–February, 9–13, 14.30–15.30; Sunday and Monday, 9–13). The ticket office closes one hour earlier.

The vast rambling mass of the Reggia is divided into three main parts: the *Corte Vecchia*, or main front wing, the *Corte Nuova*, and the *Castello*. The Corte Vecchia, or Ducal Palace proper, overlooking Piazza Sordello, consists of the low 'Domus Magna', founded by Guido Bonacolsi c 1290, and the higher Palazzo del Capitano, built a few years later by the Bonacolsi (at the expense of the Comune); the Austrians altered the windows of the façade in the Gothic style, and it was restored to its original 15C appearance at the beginning of this century by the Samuel Kress Foundation. After the sack of Mantua in 1630 a large part of the palace fell into decay, but during the Austrian occupation it was modified for use on State occasions. The restoration of the palace, begun in 1902, was completed in 1934. The Castello, the 'keep' built in the 14–15C, to defend the approach to the city from the lake, was once connected to the rest of the palace by drawbridges only. The Corte Nuova, next to the castle, was planned mainly by Giulio Romano in the 16C.—The building (which may be used to house the archaeological museum) farther along Piazza Sordella stands on the site of the *Teatro di Corte* which was burnt down. The palatine *Basilica of Santa Barbara*, built for Duke Guglielmo by Giovanni Battista Bertani in 1562–65, completes the group.

Work on the palace was carried out in the 15C by Luca Fancelli, and in the 16C and early 17C by Giulio Romano, Giovanni Battista Bertani, and Antonio Maria Viani. Painters who worked at the Court included Pisanello, Mantegna, Giulio Romano, Lorenzo Costa, Correggio, Titian, Tintoretto, Rubens, and Feti.

The palace consists of some 500 rooms and 15 courtyards. Some of these are never open to the public, while other parts are sometimes closed. The description below covers all the areas normally accessible: scholars may be given special permission to see any parts not shown on the tour. Since the order of the visit may be changed, the room numbers given below refer to the Plan on p 246–7.

The entrance to the palace is through the door on the left-hand side of the façade. The 17C *Scalone delle Duchesse* (1) by Antonio Maria Viani ascends to the First Floor. On the right are two rooms (2 and 3) which contain an interesting painting of the *Expulsion of the Bonacolsi in 1328 in Piazza Sordello*, painted in 1494 by Domenico Morone. The detail of the palace façade was used during restoration work in this century (and it also shows the Gothic façade of the Duomo, pulled down in 1761). Also here is a ruined fresco of the Crucifixion (14C).—In the following rooms of the Palazzo del Capitano (4–9) medieval and Renaissance sculptures were beautifully rearranged in 1986. The long *Corridoio del Passerino* or *Corridoio del Palazzo del Capitano* (4), designed by Viani, has interesting late-Gothic mural decorations, and painted 18C portrait medallions of the Gonzaga family from 1328 to 1708. The sculpture here includes: *Virgil, a seated figure of c 1220; a mantelpiece by Luca Fancelli, coats-of-arms, and a stemma of the Podestà Ginori (1494; recently restored) by the Della Robbia workshop.—Off the corridor is the *Appartamento Guastalla* (5–10). These rooms contain: a lapidary collection; a group of five terracotta statues attributed to the school of Mantegna; a terracotta bust of Francesco II Gonzaga by Gian Cristoforo Romano; small bronzes by l'Antico; the tomb effigy of Margherita Malatesta (wife of Francesco I) by Pier Paolo dalle Masegne; relief of Christ by the school of Donatello; classical relief attributed to Tullio Lombardo; and a 16C sleeping cupid with two serpents. Also here is a large ruined fresco lunette of the Crucifixion attributed to the 14C Bolognese school.

In the last room (10) are displayed sinopie of Arthurian scenes, by Pisanello. The *Sala del Pisanello* (11; formerly *Sala dei Principi*) is so-called from a splendid fragment of a *Mural painting discovered in the 1960s showing a battle tournament. The unfinished but vivacious composition is one of the masterpieces of Pisanello. Forming a border along the top of the painting is a beautiful frieze incorporating the Lancastrian SS collar entwined with marigold flowers, the emblem of the Gonzaga. Henry VI granted the Gonzaga the concession to use the heraldic crest of the House of Lancaster. The adjoining room (12) displays the sinopie of the painting.

The *Salette dell'Alcova* (13 and 14; not always open) contain 15C and 16C paintings including works by Francesco Bonsignori and Francesco Francia.— The *Galleria Nuova* (15; also often closed) is hung with a fine series of paintings by Domenico Feti (the Redeemer and the Apostles), and works by Girolamo Bedoli Mazzola and Lorenzo Costa the Younger.

The next four rooms form the *Appartmento degli Arazzi* (16–19), overlooking the Cortile d'Onore, with neo-classical decoration by Paolo Pozzo (1779). The Brussels *Tapestries here, designed after Raphael's cartoons of the Acts of the Apostles (now in the Victoria and Albert Museum, London), are the most important replica of the Vatican series. They were acquired by Ercole Gonzaga.—The ceiling of the *Sala dello Zodiaco* (20) has delightful frescoes by Lorenzo Costa the Younger (1580).

To the left is the *Sala dei Fiumi* (21), decorated in 1775 by Giorgio Anselmi, with a view of the 16C 'hanging garden'. Three rooms near here (22–24), known as the *Appartamento dell'Imperatrice*, with 19C furniture, are usually closed.

Beyond the Sala dello Zodiaco is the *Sala dei Falconi* (25), named after a ceiling painting of hawks, attributed to Ippolito Andreasi. The *Saletta dei Mori* (26) has a fine gilded wood ceiling and 16C and 17C paintings. In the *Loggetta dei Mori* (27) are hung works by Domenico Feti. The narrow *Corridoio dei Mori* (28; with a view of the handsome 16C campanile of the Palatine Basilica of Santa Barbara), decorated in the early 17C, leads to the *Galleria degli Specchi* (29) designed by Viani, and decorated by his pupils. The two busts are by Lorenzo Ottoni.

The *Salone degli Arcieri* (30) has an unusual frescoed frieze of horses behind curtains. Here are hung some of the most important paintings in the palace: Rubens, The Gonzaga family in adoration of the Trinity (two fragments reassembled after the painting was cut into pieces during the French occupation), and a bozzetto of the Martyrdom of St Ursula, also by Rubens. Works by Domenico Feti include a monochrome lunette showing Viani presenting a model of the church of Sant'Orsola to Margherita Gonzaga d'Este. The Nativity of the Virgin is by the school of Tintoretto.

The *Appartamento Ducale* (31–38), arranged by Duke Vincenzo shortly after 1600, has been closed since 1974. The first room (31) has a coffered ceiling with the emblem of Vincenzo I (a gold crucible). Also here are portraits of Eleonora Gonzaga and her children kneeling (attributed to Frans Pourbus the Younger) and Vincenzo II Gonzaga (Sustermans). The *Sala del Labirinto* (32) has a labyrinth carved in the wood ceiling, and paintings by Palma Giovane and Sante Peranda. The crucible motif appears again in the ceiling of R 33. Beyond are small neo-classical rooms (34–38).—The *Appartamento di Eleonora Medici Gonzaga* (39–42), wife of Vincenzo II, designed by Viani is also usually closed.—The *Scalone del Paradiso* (43) leads to the so-called *Appartamento dei*

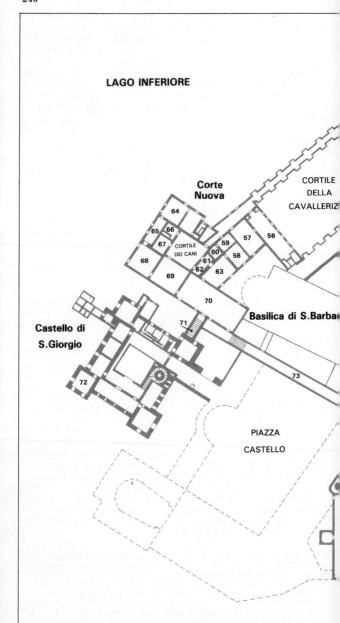

LAGO INFERIORE

Corte
Nuova

CORTILE
DELLA
CAVALLERIZ

64

65 66
67   CORTILE   59   57   56
            DEI CANI   60   58
68   61
        69   62   63

70

Basilica di S.Barba

Castello di
S.Giorgio

71

72   73

PIAZZA
CASTELLO

PALAZZO DUCALE
Mantua

Appartamento Estivale
48 – 54

Giardino Padiglione

Appartamento di Eleonora
39 – 42

PIAZZETTA PARADISO

Appartamento Ducale
31 – 38

PIAZZA
S.BARBARA

CORTILE D'ONORE

Palazzo di Corte Vecchia

PIAZZA LEGA
LOMBARDA

anging

arden

Appartamento dell'Imperatrice
22 – 24

Palazzo del Capitano

PIAZZA SORDELLO

Nani, on a mezzanine floor, which is a miniature reproduction of the Scala Santa at San Giovanni in Laterano made by Viani for Ferdinando Gonzaga c 1620.

The *Appartamento delle Metamorfosi* (44–47), with ceilings by Viani and his school, looks out onto the *Giardino del Padiglione*, recently reconstituted. Here are displayed Roman busts and reliefs.—Beyond is the *Appartamento Estivale* (48–54; usually closed), redecorated by Bertani and Viani.—The *Galleria della Mostra* (55), with a magnificent ceiling, was built by Viani for the display of the most important part of the ducal collection: it now contains original busts of Roman emperors. There is a splendid view of the *Cortile della Cavallerizza* (by Giulio Romano and Bertani) and the lake beyond.—Beyond the *Galleria dei Mesi* (56), built as a loggia by Giulio Romano, is the *Sala di Troia* (57), with frescoes designed by Giulio Romano and executed by his pupils. Beyond the pretty *Sala di Giove* or *delle Teste* (58), the *Stanza dei Cesari* (59), and the *Camerino di Ganimede* (60), the *Loggetta dei Cani* (61) opens on to the *Giardino dei Cani*.—The *Camerino degli Uccelli* (62; often closed) has a pretty ceiling and contains a statuette of Aphrodite, a Roman copy of a 3C BC original. The *Sala dei Cavalli* (63) takes its name from paintings of horses by Giulio Romano which formerly hung here. It has a fine wooden coffered ceiling. The classical sculpture includes two circular altars.

The following rooms (64–69) are normally closed. Beside the *Sala dei Duchi* (64) is the *Appartamento del Tasso* (65 and 66), the alleged lodging of Torquato Tasso when the Gonzaga received him on his flight from Ferrara, which contains more classical sculpture.—The *Stanza di Apollo* (67) has beautiful decoration traditionally attributed to Francesco Primaticcio (from a previous building).—The *Sala dei Marchesi* (68) has fine allegorical figures and busts in stucco by Francesco Segala. The beautiful Greek sculpture here includes the stele of a male figure and child (4C BC), and an Attic lute player.—The *Sala dei Capitani* (69) has a fine Hellenistic *Torso of Aphrodite.

The fine *Salone di Manto* (70) contains more good classical sculpture including a *Caryatid of the 5C BC, and the 'Mantua Apollo'.—The *Scalone di Enea* (71) leads into the CASTELLO DI SAN GIORGIO, the Castle proper (1395–1406), with a fine exterior formerly covered with frescoes. The design of the loggia of the courtyard built by Luca Fancelli is attributed to Mantegna. A spiral ramp leads up to a hall with late-16C copies of Mantegna's frescoes of the Triumph of Julius Caesar (now at Hampton Court). Beyond other rooms with detached frescoes (14–16C) is the *Camera Picta* (72), the so- called **Camera degli Sposi** (73), one of the most celebrated works of the Renaissance. The magnificent frescoes by Mantegna, his most famous work, were painted in 1465–74. They have recently been beautifully restored (since there is no electric light, they should be seen on a bright day). They illustrate the life of Marquis Ludovico and his wife Barbara of Brandenburg. Above the fireplace the Marquis and his wife are shown seated surrounded by their daughters, courtiers, a dwarf, and their dog Rubino. On the other wall are three scenes showing servants in the Gonzaga livery with hounds and a horse (the Gonzaga were famous as horse breeders and dog lovers), and Cardinal Francesco Gonzaga being met by his father the Marquis Ludovico. The group on the extreme right shows Frederick III, the Holy Roman Emperor, Christian I of Denmark, and Federico Gonzaga. The children are also members of the Gonzaga family. The landscape in the background of all three scenes is particularly beautiful and includes classical monuments (derived from buildings in Rome and Verona) and an imaginary city. In the frieze on the pilaster to the right of the door a self-portrait of the painter has been identified. The vaulted ceiling, also by Mantegna, has a trompe l'oeil oculus in the centre, one of the first examples of aerial perspective in painting, surrounded by court figures and putti, busts of Roman emperors and mythological scenes.

The exit from the palace is usually along the long Corridor (73) with modern copies of the stucco portraits of the Gonzaga in Palazzo Ducale, Sabbioneta, and down to the Cortile d'Onore.

The *Appartamento di Isabella d'Este*, off the Cortile d'Onore, is not always shown. Her *Studiolo* (for which she commissioned paintings from Mantegna, Perugino, Lorenzo Costa, and Correggio, all of them now in the Louvre) has a door by Gian Cristoforo Romano. Her *Grotta* contains intarsie by the Della Mola brothers. Both rooms have fine gilded wood ceilings.

Via Accademia leads from the Broletto to *Piazza Dante* (monument to the poet) in which is *Palazzo degli Studi*, containing the town library. In the same square is the *Accademia Virgiliana*, built by Piermarini in 1767, with the *Teatro Scientifico* by Antonio Bibiena (restored in 1972; open for concerts, etc., and 9–12, 15–17, except Sunday & festivals). Mozart gave the inaugural concert in 1770 at the age of thirteen, during his first visit to Italy. A tablet on No. 17 Via Ardigò marks the residence of St Louis Gonzaga (1583), and in Via Pomponazzo are several handsome courtyards (Nos 31, 27, 23).

On the left of the busy Piazza Martiri, a little park, above Giulio Romano's *Fish Market* (propped up with scaffolding) alongside the river, contains an old brick campanile. The main Via Principe Amedeo leads S; on the right, at No. 18 Via Carlo Poma, is *Giulio Romano's House*, designed by himself. The *Palazzo di Giustizia* opposite (No. 7), with bizarre monster caryatids, is attributed to Viani. The huge church of *San Barnaba*, with a dome and façade by Antonio Bibiena, contains works by Lorenzo Costa the Younger, and Giuseppe Bazzani (18C).—Via Acerbi continues S to the ducal church of **San Sebastiano** (1460; being cleaned in 1990) designed by Alberti on a Greek Cross plan. This unusual building with a beautiful raised vestibule, a side portico, and a ground level crypt, has been brutally altered over the centuries. The interior (for adm. apply at Palazzo Te) now contains the sarcophagus of the Martyrs of Belfiore (shot in 1851–52), and the crypt serves as a War Memorial. Opposite is the plain brick *House of Mantegna* (adm. weekdays 8–13). It was built to Mantegna's design in 1466–74 as a studio and private museum, and has a remarkable circular courtyard.

Beyond the site of the Porta Pusterla and a public garden is the ***Palazzo Te** (open 9.30–12.30, 14.30–17.30; closed Monday; the ticket office closes half an hour earlier). This delightful suburban villa was the summer residence of Federico II Gonzaga. Here he held splendid entertainments, and, in 1530, received the Emperor Charles V, on which occasion he bestowed the Dukedom of Mantua on Federico II. The name is derived from 'teieto', the name of the locality. Begun in 1525, and built of brick and stucco it is *Giulio Romano's* most famous work. He was called by Shakespeare 'that rare Italian master' ('The Winter's Tale'). In the decorative design he was helped by his pupils, including *Primaticcio*, who executed part of the stucco work. It has recently been beautifully restored.

The present entrance is through the *Loggia delle Muse* (the original entrance was on the W side of the Cortile d'Onore). The *Sala del Sole*, to the right, has a fine ceiling with stuccoes by Primaticcio and a painting of the Sun and Moon probably by Giulio Romano. The *Cortile d'Onore* is still being restored. On the left of the entrance vestibule the *Sala dei Cavalli* has frescoed portraits of horses from the Gonzaga stables by Rinaldo Mantovano (on a design by Giulio Romano)

and a carved ceiling by Gasparo Amigoni (1528).—The *Sala di Psiche* has
splendid *Frescoes (recently restored) illustrating the Story of Psyche from
Apuleius, by Giulio Romano.—The next room, the *Sala dei Venti*, was the studio
of Federico II. It has a ceiling with signs of the zodiac, and tondi illustrating
horoscopes. The room also has a fine stucco frieze and fireplace.—The *Camera
da Letto* has a fresco of the Fall of Phaeton in the centre, and stuccoes including
four eagles.—The fine *Loggia d'Onore* (or *di Davide*), with biblical frescoes, has
been restored. Beyond is the *Sala degli Stucchi*, the last work executed by
Primaticcio before his departure for France. The two classical friezes, in imitation
of a Roman triumphal column are thought to have been executed in honour of
Charles V's visit. The *Sala dei Cesari* has a trompe l'oeil frieze of putti and
Roman historical scenes in the vault.—The famous *Sala dei Giganti*, in which
painting and architecture are united in a theatrical trompe l'oeil, is the work of
Rinaldo Mantovano (on designs by Giulio Romano). It represents the fall of the
giants, crushed by the thunderbolts of Jupiter hurled from Mount Olympus. The
pavement was originally concave and was made up of large stones in imitation of
a river bed. The room has strange acoustical properties.—The rooms beyond
have recently been restored. The huge *Frutteria*, off the garden, is now used for
exhibitions.—From the Loggia (see above) there is access to the garden,
between two fishponds, closed at the end by an exedra, added c 1651 and
attributed to Nicolò Sebregondi. On the left is the little *Casino della Grotta*,
with more charming stuccoes by Giulio Romano and Primaticcio.

The upper floor contains collections from the *Museo Civico*: the Egyptian
collection of Giuseppe Acerbi has recently been beautifully arranged here. It
includes a well preserved bronze water jar, and sculptures. Another wing,
opened in 1983, displays the Gonzaga collection of weights and measures, as
well as a numismatic collection. There is also a gallery of modern art including
works by Federico Zandomeneghi and Armando Spadini.

In a remote part of the town to the SE (see the Plan) is the restored Romanesque
church of *Santa Maria di Gradaro*, with a good Gothic portal of 1295 and Gothic
frescoes in the presbytery. The adjoining conventual buildings surround a fine
cloister.

Virgil is commemorated in Mantua by the spacious PIAZZA VIRGI-
LIANA, laid out in the Napoleonic period at the beginning of the 19C,
with fine trees and a grandiose monument. At No. 55, the **Museo
Diocesano Francesco Gonzaga** was opened in 1983 (adm. in summer,
9.30–12, 15–17.30, except Monday; July and August only on Saturday
& Sunday; winter open only on Sunday, 9–12, 14–17; and closed in
February). It is still in the course of arrangement. Here are displayed
the splendid suits of armour found on the life-size ex voto statues in
the sanctuary of Santa Maria delle Grazie (see below). Recently
restored, the 15C suits are especially remarkable. The sculpture
collection includes a statuette of St George (c 1401), and 16C wood
groups of the Passion. The round sinopia of the Ascension of Christ
from Sant'Andrea is attributed to Mantegna. In a room with precious
goldsmiths' work, reliquaries, and church silver, is a German jewel
pendant belonging to Duke Guglielmo Gonzaga, and a large reliquary chest made of ebony and rock crystal (Venetian, c 1600). Also
here is a 14C French Gothic statuette in gilded silver of the Madonna
and Child.

In the church of *San Leonardo* is a Madonna and Saints over the high altar (partly
hidden by the organ), a fine work by Francia, and, in the adjoining chapel of San
Gottardo, a fresco of the Redeemer and Saints, by Lorenzo Costa the Elder.—In
Via Fernelli, farther S, is the church of *San Simone*, with a tablet (W wall) to the
Admirable Crichton who was buried here after being killed in a brawl in 1582
(perhaps by Prince Vincenzo, son of Duke Guglielmo). From the neighbouring
Chiesa della Vittoria (deconsecrated), built by Francesco IV Gonzaga to
celebrate the harrying of Charles VIII at Fornovo and despoiled by military
occupation in the 18C, Napoleon seized Mantegna's Madonna della Vittoria for
the Louvre. Farther W, in Piazza Carlo d'Arco, is the neo-classical PALAZZO
D'ARCO built by Antonio Colonna in 1784 (adm. 9–12; Thursday, Saturday, and
Sunday also 15–17; closed Monday; visitors are conducted), decorated and

furnished by the Counts of d'Arco. It includes 18C and 19C furniture, a collection of musical instruments, and numerous paintings (by Lorenzo Lotto, the local 18C painter Giuseppe Bazzani, Pietro Muttoni, Sante Peranda, Alessandro Magnasco, and many others). In the garden are the remains of a 15C palace where the Sala dello Zodiaco, has remarkable painted decoration attributed to Giovan Maria Falconetto (c 1520; including views of Rome, Ravenna, and Verona).—Nearby is the Gothic church of *San Francesco* (1304; rebuilt 1954), revealed when the Arsenal that formerly engulfed it was destroyed in 1944. The campanile and W front are original. In the Cappella Gonzaga (off the S side) where the first Gonzagas were buried with their wives, are frescoes of the life of St Louis of Toulouse by Tommaso da Modena.

Another interesting church is *Santa Maria delle Grazie*, 7km W, on the Cremona road (N10), founded by Francesco Gonzaga in 1399. The nave has two tiers of life-size statues in various materials set up as ex votos, an astonishing sight. Some of the figures bore the armour now exhibited in the Museo Diocesano. Also here is the tomb of Baldassare Castiglione (died 1529), probably by Giulio Romano.—Boat excursions may be made on the river Mincio from *Rivalta*, 3km N.

FROM MANTUA TO MODENA, 72km by road (N413), railway via Suzzara in 1–1¾hrs. Outside Porta Virgilio is the *Bosco Virgiliano*, a wood planted in 1930, extending as far as *Pietole*, 8km SE, a village usually regarded as the birthplace of Virgil. The road crosses the motorway (A22) which links the Brenner with Emilia, and then the Po. It passes *Bagnolo San Vito*, where excavations are still in progress of an Etruscan site (5C BC), the first ever discovered N of the Po, and the most ancient site in Lombardy. Finds are displayed in the Antiquarium and archaeological museum of Pietole.—22km **San Benedetto Po** grew up round the important Benedictine abbey of *Polirone*, a house protected by the Countess Matilda of Canossa (1046–1115), whose tomb here is still extant. The church was rebuilt in 1539–42 by Giulio Romano, and contains terracotta statues by Antonio Begarelli, and (in the 12C chapel of the Immacolata) a mosaic pavement of 1151. Three cloisters, a refectory of 1478 (with a fresco recently discovered and attributed to Correggio), and a Baroque staircase by G.B. Barberini remain of the partly ruined monastery. The *Museo Civico Polironiano* here contains material relating to the monastery (suppressed in 1797), including codexes, breviaries, etc., as well as an interesting collection of 19C puppets. In the neo-classical library by Giovanni Battista Marconi, and other rooms is an interesting local ethnographical collection.—2km S is the Romanesque church of Santa Maria di Valverde, altered in the Gothic period.—A by-road on the right farther on leads to *Gonzaga* (15km), the ancestral home of the famous Ducal family.—54km **Carpi**, a hosiery and shirt-making town (55,000 inhab.), of Roman origin, was a seigniory of the Pio family (1327–1525), famous as patrons of literature and the arts. Their *Castle*, in the handsome *Piazza*, houses the Museo Civico (open festivals in May–October, 10–12, 16–19, in other months on application). The *Duomo*, begun by Baldassare Peruzzi (1514) contains terracottas and sculptures by Antonio Begarelli and Clementi. The *Teatro Comunale* dates from 1857–61. Behind the Castle is the pieve of *Santa Maria di Castello*, with its tall campanile, of 8C foundation. It was rebuilt in the 12C and partly demolished in 1514. Excavations are being carried out beneath the floor and a Roman pavement has been found. It contains the sarcophagus of Manfredo Pio and a marble ambone (both 12C), and two fresco cycles of the early 15C. San Nicolò (1494, altered by Peruzzi) contains scagliola altars. In *San Francesco* is the tomb of Marco Pio attributed to the school of Jacopo della Quercia. The rococo church of the *Crocifisso* contains a Madonna by Begarelli. —72km *Modena*, see Rte 39.

FROM MANTUA TO VERONA, 38km; railway in c ¾hr. The only place of importance on this route is (22·5km) *Villafranca di Verona* which preserves a castle of the Scaligers (1202; to be restored) and gives name to the armistice of 11 July 1859 concluded between Napoleon III and Francis Joseph. 9km W of Villafranca is *Valeggio sul Mincio* with a Scaliger castle and, nearby, the ruins of the fortified Ponte Visconteo (1393) over the Mincio. On the Verona road is the unusual *Parco-Giardino Sigurtà* (open on Saturday & festivals) which can be visited by car.

III THE VENETO

Venetia today comprises three regions of very distinct character: the *Veneto* (4,123,000 inhab.; 18,365 sq. km), with the provinces of Belluno, Padua, Rovigo, Treviso, Venice, Verona, and Vicenza; and two autonomous regions, *Trentino-Alto Adige*, (841,000 inhab.; 13,613 sq. km), the mountain territory of the Upper Adige valley and South Tyrol, the modern provinces of Bolzano and Trento; and *Friuli-Venezia Giulia* (1,213,000 inhab.; 7844 sq. km), at the NE corner of the Adriatic, consisting of the provinces of Udine, Trieste, Pordenone, and Gorizia.

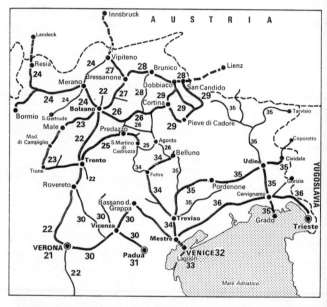

The *Veneto* consists approximately of the territory occupied by the Venetians in the 14C and early 15C when the dominion of the Milanese Visconti was coming to an end. Until then Venice had confined her interests mainly to maritime affairs, while the inland cities had been closer to Lombardy. Verona, Padua, Vicenza, and Treviso in the 12C formed the Veronese League in imitation of the Lombard League, and with the same end of checking the power of the Emperor. After the pillaging of the piratical Ezzelino da Romano, who terrorized the Adige valley in the early 13C, there following the age of the great families. The Scaligeri in Verona and Vicenza, the Carraresi in Padua and Vicenza, and the Da Camino in Treviso held their little courts, brilliant in literature and art, for about a century, but they were finally overcome by the Milanese Visconti. Meanwhile, however, the rising Turkish power had checked Venetian expansion in the East, and so they sought new expansion inland; the fall of the Visconti afforded the opportunity; and many cities, notably Treviso and Padua, came willingly into the Venetian fold, preferring the protection of the wealthy Republic to the chances of civic independence. By 1420 the whole territory from Verona to Udine and from Belluno to Padua acknowledged the Lion of St Mark. Further extensions of the Doges' dominion—to Bergamo in the west, Rimini in the south, and Fiume in the east—provoked the jealousy of the powers beyond the Alps, and the League of Cambrai (1508) put an end to Venice's imperial ambitions. But for 300 years the Venetian dominions in Italy remained united. The Napoleonic invasion of Italy saw the dismemberment of Venetia; Venice itself and Venetia east of the Adige was ceded to Austria in 1797, while the western portion also fell to the same power in 1814, after a brief union with the Cisalpine Republic. In 1859 an armistice stopped the progress of Victor Emmanuel at the Lombard frontier, and it was not until the Austrian defeat by the Prussians in 1866 that Venetia was able by plebiscite to join the Piedmontese kingdom. In the Second World War the province suffered considerably from air attack, notably at Treviso, and from German destructiveness at Verona. German resistance had practically collapsed by the time the Allied armies reached Venetia; and Udine was entered on the last day of the fighting in Italy—1 May, 1945.

Trentino-Alto Adige, a semi-autonomous region, is another totally different territory; in place of the marshy lagoons and fertile hills of the Veneto, the countryside is a labyrinth of deep valleys and snow-clad mountain ranges. Most characteristic among the mountains of this region are the fantastic pinnacles of the *Dolomites*, the strangely shaped limestone mountains disposed in irregular groups between the Adige and Piave valleys. The province of Trento is almost entirely Italian speaking, while in that of Bolzano the native language of Ladin has, except in the more remote valleys, been overlaid by the official language of the ruling power—German until 1918, and, since then, Italian or German. The two provinces represent respectively the old ecclesiastic principalities of Trent and Bressanone, or Brixen, both of which in the Middle Ages paid nominal allegiance to the Empire. In the 14–15C the prince-bishops held the balance between the rising power of Venice, on the S, and the Counts of Tyrol, on the N, while in the 16C, under the great bishops Clesio of Trent and Madruzzo of Bressanone, the valleys were practically independent. The decay of local powers prevailed here as elsewhere in the 17–18C and the Trentino and Southern Tyrol became more closely attached to the Empire. During Napoleon's campaigns the region was transferred first to Austria, then (in 1803) to Bavaria; the insurrection of Andreas Hofer in 1809 led to a return to Austria in 1814. Austrian mis-government in the 19C caused great discontent in the Trentino, and a movement for absorption into Venetia, but in 1866 Prussia discountenanced the abandonment of any Austrian territory beyond the Veneto proper, and the Triple Alliance (Germany, Austria, and Italy) of 1882 appeared to confirm Austrian possession of the territory. The denunciation of the alliance by the Italians in 1915 and the successful outcome of the First World War brought the Trentino under Italian power, and the extension of the frontier northward to the strategic line of the Brenner was an inevitable consequence, though the mountain warfare in the region produced little result for either side. In the Second World War the road and railway over the Brenner Pass, the main channel of communication between Italy and Germany, was heavily attacked from the air.

Fruili-Venezia Giulia, the easternmost portion of Venetia, is a province with a chequered career. Historically, its west part had as its centre the patriarchate of Aquileia, where an important Roman city, largely destroyed in the barbarian invasions, had risen again in the 7C in rivalry with its daughter-city on the isle of Grado. The *Friuli* also (the present province of Udine, formerly in Veneto proper) came within the patriarchs' dominion. In 1420 the Friuli, with the mountainous country of Carnia to the N and the city of Aquileia was absorbed by the Venetian power. Trieste meanwhile, an independent commune under her bishops, had been in continual rivalry with Venice for the seaborne trade of the Adriatic. Sometimes, with the help of the warlike counts of Gorizia, or the dukes of Austria, Trieste held the upper hand, but on more than one occasion the Venetians captured the port. The Istrian coast generally owed allegiance to Venice, while the hinterland and Gorizia belonged to the vassals of Austria. In the war against Austria in 1507–16 the Venetians at first made important conquests, but outside intervention forced them to withdraw their frontier W of Aquileia. Throughout the 16C disturbed conditions on the Istrian coast were fomented by the raids of Liburnian pirates nominally subject to Austria, and the power of Venice diminished. The outcome of the Napoleonic Wars here was the short-lived Kingdom of Illyria, which extended from Isonzo to Croatia, but was shattered in 1813–14 by an Austrian army and a British fleet; and from 1815 to 1918 the whole region fell under Austro-Hungarian dominion. In the First World War prolonged and fierce fighting took place fluctuating between the valleys of the Isonzo and the Piave, the Italians ultimately achieving success with the aid of the British and French detachments. The frontier was extended E and S to include the whole of Istria (including Fiume, after much negotiation), with the adjacent isles and Dalmatian Zara.

Towards the end of the Second World War, the Allied forces, advancing eastwards in May 1945, met Marshal Tito's Yugoslav forces at Cividale del Friuli and Monfalcone; and on 2 May the New Zealanders arrived at Trieste, where the occupying German force surrendered to General Freyberg. Italian and Yugoslav claims to the liberated territory came at once into conflict, and on 12 June the administration of Trieste, which had been occupied by the Yugoslavs, was taken over by Allied Military Government. In July 1946, all territory E of the so-called 'French Line' was ceded by Italy to Yugoslavia, the ceded areas including the E suburbs of Gorizia and all Istria S of Cittanova. The region around Trieste, including the coast from Monfalcone to Cittanova with a portion of the hinterland, was established as a free territory—neutral and demilitarized—by the Treaty of Paris on 10 February 1947. At the same time the province of Udine was transferred from the Veneto to Venezia Giulia and the new region, under the title *Friuli-Venezia Giulia*, was granted special measures of autonomy. A more rational adjustment of the frontier at Gorizia was undertaken in 1952, and in 1954 Trieste finally returned to Italian rule while the remainder of Istria was incorporated in Yugoslavia.

21 Verona

VERONA, surnamed 'La Degna', is a supremely beautiful and attractive city (266,000 inhab.) pleasantly situated on the rapid Adige, at the foot of the Monti Lessini. Among the cities of the Veneto it is second only to Venice for the interest of its monuments, and it is especially notable for the quantity of its Roman remains. It also has numerous handsome palaces, many with courtyards. Its modern commercial activity is in great part due to its position at the junction of two main arteries of transport: from Germany and Austria to Central Italy, and from Turin and Milan to Venice and Trieste.

Railway Stations. *Porta Nuova* (Pl. 13) for all main line services.—*Porta Vescovo* (beyond Pl. 12) is served by slow trains on the line to Vicenza and Venice.

Airport at Villafranca. Flights to Rome, Paris, Munich, and (charter services) to London. Airport bus from the station.

Theatres. Opera is presented in the ARENA (July–August). Booking office: Ente Autonomo Arena di Verona, Piazza Brà 28. *Drama festival*, including Shakespeare, in the ROMAN THEATRE (June–September).—*Teatro Nuovo*, for drama.

Tourist Information Office (A.P.T.), 42 Piazza delle Erbe; information offices also at 6B Via Dietro Anfiteatro, and on the Motorway exit ('Verona sud').—**Post Office** (Pl. 7), Piazza Viviani.

Buses from *Porta Nuova Station* via Piazza Brà to *Porta Vescovo*, and via Piazza Erbe and Teatro Romano to *San Giorgio*; from Porta Nuova to Castelvecchio (No. 4); and via Piazza Erbe and Castelvecchio to San Zeno (No. 7).—**Country buses** from Piazza Brà, Piazza Cittadella and Piazza Isolo. *Tramlines* to Domegliara, Grezzana, San Bonifacio, and Tregnano.

History. The settlement of the Euganean tribes on this site became a Roman colony in 89 BC and, because of its position (then as now at the crossing of important traffic-routes), Verona flourished under the Roman emperors. Theodoric the Ostrogoth lived in the city; and the Lombard king, Alboin, was murdered here, in his favourite residence, by his wife Rosamunda (573). Of the Frankish emperors, Pepin, son of Charlemagne, and Berengar I (who died here in 924) chose it as their seat. The free commune established here in 1107 united with Padua, Vicenza, and Treviso to form the Veronese League, the model of the Lombard League. Though always in sympathy with the Empire in its struggles against the Papacy, Verona resented Germanic attempts at conquest, defeated Barbarossa in 1164, and shared in the Lombard victory of Legnano in 1176. Family feuds within the city (on which the story of Romeo and Juliet is based) led to the calling in of Ezzelino da Romano, who established a tyranny lasting from 1231 to his death in 1259. In 1260 Mastino della Scala, the podestà, established his position as overlord of Verona, and his family held power in the city until 1387, throughout the most brilliant period of Veronese history. Dante found a refuge in the Ghibelline city under Bartolomeo (nephew of Mastino) in 1301–4, and in the reign of Cangrande I (1311–29) Verona reached its greatest period of magnificence. After the fall of the house of Scaliger, Gian Galeazzo Visconti became tyrant of the city, but in 1405 Verona placed itself under the aegis of St Mark. John Evelyn, who visited Verona in 1646, called it 'one of the delightfulest places that ever I came in'. In 1796 it was occupied by the French. Armed protest against the invader (the '*Pasque Veronesi*', 1797) was avenged by the destruction of much of the city, and Verona was several times exchanged between France and Austria by the treaties of the early 19C, until it was finally given to Austria in 1814. During the Wars of Independence it formed the strongest point of the Austrian 'Quadrilateral' (together with Peschiera, Mantua, and Legnago), but in 1866 it was united with the Italian kingdom. During the Second World War the city suffered considerably from bombing, and the bridges were all blown up.

Among the famous Veronese are Catullus (87–47 BC), Vitruvius (1C BC), the physician Girolamo Fracastoro (1483–1553), and the dramatist Scipione Maffei (1675–1755), besides the artists named below.

Art. The wonderful church of San Zeno marks Verona as a centre of architecture in the Romanesque period. Fra Giocondo and Sanmicheli were accomplished builders of the Renaissance, the latter renowned especially as a military architect. Sculpture at Verona is best represented by Pisanello, the medallist, and by Fra Giovanni da Verona, the woodcarver. Veronese painting reaches individuality with the schools of Altichiero and Jacopo d'Avanzo in the early 15C; and in later years the influences of Mantegna and especially of Venice were felt. Giovanni Badile, Stefano da Zevio, and Pisanello first distinguished Veronese art and among their successors were Francesco Bonsignori, Domenico and Francesco Morone, Girolamo dai Libri (a skilful illuminator), Liberale,

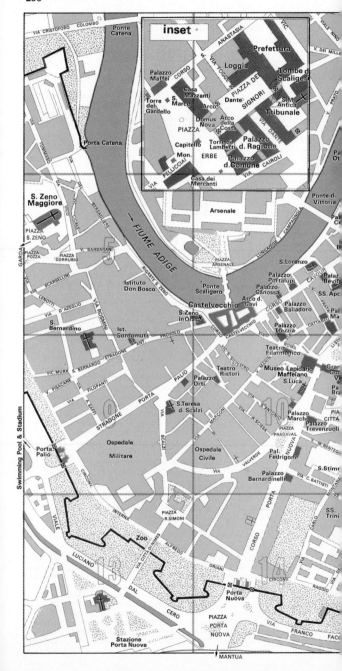

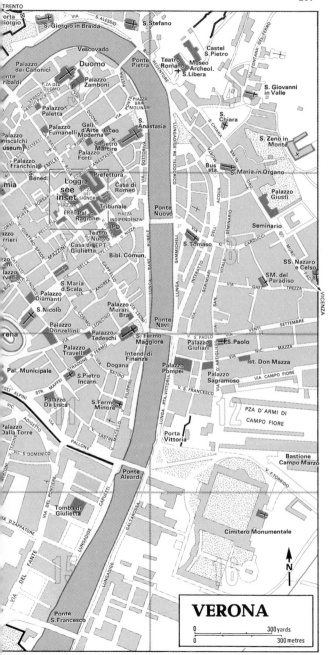

VERONA

| 0 | | 300 yards |
| 0 | | 300 metres |

Francesco Torbido, Bonifazio Veronese, Antonio Badile, and most famous of all, Paolo Caliari, called Il Veronese (1528–88). The town walls erected by Sanmicheli (c 1523) on the lines of the older ramparts of the Scaligers, are the earliest example of the new military engineering that was later developed by Vauban.

A.   Piazza Brà and the Arena

The focus of the life of Verona is the NW side of the huge PIAZZA BRÀ (Pl. 10). Corso Porta Nuova (from the Station) enters it under the *Portoni della Brà* (1389) which carried a covered way joining the Castelvecchio (see below) to the Visconti citadel: a pentagonal tower of the latter survives behind the *Gran Guardia*. This huge Doric building begun in 1609–14 by Domenico Curtoni dominates the W side of the piazza. It was built for military exercises and was completed in the same style by Giuseppe Barbieri in 1820. It is now used for exhibitions. On the other side of the Portoni della Brà is the entrance to the **Museo Maffeiano** (Pl. 10; adm. 9–19 except Monday), a lapidary museum reopened in 1982. Founded by Scipione Maffei in 1716 with material already collected in the courtyard here a century earlier, it was one of the first public museums in Italy. Goethe admired it on his visit to Verona in 1786.

The magnificent *Pronaos* with six huge Ionic columns was built by Domenico Curtoni in 1604, clearly influenced by Palladio. It was designed to be seen in conjunction with his Palazzo della Gran Guardia along the line of the medieval walls. It was to serve as the entrance to a theatre, but this was only built much later. In the courtyard Alessandro Pompei added the low Doric portico in 1739–45 to display the lapidary collection: the scale has been destroyed in this century by the addition of the two floors above.
  The collection has been restored and rearranged. In the *Pronaos* the Etruscan urns were set into the wall by Maffei. Also displayed here are Roman material from Verona including architectural fragments and funerary monuments. In the *Right Portico* and on the two small modern walls and in underground rooms are inscriptions from Verona. In the *Left Portico*, inscriptions from Istria, Brescia, Rome, etc.—From the Ticket Office a lift gives access to two rooms on the first and second floors. *First Floor.* Some 100 Greek inscriptions from Smirna, the Cyclades, Attica, the Peloponnese, etc., ranging in date from the 5C BC to the 5C AD constitute the best collection of its kind in Italy. *Second Floor.* Roman sarcophaghi, Etruscan cinerary urns, and Roman material from the Veneto. Steps lead up to the walkway over the Portoni del Brà, from which there is a delightful view.

On the S side of Piazza Brà is the huge *Palazzo Municipale* another impressive classical building (1838) by Giuseppe Barbieri (restored since the War). The *****Arena** (Pl. 7,11), is the third largest Roman amphitheatre in existence after the Colosseum and that at Capua (adm. daily except Monday, 8–dusk; during the opera season in July–August, 8–13). Its interest is lessened, however, by lack of access to the sub-vaults. It has been in the process of restoration for many years.

Built originally c AD 100, this amphitheatre is in excellent preservation, especially in the interior, and has been many times restored. Of the outermost arcade, however, which measured 152 by 123 metres, only four arches, preserving their simple decoration, were left standing by the earthquake of 1183; the inner arcade (138 by 109 metres) of two orders superimposed is almost complete. The present circumference is made up of 74 arches (80 at the Colosseum), and the floor of the arena is 73 metres long by 44 metres wide. The 44 stone stages of the cavea, restored in the 16C after medieval quarrying, provide space for 22,000 spectators; the topmost stages afford a fine view of the city. Goldoni's first successful play, 'Belisario', was produced here in 1834. The performance here of 'Aïda' in 1913 set a new standard for the production of operatic spectacle; opera season, see above.—At the back of the Arena, on the E, is a fragment of the *Wall of Gallieno*.

Piazza delle Erbe, Verona

A wide promenade known as the 'LISTON' borders the NW side of Piazza Brà and is lined with fashionable cafés and restaurants. Here also is *Palazzo Malfatti* (No. 16), by Sanmicheli (1555).

Some way to the SE of Piazza Brà, beyond the medieval walls, in an unattractive part of the town off Via del Pontiere, is the so-called **Tomba di Giulietta** (Pl. 15; adm. 7.30–19 except Monday). In a crypt off a Romanesque cloister an empty 14C tomb is called the tomb of Juliet. Also here is a small *Fresco Museum*, with

works by Paolo Farinati (c 1560); Domenico Brusasorci and Bernardo India (from
the façade of a palace, 1550–60); and 12C frescoes (very damaged) from Santi
Nazzaro e Celso.—Some way to the W is the Romanesque church of the *Trinità*
(Pl. 14).

B. Piazza delle Erbe and Piazza dei Signori

Via Mazzini (Pl. 7; usually called Via Nuova), the elegant main street
of Verona, closed to wheeled traffic, connects Piazza Brà with Piazza
delle Erbe. A side street leads down to the church of *San Nicolò*, to the
E front of which was added the imposing Ionic façade of San
Sebastiano, a church destroyed in 1945. Farther on, another side
street leads past the hotel Accademia, in an 18C palazzo by Adriano
Cristofali, to the church of *Santa Maria della Scala* with an apse and
campanile of 1324. In the S apse is a good Gothic tomb (1430) and
frescoes by Giovanni Badile. The Baroque altar on the S side,
designed by Cristofali (1751) encloses a votive fresco of the Madonna
and Child by Turone.—At the end of Via Mazzini in Via Cappello
(right), also barred to traffic, is the so-called **Casa di Giulietta** (Pl. 7;
adm. 7.30–19 except Monday), a restored 13C house once an inn with
the sign 'Il Cappello' and so identified with the Capulets.

The spacious interior (restored) is interesting for its painted walls (recently
disfigured by graffiti) and fine wood ceilings (top floor). Shakespeare's play of
Juliet Capulet (Cappello or Cappelletti) and Romeo Montague (Montecchi) is
founded on a tale by Luigi da Porto, a 16C novelist. The legend of a feud between
the two families is apocryphal; in fact, it is probable that the clans were in close
alliance.

The picturesque and irregular **Piazza delle Erbe* (Pl. inset) occupies
the site of the Roman forum and now serves as a general market. In a
line along the centre of the piazza rise the *Colonna Antica*, a Gothic
column with a stone lantern; the *Capitello*, a tribune of four columns
of uncertain date; a fountain of 1368, with a Roman statue called
'Madonna Verona'; and the *Colonna di San Marco* (1523), with a
Venetian lion (1886) replacing the original destroyed after the
'Pasque Veronesi' (see above).

The *Casa dei Mercanti*, on the W side, founded by Alberto della
Scala (1301) but now mainly a 17C building, houses the Chamber of
Commerce. It bears a Madonna by Girolamo Campagna (1595). The
statue in the adjoining piazzetta commemorates the victims of an
Austrian bomb that fell on this site in 1915. In the NW corner is the
Torre del Gardello (1370), and on the N is the splendid *Palazzo Maffei*
(1668), crowned with a balustrade bearing six statues. The *Casa
Mazzanti*, on the E, once a palace of the Scaligeri, was reduced to its
present size in the 16C and has a frescoed façade (recently restored),
and pretty balconies. On the same side is the *Domus Nova* (rebuilt in
1659), joined by the *Arco della Costa* (from a whale's rib hung
beneath the vault) to the great **Palazzo della Ragione**, founded before
1193 but much altered, with its main façade on this square rebuilt,
except for the heavy *Torre delle Carceri*, in the 19C. The 12C *Torre
dei Lamberti* (84m; adm. daily except Monday 8–14; summer 8–18.45;
lift or stairs; *View) was completed with a lantern in 1464, and the
Romanesque courtyard given a monumental Gothic staircase in
1446–50.

The Arco della Costa leads into the dignified ***Piazza dei Signori**, the centre of medieval civic life, with a monument to Dante. An arch joins the N wing of the Palazzo della Ragione (Romanesque and Renaissance; the Lion of St Mark was destroyed in 1797) to *Palazzo del Capitano* (now the *Tribunale*, or law courts) with a portal by Sanmicheli (1530–31) and a crenellated tower. In the courtyard is a bizarre portal by Giuseppe Miglioranzi (1687). Beneath the level of the piazza and in Via Dante a Roman pavement has been revealed. In the opposite corner of the piazza, through an archway (crowned with a statue of Scipione Maffei, 1756) is the back of the Casa Mazzanti with a curious outside walkway and stair. Here, too, is a Renaissance well-head. Beyond another arch, with a statue of Fracastoro (1559) is the ***Loggia del Consiglio**, an elegant Renaissance building of 1493.

The design has been wrongly attributed to Fra Giocondo. The twin windows are by *Domenico da Lugo* and *Matteo Panteo*, and the statues of famous sons of Verona in Roman times by *Alberto da Milano* (1493). Above the door an inscription records Verona's faithfulness to Venice and their mutual affection: 'Pro summa fide summus amor MDXCII'.

At the end is the *Prefettura*, originally (like the Tribunale) a palace of the Scaligeri, now restored in the original 14C style. The passage between the Prefettura and the Tribunale leads to the little early-Romanesque church of *Santa Maria Antica* with its 12C campanile. Outside are the ***Tombs of the Scaligers**, which are both historically interesting and illustrative of a century of Veronese architecture. They were shaken in the Friuli earthquake of 1976 and are still in the process of restoration.

Over the side doorway of the church is the tomb of Cangrande I (died 1329), by *Bonino da Campione* (the equestrian statue is a copy; original in the Castelvecchio). The other tombs are enclosed by a magnificent wrought-iron grille of the 14C, in which the ladder, emblem of the Della Scala, is many times repeated (this is at present locked while restoration is in progress). Against the wall of the church is the plain tomb of Mastino I the first of the Scaliger dynasty, assassinated in 1277 in the Piazza dei Signori. On the left of the entrance is the tomb of Mastino II (died 1351; covered for restoration) and in the opposite corner that of Cansignorio (died 1375), both elaborate monuments by *Bonino*, with recumbent and equestrian figures. At the back of the enclosure is the tomb of Giovanni (died 1359) by *Andreolo de'Santi*; nearby is the sarcophagus of Bartolomeo (died 1304) with bas-reliefs.
The Gothic house at the corner of the Via delle Arche Scaligere is called *Romeo's House* and is doubtless as authentic as that of Juliet.

C.   Sant'Anastasia and the Duomo

A short way NE of Piazza dei Signori is the church of ***Sant'Anastasia** (Pl. 3; closed 12–16), a fine example of Gothic brickwork of two periods, 1290–1323 and 1423–81. The W front is unfinished, but the double W door is a beautiful work; to the right are two sculptured panels from a series of the life of St Peter Martyr. The graceful tower supports an eight-sided spire.

The INTERIOR is remarkable for the short space between the springing of the vault and the apex of the arcade; the fine architectural detail throughout has been revealed to advantage by recent cleaning. The holywater stoups are upheld by two life-like crouching figures, known as the 'Gobbi' (hunchbacks). The 1st S altar is the Fregoso monument (1565), a fine marble composition by *Danese Cattaneo*. At the 3rd altar are frescoes by *Liberale* and *Benaglio* (attributed); the 6th chapel has a finely sculpted arch by *Pietro da Porlezza*: the sculptured Entombment is attributed to *Bartolomeo Giolfino*.—In the SOUTH TRANSEPT, Virgin and Saints by *Girolamo dai Libri*.—The SANCTUARY contains the grandiose tomb (1424–29) of Cortesia Serego, general of Antonio della Scala, attributed to *Giovanni di Bartolo*; it is surrounded by a delightful carved frame and frescoes by *Michele Giambono*. Opposite is a large fresco of the Last Judgement. On the jambs of the *Pellegrini Chapel, to the right, are four Apostles, by the School of *Mantegna*, and inside are two good Gothic family tombs and 24 terracotta reliefs of the life of Christ, by *Michele da Firenze*; also the effigy of Wilhelm von Bibra (died 1490), ambassador of Cologne to the Vatican. The outermost chapel on the right has frescoes by *Altichiero*. To the left of the sanctuary, beyond a chapel with 15C frescoes, is the entrance to the SACRISTY in which are fine stalls of 1490–93, 15C stained glass, and the gonfalon of the Millers' and Bakers' guild. Here, too, is displayed the celebrated fresco of *St George at Trebizond, by *Pisanello* (detached from inside the church; light; fee).—In the NORTH AISLE the 5th chapel contains a 14C fresco of the Virgin with Saints Peter and Dominic. The organ (1705) stands over the N door. At the sumptuous 4th altar is the Descent of the Holy Ghost, by *Giolfino* (1518), and around it are eight statues of saints and the Redeemer; at the 2nd, Christ in glory, by the same; above the 1st, frescoes by *Francesco Morone*.

Beyond the Gothic tomb of Guglielmo Castelbarco (died 1320), above the former convent-gate, is the little 14C church of **San Pietro Martire** (or *San Giorgietto*), now a cultural centre open for exhibitions. It contains 15C frescoes and a large frescoed lunette of the Annunciation, a very unusual allegorical composition by Giovanni Maria Falconetto with symbolic animals and idealised views of Verona. The two Veronese knights who commissioned the fresco are shown kneeling.

The road continues past the long neo-classical façade with Doric columns of the *Conservatory* (1807) to cross Via Emilei (left). Here in the 18C *Palazzo Forti* where Napoleon lodged in 1796–97 is the *Galleria d'Arte Moderna* (open 7.30–19 except Monday).

Via Emilei continues towards Ponte della Vittoria past the Venetian Gothic *Palazzo Franchini* (No. 20) to **Sant'Eufemia** (Pl. 7; closed 12–15.30), a church of 1262, rebuilt in 1375, with fine tombs on the exterior (covered for restoration in 1990). On the 3rd S altar, *Domenico Brusasorci*, Madonna and Saints and two donors; in the chapel S of the choir, frescoes by *Gian Francesco Caroto*. In the S transept, detached fresco of the Coronation of the Virgin by *Martino da Verona*. The 1st chapel on the N has a late painting of the Madonna in glory with saints by *Moretto*.

Via del Duomo continues past several Renaissance palaces to the *Duomo (Pl. 3; closed 12–15), whose reconstruction was begun in 1139. It is Romanesque below and Gothic above, while the apse is a charming classical composition. The building has been in the process of restoration for many years. The S porch, of the 12C, has a sculpture of Jonah and the whale (removed for restoration). The W entrance, another fine 12C porch, is guarded by statues of the Paladins, Roland (identified by the name carved on the sword) and Oliver. The campanile, continued above its Romanesque base by Sanmicheli, was given its incongruous bell-chamber by Ettore Fagiuoli in 1924–27.

INTERIOR. The spacious NAVE has clustered pillars with curious capitals and pointed arches. Round each chapel is a charming framework of sculptured pilasters and architectural fretwork. The walls around the first three chapels on either side are decorated with architectural frescoes by *Giovanni Maria Falconetto* (1503). In the SOUTH AISLE the 2nd chapel contains the Adoration of the Magi by *Liberale da Verona*, with a Deposition, by *Nicolò Giolfino*, above; by the nave pillar is a Romanesque marble stoup. Beyond the magnificent organ is the tomb-slab of Pope Lucius III, who died in Verona in

1185. Hanging in the aisle is a large Crucifix (early 15C). At the end is the *Cappella Mazzanti, with sculptured pilasters by *Domenico da Lugo* (1508); it contains the tomb of St Agatha (1353) by a Campionese master. The graceful curved choir-screen by *Sanmicheli* (1534) bears a Crucifixion with the Virgin and St John by *Giambattista da Verona*. The frescoes on the choir-vault are by *Francesco Torbido* (1534); the organ, on the left, has panels painted by *Felice Brusasorci*. In the NORTH AISLE the 3rd chapel contains a polyptych by *Francesco Morone* and *Antonio Brenzoni* (1533); in the 1st chapel are the Nichesola tomb and an altar-frame both by *Sansovino* (1527), the latter enclosing the *Assumption, by *Titian* (recently restored).

On the N side of the cathedral is the Cortile Sant'Elena, where the charming Romanesque cloister (with a double arcade on one side) preserves fragments of 6C mosaic pavement. Opposite is the church of *Sant'Elena*, beneath which and to the E excavations (for adm. apply at the Duomo) have revealed the church of *Santa Maria Consolatrice*, the 8C cathedral, itself a replacement of an earlier basilica. The tombs of two early bishops have come to light. Beyond is SAN GIOVANNI IN FONTE its Romanesque baptistery, with 9C capitals and a huge font hewn from a single block of marble.—In Piazza del Duomo is the **Chapter Library** (No. 21; open weekdays except Thursday 9.30–12; Tuesday and Friday also 16–18; closed August & September), founded by the archdeacon Pacificus (778–846) and containing many precious texts.

Opposite the S door of the cathedral a seated 14C figure of St Peter surmounts the doorway of *San Pietro in Archivolto*.—Behind the Duomo, beside the beautiful apse, is the *Bishop's Palace (Vescovado)* with an unusual façade of 1502 with Venetian crenellations and a graceful Madonna attributed to Fra Giovanni da Verona over the portal. The attractive courtyard with curious Romanesque capitals, is dominated by the Torrione di Ognibene (1172). Nearby is the *Ponte Pietra* over the Adige (see Rte 21F) guarded by a medieval gateway.

The Stradone Arcidiacono Pacifico leads from the piazza in front of the Duomo past *Palazzo Paletta* (No. 6; with a finely carved portal) to Via Garibaldi which leads to the left. In Via San Mammaso is **Palazzo Miniscalchi** (Pl. 3) with a beautiful façade restored in 1984. This was built in the mid-15C and has handsome marble windows and doorway. The painted decoration was carried out c 1580 by Michelangelo Aliprandi and Tullio India il Vecchio. The **Museo Miniscalchi-Erizzo** will probably be opened here in 1990 (adm. Tuesday, Thursday, Saturday, and Sunday, 10–12.30, 15–19). It contains drawings, paintings, archaeological material, sculpture, ceramics, arms, coins, etc.

D.   The Castelvecchio

From Piazza Brà Via Roma leads to Castelvecchio past (right) *Palazzo Carli*, once the residence of Marshal Radetzky, the Austrian commander. It continues a military role as NATO headquarters Allied Land Forces, Southern Europe. Here in 1859 the Emperor Francis Joseph ratified the peace of Villafranca.

The *Castelvecchio** (Pl. 6), begun by Bevilacqua for Cangrande II in 1354, was used by the Venetians first as a citadel and after 1759 as a military college. From 1796, under French, Austrians and Italians, it served as barracks until 1923. After restoration it was inaugurated as a museum in 1925 by Victor Emmanuel III. Here in 1944 Mussolini's puppet Republican government staged Ciano's trial. One wing was later damaged by bombing. In 1956–64 the structure was thoroughly restored and the museum imaginatively recreated by Carlo Scarpa. Adm. 7.30–19.30 (winter, 8–18.45), except Monday; in July–September usually open 8–23.00.

From the drawbridge, across the courtyard, is the entrance to the Napoleonic E wing. ROOM I. Sarcophagus (1179) depicting Saints Sergius and Bacchus; archivolt carved in relief, Christ between Saints Peter and Paul; male figure (13C) attributed to Brioloto; lapidary inscription dated 979; in a niche, Lombard gold burial ornaments and small marble coffer of early-Christian workmanship.—In RII, which has a fine view of the bridge, begins the 14C SCULPTURE: St Cecilia, St Catherine, from destroyed churches.—RIII. Fragmentary relief; Madonna, after the manner of Giovanni Pisano.—RIV. Relief of the Virgin (on a sarcophagus); the Two Maries; *Crucifixion, from the hospital of Tomba. RV. A glass panel in the floor shows Romanesque sub-structures incorporated into the castle. 15C SCULPTURE: two tabernacle panels; six low relief panels of the Prophets; *St Martin on horseback (1436); St Peter enthroned.—A terrace opens on the *Porta del Morbio*.

Beyond the fortress wall is the entrance to the main KEEP (1370), or *Mastio*, guarding the approach road to the bridge which passes between the two parts of the fortress.—From RVI (with 14C bells) a stair mounts to RVII with more bells. A bridge leads across to the REGIA proper. RVIII (left). Frescoes: Crucifixion, and Madonna (both 13C); Cavalry battle (fragment), from the Scaliger palace (mid-14C); the 'Via Trezza *Treasure' (removed for restoration), found in 1938, notably a jewelled gold star.—RIX. Frescoes, including a 14C Madonna and Child; also sinopie of the school of *Altichiero*.—RX. *Turone*, Polyptych of the Trinity (1360), his only signed work, and other attributed works; *Tommaso da Modena*, Saints James and Anthony with a nun; *School of Altichiero*, Boi Polyptych, from the Zanardi Boi Chapel at Caprino Veronese.—RXI. Statute-book of the Chamber of Commerce (15C, with miniatures; removed in 1986); *Jacopo Bellini*, St Jerome in the Desert, Madonna dell'Umiltà (attributed), and the risen Christ; *Stefano da Zevio*, Madonna del Roseto; *Pisanello* (attributed), Madonna della Quaglia; *Nicolò di Pietro Gerini*, Saints Gregory and Bartholomew; *Michele Giambono*, Madonna del latte.—RXII (left) Flemish painters.

RXIII, a long gallery overlooking the Adige, contains paintings of the school of Bressanone; *Jacopo Bellini*, Crucifixion (signed; removed for restoration); *Giovanni Badile*, Polyptych; Madonna with Saints Martin and George, the so-called 'Ancona Fracanzani' (1428); also Madonnas and processional crosses of the 15C.

UPPER FLOOR. RXIV. Veronese school (*Mocetto* and *Giolfino*).—RXV, at the far end, *Carlo Crivelli*, Madonna della Passione; *Mantegna*, *Holy Family, and Christ carrying the Cross.—RXVI, works by *Liberale*, including coffer with the Triumph of Love and Chastity.—RXVII. *Bonsignori*.—RXVIII. *Francesco Morone* and *Francesco dai Libri*.—RXIX. *Giovanni Bellini*, two *Madonnas.—A covered passage leads back to the Keep. RXX. *Brusasorci* (attributed, formerly thought to be by Veronese), *Portrait of Pase Guarienti in a magnificent suit of armour, and four portrait busts of Roman emperors, by the workshop of Sanmicheli. A second bridge leads to the upper floor of the Napoleonic wing; from the battlements the curve of the river is well seen and from the belvedere the *Equestrian figure of Cangrande I (14C), an evocative work strikingly displayed.

ROOM XXI. *Cavazzola*, *Passion scenes (1517) and four saints from the church of San Bernadino; *Gian Francesco Caroto*, Boy with a drawing; Benedictine monk.—RXXII. Further works by *Caroto*, including The artist and his wife; also *Girolamo dai Libri*, Holy Family with rabbits, Madonnas.—RXXIII. *Paolo Veronese*, Descent from the Cross (c 1565), Bevilacqua altarpiece (c 1548); *Jacopo Tintoretto*, Manger scene; *Sebastiano del Piombo* (attributed), St Dorothy; *Lorenzo Lotto* (?), Portrait of a man (sometimes ascribed to Titian).—RXXIV. *Brusasorci*.—RXXV. *Pietro Bernardi, Bernardo Strozzi, Marcantonio Bassetti*.—RXXVI. *Domenico Feti, Claudio Ridolfi*.—RXXVII. *Sebastiano Ricci, Gian Domenico Tiepolo*.

Approached through the S wing of the castle is *Ponte Scaligero* or *Ponte Merlato*, built by Cangrande II (1354–76). Blown up in 1944, it was rebuilt, mainly with original materials, and reopened in 1951.— The wide and busy CORSO CAVOUR (Pl. 6), lined with some very grand palaces, leads from Castelvecchio to the Porta dei Borsari. In the piazzetta beside the Castle is the *Arco dei Gavi*, a Roman arch of the 1C AD erected, astride the road, in honour of the family of the Gavii, demolished in 1805, and reconsitituted from the fragments in 1932. Among the fine palaces in Corso Cavour are *Palazzo Canossa* (No. 44; 1530–37; being restored), by Sanmicheli, with an 18C screen, and *Palazzo Portalupi* (No. 38; 1802–04) occupied by the Banca d'Italia. Farther on (left) is the finely restored Romanesque church of *San Lorenzo (c 1110). In its two cylindrical W towers were approaches to the matroneum. Opposite, is *Palazzo Bevilacqua (No. 19), an unusually ornate work by Sanmicheli (1530). Farther on (right) is the church of the **Santi Apostoli** (1194), with a Romanesque tower, apse, and cloister. From the sacristy stairs lead down to *Santi Tosca e Teuteria*, a domed cruciform shrine (5C), consecrated in 751 as a Baptistery, and reduced again to a burial chapel by the Bevilacqua (two tombs and a relief) in 1427.—No. 10 is the Venetian Gothic *Casa Pozzoni*, and, No. 11, a Renaissance palazzo of excellent design, now houses the study collections of the Museo Civico di Storia Naturale (see Rte 21F). No. 2 is the Baroque *Palazzo Carlotti* (1665). In the little piazza No. 1 is a Renaissance house, the home of the Giolfino family of artists. The ***Porta dei Borsari** (Pl. 6,7) is a Roman gateway with a double archway surmounted by two stages of windows and niches, through which passed the decumanus. It preserves only the outer front, though Roman masonry can be traced in the adjacent buildings. The gate is certainly older than the inscription affixed to it by Gallienus in AD 265.

To the right Via Diaz leads to *Ponte della Vittoria*, a stately bridge rebuilt since 1945, with four equestrian groups, by Salazzari and Bianchini, as a memorial of the First World War. The little Pilastrino dell'Agnello (16C) was erected by the Wool Guild.

E. San Zeno Maggiore

From Piazza Erbe or the Castelvecchio, bus No. 7 runs to Piazza San Zeno, in a less prosperous district of the town. The walk along the Rigaste (quay) from Castelvecchio passes the little 13C church of *San Zeno in Oratorio* (restored). The church of *San Zeno Maggiore (Pl. 5; open 8.30–12, 15–18.30) is one of the most beautiful of the Romanesque churches of Northern Italy. It dates in the lower part from 1120–38 and was completed c 1225; the apse was rebuilt in 1386–98.

EXTERIOR. The brick *Campanile was built in 1045–1149, and the *Torre del Re Pipino* (c 1300), N of the church is supposed to be a relic of the 9C palace of Pepin, but is really a fragment of the former abbey. The magnificent circular window in the upper part of the W front, by Brioloto (c 1200), depicts the Wheel of Fortune. The rich *Porch*, supported on marble lions, is decorated with sculptures by Nicolò, and on either side of the doorway are scriptural and allegorical scenes by Nicolò and Guglielmo, including the *Hunt of Theodoric*, in which the Emperor chases a stag headlong into Hell. In the tympanum is St Zeno trampling the devil and on either side is a charming row of twin arches, continued round the S side. The 11C doors (enlarged in the 12C) are decorated with remarkable bronze *Reliefs of biblical subjects from the Old and New Testaments (restored in 1988).—The little church of *San Procolo* (right; restored) is partly 9C work.

The spacious basilican INTERIOR (normally entered from the cloister), as simple as it is impressive, has a nave separated from its aisles by simple and compound piers and covered by a trifoliate wooden ceiling (1386). Some of the capitals are from Roman buildings. On the W wall to the left of the entrance hangs a 15C Crucifix. The large porphyry bowl in the NW corner is of Roman origin. In the SW corner is the large font of pink marble (12C). The walls are frescoed in layers of varying date (13–15C; being restored). The 1st S altarpiece of the Madonna and Saints is by *Francesco Torbido*; the 2nd S altar is made up of 'knotted' columns of red marble on a lion and a bull (? from an older porch).

In the raised presbytery are a further series of very old frescoes (scribbled over). On the balustrade are statues of Christ and the Apostles (c 1250). Above the high altar, in its original frame, is a *Triptych by *Mantegna* (light; fee), the Madonna with angel musicians and eight saints, the figures influenced by Donatello. The panels of the predella are copies of the originals, now in the Louvre. The frescoes on the walls include two of the school of *Altichiero* (1397): the Crucifixion (left; over the sacristy door) and Monks presented to the Virgin (over the S arcade). In the N apse is a painted figure of St Zeno (14C) and in the S apse is a statue of St Proculus (1392).

The spacious *Crypt*, supported by 49 Romanesque columns brought from other buildings, contains the tomb of St Zeno (1889) and other saints and bishops, including (it is said) Saints Cosmas and Damian. The sarcophagus of St Lucillus has good reliefs.—On the N side of the church is the charming *Cloister*, with coupled columns, built in 1123, but altered in the 14C. On the E side is *St Benedict's Chapel*, with four columns made up of ill-assorted fragments; on the N side is a projecting lavatorium; on the S side are tombs, including that of Farinata degli Uberti (died 1348) and of members of the Scaliger family.

Some way S of San Zeno is the church of **San Bernardino** (Pl. 9), an interesting example of the transition from Gothic to Renaissance (1451–66). It is preceded by a cloister and has a Renaissance portal of 1474. On the high altar is a triptych by *Benaglio* inspired by Mantegna's altarpiece in San Zeno. SOUTH SIDE. The 1st chapel is entirely frescoed by *Giolfino*, including some views of Verona (in poor condition); 2nd chapel, altarpiece by *Francesco Bonsignori*; 4th chapel, frescoes attributed to *Domenico Morone* and his son *Francesco*; and the *Cappella Pellegrini*, a refined work of the Renaissance (1557) by *Sanmicheli*. The chapel at the end of the S aisle is decorated with paintings in gilded wood frames by *Antonio Badile*, *Gian Francesco Caroto*, *Nicolò Giolfino*, and *Francesco Morone*.—NORTH SIDE. Charming organ (1481), with Saints Bernardine and Francis on the doors, by *Domenico Morone*; Baroque altar designed by *Francesco Bibbiena*.—From another cloister of the convent may be visited the *Sala Morone*, the former library, frescoed with Franciscan Saints and Martyrs, and the Madonna and Saints and Donors by *Domenico Morone* and his pupils (1503).

In the *Porta Palio* (Pl. 9), farther S (1542–57), Sanmicheli's skill in combining structural beauty with military strength is notable. In the gardens nearby is a *Zoo* (open 9–dusk), entered from Via Città di Nimes. Still farther S, near the station, is the *Porta Nuova*, a plainer work by the same artist (1535–40).

F. San Fermo Maggiore and the Left Bank of the Adige

From Via degli Alpini (Pl. 11), behind the Municipio in Piazza Brà, the Stradone Maffei leads to the left. On the right of it is *Palazzo Ridolfi* (restored as a Liceo Scientifico; no adm.), where the great hall is frescoed by Brusasorci (meeting of Charles V and Clement VII at Bologna, 1530). Opposite is the Renaissance Palazzo Maffei. Beyond the church of *San Pietro Incarnario*, built on Roman foundations with a 14C campanile, the Stradone San Fermo, lined with palazzi, leads to *San Fermo Maggiore** (Pl. 7), really one church on top of another. The lower building retains Benedictine characteristics of 1065–1138, the upper one was largely rebuilt by the Friars Minor c 1313 in a Gothic style (the different architectural styles are well seen from outside the E end).

EXTERIOR. The partly Romanesque façade has a round-headed door, to the left of which is the tomb of Antonio Fracastoro (died 1368), the physician of the Scaligeri. On the N side a 15C porch protects a fine portal of 1363 (the usual entrance). The smaller apses and the campanile date from before the rebuilding.

INTERIOR. The aisleless nave, adorned with 14C frescoes, is roofed by a very fine wooden ceiling (1314). The main doorway has a Crucifixion, attributed to Turone, in the lunette. To the left is a fresco of the Martyrdom of four Franciscans in India; and to the left of the first altar, Angels, a fresco by *Stefano da Zevio*. The marble pulpit (1396), and the tomb of the donor, Barnaba Morano (1412), in the adjoining chapel are by *Antonio da Mestre*. The 3rd S altar, beyond a 16C tomb borne by oxen, has a painting by *Francesco Torbido*.

The CHOIR has a screen of 1573 and a fresco (1320) above the triumphal arch depicting Guglielmo di Castelbarco offering the church to Prior Gusmerio. In the N apse, Saints, by *Liberale*. On the N side of the nave is a chapel containing the *Tomb of Girolamo and Marcantonio della Torre, an unusual classical work in marble and bronze by *Andrea Briosco* (c 1516); the *Lady Chapel*, with the Madonna and Saints, a vigorous work by *Caroto* (1528); and at the W end the Brenzoni Mausoleum, by *Giovanni di Bartolo* (1439), with an Annunciation by *Pisanello* above.—From the S side of the choir the Lower Church may be visited, an interesting Romanesque work. On the S side are two cloisters, recently rebuilt, with 16–17C frescoes.

Via Leoni, passing the damaged remains of the Roman *Porta dei Leoni* (1C AD), is continued by Via Cappello past the *City Library* (400,000 vols) towards Piazza delle Erbe.—In the parallel Via San Cosimo is a bizarre palace at No. 4.

From behind San Fermo the *Ponte Navi*, once a bridge of boats, crosses the Adige. To the right, overlooking the river, is **Palazzo Pompei* (Pl. 12), a fine early work by Sanmicheli (c 1530) housing the *Museo Civico di Scienze Naturale** (adm. 8–19, except Friday), one of the most interesting in Italy, beautifully arranged and well labelled. It also has extensive collections of fossils found in the locality. Ahead, Via San Paolo (with some fine palazzi) leads to SAN PAOLO (Pl. 12), a church reconstructed in 1763 and rebuilt since 1944. It contains (2nd S altar) St Anne, the Madonna, and Saints, by *Girolamo dai Libri* and (chapel to right of main altar) *Madonna and Saints by *Veronese*; and a high altarpiece by *Giovanni Caroto* (1516).—Some way along Via

XX Settembre, which has more good palaces (Nos 33, 35), as well as an amusing Art Nouveau corner house at No. 17, Vicolo Terrà leads left for **Santi Nazaro e Celso** (Pl. 8), a church built in 1463–84 near the site of a 10C shrine of the two saints, with a pretty forecourt.

The NORTH TRANSEPT, or Chapel of St Blaise (San Biagio), the saint's burial-place has a pretty vault over the apse and is noteworthy for its paintings: the altarpiece is by *Girolamo dai Libri*; on the inside of the entrance arch is an Annunciation by *Cavazzola*; and on the walls are scenes from the life of the Saint, interesting frescoes by *Bartolomeo Montagna* (suffering from humidity). In the SACRISTY is a triptych by *Francesco dai Libri*, three parts of a polyptych by *Montagna*, and 15C inlaid cupboards. Over the 2nd N altar is a Madonna with Saints, the masterpiece of *Antonio Badile*.

Via Muro Padri continues towards the celebrated **Giusti Gardens** (Pl. 8; No. 2 Via Giardino Giusti; 9–18.30 daily), the 16C green hillside pleasance of the contemporary Palazzo Giusti, praised by Coryat, Evelyn, and Goethe. With ancient cypresses, box hedges and fountains, it is beautifully kept. A path leads up through the wood to a tower (with a spiral staircase) which gives access to the upper terrace.—Via Carducci leads back towards the *Ponte Nuovo*, overlooking which is *San Tomaso Cantuariense* (St Thomas Becket), with a fine W front and rose window of 1493. It contains Sanmicheli's tomb (1884) and a painting of three saints by Girolomo dai Libri (4th N altar). The Interrato dell'Acqua Morta leads to **Santa Maria in Organo** (Pl. 4), a church perhaps of 7C foundation which received its present form from Olivetan friars in the late 15C. The façade is partly early Gothic, partly Renaissance, and the graceful campanile, ascribed to *Fra Giovanni da Verona*, dates from 1525–33.

The interior is frescoed all over; in the nave are Old Testament scenes by *Gian Francesco Caroto* (right) and *Nicolò Giolfino* (left), while outside the S transept are other works by *Caroto*, *Francesco Torbido*, and *Cavazzola* (Annunciation); inside is an altarpiece (Santa Francesca Romana) by *Guercino*. From the apse of the N transept (with a delightful Palm Sunday figure of Christ on an ass from the mid-13C, and frescoes by *Domenico Brusasorci*) is the entrance to the *SACRISTY*, notable for its cupboards, inlaid by *Fra Giovanni*. The walls are frescoed with portraits of monks by *Francesco Morone*. Here has been placed a 14C Dossal in local stone of the Madonna and Saints, attributed, since its recent restoration, to *Giovanni di Rigino*. In the main apse (unlocked by the sacristan) are *STALLS* (inlaid with street scenes and musical instruments), a lectern and candelabrum also by *Fra Giovanni*. The Crypt (apply to the Sacristan) preserves ancient capitals.—A large Renaissance cloister of the adjoining convent may be seen to the left of the church.
   The street ascending beyond Santa Maria leads to *San Giovanni in Valle*, a charming church rebuilt in the 12C with materials from an earlier structure. The crypt contains two good early-Christian sarcophagi (4C) and part of a small cloister survives.

Farther N, overlooking the river, is the *Roman Theatre** (Pl. 4; adm. 8–19; winter 8–14; closed Monday; during the summer drama season, 8–13.30), founded under Augustus and enlarged later. The cavea with its rows of seats and the arches that supported them, the scena, and the two entrances survive. In the ruins of the cavea is the little church of *Santi Siro e Libera* (920, altered 14C). At the back of the theatre a lift gives access to the convent building above, now an *Archaeological Museum*. The charming little collection includes Hellenistic bronzes, well-preserved glass, sculpture (torsos; head of the young Augustus), mosaic fragments, and, in the cloister, sepulchral monuments. From the windows are *Views of the theatre, and the city beyond.—High above stands the *Castel San Pietro*, where the Austrians built their barracks on the foundations of a Visconti castle destroyed by the French in 1801.

The ***Ponte Pietra** was blown up in 1945 but rebuilt in 1958 on the old lines by dredging the material (part-Roman and part-medieval) from the river. **Santo Stefano** (Pl. 3) is a venerable church rebuilt in the 12C. Round the apse (with a stone episcopal throne) runs a curious gallery, with 8C capitals. The 1st S chapel is a good Baroque work; on the left, the Forty Martyrs, by *Orbetto*. To the left of the sanctuary are frescoes by *Stefano da Zevio* (Annunciation) and *Altichiero* (Coronation of the Virgin). On the entrance arch above both transepts are charming frescoes of angel musicians. In the vaulted crypt (kept locked) is a raised semicircular gallery with capitals, etc., brought from older buildings.—Across the river are the cathedral, the battlemented tower of the bishop's palace, and the pretty little loggia of the chapter library.

The large church of **San Giorgio in Braida** (Pl. 3) was begun in 1477 on the site of a 12C church. The bold cupola was designed by *Sanmicheli*, who also began the unfinished campanile. The façade is of the 17C.

The aisleless nave, with side chapels, is notable for numerous fine paintings (although some of them are difficult to see). Above the W door, *Jacopo Tintoretto*, Baptism of Christ.—SOUTH CHAPELS: 3rd, *Domenico Tintoretto*, Descent of the Holy Ghost; 4th, *Francesco Brusasorci*, Three Archangels.—Beside the minstrels' gallery, *Romanino*, St George before the Judge.—At the entrance to the sanctuary, *Gian Francesco Caroto*, Annunciation.—The Sanctuary has a balustrade with bronze figures of saints: the two huge paintings are by *Paolo Farinati* (Miracle of the Loaves), and *Brusasorci* (Manna in the Desert). In the Apse, Sanmicheli's fine altar incorporates the *Martyrdom of St George, a masterpiece of colour and design by *Veronese*. North side, below the organ, *Moretto*, *Female saints; beside it, *Romanino*, Martyrdom of St George; 4th chapel *Girolamo dai Libri*, *Virgin enthroned between St Zeno and St Laurence Giustiniani–above another Sanmicheli altar; 3rd, *Caroto*, Saints Roch and Sebastian, and the Transfiguration; 1st, *Caroto*, St Ursula and her companions.

In the walls opposite the church opens the *Porta San Giorgio* (1525) by Sanmicheli, beyond which a short walk through a little public garden leads to the Ponte Garibaldi.

At *San Michele Extra*, 4km along the Vicenza road, is the *Madonna di Campagna*, a round church with a peristyle, probably designed by Michele Sanmicheli (1484–1559), who was born in the village.

The **Valpolicella**, a district famous for its wine and its marble, is reached from Verona by road from the Porta San Giorgio, keeping N of the main road to Trento. The chief village is (14km) *San Pietro in Cariano*, which preserves the old Vicariate, the seat of the Venetian district magistrates.—18km *Sant'Ambrogio* has quarries of 'rosso di Verona'. The *Church of San Giorgio*, 3km NE, dates from the 7C and has a 13C cloister.

The **Monti Lessini**, N of Verona, have become popular for winter sports, and several roads run up along the valleys of the *Tredici Comuni*, a high-lying district occupied by the descendants of Germanic settlers who migrated here in the 13C. Their dialect has practically died out. A road runs from Verona to (13km) *Negrar*, with the 15C Villa Bertoldi and the charming gardens (1783–96) of the Villa Rizzardi, at Poiega, nearby; (32km) *Sant'Anna d'Alfaedo*, with a local museum, and (35km) *Fosse*, two good walking-centres. The *Cave di Monte Loffa* may be visited (9–12, 15–18 except Monday). The road up the Val Pantena, passes just W of *Santa Maria in Stelle*, with a Roman hypogeum, to (11km) *Grezzana* (Romanesque campanile) and (15km) *Stallavena*. Near here the *Riparo Tagliente*, a shelter used by Palaeolithic hunters, has revealed numerous interesting finds from the Middle to Upper Palaeolithic periods.—(34km) **Bosco Chiesanuova**, the main resort of the Lessini. On the NE side of the Corno d'Aquilio, above Fosse, is the *Spluga della Preta*, a remarkable pothole (850m) in the limestone, which was descended in 1963.

Monte Baldo, the chain of hills separating the Adige valley from Lake Garda, is reached from Verona via (20km) *Domegliara* (see above). The road crosses the Adige and the route forks, the left-hand road descending to (35km) *Bardolino* and (38km) *Garda*, on Lake Garda (see Rte 19).—The right-hand branch mounts

the Tasso valley to (34km) **Caprino Veronese**. From there a twisty road,
bedevilled by motor-rallies in August, goes on to (10km) *Spiazzi*, and (14km)
Ferrara di Monte Baldo (856m), beneath the *Punta del Telegrafo* (c 2110m).

FROM VERONA TO BOLOGNA, 114km by direct railway in 1½–2¼hrs. The main
road (N12) follows the railway as far as Mirandola, then diverges via Modena.—
19km *Isola della Scala* (9800 inhab.) is the junction for Rovigo.—31km *Nogara* is
also on the railway from Mantua to Monselice and Padua.—Lombardy is entered
just short of (46km) *Ostiglia* (8100 inhab.), where the road crosses the Po. The
marshes here are a bird sanctuary. A short way downstream is the *Isola
Boschina*, its woods a rare survival of the vegetation which was once typical of
the Po landscape. There are plans to make the island into a nature reserve.—
48km *Revere*, on the S bank, preserves a palace of Ludovico Gonzaga with a
charming courtyard and portal by Luca Fancelli. Here the Museo del Po has
archaeological and historical material relating to the river.—56km *Poggio Rusco*
is a junction for Ferrara. The road here begins to diverge from the railway, and
(67km) **Mirandola**, the first town in Emilia, with 21,600 inhabitants, is 4km W of
its station (bus). It was a principality of the Pico family, the most famous member
of which was Giovanni Pico (1463–94), noted for his wide learning, a typical
figure of the Italian Renaissance. There are family tombs in the church of San
Francesco. A bus follows the main road to Modena; but this route soon diverges
left for (74km) *San Felice sul Panaro. Finale Emilia* (13km E) has a 14C castle,
and interesting 16–17C paintings in the Collegiata.—86km *Crevalcore* was the
birthplace of Marcello Malpighi (1628–94), the physiologist.—94km *San Giovanni in Persiceto*.—114km *Bologna*, see Rte 40.

From Verona to *Brescia* and *Milan*, see Rte 17; to *Mantua*, see Rte 20; to *Trento*
and *Bolzano*, see Rte 22; to *Vicenza, Padua,* and *Venice,* see Rte 30.

22   Verona to Trento and Bolzano

ROAD, 150km. N12.—53km *Ala.*—69km **Rovereto.**—92km
Trento.—100km *Lavis.*—107km *San Michele all'Adige.*—131km
Ora.—138km *Bronzolo.*—150km **Bolzano.**

The MOTORWAY ('Autostrada del Brennero'; A22) links the
Brenner Pass with Modena and the Autostrada del Sole. Between
Verona and Bolzano it runs parallel with the road on the
opposite bank of the Adige.

RAILWAY, following almost the same route as the roads. To
Trento, 92km in 1–2hrs; to **Bolzano**, 148km in 1½–3hrs. This
route has through carriages from Rome, Florence, and Bologna to
Munich, Hamburg and Copenhagen.

Verona, see Rte 21. The road leaves the city by the Porta San Giorgio
and traverses the Valpolicella (see above).—At (20km) *Volargne*, the
15C Villa del Bene (ring for custodian), enlarged by Sanmicheli in
1551, contains frescoes by Domenico Brusasorci. The roads, railway,
river and canal are now penned between the vertical cliffs of the
Chiusa di Rivoli. Rivoli, on the farther bank, gave Massena his ducal
title after the battle of 1797. The deep valley covered with woods and
vineyards, here called VAL LAGARINA, lies between the long ridge of
Monte Baldo, on the left, and the Monti Lessini on the right. Here
begins the region of Trentino-Alto Adige. Across the river, a little
before (48km) *Vo*, is seen the *Castle of Avio*, the home of the Counts of
Castelbarco since the 14C, with a tower of the 10C or 11C. It was the
first castle in Italy to be donated to the Fondo per l'Ambiente
Italiano (founded in 1975 on the model of the British National Trusts)
who have restored it and opened it to the public (9–dusk; winter 9–13;
closed Monday). The Casa delle Guardie has remarkable frescoes
(13–14C) of battle scenes.—The pretty campanile of the little church
of San Pietro in Bosco (13C frescoes) marks the approach to (53km)

Ala, with several Baroque palaces. It lies at the head of Val Ronchi, at the end of which the Monte Lessini are visible.—Between (59km) *Serravalle* and (62km) *Marco*, both rebuilt since the First World War, lay the front line of 1916–18. On the right are the *Slavini di Marco*, formed by landslips from Monte Zugna.

69km **Rovereto** (204m) at the mouth of the Vallarsa, is the chief town (29,600 inhab.) of the Val Lagarina. Here Paolo Orsi (1849–1925), the archaeologist, was born and died. The Corso and Piazza Rosmini commemorate Antonio Rosmini (1797–1855), the philosopher, another native. The *Cassa di Risparmio* in the piazza is a rebuilt 15C mansion. The *Municipio*, though much altered, retains some 15C portions. Nearby, the *Museo Civico* (9–11, 14.30–18; winter, mornings only; closed Monday), opened to the public in 1855, houses an archaeological collection, and exhibits of local interest including a natural history section. The 18C Corso Bettini is interesting. The *Castle* (8–12, 14–19; November–March, 9–12, 14–18; closed Monday), enlarged in the 15C, contains a large WAR MUSEUM (adm. 9–12, 14–18 or 19; in August 8–19), the most important in Italy devoted to events of the First World War. The War, which badly damaged the town, is commemorated by the *Sacrario*, erected in 1936 by Fernando Biscaccianti, on the summit of the so-called Castel Dante, rising S of the town. Nearby is the *Campana dei Caduti*, the largest bell in Italy, which tolls every evening for the fallen of all nations.

FROM ROVERETO TO RIVA, 21km; bus in 1hr. The road crosses the Adige between the station and village of (7km) *Mori*. It ascends the valley of the Cameras to (11km) *Loppio*, then crosses a huge moraine with a fine view of the Adamello on the left.—16km *Nago* commands a splendid panorama of Lake Garda and of the Sarca valley into which the road descends.—17km **Torbole** and (21km) *Riva*, see Rte 19.

From Rovereto to Monte Pasubio, Schio, and Vicenza, see Rte 30.

Beyond Rovereto the mountain views increase in grandeur. Monte Pasubio, with its oddly flat-topped spurs, is seen on the right.—75km *Calliano*. On the right rises the ruined castle of *Beseno* (being restored), with the Becco di Filadonna (2150m) behind it, and on the left is the Monte Bondone ridge.—83km *Acquaviva*. Villa Fogazzaro was the home of Emperor Karl I in 1915–18. Beyond *Mattarello* with its orchards of fruit trees, modern tower blocks announce the approach to Trento.

92km **TRENTO**, the chief town (91,700 inhab.) of its province and of the autonomous region of Trentino-Alto Adige, stands near the confluence of the Adige with the Brenta which descends from the Val Sugana on the E. Spectacular mountain ranges encircle the town which presents a cheerful air. Though it remained in Austrian hands until 1918, it is a typically North Italian city and entirely Italian speaking.

Railway Stations. *State Railways*, Piazza Dante. *Piazza Centa* for the Malè railway (bus beyond Cles).

Post Office, Via Calepina.—*Tourist Offices*, 132 Corso III Novembre and 4 Via Alfieri.

Bus Station, near the state railway station, with services to *Fai, Andalo*, and *Molveno*; to *Arco* and *Riva* (1½hrs); to *Pinzolo* (2¼hrs) going on to *Madonna di Campiglio* (3hrs); to *Borgo Valsugana* (1hr); to *Cavalese*, via Ora (going on to *Predazzo*; 2½hrs), via Cembra, or via Segonzano; to *Moena, Pozza di Fassa*, and *Canazei*.

History. *Trent*, the Roman *Tridentum*, owed its importance throughout the Middle Ages to its position on the main road from the German Empire into Italy; and in the 10C the bishops of Trent acquired the special privileges from the Emperor (probably Conrad the Salic) which they held until 1796 practically without a break. Early in the 15C the citizens rose against the overwhelming power of the bishops, but local unrest came to an end with the threat of a

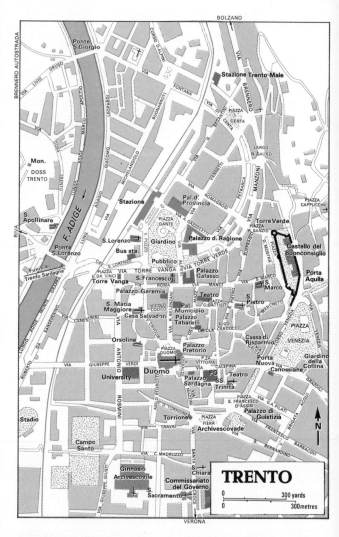

Venetian invasion, Venice having secured control of the Val Lagarina as far up as Rovereto (1416). The Tridentines asked for help from the Count of Tyrol, the Venetians were defeated in 1487, and in 1511 Austria established a protectorate over the Trentino. In the 16C the city rose to prominence under Bishop Bernardo Clesio and Bishop Cristoforo Madruzzo, and during the episcopate of the latter the famous Council of Trent met here (1545–63). The last prince-bishop escaped from the French in 1796, and the Austrians took possession of the town in 1813, holding it until 1918 through a century of great unrest.

VIA ROMA and its continuation VIA MANCI, the chief street of the old town, runs E and W. From its N side, between the Baroque church of

San Francesco Saverio and *Palazzo Galasso*, built by the banker Georg Fugger in 1602, Via Alfieri runs N, across the old course of the Adige, to the public gardens and the station. To the left is a good monument to Dante (1896, by Cesare Zocchi), behind which rises the tower of the Romanesque church of *San Lorenzo*, a fine example of 12C monastic architecture.

In Via Belenzani, opening opposite San Francesco, is (left) the 16C *Palazzo del Municipio*, with frescoes by Brusasorci in the Sala della Giunta (open only when meetings are in session). On the other side of the street are *Palazzo Geremia*, in the Venetian Renaissance style, and *Palazzo Salvadori*; the former has charming frescoes of the early 16C (restored) showing the Emperor Maximilian, who stayed here in 1508–09, and members of his court. Vicolo Colico (right) leads to the graceful and simple Renaissance church of **Santa Maria Maggiore**, by *Antonio Medeglia* (1520). The great portal of the façade dates from 1535; on the S side is a 16C Lombardesque portal. In the interior were held several sessions, including the last of the Council of Trent. The *Organ Gallery, richly carved, is by *Vincenzo Grandi* (1534).—Via Cavour, passing the old Municipio, leads to PIAZZA DUOMO, a pretty square with a handsome 18C Neptune fountain, the frescoed *Palazzo Cazuffi* (16C), and the *Torre Civica*, on the site of a Roman enceinte tower (one of the 'Trenta Torri' from which Trent is erroneously supposed to have taken its modern name). *Palazzo Pretorio*, once the episcopal palace, now houses the MUSEO DIOCESANO (adm. 9–12, 14–18; closed Wednesday), with a fine collection of paintings and sculpture from local churches, objects from the cathedral treasury, and a superb series of Flemish *Tapestries by Pieter van Aelst (1497–1532).

The ***Duomo**, a handsome and severe Romanesque building, entirely of marble, was begun by *Adamo d'Arogno* (died 1212), and not completed until 1515. The exterior, with its galleries, is impressive, especially at the E end, where the three apses and the *Castelletto* (the rear part of the adjoining Palazzo Pretorio) are effectively grouped. In the solemn interior clusters of tall columns carry the arcades, surmounted by a diminutive clerestory, and unusual arcaded staircases lead up to the galleries. It contains numerous tombs of bishops and 13–14C frescoes in the transepts. The Crucifix before which the decrees of the Council of Trent were promulgated is preserved in a large chapel on the right side. The baldacchino beneath the cupola is modelled on that of St Peter's in Rome.

Via Calepina leads E from behind the cathedral to the 18C *Palazzo Sardagna*, with the *Museo Tridentino di Scienze Naturali*, and the monumental *Post Office*, behind which Via Santissima Trinità ends at the small Baroque church of the Trinità. Via Oss-Mazzurana leads N from beside the Torre Civica, past the charming Renaissance *Palazzo Tabarelli* (No. 4; right) to rejoin Via Manci. To the right is the picturesque *Cantone*, once the chief crossroads in the town.

Via San Marco goes on to the ***Castello del Buonconsiglio**, the stronghold of the medieval prince-bishops. The N (left) portion is the Castelvecchio, dating from the 13C; the S portion is the Renaissance Magno Palazzo, built under Bishop Clesio in 1528–36 (and recently restored). It is the seat of the *Museo Provinciale d'Arte* (adm. 9–12, 14–16.30 or 18; closed Monday).

The main entrance admits to the gardens, from which are visited the cells in which Cesare Battisti, Fabio Filzi, and Damiano Chiesa (three Italian patriots, born Austrian subjects) were imprisoned in 1916 before being shot as traitors in the adjoining fosse, where modest monuments mark the site of their death.

The ATRIUM, with a collection of bells, preserves frescoes in the vault by *Romanino*. From here stairs mount to the SECOND FLOOR. The GREAT HALL has a good ceiling and a chimneypiece by *Vincenzo Grandi*. In adjoining rooms are a 17C organ from Riva, ecclesiastical sculpture, altarpieces, etc. The circular SALA DEGLI SPECCHI (unlocked by the custodian) was transformed in the rococo style in the 18C (cases of small bronzes, porcelain, glass, etc.). Across the stairway the APARTMENT OF BERNARDO CLESIO contains an archaeological collection, including the Tabula Clesiana, a bronze tablet with an edict of Claudius, dated the Ides of March, AD 46. From here a walkway (opened by the custodian) leads to the TORRE DELL'AQUILA with *Frescoes of the Months (c 1400), with delightful contemporary rural scenes.

The First Floor (shown on request) has a collection of furniture, sculpture, and paintings displayed in a series of rooms with fine ceilings (by *Fogolino, Dosso Dossi*, and *Gerolamo Romanino*). Also here is the grim courtroom where the martyrs (see above) were condemned in 1916. The Chapel has terracotta decoration by *Zaccaria Zacchi* and an altarpiece by *Girolamo Romanino*.—The LIBRARY contains a collection of 15C music manuscripts (French, German, and Italian).—The Castelvecchio, grouped round a picturesque courtyard at the N end, contains a copious collection illustrating the Risorgimento and the First World War (including the Cesare Battisti archives).

The *Torre Verde*, with its particoloured roof, formerly connected the castle with the town wall. Other relics of the ramparts are the *Torre Vanga* (c 1210), and the *Torrione*, S of the town.

Ponte San Lorenzo crosses the Adige W of the town. On the farther bank is the Romanesque and Gothic church of *Sant'Apollinare*. Behind it rises *Doss Trento* (307m), an abrupt hill crowned on its N summit by a circular colonnade commemorating Cesare Battisti (1875–1916; see above), a native of Trento. Nearby is the *Museo Nazionale degli Alpini* (9–12, 15–18; closed Monday) dedicated to the Alpine troops of Italy.—A precipitous road climbs SW to (7km) *Sardagna* (571m; view; cableway from Ponte San Lorenzo) continuing up the N ridge of *Monte Bondone*, the ski-slopes of whose crest are reached from the road by chairlifts.—15km *Vaneze*, a small resort.—On (24km) the plateau of *Viotte* is a renowned alpine Botanic Garden. A cableway mounts to the summit of Monte Bondone (1875m).

A road runs SE of Trento via (12km) *Vigolo Vattaro* (725m; road left to Lago di Caldonazzo 5km further, see below) and the imposing valley of the Centa, to (26km) **Lavarone** (1353m), a scattered community on the pine-clad slopes of the Asiago plateau. The return may be made via *Folgaria*, a winter and summer resort, to Calliano on the N12. From there to Trento, see above.

FROM TRENTO TO THE LAGO DI CALDONAZZO, local trains on Venice line to San Cristoforo and Caldonazzo in ½–¾hr. N47, the Venice road, enters the ravine of the Fersine, in which the road is cut into the rock.—10km **Pergine** (482m), well placed on the saddle between the Brenta and Fersine valleys, has a restored castle and some interesting buildings. It is a good base for walks in the Valle dei Mocheni to the NE via *Sant'Orsola* (10km), a small spa. The road bears right for (12km) *San Cristoforo* a bathing resort (water-skiing, etc.) at the N end of LAGO DI CALDONAZZO. The road circles the lake via (on the E shore) *Ischia* and *Tenna*, or follows the W shore to meet the road (right) from Vigolo Vattaro (see above) at (17km) *Calceranica* where the rustic Romanesque church (restored; 16C frescoes) has an altar stone dedicated to the goddess Diana.—19km **Caldonazzo**, another popular resort. To the W of the lake, and parallel to it, is the smaller Lago di Levico, with **Levico Terme** (506m), a spa with ferruginous waters, at its S end

(3km from Caldonazzo). A winding road leads up to *Vetriolo Terme* (1500m; 12km N), a modern spa and winter sports centre (cable car to Panarotta, 1819).

FROM TRENTO TO BASSANO DEL GRAPPA, 86km (N 47, double carriage-way in places). The road runs between Lago di Calonazzo and Lago di Lerico to by-pass (20km) Levico Terme, described above. The road enters the Valsugana.—From (30km) *Roncegno-Marter* station a road leads to *Roncegno* (535m), a small chalybeate spa.—35km *Borgo Valsugana* (386m) is the chief place in the valley. To the SW lies the Moggio valley, with the small resort of *Sella Valsugana*.— 48km *Grigno*. A road climbs to the winter and summer resorts on the Tesino plateau: 10km *Castello Tesino*, 13km *Pieve Tesino*, and (27km) the *Passo del Brocon* (1616m). From there the road continues to *Imer* (56km) on the Feltre-Fiera di Primiero road (Rte 34).—The main road enters the Veneto just before *Primolano* (217m), the junction for the road to Feltre. The Bassano road now penetrates the hills by means of the so-called Canale di Brenta, a narrow valley which the railway negotiates with many tunnels.—86km *Bassano del Grappa*, see Rte 30.

From Trento to *Tione* and *Malè* (Bolzano) see Rte 23; to *San Martino di Castrozza*, see Rte 25.

On the right beyond Trento is seen Monte Calisio, with lead mines dating from Roman times.—102km *Lavis* a vine-growing village, stands on the Avisio, at the foot of the Val di Cembra, up which runs a road to **Cavalese** (43km; Rte 25) via *Cembra* (14km), where the church has 16C wall-paintings. On the left rises the *Paganella* (2098m), reached in 8 minutes by cableway.—110km *San Michele all'Adige* is opposite the entrance of the spacious **Val di Non** (Rte 23). The railway station is at Mezzocorona, on the right bank of the Adige.—Beyond (118km) *Salorno* (with ruins of its castle on a precipitous rock), a German dialect becomes increasingly prevalent in the local speech.—133km *Ora*.

150km **BOLZANO**, in German *Bozen*, stands at the junction of the Talvera and the Isarco (265m), whose united stream flows into the Adige about 3km SW. With 105,800 inhabitants, it is the largest town in the upper basin of the Adige, and has been the capital of a province (mainly German speaking) since 1927. It has the character of a German rather than Italian town, although its population is now mainly Italian speaking. The old town, with its low-pitched Tyrolean arcades and Gothic architecture has a somewhat grim aspect; it is surrounded by extensive modern suburbs. Bolzano is a splendid centre for walks in the neighbourhood, with excellent transport facilities, though in summer the heat is apt to be oppressive.

Post Office, Via della Posta.—TOURIST INFORMATION OFFICES in Piazza Walther.—*Club Alpino Italiano*, 46 Piazza Erbe.

Buses. No. 3 traverses the town from the station to the Monumento della Vittoria and beyond (via Piazza Walther and Piazza Domenicani); No. 1 from the station to *Gries*. Other services from the coach station to *Ortisei* and *Plan*; to *Siusi*; to *Canazei* via *Nova Levante*; to *Belluno*; to *Brunico*; to *Merano*, etc. Express services to *Milan* (4hrs) via Trento; to *Trieste* (8½hrs) via Brunico and Udine; to *Cortina* (3hrs) via Dobbiaco; to *Vigo di Fassa* and *Passo Pordoi* (2¾hrs; summer only); to *San Martino di Castrozza* (3hrs).

Swimming: Lido (4 pools), Viale Trieste. *Skating* and *Ice-hockey*, at the Palazzo della Fiera, Via Roma. *Tennis Courts*.—**Theatre**. Teatro Stabile di Bolzano, 13 Galleria Telser.

Cable-way from Via Renon (near the station) to *Renon* (with connecting tramway to *Collalbo*); from Bolzano/Campiglio to *Colle* (the first cableway to be built in Italy); and from Via Sarentino to *San Genesio*.

History. An Iron Age necropolis has recently been found beneath the city, and a bridge is believed to have been built across the Isarco by Drusus somewhere in the neighbourhood of Bolzano. Bolzano became an important market in the Middle Ages, and was a bone of contention between the bishops of Trent and the counts of Tyrol until 1276. With the rest of Tyrol it was handed to the Habsburg family in 1363. Andreas Hofer led a rebellion against the Bavarian invasion from 1796–1809. In 1810–13 it was part of the Napoleonic kingdom of Italy, and from then until 1918 it belonged again to Austria. It was damaged by bombing in the Second World War.

In the central Piazza Walther stands the statue of the minnesinger Walther von der Vogelweide. On the S side of the square is the **Duomo**, a Gothic church of the 14–15C (restored since 1945) with a fine tower of 1501–19, by Johann Lutz, and a colourful roof. The former *Dominican Monastery*, a little to the W, has frescoes in the S aisle, and in the Cappella di San Giovanni (left of apse; light on wall opposite entrance), with interesting Giottesque figures (1330–40). The Gothic cloister (entrance at No. 19) and the Chapel of St Catherine (14–16C frescoes) survived the bombing which spoiled the rest of the church. To the NE is the unattractive Municipio, beyond which **Via dei Portici**, with its heavy low arcades, leads to the left. No. 39 on the left is the *Palazzo Mercantile*, in an 18C mansion. From Piazza delle Erbe (fruit market), at the end of the street, Via dei Francescani leads (right) to the *Franciscan Church*, a 14C building (restored) with an attractive cloister on the N side (interesting remains of frescoes). In a side chapel is a fine carved wooden altarpiece by Hans Klocker (1500). The N wall of the church is decorated with an entertaining frieze of celebrated Franciscans (16C). Via Dr Streiter, to the S, is typical of old Bolzano.

Via del Museo leads from Piazza delle Erbe to the Talvera bridge; on the left is the *Museo Civico* (adm. 9–12, 15–17; closed Sunday & festivals), an interesting collection of local antiquities and 'bygones'. To the right, beyond, extends the LUNGOTALVERA BOLZANO, a pleasant promenade on an embankment. On the right, below the promenade, is the *Castello Mareccio*, a 13C building with five later towers which is now a congress centre. It commands a fine view, especially of the Catinaccio.

The *Talvera Bridge*, another fine view-point, leads across the river to the MONUMENTO DELLA VITTORIA, a triumphal arch by Marcello Piacentini (1928) adorned with sculptures by various artists, with gardens behind.

Corso Libertà leads on to the garden suburb of **Gries**, in whose main square stands a Benedictine monastery and abbey church. In Via Martin Knoller, N of the square, the *Parish Church* (15–16C) contains another carved wooden altarpiece (1471–80), by Michael Pacher and his school. Above the village rises the hill of *Guncinà* which can be climbed by the winding Passeggiata, beyond the church.

Another pleasant walk leads from the Municipio along the old Via dei Bottai to Via Andrea Hofer, with an old inn on the first corner. Farther N, across Via Cavour, is the Romanesque church of *San Giovanni*. Via Monte Tondo continues N from Via Cavour past (right) the 17C mansion of *Hortenberg*. From Via Sant'Osvaldo at the end of this street, a stepped ascent leads to the *PASSEGGIATA SANT'OSVALDO, a terrace walk, with views, which descends again to the N end of the Lungotalvera promenade.

From the farther side of the Ponte Sant'Antonio (bus No. 1), which crosses the Talvera 2km N of the town, a cableway ascends to *San Genesio Atesino* (1087m), an old village with a fine view across the Val Sarentina of the Dolomites.—On the S side of the Isarco valley, reached by cableway or on foot (c 2½hrs) via Castello di Campegno and Bagni di Sant'Isidoro, is **Colle** or *Colle di Villa* (1136m), from where an easy footpath (½hr) leads up to *Col dei Signori* (1180m) a popular summer holiday centre of Bolzano.

FROM BOLZANO TO COLLALBO, 12km, cableway ascending the high plateau NE of Bolzano, with its *Views of the Dolomites.—The cableway starts from Via Renon and mounts to Soprabolzano, passing over vineyards.—On the right on the approach to (5km) *L'Assunta* some eroded earth-pyramids are seen.—6km **Soprabolzano** (1221m) is a holiday resort with views extending to the Brenta and Ortler groups. Here may be joined the rack railway from L' Assunta.—8km *Costalovara* has a small lake, on the road leading S to Bolzano.—9km *Stella Renon* and (10km) *Colle Renon* are two scattered holiday resorts.—12km **Collalbo** (1154m), the chief village of the plateau of *Renon*, is a good centre for walks and climbs. About ½hr N are the earth-pillars of Longomoso, the most remarkable of the many groups of erosion-pillars in the neighbourhood; and farther on (3½hrs by a marked path) is the *Rifugio Corno di Renon* (2259m), commanding a fine mountain view.—From Collalbo an easy path descends to Campodazzo in the Isarco valley.

FROM BOLZANO TO SARENTINO, 20km, bus in 1hr, the road mounts the narrow valley of the Talvera, to the N of Bolzano, and passes (right) *Castel Roncolo* (1237), with remarkable frescoes in the interior (10–12, 15–18 except Monday & festivals; in winter, 10–12). Farther on (left) are the ruins of *Castel Sarentino*. The road winds upward through an attractive gorge, with porphyry cliffs and two more ruined castles.—20km **Sarentino** (961m), the chief place (5800 inhab.), in the Val Sarentina, is a centre for mountain walks (marked paths).

From Bolzano to the *Brenner* (Innsbruck), see Rte 27; to *Cortina* and *Pieve di Cadore*, see Rte 26; to *Merano* and *Bormio* (Stelvio Pass), see Rte 24; to *Tione* and *Trento* via Malè, see below.

23 Bolzano to Malè, Tione, and Trento

ROAD, 164km.—25km *Passo della Mendola.*—34km *Cavareno.*—36km *Fondo.*—56km *Ponte di Mostizzolo.*—66km **Malè.**—71km *Dimaro.*—88km **Madonna di Campiglio.**—101km *Pinzolo.*—120km **Tione.**—132km *Ponte delle Arche.*—144km *Le Sarche.*—164km **Trento.**

BUSES. From Madonna di Campiglio to Tione and *Trento*, twice daily service all the year in 2¼hrs. Summer service to *Malè* and from Malè to *Trento* via Dermulo (60km in 1½hrs); and from Mendola and from Dermulo to Fondo.

This route through the W part of Tridentine Venetia traverses some of the finest country in the Italian Alps, including the Val di Non and Val di Sole and the Presanella and Brenta mountain-groups, forming part of the **Adamello-Brenta National Park**. It connects also with the main roads from Lombardy: at Malè with the Tonale road from Edolo; at Tione with the Valli Giudicarie; and at Le Sarche with the road from the Lake of Garda.

From the Druso road at Bolzano the Mendola road bears to the left and crosses the Adige, beneath (4km) the hill of *Castel Firmiano* (restored, and now a restaurant), an ancient stronghold said to have been founded in Roman times, and later the property of the bishops of Trento and the counts of Toggenburg.—At 7km a road (right) leads to *San Paolo* (2km) with a fine Gothic and Renaissance church and notable bells, and to the ruined *Castle of Appiano* (8km), founded in the 12C, and still retaining a Romanesque chapel with murals (adm. April–October except Tuesday).—10km *Appiano sulla Strada del Vino* is a scattered commune, with its principal centre at San Michele, on the main road. Several fine 17–18C houses here are in a Renaissance style peculiar to the district. The road ascends across the face of the Mendelwand (good retrospective views of Bolzano). On the left, at 15km is a road (the 'Strada del Vino') which leads S through vineyards to *Caldaro* and the Lago di Caldaro. Near here is the 14C *Castello di Monterotondo (Ringberg)* with a Wine Museum (adm. April–October, 9.30–12, 14–18; closed Monday and fest.). —The main road continues a zigzag climb through woods to end at (25km) **Mendola** (1363m), a beautifully situated resort (ski facilities) in the Passo della Mendola between the Penegal (N) and Roen (S), with a fine view of the Catinaccio and Latemar groups across the Adige valley, and of the Brenta and Adamello to the SW.

The *Penegal* (1737m) is ascended by road; the *Roen* (2116m) in 3hrs by a marked track via the *Rifugio Oltradige*, or by chairlifts.—A cableway descends from Mendola to Sant'Antonio, near Caldaro (see above).

Passing above (29km) *Ruffrè*, the road turns left at (31km) *Belvedere*. About 2km N is *Malosco* visited, like (33km) *Ronzone*, for the sake of the mountain views.—34km *Cavareno*.

Here N43, leading S, provides a short cut to Trento.—3km *Romeno* was the birthplace of the 18C painter Giovanni Battista Lampi, whose frescoes decorate the church.—6km *Malgolo* has a fine medieval castle, well restored.—9km *Sanzeno*, a pleasant village with a large Gothic church. A by road leads up to the sanctuary of *San Romedio*, a pilgrim resort on a steep rock, consisting of five old chapels connected by steps, and a modern chapel. The two upper chapels are said to represent the hermitage occupied by the tutelary saint.—12km *Dermulo* is on the main road from Trento to Malè (see below).

The main road turns N through (35km) *Sarnonico*.—36km *Fondo* (987m) is a large village divided into two by a gorge, situated at the foot of *Monte Macaion* (1866m). *Castelfondo*, 5km NW, beyond its battered old castle, is a pretty village from which the little-known valleys to the N may be explored.—The road crosses the romantic *Novella* valley and descends to (42km) *Brez.*— Beyond (49km) *Revò* it descends from the plateau to (52km) a junction above the *Ponte San Gallo*, a bridge crossing the Lago di Santa Giustina. The left branch joins the main road coming from Trento.

FROM THE PONTE SAN GALLO TO SAN MICHELE ALL'ADIGE (Trento), 30km. This road descends the lovely *VAL DI NON*, or *Anaunia*, with its woods and ruined castles.—4km **Cles** (658m), the chief place in the valley, overlooks the hydro-electric Lago di Santa Giustina. The town, with 5200 inhabitants, has a good Renaissance church and old houses. To the NE rises *Castel Cles*, the ancestral home of the famous episcopal Clesio family, rebuilt in the 16C. It stands at the foot of *Monte Peller* (2319m) the N peak of the Brenta group.
  A good alternative road to Trento keeps to the W of the main road.—4km *Tuenno*. The *Lago Tovel*, 11km SW, is a lovely lake in a deep valley beneath the Brenta range.—17km *Denno*.—At (21km) *Rocchetta* (see below) this route rejoins the main road.
  The Cles-Trento railway follows the road closely. The Noce is crossed by the bridge of Santa Giustina, 143m above the stream.—6km **Dermulo** stands at the junction of the valley road with the road to Mendola via Cavareno (N43d; see above). *Coredo* (831m), 4km NE is a summer resort, with a 15C mansion of the bishops of Trento.—8km *Taio*, for the *Castello Bragher*, 2km NE, the best preserved of the castles in the valley. Beyond the castle of *Ton*, high up on the left, is (19km) *Rocchetta*, where the valley appears closed by two huge crags. On the right is the upper road to Cles (see above); also a road to Molveno (see below). The valley opens out before (27km) *Mezzolombardo* (227m), a centre of wine production. A delightful road, starting about 1km N of Mezzolombardo, ascends to (12km) **Fai** (960m), a summer and winter resort. A cableway ascends from there to the *Paganella* (2098m), a splendid viewpoint, from which a descent may be made W to Andalo (by

chair-lift) and Molveno.— 28km *Mezzocorona* lies mainly to the left. The road crosses the Adige and joins the valley road at (30km) *San Michele all'Adige* (Rte 22).

Beyond the Ponte San Gallo the Tione road ascends the VAL DI SOLE, the upper glen of the Noce.—65km *Caldes*, with a restored castle.—66km **Malè** (738m), the chief village in the valley, has a local ethnographical museum (Museo della Civiltà Solandra). It has bus connections with the railway from Trento to Cles, and chair-lifts to the ski-slopes of Monte Peller (see above).

A narrow road ascends the Val di Rabbi to (12km) **Bagno di Rabbi** (1195m) a small spa and climbing centre, beneath the *Passo di Rabbi* (2467m).

At (71km) *Dimaro* (766m), the Tonale road (see Rte 18) to Edolo bears off to the right. This road ascends in zigzags amid pine-forests in the Val Meledrio via *Folgarida*, now developed as a winter resort (chair-lifts etc. and a modern cableway up to Malghet Haut, 1860m). Just beyond the summit-level (1682m) is (87km) *Campo di Carlo-magno*, another resort, with views of the Brenta group to the left. The road descends through forest.

88km **Madonna di Campiglio** (1522m), a famous winter and summer resort, stands in a wooded basin in the upper valley of the Sarca. It is the chief centre for climbs in the Brenta group, which lies to the E. The fashionable seasons are July–August and December–March. The winter sports facilities include a ski school, chair-lifts and cableway to the Spinale Pancugolo, and Pradalago ski-slopes, ski-jump below the Spinale, and a skating rink. A chair-lift also connects Pradalago with the ski-resorts in Val di Sole via Monte Vigo (2180m).

The Brenta mountains, an isolated dolomitic group between Madonna di Campiglio and the Adige valley, are for expert climbers only, but there are many easier walks (marked by coloured signs) in their foothills.

Monte Spinale (2104m) is almost due E (chair-lift in 20 minutes or well-marked path in c 2hrs). A road is projected up the E side of the mountain despite the fact that it would destroy the natural beauty of the area. The summit commands a splendid circular view of the Brenta, Adamello, Presanella, and Ortler mountains. A funicular continues to the *Rifugio Graffer* (2262m), on the Passo del Grost, from where the *Panorama extends to Monte Cevedale, 40km NW.—On the W side of the main valley, to the S of Madonna di Campiglio, is the magnificent *Val Brenta and the *Vallesinella*, on the 'Giro delle Cascate' walk.

A steep and winding descent carries the road from the Campiglio basin down the Val di Nambino, with the Brenta group towering above the forest on the left.—Beyond (96km) *Sant'Antonio di Mavignola* (1123m) the pines and larches gradually give way to chestnut-groves and the Val di Nambrone, and later the Val di Genova, open out on the right.

101km **Pinzolo** (770m), splendidly situated at the junction of the two main upper valleys of the Sarca, is another ski resort and climbing centre (2500 inhab.). The church of *San Vigilio, to the N, is notable for its external fresco of the Dance of Death, by Simone Baschenis (1539).

A similar painting (1519) by the same artist adorns the exterior of the church of *Santo Stefano* (which also contain frescoes inside by him), 3km up the **Val di Genova**. The magnificent valley 16km long, thickly wooded in parts, is the main approach to the Presanella and Adamello groups from the E. The peaks and spurs on the S side were the scene of some of the most difficult fighting during the First World War. On the N side of the valley, 5km from Pinzolo, is the *Cascata di Nardis*, a waterfall on the stream descending from the Nardis glacier.—The road passes the mouth of the Val Lares (left) with another waterfall.—10km *Ragada* (1278m), with a small war-cemetery. The unmade-up road ends at *Pian di Bedole* (1578m) at the head of the valley. The *Presanella* (3556m) was first ascended by the English alpinist Douglas Freshfield (died 1929) in 1864.—Chair-lifts ascend from Pinzolo to Dosso Sabion (2059m).

The road descends the Val Rendena, the valley of the Sarca, now much wider and more populous. A narrow winding road branches left about 1km before (105km) *Caderzone* to bypass Tione and rejoin the Trento road beyond Saone (see below). The villages lower down the valley have suffered greatly from forest fires. The *Carè Alto* (3462m) dominates the landscape on the right.—120km **Tione** (565m), lies at the junction of the road to the Valli Giudicarie (Rte 17) with that to Trento.

The Trento road turns E and beyond (124km) *Saone* and the newly formed Lago Ponte Pia, enters the *Gola della Scaletta*, a narrow winding gorge of the Sarca.—132km **Ponte delle Arche** (398m) is an important road centre. *Stenico* (666m), 4km NW has a medieval castle commanding a good view, and is connected with Madonna di Campiglio by a fine mountain walk.

FROM PONTE DELLE ARCHE TO MOLVENO, 20km. The road serves the scattered hamlet of *San Lorenzo in Banale*, passes the little *Lago di Nembia*, and then skirts the pleasant *Lago di Molveno*, 6·5km long. At its N end is (20km) the popular resort of **Molveno** (865m), lying under the lee of the Brenta mountains (chair-lift from the Rifugio Pradel).

Beyond Molveno the road goes on to (5km) *Andalo* (1041m), another resort with chair-lifts ascending to **Paganella** (see Rte 22). From there the road continues via Fai or via (15km) *Spormaggiore* to Rocchetta and (24km) **Mezzolombardo** (see above).

134km *Comano Terme* is a small spa treating skin complaints. Another fine gorge through the S spurs of the Brenta group ends at (144km) *Le Sarche* to meet the main road from Arco and Lake Garda. The road leaves the Sarca valley and skirts the *Lago di Toblino*, with the picturesque *Castel Toblino* on a cape on the right. On the left farther on is the *Lago di Santa Massenza*.—151km *Vezzano*.—Beyond (155km) *Vigolo Baselga* which like Baselga di Vezzano (1km right), is another small spa, a road leads to *Terlago* (3km) with an old castle and charming little lake.—At (157km) the *Passo di Cadine* (495m) the watershed into the Adige valley is crossed, and a little farther on is the entrance to the impressive gorge of the Buco di Vela.—At 160km is a turning for Sardagna and Monte Bondone (see Rte 22).—164km **Trento**, see Rte 22.

24 Bolzano to Merano and Bormio

ROAD, N38, 127km.—29km **Merano**.—43km *Naturno*.—63km *Silandro*.—78km **Spondigna**.—80km *Prato allo Stelvio*.—86km *Gomagoi*.—91km *Trafoi*.—104km **Stelvio Pass**.—127km **Bormio**.

RAILWAY to *Malles Venosta*, 92km in 2½hrs (change necessary at Merano). Frequent service to *Merano*, 32km in c 50 minutes.

BUSES daily (July–Sept) from Bolzano to the *Stelvio Pass* in 3¾hrs (several services from Spondigna to the *Stelvio Pass* in 2hrs); from the Pass to *Bormio* in 1hr.

From Bolzano N38 crosses the Ponte Druso, along Viale Druso, and ascends the left bank of the Adige; the railway keeps close to the river. Fruit trees grow on the valley floor, while vineyards cover the lower slopes with woods above. The ruined Castel Casanova appears on a spur to the right on the approach to (10km) *Terlano*.—21km *Postal* is connected by road from the station of Lana-Postal, with *Lana di Sopra* (5km), best visited from Merano (see below).

29km **MERANO** (320m), in German *Meran*, lying on the right bank of the Passirio a little above its junction with the Adige, is an ancient town (34,200 inhab.) famous as a climatic resort and spa. It is now also a climbing centre and a ski resort. Together with *Maia Alta* and *Maia Bassa (Obermais* and *Untermais)* on the opposite bank of the torrent, it consists mainly of monumental hotels and villas, many of them built at the turn of the century by Austrian architects, surrounded by luxuriant gardens in a sheltered valley. Spring and autumn are the fashionable seasons for visiting Merano. The inhabitants are mainly German speaking.

Post Office, Via Roma (beside the Ponte della Posta). *Tourist Information Office,* Corso Libertà.—*Thermal Centre,* Via Piave; *Fonte San Martino,* N of the town.
Town Buses ·from the station to (1) *Maia Alta;* (2) *Maia Bassa* and *Sinigo;* (3) *Tirolo:* (4) *Funivia Avelengo.* Country Buses from Piazza Rena to *Lana di Sopra;* to *Moso;* to *Santa Gertrude;* to *Fondo;* to *Madonna di Senales;* from Piazza Rena to *Trieste;* to *Cortina d'Ampezzo;* to *Milan;* and via the Resia Pass to *Landeck.*—COACH TOURS in summer round *Lake Garda;* round the *Cinque Pàssi;* and to *Cortina* (Grand Tour of the Dolomites).

Teatro Puccini, Piazza del Teatro; *Casino di Cura* (Kursaal), Corso Libertà; *Race-course* at Maia Bassa; *Swimming Pools*: Via delle Terme (outdoor and indoor); Via Lido (outdoor).

History. Although it is probable the area was already inhabited in Roman times, the name *Mairania* appears for the first time in 857. After the town came into the possession of the Counts of Venosta in the 13C it gradually assumed importance so that by 1317 it was designated a municipality. After 1836, under Austrian rule, its good climate began to attract visitors and it developed into one of the most celebrated climatic resorts in Italy. Radioactive springs are used in the Thermal centre.

The old main street of the medieval town is the dark and narrow VIA DEI PORTICI. Beneath its low arcades are excellent shops and the *Palazzo Municipale* (1930). Behind this is the *Castello Principesco* (adm. 9–12, 14–18; closed Sunday, festivals & in winter), built by Archduke Sigismund in 1445–80 and containing contemporary furnishings. The arms of Scotland alongside those of Austria recall the marriage of Sigismund with Eleanor, daughter of James I of Scotland. In Via Galilei, is the *Museo* (adm. 10–12, 16–18 except Sunday & Saturday afternoon), with local collections.—At the end of Via dei Portici is the DUOMO, a Gothic church of the 14–15C, with a curious battlemented façade, a tall tower (83m), 14–16C tomb-reliefs and wall-paintings on the S side. Inside are two 15C altarpieces by Martin Knoller. Behind the Duomo is a small octagonal Gothic chapel.

Along the river Passirio extend gardens and promenades laid out at the turn of the century. The *Passeggiate Lungo Passirio d'Inverno*, and *Gilf* run along the sunny N bank, in part protected by verandas. A medieval bridge crosses to the shaded *Passeggiata d'Estate*, a pleasant walk through gardens. The Gothic church of *Santo Spirito* was rebuilt in 1450.

The cheerful *Corso Libertà*, with the most fashionable shops, was laid out before the First World War. It passes the Kursaal (1914), the neo-classical Theatre, and several elaborate hotels.—The *Passeggiata Tappeiner*, on the hill above the town, passing the old Torre della Polvere, is another fine walk.—In Maia Bassa is the *Hippodrome* (1935), run in conjunction with a famous national lottery.

A.   Environs of Merano

The chief attraction of Merano is its delightful surroundings, made easily accessibly by good roads and frequent bus services.

The ROAD TO CASTEL TIROLO (bus No. 3) ascends over *Monte di Merano* to *Tirolo*, a village given over to tourism, especially favoured by Germans on walking holidays. It has a Gothic church. On the opposite side of a ravine (a walk of about 20 minutes from the bus terminal) rises *Castel Tirolo (normally open 9–12, 14–17; Monday & festivals, afternoons only), the 12C castle of the counts of Tyrol which gave its name to the whole country round. With the abdication of Margaret Maultasch, the 'ugly duchess', in 1363, the castle and province passed to the Habsburgs. Damaged by a landslip in 1680, the castle was restored in 1904, and is again being restored; it is remarkable above all for its superb position. It is now the property of the province. The Knights' Hall and the Chapel have sculptured Romanesque doorways, and the Throne Room has a fine view.

TO SAN VIGILIO. The road crosses the Adige and runs via Marlengo and Cérmes; above the latter is the 13C castle of *Monteleone*.—7km *Lana di Sopra* (328m) a resort, stands at the mouth of the Val d'Ultimo. *Lana di Sotto*, to the S, has a 13C church. A cableway ascends from Lana di Sopra to *San Vigilio* station (1485m), from where a rough road goes on to **Monte San Vigilio** (1795m), an excellent viewpoint, with an old chapel; and a chair-lift ascends to the Dosso dei Larici (1830m).

TO AVELENGO. From its lower station (350m) on the Rio di Nova, SE of Maia Alta, a cableway ascends hourly in 8 minutes to the upper station (1245m) at *Santa Caterina*, named after the 13C chapel nearby. From there a road crosses the ravine of the Sinigo and ascends to the plateau of **Avelengo** (1290m), a winter-sports ground.

The castle of *Scena* (594m) on the hill 5km NE of Maia Alta (bus) is reached by road (5km) or in 1hr on foot. The castle, a 14C building, restored by the Count of Liechtenstein in 1700, now belongs to Count Franz of Meran (adm. April–October, 10–11.30, 14.30–17). Visitors are shown an armoury, rooms with Renaissance furniture, and (on application) the neo-Gothic tomb of Archduke John (died 1859) and his wife. From near Scena a funicular ascends Monte Scena (1445m), and from Verdins, at the end of the road, another one ascends to Masodi Sopra (Oberkirn; 1441m).

From Maia Alta the cableway Ivigna ascends to (1905m) *Merano 2000*, recently developed as a ski-resort (chair-lift to *San Osvaldo*; refuge at 2302m).

FROM MERANO TO SANTA GERTRUDE, 42km (bus). —To (7km) *Lana di Sopra*, see above; this route turns right at the entrance to the village. The road ascends in zigzags to enter the VAL D'ULTIMO, the valley of the Valsura.—20km *San Pancrazio* and (29km) *Santa Valburga* (1190m) are the principal villages, with characteristic wood houses. The road ends at (42km) *Santa Gertrude* (1256m), beautifully situated beneath the E spurs of the Ortler range, on the edge of the Stelvio National Park (information office; see below).

FROM MERANO TO VIPITENO, N44, 58km (bus), ascending the pastoral VAL PASSIRIA with its scattered villages. Beyond (5km) *Rifiano*, the fine gorge of the Val Masul is seen on the right. At (9km) *Saltusio* a cableway ascends to Rifugio Hirzer (Cervina; 1983m), also developed as a ski-resort.—From (17km) *San Martino*, the road crosses the river to (18km) *Maso della Rena*, the birthplace of Andreas Hofer (1767–1810), the Tyrolese patriot, who led the successful insurrection of 1809 against Bavaria, the power to which the Tyrol had been awarded by the Treaty of Pressburg. His house is now open as a little museum.—20km **San Leonardo in Passiria** (688m), is the capital (2850 inhab.) of the valley, which here bends abruptly to the W.

An interesting road ascends the upper Val Passiria from San Leonardo to (9km) *Moso* and (16km) *Corvara in Passiria* (1419m).

Beyond San Leonardo the Vipiteno road zigzags steeply up into the Valtina valley, from which another climb leads to the road summit at (41km) the **Passo Giovo** (2099m), a good skiing centre. The descent, equally steep, leads at first through forest, but later the road commands good views of the Isarco valley and its tributaries.—58km **Vipiteno**, see Rte 27.

The Stelvio Road now begins the ascent of the **Val Venosta** or *Vinschgau*, the wide and fertile upper valley of the Adige.—43km *Naturno* (554m), a summer resort. The little Romanesque church of San Procolo (9.30–12, 14–17 or 18; if closed apply at parish church) contains remarkable mural paintings (8C).

The *Val di Senales*, on the right beyond, is a long mountain valley, dominated from the NE by the mighty pyramid of the *Similaun* (3597m), on the frontier.—10km *Certosa*. A by-road diverges right up the beautiful *Val di Fosse* as far as *Casera di Fuori*. From here a mule track (1½hrs) follows the torrent as far as Maso Gelato in front of *Monte Tessa*, a protected area since 1976 (33,000 hectares), with deer etc. The park may also be reached from

Merano via *Lagundo* (cableway to Malga Leiter).—Beyond Certosa the road
extends as far as (17km) *Vernago* (1700m) on the lake of the same name, and
(26km) *Corteraso* (2004m), recently developed as a winter and summer ski-
resort (cablecar to Croda Grigia, 3212m).

51km *Castelbello* is dominated by its ruined castle.—57km *Laces*
(1km left), on the old road, S of the river (now bypassed) is connected
by cableway with *San Martino al Monte* (1736m). From here there is
access (chairlift) to the ski slopes on the *Alpe di Tarres*.—At (59km)
the station of *Coldrano* (660m) a road on the left ascends the **Val
Martello**, in the Stelvio National Park, see below.

The road leads via (2km) *Morter*, with a triapsidal Romanesque church, and an
aviary for falcons. The Castel Montani is a ruin.—Beyond (11km) *Ganda di
Martello* is (26km) *Paradiso del Cevedale* (2088m), a climbing and cross-country
ski resort, with ascents in the Ortler group. The upper end of the valley, with the
Ortler group, forms the **Stelvio National Park**, designated a protected area in
1935 and now some 134,600 hectares. It is an area of great natural beauty around
the Ortles-Cevedale mountain ranges. Here survive mountain goats, deer,
eagles, etc. The administrative centre of the park is now at Bormio (see Rte 14);
information centres at Prato allo Stelvio, Ganda di Martello, San Gertrude,
Rabbi, and Cogolo. In the last few decades the park has been threatened,
especially in the E section (belonging to the Province of Bolzano): hunting has
been allowed, as well as the building of roads, hotels, ski-lifts etc. for the
development of tourism.

63km **Silandro** (722m), with 4680 inhabitants, is the chief place in the
valley, at the upper limit of the vine. Its tall church steeple is a
prominent landmark, and its castles are picturesque.—68km *Lasa* is a
marble-quarrying village.—77km **Spondigna** (885m) is at the junction
of the Stelvio Road with the road to Malles and the Resia Pass (see
below).

The Stelvio Road crosses the wide Adige valley to (79km) **Prato allo
Stelvio** (915m), another resort, at the foot of the Trafoi valley.—84km
Stelvio on a height above the road.—86km *Gomagoi* (1267m) lies at
the foot of the **Val di Solda**, in the Stelvio National Park.

The Solda road leads S up this side valley to (12km) **Solda** (1907m), one of the
most important climbing centres in the upper Adige and a holiday resort. The
Passeggiata di Montagna, a walk laid out up and downstream, has delightful
views of mountain and valley. It is also now visited by skiers (cableway to Rifugio
Città di Milano, 3100m). Above rise *Monte Cevedale* (3769m) and the *Ortler (or
Ortles*, 3905m), a magnificent viewpoint, famous as an Austrian strong-point
throughout the First World War.

91km **Trafoi** (1543m) is a summer and winter resort visited for its
panorama of the Ortler group. A chair-lift ascends to Rifugio Forcola
(2153m). 4km farther up the Stelvio road (good viewpoint) an obelisk
records the first ascent of the Ortler by Joseph Pichler in 1804.

A narrow road leads from Trafoi to the *Three Holy Springs*, the 'Tres Fontes' that
gave the village its name. These are made to issue from the breasts of figures of
Christ, the Virgin, and St John, in a little chapel, much visited by pilgrims.

The ascent to the pass is made by 48 serpentine loops hewn in the face
of the ravine. To the left is the huge Madaccio Glacier, descending
from the Ortler.—104km The **Stelvio Pass** (2758m), the second
highest road-pass in the Alps (12m lower than the Col d'Iseran) is
generally open only in June–October. On either side are hotels and it
is visited for summer skiing (chair-lift to 3174m). Until 1918 this was
the meeting-place of the frontiers of Italy, Switzerland, and Austria.
The best viewpoint is (¼hr N) the *Pizzo Garibaldi* (2838m), in German

called Dreisprachenspitze from the meeting of the districts where Italian, Romansch, and German are spoken. The descent on the W side of the pass into the *Val Braulio* is rarely altogether free from snow.—At (99km) the *Quarta Cantoniera* (2489m), with the Italian custom-house, the road to the *Umbrail Pass* or *Giogo di Santa Maria* (2502m), crossing the Swiss frontier, diverges on the right for Santa Maria (14km) and Zernez (49km), see 'Blue Guide Switzerland'.

Below (110km) the *Terza Cantoniera* (2320m) begins the descent of the Spondalunga ('long bank'), achieved by means of a striking series of zigzags. A wild defile protected by snow-galleries leads down to (118km) the *Prima Cantoniera* (1716m), beyond which is the valley of the Adda. On the outskirts of Bormio, at Rovinaccio, is the Botanical Garden of *Rezia*, with c 1000 species of flora from the Stelvio National Park (particularly beautiful in July and August).—127km **Bormio**, see Rte 14.

B.   Spondigna to Malles and Landeck

ROAD, 76km. N40 to the frontier; bus (July–September) in 1½–2hrs from Merano; through service; railway to Malles only.

Spondigna, see above. Road and railway ascend the left bank of the Adige.—4km **Sluderno** (921m) is commanded by *Castel Coira*, or *Churburg*, the 13C castle of the bishops of Coire, restored in the 16C by the Counts Trapp (interesting armoury).

From Sluderno an important road, leads W.—3km *Glorenza*, a typical old Tyrolean town, particularly well preserved, with medieval and 16C ramparts and three gates. The road now begins the ascent of the Val Monastero (Münster-Tal), with the *Calven* gorge, where in 1499 the Swiss defeated the Austrians and won their practical independence of the Empire.—12km *Tubre* (1240m), or *Taufers*, with the Italian custom-house, has a fine Romanesque church (good 13C frescoes).—Beyond (13km) the frontier is (15km) the village of *Münster [1248m]*, or *Müstair*, with the Swiss custom-house, in the canton of the Grisons, see 'Blue Guide Switzerland'.—25km **Santa Maria** (1375m) stands at the junction of the Umbrail Pass road (see above). *Zernez*, for Davos and St Moritz, is 35km farther (all described in 'Blue Guide Switzerland').

9km **Malles Venosta** (1051m) is an old mountain town (4700 inhab.) with an attractive array of towers and steeples rising above its roofs. Most of the churches were rebuilt in the Gothic style, but *San Benedetto* (open 9–12, 15–18, or key at No. 29 nearby) is of the 9C or earlier (important Carolingian fresco cycle).

Above Malles the valley becomes steeper. The large Benedictine abbey of *Monte Maria* (mainly rebuilt in the 17–19C; frescoes of c 1160), is conspicuous on the left on the approach to (11km) *Burgusio*, which has an old church-tower and a 13C castle. Just outside the town, the church of San Nicolò has remains of Romanesque frescoes.—Beyond the little Lago della Muta lies (18km) the ancient village of *San Valentino alla Muta* (1470m), with ski facilities (ski-lift to Alpe della Muta, 2120m). The road now skirts the Lago di Resia formed from two smaller lakes by a dam.—23km **Curon Venosta** (1520m), a pleasant summer resort at the foot of the Valle Lunga, with skiing facilities.—At the N end of the lake, below the source of the Adige, stands (26km) **Resia** (1525m), the last Italian village, commanding a splendid view down the valley of the Ortler group. Both villages were rebuilt when their original sites were submerged. The frontier, with both custom-houses, lies 1km beyond the **Passo di Resia** (1507m).—34km *Nauders* (1365m), the first Austrian village, stands at the foot of the road from the Lower Engadine in Switzerland. The route descends into the Inn valley, which is followed to (76km) *Landeck*, see 'Blue Guide Austria'.

25 Trento to San Martino di Castrozza and to Cortina

ROAD TO SAN MARTINO. 93km.—53km *Cavalese*.—68km **Predazzo**.—93km **San Martino**.

ROAD TO CORTINA, 156km. To *Predazzo*, as above.—78km *Moena*.—82km *San Giovanni*, and from there by the Pordoi and Falzarego passes to (156km) **Cortina**, see Rte 26.

BUS from Trento to San Martino in 4hrs; via Borgo Valsugana, Passo del Brocon, and Fiera di Primiero in 5 hrs.

From Trento this route follows N47 through the Fersina ravine for 5km, then turns left.

At the crossroads a road (right) ascends to the Valle di Pinè for (17km from Trento) *Baselga di Pinè* (969m), a scattered commune and summer resort on the little Lago di Serraia. Farther up are the smaller resort of (23km) *Bedollo* and (26km) *Brusago* (1103m).

Beyond (16km) *Lases*, on a small lake, the road follows the Val di Cembra, the lower course of the Avisio. Farther on, beyond the erosion pillars (*Piramidi*) and the ruined castle of (23km) *Segonzano*, it skirts the artificial Lago di Stramentizzo, at the end of which it joins the road from Lavis (Rte 22).—At (51km) *Castello di Fiemme* N48 comes in from Ora, and this route bears right to reach the summer and winter resort centre of (53km) **Cavalese** (998m), the chief village in the *Val di Fiemme*, the middle course of the Avisio. Like many of the valleys of the Pyrenees, this glen has preserved something of medieval independence, and the 'Magnifica Comunità', installed in the ancient palace of the bishops of Trento, still administers the valuable communal lands, though justice is no longer dispensed at the stone table in the municipal park. The palace contains a local museum (open 15–17 except Saturday and fest.). The Gothic parish church has a marble portal and an attractive little courtyard. A cableway ascends to *Cermis* (1980m) to the S, scene of a tragedy in 1976 when it failed leaving 42 dead.

Carano is a little spa 4km W.—A mountain road leads N via (2km) *Varena*, a small health resort with hay-baths, to (9km) the *Passo di Lavazè* (1805m), below the W slopes of Latemar, from where a precipitous descent leads in 9km to the Bolzano road at Pontenova.

59km *Tesero*, where frescoes of Sabbath-breakers decorate the church of San Rocco, stands at the foot of the pretty *Val di Stava*, traversed by a road at the end of which (7km) are several ski-lifts. The valley was the scene of a tragedy in 1985 when a dam above two reservoirs broke drowning 269 people.—From (61km) *Panchià* a road crosses the river for the Val Cavelonte.—62km *Ziano* (ski facilities).

68km **Predazzo** (1018m; chair-lifts, etc.), has a school for Alpine Frontiersmen (Guardia di Finanza). The *Museo Comunale* contains a collection of local geological specimens.

FROM PREDAZZO TO SAN GIOVANNI (Cortina), 14km. N48 ascends the Avisio valley with fine views of the mountains in front.—10km **Moena** (1184m), is a cheerful village resort with a fine view of the Catinaccio and Sella ranges to the NW and NE.—To *Belluno*, see Rte 26.

Beyond the Ladin-speaking Val di Fassa, the road from Bolzano and Carezza is joined.—14km *San Giovanni*, and from there to *Cortina*, see Rte 26.

The San Martino road (N50), from Predazzo, sharply ascends the Val Travignolo to the E.—Beyond (69km) *Bellamonte* (1372m), becoming narrow, it twists high above a ravine, and enters the **Parco Naturale Paneveggio-Pale di San Martino**, a protected area noted for its magnificent forest, wild flowers, and wild life (deer, mountain goats, etc.). Much of the wood used to build the Venetian Republic's fleet came from here. The road passes the Lago Fortebuso before (76km) *Paneveggio* (1515m) which has been rebuilt since 1918.

FROM PANEVEGGIO TO FALCADE, 18km, a road with fine views traversing the forest of Paneveggio. On the left rises the *Cima Bocche* (2745m), the chief peak of the range separating this from the San Pellegrino valley.—8km *Passo di Valles* (2033m) is on the old Austro-Italian frontier, in the heart of the war zone of 1917.—18km Falcade, see Rte 26.

A series of broad curves, with splendid views of the Pale di San Martino brings the road (still within the ancient forest of Paneveggio) up to (85km) the **Passo di Rolle** (1970m), a wide saddle with excellent ski-slopes, dominated by the Cimon della Pala. A steeper series of hairpin curves leads down through conifers on the S side.

93km **San Martino di Castrozza** (1444m), the most popular summer and winter resort in the Southern Dolomites, lies in an ample basin of the Cismon valley, with wooded slopes leading up to the towering peaks of the Pale di San Martino.

Buses all the year to Fiera di Primiero and *Feltre* in 1½hrs; from mid-July to mid-September to *Trento* in 4hrs, to Predazzo and *Bolzano* in 3 hrs.

Winter Sports. Ski-slopes at Passo di Rolle (see above; chair-lifts), on the Col Tognola, to the W (cableway and chair-lift), and at Pez Gaiard (ski-lift); bobsleigh run; skating rink. Cableway and chair-lift almost to the summit of the *Rosetta* (2743m).

The terraced village of San Martino, which arose around a small priory and hospice dating from the 15C, was demolished, except for the church, by the Austrians in 1915. It is a first-class climbing centre and also provides many easy excursions and wooded walks in the nearer environs.

FROM SAN MARTINO TO AGORDO, (45km), part of a very fine circular road-route round the Pale di San Martino, returning via Cencenighe, Falcade, and Paneveggio.—It ascends the Cismon valley for 13km almost to Fiera di Primiero and then turns left to climb to (21km) the *Passo di Cereda* (1369m).—29km *Don* is the chief village in the wooded basin of *Gosaldo*.—33km *Forcella Aurine* (1299m) commands a fine view of the Piz di Sagron to the SW. The road descends into the Sarzana valley at (37km) *Frassenè* (1080m), a summer resort (cableway to Rifugio Scarpa, 1735m, on the *Croda Grande*, 2849m).—41km *Voltago*

(858m).—At (46km) *Agordo* the road and railway from Belluno come in, see Rte 33.

From San Martino di Castrozza to *Fiera di Primiero* and *Feltre*, see Rte 33.

26　Bolzano to Cortina and to Belluno

ROAD TO CORTINA, 108km. The famous *Strada delle Dolomiti from Bolzano to Cortina, one of the most beautiful roads in the Alps, is a magnificent feat of engineering. It is followed in summer by regular coach services. —20km *Nova Levante*.—28km *Carezza*.—37km *Vigo di Fassa*.—39km **San Giovanni**.—51km **Canazei**.—63km *Passo Pordon*—72km *Arabba*.—79km *Pieve di Livinallongo*.—108km **Cortina**.

ROAD TO BELLUNO, 112km. To *San Giovanni*, see above.—44km **Moena**.—63km *Falcade*.—73km *Cencenighe*.—83km **Agordo**.— 112km **Belluno**.

BUSES on the Strada delle Dolomiti: daily express service (June– September) in 3hrs, supplemented by an ordinary service (4½hrs). Further buses run between Bolzano and Canazei; and to *Belluno* (4–4½hrs).

Bolzano, see Rte 22. The Isarco is crossed by (3km) the *Ponte di Cardano*, dominated by its 13C castle, and passing beneath the two motorways N 241 enters the wild and romantic gorge of the *Val d'Ega*, perhaps most striking at the **Ponte della Cascata*. Beyond a tunnel and another gorge the fantastic peaks of the Latemar range come into view on the right, with the *Cima della Valsorda* (2752m) especially prominent.—16km *Ponte Nova* (872m) is the junction of the road to the Passo di Lavazè and **Cavalese** (Rte 25).—The Cantinaccio chain comes into view ahead on the approach to (20km) **Nova Levante**, or Welschnofen (1182m), a winter sporting centre on the side of a wooded glen. It is also popular as a summer resort. A good path leads N to Tires (2¾hrs) and a chair-lift in two stages rises to the Rifugio Fronza (see below).—The Latemar soon appears at close quarters on the right, and the whole Catinaccio chain is seen on the left. The road skirts (26km) the tiny green Lago di Carezza to reach (28km) *Carezza al Lago* (1609m), popular as a summer and climbing resort, with winter sports facilities. A chair-lift rises to the Rifugio Paolina (2125m). The resort is dominated by the two most typical Dolomite mountain groups with their characteristic battlemented skyline, the **Latemar** (2842m) and the **Catinaccio** (2981m).

The road-summit is reached at (30km) the *Passo di Costalunga* (1745m), offering a splendid view ahead of the Val di Fassa and the Marmolada and San Martino mountains, with the imposing Punta della Vallaccia between.—37km **Vigo di Fassa** (1382m), the chief village in the Ladin-speaking Val di Fassa, and a winter sports resort, lies beneath the *Ciampediè* (1997m; cableway to Rifugio Ciampediè), a rocky spur of the Catinaccio c 2hrs N. The *Rifugio Roda di Vael* (2280m), 2¾hrs W, is a base for higher climbs.—At the church of (41km) **San Giovanni** this route joins N48.

FROM SAN GIOVANNI TO BELLUNO. The road branches right to follow N48 S to (44km) **Moena** (see Rte 25), then turns E on N346 to ascend the Val di San Pellegrino, recently developed as a fine skiing area. A track ascends to Passo di Lusia (2056m; cableway in two stages). The road reaches the summit-level at (56km) the *Passo di San Pellegrino* (cableway to Col Margherita, 2511m the biggest in the Dolomites).—

The road descends steeply to (63km) *Falcade* (1297m), a straggling village and now a ski resort.—68km *Canale d'Agordo* (976m), known until 1964 as Forno di Canale, lies at the foot of the long wild valley of *Gares*, a little-known approach to the Pale di San Martino.—71km *Celat* (971m).—At the pleasant village of (73km) *Cencenighe* (773m) this route meets the road from Alleghe and Cortina (see below).— 83km **Agordo**, in the Cordevole valley, is an excellent centre for mountain drives, with a School of Mines and a 17C palazzo in the attractive main square. Beyond Agordo, the road continues S through the magnificent gorge of the Canale d'Agordo to (91km) *La Muda*.— The valley widens and enters the Piave basin, leaving, beyond (102km) *Mas*, the road to Feltre (right, 26km; see Rte 33).—112km **Belluno**, see Rte 33.

From San Giovanni, N48 turns N up the Val di Fassa.—41km *Pozza* (1325m) and (42km) *Pera* (1326m) are both winter resorts and bases for ascents among the Catinaccio peaks and for the W side of the Marmolada group.

The **Catinaccio** is especially famous for its marvellous colouring at sunrise (from which it takes the German name *Rosengarteen*). It is approached by the Vaiolet Valley, at the head of which is the *Gardeccia Refuge* (1948m), reached by road from Pera in 2hrs, and open in July–August and New Year week only. A path goes on to (1 hr more) the *Rifugio del Vaiolet* (2243m), above which rises the curious *Torri del Vaiolet*, whose fantastic configuration is typical of the dolomitic mountains. The central peak was first ascended in 1887 by Georg Winkler at the age of 18. The *Catinaccio di Antermoia* (3002m) is the highest peak in the group.—On the E side of the valley is the *Val di San Nicolò*, followed by a bridle-path over the *Passo di San Nicolo* (2362m). To the S of it rise the *Punta Vallaccia* (2637m) and the *Costabella* (2759m).

The Sasso Piatto and Sasso Lungo come into view as the road ascends the valley, and at (45km) *Mazzin* (1372m) the Sasso di Pordoi rises ahead.—Beyond (46km) *Campestrin* and (47km) *Fontanazzo* lies (49km) **Campitello**, an old-established climbers' resort (chair-lift to the Rodella; for the Sasso Piatto and Sasso Lungo, see below).

51km **Canazei** (1465m), standing in a hollow where the Dolomites Road leaves the Val di Fassa, is a centre for climbs in the Sella group to the NE and the Marmolada group to the SE. It is well equipped with all the usual winter-sports facilities. The pyramidal Gran Vernel (3210m) hides the Marmolada itself.

THE MARMOLADA, the largest and loftiest group of peaks in the Dolomites, is approached from this side by the Avisio and Contrin valleys. A road ascends the Avisio from Canazei to (2km) *Alba* (1517m). A cableway and chair-lift ascend from the road to *Monte Brunec* (2486m). A little above this a bridle-path on the right leads into the Val Contrin, at the head of which is the *Rifugio Contrin* (2016m).—The road goes on to the refuge-inn at (9km) *Pian Trevisan* (1717m) and the *Rifugio Castiglioni alla Fedaia* (2097m) on the artificial *Lago di Fedaia*, 3hrs from Canazei. For the continuation of the road into the Val Pettorina, see below.—The *Marmolada* (3342m) is the highest peak in the Dolomites. A chair-lift ascends from the S side of the lake to the *Pian dei Fiacconi Refuge* (2520m) from where an easy glacier path (chair-lift) goes on the *Punta del Rocca* (3309m), with the small *Rifugio Marmolada* (3258m), E of the main summit.

From the steep hairpin turns above Canazei, the *View of the Sasso Lungo to the left and the Sella peaks ahead is more and more striking. This route joins (57km) the Passo di Sella road coming from Ortisei, and reaches the road summit at (63km) the **Passo del Pordoi** (2239m), an open saddle, lying between the *Sass Beccê1* (2534m), on the S, and the rocky battlements of the *Sass Pordoi* (2950m; chair-lift), on the N.

A footpath to the left provides a better sight of the Marmolada; still more rewarding is the *View from the Belvedere (½hr to the right), which may also be reached by chair-lift from Canazei.—A winding descent through high pastures brings the road into the Val Cordevole.—72km **Arabba** (1601m) at the junction of the road to the Val Badia (Rte 28); its ski-slopes are on the Due Baite (chair-lift to La Mesola, 2734m; funicular to Col Burz, 1943m). The scattered parish of Livinallongo, is dominated from the E by the *Col di Lana* (2452m), the top of which was blown off by an Italian mine in 1916.—70km **Pieve di Livinallongo** (1475m), the chief village of the district, enjoys fine views of the Civetta to the S and the Pelmo to the SE.

FROM LIVINALLONGO TO AGORDO 35km, bus in 1hr. Following the Cortina road for 2km this route turns abruptly right, descending the Cordevole valley, in which are numerous war-cemeteries.—At 12km the road divides. On the right is the *Val Pettorina*, the main approach to the E side of the Marmolada. The chief village in this valley is *Rocca Pietore*, 3km from Caprile, with an old church. There are plans to develop the village as a ski resort. From *Malga Ciapela* (1450m; chair-lift for Marmolada, 3270m), 6km farther on, beyond a fine gorge, the road turns N and continues to the *Passo di Fedaia* (2057m) and the *Rifugio Fedaia* (2004m) at the end of the Fedaia lake (see above).

The left road leads via (14km) *Caprile* (1023m), where an alternative road leads down the E side of the Cordevole valley (via Andraz) to (18km) **Alleghe** (979m), beside a small lake.—At the S end of the lake is (20km) *Masarè*.—26km *Cencenighe*, and from there to *Agordo*, see Rte 33.

The Cortina road beyond Pieve leaves the Cordevole and begins a long ascent.—84km *Andraz* lies below the road to the right. To the left, beyond a turning on the right for Caprile (see above), rises the ruined castle of Andraz. The Settass and Monte Cavallo dominate the view on the left, with the Sasso di Stria in front.—94km The **Passo di Falzarego** (2105m), between the *Sasso di Stria* (2477m) and the Nuvolau ridge, was a hotly contested strongpoint in the First World War. To the left is the Lagazuoi massif, and farther on during the descent (right), the strangely shaped Cinque Torri, with the Croda da Lago and Antelao behind them, and on the left the cliffs of the Tofane. The Boite valley soon comes into view and the road zigzags down through the outlying hamlets of Cortina.—108km **Cortina**, see Rte 29.

27 Bolzano to Innsbruck via the Brenner Pass

ROAD, N12, 125km.—23km *Ponte Gardena*.—29km *Chiusa*.—40km **Bressanone**.—50km *Fortezza*.—72km **Vipiteno**.—78km *Colle Isarco*.—86km **Brennero** (frontier).—99km *Steinach*.—125km **Innsbruck**.

The Autostrada del Brennero (A 22) follows this route.

RAILWAY, 134km in 2–3hrs; to *Fortezza*, 48km, in 1hr. Through carriages run on this route to Innsbruck and Munich from Rome, Florence, Venice, Turin, and Milan.

The road and railway from Bolzano soon descend to the Isarco and follow its banks closely. The power-station of Cardano is on the left, the castle of Cornedo on the right.—9km *Prato all'Isarco* (315m). A road ascends on the right to (7km) *Tires* (1028m), a summer resort beneath the W side of the Catinaccio.—Beyond Prato a road ascends (right) to *Fiè* (7km; 880m) and continues via *San Costantino* to **Siusi**

(17km; see below).—N12 now enters a gorge in which lies (15km) *Campodazzo*, from which steep paths ascend to the Renon plateau. Beyond a quaint covered bridge it emerges from the gorge.—23km **Ponte Gardena** (470m) or *Waidbruck*, is a road junction at the mouth of the Val Gardena. Above the village (20 minutes walk) stands the 12C *Castle* of the Wolkenstein, with a 16C hall (adm. June–September, at 11, 12, 14, 15, & 16).

FROM PONTE GARDENA TO SIUSI, 11km, bus. The road ascends S above the left bank of the Isarco to (8km) *Castelrotto* or Kastelruth (1060m), an ancient village with a 17C town hall and an 18C belfry, now visited for skiing in summer and winter.—11km **Siusi** (998m), or *Seis am Schlern*, is a well-known summer resort, visited also for winter sports on the Alpe di Siusi. It lies on a broad terrace under *Monte Castello* the NE spur of the Sciliar, in the forest beneath which is the ruined *Castelvecchio* (Havenstein castle).—The **Alpe di Siusi**, a wide upland plateau to the E is famous as a skiing ground in winter.

FROM PONTE GARDENA TO ORTISEI AND THE DOLOMITES ROAD, 37km. This route, ascending the Ladin-speaking *Val Gardena*, at first a narrow gorge, is served in summer by a bus from Bolzano to Corvara.—13km **Ortisei** (1234m) or *St Ulrich*, the chief place (4000 inhab.) in the Val Gardena, is an excellent summer and winter resort. Cableways and lifts rise to the Alpe di Siusi, the Resciesa and the Seceda. The town is a centre for the manufacture of the wooden statuettes that adorn the local churches. In the central square is a *School of Woodcarving* and *Design*, which may be visited; and here also is a table showing the chief excursions in the neighbourhood. The 18C church contains good examples of local carving. The *Museo della Val Gardena* has a collection of local interest. To the N side of the town are the wooded slopes of the Resciesa and to the SE the peaks of the Sasso Lungo dominate the view.

An even finer view is obtained from the Gothic church of *San Giacomo* (1hr E), which contains a fine carved altarpiece by Franz Unterberger (1750.—On the crest of the slopes S of Ortisei (cableway) is the famous ski ground of the *Alpe di Siusi* (see above; c 3hrs). The mountains to the N are climbed via the Rifugio Rasciesa (2170m; chair-lift).

The valley is now broader.—17km **Santa Cristina** (1428m), another wood-carving village, is a popular summer and winter skiing centre, and climbing centre. The magnificent *Sasso Lungo* (318m) and the *Sasso Piatto* (2955m) are seen to the S. To the NE of the village is the Cisles valley beneath the *Odle* group (*Sass Rigais, 3025m) and the Punta del Puez Ovest* (2913m).

20km **Selva di Val Gardena** (1563m), or *Wolkenstein in Groden*, a resort with similar attractions to those of Santa Cristina and well provided with cableways and ski-lifts, stands at the foot of the Vallunga, which penetrates the heart of the Puez and Gardenaccia mountains to the NE.—22km *Plan Val Gardena* (1614m). Beyond the ascent becomes steeper.—At (25km) *Plan de Gralba* (1810m) a road to the Val Badia bears off to the left.

This spectacular road (N243) crosses (9km) the *Passo Gardena* (2121m), the saddle between the Pizzes da Cir (left) and the N wall of the Sella group. The open slopes on the N side (chair-lift) are popular for skiing. The zigzag descent passes a path on the right leading to the *Rifugio Pisciadu* (2585m), for the N peaks of the Sella group.—17km *Colfosco* (1645m) has a splendid view of the frowning cliffs of the Sella across the valley.—At 19km this route joins the Val Badia road, c 1km below **Corvara** (Rte 28).

The main road climbs between the Sasso Lungo and the Torri di Sella to (29km) the **Passo Sella** (2213m), an open saddle affording good ski-runs. The *View on all sides is surpassed only by that from the *Rodella* (2387m; refuge-hut, chair-lift), to the SW, which is perhaps the finest in all the Dolomites, including nearly all the principal groups, with the Sasso Lungo (NW), Sella (NE), and Marmolada (SE) prominent near at hand.—The descent leads in zigzags beneath the *Piz Selva* (2940m), leaving on the left the Boè track (see above).—At 37km this route joins the Dolomites Road (Rte 26), 5km above Canazei.

THE BRENNER ROAD above Ponte Gardena reaches (29km) **Chiusa** (523m), or *Klausen*. This ancient little town is overlooked by the 17C buildings of the convent of Sabiona. Lower down is a 13C tower. By the monastery at the entrance to the town is the chapel of the Madonna di Loreto which contains a precious treasury.—At 33km a bridge crosses the Isarco for the Funès valley. The chief resorts in this valley are (2km) *Gudon* (720m), (9km) *Funès-San Pietro* (1132m), and (11km) *Santa Maddalena*.

40km **Bressanone** (559m), in German *Brixen*, is an ancient episcopal city (16,000 inhab.), for many centuries the capital of an independent state in continual dispute with the counts of Tyrol. It stands at the confluence of the Rienza (coming from the Pusteria valley) with the Isarco and preserves many ancient buildings. The CATHEDRAL, completely rebuilt in the Baroque period (1745–54), contains some good carved altarpieces, vault frescoes by Paul Troger, and altarpieces by Francesco and Cristoforo Unterberger. It is adjoined by a Romanesque *Cloister* adorned with frescoes of the 14–15C. The cathedral treasury is in the *Bishop's Palace* with the *Diocesan Museum* (adm. 10–12, 14–17 or 18; Sunday & festivals closed) which contains a collection of locally carved Presepi or cribs. The handsome courtyard of the palace has terracotta statues by Hans Reichle (1599). In the *Baptistery*, an 11C building, was held the council instigated by Henry IV in 1080 to depose Hildebrand (Pope St Gregory VII) and elect the antipope Clement III. It is decorated with interesting frescoes. To the N of the cathedral is the 15C *Parish Church* (San Michele), with a fine steeple (the 'White Tower'). *Palazzo Pfaundler*, in the square beside it, was built in 1581, and the old houses in the neighbouring arcaded Via dei Portici are typical.

The convent of **Novacella** (described in Rte 28) is 4 km outside the town on the Pusteria road. The fine 16C *Castle* (shown on guided tours, May–November, except Monday) of the Bishops at *Velturno* is 7km SW.—A cableway ascends from SE of the town to *Sant'Andrea in Monte* (958m) and *Kreuztal Valcroce* (2012m) and from there by chair-lift to the *Rifugio Plose* (2226m), a fine viewpoint visited by skiers. A road runs via Sant'Andrea to (8km) *Eores* (1503m) and (18km) *Plancios* (1911m), two resorts in the Eores valley. From Plancios, a road (left) leads to the Rifugio Plose chair-lift (see above).

Above Bressanone the valley takes on a more alpine character; from the road there is a fine view of the town and, farther on, of the Novacella convent on the right. At 44km the Pusteria road (Rte 28) bears off to the right.—45km *Varna* (left; 671m) with the ruins of a 13C castle, is on the road from the *Bagni di Scaleres* or *Schalders* (1167m), 6km W.—The road and railway from the Pusteria come in on the right by a small artificial lake on the approach to the fortifications (1833–38) that have given name to (51km) **Fortezza** (749m), or *Franzensfeste*, an important railway junction. The valley remains generally very narrow.—Between (62km) *Mules* and (67km) *Campo di Trens* is the ruined Castel Guelfo (right) and farther on two more castles (Castel Tasso or Reifenstein and Castel Pietra or Sprechenstein) dominate the open vale of Vipiteno. Castel Tasso is open to the public in May–October (except on Friday).

71km **Vipiteno** (948m), or *Sterzing*, takes its Italian name from a Roman post established here. The town (4500 inhab.) owed its importance to the mines which were worked in the side-valleys until the 18C; it is now mainly important as a road-centre. The *Palazzo Comunale* (admission granted), an attractive building of 1468–73, is the chief among the many old houses in the main street. At the end is the tall *Torre di Città*, around which are 15–16C *Mansions, many with battlements, built by the old mine-owning families. The *Museo Multscher* (9–11, 15–17; closed Sunday & festivals) in the Piazza Città contains paintings by Hans Multscher (1458). To the S of the town, on the Merano road, is the *Parish Church* (1417–1525) and nearby is the *Hospital*, founded by the Teutonic Knights in 1241, and rebuilt in the 16C.

A cableway mounts to *Monte Cavallo* (Rosskopf; 1862m; Refuge-hut).

To the NE of Vipiteno extends the long *Val di Vizze* with several mountain inns, principally at (4km) *Prati* and (20km) *San Giacomo di Vizze* (1446m), the highest village in the valley. The *Gran Pilastro* or *Hochfeiler* (3510m), the highest of the Alpi Aurine or Zillertal Alps, stands on the frontier, 12km E. To the W of Vipiteno and approached from the Merano road is the VAL RIDANNA, the main avenue of access to the Alpi Breonie. On the left at (6km) *Stanghe* is the mouth of the impressive *Val di Racines*, developed as a skiing centre. The road goes on to (13km) *Ridanna* (1342m), a quiet mountain hamlet visited by alpinists, and (17km) *Masseria*, with a chair-lift.

From Vipiteno to *Merano* by the Passo di Giovo, see Rte 24.

The valley narrows and pine-forests clothe its higher slopes; on the right is seen Castel Strada.—77km **Colle Isarco** (1098m), or *Gossensass*, a summer resort and a good winter sports centre, stands at the foot of the wooded Val di Fléres, once famous for its silver mines. A chair-lift mounts via the *Rifugio Gallina* to the *Cima Bianca* (2700m).

The railway makes a long detour into the Val di Fléres, but the road continues NE.—83km *Terme del Brennero* (1309m), a former spa surrounded by pine-forests.—86km **Brennero** (1375m), the last Italian village, with the custom-house and barracks, stands c 230 metres S of the stone pillar (1921) marking the frontier on the *Brenner Pass* (Passo di Brennero; 1375m).

The lowest of the great alpine passes, the flat broad saddle of the Brenner, first mentioned with the crossing of Augustus in 13 BC, was the main route of the medieval invaders of Italy.

From here to (38km) **Innsbruck**, see 'Blue Guide Austria'.

28 Bressanone to Lienz via Dobbiaco

ROAD, N49, 109km—34km **Brunico.**—52km *Monguelfo.*—61km **Dobbiaco.**—66km *San Candido.*—73km *Passo Drava* (custom-house).—109km **Lienz**.

RAILWAY (from Fortezza, see Rte 27), 109km in 4hrs; to *Dobbiaco*, 61km in 1½–2hrs. Through trains continue to Vienna.

The **Pusteria**, the valley of the Rienza, is one of the most attractive districts in the South Tyrol. In the gaily-coloured villages many of the churches have bulbous steeples, and often contain good local woodcarvings. The breadth of the valley allows splendid views of the mountains at the head of the side-glens on either hand. In the main valley German has replaced Ladin as the language of the people, but in one side-valley the old language has been preserved.

Bressanone, see Rte 27. The Pusteria road soon diverges to the right from the Brenner road and passes (4km) the convent of **Novacella** (adm. to the library, 10–16 except Sunday & festivals), a picturesque group of buildings mainly of the 17–18C and surrounded by 15C fortifications, but including a Romanesque steeple and other 12C portions. The Baroque church contains carved altarpieces and gives access to the *Cloister* rebuilt in the 14C, with 14–15C frescoes. The Library and Picture Gallery contain old MSS and paintings of the local 15C school. The chapel of San Michele is a circular fortified building of the 12C rebuilt in the 16C.—Beyond (7km) *Sciaves* this route joins the road from Fortezza, with the castle of Rodengo above.—11km *Rio di Pusteria* stands at the foot of the Val di Valles, and commands a fine view downstream. Its ruined 16C barrier still spans the road beyond. A cableway ascends to the ski-slopes of *Maranza* (1414m).—16km *Vandoies* (755m). To the N extends the Val di Fundres.—Farther on the valley narrows and the road passes (25km) *Chienes*, opposite *Casteldarne* (Ehrenburg) with its fine 16C castle (open in summer, except Thursday & Sunday). The convent of Castel Badia (Sonnenburg; in part restored as a hotel), with a 12C chapel, appears on the left on the approach (31km; right) to *San Lorenzo di Sebato* (810m), a village on the site of the larger Roman *Sebatum*, partly excavated (the walls are conspicuous). The 13C church contains good carvings.

FROM SAN LORENZO TO ARABBA, 44km, an important north-to-south road through the Ladin-speaking Val Badia, down which flows the Gadera. The road follows the windings of the narrowing glen.—At (10km) *Longega* a fork on the left ascends a side-valley for 4km to *San Vigilio di Marebbe* (1193m), a summer and winter resort (cable-car and chair-lift). A road continues for 11km to Pederù (1540m).—15km *Piccolino* (1115m) has a lovely view of the *Putia* (2875m) above San Martino to the right.—Beyond (23km) Pederoa a road leads left to *La Valle* (2km), also developed as a resort.—25km *Pedraces* (1315m) stands below *San Leonardo in Badia*, the communal centre of the valley; both are visited for winter sports (chair-lift to Croda Santa Croce, 1840m).—28km **La Villa in Badia** (1483m) a winter and summer resort. Skiing is practised especially at *San Cassiano* (1537m), 3km SE.—33km **Corvara in Badia** (1568m), at the junction of the Gardena Pass road to Ortisei, is another popular resort. The towering *Sass Songher* (2665m) dominates the valley from the NW and the Sella group is prominent to the SW. As the road ascends the Marmolada comes into view ahead.—From (40km) the *Passo di Campolongo* (1875m) the descent is rapid to (45km) *Arabba* on the Dolomites Road (Rte 26).

34km **Brunico** (830m) or *Bruneck*, the picturesque capital (10,100 inhab.) of the Pusteria, stands in a small upland plain clad with firs, and overlooked by the castle of Bishop Bruno of Bressanone (1251). It is the native town of Michele Pacher (c 1430–98), whose sculptured wooden crucifixes can be found in the churches of the region.

Buses to *Colfosco*; to *San Vigilio*; to *Campo Tures* and the Valle Aurina; to *Ortisei*; and to *Lago di Anterselva*. The Milan-Cortina and Innsbruck-Venice long-distance coach services pass through Brunico.

Brunico has some quaint old streets, but is principally attractive for its environs. The finest local viewpoint is the *Plan di Corones* (Kronplatz; 2273m), 3km S via Riscone (cableway). Beyond Riscone is *Castel Lamberto*, overlooking the Rienza gorge. By-roads lead N to *Teodone*, with a local museum and Villa Santa Caterina (15C).

The level TURES VALLEY, running N from Brunico, through which flows the
Aurina river, provides access to a group of thickly wooded mountain glens lying
beneath the peaks and glaciers of the Alpi Aurine on the frontier. At (12km)
Molini di Tures (856m), the first of the important side-valleys (Val dei Molini)
leads off to the W.—14km **Campo Tures** (874m), or *Sand in Taufers*, is the chief
centre in these valleys, and is commanded by the 13–15C castle (open in
summer) of the barons of Tures. It is a noted climbing centre, and has winter
sports facilities.—To the E the Val di Riva leads in 12km to *Riva di Tures* (1598m)
beneath the *Vedrette Giganti*, a group of mountains noted for their numerous
glaciers.

The main Valle Aurina, above Campo Tures, passes (20km) *Lutago* (956m)
and turns NE.—Farther on are the villages of (28km) *Cadipietra*, (33km) *San
Pietro* and (42km) *Casere*, and (44km) *Pratomagno* (1623m) the northernmost
village in Italy. The peak of the *Vetta d'Italia* (2912m) is the N point of the
frontier. The *Picco dei Tre Signori* (3498m) farther E marked the junction of the
counties of Tyrol, Salzburg and Gorizia.

45km *Rasun*, to the left, lies opposite the scattered village of *Valdaora*.
To the N extends the long *Val di Anterselva* (or Antholzer Tal) leading
to the *Lago di Anterselva* (18km; 1642m).—52km *Monguelfo* (1087m),
or *Welsberg*, a resort with a 12C castle, is at the foot of the Val
Casies.—57km **Villabassa** (1158m), or *Niederdorf*, with some good
15–16C houses.

The VAL DI BRAIES (Prags) runs S from the Pusteria for c 6km and then divides. In
the left branch are (2km) the *Bagni di Braies Vecchia*, and then (6km) *Prato
Piazza* (Plätzwiese; 1991m), beneath the Croda Rossa (3146m).—The right
branch leads to (9km) *Braies Nuova* (1327m) and (12km) the lovely *Lago di
Braies* (1493m), a vividly green lakelet surrounded by pine woods and hemmed
in by the crags of the *Croda del Becco* (Seekofel; 2810m) on the S.

61km **Dobbiaco** (1256m), or *Toblach*, on the bleak saddle dividing the
valley of the Rienza from the Danubian basin of the Drava, is divided
into two distinct portions; Dobbiaco Nuovo, to the S near the station,
and Dobbiaco Paese, with a large church and a castle built in 1500 for
the emperor Maximilian I.

The gentle slopes around Dobbiaco provide excellent skiing
grounds (chair-lift to Monte Rota, 1591m). To the Lago di Dobbiaco
and Cortina, see Rte 29B.

65km **San Candido** (1175m), or *Innichen*, with the Italian railway
custom-house, is a popular summer and winter resort on the Drava.
The fine 13C collegiate *Church* (tower 1326) is dedicated to Saints
Candidus and Corbinian, who are depicted in the fresco above the S
door, by Michele Pacher (died 1498). The Crucifixion group above the
high altar dates from c 1200. For the Cadore road, see Rte 29.

At San Candido begins the Austrian Süd-Bahn, though the station at (71km)
Versciaco is in Italian territory. The road custom-house and frontier are at (73km)
Passo Drava (1113m).—81km *Sillian*, with the Austrian railway custom-house.
—111km **Lienz** (673m), see 'Blue Guide Austria'.

29 The Cadore and Cortina

The **Cadore** is the mountainous district surrounding the upper valley of the
Piave and its western tributaries. Among its peaks it includes some of the most
famous of the Dolomites, such as the Marmarole, Sorapis, Antelao, and Monte
Cristallo. Until 1918 only the SE half of the district was Italian territory and there
was heavy mountain fighting during the First World War on the old frontier-line.
The Cadorini are mainly a Ladin-speaking people, with Ladin-Venetian dialects

in the lower valleys; but German is everywhere understood from Cortina
northwards.

A. San Candido to Pieve di Cadore

ROAD, N52, N51 bis, 60km.

From San Candido (see above) the road ascends the VAL DI SESTO
where many houses have the traditional balconies sheltered by a
wide roof.—7km **Sesto** (1310m), otherwise *Sexton*, and (9km) *San
Giuseppe* (1339m), rebuilt since the First World War, stand at the foot
of the Val Fiscalina, a magnificent alpine valley between the Cima
Undici and the Tre Scarperi, popular with skiiers and mountain
climbers.

At (15km) the *Passo di Monte Croce* (1636m) begins the descent
into the *Comelico Valley, with splendid views on the right of the
Cadore Dolomites.—25km *Padola* (1213m; a ski resort) and (28km)
Candide (1210m) are two of the scattered villages that make up the
commune of *Comelico Superiore*. The road makes a long loop to the
left, and descends to (36km) **Santo Stefano di Cadore**, the centre of
the Comelico and a winter resort, where the Padola flows into the
Piave. For the road via Sappada to Tolmezzo, see Rte 34.

The Cadore road crosses the Piave and descends its wooded valley,
which narrows into a gorge where the river has been dammed to form
a power-reservoir. The road (difficult in winter as far as Cima Gogna;
tunnel planned) penetrates a tunnel and crosses into the Ansiei
valley, with a fine backward view of Monte Tudaio (2285m).—At
(46km) *Cima Gogna* (796m) this route joins the road from Auronzo
(Rte 29C). The road crosses the Piave at Treponti and again by (49km)
the *Ponte Nuovo*.

The steep road on the left just above the bridge ascends through (6km)
Lorenzago (880m) to (14km) the *Passo della Mauria* (1295m). From there through
Forni and Ampezzo to *Villa Santina* and *Tolmezzo*, see Rte 34.—*Vigo* and *Laggio*
(944m) are little summer resorts 4km N of Ponte Nuovo.

At (50km) *Lozzo di Cadore* (756m) the road crosses the Longiarin.—
Beyond (54km) *Domegge* (775m) the Piave broadens to form the
hydro-electric *Lago Centro Cadore*. Beyond is (57km) the Valley
d'Oten, which separates the Marmarole from the Antelao. By the
bridge stands the church of Il Molinà, below **Calalzo** (806m), an
industrial village that shares with Pieve the terminal station of the
railway from the S.

60km **Pieve di Cadore** (878m) is a pleasant summer and winter
resort beneath the southern foothills of the Marmarole. The PALAZZO
DELLA MAGNIFICA COMUNITÀ CADORINA (1525; adm. in summer
9–12, 15–19) attests to its ancient importance as chief town of the
Cadore. It contains a small archaeological museum. The modest
birthplace of the painter Titian (c 1485–1576), with its museum (adm.
in summer 9–12, 15 or 16–19; closed Monday; ring in winter) should
not be confused with the 16C balconied house of his orator namesake.
A Madonna with Saints by the artist hangs in the parish church (3rd

altar on the left). The Casa di Babbo Natale in the *Park*, receives Italian mail addressed to Father Christmas.

Pozzale 2km above Pieve to the NW, has a painting by Carpaccio (1514).

B. Pieve di Cadore to Dobbiaco via Cortina

ROAD, N51, 65km.—20km *San Vito di Cadore*.—30km **Cortina**.— 49km *Carbonin*.—65km **Dobbiaco**.

Pieve di Cadore, see above. The Cortina road runs SW leaving the Belluno road on the left at (1km) *Tai*, to cross into the Boite valley.—4km *Valle di Cadore* (820m). A small power lake appears ahead as a long curve round the Vallesina valley provides a fine view of the Antelao (right). The long villages of *Venas* and *Vodo* follow in succession as the road approaches (17km) *Borca di Cadore* (942m) which faces the strangely-shaped Pelmo (see below). A summer resort, it has also been developed for skiing.—20km **San Vito di Cadore** (1011m), lying beneath a semi-circle of mountains, with the Croda Marcora (3154m) prominent to the N, is an excellent climbing and skiing centre, with a chair-lift to the Sennes plateau (1214m). To the SE is the *Antelao* (3263m), and to the SW the *Pelmo* (3168m), while to the N is the *Sorapis* (3205m) peak.

21km *Chiapuzza*. The Tofane are soon prominent in front, with the Croda da Lago on the left, and farther on Monte Cristallo appears on the right above the Cortina basin.—28km *Zuel*, with the Olympic ski-jump (see below). The first scattered hamlets of Cortina are soon passed.

30km **CORTINA D'AMPEZZO** (1210m at the church), deservedly the most popular holiday resort (8500 inhab.), both in winter and summer, in the Eastern Dolomites, lies in a sunny upland basin at the junction of the Bigontina and Boite valleys. Venue of the 1956 Winter Olympic Games, it has unrivalled facilities for winter-sports, and there are many comfortable hotels. Aldous Huxley wrote much of 'Point Counter Point' here in 1926–27.

Numerous **Hotels** (some with swimming pools and tennis courts); prices raised at Christmas, in February, and July–August. Also at *Poco*.

Buses to *Calalzo* for train connections to Milan; in the summer season several times daily to *Misurina*; to *Bolzano* via the Dolomites Road in 4½–6hrs, going on to *Merano* daily to *Bolzano* via the Val Gardena in 4¾hrs; to *Dobbiaco* and *Lienz* in 3¼hrs; to *Treviso* and *Venice* in 3hrs; to *San Martino di Castrozza*and *Fiera di Primiero* in 5hrs; to *Livinallongo*, and the *Rifugio Marmolada* in 3hrs; to *Milan* in 7hrs.—Also many circular tours are organised varying in price and distance, including the trip to the *Grossglockner Pass* and back and the celebrated *Giro dei Cinque Passi*, a magnificent round trip through the Dolomites.

Winter Sports. On the bank of the Boite, N of the town, is the magnificent *Ice Stadium* (1956), with facilities for skating, curling, ice hockey, etc. Overlooking this, on the opposite bank is a *Bobsleigh Run* with sledge-hoist. On every side ski-slopes of graded difficulty are reached by aerial ropeway or by one of numerous ski-lifts, chair-lifts or cable-ways; the Olympic ski-jump is at Zuel (see above). The *National Ski School* offers instruction privately or in groups, and hire of equipment.

The village of Cortina lies strung out along the Corso Italia, part of the main road up the Valle d'Ampezzo, or Boite valley. The centre is the Piazza Venezia, with the church, post office, tourist offices, and chief shops. A Museum contains works by Filippo de Pisis (1896–1956), who often stayed in Cortina, and other modern Italian painters. The view of the mountains on all sides is magnificent: to the W are the Tofane, NE the precipice of the Pomagagnon masks Monte Cristallo, SE rise the broken spurs of the Sorapis, and the Becco di Mezzodì and Croda da Lago fill the horizon to the S. Cortina has few old buildings (a fire in 1976 destroyed virtually the last ones), but in the numerous surrounding hamlets are some fine old wooden houses, notably at *Alverà* and *Staolin*, near the Tre Croci road.

In the immediate environs of Cortina are: *Pocol* (1539m) on the Falzarego road, a green plateau and a splendid viewpoint with a large cemetery of the First World War; and *Monte Faloria* (cableway; (2123m), above the town to the E with its extension to the *Tondi di Faloria* (2327m). A cableway rises from the town to Col Druscie, a popular skiing ground (1779m) and *Tofano di Mezzo* (3244m).

FROM CORTINA TO MISURINA (14km), a fine mountain drive which may be made part of a circular route via either Carbonin or Auronzo (see Rte 29C). The road ascends steeply E up the Val Bigontina, passing the chalets of Alverà; the view widens rapidly, and the Antelao (right) and Pelmo (behind) come momentarily into view.—8·5km **Passo di Tre Croci** (1814m), the highest point of the road, is visited for winter sports and for climbing. The Alpe Faloria on the right is a good ski ground. To the N a cableway rises to the *Som Forca* (2213m; chair-lift on to Forcella, 2989m). On the descent from Passo di Tre Croci the curiously shaped peaks of the Cima Cadin are seen ahead, with the Tre Cime di Lavaredo to the left and the deep Ansiei valley to the right.—At 13km this route joins the road from Auronzo, with *Misurina* (see Rte 29C) 2km to the left.

FROM CORTINA TO CAPRILE BY THE GIAU PASS (31km), an interesting alternative to the Falzarego-Andraz route. This route leaves the Dolomites Road near the Pocol Hotel and ascends the wooded Costeana and Cernera valleys, across which is a wall built in 1753 to mark the boundary between the Ampezzano and the Cadore.—13km *Gino Ravà Ski Hut* (1969m).—From (16km) the *Passo di Giau* (2233m; refuge), a wide saddle of the Nuvolau (chair-lifts), the road descends the Codalunga valley to (25km) *Selva di Cadore* (1335m), where it joins the road from Longarone (Rte 33). Beyond is the descent into the Valle Fiorentina, above the opposite side of which are the scattered hamlets of *Colle Santa Lucia*, noted for its view of the Dolomites.—31km **Caprile**, see Rte 26.

From Cortina to *Bolzano* by the Grand Dolomites Road, see Rte 26.

The Dobbiaco road ascends the Ampezzo valley, with the Tofane towering on the left above its wooded slopes, and the Pomagagnon rock-wall on the right. It makes a long detour round the hill of Podestagno, which is crowned by the remains of a castle, and leaves the Boite near the ruins of Castel Sant'Uberto where the united Travenanzes and Fanes valleys come in on the left, opposite Monte Cadin (2367m). The wooded Val Grande opens on the right on the approach to (42km) *Ospitale* to the N of which towers the *Croda Rossa* (3146m). To the right are the tiny Lago Nero and Lago Bianco.—46km *Cimabanche* (1529m) is the highest point on the road.—48km **Carbonin** (1432m), or *Schluderbach*, is the junction of the road from Auronzo (Rte 29C). The road turns N and crosses what was approximately the front-line in 1916–17; the *Lago di Landro* (right) has a fine view S of *Monte Cristallo* (2918m).—61km *Lago di Dobbiaco* (1256m) lies amid woods.—65km **Dobbiaco**, see Rte 28.

C.   Pieve di Cadore
to Dobbiaco via Auronzo

ROAD, 66km.—20km **Auronzo**.—45km *Misurina*.—50km *Carbonin*.—66km **Dobbiaco**.

From Pieve di Cadore to (14km) *Cima Gogna*, see Rte 29A. This route leaves the Santo Stefano road on the right and continues to ascend the tributary Ansiei valley. Soon it reaches the outskirts of Auronzo, which extends for 4km along the road, with a power-reservoir on the left.

20km **Auronzo** (864m), with 3950 inhabitants, is commanded from the N by the pointed Aiarnola. A cablecar for skiers rises to *Monte Agudo* (1585m).—Beyond the NW hamlets of Auronzo the wooded valley is thinly populated. Monte Popera, and the Croda dei Toni dominate the view on the right and the Marmarole peaks on the left. Beyond the spoil-heaps of some old zinc mines is the approach to the MARMAROLE, a fine dolomitic mass rising to 2932m in the *Cimon del Froppa*.—After (34km) *Palus* (1112m) the Sorapis and Cadin groups come into prominence, and on the left is the *Corno del Doge* (2615m) shaped like a huge Doge's cap. The ascent becomes steeper, and the Tre Croci road from Cortina is joined.

44km **Lago di Misurina** (1737m), one of the most beautifully situated lakes in the Dolomites (although now sadly polluted) lies in the broad valley between the Cadin (E) and the Cristallo group (W), but the finest peaks in view are the Tre Cime di Lavaredo and the Sorapis, to the NE and S respectively. Misurina is an excellent centre for winter sports (especially skating), and for mountain climbing in the Dolomites. A chair-lift rises to Col de Varda (2201m).

Monte Piana (2324m), 6km N of Misurina by mountain road, is a fine belvedere fiercely contested in 1916–17. The pyramid at its N end commemorates the poet Carducci (1835–1907).—A still finer road, not always passable, leads NE to (7km) the *Rifugio Auronzo* (2320m), at the foot of the beautiful *Tre Cime di Lavaredo (Cima Grande, 2999m). From there a marked path goes on to a chapel and the *Rifugio Lavaredo* from where a side path on the right leads to the *Bersaglieri Memorial, by Vittorio Ancona (1916).

Beyond the lake soon begins a rapid ascent into the Valle Popena, and at (49km) *Ponte della Marogna* the road crosses the old frontier.—50km **Carbonin**, and from there to (67km) *Dobbiaco*, see Rte 28.

30   Verona to Vicenza

ROAD, 83km, N11 (PADANA SUPERIORE), leaving Verona by Via Venti Settembre (Pl. 8).—50·5km **Vicenza**, entered by the Corso San Felice and left by the Porta Padova (or bypassed to the S).—83km **Padua**, entered by the Porta Savonarola.
    The busy AUTOSTRADA, A4 (SERENISSIMA), follows the same route and is 4km shorter.

RAILWAY, 82km, in 45–60 minutes; to *Vicenza*, 52km, in 30–50 minutes. Frequent services, mostly starting in Milan.

Leaving Verona, there is a view of the Madonna di Campagna on the right, and on the left the valleys of the Tredici Comuni (see above) leading up into the Monti Lessini.—11km *Vago. Zevio*, a fruit-growing town of Roman foundation, 5km S on the Adige, is the reputed home of the painter Stefano da Zevio.—15km *Caldiero* has hot springs (perhaps the Roman Fontes Junonis).

On the left is the road up the Val d'Illasi, at the head of which is the village of *Giazza* (29km) where a Germanic dialect is still spoken. An Ethnographical Museum has been opened at Selva di Progno (9–12, 15–18 except Monday). On the way is (6km) *Illasi*, where the church has a fine frescoed Madonna by Stefano da Zevio, and there are two villas.

On the left farther on rises the fortified townlet of *Soave*, famous for its white wine, with battlemented walls, a conspicuous 14C castle (9–12, 15–18 except Monday) of the Scaligers, and several old palazzi of the period.—At (22km) *Villanova*, an outlying part of *San Bonifacio* (right), is the Romanesque abbey of San Pietro Apostolo (1131–39), many times restored.

At *Arcole*, 7km S, Napoleon defeated the Austrians under Alvinczy in November 1796.—At *Locara*, 5km farther along the main road, is the station for **Lonigo** (6km S), a little town (11,500 inhab.) at the foot of the Monti Berici, where the *Town Hall* occupies a mansion of 1557. On the outskirts stands the *Rocca*, or *Villa Pisani* (1576), a charming work by Andrea Scamozzi (recalling Palladio's Villa Rotonda) on the site of an old castle, with a park (adm. on request at the local tourist office).

32km The *Villa da Porto* ('La Favorita') by Francesco Antonio Muttoni (1714–15; open Sunday 8–12, 15–18), is prominent to the right. The road traverses a wide valley between the foothills of the Monti Lessini (left) and the volcanic Monti Berici.—33km *Montebello Vicentino* preserves some remains of a castle. On the right rise the ruins of the castle of *Brendola*, slighted in 1514; on the left opens the Val d'Agno, with the castles of **Montecchio** (see below).—42km *Tavernelle*.

51km **VICENZA**, the city of Palladio, is a thriving provincial capital (116,600 inhab.) with many beautiful buildings. It lies in a pleasant position beneath the foothills of the green Monti Berici and is traversed by two sluggish little streams, the Retrone and the Bacchiglione. The streets are cheerful, and the Venetian dialect word *Contrà* or *contrada* replaces the more usual 'Via' in the older districts of the town. Much of the centre has been closed to traffic.

A.P.T. Tourist Information Office, 12 Piazza Matteotti.—**Amministrazione Provinciale, Assessorato al Turismo (Provincial Tourist Office)**, 1 Contrà Gazzolle.—**Post Office**, Piazza Garibaldi.

Buses. No. 8 from Viale Roma and the Station for *Villa Rotonda* and *Villa Valmarana*.—The TRAMVIE VICENTINE company runs a service (blue coach) from Piazza Castello and the Bus Station (W of the Railway Station) to *Monte Berico*.—Long distance coaches from the Bus Station to: *Marostica* and *Bassano*; *Asiago*; *Padua*; *Treviso*; *Montecchio*, *Valdagna* and *Recoaro*, etc.

Car Parking. Large car parks (with a mini-bus service for the historical centre) near the wholesale fruit market (N of the Verona road) and beyond the Stadium. In the centre of the town, limited parking is available in Viale Roma and Piazza Matteotti.

History. The Roman municipium of *Vicetia*, the successor of a Gaulish town, was destroyed during the barbarian invasions, but rose to importance again in the later Middle Ages, and became in turn an episcopal city and a free commune, and a member of the Veronese League against Barbarossa (1164). Following the usual series of petty wars against its neighbours, Verona and Padua, Vicenza reached a certain stability under the Veronese Scaligers after 1314. In 1404 it joined itself to the Venetian dominion, and its chief architectural glories, both Gothic and Renaissance, date from the Venetian period. Like the rest of Venetia, it passed under Austrian dominion in 1813; the insurrection of 1848 was unsuccessful, but in 1866 Vicenza was united to the Italian kingdom. The town was bombed and the centre much damaged in the Second World War.

The greatest name in the history of Vicentine art is that of Andrea di Pietro della Gondola (1508–80), nicknamed Palladio by his patron the poet Gian Giorgio Trissino (died 1550). Born in Padua, he settled in Vicenza where he practically rebuilt the town in his distinctive classicizing style. His work was carried on by Vincenzo Scamozzi (1552–1616). The most illustrious painter of Vicenza is Bartolomeo Montagna (c 1450–1523), a native of the province of Brescia; he was followed by his son Benedetto, by Giovanni Buonconsiglio, and by Marcello Fogolino. Among other famous Vicentines are Antonio Pigafetta (1491–1534), the fellow-voyager of Magellan, Giacomo Zanella (1820–88), the poet, and Antonio Fogazzaro (1842–1911), the novelist.

The road from Verona meets Viale Roma (coming from the station) at *Porta Castello*. The massive 11C tower here is a fragment of the Scaligers' stronghold, destroyed in 1819. Here is the 17C entrance to the *Giardino Salvi*, with the Palladian Loggia Valmarana (1592) at the end of a canal. Nearby is a loggia by Baldassarre Longhena (1649). On the right in Piazza Castello, just inside Porta Castello, are the three huge

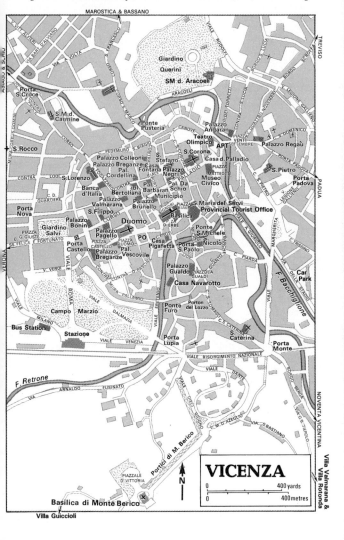

columns of *Palazzo Breganze*, probably designed by Palladio, and left unfinished by Vincenzo Scamozzi (c 1600; covered for restoration in 1989). Here begins the handsome CORSO PALLADIO, the principal street of Vicenza, notable for its many fine palaces. At the beginning, on the left, No. 13 is *Palazzo Bonin*, probably by Scamozzi; Nos 38–40, the *Palazzo Pagello*, is by Ottavio Bertotti Scamozzi (1780). Opposite is the handsome neo-classical façade of the church of *San Filippo Neri* by Antonio Piovene (1824; on a design by Ottone Calderari). It contains a good 18C organ by the Favorito brothers. Beyond the Gothic *Palazzo Thiene* (No. 47), No. 67, *Palazzo Brunello*, is a charming example of 15C Venetian Gothic art. At No. 98 is the imposing **Palazzo del Comune**, formerly a private palace, begun by Vincenzo Scamozzi in 1592 and finished in 1662.

In the huge and dignified *PIAZZA DEI SIGNORI, behind the Municipio, is the majestic **Basilica** (1549–1614), Palladio's masterpiece, with two open colonnaded galleries, Tuscan Doric below and Ionic above. The nucleus of the building is the beautiful 15C hall (with a remarkable roof) of the *Palazzo della Ragione* (adm. 9.30–12, 14.30–17; Sunday 10–12; closed Monday; used for exhibitions), and the skill with which Palladio adapted a Renaissance shell to this Gothic core is especially notable. Its name 'Basilica' is derived from its original function as a place in which justice was to be administered. It is in need of restoration, but an ambitious project to adapt it for use as a 'cultural centre' has met with justifiable opposition. Near the N corner rises the slender *Torre di Piazza* (12C), to which additional stories were added in 1311 and 1444. Facing the basilica are the brick *Loggia del Capitaniato* (1571) by Palladio, and the *Monte di Pietà*, in two parts (left, 1500; right, 1553–57) separated by the church of *San Vincenzo*, by Paolo Bonin (1614–17). Two graceful columns (being restored) at the E end of the piazza bear the Lion of St Mark (1520; restored after bombardment in 1945) and the Redeemer (1640). In the adjacent Piazza delle Biade, *Santa Maria dei Servi*, a Gothic church of 1407 enlarged in 1490, has an altarpiece by Benedetto Montagna (1st on the right), and a Lombardesque altar (2nd on left). A late-15C cloister (S side) has capitals of varying origin.

Piazza delle Erbe, behind the Basilica, is a quaint market square with a medieval prison-tower; and in the narrow streets to the SW are several old mansions, notably *Casa Pigafetta* (1481), in an early Renaissance style seemingly influenced by Spanish Gothic, and with a French motto. On the adjacent house a plaque records Antonio Pigafetta, one of Magellan's company in 1519–22. Contrà dei Proti (and its continuations to the W) leads to Piazza del Duomo. Here is the *Palazzo Vescovile*, well rebuilt after 1944, and preserving a charming courtyard-loggia (1494) by Bernardino da Milano.

The Gothic **Duomo**, largely rebuilt in the 14–16C, was practically destroyed in 1944; the façade (1467) and some chapels remained and it was carefully rebuilt. The beautiful Renaissance Tribune also survived: it was begun in 1482 by Lorenzo da Bologna, and the cupola is by Battista and Francesco Della Porta on a Palladian design (1558–74). The sturdy detached campanile (11C), also at the E end, stands on a ruined Roman building. In the Interior, North side: in the 4th chapel, Madonna, by *Bartolomeo Montagna*; 5th chapel, Coronation of the Virgin, with figures of painted stone, by *Antonino da Venezia* (1448) and two 16C tombs. South side: 5th chapel, Polyptych, by *Lorenzo Veneziano* (1356; removed for restoration); 1st chapel, 8C sarcophagus, and, outside, pretty stoup. Beneath the crypt excavations (closed since 1973) have revealed part of a Roman street and considerable remains of a 9C double-aisled basilica, and of a still earlier cathedral.—On the S side of the square, beneath Palazzo Proti, is a Roman criptoporticus probably part of a 1C AD palace (for adm. apply at No. 2 in the piazza, Thursday & Saturday 10–11.30).

From the E end of the Duomo, Contrà Pasini leads S past the two attractive *Case Arnaldi*, one Gothic, the other Renaissance. In the Contrà Carpagnon (left) is a house (No. 11) occupied by Frederick IV of Denmark in 1709. In Viale Eretenio, along the river, is the *Casa Civena* (Trissino) built in 1540–46 by Palladio. *Ponte Furo* crosses the little Retrone; there is a good view (left) of the Basilica and Torre di Piazza, and (right) of Monte Berico. On the left (No. 2 Piazzetta Santi Apostoli) is the fine Gothic *Casa Navarotto* (14C). Leaving the neo-classical Palazzo Gualdo (by Giovanni Miglioranza, 1838) and the *Porton del Luzzo*, a 13C gateway, to the right, the street continues past an unusual house with brick columns above a rusticated ground floor, to Piazzola dei Gualdi with the two Renaissance *Palazzi Gualdo* (in very poor repair). On the left, in Via Paolo Lioy, is the charming Gothic *Casa Caola*. The river may be recrossed by the hump-backed *Ponte San Michele* (1620). At the end of Contrà Ponte San Michele is Contrà Piancoli with several interesting houses. Contrà delle Gazzolle leads back to the centre.

In Corso Palladio, beyond Palazzo del Comune, are *Palazzo da Schio* (No. 147; 15C Venetian Gothic, restored), known as the 'Ca d'Oro'. Beyond the raised garden railing of Santa Corona (see below) is the simple little '*Casa del Palladio*' (Palazzetto Cogollo; No. 165–7), with a portico and two Doric and two Corinthian columns, traditionally thought to have been built by the architect for Pietro Cogollo, but now not generally ascribed to Palladio. It was greatly admired by Goethe on his visit to the city in 1786. At the end, in Piazza Matteotti is *Palazzo Chiericati*, an excellent example of Palladio's work (1550–57), in which is housed the **Museo Civico** (9.30–12, 14.30–17; Sunday 10–12; Monday closed).In 1989 the palace was being restored, and the works from the 16C onwards had not yet been rearranged here. In 1987 the earlier works, many of them recently restored, were arranged in the adjoining palace. The modern rooms (un-numbered) are designed in a severe anaesthetic style, but the works are well labelled.

Room 1 has scuptural fragments.—Room II. *Paolo Veneziano*, Transition of the Virgin, signed and dated 1333; fresco fragments of the late 14C; pulpit of 1346 with a relief of St Michael.—Room III. Works by *Battista da Vicenza*; *Giovanni Badile*, St Christopher.— Room IV. Stone carved tabernacle by *Nicolò* and *Antonino da Venezia* (1427).—Room V. *Pietro Lombardo*, marble portrait of a man in profile; *Domenico Morone* (attributed), Scenes from the life of St Blaise; *Francesco Marmitta* (formerly attributed to Gian Francesco De Maineri), St Thomas as a child; *Hans Memling*, Calvary.—Room VI. *Venetian painter of the early 16C*, Archers;medals by *Pisanello*, and a collection of coins; *Francesco* and *Bernardino Zaganelli*, Madonna in Glory with angels and cherubs; *Marco Palmezzano*, The Dead Christ with St Joseph of Arimathea, Nicodemus, and Mary Magdalene.— Room VII. Fine works by *Bartolomeo Montagna*, including Christ carrying the Cross, and the Madonna in adoration of the Child with Saints Monica and Mary Magdalene.—Room VIII. Works by *Marcello Fogolino* (including Epiphany) and paintings by *Giovanni Buonconsiglio* (Deposition).

The later works which are to be rearranged in Palazzo Chiericati include: *Sansovino*, *Madonna and Child (terracotta) in its original wood frame;*Tintoretto*, A miracle of St Augustine; *Veronese*, Madonna and Child with Saints; *Marcello Venusti*, Shepherds; *Bernardino Licinio*, Portrait of a Fieramosca; works by *Pietro Vecchia*;

paintings by *Jacopo Bassano* (including three Portraits, and Madonna with Saints); *Brueghel the Elder*, Madonna and Child (with beautiful landscape), and scenes from the life of Christ around the border; *Van Dyck*, Three ages of man; works by *Francesco Maffei*, *Pittoni*, *Giuseppe Zais*, *Sebastiano* and *Marco Ricci*; *Giovanni Battista Tiepolo*, Immaculate Conception; large works by *Luca Giordano* and *Bellucci*, and 17C civic paintings.—The Museum also owns 33 drawings by *Palladio*, facsimiles of which are to be exhibited.

The **Archaeological Section** of the museum is to be moved to the cloisters of Santa Corona (see below). This includes prehistoric finds from the province, including a Venetian inscription and objects from lake dwellings at Fimon; Roman tombs and sculpture (head of a Faun), and a mosaic hunting scene (4C); and Lombard relics (6–7C).

On the opposite side of the square is the *Territorio*, a defensive work transformed during the centuries with a tower rebuilt since the bombing. Inside stands the *Teatro Olimpico* (9.30–12.20, 15–17.20; winter, 9.30–12, 14–16; Sunday 9.30–12), the last work of Palladio (1580; finished by Scamozzi), a fascinating structure of wood and stucco with fixed scenery representing a piazza and streets in perfect perspective. It was restored in 1985–87. The opening play, given by the Accademia Olimpica in 1585, was Sophocles' 'Oedipus Tyrannus'.

Just across the bridge over the Bacchiglione is Piazza Venti Settembre with the 15C *Palazzo Angaran* (rebuilt), and in Contrà Venti Settembre is the fine *Palazzo Regaù* (15C Gothic). To the right is the 14C church of *San Pietro*, with a 15C brick cloister (apply at the hospice next door). N of Piazza Venti Settembre, at the end of Contrà Torretti, is the unusual Baroque church of *Santa Maria d'Aracoeli*, on the edge of the Giardino Querini. Elliptical in plan it is perhaps based on designs by Guarino Guarini (1675–80).

Contrà Santa Corona leads N from the Corso to the Dominican church of **Santa Corona** (closed 12.30–15 or 15.30 and on Monday morning), early Gothic in style (1261) with a.Renaissance E arm of 1482–89.

INTERIOR. N side: 2nd altar, Glorification of St Mary Magdalene, by *Bartolomeo Montagna*; 3rd, *Leandro Bassano*, St Anthony; 4th, Madonna delle Stelle, a late-Gothic votive image of the Virgin with an early-16C landscape view of Vicenza by Fogolino. 5th, *Giovanni Bellini*, *Baptism of Christ*, a superb late work, in a splendid altar of 1501. NORTH TRANSEPT. Derision of Christ, by *Tentorello* (late 14C; restored). The colourful high altar (1669) is inlaid with marble. The choir stalls are finely inlaid (end of 15C). In the chapel N of the sanctuary is kept the gold reliquary of the Holy Thorn (14C; displayed only on Good Friday on the high altar). A plaque on the nave pillar records the burial of Palladio here in 1580; his remains were later removed to the cemetery of Santa Lucia. To the S of the choir is the THIENE CHAPEL, with two splendid Gothic family tombs (restored in 1976). The chapel's altarpiece is by *Giovanni Battista Pittoni* (1723). The 4th S chapel is sumptuously decorated by *Giovanni Battista* and *Alessandro Maganza*. In the 3rd chapel is *Veronese*'s *Adoration of the Magi*, with superb colouring.—The Archaeological Section of the Museo Civico (see above) is to be displayed in the cloisters of the church.

In the N transept of the church of SANTO STEFANO (open early morning or late evening) to the W, is a beautiful painting of the *Madonna with Saints George and Lucy* by *Palma Vecchio*. Opposite are the *Casa Fontana*, the most successful Gothic building in the city, and the Renaissance *Palazzo Negri* (in poor repair). The *Palazzo della Banca Popolare*, or Palazzo Thiene, to the left, has a courtyard and E façade by Palladio (1558) and the main façade, with remains of frescoes, by Lorenzo da Bologna (1489) and a fine portal, in the Contrà Porti.

Also in *Contrà Porti are: (left) No. 8, the Gothic *Palazzo Cavalloni*; (right) No. 11, the dignified *Palazzo Porto Barbaran* (1570) by Palladio, recently acquired by the State and being restored; No. 15, where Luigi Da Porto, author of the story of 'Romeo and Juliet' died in 1529; No. 17, *Palazzo Porto Breganze*, Gothic with a Renaissance doorway; No. 19, the magnificent 15C *Palazzo Colleoni Porto*; and No. 21, *Palazzo Iseppo Da Porto* (1552), by Palladio.

Contrà Riale runs SW; No. 12 (right), the sumptuous *Palazzo Cordellina*, is by Calderari (1776), and at No. 9 in the former 17C convent of San Giacomo is installed the fine *Biblioteca Civica Bertoliana*, left to the city by Giovanni Maria Bertolo in 1702. To the right is the animated Corso Fogazzaro, in which, beyond the *Banca d'Italia* (Palazzo Repeta; 1701–11), by Francesco Muttoni, stands the majestic 13C brick church of **San Lorenzo**. The W front is the finest in Vicenza, with a splendid marble portal of the mid-14C (covered for restoration), and sculptures in a good state of preservation although the church was secularised from 1797 to 1927.

INTERIOR (vista spoilt by the glass at the E end). Above the door, Monument to General Da Porto (1661), with a remarkable collection of military emblems. South Transept: Altar of the Trinity, with coloured reliefs (15–16C) and frescoes. On the N side: against the W wall, tomb of Scamozzi (died 1616); 2nd bay, Volpe tomb, once ascribed to Palladio (1575); 3rd bay, remains of 14C frescoes (very ruined). The Choir and its flanking chapels contain interesting tombs, notably a fine Gothic tomb of the Da Porto family, on the left; opposite, Beheading of St Paul, a large fresco, by *Bartolomeo Montagna* (detached and very ruined).
   Santa Maria del Carmine, farther on, has good Renaissance sculptured details inside; beyond is *Porta Santa Croce*, a well-preserved gateway of 1381.

In the opposite direction Corso Fogazzaro leads back to the Corso, passing *Palazzo Valmarana-Braga* (No. 16), by Palladio (1566).

Outside Porta Castello Contrà Santi Felice e Fortunato leads past the Giardino Salvi (see above) to the remarkable church of **Santi Felice e Fortunato**, with a curious fortified campanile (1166), a fragmentary mosaic pavement, partly Constantinian, partly Theodosian, a Martyrion of the 4C, and parts of its cloister.
   In the NW outskirts of the town (just within the walls) the church of *San Rocco* (see the Plan) preserves an elegant interior of the early Renaissance (if closed, ring at No. 22 Contrada Mure San Rocco).
   4km S of the town, reached via Porta Castello, just by the motorway, is the church of *Sant'Agostino*. It was built in 1322 on the site of an 8C chapel. Over the main altar, Polyptych by Battista da Vicenza (1404); 14C frescoes decorate the apse and nave walls.

Monte Berico, Villa Valmarana, and Villa Rotonda

The green hillside of Monte Berico has been preserved almost entirely from modern building. For those with time, the best way of visiting the basilica and the villas is on foot as described below (the return may be made by bus); the pleasant walk takes about 1½hrs.—By BUS, the Basilica can be reached by a half-hourly coach service run by the Tramvie Vicentine from Piazza Castello and the Station. The Villa Valmarana is reached in c 15 minutes by Bus No. 8 from Viale Roma on the Noventa Vicentina road (N 247; request stop at Via Tiepolo, 500 metres below the villa); No. 8 continues along the Viale Riviera Berica to another request stop at the foot of Via della Rotonda, 200 metres below Villa Rotonda.—By CAR the Basilica is reached by Viale Dante, which winds uphill from the road junction E of the

VILLA ROTONDA
Vicenza

Station (see the Plan); the Villa Rotonda and Villa Valmarana
are reached by the same route as Bus No. 8 (see above).

The **Basilica di Monte Berico** (*Madonna del Monte*), conspicuous
from all parts of the town, on a hill S of the station, is approached by
the *Portici*, a covered ascent with 150 arches and 17 chapels, designed
by Francesco Muttoni (1746–78) and erected by various pious citizens
or guilds. Viale X Giugno (closed to cars; see the Plan) skirts the
portici steeply uphill. There is a fine view (E) of the Villa Rotonda from
just below the basilica.

The BASILICA (closed 12–14.30) replaces a chapel built to commemorate two
apparitions of the Virgin (1426–28); it was enlarged in 1476 and finally
completely rebuilt, apart from the campanile, by Carlo Borella in 1688–1703. It is
a pilgrim shrine (festival on 8 September). Lorenzo da Bologna's façade of 1476
has been re-erected alongside the present S front. The interior contains (to the
right of the altar) a *Pietà, by *Bartolomeo Montagna* (1500); from the Sacristy
(left of the altar) steps descend to the Gothic cloister where the refectory contains
the *Supper of St Gregory the Great, by *Veronese*, repaired at the expense of the
Austrian emperor Francis Joseph after having been hacked to pieces by his
soldiery in 1848 (and restored in this century).

The *Piazzale della Vittoria*, beside the church, built as a memorial of the First
World War, commands a magnificent view of Vicenza, and of the mountains that
once marked the front-line. Viale X Giugno continues beyond the basilica to the
Villa Guiccioli, with a beautiful park (open 9–17.30 or 18 except Monday) and a
Risorgimento Museum (open 9.30–12, 14.30–17.30;fest. 9.30–12; closed
Monday).

From the Basilica Villa Valmarana can be reached by following the Portici down-hill again, and (half-way down) taking Via Massimo d'Azeglio to the right (good view of Vicenza). Just beyond a Carmelite monastery the narrow cobbled Via San Bastiano (closed to through traffic) diverges right. It leads downhill past a charming dovecote to (15 minutes) **Villa Valmarana** called *dei Nani* from the dwarfs decorating its garden wall (adm. March–November, 14.30 or 15–17.30 or 18; Thursday, Saturday & festivals, also 10–12). It consists of the Palazzina, built in 1668, probably by Antonio Muttoni, and the Foresteria added by Francesco Muttoni. In both buildings are remarkable *Frescoes by *Giovanni Battista Tiepolo* and his son *Gian Domenico*.

The stony path (Stradella Valmarana) on the right beyond the villa continues downhill to the *Villa Rotonda* (*Almerico-Capra*), the most famous of Palladio's villas (adm. to exterior, Tuesday & Thursday 10–12, 15–18; other days usually on request; to the interior, 15 March–15 October, Wednesday only, 10–12, 15–18; always closed Monday). Built as a belvedere for Cardinal Capra on a charming hill-top site, its central plan consists of a circular core (domed) within a cube. The four classical porticoes complete its symmetry. Begun c 1551 by Palladio it was taken over at his death by Scamozzi and finished in 1606. It has been copied at Chiswick House, London and elsewhere.

The return may be made by following Via Rotonda to the bottom of the hill (200 metres), where Bus No. 8 can be taken back to the centre of Vicenza.—From Villa Valmarana Via Giovanni Battista Tiepolo descends to the Porta Monte, just above which is a charming little arch by Palladio (?) dated 1595. Bus No. 8 may be taken back along the main road into Vicenza.

The Ville Vicentine

The first two routes described below can each be travelled in a day from Vicenza and include some of the most spectacular villas in the environs of the city; others can be seen on the way to Verona (see above), Recoaro, and Padua (see below). Many of the interiors of the villas are closed to the public (except with special permission), but the exteriors and gardens are often the most important features. Opening times change frequently and accessibility varies; it is therefore advisable to consult the Provincial Tourist Office (Assessorato Turismo, Contrà Gazzolle) in Vicenza before starting a tour. The names of the villas change with each new owner, but they generally carry also the name of the original proprietor. Concerts are organised in some of the villas in July.

ROUND TRIP FROM VICENZA TO THIENE AND MAROSTICA, 63km N349 leads N from Vicenza.—8km *Caldogno* (right), with the Villa Caldogno-Nordera (1570; adm. by appointment, July–October, Tuesday & Saturday, 9–12; Thursday, 15–18), designed by Palladio.—14km *Villaverla* has two fine villas: the Villa Verlato (1576 by Scamozzi), and the decayed Villa Ghellini (1664–79) by Pizzocaro.—At (20km) **Thiene** (17,300 inhabitants) is the *Villa Porto-Colleoni* (begun after 1440, and altered in 1521), an early castellated villa with a charming contemporary chapel adjoining (adm. 15 March–31 October, Tuesday, Saturday, and fest. 9–12, 15–18.30). N248 continues E from Thiene past (25km) *Sarcedo* (left of the road), with the Villa Capra (1764; adm. sometimes on request in summer). Just beyond the Astico, a road leads to *Lonedo di Lugo* (4km N). Here the *Villa Godi-Valmarana*, now *Malinverni* (open March–October, Tuesday, Saturday, & Sunday 14–18) is one of the earliest known works by Palladio (1540–42); it is frescoed by Giovanni Battista Zelotti. The small Modern Art Gallery has a representative collection of 19C Italian paintings, including works by Francesco Hayez, Tranquillo Cremona, the Indunno brothers, Segantini, De Nittis, Domenico Morelli, the 'Macchiaioli' painters, Giovanni Boldini, etc. A

Fossil Museum has local exhibits including a palm tree 5 metres high. The *Villa Piovene*, close by (adm. to garden only; 14.30–19), has a Palladian core, altered in the 18C by Muttoni.—28km *Breganze*, with several villas including the Villa Diedo-Malvezzi (1664–84, with additions).—For (37km) **Marostica**, and the return to Vicenza, see below.

ROUND TRIP FROM VICENZA TO ORGIANO AND LONGARE, 84km. This route traverses the 'Riviera Berica' S of Vicenza. N11 leads W from Vicenza. At (5km) *Olmo*, a by-road (2km) leads SW towards the motorway and *Altavilla*, where the *Villa Valmarana* (1724) has been restored by the University (adm. on application). North of Olmo (on the Monteviale road), *Villa Zileri* has a fine park with exotic trees. Visitors are admitted on request to see the frescoes by Giovanni Battista Tiepolo (1734; the earliest known by him outside Venice). At Sovizzo, to the W, *Villa Bissari Curti* (being restored) has a garden with antique fragments and an amphitheatre.—Just before (13km) *Montecchio Maggiore*, the road passes the *Villa Cordellina-Lombardi*, by Massari, now owned by the province of Vicenza and used for conferences, courses, etc. (usually open April–October, Wednesday, Saturday, and Sunday, 9–12, 15–18). It is particularly interesting for its fine frescoes (1754) by Giovanni Battista Tiepolo in the entrance hall (restored in 1984). The picturesque village of Montecchio has two restored Scaliger castles, a legendary stronghold of the 'Montagues' of 'Romeo and Juliet'.—N500 leads S to (27km) *Sarego*. The Villa da Porto 'La Favorita' is the work of Francesco Muttoni (1714–15).—29km *Lonigo* (see the beginning of Rte 30).—38km **Orgiano**. Here the *Villa Piovene*, built by Muttoni in 1710, has a notable garden open to the public.—52km *Noventa Vicentina* where the town hall occupies the Villa Barbarigo (early 17C; adm. during office hours). Just to the E of the town N247 leads back towards Vicenza via (75km) **Longare**. Here are three villas: Villa Trento-Carli (1645), and Villa Garzadori-da Schio, with frescoes attributed to Dorigny, both open only by previous appointment; and the Villa Eolia (now a restaurant, closed Tuesday).—84km **Vicenza**.

FROM VICENZA TO RECOARO, 42km. Bus in c 1hr. N246 ascends the Val d'Agno.—19km *Trissino* (left), with the Villa Marzotto, whose delightful park is open to visitors by previous appointment.—At (22km) *Castelgomberto* (right) is the Villa Piovene da Schio of 1666 (chapel of 1614), with 18C additions (no adm.).—32km **Valdagno** (28,400 inhab.) has woollen mills. *Castelvecchio* (794m), 6km W, is a summer resort in a pleasant position.—42km **Recoaro Terme** (445m) is a finely situated spa with ferruginous springs. The road goes on to (53km) *Valli del Pasubio* (see below), while a chair-lift ascends to *Recoaro-Mille* (1021m) and *Monte Falcone* (1700m), popular with skiers.

FROM VICENZA TO ROVERETO, 72km, railway via Thiene as far as Schio (32km in ¾hr), bus from there in summer. The road runs via Isola Vicentina and Malo through spectacular countryside.—24km **Schio** is a well-situated town (35,000 inhab.) with wool manufacturers. It has a cathedral begun in 1740, a good 15–16C church (*San Francesco*) and beyond it, on the Asiago road, an *Ossuary-Cloister*, with 5000 graves of soldiers who fell in 1915–18. Buses run to Thiene and in summer to Recoaro.—28km *Torrebelvicino*.—33km *Valli del Pasubio* (338m) is at the junction of the road from Recoaro (see above).—At (42km) *Ponte Verde* a poor road on the right (28km) ascends to the Colle di Xomo and, (right), **Monte Pasubio** (2235m). The road ends about 150m below the flat summit, which is easily reached from there in ½ hour. The massif was hotly contested in 1916–18 and a ring of boundary-stones defines the 'Zona Sacra', dedicated to those who died here.—45km *Pian delle Fugazze* (1159m), the highest point on the road, is 1·5km from the *Sacello del Pasubio* (left), an imposing war memorial with a battle museum. The descent is made through dolomitic country, amid villages rebuilt since the First World War.—72km *Rovereto*, see Rte 22.

FROM VICENZA TO ASIAGO, 55km, railway to Thiene in ½hr; bus from there in 1½hrs; more frequently to Piovene. The motorway from Vicenza to Trento is open as far as Rochetta, which is connected by a fast road to Asiago. From Vicenza to (20km) Thiene, see above.—Beyond (27km) *Chiuppano* the road ascends to the right in zigzags.—54km **Asiago** (998m), rebuilt since 1919 (6700 inhab.), is near the centre of the plateau of the *Sette Comuni*, which has a good climate, and is a popular summer resort of the Milanese and Venetians. The inhabitants were of Germanic origin. There are good winter sports facilities in the area. In the BATTLE OF ASIAGO (15–16 June 1918), the British XIV Corps was heavily engaged and the dead are buried in five cemeteries: *Barenthal*,

Granezza and *Cavalletto*, S of Asiago; and *Boscon* and *Magnaboschi*, E and S of *Cesuna*, to the SW. The Italian dead lie in the Sacrario Militare, E of the town, near the Astrophysical Observatory of Padua University.—*Gallio*, 4km E on the mountain road to Primolano (42km) is a summer and winter resort (ski-lifts, etc).

FROM VICENZA TO PADUA, N11, 32km. The road passes (11km) the Villa Da Porto Rigo, by a follower of Palladio, in *Vancimuglio*, and, just short of (15km) *Grisignano di Zocco*, the Villa Ferramosca-Beggiato, by Gian Domenico Scamozzi (c 1560).—About 4km SW, on either side of the Bacchiglione, are *Montegalda* and *Montegaldella*, the former with a 12C castle adapted as a villa in the 18C, the latter with the 17C *Villa Campagnolo 'La Deliziosa'*, decorated by Orazio Marinali, with a garden and collection of statues (closed to the public in 1989).—32km **Padua**, see Rte 31.

ROUND TRIP FROM VICENZA TO BASSANO DEL GRAPPA AND ASOLO, CASTELFRANCO VENETO AND CITTADELLA, 97km (N248, & N53). The road leaves Vicenza along the river and passes *Villa Trissino* (no adm.) where Palladio worked as a young artist for his first patron, Gian Giorgio Trissino.—10km A by-road leads W to *Dueville*. Here are the Villa Da Porto dei Pilastroni (now Casarotto), by Ottone Calderari (1770–76; adm. to the exterior only, Sunday 9–11, 15–18), and the *Villa Da Porto del Conte*, at Vivaro.—At (15km) *Sandrigo*, the Villa Sesso (open 9–12, 15-18) was built by a follower of Palladio in 1570 and has contemporary frescoes.—18km *Longa di Schiavon*. The Villa Chiericati-Lambert (adm. only to the exterior with special permission) has frescoes formerly attributed to Paolo Veronese, but now thought to be by Ludovico Pozzoserrato.—24km **Marostica**, a charming old fortified townlet preserving its Medieval *Ramparts.

From the piazza, where a 14C battlemented castle serves as town hall (adm. during office hours), there is a fine view of the walls and the upper castle of the Scaligers (1372). The 'Partita a Scacchi', a chess match with human combatants, is played here in alternate years in early September (next in 1990). The match commemorates and reproduces a 'Duel' fought between Rinaldo da Angarano (white) and Vieri da Vallonara (black) for the hand of Lionora, daughter of Taddeo Parisio, the local Venetian governor. The herald's announcements are made in Venetian dialect.—4km S of Marostica is *Nove*, a ceramics centre (museum in the Istituto Statale d'Arte Ceramica, adm. 8–12), with the Villa Macchiavello (restored 17C frescoes).

31km **Bassano del Grappa**, standing at the point where the Brenta emerges from the hills, is a cheerful little town (35,000 inhab.) with arcaded streets and a fine view N from the old ramparts (Viale dei Martiri), on which stands a statue of General Gaetano Giardino (1864–1935), defender of Monte Grappa in 1918.

Bassano was a dependency of Venice from the 15C onwards. Napoleon's victory over the Austrians here in 1796 was overshadowed by the campaign on Monte Grappa in 1917–18 (see below) in which the town was considerably damaged. It was again damaged in the Second World War. Famous for its mushrooms, grappa, ceramics, and wrought-iron work, it has recently also become an industrial centre. The famous Da Ponte family of painters (notably Jacopo and Leandro) were surnamed Bassano from this their native town. Tito Gobbi (1913–84), the great baritone, was born here.

In the central Piazza Libertà are the 18C church of *San Giovanni Battista* and the *Loggia Comunale* (1582) with a fresco of St Christopher attributed to Jacopo Bassano; the fresco (badly faded) on the building opposite is probably by his father, Francesco il Vecchio (dated 1522). The neighbouring Piazza Garibaldi is dominated by the 13C *Torre di Ezzelino* and the campanile of the Gothic church of *San Francesco*. The MUSEO CIVICO (adm. 10–12.30, 14.30–18.30; closed

Monday; Sunday 10–12.30) behind the latter in its former monastery (15C cloister) contains a notable collection of paintings by *Jacopo*, *Francesco*, and *Leandro Bassano*, including Jacopo's early masterpiece, the Flight into Egypt, and a detached façade fresco by him; important busts by *Danese Cataneo* and *Girolamo Campagna*; casts and sketches by Canova; a fine collection of engravings for which Bassano was renowned in the 18C; ceramics; and local archaeological material (Roman and Lombard periods).

Ponte degli Alpini, Bassano del Grappa

Below Piazza Libertà, the Piazzetta Monte Vecchio, with the old *Monte di Pietà* and a house frescoed by the Bassano and Nasocchio families (the frescoes have been detached and restored), leads down to the *PONTE DEGLI ALPINI, a covered wooden bridge across the Brenta (small museum in the Taverna al Ponte). Although many times rebuilt, it retains the form designed for it by Palladio in 1569. Beside it is a grappa distillery of 1769. At the N end of the town are the ruins of the *Castello degli Ezzelini*, a tower of which serves as a belfry for the Duomo, a 15C church much restored. North of the cathedral, in the Salita Margnan, is the 15C Capuchin church of *San Sebastiano*.

Monte Grappa (1775m) N of Bassano, is ascended by road (31km, bus in July–September in 2 hours). It was the scene of heavy fighting between Austrians and Italians in 1917–18. On the summit are a votive chapel crowned by a figure of the Madonna, and a cemetery.

A road leads NE out of Bassano to *Romano d'Ezzelino* (4km) with traces of the castle of the Ezzelini, most notorious of whom was Ezzelino III (1194–1259), the terror of the countryside. The Villa Cornaro here may be visited on application.—The road continues to *Possagno* (18km), the birthplace of Antonio Canova (1757–1822), the sculptor. Adm. to his house and the Museum of casts, 9–12, 15–18; in winter, 9–12, 14–17; closed Monday. The *Tempio*, now the parish church, in which Canova is buried, was designed by himself (for adm. to the Cupola, apply to the sacristan).

N47 leads S from Bassano past the Ca'Rezzonico, an early work by Longhena to *Rosà* (5km), where the park of the 18C Villa Dolfin-Boldù may be visited by previous appointment.

N248 continues E from Bassano (bus) for (45km) **Asolo**, a charmingly situated town with interesting old houses. It was presented by Venice to Queen Catherine Cornaro in exhange for her dominions of Cyprus and here in the *Castello* she lived in 1489–1509. A bus ascends to the centre of the little town from the main road (bus stop) and car park. The small museum (adm. 9.30–12, 16–19; closed Monday) in the 15C *Loggia del Capitano*, with a façade frescoed by Antonio Contarini (1560), contains memorials of Queen Cornaro and of Browning, as well as paintings, sculpture, and archaeological exhibits. The Cathedral, rebuilt in 1747 on remains of Roman baths, contains two paintings of the Assumption, one by Lorenzo Lotto, and the other by Jacopo Bassano.

From the name of this town Cardinal Bembo (who frequented Queen Catherine's court) coined the term 'asolare' (to gambol, amuse oneself at random), from which is derived 'Asolando', the name chosen by Robert Browning 'for love of the place' for his last volume of poems (1899). Browning's first visit to Asolo was in 1838, and it is the scene of his 'Pippa Passes', published five years later. Eleonora Duse (1850–1924), the actress, and Browning's son (1849–1912) are buried at Asolo in the cemetery of Sant'Anna. Another distinguished resident, the writer and traveller Dame Freya Stark received the keys of the town in 1984 on her nintieth birthday. An important annual chamber music festival is held in the Teatro Duse (in the castle) in September.—The Villa Barbaro at Maser, described in Rte 34B, is 7km E.

The road runs S to (60km) **Castelfranco Veneto** (26,200 inhab.), founded in 1199 by Treviso as a bulwark against Padua. It is famous as the birthplace of Giorgione (c 1478–1510). The old town, or 'Castello', is surrounded by a moat and a battlemented brick wall, one tower of which serves as a belfry. The main *Torre Civica* is the N gate of the 'Castello'. In the centre is the neo-classical *Cathedral* by Francesco Maria Preti, which contains a famous *Madonna and Child with Saints (c 1500), generally attributed to Giorgione, in the chapel to the right of the presbytery (apply to sacristan). In the sacristy are frescoes by Veronese. The so-called *Casa del Giorgione* (9.30–12.50, 15.30–18.30; closed Wednesday) contains a small museum and a chiaroscuro frieze on the first floor thought to be by Giorgione. The 18C *Teatro Accademico*, also by Francesco Maria Preti, in Via Garibaldi (adm. 9–12.30, 14–18) has been restored. The park of Villa Revedin-Bolasco, with 17C statues, in Borgo Treviso may be visited in summer (Wednesday, Saturday & Sunday 15.30–18.30).

At Sant'Andrea, 4km SW of Castelfranco, the *Villa Corner* (now Chiminelli; adm. June–September, Saturday 15–18; or by appointment) has frescoes of the school of Veronese.—At *Piombino Dese*, 9km SE of Castelfranco, is the Villa Cornaro built for Doge Giorgio Cornaro by Palladio (1566–76) and containing stuccoes by Vittoria (adm. Saturday in summer, 15.30–18).

N53 leads W to (73km) **Cittadella** (15,900 inhab.), built by the Paduans as a reply to Castelfranco (see above). The tiny town is enclosed in medieval *Walls, remarkably well preserved with numerous towers and gates. The moated fortifications, designed in an unusual elliptical shape, surround a simple and symetrically planned town, with a neo-classical Duomo and Theatre (1820–28, by Giuseppe

Japelli).—N53 continues across the Brenta and leads straight back
across the plain to (97km) **Vicenza**.

31 Padua

PADUA, in Italian **Padova** (231,000 inhab.), is one of the most ancient
cities in Italy. Above all visited for its famous frescoes by Giotto in the
Cappella degli Scrovegni, it also preserves some masterpieces by
Donatello and other sculptors at the great pilgrim church of Il Santo.
Although some pretty arcaded streets survive in the old town, the
northern part of the city, rebuilt since war damage, is unattractive.
Padua university is one of the oldest and most famous in Europe.

A.P.T. Tourist Information Office at the Railway Station (Pl. 2). The headquarters of the A.P.T. is at No. 8 Riviera Mugnai.—**Post Office**, 5 Corso Garibaldi.

Town Buses. Nos 18, 8, & 3 from the Station to Corso Garibaldi (for the Cappella
degli Scrovegni), Riviera Businello (for the Basilica del Santo), and Prato della
Valle (for Santa Giustina).—No. 6 from the Station via Viale Mazzini and Via
Dante to Corso Milano (for Piazza dei Signori and Piazza del Duomo).—
COUNTRY BUSES from Piazzale Boschetti (Pl. 7) to *Mestre* and *Venice*; to *Piove di
Sacco* for Adria; to *Bassano*; to *Chioggia*; to *Monselice* and *Este* or *Rovigo*; to
Treviso via Noale to *Vicenza*; and to *Bologna*; from the Station to *Montegrotto*,
Abano and *Torreglia*.

Car Parking. Large car parks (with hourly tariff) near the Railway Station (Pl. 3)
and at Prato della Valle (Pl. 14).—Smaller car parks at Piazza Insurrezione (Pl. 6)
and Piazzale Boschetti (Pl. 7).

Il Burchiello Motor-Launch. Wednesday, Friday, & Sunday usually in April–
October, via the Brenta Canal to Venice in 8½hrs with stops at Strà, Mira,
Oriago, and Malcontenta (return from Venice by bus). In 1989 the departure was
by bus (A.T.P.) from Piazzale Boschetti for Villa Pisani, where the boat was
boarded. Bookings at SIAMIC Express Office, Piazzale Boschetti.

History. According to the Roman historian Livy (59 BC–AD 18), the most famous
native of Padua (he was actually born at Teolo, in the Euganean Hills), *Patavium*
was founded by the Trojan Antenor. At any rate it was an important settlement of
the Euganei and Veneti, and received full Roman franchise in 89 BC. After the
barbarian invasions it rose again to prosperity under the Byzantine and Lombard
domination, finally declaring itself an independent republic in 1164. In 1237–54
Ezzelino da Romano was tyrant of Padua, and the suzerainty of the Carraresi
(1318–1405), though more auspicious, was ended by the Venetian conquest.
From 1405 until the fall of Venice, Padua remained faithful to St Mark. The
foundation of the University in 1222 attracted many distinguished men to Padua,
including Dante and Petrarch, as well as innumerable students from England,
earning for the city the surname of 'la Dotta' (the learned).

St Anthony of Padua (1195–1231), a native of Lisbon, driven, on a missionary
journey, by a chance tempest to Italy, settled at Padua, where he preached and
wrought miracles under the guidance of St Francis. He died at Arcella, 1·5km N
of Padua, and was canonised in the following year. Famous natives include
Bartolomeo Cristofori (1655–1731); Giovanni Battista Belzoni (1778–1823), actor,
engineer, and egyptologist (the first European to enter the tomb of Ramesses II at
Abu Simbel, he also supplied the British Museum with many of its largest
Egyptian statues); Ippolito Nievo (1831–61), the patriot novelist; and Arrigo
Boito (1842–1918), the composer.

Art. Paduan painting was first inspired by Giotto's frescoes in the Cappella
Scrovegni, which gave rise to a flourishing local school of 'Giottesque' painters
(Pietro da Rimini, Guariento, Giusto de'Menabuoi, etc). The Veronese Altichiero
(c 1330–c 1395), who was active in Padua in the 1380's, was one of the most
creative interpreters of Giotto's achievements before Masaccio. The birth of an
individual school is especially connected with the name of Francesco Squarcione
(1397–1468), who influenced a great number of disciples. Foremost among these
was Andrea Mantegna (1431–1506), who, however, soon loosed himself from his
master's control. The arrival of Donatello at Padua in 1443 opened a new

horizon; and the native artists, notably Mantegna, were quick to range themselves behind him. In the late 15C Bartolomeo Bellano (1434–1496), who had been Donatello's pupil, and Andrea Briosco ('Il Riccio', 1470–1532), who was in turn Bellano's pupil, were the creators of some of the finest small bronze sculpture of the Renaissance. From the beginning of the 16C the school of Padua is merged in the Venetian, and many Venetian artists worked in the city. The best known local painter was Alessandro Varotari, known as Il Padovanino.— The Byzantinesque basilica of St Anthony and church of Santa Giustina appear not to have inspired a continuous tradition of building.

The centre of city life is Piazza Cavour, the adjacent piazzetta, and Via 8 Febbraio (Pl. 10,6), all now rather pretentiously designed pedestrian precincts, lacking in character. The female bronze statue by Emilio Greco dates from 1973. The large CAFFÈ PEDROCCHI (Pl. 6) is one of the most celebrated cafés in Italy, and was famous in the 19C as a meeting place for intellectuals. The neo-classical building was design-ed in 1831 by Giuseppe Japelli, who added in 1837 the little mock-Gothic wing. For many years the café was kept open twenty-four hours a day. It was left to the city in 1891. The interesting upper floor, with decorations by Ippolito Caffi is used for exhibitions. On the opposite side of Via 8 Febbraio is the **University** (Pl.10), famous as a medical school, nicknamed 'il Bo' (the ox) from the sign of an inn on whose site it stands. It was founded in 1222.

The older façade (recently cleaned) dates from 1757, and the tower from 1572. The dignified courtyard (1552) by Andrea Moroni, with armorial bearings and busts, is entered from the adjoining university building to the right, which was reconstructed in 1938–39 (the façade is covered for restoration). From the old courtyard, stairs (at the foot of which is a statue of Elena Cornaro Piscopia, 1646–84, who was the first woman to take a doctor's degree, in philosophy) lead up to the loggia where guided tours begin of the University (Monday, Wednes-day, and Friday 9.30, 10.30, 11.30, 15.30, and 17.30; in August only in the morning). Visitors are shown the *Museum*, with Galileo's 'cattedra', etc. and the *Anatomical Theatre* (1594), the most ancient in Europe, built by the surgeon Fabricius, master of William Harvey who took his degree here in 1602. Thomas Linacre (1492) and John Caius (1539) also qualified here as doctors. Among the famous medical professors were Vesalius (1540) and Fallopius (1561), and Galileo was teacher of physics from 1592 to 1610, among his pupils being Gustavus Adolphus of Sweden.

Opposite the University the E façade (1928–30; recently cleaned) of the *Municipio* disguises a 16C building, by Andrea Moroni, that incorporates a tower of the 13C Palazzo del Podestà. Beyond the Municipio, separating Piazza delle Erbe from Piazza delle Frutta stands *Palazzo della Ragione*, commonly called **Il Salone** (Pl. 10), a building of 1219, rebuilt in 1306 by *Fra Giovanni degli Eremitani*. The immense roof was reconstructed in 1756 after storm damage. A busy market now occupies part of the ground floor (and the adjoining piazze).

The entrance (open 9.30–12.30, 14.30–17.30; festivals 9.30–12.30; closed Mon-day, except when exhibitions are being mounted or dismantled) is by the right-hand staircase, towards the Municipio. The interior is one vast hall, 79 metres long, 27 metres wide, and 26 metres high. It contains a block of stone the 'pietra del vituperio', which once served as a stool of repentance for debtors, and a giant wooden horse, copied from that of Donatello (see below), made for a fête in 1466. On the walls are 333 interesting frescoes of religious and astrological subjects, by *Nicolò Miretto* and *Stefano da Ferrara*. These are reproductions painted shortly after a fire in 1420 had destroyed the originals by Giotto in 1420.

In Piazza delle Frutta are remains of the *Palazzo Consiglio* (1283), with two good Byzantine capitals, and *Palazzo degli Anziani* (1285). Via San Clemente leads W to PIAZZA DEI SIGNORI (Pl. 6), attractively enclosed by old buildings. To the left is the *Loggia della Gran*

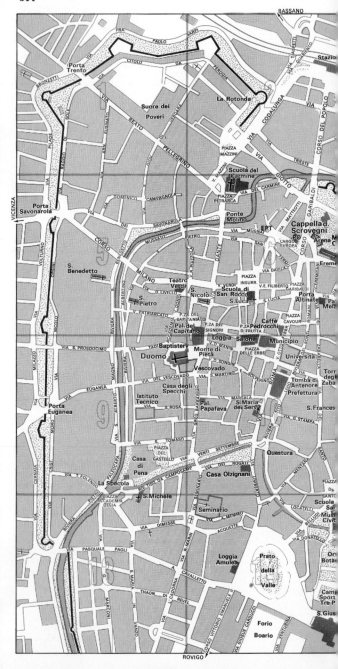

PADUA

| 0 | | 400 yards |
| 0 | | 400 metrès |

Guardia, a pretty Lombard edifice begun by Annibale Maggi (1496) and finished in 1523. On the W side of the square *Palazzo del Capitanio* (1599–1605) occupies the site of the castle of the Carraresi, of which a 14C portico survives just off Via Accademia (at No. 11). The palazzo incorporates a tower, adapted in 1532 by Giovanni Maria Falconetto to accommodate an astronomical clock dating from 1344 (the oldest in Italy). Beyond the Arco dell'Orologio lies the Corte Capitaniato, with the buildings of the arts faculty, the *Liviano* by Gio Ponti (1939). The entrance hall was frescoed by Massimo Campigli.

The building incorporates the *Sala dei Giganti* (open only by appointment, or for concerts) with frescoes of famous men by Domenico and Gualtiero Campagnolo, and Stefano dell'Arzere (1539). These were painted over earlier 14C frescoes, a fragment of which remains showing Petrarch reading in his study, possibly drawn from life since Petrarch lived nearby in Arquà in 1368–74. Formerly thought to be by Avanzo, this has recently been attributed to Altichiero.—On the top floor is the *Museo di Scienze Archeologiche e d'Arte* (closed since 1986), containing a headless Athena (4C BC), a wax mould after Donatello, and plaster statuettes by Ammannati.—Nearby, in Via Accademia (Pl. 5) is the beautiful *Loggia Carrarese*, seat of the *Accademia Patavina di Scienze, Lettere, ed Arti*. The former chapel here has frescoes of Old Testament scenes by Guariento (c 1360).

From Piazza Capitaniato, with a 16C Loggia and ancient acacias, the Corte Valaresso (fine staircase of 1607) leads under an arch of 1632 to Piazza del Duomo, with the Cathedral, Baptistery, and the Monte di Pietà of the 13–14C, remodelled with a portico by Giovanni Maria Falconetto in 1530. The **Cathedral** (Pl. 9) was reconstructed in 1552 by Andrea da Valle and Agostino Righetti to a design, much altered, of Michelangelo.

In the ponderous interior, the most interesting parts are the SACRISTY and crypt, shown by the sacristan. The former contains four Saints, from a triptych by *Giorgio Schiavone*, and a Descent from the Cross, by *Jacopo da Montagnana*. The TREASURY (adm. only with special permission from the Curia) here contains illuminated *MSS (12C and 13C), a Byzantine thurible (censer) of the 11C, a fine processional cross of 1228, and the large *Reliquary of the Cross, of silver gilt, with enamels, dating from c 1440.

The **Baptistery** (open 9.30–12.30, 14.30–17.30; fest. 9.30–12.30; closed Monday; summer: 9.30–12.30, 15–19; Sunday & Monday, 15–19) was built at the end of the 12C, and has Romanesque additions. The interior is entirely covered with *Frescoes by *Giusto de'Menabuoi*, his best work (beautifully restored in 1985). Carried out in 1378, this is one of the most interesting medieval fresco cycles in Italy. In the dome is Christ Pantocrater surrounded by angels and the Blessed; in the drum, scenes from Genesis; in the pendentives, the Evangelists; and on the walls, scenes from the life of Christ and St John the Baptist. In the apse, scenes from the Apocalypse. On the altar is a polyptych, also by *Giusto*.

To the S of the cathedral is the **Bishop's Palace**, with the *Museo Diocesano d'Arte Sacra* (open 9–12.30, except Thursday & festivals & in July & August). Here are portraits of bishops by *Montagna*, one of Petrarch, bronze reliefs by *Tiziano Aspetti* from the crypt of the cathedral, and a chapel with the *Annunciation, a fresco by *Jacopo da Montagna*. The adjoining *Chapter Library* preserves the treasury from the old cathedral at Monselice.—No. 79 in the neighbouring Via del Vescovado is the *Casa degli Specchi* or 'House of the Mirrors', so called from its tondi of polished marble, an early 16C Lombardesque building by Annibale Maggi.

Via Dante, with several good palazzi, passes E of the Romanesque church of *San Nicolò* and the *Teatro Verdi*. In Via Santa Lucia to the right are the church of *Santa Lucia* and the SCUOLA DI SAN ROCCO (Pl. 6), dating from 1480–1525 (reopened in 1990 after restoration), an attractive Renaissance building containing *Frescoes illustrating the life of St Roch, mainly by *Domenico and Gualtiero Campagnola*. The modern Piazza Insurrezione, beyond, is the centre of a rebuilt business quarter. Among the old houses in Via Santa Lucia, the so-called *Casa di Ezzelino*, on the right at the corner of Via Marsilio, is an interesting example of 12C work.

On the far side of Piazza Garibaldi opens the *Porta Altinate*, a gateway of the 13C town wall. The Augustinian church of the **Eremitani**, to the NE (Pl. 6), was built in 1276–1306, the façade being added in 1360. It was almost completely destroyed by bombing in 1944, but has been well rebuilt.

INTERIOR (usually entered from the S side; closed 12–15.30) contains some 14C tombs, and fragmentary remains of frescoes. SOUTH SIDE. 1st chapel, fresco fragments by *Giusto de'Menabuoi* (c 1370); 4th chapel, Madonna and Child and Ecce Homo by *Guariento*. The OVETARI CHAPEL, S of the sanctuary, contains all that remains of the famous frescoes by *Mantegna* (light on right), the destruction of which was the greatest individual disaster to Italian art in the Second World War. Behind the altar, *Assumption; (left) Martyrdom of St James (recomposed from the shattered fragments) and two fragmentary frescoes by *Giovanni di Camerino*; (right) *Martyrdom of St Christopher (detached and removed to safety before the War). Mantegna worked on them between 1454 (when he was only 23) and 1457. Here, too, is an altarpiece of the Madonna and Saints in the style of Donatello.—In the SANCTUARY, the frescoes on the left wall of Saints Philip, James, and Augustine, are by *Guariento*. The Giottesque frescoes in the CAPPELLA SANGUINACCI left of the sanctuary, include some by *Giusto de'Menabuoi* (1373).—On the NORTH SIDE are two polychrome altarpieces by *Giovanni Minello* and his school (early 16C), and the mausoleum of the law-professor Marco Benavides (1489–1582), by *Bartolomeo Ammannati* (1546).

The convent of the church was rebuilt and modernised in 1985, after years of controversy, to house the **Museo Civico** (adm. 9–dusk; closed Monday; inclusive ticket with the Cappella degli Scrovegni, see below), which is in the process of being transferred from its old seat near the Santo. So far only the archaeological section, the collection of Renaissance bronzes, and the Museo Bottacin are on view here. The important large collection of *Paintings will probably be on display here by the end of 1990; meanwhile they are still on view at the old museum in Piazza del Santo (see below). Beside the church façade, the construction of a big new entrance was blocked by the Italian authorities; it is to be hoped that the shell, half-built, will be demolished.

The museum is on two floors and is still in the course of arrangement (the exhibits are well labelled). GROUND FLOOR. Rooms 5–21 contain the Archaeological Collections. Rooms 5 and 6. Finds from pre-Roman and Roman tombs in Padua. These include *Stele, vases, and small bronzes (6C–2C BC). Room 9 contains statues from 3C AD, and a notable *Bust of Silenus (2C AD). Room 11 has several large mosaics from Roman Padua (1C–6C AD). The next room (12) has an imposing aedicular *Tomb of the Volumnii family, dating from the Augustan period (restored in 1988).—Rooms 13 and 14 contain a small but interesting collection of Egyptian antiquities including two *Statues of the Goddess Sekhmet in black basalt, given to the city by Giovanni Battista Belzoni in 1819, and a display relating to his activities in Egypt (see above).—Rooms 15–18 contain Etruscan pottery, and in Room 20 are paleochristian artefacts.

FIRST FLOOR. The **Museo Bottacin** here, in a temporary arrangement, contains coins and Renaissance medals (including works by Pisanello); also a number of 19C paintings and sculptures purchased by Nicola Bottacin between 1850–75, interesting as a reflection of Italian taste of the period.— The collection of Renaissance bronzes contains notable works of the 15–16C by l'Antico, Il Riccio (*Drinking Satyr), Desiderio da Firenze (voting urn for the city council of Padua), and Francesco Segala. The **Museo Emo Capodilista**, an eclectic collection of Venetian and Flemish works (16–18C), is soon to be displayed here.

Beside the Museo Civico, in a garden enclosed by the ruined walls of a Roman amphitheatre (1C AD), is the ****Cappella degli Scrovegni** (Pl. 6; adm. through the Museo Civico with an inclusive ticket; for opening times, see above). This simple little chapel (also known as the *Arena Chapel*) was built for Enrico Scrovegni in 1303 in expiation for his father's usury (see Dante, 'Inferno', xvii, 64–75), adjoining the Scrovegni Palace, demolished in the last century. The façade is covered for restoration in 1989. It contains famous frescoes painted by *Giotto* at the height of his power (1303–05). Giotto may have designed the chapel himself to contain the fresco cycle, which is the only one by him to survive intact.

Giotto's influence on all subsequent Italian painting can here be understood to the full: his painting has a new monumentality and sense of volume which had never been achieved in medieval painting. The Biblical narrative is given here for the first time an intensely human significance. Bernard Berenson pointed out that his figures have remarkable 'tactile values'. The superb colouring is extremely well preserved (the frescoes were last restored in 1887). The frescoes are arranged in three bands and depict the history of Christian redemption through the life of Mary and Christ. They were painted in chronological order: the cycle begins on the top band of the S wall (nearest to the triumphal arch). The subjects are: 1. Expulsion of Joachim from the Temple; 2. Joachim among the shepherds; 3. Annunciation to Anna; 4. Sacrifice of Joachim; 5. Vision of Joachim; 6. Meeting of Joachim and Anna at the Golden Gate.—N Wall (W end): 7. Birth of the Virgin; 8. Presentation of the Virgin in the temple; 9. Presentation of the Rods to Simeon; 10. Watching of the Rods; 11. Betrothal of the Virgin; 12. The Virgin's return home.—Triumphal Arch: 13. God the Father dispatching Gabriel; 14. Annunciation; 15. Visitation.—S Wall (middle band): 16. Nativity; 17. Adoration of the Magi; 18. Presentation of Christ in the Temple; 19. Flight into Egypt; 20. Massacre of the Innocents.—N wall: 21. Christ disputing with the Elders; 22. Baptism of Christ; 23. Marriage at Cana; 24. Raising of Lazarus; 25. Entry into Jerusalem; 26. Expulsion of the money-changers from the Temple.—Triumphal arch: 27. The pact of Judas.—S wall (lower band): 28. Last Supper; 29. Washing of the Feet; 30. Betrayal of Christ; 31. Christ before Caiaphas; 32. Mocking of Christ.—N wall: 33. Way to Calvary; 34. Crucifixion; 35. Deposition; 36. Angel at the empty tomb and Noli me tangere; 37. Ascension; 38. Pentecost.—On the entrance wall, Last Judgement (covered in 1989). The bands at the end and separating the panels are decorated with busts of Saints and Doctors, and Scenes from the Old Testament, mainly by Giotto's assistants; the ceiling medallions show Jesus, the Virgin, and the Prophets. The lowest range of paintings consists of beautiful monochrome allegorical figures of Virtues and Vices, also by Giotto.—In the apse are frescoes by followers of Giotto; on the altar are statues of the Virgin and two saints, by *Giovanni Pisano*. Behind the latter is the tomb of the founder, Enrico Scrovegni, by *Andreolo de'Santi*.

From Piazza Garibaldi (see above) Via Altinate leads E past *Palazzo Melandri* (No. 18), with a beautiful four-light window, and *San Gaetano*, a pleasant church by Scamozzi (1586), to **Santa Sofia** (Pl. 11), the oldest church in Padua. Founded in the 9C on an earlier structure, it was rebuilt in the 11–12C in a Romanesque style recalling earlier churches of the Adriatic exarchate. The apse is remarkable.

From the Eremitani, Corso Garibaldi and Corso del Popolo continue N to the Station. To the left Via Giotto and Via del Carmine lead to the church of the *Carmini* (Pl. 2, 6) at the top of Via Dante. The sacristan will show the adjacent **Scuola del Carmine** (1377), with frescoes attributed to *Giulio* and *Domenico*

Campagnola, notably the *Meeting of St Anne and St Joachim.—The road from the Carmini to the station passes the *Bastione della Gatta*, where the Paduans made a heroic resistance to the Austrians in the siege of 1509.—A little N of the station (to the right of the Castelfranco road) is the *Santuario dell'Arcella*, with a 19C church enclosing the cell where St Anthony died in 1231.

The Riviera dei Ponti Romani, from the Eremitani, meets Via San Francesco at the SE corner of the University. At their junction stands the alleged *Tomb of Antenor*, a marble sarcophagus erected in 1233 on short columns; another sarcophagus (1309) was set up here on the 2000th anniversary of Livy's birth. Straight ahead, beyond Via del Santo, are the 13C *Torre degli Zabarella* and the church of *San Francesco* (Pl. 10; 1416; restored), containing the *Monument of Pietro Roccabonella, natural philosopher, by Bartolomeo Bellano and Il Riccio (1496–7; SE chapel).—Via del Santo leads S to PIAZZA DEL SANTO (Pl. 10, 14) in which stands the equestrian *Statue of Gattamelata** (Erasmo da Narni, the Venetian condottiere, died 1443), a masterpiece by *Donatello* (1453), and the first great Renaissance bronze equestrian monument cast in Italy.

The *Basilica of Sant'Antonio** (Pl. 11; open all day, 6.30–19), usually called simply *Il Santo*, was begun in 1232 (on the site of the 12C church of Santa Maria Mater Domini) as a temple for the tomb of St Anthony of Padua, and finished in the 14C. It is now one of the great pilgrim shrines of Italy.

EXTERIOR. The six spherical domes in the Byzantine manner, the cone of the central cupola, and the two minaret-like campanili give an oriental appearance to the church. The bronze doors (1895) and the frescoes of Franciscan saints in the portal are recent additions and the fresco above the principal doorway is a modern copy (see below).

The magnificent INTERIOR, though Gothic in plan and detail, is Byzantine in inspiration. It contains many important sculptures. In the NAVE the first two piers on either side have holy-water stoups with statues of Christ, by *Aspetti* (left) and St John the Baptist (right), by *Tullio Lombardo*; against the left pier, tomb of Alessandro Contarini (died 1553), the Venetian general, an elaborate work by *Sanmicheli*, with a bust by *Danese Cattaneo* and statues by *Vittoria*. Opposite (on the inside of the pillar) is the tomb of Cardinal Bembo, who died in 1547, recently attributed to *Palladio*, with a bust by *Danese Cattaneo*.—On the S side: 1st chapel, monuments of Erasmo Gattamelata (died 1443), by *Bellano*, and of his son Giannantonio (died 1455) by *Pietro Lombardo*. In the S transept is the *CHAPEL OF ST FELIX, designed in 1372–77 by *Andriolo* and *Giovanni De Santi*, with *Frescoes by *Altichiero*. —In the N transept is the *CHAPEL OF ST ANTHONY, with the tomb (much revered) of St Anthony of Padua (died 1231) behind the altar. Pilgrims come from all over Italy to touch the green marble sarcophagus, and many leave ex votos in the chapel.

The chapel was probably designed by *Tullio Lombardo* in 1499, but executed by *Giovanni Minello*, and completed by *Falconetto* in 1546. High up on the entrance-screen are statues of the patron saints of Padua, among which that of St Justina, on the left, by Giovanni Minello, is particularly fine. The nine large classical *Reliefs of the miracles of St Anthony (with perspectives of Padua above) which line the walls are (left to right) by *Antonio Minello*; *Giovanni Rubino* and *Silvio Cosini*; *Girolamo Campagna*; *Jacopo Sansovino*; *Antonio Minello* and *Sansovino*; *Tullio Lombardo* (two); *Giovanni Maria Mosca* and

Paolo Stella; and *Antonio Lombardo. Tiziano Aspetti* made the statues on the altar (1593).

The adjoining CONTI CHAPEL is dedicated to the Blessed Luca Belludi, St Anthony's companion, who is buried here. It is decorated with frescoes (damaged, but recently restored) by *Giusto de'Menabuoi.*—In the N aisle are the Baroque tomb of General Caterino Cornaro, by *Juste le Court* (1674) and that of Antonio Roselli (died 1466), by *Pietro Lombardo*; and in the westernmost bay is a Madonna, painted by *Stefano da Ferrara* (?) facing the tomb of Antonio Trombetta (died 1518), by *Il Riccio*.

The bronze doors of the CHOIR are by *Camillo Mazza* (1661), the four statues on the balustrade by *Aspetti* (1593). The magnificent *HIGH ALTAR (the sanctuary gates are unlocked on request by the uniformed custodians), sculpted by *Donatello* and his assistants in 1445–50, has suffered many vicissitudes and its present arrangement dates from 1895.

Above 12 reliefs of angel musicians and a Pietà, are four reliefs (two on the front and two on the back) of *Miracles of St Anthony, and a small Christ in Pietà. At the ends, symbols of the Evangelists. The altar is crowned with the Madonna enthroned surmounted by the *Crucifixion, between statues of the six patron saints of Padua (left to right: St Louis of Anjou, St Giustina, St Francis, St Anthony, St Daniel, and St Prosdocimus). Behind is a *Deposition in stone.—On the left of the altar is a paschal *Candelabrum, the most important work of *Il Riccio* (1507–15). On the wall of the choir are 12 small bronze *Reliefs of Old Testament scenes by *Bellano* and *Il Riccio*. The decorations of the apse date from 1926.

A Rococo chapel at the E end of the ambulatory houses the *Treasury (open 8–12, 14.30–19) containing more than 100 reliquaries.—The ceiling-painting in the SACRISTY, by *Pietro Liberi* (1615), shows the Entry of St Anthony into Paradise. In the adjoining *Chapter House* are fragmentary frescoes after *Giotto.*—To the S of the church are four CLOISTERS (entered from the N side of the church), with many tombstones and monuments. In the first cloister a modest slab on the N side marks the burial-place of the entrails of Thomas Howard (1586–1646), earl of Surrey and Arundel, collector of the 'Arundel Marbles'; in the second a bust commemorates Giuseppe Tartini (1692–1770) who returned to die in Padua from where he had eloped in 1713 with a daughter of the Premazzone family. From here steps lead up (past the original stone reliefs from the base of the Gattamelata monument, see above) to the **Biblioteca Antoniana** (9–12, 14.30 or 15–16.30 or 17; closed Saturday & Sunday) which contains many MSS and incunabula, including a MS of sermons annotated in St Anthony's handwriting. The *Museo Antoniano* has been closed indefinitely, although a collection of ex votos is on view in the cloisters. The fresco of Saints Anthony and Bernard adoring the monogram of Christ, by Mantegna (1452) from the lunette of the main W door, is preserved in the *Presidenza* (First Cloister; sometimes shown on request).

In Piazza del Santo are the **Scuola del Santo** and the **Oratorio di San Giorgio** (Pl. 14; inclusive ticket; 9–12.30, 14.30–16.30 or 18.30). A hand-list is lent to visitors. The Scuola, built in 1427–31 (with an upper storey of 1504) is approached by a pretty flight of stairs (1736). The paintings (1511) of the life of St Anthony are by *Francesco Vecellio, Girolamo Tessari, Filippo da Verona, Bartolomeo Montagna, Gianantonio Corona, Domenico Campagnola*, and others. Nos 12 and 13 are early works by *Titian* (and Nos 1 and 2 are attributed to him). The seated statue of the Madonna and Child in polychrome terracotta is by *Il Riccio* (1520). The *Oratory next door (unlocked on request by the custodian), originally the mausoleum of the Soranzo family, is entirely covered with *Frescoes by *Altichiero di Zevio* and *Jacopo Avanzo* (Lives of Saints George, Catherine, and Lucy, and scenes from the life of Christ, 1378–84).

In the corner of the piazza is the ***Museo Civico** (Pl. 14; open 9–13.30; fest. 9.30–13; closed Monday), in an unusual building of 1870–80, with a façade by Camillo Boito. The museum is in the process of being transferred to a new building near the Cappella degli Scrovegni (see above). In 1989 the paintings were still in this building; when they are moved to the new site, this building, part of the convent of Sant'Antonio, may be used for the Museo Antoniano (see above).

In the entrance hall and on the stairs are three frescoes detached from the Oratorio di San Michele (see below) by *Jacopo da Verona*. FIRST FLOOR. ROOM 1. Frescoes (very ruined) attributed to *Pietruccio da Rimini*, from the Eremitani convent; *Paolo Veneziano*, Madonna and Child; *Giotto*, *Crucifix (from the Scrovegni Chapel); *Guariento*, *Angel panels; *Michele Giambono*, Saints; *Francesco dei Franceschi*, Polyptych; *15C Paduan School*, Madonna and Child.—RII. 15C tapestry from Arras; Faience ware.—Works by Paduan and Venetian painters of the 15C and early 16C: *Lorenzo Costa* (attributed), The Argonauts; *Alvise Vivarini*, Portrait of a man; *Giovanni Bellini* (attributed), Madonna and St John the Baptist; *Andrea Previtali*, Madonna and donor (1502); *Giorgione* (attributed), two tiny paintings: *Leda and the Swan, and *Figures in a landscape; *Giovanni Bellini*, Portrait of a young senator, St Catherine; *Palma Vecchio* (attributed), Portrait of a Poetess; *Titian* (attributed), Two cassone panels with mythological scenes.—Works by *Boccaccio Boccaccino*; *Francesco Torbido*, Portrait of a shepherd.—*Bonifazio Veronese*, Madonna and Saints.—RIII. *Veronese*, Last Supper; *Leandro Bassano*, several typical works.—RIV. Works by *Padovanino*, and a fine collection of Venetian ceramics.—RV. Works by *Pietro Liberi*, *Pietro Vecchia*, *Monsù Bernardo*, and *Onofrio Gabrielli*. Between this and RVI, terracottas by *Briosco* and *Guido Mazzoni*.—RVI, a large hall with a huge 15C tapestry has large works by *Campagnola*, Baptism of St Justina, Madonna and Saints; *Girolamo del Santo*, Descent from the Cross; and works by *Giovanni da Asola* and *Stefano dell'Arzere* (Calvary). *Palma Giovane*, Two magistrates of the Soranzo family, an allegory; *Tintoretto*, Jesus in the Pharisee's house (signed and dated); and *Veronese*, Martyrdom of St Justina; *Romanino*, Madonna enthroned; portraits by *Domenico Tintoretto* and *Leandro Bassano* (Doge Andrea Memmo).—A small room contains eight paintings of mythological subjects by *Jacopo Tintoretto*, restored in 1980 and left to the museum in 1984.—RRVIII–IX. Works by *Zais*, *Giovanni Battista Piazzetta*, and *Antonio Marini*.—RX. *Giovanni Battista Tiepolo*, St Patrick casting out a devil; *Alessandro Longhi*, Jacopo Gradenigo (c 1778), a typical Venetian of the decadence; *Pietro Longhi*, Geography lesson.—The Museum Library (200,000 volumes) has been moved to No. 5 Via Orto Botanico.
In Via Cesarotti is Palazzo Giusti del Giardino, with the *Loggia and Odeon Cornaro* by Falconetto (1524–30); closed for restoration in 1990.

Beyond the Museum is the ***Botanic Garden** (Pl. 14; open 9–13; May–September, also 15–18; fest. closed except in April–September when it is open 9.30–13; Saturday and fest. afternoons always closed), the most ancient in Europe, founded in 1545, and retaining its original form and structure. It has a charming circular walled garden and some fine old trees and interesting hothouses. A palm-tree, planted in 1585, and known as 'Goethe's palm' (he visited the garden in 1786) survives in a little greenhouse. Here the lilac was first cultivated in 1565, the sunflower in 1568, and the potato in 1590.—Via Beato Luca Belludi leads W (with an interesting Art Nouveau house at No. 3) to the pleasant PRATO DELLA VALLE (Pl. 14), the largest 'piazza' in Italy surrounded by a miscellany of arcaded buildings. This huge area has been used since Roman times for public spectacles, fairs, etc. In the centre is the *Isola Memmia*, encircled by a canal bordered by 18C statues (some of them being restored) of famous citizens, professors, and students of the University. On the W side of the Prato is the two-storeyed *Loggia Amulea*

(1861) with statues of Giotto and Dante by Vincenzo Vela (1865), and
on the S side the monumental entrance to the former Foro Boario, now
used as a car park and stadium.

The Benedictine church of **Santa Giustina** (Pl. 14), designed by *Il
Riccio* in 1502 but modified by its builder *Andrea Moroni*, recalls by its
eight cupolas the exotic aspect of Sant'Antonio.

The huge cruciform interior is decorated in the Baroque manner, with altarpieces to match, and presents an epitome of 17C Venetian art. In the nave, model
15C Crucifix. SOUTH AISLE. 2nd chapel, *Pietro Liberi*, Ecstasy of St Gertrude; 3rd
chapel, *Carlo Loth*, Martyrdom of St Gerard; 4th chapel, *Luca Giordano*, Death
of St Scolastica; 6th chapel (behind the altar), reliefs by *Giovanni Francesco de
Surdis*.—SOUTH TRANSEPT. Arca of St Matthew, with reliefs by *Giovanni
Francesco de Surdis*. Behind is a corridor which leads to a well beside an unusual
iron sarcophagus beneath a cupola frescoed by *Giacomo Ceruti*. In the niches
are four terracotta statues by *Francesco Segala* (1564–5). Beyond a painting of
the Discovery of the well here by *Pietro Damini* and two more statues by
Francesco Segala, is the domed cruciform CHAPEL OF SANTA MARIA (also
dedicated to St Prosdocimus, first bishop of Padua), an oratory built c 520, with a
rare contemporary iconostasis, with an inscription. Also here are a double
pluteus and tympanum (both 6C). On the altar, effigy of St Prosdocimus (1564),
and above, a relief of the Saint (late 5C or early 6C).—From the 9th chapel
(beyond the transept) a door leads into another corridor, off which is the
CAPITOLO VECCHIO with fragmentary frescoes of the translation of the body of St
Luke by *Giovanni Storlato*, the only known work by this artist (1436–41). Here
Elena Cornaro Piscopia (see above) is buried.—From the corridor a door (not
always open) leads to the long Monks' corridor with sculptural fragments. Off
this is the CORO VECCHIO, the old choir built in 1472, with inlaid stalls, and a fine
15C statue of St Justina. Beyond, in the Ante-Sacristy is a fine terracotta seated
statue of the Madonna and Child (late 15C), and the carved architrave of a 13C
door.—In the chapel to the right of the Sanctuary (restored in 1990), Pietà,
carved by *Filippo Parodi*.—In the SANCTUARY the *Choir-stalls are elaborately
carved by the Norman *Riccardo Taurigny*, with the help of Vicentine craftsmen.
The high altarpiece of the Martyrdom of St Justina, is by *Paolo Veronese*
(1575).—In the chapel left of the Sanctuary, the Baroque altar is by *Giuseppe
Sardi*, and the frescoes in the apse by *Sebastiano Ricci*.—In the SOUTH TRANSEPT,
carved arca of St Luke, dating from 1313, and (left wall), Fall of Manna, by
Francesco Maffei.—SOUTH AISLE. 4th chapel, *Luca Giordano*, Martyrdom of St
Placido; 2nd chapel, *Sebastiano Ricci*, St Gregory the Great.

In Via Umberto I (Pl. 10), leading back from the piazza towards the
centre, No. 82 is the old feudal palace of the Capodilista, with high
arcades and a tower, and No. 8 is the *Casa Olzignani*, a fine example
of early Lombardesque architecture (1466; in poor repair). Across a
bridge is Via Roma and (left) the Gothic church of *Santa Maria dei
Servi* (1372–92, restored 1930), with a fine doorway and a 16C portico.
It contains (in a small tabernacle to the right of a Baroque altar by
Giovanni Bonazza) a frescoed Pietà by Jacopo da Montagnana, and
the monument of the brothers De Castro, by Bartolomeo Bellano,
above the sacristy entrance. Via Marsala leads left to (No. 35) the
Baroque *Palazzo Papafava*, now a police station.

Via Giovanni Barbarigo, to the left beyond the palazzo, leads to the SW district,
which contains some buildings of interest. Via Venti Settembre ends (right) at
Piazza del Castello (Pl. 9), with some remains of the *Castle* (now a prison) built by
Ezzelino da Romano; one tower is surmounted by an observatory ('La Specola';
1767). Beyond the bridge, in the Riviera Tiso, is the *Oratorio di San Michele* (if
closed, ring at No. 27), with remains of frescoes by Jacopo da Verona (1397).
Three of the best preserved frescoes have been detached and are now in the
Museo Civico.

FROM PADUA TO VENICE the motorway (20km) and the main railway to Venice
follow a dead straight line across the plain towards Mestre. Much more
interesting is the old road along the Brenta described in Rte 33.

The railways from Padua to *Cittadella* (33km) and *Bassano* (48km in c 1hr), and to *Castelfranco* (31km) and *Montebelluna* (48km in 1hr) diverge at (19km) *Camposampiero*.—The bus to *Carmignano*, serves (18km) the modern industrial town of *Piazzola sul Brenta*, with the imposing Villa Camerini (in the Palladian style, with a fine park; adm. on application), and (25km) *Isola Mantegna*, the birthplace of Andrea Mantegna (1431–1506).

From Padua to *Abano* (for the Euganean Hills) and *Ferrara*, see Rte 37.

32   Venice

VENICE, in Italian **Venezia**, with 334,000 inhabitants, stands on an archipelago of 117 islets or shoals, 4·2km from the mainland and 2km from the open sea, whose force is broken by the natural breakwater of the Lido. The population of the commune includes Mestre; that of the historic centre being now only 80,000 compared with the 200,000 it had when the republic was at its zenith. A unique position, the grace of her buildings, the changing colours of the lagoon, and not least the total absence of wheeled transport make Venice the most charming and poetic city in the world. The Republic of the 'Serenissima' founded in the 8C survived until 1797, and was one of the most glorious in history. The city is subject to periodic floods from exceptionally high tides (the 'acque alte'), and the delicate ecological balance of the lagoon is threatened by pollution. A special law was passed in 1973, and renewed in 1984, by the Italian government to safeguard the city, but in 1990 measures to prevent the flood tides, and clean the polluted lagoon, were still at an experimental stage. Meanwhile committees funded from various countries have been working in conjunction with the Italian authorities for many years on the restoration of buildings.— **For a full description of the city, see 'Blue Guide Venice'.**

Topography. The irregular plan of Venice is traversed by some 100 canals of which the *Grand Canal* divides the city into two unequal parts. The other canals, called *Rii* (singular, *Rio*), with the exception of the *Cannaregio*, have an average breadth of 4–5 metres and are spanned by c 400 bridges, mostly of brick or stone. The streets, nearly all very narrow, are called *Calle*; the more important thoroughfares, usually shopping streets, are known as *Calle Larga*, *Ruga*, or *Salizzada*. Smaller alleys are called *Caletta* or *Ramo*. A street alongside a canal is called a *Fondamenta*; a *Rio terrà* is a street on the course of a filled-in rio. A *Sottoportico* or *Sottoportego* passes beneath buildings. The only *Piazza* is that of St Mark; there are two *Piazzette*, one in front of the Doges' Palace, the other the Piazzetta dei Leoncini (now Giovanni XXIII). Other open spaces are called *Campo* or *Campiello*, according to their size. Names of streets and canals are written up on the walls in the Venetian dialect.—Houses are numbered consecutively throughout each of the six 'sestieri' into which the city is divided (San Marco, Castello, Dorsoduro, San Polo, Santa Croce, and Cannaregio).

The city is supported on piles of Istrian pine, driven down about 7·5m to a solid bed of compressed sand and clay, and many of her buildings are built upon a foundation course of Istrian limestone, which withstands the corrosion of the sea. Her prosperity as a port is due to the diversion of silt-bearing rivers to N and S of the lagoon, still effected by channels dug in the 14–15C; and her very existence depends on the control of the eroding waters of the Adriatic, which are allowed to flow into the lagoon by only three channels. This work, under special supervision as early as the 12C, has been performed since 1501 by a board presided over by the Magistrato alle Acque. Despite these precautions, the city suffered the worst flood for nearly a century in 1966. There is a long-term plan to control the flood tides by moveable barriers at the three entrances to the lagoon, and in 1988 an experimental model of a flood prevention gate was installed on the bed of the lagoon at the Lido entrance.

Information Office. *A.P.T.* (Pl. 11), 71C Calle Ascensione (on the corner of Piazza San Marco); branch offices at the Railway Station, and the Marghera exit from the Milan autostrada.

Airport. *Marco Polo* on the lagoon, 9km N of Venice. *Terminal* at Piazzale Roma (coach service); motor-boats are usually run in connection with scheduled flights to the Giardinetti (near San Marco). Taxis also available to Piazzale Roma.

Railway Station. *Santa Lucia* (Pl. 5) near the W end of the Grand Canal, with 'albergo diurno', left luggage office, etc. Water-buses, motor-boat taxis, and gondolas from the quay outside.

Car Parks and Bus Station. Motorists approaching the city have to leave their vehicles in a multi-storey garage or an open-air car park (charges according to the size of the vehicle; the rates are per day). *Parking space is very limited especially in summer.* The most convenient multi-storey garages are at *Piazzale Roma*; garages and huge open-air car parks also at *Isola del Tronchetto*. Frequent vaporetti services (see below) serve all of these. In summer, at Easter, and Carnival time open air car parking is usually available also at *San Giuliano* and *Fusina* (with vaporetto services).—The BUS STATION is at Piazzale Roma.

Porters (distinguished by their badges) are available in various parts of the city; tariffs should be established before engaging one.

Water-buses. An excellent service is run by A.C.T.V. Tickets can be bought at landing-stages; the most convenient way is to purchase a book of tickets which have to be stamped at automatic machines on the landing-stages before each journey. The **'Vaporetti'** are more comfortable and provide better views for the visitor than the smaller and faster **'Motoscafi'**. Most of the services run at frequent intervals (every 10 minutes). Tourist tickets may be purchased giving free transport on any line for one day. A 'Carta Venezia', which entitles the holder to greatly reduced fares, can be purchased (photograph necessary) at the A.C.T.V. office in Corte dell'Albero, Sant'Angelo. The main services include:

1. 'ACCELERATO'; the line most frequently used which runs along the Grand Canal. It operates every 10 minutes by day, and also throughout the night c every hour. It takes c 1hr with 22 stops between Tronchetto and the Lido: *Tronchetto A Car Park–Tronchetto B Car Park–Piazzale Roma* (Car Park)*–Ferrovia* (Railway Station)*–Riva di Biasio–San Marcuola–San Stae* (Ca' Pesaro)*–Ca' d'Oro–Rialto–San Silvestro–Sant'Angelo–San Tomà* (Frari)*–Ca' Rezzonico–Accademia–Santa Maria del Giglio–Santa Maria della Salute–San Marco* (Vallaresso)*–San Zaccaria–Arsenale–Giardini–Sant'Elena–Lido.*

2. 'DIRETTO', the motoscafo which takes the short cut to the Station and Piazzale Roma along the Rio Nuovo (every 10 minutes; night service in summer only at less frequent intervals). *Rialto–San Marcuolo–Ferrovia–Piazzale Roma–San Samuele–Accademia–San Marco* (Vallaresso)*–San Zaccaria–Sant'Elena–Lido.*

5. 'CIRCOLARE SINISTRA' and 'CIRCOLARE DESTRA'. Two services which provide a left circular and a right circular route of the city: *Murano–San Michele* (Cimitero)*–Fondamente Nuove–Ospedale Civile–Celestia–Campo della Tana* (Arsenal)*–San Zaccaria–Isola di San Giorgio Maggiore–Zitelle–Redentore–Sant'Eufemia–Zattere–San Basilio–Sacca Fisola–Santa Marta–Piazzale Roma–Ferrovia–Ponte Guglie* (Cannaregio Canal)*–Ponte Tre Archi–Sant'Alvise–Madonna dell'Orto–Fondamente Nuove–San Michele* (Cimitero)*–Murano.*

6. *Riva Schiavoni–Lido* (direct), by steamer.

8. *San Zaccaria–Isola di San Giorgio Maggiore–Zitelle–Traghetto–Zattere–Sant'Eufemia–San Basilio–Sacca Fisola–Santa Marta.*

9. 'Traghetto', the ferry across the Giudecca canal: *Zattere–Giudecca* (near Sant'Eufemia).

12. The regular service for the islands of Burano and Torcello, every 1–1½hrs in c 40 minutes: *Fondamente Nuove–Murano* (Faro)*–Mazzorbo–Torcello–Burano–Treporti.*

Other less frequent services run to the minor islands.—Among the summer services is the 'TURISTICO' (No. **34**), a service for visitors from Tronchetto along the Grand Canal to the Lido (but with fewer stops than the Accelerato No. 1). Every 20 minutes in c 40 minutes. *Tronchetto–Piazzale Roma–Ferrovia–Rialto–San Tomà* (Frari)*–Accademia–San Marco* (Vallaresso)*–San Zaccaria–Giardini* (when the 'Biennale' is open)*–Lido.*

CAR FERRY (No. **17**) from *Piazzale Roma* (Tronchetto) via the Giudecca canal to the *Lido* (San Nicolò), c every hour in 30 minutes.

Taxis (motor-boats) charge by distance and tariffs are officially fixed, although it is always wise to establish the fare before hiring one. Taxi-stands on the quays in front of the Station, Piazzale Roma, Rialto, San Marco, etc.

Gondolas are now almost exclusively used for pleasure (mostly by visitors). They are for hire for 50 minute periods and the tariffs are fixed, but it is advisable to establish the fare before starting the journey. Gondola stands at the Station, Piazzale Roma, Calle Vallaresso (San Marco), Riva degli Schiavoni, etc.

Gondola ferries (*Traghetti*) cross the Grand Canal in several places. They are a cheap and pleasant way of getting about in Venice and provide the opportunity to board a gondola to those who cannot afford to hire one (passengers usually stand for the short journey).

Hotels near San Marco, the Rialto bridge, and the Station. Others in quieter and often more attractive positions away from these areas (i.e. Dorsoduro). Prices are raised from 1 April and at Christmas. Booking facilities at the *Associazione Veneziano Albergatori (A.V.A.)* offices on arrival at the Station and Piazzale Roma. It is advisable to book well in advance, especially in summer and at Easter.—The *Venice Youth Hostel* is on the Giudecca (Fondamenta Zitelle) in a good position.

Local Buses from Piazzale Roma to *Mestre, Marghera*, the *Airport*, and *Malcontenta*. Long-distance coaches to *Padua* (via the autostrada or via the Brenta) *Asiago, Trieste, Vicenza*, etc.—For the '*Burchiello*' motor-launch to *Padua*, see Rte 31.

Theatres. *La Fenice*, Campo San Fantin, one of the most famous opera-houses in Italy.—PROSE THEATRES: *Goldoni, Del Ridotto, L'Avogaria*. Concerts are often given in churches (including La Pietà), and organ recitals held in St Mark's in summer.

The BIENNALE (held in even years) is one of the most famous international exhibitions of Modern Art; it is held in the Giardini Pubblici in permanent pavilions. Every other year smaller exhibitions are held.

The CASINÒ is open in summer at the Lido, with gaming rooms. In winter it operates at Palazzo Vendramin on the Grand Canal.

Annual Festivals. *Carnival time*, the period preceding Shrove Tuesday and Lent, is now celebrated for about a month by merrymakers in fancy-dress and masks. Numerous theatrical and musical events also take place in this period. In the last week the city is exceptionally crowded. The '*Vogalonga*' takes place on a Sunday in May. Any type or size of boat may participate with any number of oarsmen in each boat along the course of 32 kilometres.—On the *Festa del Redentore* (3rd Sunday in July) a bridge of boats is usually constructed across the Giudecca canal. Its vigil is celebrated with a firework display.—The *Festa della Salute* (21 November) is also usually celebrated by a bridge of boats across the Grand Canal. At the *Regata Storica* (1st Sunday in September) processions and races are held.

A. Piazza San Marco, the Basilica of San Marco, and the Palazzo Ducale

In ****Piazza San Marco** (Pl. 11) some of the most important events in the history of the Venetian Republic were celebrated and it remains the centre of Venetian life. Napoleon commented that it was 'the finest drawing room in Europe'. It is enclosed on three sides by the uniform façades of stately public buildings; in the arcades beneath, the elegant cafés have tables outside grouped around their orchestra podiums. The colonnades open out towards the east end of the Piazza and the fantastic façade of the Basilica of San Marco. In front of the church tall flagstaffs rise from elaborate pedestals cast in bronze by Alessandro Leopardi (1505). Near the Piazzetta Giovanni XXIII the

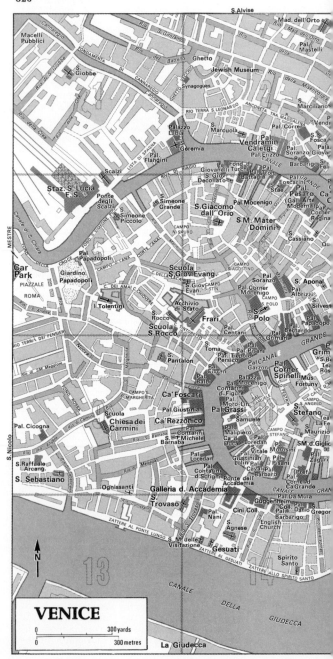

VENICE

0 _____ 300 yards
0 _____ 300 metres

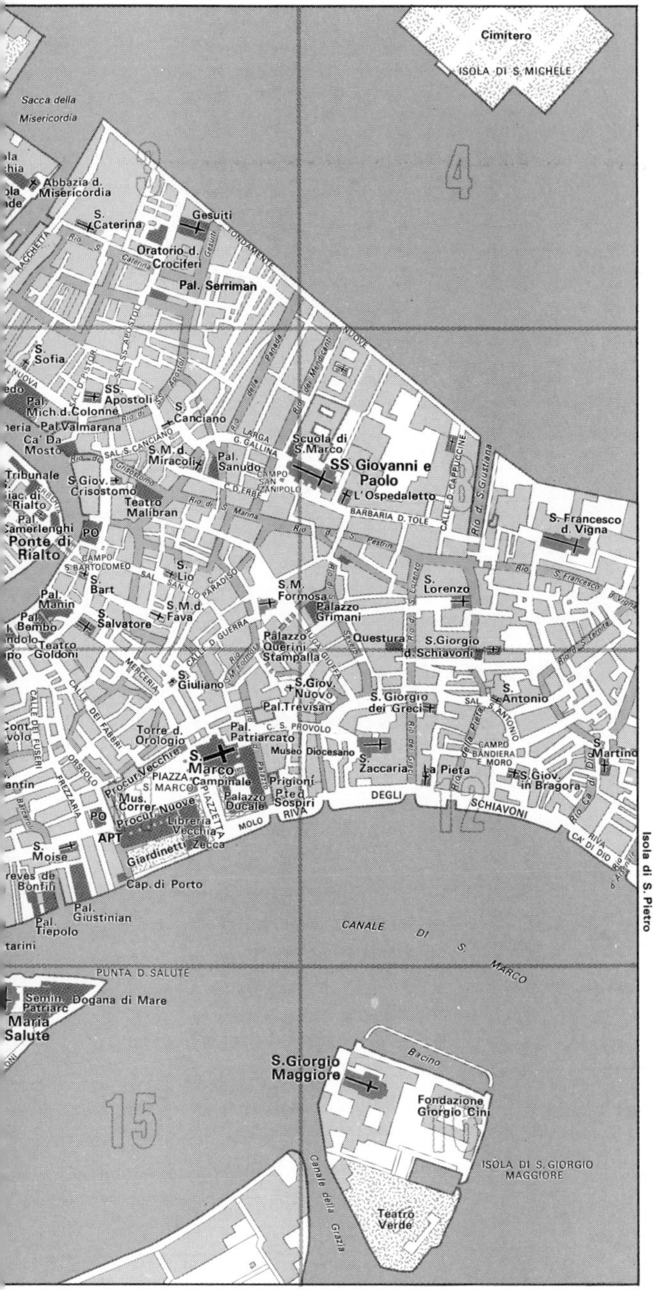

Cimitero
ISOLA DI S. MICHELE

Sacca della Misericordia

Abbazia d. Misericordia

S. Caterina
Gesuiti
Oratorio d. Crociferi
Pal. Serriman

S. Sofia
SS. Apostoli
Pal. Mich. d. Colonne
Pal. Valmarana
Ca' Da Mosto
S. M. d. Miracoli
Pal. Sanudo
S. Canciano
S. Giov. Crisostomo
Teatro Malibran

Scuola di S. Marco
SS Giovanni e Paolo
L'Ospedaletto
BARBARIA D. TOLE

S. Francesco d. Vigna

Tribunale
Fabb. di Rialto
Camerlenghi
Ponte di Rialto

CAMPO S. BARTOLOMEO
S. Bart.
SAL. S. Lio
S. Lio
S. M. d. Fava
S. M. Formosa
Palazzo Grimani
S. Lorenzo

Pal. Manin
Pal. Bembo
Teatro Goldoni

S. Salvatore

Palazzo Querini Stampalia
Questura
S. Giorgio d. Schiavoni

S. Giuliano
S. Giov. Nuovo
S. Giorgio dei Greci
S. Antonio

Torre d. Orologio
Pal. Patriarcato
Museo Diocesano
S. Martino

S. Marco
PIAZZA S. MARCO
Campanile
Procuratie Vecchie
Mus. Correr
Procuratie Nuove
APT
Libreria Vecchia
Giardinetti
Zecca

C. S. PROVOLO
Prigioni
Pte d. Sospiri
Palazzo Ducale
Pal. Trevisan
S. Zaccaria
La Pietà
S. Giov. in Bragora

RIVA DEGLI SCHIAVONI

S. Moise
reves de Bonfili
Pal. Tiepolo
Pal. Giustinian
tarini

Cap. di Porto

CANALE DI S. MARCO

PUNTA D. SALUTE
Semin. Patriarc.
Maria Salute
Dogana di Mare

Bacino

S. Giorgio Maggiore
Fondazione Giorgio Cini
ISOLA DI S. GIORGIO MAGGIORE

Teatro Verde

Canale della Grazia

Isola di S. Pietro

gay Torre dell'Orologio provides an entrance from the Piazza to the Merceria, the main pedestrian thoroughfare of the city which leads to the Rialto. Opposite, beyond the tall isolated campanile, the Piazzetta with the Palazzo Ducale opens on to the water-front, the entrance to the city in Republican days. The famous pigeons of St Mark still flock to the square.

The ****Basilica of San Marco** (Pl. 11) stands high in importance among the churches of Christendom. Founded in 832, its sumptuous

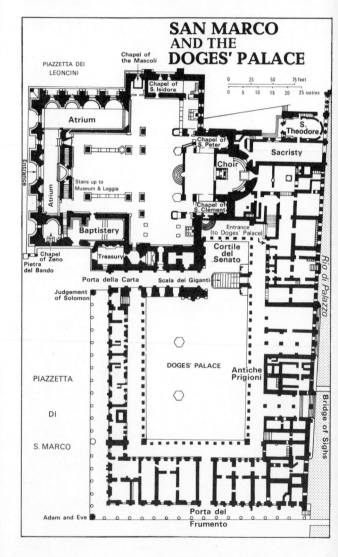

architecture retains the original Greek-cross plan derived from the great churches of Constantinople, and in particular from the (destroyed) church of the Holy Apostles. Its five domes are Islamic in inspiration. This famous shrine has been embellished over the centuries by splendid mosaics, marbles, and carvings; numerous different styles and traditions have been blended in a unique combination of Byzantine and Western art.

Admission. The church is open all day, but tourists are asked to visit the church between 9.30 and 17.30 in order not to disturb religious services. The Treasury and Pala d'Oro may be seen 9.30–17 (fest. 14–17). The Loggia on the façade and the Museo Marciano are open 9.30–17.30 (fest. 14–16.30).

History. Legend tells how St Mark the Evangelist on a voyage from Aquileia to Rome anchored off the islands of the Rialto where he had a vision of an angel who greeted him with the words 'Pax tibi, Marce evangelista meus. Hic requiescet corpus tuum'. This portent was fulfilled in 828 when two Venetian merchants brought the body of St Mark from Alexandria and placed it in charge of Doge Giustiniano Participazio who caused the first church on this site to be built. The name and symbol of St Mark (a winged lion) have been emblematic of Venice since this time. Although it was rebuilt twice in the 10C and 11C, the church consecrated in 1094 by Doge Vitale Falier is thought to have had basically the same form as the first church, and is that which exists today. As the Doge's Chapel the basilica was used throughout the Republic's history for State ceremonies; it became the cathedral of Venice only in 1807. The music school of the Ducal Chapel of St Mark was famous in the 16C and 17C.

EXTERIOR. The *MAIN FAÇADE is supported by columns of different kinds of marble, many from older buildings, and most of them with fine capitals. Between the arches are six bas-reliefs: the first on the left is a Roman work; the second, of St Demetrius, is by Byzantine craftsmen (late 12C); and the others are 13C in the Veneto-Byzantine style. Above the door of Sant'Alipio (1) at the left end, is a *Mosaic of the Translation of the body of St Mark to the Basilica (1260–70). This is the only original mosaic left on the façade, and is the earliest representation known of the exterior of the basilica (the bronze horses are already in place). In the fine lunette above are the symbols of the Evangelists (early 14C) and a 13C bas-relief in the Paleochristian style. The doors, by Bertuccio, date from 1300.— The central doorway (2) has three beautifully carved *Arches dating from c 1240–65 (restored in 1988), one of the most important examples of Romanesque carving in Italy. The Byzantine doors date from the 6C. In front of the central window, above the central doorway, stand copies (made in 1980) of the famous gilded bronze *Horses, a symbol of Venetian power during the Republic; the originals are now displayed in the Museo Marciano. The façade is crowned by fine Gothic sculpture, begun by the Dalle Masegne and continued by Lombard and Tuscan artists (including the Lamberti). The two outer tabernacles contain the Annunciatory Angel and the Virgin Annunciate recently attributed to Jacopo della Quercia. At the SW angle of the balcony, was a porphyry head (8C), said to be a portrait of Justinian II (died 711); it has been removed to a locked room in the Treasury.

The SOUTH FAÇADE (towards the Palazzo Ducale) continues the design of the W façade, and the two upper arches are finely decorated. The two rectangular walls of the Treasury (3) are richly adorned with splendid marbles and fragments of ambones and plutei (9–11C). On the corner are two quaint sculptured groups in porphyry known as the 'Tetrarchs', thought to represent Diocletian and three other emperors, Egyptian works of the 4C. The two

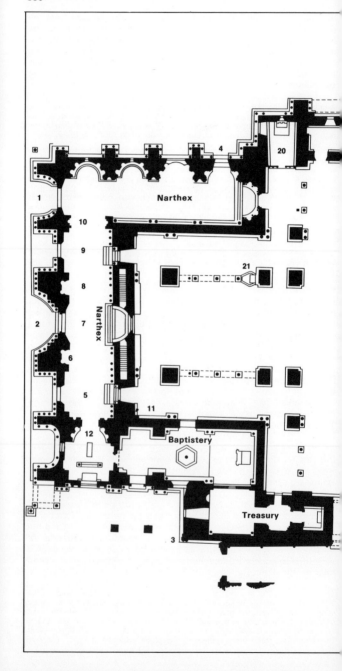

1

10

9

8

2

7

6

5

4

20

21

11

12

3

Narthex

Narthex

Baptistery

Treasury

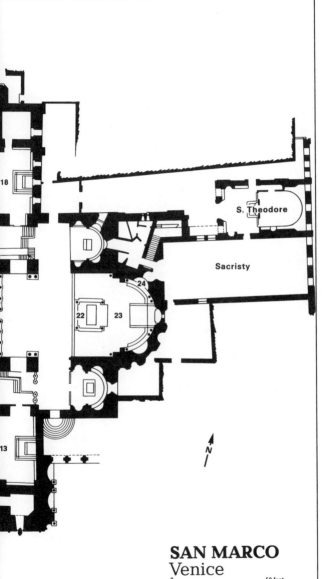

18

S. Theodore

Sacristy

24

22 23

13

N

SAN MARCO
Venice

0   50 feet

0   15 metres

isolated pillars in front of the Baptistery door are thought to have been brought from Constantinople at the time of the Fourth Crusade. They are rare examples of Syrian carving of the 5–6C.—The NORTH FAÇADE (facing the Piazzetta dei Leoncini) was probably the last to be finished. It bears interesting bas-reliefs and the Porta dei Fiori (4) has beautifully carved 13C arches. The upper part of the façade has statues by the Lamberti.

The NARTHEX provides a fitting vestibule to the Basilica. The slightly pointed arches, probably the earliest of their kind in Italy, support six small domes. The fine columns of the inner façade were either brought from the East or are fragments of the first basilica. The lower part of the walls is encased in marble; the upper part and the pavement are mosaic. The Romanesque *Mosaics of the domes and arches represent stories from the Old Testament, and are mainly original work of the 13C.—The mosaics in the first bay on the right (5) illustrate the Story of Genesis to the Death of Abel (1200–1210). The Door of San Clemente, cast in the East, is traditionally supposed to be a gift from the Byzantine Emperor Alexius Comnenus. The arch has mosaics showing the story of Noah and the Flood. Here is the tomb (6), made up of Byzantine fragments, of Doge Vitale Falier (died 1096) who consecrated the basilica in 1094, and who was responsible for much of the work on it. This is the oldest funerary monument which survives in the city.—The Bay (7) in front of the main door has two tiers of niches containing unrestored *Mosaics, the earliest in the basilica (c 1063). In the semi-dome, St Mark in Ecstasy (cartoon attributed to Lotto, 1545). The great door was executed by order of Leone da Molino (1113–18) and modelled on the Byzantine doors of San Clemente (see above). The slab of red Verona marble with a white marble lozenge in the pavement traditionally marks the spot where Barbarossa did obeisance before Alexander III in 1177.—The second arch (8) has mosaics showing the Death of Noah and the Tower of Babel. The tomb of the wife of Doge Vitale Michiel (died 1101) is made up of plutei and transennae of the 11C.—In the third bay (9), mosaics of the story of Abraham (c 1230), and in the lunette above the door, Byzantine mosaic of St Peter.—The third arch (10) has mosaics of Saints Alipio and Simon, and a tondo with Justice (c 1230).—The mosaics along the side of the narthex were partly re-made in the 19C; they portray the story of Joseph, and of Moses.

INTERIOR. Five great domes cover the Greek-cross of the interior, alternating with barrel vaults; each of the four arms has vaulted aisles in which the numerous columns with exquisite foliated capitals support a gallery (formerly the matroneum) fronted by a parapet of ancient plutei (dating from the 6C–11C). The Sanctuary, where the religious and political ceremonies of the Republic were held, is raised above the crypt, and separated from the rest of the church by a rood screen. The whole building is encased by eastern marbles below, and splendid mosaics on a gold ground above, illuminated high up by small windows. At the centre of the nave hangs a huge Byzantine chandelier. The 12C *Pavement, which has subsided in places, has a geometric mosaic of antique marble with representations of beasts, birds, etc.

The MOSAICS were begun after 1063 and were badly damaged in a fire of 1106. The original medieval iconographical scheme has been largely preserved, although renewal and repair work on them continued up until the present century. In the 12C and 13C the Venetian school of mosaicists flourished, and in the 14C and 15C Tuscan artists, including Paolo Uccello and Andrea del Castagno added mosaics to some of the chapels. From the early 16C onwards the work of restoration was begun and the partial replacement of the mosaics took place. Cartoons by Tintoretto and the famous artists of the time were used to reproduce paintings in mosaic, and the art of true mosaic decoration was lost.—The central *Dome of the Ascension is the work of Venetian masters of the late 12C. The *Mosaics on the arch towards the nave also date from this time and portray Scenes of the Passion. Over the nave rises the *Dome of the Pentecost, dating from the early 12C and probably the first of the five domes to be decorated with mosaics. Above the W door into the Narthex, *Lunette of Christ enthroned between the Madonna and St Mark (13C; restored). In the barrel vault stretching to the façade are scenes of the Last Judgement and Paradise from a cartoon by Tintoretto and others (1557–1619; restored in the 19C). In the right aisle, frieze of five mosaic *Rectangles with the Madonna and four Prophets (c 1230). On the wall above, *Agony in the Garden (early 13C), a splendid large composition, and the Acts of the Apostles (end of 12C, beginning of 13C). In the left aisle, Frieze of five mosaic *Rectangles with a beardless Christ and four Prophets.

RIGHT TRANSEPT. The Dome of St Leonard is decorated with four lone figures of Saints (early 13C). In the arch towards the nave, *Scenes from the Life of Christ (early 12C). The narrow arch in front of the rose window bears four Saints showing Tuscan influence (1458). On the right wall: *Prayers for and the Miraculous Discovery of the Body of St Mark (second half of the 13C) with interesting details of the interior of the basilica. On the arch above the Altar of the Sacrament, the Parables and Miracles of Christ (end of 12C or beginning of 13C).—The *Dome of St John in the left transept was executed in the first half of the 12C with stories from the Life of St John the Evangelist. The *Dome at the East end of the church over the Presbytery is a superb work of the 12C showing the Religion of Christ as foretold by the Prophets. In the apse, Christ blessing, and the four Patron Saints of Venice; St Nicholas, *St Peter, *St Mark, and St Hermagorus, among the earliest mosaics in the basilica.

THE LOWER PART OF THE CHURCH. RIGHT AISLE. There is a 12C Byzantine relief (11) by the BAPTISTERY (closed while the mosaics are being restored). The font was designed by Sansovino (c 1545). The fine Gothic sarcophagus of Doge Andrea Dandolo (died 1354) is by Giovanni de'Santi. At the E end a slab in the pavement marks the resting place of Jacopo Sansovino (died 1570). The huge block of granite (with an ancient inscription) is said to have been brought from Tyre in 1126. Beneath it have been discovered traces of a rectangular font, thought to have belonged to the first church. On the wall are three reliefs (13–14C). On the left wall 13C fresco fragments have been revealed. The Baptistery *Mosaics, carried out for Doge Andrea Dandolo (c 1343–44), illustrate the life of St John the Baptist and the early Life of Christ.

The Cappella Zen (12; closed while the Baptistery is being restored) was built in 1504–22 in honour of Cardinal Giovanni Battista Zen, who is buried here in a bronze tomb. Noteworthy are the *Doorway into the Narthex, the statue of the Madonna ('of the Shoe'), by Antonio Lombardo (1506), and the late 13C vault mosaics (restored).

RIGHT TRANSEPT. The bas-relief here of the Madonna and Child is thought to date from the 12C. The TREASURY (adm. see above) contains a rich store of booty from the sack of Constantinople in 1204. Many of its most precious possessions were melted down in 1797, but it retains one of the most important *Collections of Byzantine goldsmiths' work of the 12C. Also here; the marble Chair of St Mark (Alexandrine, 6–7C); reliquaries, icons, chalices in precious stone, etc.—Near the altar (13) a rectangle of fine marble inlay on a pilaster marks the place where St Mark's body was hidden during reconstruction work on the church, and miraculously re-discovered on 24 June 1094. The mosaic pavement bears palaeochristian motifs. The Altar of St James (14), is a charming work in the 15C Lombardesque style.

Here is the entrance to the Sanctuary (see below). From the polygonal pulpit (15) the Doge traditionally showed himself to the people after his coronation in the sanctuary. Above it, Madonna and Child, statue attributed to Giovanni Bon. The *Rood Screen (16) with eight columns of dark marble, bears the great Rood, a work in silver and bronze by Iacopo di Marco Benato of Venice (1394), and marble *Statues of the Virgin, St Mark the Evangelist, and the Apostles, signed by Jacobello and Pier Paolo Dalle Masegne (1394). The second pulpit (17) is supported by precious marble columns, and is crowned by a little oriental cupola. At the spring of the pendentives of the central cupola are four gilded marble *Angels (Romanesque works showing the influence of Antelami). In the pavement is a large rectangle of veined Greek marble on the site of the old choir (11–12C).

LEFT TRANSEPT. The CHAPEL OF THE MADONNA OF NICOPEIA (18) contains a precious *Icon said to have been brought from Constantinople in 1204. It is the most venerated image in the basilica and considered the Protectress of Venice. It was carried by the Byzantine emperor into battle at the head of his army and dates from the 12C. It is surrounded by a fine enamelled frame encrusted with jewels. It was badly damaged in 1979 when the jewels were stolen (they were later recovered) and it has been restored. The CHAPEL OF ST ISIDORE (19) was constructed by Doge Andrea Dandolo in 1354–55. The upper part of the walls and the barrel vault are completely covered by mosaics in a beautiful decorative scheme depicting the history of the saint (whose 14C statue is in a niche behind the altar). The CHAPEL OF THE MADONNA DEI MASCOLI (20) contains *Mosaics (1430–50) on the barrel vault of the Life of the Virgin. They were carried out under the direction of Michele Giambono, using cartoons by Andrea del Castagno and probably also Jacopo Bellini, and are one of the earliest examples of Renaissance art in Venice. Those on the left wall bear the signature of Michele Giambono. The carved Gothic altar (1430) with statues by Bartolomeo Bon is set in to the end wall encased in splendid marbles.—The LEFT AISLE contains the little *CHAPEL OF THE CRUCIFIX (21), with a pyramidal marble roof surmounted by a huge oriental agate and supported by six columns of precious marble with gilded Byzantine capitals. It contains a painted wood Crucifix thought to have been brought from the East in 1205.

The SANCTUARY (entrance from the right transept; adm., see above). The baldacchino (22) of the high altar is borne by four *Columns of eastern alabaster sculpted with New Testament scenes. It is still uncertain whether these are Byzantine works of the early 6C or even 5C, or Venetian works of c 1250. The sarcophagus of St Mark is preserved beneath the altar. Over the altar has been placed an altarpiece attributed to Michele Giambono. Behind this is the *Pala d'Oro (23), glowing with precious stones, enamel, and old gold. This is one of the most remarkable works ever produced by medieval goldsmiths.

The first Pala was ordered in Constantinople by Pietro Orseolo I (976–978). Enriched in 1105 for Doge Ordelafo Falier, it was enlarged by Doge Pietro Ziani in 1209, and finally re-set in 1345 by Gian Paola Boninsegna. The scenes in the upper part may come from the church of the Pantocrator in Constantinople. In the lower part, the Pantocrator (a 12C work also from Constantinople?) is surrounded by 14C Venetian panels. In the border are scenes from the Life of the Evangelists, thought to survive from the Pala of Doge Falier. The precious stones used to decorate the work include pearls, sapphires, emeralds, amethysts, rubies, and topaz.

The Apse, with two fine gilded capitals from Orseolo's basilica, has three niches. In the central one is an altar with six precious columns, including two of unusually transparent alabaster. The gilded door of the tabernacle is by Sansovino, and the statues by Lorenzo Bregno. The Sacristy door (24) is also by Sansovino, with fine bronze *Reliefs.—The *Crypt* is being restored in 1990.

From a small door to the right of the main W door of the basilica is access to the MUSEO MARCIANO and the LOGGIA (adm. see above). The museum contains the four gilded bronze *Horses removed from the façade of the basilica since their restoration.

They were brought here from Constantinople (where they had probably adorned the Hippodrome) at the time of the Fourth Crusade in 1204, and they were already in place on the façade of the Basilica by the middle of the century. Discussion continues about their origin; recent scholarship tends to assign them to the 2C AD, and therefore to a Roman rather than a Greek sculptor. In 1797 they were carried off to Paris by Napoleon where they remained until 1815. They were beautifully restored in 1978–81 and the original gilding revealed. After much controversy it was decided to replace them on the façade by copies.

The museum also contains mosaic fragments, several covers for the Pala d'Oro (one painted by Paolo Veneziano and his sons Luca and Giovanni in 1345), embroideries, carpets, and tapestries.—From here there is access to the LOGGIA on the façade which commands a fine view of the Piazza and allows a close examination of the Gothic sculpture.—The *GALLERIES, which offer a superb opportunity to study the mosaics inside the basilica, have been closed to the public indefinitely.

To the left of the Basilica is the Piazzetta Giovanni XXIII, with a fountain and two red marble lions. The Palazzo Patriarcale was begun in 1834–43 by Lorenzo Santi. The church of SAN BASSO, with a façade by Longhena (1675), is sometimes used for exhibitions. Above the entrance to the Merceria (Rte 32E) rises the **Torre dell'Orologio**, probably by Mauro Coducci (1496–99); the wings were added in 1506 perhaps by Pietro Lombardo. Above the great clock-face, brightly decorated with gilding and enamels is the figure of the Madonna. On the top of the tower two bronze figures (1497), known as the 'Mori', strike the hours. The tower is closed for restoration, but may usually be climbed. The rest of the N side of the Piazza is occupied by the arcades of the **Procuratie Vecchie** by Mauro Coducci, reconstructed after a fire in 1512 by Guglielmo dei Grigi Bergamasco, Bartolomeo Bon the Younger, and Sansovino. These were built as the residence and offices of the Procurators who had charge of the fabric of St

Mark's. Beneath the portico is the Caffè Quadri. At the W end of the
Piazza is the so-called ALA NAPOLEONICA of the Palazzo Reale, by
Giuseppe Soli (1810).

The **Procuratie Nuove**, on the S, were planned by Sansovino to
continue the design of his Libreria Vecchia which faces the Doges'
Palace. Up to the tenth arch from the left they are the work of
Scamozzi (1582–86), and they were completed by Longhena c 1640.
They were a later residence of the Procurators (see above), and
became a royal palace under Napoleon. The Caffè Florian, named
after its first proprietor in 1720 retains a charming old-fashioned
interior. Since 1923 the Procuratie Nuove have been occupied by
the **Museo Correr** (Pl. 11; adm. 10–16; festivals 9–12.30; closed
Tuesday), the city museum of art and history, which was founded by
the wealthy citizen Teodoro Correr (1750–1830). The entrance is
usually from the Ala Napoleonico.

The First Floor has neo-classical decorations and works by *Antonio Canova*.
The **Historical Collections** include old views and plans of Venice, historical
paintings, documents and portraits of the Doges, a good collection of coins
from the 9C to the fall of the Republic, material relating to commerce and
navigations, arms and armour, etc.—On the Second Floor the MUSEO DEL
RISORGIMENTO (often closed) continues the history of Venice to the present
day.—The **Picture Gallery** is arranged strictly chronologically. It includes
works by *Paolo, Lorenzo* and *Stefano Veneziano, Michele Giambono, Cosmè
Tura* (Pietà), *Bartolomeo Vivarini, Antonello da Messina* (*Pietà), Flemish and
German painters, *Giovanni, Gentile,* and *Jacopo Bellini, Bartolomeo Montagna, Vittore Carpaccio* (*Two Venetian ladies), etc. The last section of the
museum has been closed for many years: it displays the minor arts (small
bronzes, materials, lace, etc.), and plans and maps, including the famous huge
wood engraving (with the original six *Blocks) of Venice in 1500 by *Jacopo
de'Barbari*.

At the corner of the Procuratie Nuove rises the **Campanile of San
Marco**, over 98·5 metres high, first built in 888–912, and completed
in 1156–73. It was later restored, the last time by *Bartolomeo Bon the
Younger* in 1511–14. On 14 July 1902 it collapsed, causing little
damage (except to the Loggetta, see below) and no human casual-
ties. An exact reproduction of the original was immediately begun
and opened on 25 April 1912. The bell-chamber reached by a lift
(adm. 10–dusk; summer 10–20.30), commands a magnificent *View
of the town and lagoon.—At the base of the campanile is the
***Loggetta**, a fine work by *Jacopo Sansovino* (1537–49), which was
crushed by the fall of the tower, but has been carefully restored. Its
form is derived from the Roman triumphal arch and its sculptures
celebrate the glory of the Republic. The bronze statues in the niches
are by *Sansovino*.—The ***Piazzetta**, with the Doges' Palace on the
left, and the old Library on the right, extends from St Mark's to the
water-front. Near the water's edge are two huge monolithic columns
brought to Venice from the east by Doge Vitale Michiel II, and
erected here at the end of the 12C. One bears a winged lion
(removed for restoration) adapted as the symbol of St Mark from a
Persian, Syrian, or even Chinese chimera; the other a statue of St
Theodore and his dragon, the first patron saint of Venice. The torso
is a fragment of a Roman statue of the time of Hadrian, and the head
a fine portrait in Parian marble (the original has been replaced by a
copy).

The ****Doges' Palace**, or *Palazzo Ducale* (Pl. 11; adm. daily 8.30–
dusk) the former official residence of the doges and chief magistrates, was founded on this site in the 9C. The present building dates

from the 14C and the two façades overlooking the Bacino di San Marco and the Piazzetta are magnificent examples of florid Gothic architecture. The decoration of the interior by Venetian painters of the 16C and 17C (after fires in 1574 and 1577) survives intact.

History. The palace rebuilt in the 12C was destroyed by fire. In 1340–1419 a large hall was built for the Maggior Consiglio, and in 1422 part of the old building was demolished in order to extend the façade in the same style. It is thought the building was constructed by a group of master-masons, including Filippo Calendario (died 1355), under the direction of officials of the Republic. The interior façade and the courtyard were continued in the 15–17C. The palace contained a vast number of public offices, law courts, etc., as well as the doge's residence.

The numbers in the text refer to the Plans on pp 338–9. A guide giving details of every painting is displayed in each room.

The MAIN FAÇADE (overlooking the Bacino di San Marco) is a superb Gothic work. Each arcade of the portico supports two arches of the loggia decorated with quatrefoil roundels. Above rises a massive wall lightened by a delicate pattern of white Istrian stone and pink Verona marble. In the centre is a balconied window (restored in 1989) by *Pier Paolo Dalle Masegne* (1404). On the corner nearest to the Ponte della Paglia are statues of the Drunkenness of Noah and the archangel Raphael; on the corner nearest to the Piazzetta, Adam and Eve, with the archangel Michael above. Of uncertain attribution, these carvings date from the mid 14C. The *Capitals (36 in all) are superb examples of medieval carving; some were replaced by copies c 1880.—The Façade towards the Piazzetta repeats the design of the main façade. On the corner nearest the Basilica is the *Judgement of Solomon, with the archangel Gabriel above, a beautiful sculptural group recently attributed to *Jacopo della Quercia* (c 1410).—The *PORTA DELLA CARTA (1438–1443; restored 1976–79) is an extremely graceful gateway in the florid Gothic style, by *Giovanni* and *Bartolomeo Bon*. The fine *Statues of Temperance, Fortitude, Prudence and Charity are attributed to the Bon workshop. The gateway is crowned by a figure of Venice as Justice attributed to *Bartolomeo Bon*. The group of Doge Francesco Foscari and the Lion of St Mark is a reproduction (1885) of the original destroyed in 1797.

The entrance to the COURTYARD is through the Porta della Carta. The magnificent E side was rebuilt after the fire by *Antonio Rizzo* (1483–98), with carvings by the *Lombardo* family. The lower storeys of the other two sides were completed in the same style in the 17C by *Bartolomeo Monopola*. In the centre are two splendid well-heads in bronze by *Alfonso Alberghetti* (1559) and *Niccolò dei Conti* (1556). On the last side towards the Basilica is a Baroque façade by *Monopola* and the Arco Foscari, a triumphal arch attributed to *Antonio Rizzo* (the fine statues have been removed to the inside of the palace, and replaced by copies).—The *SCALA DEI GIGANTI, designed by *Antonio Rizzo* (1484–1501) is decorated with delicate reliefs and elaborate sculpture. The colossal statues of Neptune and Mars are late works by *Jacopo Sansovino*. On the wide landing at the top the doges used to be crowned with the jewelled 'beretta'. The small Cortile dei Senatori, beyond, is a charming Renaissance work by *Spavento* and *Scarpagnino*.

INTERIOR. The SCALA D'ORO (1), built in 1538–59, to the design of *Sansovino*, and decorated with gilded stuccoes by *Vittoria*,

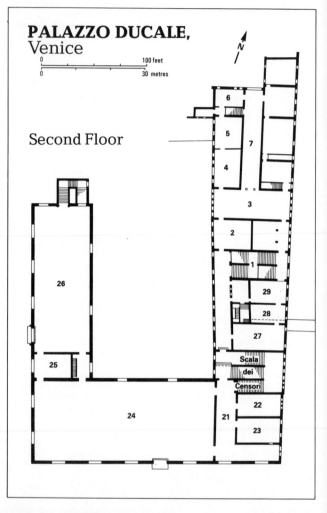

PALAZZO DUCALE,
Venice

| 0 | | 100 feet |
| 0 | | 30 metres |

Second Floor

leads up to the PRIMO PIANO NOBILE (or second floor). Here are the
Doges' Private Apartments (Rooms 2–7), since 1980 only open for
exhibitions. They were reconstructed after a fire in 1483, and contain
good ceilings and chimneypieces, as well as a ruined fresco of St
Christopher by *Titian*.—The Scala d'Oro continues to the SECONDO
PIANO NOBILE, or third floor. The Atrio Quadrato (8) has a ceiling
painting by *Tintoretto*. The *Sala delle Quattro Porte (9) is by *Antonio
da Ponte* (1575), after a plan of *Palladio* and *Rusconi*. Here there are
paintings by *Titian* and *Marcello Vecellio* (Doge Antonio Grimani
before the Faith), and *Giovanni Battista Tiepolo* (Venice receiving

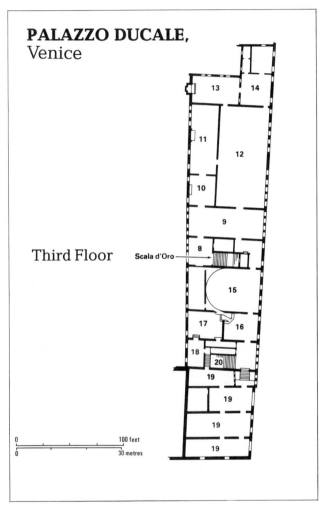

PALAZZO DUCALE, Venice

Third Floor

Scala d'Oro

13 14

11

12

10

9

8

15

17 16

18

20

19

19

19

19

0 _____ 100 feet
0 _____ 30 metres

homage of Neptune). The Anticollegio (10) has a good ceiling by *Marco del Moro*, and paintings by *Veronese* (*Rape of Europa), *Tintoretto* (*Vulcan's Forge, *Bacchus and Ariadne, etc.), and *Jacopo Bassano*. The Sala del Collegio (11; 1577–78) is a treasure-house of art. The *Ceiling, by *Francesco Bello*, the finest in the palace, contains a wonderful series of paintings by *Veronese* (c 1577), including Justice and Peace offering the Sword, the Scales, and the Olive-branch to triumphant Venice. Above the throne, *Veronese*, *Doge Sebastiano Venier offering thanks to Christ for the victory of Lepanto. Also here are four splendid paintings by *Tintoretto*. The *Sala del

Senato (12) has more fine works by *Tintoretto*, including the
*Descent from the Cross, with Doges Pietro Lando and Marcanto-
nio Trevisan.

From the Sala delle Quattro Porte a corridor leads into the Sala
del Consiglio dei Dieci (15), the seat of the Council of Ten. In the
ceiling is an *Old Man in Eastern costume with a Young Woman
by *Veronese*, and on the walls paintings by *Francesco* and *Leandro Bassano, Aliense*, and *Marco Vecellio*. The Sale d'Armi del
Consiglio dei Dieci (19) contain the Council's private armoury and
the state arms and armour were stored here until the fall of the
Republic. The rooms still contain a fine display of arms and
armour (14–17C).

The Scala dei Censori (20) redescends to the PRIMO PIANO
NOBILE. Off the Andito del Maggior Consiglio (21) with a good
16C ceiling is the Sala del Guariento (23; closed for restoration)
with the remains of a huge fresco of the *Coronation of the Virgin
by *Guariento* (1365–67) which used to adorn the Sala del Maggior
Consiglio. This famous work was ruined by the fire of 1577; it was
discovered in 1903 beneath Tintoretto's painting (see below). In
the veranda are displayed the marble statues of Adam and Eve by
Antonio Rizzo (c 1470), and of the condottiere Francesco Maria I
della Rovere, Duke of Urbino, by Giovanni Bandini, removed from
the Arco Foscari. The *SALA DEL MAGGIOR CONSIGLIO (24) was the
seat of the governing body of the Republic.

This vast hall, first built on this scale in 1340, was large enough to hold the
assembly of Venetian patricians (which reached a maximum of 1700
members). Here laws were ratified and the highest officials of the Republic
were elected. The paintings by Venetian artists, carried out in 1578–95 after
a fire, illustrate the Meeting in Venice between Barbarossa and Pope Alexander III in 1177; the Fourth Crusade in 1202; and the triumph of Doge
Contarini after the victory at the Battle of Chioggia in 1379. The hall is 52m
long, 24m wide, and 11m high.

On the entrance wall is *Paradise by *Jacopo* and *Domenico
Tintoretto*, the largest oil-painting in the world (7 × 24m), recently
restored. The *Ceiling is divided into 35 compartments; the three
central panels are by *Palma Giovane, Tintoretto*, and *Veronese*
(*Venice surrounded by gods and crowned by Victory). The large
historical canvases on the walls are the work of *Benedetto* and
Carletto Caliari, Leandro and *Francesco Bassano, Jacopo
Tintoretto, Paolo dei Franceschi, Andrea Vicentino, Palma Gio-
vane, Federico Zuccari, Girolamo Gambarato, Giulio del Moro,
Carlo Saraceni, Jean Leclerc, Aliense*, and *Paolo Veronese*. The
frieze of the first 76 Doges (from Obelario degli Antenori, c 804 to
Francesco Venier, died 1556) begins in the middle of the wall
overlooking the Courtyard and runs left to right. It is the work of
Domenico Tintoretto and assistants; the space blacked in on the
wall overlooking the Piazzetta takes the place of the portrait of
Marin Falier; an inscription records his execution for treason in
1355.

Beyond the Sala della Quarantia Civil Nuova (25) is the Sala
dello Scrutinio (26; closed for restoration), used to record the votes
of the Great Council for the new doge. It contains historical paintings by *Andrea Vicentino, Francesco Bassano, Aliense, Palma Giovane, Sante Peranda, Marcello Vecellio, Jacopo Tintoretto, Pietro
Bellotti*, and *Pietro Liberi*. The frieze continues the series of portraits of the doges down to the last one, Lodovico Manin; each one

was painted by a contemporary artist.—From the Scala dei Censori is reached the Bridge of Sighs (by *Antonio Contino*, 1603) and the new prisons.

Some of the most precious paintings in the palace, including the three winged lions of St Mark by *Jacobello del Fiore*, *Carpaccio*, and *Donato Veneziano*, and a Pietà by *Giovanni Bellini*, can be seen only by special request.

Interesting guided tours are given of the **'Itinerari Segreti del Palazzo Ducale'** daily except Sunday at 10 and 12, by appointment at the ticket office. The lesser known parts of the palace are shown, including the administrative offices of the Republic, the chancellery, law courts, Sala dei tre Capi del Consiglio dei Dieci (with four paintings by *Hieronymus Bosch*), the prison cells known as the 'Piombi' (from which Casanova made his famous escape), and the roof of the Sala del Maggior Consiglio.

The ***Libreria Sansoviniana** (Pl. 11; *Library of St Mark*), opposite the Ducal Palace, is the masterpiece of *Sansovino* (begun 1537). It was finished by *Scamozzi* (1588–91). Built of Istrian stone, its design is derived from Roman classical architecture. It was considered by Palladio to be the most beautiful building since the days of antiquity.

Petrarch gave his books to Venice in 1362, but it was not until Cardinal Bessarion presented his fine collection of Greek and Latin MSS in 1468 that the library was formally founded. Today the library (open to students) contains about 750,000 vols and 13,500 MSS (many Greek). The **Libreria Marciana** (or Old Library), can only be seen with special permission, or when exhibitions are being held. In the anteroom is a beautiful fresco of Wisdom by *Titian*. The Great Hall (restored in 1986) has a Mannerist ceiling of 1557 and paintings of Philosophers by *Tintoretto*, *Veronese*, and *Andrea Schiavone*. The ancient books include a late–14C Dante with illuminations; evangelisteries dating back to the 9C; the *Grimani Breviary illuminated by Flemish artists of c 1500; *Fra Mauro's Map, a celebrated world-map of 1459; Marco Polo's will; a MS. in Petrarch's hand, etc.

The **Archaeological Museum** (Pl. 11; open 9–14; fest. 9–13) was founded in 1523 from a bequest of Greek and Roman sculptures made by Cardinal Domenico Grimani to the Republic. It is especially remarkable for its ancient Greek *Sculpture, including the *Abbondanza Grimani, an original of the 5C BC. Also noteworthy are three Gallic *Warriors, copies of a group presented by Attalus of Pergamum to Athens, and *Vitellius (?), a particularly fine Roman portrait of the early 2C AD.

At the seaward end of the Piazzetta is the MOLO, on the busy water-front. To the right is the severe façade of the old **Zecca**. This rusticated Doric building was finished in 1547 by Sansovino on the site of the 13C mint.—In the other direction the quay extends in front of Palazzo Ducale as far as the *Ponte della Paglia*, from which may be seen the Renaissance E front of the palace (begun by Antonio Rizzo), and the famous **Bridge of Sighs** or *Ponte dei Sospiri* (Pl. 11), a flying bridge in Istrian stone by Antonio Contino (c 1600), named from the fact that it was used for the passage of prisoners from the Prigioni to be examined by the Inquisitors of State. The *Prigioni* (being restored), on the other side of the bridge, were begun by Giovanni Antonio Rusconi (1560).

B.   The Grand Canal

The ****Grand Canal** (*Canal Grande*), over 3km long, is the main thoroughfare of Venice. In its course through the city winding like a reversed S, it passes more than 100 marble palaces, mostly dating

from the 14–18C, though a few date back to the 12C. The wonderful
views afforded by every turn of this splendid waterway are unequalled in the world.

The best way to see the Grand Canal is by gondola; otherwise the slow vaporetto
(water-bus) No. 1 ('accelerato'). In the itinerary which follows the right bank is
described from San Marco to the Station, and the opposite bank on the way back
from the Station to San Marco.

San Marco to the Station: The Right Bank

From Riva degli Schiavoni (SAN ZACCARIA landing-stage) the boat
steers out into the Canale di San Marco with a good view of Palazzo
Ducale. Beyond the landing-stage of SAN MARCO (Calle Vallaresso)
is the 15C Gothic *Palazzo Giustinian*, with the municipal tourist
offices, and the 'Biennale' headquarters. It was a noted hotel in the
19C; Giuseppe Verdi, Théophile Gautier, and Marcel Proust all
stayed here.—On Rio di San Moisè is the plain classical façade of
Palazzo Treves de'Bonfili, attributed to Bartolomeo Monopola (17C).
The tiny *Palazzo Contarini-Fasan* has just three windows on the
piano nobile and two on the floor above. The charming 15C decoration includes a balcony with wheel tracery.—Beyond the rio is the
15C *Palazzo Pisani*, now the Gritti Palace Hotel with a terrace
restaurant on the canal. John and Effie Ruskin stayed here in
1851.—Beyond the landing-stage of SANTA MARIA DEL GIGLIO rises
the huge *Palazzo Corner*, called *Ca' Grande*, a dignified edifice in
the full Renaissance style by Sansovino (begun after 1545). It is now
occupied by the Prefecture.—Farther on are the two *Palazzi Barbaro*,
one 17C, and the other, on Rio dell'Orso, 15C Gothic decorated with
marbles and carvings. This is still owned by the Curtis family; in the
19C they here entertained John Singer Sargent, Henry James (who
wrote 'The Aspern Papers' during his stay), James Whistler, Robert
Browning, and Monet.—Across the rio is *Palazzo Franchetti*, a
sumptuous 15C building, arbitrarily restored (and a wing added) in
1896.

The wooden **Ponte dell'Accademia** is an exact replica made in 1986
of the bridge built in 1932 to replace a 19C iron bridge. *Palazzo
Giustiniani-Lolin*, with two pinnacles, is an early work by Longhena
(1623). *Palazzetto Falier* (15C Gothic) has two protruding loggie, rare
survivals of the 'liagò' which used to be a characteristic feature of
Venetian houses. Across the rio is a palace which incorporates the
rusticated corner of the *Ca' del Duca*, begun by Bartolomeo Bon in the
mid-15C but never completed.—The vast *Palazzo Grassi* was begun
in 1748 by Giorgio Massari. It has been restored by the Fiat
organisation and they use it for exhibitions. *Palazzo Contarini delle
Figure* is a graceful Lombardesque building by Scarpagnino (16C)
decorated with heraldic trophies. The four *Palazzi Mocenigo* consist
of two palaces on either side of a long double façade. In the first
Emmanuel Philibert of Savoy was a guest in 1575, and Giordano
Bruno in 1592 (when he was betrayed by his host); in the third
(plaque) Byron wrote the beginning of 'Don Juan' (1818) and
entertained Thomas Moore.

Beyond the SANT'ANGELO landing-stage is *Palazzo Corner-
Spinelli*, by Mauro Coducci (1490–1510), a particularly successful
Renaissance palace, with a rusticated ground floor.—On Rio di San
Luca stands *Palazzo Corner Contarini dei Cavalli*, an elegant Gothic
work of c 1450 with two coats-of-arms and a fine central six-light

window. Across the rio rises ***Palazzo Grimani**, a masterpiece designed by Sanmicheli before his death in 1559, and built by Giangiacomo dei Grigi. It is now the seat of the Court of Appeal. The *Casa Corner-Martinengo-Ravà* was owned by the distinguished Morosini family who were visited by Paolo Sarpi, Galileo Galilei, and Giordano Bruno. The Fondamenta del Carbon now skirts the Grand Canal as far as the Rialto bridge. The 12–13C Veneto-Byzantine *Palazzi Farsetti and *Loredan* are occupied by the town hall. The Palazzo Loredan has a double row of arches and statues of Venice and Justice beneath Gothic canopies and bears the arms of the famous Corner family. Elena Corner Piscopia (1646–84), who lived here, was the first woman to receive a degree (from Padua University in Philosophy). In the middle of the next group of houses is the tiny Gothic *Palazzetto Dandolo*, with a double row of four-light windows. Across the rio stands the white *Palazzo Dolfin-Manin* by Sansovino, begun in 1538 for a Venetian merchant, Zuanne Dolfin.

The famous **Ponte di Rialto**, built by Antonio da Ponte in 1588–92 replaced a wooden bridge, which had in turn superseded a bridge of boats in 1264. Its single arch, 48 metres in span and 7·5 metres high carries a thoroughfare divided into three lanes by two rows of shops. It bears high reliefs of the Annunciation by Agostino Rubini (16C). Just beyond the bridge is the **Fondaco dei Tedeschi**, the most important of the trading centres on the Grand Canal leased by the Venetians to foreign merchants. By the mid-13C the Germans, Austrians, Bohemians, and Hungarians had their warehouses, shops, offices, and lodgings here. The building was reconstructed in 1505 by Spavento and completed by Scarpagnino from the designs of Girolamo Tedesco, and the exterior frescoed by Giorgione and Titian (this has entirely disappeared; detached fragments survive in the Ca' d'Oro). It is now the central post office.—Farther on stands *Ca' da Mosto*, a 13C Veneto-Byzantine building decorated with paterae above the windows. This was the birthplace of Alvise Da Mosto (1432–88), discoverer of the Cape Verde Islands. Across Rio dei Santi Apostoli stands *Palazzo Mangilli–Valmarana*, a classical building built on a design by Antonio Visentini for the English consul Joseph Smith (1682–1779), patron of Canaletto and other Venetian artists. In Campo Santo Sofia is the red *Palazzo Morosini-Sagredo* with a pretty balconied Gothic window and a variety of arches on its interesting façade.

By the next landing-stage is the ***Ca' d'Oro** (see Rte 32/J), with the most beautiful Gothic façade in Venice (1425–c 1440), famous for its elaborate tracery. —Farther on, on a rio, stands the handsome *Palazzo Gussoni Grimani della Vida* attributed to Sanmicheli (1548–56), formerly decorated with frescoes by Tintoretto. Sir Henry Wotton, the English ambassador, lived here in 1614–18.—The 16C *Palazzo Barbarigo* has almost lost its façade frescoes by Camillo Ballini. Beyond the bend in the canal is *Palazzo Soranzo*, with a fine façade probably by Sante Lombardo.—The imposing edifice in Istrian stone beyond its garden is ***Palazzo Loredan Vendramin Calergi**, almost certainly designed by Mauro Coducci in the first decade of the 16C. It is a masterpiece of Renaissance architecture, with a noteworthy cornice and finely carved frieze. Wagner died here on 13 February 1883. It is now the winter home of the Casinò. Beyond the rio, ***Casa Gatti-Casazza**, with a roof garden (the typical Venetian 'altane') has been restored in the 18C style.

Beyond the landing-stage of SAN MARCUOLA are several 17C palaces. The CANNAREGIO, the second largest canal in Venice, diverges right. Beyond the church of San Geremia is the little *Scuola dei Morti* (rebuilt after 1849), and the stone façade of *Palazzo Flangini*, left unfinished by Giuseppe Sardi.—The bridge which serves the Station was built by Eugenio Miozzi in 1934. Just before the FERROVIA landing-stage is the Baroque façade of the church of the *Scalzi* by Giuseppe Sardi. The railway station was built in 1955.—The landing-stage of PIAZZALE ROMA is at the terminus of the road from the mainland.

Piazzale Roma to San Marco: The Right Bank

From PIAZZALE ROMA the boat steers out into the Grand Canal and soon passes the mouth of the *Rio Nuovo*, a canal cut in 1933 as a short route from the Station to Piazza San Marco. Beyond the *Giardino Papadopoli* is the church of *San Simeone Piccolo*, with a lofty green dome and Corinthian portico.—Beyond the station bridge and the RIVA DI BIASIO landing-stage is the 15C Gothic *Palazzo Giovanelli*.— The **Fondaco dei Turchi** is an impressive Veneto-Byzantine building, unfeelingly restored in the 19C. It was the Turkish warehouse from 1621–1838, and is now the Natural History Museum. Beneath the portico are several sarcophagi; one is that of Doge Marin Falier, beheaded in 1355. Across the rio is the plain brick façade of the *Granaries* of the Republic. This 15C battlemented edifice bears a relief of the Lion of St Mark.—*Palazzo Belloni-Battagià* has two tall obelisks crowning its façade; it was built by Baldassarre Longhena in 1647–63, with a fine water-gate. Across the rio stand *Palazzo Tron* (1590) and *Palazzo Duodo* (Gothic). Beyond a garden is *Palazzo Priuli Bon*, with 13C Veneto-Byzantine traces on the ground floor.

The SAN STAE landing-stage is next to the church of *San Stae* with a rich Baroque façade (c 1709) by Domenico Rossi. It is adjoined by the pretty little *Scuola dei Battiloro e Tiraoro* (goldsmiths), attributed to Giacomo Gaspari (1711). The grand ***Palazzo Pesaro** is a fine Baroque palace by Baldassarre Longhena decorated with grotesque masks. The façade has recently been cleaned. It now contains the Gallery of Modern Art.— *Palazzo Corner della Regina* by Domenico Rossi (1724) stands on the site of the birthplace of Caterina Cornaro, queen of Cyprus (1454–1510).—A bridge connects Fondamenta dell'Olio with the *Pescheria*, a graceful Gothic market hall built in 1907 on the site of the 14C fish-market. Here begin the **Rialto markets**, the busy wholesale markets of the city, the buildings of which continue right up to the Rialto bridge. The long arcaded *Fabbriche Nuove di Rialto* is a serviceable market building which follows the curve of the Grand Canal, begun by Sansovino in 1554. Beyond the *Erberia*, the fruit and vegetable market, is *Palazzo dei Camerlenghi*, restored by Guglielmo dei Grigi (il Bergamasco) in 1523–25.

The boat passes beneath the **Rialto bridge** (see above). The reliefs of St Mark and St Theodore are by Tiziano Aspetti. At its foot is *Palazzo dei Dieci Savi*, a building of the early 16C by Scarpagnino.— Beyond SAN SILVESTRO landing-stage *Palazzo Barzizza* bears remarkable reliefs on its façade (12C Veneto-Byzantine). On the rio stands *Palazzo Coccina-Tiepolo Papadopoli*, a good Renaissance palace by Giangiacomo Grigi of Bergamo (early 1560s). *Palazzo Donà* and *Palazzo Donà della Madonnetta* are both interesting palaces with good windows. Across the rio stands **Palazzo Bernardo* with a lovely Gothic façade, especially notable for the tracery on the second piano nobile. *Palazzo Grimani* (now *Sorlini*) is an elegant Lombardesque building of the early 16C. The *Palazzo Cappello-Layard* was the residence of the English diplomat Sir Henry Layard (1817–94), the discoverer of Nineveh, whose fine collection of paintings was left to the National Gallery of London in 1916.—The *Palazzo Pisani-Moretta* has graceful Gothic tracery of the second half of the 15C.—After SAN TOMA (FRARI) landing-stage rises the grand *Palazzo Balbi*, probably by Alessandro Vittoria (1582–90). The beautifully proportioned **Ca' Foscari* (1428–37) was built for Francesco Foscari, doge for 34 years. It has notable tracery, fine marble columns, and a frieze of putti bearing the Foscari arms. It is now part of the University. The *Palazzi Giustinian* were begun c 1452 by Bartolomeo Bon. Wagner stayed here in 1858–59 and wrote the second act of 'Tristan'. The **Ca' Rezzonico** was begun by Longhena c 1667, and a storey was added by Giorgio Massari in 1745. It now houses an 18C museum.

Behind CA' REZZONICO landing-stage is the 17C Lombardesque *Palazzo Contarini-Michiel.—Palazzo Loredan dell'Ambasciatore* is a Gothic building of the 15C with two shield-bearing pages, fine Lombard works from the circle of Antonio Rizzo. Beyond Rio San Trovaso stand the *Palazzi Contarini Corfù* and *Contarini degli Scrigni*. The former is 15C Gothic with vari-coloured marbles, while the second was built in 1609 by Vincenzo Scamozzi. Beyond the **Accademia Bridge** is *Palazzo Contarini Dal Zaffo (Polignac)*, a graceful Lombardesque building with fine marble roundels, next to its garden. Beyond *Palazzo Barbarigo*, with a harshly coloured mosaic façade (by Giulio Carlini, died 1887) stands *Palazzo Da Mula* (15C Gothic). *Palazzo Venier dei Leoni* was begun in 1749 and only the ground-floor was completed. It was owned by Mrs Peggy Guggenheim from 1949 until her death in 1979, and still houses her collection of modern art. Beyond is **Palazzo Dario*, a charming Lombardesque building of 1487 in varicoloured marble, with numerous chimney-pots. Its outside walls incline noticeably.—The Salviati glass company, founded in 1866, occupies *Palazzo Salviati* with a harsh modern mosaic on its façade. A splendid water-gate crowned by a large relief of St Gregory gives on to the cloister of the ex-abbey of *San Gregorio*.

At the SALUTE landing-stage a marble pavement opens out before the grandiose church of ****Santa Maria della Salute**, a masterpiece of Baroque architecture by Longhena which dominates this part of the canal. It is adjoined by the 17C *Seminario Patriarcale*. The *Dogana di Mare*, the customs house, a Doric construction by Giuseppe Benoni (1676–82), extends to the end of the promontory. The picturesque turret has two telamones who support a golden globe on which is balanced a weathervane of Fortune. The boat re-crosses the Grand Canal (with a fine view of the island of San Giorgio Maggiore) to the SAN MARCO (VALLARESSO) landing-stage.

C. Riva degli Schiavoni to Castello

Riva degli Schiavoni (Pl. 12) is a wide and busy quay on the basin of St Mark's with numerous moorings and landing-stages for vaporetti, gondolas, and steamers. The *Danieli*, which has been a hotel since 1822, occupies the Gothic Palazzo Dandolo. It numbers among its distinguished visitors George Sand, Alfred de Musset, Charles Dickens, Ruskin, Wagner, and Proust. Its disappointing extension was built in 1948. Across *Ponte del Vin* towers the Victor Emmanuel

Monument by Ettore Ferrari (1887). At a house on the quay here (no. 4161) Henry James finished 'The Portrait of a Lady' in 1881. Sottoportico San Zaccaria leads to the church of *San Zaccaria (Pl. 12), built in a remarkably successful mixture of Gothic and Renaissance styles (1444–1515), begun by *Antonio Gambello*, and finished by *Mauro Coducci* (who completed the upper part of the tall façade). Over the doorway is a statue of the patron saint, by *Alessandro Vittoria* (in poor condition).

The church was founded by Doge Giustiniano Participazio in the 9C. The elegant INTERIOR has a multiple apse with an ambulatory and coronet of chapels lit by long windows, unique in Venice. On the 2nd N altar, *Madonna and four Saints by *Giovanni Bellini*, signed and dated 1505. The CHAPEL OF ST ATHANASIUS (opened by the sacristan) leads to the CHAPEL OF ST TARASIUS which has three fine *Anconas by *Antonio Vivarini* and *Giovanni d'Alamagna* (1443). In the fan vault are frescoes by *Andrea del Castagno* and *Francesco da Faenza* (signed and dated 1442). The mosaic pavement and the crypt are thought to date from the 9C.

Beyond the next bridge is LA PIETÀ, the church of an orphanage for girls which achieved European fame for its music in the 17–18C. Vivaldi was violin-master in 1704–18 and concert-master in 1735–38. The bright oval *Interior was rebuilt by Massari (1745–60), and the contemporary decorations remain intact (including a fine ceiling fresco of the Triumph of Faith by Giovanni Battista Tiepolo).—Several Calle lead N to the Orthodox Greek church of *San Giorgio dei Greci* (Pl. 12), begun in 1539 on a design by Sante Lombardo, with a leaning campanile of the 16C. It contains an iconostasis with late-Byzantine figures. Next door is the *Scuola di San Nicolò dei Greci*, by Baldassarre Longhena (1678) with a MUSEUM OF ICONS (mostly 16–17C).—To the NE on a rio is the little **Scuola di San Giorgio degli Schiavoni** (Pl. 12; 8; adm. 10–12.30, 15.30–18; Sunday 10.30–12.30; closed Monday), founded in 1451 by the Dalmatians. The *Interior is one of the most evocative in the city, decorated with a delightful series of *Paintings by Carpaccio (1502–08), relating to the lives of the three Dalmatian patron saints, Saints Jerome, Tryphon, and George.

At the end of Riva degli Schiavoni Calle del Dose leads into Campo Bandiera e Moro with the church of **San Giovanni in Bragora** (Pl. 12), rebuilt in 1475. It contains (by the Sacristy door), Constantine and St Helena by Cima da Conegliano (1502), and The Risen Christ by Alvise Vivarini (1498). In the Sanctuary is the *Baptism of Christ by Cima da Conegliano (1494). In the chapel to the left of the apse is a triptych by Bartolomeo Vivarini. In the lovely 15C font Vivaldi was baptised in 1678.—On the next rio is the *Ca' di Dio* (restored) a pilgrim hospital founded in the 13C for Crusaders. On the Riva are the *Forni Pubblici* (1473) with an ornamental marble frieze. These were the bakeries of the Republic which supplied the ships as they set sail from the Arsenal. The Canale dell'Arsenale leads up to the splendid Arsenal Gateway, the land entrance to the **Arsenal** (beyond Pl. 12), beside two massive towers which protect the entrance from the lagoon. The arsenal remained for centuries the symbol of the economic and military power of the Venetian Republic.

The Arsenal was founded in 1104 and was enlarged from the 14–16C. It gave its name (from the Arabic 'darsina 'a', meaning 'workshop') to all subsequent dockyards. Dante visited it in 1306 and again in 1321 (see 'Inferno', xxi). At the height of Venetian prosperity it employed 16,000 workmen.—The interior is still used by the armed forces and is open to the public only on 4 November; there are long-term plans to convert this huge area of the city to civil use. Part of it can be seen from vaporetto No. 5 which runs through the main canal of the Arsenale Vecchio (closed to private vessels) on its circular route of the city. The GREAT GATEWAY, in the form of a triumphal arch, is one of the earliest works of the Renaissance in the city. It was built in 1460 probably by Gambello who re-used Greek marble columns with Veneto-Byzantine capitals. The doorway is flanked by two colossal lions sent by Francesco Morosini from Pireaus as spoils of war and placed here in 1692; the two smaller lions, added in 1718 after the relief of Corfu may have come originally from the Lion Terrace at Delos.

The wooden bridge leads across to Rio dell'Arsenale on which is the church of *San Martino* built in 1553 by Jacopo Sansovino on a Greek cross plan.

On the quay at the other end of the Arsenal canal is the MUSEO STORICO NAVALE (adm. 9–13; Saturday 9–12; closed fest.), well arranged on four floors. It contains models of boats and interesting material relating to the naval history of the Republic. An extension of the museum has recently been opened in the 16C 'Officina Remi' on the Arsenal Canal, where the oars were made for the Venetian fleet. Here are preserved a miscellany of boats.—Across the bridge the long broad VIA GARIBALDI leads away from the water-front. This was laid out by Napoleon in 1808 by filling in a canal. The house at the beginning on the right was the residence of John and Sebastian Cabot in 1581. The church of *San Francesco di Paola* has 18C paintings. At the end of Via Garibaldi, Fondamenta di Sant'Anna continues to a bridge over the wide Canale di San Pietro. On the solitary Isola di San Pietro, near the E limit of the city is the church of **San Pietro di Castello**, the cathedral of Venice from the 11C until 1807.

The present church was built on a Palladian design of 1557. It contains a venerable marble throne from Antioch with a Muslim funerary stele. The sumptuous high altar was designed by Longhena; behind it is the organ by Nacchini (1754). The Cappella Lando contains a 6C pluteus, and an interesting mosaic fragment thought to date from the 5C.—The isolated campanile by Mauro Coducci dates from 1482–88.

The pleasant public gardens to the S of Via Garibaldi (the 'GIARDINI PUBBLICI') contain the pavilions of the *International Exhibition of Modern Art*, known as the 'BIENNALE' since it is held every two years (the first exhibition was held in 1895). On the N side is the interesting church of *San Giuseppe di Castello*.—Farther out is a residential quarter spaciously laid out in this century, the sports stadium, and the island of Sant'Elena. Here the church of SANT'ELENA (early 13C; rebuilt in 1435) has a sculpted *Group over the doorway attributed to Antonio Rizzo or Nicolò di Giovanni Fiorentino (c 1467) representing admiral Vittorio Cappello kneeling before St Helena.

D. Santa Maria Formosa, Santi Giovanni e Paolo, and San Francesco della Vigna

Behind Piazzetta Giovanni XXIII and Palazzo Patriarcale a bridge leads over Rio di Palazzo to the CLOISTER OF SANT'APOLLONIA, the only Romanesque cloister in the city. The MUSEO DIOCESANO D'ARTE SACRA has recently been opened here (adm. weekdays 10.30–12.30).

It contains paintings and sculpture from churches either closed permanently or unable to provide safe-keeping for their treasures, as well as vestments, missals, candlesticks, church plate, crucifixes, and reliquaries. Among the paintings are works by *Palma Giovane* and *Luca Giordano* (*Paintings from Sant'Aponal); the patriarch's late-15C processional Cross is from San Pietro di Castello.

From here various Calle and Fondamente (sign-posted) lead N to the 16C **Palazzo Querini-Stampalia** (Pl. 7; adm. 10–16; fest. 10–15; winter: 10–13; fest. 10–12.30; closed Monday), which contains (on the second and third floors) an interesting collection of Venetian paintings, and 18C material illustrating the history of the family.

The paintings include: 18C views of Venice by *Gabriele Bella;* Coronation of the Virgin, by *Donato* and *Caterino Veneziano* (1372); portraits by *Sebastiano Bombelli;* *Presentation in the Temple by *Giovanni Bellini* (a copy from Mantegna); *Francesco Querini and *Paola Priuli Querini, two unfinished portraits by *Palma Vecchio;* *Judith by *Vincenzo Catena;* Giovanni Dolfin by *Giovanni Battista Tiepolo;* and genre paintings by *Pietro Longhi.*

The pretty CAMPO SANTA MARIA FORMOSA has a number of handsome palaces. The church of **Santa Maria Formosa** (Pl. 7) was rebuilt by Mauro Coducci in 1492. The name is derived from the tradition that the Madonna appeared to its founder San Magno in the 7C in the form of a buxom matron.

INTERIOR. The Greek-cross plan of the primitive church, derived from Byzantine models, was preserved by Coducci when he gave the interior its beautiful Renaissance form. The Chapel of the Bombardieri has a composite *Altarpiece by *Palma Vecchio*, notable especially for the colourful and majestic figure of St Barbara in the centre. In the 1st chapel on the right, Madonna della Misericordia, by Bartolomeo Vivarini (1473).

A calle (sign-posted) leads out of the piazza to CAMPO SANTI GIOVANNI E PAOLO (*San Zanipolo;* Pl. 7,8), historically one of the most important campi in the city. On a fine pedestal rises the equestrian *Statue of Bartolomeo Colleoni**, the famous condottiere, begun by *Verrocchio* in 1481. This masterpiece of the Renaissance was finished after Verrocchio's death by Alessandro Leopardi.—The church of *Santi Giovanni e Paolo** (*San Zanipolo;* Pl. 8) disputes with the Frari the first place among the huge Gothic brick churches of Venice. It was begun by the Dominicans in 1246. It is the burial place of 25 doges, and after the 15C the funerals of all doges were held here.

The main *DOORWAY is attributed to *Bartolomeo Bon.*—The vast solemn INTERIOR is notable for the slenderness of its arches and its beautiful luminous choir. Among the impressive series of funerary monuments to doges and heroes of the Republic are some masterpieces of Gothic and Renaissance sculpture, many of them recently beautifully cleaned.—On the W WALL is a monument to Doge Giovanni Mocenigo (died 1485), by *Tullio Lombardo*, and a *Monument to Doge Pietro Mocenigo (died 1476), a masterpiece by *Pietro Lombardo*.—SOUTH AISLE. Beyond the 1st altar, monument to Marcantonio Bragadin, the defender of Famagusta (1571) flayed alive by the Turks (his bust surmounts an urn which contains his skin); 2nd altar, *Giovanni Bellini*, (recently reattributed to *Lauro Padovano*) *Polyptych of St Vincent Ferrer, a beautiful work in its original frame. In the pavement in front of the next chapel, Tombstone of Ludovico Diedo (died 1466) a masterpiece of niello work.—The Chapel of St Dominic has a ceiling painting of the *Saint in Glory by *Giovanni Battista Piazzetta* (1727).—The stained *Glass in the great window in the SOUTH TRANSEPT was made in Murano from cartoons by *Bartolomeo Vivarini* and *Girolamo Mocetto* (1473), and possibly also *Cima da Conegliano.*—In the CHOIR is the Gothic *Tomb of Doge Michele Morosini (died 1382), with carving attributed to the *Dalle Masegne* school. Opposite is the *Tomb of Doge Andrea Vendramin (died 1478), a masterpiece of the Renaissance by *Tullio* and *Antonio Lombardo.* Next to it is the Gothic tomb of Doge Marco Corner (died 1368) with a *Madonna signed by *Nino Pisano.*—The CHAPEL OF THE ROSARY, off the N transept, contains ceiling *Paintings by *Paolo Veronese.*—Among the fine funerary monuments in the NORTH AISLE are the *Monument to Doge Pasquale Malipiero by *Pietro Lombardo*, the *Tomb of Doge Tommaso Mocenigo (died 1423) by *Piero di

Niccolò Lamberti and *Giovanni di Martino*, and the *Monument to Doge Nicolò Marcello (died 1474) by *Pietro Lombardo*.

Beside the church is the **Scuola Grande di San Marco** (Pl. 7,8), one of the six great philanthropic confraternities of the Republic, now occupied by the civic hospital. The sumptuous *FAÇADE by *Pietro Lombardo* and *Giovanni Buora* was finished by *Mauro Coducci* (1495). The sculptures are by *Tullio Lombardo* and *Bartolomeo Bon*. The interior incorporates the church of San Lazzaro dei Mendicanti by *Vincenzo Scamozzi*.

Beyond the S flank of Santi Giovanni e Paolo the salizzada continues to the heavy Baroque façade of the OSPEDALETTO, rebuilt by Longhena, with a fine interior. In the nearby hospital is an elegant Music Room with frescoes by Jacopo Guarana (being restored).— Farther E, across Rio di Santa Giustina, is **San Francesco della Vigna** (Pl. 8). The foundation stone of the present church was laid in 1534 by Doge Andrea Gritti, and the building begun by his friend *Jacopo Sansovino*. *Palladio* added the façade in 1568–72.

The dignified Interior has a broad nave with side chapels and a long chancel. In the S transept is a *Madonna and Child enthroned, a charming large composition by *Antonio da Negroponte* (c 1450). The Giustiniani Chapel (left) is beautifully adorned with 15C *Sculptures by *Pietro Lombardo* and his school. In the Cappella Santa is a Madonna and Saints by the school of *Giovanni Bellini*. In the chapels on the N side are chiaroscuri by *Giovanni Battista Tiepolo*, statues of three saints by *Vittoria*, and an altarpiece by *Federico Zuccari*.

E. San Marco to the Rialto via the Merceria

The narrow **Merceria** (Pl. 11,7) is the shortest route from Piazza San Marco to the Rialto. It is the busiest thoroughfare of the city and always crowded. It leaves Piazza San Marco under the Torre dell'Orologio. At the first bend (right) is the church of **San Giuliano** (*San Zulian*; Pl. 11), rebuilt in 1553 by *Iacopo Sansovino* with a seated *Statue by him on the façade of Tommaso Rangone, the scholar from Ravenna who paid for the rebuilding of the church. The fine interior has a ceiling painting by *Palma Giovane*, and works by *Girolamo da Santacroce*, *Alessandro Vittoria*, *Paolo Veronese*, and *Boccaccio Boccaccino*.—The Merceria continues to the church of **San Salvatore** (Pl. 7), begun by *Giorgio Spavento* (1508), continued by *Tullio Lombardo*, and finished by *Vincenzo Scamozzi*.

In the handsome Renaissance *INTERIOR is a Monument to Doge Francesco Venier with statues by *Sansovino*, and a splendid *Annunciation, painted in 1566 by *Titian*. In the S Transept, Tomb of Caterina Cornaro, queen of Cyprus (died 1510), by *Bernardo Contino*. Over the high altar a Transfiguration by *Titian* screens a silver reredos, a masterpiece of Venetian goldsmith's work (14C). In the chapel to the N, Supper at Emmaus by the school of *Giovanni Bellini*.

The Merceria continues (right) into CAMPO SAN BARTOLOMEO (Pl. 7), the crowded business centre of Venice. It is at the cross-roads of the city. The spirited statue of Goldoni, the dramatist of Venetian life, is by Antonio Dal Zotto (1883). Salizzada Pio X leads to the foot of the Rialto bridge.

From the other side of Campo San Bartolomeo several calle lead to the church of *San Lio*, with lovely sculptural details by Pietro and Tullio Lombardo in the Gussoni chapel, and a ceiling painting by Gian Domenico Tiepolo.—A short way to the S is the church of *Santa Maria della Fava* (or Santa Maria della Consolazione) with altarpieces by Giovanni Battista Tiepolo and Giovanni Battista Piazzetta.

F.   San Marco to the Rialto via Santo Stefano

Beneath the Ala Napoleonica at the W end of Piazza San Marco, Salizzada San Moisè leads to the campo in front of the elaborate Baroque façade of **San Moisè** (Pl. 11), by Alessandro Tremignon (1668). The interior contains some good 17–18C paintings and (in the sacristy) a remarkable bronze altar front of the Deposition, by Nicolò and Sebastiano Roccatagliata (1633).—Across the rio is the broad Calle Larga 22 Marzo, from which a calle diverges right for CAMPO SAN FANTIN, crowded with monumental buildings, including **La Fenice** (Pl. 10), one of the most important opera-houses in Italy.

It was built in 1792 by Giovanni Antonio Selva, and, after a fire in 1836, rebuilt on the same lines by Giovanni Battista Meduna (adm. to the fine interior is granted on request). Many of Verdi's operas had their opening nights here.—Opposite is the charming Renaissance church of *San Fantin*, with a domed sanctuary and apse attributed to Sansovino. The *Scuola di San Fantin* (now the Ateneo Veneto), with an Istrian stone façade, contains paintings by Paolo Veronese and his school.

The Calle returns to Calle Larga 22 Marzo which continues to Campo Santa Maria Zobenigo which opens on to the Grand Canal. Here stands the church of **Santa Maria del Giglio** (Pl. 10), with a fine Baroque façade by Giuseppe Sardi. It contains paintings by Antonio Zanchi, Johann Karl Loth, and Jacopo Tintoretto, and sculptures by Morleiter and Meyring. In the Cappella Molin is a Madonna and Child with the young St John attrib. to Rubens.—Beyond the Campo San Maurizio is the huge CAMPO SANTO STEFANO (Pl. 10; also called Campo Morosini), one of the pleasantest squares in the city. Here are the 17C *Palazzo Morosini*, the long *Palazzo Loredan*, with a Palladian façade on the N end, and the imposing *Palazzo Pisani*, one of the largest private palaces in the city begun by Bartolomeo Monopola in 1614. The other end of the campo is occupied by the early Gothic church of *****Santo Stefano** (Pl. 10).

The Gothic INTERIOR has a fine wood tricuspid *Roof in the form of a ship's keel. In the Sacristy are three paintings by Jacopo Tintoretto. In the church are a number of 18C altarpieces, and wooden choir stalls by Leonardo Scalamanzo and Marco and Francesco Cozzi (1488).

At the other end of the campo stands the monumental façade of *San Vitale* (deconsecrated) which contains a painting of San Vitale by Carpaccio. To the right a calle leads over several bridges to emerge in *Campo San Samuele* on the Grand Canal. The church contains frescoes by the 15C Paduan school. The 18C PALAZZO GRASSI (see Rte 32B) is used for exhibitions.

Just beyond Santo Stefano Calle dei Frati leads across a rio into the pretty CAMPO SANT'ANGELO (Pl. 10), with a view of the fine tower of Santo Stefano, the most oblique of the many leaning towers of Venice, and several fine Gothic palaces.—Calle del Spezier (sign-posted 'Rialto') leads out of the Campo. A calle diverges left for the MUSEO FORTUNY (Pl. 10; adm. 8.30–13.30 except Monday) in the 15C *Palazzo Pesaro degli Orfei*, the home of the Spanish painter Mariano Fortuny (1871–1949) who here designed the famous Fortuny silks. The house, with a remarkable 'fin de siècle' atmosphere, is filled with curios and the artist's own works. It is frequently used for exhibitions. The fine main façade of the palace gives on to *Campo San Benedetto*, where the church has paintings by Bernardo Strozzi, Carlo Maratta, Sebastiano Mazzoni, and Giovanni Battista Tiepolo.—Across Rio di San Luca is *Campo Manin*, near which (signposted) is *Palazzo Contarini del Bovolo*, celebrated for its graceful spiral *Staircase and loggia by Giovanni Candi (c 1499) in an open courtyard.—From here the Rialto bridge is soon reached along Riva del Carbon which skirts the Grand Canal.

G.   Dorsoduro

On the Grand Canal is the grandiose façade of **Ca' Rezzonico** (Pl. 9,10). It was begun by Longhena (c 1667) and completed by Massari (1756). The palace contains the **Museo del Settecento Veneziano** (adm. 10–16; fest. 9–12; closed Friday), the city's collection of 18C art, displayed in rooms decorated in the most sumptuous 18C style with superb views over the Grand Canal.

This was the last home of Robert Browning and he died in 1889 in the small apartment (not open) on the first floor. The rooms on the first floor contain furniture by *Andrea Brustolon*; frescoes by *Giovanni Battista Tiepolo*; and pastels by *Rosalba Carriera*. On the second floor are frescoes by *Francesco Guardi, Gian Domenico Tiepolo* (*Frescoes from the Villa di Zianigo); and genre paintings by *Pietro Longhi*. The third floor, with a puppet theatre, an 18C pharmacy, etc. was reopened in 1989.

The fondamenta leads along the rio to a bridge which crosses to CAMPO SAN BARNABA, where the church contains a Holy Family attributed to Veronese (restored in 1989). Fondamenta della Toletta leads out of the campo; across a rio, a calle (left) continues to the campo on the Grand Canal beside the Accademia bridge. Here the former church of Santa Maria della Carità, the ex-convent, and the Scuola della Carità are now occupied by the Accademia di Belle Arti and the ****Galleria dell'Accademia**; (Pl. 10,14; adm. daily, 9–14; fest. 9–13) which contains by far the most important collection of Venetian paintings in existence. The works cover all periods from the 14C, and the 15C art of Giovanni Bellini, through the wonderful era of Titian, Tintoretto, and Veronese, down to Tiepolo and the 18C. The paintings are well labelled.

ROOM I. *Altarpieces by *Paolo* and *Lorenzo Veneziano*, and works by *Jacobello del Fiore, Michele Giambono*, etc. The wooden ceiling is ascribed to *Marco Cozzi* with paintings by *Alvise Vivarini* and *Domenico Campagnola*.—R2 contains a superb group of large altarpieces by *Carpaccio* (Presentation of Christ in the Temple), *Marco Basaiti* (*Calling of the sons of Zebedee), *Giovanni Bellini* (*'Pala di San Giobbe'), and *Cima da Conegliano* (Madonna 'of the Orange Tree').—RIV. Among the exquisite small paintings here are *Madonnas by *Giovanni Bellini*, and *Jacopo Bellini*, and works by *Piero della Francesca* (St Jerome in the desert), and *Andrea Mantegna* (*St George).—RV. *Giorgione*, *Old Woman, and *'La Tempesta'; *Giovanni Bellini*, *Madonnas.—RVI contains works by *Paris Bordone* (The fisherman presenting St Mark's ring to the Doge), *Bonifazio* (Dives and Lazarus the beggar), and *Titian* (St John the Baptist).— RRVII & VIII. Works by *Lorenzo Lotto* (Gentleman in his Study), *Andrea Previtali, Palma Vecchio* (Holy Family), etc.—In RRX & XI are some famous works by *Paolo Veronese* (*Christ in the House of Levi and *Allegory of Venice), *Tintoretto* (*Transport of the body of St Mark, *Miracle of St Mark, Creation of the Animals), and *Titian* (*Pietà).

RXIII is devoted to *Tintoretto* (fine *Portraits), *Andrea Schiavone*, and the *Bassano* family.—RRXIV, XV and XVI contain works by *Domenico Fetti*, *Giovanni Battista Tiepolo*, *Domenico Pellegrini*, and *Giovanni Battista Piazzetta* (*Fortune-teller).—RXVII has a number of Venetian scenes including works by *Canaletto* and *Guardi*, interiors by *Pietro Longhi*, and portraits by *Rosalba Carriera*.—RXIX displays paintings by *Marco Basaiti*, *Antonello de Saliba*, etc.—In RXX is a charming series of *Paintings from the Scuola di San Giovanni Evangelista by *Carpaccio*, *Giovanni Mansueti*, *Gentile Bellini*, *Benedetto Diana*, and *Lazzaro Bastiani*, many of them with interesting views of 15C Venice, including Piazza San Marco as it was in 1496.—Paintings illustrating the *Legend of St Ursula from the Scuola di Sant'Orsola by *Carpaccio* fill RXXI.— RXXIII (opened periodically) forms part of the elegant Gothic ex-church of Santa Maria della Carità. It contains fine 15C Venetian paintings by *Giovanni* and *Gentile Bellini*, *Crivelli*, *Lazzaro Bastiani*, *Bartolomeo* and *Alvise Vivarini*.— RXXIV, the former 'albergo' of the Scuola della Carità, contains the *Presentation of the Virgin by *Titian*, and a large *Triptych by *Antonio Vivarini* and *Giovanni d'Alemagna*, both painted for this room.

Rio Terrà di Sant'Agnese leads out of the campo, and Calle Nova continues left past PALAZZO CINI (No. 864) which houses the Vittorio Cini Collection of Tuscan paintings (open June–October, 14–19, except Monday). It includes works by Botticelli, Piero di Cosimo, and Pontormo. Across Rio di San Vio is the little campo on the Grand Canal with the Anglican church of ST GEORGE, given to the English community in Venice in 1892 by Sir Henry Layard. A calle continues to *Palazzo Venier dei Leoni*, which houses the *PEGGY GUGGENHEIM COLLECTION (Pl. 14; adm. 11–18 except Tuesday; Saturday 11–21), one of the most representative displays of modern art (after 1910) in Europe (since Peggy Guggenheim's death in 1979 it has been owned by The Solomon R. Guggenheim Foundation). It includes works by Picasso, Braque, Gris, Kandinsky, Klee, Calder, Giacometti, Mondrian, Ernst, Mirò, Dali, De Chirico, Brancusi, Pollock, Rothko, Bacon and Dubuffet.—The calle continues past the Gothic church (now used as a restoration centre) of *San Gregorio* to a campo on the Grand Canal in front of *Santa Maria della Salute** (Pl. 15). The church was built in 1631–81 in thanksgiving for the deliverance of Venice from the plague. It is a beautiful octagonal building built partly of Istrian stone by Baldassarre Longhena. It is particularly well adapted to its impressive site at the entrance to the city, and dominates the view of the Grand Canal from the lagoon.

The INTERIOR contains altarpieces by *Luca Giordano*, *Pietro Liberi*, and *Titian*. The high altar, by *Longhena* bears good sculptures, some by *Juste Le Court*.— The GREAT SACRISTY contains a remarkable series of paintings: *St Mark enthroned between Saints, tondi of the Evangelists and Doctors of the church, and three ceiling *Paintings, all by *Titian*; and the *Marriage at Cana by *Tintoretto*. The 15C tapestry altar-frontal is notable.

Next to the church is the SEMINARIO PATRIARCALE (Pl. 15) which contains the **Manfrediniana Picture Gallery** (adm. by appointment only). This contains sculptures by the *Dalle Masegne*, *Pietro Lombardo*, *Alessandro Vittorio*, *Gian Lorenzo Bernini*, and *Canova*; and paintings by *Temporello*, *Boltraffio* (attributed), *Filippino Lippi*, *Paolo Veronese*, etc.

The DOGANA DI MARE, the customs house, with a low Doric façade by Giuseppe Benoni extends to the end of the promontory where there is a little turret surmounted by a golden ball and a weather vane supported by two telamones. The FONDAMENTA DELLE ZATTERE (Pl. 13, 14, & 15) skirts the wide Giudecca canal, busy with shipping including the large ocean-going vessels bound for the industrial port and oil refinery of Marghera. On the Zattere are the *Magazzini del Sale* with a neo-classical exterior and splendid 15C interior (used for exhibitions), and, farther on, the *Incurabili*, a huge classical building.—Beyond the Rio San Vio, the Zattere becomes more animated. On the corner is a house (now a hotel) where John Ruskin stayed in 1877. The church of the **Gesuati** (Pl. 14) is a fine building by Giorgio Massari. The interior has ceiling frescoes and an *Altarpiece (1st on right), both by Giovanni Battista Tiepolo, and altarpieces (Three Saints) by Sebastiano Ricci and Giovanni Battista Piazzetta.— The Renaissance church of SANTA MARIA DELLA VISITAZIONE has a charming wood roof with painted panels by the 16C Umbrian school. On Rio di San Trovaso is a picturesque old boat-building yard ('squero'), and the church of **San Trovaso** (Pl. 13, 14), which contains several works by Jacopo Tintoretto, a painting of St Chrysogonus on horseback by Michele Giambono, and an interesting marble bas-relief attributed to the 'Maestro di San Trovaso'.—Farther W, on Rio di San Basilio is the church of *San Sebastiano* (Pl. 9), famous for its decorations (1555–70) by Paolo Veronese who lived nearby and is buried in the church.

INTERIOR (open 10–12, 14–16). The beautiful ceiling contains panels of the *Story of Esther painted by *Veronese* surrounded by decoration by his brother *Benedetto Caliari*. The altarpiece of St Nicholas (S side) is a late work by *Titian*.—In the Choir are three more *Paintings by *Veronese*. In the chapel to the N of the choir is the tomb of Veronese and his brother Benedetto Caliari. The organ (1558) has painted panels by *Veronese*.—The ceiling of the SACRISTY is among the earliest of Veronese's works in Venice (1555); here also are paintings by *Brusasorci* and *Bonifazio*.—The NUNS' CHOIR has more frescoes by *Veronese*, and over the 3rd N altar is an early altarpiece, also by *Veronese*.

Nearby is the church of the ANGELO RAFFAELE, with a sculpture over the main portal attributed to Sebastiano Mariani da Lugano, and organ paintings by Francesco or Giovanni Antonio Guardi.—A fondamenta follows the rio (left) to the church of SAN NICOLÒ DEI MENDICOLI (beyond Pl. 9), founded in the 7C. The charming interior has interesting wood sculptures, including a statue of the titular Saint by the workshop of Bartolomeo Bon and paintings by Alvise Dal Friso, Montemezzano, and Leonardo Corona.—The fondamenta leads back along the rio past the Angelo Raffaele to the little campo in front of the church of the **Carmini** (Pl. 9).

The spacious basilican INTERIOR contains gilded wooden sculptural decoration beneath a frieze of 17–18C paintings. The altarpieces include works by *Cima da Conegliano* (*Nativity), *Antonio Corradini*, and *Lorenzo Lotto*. In the chapel to the right of the chancel is an interesting small Relief of the Deposition attributed to *Francesco di Giorgio Martini*.

The SCUOLA GRANDE DEI CARMINI (9–12, 15–18 except fest.), beside the church, is attributed to Baldassarre Longhena (1668). The salone contains fine ceiling paintings by Giovanni Battista Tiepolo, including the *Virgin in Glory.—Beyond the Scuola opens the huge *Campo di Santa Margherita*, at the end of which a bridge leads across to the church of SAN PANTALON (Pl. 9), with a huge *Painting on the nave roof by Gian Antonio Fumiani (1680–1704).

H.   San Polo and Santa Croce

The church of the ***Frari** (Pl. 6; properly *Santa Maria Gloriosa dei Frari*) contains remarkable sculptures and paintings. Its size rivals that of Santi Giovanni e Paolo. The Franciscan church was founded c 1250. The present church, built of brick in the Italian Gothic style, was begun c 1330 and not finished until after 1443. The majestic tall campanile dates from the 14C. The sculptured portals on the N and W sides are notable.

In the centre of the imposing *INTERIOR is the Monks' Choir, the arch of which frames *Titian*'s magnificent Assumption in the apse.—On the W wall are monuments attributed to *Tullio Lombardo* and *Lorenzo Bregno*.—An ungainly 19C mausoleum in the S aisle marks the spot where Titian is believed to be buried. The statue of St Jerome on the 3rd altar is by *Vittoria*—The S transept has interesting sepulchral monuments including one to Jacopo Marcello recently attributed to *Giovanni Buora*, and the tomb of Benedetto Pesaro by *Lorenzo Bregno*. The Gothic tomb (c 1406) of Paolo Savelli is the first in Venice to include an equestrian statue.—In the SACRISTY is a *Triptych of the Madonna and Child between Saints by *Giovanni Bellini*, one of his most beautiful works. The CHAPTER HOUSE contains the sarcophagus of Doge Francesco Dandolo (died 1339) with an interesting lunette by *Paolo Veneziano*.—In the CHOIR CHAPELS: an altarpiece by *Bartolomeo Vivarini*; and a wooden statue of *St John the Baptist by *Donatello*. Titian's huge *Assumption (1518) in the SANCTUARY is celebrated among his masterpieces. Here the *Tomb of Doge Nicolò Tron (died 1473) by *Antonio Rizzo* is one of the finest Renaissance funerary monuments in Venice. In the other CHOIR CHAPELS: altarpiece begun by *Alvise Vivarini* and finished by *Marco Basaiti*; and the grave of Claudio Monteverdi.—The *Stalls in the CHOIR are carved by *Marco Cozzi* (1468) with intarsia by *Lorenzo* and *Cristoforo Canozzi*. The Choir Screen has carvings by *Bartolomeo Bon* and *Pietro Lombardo*.—In the N aisle is the *Madonna di Ca' Pesaro, by *Titian*.—The convent buildings contain the **State Archives**, which provide a remarkably full documentation of the Venetian Republic.

Beside the Frari is SAN ROCCO (Pl. 5), a church designed by Bartolomeo Bon the Younger but almost entirely rebuilt in 1725. It contains paintings by Sebastiano Ricci, Francesco Solimena, Pordenone, and Jacopo Tintoretto (on the W wall, on the S side, and four stories of St Roch in the sanctuary).—Beside the church is the *Scuola Grande di San Rocco (Pl. 5; adm. 9–13, 15.30–18.30; winter: weekdays 10–13, Saturday & Sunday, 10–16), begun by *Bartolomeo Bon the Younger*, continued by *Sante Lombardo*, and finished by *Scarpagnino*, who added the splendid main façade. The interior is famous for its works by *Tintoretto*, who here, in over fifty **Paintings produced one of the most remarkable pictorial cycles in existence.

Tintoretto, a brother of the Confraternity of St Roch, spent 23 years (without the help of assistants) working on the paintings (beautifully restored in 1974). The paintings of the Life of the Virgin in the GROUND FLOOR HALL were the last to be painted in the School by Tintoretto. The *GRAND STAIRCASE by *Scarpagnino* leads up to the huge CHAPTER HOUSE where the paintings by *Tintoretto* represent Old and New Testament subjects. Here, too are displayed paintings (on easels) by *Titian, Tintoretto*, and *Giovanni Battista Tiepolo*. The vast Crucifixion in the SALA DELL'ALBERGO can perhaps be considered *Tintoretto*'s masterpiece. The easel painting of Christ carrying the Cross here is now usually attributed to *Titian*.

To the N of the convent buildings of the Frari is the **Scuola di San Giovanni Evangelista** (Pl. 5,6), with a beautiful marble screen and portal in the first court by Pietro Lombardo. Inside, the double *Staircase by Mauro Coducci leads up to the 18C Salone with paintings by Sante Peranda, Domenico Tintoretto, and Andrea Vicentino, and a ceiling painted in 1760.—From Campo dei Frari, Calle Larga Prima leads into *Campo San Tomà* with the 15C Scuola dei Calegheri. A bridge leads over the rio to Calle dei Nomboli with Palazzo Centani, the birthplace of Carlo Goldoni (1707–93), the playwright. Known as the CASA GOLDONI (open 8.30–13 except Sunday), the picturesque interior contains Goldoni relics.—Calle dei

Saoneri leads across another rio into CAMPO SAN POLO (Pl. 6), one of the largest and most attractive in the city, with some fine palaces. Here the church of **San Polo** (Pl. 6) has a good S doorway attributed to Bartolomeo Bon.

The INTERIOR contains paintings by *Jacopo Tintoretto* (Last Supper), *Veronese*, *Paolo Piazza*, and *Giovanni Battista Tiepolo*.—In the ORATORY OF THE CRUCIFIX are the *Stations of the Cross by *Gian Domenico Tiepolo*, and, on the ceiling a Glory of Angels, and *Resurrection, also by him.

Farther E, across Rio dei Meloni is *Campo Sant'Aponal* where the church has a Gothic façade. Calle del Traghetto leads to the peaceful Campo San Silvestro. The neo-classical interior of SAN SILVESTRO (Pl. 6) by Lorenzo Santi contains altarpeices by Tintoretto, Johann Karl Loth, and Girolamo da Santacroce (St Thomas Becket enthroned). Fondamenta del Vin skirts the Grand Canal as far as the **Rialto Bridge** (Pl. 7) which stands at the topographical centre of the city. A bridge has existed at this point since earliest times, and it remained the only bridge across the Grand Canal throughout the Republic. The area known as the Rialto has been the commercial and economic centre of Venice since the beginning of the Republic. The markets, established here as early as 1097, were reconstructed by Scarpagnino after a disastrous fire in 1514. The busy Ruga degli Orefici leads through the colourful market past the Campo San Giacomo. Here the little church of **San Giacomo di Rialto** (Pl. 7), founded in the 5C, is traditionally considered the oldest church in Venice. Its domed Greek-cross plan, derived from Byzantine models, was preserved in the rebuilding of 1601.—Across the campo is the *Gobbo di Rialto* by Pietro da Salò (16C), a crouching figure which supports a flight of steps leading to a rostrum of Egyptian granite from which the laws of the Republic were proclaimed. The *Erberia*, the wholesale market for fruit and vegetables, opens on to the Grand Canal.

In Ruga Vecchia San Giovanni (left) is SAN GIOVANNI ELEMOSINA-RIO (Pl. 7; it has been closed for many years), a church rebuilt by Scarpagnino in 1527. It contains works by Leonardo Corona, Titian, Pordenone, and Marco Vecellio.—Ruga dei Spezieri continues past the *Pescheria* (fish market); farther on is the church of **San Cassiano** (Pl. 6). In the chancel are three remarkable paintings (including a *Crucifixion) by Tintoretto; the altarpieces are by Rocco Marconi, Leandro Bassano, and Matteo Ponzone.—Beyond two more rii, on the Grand Canal, is the Renaissance **Palazzo Pesaro** (Pl. 6) which contains the *Galleria d'Arte Moderna* (closed since 1981) and the *Museo Orientale* (adm. 9–14; Sunday 9–13; closed Monday).

The **Gallery of Modern Art** contains a large collection of paintings and sculptures, mostly purchased at the 'Biennale' art exhibitions, including works by *Arturo Martini, Emilio Greco, Francesco Hayez, Telemaco Signorini, Giovanni Fattori, De Chirico, Carlo Carrà, Filippo de Pisis, Felice Casorati, Kandinsky, Paul Klee, Max Ernst, Matisse, Corot, Dufy*, and *Marc Chagall*.—The **Museum of Oriental Art** (which is to be moved to Palazzo Marcello on the Grand Canal) is devoted principally to Japanese and Chinese art, with specimens of Siamese and Javanese work.

Nearby, also on the Grand Canal, is the church of SAN STAE, with a splendid Baroque façade by Domenico Rossi. The interior (used for exhibitions) contains an interesting collection of 18C paintings, including works by Giovanni Battista Tiepolo, Sebastiano Ricci, and Giovanni Battista Piazzetta.—At No. 1992 Salizzada San Stae is *Palazzo Mocenigo* where the late-17C family residence is open to the public on Saturday (8.30–13.30).—To the S, on Rio Pesaro, is SANTA MARIA MATER DOMINI (Pl. 6), a Renaissance church which was reopened in 1989 after restoration (10–12, 15–17). It contains paintings (some of them still removed for restoration) by Vincenzo Catena, Francesco Bissolo, Bonifazio, and Tintoretto (*Invention of the Cross), and sculptures by Lorenzo Bregno. In the campo are some interesting old palaces.—Farther on, on the Grand Canal is the **Fondaco dei Turchi** (Pl. 2), from 1621–1838 the warehouse of the Turkish merchants. One of the most characteristic Veneto-Byzantine palaces (12–13C) in the city, it was virtually rebuilt after 1858. It now contains a *Natural History Museum* (9–13, except Sunday and Monday).— Nearby is the deconsecrated church of SAN GIOVANNI DECOLLATO with Greek marble columns and a ship's keel roof.—To the S is the large Campo and church of **San Giacomo dell'Orio** (Pl. 6; being restored).

The interesting INTERIOR contains massive low Byzantine columns, and a beautiful ship's keel roof. In the NEW SACRISTY is a ceiling painting by *Veronese*, and paintings by *Francesco Bassano, Palma Giovane,* and *Bonifazio Veronese.* In the SANCTUARY are works by *Lorenzo Lotto* and *Lorenzo Veneziano.* The OLD SACRISTY has paintings by *Palma Giovane.*

Farther on, nearer the Grand Canal, is the church of **San Simeone Grande** (Pl. 5), with an *Effigy of St Simeon attributed to Marco Romano, and paintings by Tintoretto, Palma Giovane, and Giovanni Mansueti (attributed).—Across the rio Marin, on the Grand Canal, is the church of SAN SIMEONE PICCOLO (Pl. 5), on a stylobate with an interesting pronaos with Corinthian columns and a high green dome. The fondamenta leads along the canal to the *Giardino Papadopoli*, behind which is the church of **San Nicola da Tolentino** (Pl. 5), with a Corinthian portico, and a classical interior by Vincenzo Scamozzi. It contains paintings by Padovanino, Camillo Procaccini, Girolamo Forabosco, Luca Giordano, Johann Lys (St Jermome visited by an angel), Bernardino Strozzi, and Palma Giovane.—On the other side of the public gardens is **Piazzale Roma** (Pl. 5) the terminal of the road from the mainland with its huge multi-storey car parks and bus stations.

I. Cannaregio

From the Rialto bridge a salizzada skirts the back of the huge *Fondaco dei Tedeschi* (see Rte 32B; now the central post office) to the church of **San Giovanni Crisostomo** (Pl. 7) which almost fills its small campo. The last work of Mauro Coducci, it is a masterpiece of Venetian Renaissance architecture. In the Greek-cross interior is a late work by Giovanni Bellini (*Three saints), and the high altarpiece of seven *Saints is by Sebastiano del Piombo.—Behind the church is the Corte Prima del Milion and (beyond) the CORTE SECONDA DEL MILION, with ancient houses and a carved Byzantine arch. The courtyards bear Marco Polo's nickname, the famous traveller and writer who lived in this area.—To the N is the church of ***Santa Maria dei Miracoli** (Pl. 7), a masterpiece of the Renaissance by Pietro Lombardo (1481–89), with its N flank set on a canal.

The EXTERIOR has exquisite carved details, and a beautiful façade with marble inlay and carved friezes.—The INTERIOR, with its simple clean lines and marble walls, has a raised choir and domed apse. The exquisite *Carving in the CHOIR is by *Pietro* and *Tullio Lombardo*. Over the high altar is a charming Madonna by *Nicolò di Pietro Paradisi*, and the ceiling panels were painted by *Pier Maria Pennacchi*.

Beyond Campiello Santa Maria Nova with a Gothic palace, and San Canciano, a bridge leads over Rio dei Santi Apostoli to (left) the pleasant campo of the church of **Santi Apostoli** (Pl. 7). The interior contains paintings by Giovanni Battista Tiepolo, Giovanni Contarini, and Francesco Maffei, and interesting sculptures and frescoes. Across the rio can be seen the late-13C *Palazzo Falier*, a characteristic merchant's house, traditionally thought to be the home of Doge Marin Falier, executed in 1355.—The wide STRADA NUOVA, a busy shopping street, continues to (left) the *Ca' d'Oro* (Pl. 6), famous as the most beautiful Gothic palace in Venice. It received its name, the 'Golden House' from the splendid polychrome and gilded decoration carried out in 1431 which used to adorn the sculptural details of the façade. It was presented to the State, together with a magnificent collection of works of art, by Baron Giorgio Franchetti in 1916, and was reopened in 1984 after restoration and modernisation. Adm. daily, 9–14; Sunday 9–13.

The palace was built between 1420 and 1434 by *Matteo Raverti, Giovanni* and *Bartolomeo Bon*, and others. The splendid façade is best seen from the Grand Canal. The contents of the *Galleria Franchetti* are well labelled. FIRST FLOOR. *Mantegna*, *St Sebastian; *Sculptures by *Antonio Rizzo, Tullio Lombardo* (*Double Portrait), *Andrea Briosco, Vittore Gambello, L'Antico* (Apollo); small bronzes and medals.—SECOND FLOOR. Portrait busts by *Alessandro Vittoria*; a portrait by *Van Dyck*; Flemish paintings; *Fresco fragments by *Giorgione* and *Titian* (from the exterior of the Fondaco dei Tedeschi); detached frescoes by *Pordenone*; Venetian views attributed to *Francesco Guardi*.—The gallery is to be extended, and a ceramics collection exhibited in the adjoining Palazzo Duodo.

A little farther on a fondamenta diverges right along the Rio di San Felice; to the NW is the church of the **Gesuiti** (Pl. 3), with a monumental Baroque façade. The highly elaborate interior has decorative grey and white marble intarsia in imitation of wall hangings. It contains an Assumption by Jacopo Tintoretto, and the *Martyrdom of St Laurence (1st N altar) by Titian. Near the church is the little *Oratorio dei Crociferi* (only open in summer) with a cycle of *Paintings by Palma Giovane (1583–92).—On the other side of Rio di San Felice a bridge leads over to the huge *Scuola Grande della Misericordia*, begun in 1532 by Sansovino, but left unfinished at his death. The fondamenta leads N to the *Scuola Vecchia della Misericordia* (founded 1308), with a worn Gothic façade, next to the 17C façade of the church. The abbey buildings are used as a restoration centre. Sottoportico dell'Abbazia leads along the rio; to the S across two rii is the church of SAN MARCILIANO, with paintings by Sebastiano Ricci, Jacopo and Domenico Tintoretto, and Titian.—Corte Vecchia leads up to the Sacca della Misericordia which opens onto the lagoon in this remote part of the town. Fondamenta Gasparo Contarini leads past several interesting palaces and, on the opposite side of the canal can be seen Palazzo Mastelli with a charming relief of a man leading a camel. At the end is the pretty paved campo in front of the church of the *Madonna dell'Orto** (Pl. 2), which contains important works by Tintoretto who is buried here in his parish church.

The FAÇADE is a fine example of Venetian Gothic, with good early-15C tracery in the windows. The sculptures are attributed to *Antonio Rizzo, Bartolomeo Bon*, and the *Dalle Masegne*. INTERIOR. In the S aisle are *Cima da Conegliano's* masterpiece of *St John the Baptist and four other Saints (c 1493), and the *Presentation of the Virgin in the Temple, by *Tintoretto*. A modest slab in the chapel on the right of the choir marks *Tintoretto's* burial place; the CHOIR contains two huge paintings by him, the *Last Judgement and the *Making of the Golden Calf. The apse and vault bear more paintings by *Tintoretto*.—The CAPPELLA CONTARINI contains family busts (two by *Vittoria*) and an altarpiece by *Tintoretto*. The CAPPELLA VALIER is an elegant Renaissance work completed by *Andrea* and *Antonio Buora*; the altarpiece of the Madonna is by *Giovanni Bellini* (recently restored).

Some way to the W, in a remote part of the city, is the church of **Sant'Alvise** which has been undergoing restoration for years. It contains a *Calvary by *Giovanni Battista Tiepolo*.

In front of the church a bridge leads over to Campo dei Mori with three statues of Moors popularly supposed to be the Levantine merchants of the Mastelli family. On the fondamenta (left) a plaque marks the residence of Tintoretto from 1574 to his death in 1594; the façade bears a quaint figure in a turban and several sculptural fragments.—Various calli lead back across three rii to *Campo Santa Fosca* (Pl. 2), near the large 15C Palazzo Giovanelli. Ponte Sant'Antonio leads to the pretty Campo della Maddalena with quaint old houses, and the round neo-classical church of the MADDALENA. Rio Terrà della Maddalena continues past several handsome palaces to Calle Larga Vendramin (left) which leads towards the Grand Canal and the land entrance to *Palazzo Vendramin* (the winter home of the Casinò). In the courtyard is a fine Byzantine well-head. A plaque records Wagner's death here in 1883. Nearby, on the Grand Canal is the church of **San Marcuola** (Pl. 2). The interior contains statues by Giovanni Maria Morleiter, and paintings by the school of Titian, Tintoretto, and Francesco Migliori.—The wide Rio Terrà di San Leonardo, to the N, leads to the CANNAREGIO CANAL (Pl. 1), a busy waterway with two broad fondamenta, which traverses a distinctive part of the city. The stone *Ponte delle Guglie* dates from 1580. A sottoportico diverges right from the fondamenta into the **Ghetto** (Pl. 1,2).

The word 'ghetto' is derived from 'getto', to 'cast' metals; there was an iron foundry here until 1390. In 1516 Jews were given permission to inhabit this area, and not until 1797 were they allowed to live in other parts of the city. In the Campiello delle Scuole are the *Scola Spagnola*, with an interior by Longhena, and the *Scola Levantina*, with an exterior attributed to pupils of Longhena (both synagogues are still in use, and shown on tours from the Jewish Museum). The island of the GHETTO NUOVO is the oldest area of the ghetto. Here are characteristic tall houses, three more synagogues, and the JEWISH MUSEUM (adm. July–October, 9.30–17; March–June, 10.30–13, 14.30–17; winter 10–12.30; always closed on Saturday, and Sunday afternoon). On the upper floor is the *Scola Tedesca*, the oldest synagogue (1528). Guided tours of the ghetto and three synagogues are given from the Museum at 10.30 and 11.30.

The fondamenta continues along the Cannaregio canal to the next bridge, across which is the church of **San Giobbe** (Pl. 1), built after 1450 by Antonio Gambello and enlarged by Pietro Lombardo who designed the fine *Doorway.

INTERIOR. The domed *SANCTUARY is a masterpiece of Renaissance architecture and carving by *Pietro Lombardo* and assistants. The altarpieces on the S side are by *Lorenzo Querena* and *Paris Bordone*. On the N side is a statue of St Luke by *Lorenzo Bregno*, and the CAPPELLA MARTINI, a 15C Tuscan work. The vault contains five Roundels by the Della Robbia workshop, and on the altar are statuettes by a follower of *Antonio Rossellino*. The ANTE-SACRISTY contains a Nativity by *Girolamo Savoldo*, and the SACRISTY paintings by *Andrea Previtali*, and *Antonio Vivarini* and *Giovanni d'Alamagna*.

The fondamenta leads back along the canal past several large palaces. By Ponte delle Guglie is PALAZZO LABIA, with two 18C façades. The Ballroom has trompe l'oeil frescoes by Gerolamo

Mengozzi-Colonna, and *Frescoes of Antony and Cleopatra by Giovanni Battista Tiepolo.—In Campo San Geremia is the church of SAN GEREMIA (Pl. 1,2). The relics of St Lucy (martyred in Syracuse in 304), stolen from Constantinople in 1204 by Venetian crusaders, are preserved here. The garish *Lista di Spagna* (given over to the tourist trade) leads to the Station, past the church of the SCALZI (Pl. 1,5), a good Baroque building by Longhena (1670–80), with a façade by Giuseppe Sardi. It contains damaged frescoes by Giovanni Battista Tiepolo.

J.   The Island of San Giorgio Maggiore and the Giudecca

The island of SAN GIORGIO MAGGIORE (Pl. 16) can be reached by vaporetto from San Marco, or from the Zattere and the Giudecca. This lovely small island was for long occupied by an important Benedictine convent. In 1951 the Giorgio Cini Foundation was established here and the buildings beautifully restored. The church of *San Giorgio Maggiore* (Pl. 16) is one of the most conspicuous in Venice, in a magnificent position facing St Mark's. The white façade, tall campanile, and brick building reflect the changing light of the lagoon, and are especially beautiful at sunset. The building was begun in 1566 by *Palladio* and finished in 1610 by *Simone Sorella*.

The FAÇADE was designed by Palladio in 1565 and built after his death.—The white INTERIOR is remarkable for its clean architectural lines. It contains a monument to Doge Leonardo Donà by *Alessandro Vittoria*, and altarpieces by *Jacopo Bassano, Jacopo Tintoretto*, and *Sebastiano Ricci*.—In the chancel is the high altar by *Aliense*, and *Gerolamo Campagna*, and two good late works by *Tintoretto*, *The Last Supper, and *The Shower of Manner. The Baroque *Choir stalls are by *Albert van der Brulle* and *Gaspare Gatti*.—In the CHAPEL OF THE DEAD is a *Deposition by the *School of Tintoretto*.—The view from the CAMPANILE (lift) is one of the best in Venice.

The adjoining *Monastery, now part of the Giorgio Cini Foundation, may be visited when exhibitions are being held, or by previous appointment. The Foundation includes a Centre of Culture and Civilization, an Arts and Crafts Centre, and a Naval Training School. The *First Cloister* was designed by Palladio; beyond the *Library* wing by Longhena, is the *Second Cloister* by Andrea Buora. Off it is the handsome *Refectory*, a splendid work by Palladio.

From the island of San Giorgio Maggiore the vaporetto crosses to **La Giudecca** (Pl. 13,14), occupying eight islands, also connected directly by a ferry with the Zattere. It is one of the most characteristic parts of the city, and less visited by tourists. The church of LE ZITELLE was planned by Palladio and built after his death. The fondamenta continues past ship-building warehouses and the Venice Youth Hostel to the Franciscan church of the *Redentore*, the most complete and perhaps the most successful of *Palladio*'s churches, with a good façade.

The church was built in thanksgiving for the deliverance of Venice from the plague in 1575–76, and the doge vowed to visit the church annually across a bridge of boats which united the Zattere with the Giudecca. The feast of the Redentore remains one of the most popular Venetian festivals.—The splendid INTERIOR has elements derived from Roman classical buildings, and the design of the chancel is particularly fine. It contains paintings by *Francesco Bassano*, the workshop of *Jacopo Tintoretto*, and *Palma Giovane*, and (in the Sacristy) works by *Carlo Saraceni* and *Alvise Vivarini*. The main altar has bronzes by *Campagna*.

The long fondamenta ends at the church of SANT'EUFEMIA with a rococo interior and a painting of St Roch and the Angel by Bartolomeo Vivarini (recently restored). At the W extremity of the island rises the huge *Mulino Stucky*, a neo-Gothic flour-mill built by Ernst Wullekopf in 1895, which has been abandoned for years.

The Venetian Lagoon

The Venetian Lagoon, separated from the Adriatic by the low and narrow sand-bars of the Lido and Pellestrina which are pierced by three channels, the Porto di Lido, the Porto di Malamocco, and the Porto di Chioggia, is a shallow expanse of water, 210 square miles in area. Rather more than half of this is the *Laguna Morta*, under water only at high spring tides; the remainder is the *Laguna Viva*, perennially flooded. On some of the islands townships and monasteries were established in the Middle Ages. The future of many of the smaller islands, abandoned in the 1960s and 1970s is uncertain. The hauntingly beautiful but desolate lagoon today supports a few small fishing communities and market gardens, apart from the famous Lido and the glass manufactories of Murano. Motor-launches provide an excellent service between the main islands. Plan on p 362.

K. The Islands of San Michele, Murano, Burano, and Torcello

Vaporetto No. 5 serves the islands of San Michele and Murano; a vaporetto or steamer service (No. 12) from Fondamenta Nuove calls at Murano, Mazzorbo, Torcello, and Burano (c every 1–1½ hrs; to Torcello and Burano in 40–50 minutes).

The walled **Island of San Michele** is the Cemetery of Venice. SAN MICHELE IN ISOLA by Mauro Coducci (1469–78) is the earliest Renaissance church in the city. The elegant and well-sited Façade has a good doorway with a 15C statue of the Madonna and Child.

INTERIOR. A marble lozenge in the floor marks the burial place of Fra Paolo Sarpi (died 1623). The Monument to Cardinal Giovanni Dolfin (died 1622) is by *Pietro Bernini*, with a bust by his son *Gian Lorenzo*. The stone statue of St Jerome is by *Juste Le Court*. In the left apse chapel is an altarpiece by *Gian Domenico Tiepolo* (removed for safety).—The charming little Renaissance CAPPELLA EMILIANA by *Guglielmo dei Grigi Bergamasco* contains fine marble inlay and reliefs by *Giovanni Antonio da Carona*.

In the Camaldolensian monastery Fra Mauro (1433–59), the cartographer, was a monk.—In the **Cemetery**, planted with magnificent cypresses, the writer Baron Corvo (Frederick Rolfe; died 1913) is buried. In the Protestant enclosure lies the poet Ezra Pound, and in the adjacent Orthodox cemetery are buried Serge Diaghilev (1872–1929), and near him his composer protégé Igor Stravinsky (1882–1971; died in New York).

The boat continues to the **Island of Murano**, about 1·5km from Venice. Since 1292 it has been the centre of the Venetian glass industry. The art of making crystal glass was rediscovered by the Venetians who retained the monopoly throughout the 16C. The special characteristics of Venetian glass are its elaborate design, lightness, and bright colour. After a period of decline the industry was revived at the end of the 19C, and the production of artistic glass is still thriving, and the numerous glass factories all welcome visitors. Near the centre of the island is **San Pietro Martire**, a Dominican Gothic church.

INTERIOR. On the S side are an Immaculate Conception (removed for restoration) and *Madonna with angels and saints, both by *Giovanni Bellini*. In the chapel to the left of the high altar, paintings by the school of *Pordenone*, *Agostino da Lodi*, *Francesco di Simone da Santacroce*, *Nicolò Rondinelli*, and *Domenico Tintoretto*.—The elaborate panelling in the SACRISTY is by *Pietro Morando*.

Ponte Vivarini crosses the main Canale degli Angeli near the restored *Palazzo Da Mula*, one of the few traces of Murano's ancient splendour. A fondamenta leads left to SANTA MARIA DEGLI ANGELI, with an Annunciation attributed to Antonio Rizzo, a ceiling painted by Pier Maria Pennacchi, and an altarpiece by Pordenone.—In the other direction the fondamenta leads to PALAZZO GIUSTINIAN which contains the **Museo Vetrario** (Glass Museum; adm. 10–16; festivals 9.30–12.30; closed Wednesday).

The good collection of glass from the oldest Roman period to the 18C is beautifully displayed. The earliest Murano glass to survive (15C) includes the famous *Barovier Marriage Cup. There is also an excellent display illustrating how glass is made.—The modern and contemporary glass is now exhibited in the Consorzio Vetraio on Rio dei Vetrai (near the vaporetto landing stage of 'Colonna').

A little farther on the magnificent *Apse of the Venetian Byzantine basilica of ***Santa Maria e Donato** fronts the canal.

The church, founded in the 7C, was rebuilt in the 12C, and was restored in 1979. The FAÇADE incorporates Roman columns. The splendid *PAVEMENT in the interior dates from 1141. In the apse is a Byzantine mosaic of the Virgin. In the N aisle is a wooden ancona of St Donato (1310), and a Madonna by Lazzaro Bastiani.—The BAPTISTERY contains a Roman sarcophagus from Altino (2C), once used as a font.

The boat for Torcello skirts the E side of Murano and then steers out into the lagoon along a channel marked by piles. Ahead, the green island of San Francesco del Deserto and the leaning campanile of Burano soon come into view, and in the far distance, the cathedral and campanile of Torcello. The boat passes *San Giacomo in Palude*, an island abandoned in 1964. The cypresses of *San Francesco del Deserto* are now prominent to the right. After passing the abandoned ammunition factory on the island of the *Madonna del Monte*, the boat enters the pretty canal of MAZZORBO, lined with a few villas and a boat-yard. The little settlement is connected by a long bridge with Burano (the boat usually calls first at Torcello).

***Torcello**, though now a small group of houses in a lonely part of the lagoon, still preserves some lovely relics of its days of splendour, when, from the 7C to the 13C, it was the insular stronghold of the people of Altinum, who were driven from the mainland by the Lombard invaders. At one time Torcello is said to have had 20,000 inhabitants, but by the 15C the rivalry of Venice and the malaria due to the marshes formed by the silting up of the Sile had brought about its downfall.

A pleasant walk leads along a canal from the landing-stage (c 10 minutes) to the ***Cathedral** (closed 12.30–14), founded in 639. This

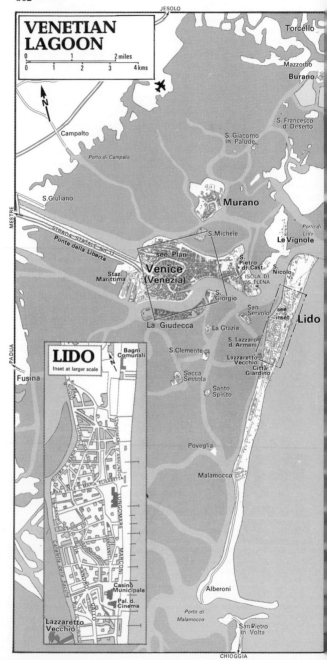

VENETIAN LAGOON

0   1   2 miles
0   1   2   3   4 kms

JESOLO

Torcello

Mazzorbo

Burano

S. Francesco
d' Deserto

Campalto

Porto di Campalo

S. Giacomo
in Palude

S.Giuliano

Murano

MESTRE

STRADA STATALE No.11
Ponte della Libertà

S.Michele

Porto di
Lido

Le Vignole

see Plan

S. Pietro
di Cast.

S. Nicolò

Staz.
Marittima

Venice
(Venezia)

ISOLA DI
S.ELENA

PADUA

S. Giorgio

San
Servolo

see
inset

Lido

La Giudecca

La Grazia

S. Lazzaro
d. Armeni

Fusina

LIDO
Inset at larger scale

Bagni
Comunali

S. Clemente

Lazzaretto
Vecchio

Città
Giardino

Sacca
Sessola

Santo
Spirito

LUNGOMARE G. D'ANNUNZIO

GRAN VIALE S. MARIA ELISABETTA

LUNGOMARE MARCONI

RIVIERA S. NICOLO

Poveglia

Malamocco

CASERMA DELLE SACCHE

Casino
Municipale

Pal. d.
Cinema

Lazzaretto
Vecchio

Alberoni

*Porto di
Malamocco*

San Pietro
in Volta

CHIOGGIA

Veneto-Byzantine building, derived from the Ravenna-type basilicas was rebuilt in 1008. At the W end are remains of the 7C Baptistery.

The INTERIOR has eighteen slender marble columns with good capitals and a superb pavement of 'opus Alexandrinum'. An elaborate Byzantine *Mosaic (11–12C; restored) of the Last Judgement covers the W wall. The marble pulpit and ambo are made up from fragments from the earliest church. The four elaborately carved *Transennae (11C) are fine examples of late-Byzantine design; above the columns are 15C local paintings. There is an interesting 7C marble Synthronon in the apse. Below the high altar is a pagan sarcophagus (3C), which contains the relics of St Heliodorus, first bishop of Altinum. Set in to the wall is the foundation stone of the church (639). In the apse, on a stark gold ground, is a mosaic of the *Madonna, one of the most striking figures ever produced in Byzantine art. The other ancient mosaics here are also of the highest interest.—The tall detached CAMPANILE (11–12C; no adm.) is a striking land-mark in the lagoon.

The church of *SANTA FOSCA dates from the 11C but it has been drastically restored. It is built on a Greek-cross plan, and is surround-ed by an octagonal portico on three sides. It has a conical wooden roof.— On the grass outside is a primitive stone seat known as 'Attila's chair'. In the loggia of the *Palazzo dell'Archivio* are fine Roman sculptural fragments dating from the late Empire, from Torcello and Altinum. The *Palazzo del Consiglio* now houses the MUSEO DI TOR-CELLO (adm. 10–12.30, 14–17.30) which contains an interesting and well displayed collection of objects from the demolished churches of Torcello and archaeological material.

Burano is a cheerful little fishing village of great charm with brightly painted houses and miniature canals. It was for long celebrated as the centre of the Venetian lace industry, and lace is still made and sold on the island. The parish church contains paintings by Girolamo da Santacroce, Giovanni Battista Tiepolo, and Giovanni Mansueti. The Scuola dei Merletti has a delightful Museum of Lace (adm. 9–18; Sunday 10–16).

San Francesco del Deserto, an island to the S in a deserted part of the lagoon, can be reached by hiring a boat on Burano from the local fishermen near the parish church (the journey takes about 20 minutes). It is said to have been a retreat of St Francis in 1220, and visitors (admitted 9–11, 15–17 only) are shown the church and gardens by one of the ten friars who still live here.

L. The Lido

The island of the Lido is reached from Venice by numerous water-buses (frequent service; see p 324).

The N end of the **Lido**, the largest of the islands between the Lagoon and the Adriatic, had, by the beginning of this century, become the most fashionable seaside resort in Italy. It bequeathed its name to numerous bathing resorts all over the world. The Adriatic sea-front consists of a group of luxurious hotels and villas bordering the fine sandy beach, which is divided up into sections, each belonging (except at the extreme ends) to a particular hotel or bathing establish-ment. The rest of the N part of the island has become a residential district of Venice, with fine trees and gardens, and traversed by several canals. The atmosphere on the Lido is very different from that in the city of Venice itself, not least because of the presence of cars.

The *Gran Viale Santa Maria Elisabetta*, the main street traversing the widest part of the island leads from the lagoon to the sea-front. Here is the *Grand Hotel des Bains* which provided the setting for Thomas Mann's 'Death in Venice'. Farther S is the CASINÒ and the Excelsior Palace Hotel (built by Giovanni Sardi).—At the N end of the island is the church of SAN NICOLÒ AL LIDO, used by the Doge as the official place to receive visitors. The N tip of the island overlooks the PORTO DI LIDO, the main entrance to the lagoon and always strongly defended in Republican days. On the island of Le Vignole is the *Forte di Sant'Andrea*, the masterpiece of Sanmicheli (1543). In the channel here the Doge performed the annual ceremony of the marriage with the sea, when he threw his ring into the sea from the Bucintoro and it was retrieved by a young fisherman.

Across the channel is *Punta Sabbioni* on the mainland, connected by road with **Lido di Jesolo**, a huge bathing resort, between the old and new mouths of the Piave. It may be reached by water-bus in summer from the Riva to Punta Sabbioni in connection with a bus (c ½hr). The old village of *Iesolo*, formerly Cavazuccherina, 1·5km N of the E end, perpetuates the name of an early-medieval centre, known also as *Equilium*, the rival of Heraclea in the affairs of the lagoon. Here some remains of a Romanesque church survived until the Austrian offensive of June 1918.—The bus goes on to San Donà (Rte 36).

On the narrow S end of the Lido is **Malamocco**, a quiet fishing village; the ancient *Metamauco* was one of the first places to be inhabited in the lagoon, and it was the scene of the famous defeat of king Pepin who had laid siege to the city in 810.—Beyond ALBERONI, a little bathing resort with the LIDO golf course, a car ferry crosses the *Porto di Malamocco* to the thin Island of **Pellestrina**, with several fishing villages. To the S stretch the famous *Murazzi*, a great sea wall built in 1744–82 by Temanza on either side of the Porto di Chioggia, the third and last entrance to the lagoon.

The island of **San Lazzaro degli Armeni**, just off the Lido, is reached by vaporetto from Riva degli Schiavoni. The boat first calls at the island of *San Servolo*, once an important Benedictine convent, later used as a hospital, and since 1980 occupied by a European foundation for the training of craftsmen in restoration work, funded by the Council of Europe. San Lazzaro is distinguished by its tall campanile crowned by an oriental cupola. It was used from 1182 as a leper colony. Since 1717 it has been the seat of a Roman Catholic Armenian monastery; the community is celebrated for its polyglot printing press. Visitors (admitted Sunday and Thursday, 15–17) are shown the fine collection of illuminated manuscripts, a fresco by Giovanni Battista Tiepolo, a small museum, and Byron's room which he used when he came here to study Armenian as a means of conquering his boredom.

Many of the other small islands in the lagoon, formerly used as hospitals or military deposits, have recently been abandoned, and plans for their future are uncertain.

33 Environs of Venice

A. Chioggia

Chioggia may be reached by bus (No. 11) and ferry from the Lido, or (via the mainland) by bus from Piazzale Roma.

Chioggia, one of the main fishing ports on the Adriatic (particularly famous for mussels), is situated at the S extremity of the Venetian lagoon, connected to the mainland by a bridge (1921). The most important town after Venice on the lagoon, its remarkable longitudinal urban structure survives. It is traversed by three canals running N–S and a parallel wide main street.

Its early importance was due to the producion of salt, and its position as a port. The history of Chioggia has been intimately involved with that of Venice since it was first settled by inhabitants of Este, Monselice, and Padua, in the 5–7C. The defeat of the Genoese here in 1379 by the Venetians under Vettor Pisani marked the end of the struggle between the two rival maritime powers.

Near the quay is the church of *San Domenico* with paintings by Pietro Damini, Andrea Vicentino, Carpaccio (St Paul, signed and dated 1520), and Leandro Bassano. The CORSO DEL POPOLO, the lively main street, with porticoes and cafés, traverses the town parallel to the picturesque *Canale della Vena* used by the fishing fleet. The church of *Sant'Andrea* has a Veneto-Byzantine campanile and a painting by Il Chioggiotto. The *Granaio* (1322; restored), now the market hall, bears a Madonna and Child by Jacopo Sansovino. On the canal behind is the picturesque fish market. The church of *Santissima Trinità* was rebuilt by Andrea Tirali in 1703. The ceiling of the Oratory has paintings by the School of Tintoretto. The churches of the *Filippini* and *San Giacomo* contain interesting paintings. The early Gothic church of *San Martino* (disused) has an interesting exterior. In the piazza stands the **Duomo**.

The INTERIOR was reconstructed by *Longhena* in 1624. It contains paintings by the *School of Bellini, Andrea Vicentino, Alvise dal Friso, Pietro Malombra, Benedetto Caliari, Il Chioggiotto, Giovanni Battista Cignaroli, Gaspare Diziani, Giovanni Battista Tiepolo, Giovanni Battista Piazzetta, Pietro Liberi*, and *Gian Mattei*.

A long bridge connects Chioggia with **Sottomarina**, now a seaside resort.

B. The Brenta Canal

The best way of seeing the Brenta Canal is from the 'Burchiello' motor-launch, see the beginning of Rte 31.— *Malcontenta* can be reached easily by bus from Piazzale Roma.

Venice is connected to the mainland by a road bridge (over 3·5km long), Ponte della Libertà, built in 1931–32, and a (parallel) railway bridge (1841–42). On the left the commercial port of MARGHERA, built in 1919–28, with an oil depot, is conspicuous.—8km Motorway junction and flyover for **Mestre** (184,000 inhab.), a dull modern town and important rail junction, now incorporated in Venice, which it has outgrown.—12.5km Turning right for **Malcontenta** with the famous *Villa Foscari* (adm. 1 May–30 October, Tuesday, Saturday, and the first Sunday of the month, 9–12), one of the most beautiful of the Venetian villas, built in 1555–60 by Palladio.

The road (N 11) now follows the Brenta Canal lined with numerous villas built by the Venetian aristocracy.—Near (16km) *Oriago* is *Villa Costanzo (Widmann-Foscari)* dating from 1719 but transformed in the French Baroque style (adm. daily except Monday, 9–12, 15–18).—The long village of (20km) **Mira** is one of the most attractive places on the Brenta. Here the post office occupies the *Palazzo Foscarini* where Byron, between 1817 and 1819, wrote the fourth canto of 'Childe Harold' and was visited by Thomas Moore. Here, too, he first met Margherita Cogni, whom he called 'la bella Fornarina'. Beyond Dolo is (30km) **Strà**, famous for the *Villa Nazionale* (or *Pisani*), the largest of the 18C Venetian villas, with *Frescoes by Giovanni Battista Tiepolo (adm. 9–13,30 except Monday; the park is open 9–dusk). It was bought from the Pisani in 1807 by Napoleon, who presented it to Eugène Beauharnais, and it was the scene of the first meeting between Hitler and Mussolini in 1934.—Beyond Strà the road crosses the Brenta river and leaves the canal. Just before (36km) *Ponte di Brenta* is *Noventa Padovana*, with the *Villa Valmarana* (now an institution) and other villas. The road passes under the motorway and soon joins the Padua ringroad.—42km **Padua**, see Rte 31.

34   Venice to Treviso, Belluno, and Pieve di Cadore

A.   Via Vittorio Veneto

ROAD, 133km. N13. 30km **Treviso**.—58km **Conegliano**.—N51. 71km **Vittorio Veneto**.—100km *Ponte nelle Alpe*.—133km **Pieve di Cadore**.—The MOTORWAY (A 27) follows this route as far as the N outskirts of Vittorio Veneto.

RAILWAY, 135km in 2½ hours.

From the landward end of the Venice road bridge, the Mestre by-pass diverges right to join N13 north of the town beyond the motorway junction for Trieste. The road, with the railway on the left, drives due N across the *Terraglio*, a plain once dotted with aristocratic Venetian villas, via (18km) *Mogliano Veneto* and (23km) *Preganziol*. At Zerman, to the right of the road, is the Villa Condulmer (now a hotel, but adm. freely granted).

30km **TREVISO** is a bright and attractive provincial capital (90,400 inhab.) traversed by several branches of the Sile and the Cagnan. The canals give it an atmosphere reminiscent of Venice. Many of its narrow streets are lined with arcades and the older houses often overhang the pavement (their exterior frescoes have now mostly disappeared). The streets are decorated with numerous fountains. New building following severe war-damage, avoiding extremes of preservation or innovation, did not rob the old town of its character.

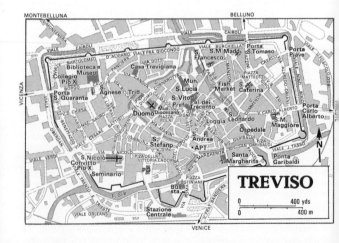

Post Office, Piazzale della Vittoria.—**Tourist Office**, Palazzo Scotti, 41 Via Toniolo.—**Buses** from the station to Piazza Indipendenza, etc.; also to Mestre and Venice.—**Teatro Comunale**, Corso del Popolo, Music Festival, October–January.—**Airport** (*San Giuseppe*) at Sant'Angelo (charter flights).

History. Treviso in the Middle Ages, as capital of the Marca Trevigiana, was well known for its hospitality to poets and artists, especially under the dominion of the Da Camino family (1283–1312). From 1389 to 1796 it was loyal to the Venetian Empire. During both world wars it suffered from air raids, notably on Good Friday, 1944, when half the city was destroyed in a few minutes. Treviso was the birthplace of the painters Pier Maria Pennacchi (1464–c 1528) and Paris Bordone (1500–71), and of Pope St Benedict XI (Nicolò Boccasini, 1240–1303), a great Dominican.—The works of Tomaso da Modena, a brilliant successor of Giotto, are best studied in this city.

Travellers from Venice by road or rail enter the town by Via Roma and Corso del Popolo, crossing the Sile, with the Romanesque tower of *San Martino* (church modernised) on the left. Via Venti Settembre, bearing left, leads on to PIAZZA DEI SIGNORI, the animated centre of the town, where many streets converge. To the right here is *Palazzo dei Trecento* (restored), the 13C council house, and the adjoining *Palazzo del Podestà* (now the Prefecture) rebuilt in antique style in 1874–77, with a tall battlemented tower. Behind them, in a little cobbled piazza, is the *Monte di Pietà* (ring for adm. at No. 2; weekdays 8.30–13), with the charming 16C Cappella dei Rettori (works by Francesco Vecellio and Pozzoserrato). Beyond, through an archway, are *San Vito* and *Santa Lucia*, two adjoining medieval churches. Santa Lucia has good frescoes by Tomaso da Modena and pupils, and a charming balustrade around the altar with half-figures of Saints, probably dating from the late 14C. In San Vito are Veneto-Byzantine frescoes of the 12–13C.

The Calmaggiore, an arcaded street, leads from Piazza dei Signori to the **Duomo** (*San Pietro*), an attractive building with seven domes beside the little 12C church of San Giovanni Battista (called the Baptistery), and the detached Campanile. Founded in the 12C, the cathedral underwent repeated alterations and extensions, down to the W portico, added in 1836 (retaining two Romanesque lions). It was restored after severe war damage.

INTERIOR. South Aisle. In a niche on the second pilaster, *Lorenzo Bregno*, relief of the Visitation. At the end of the aisle is the MALCHIOSTRO CHAPEL (light to right of the altar), added in 1519, with frescoes (restored in 1982) by *Pordenone* and assistants, notably the *Adoration of the Magi (1520). The *Annunciation is by *Titian* (restored in 1976); the figure of Broccardo Malchiostro is a later addition. In the vestibule of the chapel are the jambs of the 12C W portal, the *Adoration of the shepherds by *Paris Bordone*, the 'Madonna del Fiore', by *Girolamo da Treviso il Vecchio*, the tomb of Bishop Castellano (1332), and a Romanesque relief of the Redeemer.—In the retro-choir, frescoes by *Lodovico Seitz* (1880); on the right, tomb of Pope Alexander VIII (died 1691), with a remarkable portrait-statue by *Giovanni Bonazza*; on the left, *Monument of Bishop Zanetto (1485), by *Antonio* and *Tullio Lombardo*, in collaboration with their father *Pietro*. On the high altar is the urn of Saints Teonisto, Tabra, and Tabrata, with sculpted portraits attributed to *Tullio Lombardo*. The Chapel of the Sacrament (1513–14) at the end of the N aisle, has good sculptures by *Giovanni Battista* and *Lorenzo Bregno*. In the vestibule is the fine *Tomb of Bishop Franco (1501). North Aisle. 3rd chapel, *Francesco Bissolo*, Santa Giustina and Saints. The figure of St Sebastian, against the pillar of the nave, is by *Lorenzo Bregno*. The interesting crypt, beneath the choir (apply to the sacristan) has 68 columns and fragmentary 14C mosaics (recently restored). The sacristan also unlocks the so-called Baptistery, a little rectangular church (see above) dating from the 12C. It contains two 13C fresco fragments of the Madonna and Child. On the exterior wall is a Roman funerary stele (3C AD) with two male half-figures.

From Piazza Duomo (right of the façade) Via Canoniche leads under an arch to a circular Roman mosaic, a paleochristian work of the early 4C AD, probably belonging to a baptistery. Beyond (left) the Gothic *Canoniche Vecchie* have been restored to house the **Museo Diocesano d'Arte Sacra**, reopened in 1988 (adm. Tuesday, Thursday, & Saturday 9–12). It contains archaeological material, two frescoes of the Martyrdom of St Thomas Becket and Christ in Limbo (c 1260), a detached fresco lunette by Tomaso da Modena from the Palazzo Vescovile, Romanesque and Gothic sculpture, church silver and vestments, a tapestry of 1500, and 17C and 18C paintings and sculpture.

Via Canova and Borgo Cavour prolong the Calmaggiore to the city wall. To the right in Via Canova, beyond two pleasant cloistered courts, is the *Museo della Casa Trevigiana* (closed for restoration for a number of years), a decorative building of the 14C (enlarged in the 16C) with a collection of applied art (including a remarkable display of wrought iron work), and musical instruments. In the garden (removed from nearby) is the quaint 14C Municipio. In Borgo Cavour are the *Library* and **Museo Civico** (adm. 9–12, 14–17, holidays 9–12; closed Monday). The room numbers are eratic, but the works are well labelled.

The ground floor (9 rooms and the cortile) contains (R. 2) the remarkable bronze ritual discs (5C BC) from Montebelluna and (R. 1) a unique collection of bronze sword-blades dredged from the Sile and its tributaries (Hallstatt period). The Roman relics include the tomb of a citizen of Tarvisium (Treviso) and statuettes from Oderzo. Early-Christian and Byzantine sculptures.

The PICTURE GALLERY is on the first floor. At the top of stairs, *Giovanni Battista Tiepolo*, Flora (detached fresco from Villa Corner at Merlengo). The chronological display starts in the room to the right (R 8). Here are exhibited: sculpture, including works by *Pietro Lombardo*, and paintings by *Giovanni Bellini* and bottega, and *Cima da Conegliano* and bottega.—R. 9. Works by *Girolamo da Treviso* and *Girolamo da Santacroce*.—R. 10. Works by *Paris Bordone*.—R. 11. *Titian*, Portrait of Sperone Speroni; *Lorenzo Lotto*, *Portrait of a dominican; *Jacopo Bassano*, Crucifixion.—R. 12. *Pordenone*, St Anthony Abbot.—R. 13. Frescoes of Pages attributed to *Benedetto* and *Carletto Caliari*; *Arminio Zuccato*, Mosaic. Outside the door are two wooden statues of Patriarchs (17C, Venetian).—In the group of seven rooms beyond (across the stair landing) are exhibited 16–18C works by *Salvatore Rosa*, *Pietro Muttoni*, *Pozzoserrato* (Fire in the Doges' Palace in 1577), *Borgognone*, Flemish and German painters, *Giuseppe Cignaroli*, *Antonio Molinari*, *Giuseppe Zais*, *Francesco Guardi*, *Gian Domenico Tiepolo*, *Pietro Longhi*, and *Rosalba Carriera*.—In the last group of rooms off the stair landing is a large collection of 19C and 20C works including paintings by *Guglielmo Ciardi* (1842–1917), and a good group of sculptures and charcoal drawings by the native artist *Arturo Martini* (1889–1947), including 'La Pisana' (1930). There is also a portrait of Canova by *Sir Thomas Lawrence*.—Also in the museum (but not on display) are the prisms with which Newton made his experiments with the refraction of light, which passed into the hands of his disciple Count Algarotti.

At the end of the street is *Porta dei Santi Quaranta*, a town-gate of 1517. To the N is the most interesting stretch of city wall, built by Fra Giocondo and others in 1509–18, the top of which has been laid out as a promenade almost as far as *Porta San Tomaso*, another fine gateway. The wall itself is better seen from the *Gardens* outside.

In the SW district is the large Dominican church of *San Nicolò**, built in brick in the 13–14C, with a fine triple polygonal apse. The massive columns inside are frescoed with *Saints by *Tomaso da Modena* (St Agnes, on the N side is especially charming). On the S wall the 15C altars have good decoration. The huge fresco of St Christopher (1410) is attributed to *Antonio da Treviso*. In the apse is a *Madonna and saints by *Marco Pensaben* and *Savoldo* (1521; being restored in situ in 1990); on the right is a memorial (1693) to St Benedict XI, the chief founder of the church; on the left the tomb of Agostino d'Onigo (c 1500), with sculptures by *Antonio Rizzo*, and *Pages, frescoed by *Lorenzo Lotto*. The fine altarpiece in the chapel to the right of the high altar has portraits of members of the Monigo commission attributed to *Lotto*. On the walls are frescoes by the Sienese school (c 1370; Adoration of the Magi, St Margaret of Hungary) and the contemporary Riminese school (votive image of the Madonna and Saints. The chapel to the left of the presbytery has an altarpiece of the Risen Christ by *Giovanni Battista Bregno*. The 16C organ by *Gaetano Callido* was decorated by *Antonio Palma*.

A door leads into the cloister of the adjoining *Seminario* (adm. also from Via San Nicolò; ring for the porter) where the chapter house contains delightful *Frescoes of 40 leading Dominicans, by Tomaso da Modena (1352). Several interesting frescoes in the Byzantine style are temporarily stored here. There is also an ethnographical museum.

In Via Martiri della Libertà, leading NE from the Corso, is the *Loggia dei Cavalieri*, a Romanesque building of 1195. Near San Leonardo, beyond remains of an old water-mill beneath a modern building, is the picturesque *Fishmarket* on an island in the Cagnan. Via San Parisio continues left to *San Francesco*, a large brick church of the 13C, restored in 1928 after many years' use as an army store. In the floor near the S door is the tomb slab of Francesca, daughter of Petrarch, who died in child-birth in 1384; in the N transept, that of Pietro Alighieri (died 1364), the son of Dante; and, in the chapel to the left of the high altar, Madonna and Saints, a fresco by Tomaso da Modena (1351). Opposite the S door is part of a huge fresco of St Christopher.

The deconsecrated church of *Santa Caterina* (closed for restoration), stands a little to the E of the Fishmarket (see above). In the Cappella degli Innocenti are frescoes by Tomaso da Modena. The Virgin Annunciate and *Story of the life of St Ursula, a splendid series of frescoes, by *Tomaso da Modena* are now also displayed here. They were detached in 1882 from Santa Margherita sul Sile before it was demolished. Via Carlo Alberto leads to *Santa Maria Maggiore*, a church of 1474 containing a tomb by Bambaia and a much-venerated Madonna originally frescoed by Tomaso da Modena. The delightful Riviera Garibaldi (reminiscent of Amsterdam), alongside the Sile, returns towards the centre.

At *Istrana*, 10km W of Treviso on the Castelfranco road, the 18C Villa Lattes, now part of the Museo Civico of Treviso (open Tuesday, Friday, Saturday, and Sunday, 9–12), has a collection of furniture, oriental art, musical boxes, 19C dolls, etc.
    From Treviso to *Castelfranco* and *Vicenza*, see Rte 30A, to *Udine*, and to *Oderzo*, see Rte 35.

From Treviso N13 continues due N, crossing the Piave at *Ponte della Priula*, with a votive temple commemorating the BATTLE OF THE PIAVE, where in 1918 the Italians withstood the last Austro-Hungarian attack and launched their successful counter-offensive. There are British war cemeteries at *Tezze* (8km E) and at *Giavera* (9km W).—58km **Conegliano** is a wine-growing town (31,500 inhab.), noted also as the birthplace of the painter Giovanni Battista Cima (c 1459–1518), and has many attractive 16–18C houses (notably in Via XX Settembre). The *Casa di Cima* (24 Via Cima; open Saturday and Sunday 16 or 17–18 or 19), is the seat of the Fondazione Giovanni Battista Cima with an archive, reproductions of his paintings, and archaeological material found during the restoration of the house. The *Cathedral* (14–15C) contains a fine altarpiece by Cima (1492); the adjacent guildhall ('Scuola dei Battuti'; adm. on request to sacristan 9.30–12, 15–19 except Wednesday) is covered with 16C frescoes attributed to Pozzoserrato, and inside are frescoes by Andrea Previtali, Jacopo da Montagnana, Francesco da Milano, and Gerolamo da Treviso (restored in 1962). In the main piazza is the neo-classical *Theatre* (1846–68). Above rises the ruined *Castello*, with a museum in one tower (adm. 8 or 9–12, 14 or 15.30–17.30 or 19 except Monday), and the Oratorio di Sant'Orsola.

Outside Conegliano N51 continues N to (71km) **Vittorio Veneto** (30,800 inhab.), the town that gave its name to the final victory of the Italians over the Austrians in October 1918. It was created in 1866 by merging the lower (now industrial) district of *Ceneda* with the old walled town of *Serravalle* which has many old houses and churches. Ceneda has a museum (10–12, 15 or 16–17 or 18; closed Monday and Friday) relating to the battle in the former Town Hall (1537–38) and a dramatic memorial of 1968. In Serravalle the *Ospedale Civile* contains the chapel of San Lorenzo (10–12, 16–19) with 15C frescoes. In the fine main piazza is the *Loggia di Serravalle* (1462), the old town hall, with the *Museo del Canedese*, which contains local archaeological finds, paintings, frescoes etc. (open 15–18; in winter 9–12; Saturday and fest. 9–12, 15–17.30). The 14C *Duomo* (rebuilt in 1776) contains a fine altarpiece by Titian (Madonna with Saints Peter and Andrew; 1547). The church of *San Giovanni Battista* (1357) contains 15C frescoes (some attributed to Jacobello del Fiore), and *Santa Giustina* contains the good tomb (1336–40) of Rizzardo IV da Camino.

Above Vittorio Veneto is the *Bosco del Cansiglio*, a high-lying plateau with forests of beech and fir (1120m) to the E. There is a natural history museum (open in summer, fest. 14.30–19; Saturday 9–12; Thursday 15–18) here.

Beyond Vittorio the road ascends the Meschio valley passing three power-reservoirs.—85km *Fadalto* lies just below the *Lago di Santa Croce*, now a supply reservoir, which the road skirts.—100km *Ponte nelle Alpi* is at the junction of two routes to the Cadore from the S. The road turns N and on the right, below the pyramidal *Piz Gallina* (1545m), is the dam of the hydro-electric system of Piave-Santa Croce. Beyond *Monte Toc* (right; 1921m) it reaches (133km) *Longarone*, almost totally wiped out by a disastrous flood.

In 1963 a landslide from Monte Toc into the basin of the Vaiont dam caused a huge water displacement to sweep through the Piave valley, destroying five villages and killing 1899 people. The dam, 6km E, now largely filled with rubble and a scene of desolation, is reached via the spectacular *Gola del Vaiont*.

The *Valle di Zoldo*, traversed by the Maè and a narrow road, ascends NW towards the Pelmo massif. The local dialect approaches the Ladin of the Cadore valleys. The chief centre is (17km) *Forno di Zoldo* (810m) at the junction of the Maè with several smaller torrents. Nearby is the 15C church of *San Floriano*, containing a 13C stone triptych and an altarpiece by Brustolon. The church of *Zoppè di Cadore*, 8km N beneath the Pelmo, has a Madonna by Titian. A good mountain road (20km) leads N into the Ampezzo valley.—At (21km) *Dont* (935m) is a monument to Andrea Brustolon (1662–1732), the famous woodcarver, whose work may be seen in many of the old village churches. The road on the left leads over the *Passo Duran* (1601m) to (21km) *Agordo*. Above Dont there is a splendid view of the Civetta (left) and Pelmo (right).—25km *Fusine* (1177m) is the chief centre of the upper valley which is visited for winter sports, beneath *Monte Civetta* (3220m).—27km *Pecol*, is another small summer and winter resort.—The valley road now ascends to (33km) the *Forcella Staulanza* (1773m), in full view of *Monte Pelmo* (3168m), then descends rapidly to (42km) *Selva di Cadore* (see Rte 29B).

113km *Castellavazzo*, the Roman Castrum Laebatii, dominated by the ruined castle-tower of Gardona, commands a fine view of the mountains upstream.—118km *Ospitale*, named from an ancient hospice.—127km *Peràrolo* stands at the confluence of the Boite and the Piave; the railway makes a circuit of the side-valley high above the village, and Monte Antelao is prominent to the left. Farther on the valley opens out, and at (132km) *Tai* the road reaches the upland basin of Pieve di Cadore and joins the Cortina road. From here to (133km) **Pieve di Cadore**, see Rte 29A.

B.   Via Feltre and Belluno

ROAD, 158km.—To (30km) **Treviso**, see Rte 34A. Leave by Borgo Cavour and turn right, N348.—50km Turning for *Montebelluna* (2km left).—85km **Feltre**, junction with the road from Trento.— N50. 115km **Belluno**.—123km *Ponte nelle Alpi*, and from there to **Pieve di Cadore**, see Rte 34A.

RAILWAY, 160km. Through trains daily to Calalzo-Pieve di Cadore in 3½–4hrs.

The Villa Barbaro at Maser, by Palladio

To (30km) **Treviso**, see Rte 34A. The Feltre road leaves Treviso by the Borgo Cavour, then bears right, crossing the Roman Via Postumia at (40km) *Postioma*, with the Montello in front.—49km A little to the left is seen **Montebelluna**, a modern town (22,300 inhab.) at the foot of the Montello, with a pleasant 17C church on a hill contrasting with the unattractive new cathedral below. It has a Museo Civico. At *Biadene*,

1km N of the town, in the former parish church (deconsecrated) a fresco of the Assumption of the Virgin has recently been attributed to Giovanni Battista Tiepolo, thought to be his earliest work in fresco.

The lovely old town of **Asolo** (described in Rte 30) is 13km W of Montebelluna. At (7km) *Maser* (easily reached by the Cornuda bus from Bassano del Grappa, see Rte 30), at the foot of the hills of Asolo, is the *Villa Barbaro, now *Villa Luling Buschetti*, built by Palladio in 1560–68 for Daniele Barbaro, patriarch of Aquileia. The house (adm. Tuesday, Saturday, Sunday, and fest. 15–18; October–May, 14–17; closed January and February) contains brilliant frescoes by Veronese and stuccoes by Alessandro Vittoria. In the grounds are a Carriage Museum and a fine Palladian *Temple.*—*Villa Emo at *Fanzolo*, 10km SW of Montebelluna, is open Saturday, Sunday, and fest. 15–18 (winter 14–17). Built by Palladio (1550–60) it has frescoes by Giovanni Battista Zelotti, and is well worth a visit.

Beyond Montebelluna rise (left) the Colli Asolani with the castle of Asolo, with Monte Grappa behind; to the right is the distant Monte Cavallo, then the nearer Monte Cesen shuts in the view.—57km *Cornuda*. The chapel of Santa Maria della Rocca crowns a prominent hill to the left. The road descends to the Piave and follows its right bank.—Opposite (64km) *Pederobba* is *Valdobbiadene* rebuilt since 1918. It has an ossuary containing the remains of Frenchmen who fell in Italy in the First World War. A road mounts to *Pianezze* (1070m), with winter sports facilities (chair-lift to Monte Barbaria, 1465m). The road from Valdobbiadene to Conegliano (34km; Rte 34A) is known as the 'Strada del Vino Bianco'.—Beyond (67km) *Fener* the valley narrows to form the Stretta di Quero; on the left rise the steep wooded slopes of Monte Tomatico; on the right, as the road recedes from the Piave valley, is *Santi Vittore e Corona*, an interesting Romanesque church of 1100 beside a 15C monastery, a pleasant walk from Feltre (½hr).

85km **Feltre** is an upland town (21,600 inhab.) whose ancient centre, largely rebuilt after a sack in 1509, rises above its modern extensions. Gateways survive at either end of the old main street, in which external frescoes by Morto da Feltre (? Leonardo Luzzo, died 1512) and his pupils adorn many houses, including the painter's own. Midway along Via Mezzaterra, opens *Piazza Maggiore* where stand the *Castle*, the 19C *Palazzo Guarnieri*, and the 16C *Palazzo della Ragione*, with a Palladian Loggia (1558). Inside is a little wooden *Theatre* rebuilt by Gian Antonio Selva in 1802 and recently restored. A 16C Fountain by Tullio Lombardo stands in the forecourt of *San Rocco* (1599). Via del Paradiso, with the decorated façade of the *Monte di Pietà* leads from the piazza to the *Museo Rizzarda*, notable for its superb wrought-iron work and housing the Galleria d'Arte Moderna. The *Museo Civico* (adm. 9–12; Saturday and Sunday also 16–18; closed Monday), within the E gate, contains Roman and Etruscan remains, a portrait by Gentile Bellini, a triptych by Cima da Conegliano, the Mystic Marriage of St Catherine and Portrait of Zaccaria dal Pozzo, both by the native artist Pietro de Mariscalchi, as well as examples of Morto da Feltre's work. The masterpiece of Morto (a Transfiguration) is in the sacristy of the *Ognissanti*, beyond the gate. From the square a 16C stairway descends to the S gate (1494) and to the *Cathedral*, which has a 15C apse and a campanile of 1392, heightened in 1690. It contains an Adoration of the Shepherds and St John the Baptist both by Pietro de Mariscalchi, and the tomb of Matteo Bellati designed by Tullio

Lombardo (1528). Also preserved here is a carved Byzantine cross of 542. Near the Renaissance Baptistery, remains of the paleochristian baptistery have been found.

Pedavena 4km N, noted for its beer, is a centre for easy climbs to the Feltrino peaks.

FROM FELTRE TO SAN MARTINO DI CASTROZZA. N50, 48km, bus in 1½hrs, a fine approach to the Southern Dolomites. This route follows the Primolano road to (6km) *Arten* and then bears right up the narrow and picturesque Cismon valley.—9km *Fonzaso*.—At (13km) *Ponte della Serra* it passes between two artificial lakes below (17km; left) *Lamon*.—An attractive by-road on the left at 21km ascends the Val Cortella to *Canale San Bovo* (8km) and *Caoria* (14km).— 30km *Imer* stands at the foot of the attractive Val Noana (right).—31km *Mezzano*. An important road ascends left in 5km to *Gobbera* (998m) and from there down to Canal San Bovo (4km farther; see above). For its continuation to the Valsugana, see Rte 22.

35km **Fiera di Primiero** (710m), with a Gothic church, is a climbing centre and a resort with winter sports facilities. It stands at the confluence of the Cismon and Canali. In the Val Canali is the ruined Castel Pietra.—Crossing the Cismon at (36km) *Siror*, another winter resort, the road ascends the left bank.—48km *San Martino di Castrozza*, see Rte 25.

From Feltre N50 turns NE and descends again to the Piave valley. At (92km) *Busche* the road divides to follow both banks of the river to Belluno. At 3km along the right branch is *Lentiai*, where the unexpectedly fine church contains paintings by the Vecellio family, perhaps including Titian himself. From the left branch, *Monte Pizzocco* (2186m), shaped like a doge's cap, comes into view on the left.—99km *Santa Giustina*, is an important agricultural centre on a fertile upland basin.—At 100km a by-road (left) leads to *Lago di Mis* (11km N), at the foot of the wild and rugged CANALE DEL MIS, in an area of the Dolomites destined to become part of the *Parco Nazionale delle Dolomiti Bellunesi*.—At (104km) *Sedico*, the road to Agordo and Cortina (through a protected area of natural beauty; see Rte 26) diverges; this route passes N of the Villa Pagani-Gaggia where Hitler met Mussolini in July 1943. On the approach to Belluno, *Monte Schiara* (2563m) becomes prominent at the head of the Ardo valley (left).

115km **BELLUNO** is an old mountain capital (34,400 inhab.) splendidly situated above the junction of the Ardo and the Piave. It was the birthplace of Sebastiano Ricci (1659–1734), the painter, of Pope Gregory XVI (1765–1846), and of Girolamo Segato (1792–1836), a pioneer of Egyptian archaeology. The *Duomo*, by Tullio Lombardo (16C), was partly rebuilt after earthquakes in 1873 and 1936; the campanile by Juvarra (1743) is worth ascending for the view. In Piazza del Duomo are the *Town Hall* (1838) and the *Palazzo dei Rettori*, now the Prefettura, a Renaissance building of 1492–96, to the right of which are the old town belfry and the *Museo Civico* (weekdays except Monday 9–12 on request), in a building of 1664. Beyond the last opens Piazza del Mercato, with a fountain of 1410 and the *Monte di Pietà* (1501). From there Via Mezzaterra, the main street of the old town, extends to the S. From it Vicolo San Pietro leads (left) to the church of *San Pietro*. It contains carved panels by Brustolon, a high-altarpiece by Sebastiano Ricci, and paintings of the Annunciation and Saints Peter and Paul by Andrea Schiavone. Via Santa Croce, farther down Via Mezzaterra (left), leads to *Porta Rugo* (12C; restored 1622), commanding a splendid *View of the Piave valley and the Dolomites.—From the N end of Piazza Mercato a 16C gate admits to Piazza Vittorio Emanuele. To the left opens the spacious main square of the modern town; to the right, Via Roma leads to *Santo Stefano*, a church of 1486. The Roman sarcophagus formerly here has been removed to the 'Crepadona' cultural centre. The lofty interior retains frescoes by Jacopo da Montagnana (c 1487; restored) and a fine wooden altarpiece by the Bellunese, Andrea di Foro (16C).

The *Alpe del Nevegal* (1030m), 11km S is a ski-resort; a chair-lift rises to the *Rifugio Brigata Alpina Cadore* (1600m), with a botanical garden nearby.

As the road leaves Belluno it crosses the Ardo with a good retrospect of the city. On the left rises *Monte Serva* (2132m) and ahead, up the Piave valley, is the fine pyramid of *Monte Dolada* (1939m).—123km *Ponte nelle Alpi*. From here to (158km) **Pieve di Cadore**, see Rte 34A.

35 Venice to Udine. The Friuli and Carnia

ROAD, 137km. N13. To (58km) **Conegliano**, see Rte 34A. Alternative route from Treviso to Codroipo, see below.—88km **Pordenone** (by-pass, left).—113km *Codroipo* (by-pass, left).— 137km **Udine**.

MOTORWAY to Pordenone, 77km, A4 (see Rte 36) to Portogruaro, then A28. To Udine, 129km, A4 to Palmanova, then A23.

RAILWAY, 136km in c 2hrs. This is part of the international route between Italy and Austria via Villach, with through carriages via (230km), *Tarvisio* (frontier) from Marseille to Vienna, Rome to Vienna (and Moscow), Trieste to Munich, etc. The line between Udine and Tarvisio (94km) is being modernised.

Many places in this region were severely damaged in the Friuli earthquake in May and September 1976. The epicentre was NW of Udine: the communes of Gemona, Tarcento, San Daniele, Maiano, and many others were devastated. Earth tremors continued for two years and the final toll was nearly 1000 dead, and over 70,000 homeless. Reconstruction is still under way.

From Venice to (58km) **Conegliano**, see Rte 34A.

FROM TREVISO TO CODROIPO VIA ODERZO, 75km. The route leaves Treviso by Via Carlo Alberto, and after 17km just beyond a huge battle memorial, crosses the Piave.—28km **Oderzo**, the Roman *Opitergium*. Finds exhibited in the Museo Civico (8–13, 15–18; Saturday 10–12; closed Monday) include mosaics with hunting scenes and sculptural fragments. The Duomo, founded in the 10C, was rebuilt in Gothic style in the 14C.—At (36km) *Motta di Livenza* the 16C cathedral has a good façade. This was the birthplace of Pomponio Amalteo (1505–88), the painter. The road passes to the left beyond the town for (63km) *San Vito al Tagliamento*. The cathedral has a tall campanile, Romanesque below, Renaissance above, and contains some of Amalteo's works. A small local museum has archeological material from the prehistoric to Roman periods.—At 69km the route strikes the main road to Udine, and then turns right for (75km) *Codroipo* (see below).

75km *Sacile*, placidly reflected in the waters of the Livenza, was hit by the earthquake in 1976 when its 15C cathedral was damaged (since restored).—88km **Pordenone** (*Azienda Autonoma del Turismo*, 13 Piazza della Motta), the industrial centre of Friuli (47,300 inhab.). It became the chief town of a new province in 1968. Many of the buildings in the city, especially the newer ones, were severely shaken by the 1976 earthquake. It was the birthplace of the painter Giovanni Antonio de'Sacchis (c 1483–1539), called 'Il Pordenone'. The old centre consists mainly of one long winding Corso with arcades and some painted house fronts. At its S end is the eccentric *Palazzo Comunale*, with a projecting clock tower in a Venetian Renaissance style (16C) at odds with the 13C Emilian Gothic core. The side towers were restored after earthquake damage. Nearby, in *Palazzo Ricchieri*, the MUSEO CIVICO is closed for restoration. The palace dates from the 15C and has fine painted wood ceilings and some remains of mural paintings.

The collection consists mainly of 16–18C works by regional artists: *School of Pordenone*, Head of a Friar; *Pordenone*, Finding of the True Cross, and the painted organ doors from the Duomo; *Luca Giordano*, Judgement of Paris, etc.—On the Second Floor are 19–20C works by local artists including *Antonio Marsure* and *Michelangelo Grigoletti*.

The DUOMO (*San Marco*), with a Romanesque *Campanile and good W portal by Pilacorte (1511), has been restored since the earthquake. South Aisle. 1st altar, *Pordenone*, *Madonna of the Misericordia, with Saints Joseph and Christopher and donors (1515); 3rd altar, *Marcello Fogolino*, St Francis between St John the Baptist and the Prophet Daniel. In the next chapel, *Pomponio Amalteo*, Flight into Egypt, and frescoes by *Calderari*. 3rd N altar, *Marcello Fogolino*, Madonna with Saints Blaise and Apollonia (1533). The Treasury of the Duomo contains sixteen precious Gothic reliquaries (at present not on view).—Just N of the Corso (reached by Via Mercato) the church (deconsecrated) and conventual buildings of *San Francesco* have been restored as a cultural centre. The exterior has notable brickwork decoration. The *Natural History Museum* is to be moved from Piazza Giustiniano to No. 16 Piazza della Motta; meanwhile it is closed. Farther along the Corso, Via del Cristo leads N to the *Chiesa del Cristo*, with a portal by Pilacorte. The interior has been stripped of its Baroque decoration to reveal its earlier origins. *San Giorgio* (16C), at the other end of the town, has a giant Tuscan column (1852) for campanile.

Maniago (26km N), which once supplied Venice with daggers, now makes cutlery. The cathedral, rebuilt in the 15C, and a market-hall, both frescoed by Amalteo, were damaged in 1976.

Beyond (103km) *Casarsa della Delizia* this route joins the road from San Vito (see above) and crosses the sandy bed of the Tagliamento on the long Ponte della Delizia.

Roads ascend both banks of the Tagliamento. Above the W bank is (18km) *Spilimbergo*, severely damaged in 1976. The Romanesque and Gothic cathedral has been restored. It contains 14C frescoes attributed to the school of Vitale da Bologna, and organ doors painted by Pordenone (1515). There is a Mosaic School here.—2km N of Spilimbergo is *Vacile* where the parish church of San Lorenzo has apse frescoes by Pordenone (restored in 1980).—N463 follows the E bank to (42km) *Gemona* (see the end of this route). The chief place on the way is (23km) *San Daniele del Friuli*, noted for ham. The town was devastated in the earthquake, but the frescoes (1487–1522) by Pellegrino da San Daniele in the ex-church of Sant'Antonio Abate were miraculously saved. A local museum has been opened here.

113·5km *Codroipo* was the Roman *Quadrivium*, on the Via Postumia. About 3km SE on the old Palmanova road is *Passariano* with the vast VILLA MANIN (altered c 1650 perhaps by Giuseppe Benoni, and later by Domenico Rossi) that belonged to Lodovico Manin, last of the Venetian doges. It was restored by the Ente delle Ville Venete, and is now a cultural centre (exhibitions, concerts, etc.). In 1976 it also became a centre for the recuperation of works of art damaged in the

Friuli earthquake. The interior (frescoes by Ludovico Dorigny and Amigoni) may be visited (9.30–12.30, 14 or 15–17 or 18 except Monday). The fine park is open on Sundays. The villa was occupied by Napoleon in 1797 when he concluded the shameful treaty of *Campo Formio*, which sacrificed Venice to Austria. The village after which it is named is now called *Campoformido*, 7km short of Udine on the main road.

137km **UDINE**, with 100,700 inhabitants, the historical centre of Friuli, became the focus of the rescue operations after the earthquake in 1976, which, however, left the city itself remarkably unharmed apart from the buildings on the Castle hill. It is the see of an archbishop, and has spinning and weaving mills and iron foundries. The old streets, mostly arcaded, fan out round the castle hill. Some splendid examples of Tiepolo's work are preserved in the city.

Post Office, Via Vittorio Veneto.—**Azienda Autonoma del Turismo**, Piazza 1 Maggio.

Buses. No. **1** from the station via Piazza Libertà to beyond Porta Gemona; No. **4** from Piazza Libertà to Porta Venezia and Santa Caterina. COUNTRY BUS STATION, Viale Europa Unita: services to *Cividale*; to *Aquileia* and *Grado*, to *San Daniele*, etc.

The Porticato di San Giovanni and the Torre dell'Orologio, Udine

History. A Roman station called *Utina* is alleged to have occupied the site of Udine, and a 10C castle here is recorded as part of the domain of the patriarch of Aquileia. In the 13C Udine, appointed the seat of the patriarch, became the bitter rival of Cividale, but the attacks of the counts of Gorizia and Treviso (c 1300) and of Philip of Alencon (c 1390) unified the Friuli. In 1420, after nine years' resistance, Udine surrendered to Venice, the fortunes of which it followed from then on. It was occupied by Bernadotte in 1797, and by Massena in 1805. In the First World War it was Italian General Headquarters until October 1917, and then was held by the Austrians for a year. In the Second World War, after considerable damage from air raids, it was entered by South African troops on 1 May 1945, the day before the official end of the campaign. The painter and architect Giovanni da Udine (1487–1564) is the best-known native of the city.

*PIAZZA DELLA LIBERTÀ, a picturesque square in the Venetian manner, is a worthy centre of the city. The particoloured **Palazzo del Comune**, or *Loggia del Lionello*, a typical Venetian Gothic building, dates from 1448–56 and was rebuilt after a fire in 1876; the statue of the Madonna at the corner is by Bartolomeo Bon. Opposite is the Renaissance *Porticato di San Giovanni* (1533), with a chapel that has been converted into a war memorial, and the *Torre dell'Orologio*, by Giovanni da Udine (1527; the 'mori' on the clock are 19C). In the piazza are a fountain of 1542, two columns with the Lion of St Mark and Justice, and colossal statues of Hercules and Cacus (called by the Udinese Florean and Venturin) from a demolished 18C palazzo. The statue of Peace (with a sarcastic inscription) commemorates the Treaty of Campo Formio.—The *Arco Bollani*, by Palladio (1556) serves as the entrance to the CASTLE HILL (60m), which rises unexpectedly out of the plain. All the buildings have had to be restored since they were damaged in the earthquake, and the museums are still closed, although they may reopen in 1990.

The path leads up alongside a graceful Gothic portico (1487) and past the church of *Santa Maria di Castello* (13C) whose contemporary frescoes were badly damaged in 1976. The **Castle** was the seat of the patriarchs and Venetian governors; the present main building dates from 1517. It now houses the **Museo Civico**, the **Galleria d'Arte Antica e d'Arte Moderna**, and the **Museo del Risorgimento** (all the contents have been removed while the building is in restoration). Beside an archaeological collection and an armoury, the works of art include: *Giovanni Battista Tiepolo*, the 'Consilium in Arena'; *Canova*, Plaster sketch for a Crucifixion; *Pordenone*, Eternal Father; *Giovanni Martini*, St Peter Martyr; *Pellegrino di San Daniele*, Annunciation; *Jacques Callot*, Udine in the 17C; *Carpaccio*, Christ and four angels; *Domenico da Tolmezzo*, Polyptych; works by *Antonio Carneo*, *Palma Giovane*, (Mauroner Collection) *Baciccia*, *Fra Galgario*, *Marco* and *Sebastiano Ricci*. The classical and historical frescoes by *Amalteo* in the Sala del Parlemento Friulano were badly damaged in 1976.—On the esplanade, which commands a fine view of the Alps, the old (reconstructed) buildings include the *Casa della Contadinanza*.

The **Duomo**, backing on to the busy Via Vittorio Veneto, was consecrated in 1335 and completed in the mid-15C. Much altered later, it retains a heavy octagonal campanile of 1441 above the 14C baptistery (entered from the church, see below). On the E side (seen from Via Vittorio Veneto) are two statues (the Annunciation) of the 14C. By the door of the baptistery, on the N wall of the church is a blocked portal (in poor condition) dating from the late 13C. The brick W front (late 14C) has been well restored.

INTERIOR. The transepts and choir, designed by *Domenico Rossi* and assistants (1678–1742), the frescoes by *Ludovico Dorigny*, and the carved choir-stalls

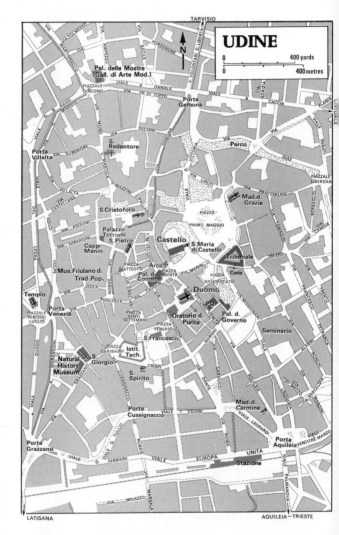

form an admirable Baroque ensemble. NORTH AISLE. 1st Chapel (light on
right) *Giovanni Martini* (1453–1535), St Mark and other Saints; 2nd Chapel,
Pellegrino di San Daniele, St Joseph. SOUTH AISLE. 1st Chapel, *Giovanni
Battista Tiepolo*, Holy Trinity; 2nd Chapel, Saints Hermagoras and Fortunatus, also attributed to *Tiepolo*, 4th Chapel. The Baroque altar encloses a small
painting of the Risen Christ by *Tiepolo*, who also frescoed the walls. The
elaborate organ in this aisle has paintings attributed to *Pordenone* (1528).—
The *Museo del Duomo* (closed for restoration) is arranged in the chapel with
frescoes of the funeral of St Nicholas (1349; restored in 1989) by *Vitale da
Bologna*, and an adjoining chapel, with detached frescoes and their sinopie,

as well as in the 14C Baptistery. Here a charming 14C tomb carried by five caryatids contains the relics of Saints Hermagoras and Fortunatus.

The ORATORIO DELLA PURITÀ, on the S side of Piazza del Duomo, contains a frescoed and painted *Assumption, by *Giovanni Battista Tiepolo*.—Via Lovaria leads E to the *Palazzo Arcivescovile* (ring at Curia; weekdays 9–12; Saturday and Sunday closed) with more *Frescoes by Giovanni Battista Tiepolo. On the stairs, Fall of the Angels; in the gallery, Old Testament scenes; in the Sala Rossa, Judgement of Solomon and four Prophets (in the lunettes). Another room is frescoed by Giovanni da Udine.

The streets of old Udine, sometimes skirted by rushing streams, are well worth exploring, although the mural paintings on the house-fronts have now sadly all but disappeared. From Piazza Libertà, Via Mercato Vecchio, Via Palladio (with the Palazzo Antonini, now the seat of the Banca d'Italia, by Palladio) and Via Gemona (see the Plan) are all within easy reach. Via Paolo Sarpi leads left off Via Mercato Vecchio past *San Pietro* with a good side portal, to PIAZZA MAT-TEOTTI, a large arcaded market-place with attractive houses. The fountain was designed by Giovanni da Udine (1542). Near the church of *San Giacomo*, with an early 16C Lombard façade, is a pretty well of 1486. A passageway leads from the piazzetta to Via Zanon with the tower of the 13C town wall and the Baroque *Cappella Manin* (attributed to Domenico Rossi). In Via Viola, to the W is the *Museo Friulano delle Arti e delle Tradizioni Popolari*, an important local ethnographical museum arranged in twenty rooms (open 9–12, 16–19; fest. 9–12; closed Monday). Farther SE, in Piazza Venerio, the church of **San Francesco**, was restored to its 13C appearance, for use as an auditorium and for exhibitions. To the SW, beyond Piazza Garibaldi, in Palazzo Giacomelli in Via Grazzano, is the interesting *Museo Friulano di Scienze Naturali* (closed for rearrangement).

From Piazza Libertà Via Manin leads NE through another town gate to the large Piazza Primo Maggio. Here the 16C *Madonna delle Grazie*, a popular votive church, has a cloister covered with ex votos.—In Piazzale Diacono (see the Plan) the *Palazzo delle Mostre* houses a modern art gallery (9.30–12.30, 15–18; closed Sunday and Monday).

FROM UDINE TO GORIZIA. 36km; railway in 20–40 minutes (through trains to Trieste in 1–1½hrs).—23km *Cormons*, an ancient seat of the patriarchs of Aquileia, is the only intermediate place of importance.

FROM UDINE TO CIVIDALE, 17km. Train every hour in 20 minutes. **Cividale del Friuli** is a very old town (11,000 inhab.) pleasantly situated at the point where the Natisone emerges into the plain. It was badly shaken in the earthquake of 1976.

Founded as *Forum Iulii*, perhaps by Julius Caesar, it gave its name to the *Friuli*, the first Lombard duchy to be formed in Italy. Later it was the capital of a free duchy of which Berengar I, afterwards King of Italy (888–924), was the most distinguished lord. From the 8C until 1238 Cividale was the chief seat of the patriarchs of Aquileia. It was the birthplace of Paul the Deacon (Warnefride; 723–799), historian of the Lombards, and of Adelaide Ristori (1821–1906), the tragedienne (monument in Piazza Giulio Cesare).—*Azienda di Soggiorno*, 4 Largo Boiani.

From the station and the main road from Udine, Viale Libertà leads E to Corso Alberto which continues S to the pretty Piazza Diacono. Corso Mazzini leads on to the DUOMO (*Santa Maria Assunta*). It was begun in its present form in 1453 and continued in 1503–32 by Pietro Lombardo. In the austere interior the 12C silver gilt *Altar (set within the Baroque high altar) is magnificent. On the N wall is the sarcopha-

gus of the Patriarch Nicolò Donato, by *Antonio da Carona*; above the
W door, equestrian monument to Marco Antonio di Manzano, killed
in 1617 in the Turkish wars. At the end of the S aisle hang fragments of
a processional standard with the Annunciation, attributed to *Giovanni da Udine*. On the S side is a small *Museo Cristiano* (adm.
9.30–12, 15–18.30; fest. 11.30–12, 16.30–18.30; in winter it closes at
17.30) containing an octagonal *Baptistery (8C) reconstructed from
Lombardic fragments, a marble Patriarchal throne (11C), and the altar
of Duke Ratchis (744–49) with sculptured panels. Also, Lombardic
sculptural fragments and interesting detached frescoes. The *Treasury*, with the great sword of Marquedo (Patriarch, 1368–81), is kept
in the Sacristy (not open to the public).

*Detail of the altar of Duke Ratchis (744–49) in the Museo
Cristiano, Cividale del Friuli*

The ARCHAEOLOGICAL MUSEUM, across the square, was founded in
1817. It is in the process of being transferred to Palazzo dei Provveditori Veneti (see below), and meanwhile only part of the collection is on
display (open daily 9–13.30; fest. 9–12.30). It contains numerous
Roman remains and later material, but is especially famous for its
early medieval treasures.

The collection includes: the Sarcophagus of Duke Gisulphus (I or II; died 568 or
610); Roman mosaic with Head of Oceanus; early Christian reliefs, one with a
mermaid (8C); 12C sarcophagus, from the cathedral; wayside Madonna, a
provincial 16C work; stone with the Lion of St Mark, commemorating the
stubborn defence of Cividale in the siege of 1509. In the court, Jewish
tombstones (13–18C). A noble staircase of 1530, with 16C frescoes and an

altarpiece (Descent of the Holy Ghost) by *Andrea Vicentino*, ascends to the FIRST FLOOR. Here is the Chapter Library, with coins, Roman remains, etc. The contents of a warrior's tomb, with his arms, gold and silver ornaments, and ivory chessmen; also the rare embroidered linen *Altar Cover (c 1400) from San Pietro, with the Annunciation, Crucifixion, and Saints, popularly ascribed to the Blessed Benvenuta Boiani (died 1292). The 6C–9C works include the *Treasure of Duke Gisulphus found in his sarcophagus (see above), including a fine bracteate cross (with portrait gems), a ring, and an enamelled fibula, all of gold. Also, gold ornaments, including a remarkable filigree disc, and the *Pax of Duke Ursus (c 800), an ivory Crucifixion in a jewelled silver frame. The treasures of the cathedral and of Santa Maria in Valle, include the Grimani pax (mid-4C); ivy-leaf *Reliquary, apparently a wedding gift from Philip II, prince of Taranto, to his bride (French; c 1294); 10C ivory casket (Byzantine); silver cross of Patriarch Pellegrino II (c 1200); processional cross of c 900, in provincial style. Among the MSS the following are outstanding: 'Bible of Aquileia' in 2 volumes (12C); *Psalter of Bishop Egbert of Trèves (977–93), and another of the 13C; both belonged to St Elizabeth of Hungary and were presented to the cathedral by her uncle Patriarch Berchtold von Andecht; History of the Lombards, by Paul the Deacon (Montecassino; 8C). Triptych by *Pellegrino da San Daniele* (1501; his masterpiece) and *Girolamo da Udine* (1539); *Pordenone*, Noli me tangere.

Palazzo dei Provveditori Veneti (formerly Palazzo Pretorio), closing the E side of the square, was begun by Palladio in 1564. The Archaeological Museum is being transferred here. The *Palazzo Comunale* dates from the 14C, but it was virtually rebuilt in the 15–16C (and has a modern extension). Corso Ponte d'Aquileia leads down to the *Ponte del Diavolo* (15C; restored) crossing the impressive limestone gorge of the Natisone. From the N side of the bridge Via Monastero Maggiore, once the main street of the town, leads E. At No. 2 (right) are remains of the so-called *Ipogeo Celtico* (key at the Azienda di Soggiorno). Farther on the road passes through a Roman arch (note the medieval house on the left, in Stretta Santa Maria di Corte) and, beyond Porta Patriarchale (surmounted by a Romanesque house) opens the Piazzetta San Biagio on the banks of the Natisone. Here is the celebrated *TEMPIETTO LONGOBARDO (open 9–12, 15–18; winter 9–12, 14–17; fest. & Monday 9–12). This was part of a Lombardic church (8C) constructed of earlier fragments, and decorated with fine contemporary stucco reliefs of female saints; it contains a sarcophagus of Lombardic work, and 14C stalls. It was severely damaged in 1976 and has been restored. The church of *San Biagio* (ask locally for the key) has a badly faded painted façade. The frescoes in the interior are particularly notable in the domed chapel in the S aisle.

On the S side of the town, beyond the *Porta San Pietro* (used by the Venetians as a store) is the church of *San Pietro*, with a good altarpiece by Palma Giovane.
   From Cividale the road goes on up the Natisone valley, Slovene-speaking in its upper reaches, to (15km) *Stupizza*, the last Italian village. *Caporetto*, 15km farther on over the Yugoslav frontier, is memorable for the disaster to the Italian armies in October 1917.

FROM UDINE TO TARVISIO, 91km, N13, part of the main road to Vienna; railway, see above. The motorway (A23) from Udine to Tarvisio (100km), which follows close to the road, has recently been completed; it continues to the Austrian frontier where it connects with the A2 autobahn for Klagenfurt in Austria (see 'Blue Guide Austria'). This route traverses the area devastated by the 1976 earthquake (see above). The main road to Tarvisio runs N from Udine, parallel with the railway. As far as (12km) *Tricesimo* it is followed by buses, some of which go on to *Tarcento*, a little town among the foothills, damaged in 1976, 4km right of the road.—At 20km N13 bears away to the left, by-passing *Artegna* (2km) and **Gemona** (6km), one of the worst hit towns in 1976 when over 300 people lost their lives. Several monuments were destroyed including the church of San Giovanni Battista and the sanctuary of Sant'Antonio. The fine Romanesque and Gothic Cathedral and its 14C campanile have been restored, leaving the pilasters strengthened but leaning out of line.

At (27km) *Taboga* this route is joined by the road from Casarsa (see above), on which, 2km left, stands *Osoppo*, a medieval fortress strengthened by Napoleon, virtually wiped out in 1976. The main road now approaches the wide bed of the Tagliamento.—35km *Venzone*. Its Medieval walls, beautiful Duomo of 1308, and fine old houses, were reduced to rubble by the earthquake. The Palazzo Municipale has been rebuilt.—Beyond the confluence of the Fella with the Tagliamento the road reaches (40km) *Carnia* the junction for Tolmezzo and the Carnic Alps (see below), with the pyramidal *Monte Amariana* (1906m) prominent on the left.

N13 ascends the narrowing valley of the Fella and, beyond (45km) the Valle d'Aupa (left), in which is seen the old village of *Moggio Udinese*, the road passes (48km) *Resiutta*, at the foot of the Valle di Resia.—56km *Chiusaforte* stands at the foot of the gorge, once fortified, from which it is named. The railway traverses a succession of tunnels high up on the E side of the valley.—61km *Dogna* stands at the foot of the Valle di Dogna, dominated by the Iôf di Montasio (2754m), the highest peak in a forested area of c 40,000 hectares, destined to become the *Parco Nazionale del Tarvisiano*. The park extends N to the Austrian border, and E to the Yugoslav border beyond Tarvisio (see below).—68·5km *Pontebba* was on the old Austro-Italian frontier, marked by the stream which traverses the village. The valley widens as the route enters the Valcanale, a Slovene-speaking region.—75km *Bagni di Lusnizza* is a small sulphur spa.—79km *Malborghetto-Valbruna* is the chief centre of the valley.—82km *Ugovizza* has a few visitors, and Valbruna itself, in a valley to the S, has hotels at the lower and upper ends of a cableway to *Monte Santo di Lussari* (1766m). The chief summer and winter resort here is (87km) *Camporosso in Valcanale* (816m), where the road crosses the watershed and descends into the basin of Tarvisio, with waters flowing towards the Drava.—91km **Tarvisio** (741m), the frontier station and Italian custom-house, with 6400 inhabitants and two railway stations, is divided into an old lower town and a modern upper town. It stands at the junction of main roads to Vienna via Arnoldstein and Villach (see 'Blue Guide Austria'), to Ljubljana (see 'Blue Guide Yugoslavia') via Kranjska Gora, and to Caporetto. The last crosses the Yugoslav frontier at (14·5km) the *Passo del Predil* (1156m); at *Cave del Predil*, 3km short of this, once noted for its lead and zinc mines, a road bears right for the charming *Lago del Predil* or *Raibl-See* (to become part of the Parco Nazionale del Tarvisiano), dominated from the E by *Monte Mangant* (2678m), where a road leads on to Chiusaforte (see above). The *Laghi di Fusine*, two charming little lakes 10km SE of Tarvisio, off the Ljubljana road, are also included in the area of the park.—A chair-lift ascends from Tarvisio to the ski-slopes on the Monte Priesenig at 1289m.

FROM UDINE TO THE CARNIC ALPS AND CADORE; railway to *Carnia* (c 40 minutes) in connection with bus from there to *Villa Santina* in 30 minutes more.—For *Carnia*, see above. From there road and railway ascend the left bank of the Tagliamento to (12km) **Tolmezzo** (10,000 inhab.) the chief centre of Carnia, damaged in 1976, with a museum of local handicrafts (9–12, 14 or 15–17 or 18 except Monday).—From Tolmezzo a fine cross-country road leads to (75km) *Calalzo* (Rte 29A) via (19km) *Villa Santina*, (32km) *Ampezzo*, (46km) *Forni di Sotto*, and (55km) *Forni di Sopra*. All these are summer resorts, offering varied excursions among the Carnic Alps. The descent into the Cadore valley beyond (64km) the *Passo della Mauria* (1295m) is steep and winding.

The road running N from Tolmezzo leads via (7km) *Cedarchis* and (16km) *Paluzza* to (23km) *Timau* (custom-house) and (33km) the *Passo di Monte Croce* (1362m) on the Austro-Italian frontier. The descent leads to (45km) *Kötschach-Mauthen*, in the Ober-Gailtal (see 'Blue Guide Austria').—On the right of the road, just beyond Cedarchis, are *Arta Terme* and *Piano d'Arta*, ½hr higher up, two little summer resorts with mineral waters. Opposite them is the village of *Zuglio*, the ancient Forum Iulii Carnicum which guarded the Roman road over the pass. Above it (c 1hr) is the little church of San Pietro di Carnia, the oldest in the district (? 14C).

Paularo (648m), a summer resort with some ancient chalets, is reached by road (14km) NE from Cedarchis up the Canale d'Incaroio; while another road to the W connects Paluzza with Comeglians (16km; see below), with a branch to (10km) *Ravascletto* (950m), on an open terrace, visited both in summer and winter (chair-lift).

The Cadore can be reached also by road from Villa Santina by the Gorto valley, and from there via (14km) *Comeglians* (bus from Villa Santina), *Rigolato*

(18km) *Forni Avoltri* (26km) and (37km) *Sappada* (see below), a fine run of 50km to *Santo Stefano di Cadore* (Rte 29A); or (diverging before Comeglians) by a hilly road via Prato Carnico and the *Forcella Lavardet* (1542m), again a distance of 50km to Santo Stefano.

Sappada (1217m) has become a popular summer and winter resort; it extends for 4km along the uppermost valley of the Piave, from Cima Sappada at the E end down to Palù and beyond. There are two chair-lifts, one rising S from Cima, the other N from Palù, numerous ski-lifts, and mountain refuges as well as tennis-courts; and there are daily bus services to Villa Santina, Calalzo, and San Candido.

36 Venice to Trieste

ROAD, 162km, N14.—37·5km *San Donà di Piave.*—66km *Portogruaro.*—80km *Latisana.*—108km *Cervignano* (right for **Aquileia**, 8km and *Grado*, 18km).—126km *Monfalcone.*—162km **Trieste** (158km by the coast road).

MOTORWAY, A4, between Mestre and Monfalcone (119km), running farther N all the way, shortens the total distance by 3km.

RAILWAY. 157km, several expresses daily in c 2hrs.

From the lagoon bridge of Venice N14 turns E skirting (12km) the airport of Venice (Marco Polo).—18km *Altino* (left), already settled by the 7C BC, represents the Roman *Altinum* built at the junction of several Roman roads, and where the Dese, Sile, and Piave rivers enter the lagoon. The beauty of its country villas was admired by the Latin poet Martial; some of their fine mosaic pavements have been uncovered. A Roman road, thought to be part of the Via Claudia, has been exposed, and excavations of the city continue. The town was destroyed by Attila and the Lombards, and, after floods and malaria, had been abandoned by the mid-7C. The people took refuge at Torcello and are thus directly involved with the early history of Venice (and many Roman stones from Altino were reused in the buildings of Venice, Torcello, and Murano). A small Museum (9–14; except Monday; fest. 9–13) contains mosaic pavements, stelai, Roman portrait busts (1–2C AD), glass, amphorae, and architectural fragments.—The road crosses the Sile and leaves on the right the shortest road to Lido di Iesolo (Rte 33M) along the canal that carries the Sile's waters outside the Venetian lagoon. It reaches the *Piave*, a river famous as the line of Italian resistance after the retreat from the Caporetto (monument on the bridge), just before (37·5km) *San Donà di Piave*, rebuilt since its ordeal in 1917–18. At *Fossalta di Piave*, 6km N, Ernest Hemingway, as a member of the US Red Cross, was wounded in 1918 at the age of nineteen (see 'A Farewell to Arms'). A memorial stele was set up here in 1979.

A road runs S to (20km) *Lido di Iesolo* (Rte 33M) via (11km) *Eraclea*, a modern village (formerly Grisolera) on the Piave which has assumed the title of the ancient **Heraclea** (called after the Emperor Heraclius), the episcopal and administrative centre of the lagoon in the 7–8C after the sack of Oderzo by the Lombards. The site of the ancient city was identified by aerial photography in 1984 near *Cittànova* (7km E of San Donà) and it is to be excavated. It was formerly surrounded by a lagoon, and in plan it recalls Venice, with a central canal and many smaller canals. From 750 onwards the inhabitants migrated to the safer islands of Malamocco and Rialto, and a leader from Heraclea is thought to have become the first Doge of Venice. Heraclea rapidly declined as its lagoon silted up and Venice grew in importance.

Beyond (41km) *Ceggia* the road crosses the Livenza and there is a magnificent distant view of Monte Civetta and the Cadore Alps. Two kilometres beyond the river the main road to Caorle (21km) diverges (right); Caorle is reached also by bus from San Donà or from Portogruaro in connection with trains.

Caorle is an ancient fishing village, and now a seaside resort with two beaches near the mouth of the Livenza. Founded by refugees from Concordia (see below), it was a bishop's see for twelve centuries and preserves a cathedral of 1048 with a fine detached round tower. Above the high altar is a celebrated Venetian pala of gilded silver. The beautiful lagoon to the N (Valle Vecchia, etc.), with its fishing huts and interesting wildlife, may become a protected area.

66km **Portogruaro**, a medieval town (22,800 inhab.) at the junction of the main road from Treviso to Trieste, has an interesting urban plan with its two main streets running parallel on either side of the river Lemene, which is still navigable from here to Caorle on the sea. Many of its buildings are Venetian in inspiration. By Ponte Sant'Andrea is the *Duomo*, rebuilt in 1793, with a Romanesque campanile. In Piazza della Repubblica is the handsome *Loggia Municipale* (14C, enlarged 1512), with Venetian-type crenellations. The arcaded Via Martiri della Libertà is lined with 14–15C houses; the parallel street on the other side of the river is also interesting. Here, in Via del Seminario, is the *Museum* which contains finds from the Roman station of *Concordia Sagittaria*. The present village of **Concordia**, 2km S, has a 15C Duomo above remains of a palaeochristian church, and a fine 11C Baptistery with a triple apse and contemporary frescoes. Along the S side excavations have revealed a 4C martyrium and basilica (with a mosaic).— NW of Portogruaro are the fine Romanesque churches of two early Benedictine abbeys, at *Summaga* (6km) and *Sesto al Reghena* (13km), with 13–16C frescoes and 8C reliefs in the crypt.— At (80km) *Latisana*, where the parish church has a Baptism of Jesus by Veronese (1567), the road crosses the broad gravelly bed of the Tagliamento and from there follows the railway closely.

A road (N354) leads S along the river to **Lignano Pianeta, Sabbiadoro**, and **Riviera** forming a huge and continuous planned tourist resort with some 400 hotels along a sandy spit at the mouth of the Laguna di Marano.—*Bibione* is another resort.

98km *San Giorgio di Nogaro* is connected by rail with Palmanova and Udine. Beyond the tiny Ausa river, the Austro-Italian frontier of 1866–1918, the countryside becomes more wooded.—At (108km) *Cervignano del Friuli*, also connected by rail with Udine, the road to Aquileia and Grado (bus from Cervignano station) diverges right.

A road leads N from Cervignano to **Palmanova** (9km), an old Venetian fortress built on a regular plan (1593), with symmetrical brick bastions, moated and grassgrown, and a hexagonal central piazza. The three chief gates are by Scamozzi, the Duomo by Longhena. The Civico Museo Storico is usually open 10–12, except Monday.

FROM CERVIGNANO TO AQUILEIA AND GRADO, N352, 19km.—8km **AQUILEIA** now a village of 3000 inhabitants, preserves magnificent and evocative remains of its great days both as a Roman city and as an early medieval capital, including some splendid mosaics. It is situated in a fertile plain. There are still large areas of the Roman city being excavated.

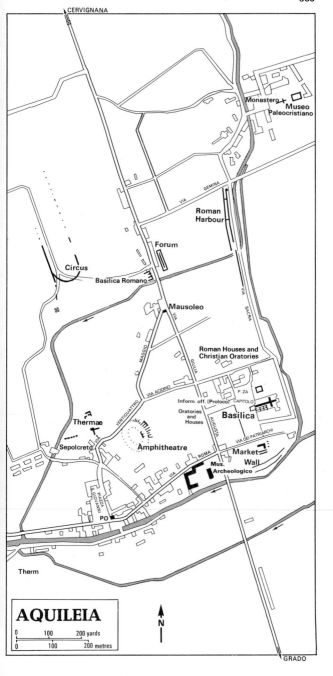

CERVIGNANA

Monastero
Museo Paleocristiano

VIA GEMINA

Roman Harbour

VIA SACRA

Forum

Circus

Basilica Romano

Mausoleo

VIA MAGGIO

VIA GIULIA

Roman Houses and Christian Oratories

P.ZA CAPITOLO

VIA ACIDINO

Inform. off. (Proloco)

Oratories and Houses

Basilica

Thermae

VENTIQUATTRO

VIA AUGUSTA

VIA DEI PATRIARCHI

Amphitheatre

Sepolcreto

VIA ROMA

Market

Wall

Mus. Archeologico

PIAZZA GIOVANNI

PO

Therm

AQUILEIA

| 0 | 100 | 200 yards |
| 0 | 100 | 200 metres |

N

GRADO

History. Aquileia was founded as a Roman colony in 181 BC and soon rose to prominence. In 10 BC Augustus was in residence here and received Herod the Great. In AD 238 the 'Emperor' Maximinus was murdered by his troops when besieging the city, and in 340 Constantine II was killed on the banks of the Aussa (a little W) by his brother Constans in their struggle for imperial power. The bishopric or patriarchate was founded soon after 313; but civil wars and barbarian incursions, culminating in the Lombard sack of 568, led to the transference of the see to Grado, which had become the foreport of Aquileia. After 606 there were two rival patriarchs, but in 1019 Poppo united the sees and rebuilt the basilica. Slow decadence, due to malaria, followed; in 1420 the civil power passed to Venice; the Austrians seized the place in 1509; and in 1751 the patriarchate was merged in the archbishoprics of Udine and Gorizia.

The approach road follows exactly the line of the Roman cardo. Car Park by the Basilica (if full, in the village by the post office). A whole day is needed to visit the site, Basilica, and two museums.

Admission times. The *Basilica* is open daily 9–12, 15–19 (sometimes all day in mid summer). The *Archaeological Museum*, the *Palaeochristian Museum* and *Crypt of the Basilica*, every day 9–14, fest. 9–13. The *Excavations* are open from 9 to one hour before sunset.

The ****Basilica**, built soon after 313 by the first patriarch Theodore, was the scene of a historic council in 381, attended by Saints Ambrose and Jerome. It was extended soon afterwards and was reconstructed in its present form by the patriarch Poppo in 1021–31.

A portico, probably dating from the beginning of the 9C, extends from the W front to the 'Chiesa dei Pagani', a rectangular 9C hall for catecumens, with remains of 13C frescoes, to the much altered remains of the *Baptistery*. Beneath the font, an earlier octagonal font was discovered in 1982 above remains of a Roman house.—The tall *Campanile* (73m) was built by Poppo; the upper part dates from the 14C, the bell-chamber and steeple from the 16C. On a Roman column facing it is a figure of the Capitoline Wolf, presented by Rome in 1919.

Detail of the mosaic floor of the Basilica at Aquileia

Inside the basilica, the arcades surmounting the fine Romanesque capitals date from the patriarchate of Markward (1365–81), the nave ceiling from 1526. The huge colourful mosaic *Pavement* (700 square metres), discovered at the beginning of this century, dates from Theodore's basilica. It is one of the most remarkable palaeochristian monuments in Italy, combining Christian images (story of Jonah, the Good Shepherd, etc.) with pagan symbols (the cock, tortoise), and the portrait heads of donors, etc. At the end of the S aisle is the Gothic chapel of St Ambrose, built by the Torriani in 1298; it contains four family tombs (1299–1365) and a polyptych by Pellegrino da San Daniele (1503) in a fine frame; the SE chapel has a 9–10C transenna and a fresco of Christ blessing (14C), and detached frescoes from Theodore's period. To the left of the chapel is the sarcophagus of Pope St Mark (14C, Venetian Gothic), and in front of the tomb is a fragment of 5C mosaic pavement (discovered in 1972). The central Renaissance tribune and the altar to the right of it, with a good Pietà, are the work of Bernardino da Bissone. The high altar was carved by Sebastiano and Antonio da Osteno (1498). In Poppo's apse are faded frescoes, with a dedicatory inscription (1031), showing the patriarch (with a model of the church), the Emperor Conrad II with Gisela of Swabia and Prince Henry (later Henry III) before the Madonna and six patron saints. The bishop's throne is probably somewhat earlier. In the NE chapel are interesting frescoes and (N wall) a bas-relief with Christ between St Peter and St Thomas of Canterbury, sculptured soon after St Thomas's martyrdom in 1170. Outside the chapel is a bust of Christ (1916) by Edmondo Furlan. In the N aisle are fresco fragments (Madonna enthroned, 15C) and statuettes from a Deposition group. Near the W end of the N aisle is the *Santo Sepolcro*, an 11C reproduction of the Holy Sepulchre at Jerusalem.—The *Crypt*, beneath the presbytery, has frescoes of great interest, thought to date from the mid-12C. They depict scenes from the life of Christ (including a fine Deposition), and of the Madonna, and scenes relating to Saints Hermagoras and Fortunatus.

The CRIPTA DEGLI SCAVI (adm. with the same ticket as for the Museum, for opening times, see above) is entered from beside the Santo Sepolcro. It is remarkable for three levels of *Mosaics: those of a Roman house of the Augustan period (to the left on entering); the magnificent floor of a second basilica of the time of Theodore, encircling the foundations of Poppo's campanile; and parts of the floor of the late-4C basilica, as well as its column-bases. The frescoes have been detached for restoration.

Behind the church is the cypress-girt *Cimitero degli Eroi*, dedicated to the victims of the First World War.

The ***Archaeological Museum*** (adm., see above) is reached by the main road (Via Giulia Augusta) and Via Roma (right). It has a good collection of finds made in and around Aquileia. Part of the museum was temporarily closed in 1989.

On the GROUND FLOOR (and in the garden) are the larger sculptures and mosaic pavements of 2–4C. In a garden pavilion is exhibited the Roman ship found in 1982 in the locality of Monfalcone. Its careful excavation and preservation represent one of the most sucessful archaeological operations in recent years. ROOM I. Interesting collection of portrait busts of the Republican era, including the 'Old Man of Aquileia'; an inscription with the name of L. Manlius Acidinus, one of the city's founders; bas relief relating to the elevation of Aquileia to a Roman colony in the first century AD.—R.II. Statues of Tiberius, Claudius, etc.—R. III. Finds from the necropolis; tomb stones, including one showing a smithy.—R. IV. Roman copies of Greek originals (Head of Jove, Venus, of the Medici type, etc.); Relief of the river god Æsontius (Isonzo).—FIRST FLOOR. R. V. Semi-precious gems (mostly of local make), cameos, intaglios (fine Farnese bull), objects in amber and gold (notably the golden flies, ornaments from a lady's veil).—R. VI. Egyptian fragments; Head of a Child (1C AD).—R. VII. Terracottas. R. VIII. Small bronzes.—R. IX. Fine collection of *Glass, with some unique specimens.—On the floor above, domestic utensils, coins, and a lapidary collection.

The TOUR OF THE EXCAVATIONS is most easily made on foot. Near the Basilica, across Via dei Patriarchi (see the Plan) are the foundations of late Roman *Market-Halls*, with the town walls beyond. On the other side of the Basilica, reached from Piazza Capitolo, are the remains of *Roman Houses and Christian Oratories* with superb mosaic pavements. To the E, clearly marked by a noble avenue of cypresses, is the *Via Sacra* which follows the Natissa stream N. It is lined with architectural fragments of the 1–4C (architraves, columns, capitals, etc.) found here. After some 500m it reaches the little **Roman Harbour**, where a finely-wrought quay still skirts the sadly diminished waters of the Natissa, once a navigable river as far as Grado. Across Via Gemina a road leads past a group of modern houses to the former Benedictine Monastery of Santa Maria in which are the remains of another large early-Christian *Basilica* (mosaic floor) and the **Museo Paleocristiano** (adm., see above). It contains a good collection of sarcophagi, transennae, and mosaic panels showing the transition of art from the classical Roman period to the new Christian era. In the piazza in front of the monastery is a fragment of Roman road.

Via Gemina leads (right) to Via Giulia Augusta, which passes several Roman monuments on its way back towards the Basilica. On the right can be seen a fine stretch of Roman road, and beyond, traces of the *Circus*. On the left of the road, a row of fluted composite columns belong to the **Forum** of Aquileia (still being excavated). The sculptural fragments include a fine Gorgon's head. The W and E porticoes, as well as part of the pavement, have been uncovered. On the other side of the road the Roman basilica of the Forum has been discovered. There are long term plans to arrange an Antiquarium here. At the road fork (with Via XXIV Maggio) is the *Grande Mausoleo*, an imposing (reconstructed) family tomb (1C AD), brought from its original site in the suburbs. Farther on, on the right of the main road (opposite the church) is a large area still being excavated of *Roman Houses and Palaeochristian Oratories* (2–4C AD) with good pavements (especially W of the vineyard). The polychrome mosaic floor under cover belonged to an oratory. Via Acidino leads W past (left) the scanty remains of the *Amphitheatre* and (right) the site of the *Thermae* (still being excavated) towards the *Sepolcreto* (key at No. 17), a row of five family tombs of the 1–2C. Via XXIV Maggio returns S to Piazza Giovanni, the village square.

Beyond (12·5km) *Belvedere* the causeway crosses the lagoon, with islets on either hand, to the island-city of Grado.

18km **GRADO** is a seaside resort (10,000 inhab.) with a very popular sandy beach equipped with thermal and sand baths, joined to a town of ancient origin, the foreport of Aquileia after the 2C. Grado, despite its island site, was many times plundered in the Middle Ages, but it retains some fine old buildings in its narrow streets. The monuments are open all day in summer.

In the centre of the old fishing town is the **Duomo* (Santa Eufemia) founded as the seat of the patriarchate of Nova Aquileia by Patriarch Elias in 579; after the union of the sees these rival patriarchs moved to Venice, and in 1451 the title was finally abolished. The campanile is crowned by a statue of St Michael (1462). The church, a basilica of the Ravenna type, preserves twenty different columns with Byzantine capitals, and a fine 6C mosaic *Pavement. The ambo is made up of numerous 11C fragments. On the high altar is a Venetian pala of beaten silver (1372). In the apse is an early 15C fresco. The Cathedral has a precious treasury. Beneath the church remains have been revealed of a 4C oratory. On either side of the apse are more ancient remains, including mosaics.

To the right of the basilica is a *Lapidary Collection* with Roman and palaeochristian sculpture and inscriptions. The restored octagonal *Baptistery* is approached by an avenue of sarcophagi found in Grado. It contains a hexagonal font. The church of *Santa Maria delle Grazie*, a little to the left of the cathedral, is another basilica of the 4–5C, rebuilt in the 6C, on a small scale, with an even more miscellaneous assortment of ten columns, a restored marble transenna, and an apsidal bench and throne with passage behind. Excavation has revealed some good 6C floor-mosaics. Remains of another early-Christian basilica have been found in Piazza della Vittoria, to the SE.

The islet of *Barbana*, in the lagoon to the NE, can be reached by boat every afternoon in summer. The church was built in 1593 and rebuilt since 1918, with a venerated statue of the Virgin (procession of boats on the 1st Sunday in July).

FROM CERVIGNANO TO GORIZIA. N351, 28km. Beyond (5km) *Ruda* the road crosses the motorway and approaches the W bank of the Isonzo, parallel to the motorway branch (from Villesse) to the new frontier station with Yugoslavia at Sant'Andrea-Vertoiba.—16km *Gradisca* is an old Venetian fortress still preserving many of its 15C watch-towers against the Turks and some good Baroque mansions, and a lapidarium. The county was ceded to Austria in 1511, and in 1615–17 was the occasion of the War of Gradisca, between Austria and Venice. Opposite rises Monte San Michele, a ridge hotly contested in the Carso campaign (museum).—The road crosses the Isonzo.

28km **Gorizia** (Azienda Autonomo del Turismo, 100 Corso Verdi), with 42,700 inhabitants, is a provincial capital standing in an expansion of the Isonzo valley hemmed in by hills. After the fall of the independent counts of Gorizia in the 15C, the city fell into the hands of Austria, and it remained an Austrian possession almost continuously from 1509 to 1915. In the First World War it was the objective of violent Italian attacks in the Isonzo valley, and eventually was captured on 9 August 1916. Lost again in the autumn of 1917, it was finally taken in November 1918. The Treaty of Paris (February 1947) brought the Yugoslav frontier into the streets of the town, cutting off its E suburbs, the subsidiary railway stations of Monte Santo and San Marco, and the old cemetery. The town, and the country on both sides, were threatened with complete ruin, but in 1952, and again in 1978–79, more reasonable readjustments were made, including a ten-mile-wide zone in which local inhabitants may circulate freely.

The road passes the railway station on the way in to the town. The chief buildings of interest are towards the N end. To the right of the *Post Office* in the main Corso Giuseppe Verdi is the central Piazza della Vittoria in which are the handsome church of *Sant'Ignazio* (17–18C) and the *Prefettura*. From there the old Via Rastello leads to the *Duomo*, a 14C building much restored, containing the treasury brought from Aquileia in 1752. Above it stands the Borgo Castello of the Venetians (1509); within its wards are the *Museo di Storia e Arte* (9–19 except Monday), the little church of Santo Spirito (1398), and the KEEP (9–12.30, 14 or 15–17 or 18.30, except Monday), a 12C castello of the counts of Gorizia, remodelled in 1508. Important exhibitions are held here. The rampart walk commands a wide view. In the Baroque Palazzo Attems (1745) near the N end of the main street is the *Museo Provinciale* (open 9–19 except Monday) with a pinacoteca of local paintings. The Museum of the First World War here has been closed indefinitely.—Across the river, 4km to the NW at *Oslavia*, a 'Gothic' castle (open 9–19) holds the graves of 57,000 men of the 2nd Army who fell in 1915–18.

From Gorizia to *Udine*, see Rte 35.—The *Bainsizza Plateau*, to the E, the scene of a brilliant Italian offensive in May–August 1917, is now Yugoslav territory.

At (114km) *Villa Vicentina* (2km left) is a villa built by Elisa Bonaparte Baciocchi in 1815, where in 1869–70 Pasteur saved the silk industry of Italy, as he had that of France. The road crosses the Isonzo, and at (123km) *Ronchi dei Legionari* reaches the edge of the Carso and the region of the battle-front of 1915–17.

The town has a special place in Italian patriotic sentiment: here Guglielmo Oberdan was arrested in 1882 and from here in 1919 D'Annunzio set out to occupy Fiume. It now has an important civil airport serving Udine, Gorizia, and Trieste (flights to London, Madrid, Frankfurt, Athens, etc.). The **Carso** (German *Karst*, Slav *Kras*), a curiously eroded limestone plateau, was the scene of the most violent struggles in the Austro-Italian campaign. Vast trenches and veritable caverns were easily constructed by widening the existing crevasses in its surface; and although large-scale operations were made difficult by the nature of the ground, immense concentrations of artillery were brought up by both sides for the defence of this key position. It was the Duke of Aosta's stand here with the 3rd Italian Army that averted complete disaster after Caporetto (October 1917).—The *Bora* (NE wind) sweeps the plateau with great fury at some seasons.

126km **Monfalcone**, an industrial town (29,600 inhab.) with large and conspicuous naval shipyards, has been completely rebuilt since 1918.

FROM MONFALCONE TO GORIZIA. Railway, 22km; frequent service to Gorizia Centrale in 20 minutes, going on to Udine. Bus, 4–8 times daily, in 35 minutes. The Udine road follows the railway past (3km) *Ronchi* (see above) which it leaves on the left. 6km *Redipuglia* has the huge war cemetery of the 3rd Army, with over 100,000 graves, including that of the Duke of Aosta (1869–1931), the heroic defender of the Carso.—At (9km) *Sagrado* the railway keeps to the left bank but the road crosses the Isonzo for (12km) *Gradisca* (to Gorizia, see above).

Outside the town the way divides. To the left is a road (N55) to Gorizia across the Carso; in the centre the main road (N202), an extension of the motorway with few intermediate exits, runs farther inland direct to (151km) *Poggioreale del Carso* (see below), from where alternative hilly spurs enter **Trieste** from the E (162km) or SE (168km).—N14 keeps to the right along the coast.

At (132km) *San Giovanni al Timavo* it passes the mouth of the Timavo, which emerges here from an underground course of over 134km. *Duino* is a fishing village with the ruined Castello Vecchio. The imposing Castello Nuovo was built in the 15C on the ruins of a Roman tower. Rainer Maria Rilke stayed here as a guest of Maria von Thurn und Taxis in 1910–14; it is now a study centre dedicated to the poet.—137km *Sistiana*, on a delightful bay known to the Romans as Sextilianum. Here the coast road (fine sea views) bears to the right, via Miramare (see below), for (158km) **Trieste**.

The old road (1·5km farther) runs inland, through (4km) *Aurisina*, where the quarries of fine white stone have been worked since Roman times.—At (10·5km) *Prosecco*, known for its wine, it turns right to descend into *Trieste*.

TRIESTE, the most important seaport of the northern Adriatic, although its commercial traffic has diminished in recent years, commands a pretty gulf backed by the low rolling hills of the Carso. It is an attractive provincial capital (271,800 inhab.), mainly modern in appearance, with lively streets, and a harbour of which the principal quays, unlike those of Genoa, are generally open. A few streets of the old town retain their character and the environs are pleasant. Trieste was the centre of Irredentism in Istria during the period of Austrian rule.

Tourist Information Offices. *Azienda Autonoma di Soggiorno e Turismo*, Castello di San Giusto; information office at the central railway station.—**Post Office**, Piazza Vittorio Veneto.—POLICE STATION (Questura), 6 Via Tor Bandena.

Car Parking in the centre is particularly difficult; best on the Rive or near the cathedral. A multi-storey car park is under construction beside the station.— **Airport** at *Ronchi*, 35km NW; terminal at Stazione Centrale (Viale Miramare), coach in 60 minutes. International services daily to Athens, Brussels, Frankfurt, London, Madrid, etc.

Local Buses from Piazza Oberdan to *Barcola, Miramare, Grignano*, and *Sistiana*; to *Duino*; to *Prosecco*; to *Aurisina:* to *Opicina*. Other **Buses** from Stazione Largo Barriera Vecchia to *Muggia*; to *Koper, Piran, Porec*, and *Pula*. From main Bus Station in Piazza della Libertà to *Muggia*; to *Sistiana*; to *Postojna* and *Ljubljana*; to *Rijeka*; to *Sežana*; to *Zagreb* and *Belgrade*, etc. Coaches to Venice, Milan, the Dolomites, etc.—RACK TRAMWAY from Piazza Oberdan to *Opicina*.

Maritime Services. International liners moor at the *Stazione Marittima*. Regular steamer service for *Istria, Dalmatia*, and *Greece* (information at Molo Audace).—TOURS of the port and gulf by motor launch are organised in summer. from Riva del Mandracchio.

Theatres. *Politeama Rossetti*, Viale Venti Settembre. *Teatro Comunale Giuseppe Verdi*, Piazza Verdi (opera season in November–March, concerts in May and October). Open-air theatre (July–August) in the *Castle*.—**Sport**. *Golf Course*, 9 holes, at Padriciano (6·5km E).—Trotting Races at Montebello stadium.—*Sea Bathing*. Riviera di Barcola; Grignano and Sistiana (sand); Duina (rocks).—SWIMMING POOL (covered), Riva Gulli.

History. The settlement of *Tergeste*, already an important outlet into the Adriatic for the produce of the middle Danube and its tributaries, was absorbed into the Roman dominion early in the 2C BC. From the 9C to the 13C the city was ruled by its bishops, with various nominal overlords, and at the beginning of the 13C, with the rise of the independent Commune of Trieste, began also the age-long rivalry with Venice for the commerce of the Adriatic. The Venetians generally had the upper hand, and in 1382 Trieste came under the protection of the Austrian Emperor Leopold III. The strife with Venice, however, continued, and in 1463 Trieste, reduced to desperate straits by a blockade, was saved only by the intervention of Pius II. In 1470 Frederick III rebuilt the ruined city, but its latter-day prosperity dates from Charles VI, who declared it a free port in 1719, a privilege followed by further favours from Maria Theresa. Later emperors, however, though fostering the commerce of Trieste, paid less attention to its liberty of sentiment, and despite the increased prosperity brought about by the opening of the Suez Canal (1869) the Triestines leant more and more towards the cause of Italian unity. Italian troops entered Trieste in 1918 and the city, together with the Carso and Istria, was ceded to Italy by the Treaty of Rapallo in 1920. These territories fell in 1945 to Yugoslav forces and the Carso was incorporated into Yugoslavia. By the Italian peace treaty (1947) Trieste and Istria were created a Free Territory, with Anglo-American trusteeship of the city and a Yugoslav zone in Istria, until in 1954 the existing frontier was agreed at a further four-power conference in London. Trieste remains a free port.

Charles Lever was British consul at Trieste from 1867 until his death in 1872, and he was succeeded by Sir Richard Burton, who also died here in 1890. J.J. Winckelmann (1717–68), the archaeologist, was murdered at Trieste under the assumed name of 'Signor Giovanni' by a thief whose cupidity he had excited by displaying some ancient gold coins. James Joyce (1882–1941) lived in the city in 1905–14 and 1919–20.

The life of Trieste centres on the **Harbour**, fronted by the pleasant broad quay, or Riva, and always animated by the movement of ships. The modern deep-sea harbour of Trieste was engineered in the Vallone di Muggia (in Istria 'vallone' means a wide bay, while 'val' or 'valle' is applied to the narrower fiords of the W coast). Its N limit (beyond which extend the quays and warehouses of the Punta Franco) is marked by the *Canal Grande*, which serves as a mooring for small boats, the end of which is closed scenographically by the church of Sant'Antonio (see below). Then beyond the Greek Orthodox church of San Nicolò comes the *Molo Audace*, commemorating the

Trieste from the harbour

name of the destroyer from which the first Italian troops landed on 3 November 1918. On the left is the *Teatro Verdi*, with an excellent *Theatre Museum* and Library (open 9–13 except Monday), founded in 1924. Beyond opens the handsome PIAZZA DELL'UNITÀ D'ITALIA, the centre of the city. Facing the sea is *Palazzo Comunale* built by Giuseppe Bruni in 1875, with a statue of Charles VI nearby. On the left is the *Palazzo del Governo* (1904–05) by the Austrian architect Emil Artmann, and on the right the huge offices built in 1883 by the Austrian Heinrich Ferstel for the famous *Lloyd Triestino Shipping Company*, founded in 1830. The Caffè degli Specchi, one of the city's famous cafés, was founded in the square in 1840. The name of Riva Mandracchio is suggestive (Mandraki, in Greek 'sheepfold', commonly denotes an ancient galley port; as at Rhodes, Kos, and also Hvar). On the Molo Bersaglieri is the *Stazione Marittima*. Beyond the next jetty is the *Pescheria* with its spacious market hall (1913, by Giorgio Polli) open to the sea. Nearby is the fine *Aquarium* (daily 9–13, except Monday), founded in 1933, with fish from the Adriatic and tropics, as well as two penguins. In Piazza Venezia (left) is the *Museo Revoltella* (closed indefinitely; entrance at No. 27 Via Diaz) with a collection of 19C paintings displayed on the first floor. The later works of modern art are to be arranged in the adjacent palazzo. In Piazza Attilio Hortis, in a palazzo built in 1816 by Pietro Nobile, are the *Natural History Museum* (open 9–13, except Monday), founded in 1846, and the Public Library. Nearby, in Via Madonna del Mare, are remains of a palaeochristian basilica (open Thursday 10–13).

On a rise to the SW stands the·*Museo Sartorio* (9–13, except Monday) with a collection of decorative arts arranged in 19C period rooms. Some paintings from the Museo di Storia ed Arte (see below) are displayed permanently here. The villa also serves as an exhibition centre. Nearby, the *Villa Necker* was occupied by Jerome Bonaparte after 1815.—At the end of Riva Grumula, in Via Campo Marzio (see the Plan), is the MUSEO DEL MARE (9–13, except Monday) with sections devoted to harbours, navigation, and fishing.

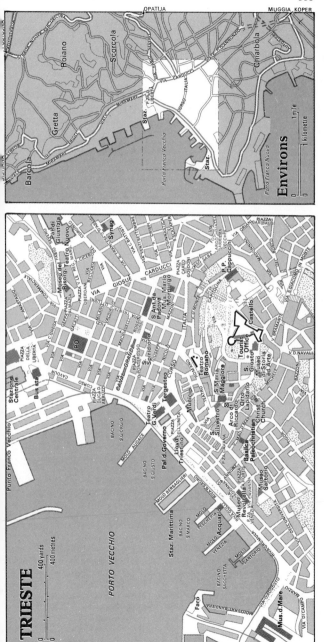

Environs

1 mile
1 kilometre

OPATIJA
MUGGIA, KOPER

Roiano
Scorcola
Chiarbola
Gretta
Barcola

VIA CARDUCCI
CORSO ITALIA

Staz.
Staz.

Porto Franco Vecchio
Porto Franco Nuovo

TRIESTE

400 yards
400 metres

PORTO VECCHIO

Punto Franco Vecchio

BACINO S. GIORGIO
BACINO S. MARCO
BACINO VENEZIA
BACINO SACCHETTA

MOLO AUDACE
MOLO BERSAGLIERI
MOLO S. MARCO
MOLO VENEZIA
MOLO SARTORIO

Staz. Marittima

Faro

Mus. d. Mare

Museo del Risorg
Teatro Nuovo
Synag.
PIAZZA S. Spiridi
GIUSTIZIE
PIAZZA GARIBALDI

VIA GIOSUÈ CARDUCCI
VIA GIOSUÈ

S. Ant. da Padova
P.P. Cappuccini

Castello
Tourist Office

Mus. Mario Morpurgo
S. Maria Maggiore
Teatro Romano
Museo di Storia ed Arte
S. Giusto
Orto Lapidario
V.D. NAVALI
BRAMANTE

PIAZZA DELLA LIBERTÀ
PIAZZA OBERDAN
PIAZZA DUCA DEGLI ABRUZZI

Stazione Centrale
Bus stn.

Teatro G. Verdi
PIAZZA DELL'UNITÀ
Pal. d. Governo
Lloyd Triestino
Municip.
Arco di Riccardo
S. Silvestro
Basilica
Paleochristian Church

Acquario
Pescheria
PIAZZA VENEZIA
Museo Sartorio
Revoltella

CORSO ITALIA
VIA CARDUCCI

MuS. Marzio

Via and Piazza Cavana and Via San Sebastiano (all closed to traffic) penetrate the dwindling area of the old town. To the E, in Via del Teatro Romano, demolitions in 1938 revealed the remains of a *Roman Theatre* endowed in the late 1C by a certain Q. Petronius Modestus. Behind the theatre rises the hill of San Giusto, reached by narrow lanes and steps through the *Parco della Rimembranza*, or with a car by Via Capitolina.

On the hilltop, planted with trees and with a pleasant view out to sea, is the *Cathedral of San Giusto* (closed 12–15), a venerable building of irregular plan and in several styles.

Between the 5C and the 11C two aisled basilicas arose, one dedicated to San Giusto, the other smaller, alongside it to the left, dedicated to Santa Maria Assunta. Still more to the left is a third Romanesque church, now the baptistery. In the 14C the two larger churches were made into one, and the whole dedicated to Justus, a Christian martyr who was hurled into the sea during the persecution of Diocletian.

EXTERIOR. The irregular façade incorporates five Roman Corinthian columns in its projecting campanile (1337), and the pillars of the main doorway are fragments of a Roman tomb, with six busts. Above the latter are three modern busts of bishops of Trieste (including Pope Pius II) and a splendid rose-window. Over the campanile door is a 14C statue of St Justus.

INTERIOR. The nave is made up of the N aisle of San Giusto and the S aisle of the Assunta and has a 14C roof. The central apse, disfigured in 1842, was restored on the 14C lines. The mosaic is by Guido Cadorin (1932). The Madonna on the wall is by Benedetto Carpaccio (1540). The two aisles on the right preserve the dome of San Giusto and in the chapels are a polychrome Pietà (15C), a 14C Crucifixion on a gold ground, and the tomb of Don Carlos of Spain (died 1855). The apse preserves its old choir-bench and some good Byzantine pillars and capitals between which are 13C frescoes of the life of St Justus. The 13C *Mosaic above depicts Christ between Saints Justus and Servulus, and has a beautifully decorated border. The apse of the Assunta on the left also has fine and well preserved mosaics (12–13C), while at the end of the outer left aisle is the good Renaissance grille of the treasury. The Baptistery (entered from the N aisle) has a 9C immersion font.

In the piazza outside is a Venetian column (1560). Down the hill from the cathedral is the entrance to the **Museo di Storia ed Arte** and **Orto Lapidario** (9–13, except Monday), which has been undergoing rearrangement for years. In the garden, the cenotaph of Winckelmann (see above), in a little chapel, stands among Roman altars, stelae, and inscriptions, Egyptian and Gandhara sculptures, etc. The most interesting objects in the museum are the prehistoric and Roman antiquities from Tergeste and its neighbourhood, including finds relating to the Castellieri civilisation, Roman glass and small bronzes, and red-figure vases. However, the two most precious objects are no longer displayed for safety reasons: a silver-gilt *Rhyton, in the form of a deer's head, and a bronze wine-vessel, both from Tarentum (5C BC). The paintings (including works by Magnasco and Tiepolo, a 14C Venetian triptych, and a Limoges enamel of the Last Supper) have been removed to the Museo Sartorio (see above).

To the left of the cathedral rises the castle, in front of which may be seen the paved floor and column bases (restored) of a large Roman *Basilica* of c AD 100, and a good War Memorial of 1935 by Attilio Selva. The 15–16C **Castello** (open during daylight hours) was begun by the Venetians in 1368 and later altered and enlarged by the

Austrians. In summer plays are given in the courtyard. Part of the building houses the *Museo Civico* (9–13; closed Monday) with an interesting collection of arms and armour. The Cappella di San Giorgio may also be visited. Exhibitions are held annually in the Sala del Capitano. There is a fine view from the ramparts.

The steep Via della Cattedrale descends to the ARCO DI RICCARDO, a vaulted Roman arch erected to honour Augustus in AD 33; its name survives from a belief now discounted that Richard I was confined here after his return from the Holy Land. Just below are (left) the little church of *San Silvestro* (open Thursday and Saturday 10–12, Sunday at 11) of the 12C but remodelled in the 18C, now occupied by the Waldensians. The porch over the N door supports the quaint campanile. To the right is the Baroque church of *Santa Maria Maggiore*. Steps lead down towards the centre of the city.

Beyond the Capo di Piazza opens the triangular Piazza della Borsa. On the left are the *Tergesteo* (1840), a neo-classical building containing the stock exchange, and the *Borsa Vecchia* (1806, by Antonio Molari), now the chamber of commerce. A bronze statue of Leopold I (1673) faces up the busy CORSO ITALIA, the main street with elegant shops, which leads to Piazza Carlo Goldoni. In Via Imbriani (left), before the square, is the small *Museo Morpurgo e Stavropoulos* (9–13, except Monday) with 19C collections. Beyond is the broad Via Giosuè Carducci which descends left to PIAZZA OBERDAN, laid out in the 1930s, from which, at the end of Viale Regina Margherita, is seen the *Palazzo di Giustizia* (by Ernesto Nordio; 1933); to the left is the *Museo del Risorgimento* (9–13, except Monday) in a fine palazzo by Umberto Nordio (1934), which incorporates the cell of Guglielmo Oberdan, hanged in 1882 by the Austrians in the old barracks on this site. In Via San Francesco the **Synagogue**, built by the local architect Ruggero Berlam and his son Arduino (1910), is one of the finest in Europe. From Piazza Oberdan Via Trenta Ottobre leads back to Piazza Sant'Antonio (formed by filling in part of the Canal Grande) before the large neo-classical church of *Sant'Antonio* (1827–47, by Pietro Nobile). On the S side of this square is *San Spiridione*, the Serbian church, with a fine interior (1868, by Carlo Maciachini and Pietro Palese). From here Via Filzi continues S to the Corso Italia.

Environs of Trieste

The park of **Miramare** (open 9–one hour before sunset), is beautifully situated above the Adriatic, 7km NW of Trieste. It is reached by bus (No. 6 and 36) from Piazza Oberdan, or by railway. The road passes the *Faro della Vittoria*, a beacon erected in 1927 in memory of the victims of the First World War who died at sea. The white stone tower (closed since 1979) is by Arduino Berlam, the bronze Victory and the sailor are by Giovanni Mayer. Beyond the resort of *Barcola* are the park and **Castle** of Miramare, built in 1856–60 for Archduke Maximilian of Austria, who became Emperor of Mexico and was shot in 1867; its *Museo Storico* (9–13) contains a few souvenirs. In June–September son-et-lumière pageants are held nightly. The *Castelletto*, where Maximilian lived during the construction of the palace, houses a Gallery of paintings (adm. as for the Museum).— *Grignano*, is a few minutes below the park to the N.

THE VEDETTA D'OPICINA AND THE GROTTA DEL GIGANTE, ½ day. The Opicina tramway from the Piazza Oberdan runs to (5km) *Poggioreale* (360m), from where a lane ascends to the *Vedetta* (396m), a splendid viewpoint, with a panorama ranging from the Punta Salvore in Istria to the Carnic Alps. Another good viewpoint is the *Vedetta Italia*, ¾hrs walk NW of Poggioreale.—7km **Villa Opicina** or *Opicina*, the terminus of the tramway, has also a station on the railway to Gorizia. Here a plaque on the Albergo Obelisco records Richard Burton's completion of the translation of the 'Thousand and one Nights'. *Borgo Grotta Gigante*, ½hr NW on foot, may be more closely approached by taking the Prosecco bus from Piazza Oberdan. The *Grotta del Gigante* (9–12, 14–19; winter 10–12.30, 14–16.30; closed Monday), ¼hr's walk farther, is the largest single cave yet discovered in the Carso (238m long, 137m high); its stalactitic formations are famous.—*Monrupino* (421m), 3km to the E, affords a superb view of the Carso plateau. A local museum here is open on Sunday.

The road-route to Opicina follows the Via Fabio Severo and passes the buildings (1940–50, by Umberto Nordio and Raffaello Fagnoni) of the *University* founded in 1919.

TO MUGGIA, 11km S, bus No. 20 (½hr) from Largo Barriera Vecchia. **Muggia**, a flourishing fishing-port (13,100 inhab.) of Venetian aspect, the only Istrian town remaining within Italy, lies at the base of the hill which bears the Roman and medieval settlement of Muggia Vecchia. The *Duomo* is a 13C foundation with a 15C Gothic façade, while the *Palazzo dei Rettori*, rebuilt after a fire in 1933, was once a palace of the patriarchs of Aquileia. An ascent on foot of rather more than ½hr (also reached by road) leads to **Muggia Vecchia**, now in ruins except for the *Basilica*, a 9C building with an ambo of the 10C, transennae in the Byzantine style, and remains of early frescoes.

By far the most interesting of the longer excursions that can be made by bus are across the Yugoslav frontier (passports) to the splendid **Caverns of *Postojna* (50km; Postumia) and to the *Basilica at *Poreč* (Parenzo); for both see the 'Blue Guide Yugoslavia'.

IV EMILIA

Emilia-Romagna as the name of a district dates only from the Risorgimento (c 1860) but its use is derived from the Via Aemilia, the great Roman road built by M. Aemilius Lepidus, that traverses the country from end to end. Emilia occupies the region between the middle and lower Po, the Apennines, and the Adriatic. Its area is 22,122 square kilometres with a population of 3,846,000. The modern provinces are those of Bologna, Ferrara, Forlì, Modena, Parma, Piacenza, Ravenna, and Reggio nell'Emilia; and Bologna is the chief town. The eastern part of Emilia, coinciding roughly with the modern provinces of Ravenna and Forlì, is known as the *Romagna*. Extending as it does from the summits of the Apennines to the plain of the Po, Emilia has a very varied landscape. The mountain country, centring round the *Frignano*, is a region of chilly winters with periodic streams liable to sudden floods. All the principal towns except Ferrara and Ravenna lie along the line of the Via Aemilia at the foot of the mountains; the climate here is subject to extremes, and the summers are often unpleasantly hot.

The history of Emilia is a confused one. The *Romagna* in the E followed a separate destiny. Ravenna was the capital of the Western Roman Empire from 402, after the fall of Rome, until it was taken by Odoacer, who, like his successor Theodoric, made it capital of a short-lived Gothic Empire. It was conquered by the Byzantines in 540, and was governed by Exarchs of the Eastern Empire for two centuries.

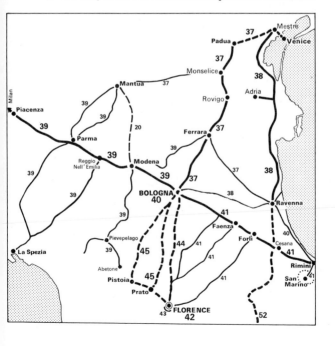

In 757 the Romagna came into possession of the Popes, who maintained at least a nominal suzerainty here until 1860; in the 13–15C, however, the effective rule of the Da Polenta clan gave Ravenna a pre-eminent position in the world of learning. Parts of historic Romagna are now included in the modern provinces of Tuscany and the Marches.

The other districts of Emilia emerged disunited after the barbarian (Gothic, Lombard, Frankish) incursions of the 5–8C; and the cities spent themselves in internecine warfare. In the early Middle Ages Guelfs and Ghibellines held now one city, now another; but Piacenza and Parma later tended to be absorbed into the orbit of Milan, Ferrara felt the proximity of Venice, and Bologna was always open to incursions from the Papal dominions. The dominion of the Este family at Ferrara in the 13C extended over Modena and Reggio, while the Pepoli and Bentivoglio at Bologna, the Ordelaffi at Forlì, and the Malatesta at Rimini held temporary local sway for varying periods up to the 16C. After the 16C wars the Papal power was firmly established in Romagna and at Ferrara and Bologna; while the Farnese family, descended from the son of Pope Paul III, made Modena the capital of a new duchy and the centre of a court of some pretensions. New dispositions followed the Napoleonic disturbances. The Empress Marie-Louise emerged as Duchess of Parma, with Piacenza and Tuscan Lucca subjoined; the rest of Emilia went to Austria, as successors of the Este dynasty, and Romagna remained papal land. In 1848 the ferment of the Risorgimento began to take effect; the ducal rulers were expelled, though only temporarily, from Parma and Bologna; in 1859 Carlo Farini announced the union of Emilia and Romagna with Piedmont, and in 1860 the union became effective.

Emilia, and especially the Romagna, played an important part in the Second World War. In 1944 the Allies occupied San Marino, Rimini, Cesena, Forlì, Ravenna, and Faenza. The Romagnole partisans were particularly active in 1945 and by the Spring, after Modena, Reggio, Parma, and Piacenza were taken, the advance had reached Verona.

37 Venice to Bologna

ROAD, 168km. To (42·5km) *Padua*, see Rte 33. N16 leaves the city by the Corso Vittorio Emanuele.—63km *Monselice.*—84km **Rovigo.**—121km **Ferrara.**—N64. 168km **Bologna**.

AUTOSTRADA (152km), A4 to Padua; then A13 to Bologna, with exits at the Eugenean Hills, and all the main towns.

RAILWAY, 160km, several expresses daily in 1½–2¼ hours; to *Ferrara*, 113km in 1–1½ hours. Through carriages from Trieste to Rome run on this line.

From Venice to (42·5km) *Padua*, see Rte 33. A short way beyond Padua a road to Mandria diverges on the right giving access to the **Euganean Hills**.

The road passes (right) the *Villa Giusti*, where the armistice between Italy and Austria was signed on 3 November 1918.—Just short of (8km) Abano Terme Station, the road turns right for (11km) **Abano Terme**, one of the most well-equipped thermal spas in Europe, with numerous hotels (catering especially for German visitors). The springs (80–87°C) which have been known since Roman times, are used mainly for baths, but Abano is principally noted for its mud therapy, effective especially in cases of rheumatism and arthritis. In the season (March–October) Abano and the neighbouring spas are crowded with visitors.—*Monteortone*, 2km farther on, is another mud spa, with an interesting church built from 1435 to 1497, containing frescoes by Jacopo da Montagnana.—5km NW is *Praglia*, with a Benedictine abbey and church (rebuilt 1490–1548), by Tullio Lombardo. The refectory has paintings by Giovanni Battista Zelotti, and a fresco by Bartolomeo Montagna. The monks are renowned for their skill in restoring books (their laboratory is off the beautiful cloisters).— 14km *Montegrotto*, another small spa, with extensive remains of Roman baths, and a theatre. There is now a by-pass to Montegrotto which will be opened as far as Battaglia Terme (see below).

Just before (19km) this road rejoins the N16, stands the curious castle of the *Cataio*. It was built in 1570 by Pio Enea degli Obizzi, and afterwards became the property of the dukes of Modena. The frescoes by Giovanni Battista Zelotti on the first floor (permission to view them granted on request by the proprietor) depict the exploits of members of the Obizzi family, including one who attended Richard I of England to the Crusades, and another who perhaps fought for Edward III at Neville's Cross.

At (53km) *San Pelagio* the castle has an 'Air Museum'. The display, in 33 rooms, is arranged chronologically from the experiments of Leonardo to the era of space travel. The exhibits include material relating to d'Annunzio's flight to Vienna in 1918, planned in the castle; a model of the first helicopter designed by Forlanini in 1877; planes used in the Second World War, etc.—57km *Battaglia Terme* is yet another spa.—At *Valsanzibio*, 5km W, is the *Villa Barbarigo*, now Pizzoni Ardemagni, with a fine garden (1699) and maze.

64km **Monselice** (17,600 inhab.) lies at the foot of a conspicuous hill (*mons silicis*) with a huge trachyte quarry and a ruined Rocca. It is a Lombard city of ancient foundation. The approach from the Station crosses the canal by an iron swing-bridge beside *Villa Pisani* (on a design by Palladio), being restored as the Museo Civico. A stretch of 14C walls can be seen here. Via XI Febbraio and Via XXVIII Aprile continue to Piazza Mazzini, the centre of the medieval town. In Piazza Vittoria to the S are the Duomo Nuovo (1957) and the Municipio (1965). Via del Santuario ascends from Piazza Mazzini past the 15C Monte di Pietà, the church of San Paolo, and remains of the Palazzo Pretorio. Above is the *Castello di Ezzelino*, restored in 1939 for Count Vittorio Cini who transformed it into a museum of medieval and Renaissance works of art, now the property of the Region. The road continues past monumental edifices including the Baroque *Palazzo Nani-Mocenigo*, the 13C *Duomo Vecchio*, and the 18C *Santuario delle Sette Chiese*. At the top is *Villa Duodo* by Vincenzo Scamozzi and Andrea Tirali, preceded by four statues of the seasons.

At *Arquà Petrarca* (6·5km NW), Petrarch lived from 1370 until his death in 1374. His house (9.30–12.30, 13.30 or 15–16.30 or 19.30; ring), in a pretty setting, contains visitors' books with Byron's signature. Petrarch's plain marble sarcophagus, in front of the church, has an epitaph composed by himself.

FROM MONSELICE TO MANTUA. Road, 85km; railway, following the road, in 1¾–2¼hrs.—9km **Este** (17,000 inhab.), a centre of the ancient Veneti, and then the Roman *Ateste*, became the stronghold of the Este family who afterwards became dukes of Ferrara. It was under Venetian dominion from 1405 onwards. The huge battlemented *Castle* dates mainly from 1339 and encloses a public garden. Here, in *Palazzo Mocenigo* (16C), is the MUSEO NAZIONALE ATESTINO (adm. 9–13, 15–19; winter 9–13, 14–17; fest. 9–14; closed Monday) a remarkable collection of pre-Roman and Roman antiquities, especially famous for its bronzes. These include the Benvenuti *Situla (6C–5C BC); remains of a temple of the Veneti; the Lex Rubria, a bronze tablet of 49 BC; a fine *Medusa's Head, in bronze, of the 1C AD; and a collection of votive statuettes found in the sanctuary of Reitia. The collection of ceramics dates from the 8C–3C BC. A room dedicated to the medieval and Renaissance periods includes a Madonna and Child by Cima da Conegliano.— Behind the castle (Via Cappuccini) are the fine parks of several villas, including the *Villa De Kunkler*, occupied by Byron in 1817–18, where Shelley composed his 'Lines written among the Euganean Hills'. The *Duomo* (rebuilt 1690–1708) contains a painting by Giovanni Battista Tiepolo. The Romanesque church of *San Martino* (1293) has a leaning campanile. Remains of the Roman city (including a stretch of road, houses with mosaic pavements, and fragments of a public building) have been found near the church of the Salute.—24km **Montagnana** (10,100 inhab.) preserves its medieval *WALLS intact, with two splendid fortified gate-castles, the Rocca degli Alberi, restored in the 1960s as a Youth Hostel, and the Castello di San Zeno (1242; being restored). The Gothic *Duomo* has a portal attributed to Sansovino, and an interesting interior. The *Palazzo del Municipio* is by Sanmicheli (c 1550). Just outside the walls to the E is *Palazzo Pisani* (adm. by previous appointment), built in 1552 to a design by Palladio.—Another Palladian villa can be visited (daily 15–16) at *Poiana*, 7·5km N of Montagnana.—40·5km *Legnago* was once one of the fortresses of the 'Quadrilateral'.—49km *Cerea*, for the railway to Verona.— 54·5km *Sanguinetto* has an old castle, now the town hall.—61·5km *Nogara* is on the route from Verona to Bologna.—84·5km *Mantua*, see Rte 20.

The road now runs due S crossing the Adige.—84km **Rovigo** the growing chief town (49,800 inhab.) of the Polesine, the fertile strip of land between the lower Adige and Po, has a *Cathedral* of 1696 and some towers of its old defences. In the central piazza are *Palazzo Roncale* by Sanmicheli (1555), the *Municipio* (16C, restored in 1765), *Palazzo Roverella*, begun in the early 15C, and the PINACOTECA DEI CONCORDI (adm. 10–12, 16–18.30; Sunday 10–12; closed Saturday) which contains some good pictures, including: *Quirizio da Murano*, Triptych of St Lucy; *Palma Vecchio*, Scourging of Christ, Madonna and Saints; *Giovanni Bellini*, Madonna, Christ Carrying the Cross; *Dosso Dossi*, Saints Benedict and Bartholomew, Saints Lucy and Agatha; *Giovanni Battista Tiepolo*, Portrait of Antonio Riccoboni. The 17–18C paintings from the Seminary are now also displayed here. There is also an archaeological section. The octagonal church ('La Rotonda') of the *Beata Vergine del Soccorso* by Francesco Zamberlan (1594–1602), pupil of Palladio, has a campanile by Longhena (1655).

The road (N499) which runs W from Rovigo to Legnago (see above) passes (15·5km) **Lendinara**, an ancient city with fine palaces, and, in the Duomo, a Madonna enthroned with an angel musician, signed by Domenico Mancini (the head of the angel has recently been attributed to Dosso Dossi). 10km S is *Fratta Polesine*, with the beautiful Palladian *Villa Badoer* (1570; open 14 or 15–17 or 19). The main road continues from Lendinara to (24km) *Badia Polesine* with remains of the Abbey of Vangadizza, founded in the 10C, and the Museo Civico Baruffaldi. 8km S is *Canda* on the Bianco canal, with the *Villa Nani-Mocenigo*, by Vincenzo Scamozzi (1580–84), enlarged in the 18C.

The road E from Rovigo to (66·5km) *Chioggia* (railway also in 1¼hrs) passes (27·5km) *Adria* (see Rte 38).

At (96·5km) *Polesella* the road reaches the Po (where a pontoon bridge to Ro was substituted in 1980 by a new bridge), and follows its left bank. It crosses the Po to enter Emilia at (113·5km) *Pontelagoscuro*, a river-harbour and industrial centre.

121km **FERRARA** (154,000 inhab.), a cheerful city situated in a fertile plain near the right bank of the Po, is principally famous as the residence of the Este dukes, whose court was one of the most illustrious of the Italian Renaissance, when 'Ferrara blades' rivalled the swords of Toledo. The city is divided into two distinctive parts: the S district retains many attractive cobbled streets and medieval houses, while the area to the N, defined by Jacob Burckhardt as the first modern city of Europe, was laid out with spacious streets and fine palaces in the 15C. Extensive land-reclaiming operations in the environs brought back to Ferrara much of its old prosperity, and it is now an important market for fruit. Since the closure of the centre to motor traffic, bicycles appear to be the most popular form of transport.

A.P.T. Information Office, 19 Piazza Municipale (in the courtyard of Palazzo del Comune: Pl. 11).—**Post Office**, Via Cavour (Pl. 6).—**Buses** from the Station (Nos 1 & 9) to Piazza Castello, etc. COUNTRY BUSES from Corso Isonzo (Pl. 6) to *Bologna, Modena, Rovigo*, and the *Lidi Ferrarese*.—**Car Parking.** Largo Castello, Piazza Repubblica, Piazza Travaglio, and (for cars with foreign number plates) Corso Portareno (Pl. 10,11).—**Teatro Comunale** (closed for restoration in 1989), Corso Martiri della Libertà (opera and concert season November–May). In summer concerts are held in the courtyards of various palazzi.

History. Originating probably as a refuge of the Veneti in the marshes of the Po, Ferrara first became important under the Exarchate of Ravenna (6C), but its main interest dates from the rise of the House of Este, the Guelf family that established the earliest and one of the greatest of the North Italian principalities. Though the family had been of municipal importance for many years, their princely power dates in reality from the crushing defeat of the Ghibellines by Azzo Novello at Cassano in 1259. Ferrara remained under the sway of the Este dukes until 1598, and their court attracted a great many poets, scholars, and artists, while trade and commerce flourished. Nicolò II (1361–88) gave hospitality to Petrarch; Alberto (1388–93) founded the university; Nicolò III (1393–1441) was the patron of Guarino da Verona and of Pisanello, and in his city (1438) the eastern Emperor John VI Palaeologus met Pope Eugenius IV for the ecumenical council, later transferred to Florence; Lionello (1441–50) inaugurated the age of artistic pre-eminence that Borso (1450–71) continued; Ercole I (1471–1505) laid out the northern district of the city; Alfonso I (1505–34), husband of Lucrezia Borgia, was the patron of Ariosto and Titian; Ercole II (1534–59) exiled his wife Renée, the daughter of Louis XII of France and the protectress of John Calvin, who lived for a while in Ferrara under the assumed name of Charles Heppeville; Alfonso II (1559–97) was the patron of Tasso and Guarini and began the reclamation of the marshes which still continues. In 1598 the city was annexed to the States of the Church on the pretext that Cesare d'Este, heir apparent to the duchy in a collateral line, was illegitimate, and the city decayed under 250 years of neglect. Ferrara suffered widespread bomb damage in the Second World War.

Ferrara had a productive school of painting, its leaders having been influenced in turn by the schools of Padua, Bologna, and Venice. The most eminent were Cosmè Tura, 'the Mantegna of Ferrara', Francesco del Cossa, Ercole de'Roberti, Lorenzo Costa, Dosso Dossi and his brother Battista Luteri, and Benvenuto Tisi, surnamed Il Garofalo, pupil of Raphael. The Metaphysical school of painters was founded here c 1917, and Giorgio De Chirico (1888–1978) spent much time in the city.—Ferrara was the birthplace of a great sculptor, Alfonso Lombardi (1497–1537), and of a great architect, Biagio Rossetti (c 1447–1516), as well as of the reformer Girolamo Savonarola (1452–98), the poets Giambattista Guarini (1538–1612) and Fulvio Testi (1593–1646), and the composer Girolamo Frescobaldi (1583–1643). At the end of the 16C the 'concerto delle donne' at the Este court had an important influence on the development of the madrigal. Robert Browning wrote several poems about Ferrara, and 'My Last Duchess' (written in 1842) probably refers to Alfonso II and his wife. The writer Giorgio Bassani was born here in 1916.

The **Walls of Ferrara** (see the Plan) are among the most extensive and interesting in Europe. Recent studies have awoken interest in their preservation and restoration. They were begun in 1451 at the S limit of the city, and in 1492 Biagio Rossetti was commissioned to build the walls around Ercole I's new extension to the city to the N. Alfonso I and Alfonso II strengthened the fortifications and more work was carried out on them by the popes in the 17C and 18C. Their total length is c 9·2km, and paths and avenues surmount them for some 8·5km. The most interesting stretch is in the NE corner, between the ex Porta degli Angeli and the Porta Mare (see below).

In the centre of the city rises the *Castello Estense (Pl. 7; adm. 9–12.30, 14.30–17; closed Monday) the former palace of the dukes, a massive quadrilateral surrounded by a moat and approached by drawbridges. It houses the administrative offices of the province. The entrance to the upper floor is in the centre of the building.

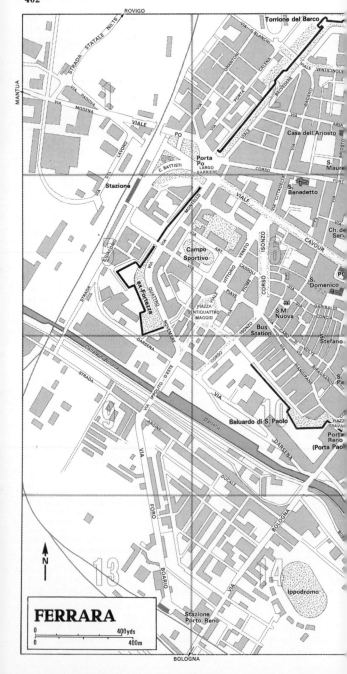

FERRARA

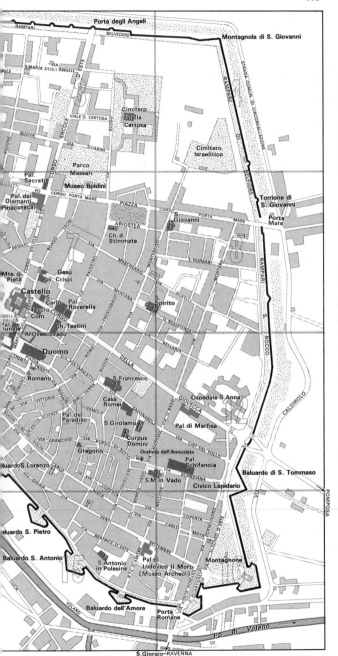

Porta degli Angeli
RAMPARI
BELVEDERE
Montagnola di S. Giovanni
STRADA COMUN. DI CIRCONVALLAZIONE
RILE
S.MARIA DEGLI ANGELI
VIA
RAMPARI
D'ESTE
ERCOLE
Cimitero della Certosa
Viale D. Certosa
BORGO
Cimitero Israelitico
BELFIORE
NUOVA
VIA
GUABINI
PAVONE
Parco Massari
Pal. Sacrati
CORSO
Museo Boldini
Torrione di S. Giovanni
OSSETTI
PO
CORSO PORTA MARE
Pal. dei Diamanti (Pinacoteca)
PIAZZA
CORSO
PORTA
MARE
Porta Mare
ARIOSTEA
S. Giovanni
RAMPARI
BORGO
LEON
Ch. d. Stimmate
MONTEBELLO
L. BORSARI
S.
PALESTRO
MORTARA
Mte. di Pietà
ERCOLE
BORGO
VIA
MASCHERAIO
VIA
BOVELLI
ROCCO
Gesù
Pal. Crispi
MENTANA
VIA
D'ESTE
Castello
S. Carlo
Pal. Roverella
FRESCOBALDI
S. Spirito
D. RESISTENZA
DELLA BBLICA
Teatro Com.
CORSO
Gh. Teatini
CALDIROLO
unale
Arcivescovado
BELLARIA
Duomo
ROMEI
DELLA
MARTIR
TRENTO E TRIESTE
VIA
VOLTAPALETTO
NUOVA
S. Francesco
ROMANO
Romano
MAZZINI
SAVONAROLA
GIOVECCA
Ospedale S. Anna
VITTORIA
VIA
Casa Romei
DELLE SCIENZE
ZEMOLA
Pal. del Paradiso
S. Girolamo
Pal. di Marfisa
VIA GRANCHIO
VIA
BORGO DI SOTTO
Corpus Domini
VIA CIST. DEL FOLLO
Baluardo di S. Tommaso
luardo S. Lorenzo
CARLO
S. Gregorio
Oratoria dell'Annunziata
POMPOSA
VIA GHIAIA
VIA
COPERTA
Pal. Schifanoia
S.M. in Vado
BORGO
SCANDIANA
Civico Lapidario
MAYR
VIA
VENTI
S. VIA
MELLONE
COPERTA
Baluardo S. Pietro
CARLO
MAYR
FORMIGNANA
luardo S. Antonio
BEATRICE D'ESTE
SETTEMBRE
Montagnone
S. Antonio in Polesine
Pal. di Lodovico il Moro (Museo Archeol.)
LUCA
VOLANO
Baluardo dell'Amore
Porta Romana
Po di Volano
S. Giorgio–RAVENNA

It was begun in 1385 by Bartolino da Novara for Duke Nicolò II; he incorporated the 13C 'Torre dei Leoni' into the N corner of the fortress, and added three more identical towers. It was altered by Girolamo da Carpi in the 16C. Of the decorations by early Ferrarese masters which formerly adorned its rooms, the only important survivals are in the Sala dell'Aurora, the Salone and Saletta dei Giochi, and the Camerina dei Bacchanali, which are frescoed by *Camillo Filippi* and his sons *Cesare* and *Sebastiano (Il Bastianino)*. The tiny *'Stanzina delle Duchesse' (adm. on request at the administrative offices) was entirely decorated with grotteschi by the Filippi c 1555–65. The Chapel of Renée de France, with marble decoration, was one of the few Calvinist chapels in Italy to survive the Counter-Reformation. The underground rooms are also usually open (entrance off the courtyard). In the dungeons beneath the 'Torre dei Leoni', Parisina, wife of Nicolò III, and her lover Ugo, his illegitimate son, were imprisoned and murdered; the cells were last used for political prisoners in 1943. Here also are the kitchens, and an artillery ramp by which the cannons were taken up to the bastions.

In the piazzetta on the W side of the castle stands the chapel of *San Giuliano* (1405), its charming exterior unaffected by the reconstruction within.

Corso Martiri della Libertà leads S along the E side of the castle; on the right opens Piazza della Repubblica, with a monument to the great reformer, Savonarola, by Stefano Galletti (1875). Beyond is the **Palazzo del Comune** (Pl. 7), built for Azzo Novello (1243), considerably altered in the late-15C by Pietro Benvenuti and Biagio Rossetti, and skilfully restored in 1924. The bronze statues of Nicolò III and Borso, on the classical arch (on a design attributed to Leon Battista Alberti) and column in front, are reproductions (by Giacomo Zilocchi; 1926) of the 15C originals destroyed in 1796. The arcaded courtyard has a fine staircase by Pietro Benvenuti (1481).

The *Cathedral (Pl. 11), begun in 1135 by the architect Wiligelmo and the sculptor Nicolò, was almost complete by the end of the 13C. The very fine W front is divided into three arcaded bays separated by buttresses beneath a low-pitched gable. The projecting great portal by Nicolò (1135) is crowned with an elaborate *Tribune uncovered in 1982 after fourteen years of careful restoration. In the tympanum is the Last Judgement in high relief executed by an unknown Romanesque sculptor in the mid-13C. In the loggia beneath stands a statue of the Madonna and Child by Cristoforo da Firenze (1427). To the right of the side door is a statue of Alberto d'Este (1393). The N side shows the original arcading; that on the S is partly obscured by a charming little portico of shops added in 1473. The massive campanile (covered for restoration), SE of the church, was built from 1412 to 1514.

The INTERIOR (closed 12–15), remodelled in 1712–18, is preceded by a narthex in which a fine 5C sarcophagus (the other dates from the 14C), and the original pilasters of the main portal have been placed. On the W wall are two detached frescoes of Saints Peter and Paul by *Garofalo*. In the 3rd chapel of the N aisle is a Madonna and Saints, by Garofalo (1524); in the 6th chapel a Coronation of the Virgin, a late work by *Francesco Francia*. In the N transept are terracotta busts of Christ and the Apostles by *Alfonso Lombardi*. In the S transept are similar busts, a Martyrdom of St Laurence (over the altar), by *Guercino* (1629), and, facing the S aisle, the *Altar of the Calvary, composed in 1673 from large bronze groups of statuary (15C; including the Virgin and St John, by *Niccolò Baroncelli*, Saints George and Maurelius, by *Giovanni Baroncelli* and *Domencio Paris*). Below is the good effigy tomb of Bishop Bovelli (died 1954). In the apse is the Last Judgement, by *Bastianino* (1580–83).

The MUSEO DELLA CATTEDRALE (in a room entered from the narthex up a long staircase) is open from 10–12, 15–17 (except Sunday and fest.). It contains good Flemish tapestries and illuminated choir books; St George and an *Annunciation, by *Cosmè Tura* (1469; restored), from the old organ-case; *Madonna of the Pomegranate, and a statuette of St Maurelius, both by *Jacopo della Quercia* (1408); charming *Reliefs of the Months, from the old S doorway; and an elaborate paliotto in gold thread.

To the NE of the cathedral (entrance 32 Via Cairoli) the *Seminario* occupies the 16C Palazzo Trotti, which contains two rooms frescoed by Garofalo (1519–20), with remarkable perspectives.

In the piazza S of the cathedral are the *Torre dell'Orologio* and a department store in an ugly building of 1957 on the site of the 14C Palazzo della Ragione. At No. 7 Via San Romano are the Romanesque cloisters of the disused church of *San Romano* (restored). The pretty arcaded Via San Romano (closed to traffic) leads S through an interesting medieval part of the town (described below).

The attractive Via Voltapaletto (Pl. 11), E of the Cathedral, leads past the handsome Palazzo Costabili (No. 11; 17C), decorated with busts and trophies, to the spacious church of *San Francesco* (closed for restoration), partly rebuilt in 1494 by Biagio Rossetti. The frescoes above the arches (Franciscan saints) and on the vault are good Ferrarese works of the 16C. In the 1st chapel in the N aisle the fresco of the seizure of Christ in the Garden (1524) by Garofalo has been detached and the sinopia exposed. In the 7th N chapel, Scarsellino, Rest on the Flight (restored).—Via Savonarola continues to the *CASA ROMEI (Pl. 11; No. 30; adm. 9–14, fest. 9–13, except Monday). Begun c 1442 it retains two graceful courtyards, its original ceilings, and (in a room off the second courtyard) delightful contemporary mural paintings and a fine fireplace. The grotteschi decorations on the upper floor are by the Filippi. The sculptures of the 13–15C and detached frescoes have been collected from destroyed churches.—Farther on, to the right, the church of *San Girolamo* (1712) faces the house (No. 19) where Savonarola passed the first twenty years of his life. Near San Girolamo is the church of *Corpus Domini* (ring at No. 4 Via Pergolato at the closed order of nuns; the door at No. 1 Via Campofranco is opened by them with an automatic bell), with a 15C façade. From the church a second door is opened into the nuns' choir, with the tomb slabs in the floor of Alfonso I and II d'Este and (in the centre) of Lucrezia Borgia (died 1519) and two of her sons. Via Savonarola ends at the severe *Palazzo Saracco*.

To the left, Via Ugo Bassi leads to the Corso della Giovecca (see below), No. 174 in which is the *Palazzina di Marfisa d'Este* (Pl. 12; 9–12.30, 14 or 15–17 or 18; fest. 9–12.30). Built in 1559 it was restored in 1939. It has admirable ceilings and contemporary furniture, a supposed portrait of James I of England, and a damaged bust in profile of Ercole I d'Este, by Sperandio. The 'Loggia degli aranci' in the garden, with a vault painted with trelissed vines and birds, is used for exhibitions.

To the right, Via Madama continues as Via Borgo Vado, where the church of *Santa Maria in Vado*, another work of Rossetti (1495–1518), has a handsome interior. Nearby at No. 47 Via Borgo di Sotto, is the *Oratorio dell'Annunziata* (Pl. 11; ring for adm. at the convent at No. 49) decorated in 1548 with frescoes attributed to Camillo Filippi, Pellegrino Tibaldi, and Nicolò Rosselli, and trompe l'oeil perspectives by Francesco Scala. On the altar wall is a fine Resurrection with members of the Confraternità della Morte (who assisted the condemned), and on the opposite wall an Assumption signed by Lamberto Nortense (restored). In Via Scandiana is **Palazzo di Schifanoia** (entrance at No. 27; Pl. 12; open daily 9–19), begun in 1385, and enlarged in 1391, 1458, and in 1469 by Pietro Benvenuti and Biagio

Rossetti. A selection of material from the MUSEO CIVICO is displayed here, including Greek and Roman coins, Egyptian statuettes, Greek vases, Roman glass , and wood carvings from a Venetian galley of c 1500; and ceramics and glass (mostly 15C) found in excavations beneath Palazzo Paradiso. A room of bronzes displays numerous 16C Paduan pieces, and the head of an angel by Alessandro Algardi. The sculpture includes two half-figures of Saints by Andrea della Robbia, a bust in polychrome terracotta of the Addolorata by Guido Mazzoni, and two polychrome terracotta Madonnas by Domenico di Paris.— The *SALA DEI STUCCHI (1468–70) has a delightful ceiling attributed to Domenico di Paris. The scenes of the Passion in alabaster were made in Nottingham in the early 15C.—The *SALONE DEI MESI was decorated for Duke Borso d'Este with delightful frescoes of the Months, one of the most renowned fresco cycles of the Renaissance of profane subjects. They were painted by *Francesco Cossa*, with the help of *Ercole de'Roberti* and other (unidentified) masters of the Ferrarese school.

The present entrance is on the W wall; it was formerly on the long N wall. The frescoes follow a complicated decorative scheme referring to the months of the year in three bands: above are twelve scenes illustrating the triumph of a divinity; the middle band has the sign of the zodiac for that month, flanked by two symbolic figures, and the lower part of the walls are decorated with scenes from the court of Duke Borso. The W wall, with January and February is very ruined. The wall opposite the present entrance is known to have been decorated by *Francesco Cossa*. March: Triumph of Minerva, showing her on a chariot drawn by two unicorns; the sign of Aries; hawking scenes.—April: Triumph of Venus (her chariot drawn by swans); Taurus; Duke Borso returning from the hunt and the Palio of St George.—May: Triumph of Apollo; Gemini; fragments of farming scenes.—North Wall. June: Triumph of Mercury; cancer; scenes of the Duke in a landscape.—July: Triumph of Zeus; Leo; the Duke receiving visitors, and scenes of women working hemp.—August: Triumph of Ceres; Virgo.—The scenes for September are usually attributed to *Ercole de'Roberti*: Triumph of Vulcan, with Vulcan's forge, and a love scene in bed thought to represent Mars and the vestal Virgin Silvia, from whom Romulus and Remus were born; Libra; Borso receivng Venetian ambassadors.—The West Wall with the last three months is almost totally obliterated.

Across the road (on the corner of Via Camposabbionario) is the *Civico Lapidario* (adm. as for Palazzo Schifanoia), recently opened in the 15C ex church of Santa Libera. The collection of Roman works was formed in 1735 by Marchese Bevilacqua, and includes funerary stelae and sarcophagi, including those of Annia Faustina and of the Aurelii (both dating from the 3C AD).

Via Mellone leads S from Palazzo Schifanoia to Via XX Settembre, with (at No. 124) **Palazzo di Lodovico il Moro** (Pl. 15), a masterpiece by *Biagio Rossetti*, which he left unfinished in 1503. There is an admirable courtyard and a ground-floor chamber decorated by *Garofalo*. Beneath a small loggia are displayed two remarkable archaic dug-out canoes from Comacchio (late Roman period). The Piano Nobile is occupied by the *MUSEO ARCHEOLOGICO NAZIONALE DI SPINA (closed since 1987). Founded in 1935, this contains a superb collection of objects discovered in the necropolis of Spina, near Comacchio, a Greco-Etruscan port that flourished in the 6C–3C BC. The collection consists principally of vases, including many fine specimens of the 5C BC, as well as ornate coloured ware of the 4C, of which the two rhytons in the shape of a mule's and a ram's head are striking examples. The most important items are displayed in the five rooms (10–14), with good ceilings, that overlook the garden; special mention may be made of a gold diadem (4C BC) and earrings.

Via XX Settembre leads right past the house (No. 152) built for himself by Biagio Rossetti, to the shady gardens crowning the ramparts of *Montagnone* (Pl. 16). The park extends N above the walls built by Alfonso I (1512–18). Paths continue from here for c 5km around the walls as far as Porta Po (see the Plan), only interrupted at Porta Mare.

Via Porta Romana leads S through the walls and across the Po di Volano canal to Piazzale San Giorgio and the church of *San Giorgio* (beyond Pl. 16), which was the cathedral of Ferrara in the 7–12C, then rebuilt in 15C and partly renovated in the 18C. The campanile is by Rossetti (1485). Inside, in the choir, is the magnificent *Tomb of Lorenzo Roverella, physician to Julius II and afterwards Bishop of Ferrara, by Ambrogio da Milano and Antonio Rossellino (1475). The tomb slab of Cosmè Tura is in the left aisle.

From Porta Romana there is a path along a good stretch of walls built by Alfonso II d'Este, passing the well-preserved Baluardo dell'Amore and Baluardo di Sant'Antonio.

Near Palazzo di Lodovico il Moro, off Via Beatrice d'Este, is the Convent of *Sant'Antonio in Polesine* (ring for adm. 9–11.30, 15–17 except fest.) with some good 13–15C frescoes (partly restored).

From Palazzo di Lodovico il Moro, Via Mellone runs NE. The first turning on the left, Via Carlo Mayr (busy with traffic), leads back towards the centre. After some 500m Via Gioco del Pallone diverges right passing the house of Ariosto's family (No. 31). At No. 17 Via delle Scienze PALAZZO PARADISO (being restored) houses the *Biblioteca Comunale Ariostea*. The building dates from 1391, and has a façade of 1610 by Giovanni Battista Aleotti. The courtyard contains Roman and Renaissance marbles, and in the library are the tomb of Ariosto, MS pages of the 'Orlando Furioso', and autographs of Ariosto and Tasso.

A good idea of the old city, with its well-preserved houses and little churches, may be obtained from a stroll through the narrow lanes lying between Via Scienze and Via Borgo Vado (Pl. 11). Via delle Volte (which runs beneath numerous arches) leads from Via delle Scienze to Via San Romano (a pedestrian street), with porticoes with good capitals. Via San Romano connects the Porta Reno (or Porta Paolo; built in 1612 on a design by Giovanni Battista Aleotti) with the Duomo.

The area of the city N of the Castello and the broad and busy Corso della Giovecca (Pl. 7,11, & 12), was planned by Ercole I in the early 15C with wide thoroughfares and fine palaces and gardens.

In Corso Giovecca, No. 37 is a fragment of the old *Arcispedale Sant'Anna* where Tasso was confined as a lunatic in 1579–86; behind is a 15C cloister of the former Basilian convent. Beside it is the fine church of *San Carlo* by Giovanni Battista Aleotti (1623). To the N, on via Borgo Leoni, is the church of the *Gesù* (Pl. 7), which contains a *Pietà in terracotta by Guido Mazzoni (1485). On Corso Giovecca the *Palazzo Roverella* (No. 47) has a beautiful terracotta façade (1508), attributed to Biagio Rossetti. Opposite is the church of the *Teatini* (1653) which contains the Presentation in the Temple by Guercino. The *Teatro Comunale* (closed for restoration), without a monumental façade, is attributed to Antonio Foschini (c 1780).

The handsome cobbled CORSO ERCOLE I D'ESTE (Pl. 7,3) named after the Duke who laid out this part of the city, leads N past several palaces and garden walls to **Palazzo dei Diamanti** (Pl. 7) begun by Rossetti for Sigismondo d'Este c 1492 and remodelled around 1565. It takes its name from the diamond emblem of the Estes, repeated 12,600 times on its façade. It contains a **Pinacoteca**, especially notable for its paintings of the Ferrarese School. Admission 9–14; fest. 9–13; closed Monday.

The room numbers are erratic, but the works are all labelled. Room 1 (left) contains the Vendeghini-Baldi collection, including: *Garofalo*, Head of a woman; *Michele Coltellini*, The Redeemer; *Bartolomeo Vivarini*, St Jerome; *Andrea Mantegna*, The Redeemer; *Ercole de'Roberti*, St Petronius (a tiny work); works by the 15C Veneto and Ferrarese school (notably, St John the Baptist);

Ercole de'Roberti, Madonna and Child; *Jacopo Bellini*, Madonna and Child (very damaged).—Room 2. *'Maestro di Figline'*, St John the Baptist (being restored); 15C detached frescoes of the Story of St John the Evangelist (from San Domenico); *Simone de'Crocefissi*, Coronation of the Virgin, Dream of the Virgin.—Room 3. *Ercole de'Roberti* and *Giuseppe Mazzuoli*, Deposition; detached frescoes of Saints Sebastian and Christopher, both by the school of *Piero della Francesca*; *Cosmè Tura*, Martyrdom of St Maurelius (tondo); *Francesco Cossa* (attributed), St Jerome; *Cosmè Tura*, Judgement of St Maurelius (being restored).

On the other side of the entrance hall, the Salone has a fine wood ceiling of 1567–91. Here are displayed detached frescoes: on the two end walls: *Apotheosis of St Augustine by *Serafino Serafini* (very damaged) and Allegory of the Old and New Testament by *Garofalo* (both from Sant'Andrea). Opposite the windows are huge late-13C frescoes from the Abbazia di San Bartolo. Four more rooms off the far end of the Salone contain works by 16C Ferrara painters, especially *Dosso Dossi* (Polyptych of Sant'Andrea) and *Garofalo* (Massacre of the Innocents). *Scarsellino*, *Carlo Bononi*, and the Bolognese *Guercino* dominate the late 16C and early 17C works. Paintings of other schools include: *Carpaccio*, Transition of the Virgin; *Early 16C Venetian School*, The Tribute-Money. Three rooms off the other end of the Salone contain the collection of the Cassa di Risparmio. The gallery also owns a good collection of etchings and engravings.

On the Ground Floor (entrance in Corso Ercole d'Este) is a *Museo del Risorgimento e Resistenza* (9–12.30, 15–18; fest- 9–12.30). There is also a Modern Art gallery (9.30–13, 15–18.30) which displays works by Ferrarese artists of the 19C and 20C.

At the end of Corso Ercole I d'Este the ex *Porta degli Angeli* (Pl. 3) in the walls of Ercole I is being restored. This was the gate by which the Estensi left Ferrara in 1598, and it was closed the following year. To the left eight semicircular towers survive and at the NW angle the Torrione del Barco is also being restored. From Porta degli Angeli a walkway (open to cyclists) follows the most picturesque stretch of walls E and S as far as Porta Mare (Pl. 8). The view N extends across the former 'Barco', the ducal hunting reserve, as far as the Po, an area of some 1200 hectares destined to become a park. Inside the walls can be seen the orchards which surround the Certosa (see below) and the Jewish Cemetery, and in the distance are the towers of the Castello.

Opposite Palazzo dei Diamanti stands *Palazzo Sacrati*, with an elaborate 16C portal. Corso Porta Mare leads E to the Parco Massari where the Palazzine dei Cavalieri di Malta provides a fit setting for the *Museo Boldini* (Pl. 7; adm. 10–13, 15–18.30), devoted to works by the Ferrarese painter Giovanni Boldini (1842–1931) and other local painters of the 19C and 20C (including Giorgio De Chirico). Farther on, on the right is PIAZZA ARIOSTEA (Pl. 7) (Pl. 7), with two Renaissance palaces, and a statue of Ariosto (19C) on a column which in turn has carried statues of Duke Ercole I, Pope Alexander VII, Liberty, and Napoleon. In Via Borso (N) the **Certosa** (Pl. 3; 1452–61), straight ahead, has interesting cloisters, and is now occupied by the cemetery. The adjoining church of *San Cristoforo*, begun in 1498, probably by Rossetti, has good terracotta decoration.

Off Via Borso Via Guarini and Via Aria Nuova lead due W to the *Casa dell'Ariosto* (Pl. 2; No.67 Via Ariosto), the house built for himself by the poet, who died here in 1533 (open weekdays 8–12, 15–18). To the S, in Corso Porta Po is the Capuchin church of *San Maurelio*, with terracotta and wooden statues and bas-reliefs.

FROM FERRARA TO RAVENNA. 74km; branch railway, 74·5km in 1–1¼hrs. A new straight road is being constructed across the reclaimed marshland alongside the twisty old road (N16) as far as San Biagio, and the first 19km are open. The little town of (35·5km) *Argenta*, was flooded by the Germans in the winter of 1944–45.—42km *Alfonsine*, another small town, was the centre of German resistance to the British Eighth Army's advance on the Po. The British Military Cemetery (78th Division) is c 2km N.—74·5km *Ravenna*, see Rte 38.

From Ferrara to *Modena*, see Rte 39.

The road to Bologna crosses the plain watered by the canalised Reno, on which stands (137km) *Malalbergo*, the only village of importance.—At (151km) *Ca'de'Fabbri*, a road leads right to Bentivoglio, where the Museo della Civiltà Contadina illustrates local peasant culture.—168km **Bologna**, see Rte 40.

38 Venice to Ravenna

ROAD, N309, the VIA ROMEA. 147km. 51km *Chioggia.*—72km *Contarina.*—97km *Pomposa.*—116km *Porto Garibaldi.*—147km **Ravenna**.

The road, in parts a post-war revival of the long decayed Roman *Via Popilia*, runs dead flat and just above sea-level through an evocative landscape of deserted reclaimed marshes divided up by canals and canalised streams. The POLESINE, round the Po delta, is succeeded by the Valli di Comacchio, reclaimed from the drained lake. The whole region is much visited by fishermen and by 'sportsmen' after duck and other birds, although part of the area is protected as a nature reserve. Though torrid in summer and damp in winter, the route provides the shortest E approach to the Adriatic coastal resorts.

From Venice the road crosses the Ponte della Libertà, bears left and, just before the motorway entrance, left again on N309, soon crossing the Fusina road. The industries of Marghera dominate the E skyline. The road runs dead straight between the Taglio di Brenta and the Laguna Morta then joins the Padua-Chioggia road to cross the most southerly inlet of the Venetian Lagoon; striking *View of (51km) Chioggia* (2km left; see Rte 33). It crosses the mouth of the Brenta alongside the branch railway linking Chioggia with Rovigo.—At (62km) *Cavanella*, the Adige is crossed, and the land becomes more intensely cultivated. Farther on the Po di Levante is also crossed.— 72km *Contarina* (7600 inhab.) and (73km) *Taglio di Po* (7700 inhab.), both industrial, lie N and S of the main channel of the Po, the largest river in Italy (678km) whose waters are now sadly polluted with chemicals.

Recent scientific studies have shown that the river feeds some 243 tons of arsenic into the Adriatic every year, and, according to Common Market regulations, none of its waters should be used for drinking, swimming, or irrigation. Urgent measures are needed to regulate the waters (in 1951 the Polesine area was devastated by a flood); to prevent industrial pollution (which reached frightening proportions in 1980 when petrol was spilled into the river from an oil refinery on its banks); and to resolve the problem of nuclear hydroelectric plants. In 1599 the Venetian Republic carried out major works of canalisation in the delta area in order to deviate the course of the river S to prevent it silting up the Venetian lagoon. It now reaches the sea by seven different rivers, the largest of which is called the 'Po di Venezia'. In the last few decades the delta area has sunk below sea level because of drilling operations for natural gas and quarrying in the area. The long-term project to make the Po Delta into a National Park is still in the planning stage; the marshes are on the migratory bird routes from Northern Europe. There are also plans to make the river navigable again all year round, as it was in the late Middle Ages, when it was one of the principal waterways of Europe.
    Porto Tolle, 14km to the E, lies in a protected are of natural beauty, and *Scardovari* (29km), at the mouth of the Po, has important fisheries.

A diversion may be made W from Contarina to (18km) **Adria**, the ancient capital (21,300 inhab.) of the Polesine, that gave its name to the Adriatic (to which it is now joined only by canal). The 17C church of *Santa Maria Assunta della Tomba* preserves an octagonal font of the 8C, and a terracotta Dormition of the Virgin (15C). The MUSEO ARCHEOLOGICO (9–14; fest. 9–13; closed Monday) contains proof of the city's Greco-Etruscan origins (bronzes, vases, jewellery, etc.; 6–2C BC) and the famous iron chariot of a Gaulish chieftain (4C BC) found with the skeletons of its two horses. The blocks of masonry found in the Etrusco-Roman necropolis are probably foundations of a temple. Recent excavations have brought to light an Archaic village and Roman ovens.

84km *Mesola*, just beyond the crossing of the Po di Goro, has a hunting lodge of Alfonso II d'Este (1583). On the right extends the *Grande Bonifica Ferrarese*. The once marshy country between Ferrara and the sea, where the Po enters the Adriatic, has many times been the subject of land-reclamation schemes. The first real efforts were due to Alfonso II d'Este, but the present scheme dates from 1872. The dunes in the Po di Goro delta are of great interest to naturalists. The Boscone della Mesola on the Volano delta, one of the last wooded areas in this plain, has been designated a nature reserve (adm. fest., 8–dusk). The hunting lodge of the Estense is being restored.—97km. The isolated Benedictine *Abbey of Pomposa, which was founded in the 7–8C on what was then an island and gradually deserted in the 17C because of malaria. The CHURCH (closed 12–14) dates from the 8–9C, and was enlarged in the 11C. It is preceded by an atrium with beautiful Byzantine sculptural decoration. The fine basilican interior (good capitals) is covered with charming 14C frescoes, some attributed to *Vitale da Bologna* (including the Christ in glory in the apse). Most of the mosaic pavement survives. The monastic buildings include the CHAPTER HOUSE and REFECTORY, both with important frescoes of the Bolognese school. Guido d'Arezzo (c 995–1050), inventor of the modern musical scale, was a monk here. The PALAZZO DELLA RAGIONE (abbot's justice-court) is a beautiful 11C building (altered in 1396). The fine campanile is 48m high.

The road traverses fields where rice is cultivated and skirts the marshes of the Valle Bertuzzi (inhabited by migratory birds). It then approaches the sandy coast, passing between a line of seven resorts (*Lido delle Nazioni, Lido degli Estensi,* etc.) known as the *'Lidi Ferraresi'* and (114km) *Comacchio*, 4km W, an interesting little town which grew to importance because of its salt-works. It was continuously attacked by the Venetians and destroyed by them in 1509. The pretty canal-lined streets are crossed by numerous bridges (notably the 17C Trepponti, which traverses no less than four canals). The Loggia dei Mercanti, Duomo, and Loggiata dei Cappuccini, all date from the 17C. Most of the 18,700 inhabitants are engaged in the fishing and curing of eels. The fishing season is in October–December, when the huge shoals of eels rushing seawards are caught in special traps.

In the drained lagoon NW of Comacchio the burial-ground of the Greco-Etruscan city of **Spina** has yielded a large quantity of vases and other pottery, now at Ferrara. Founded c 530 BC, it was a port carrying on a lively trade with Greece, but it barely outlasted the 4C BC. Part of the city itself was located by aerial survey in 1956 and excavations continue.

The road skirts the dwindling LAGO DI COMACCHIO, now more than two-thirds drained to the detriment of the egrets, herons, stilts, terns, and avocets that were once found in profusion. It has, however, now become a protected area. At *Porto Garibaldi* (formerly Magnavacca) the Austrian navy captured the last 200 'Garibaldini', leaving Garibaldi alone with Anita and his comrade Leggero. Anita died at *Mandriole*, on the S shore of the lake (monument). On the left the sea is hidden by the vast pinewoods of San Vitale.—Conspicuous industrial buildings on the sky-line announce the arrival at Ravenna.

147km **RAVENNA** is unique in western Europe for the profusion of its Byzantine remains. Now 10km from the sea, it was once a flourishing Adriatic port and the capital of the Byzantine exarchs, whose semi-oriental power is reflected by the magnificently coloured mosaics and imperial tombs. The cylindrical campanili of the 9–10C are characteristic of the city. The modern town (131,900 inhab.), in which the great monuments are scattered, is without distinction and is surrounded by extensive industrial suburbs.

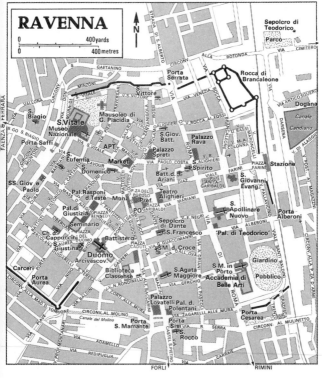

Tourist Office (A.P.T.), 2 Via San Vitale; *I.A.T. Information Office*, 8 Via Salara.—*Post Office*, Piazza Garibaldi.—**Buses** traverse the town. Country services to *Marina di Ravenna, Punta Marina, Forlì, Rimini, Bologna, Cesena, Faenza*; and to *Venice*, and *Florence*.

History. The importance of Ravenna begins with the construction, by Augustus, of the imperial port of *Classis*, to which the town was united by the Via Caesarea. Its greatest period, however, began with the 5C, when Honorius removed the imperial court from Rome to Ravenna. His sister, Galla Placidia, was the first to adorn the city with splendid monuments, and her example was followed by the Gothic kings Odoacer (473–93) and Theodoric (493–526). The capture of Ravenna by Belisarius in 540 led to a period of renewed prosperity under the

Eastern Empire, and Justinian and his empress Theodora embellished the
capital of the new Exarchate with unbounded magnificence. The inevitable
decadence followed, and the province came into the hands of the Church in 757;
sufficient vitality, however, was left for Ravenna to proclaim its independence as
early as any town in Italy (1177). Another period of changing mastery followed,
and in the 13–14C the city was governed by the Da Polenta family, distinguished
for their hospitality to Dante. Francesca da Rimini belonged to this family. From
1441 to 1509 the domination of Venice brought renewed prosperity to Ravenna,
but the renewal of Papal domination and the sack of the city in 1512, after the
battle between Louis XII of France and the Holy League outside its walls,
marked the beginning of its final decline. In 1849 Garibaldi found a brief refuge
in the pine-forest near the town, though his wife Anita died from the hardships of
her flight from the Austrians; and in 1860 the city was finally united with the
kingdom of Italy. It was captured from the Germans in December 1944. Since the
war a busy industrial area has risen beyond the railway and the port is again
flourishing.—Nicolò Rondinelli (1450–1510), the painter, was a native of
Ravenna, and Byron lived here in 1819– 21.

Art. Ravenna is unequalled in western Europe as a centre for the study of
Byzantine architecture, sculpture, and mosaic. The plan of the churches had a
widespread influence on later building, and the storied capitals at San Vitale
are equal to the finest work in Constantinople itself. The mosaics show a
progressive movement from the naturalism of the earlier work inspired by
classical ideals (Tomb of Galla Placidia, the Baptisteries, Sant'Apollinare in
Classe) to the hieratic decorative quality of the purely Byzantine style (San
Vitale; processional mosaics in Sant'Apollinare Nuovo).

In the central PIAZZA DEL POPOLO are two Venetian columns with
bases (much worn) decorated by Pietro Lombardo (1483) now bearing
statues of St Apollinaris and St Vitalis (1644). On the left of the
crenellated *Municipio* is a portico of eight 6C columns (four bearing
the monogram of Theodoric), which perhaps came from the church of
Sant'Andrea destroyed in 1457. In the *Palazzo Guiccioli*, at No. 54 Via
Cavour to the NW, Byron lived with the Count and Countess
Guiccioli, and wrote the end of 'Don Juan', 'Marino Faliero', and other
poems. Just off Via San Vitale, to the N of this beyond a 17C archway,
are the precincts of the church of ****San Vitale** (open all day
8.30–dusk), the most precious example of Byzantine art extant in
western Europe.

Founded by Julianus Argentarius for Bishop Ecclesius (521–34), the church was
consecrated in 547 by Archbishop Maximian. The octagonal building is surrounded by a double gallery and surmounted by an octagonal cupola. The
narthex, which stands obliquely to the church, was formerly preceded by an
atrium; it can best be seen from the second cloister (see below).

The entrance is through the Renaissance south portal. The impressive
INTERIOR is famous for its decoration in marble and mosaics. The
remarkable plan—two concentric octagons with seven exedrae or
niches and an apsidal choir—may have been suggested by Saints
Sergius and Bacchus at Constantinople. The eight pillars which
support the dome are encased in marble (largely renewed), and are
separated by the exedrae with their triple arches. Higher up is the
matroneum, or women's gallery, and above all is the dome, built, for
lightness, of two rows of terracotta tubes laid horizontally and fitting
into one another. The vault-paintings are of the 18C; the intended
mosaic decoration was probably never executed. The modern pavement has been in great part removed to reveal the original floor.

The chief glories of the church are in the *CHOIR and *APSE. On the
triumphal arch are mosaics of Christ and the Apostles with Saints
Gervasius and Protasius, the sons of the patron saint. On either side
are two constructions of antique fragments patched together in the

16–18C, including four columns from the ancient ciborium (the first on the left is of rare green breccia from Egypt), and a fragment with putti of a Roman frieze known as the 'Throne of Neptune'. Within the arch, on either side, are two *Columns with lace-work capitals and impost-blocks bearing the monogram of Julianus. In the lunettes are mosaics; on the right, Offerings of Abel and of Melchisedech; in the spandrels, Isaiah and the Life of Moses; on the left, Hospitality and Sacrifice of Abraham, at the sides, Jeremiah and Moses on the Mount. The upper gallery has magnificent capitals and mosaics of the Evangelists; and the vault-mosaics of Angels and the Paschal Lamb amid foliage are also very fine. The stucco decoration beneath the arches is beautiful. In the centre is the altar, reconstructed, with a translucent alabaster top (usually covered).

The apse has the lower part of its walls covered with marble inlay, a modern reconstruction from traces of the original plan. In the centre of the *Mosaic, in the semidome, Christ (beardless) appears between two Angels who present St Vitalis and Bishop Ecclesius (with a model of the church). On the side-walls are two fine processional pieces: (left) *Justinian with a train of officials, soldiers, and clergy, among whom are Archbishop Maximian and Julianus Argentarius or Belisarius; (right) *Theodora with her court. In front of the apsidal arch are Jerusalem, Bethlehem, and two angels.

To the right of the apse, beyond an apsidal chamber, is the Sancta Sanctorum, containing two early sarcophagi. Farther on is the former entrance to the campanile (originally one of the staircase towers giving access to the matroneum); beneath an adjoining stair are some fine stuccoes. On the other side of the narthex (the former entrance to the church; best seen from the cloister outside, see below) is the second staircase tower, still preserving some original work, with a stair ascending to the matroneum.

From the N side of San Vitale a pathway leads towards the charming ***Tomb of Galla Placidia** (open as for San Vitale), a small cruciform building erected by the sister of Honorius towards the middle of the 5C. The plain exterior is decorated with blind arcades and pilasters. The interior, lit by alabaster windows, is famous for its magnificent *Mosaics, predominantly blue, especially interesting for the classic character of the figures and for their excellent state of preservation (although they are restored periodically).—Over the entrance is the Good Shepherd; in the opposite lunette, St Laurence with his gridiron; in the side lunettes, Stags quenching their thirst at the Holy Fount. The vaults and arches of the longer arm of the cross are decorated to represent rich hangings and festoons of fruit. In the shorter arm are four Apostles; the other eight are on the drum of the cupola. In the pendentives are the Evangelists, and, above all, the Cross in a star-strewn sky. The three empty sarcophagi are no longer considered to have held the remains of Placidia, Constantius, and Valentinian III; only one of them is of 5C workmanship.

Between the tomb of Galla Placidia and San Vitale is the entrance to the ***Museo Nazionale**, recently enlarged and beautifully re-arranged around three cloisters of the ex-Benedictine convent here. Admission 8.30–13.30; closed Monday. In summer, usually open 8.30–19, except Monday.

On the right of the ticket office a mezzanine floor exhibits Arms and Armour (16–17C), and a marble head perhaps of Gaston de Foix, attributed to Tullio Lombardo.—To the left of the ticket office a door leads (right) into a room with interesting funerary Stele (1C BC–1C AD), many of them belonging to sailors, and finds (6–5C BC) from the necropolis of San Martino in Gattara including a large Greek Krater.—The **Refectory** (used for exhibitions and not always open) contains important detached *Frescoes* from Sant Chiara by Pietro da Rimini (mid–14C).—The 18C **Third Cloister** (at present closed for restoration) contains a statue of Alexander VII (1699).—In the middle of the **Second Cloister** (by Andrea da Valle, 1562) is a seated statue of Clement XII by Pietro Bracci (1738). Here can be seen the narthex of San Vitale, the former entrance to the church. Beneath the porticoes are interesting sculptural fragments: octagonal well-head from Classe; sarcophagus of Caio Sosio Giuliano, an oculist; statue of a warrior attributed to the workshop of Antonio Bregno; 6C capitals; and a 5C sarcophagus showing Christ between Saints Peter and Paul and two date palms. (The First Cloister may be visited from outside San Vitale, see below).

A fine staircase by Benedetto Fiandrini (1791) leads up to the **First Floor** and the series of rooms around the Second Cloister. On the landing is a fine Byzantine capital probably made in Constantinople. There follow three small rooms with local *Archaeological Material* (prehistoric, Etruscan, and Roman); and a room of *Roman Herms* and portrait heads.—*Roman glass; Transennae*, a 6C group of Hercules and the stag, and the Cross from the top of San Vitale; and finds from the so-called *Palazzo di Teodorico* (in Via di Roma).—To the left is a room of *Fabrics* including some precious examples from the tomb of St Julian at Rimini, and the so-called 'Veil of Classis' with embroideries of Veronese bishops of the 8–9C. The *Ivories* include a relief of Apollo and Daphne (530 AD), a 6C diptych from Murano, and evangelistary covers.—On the last side of the cloister are five small rooms of *Furniture* (16C–18C) including an inlaid 16C cupboard.—It is necessary to return through the rooms of furniture and ivories to reach the room of finds from *Sant'Apollinare in Classe*. Here is displayed a large sinopia found beneath the apse mosaic, and epigraphics.—Beyond is an L-shaped hall with an interesting collection of *Icons* dating from the 14C to the 17C of the Cretan-Venetian school, which combine Byzantine traditon with local schools of painting. They are arranged iconographically by type. Also here, Paolo Veneziano, Crucifixion.—The so-called 'Manica Lunga' beyond, contains a large collection of *Ceramics* (Ravenna, Deruta, Faenza, Urbino, Castelli, etc.).—A modern staircase leads down to a mezzanine floor where a splendid collection of *Coins* is beautifully displayed in chronological order from the Roman period onwards.—The stairs continue down to the entrance hall with a marble statue of Venice by Enrico Pazzi (1884), the first director of the Museum.

The **First Cloister** is entered through a little Renaissance portico near the E end of San Vitale (where the terracotta frieze on the wall below the campanile can be seen). It contains Roman remains including epigraphics, funerary stele (including one of the 1C AD showing a carpenter building a boat), and the Apotheosis of Augustus, a relief with idealised portraits of the Imperial family. Small rooms off the cloister exhibit remains of the 'Porta Aurea' of Ravenna, and finds from the Roman Villa of Russi excavated near Ravenna.

Nearly opposite the apse of San Vitale is the church of *Santa Maria Maggiore* (525–532, rebuilt 1671), preserving Byzantine capitals above Greek marble columns, and a tiny cylindrical campanile (9–10C).—Via Barbiani, on the other side of Via Cavour, leads S to Via Cura, in which the small church of *Santi Giovanni e Paolo* (locked), rebuilt in 1758, retains a tiny 10C campanile.

To the SE of Via Cavour various streets (see the Plan) lead to Piazza del Duomo via Piazza Kennedy in which is the 18C *Palazzo Rasponi dalle Teste*. The **Cathedral**, founded early in the 5C by Bishop Ursus, and often known as the *Basilica Ursiana*, was practically all destroyed in 1733 and immediately rebuilt. The columns of the central arch of the portico and those on either side of the central door are from the original church. The round campanile, many times restored (last in 1986), dates from the 10C.

In the nave is the 6C *Ambo of St Agnellus, pieced together in 1913. In the S transept, two fine 6C sarcophagi; in the ambulatory, St Mark, a relief of 1492 ascribed to Pietro Lombardo. The Chapel of the Sacrament has frescoes by Guido Reni and his school.

Adjoining the cathedral is the octagonal *Battistero Neoniano* (or *degli Ortodossi*), converted from a Roman bath-house, perhaps by

Bishop Neon (mid-5C), perhaps 50 years earlier. The plain exterior is decorated with vertical bands and small arches. Admission 9–12, 14.30–17 or 18; fest. 9–12.

The remarkable interior is entirely decorated with mosaics and sculptural details which blend with the architectural forms. The original floor is now over 3m below the present surface. Eight corner columns support arches decorated with mosaics of prophets. In the niches and on the wall-spaces which are arranged alternately beneath the arches are mosaic inscriptions and marble inlaid designs from the original Roman baths. Each arch of the upper arcade encloses three smaller arches; the stucco decoration is very fine. In the dome, built of hollow tubes, like that of San Vitale, are mosaics of the Baptism of Jesus (the old man with the reed represents the Jordan), the Apostles, the Books of the Gospel, and four Thrones, remarkable for their contrasting colours. The font is of the 12–13C. In the niches are a Byzantine altar and a pagan marble vase.

In the *Arcivescovado*, behind the cathedral, is the interesting **Museo Arcivescovile** (adm. 9–12, 14.30–17 or 18; fest. 9–12). The *Sala Lapidaria* contains fragments and mosaics from the original cathedral and from San Vitale; the marble pulpit from Santi Giovanni e Paolo (596); a 6C porphyry statue (? Justinian); and in the farthest room the famous *Ivory Throne of Maximian, an Alexandrine work of the 6C, carved with the story of Joseph, the Life of Christ, and figures of St John the Baptist and the Evangelists and a 6C Paschal calendar incised on marble.—The *Cappella Arcivescovile* (Oratorio di Sant'Andrea) is preceded by an atrium with a barrel vault covered with a delightful mosaic of birds. The chapel, built by Bishop Peter II (494–519), contains good *Mosaics and the silver *Cross of St Agnellus (? 11C; many times restored). In an adjoining room is the so-called chasuble of St John Angeloptes, probably 12C work.

The **Biblioteca Classense** (entered from Via Baccarini), in a 16–17C building, contains a library (8–13, 14–19, except Saturday afternoon and fest.) with some valuable codexes, including an 11C text of Aristophanes.

In Piazza San Francesco, to the NE, is the church of **San Francesco**, built by Bishop Neon in the 5C, remodelled in the 10C, but almost entirely rebuilt in 1793. The 10C campanile was restored in 1921. The interior has 22 columns of Greek marble. North aisle: Tomb of Luffo Numai, by *Tommaso Fiamberti* (1509); tombstone of Ostasio da Polenta (1396); and a 5C sarcophagus with Christ and the Apostles. The 1st chapel on the S side is decorated by *Tullio Lombardo* (1525). The high altar is made from the 4C *Tomb of St Liberius. In the 9–10C Crypt (almost always flooded; light outside) can be seen the foundations of an earlier church with its mosaic pavement (restored).—On the left of San Francesco is the so-called *Braccioforte Mausoleum* (1480), containing several early Christian sarcophagi.

To the left again is the **Tomb of Dante** (open 9–12, 14 or 14.30–17 or 19), a building by *Camillo Morigia*, erected at the instance of Cardinal Luigi Gonzaga in 1780 to enshrine the older tomb by *Pietro Lombardo* (1483). This in turn covers the antique sarcophagus in which the poet's remains were originally interred in the old portico of San Francesco.

Exiled from Florence and harried by his political enemies, the poet found refuge, in 1317, with the Da Polenta family of Ravenna, and with them he spent his last years, finishing the 'Divine Comedy'. He died on the night of 13–14 September 1321.

His effigy is by Pietro Lombardo, and the epitaph by Bernardo Canaccio (1357). The *Museo Dantesco*, approached by steps by the little (modern) memorial bell-tower, has been closed since 1970.—To the N are two fine 15C Franciscan cloisters (restored).

At the corner of Piazza San Francesco and Via Ricci stood *Palazzo Rasponi*, Byron's first home in Ravenna (1819); and farther S is the 5C basilican church of *Sant'Agata Maggiore* (closed for restoration), which has a squat round campanile completed in 1560, and contains

Roman and Byzantine capitals, a 7C pulpit, and two Renaissance baldacchini.—Via Cerchio, to the left, ends opposite *Santa Maria in Porto*, a church begun in 1553, with a sumptuous façade by Morigia (1780). It contains fine stalls by Mariano (1576–93), and other French craftsmen, and (over the altar in the N transept), a marble Byzantine relief called 'La Madonna Greca' (probably 11C). In the public gardens behind is the *Loggetta Lombardesca* (early 16C; recently restored).

Adjoining the church is the ex *Monastero dei Canonici Lateranensi* restored as the seat of the **Accademia di Belle Arti**. Its fine large **Pinacoteca** (open 9–13, 14.30–17.30, except Monday) is spaciously arranged around a pretty cloister in the well-lit rooms of the convent.

The collection includes: *Taddeo di Bartolo*, Annunciation; *Paolo di Giovanni Fei*, Crucifixion; *Lorenzo Monaco*, Crucifixion; *Marco Palmezzano*, Nativity, Presentation in the Temple, etc.; *Bernardino Zaganelli*, Prayer in the Garden of Gethsemane; *16C Venetian school*, Last Supper (a tiny work); *Ludovico Brea*, Madonna and Child; *Antonio Vivarini*, St Peter; *Gentile Bellini*, Saints Ludovic and Peter.—Works by *Luca Longhi*, *Nicolò Rondinelli*, *Francesco di Santacroce*, *Palma Giovane* (Creation of Man), and *Paris Bordone* (the Redeemer). The effigy of Guidarello Guidarelli, killed at Imola in 1501, is the work of *Tullio Lombardo* (1525).—The modern section includes works by *Armando Spadini*, *Felice Carena*, *Giuseppe Abbati*, and *Arturo Moradei*. Off the cloister there is also an *Ornithological Museum*.

In Via di Roma, to the N, is the building known as the *'Palazzo di Teodorico'* or *Palazzo di Calchi* or *degli Esarchi* (no adm.), perhaps a military post constructed by the exarchs to protect their own court against the townspeople. It is being restored. Beneath the arches are mosaic fragments from a palace, nearer the railway, the foundations of which were excavated in 1908–14.

The church of **Sant'Apollinare Nuovo** (open 8.30–17.30 or 19.30) almost next door, one of the finest in Ravenna, was built by Theodoric in the early 6C; the mosaics are partly of this time, partly of the mid-6C.

Dedicated originally to Jesus and later to St Martin, the church passed from the Arians to the orthodox Christians under Archbishop Agnellus. Its present dedication dates only from the 9C. The façade with its portico was rebuilt in the 16C; adjacent is a fine 10C campanile.

INTERIOR. The floor and the 24 Greek marble columns were raised in the 16C and are surmounted by a panelled ceiling of 1611; the arcades bulge noticeably to the N. Along the nave walls are two magnificent bands of *Mosaic; that on the N side represents the port of Classis, with a procession of 22 virgin martyrs preceded by the Magi who offer gifts to the Infant Jesus seated on His mother's lap between four angels. On the S side are Ravenna, showing the façade of Theodoric's palace, and a procession of 26 martyrs approaching Christ enthroned. Above, on either side, are sixteen fathers of the Church, or prophets; higher still, thirteen scenes from the Life of Christ. The stucco decoration beneath the arches is very fine. The Ambo in the nave dates from the 6C. In the apse, reconstructed in 1950, are the recomposed altar, transennae, four porphyry columns, and a marble Roman chair.

At the corner of Viale Farini, leading to the station, is Piazza Anita Garibaldi, with a monument to the martyrs of the Risorgimento (with engaging lions). In Viale Farini is the church of **San Giovanni**

Evangelista built by Galla Placidia in fulfilment of a vow made in 424 during a storm at sea. It was well restored after war damage.

Most of the façade and the first four bays were destroyed and the notable galleried apse, as well as the aisles, seriously damaged. The 10–14C campanile survives (leaning to the W); two of the bells date from 1208. The main 14C portal has been reconstructed on the new wall which encloses the church precincts. Inside, some columns, with their capitals and impost blocks, are original. Round the walls are displayed mosaics from the 13C floor, their naïve designs illustrating episodes from the 4th Crusade. The carving on the 8C altar in the S chapel is notable. In a chapel in the N aisle are fragments of frescoes (on the vault and walls) of the 14C Riminese school.

To the left, beyond the cross-roads, is Via Paolo Costa. The first lane on the left (Via degli Ariani) leads to the church of *Santo Spirito* (usually locked), converted, like Sant'Apollinare, to the orthodox cult by Agnellus in the mid-6C. Fourteen columns and an ambo from the original church were retained after a rebuilding in 1543. Beside it is the BATTISTERO DEGLI ARIANI (now Santa Maria in Cosmedin; open 8.30–12.30, 14.30–17). It contains splendidly preserved *Mosaics (6C) of the Baptism of Christ and of the Apostles in the dome.—In Via Costa, No. 8 is the *Casa Stanghellini*, a charming 15C Venetian house, and at the end is the leaning 12C *Torre Comunale*. From here Via Rossi (right) leads to the church of *San Giovanni Battista*, with a cylindrical campanile; the interior, a 17C reconstruction, retains its ancient marble columns.

At the N end of Via di Roma is *Porta Serrata* (1582). The Circonvall-azione Rotonda leads E through unattractive suburbs past the rugged bastions of the Venetian *Rocca di Brancaleone* (opera performances are held here in summer). Beyond the railway (c 20 minutes walk from the gate), in a clump of trees to the left of the road, is the ***Mausoleum of Theodoric** (adm. 8.30–dusk).

For those without a car, the Mausoleum is not very conveniently reached by bus (No. 2 from the station; infrequent service). The walk from Porta Serrata, along a busy trunk road, is not a pleasant one.

The unfinished building, begun by the great Ostrogoth himself, is of hewn stone without mortar and is crowned by a monolithic roof. For a time, until 1719, it was used as a monastic church (Santa Maria al Faro). The ten-sided lower storey has a deep recess on every side. The upper floor, which is decorated with unfinished arcading, was approached by two 18C staircases, which collapsed in 1921. The monolithic cupola of Istrian limestone from Pola has a diameter of 11m, and weighs about 300 tons. The crack, which is clearly visible, was probably the result of a harsh knock received during its installation. The problem of the methods of construction and the transport of the monolith is still unsolved. Inside is a porphyry bath which was used as the royal sarcophagus.

About 5km S of Ravenna and reached either by rail (Classe station, on the Rimini line), or (better) by road (frequent bus service from Ravenna station) across the *Ponte Nuovo* (1736) and the site of Classis, is the basilica of *Sant'Apollinare in Classe** (closed 12–14), built for Bishop Ursicinus by Julianus Argentarius in 535–38, and consecrated by Archbishop Maximian in 549. The narthex, which preceded the church, has been reconstructed. The magnificent late-10C *Cam-panile is the tallest and most beautiful of all the towers of Ravenna.

The wide INTERIOR has 24 Greek marble columns with Byzantine bases and capitals. In the centre of the nave is the altar of Archbishop Maximian, restored in 1753. At the W end of the church are eight columns from the two original ciboria. In the aisles are a series of magnificent sarcophagi, complete with lids, dating from the 5C to the 8C. At the end of the N aisle is a 9C ciborium and an interesting altar with a 5C relief of Christ and the Apostles. The *Mosaics of the apse are extremely interesting, though much altered; in the centre, the Transfiguration, with St Apollinaris in prayer below; at the sides, Sacrifices of Abel, Melchizedech, and Abraham; and Constantine IV granting privileges for the church of Ravenna to Archbishop Reparatus (7C); between the windows Bishops Ursicinus, Ursus, Severus, and Ecclesius (6C). On the front of the arch are five rows of symbolic mosaics.

The Pineta di Classe, E of the basilica beyond the railway, whose sylvan grandeur was sung by Dante and Byron, is now sadly diminished. Although designated a nature reserve it is threatened by the industrial development on the outskirts of Ravenna.

The road to the Marina (buses in summer) follows the Candiano Canal which links the *Darsena* with the sea. In the busy suburb beyond the station is the polygonal church of *San Pier Damiano*, by Giovanni Gandolfi (1958), with a striking hexagonal cupola and campanile.—13km *Marina di Ravenna*, a sandy bathing resort, has developed round the Porto Corsini (1736). Across the canal is *Marina Romea*, reached by the Strada del Cimitero. *Garibaldi's Hut*, in the Pineta di San Vitale, off this road (c 7km from Ravenna), may also be reached by ferry from the Marina road. This is a reconstruction of the hut where the great patriot lay in hiding in 1849; the original was burned in 1911.—The *Colonna dei Francesi* (1557), 4km SW along the Forlì road, marks the spot where Gaston de Foix fell mortally wounded in 1512 in the battle between the French and Julius II.—There is a *British Military Cemetery* 8km NW of Ravenna by the Ferrara road and a lane leading left to *La Tagliata*. About 2km farther on the Ferrara road, across the Lamone river, a road goes left for *Villanova* and a *Canadian Military Cemetery*.

FROM RAVENNA TO RIMINI, 52km. A new road is under construction parallel to the old road (N16). Railway (line recently modernised) parallel.—5km *Classe*, with the basilica of Sant'Apollinare (see above). 21km **Cervia**, approached through pinewoods, is a small town (23,000 inhab.), built in 1698 on a regular plan and surrounded with walls round which has developed a large seaside resort and spa extending northwards as *Milano Marittima* and southwards as *Pinarella*. The road crosses a stretch of salt-marshes with Cervia and Cesenatico located by conspicuous skyscrapers.—30km **Cesenatico**, another popular bathing resort, is the port of Cesena, designed in 1502 by Leonardo da Vinci for Cesare Borgia, from which Garibaldi and his wife Anita set sail on their ill-omened flight towards Venice in August 1849.

There are numerous summer hotels also at *Zadina Pineta*, its N extension, and in *Valverde* and *Villamarina* on the way S towards (35km) *Gatteo a Mare*. The road crosses the Rubicone, the fateful Rubicon which Caesar crossed in defiance of Pompey in 49 BC. The line of seaside resorts, with innumerable summer hotels, is virtually continuous for 30km. Since 1988 the pollution of the Adriatic here has become increasingly evident with the presence of tons of seaweed (and micro-algae) all along the coast. The main road runs a little farther inland to (52km) *Rimini*, see Rte 41.

FROM RAVENNA TO BOLOGNA, N253. 76km, traversing level country all the way. Motorway (77km) A14 dir, and A14.—19·5km *Bagnacavallo*, the native town of the painter Bartolomeo Ramenghi (1484–1542), called 'Il Bagnacavallo', some of whose paintings are exhibited in the local pinacoteca. Allegra, infant daughter of Byron and Claire Clairmont, died in the capuchin nunnery in 1821. The church of San Pietro in Silvis is a building of the Ravenna type probably dating from the early 7C. The restored frescoes in the apse are attributed to a Riminese master, c 1323.—25km *Lugo* (34,600 inhab.) has a 14C castle and an arcaded market-place (1783–1889). The Rossini theatre built by Antonio Bibiena in 1758–61 was restored in 1987. This area was the scene of severe fighting in 1944–45. *Fusignano*, 7km N, was the birthplace of Arcangelo Corelli (1653–1713), the composer, and of *Cotignola*, 6km SE, that of Attendolo Sforza (1369–1424), founder of the ducal family.—32km *Massalombarda* takes its name from some Lombard fugitives who sought refuge here in 1251.—51km *Medicina*.—76km **Bologna** (see Rte 40) is entered by Porta and Via San Vitale.

39 Milan to Bologna

ROAD, N9, 219km. 32km *Lodi* (by-pass).—52km *Casalpusterlengo*. The road keeps to the right on leaving the town.—68km **Piacenza**, from where the route follows the Roman Via Aemilia.—90·5km *Fiorenzuola*.—104.5km *Fidenza*.—127·5km **Parma**.—155km **Reggio**.—180km **Modena**.—193km *Castelfranco*.—219km **Bologna**.

The AUTOSTRADA DEL SOLE (A1) links Milan with Rome, with continuations to the S. It follows a course to Bologna roughly parallel to N9, but avoiding towns, it crosses the Po NE of Piacenza by a bridge with the longest pre-stressed concrete spans in Europe; from there it runs N of the Via Aemilia as far as Modena where it crosses to the S. Beautifully engineered and constructed, the motorway has convenient exits to all the main towns on the Via Emilia.

RAILWAY, 219km; many expresses daily in 1¾–3hrs. To *Piacenza*, 72km in c 1hr; to *Parma*, 129km in 1½–2hrs; to *Modena*, 182km in 2–2½hrs.

The Via Emilia runs SE through the suburbs of Milan and crosses the railway at (6km) *Rogoredo*.—18km *Melegnano*, at one time known as *Marignano*, gives name to the battle of 14 September 1515, in which Francis I won a transient and delusive victory over the Swiss mercenaries of Massimiliano Sforza (among whom was numbered the young Zwingli); but at *Landriano*, 6·5km SW, he was defeated in 1528. In the church of San Giovanni Battista is a Baptism of Christ by Bergognone.—At (24km) *Tavazzano* a road on the right leads to Lodi Vecchio (see below).

32km **Lodi**, an important centre (44,400 inhab.) for dairy produce, on the right bank of the Adda, in the fertile and well-irrigated Lodigiano district. It was founded in 1158 by Frederick Barbarossa after the destruction of Lodi Vecchio (see below). At the bridge over the river here Napoleon had a victory over the Austrians in 1796.

Here Maria Cosway (1759–1838), widow of Richard Cosway, and herself a painter, retired in 1821, to found the *Collegio delle Dame Inglesi*, where she is buried. It contains relics of the Cosways.

The Corso Adda and the Corso Vittorio Emanuele (coming from the station) meet in the large arcaded Piazza della Vittoria. Here rise the *Broletto*, with an 18C façade and vestiges of the original 13C building, and the *Duomo*, with a 12C façade (altered in the Renaissance). The neo-classical interior was 'restored' in the 1960s in the Romanesque style. On the walls are fragments of 14C and 15C frescoes, and in the nave, a 13C gilt statue of San Bassiano. The 1st S Chapel has a fine tomb by Andrea Fusina (1510). The *Museo Civico* in Corso Adda has an archaeological section and a Pinacoteca (14–15C detached frescoes, paintings by Callisto Piazza, Cesare da Sesto, etc.), and an interesting collection of local ceramics.

In Via Incoronata (running N from Piazza della Vittoria) is the church of the *INCORONATA. Constructed in 1488–94 by Giovanni Battagio and Gian Giacomo Dolcebuono, this is a gem of Renaissance architecture. It has a well-preserved octagonal interior, with four fine paintings by Bergognone (in the chapel of St Paul, S side), and others by Martino, Albertino, and Callisto Piazza ('Callisto da Lodi'), the last an imitator of Titian. The early 18C stalls are finely carved.

From the other side of Piazza della Vittoria Via Marsala leads to *Sant'Agnese* (left), a 15C church with a good polyptych by Albertino Piazza. From here Via Venti Settembre, with the fine 15C *Palazzo Varesi* at No. 51, leads E to *San Francesco* (1289), a church with an unusual façade, and decorated inside with 14–15C frescoes. In Piazza Vittorio Emanuele (or del Castello), on the way to the station, are some remains of a castle erected in 1370 by Bernabò Visconti.

Lodi Vecchio (5km E; 5100 inhab.), the Roman *Laus Pompeia*, mentioned by Cicero, was a constant rival of Milan until its total destruction in 1158. Only the church of *San Bassiano* (8C and 12C with 14C additions), dedicated to a 4C bishop, was left standing (restored in 1960). The site of the Roman city was identified in 1987 by aerial photography.—At *Pandino*, 12km N, stands a 14C castle of the Visconti.—At *Sant'Angelo Lodigiano*, 13km SW (on the Pavia road) the restored Visconti castle may be visited (fine armoury).

At (52km) *Casalpusterlengo* (12,900 inhab.), the road to Cremona diverges to the left.

FROM CASALPUSTERLENGO TO CREMONA, 33km, N234.—4.5km *Codogno* has some importance as an agricultural centre (14,900 inhab.) and as the junction of the Cremona line with the main Milan-Bologna railway. In the 16C church of San Biagio are paintings by Marco d'Oggiono, Callisto Piazza, and Camillo Procaccini.—The road turns N to reach the swift-flowing Adda to (69.5km) *Pizzighettone*, an old town (7000 inhab.) preserving important remains of its old fortifications, including the Torrione, in which Francis I was imprisoned after the battle of Pavia (1525). The church of San Bassano dates from the 12C, but has been greatly altered.—From there to (33km) *Cremona* (see Rte 20).

Near *Guardamiglio*, the road crosses over the motorway and traverses the Po on a long bridge to enter Emilia.

67.5km **PIACENZA**, an important centre (106,900 inhab.) of internal trade, situated at the strategic point where the Via Aemilia touches the Po, possesses several fine churches. Its name (the French of which is *Plaisance*) is derived from the Latin *Palacentia*.

A.P.T. Tourist Information Office, Piazzetta dei Mercanti (near Piazza Cavalli).—**Post Office**, 38 Via Sant'Antonino.—**Buses** from the station to the centre, etc.—COUNTRY BUSES from Piazza Cittadella to *Cremona*, *Bologna*, and principal cities.

History. In the church of Sant'Antonio were conducted the peace negotiations, ratified at Constance (1183), between Frederick Barbarossa and the Lombard League; but the most outstanding event in Piacenza's typical history was the plebiscite of 1848, by which she joined Piedmont, the first city so to do.

The centre of the old city is *Piazza Cavalli*, named from its pair of bronze equestrian *Statues* (removed for restoration) of dukes Alessandro (1625) and Ranuccio Farnese (1620) designed by Francesco Mochi, a pupil of Giambologna. Alessandro Farnese (1545–92) is better known as the 'Prince of Parma', governor of the Low Countries from 1578 till his death; Ranuccio was his son and successor in the dukedom. The **Palazzo del Comune**, called 'Il Gotico', in the same square, is a fine Gothic building begun in 1280, in which brick, marble, and terracotta are harmoniously blended. Via Venti Settembre leads from the square, past *San*

Francesco, a church begun in 1278 with a transitional façade. The fine Gothic interior has a pretty apse (with an ambulatory).

At the end of the street stands the *Duomo*, an imposing Lombard Romanesque church (1122–1233), with two of its projecting W porches supported by atlantes instead of the more usual lions, which support the central porch. The 14C campanile is crowned by a gilded angel. In the beautiful interior massive cylindrical pillars divide the nave and aisled transepts. Set into the pillars are little square reliefs showing the work of the Guilds which paid for the erection of the column, by a follower of *Wiligelmus*. Above the arches are 12C figures of Saints and prophets. The vault of the central octagon is decorated with frescoes by *Morazzone* and *Guercino* (restored in 1986). On a nave pillar near the W end are three votive frescoes (14–15C); the transepts also have interesting frescoes (and the apses are decorated by *Eugenio Cisterna* (1862–1933). In the raised choir the high altar has a gilded reredos (1447; difficult to see), behind which are good stalls of 1471. The frescoes here are by *Camillo*

Procaccini and *Ludovico Carracci*. The two ambones are modern reconstructions (using some original reliefs). The crypt has a forest of slender columns. The apses and octagon, with their characteristic arcading, are well seen from the street behind the bishop's palace.

To the SW Via Chiapponi leads to the church of *Sant'Antonino* rebuilt in the 11C with an octagonal lantern tower (being restored), claimed to be the earliest in Italy, supported inside on a group of massive pillars. The huge N porch (called 'Paradiso') was added in 1350. The large paintings in the sanctuary are by Roberto De Longe (1693). A small Museum (adm. only with special permission) contains pergamenes, illuminated codexes, and 15–16C paintings.

Nearby is the *Teatro Municipale* (1803–10) with a little museum (ring for adm. at 41 Via Verdi). Farther SW is the charming GALLERIA RICCI-ODDI, with a representative collection of Italian 19–20C painting (adm. 10–12, 15–17 or 18; winter, 10–12, 14–16; closed fest. & Monday). Artists represented include: Vito d'Ancona, Telemaco Signorini, Giovanni Boldini, Giovanni Fattori, Giuseppe Abbati, Vincenzo Cabianca, Francesco Hayez, Gerolamo Induno, Vincenzo Gemito, Antonio Mancini, Filippo Palizzi, Edoardo Dalbono, Domenico Morelli, and Ettore Tito.

Via Sant'Antonino, passing the Post Office, is prolonged by the busy Corso Garibaldi in which are (right) the 12C front (recently restored) of *Sant'Ilario* (closed), with a relief of Christ and the Apostles on the architrave, and, at the end of the street, *Santa Brigida*, also 12C. A little to the left is *San Giovanni in Canale*, a 13C and 16C church, well restored. Nearby in Via Taverna, at the Collegio Morigi, a *Natural History Museum* is to be opened.

Via Campagna leads NW from beyond Santa Brigida to (15 minutes walk) the church of the **Madonna di Campagna** (closed 12.30–15), a graceful Renaissance building by *Alessio Tramello* (1522–28). On a Greek-cross plan, it has four little domed corner chapels. The central *Dome, beautifully lit by small windows in a loggia, has frescoes by *Pordenone* (1528–31). The decoration of the drum and the pendentives was completed by *Bernardino Gatti* (1543). To the right of the entrance, St George and the Dragon by *Gatti*, and (left) St Augustine by *Pordenone* (restored). In the 1st left corner chapel the frescoes by *Pordenone* include an Adoration of the Magi, and (in the lunette), Adoration of the Shepherds and the Flight into Egypt. In the left arm are canvases by *Camillo Procaccini*. In the 2nd left corner chapel are more works by *Pordenone*: *Mystical marriage of St Catherine and *Frescoes of scenes from her life.—Above the arch of the opposite corner chapel is an oblong painting of an angel announcing the birth of Samson to Manoah by *Guercino*. The organ was built by the Serassi of Bergamo. In the presbytery (added in 1791), behind the high altar, Annunciation by *Camillo Boccaccino* and St Catherine attributed to *Giulio Cesare Procaccini*. On the altar, 14C polychrome wood statue of the venerated Madonna di Campagna, between Saints Catherine and John the Baptist.

Via Sant'Eufemia leads NE past the church of *Sant'Eufemia*, with an early 12C front (restored); straight ahead is *San Sisto*, another pretty church by Tramello (1499–1511), preceded by a courtyard. It was for this church that Raphael painted his famous 'Sistine Madonna' sold by the convent to the elector of Saxony in 1754, and now at Dresden. On the N choir pier is the monument of Duchess Margaret of Parma (1522–86), governor of the Netherlands in 1559–67; the fine stalls date from 1514.

Via Borghetto leads back towards the centre: on the left, in Piazza

Cittadella, is the huge **Palazzo Farnese** begun for Duchess Margaret
in 1558 by Francesco Paciotto and continued after 1564 by Vignola,
but left only half finished. It has a grand if plain exterior, divided in
three floors by protruding cornices and numerous well-proportioned
windows. Adjoining to the left is the smaller 14C *Rocca Viscontea*,
recently restored. In the courtyard can be seen the 15C loggia of the
castle, and a huge double loggia with niches of the Palazzo Farnese. It
was reopened in 1988 after years of closure for restoration, and part of
the **Museo Civico** is exhibited here (adm. 9–12.30; Thursday, Saturday, & Sunday, also 15.30–17.30; closed Monday). So far (in 1990)
some 14 rooms are open and the exhibits include: the famous 'Fegato
di Piacenza', an Etruscan divination bronze representing a sheep's
liver, marked with the names of Etruscan deities; a tondo by Botticelli,
paintings by Bonifacio Veronese, Mattia Preti, and Sebastiano Ricci; a
Crucifix attributed to Giotto; and works by the 16C local school. The
Museo Risorgimento may be seen on request. Other sections will be
devoted to the Middle Ages; Archaeology; carriages; glass and
ceramics; and arms and armour.

Near the palace scanty remains of the Roman amphitheatre have been
discovered. From Piazza Cittadella Via Gregorio X, named after Pope Gregory X
(Teobaldo Visconti of Piacenza, pope in 1271–76), leads to *Palazzo dei Tribunali*,
a 15C building with a good sculptured doorway, and a pretty garden. In Via
Roma, to the right, is the *Biblioteca Comunale Passerini-Landi* (adm. 9–12,
14.30–17.30) with over 170,000 vols, and 3000 MSS. (interesting psaltars and
codexes). To the left in Via Roma is *San Savino*, a 12C church with two mosaics of
the 13C or earlier. Nearby is a pleasant public park in front of the Station.

At *San Lazzaro Alberoni*, c 2.5km SE of the town, the important Collegio
Alberoni has a gallery (adm. by appointment Sunday, 15–18) with 18 Flemish
tapestries and a Christ at the Column by Antonello da Messina.—In the environs
are *Grazzano Visconti* (14km S; bus), a village rebuilt in medieval style; and
(reached via San Giorgio Piacentino) *Velleia* (33km S; bus), where the attractive
ruins of a small Roman town, excavated in the 18C, stand amid rolling
countryside.

FROM PIACENZA TO CREMONA, 32·5km. N10 (or motorway, A21).—13km *Caorso*,
where the largest nuclear energy plant in the country is now in operation.—
20·5km *Monticelli d'Ongina* on the Po, which here makes wide serpentine loops.
The 15C castle has frescoes by Bonifacio Bembo and an Ethnographical Museum
of the Po.—32·5km **Cremona**, see Rte 20.

FROM PIACENZA TO GENOA, 145km, N45. This is the direct road across the hills
(Genoa can also be reached via Voghera on the N10).—46km *Bobbio*, noted for
the learned monastery founded in 612 by the Irish saint, Colombanus, who died
here in 615. The Basilica (15–17C), has a crypt with some traces of the primitive
church and the tomb of St Colombanus (1480). The Museum contains a
remarkable ivory Roman bucket with David in high relief (4C).—145km **Genoa**,
see Rte 6.

The route now follows the VIA AEMILIA, a Roman road constructed in
187 BC by M. Aemilius Lepidus as a military thoroughfare from which
to guard the newly-conquered lands of Cisalpine Gaul.—90·5km
Fiorenzuola d'Arda, with 14,100 inhabitants, was the birthplace of
Giulio Alberoni (1664–1752), the gardener's son who rose to be a
cardinal and the able minister of Philip V and Charles III of Spain. To
the N rise the huge refineries that extract petrol from the mineral oils,
discovered in 1949, of *Cortemaggiore*, 6·5km N. Production has
diminished since 1960.

A pleasant road ascends the Arda valley.—9.5km **Castell' Arquato**, a picturesque hill-town with double walls. In the pretty Piazza stand the *Palazzo Pretorio* of
1293 and the Romanesque *Collegiata* with a 14C cloister, off which is entered the
Museum with church silver, sculpture, and paintings. In the 16C Torrione

Farnese a *Geological Museum* houses local finds, including marine fossils etc. (adm. 9–12; Sunday 15–18).

96km *Alseno*. About 4km left of the road is the abbey of *Chiaravalle della Colomba*, with a fine Romanesque church and a 13C Gothic *Cloister, with coupled columns, off which open the restored chapter-house and an octagonal chapel.

104km **Fidenza** (23,000 inhab.), known as *Borgo San Donnino* from the 9C to 1927, occupies the site of the Roman *Fidentia Iulia*, where St Domninus was martyred by the Emperor Maximian in 291. The *Cathedral*, built during the 13C, has a particularly fine porch with *Statues of David and Ezekiel from the workshop of Antelami.

Over 10km SW of Fidenza and connected with it by railway and bus, lies **Salsomaggiore Terme** (160m), one of the most famous spas of Italy, with saline waters used in rheumatic, arthritic, and post-inflammatory disorders. From the Roman era until the mid-19C salt was extracted from the waters. The *Giardino Poggio Diana* has tennis-courts and a swimming pool.—*Tabiano*, 6·5km SE, is a smaller spa with sulphur springs beneficial to skin complaints.—*Sant'Andrea Bagni* is another spa in the pretty valley of the Dordone, 21km SE of Fidenza, reached via *Felegara* on the road and railway to **Fornovo**, see below.

116km *Castelguelfo* preserves a castle (no adm.) of the Ghibelline Pallavicini which was called the Torre d'Orlando until its capture in 1407 by the Guelf, Ottobono Terzi, who gave it its present name. The road crosses the Taro (view on the right).

127km **PARMA**, on the seasonal river Parma, is the second city of Emilia (172,200 inhab.), famous for its ancient buildings, the spires and domes of which give it a characteristic skyline, and for the paintings of Correggio. Parmesan cheese is a staple product of the surrounding countryside. The town was badly shaken in an earthquake in 1983.

A.P.T. Tourist Information Office, 5 Piazza Duomo.—**Post Office**, Strada Pisacane.—**Buses** from the station to Piazza Garibaldi and Villetta (No. 1), etc. COUNTRY BUSES from Viale Toschi to *Busseto, Montecchio, Fonovo, Salsomaggiore Terme, Fidenza*, etc.—**Teatro Regio**, Via Garibaldi (famous for opera; also plays and concerts).—*Swimming Pools*, Viale Rustici, Viale Piacenza, Via Zarotto.

History. Little is known about the Roman station that was established here on the Via Aemilia, and Parma emerges in the early Middle Ages as a pawn in the struggles between the various lords who held sway over Emilia. In the wars between Pope and Emperor it was on the Ghibelline (Imperial) side, and in the 12–14C it had a republican constitution. From c 1335 onwards, however, it was ruled by a succession of ducal families, the Visconti, Terzi, Este, and Sforza; in 1531 it became a papal dominion and in 1545 Paul III made it over, along with Piacenza, to his illegitimate son Pier Luigi Farnese, with the title of duke. The house of Farnese, and their heirs, the Spanish house of Bourbon-Parma, held the duchy until 1801. In 1815 the Vienna Congress assigned Parma to the ex-Empress Marie Louise, but in 1859 the widow of her son Charles III was obliged to hand it over to the King of Italy. It was heavily bombed in the Second World War.

Artistically Parma was more or less subject to Lombardy until the arrival of Correggio c 1520; and from him developed the Parma school of painting, including Parmigianino and Girolamo Mazzola, as his most successful disciples.—Arturo Toscanini (1867–1957), the conductor, was born at No. 3 Borgo Rodolfo Tanzi and played in the orchestra of the Teatro Regio.

The main streets of the city meet at the central PIAZZA GARIBALDI with the *Municipio* (S side) and *Palazzo del Governatore* (N side), both of the 17C. Here also are monuments to Garibaldi and Correggio. To the N is the church of the **Madonna della Steccata**, built in 1521–39 by Bernardo and Giovanni Francesco Zaccagni, on the plan, it is said, of Bramante's original model for St Peter's at Rome. In the richly decorated interior (left of the entrance) is the tomb, by Lorenzo Bartolini (1840), of Field-Marshal Count Neipperg (1775–1829), husband of Marie Louise. The frescoes in the chapels (coin-operated light) by Bernardo Gatti, Parmigianino, Michelangelo Anselmi, and Girolamo Mazzola Bedoli, as well as several fine tombs, are excellent examples of the 16C Parma school. The Sagrestia Nobile (1670) and the tombs of the Farnese may be seen on request.—Strada Cavour leads to Strada al Duomo which passes between the birthplace (right) of Frate Salimbene (1221–c 1290), the chronicler, and the side of the *Archbishop's Palace*, whose well-restored façade shows successive additions of 1175 and 1234.

The handsome Piazza Duomo is dominated by the **Duomo* (closed 12–15; in July and August 12.30–15.30), a splendid 11C church with a campanile (1284–94) and a projecting porch supported by two lions, with reliefs of the Months added around the arch in 1281. The nave is decorated with frescoes by pupils of Correggio (1555–70), and in the cupola (coin-operated light) is the celebrated *Assumption by *Correggio* (1520–30, recently restored); access to the cupola to examine the fresco has been closed for several years. In the last chapel in the S aisle is a Crucifixion with saints, by *Bernardo Gatti*; the chapel opposite, in the N aisle, contains interesting frescoes. On the W wall of the S transept is a famous *Deposition by *Benedetto Antelami* (1178).

The adjacent Romanesque *Baptistery (9–12, 15–17 or 18.30), one of the finest in Italy, is a splendid octagonal building in red Verona marble, begun in 1196 by *Benedetto Antelami*, who executed the three portals and the frieze that almost girdles the edifice. Restoration is still in progress of the exterior; the restoration of the interior (which has aroused some controversy) has recently been completed. The interior has a magnificent series of 13C frescoes (coin-operated light) in the vault and lunettes, reliefs over the doors by Antelami, and a series of 14 *Statues of the months, and winter and spring, by Antelami (formerly in the wall niches). Immediately E of the cathedral is the church of **San Giovanni Evangelista** (closed 12–15.30), rebuilt in 1498–1510, with a façade of 1604–7, and containing in its dome a splendid fresco by *Correggio*, the *Vision of St John at Patmos (light in N transept), as well as frescoes of St John writing, by the same painter (N transept), and others by *Parmigianino* (1st and 2nd N chapels). The walls of the nave have a beautiful frieze of prophets and sibyls, also by *Correggio*. In the S transept are statues of St Felicity and St Benedict by *Antonio Begarelli*.—The *Spezieria di San Giovanni Evangelista*, founded in 1298, preserves its 16C decoration (entrance at No. 1 Borgo Pipa; 9–14; fest. 9–13; closed Monday). *Sant'Antonio Abate*, to the S, was begun by Francesco Bibbiena in 1712, and finished in 1766.

On the other side of Strada Garibaldi, on the bank of the river, is the **Palazzo della Pilotta**, a gloomy and rambling palace built for the Farnese family in c 1583–1622, but left unfinished; it was badly bombed and half of it demolished. Here are installed the important collections of the city (in the course of rearrangement), including the museum of antiquities, the large library, and the picture gallery containing Correggio's masterpieces. The *Museo Nazionale di Antichità (in 1990 visible only on guided tours by appointment daily except Monday at 9, 10.30, & 12; Thursday, Saturday, & Sunday also 15 & 16.30), founded in 1760, is interesting chiefly for the bronze and other objects excavated at Velleia (see above).

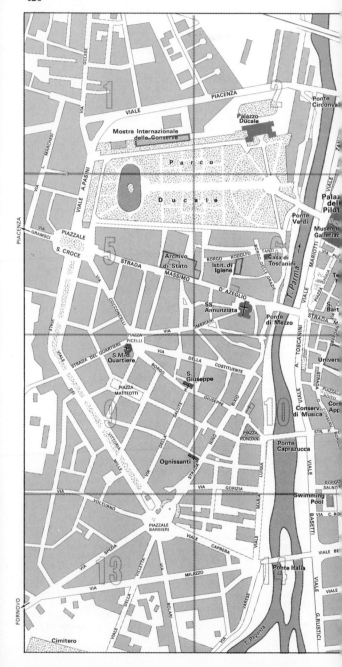

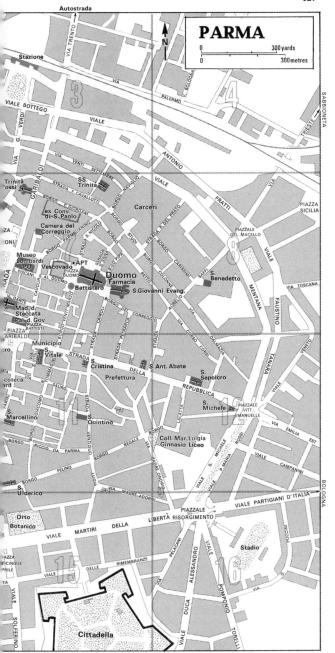

PARMA

0   300 yards
0   300 metres

Autostrada

Stazione

VIA TRENTO

VIALE BOTTEGO

VIA G. VERDI

VIA GARIBALDI

VIALE

VIA

PALERMO

VIA B. BOLOGNA

SABBIONETA

TRIESTE

PIAZZA SICILIA

VIA VENTI SETTEMBRE

VIALE ANTONIO

FRATTI

Trinità
rossi

SS. Trinità

STRADA F. CAVALLOTTI

BORGO P. GIORDANI

BORGO NAVIGLIO

Carceri

STRADA D. DEL PRATO

PIAZZALE DEL MACELLO

ex Conv.
di S.Paolo

Camera del
Correggio

BORGO FARMIGIANINO

BORGO STUDI

STRADA S. NICOLO

BORGO COLONNE

BORGO CARISSIMI

VIALE MENTANA

ZA

ONI

Museo
Lombardi
PO

Vescovado

APT

PIAZZA DUOMO

STRADA AL DUOMO

S. BENEDETTO

VIA TOSCANA

MADA

PISCANI

VIA CAVOUR

PIAZZA

Duomo

Farmacia

Battistero

S.Giovanni Evang.

BORGO DEL CORREGGIO

S. Benedetto

SAFFI

AURELIO

VIA CORSO CORSI

FAUSTINO

VIA DANTE

Mad. d.
Steccata
Pal. d. Gov

STRADA PETRARCA

BORGO XX MARZO

CAIROLI

STRADA D. REPUBBLICA

VIA DALMAZIA

TANARA

VENETO

PIAZZA
GARIBALDI

ro

Municipio

S. Vitale

STRADA

S. Cristina

STRADA TOMMASINI

VIA SAURO

DELLA

S. Ant. Abate

S. Sepolcro

REPUBBLICA

coteca
ard

S.
Marcellino

BORGO GIACOMO TOMMASINI

S. Quintino

BORGO REGALE

BORGO

PIAZZA
FABIO

BORGO RICCIO DA PARMA

FELINO

S.
Michele

PIAZZALE
VITT.
EMANUELE

VIA EMILIA EST

BORGO
S.
Ulderico

BORGO LUIGIA

VIA MADRE ADORNI

Coll. Mar. Luigia
Ginnasio Liceo

BORGO PADRE ONORIO

VIALE S. MICHELE

VIALE P. MARIA ROSSI

VIALE CAMPANINI

BOLOGNA

Orto
Botanico

VIALE MARTIRI DELLA

PIAZZALE
LIBERTÀ RISORGIMENTO

VIALE PARTIGIANI D'ITALIA

PIAZZA
CINQUE
APRILE

TA

VIALE SOLFERINO

VIALE DELLE RIMEMBRANZE

VIALE PELACANI

VIALE ALESSANDRO

VIALE DUCA

VIALE POMPONIO

VIALE TORELLI

Stadio

VIA PICCININI

VIA G.

Cittadella

FIRST FLOOR. Classical sculpture (statues and architectural fragments which belonged to the Farnese, Gonzaga, and other collections, including a fine bronze head of a boy), Egyptian works, and medals. Objects excavated at Velleia (among which the famous Tabula Alimentaria, bronzes and statues). Greek, Italiot, and Etruscan pottery and small Etruscan funerary urns.

GROUND FLOOR. Prehistoric objects from the region around Parma: terracottas and other objects from the pile-dwellings of Parma and the lake-villages of Castione dei Marchesi, Castellazzo, etc. Works from the palaeolithic and neolithic periods, as well as the Iron and Bronze Ages. Lapidary collection. Roman bronzes and architectural fragments. Goldsmiths' work from the region, and from Lombardy.—The TEATRO FARNESE, built of wood by *Giovanni Battista Aleotti* in 1618–28, was modelled on Palladio's theatre at Vicenza, but made use of movable scenery; it was almost entirely destroyed in the war, but has been partly reconstructed.—The PALATINE LIBRARY, adjoining, houses about 600,000 volumes, with editions and matrices of Giovanni Battista Bodoni, the printer, whose office was in the palace in 1768–1813, and a section with musical MSS. Here also is a fresco by *Correggio* (Coronation of the Virgin), from San Giovanni.

Opposite the library, on the second floor of the Palazzo, is the **Galleria Nazionale** (adm. 9–14; fest. 9–13; closed Monday), founded by Philip of Bourbon-Parma in 1752. It was partly reopened in 1986; when the entire gallery is open the arrangement may change and no longer correspond to the description given below.

ROOM I. 15C–early 16C Emilian School. Paintings by *Jacopo Loschi, Cristoforo Caselli, Alessandro Araldi*, and *Francesco Francia*.—RII. Detached frescoes by local artists.—RIII. Works by the Tuscans *Bernardo Daddi* and *Agnolo Gaddi*, the Venetian *Paolo Veneziano*, and the Emilian *Simone dei Crocifissi*.—RIV. Tuscan paintings by *Spinello Aretino; Giovanni di Paolo*, the Redeemer and Saints; *Fra Angelico*, Madonna and Child with Saints.—RV. *Works by *Cima da Conegliano* (Madonna and Child with Saints; Endymion, Apollo, and Marsyas); *Leonardo da Vinci*, *Head of a young girl (sketch); *Sebastiano del Piombo*, Clement VII.—RVI. Works by *Garofalo*, and the Lombard and Roman schools.—RVII. *Correggio*, *Madonna di San Gerolamo, Madonna della Scala (detached fresco).—RVIII. *Anthony Mor*, Alessandro Farnese; *Correggio*, Deposition, Martyrdom of a Saint.—RIX. *Murillo*, Job; *El Greco*, Healing of a blind man; *Correggio*, *Madonna della Scodella ('Madonna of the Bowl').—In the oval hall (near the entrance): Portraits by *Frans Pourbus the Younger*, and works by *Michelangelo Anselmi*. Flemish masters exhibited here include *Paul Brill*, *Brueghel the Elder*, and *Van Dyck* (Clara Eugenia of Spain, Madonna and Child).—The long gallery has works by *Annibale* and *Lodovico Carracci*, *Sebastiano Ricci, Bernardo Bertoldo, Zoffany*, and *Canaletto*.—Other rooms contain works by *Parmigianino* (Marriage of St Catherine, Turkish slave); *Bronzino, Guercino, Holbein* (Erasmus), and numerous others.

The PRINTS AND DRAWINGS ROOM (with 23 drawings by *Parmigianino*), the SALA ICONOGRAFICA (portraits of the Dukes of Parma from the 16C to the 19C) and the SALONE FARNESE (contemporary art) are opened on request.

In the former Convent of San Paolo (across Piazza Marconi in Via Melloni) is the ***Camera del Correggio** (adm. as for the Galleria Nazionale), the refectory of the abbess, frescoed by *Correggio* in 1518, at the order of the abbess of the day, Giovanna Piacenza. The celebrated decoration of the vault has a most original design. The adjoining room is adorned with grotteschi and other frescoes by *Alessandro Araldi* (1514).—Nearby, at No. 15 Via Garibaldi, is the *Museo Glauco Lombardi* (open 9.30–12.30, 15 or 16–17 or 18; fest. 9.30–13; closed Monday) with a collection relating to the Empress Marie Louise of Austria. Also in Via Garibaldi is the *Teatro Regio* (adm. 9–12 by arrangement), which opened in 1829 with Bellini's 'Zaira'. It is one of the most famous opera houses in Italy.

On the other side of the river is the *Parco Ducale* created in 1560, in which is *Palazzo Ducale* built as a summer residence for Ottavio Farnese by Giovanni Boscoli in 1564. A wing, furnished in the neo-classical French style, has been restored and opened to the public (adm. on request to the Carabinieri who now occupy the building). To the S, in Borgo Rodolfo Tanzi, is the birthplace of Toscanini, now a small museum relating to the conductor (adm. 9–12 by appointment). The church of the *Annunziata*, in this part of the town, is an impressive Baroque building (1566), beyond which the graceful *Ospedale della Misericordia*, begun c 1214 and enlarged in the 16C, houses the archives of the Duchy (open 9–14). About 1km to the S in the *Villetta Cemetery* the embalmed body of Paganini rests beneath a classical canopy.—Also of interest is the *University*, in a 16C building ascribed to Galeazzo Alessi and Vignola, which has faculties of law and medicine and contains natural history collections. Nearby, at No. 14 Via Cavestro, is the *Pinacoteca Stuard* (8.30–12; Monday & Thursday, also 15–17; closed Saturday & fest.), with 14–19C paintings (including works by Paolo di Giovanni Fei, Bernardo Daddi, Lanfranco, and Guercino).—On the S outskirts of the town, in Via San Martino, is the *Museo d'Arte Cinese* (open 15–18 except Monday and Tuesday), founded in 1900, and an *Ethnographical Museum*.

The province is rich in feudal strongholds. A road leads to *Montechiarugolo* (16km SE), with a good castle of 1406 and *Montecchio Emilia* (2·5km farther, across the Enza), which preserves parts of the old ramparts; or to *Torrechiara* (19·5km S) with its *Castle, the finest in the province, built for Pier Maria Rossi (1448–60) and noteworthy for its 'golden room' frescoed by Benedetto Bembo (c 1463). Other rooms are decorated by Cesare Baglione and his followers. It is open 9–12.30, 15.30–19; winter, 9–13, 14–16; fest. 9–13; closed Monday. On the other side of the Parma river is *Mamiano* (reached also by a direct road from Parma in 17km). Here, surrounded by a beautiful park is the *Villa Mamiano*, seat of the **Fondazione Magnani-Rocca**. This was the residence of the connoisseur, musicologist, and art historian Luigi Magnani until his death in 1984. It is hoped that his remarkable private museum here will be opened to the public in 1990. The *Paintings include works by: Dürer (Madonna and Child); Carpaccio (Pietà); Filippo Lippi (Madonna and Child); Gentile da Fabriano (St Francis receiving the Stigmata); Van Dyck (equestrian portrait of Giovanni Paolo Balbi); Goya (Allegorical family portait of the Infanta Luis de Bourbon, a conversation piece of 1789). The later paintings include works by Monet, Renoir, Cézanne, and Giorgio Morandi.— The road continues beyond Torrechiara along the Parma river to Pastorello (31km) where a by-road crosses the river and mounts to *Schia* (49km) with ski-ing facilities on Monte Caio (1580m).

The road to Busseto leaves the Via Aemilia at Castelguelfo (see above) and passes (19·5km) *Fontanellato* with a moated 13C *Castle of the Sanvitale family (guided tours 9.30–12.30, 15 or 15.30–18 or 19; closed Monday), preserving furnishings and a fresco (1533) by Parmigianino.—At (27·5km) *Soragna* other 16C works of art are preserved in the castle (guided tours 9–12, 14 or 15–17 or 19; closed Monday & Tuesday) of the Meli Lupi.—At (33km) *Roncole Verdi* is the simple birthplace of Giuseppe Verdi (1813–1901), the composer. His house is open 9.30–12, 14 or 15–17.30 or 18.30 except Monday.—38km *Busseto*, a charming little town, was the lordship of the Pallavicini in the 10–16C. It has many buildings adorned with terracotta in the Cremonese manner. The battlemented Castle contains the town hall and the little Teatro Verdi (adm. as above), and the Villa Pallavicino (attributed to Vignola) houses the Museo Civico with mementoes of Verdi (adm. as above). A road continues N of the town, passing *Sant'Agata di Villanova sull' Arda* where the *Villa Verdi* was built by Verdi in 1849 as a summer residence. The Verdi Museum here is open April–October, 9–12, 15–19 except Monday; it contains relics and a bust by Vincenzo Gemito. The road then turns E along the Po, making a slightly longer return (48·5km) past the fortresses of the Rossi family at *Roccabianca* and *San Secondo* (frescoes by the Campi).

FROM PARMA TO LA SPEZIA, 124km by N62; motorway, A15; railway, 120km in 2¾hrs (many tunnels). Beyond (10·5km) *Collecchio* the road ascends the broad valley of the Taro as far as (23km) *Fornovo di Taro*, a village noted as the scene of the battle of 1495, in which the retreating Charles VIII of France defeated the Milanese and Venetians. The Romanesque church has fine 13C sculptures on its façade. (The railway here leaves the road and runs via (61·5km) Borgo Val di Taro, traversing the Apennines by the Borgallo Tunnel, 8km long, and rejoining the road at Pontremoli.) The road ascends rapidly.—52·5km *Berceto* (800m) with a 13C church.—Beyond (62km) *Passo della Cisa* (1039m), the road summit, the descent begins into the Magra valley.—80km **Pontremoli** (236m) lies in a strategic position among the chestnut-clad foothills of the Apennines. There was a castle here in 990, and a medieval Borgo grew up between the Magra and Verde rivers. The ancient castle of Piagnaro on a hill houses a Museum which contains remarkable Bronze Age statue-stelae of the Lunigiana cult (see Rte 7). Via Cavour and Via Mazzini traverse the old town with some 17C and 18C palaces from the Porta Parma to the Porta Fiorentina, on the line of the ancient Via Francigena. The rococo oratory of the Madonna del Ponte stands beside the bridge over the Magra.—The church of the Annunziata, S of the town, contains an octagonal tabernacle attributed to Jacopo Sansovino (1527), and San Francesco (across the Verde river) contains a bas-relief attributed to Agostino di Duccio.

92km *Villafranca in Lunigiana*, with a local ethnographical museum in an old mill (adm. 9–12, 15 or 17–18 or 19 except Monday).—103km *Aulla*, beneath the picturesque 16C fort of Brunella (recently the subject of a controversial restoration; there are long-term plans to open a Natural History Museum here). This route leaves the Sarzana road and railway on the left, and crosses the Magra.—124km *La Spezia*, see Rte 7. For the road from Berceto and Borgotaro to Sestri Levante, see Rte 7.

FROM PARMA TO MANTUA (57·5km); railway via Piadena (where a change is necessary) in 1½hrs. N343 runs N via (16km) *Colorno*. Here the ducal palace of the Farnese, with its park and orangery, may be visited on request at the Comune. The church of San Liborio (begun in 1777) and several 18C oratories are also of interest.—The road crosses the Po on a long bridge near *Casalmaggiore* (Rte 17).—29km **Sabbioneta** (5100 inhab.), built by Vespasiano Gonzaga, Prince of Bozzolo (1531–91) as an ideal fortified city, with regular streets within hexagonal walls. The centre of the city, suffering from depopulation, retains some splendid monuments built by the Duke. *Palazzo Ducale* (1568) contains four wooden equestrian statues of Vespasiano and members of the Gonzaga family, as well as fine carved ceilings and frescoes. In the church of the *Incoronata* is the tomb of Vespasiano by Giovanni Battista Della Porta, and his statue by Leone Leoni (1588). The *Teatro Olimpico* (1590; restored), by Vincenzo Scamozzi, resembles Palladio's more famous theatre at Vicenza. The *Palazzo del Giardino* built in 1584 as the Duke's private residence, contains frescoed rooms by Bernardino Campi and the school of Giulio Romano (recently restored). The monumental *Galleria degli Antichi*, where the Duke's treasures were kept, connects the palace with Piazza Castello. It is now used for exhibitions.—From here to Mantua, see Rte 20.

An alternative route from Parma (68km) is the N62; railway via Suzzara (where a change is necessary) in 1½–2hrs. On this road, 4km outside the town, a by-road leads right for the *Certosa di Parma*, first built in 1282, which gave its name to Stendhal's famous novel. The present church contains frescoes by Sebastiano Galeotti, Francesco Natali, etc.—20·5km *Brescello*, a town of Roman origins. The church of Santa Maria Maggiore (1830–37) is known as the church of Don Camillo since the stories written by Giovanni Guareschi in 1950 are thought to have taken place here. In the central piazza is a statue of Hercules by Jacopo Sansovino. Sir Anthony Panizzi (1797–1879), librarian of the British Museum, was born in the town.—30km *Gualtieri* has the vast *Piazza Bentivoglio as its main square (with a garden in the centre). It was begun in 1580 by Giovanni Battista Aleotti.—33·5km **Guastalla** (14,200 inhab.) was once the capital of a duchy of the Gonzagas. In the square is a statue of Ferrante Gonzaga (died 1457), the condottiere, by Leone Leoni. The *Basilica della Pieve*, 10 minutes beyond the railway, is an interesting Romanesque church.—The road leaves Suzzara on the right, and crosses the Po at (55km) *Borgoforte*, with an 18C castle and a Baroque parish church. On the S bank of the Po is a 15C fortified villa at *Motteggiana*.—68km *Mantua*, see Rte 20.

Beyond Parma the Via Aemilia crosses the Enza just before Sant'Ilario, with a good view of the mountains on the right.

153·5km **REGGIO NELL'EMILIA** (now usually shortened to 'Reggio Emilia'), the large and flourishing centre (128,700 inhab.) of an important agricultural area, is especially noted for the manufacture of Parmesan cheese ('parmigiano-reggiano'). The *Regium Lepidi* of the Romans, it is divided in two by the Via Aemilia; the S part of the town retains a medieval pattern, while to the N are broad streets and open squares.

Post Office, 3 Via Sessi (E of Piazza Cavour).—**Tourist Information Office**, 1 Piazza Battisti.—**Theatres**. *Municipale*, Piazza Cavour. Opera season, December–March; plays and concerts throughout the year. *Teatro Ariosto*, Piazza Vittoria, for music and prose.—**Buses**. From Piazza Vittoria to all the main towns in the province; and for *La Spezia* and *Mantua*; from Piazza Battista for *Parma* and *Modena*.

The most settled period of Reggio's turbulent history was under the Este domination (1409–1796).—Reggio was the birthplace of Lodovico Ariosto (1474–1533), and here in 1741 Horace Walpole quarrelled with Gray and was nursed by Joseph Spence through an attack of quinsy.

Via Emilia widens to form the little Piazza Battisti where the Albergo Posta and the Tourist Office occupy the restored *Palazzo del Capitano del Popolo* (1281). The **Duomo**, in the piazza adjoining to the S, is a Romanesque church, remodelled except for the apse and crypt. The unfinished façade was added in 1544 by Prospero Spani and the statues, notably Adam and Eve above the central door, are by him (1557). The curious tower bears a group of the Madonna and donors, in copper, by Bartolomeo Spani (1522). In the 3rd chapel of the S aisle is the tomb of Valerio Malaguzzi, uncle of Ariosto, also by Spani, and in the E chapels are (right) the tomb of Bishop Rangone, and (left) a marble ciborium, both by Prospero Spani. In the piazza is *Palazzo Comunale*, begun in 1414, where in 1797 the green, white, and red tricolour of the Revolution was proclaimed the national flag of Italy. The Sala del Tricolore, with a small museum, is shown on request. Behind the cathedral lie the market and the church of *San Prospero* (recently restored), guarded by six red marble lions. It was rebuilt in 1514–27, with a choir frescoed by Camillo Procaccini and fine inlaid stalls. In the broad Corso Garibaldi to the W (reached via Piazza Vittorio Emanuele and Via San Pietro Martire), is the ornate but graceful church of *Madonna della Ghiara* (1597–1619), with a well-preserved interior decorated with frescoes and altarpieces by 17C Emilian painters. A Museum here displays the cathedral treasury (open Sunday 15.30–18.30).

To the N of Via Emilia opens the huge Piazza Cavour, bounded on the N side by the elegant *Teatro Municipale* (1852–57; with a high theatrical reputation), and extending W as Piazza della Libertà. To the right, beyond a harrowing bronze monument (1958) to Resistance martyrs, are the MUSEI CIVICI (adm. 9–12, except Monday; Tuesday & Friday also 15–18; fest. 10.30–12.30, 16–18). From the vestibule (with fragments of mosaic pavements) are the entrances to the various collections. The *Museo Spallanzani* has a delightful natural history display (including a room of fossils). Another gallery has been arranged as a *Museo del Risorgimento e della Resistenza*. The *Museo Chierici* consists of archaeological material (including Etruscan finds), arranged for study purposes. The *Numismatic Collection* shows examples from the Reggio mint. In the basement (entrance in Via Secchi) the prehistoric collection is well displayed, with finds from the locality including a 5C treasure dug up in 1957 (fine gold fibula). The *Galleria Fontanesi*, with pictures by Emilian painters from the 15C to the 19C is open as for the Musei Civici.

In the public garden behind the theatre has been erected the *Monument of the Concordii*, a Roman family tomb of c AD 50 discovered in 1929 near Boretto, on the bank of the Po, 27·5km NW of Reggio. To the SW rises the 'Gothick' spire of the *Galleria Parmeggiani* (reopened in 1988 after restoration), entered through a fine 16C Hispano-Moresque doorway brought from Valencia. The eclectic collections include medieval metal-work, 14–16C paintings of the Flemish and Spanish schools, a Christ Blessing by El Greco (recently restored), and an imaginative Abdication of Charles I of England by León y Escosura (1836–1902).

The best surviving palazzi (15–16C) are in Via Emilia towards the station (E) and Via Roma leading N from it. A frequent bus service (No. 7, and for the return No.

77) runs along the Modena road past the modern buildings of the asylum of *San Lazzaro*, a foundation dating back to the Middle Ages, to (2·5km) *San Maurizio*, just beyond which is the *Mauriziano* (closed for restoration), the country villa of the Malaguzzi family, where Ariosto often visited his relatives. Three frescoed rooms on the first floor have been restored to their appearance in the poet's time.

ENVIRONS OF REGGIO. About 16km NE is **Correggio** the birthplace of Antonio Allegri (1489–1534) surnamed Correggio, whose house (reconstructed) is in Borgovecchio. The *Palazzo dei Principi*, begun in 1507, contains the Museo Civico with twelve Flemish tapestries (16C). Next door the *Istituto Contarelli* has a tempera head of Christ by Mantegna (to be moved to the new Museo Civico). The *Teatro Asioli* (18C) has been restored. *San Quirino* (1516–87) has an interesting interior.—*Scandiano*, 13km SE, is a picturesque little town, with the old castle of the Boiardi, famous among whom was the poet Matteo Maria Boiardo (1434–94). It was the birthplace of Abate Lazzaro Spallanzani (1729–99), the great experimental physiologist.—To the N of Reggio is (17·5km) *Novellara*, notable for a castle (now town hall) of the Gonzaga, dating in part from the 14C. It contains a small museum (open 9–12) with detached frescoes of 13–16C, and a remarkable series of ceramic jars made for a pharmacy in the 15–16C.

The road from Reggio to (25·5km) *Ciano d'Enza* is the best approach to the castle of Canossa.—At (23km) *San Polo d'Enza* a by-road on the left ascends to (32·5km) the ruined **Castle of Canossa** (adm. 9–12, 15–18.30; closed Monday), the home of the great Countess Matilda of Tuscany, famed for the submission of the Emperor Henry IV to Pope Gregory VII in 1077. Only the foundations of the castle of that time remain; the ruins above ground date from the 13C and later. The return may be made to Ciano (8km) via the castle of *Rossena*.

FROM REGGIO TO LA SPEZIA, 134km. N63 ascends steadily to (27.5km) *Casina*, beyond which a road on the left leads to *Carpineti* (9km), visited in summer (view from castle).—46km **Castelnovo ne' Monti** (702m) is a pleasant hill resort. The *Pietra di Bismantova*, a fine viewpoint, was mentioned by Dante in the 'Purgatorio'.—66·5km *Collagna* (830m) stands among chestnut-woods.—From (77·5km) the *Passo del Cerreto* (1261m) the road descends rapidly.—96km *Fivizzano* (326m) is a small Tuscan town enclosed in ramparts by Cosimo I Medici. The rapid descent continues into the Aulella valley and to (113km) *Aulla* (see above)—134·5km *La Spezia*, see Rte 7.

Beyond Reggio the Bologna road crosses the Rodano, leaves the Mauriziano (see above) on the left and reaches (167km) *Rubiera*, with its ruined castle, on the Secchia.

179km **MODENA**, an extremely prosperous town (171,000 inhab.), that has figured prominently in Italian history, is an important market for the produce of the rich plain at the foot of the Apennines. The Maserati motor-works are sited in the town, and the Ferrari works, founded by Enzo Ferrari (1898–1989) outside on the Abetone road.

Railway Stations. *FF.SS.*, for all mainline services, Piazza Dante.—*Ferrovie Provinciali*, Piazza Manzoni, for local trains to Fiorano and Sassuolo.

Post Office. 68 Via Emilia.—**Tourist Information Office**, 179 Via Emilia (Piazza Mazzini).

Buses link the stations with the centre.—*Country Buses* from the Bus Station (Via Bacchini, and Largo Garibaldi) to *Bologna, Cento, Ferrara*, etc.

Swimming Pools. Via Montecuccoli (indoor and outdoor).—*Horse Racing* (in April) at the *Ippodromo*, Via Ragazzi del '99 (S of the town).

History. The Roman colony of *Mutina*, established in the 2C BC on a site already inhabited by Gauls and Etruscans, diminished in importance under the Empire, and the present city dates its prosperity from the time of Countess Matilda of Tuscany (died 1115), the loyal supporter of the Guelfs and the Pope's authority. After her death Modena became a free city and, in rivalry with Bologna, inclined more to the Ghibelline faction. In 1288 the Este family gained control of the city, and the duchy of Modena was created for Borso d'Este in 1452. It lasted until 1796, and was reconstituted in 1814–59 through an alliance of the Estes with the house of Austria. Air-raid damage in the Second World War was mostly concentrated in an attack of May 1944.—Modena was the birthplace of the sculptors Guido Mazzoni (c 1450–1518), and Antonio Begarelli (1498–1565), the former known as 'Il Modanino', of the physiologist Gabriele Falloppio (1523–63), and of Giovanni Battista Bononcini (1672–1750), Handel's rival in London. Mary of Modena (1658–1718), queen of James II of England, was the daughter of Alfonso IV d'Este.

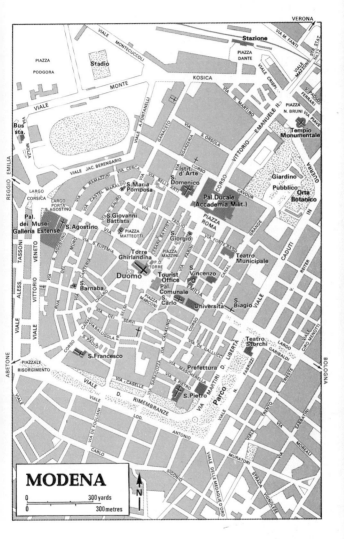

Via Emilia forms the main thoroughfare of the city, and at its centre is Piazza della Torre, in which rises the *Torre Ghirlandina* (adm. on request at Palazzo Comunale), the beautiful detached campanile of the cathedral, 86m high and slightly inclined. Begun along with the cathedral, it was completed in 1319. The splendid Romanesque

*Duomo was begun in 1099 on the site of an earlier church built over the tomb of St Geminianus (died 397), patron of Modena. The architect *Lanfranco* worked together with *Wiligelmus* who here produced some remarkable Romanesque sculpture. The building was continued by Campionese artists in the 12C–14C. The sculptures on the white façade were beautifully restored and cleaned in 1972–84. The *WEST PORTAL is a splendid work by *Wiligelmus* (the two lions are restored Roman works). The four large reliefs of the story of Genesis are also fine works by *Wiligelmus* (1100). Above the blind arcade are *Wiligelmus* and Campionese artists, is a large rose window by *Anselmo da Campione* (1200). On the S side (in need of cleaning) the PORTA DEI PRINCIPI is attributed to *Wiligelmus* or his school. Above to the right is a fine (damaged) bas relief of Jacob and the Angel. The 12C PORTA REGIA is by the Campionese school. In the last arch on the S side are four reliefs of the Life of St Geminianus by *Agostino di Duccio* (1442). The exterior of the apse is very fine. On the N side, the PORTA DELLA PESCHERIA is by a follower of Wiligelmus.

The beautiful *INTERIOR (closed 12.30–15.30) is of pale red brick with a red marble floor. The Romanesque arcades have alternate slender columns and composite piers which support an early-15C vault. In the S aisle are remains of 15C frescoes by local artists, and a small terracotta Adoration of the Shepherds by *Begarelli* (1527; restored 1976). In the N aisle the wood statue of St Geminianus probably dates from the 14C. The elaborately carved ancona, attributed to *Michele da Firenze*, was restored in 1977. The Pulpit is by Arrigo da Campione (1322). On the 2nd altar is a painting of the Virgin and Saints by *Dosso Dossi*. The *Tribuna (covered by two tapestries during restoration work) and Ambo, supported by lions and crouching figures, form the approach to the raised choir. The coloured sculptures of campionese workmanship represent the Evangelists (on the pulpit), the Washing of the Feet, the Last Supper, the Kiss of Judas, Christ before Pilate, the Via Dolorosa, and the Crucifixion. Above hangs a fine wood Crucifix with high reliefs (1200). In the Choir a screen of slender red marble coupled columns in two tiers surrounds the beautiful altar table by Campionese artists. In the apse is a restored statue in bronze and copper of St Geminianus by *Geminiano Paruolo* (1376; removed from the Porta Regia). The stalls are by *Cristoforo* and *Lorenzo da Lendinara*. On the right wall of the choir are fresco fragments (Tuscan school, late 13C), and in the left apse is a fine polyptych of the Coronation of the Virgin by *Serafino Serafini*. The four inlaid panels of the Evangelists are by *Cristoforo da Lendinara* (1477), and there is more inlaid work by him in the interesting Sacristy. In the Crypt (with remarkable capitals, some attributed to *Wiligelmus*) is the tomb of St Geminianus, and an expressive sculptured group of five terracotta statues by *Guido Mazzoni* (1480; to be restored).

Near the left side of the Duomo is the **Museo Lapidario** (adm. on request at the sacristy in the Duomo). It contains about 100 Roman marbles, epigraphs, stelae, and sarcophagi from the necropolis of Mutina; and medieval, Renaissance, and later sculpture.

The *Palazzo Comunale* in the Piazza Grande, founded in the 12C, dates in its present form from a reconstruction of 1624. The bucket carried off by the Modenese in a raid on Bologna in 1325 (described by Tassoni in his poem 'La Secchia Rapita'), formerly in the Torre Ghirlandina, is kept here and can be seen on request. The arcaded Corso Canal Chiaro leads SW to the church of *San Francesco* (1244), which contains a fine terracotta *Descent from the Cross, by Begarelli (end of N aisle). Rua del Muro leads back to Via Emilia and the church of *Sant'Agostino* which has another *Deposition by Begarelli in stucco, with traces of polychrome. Next door is the **Palazzo dei Musei**, containing interesting art collections.

The Palazzo Comunale in Piazza Grande, Modena

On the ground floor is the MUSEO DEL RISORGIMENTO (9–13 except Monday; on Tuesday, Wednesday and Thursday also 14.30–17.30). In the courtyard is a collection of Roman sarcophagi, mosaics and architectural fragments.—On the first floor is the ARCHIVIO STORICO (Monday–Saturday 8–13; Tuesday and Thursday also 15.30–18.30; closed fest.) and the **Biblioteca Estense** (10–13; closed fest.), with a fine exhibition of illuminated MSS, notably the *Bible of Borso d'Este, illuminated by *Taddeo Crivelli* and *Franco Russi*; a 14C edition of Dante; and the missal of Renée of France, by *Jean Bourdichon* (16C). On the floor above is the **Museo Civico** (reopened in 1990; 9–13; Tuesday & Thursday & fest. also 15–18; closed Monday) a collection of local interest. It includes: a 14C fresco from the Duomo; medieval sculptures; terracotta Madonna, by *Begarelli*; glass; weights and measures; scientific instruments; majolica; arms and armour; embroidered silks, textiles; applied arts; musical instruments. There is also an Archaeological section.

The **Galleria Estense** (adm. 9–14, fest. 9–13; closed Monday) is a fine collection of pictures formed by the Este family in the early 16C, notable especially for its examples of the 15–17C Emilian schools. It has been beautifully rearranged to include objects from the Museo Estense of applied arts. The rooms are not numbered, but the collection is displayed in roughly chronological order. The paintings are sometimes moved around. VESTIBULE. Islamic ceramics, 16C Venetian enamels. Head of Jove (?), 2C AD. Emilian Romanesque sculpture. Small bronzes (Etruscan, Italic, Greek). At the end, marble *Bust of Francesco I d'Este, founder of the collection, by *Gian Lorenzo Bernini* (1652).

LONG GALLERY. Portable altars (*Venetian, late 14C, Tommaso da Modena); Barnaba da Modena*, Madonna and Child with Saints, Crucifixion.—*Cristoforo da Lendinara*, Madonna and Child (removed for restoration); *Agnolo* and *Bartolomeo Erri*, Triptych; *Cosmè Tura*, St Anthony of Padua, *Bartolomeo Bonascia*, Pietà and symbols of the passion; *Bartolomeo Erri*, Madonna and Saints (4 panels).—Works by *Francesco Bianchi Ferrari*.—Lombard, French, Spanish, and Byzantine sculptures in ivory and marble, including a bas-relief of Mars, attributed to *Antonio Lombardo* or *Simone Mosca*. Busts by *L'Antico* and *Tullio Lombardo*. Bronzes by *Il Riccio*.—*Francesco Botticini*, *Adoration of the Child; *Apollonio di Giovanni*, Story of Griselda; *Antoniazzo Romano*, Pietà; *Giuliano Bugiardini*, Birth of St John the Baptist.—Flemish works: *Albrecht Bouts*, St Christopher; *Joos van Cleve*, Madonna and Child and St Anne.—*Palma Vecchio*, *Portrait of a lady; *Cima da Conegliano*, Deposition; *Vincenzo Catena*, Madonna and Child with Saints and donors.—Estense harp with rich painted decoration (end of 16C); *Gian Francesco Maineri*, Christ carrying the Cross; *Girolamo da Carpi*, Portrait of a gentleman; *Domenico Panetti*, Madonna and Child (formerly attributed to Garofalo).—At the end, *Correggio*, *Madonna Campori. Sculptures by *Guido Mazzoni, Nicolò dell'Arca*, and *Antonio Begarelli* (large terracotta of the Madonna and Child).

Works by *Girolamo da Carpi* (Portrait of a man); *L'Antico*, Bust of Ceres; *Dosso Dossi*, Adoration of the Shepherds, Portrait of Alfonso I d'Este (with *Battista Dossi*), Portrait of Hercules I d'Este (attributed).—Ceramics from Urbino. *Francesco Duquesnoy*, Bust of a woman. Small bronzes by *Pietro Tacca, Giambologna*, and *Jacopo Sansovino*.—Works by *Lelio Orsi, Giovanni Gherardo delle Catene*, and *Marco Meloni*.—*Rosalba Carriera*, Portrait; *Velazquez*, Portrait of Francesco I d'Este (removed for restoration); small works by *Bartolomeo Schedoni*.—*Lelio Orsi*, Rape of Ganymede (ceiling); series of paintings by *Nicolò dell'Abate*.—*Mabuse*, Madonna and Child; *Hans Baldung Grien*, Head of an old man; *El Greco*, *Portable altar, a youthful work; *Pieter Brueghel the Younger*, Calvary; *Charles Le Brun*, Scenes from the life of Moses; *Rubens* (workshop), Adoration of the Magi; *Frans Pourbus*, Portrait of a woman.

The remainder of the collection is displayed in four large rooms. ROOM I. *Paolo Veronese*, 3 paintings of Saints; *Palma Giovane*, Adoration of the Magi (2 paintings); *Tintoretto*, Rape of Europa, Madonna and Child with Saints; *Bonifazio Veronese*, the Virtues, *Domenico Tintoretto*, Giving of the keys to St Peter.—RII. *Carlo Cignani*, Flora; *Sassoferrato*, Madonna and Child; *Guercino*, Marriage of St Catherine; *Guido Reni*, Crucifixion; *Annibale Carracci*, Venus; *Lodovico Carracci*, Assunta, Galatea; *Guido Reni*, St Roch in prison; *Lavinia Fontana*, Portrait; *Garofalo*, Madonna enthroned with Saints.—RIII. Works by *Luca Ferrari* and *Guercino*.—RIV. Works by *Pomarancio* and *Daniele Crespi*. Huge canvases by *Giulio Cesare* and *Camillo Procaccini*. Seascapes by *Salvator Rosa*.

The *Galleria Campori*, with a good collection of paintings chiefly of the 17–18C has been closed since 1970 (it is to be exhibited in the Museo Civico, see above). In the GALLERIA CIVICA (adm. 9.30–12.30, 15.30–19.30; fest. 10–13, 16–19; closed Monday; entrance on Viale Vittorio Veneto) frequent exhibitions are held.

Via Sauro leads NE off Via Emilia (see the Plan) to *Santa Maria Pomposa*; here is buried Lodovico Antonio Muratori (1672–1750), provost of the church from 1716 and 'father of Italian history'. He lived and died in the adjacent house, now the *Museo Muratoriano* (apply to custodian of church 9–12), which preserves his autograph works and other mementoes. *San Giovanni Battista* contains a life-sized polychrome *Descent from the Cross by Guido Mazzoni (1476).—Via Cesare Battisti, on the left farther on, leads to the old church of *San Domenico* rebuilt in 1708–31. In the Baptistery (left of the entrance) is a colossal terracotta statuary *Group by Begarelli (recently restored), thought to represent Christ in the house of Martha. The huge **Palazzo Ducale** (no adm.; now the Accademia Militare), was begun in 1634 for Francesco I on the site of the old Este castle. From the other side of the palace Corso Vittorio Emanuele leads towards the station; on the right is the imposing *Tempio Monumentale*, by Achille Casanova and Domenico Barbanti (1923), a large church in the Romanesque style erected as a war memorial. In the public garden beyond is a Botanical Garden founded by Francesco III in 1772.

In the SE part of the town are the *University*, and the church of **San Pietro** (rebuilt in 1476), with a well ornamented brick front and a garishly decorated interior. It contains a notable Pietà, six statues in the nave, and a group of the Virgin and saints all by *Antonio Begarelli*, the latter completed by his nephew Lodovico for the master's tomb. In this church was buried also Alessandro Tassoni (1565–1635), author of 'La Secchia Rapita' (see above). Beyond the church is a pleasant park, with a war memorial (1926).—To the E of the Pistoia road is the *Città dei Ragazzi*, or Boys' Town, founded by Father Rocchi; one of its houses was the gift of British ex-prisoners of war rescued by the founder in 1943–45.

FROM MODENA TO FERRARA, 74km (N255).—9km *Nonantola*, with two 14C towers, is famous for its Abbey (open 9.30–12.30, 15.30–17), founded in 752 and rebuilt in brick in the 13C. The portal has reliefs by the school of Wiligelmus (1121). The church contains the tombs of Popes St Sylvester (in the choir) and Adrian III (in the crypt). In the Refectory fresco fragments attributed to the early 12C, with the story of St Benedict have recently been found. The treasury is also interesting.—At (22·5km) *San Giovanni in Persiceto* this route crosses the road from Bologna to Verona.—40·5km **Cento** was the birthplace of Giovanni Francesco Barbieri, called Il Guercino (1591–1666), of Ugo Bassi (1801–49), a priest martyred in the cause of Italian freedom, and of Isaac Israeli, great-grandfather of Benjamin Disraeli. Guercino's painting is well represented in the *Pinacoteca Civica* (adm. 9.30–12 except Monday), which, together with the Galleria d'Arte Moderna Bonzagni, is at No. 10 Via Matteotti. The church of the *Rosario* contains a chapel built for Guercino and with a fine Crucifixion by him, and above the town rises the 14C *Rocca*. At *Pieve di Cento*, 2km outside the town, is a small Pinacoteca Civica in the main square (open every morning, and all day Saturday and Sunday). It contains paintings of the Bolognese and Ferrarese schools (15–19C), a wood 14C Madonna, 18C reliquaries, etc.—74km *Ferrara*, see Rte 37.

FROM MODENA TO ABETONE, 91km , a fine road across the Apennines, recently improved as far as (42km) *Pavullo nel Frignano* (682m) in the centre of the hilly Frignano, with a 19C residence of the dukes of Modena.—Rounding the hill on which stands the old castle of *Montecuccolo* (gutted) the road continues to climb past the old tower of *Montecenere*, with fine views, to (80km) *Pievepelago* (781m), an important road junction.—85km *Fiumalbo* (935m), with an old tower, is visited for winter sports, beneath *Monte Cimone* (2165m), the highest peak in the northern Apennines, which rises to the NE (rough track; from the summit, on a clear day, can be seen the E and W coasts of Italy). It is ascended part way from Sestola by funicular. The boundary between Emilia and Tuscany is crossed just short of the road summit.—91km *Abetone*, and from there to Pistoia, see Rte 45.

From Pievepelago a steep road to *Castelnuovo di Garfagnana* (45·5km), joins an alternative road from Modena (84·5km), via the Secchia valley, just below the *Foce delle Radici* (1529m). A little below the pass on the Tuscan side is *San Pellegrino in Alpe*, with a museum illustrating the peasant life of the area.

From Modena, N623 leads SE via (16km) Spilamberto to (22km) *Vignola*, a fruit-growing centre, famous for its cherries. It is the birthplace of Jacopo Barozzi, called Il Vignola (1507–73), the architect. The fine castle was built by Uguccione Contrari between 1401 and 1435. The chapel has interesting late-Gothic frescoes (1401–48) by an unknown artist, influenced by Giovanni da Modena.

From Modena to *Mantua* via Carpi, see Rte 20; to *Mirandola*, see Rte 21.

Beyond Modena the Via Aemilia crosses the Panaro. To the left is the Forte Urbano, built by Urban VIII (1528) to mark the papal frontier of his time.—192km *Castelfranco Emilia*.—At (217km) *Lavino di Mezzo*, a by-road (5km) leads S to Lavino di Sopra. Nearby, in the commune of

Zola Predosa, is *Palazzo Albergati*. It unusual plain rectangular exterior was built in 1659–94 on a plan by Giovanni Giacomo Monti. The huge salone has stuccoes by Gian Filippo Bezzi, and other rooms have elaborate 17–18C frescoes.—On the approach to Bologna the Madonna di San Luca is seen on a hill to the right. The road crosses the Reno a little above the island on which Octavius, Mark Antony, and Lepidus met to form the Second Triumvirate (43 BC).—218km **Bologna**, see below.

40 Bologna

BOLOGNA (490,500 inhab.), the capital of Emilia and one of the oldest cities of Italy, the seat of a famous university, is situated at the S verge of the plain of the Po, at the NE foot of the slopes of the Apennines. The old town, built almost exclusively of pink brick, is particularly remarkable for its attractive porticoes which line each side of almost every street. With Romanesque and Gothic churches, and handsome public monuments, it is one of the most beautiful cities in Northern Italy, often unjustly left out of the usual tourists' itinerary. The famous Bolognese school of painting is well represented in its picture gallery. Bologna is a good centre for visiting other cities in Emilia Romagna (excellent bus services).

Post Office (Pl. 11), Piazza Minghetti.—**Tourist Information Office** *(Informazione Accoglienza Turistico)*, 6 Piazza Maggiore (Pl. 10); Information office also at the Station.—*A.P.T.*, 45 Via Marconi (Pl. 6).

Transport. The centre of the city is normally open only to motorists with special permits (although an exception is made for those going to hotels). On Saturdays and Sundays it is usually closed to motor traffic (including buses). **Buses.** From the *Station* to *Piazza Maggiore* (**21** & **22**); to the *Zona Fieristica and Gallery of Modern Art* (**3, 38,** & **91**); for *San Michele in Bosco* (**28**). From *Piazza Galvani* to *San Mamalo* (**12**) and to the *Certosa* (**43**).—COUNTRY BUSES from Piazza Venti Settembre (Pl. 3); an excellent comprehensive network which serves nearly all places of interest in the region.

Airport at Borgo Panigale, 7km NW (Airport Bus No.**91** from Piazza Stazione, 10 & 40 minutes past the hour). Flights to London, Paris, and Frankfurt, as well as internal services.

Theatres. *Comunale.* Opera and Ballet season, December–April; concerts throughout the year. Plays and concerts in *Palazzo dei Congressi (Sala Europa)* in the Zona Fieristica. *Teatro Duse*, Via Cartoleria; *Teatro Testoni*, 2 Via Tiarini.—**Swimming Pools** (open and indoor) at the Stadio Comunale, etc.

History. *Felsina,* an important Etruscan city on the site of Bologna, was overrun by the Gauls in the 4C BC. They named their settlement *Bononia*, and the name was retained by the Romans when they conquered the plain of the Po in 225–191 BC. After the fall of the Western Empire, Bologna became subject to the Exarchs of Ravenna, and later formed part of the Lombardic and Frankish dominions. In 1116 it was recognised as an independent commune by the Emperor Henry V. Its university first becomes prominent at about this time.

One of the foremost cities of the Lombard League (1167), it reached the summit of its glory after the peace of Constance (1183), and sided with the Guelfs, the papal party, against the Ghibellines, the emperor's party. In the struggles which followed the Bolognese won the fierce battle of Fossalta (1249). Enzo (1225–72), King of Sardinia, illegitimate son of the Emperor Frederick II, taken prisoner in the fight, was imprisoned in Bologna for the remaining twenty-two years of his life. In 1325 the Bolognese were defeated in their turn at Zappolino (the scene of 'La Secchia Rapita'—see under Modena), but the papal legate sent to their assistance was not welcomed, and c 1337, Taddeo Pepoli, a popular champion, founded a lordship, held in turn by the Visconti, the Pepoli, and finally the unlucky Bentivoglio, under the last of whom (Giovanni II Bentivoglio; 1463–1506) Bologna reached great fame and prosperity. In 1506 Pope Julius II reconquered the city, and for three centuries Bologna was incorporated with the Papal States, except for a brief interval (1796–1814) when it was part of Napoleon's Cisalpine Republic. In 1814 Bologna was occupied by a British force under General Nugent, in support of the Austrians against Napoleon. Unsuccessful insurrections broke out in 1831 and 1848 (the latter inspired by the eloquence of Ugo Bassi), and from 1849 until the formation of the Kingdom of Italy in 1860 the town was held by an Austrian garrison. In the Second World War Bologna was for months the focal point of German resistance, but it escaped serious artistic damage. It was entered on 21 April 1945, by the Polish Second Corps.

Bologna, the seat of a bishop since the 3C, and of an archbishop since 1583, has contributed more prelates to the sacred college than any other city except Rome, and six of its natives have been popes: Honorius II, Lucius II, Gregory XIII, Innocent IX, Gregory XV, and Benedict XIV. Among painters born in Bologna were Francesco Primaticcio (1504–70), the three Carracci (16C), Domenichino (1581–1641), Guido Reni (1575–1642), and Francesco Albani (1578–1660), the 'Anacreon of painting'. Other famous Bolognese are Cardinal Mezzofanti (1774–1849), Ottorino Respighi (1879–1936), the composer, Luigi Galvani (1737–98), and Guglielmo Marconi (1874–1937). Giosuè Carducci, the poet, spent the last years of his life in a suburban villa. Charlotte Stuart (1753–89), only daughter of Charles Edward, the 'Young Pretender', died at Bologna, and was buried in San Biagio, a church destroyed in 1797.

Art. In the architecture of Bologna the predominant material has always been brick, for both constructional and decorative purposes, and the late-Gothic buildings of the 14C show the height to which skill in brick designing attained. In the 15C the forms of the Tuscan Renaissance came to Bologna, and in the following century many great masters of the Renaissance—Formigine, Baldassarre Peruzzi, Vignola, and others—were at work in the city. The art of sculpture in Bologna is represented instead mainly by masterpieces of visiting craftsmen, from Nicolò Pisano to Jacopo della Quercia and Giambologna, than by any strongly individual local school; but in painting, after a rather sparse early period up to the end of the 15C, when Marco Zoppo stands out as an interpreter of the Paduan style, Bologna claims a very distinctive school, which continued to have an important influence throughout Italy during the 17C and 18C. The wealthy court of the Bentivoglio attracted Franceso Cossa, Ercole de'Roberti, and Lorenzo Costa from Ferrara (c 1490), and the last especially influenced Francesco Francia, the real founder of the Bolognese school, who had begun life as a goldsmith, and later came under the influence of Perugino. Costa's most faithful pupil was the Bolognese Amico Aspertini, while among Francia's numerous followers were Timoteo Viti of Urbino. Another revival at the end of the 16C was fostered by the Carracci (Lodovico and his cousins Annibale and Agostino), who founded the 'Eclectic School', animated by a rebellion against formalism. Their influence extended into the 18C, through Francesco Albani, Guido Reni, Domenichino, and Guercino, to Carlo Cignani, Elisabetta Sirani, and their followers.

A. Piazza Maggiore, San Petronio, and Piazza Nettuno

In the centre of the city is the large and peaceful *Piazza Maggiore (Pl.11), known simply as the 'Piazza' to the Bolognese. PIAZZA NETTUNO adjoins it at right angles, and both are surrounded by splendid public buildings. Facing the dignified raised façade of the great church of San Petronio is *PALAZZO DEL PODESTÀ (Pl. 11), begun at the beginning of the 13C, but remodelled in 1484. The restoration of the façade, still in progress in 1989, has been much criticized. At the centre of the building is the tall *Tower* (Arengo) of 1212: two passageways run beneath it and in the angles of the vault are statues

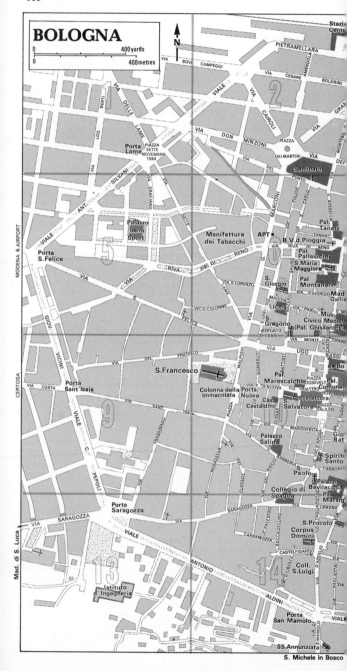

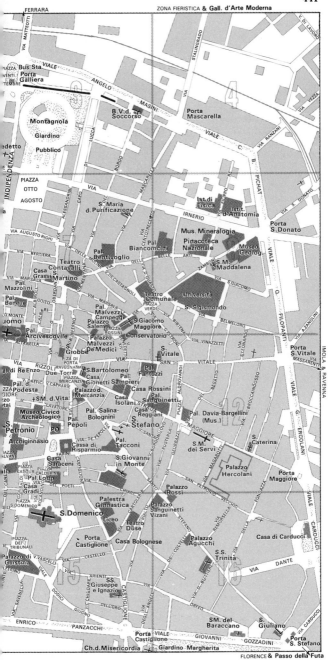

of the patron saints of the city (Saints Petronius, Florian, Eligius, and Francis) by Alfonso Lombardi (1525).—Fronting Via dell'Archiginnasio (busy with buses), skirting the E side of the piazza, is the handsome long façade of *Palazzo dei Banchi* (1412) remodelled by Vignola (1565–68), once occupied by the moneylenders. On street level is the Portico del Pavaglione, and two tall arches that give access to side streets. Above the roof of the palace can be seen the dome of Santa Maria della Vita and the top of the Torre degli Asinelli.—On the other side of San Petronio is *Palazzo dei Notai*, or the old College of Notaries, part of which was begun in 1381 by Berto Cavalletto, Lorenzo da Bagnomarino, and Antonio di Vincenzo, and the rest completed by Bartolomeo Fieravanti (1422–40).

*San Petronio (Pl. 11), the most important church in Bologna, even though never the cathedral, is one of the finest brick Gothic buildings in existence. Founded in 1390 on the designs of *Antonio di Vincenzo*, it is dedicated to St Petronius, bishop of Bologna in 431–450 and patron saint of the city. Houses and churches were demolished on this site so that the church could take its place at the political centre of the city and it soon became a symbol of civic pride and independence. Its construction went on until 1659, when the nave-vault was completed. The church is orientated almost N and S.

EXTERIOR. The immense incomplete FAÇADE (restored 1973–79) has a beautiful pink and white marble lower storey with three canopied doorways with exquisite reliefs illustrating Biblical history from the Creation to the time of the Apostles. The *Central Doorway* is famous for its *Sculptures by *Jacopo della Quercia* (1425–38), his masterpiece begun in 1425 and left unfinished at his death in 1438. On the pilasters are ten bas-reliefs illustrating the Story of Genesis, and a frieze of half-figures of Prophets. On the architrave, five scenes from the New Testament. In the lunette are statues of the Madonna and Child with St Petronius (the St Ambrose, by *Varignana*, was added in 1510). Above them the archivolt is decorated with panels of prophets carved in 1510–11 by *Antonio Minello* and *Antonio da Ostiglia*. The central figure is by *Amico Aspertini*.—The two lateral doorways were designed by *Ercole Seccadenari* and executed by numerous sculptors in 1524–30 including *Nicolò Tribolo, Alfonso Lombardo, Girolamo da Treviso, Amico Aspertini*, and others.—The two sides of the building have a high marble basement beneath the large Gothic traceried windows.

INTERIOR (open all day, 7.30–18 or 19). The great white and pink nave, 41m high, is lit by round windows, and is separated from the aisles by ten massive compound piers. Because of its orientation, the church is unusually light. The splendid Gothic vaulting of the nave was only completed in 1625 by *Girolamo Rainaldi*. The side chapels are closed by beautiful screens, many of them in marble dating from the late 15C, and others in ironwork. These are kept locked and so it is difficult to see some of the works of art at close range. Outside the chapels have been placed four 11–12C Crosses which marked the limits of the late medieval city.

SOUTH AISLE. 1st chapel, Madonna della Pace, a sculpture by *Johannes Ferrabech* (German, 1394, intended for the façade), framed by a painting by *Giacomo Francia*.—2nd chapel, polyptych by *Tommaso Garelli* (1477), and early 15C frescoes.—3rd chapel, frescoed polyptych of the school of the *Vivarini*.—4th chapel, Crucifix, attributed to *Ercole Banci* (early 16C), and further 15C frescoes; the stained glass is by *Jacob of Ulm* (1466).—5th chapel, *Amico Aspertini*,

Pietà (1519).—6th chapel, *Lorenzo Costa*, St Jerome.—8th chapel, *Carved and inlaid stalls, by *Raffaello da Brescia* (1521).—9th chapel, Statue of St Anthony of Padua, by *Girolamo da Treviso*, formerly attributed to Jacopo Sansovino; Miracles of the Saint, monochrome works also by *Girolamo da Treviso* (1526). The design of the stained glass is attributed to *Pellegrino Tibaldi*.—The screen of the 10th chapel is particularly beautiful (c 1460). The altarpiece is by *Bartolomeo Passarotti*.—11th chapel. On the left wall is a framed high relief of the *Assumption, by *Nicolò Tribolo* (with 18C additions). Here has been placed a recently restored female *Figure in polychrome wood which was formerly displayed in the Lamentation group by *Vincenzo Onofrio* (1480) beneath the organ, opposite.—The CHOIR contains carved stalls by Agostino de'Marchi (1468–77; restored). Of the two organs the one on the right was built by *Lorenzo di Giacomo da Prato* in 1470–75. Before the high altar Charles V was crowned emperor in 1530 by Clement VII.

NORTH AISLE. At the E end is a small MUSEUM (open 10–12 except Tuesday and Thursday). In the first room are preserved numerous interesting drawings for the completion of the façade of the church, submitted up until 1933. These are displayed on sliding glass panels and include works by Baldassarre Peruzzi, Domenico Tibaldi, and Palladio. Plans and models of the church by Baldassarre Peruzzi and Girolamo Rainaldi show the various projects for the church in the 16–17C. In the 2nd room are 17–18C church vestments, reliquaries, church silver, and illuminated choir books (some by Taddeo Crivelli).—In the 11th chapel two large painted panels by *Amico Aspertini* from the 15C organ have been placed since their restoration.—9th chapel, St Michael, by *Denys Calvaert* (1582), and the Barbazzi monument with a bust by *Vincenzo Onofrio* (1479).—8th chapel. *Parmigianino*, St Roch (recently restored).— In front of the monument of Bishop Cesare Nacci, by *Vincenzo Onofrio* (1479) begins the meridian line, nearly 67m long, traced in 1655 by the astronomer Gian Domenico Cassini, in substitution for an earlier one of 1575. It has since been several times adjusted; a hole in the roof admits the sun's ray.—The 7th chapel has a particularly fine screen attributed to *Pagno di Lapo*. The Altarpiece with the Madonna and Saints Sebastian, George, James and Jerome is by *Lorenzo Costa* (1492). Here are neo-classical funerary monuments of Felice Baciocchi and his wife Elisa Bonaparte by *Cincinnato Baruzzi* (1845; with two putti by *Lorenzo Bartolini*), and of their children.—6th chapel. Assumption by *Scarsellino* and a statue of Cardinal Giacomo Lercaro by *Giacomo Manzù* (1954).—The huge wooden pulpit of unusual design is attributed to *Agostino de'Marchi* (c 1470).—The 5th chapel was decorated in 1487–97. The *Altarpiece of the Martyrdom of St Sebastian with a donor is by an artist of the late-15C Ferrarese school. At the sides, Annunciation by *Francesco Francia* and *Lorenzo Costa*, who probably also painted the Apostles on the walls. The stalls date from 1495, and in the pavement is enamelled tilework by *Pietro Andrea da Faenza* (1487).—Between this chapel and the next is a fine statue of St Petronius in gilded wood (late 14C).—The 4th chapel (Cappella Bolognini) has another fine marble balustrade. The gilded polychrome wood Gothic *Altarpiece was painted by *Jacopo di Paolo* in 1410 (restored in 1988). The remarkable *Frescoes (Heaven and Hell, Life of St Petronius, and the Story of the Magi) are by *Giovanni da Modena* (being restored in 1988). Above the interesting 18C clock outside the chapel is a huge fresco of St Christopher.—The 2nd chapel is a good Baroque work by *Alfonso Torreggiani* (1743–50) with a fine grille, and the tomb of Benedict XIV. Outside the chapel (right): 15C fresco of St Bridget of Sweden, and Christ enthroned, by *Lippo di Dalmasio*, and (left) Madonna and Saints, attributed to *Giovanni da Modena*.—1st chapel, restored allegorical frescoes by *Giovanni da Modena*.—Above the right door on the inside façade, Adam and Eve attributed to *Alfonso Lombardi*.

In **Piazza Nettuno** (Pl. 11) is the famous *NEPTUNE FOUNTAIN (or *Fontana del Gigante*) designed by Tommaso Laureti and decorated with a splendid figure of Neptune and other bronze sculptures by Giambologna (1566). Neptune was removed for restoration in 1989 to the courtyard of Palazzo Comunale. Fronting both Piazza Nettuno and Piazza Maggiore is the long façade of the huge **Palazzo Comunale** (Pl. 11), which incorporates **Palazzo d'Accursio**, and is made up of several buildings of different dates, modified and restored over the centuries. The entrance gateway is by *Galeazzo Alessi* (c 1555), and the bronze statue above it of Pope Gregory XIII (Ugo Buoncompagni of Bologna, the reformer of the calendar), is by *Alessandro Menganti* (1580). To the left, under a canopy, is a *Madonna in terracotta by *Nicolò dell'Arca* (1478).

Palazzo d'Accursio, to the left, with a tower (and clock of 1773) was acquired by the Comune in 1287 from Francesco d'Accursio on his return from the court of King Edward I of England. The loggia was used as a public granary. In 1336 Taddeo Pepoli began to unite various palaces on this site as a palazzo pubblico, and in 1425–28 Fieravante Fieravanti rebuilt the palace to the right of the main entrance. In the 16C the whole edifice was fortified by the Papal legates as their residence: the impressive battlemented walls (restored in 1887) extend along Via Ugo Bassi and Via IV Novembre.

From the Courtyard the grand *Staircase*, a ramp ascribed to Bramante, leads up to the *First Floor*, with the *Chamber of Hercules*, named after the colossal terracotta statue here by Alfonso Lombardi, and the Madonna 'of the earthquake' by Francesco Francia (1505). The stairs continue up to the *Second Floor* with the *Sala Farnese* containing frescoes by Carlo Cignani and others and a copper statue of Pope Alexander VII by Dorastante d'Osio (1660). Off this room (left) is the entrance to the **Collezioni Comunali d'Arte** (adm. 9–14; Sunday 9–12.30; closed Tuesday & fest.), a well displayed collection of paintings and furniture in rooms of a wing of the Palazzo d'Accursio, used by the Cardinal legates of the city from 1508 up to the 19C. The works are well labelled.

ROOM 1. *Carlo Francesco Nuvolone*, Portrait of a lady; *Artemisia Gentileschi*, Portrait of a condottiere; *Teophime Bigot*, St Sebastian healed by St Irene.—R. 2. *Ubaldo Gandolfi*, Diana and Endymion.—R. 4, a long gallery decorated in the 17C by the papal legate Pietro Vidoni, displays a good collection of works by *Donato Creti*, mostly painted in 1710–20. Two small doors lead off the gallery (right) into R. 5 with 14C and 15C works including a number of Crucifixes: *Vitale da Bologna*, Saints; *Jacopo di Paolo*, Crucifix; *Follower of Giunta Pisano*, *Crucifix; *Simone da Bologna*, Crucifix sculpted in wood; *Luca Signorelli* (attributed), Head of a female saint; (in centre) *Francesco Francia*, *Crucifixion.—R. 6. *Bartolomeo Cesi*, small detached fescoes of the life of the Virgin; *School of Guercino*, St John the Evangelist at Patmos; *Guido Cagnacci*, Death of Cleopatra; *Annibale Carracci* (attributed), Hercules; *Jacopo Tintoretto*, Head of an old man; *Bartolomeo Passarotti*, Crucifix, Saints and donors; portraits by *Pelagio Pelagi*; *Giuseppe Maria Crespi*, Portrait of Cardinal Lambertini (a bozzetto).—R. 8, with a pretty vault, contains a painting of Ruth by *Francesco Hayez*, and R. 9 displays a collection of lace.—It is now necessary to return to R. 4. At the end (right) are Rooms 11–16 with the Rusconi collection. RR. 11 & 12 have good 16C ceilings and 18C furnishings.—R. 13 has works by *Giovanni Boulanger* and in R. 14 are 18–19C miniatures and a portrait of Marco Marchini by *Baciccia*. R. 15 contains majolica, glass, etc., and R. 16 was delightfully decorated by *Giuseppe Valliani* and *Vincenzo Martinelli* at the end of the 18C.—It is now necessary to return to R. 4. To the right is R. 17 with a good trompe l'oeil ceiling by *Dentone, Angelo Michele Colonna* and *Agostino Mitelli*, and painted coats-of-arms. RR. 18 & 19 are closed. R. 20 contains a collection of pictures from the Istituto Giovanni XXIII including a Madonna and Child by *Amico Aspertini.*

Adjoining Palazzo del Podestà (see above) in Piazza Nettuno is the battlemented **Palazzo di Re Enzo** built in 1246 which was the prison of King Enzo (see above) from his capture at Fossalta in 1249 until his death in 1272. The courtyard has a well and outside stair, and the palace was radically restored in 1905–13.

B. Museo Archeologico, the Archiginnasio, and San Domenico

Via dell'Archiginnasio skirts the left flank of San Petronio. Beneath the marble paved *Portico del Pavaglione*, with elegant uniform shop fronts, the windows enclosed in tall wooden frames, is the entrance to the **Museo Civico Archeologico** (Pl. 11), which is especially important for its Etruscan antiquities (adm. 9–14, except Monday; fest. 9–12.30).

Ground Floor. VESTIBULE: two large cylindrical Etruscan sandstone monuments of uncertain significance (found in Bologna in 1985); Roman tombs; well-head; torso of an Imperial statue; Roman mosaic floors.— COURTYARD (the former cloister of Santa Maria della Morte): Milestone from the Via Aemilia; blocks from Roman bridges; slab inscribed with an electoral programme. A door off the courtyard (left) admits to the *Museo del Risorgimento* and an exhibition gallery. At the foot of the stairs, reached through a glass door (unlocked on request) a second courtyard has architectural fragments of the 14–15C.
First Floor. ROOM 1: Remains from caves, lake dwellings, etc., in the neighbourhood of Bologna.—RII: Prehistoric objects, comparatively arranged.—RRIII–V: *Egyptian Antiquities.*—RVI: *Greek Antiquities,* including a *Head of Minerva, said to be a copy of the Athena Lemnia of Pheidias; head of a Greek; Attic sepulchral bas-relief (5C BC); fragment of an Augustan relief, showing a figure with a ram's head; the 'Cup of Codrus', a fine red-figured Attic vase, etc.—RVII: *Graeco-Roman Antiquities.*—RVIII: *Etruscan Antiquities,* including realistic terracottas from a temple at Città Alba, near Sassoferrato (2C BC).—RIX: Smaller Roman antiquities, including ivory reliefs, bronze statuettes, utensils, etc.

ROOM X. *Antiquities from the burial-grounds of Felsina, the Umbro-Etruscan predecessor of Bologna, and other Etruscan remains. In the first section, tombs from various Etruscan sites around Bologna. In the main section is tomb-furniture illustrating the development of the Umbrian (9–6C BC) and Etruscan (6C–mid-4C) civilisation. The Umbrian tombs contain urns with scratched, painted, and (later) stamped geometric decoration, while the Etruscan tombs bear reliefs in sandstone, and contain Greek vases (the so-called 'Etruscan' ware) and various objects of daily use in bronze, bone, etc. Along the window-wall are vessels from the tombs, including the best Attic vases, and a bronze *Situla (5C BC), from the Certosa of Bologna, with a ceremonial procession. In the left wing are objects showing relations with foreign races, and the oldest Umbrian tomb (? 9C BC), with contents of a Late Bronze Age type.

ROOM XI. Recent excavations, including finds from the necropolis of Giardini Margherita.—RXII displays Gaulish tombs with weapons and ornaments, and Roman objects. Also, mosaic panel of 1C AD from Claterna.
  The MEDIEVAL AND RENAISSANCE sections of the museum have been removed to Palazzo Fava (see Rte 40F).

In the narrow road to the left of the museum, next to the indoor market, is the church of **Santa Maria della Vita**, rebuilt in 1687–90 with a cupola. On the right of the high altar is the dramatic *Lamentation over the Dead Christ, in terracotta, a superb work by Nicolò dell'Arca, thought to date from 1463 (recently restored). In an oratory of the hospital administration on the first floor is a Dormition of the Virgin, an early work in terracotta by Alfonso Lombardi.

Farther along the Portico del Pavaglione is the **Archiginnasio** (Pl. 11), built by Antonio Morandi in 1562–65 to accommodate in one building the various schools of the University, which had its seat here until 1800. The upper floor is shown by the porter on request (9–13).

The courtyard, corridors, and stairways, as well as the classrooms are covered with escutcheons of former rectors and professors, in relief or fresco. The *Anatomical Theatre was built in 1637 by Antonio Levanti. By the 14C the university had acquired notoriety as the first school where the dissection of the human body was practiced. The theatre, entirely built and decorated in wood, was seriously damaged in the last War, but it has been beautifully restored using the original material. The baldacchino over the reader's chair is supported by two remarkable anatomical figures by Ercole Lelli (1734).—In the Aula Magna Rossini's 'Stabat Mater' was given its first performance under the direction of Donizetti. From here can be seen the long series of school rooms, now part of the **Biblioteca Comunale** (adm. Monday–Friday 9–18.45) with c 700,000 vols and 12,000 MSS.

In front of the building are a piazza and a monument commemorating Luigi Galvani (1737–98), the physicist. Across Via Farini, Via Garibaldi (left) continues to the cobbled PIAZZA SAN DOMENICO (Pl. 15). Here are tall columns bearing statues of St Dominic (1627) and the Madonna (1633), and the tombs (being restored) of Rolandino de'Passeggeri (1300) and Egidio Foscherari (1289), with their original canopies restored. The church of *San Domenico (Pl. 15; closed 12–15.30) was dedicated by Innocent IV in 1251 to St Dominic, founder of the order of Preaching Friars, who died here in 1221 two years after establishing the convent on this site. The church, several times enlarged, is interesting chiefly for the works of art in its interior, remodelled by Carlo Francesco Dotti (1728–31).

INTERIOR. 6th chapel (S aisle), dedicated to St Dominic, was rebuilt in 1597–1605, and restored in 1843 and again in 1883 (if closed, apply to the sacristan). In the centre is the *ARCA DI SAN DOMENICO a masterpiece of sculpture to which many artists contributed. The monumental sarcophagus of St Dominic (died 1221) was carved with scenes from the Saint's life in high relief in 1267 on a design by Nicolò Pisano, mostly by his pupils, including Fra' Guglielmo and Arnolfo di Cambio. The lid of the sarcophagus is decorated with statuettes and festoons by Nicolò dell'Arca who took his name from this work. After Nicolò's death in 1492, Michelangelo, who was staying for a year in the city in 1495 (at the age of 20) with Gianfrancesco Aldovrandi, carved three statuettes: the right-hand angel bearing a candelabrum (the other is by Nicolò dell'Arca), St Petronius holding a model of Bologna, and (behind) St Proculus (with a cloak over his shoulder). Girolamo Corbellini carved the last statue (St John the Baptist) in 1539. The sculpted scenes in relief below the sarcophagus and between the two kneeling angels are by Alfonso Lombardi (1532). The altar beneath dates from the 18C. Behind the tomb in a niche is a reliquary by Jacopo Roseto da Bologna (1383) which encloses the Saint's skull. In the apse of the chapel is the *Glory of St Dominic, by Guido Reni; on the right of the entrance, St Dominic raising a dead child, by Alessandro Tiarini; on the left, St Dominic burning heretical books, by Lionello Spada.—SOUTH TRANSEPT. Guercino, St Thomas

Aquinas. Here marquetry doors by *Fra' Damiano Zambelli* (1538) lead into the SACRISTY.

From the Sacristy there is access to the Choir via a room of the MUSEUM (seen through glass doors), closed indefinitely. It contains a *Bust of St Dominic (1474), a very fine work in polychrome terracotta by *Nicolò dell'Arca*, and paintings (including *Lippo di Dalmasio*, Madonna del Velluto, and a detached fresco of Charity and St Francis by *Lodovico Carracci*), as well as church vestments, hangings, and books of anthems.—The CHOIR has *Stalls in marquetry by *Fra' Damiano da Bergamo* (1541–51). The painting of the Magi is by *Bartolomeo Cesi*.—A marquetry door opposite the sacristy (usually unlocked) admits to the charming CLOISTER OF THE DEAD, its fourth side closed by the exterior of the apse and cupola of the chapel of San Domenico. Here is a much ruined fresco of the Holy Trinity by *Pietro Cianori*. Off the Chiostro Maggiore is ST DOMINIC'S CELL (normally shown on request by a monk), with relics of the Saint and a 13C painting of him.

In the little chapel to the right of the Choir, Marriage of St Catherine, signed by *Filippino Lippi* (1501).—NORTH TRANSEPT. Inscription (1731) marking the tomb of King Enzo. In the adjoining chapel is a 14C wall monument (altered in the 16C) to Taddeo Pepoli, and a painted Crucifix signed by *Giunta Pisano*. On the wall of the transept has been placed a detached fresco fragment of the Madonna and Saints by the late-14C Emilian school, found on a pilaster in the apse (and restored). In the Chapel of the Relics at the end of the transept is the tomb of Beato Giacomo da Ulma (Jacob of Ulm), the painter on glass, who died at Bologna in 1491.—NORTH AISLE. In the chapel opposite the chapel of San Domenico is an altarpiece of fifteen small paintings of the Mysteries of the Rosary by *Ludovico Carracci*, *Bartolomeo Cesi*, *Dionigi Calvaert*, *Guido Reni*, and *Francesco Albani*. Reni and Elisabetta Sirani are buried in this chapel (inscription on the left wall). In the porch leading to the side door is the funerary monument of Alessandro Tartagni by *Francesco Ferrucci* (1477).—On the 2nd altar, St Raimondo by *Ludovico Carracci*.

To the S of San Domenico, at the end of Via Garibaldi is the *Palazzo di Giustizia* occupying Palazzo Ruini, with an imposing Palladian façade and courtyard (1584).

To the N of San Domenico is Via Rolandino. On the left is the charming *Casa Gradi* or *dei Carracci* (15–16C); No. 2, opposite, has a curious trompe l'oeil niche in the courtyard. Beyond Piazza Calderini, at No. 15 Via Farini (right) is the *Casa Saraceni*, a gracious building of the late 15C. **Via Castiglione** (Pl. 11,15) is a fine old street which leads away from the centre of the city to an old city gate. Here at No. 47 is the 15C *Casa Bolognesi*.

From San Domenico, San Giovanni in Monte (see below) is a short way E.

C. The Due Torri, Santo Stefano, and San Giovanni in Monte

PIAZZA DI PORTA RAVEGNANA is dominated by the famous ***Due Torri** (Pl. 11), two leaning towers one of which is exceptionally tall. At one time some 180 towers existed in the city.

The **Torre degli Asinelli**, thought to have been built by the Asinelli family, or by the Comune (1109–19), is 97·5m high and leans 1·23m out of the perpendicular (to the W). The masonry at the base was added in 1488. A flight of 500 steps leads up to the top (open every day 9–19).—The *Torre Garisenda*, built by the Garisendi family at the same time as the other, was left unfinished owing to the subsidence of the soil, and was shortened for safety in 1351–60. It is now only

48m high and leans 3·22m out of the perpendicular (to the S); but it was higher when Dante wrote the descriptive verses ('Inferno', xxxi, 136) inscribed at the base of the tower.—No. 1 in the piazza is the *Casa dei Drappieri* (1486–96), with a balcony added in 1620.

Five old roads lead from here out of the city; each one ends in a gate on the line of the old city walls. The towers are now isolated by traffic; especially busy is the wide Via Rizzoli, one of the least attractive streets in the centre of Bologna. The subway beneath preserves Roman mosaics found during its construction. Adjoining Piazza di Porta Ravegnana is Piazza Mercanzia with the *PALAZZO DELLA MERCANZIA, or Chamber of Commerce, perhaps the best-preserved example of ornamented Italian-Gothic in the city. It was built in 1382–84 from the plans of Antonio di Vincenzo and Lorenzo da Bagnomarino, and has been several times skilfully restored, though the wing (1840), overlooking Via Castiglione, is not in harmony. VIA SANTO STEFANO (Pl. 11, 16) is lined by some fine 15–16C *Mansions, notably Nos 9–11 *Palazzo Salina-Bolognini*, begun in 1525, in the style of Formigine, and No. 16–18 *Palazzo Isolani* by Pagno di Lapo Portigiani (1455). In Via de'Pepoli (right) is the 17C *Palazzo Pepoli-Campogrande* (with frescoes by Donato Creti and Giuseppe Maria Crespi) which houses some 18C paintings from the Pinacoteca (see Rte 40E), open to the public in July and August. Adjoining is Palazzo Pepoli (Nos 6–10 Via Castiglione), a huge Gothic building begun in 1344 by Taddeo Pepoli and restored in 1925.

The basilica of Santo Stefano in Bologna

The street opens out in front of the basilica of ***Santo Stefano** (Pl. 11), an ancient and picturesque group of monastic buildings, mentioned as early as 887, and dedicated as a whole to St Stephen the Martyr. Three churches face the piazza: Santi Vitale e Agricola, the oldest ecclesiastical building in the city, San Sepolcro, and the Crocifisso, with a 12C pulpit on its front.

The CROCIFISSO, restored in 1924, has a painted Crucifix by Simone de'Crocifissi (c 1380) hanging in the raised Choir. The crypt has some 11C details and a jumble of capitals. The 18C Pietà is the work of Angelo Piò, and the Aldrovandi tomb dates from 1438.—On the left is the entrance to the polygonal church of SAN SEPOLCRO, perhaps founded as a baptistery in the 5C, but dating in its present form from the 11C. It has a brick cupola and interesting architectural details. In the centre is an imagined imitation of the Holy Sepulchre at Jerusalem, difficult to appreciate since the Romanesque pulpit and 19C stair and altar were placed against it in the 19C. In the centre, behind a grille, is the tomb of St Petronius.—To the left again is the church of SANTI VITALE E AGRICOLA, a venerable building perhaps of the 5C, with massive columns and capitals, incorporating many fragments of Roman buildings. The three apses (rebuilt in the 8C and 11C) are lit by tiny alabaster windows. The altars in the side-aisles are the original sarcophagi of the 4C martyrs, Saints Vitalis and Agricola (the one in the right apse was removed in 1988).—From San Sepolcro the entrance to the CORTILE DI PILATO (12C), an open court with colonnades; in the middle is 'Pilate's Bowl' (8C) bearing an obscure inscription relating to the Lombard kings Luitprand and Ilprand. The beautifully patterned brickwork of the exterior of San Sepolcro can be seen here. On a pillar in a little window is a delightful cockerel sculpted in the 14C.—Off the court is the church of the MARTYRIUM (also called *Santa Croce* or *Santa Trinità*), with a façade reconstructed in 1911. The chapel, much altered, has good capitals and remains of 14–15C frescoes. In the end chapel is a charming group of wood statues of the Adoration of the Magi painted by Simone dei Crocifissi (c 1370).—A door from the Cortile leads into the *CLOISTER, which has two beautiful colonnades, the lower one dating from the 11C, and the upper from the 12C, with fine capitals. Here can be seen the Romanesque Campanile.

There is a small MUSEUM off the cloister (adm. 9–12, 15.30–17.30). In the room to the right: *Jacopo di Paolo*, Triptych; *Michele di Matteo*, Scenes from the life of Saints Petronius and Stephen (fresco); works by *Simone dei Crocifissi*, the *Ferrarese school*, and *Lippo di Dalmasio* (Madonna and Child).—To the left is the Cappella della Benda, with reliquaries including that of St Petronius (by *Jacopo di Roseto*, 1370), and a detached 13C fresco of the Massacre of the Innocents with St Julian.

Across Via Santo Stefano and Via Farini, on a little hill stands the church of ***San Giovanni in Monte** (Pl. 11; closed 12–15.30). The church can be approached either by the side entrance off Via Santo Stefano through an impressive long 17C vaulted gallery which rises to the door in the N aisle, or from Via Farini and the piazza. The church is of ancient foundation attributed to St Petronius, but in its present form it is a 13C Gothic building with extensive 15C additions. The façade is in the Venetian-Gothic style, with a great portal by *Domenico Berardi* (1474), and above it an eagle in painted terracotta by *Nicolò dell'Arca*. Three of the N chapels were destroyed in the last War. The campanile dates from the 13–14C.

The pleasant INTERIOR consists of a nave and aisles separated by columns partly decorated with frescoes by *Giacomo* and *Giulio Francia*. Light switches can be turned on in each chapel to see the fine works of art. On the W wall the stained glass tondo of St John the Evangelist is a good work by the *Cabrini* on a design by *Lorenzo Costa* or *Francesco del Cossa* (1481). On the left of the entrance is another window with the Madonna and Child designed by *Francesco del Cossa*. In the centre of the church rises a Romanesque Cross on an inverted Roman pillar capital, with a figure of Christ in figwood attributed to *Alfonso Lombardi*.

SOUTH AISLE. 1st chapel, *Girolamo da Treviso* (also attributed to *Giacomo Francia*), Noli me tangere; 2nd chapel, *Bartolomeo Cesi*, Crucifix, and a terracotta statue of St Thomas Becket.—3rd chapel, *Pietro Faccini*, *Martyrdom of St Lawrence. On the pillar between the 4th and 5th chapel is a simple sculpted 15C Pietà in a frescoed niche.—6th chapel, *Lippo di Dalmasio*, Madonna 'della Pace' (fresco).—The 7th chapel, built in c 1497, contains a *Madonna enthroned with saints, by *Lorenzo Costa* (1497).—In the Sacristy and parish offices is a precious collection of reliquaries, church silver, vestments, etc, as well as some paintings and sculptures (adm. only to scholars).—CHOIR. The inlaid stalls are by *Paolo Sacca* (1523), and the busts of apostles above them, by *Zaccaria da Volterra*. The *Madonna in glory on the E wall is another fine work by *Lorenzo Costa*. On the left wall has been hung a *Crucifix by *Jacopino da Bologna*. The NORTH TRANSEPT is a good architectural work of 1514 showing Tuscan influence, built for the blessed Elena Duglioli Dall'Oglio (1472–1520) who is buried here. She also commissioned the famous St Cecilia altarpiece for the chapel from Raphael (now in the Pinacoteca, see Rte 40E), substituted here by a poor copy still enclosed in the original frame by *Formigine*. The four gilded angel candelabra are attributed to the bottega of *Francia*.

NORTH AISLE. On the pillar outside the 6th chapel, *Ercole de'Maria*, Annunciation. On the pillar between the 6th and 5th chapel, *Francesco Gessi*, Christ calling the Apostles.—5th chapel, *Luigi Crespi*, Holy Family; 4th chapel, gilded wood bust of St Petronius (15C). Set into the pilaster, small relief depicting the Martyrdom of St Thomas Becket.—2nd chapel, a fine Baroque work. St Francis and (at the sides) Saints Jerome and Mary Magdalene, all by *Guercino*.

Vicolo Monticelli descends to **Via Castiglione**, described in Rte 40B.

D.   The Strada Maggiore

From the Due Torri (see above) the STRADA MAGGIORE (Pl. 11, 12), one of the most attractive old streets of the city, runs SE on the line of the Via Aemilia. At the beginning, beside the Due Torri, is the church of **San Bartolomeo** (Pl. 11). The portico was richly decorated by *Formigine* in 1515 but it is now very ruined and the decoration is almost totally worn away. A 16C portal is in better condition. The ornate interior, with small domes over the side aisles, is largely the work of *Giovanni Battista Natali* (1653–84). In the fourth chapel of the S aisle is an *Annunciation by *Francesco Albani* (1632). The tondo of the Madonna in the N transept is by *Guido Reni*.—Farther on in the Strada Maggiore is a series of characteristic Bolognese mansions, of all periods from the 13C to the 19C, some of them restored. Among the finest are the *Casa della Fondazione Gioannetti* (No. 13), with Gothic windows and polychrome decoration; *Casa Gelmi* (No. 26), built for Gioacchino Rossini, the composer, from designs by Francesco Santini (1824–27); *Casa Isolani* (No. 19), a characteristic 13C dwelling-house, with a tiny upper storey on tall wooden brackets; *Palazzo Sanguinetti* (No. 34) with a rich 16C cornice; and *Casa Reggiani* (Nos 38–40), a large 15C mansion with an arcaded court.

Beyond opens the PIAZZA DEI SERVI (Pl. 12), with its porticoes. Here, at No. 44, is **Palazzo Davia-Bargellini**, built in 1638, and known as the 'Palazzo dei Giganti' from the two atlantes flanking the gateway. The fine staircase dates from 1730. It contains, on the ground floor, the **Museo Civico d'Arte Industriale** and the **Galleria Davia-Bargellini** (Pl. 12; adm. Tuesday–Saturday, 9–14; fest. 9–12.30).

The museum was founded in 1924 by Malaguzzi Valeri and it still preserves the character of its original arrangement. The museum of decorative arts includes domestic artefacts, wrought-iron work, ceramics, an 18C puppet theatre, wood carvings, Emilian furniture, etc. The paintings include works by *Vitale da Bologna, Bartolomeo Vivarini, Giuseppe Maria Crespi, Garofalo, Marcantonio Franceschini, Marco Meloni*, and *Joseph Heintz the Younger*. There is also a good collection of terracottas by *Giuseppe Maria Mazza*.

The four porticoes of Piazza dei Servi, built in a consistent style at various periods from the 14C to 1855 are a continuation of the wide arcades in the Strada Maggiore alongside the church of **Santa Maria dei Servi** (Pl. 12), begun in 1346 and enlarged after 1386, one of the most attractive Gothic buildings in Bologna.

INTERIOR (very dark). SOUTH AISLE. 4th chapel, *Denys Calvaert*, Paradise (1602). On the left pillar outside the 6th chapel, Madonna and Child, a fragment of a fresco attributed to *Lippo di Dalmasio*. The finely carved MAIN ALTAR is the work of *Giovanni Antonio Montorsoli* (1558–61). The CHOIR (entered by a door off the ambulatory) contains good Gothic stalls (1450; completed in 1617).—Outside the door into the Sacristy, frescoes by *Vitale da Bologna* have been uncovered on the vault and walls (restored), which survive from the 14C church. AMBULATORY. *Lippo di Dalmasio*, Polyptych of the Madonna enthroned with Saints; *Vincenzo Onofri*, Madonna and Child between Saints Laurence and Eustace, with the Deposition above, a delightful high relief in terracotta. In the chapel to the left of the E chapel, *Cimabue*, *Madonna enthroned (light on the right). On the choir wall, Grati monument by *Vincenzo Onofrio*.—NORTH AISLE. 6th chapel, Annunciation by *Innocenzo da Imola*, in a frame by *Formigine*. 5th chapel, Byzantine Madonna and Child (c 1261). Around the side door, elaborate monument to Cardinal Gozzadini (died 1536) by *Giovanni Zacchi*. 2nd chapel, *Francesco Albani*, Noli me tangere.

In Via Guerrazzi to the S are (No. 13) the *Accademia Filarmonica*, founded in 1666, to which Mozart was elected in 1770 at the age of fourteen, and (No. 20) the *Flemish College* (1650).

At No. 5 in Viale Carducci, on the right beyond Porta Maggiore, is the *Casa di Carducci* (open 9–12, Sunday and festivals 9–13), where the poet Giosuè Carducci lived in 1890–1907. There is a collection of MSS, and a library of over 40,000 vols. Outside is a monument by Leonardo Bistolfi (1928).

Piazza Aldrovandi, with chestnut trees and a street market, leads N to Via San Vitale. Here on the left, beyond an old city gate (11–12C) is the church of *Santi Vitale ed Agricola* (Pl. 12), rebuilt in 1824, except for its 12C crypt (unlocked on request). It is dedicated to two saints martyred under Diocletian in the Arena, thought to have been in this area. Inside, the large 15C chapel on the left contains a Crucifix and Flight into Egypt (right wall) by Alessandro Tiarini, and (right and left of the altar), frescoes of the Nativity (attributed to Giacomo Francia) and of the Visitation (by Bagnocavallo).—Opposite is the long oddly proportioned façade of *Palazzo Fantuzzi* (begun in 1517), decorated with two elephants in relief, and with a fine Baroque staircase.—It is a short way back from here, by Via San Vitale, to the Due Torri.

E. San Giacomo Maggiore, the University, and the Pinacoteca Nazionale

From the Due Torri Via Zamboni (Pl.11,7 & 8) leads away from the centre of the city. A short way along opens PIAZZA ROSSINI (Pl. 7) with the church of San Giacomo next to the *Conservatorio Giovanni*

Battista Martini where Rossini studied in 1806–10, with one of the most important music libraries in Europe, and a portrait gallery (adm. 8.30–13; closed Sunday and fest.). Opposite is *Palazzo Malvezzi de'Medici*, by Bartolomeo Triachini (1560). On Via Zamboni, facing the piazza, is *Palazzo Salem (Magnani)* by Domenico Tibaldi (1577–87), now the headquarters of a bank. In the salone are beautiful frescoes of the Founding of Rome by the Carracci (1588–91). These are at present covered for restoration, but are normally shown on request. Next door is *Palazzo Malvezzi-Campeggi* (No. 22), by Formigine, with a good courtyard. The Romanesque church of *San Giacomo Maggiore* (Pl. 7), was begun in 1267 and enlarged in succeeding centuries (restored in 1915). The top of the façade has majolica decoration, and on either side of the canopied doorway are recesses for tombs.

INTERIOR (closed 12–15.30). The aisleless NAVE is surmounted by a bold vault of unusually wide span. The side chapels are crowned by a terracotta frieze of statues and urns (by Pietro Becchetti, 1765). On the W wall a fresco of the Adoration of the Magi, with Christ in Pietà in the lunette above, was discovered in 1986 and attributed to the school of *Francia* (still covered for restoration). SOUTH SIDE. In the 5th chapel, Madonna and Saints, by *Bartolomeo Passarotti* (1565); 7th chapel, Marriage of St Catherine, by *Innocenzo da Imola*, in a frame by Formigine; 9th chapel, St Roch comforted by an angel, by *Ludovico Carracci*; the 11th chapel was designed by *Pellegrino Tibaldi*, who also painted the frescoes.—Beyond the Sacristy steps lead up into the AMBULATORY. On the left wall, *Jacopo di Paolo*, large painted Crucifix (c 1420). 2nd chapel, *Lorenzo Veneziano*, Polyptych (1368; removed for restoration), a part of which is now in the Brera in Milan. On the walls, damaged frescoes of the life of St Mary of Egypt by *Cristoforo da Bologna*. 3rd chapel, *Jacopo di Paolo*, Polyptych, and (on the wall), Crucifix, signed by *Simone de'Crocifissi* (1370). In the 4th chapel have been temporarily placed four detached frescoes from the tomb recesses on the façade: very damaged these date from the late 13C.—Opposite, on the choir wall is the funerary monument of a philosopher and a doctor, both called Nicolò Fava, by a follower of Jacopo della Quercia.—The *CAPPELLA BENTIVOGLIO at the end of the N aisle, was founded in 1445 by Annibale Bentivoglio, and enlarged for Giovanni II, probably by *Pagno di Lapo Portigiani* (restored in 1952–53). Its altarpiece is a *Virgin with four saints and two angel musicians, by *Francesco Francia* (c 1488). The *Frescoes from the Apocalypse (in the lunette above the altar; removed for restoration), of the Triumph of Death (left wall), and the Madonna enthroned (right wall) with charming portraits of Giovanni II Bentivoglio and his family, are all by *Lorenzo Costa*. On the right wall is a relief of Annibale I on horseback, by an Emilian artist (1458). The worn floor-tiles date from 1489.— Opposite the chapel is the *Tomb of Anton Galeazzo Bentivoglio, father of Annibale, one of the last works of *Jacopo della Quercia* and assistants (1435).

The ORATORY OF SANTA CECILIA (entered from No. 15 under the side portico of the church; unlocked on request by the sacristan) has interesting *Frescoes of the lives of Saints Cecilia and Valerian, by *Francesco Francia* and *Lorenzo Costa*, and their pupils, including *Amico Aspertini*. They were painted in 1504–6 by order of Giovanni II Bentivoglio. They have been recently detached and restored. The altarpiece of the Crucifixion is also by *Francesco Francia*.

Along the side of the church a delightful vaulted portico of 1477–81, with good capitals and decorated with terracotta, perhaps by Sperandio, connects Piazza Rossini with Piazza Verdi. Here is the best view of the fine brick campanile (1472). The *Teatro Comunale* by Antonio Bibbiena (1763; façade 1933) here occupies the site of the great palace of the Bentivoglio, which was destroyed in a riot in 1507 and left in ruins until the 18C ('il Guasto'). Beyond, Via Zamboni is now lined with buildings used by the various faculties of the **University**. Its headquarters have been installed since 1803 in *Palazzo Poggi* (No. 33; Pl. 8), built by Pellegrino Tibaldi (1549). The courtyard is ascribed to Bartolomeo Triachini. The palace contains frescoes of Ulysses by Pellegrino Tibaldi.

The university ('Studio'), the oldest in Italy, was founded in the second half of the 11C, and was already famous a century later, especially after Irnerius, chief of the Glossators, had taught here between 1070 and 1100. He revived the study of the Roman system of jurisprudence, which his disciples spread over Europe, sending in 1144 to England Vacarius, founder of the law school at Oxford. In return, many Englishmen and Scotsmen served as rectors at Bologna. Petrarch was taught here, and here Copernicus started on the study of astronomy; and in 1789 it became renowned for the discovery of galvanism. The number of its female professors is remarkable, among them being the learned Novella d'Andrea (14C), Laura Bassi (1711–88), mathematician and scientist, and mother of twelve, and Clotilde Tambroni, professor of Greek in 1794–1817.

The UNIVERSITY LIBRARY (No. 35 Via Zamboni, October–June: 9–19, Saturday 9–14; July–September: 9–14, Saturday 9–12; closed 1–15 September and on Sunday) contains over 800,000 vols and 9000 MSS and autographs and has a fine 18C reading-room. Here Cardinal Mezzofanti (1774–1849), who spoke 50 languages and was called by Byron 'the universal interpreter', was librarian, and his own library is added to the collection.

The *Museo Storico dello Studio*, and numerous other scientific collections belonging to the University can be seen by previous appointment (Tel. 512151), daily except Monday, 9.30–12.30, 15.30–18.30. The curious *Torre dell'Osservatorio* dates from 1725. Other faculty buildings are in Via San Giacomo, and in Via Irnerio, to the N.

On Via delle Belle Arti is the *Accademia di Belle Arti* installed in an old Jesuit college, with a handsome courtyard containing a good 16C well-head. In this building is the ***Pinacoteca Nazionale** (Pl. 8) one of the most important collections of painting in northern Italy (adm. 9–14; Sunday and fest. 9–12.30; closed Monday). The gallery is especially important for its pictures of the Bolognese school. It also has paintings by artists who worked in Bologna (including Giotto, Raphael, and Perugino). Acquisitions have augmented the 17C and 18C works. The paintings are arranged by period and school. The room numbers follow those on the Plan on p 454.

At the top of the entrance stairs three galleries (4) around the cloister display the BOLOGNESE SCHOOL OF THE 14C. Several works by *Vitale da Bologna*, including *St George and the dragon; *Jacopino da Bologna*, Polyptych; *Giovanni da Modena*, Crucifix; works by *Simone de'Crocifissi*.—In R. 5 (off the last gallery) are works by *Giotto* and his school (fine polyptych); *Lorenzo Monaco*, Madonna enthroned; *Byzantine School (late 13C)*, Three panels of the life of Christ.—Up a short flight of steps, R. 6 has local 14C works, and in R. 7 begins the 15C BOLOGNESE SCHOOL, including two Crucifixes by *Michele di Matteo*.—Rooms 8–10 display detached *Frescoes (and sinopie) by *Vitale da Bologna* and his pupils from Mezzaratta.—The most important works of the 15–16C are displayed in the Long Gallery (11), reached by steps up from R. 8. In the first section, the VENETIAN SCHOOL (A): *Antonio and Bartolomeo Vivarini*, Polyptych; *Cima da Conegliano*, *Madonna; *Marco Zoppo*, St Jerome.—FERRARESE SCHOOL (B): *Franceso del Cossa*, *Madonna enthroned.—Section C:

PINACOTECA NAZIONALE
Bologna

Ercole de'Roberti, *St Michael Archangel, a Mary in mourning (fresco fragment); *Lorenzo Costa*, Madonna enthroned with Saints, Saints Petronius, Francis, and Dominic.—BOLOGNESE SCHOOL (D). *Francesco Francia*, *Felicini altarpiece, Dead Christ, two paxes.—Section E: *Francesco Francia*, Annunciation and Saints.—Section F: *Amico Aspertini*, Adoration of the Child and Saints.—At the end (G), *Raphael*, *Ecstasy of St Cecilia, one of his most famous works. It was commissioned for San Giovanni in Monte, see Rte 40C. *Perugino*, Madonna and Saints; *Giulio Romano* (?) St John the Baptist (a copy from Raphael); *Franciabigio*, Madonna and Child; *Giuliano Bugiardini*, Madonna and Child with St John.—Section K: *Parmigianino*, *Madonna and Saints from the church of St Margaret; works by the 16C Emilian mannerists, including *Bartolomeo Passarotti*, *Camillo Procaccini*, and *Pellegrino Tibaldi*.—Section M: 15–16C FOREIGN SCHOOLS. Pseudo *De Bles*, Esther and Ahasuerus; *El Greco*, Last Supper, an early work. *Titian*, Crucifixion (a fragment, recently restored).

Beyond a long narrow corridor (12) used for exhibitions, steps descend into R. 13 with Mannerist paintings including the Dinner of St Gregory the Great by *Giorgio Vasari* and frescoes from Palazzo Fava with scenes from the story of Jason by *Annibale* and *Agostino Carracci*, and the Trojans attacked by Harpies, by *Annibale* (1587). In the little R. 13A, Annunciation by *Annibale Carracci*.—R. 14 contains large works by *Annibale*, *Ludovico*, and *Agostino Carracci*, including the Madonna Bargellini by *Ludovico* and the last Communion of St Jerome by *Agostino*.—At the bottom of another short flight of steps (which encircle a model by *Bernini* for his famous fountain in the centre of Piazza Navona, Rome), R. 15 displays works by *Guido Reni*, notably the large *Pietà dei Mendicanti, with a model of Bologna.—To the left is R. 21, a gallery of Bolognese 17–18C paintings (works by *Francesco Albani* and a supposed portrait of his mother by *Guido Reni*). The small rooms off the gallery (16–19) contain works by *Guercino Domenichino*, and *Francesco Albani*; *Giuseppe Maria Crespi*, the *Gandolfi*, and *Donato Creti*. etc. The hall at the end (used for lectures, etc.) is hung with six huge altarpieces: *Domenichino*, Martyrdom of St Agnes; *Ludovico Carracci*, Birth of St John the Baptist; *Guercino*, St Bruno; *Franceso Albani*, Baptism of Christ; *Domenichino*, Madonna of the Rosary; *Ludovico Carracci*, Transfiguration; *Carlo Cignani*, Madonna and Child with Saints.—There is also a small room with frescoes by *Nicolò dell'Abate* from the Palazzo Zucchini-Solimei.

The rest of the collection of 18C paintings is housed in Palazzo Pepoli-Campogrande, see Rte 40C, only open in July and August. The 19C works have been moved to the Galleria d'Arte Moderna, see Rte 40G.

Near the other end of Via delle Belle Arti is (No. 8) the majestic *Palazzo Bentivoglio* (No. 8; Pl. 7), built to a design perhaps by Bartolomeo Triachini in 1550–60 (it is in very bad condition). From here Via Mentana (left) leads to the basilica of SAN MARTINO (Pl. 7), founded in 1217. It was remodelled in the mid–15C, and the façade rebuilt in 1879, and the apses restored in 1929.

INTERIOR. South Side. In the 1st chapel, Adoration of the Magi, by *Girolamo da Carpi*; and on the last altar, *Amico Aspertini*, Madonna and Saints. On a pilaster here, fragment of a head of Christ from a Crucifixion by *Vitale da Bologna*. In the Sanctuary, the pretty organ by Giovanni Cipri dates from 1556. North Side. Beside the Sacristy door, fresco fragments, including a figure of Abraham, and a Madonna by *Simone de'Crocifissi*. 5th altar, *Lorenzo Costa*, Assumption; 4th altar, *Ludovico Carracci*, St Jerome; 3rd altar, *Bartolomeo Cesi*, Crucifixion. The 1st chapel was built in 1506. *Francesco Francia*, Madonna and Saints, and (above, in the same frame), *Amico Aspertini*, Deposition. The statue of the Madonna is attributed to *Jacopo della Quercia*. Here also is a fresco fragment of the Nativity, recently uncovered and attributed to *Paolo Uccello* (very difficult to see).
    The interesting Via Marsala, across Via Oberdan, has good medieval houses, one with high wooden brackets. At No. 12 is *Casa Grassi* (late 13C).
    The Cathedral (see below) is a short way to the South (see the Plan).

F. The Duomo, Museo Medievale, and San Francesco

From Piazza Nettuno and Via Rizzoli (Pl. 11) VIA DELL'INDIPENDENZA, the busy long main street, opened in 1888, leads N towards the Railway Station.

Via dell'Indipendenza ends at the *Montagnola* (Pl. 3), a public garden laid out around the mound formed over the ruins of the citadel of Galliera. Beyond it is *Porta Galliera* (1661). The *Railway Station* (Pl. 2) is just to the W. A bomb placed by right-wing terrorists in the station waiting-room in August 1980 killed 85 people and wounded 200 others. On the other side of the railway is the *Sacro Cuore*, a large church in the Byzantine style (begun in 1877 and completed in 1912; the dome was rebuilt in 1934).

A short way up Via dell'Indipendenza, on the right, is the **Cathedral**, or *Chiesa Metropolitana* (Pl. 7), dedicated to St Peter. Founded very early (probably before the 10C), it was rebuilt several times after 1605, and exists now in the form of a Baroque building of the 17C, though the elaborate W front is by *Alfonso Torreggiani* (18C). The nave is by *Floriano Ambrosini* from designs by *Giovanni Magenta*, and the choir is the work of *Domenico Tibaldi* (1575). The crypt and the fine campanile are the sole remains of the Romanesque building, except for the two delightful lions of red Verona marble (1220), inside the W door, which once supported the porch, and the stoup at the E end of the S aisle, which has been hollowed out of an old capital.

In the second chapel of the S aisle is preserved the skull of St Anne, presented in 1435 by Henry VI of England to Nicolò Albergati, better known as the Cardinal of Santa Croce. Above the inner arch of the choir is an Annunciation, frescoed by *Ludovico Carracci*, and in the crypt (unlocked by the sacristan) are a 12C Crucifixion group carved in cedar-wood and a large terracotta group in the manner of *Alfonso Lombardi*.

The area behind the cathedral is an interesting survival of medieval Bologna, with many old houses and remains of the towers erected by patrician families. Via Altobello follows the right side of the cathedral past the tall Campanile (begun 1184) and an old tower on the corner of another road of old houses. Via Sant'Alò continues left with another tower and Via Albiroli has a shorter tower and a pretty house on the corner of Via Goito.

On the opposite side of Via dell'Indipendenza is the Hotel Baglioni with interesting frescoes and remains of Roman buildings. Via Manzoni leads to Via Galliera past the *Madonna di Galliera*, a church remodelled in 1479, with a fine Renaissance façade (restored in 1906, but in poor condition). Opposite, beneath a raised portico is the entrance to *Palazzo Ghisilardi-Fava*, begun in 1483. Here is the **Museo Civico Medievale e del Rinascimento** (Pl. 6; adm. 9–14, Sunday 9–12.30; closed Tuesday & fest.). The city's important collection of medieval and Renaissance sculpture and applied arts has recently been beautifully rearranged here.

GROUND FLOOR. Off the attractive courtyard, with four unusual large carved brackets, are Rooms 1 & 2 with an interesting display illustrating the origins of the collections in the 17C and 18C, prior to the founding of the Museo Civico in 1881.—On the other side of the courtyard is R. 4 with imposing 14C tombs by the *Dalle Masegne* and others. RR. 5 & 6 display late Antique and medieval metal work and ivories including a bronze 13C Mosen *Ewer in the shape of a horse and rider. In R. 5 can be seen remains of the Imperial 'Palatium' in the first city walls, destroyed in 1116, found during restoration work on the palace.—R. 7 is dominated by the over life-size bronze and beaten copper statue of Pope Boniface VIII by *Manno Bandini* (1301), formerly on the façade of Palazzo Pubblico. The English 14C embroidered *Cope in 'opus anglicanum' has scenes from the lives of Christ and the Virgin.—Stairs lead down to the LOWER GROUND FLOOR. R. 9 has sculptural fragments and a statuette of St Peter Martyr by *Giovanni di Balduccio*.—R. 10 has remains of a Roman building on this site, and charming 14C tombs of university lecturers.—In R. 11 is the red marble tomb slab of Bartolomeo da Vernazza (died 1348).—R. 12. *Triptych of the Madonna and Child with Saints George and Peter, carved in bas-relief by *Jacopo della Quercia* (and his bottega), and an interesting recumbent image of a saint in stuccoed and painted wood by *Antonio Federighi*.—R. 13 displays several 15C floor tombs, and the tomb of Pietro Canonici (died 1502) attributed to *Vincenzo Onofrio*.—Stairs (or a lift) lead up to the FIRST FLOOR. Room 15 has a major collection of bronzes which include (on pedestals), the *Model for the Neptune Fountain by *Giambologna*, the first version of the famous *Mercury by the same artist, *St Michael and the devil, by *Alessandro Algardi*, and a bronze bust of Gregory XV by *Gian Lorenzo Bernini*.—RR. 17 & 22 contains the collection of applied arts. Among the more notable items are: a ceremonial sword and sheath given to Lodovico Bentivoglio by Pope Nicholas V (R. 17); a collection of European armour (R. 18); an ivory parade saddle (German, 15C) in R. 19; Turkish armour and *Bronzes from the 13C–15C (R. 20); RR. 21 & 22, Northern European ivories, and Venetian and German glass, including a rare blue glass *Cup with a gilt enamelled frieze, perhaps from the Barovier workshop in Murano (mid-15C), and two vessels probably made for the wedding of Giovanni Bentivoglio and Ginevra Sforza in 1464.—More rooms, frescoed by the *Carracci*, are to be opened to display the collection of musical instruments, and the Museum's celebrated holdings in majolica, including plates with the arms of Este-Gonzaga and the fable of Myrrha, with the coronation of Charles V, with the Farnese arms, and with those of Leo X; also the Presentation of the Vigin in Gubbio ware, by Maestro Giorgio (1542).

Via Manzoni enters **Via Galliera* (Pl. 6,3), the main N-S artery of the city before Via dell'Indipendenza was built (see above). It has been called, from the splendour of its palazzi, the 'Grand Canal' of Bologna. A short way to the right is *Palazzo Montanari* (1725) next to the church of *Santa Maria Maggiore*, with two 16C statues of Mary Magdalen and St Roch attributed to Giovanni Zacchi (recently restored). In the other direction Via Porta di Castello ascends through an archway across Via Monte Grappa into the busy Via Ugo Bassi. Straight across a road skirts the interesting exterior of the huge Palazzo Comunale (described in Rte 40A) into Piazza Roosevelt.

An interesting detour may be made from here to the S, via Piazza Galileo and Via Val d'Aposa, where the charming little façade of **Santo Spirito** (Pl. 10), a gem of terracotta ornament, is in very good condition (well restored in 1893). Beyond is the church of *San Paolo*, by Giovanni Magenta (1611), with a façade of 1636. The Collegio di Spagna leads along the right side of the church to the ***Collegio di Spagna** (Pl. 10,14; adm. only with special permission), founded by Cardinal Albornoz in 1365 for Spanish students—the last survivor of the many colleges, resembling those at Oxford and Cambridge, which existed at Bologna in the Middle Ages. It still has a high scholastic reputation. Among its famous students were Ignatius Loyola and Cervantes. The main building is by Matteo Gattapone (1365); the gateway (1525; being restored) is probably the work of Bernardino da Milano (formerly attributed to Andrea da Formigine). The handsome courtyard has a double gallery; the chapel has an altarpiece by Marco Zoppo. Via Urbana follows the delightful garden wall of the College (part of the external painted decoration on the building can be seen from here), back to Via Tagliapietre. Here on the right is the church of CORPUS DOMINI, or *La Santa* (Pl. 14) built in 1478–80. The terracotta portal by Sperandio was reconstructed after its destruction in the last War. The only frescoes to survive in the interior are those by Marcantonio Franceschini in the cupola. In a 17C chapel (opened by a closed order of nuns) are preserved the relics of St Catherine de'Vigri (died 1463), an erudite ascetic of Bologna, greatly venerated.—Nearby, at No. 54 Via d'Azeglio, is **San Procolo** (Pl. 14), a church of ancient foundation, with a Romanesque façade. In the choir is an interesting Roman sarcophagus, probably decorated in the late 15C. The much faded lunette, formerly above the portal, with a Madonna and Saints by Lippo di Dalmasio, is now exhibited inside the church.—Farther on, in Via d'Azeglio, on the left is **Palazzo Bevilacqua** (Nos 31–33; Pl. 10; no adm.), a good example of the imported Tuscan style of 1474–82 (but in very bad condition). The splendid courtyard is surrounded by a double colonnade. The Council of Trent held two sessions in this building in 1547 having moved to Bologna to escape an epidemic. Beyond Via Farini, the attractive and peaceful Via d'Azeglio, one of the few old main streets without arcading, continues back to Piazza Maggiore.

In Piazza Roosevelt is the enlarged Palazzo della Prefettura (No. 26), of 1561–1603, perhaps by Terribilia. Via Quattro Novembre continues left past Palazzo Marescalchi (No. 5), in the early 17C manner, and (No. 7) the birthplace of Guglielmo Marconi. Opposite is the huge classical exterior of the flank of **San Salvatore** (Pl. 10), with its façade on Via Battisti, by Giovanni Magenta and Tommaso Martelli (1605–23; restored).

INTERIOR. In the centre of the pavement is the tomb of *Guercino*. South Side. 3rd chapel, *Lippo di Dalmasio* (attributed), Madonna and Child. South Transept. High up above the Sacristy door on the right, *Girolamo da Treviso*, Presentation of the Virgin in the Temple and St Thomas Becket; on the left wall, *Girolamo da Carpi*, Madonna and Child with Saints Catherine, Sebastian, and Roch. The Coronation of the Madonna, by *Vitale da Bologna*, has been removed from the wall below. North Aisle. 3rd chapel, *Innocenza da Imola*, Crucifix and Saints; 2nd chapel, *Carlo Bononi*, Ascension; 1st chapel, *Garofalo*, Saints Zaccharias and John the Baptist.

Via Portanuova continues to emerge beneath the *Porta Nuova*, one of the old city gates, into the long Piazza Malpighi beside the Colonna dell'Immacolata, with a copper statue designed by Guido Reni. Here is the church of *San Francesco* (Pl. 10), in many ways the most attractive church in Bologna, with its two towers and chapel-girdled apse. In the churchyard are the *Tombs of the Glossators*, Accursio (died 1260), Odofredo (died 1265) and Rolandino de'Romanzi (died 1284), restored in 1904. The church is in a more or less French Gothic style, begun in 1236, completed early in 1263, but considerably altered since. It was skilfully restored after war damage. The façade (c 1250), looking on to Piazza San Francesco has two carved 8C plutei and 13–14C majolica plaques in the pitch of the roof. The smaller of the two towers was completed in 1261; the larger and finer, the work of *Antonio di Vincenzo* (1397–c 1402; restored 1950), is surrounded by decorative terracotta.

There is an entrance through the vestibule (right) between the towers. In the N aisle are the terracotta Tomb of Pope Alexander V, completed by *Sperandio* (1482); in the S aisle is the Fieschi tomb (1492); and on both sides are several 16C monuments. The choir has fine carved stalls and a marble *Reredos by *Iacobello* and *Pier Paolo dalle Masegne* (1388–92), with busts of saints curiously perched on the pinnacles crowning the structure. In the E chapel of the ambulatory hangs a Crucifix attributed to *Pietro Lianori*.

At No. 23 Via dei Gombruti (off Via Portanova) the 'Old Pretender' stayed during several visits to Bologna.

The most pleasant way back to Piazza Maggiore is to return along Via Portanuova and Via Quattro Novembre.

G.   The outskirts of Bologna

In the southern part of the town are the pleasant *Giardini Margherita* (Pl. 16), laid out in 1875. By the entrance is the church of *Santa Maria della Misericordia* (Pl. 15), enlarged in the 15C, with stained-glass windows by Francesco Francia in the 2nd and 6th S chapels; the little church of the *Madonna del Baraccano* (Pl. 16), farther along Viale Gozzadini, has a good fresco by Francesco Cossa behind the high altar.

On a hill to the SW (bus No.28) stands the former Olivetan convent of **San Michele in Bosco** (134m; beyond Pl. 14), commanding a splendid *View of Bologna. Here on 1 May 1860 took place the meeting between Cavour and Victor Emmanuel II at which approval was given for the sailing of the 'Thousand' to Sicily. The convent buildings are now occupied by an orthopaedic hospital. The church (for adm. apply at the building on the right), rebuilt since 1437, and completed in the early 16C, has a façade ascribed to *Baldassarre Peruzzi* (1523) and a portal by *Giacomo Andrea da Ferrara* and *Bernardo da Milano*. It contains the tomb of Armaciotto de'Ramazzotti, the condottiere, by *Alfonso Lombardi* (1526). The frescoes on the triumphal arch of the Fall of the Angels are by Domenico Maria Canuti. In the adjacent cloister are the remains of a famous fresco cycle by *Ludovico Carracci*, *Guido Reni*, and others.—The primitive church of *San Vittore*, on the next hill to the S (at No. 40 Via San Mamolo) is of the 11C, enlarged in the 12C. It was altered in 1864, and partly restored afterwards. The cloister (right) was rebuilt in the 15C.

Just outside the Porta San Mamolo (bus No. 12 from Piazza Galvani or Via Rizzoli) stands the Observantine church of the *Annunziata* (Pl. 14), beautifully restored. The Renaissance portico (visible from the road) precedes the austere basilica of c 1475, constructed in the style of the century before. Via dell'Osservanza, opposite, ascends, with pleasant views, to the *Osservanza* convent. To the right, about 400m short of the convent, is the classical *Villa Aldini* (1811–16). Between Via dell'Osservanza and Via San Mamolo the park of *Villa Ghigi* has recently been opened to the public.—A bus runs from the railway station via Piazza Maggiore and Via Saragozza (Pl. 13) to the Madonna di San Luca. Beyond the public park of Villa Spada is the entrance to *Villa delle Rose* (reopened in 1989 as an exhibition centre). The sanctuary of the **Madonna di San Luca**, a famous viewpoint, is connected with Porta Saragozza (Pl. 13), just over 3km away, by a *Porticus of 666 arches (1674–1793). Where the porticus begins the ascent of the hill is the *Arco del Meloncello*, by Carlo Francesco Dotti (1718), formerly connected with the Certosa by another porticus. The sanctuary (290m), built by Dotti in 1725–49, derives its name from one of the numerous paintings of the Virgin ascribed to St Luke, which is said to have been brought from Constantinople by a 12C pilgrim and is preserved above the high altar. The church also contains a Noli me tangere by Guercino, and paintings by Calvaert.—The return may be made by descending the porticus to Meloncello, and then diverging left to Porta Saragozza.

Over 1·5km beyond Porta Sant'Isaia (Pl. 9), on the left, is the *Stadio*, a huge sports stadium built in 1926, reached by bus No. 43. On the right is the *Certosa*, founded in 1334, suppressed in 1797, and consecrated in 1801 as the public cemetery of Bologna. It was much admired by Byron. The 14–16C church contains good marquetry stalls (1539) and frescoes by *Bartolomeo Cesi* in its choir. Behind the church is the old cloister, and in the farther right-hand corner of this is the columbarium, with a statue of Murat, by *Vincenzo Vela* (1865); beyond, to the left, is the tomb of Carducci. The Etruscan necropolis of Felsina (see the Museo Archaeologico, Rte 40B) was discovered in the precincts of the Certosa in 1869.

In the NE part of the town (buses 3, 38 and 91) lies the **Zona Fieristica** with permanent exhibition halls, a conference centre, and a theatre. The international Childrens' Book Fair is held annually in spring. Here, too, is the **Galleria d'Arte Moderna**, opened in 1975 (adm. 10–20, except Tuesday). On the top floor is a permanent collection of 20C works by artists from the region, most of which have been donated by the artists themselves. There is a good collection of works by Giorgio Morandi. On the second floor frequent exhibitions are held; the ground floor is reserved for didactic purposes. There are long-term plans to move the gallery to the area of the ex-Tobacco Manufacturies, off Via Riva di Reno.

Off Via Aemilia (left), 5km SE of Bologna, is a *British Military Cemetry*. From Bologna to *Ferrara* and *Venice*, see Rte 37; to *Florence*, see Rte 44; to *Ravenna*, see Rte 38; to *Rimini*, see Rte 41.

41 Bologna to Rimini

ROAD, 113km, the SE section of the Via Aemilia (N9) almost flat and dead straight until Cesena with views of the Apennine foothills on the right; a nerve-racking road recommended only for short distances between intermediate towns.—22km *Castel San Pietro*.—33km **Imola**.—41km *Castel Bolognese*.—49km **Faenza**.—63km **Forlì**.—71km *Forlimpopoli*.—82km **Cesena**.—96km *Savignano*.—113km **Rimini**.

MOTORWAY, A14, 113km almost parallel 3–5km to the N.

RAILWAY, 112km, many expresses daily in 1¼–1½hrs; to *Faenza*, 50km in 30–50 minutes. The line keeps parallel to and N of the road.

Bologna, see Rte 40. The road leaves by the Porta Maggiore and proceeds SE.—22km *Castel San Pietro* preserves a tower and gateway of its 13C castle.—33km **Imola** (57,200 inhab.), on the Santerno, occupies the site of the Roman *Forum Cornelii*, founded by L. Cornelius Sulla in 82 BC, and still preserves the main outlines of its Roman plan.—The Via Emilia divides the town in half, and the Via

Appia, from the station, meets it at a double gate beneath a clock-tower, just W of the central Piazza Matteotti. In Via Aemilia, to the W, are the *Palazzo Della Volpe* (1482) and the former convent of San Francesco, now containing a *Museum*, with a Science section. The street opposite leads to the *Cathedral*, entirely rebuilt in the 18C, containing the tombs of St Cassian, patron of the town (a teacher who was stabbed to death by the pens of his pupils), and St Peter Chrysologus, the eloquent archbishop of Ravenna (died 450), a native of Imola. In the Bishop's Palace, opposite, is a small Diocesan Museum. Farther SW rise the towers of the early–14C *Castle*, rebuilt by Gian Galeazzo Sforza, whose daughter Caterina married Girolamo Riario, lord of Imola, and held the fortress after his death until her defeat by Cesare Borgia (1500). It contains a collection of arms and armour.—To the left of Via Emilia is the 18C church of *San Domenico* (Via Quarto, off Via Orsini), with its 14C brick portal, and fine cloister. The Pinacoteca Comunale was reopened here in 1989; the paintings include a Madonna with Saints Cassian and Peter Chrysologus, by Innocenzo Francucci (da Imola; 1494–1550). Controversial restoration and reconstruction is in progress in the church and adjoining buildings. The *Pretura* (68 Via Cavour, off Via Appia) is a fine palazzo of the Florentine Renaissance (1480). The 15C *Osservanza*, near Porta Montanara, contains works by Antonio da Imola. On the outskirts of the town rises the 12C campanile of *Santa Maria in Regola*.

A road runs from Imola to Florence, ascending the valley of the Santerno, and followed by a bus as far as Firenzuola.—26km *Castel del Rio* is dominated by its huge 13C castle (of the Alidosi; containing a War Museum), and possesses a 16C palazzo (now the town hall) of the same family.—Beyond (32km) *Moraduccio* is a *British Military Cemetery* (left). There are quarries of pietra serena in the hills, which have interesting rock formations.—47.5km *Firenzuola*, a 14C Florentine colony, has a gateway at either end of its arcaded main street. The German 'Gothic' line was pierced by the taking of Firenzuola by the American Fifth Army in September 1944, after heavy fighting. The road ascends to the left, up a side valley, past *Rifredo*, to (58·5km) the *Giogo di Scarperia* (882m) on the Apennine watershed, then descends steeply with many turns into the Tuscan Mugello via (68km) *Scarperia*, with a Palazzo Pretorio of 1306 (famous for its manufacture of knives).—74km *San Piero*, and from there to (98km) *Florence*, see Rte 44.

41km *Castel Bolognese* (6700 inhab.) preserves only one tower of the castle built by the Bolognese in 1388 and destroyed by Cesare Borgia in 1501.

It is the railway junction for Ravenna via Lugo, and is connected by road with *Riolo Terme*, a small summer spa (9km SW) with a castle enlarged by Caterina Sforza.

49km **FAENZA**, a pleasant old walled town (54,700 inhab.) on the Lamone, has long been famous for its manufacture of the glazed and coloured pottery known as majolica or 'faience'. The street names are indicated by faience plaques, and several houses have ceramic decoration. The town, still with its Roman plan, is divided into halves by the Via Aemilia (Corso Mazzini and Saffi).—*Pro Loco Tourist Information Office*, 1 Piazza del Popolo.

History. From the early 13C until 1501 the powerful Manfredi family played a leading part in Faentine affairs, though their city was severely damaged in 1241 by Frederick of Hohenstaufen and again sacked in 1376 by Sir John Hawkwood, then in the papal service. In 1501 Cesare Borgia took the town and killed the last of the Manfredi, and from 1509 Faenza was included in the States of the Church. It was damaged in the Second World War.—Evangelista Torricelli (1608–47), the inventor of the barometer, was born at Faenza.

The great period of Faentine majolica was 1450–1520, when the most famous of 40 potteries was that of the brothers Pirotti (the Ca' Pirota). The earliest authenticated specimen is a votive plaque dated 1475, in the Cluny Museum at Paris, though its manufacture is documented in 1142. Baldassare Manara (first half of the 16C) and Virgilio Calamelli (Virgiliotto da Faenza; second half) are also distinguished names. The art had a second revival in the early 18C.

In the broad Viale Baccarini, which connects the station with the town, is the *Museo Internazionale delle Ceramiche (adm. in summer: 9–19; fest. 9.30–13; closed Monday; winter: 9.30–13, 15–18) the best and most extensive collection of Italian majolica in Italy. It covers all periods, and is beautifully displayed and well labelled (and an excellent catalogue is available). In 1985 an extension of the museum was opened to house the splendid Galeazzo Cora donation of majolica. The museum includes 20C Italian ceramics, and modern works from all countries, including pieces by Picasso and Matisse. There is also a small Oriental and Middle Eastern collection. The collection is complemented by a good library and photographic collection.—Nearby is the *School of Ceramics* founded in 1916.

At the end of Corso Baccarini, Corso Mazzini leads left to the centre of the town, formed by Piazza della Libertà and Piazza del Popolo, left and right of the Via Aemilia. In the former, with its fountain of 1619–21, is the **Duomo**, begun by *Giuliano da Maiano* in 1474, a Renaissance building with an unfinished front.

The graceful interior contains many works of art. South side, 1st chapel, Annunciation, relief by *Sperandio* (?; 1477), and Bosi monument by the local sculptor *Pietro Barilotti* (1542); 4th chapel, Madonna and Saints, by *Innocenzo da Imola*; 5th chapel, sculptures by *Barilotti* and *Pietro Lombardo*. In the chapel to the left of the apse (lights on right) is the *Tomb of St Savinus (first bishop of Faenza, early 4C), with exquisite reliefs by *Benedetto da Maiano* (1474–76).

In the picturesque arcaded Piazza del Popolo are the old *Clock Tower*, by Aleotti (1606–7), the *Palazzo del Podestà* (partly of the 12C), and the *Municipio*, once the palace of the Manfredi. Via Severoli leads right to the town **Pinacoteca** (closed since 1982), with an interesting collection of works of art, some of which are listed below.

ROOM I. Sculptural fragments and Roman mosaics. *Romagnole School of 14C*, Polyptych; *Giovanni da Rimini* (attributed), Madonna and Child and Saints; Crucifix carved by *Fra Damiano* of Bergamo; Madonna enthroned with Saints, a large terracotta group sculpted by *Alfonso Lombardi*.—RII. *Giovanni Battista Bertucci*, Triptych; good *Works by *Marco Palmezzano*; terracotta bust of an old man by *Lombardi*. The wood statue of St Jerome, once attributed to *Donatello*, is now thought to be by his school.—RIII. Works by *Bertucci* and *Biagio d'Antonio da Firenze*; *Ferrarese School of 15C*, Madonna enthroned with Saints.—RIV. The Bust of young St John, formerly attributed to Donatello, is probably the work of *Antonio Rossellino*; *Biagio d'Antonio da Firenze*, Annunciation.—RV. *Dosso* or *Battista Dossi*, Head of Mary Magdalene.—On the lower floor the 18C collection includes a watercolour by *Victor Hugo*.—The Modern Art collection (also closed) has been removed to the nearby Palazzo Zauli Naldi, in Corso Matteotti. The works include two busts by *Rodin*, and paintings of the 'Macchiaioli' school. Next to the Pinacoteca is the church of *Santa Maria dell'Angelo* (1621, by Girolamo Rainaldi) with a Spada tomb by Francesco Borromini, and busts by Alessandro Algardi.

Farther SW, reached by Via Cavour, is *Palazzo Milzetti*, a fine building by Giovanni Pistocchi (1794–1802), with a good interior, and appropriately the seat of a Neo-classical Museum (adm. by appointment). A Theatre Museum is also to be opened here. Nearby rises the 10C campanile of *Santa Maria Vecchia*.—In Corso Mazzini, with a number of 18C and early 19C buildings, *Palazzo Mazzolani* is to house a local archaeological museum. In Borgo Durbecco, beyond the Lamone bridge, is the small Romanesque church of the *Commenda* (restored), with a remarkable fresco by Girolamo Pennacchi the Younger (1533) in the apse. The next road to the right, beyond the Barriera, leads (500m farther) to a *British Military Cemetery*.

FROM FAENZA TO FLORENCE, 103km; railway, 120km in 2¼–2½hrs. This interesting cross-country route ascends the Lamone valley. An annual race is held on this road in spring known as '100km del Passatore'.—12·5km *Brisighella*, a spa in a pleasant site, is noted for its church, which contains fine Baroque stucco-work and a painting by Marco Palmezzano. The Museo Civico della Val Lamone displays local archaeological material. Above the town stands a clock-tower erected in 1290 on a rocky spur, and a castle with two drum towers.—On the left, below the next railway bridge, is the curious *Pieve del Tho* (San Giovanni in Ottavo), a Romanesque church incorporating some Roman fragments.—25km *San Cassiano*, with 13C castle-ruins.—36km *Marradi* lies in a narrow stretch of valley. Its capture by the British 13th Corps in September 1944 made a breach in the German 'Gothic' line.—From (54km) *Colla di Casaglia* (913m) the road begins the descent into the Mugello.—62km *Ronta* is a summer resort.—72km *Borgo San Lorenzo*, and from there to (103km) *Florence*, see Rte 44.

A railway connects Faenza with (30–35 minutes) *Ravenna* via Granarolo.

63km **FORLÌ**, a flourishing provincial capital (104,900 inhab.) and agricultural centre, takes its name from the Roman *Forum Livii*, a station on the Via Aemilia, which bisects the town. Its urban architecture suffered under the influence of Mussolini, born nearby at Predappio.

Tourist Office, 23 Corso della Repubblica.—**Airport.** *Ridolfi* at Ronco, c 5km SE with internal flights (to Rome, Milan, and Sardinia).

In later years Forlì was ruled by the Ordelaffi family (1315–1500), but after the successful campaign of Cesare Borgia it remained under the sway of Rome until the rise of the Italian kingdom in the 19C.—The Forlivese school of painting has Melozzo degli Ambrogi (1438–94) as its leader, with Marco Palmezzano as his chief disciple. Among other famous natives of the town are Giovanni Battista Morgagni (1682–1771), the anatomist, and Aurelio Saffi (1819–90), one of the builders of Italian liberty.

In the central piazza, named after Saffi, is the Romanesque church of **San Mercuriale** (12–13C but altered later) dedicated to the first bishop of Forlì. It has a fine contemporary *Campanile, 76m high, a high relief of the school of Antelami above the W door, and a graceful cloister, with an open loggia at either end. In the bold red-brick interior the S and N nave chapels have paintings by *Palmezzano* and architectural decoration by *Giacomo Bianchi* (1536). In the S aisle is the *Tomb, by *Francesco Ferrucci*, of Barbara Manfredi (died 1466) wife of Pino II Ordelaffi, moved here from San Biagio (destroyed in 1944). Excavations beneath the apse have brought to light remains of the 11C church and crypt of 1176.—*Palazzo del Municipio*, opposite the church, dates in its present form from 1459, and was altered in 1826.

Corso Garibaldi, with some 15–16C mansions, leads NW to the **Duomo** (right), mainly a rich reconstruction of 1841, but preserving in its apse a huge tempera painting of the Assumption, the masterpiece of *Carlo Cignani* (1681–1706); the 2nd chapel in the N aisle has a St Sebastian, by *Rondinelli*. The campanile, in Piazza Ordelaffi, was formerly the watch-tower of the Orgogliosi, a rival family to the Ordelaffi.

At the S end of the town is the **Rocca di Ravaldino** (1472–82; now a prison), where Caterina Sforza was besieged by Cesare Borgia in 1499–1500. It was the birthplace of her famous son Giovanni delle Bande Nere (1498–1526).

In Corso della Repubblica, leading SW from Piazza Saffi, the former hospital (1772) houses the **Archaeological Museum and Pinacoteca Saffi** (adm. 9–14, Sunday 10–13; closed Saturday and fest.).

The Ground Floor contains finds from prehistoric sites at Vecchiazzano, Villanova, and San Varano; and Roman material from the province. On the 1st floor are the works of art, including: *Guercino*, Annunciation; *Antonio* and *Bernardino Rossellino*, Tomb of 1458; Flemish tapestries; and several paintings by *Palmezzano*, including a fine *Annunciation, an early work inspired by Melozzo, and the Apostles' Communion. Noteworthy, also, are a Nativity and Agony in the Garden, both by *Fra Angelico*. There is a fine portrait (no longer believed to be Caterina Sforza) by *Lorenzo di Credi*; but *Melozzo* is represented only by a druggist's sign ('Il Pestapepe'). On the 2nd floor is the *Ethnographic Museum*, with interesting interiors, an Armoury, and a *Ceramics Museum*, with material from local potteries of 15C–19C.

In the church of *Santa Maria dei Servi*, just to the S, the tomb of Luffo Numai (1502) has good reliefs by Tommaso Fiamberti.

The south-eastern district of the town includes Piazzale della Vittoria, with a tall memorial column (1932). Viale della Libertà connects the piazza with the station.

A road from Forlì follows the Rabbi valley past (3km) a *British Military Cemetery* to (15km) **Predappio**, the birthplace of Benito Mussolini (1883–1945). The village, originally a hamlet called *Dovia* in the commune of *Predappio Alta* (2km farther on), received communal rank in 1925, and many new public buildings were erected. In the cemetery, Mussolini's remains were finally interred in 1957, and his wife 'Donna Rachele' (Rachele Guidi) was buried in 1979. The little church of *San Cassiano in Appennino* has some 10–11C portions (restored). Predappio was taken from the Germans by Poles of the Eighth Army in October 1944.—There is an *Indian Military Cemetery* 2km NE of Forlì, on the right of the Ravenna road.

FROM FORLÌ TO FLORENCE (N67), 119km.—11km *Castrocaro Terme*, a small spa with alkaline and sulphurous waters, is dominated by its large ruined castle.— 18km *Dovàdola* has an old castle and an 11C church.—28km *Rocca San Casciano* retains only fragments of its rocca. 1·5km N is another *British Military Cemetery*.—55km *Passo del Muraglione* (907m), on the watershed.—63km *San Godenzo* is noted for its *Abbey church, a massive Romanesque building founded in 1029 by Jacopo il Bavaro, Bishop of Fiesole. It stands above the main street of the town, in Piazza Dante Alighieri. The plain stone interior has the presbytery raised above the crypt. On the parapet is a pretty frieze of inlaid marble. The wooden statue of St Sebastian by Baccio da Montelupo (1506) was restored in 1988.—73km *Dicomano*, and from there to (119km) *Florence*, see Rte 44.

The main road goes on to (71km) *Forlimpopoli* where the castle of the Ordelaffi now contains a theatre, and an archaeological museum.

Bertinoro, 6km S, is an old-walled town on a hill, famous for its wine, with a 14C *Palazzo Comunale*. The *Rocca*, erected in the 12C by the belligerent Countess Aldruda Frangipane, was occupied later by the Mainardi, by the Ordelaffi, and by Cesare Borgia. 6km farther S is the 9C or 10C church of *Polenta*, celebrated in an ode by Carducci (threatened by a landslide, but being restored), with the ruined castle from which sprang the famous Da Polenta clan of Ravenna.

82km **CESENA**, an ancient arcaded town (86,500 inhab.) on the Savio, enjoyed a period of brilliance under the Malatesta family (1379–1465). Pius VI (1717–99) and Pius VII (1742–1823), whose smile fascinated Napoleon, were born here. The town is a centre for the export of fruit and jam, and the European trotting championships are held in August on its racecourse. The ***Biblioteca Malatestiana** (open 8–13, Monday 16–20), a lovely aisled basilica, built in 1447–52 by *Matteo Nuti* for Domenico Malatesta Novello (note his heraldic elephants), contains 340 valuable MSS and 48 incunabula in original presses. In the Refectory beneath is a Museum with prehistoric, Etruscan, and Roman finds (including two Roman silver plates with banquet scenes in gold and niello). The *Cathedral*, begun in 1385, contains good 15C sculpture. The 18C churches of *San Domenico* and

Sant'Agostino (with an Annunciation by Girolamo Genga) are interesting. The *Rocca Malatestiana* (mainly 1466, restored), dominating the town from a wooded hill to the S, succeeds an earlier castle destroyed by Cardinal Albornoz in 1377. It contains a local ethnological museum. It is well seen from the attractive bridge (1772) that crosses the river SW of the town.

A *British Military Cemetery*, 2·5km NE of Cesena, on the right of the road to Cervia, recalls the severe fighting in this area in October 1944 by the Eighth Army.

From Cesena to Bagno di Romagna, Bibbiena, and Sansepolcro, see Rte 52.

Bus services connect Cesena with *Cesenatico* (½hr), and with *Cervia* (50 minutes), on the coast (see Rte 38).

Beyond Cesena, on a hill to the right, is the *Madonna del Monte*, a Benedictine abbey rebuilt in the 15–16C with a famous collection of ex-votos, and a Presentation in the Temple by Francesco Francia. Just before (96km) *Savignano sul Rubicone* the Rubicon is crossed on a Roman bridge dating from c 186 BC. The identification of the stream here, once known as the Fiumicino, with the Rubicon, was long a matter of doubt, but accords well enough with the evidence of the Peutinger table.—102km *Santarcangelo di Romagna* was the birthplace of Clement XIV (1705–74). On the right rises Monte Titano.

113km **RIMINI** (118,400 inhab.), first visited for its bathing beaches in the mid-19C, became the largest seaside resort on the Adriatic in the 1950s. Its beaches, especially popular with German and British holiday-makers, extend along the shore in either direction. However, in the last few years this coast has become far less attractive because of the pollution of the Adriatic. The old city, over a kilometre from the sea front, is separated from it by the railway. Standing at the seaward end of the Via Aemilia it preserves some Roman remains, but is above all famous for the Renaissance Tempio Malatestiano.

A.P.T. Information Office, outside the station.—*Post Office*. Piazzale Giulio Cesare.—**Trolley-Buses** from Piazza Tre Martiri to the station and the shore, from where there are frequent services via Bellariva and Miramare to *Riccione*.—BUSES to *San Marino*; to *Ancona*, to *Cesena*, *Forlì* and *Faenza*; to *Cattolica*; to *Cervia* and *Ravenna*, etc.—**Airport** at Miramare, c 6km S with summer services from all over Europe.

History. Rimini occupies the site of the Umbrian city of *Ariminum*, which became a Roman colony c 268 BC and was favoured by Julius Caesar and Augustus. In the 8C, it became a papal possession, and after the struggles between the papal and imperial parties in the 12–13C, the Guelf family of Malatesta emerged as overlords. Malatesta di Verucchio (1212–1312), Dante's 'old mastiff', was the founder of a powerful dynasty of overlords, most famous of whom was Sigismondo (1417–68), a man of violent character and yet an enthusiastic protector of art and learning. Malatesta's son, Giovanni the Lame, was the husband of the beautiful Francesca da Rimini (died 1258), whose love for her brother-in-law Paolo inspired one of the tenderest passages in Dante's 'Inferno' ('we read no more that day'). Pandolfo (died 1534) surrendered the town to Venice, but after the battle of Ravenna (1512) it fell again into papal hands. Rimini, bombarded from sea or air nearly 400 times, was the scene of heavy fighting between the Germans and the Eighth Army, and was captured by Canadians in September 1944.

The road from Bologna enters the old town by the **Ponte di Tiberio**, across the Marecchia, a bridge begun by Augustus in the last year of his life and finished by Tiberius (AD 21). The N arch was rebuilt after the Goths destroyed it in order to cut Narses off from Rome in 552.

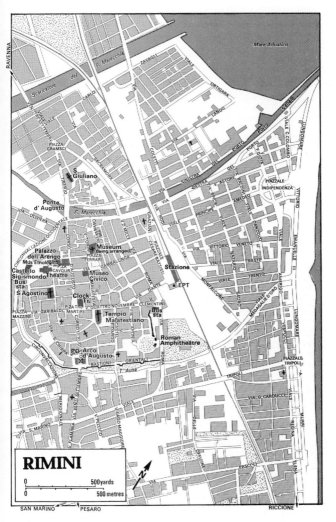

RIMINI

| 0 | 500 yards |
| 0 | 500 metres |

SAN MARINO   PESARO   RICCIONE

The church of *San Giuliano*, in the suburb beyond the bridge, contains a fine painting by Paolo Veronese, the Martyrdom of St Julian, and an interesting polyptych of the early 15C.

The Corso di Augusto leads from the bridge through the town. On the right is PIAZZA CAVOUR with a 17C statue of Paul V and a fountain of 1543 incorporating Roman reliefs. The *Palazzo dell'Arengo* is a battlemented building of 1204, aΩ,oining the 14C *Palazzo del Podestà*. To the S, behind the Theatre of 1857 (at present used for exhibitions), is the **Rocca Malatestiano** (or *Castello Sigismondo*) which dates from 1446. The Ala di Isotto is the seat (since 1988) of the

MUSEO CULTURALE EXTRAEUROPEE, founded by Delfino Dinz Rialto
(adm. 8–19; winter 8–13; closed Sunday). It contains a remarkable
ethnological collection from Africa, Oceania, and pre-Columbian
America. To the left, in Via Sigismondo, is the Romanesque church of
Sant'Agostino, with a fine campanile and remarkable 14C frescoes by
local artists (including Giovanni da Rimini) in the sanctuary and
adjoining chapel (restored). In the Bell-tower is a huge 14C Crucifix.

From the other side of the Corso roads lead towards the Station and the sea. In
Via Gambalunga is the *Biblioteca Gambalunga* which at present houses the
Pinacoteca and **Museo Civico** (adm. 8–13, except Sunday). Both museums are to
be moved to a new building near Piazza Ferrari (see the Plan). The prehistoric
and archaeological collection has been closed for many years: it includes
Etruscan tomb-furniture of the Villanovan period, with a remarkable axe-mould,
and material found during excavations which are continuing in several parts of
the city. The Roman section has mosaics (including one, dating from the early
2C, showing boats in the port of Rimini), sculpture, and a collection of the
coinage of Ariminum. The paintings include: *The Dead Christ supported by
four angels, by *Giovanni Bellini*; Three Saints, by *Ghirlandaio*; and a Crucifix by
Giovanni da Rimini.—To the N, in Via Cavalieri, is the *Roman Lapidarium* (adm.
as above).

In Piazza Tre Martiri is the little *Oratory of St Anthony* (being
restored) on the spot where the saint's mule miraculously knelt in
adoration of the Sacrament. At the end of the Corso is the ugly Piazza
Giulio Cesare, in which stands the **Arco d'Augusto**, a single archway
(c 27 BC; restored) with composite capitals, marking the junction of
the Via Aemilia with the Via Flaminia.

Via Quattro Novembre leads from Piazza Tre Martiri to the
**Tempio Malatestiano (open 7–12, 15.30–19), one of the outstanding
productions of the Italian Renaissance, in a disappointing setting.
Very seriously damaged in the fighting of 1944, it was carefully
restored in time for its quincentenary. Since 1809 it has served as the
cathedral of Rimini, with the title of Santa Colomba, transferred from
the demolished old cathedral near the Castello.

The original building was a Franciscan church, built in the late 13C, which in
1450 Sigismondo Malatesta determined to transform into what can only be
described as a combination of a religious edifice and a personal monument. The
decline of his fortunes caused the suspension of the work in 1460, and the
completion of the building is due to the Franciscans. Under Sigismondo the
rebuilding of the interior was entrusted to *Matteo de'Pasti* and the exterior to
Leon Battista Alberti, while *Agostino di Duccio* executed the sculptures.
Remains of a 9C church have recently been found beneath the edifice.

EXTERIOR. The front, inspired by the form of the Roman triumphal
arch, is one of the masterpieces of *Alberti*. The upper part is
incomplete. Each side is relieved by wide arches surmounting the
stylobate, beneath which (on the S side) are seven plain sarcophagi
containing the ashes of eminent men who died in Rimini in the
15–16C.

INTERIOR. The spacious nave is flanked by a series of deep side
chapels connected by sculptural decoration and closed by fine
balustrades. The sculptural detail (including the vaults and window
frames) is of the highest quality. On the right of the entrance is the
tomb of Sigismondo, whose armorial bearings (the elephant and rose)
and initials interlaced with those of Isotta (see below) recur
throughout the church. SOUTH SIDE. 1st Chapel (being restored),
Statue of St Sigismund supported by elephant's heads, and very low
reliefs of angels (side walls), all works of *Agostino di Duccio*. In the

niches, statues of the Virtues and armour-bearers.—2nd chapel (of the Relics; unlocked by the sacristan) has a damaged fresco (inside, above the door) by *Piero della Francesca* (1451), representing Sigismondo kneeling before his patron, St Sigismund of Burgundy, and relics found in Sigismondo's tomb.—3rd chapel. On the entrance arch, friezes of putti playing, and (over the altar), St Michael, by *Agostino*. Tomb of Isotta degli Atti, Sigismondo's mistress and later his third wife. The Crucifix (c 1310) is now attributed to *Giotto*.—The 4th chapel has superb decoration representing the planetary symbols and signs of the Zodiac, also by *Agostino*.—The 4th N chapel, opposite, the masterpiece of *Agostino*, has reliefs representing the Arts and Sciences.—The end chapels and presbytery do not belong to the original Malatesta building.—NORTH SIDE. The 3rd chapel has particularly charming putti.—In the 1st chapel (of the Ancestors) are figures of Prophets and Sibyls, a tiny Pietà (15C, French), above the altar, and the Tomb of the Ancestors, with splendid reliefs by *Agostino*.

A little to the E is the *Roman Amphitheatre*, of which only two brick arches remain above the foundations.

The sandy beaches along the coast NW and SE of Rimini, ruined by uncontrolled new building begun in the 1950s, continue to attract millions of holiday-makers every year from all over Europe. The sands are being eroded, and the sea has been declared polluted and unsuitable for bathing in many stretches. Thousands of hotels and tourist attractions line the coast at *Rivabella*, *Viserba*, *Torre Pedrera*, *Igea Marina*, and *Bellaria* to the NW, and *Bellariva*, *Marebello*, *Rivazzurra*, and *Miramare* to the SE. The sands are continued to the SE by those of **Riccione**, another internationally known resort (28,700 inhab.), beyond which again stands *Cattolica* with many more hotels.

A *Gurkha Military Cemetery* lies 3·5km S of Rimini on the San Marino road (right).

A road from Rimini (bus from Piazza Clementini) ascends the Marecchia Valley to (32km) *Novafeltria*, until recently called *Mercatino*, passing (14km) *Verucchio*, the attractive hill-town from which came the Malatesta clan, where the Collegiata has a Crucifixion (1404) by Nicolò di Pietro Paradisi. The Museo Civico, opened in 1985 in the ex-Convent of Sant'Agostino, displays local archaeological finds from a necropolis of the Villanovan period (9C–7C BC). On the opposite hill rises the old Malatesta castle of *Scorticato*. Beyond Verucchio the road ascends the Marecchia valley to its head at (72km) the *Passo di Viamaggio* (987m). The descent on the SE side leads into the Tiber valley on the road between Pieve Santo Stefano and Sansepolcro, see Rte 51.

From Rimini to *Ravenna*, see Rte 38; to *Pesaro*, *Ancona*, etc., see Rte 60.

SAN MARINO, SW of Rimini, is reached by an ugly fast road (drive with care) from Piazza Giulio Cesare, following a hilly course (27km). Cars are not permitted in the narrow streets of the town itself, which is totally given over to the tourist trade.

The little town (4600 inhab.) is interesting as being the capital of the diminutive REPUBLIC OF SAN MARINO (61 sq. km; 20,900 inhab.), which has preserved its independence for more than sixteen centuries. It is said to have been founded c 300 by Marinus, a pious stonemason from Dalmatia, who fled to the mountains to escape Diocletian's second persecution. The legislative power is vested in a Council General of 60 persons from whom ten (the Congress of State) are chosen as an executive, and twelve as a Council that functions as a Court of Appeal; the chiefs of state are two 'regent captains' who hold office for six months (investiture 1 April and 1 October). San Marino has its own mint, postage stamps, police force, etc., and an army of about 1000 men. Most of its territory consists of the peaks and slopes of the limestone *Monte Titano* (739m; *View). In the capital the church of San Francesco possesses a pinacoteca (St Francis by Guercino, and a Madonna and Child attributed to Raphael). The *Palazzo del Governo* dates from 1894, and the three citadels (*Rocca*, *Cesta*, *Montale*) command a panorama of Rimini and the Adriatic. The principal market town of the Republic is *Borgomaggiore*, about 1·5km lower down.

About 11km farther SW by a winding road is the fortress town of *San Leo*, on an impregnable rock guarded by a fortress restored in 1475 by Francesco di Giorgio Martini. Here Giuseppe Balsamo (Cagliostro) died in exile in 1795 after four years of imprisonment. The Duomo, dating from the 12–13C, is dedicated to Leo, the companion of Marinus (see above). The Pieve probably dates from the 9C, and has an early ciborium. The return to Rimini may be made by the Marecchia valley (see above).

V TUSCANY AND UMBRIA

Tuscany (in Italian, *Toscana*) is a mountainous region with an area of 22,991 sq. km and a population of 3,473,000 lying between the Apennines and the Tyrrhenian Sea, bordered on the N by Emilia and Liguria, on the E by the Marches and Umbria, and on the S by Lazio. In the Tyrrhenian Sea, between the mainland of Italy and Corsica, are the islands of the Tuscan archipelago, chief of which is Elba. To the N of the Arno, whose valley divides Tuscany into two unequal parts, it includes the main ridge and W slopes of the Central Apennines. Here it is in the main a district of broken hills and irregular valleys, the only levels of any extent being the coastal strip, called *Versilia*, between Carrara and Livorno, and the plain between Florence and Pistoia. The so-called Apuan Alps, above the Versilian coast, are separated from the main chain of the Apennines by the deep vales of the Garfagnana and Lunigiana. Though southern Tuscany lies well to the W of the main Apennine range, its only relatively flat areas are the Val di Chiana, S of Arezzo, and the coastal *Maremma*, a once malarial region now largely drained. The region comprises the nine provinces of Arezzo, Firenze, Grosseto, Livorno, Lucca, Massa-Carrara, Pisa, Pistoia, and Siena. Tuscany is renowned for its fertility; it produces wines, olives, potatoes, and cereals. The mineral wealth includes mines of iron, copper, mercury, and antimony.

Tuscany derives its name from the inhabitants of ancient **Etruria**, known as *Tusci* or *Tyrrheni*, who probably landed at Tarquinii in the 8C BC. In *Etruria Propria* they formed themselves into a CONFEDER-

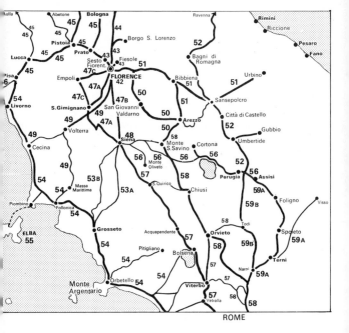

ATION of twelve principal cities, not yet certainly identified, but probably comprising Tarquinii, Veii, Caere (Cerveteri), Camars (Chiusi), Cortona, Perusia (Perugia), Vulci, Volsinii or Velsina (Orvieto), Vetulonia, Felathri (Volterra), Arretium (Arezzo), and either Rusellae or Falerii or Populonia. By the 6C or 5C *Etruria Circumpadana*, in the Po Valley, also had its confederation of twelve cities, with Felsina (Bologna) at the head. Etruria Propria was dealt its death-blow by the conquest of Veii by the Romans in 396 BC, while the Gauls also invaded from the N. The Roman conquest was completed by the 3C BC.

The Lombardic duchy of Tuscany, with its centre at Lucca, emerged after the decline of the Roman Empire, and survived in a more or less stable form until the rise of the various civic states in the 12C and the Guelf-Ghibelline struggles. Florence, supporting the famous Countess Matilda, inclined to the Guelf, or papal, side; Siena, with Lucca, Pisa, and Pistoia were Ghibelline, and upheld the emperor. By the beginning of the 15C Florence had established a hegemony in the province, the seapower of her most dangerous rival, Pisa, having been shattered by the Genoese. The great age of Florence began in the 14C, with the artists and writers of the early Renaissance; and it continued under the rule of the famous Medici family, patrons of art and learning. Only Siena rivalled the position of Florence, and was victorious in a battle against the city and Clement VII in 1526. However, Cosimo de'Medici led Florence in a decisive battle against Siena in 1555, and from then on Medici rule continued, with only short interruptions, until 1737, when it was succeeded by Austrian grand-dukes of the House of Lorraine. Lucca meanwhile, alone of the other Tuscan cities, maintained its independence, and after the Napoleonic wars was incorporated in the Duchy of Parma. The Lorraine dynasty, restored at Florence after 1815, maintained a liberal form of government remarkable among the foreign rulers of Italy in the early 19C, but even so it was unable to maintain its position in the face of the rising will towards unity of the Italian people, and in 1860 Tuscany declared itself united to Piedmont, with Victor Emmanuel as king. In 1865 the capital of Italy was transferred from Turin to Florence, as a preliminary step towards its final triumphant establishment at Rome.

In the Second World War the Allies reached Tuscany in July 1944. The Germans retreated from Florence before the Eighth Army on 3 August, and the autumn was mainly occupied in the capture of the 'Gothic Line', the strong fortification erected by the Germans in the Tuscan Apennines. The following months were spent in the hills above Bologna, and a strong German counter-attack from N of Lucca on 19 November virtually put an end to the 1944 campaign here. In April 1945, the Allied attack was resumed; Massa was occupied on the 5th, and a strenuous advance through the Apennines to the NE led down to the Emilian plain and the capture of Bologna on the 21st, bringing about the final liberation of Tuscany.

Umbria, an inland region of Italy, perhaps named after the shady forests (umbra) of the Apennines, includes the picturesque middle basin of the Tiber and its tributaries the Chiaggio, Nera, and Paglia. It consists of two provinces—Perugia and the much smaller Terni, making a total area of 8,456,000 sq. km, and a population of 775,000.

Agriculture is the chief industry of the valleys, though there are some lignite mines and stone quarries. Umbria rivals Tuscany for its artistic treasures; as well as Perugia, Assisi, Orivieto, and Spoleto, many lesser cities attract the discriminating traveller. The primitive race of the *Umbri*, regarded by Pliny as the most ancient inhabitants of Italy, originally occupied a territory far more extensive than the modern region. They appear to have yielded ground to the Etruscans and to have fled before them to the mountain fastnesses of the Apennines. In general culture they seem to have been deficient, for they did not evolve an alphabet of their own but borrowed the Etruscan and Latin characters. In 295 BC they submitted to the Roman consul Fabius. In the Middle Ages the republican communes and seignories which arose lasted only for short periods, for, from its proximity to Rome, Umbria was always more or less under the sway of the Church, which enjoyed undisputed domination from the 16C until the unification of Italy in 1860.

42 Florence

FLORENCE, in Italian **Firenze**, has been famous for centuries as one of the principal centres of art and learning in Italy. In the later Middle Ages and the early Renaissance it was the intellectual capital of the peninsula, well meriting its designation 'the Italian Athens'. The city remains a treasury of art, not only on account of the priceless collections in its museums and galleries, but also because of its rich endowment of medieval monuments and Renaissance buildings, in which it is rivalled by Rome alone. Today, Florence, with 457,800 inhabitants, is still one of the most beautiful cities in Italy, and the historical centre and the hills in the immediate vicinity have been largely preserved from new buildings. It lies in a delightful position in a small basin enclosed by low hills (which accounts for its changeable climate and high temperatures in summer). The river Arno, a special feature of the city, is a mountain torrent, subject to sudden floods and droughts.—**For a fuller description of the city, see 'Blue Guide Florence'.**

Hotels all over the city, and in the environs (particularly Fiesole), but it is essential to book well in advance in summer and at Easter. Booking Office (ITA) at the station.

Station. *Santa Maria Novella* (Pl. 6) for nearly all services; a few fast trains stop only at *Campo di Marte* (beyond Pl. 8) or *Rifredi* (beyond Pl. 2) stations.

Airport at *Pisa* (85km W; see Rte 46) with flights to London, Paris, Frankfurt, etc. Train service between the airport and Florence c every hour (in 1 hour); otherwise there are city buses from the airport to Pisa station. Air Terminal (with checking-in facilities) at Florence Railway Station.—The small airport of *Peretola*, 6km NW of Florence, serves some European cities.

Car Parking. Most of the centre of Florence (within the 'Viali', and in the Oltrarno; see the Plan) has been closed to private cars (from 7.30–18.30), except for access (which includes hotels in the area). CAR PARKS (with hourly tariff) at the Fortezza da Basso (Pl. 2; Bus No. 15).

Post Office. 53 Via Pietrapiana, and Via Pellicceria, with the telephone exchange and 'Poste Restante'.

Information Offices. *A.P.T.* (Pl. 6), 15 Via Tornabuoni and 16 Via Manzoni (Pl. 8); information offices at No. 7 Via Cavour, and off Piazza Signoria (19 Chiasso Baroncelli).

Bus Services (principal services only). Tickets must be purchased at tobacconists or ATAF offices, etc. (for 70 minutes, 120 minutes, or for 24hrs). **15** Fortezza da Basso (car park)—Piazza San Marco—Via Proconsolo—Ponte alle Grazie—Piazza Pitti—Piazza Santo Spirito—Piazza del Carmine—Viale Petrarca—Porta Romana—Ponte Santa Trìnita—Via Cavour—Fortezza da Basso. **11** Via Cavour—Piazza Duomo— Ponte alla Carraia—Via Serragli—Porta Romana. **17C**

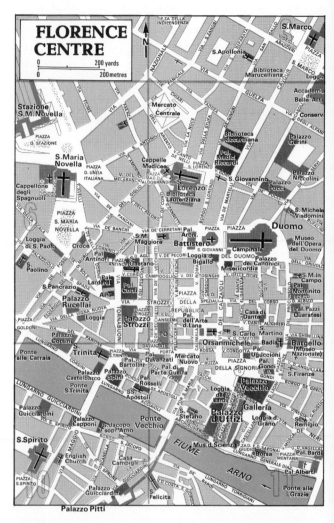

Cascine—Piazza Stazione—Piazza Duomo—Via Lamarmora—Viale dei Mille—Salviatino (Youth Hostel). **13 red** (circular) Piazza Stazione—Ponte alla Vittoria—Porta Romana—Viale Michelangelo—Piazzale Michelangelo—Ponte alle Grazie—Via dei Benci—Piazza Duomo—Piazza Stazione. **13 black** as above, but in the opposite direction. **7** Piazza Stazione—Piazza Duomo—Piazza San Marco—San Domenico—Fiesole.

Country Buses. A wide network of bus service in Tuscany is operated by *Lazzi*, (4 Piazza Stazione; Pl. 2, 6) and *S.I.T.A.*, 15 Via Santa Caterina da Siena (Pl. 6), etc.

British Consulate, 2 Lungarno Corsini (Pl. 10); **American Consulate**, 38 Lungarno Vespucci (Pl. 5).—*Anglican Church*, St Mark's, 16 Via Maggio; *American Episcopalian*, St James, 13 Via Rucellai.

Institutes. *British Institute*, 2 Via Tornabuoni (Italian language courses), with an excellent library and reading room at 9B Lungarno Guicciardini. *Institut Français*, 2 Piazza Ognissanti; *German Institute of Art History*, 44 Via Giuseppe Giusti, with the best art history library in Florence (post-graduate students only); *Dutch Institute*, 5 Viale Torricelli; *Harvard University Center for Italian Renaissance Studies*, Villa I Tatti, Ponte a Mensola, Settignano (with a good library, open to post-graduate students). *Centro Linguistico Italiano 'Dante Alighieri'*, 12 Via de'Bardi (Italian language courses).

Concerts and Drama. *Teatro Comunale* (Pl. 5), 16 Corso Italia, symphony concerts and opera. Here is held the MAGGIO MUSICALE, an annual music festival (May–July). *La Pergola* (Pl. 7), 12 Via della Pergola (drama season, and chamber music concerts organised by the 'Amici della Musica' in January–April and October–December). Concerts by the 'Orchestra Regionale della Toscana' in the church of Santo Stefano al Ponte. Chamber music concerts also held by the '*Musicus Concentus*'.—The ESTATE FIESOLANA is an annual festival of music, drama, and films (July and August).

Sport. *Swimming-pools:* Le Pavoniere, Viale degli Olmi (Cascine); Costoli, Viale Paoli (Campo di Marte); Bellariva, 8 Lungarno Colombo.— *Tennis*, Viale Michelangelo, the Cascine, etc.— *Golf Course* (18 holes) at Ugolino, 12km SE of Florence.

Annual Festivals and exhibitions. *Scoppio del Carro*, on Easter Day, a traditional religious festival held in and outside the Duomo at mid-day. On 24 June, St John's Day, the patron saint of Florence, a local holiday is celebrated with fireworks at Piazzale Michelangelo. A 'football' game in 16C costume ('Calcio in costume') is held in three heats during June.—An Antiques Fair (the *Mostra Mercato Internazionale dell'Antiquariato*) is held biennially (next in 1991) in the autumn, in Palazzo Strozzi.

A.   The Baptistery and the Duomo

The ****Baptistery of San Giovanni** (Pl. 7; open 13–18; fest. 9.30–12, 14.30–17) is one of the oldest and most revered buildings in the city, called by Dante his 'bel San Giovanni'. It was probably built in the 6C or 7C, or even as early as the 4–5C; but in any case not later than the 9C. It is a domed octagonal building of centralised plan derived from Byzantine models. In the 11–12C the EXTERIOR was entirely encased in white and green marble from Prato in a classical geometrical design, which became a prototype for numerous other Tuscan Romanesque religious buildings. The cupola was concealed by an unusual white pyramidal roof, probably in the 13C (and the 12C lantern placed on top). The building is famous for its three sets of gilded bronze doors. The two doors by Lorenzo Ghiberti were erected after he won a competition in 1401, often taken as a convenient point to mark the beginning of the Florentine Renaissance.

The **South Door* (1336) is by *Andrea Pisano* with reliefs illustrating the history of St John the Baptist. The bronze frame was added by *Vittorio Ghiberti* (1452–64).—Over the doorway are statues of the Baptist, the Executioner, and Salome, by *Vincenzo Danti* (1571).—The **North Door*, by *Lorenzo Ghiberti* (1403–24) contains scenes of the Life of Christ, the Evangelists, and the Doctors of the Church. The beautiful frame is also by Ghiberti, and his self-portrait appears in a head on the left door.—The sculptures above of St John the Baptist, the Levite, and the Pharisee are by *Francesco Rustici* (1506–11), from a design by *Leonardo da Vinci*.

The ****East Door** is the most celebrated work of *Lorenzo Ghiberti*, the completion of which took him most of his life (1425–52). It is said to have been called by Michelangelo the 'Gate of Paradise'. The pictorial reliefs, no longer restricted to a Gothic frame, depict each episode with great conciseness, and the workmanship of the carving is masterly. A copy of the door was installed here in 1990; the original panels are being restored and exhibited in the Museo

The cupola of the Duomo by Brunelleschi, Florence

dell'Opera del Duomo. The subjects are: 1. The Creation and Expulsion from
Paradise; 2. Cain and Abel; 3. Noah's Sacrifice and Drunkenness; 4. Abraham
and the Angels and the Sacrifice of Isaac; 5. Esau and Jacob; 6. Joseph sold and
recognised by his Brethren; 7. Moses receiving the Tables of Stone; 8. The Fall of
Jericho; 9. Battle with the Philistines; 10. Solomon and the Queen of Sheba. The
frame contains beautiful statuettes of Prophets and Sibyls, and medallions with
portraits of Ghiberti himself and his contemporaries. The splendid bronze door-
frame is by Ghiberti also.—Above, the sculptural group of the Baptism of Christ,
attributed to *Andrea Sansovino* and *Vincenzo Danti*, with an Angel added by
Innocenzo Spinazzi (18C), has been removed and restored.

The harmonious INTERIOR is designed in two orders, of which the lower has huge granite columns from a Roman building, with gilded Corinthian capitals, and the upper, above a cornice, a gallery with divided windows. The walls are in panels of white marble divided by bands of black, in the dichromatic style of the exterior. The oldest part of the splendid mosaic *Pavement in 'opus tessellatum' (begun 1209) is near the Gothic font. Beside the 13C high altar is an elaborate paschal candlestick delicately carved by *Agostino di Jacopo* (1320). The *Tomb of the antipope John XXIII (Baldassarre Cossa, who died in Florence in 1419) by *Donatello* and *Michelozzo* is one of the earliest Renaissance tombs in the city. This beautifully carved monument in no way disturbs the architectural harmony of the building.—The *MOSAICS (light) in the vault are remarkably well preserved. The earliest (c 1225) are in the 'scarsella' above the altar; they are signed by the monk *'Jacopo'*, who is also thought to have begun the main dome, the centre of which is decorated with paleochristian motifs. Above the apse is the Last Judgement with a huge figure of Christ (8m) attributed to *Coppo di Marcovaldo*. The four bands of the cupola illustrate the Story of Genesis, the Story of Joseph (the design of some of the scenes is attributed to the *'Maestro della Maddalena'*), the Story of Christ, and the Story of St John the Baptist (some of the early episodes are attributed to *Cimabue*). Work on the mosaics was well advanced by 1271, but probably continued into the 14C.

The ***Duomo** (Pl. 7; open all day), the cathedral dedicated to the Madonna of Florence, *Santa Maria del Fiore*, fills Piazza del Duomo; a comprehensive view of the huge building is difficult in the confined space. It produces a memorable effect of massive grandeur, especially seen from its southern flank, lightened by the colour and pattern of its beautiful marble walls (white from Carrara, green from Prato, and red from the Maremma). The famous dome, one of the masterpieces of the Renaissance, rising to the height of the surrounding hills (from which it is nearly always visible), holds sway over the whole city.

History. The paleochristian church, dedicated to the Palestinian saint Reparata, is thought to have been founded in the 6–7C, or possibly earlier. The Bishop's seat, formerly at San Lorenzo, was probably transferred here in the late 7C. By the 13C a new and larger cathedral was deemed necessary, and in 1294 *Arnolfo di Cambio* was appointed as architect. In 1355 *Francesco Talenti* continued work on the building, probably following Arnolfo's original design of a vaulted basilica with a domed octagon flanked by three polygonal tribunes. By 1417 the octagonal drum was substantially finished. The construction of the cupola had for long been recognised as a major technical problem, and after a competition *Brunelleschi* was appointed to the task, and had erected the dome up to the base of the lantern by 1436 when Pope Eugenius IV consecrated the cathedral.

EXTERIOR. The majestic **CUPOLA, the greatest of all *Brunelleschi*'s works (1420–36), is a feat of engineering skill. It was the first dome to be projected without the need for a wooden supporting frame to sustain the vault during construction, and was the largest and highest of its time. The cupola has two concentric shells, the octagonal vaults of which are evident both on the exterior and the interior of the building; the upper section is built in bricks in consecutive rings in horizontal courses, bonded together in a herring-bone pattern. The lantern was begun a few months before the architect's death in 1446, and carried on by his friend *Michelozzo*. In the late 1460s *Verrocchio* placed the bronze ball and cross on the summit. Brunelleschi also designed the four decorative little exedrae with niches which he placed around the octagonal drum between the three domed tribunes. The balcony at the base of the cupola added by *Baccio d'Agnolo* was never completed, according to Vasari, because of Michelangelo's stringent criticism. The dome has been under constant surveillance since 1980 when alarm was raised about its stability (the main problem seems to be the weight of the dome which has caused fissures in the drum).

The building of the cathedral was begun on the S side where the decorative pattern of marble can be seen to full advantage. The PORTA DEI CANONICI has fine sculptural decoration (1395–99). On the N side, the *PORTA DELLA MANDORLA (1391–1405) is by *Giovanni d'Ambrogio, Piero di Giovanni Tedesco, Jacopo di Piero Guidi,* and *Nicolò Lamberti.* In the gable is an *Assumption of the Virgin in an oval almond-shaped frame by *Nanni di Banco* (c 1418–20) which had an important influence on early Renaissance sculpture.—The FAÇADE, erected to a third of its projected height by 1420 was demolished in 1587–88, and the present front in the Gothic style was designed by *Emilio De Fabris* and built in 1871–87.

The Gothic INTERIOR is somewhat bare and chilly after the warmth of the colour of the exterior, whose splendour it cannot match. The huge grey stone arches of the nave reach the clerestory beneath an elaborate sculptured balcony. The massive pilasters which support the stone vault have unusual composite capitals. Three dark tribunes with a Gothic coronet of chapels surround the huge dome. The beautiful marble pavement was designed by *Baccio d'Agnolo, Francesco da Sangallo* and others.—WEST WALL. Mosaic of the Coronation of the Virgin, attributed to *Gaddo Gaddi. Ghiberti* designed the three stained glass windows. The huge clock was decorated with four heads of prophets by *Paolo Uccello* in 1443. The recomposed tomb of Antonio d'Orso, Bishop of Florence (died 1321) by *Tino da Camaino* includes a fine statue.—SOUTH AISLE. In a tondo is a bust of Brunelleschi by *Buggiano,* his adopted son (1446). On the side altar, statue of a Prophet attributed to *Nanni di Banco.* The bust of Giotto by *Benedetto da Maiano* bears an inscription by Poliziano. On the 2nd altar, statue of Isaiah by *Ciuffagni.*

Steps lead down to the **Excavations of Santa Reparata** (open 10–17; closed fest.). Through a grille to the left at the bottom of the steps can be seen the simple tomb slab of Brunelleschi, found here in 1972. The architect of the cupola was the only Florentine granted the privilege of burial in the cathedral. The complicated remains of Santa Reparata (explained by a model), on various levels, include Roman edifices on which the early Christian church was built, a fine mosaic pavement of the paleochristian church, and remains of the pre-Romanesque and Romanesque reconstructions. Here are displayed finds from the excavations, fresco fragments, plutei, etc.

EAST END OF THE CHURCH (open to visitors only when services are not in progress). Above the octagon the great dome soars to a height of 91 metres. The fresco of the Last Judgement by *Vasari* and *Federico Zuccari* (1572–79) has been covered for years for restoration. The stained glass in the roundels of the drum was designed in 1443–45 by *Paolo Uccello, Andrea del Castagno, Donatello,* and *Ghiberti.* Against the pillars stand 16C statues of Apostles by *Jacopo Sansovino, Vincenzo de'Rossi, Andrea Ferrucci, Baccio Bandinelli, Benedetto da Rovezzano, Giovanni Bandini,* and *Vincenzo de'Rossi.*—The marble SANCTUARY by *Bandinelli* (1555), with bas-reliefs by himself and *Bandini,* encloses the High Altar, also by *Bandinelli,* with a wood crucifix by *Benedetto da Maiano.*—Each of the three apses is divided into five chapels with stained glass windows designed by *Lorenzo*

Ghiberti. Above the entrance to the South Sacristy is a large lunette of the Ascension in enamelled terracotta by *Luca della Robbia.* In the central apse are two graceful kneeling angels also by *Luca,* and a bronze reliquary *Urn by *Lorenzo Ghiberti* with exquisite bas-reliefs. Over the door into the North Sacristy is another fine relief by *Luca della Robbia* of the *Resurrection. This was his earliest important work (1442) in enamelled terracotta. The doors were his only work in bronze. It was in this sacristy (reopened after restoration) that Lorenzo il Magnifico took refuge on the day of the Pazzi conspiracy in 1478 in order to escape the death which befell his brother, Giuliano. The inlaid cupboards were begun by *Antonio Manetti* and continued by *Giuliano* and *Benedetto da Maiano, Alesso Baldovinetti,* and *Antonio del Pollaiolo.* The lavabo was designed by *Brunelleschi* and made by *Buggiano.*—In the pavement of the left apse is Toscanelli's huge Gnomon (1475) for solar observations.

The *Ascent of the Dome (entrance in N aisle; adm. 10–17.40; closed fest.) is highly recommended. The climb (463 steps) is not especially arduous, and it follows a labyrinth of corridors, steps, and spiral staircases (used by the builders of the cupola) as far as the lantern at the top of the dome. During the ascent the structure of the dome can be examined, and the views of the inside of the cathedral from the balcony around the drum (45·5m in diameter), and of the city from the small windows and from the lantern, are remarkable. On the way down, there is a room with instruments used during the construction of the dome.

In the N aisle is a painting of Dante with the *Divina Commedia* which illuminates Florence (1465) by *Domenico Michelino.* On the side altar, *Bernardo Ciuffagni,* King David. The two splendid frescoed *Equestrian memorials to the famous 'condottieri', the Englishman Sir John Hawkwood ('Giovanni Acuto') who commanded the Florentine army from 1377 until his death in 1394, and Nicolò da Tolentino (died 1434), are by *Paolo Uccello* and *Andrea del Castagno.* The bust of the organist Antonio Squarcialupi is by *Benedetto da Maiano.* On the last altar, *Donatello* (attributed), the prophet Joshua (traditionally thought to be a portrait of the humanist friend of Cosimo il Vecchio, Poggio Bracciolini), originally on the façade of the Duomo.

The *Campanile (Pl. 7; nearly 85m high) was begun by *Giotto* in 1334 when, as the most distinguished Florentine artist, he was appointed city architect. It was continued by *Andrea Pisano* (1343), and completed by *Francesco Talenti* in 1348–59. It is built of the same coloured marbles as the Duomo, in similar patterns, in a remarkably well-proportioned design. The original bas-reliefs and statues of Prophets and Sibyls in the niches have been removed to the Museo dell'Opera and have been replaced by copies. The ascent of the bell-tower (adm. daily 9–sunset) by 414 steps is interesting for its succession of views of the Duomo, the Baptistery, and the rest of the city. Although lower than the cupola, the climb is steeper.

Between the Baptistery and the Campanile is the little Gothic *LOGGIA DEL BIGALLO built in 1351–58 probably by *Alberto Arnoldi,* who carved the reliefs. Beneath the loggia lost and abandoned children were exposed for three days before being consigned to foster-mothers. The MUSEO DEL BIGALLO (usually closed) is the smallest museum in the city, but one of the most charming. It preserves most of the works of art commissioned over the centuries by the Misericordia and the Bigallo from Florentine artists, including a portable triptych by Bernardo Daddi.

FLORENCE

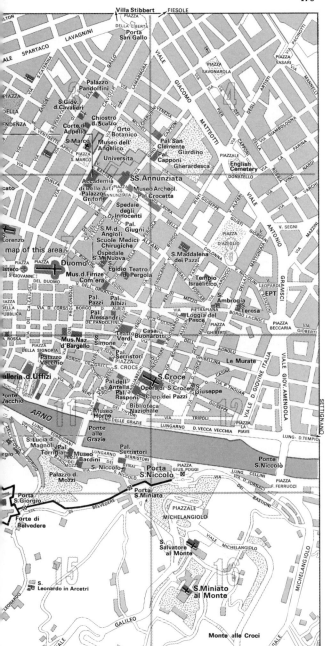

Across Via dei Calzaiuoli is the *Misericordia*, a charitable institution which gives gratuitous help to those in need, and runs an ambulance service. The lay confraternity, thought to have been founded in the 13C, continues its work through some 2000 volunteers who are a characteristic sight of Florence in their black capes and hoods. The Oratory contains an altarpiece by Andrea della Robbia and a statue of St Sebastian by Benedetto da Maiano.—At No. 9 Piazza del Duomo is the **Museo dell'Opera del Duomo* (Pl. 7; adm. daily 9–18; Summer 9–20; fest. 10–13), in a building which has been the seat of the Opera del Duomo (responsible for the maintenance of the cathedral) since the beginning of the 15C. One of the pleasantest museums in the city, it contains material from the Duomo, the Baptistery, and the Campanile, including important sculpture.

In the COURTYARD are two Roman sarcophagi (mid-3C) from the Baptistery.—In the ENTRANCE HALL, marble bust of Brunelleschi attributed to *Giovanni Bandini*, and fine marble panels from the choir of the Duomo by *Baccio Bandinelli* and *Giovanni Bandini*.—ROOM I. The drawing of the old façade (never completed) of the Duomo designed by Arnolfo di Cambio was made shortly before its demolition in 1587 by *Bernardino Poccetti*. Here are displayed numerous **Sculptures from the old façade by *Arnolfo di Cambio*, and four seated statues of the Evangelists added to the lower part of the façade by *Nanni di Banco* (St Luke), *Donatello* (*St John the Evangelist), *Bernardo Ciuffagni* (St Matthew), and *Niccolò di Piero Lamberti* (St Mark).—Two small rooms are devoted to *Brunelleschi*, with his death mask and a model of the lantern, and the apparatus which may have been used in the construction of the cupola, together with the original brick moulds.—On the STAIR LANDING is the **Pietà of *Michelangelo*, removed from the Duomo in 1981. A late work, it was intended for the sculptor's own tomb. According to Vasari, the head of Nicodemus is a self-portrait. Unsatisfied with his work, Michelangelo destroyed the arm and left leg of Christ, and his pupil *Tiberio Calcagni* restored the arm and finished the figure of Mary Magdalen.

FIRST FLOOR. ROOM I is dominated by the two famous **Cantorie made in the 1430s by *Luca della Robbia* and *Donatello* for the Duomo. The original sculptured panels by *Luca* are displayed beneath the reconstructed Cantoria. The children (some of them drawn from Classical models), dancing, singing, or playing musical instruments, are exquisitely carved within a beautiful architectural framework. *Donatello*'s Cantoria provides a striking contrast, with a frieze of running putti against a background of coloured inlay. Beneath it is displayed his expressive statue in wood of **St Mary Magdalen (formerly in the Baptistery), thought to be a late work. Around the walls are the sixteen statues from the niches on the Campanile by *Donatello* (two Prophets, Abraham and Isaac, 'Geremiah', **Habbakuk), *Nanni di Bartolo*, and *Andrea Pisano*.—Next door are the original **Bas-reliefs from the Campanile. The lower row are charming works by *Andrea Pisano* (some perhaps designed by *Giotto*) illustrating the Creation of Man, and the Arts and Industries. The last five reliefs (on the right wall) were made in the following century by *Luca della Robbia*. The upper row of smaller reliefs by pupils of *Pisano* illustrate the seven Planets, the Virtues, and the Liberal Arts. The Seven Sacraments are by *Alberto Arnoldi*. The lunette of the Madonna and Child is by *Andrea Pisano*.

In ROOM II are four gilded bronze **Panels by *Lorenzo Ghiberti*, removed from the East Door of the Baptistery (described above), and displayed here since their restoration. The magnificent **Altar of silver-gilt from the Baptistery, is a Gothic work by Florentine goldsmiths finished in the 15C. The statuette of the Baptist is by *Michelozzo*; the reliefs (at the sides) of the Beheading of the Saint, and of his birth are by *Verrocchio* and *Antonio del Pollaiolo*. The silver **Cross is the work of *Betto di Francesco, Antonio del Pollaiolo*, and others.—Also displayed here are needlework **Panels from a liturgical tapestry worked by the craftsmen of the 'Arte di Calimala' and designed by *Antonio del Pollaiolo*; sculptures by *Andrea Pisano, Jacopo della Quercia* (?), *Tino da Camaino*, and *Pagno di Lapo Portigiani* (attributed), and paintings of the 14–15C Florentine school.

Beside the Baptistery is the *Pillar of St Zenobius*, erected in the 14C to commemorate an elm which came into leaf here when the body of the bishop saint (died c 430) was translated from San Lorenzo to Santa Reparata in the 9C.

B.   Piazza del Duomo to Piazza della Signoria

VIA DE'CALZAIOLI (Pl. 7), on the line of a Roman road, was the main thoroughfare of the medieval city, linking the Duomo to Palazzo Vecchio and passing the guildhall of Orsanmichele. On the right is PIAZZA DELLA REPUBBLICA (Pl. 7), on the site of the Roman forum, and still in the centre of the city. It was laid out at the end of the 19C after the demolition of many medieval buildings. Much criticised at the time, it remains a disappointing intrusion into the historical centre of the city. It has several large cafés with tables outside.—The tall rectangular church of *Orsanmichele (Pl. 7) was built as a market by *Francesco Talenti, Neri di Fioravante*, and *Benci di Cione* in 1337. The arcades were enclosed by huge Gothic windows by *Simone Talenti* in 1380. The upper storey was intended to be used as a granary. The decoration of the exterior was undertaken by the Guilds (or 'Arti') who commissioned statues of their patron saints for the canopied niches. They competed with each other to command work from the best artists of the age, and the statues are an impressive testimony to the skill of Florentine sculptors over a period of some 200 years. Since 1984 restoration of the statues and niches has been underway. So far three statues have been restored and it has been decided that they cannot be returned to the exterior for conservation reasons. A copy of Donatello's St Mark has been made and will soon be exhibited in situ. It is not known where the originals will be kept.

The statues, beginning at Via de'Calzaioli (corner of Via de'Lamberti) and going round to the right are: St John the Baptist (1414–16), by *Lorenzo Ghiberti*, the first life-size statue of the Renaissance to be cast in bronze; *Incredulity of St Thomas (1466–83), by *Verrocchio* (removed), in a tabernacle by *Donatello* (the 'stemma' above is by *Luca della Robbia*); St Luke, by *Giambologna* (1601), in a tabernacle by *Niccolò Lamberti*; St Peter (1408–13) attributed to *Donatello*; tabernacle and St Philip (c 1415) by *Nanni di Banco*; tabernacle, relief, and statues of *Four soldier saints (the 'Quattro Santi Coronati'), modelled on Roman works, by *Nanni di Banco* (c 1415), and 'stemma' above by *Luca della Robbia*; St George by *Donatello* (copies of the statue and relief removed to the Bargello); tabernacle and *St Matthew (1419–22) by *Ghiberti*; *St Stephen by *Ghiberti* (1428); St Eligius (removed) and bas-relief by *Nanni di Banco*; *St Mark by *Donatello* (removed and restored); St James the Greater (removed) and bas-relief attributed to *Niccolò Lamberti*; Gothic tabernacle attributed to *Simone Talenti*, with a *Madonna and Child attributed to *Giovanni Tedesco*, and 'stemma' by *Luca della Robbia*; St John the Evangelist by *Baccio da Montelupo* (1515).

The INTERIOR of the dark rectangular hall now serves as a church, and it contains interesting frescoes (14C–16C), and fine Gothic stained glass windows. The Gothic *Tabernacle by *Andrea Orcagna* (1349–59) is a masterpiece of all the decorative arts. A beautiful frame of carved angels encloses a painting on the altar of the *Madonna by *Bernardo Daddi*. On the other altar is a statue of the Madonna and Child with St Anne, by *Francesco da Sangallo* (1522).—The two large Gothic halls on the upper floors are used for exhibitions.

An overhead passageway connects Orsanmichele to *Palazzo dell'Arte della Lana*, built in 1308 by the Guild of Wool Merchants but arbitrarily restored in 1905. At the base of the tower is the little 14C oratory of Santa Maria della Tromba, with a painting of the Madonna by Jacopo del Casentino.—*Palazzo dell'Arte dei Beccai*, also facing Orsanmichele, the headquarters of the Butchers' Guild until 1534, is now the seat of the Accademia delle Arti del Disegno founded in 1563 by Vasari and his contemporaries.

On Via Porta Rossa is the 16C loggia of the MERCATO NUOVO (Pl. 11), the Florentine straw-market (with stalls also selling leather goods, cheap lace, and souvenirs). It is known to Florentines as 'Il Porcellino' from the popular statue here of a bronze boar (a copy by Tacca from an antique statue in the Uffizi). Via Porta Rossa continues to **Palazzo Davanzati** (Pl. 11), now the MUSEO DELL' ANTICA CASA FIORENTINA (adm. 9–14; fest. 9–13; closed Monday), and the best surviving example of a medieval nobleman's house in Florence (despite numerous restorations). It is particularly interesting as an illustration of Florentine life in the Middle Ages.

The typical 14C façade consists of three storeys above large arches on the ground floor.—The INTERIOR, of great interest for its architecture and contemporary wall paintings (rare survivals of a decorative form typical of 14C houses) has been beautifully arranged with the furnishings of a Florentine house of 15C–17C (including tapestries, lacework, ceramics, sculpture, paintings, decorative arts, domestic objects, etc.). The 16–17C furniture is a special feature of the house.

Via Pellicceria leads to *Palazzo di Parte Guelfa*, built as the official residence of the Captains of the Guelf party in the 13C. The palace was enlarged by Brunelleschi who added a hall.—Nearby is *Palazzo dell'Arte della Seta*, with a beautiful 'stemma' in the style of Donatello.

VIA DELLE TERME, and the parallel BORGO SANTI APOSTOLI to the S, are both pretty medieval streets with numerous towers and old palaces. **Santi Apostoli** (Pl. 10), one of the oldest churches in the city, has a Romanesque stone façade.

The basilican INTERIOR (not always open) has fine green marble columns and capitals. It contains a *Sinopia of a fresco of the Madonna by *Paolo Schiavo* formerly on the façade; the Tomb of Prior Oddo Altoviti by *Benedetto da Rovezzano*; and a *Tabernacle by *Andrea della Robbia*.

Across Via Por Santa Maria (rebuilt since 1944) is the church of SANTO STEFANO AL PONTE (Pl. 11; open for concerts), another very old church. The interior was altered by Ferdinando Tacca in 1649. The altar-steps are by Buontalenti, and the altarpieces by Santi di Tito, Matteo Rosselli, and others.

Piazza della Signoria (Pl. 11), dominated by Palazzo Vecchio, the town hall, has been the political centre of the city since the Middle Ages. Here, from the 13C onwards, the 'popolo sovrano' met in 'parlamento' to resolve crises of government. In the life of the city today, the piazza is still the focus of political manifestations. It is now a pedestrian precinct and usually crowded with tourists as well as Florentines. By 1385, when it was paved, the piazza had nearly reached its present dimensions. During the 'restoration' of the 18C pavement of the square archaeological excavations interrupted the work. In 1990 the controversy continued about the laying of the pavement, and the end result is far from satisfactory.—The huge *Loggia della Signoria** (Pl. 11; also known as *Loggia dei Lanzi* and *Loggia dell'Orcagna*; covered for restoration in 1990), with three beautiful lofty arches, was built in 1376–82 by *Benci di Cione* and *Simone Talenti* (probably on a design by *Orcagna*) to be used by government officials during public ceremonies and as an ornament to the square.

Since the end of the 18C the loggia has been used as an open-air museum of sculpture. The magnificent bronze *Perseus trampling Medusa and exhibiting her severed head was commissioned from *Cellini* by Cosimo I in 1545. The original bas-relief and statuettes from the pedestal are now in the Bargello. The *Rape of the Sabine (1583), a three-figure group, is *Giambologna*'s last work, and one of the most successful Mannerist sculptures. Also here are two lions, one a Greek work, the other a 16C copy; Hercules and the Centaur, by *Giambologna*; the Rape of Polyxena, by *Pio Fedi*; and Roman statues.

Michelangelo's famous DAVID was commissioned by the city of Florence in 1501 and set up here in 1504 as a political symbol representing the victory of Republicanism over tyranny. It was removed to the Accademia in 1873 and here replaced by a copy.—The colossal statue of Hercules and Cacus, an unhappy imitation of the David, was sculpted in 1534 by *Bandinelli*. Donatello's statue of Judith and Holofernes has been replaced by a copy (original inside Palazzo Vecchio, see below). The NEPTUNE FOUNTAIN, by *Ammannati*, is dominated by a colossal flaccid figure of Neptune, known to Florentines as 'il Biancone'. The more successful elegant bronze groups on the basin were carved by *Giambologna, Andrea Calamech*, and others. The porphyry disk in the pavement in front of the fountain marks the spot where Savonarola was burnt at the stake as a heretic in 1498. The fine bronze equestrian monument to Cosimo I is by *Giambologna*. At the end of the piazza, towards Piazza San Firenze, is the *Tribunale di Mercanzia* (or Merchants' Court), founded in 1308 and established in this building in 1359. *Palazzo Uguccioni* (No. 7) has an unusual but handsome façade attributed to Mariotto di Zanobi Folfi (1550), with a bust of Francesco I by Giovanni Bandini. Above a bank at No. 5 is displayed the COLLEZIONE DELLA RAGIONE (adm. 9–14 except Tuesday, and fest. 9–13), a representative collection of 20C Italian art left to the city in 1970 by Alberto Della Ragione.

***Palazzo Vecchio** (Pl. 11; also known as *Palazzo della Signoria*), the medieval Palazzo del Popolo, is still the town hall of Florence. On a design traditionally attributed to *Arnolfo di Cambio* (1298–1302), it is an imposing fortress-palace built in pietra forte on a trapezoidal plan. The façade has remained virtually unchanged: it has graceful two-light windows and a battlemented gallery. It became the prototype of many other Palazzi Comunali in Tuscany. It was the tallest edifice in the city until the 15C; the tower (1310), asymmetrically placed, is 95m high. Many of the rooms on the upper floors are open to the public, or used for exhibitions. Adm. 9–19; fest. 9–13; closed Saturday).

The palace stands on part of the site of the Roman theatre of Florence built in the 1C AD. Here the 'priori' lived during their two months' tenure of office in the government of the medieval city. Cosimo il Vecchio was imprisoned in the 'Alberghetto' in the tower in 1433 before being exiled. In 1540 Cosimo I moved here from the private Medici palace in Via Larga. It became known as Palazzo Vecchio after 1549 when the Medici grand-dukes took up residence in Palazzo Pitti. From 1865 to 1871 it housed the Chamber of Deputies and the Foreign Ministry when Florence was capital of the Kingdom of Italy.

Above the ENTRANCE is a frieze (1528) dedicated to 'Cristo Re'. The CORTILE (being restored) was reconstructed by *Michelozzo* (1453), and the elaborate decoration added in 1565 by *Vasari* on the occasion of the marriage between Francesco, son of Cosimo I, and Joanna of Austria. The fountain bears a copy of *Verrocchio*'s putto, now inside the palace. The statue of Samson killing the Philistine is by *Pierino da Vinci*. In the 14C SALA D'ARME exhibitions are held. The rest of the ground floor is taken up with busy local government offices.—A monumental double GRAND STAIRCASE by *Vasari* ascends to the immense ***Salone dei Cinquecento**, built by *Cronaca* in 1495 for the meetings of the Consiglio Maggiore of the Republic. *Leonardo da Vinci* and *Michelangelo* were commissioned to paint huge murals of the battles of Anghiari and Cascina on the two long walls. Only the cartoons and a fragment by Leonardo were ever completed; these were copied and studied by contemporary painters before they were lost. The room was transformed by *Vasari* in 1563–65 when the present decoration was carried out in celebration of Cosimo I, and the Florentine victories over Siena and Pisa, by *Giovanni Stradano*, *Jacopo Zucchi*, and *Giovanni Battista Naldini*. *Michelangelo*'s *Victory, a strongly knit two-figure group, was intended for a niche in the tomb of Julius II in Rome. *Giambologna*'s Virtue overcoming Vice was commissioned as a 'pendant' (the original plaster model is displayed here). The statues of the Labours of Hercules are *Vincenzo de'Rossi*'s best works.

An inconspicuous door gives access to the charming *STUDIOLO OF FRANCESCO I (closed on Sunday). This tiny study is a masterpiece of Florentine Mannerist decoration created by *Vasari* and his school. It is entirely decorated with paintings and bronze statuettes celebrating Francesco's interest in the natural sciences and alchemy, by *Il Poppi*, *Bronzino, Vincenzo Danti, Vasari, Santi di Tito, Giovanni Battista Naldini, Giovanni Battista Stradano, Alessandro Allori, Giovanni Bandini, Maso di San Friano, Giambologna, Vincenzo de'Rossi, Giovanni Maria Butteri, Alessandro Fei, Bartolomeo Ammannati*, and *Jacopo Zucchi*.—The Town Council meets in the SALA DEI DUGENTO, reconstructed in 1472–77 by *Benedetto* and *Giuliano da Maiano*, who also executed the magnificent wood ceiling (with the help of *Domenico Marco*, and *Giuliano del Tasso*). On the walls are *Tapestries (removed for restoration) made in Florence by *Bronzino, Pontormo, Salviati*, and *Allori*.

The **Quartiere di Leone X** (mostly now kept closed) was decorated by *Vasari, Marco da Faenza, Giovanni Stradano*, and others for Cosimo I with paintings illustrating the political history of the Medici family. The Chapel contains an old copy of the Madonna dell'Impannata by Raphael (now in the Pitti), and portraits of Duke Cosimo and Cosimo il Vecchio as St Damaian and St Cosma, by *Vasari*. In the Sala di Clemente VII is an interesting mural painting of the siege of Florence by Charles V.

Stairs lead up to the **Quartiere degli Elementi**, also decorated by *Vasari* and assistants. The Terrazza di Saturno (closed for restoration) has a good view of Florence. In a little room here is displayed the original of *Verrocchio*'s *Putto with a dolphin, removed from the courtyard.—A balcony leads across the end of the Sala dei Cinquecento, where a painting of 1557 shows the lost fragment of the Battle of Anghiari by Leonardo, probably the best copy that has survived. The apartments of the wife of Cosimo I are known as the **Quartiere di Eleonora di Toledo**. The *Chapel was entirely decorated by *Bronzino*. Beyond the Cappella della Signoria decorated by *Ridolfo del Ghirlandaio* is the SALA D'UDIENZA with a superb *Ceiling by *Giuliano da Maiano* and assistants. The *Doorway crowned by a statue of Justice is by *Benedetto* and *Giuliano da Maiano*. The mural paintings (1545–48) are by *Salviati*.—The SALA DEI GIGLI has another magnificent *Ceiling, and frescoes by *Domenico Ghirlandaio*. Here is displayed *Donatello*'s bronze statue of *Judith and Holofernes, removed from Piazza della Signoria and recently restored. It is one of his last and most sophisticated works. The Cancelleria was Niccolò Machiavelli's office when government secretary.—The Guardaroba contains 57 maps illustrating the entire known world by *Fra Egnazio Danti* and *Stefano Bonsignori* (1563–81).— The COLLEZIONE LOESER in the Quartiere del Mezzanino is at present closed to the public. It includes a *Portrait of Laura Battiferri, wife of Bartolomeo Ammannati, by *Bronzino*; a tondo of the Madonna and Child with St John, by Alfonso Berruguete, and a 16C bust of Machiavelli.—Also here the musical instruments from the Conservatorio Cherubini have been temporarily housed (stringed instruments by Stradivari, Guarneri, Arnati, and Ruggeri; a harpsichord by Cristofori, etc.).

C. Galleria degli Uffizi

The massive **Palazzo degli Uffizi* (Pl. 11) extends from Piazza della Signoria to the Arno. The unusual U-shaped building with a short 'façade' on the river front was begun in 1560 by *Vasari*, and completed according to his design by *Alfonso Parigi the Elder* and *Bernardo Buontalenti*. It was commissioned by Cosimo I to serve as government offices ('uffici', hence 'uffizi'). Resting on unstable sandy ground, it is a feat of engineering skill. The use of iron to reinforce the building permitted extraordinary technical solutions during its construction, and allowed for the remarkably large number of apertures.

The ****Galleria degli Uffizi** is the most important collection of paintings in Italy and one of the great art collections of the world. The origins of the collection go back to Cosimo I, and numerous members of the Medici dynasty continued to add works of art in the following centuries. The last of the Medici, Anna Maria Lodovica, settled her inheritance on the people of Florence in 1737. All the works are well labelled and the collection is arranged chronologically by schools. Work has been underway for years to move the exit to Via de'Castellani, and 'restructure' the gallery, using the second floor. Admission 9–18.45; fest. 9–12.45; closed Monday.

Ground Floor. In a room (not always open) which incorporates the remains of the church of San Pier Scheraggio (founded c 1068) a series of *Frescoes of illustrious Florentines by *Andrea del Castagno* are displayed. Nearby is a detached fresco of the *Annunciation by *Botticelli*.—There is a LIFT for the picture galleries on the third floor; the STAIRCASE, lined with antique busts and statues, leads up past the **Prints and Drawings Room**, with one of the finest collections in the world, particularly rich in Renaissance and Mannerist works (shown in *Exhibitions).

On the **Third Floor** the VESTIBULE (A) contains good antique sculpture. The long U-shaped gallery, once lined with tapestries by *Bachiacca* and the 16C Flemish school (now removed for conservation reasons) provides a fine setting for the superb collection of antique sculptures (mostly Hellenistic works). ROOM 1 (right), has fine antique reliefs.

R. 2 contains three famous paintings of the *Maestà by *Cimabue*, *Duccio di Boninsegna* (both c 1285), and *Giotto* (painted some 25 years later). Duccio's Madonna was beautifully restored in 1989.—R. 3 displays works of the 14C Sienese school including, the *Lorenzetti* brothers, and an *Annunciation, one of *Simone Martini*'s most famous works.—R. 4. Florentine school of the 14C (*Bernardo Daddi, Nardo di Cione, Giovanni da Milano*, etc.).—RR. 5 & 6. Works by *Lorenzo Monaco* and *Gentile da Fabriano*, including two charming representations of the *Adoration of the Magi.

R. 7 (Florentine School of the early 15C). *Domenico Veneziano*, *Madonna enthroned with Saints; *Piero della Francesca*, *Portraits of Federico di Montefeltro and Battista Sforza; *Paolo Uccello*, *Battle of San Romano.—R. 8 contains some lovely *Works by *Filippo Lippi* (Coronation of the Virgin, Madonna and Child with two Angels, etc.).—R. 9. Paintings by *Piero* and *Antonio del Pollaiolo* (Six Virtues, and Saints Vincent, James, and Eustace, from San Miniato) and *Botticelli* (Story of Holofernes).—RR. 10–14 have been converted into

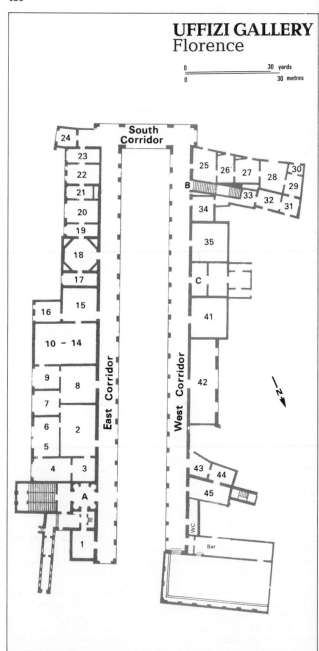

UFFIZI GALLERY
Florence

0   30 yards
0   30 metres

one huge room to display the masterpieces of *Botticelli*, including the famous *Primavera and *Birth of Venus, as well as his *Adoration of the Magi, Calumny of Apelles, *Pallas and the Centaur, and *Madonna of the Magnificat. The Primavera, an allegory of Spring richly painted on poplar wood was beautifully restored in 1982. The Birth of Venus may illustrate a poem by Poliziano and is painted with a remarkable lightness of touch. Also here, *Lorenzo di Credi*, Venus; *Filippino Lippi*, Self-portrait; and *Hugo van der Goes*, *Triptych commissioned by the Portinari family.

R. 15 displays the early Florentine works of *Leonardo da Vinci* (*Annunciation, and the *Adoration of the Magi, an unfinished composition), together with paintings by his master *Verrocchio* (Baptism of Christ, and *Tobias and three Archangels). Also works by *Luca Signorelli*, *Piero di Cosimo*, and *Lorenzo di Credi*.—The beautiful octagonal *TRIBUNA (18) was designed by *Buontalenti*, and contains the most important *Sculptures owned by the Medici (the famous Medici Venus, a copy of the Praxitelean Aphrodite of Cnidos; the 'Arrotino'; the Dancing Faun; and 'Apollino'). Around the walls are a remarkable series of distinguished court *Portraits, many of them of the family of Cosimo I commissioned from *Bronzino*.

R. 19. *Perugino*, Madonna enthroned with Saints, and Portraits; *Signorelli*, *Tondi of the Madonna and Child and Holy Family.—R. 20 is devoted to *Dürer* (Adoration of the Magi) and the German School, including *Cranach* (Adam and Eve).—R. 21 (Venetian School). Works by *Giovanni Bellini*, (*Sacred Allegory), *Giorgione*, *Cima da Conegliano*, etc.—R. 22 contains German and Flemish works. *Portraits by *Holbein*, *Hans Memling* and *Joos van Cleve the Elder*; and works by *Albrecht Altdorfer*, *Gerard David* (Adoration of the Magi), etc.—R. 23. *Triptych by *Mantegna*; and works by *Bernardo Luini*, *Giovanni Antonio Boltraffio*, etc.

The short SOUTH CORRIDOR (good view of the Arno) displays some more fine sculpture (Roman matron, Crouching Venus, etc.).—R. 25 contains the famous *Tondo Doni of the Holy Family, the only finished oil painting by *Michelangelo*, and works by *Mariotto Albertinelli*, and *Rosso Fiorentino*.—In R. 26 are some famous works by *Raphael:* *Madonna del Cardellino, *Leo X with Cardinals Giulio de'Medici and Luigi de'Rossi; works by *Andrea del Sarto*; and portraits by *Pontormo*.—More good works by *Pontormo* are displayed in R. 27, together with works by *Franciabigio* and *Bronzino*. R. 28 is devoted to *Titian:* *Flora, *Venus of Urbino, *Knight of Malta, Venus and Cupid, etc.—RR. 29–33 were closed in 1990. In RR. 29 & 30 are works of the 16C Emilian School, notably *Parmigianino* (*Madonna 'dal collo lungo').—RR. 31 & 32 (Veneto School). *Sebastiano del Piombo* (Portrait of a sick man, *Death of Adonis).—R. 33 (French School). *François Clouet*, Equestrian portrait of Francis I.—R34. Venetian School, including works by *Paolo Veronese* (*Annunciation, *Holy Family with St Barbara), and *Giovanni Battista Moroni* (*Count Pietro Secco Suardi).

The **Corridoio Vasariano** (B) can usually be visited by previous appointment (but it was closed in 1990 for structural repairs). It was built by *Vasari* in 1565 to connect Palazzo Vecchio via the Uffizi and Ponte Vecchio with Palazzo Pitti, in the form of a covered passage-way. It affords unique views of the city, and is hung with notable paintings including a celebrated collection of *Self-portraits (begun by Cardinal Leopoldo), by *Vasari, Bronzino, Salvator Rosa, Rubens, Rembrandt, Van Dyck, Velasquez, Hogarth, Reynolds, David, Delacroix, Corot, Ingres*, and many others.

R. 35 contains fine works by *Tintoretto* (Portraits, *Leda), *Jacopo Bassano*, and *Federico Barocci* (Noli me tangere, Portraits).—R. 41. *Rubens*, huge canvases illustrating the history of Henri IV, Philip IV of Spain, *Isabella Brandt; *Van Dyck*, Portraits, including an equestrian portrait of the Emperor Charles V; *Sustermans*, Galileo Galilei.—The Niobe Room (42; often closed) contains Roman statues of Niobe and her children and the neo-Attic Medici vase.—R. 43. Works by *Caravaggio* (Young Bacchus, *Sacrifice of Isaac), *Annibale Carracci* (Bacchic scene), and *Claude Lorraine* (seascapes).—R. 44 has three *Portraits by *Rembrandt* (two of them self-portraits), and Dutch and Flemish works (*Jan Steen, Jacob Ruysdael*, etc.).—R. 45 contains 18C works by *Piazzetta, Giovanni Battista Tiepolo, Francesco Guardi, Canaletto, Alessandro Longhi*; and portraits by *Jean-Marc Nattier, Etiene Liotard, Francesco Xavier Fabre, Chardin*, and *Goya*.—On the landing by the STAIRS (C) down to the exit is a sculptured Boar (copy of a Hellenistic original; see Rte 42B).

D. Ponte Vecchio, Palazzo Pitti, and the Boboli Gardens

The fame of **Ponte Vecchio** (Pl. 11; open to pedestrians only), lined with quaint medieval-looking houses, saved it from damage in 1944. It was the only bridge over the Arno until 1218. The present bridge of three arches was reconstructed after a flood in 1345 probably by Taddeo Gaddi (also attributed to Neri di Fioravante). The jewellers' shops have pretty fronts with wood shutters and awnings; they overhang the river supported on brackets. The excellent jewellers here continue the traditional skill of Florentine goldsmiths whose work first became famous in the 15C. Above the shops on the left side can be seen the round windows of the Corridoio Vasariano. From the opening in the centre there is a view of Ponte Santa Trìnita.—In the Oltrarno Via Guicciardini continues towards Piazza Pitti; on the left opens Piazza Santa Felicita with a granite column of 1381 marking the site of the first Christian cemetery in Florence. Here is **Santa Felicita** (Pl. 11), probably the oldest church in Florence after San Lorenzo. The paleochristian church, dedicated to the Roman martyr, St Felicity, was last rebuilt in 1736 by Ferdinando Ruggieri in a 15C style.

The fine INTERIOR is chiefly notable for the superb *Works (1525–27) by *Pontormo* in the Cappella Capponi (an altarpiece of the Deposition, and frescoes of the Annunciation, and the Evangelists). The church also contains altarpieces by *Antonio Ciseri, Simone Pignone*, and *Francesco Brina*.—In the SACRISTY are works by *Taddeo Gaddi, Neri di Bicci*, and *Niccolò di Pietro Gerini*.

*Palazzo Pitti (Pl. 10) was built by the merchant Luca Pitti, an effective demonstration of his wealth and power to his rivals the Medici. The majestic golden-coloured palace is built in huge rough-hewn blocks of stone of different sizes. Its design is attributed to *Brunelleschi* although it was begun c 1457, after his death. *Luca Fanelli* is known to have been engaged on the building, but it is generally considered that another architect, whose name is unknown, was also involved. The palace remained incomplete on the death of Luca Pitti in 1472; by then it consisted of the central seven bays with three doorways. *Bartolomeo Ammannati*, and then *Giulio* and *Alfonso Parigi the*

Younger completed the building, and the two 'rondò' were added in the 18C and 19C.

In 1549 the palace was bought by Eleonora di Toledo, wife of Cosimo I. It became the official seat of the Medici dynasty of grand-dukes after Cosimo I moved here from Palazzo Vecchio. The various ruling families of Florence continued to occupy the palace, or part of it, until 1919 when Victor Emmanuel III presented it to the State.

The splendid *COURTYARD by Ammannati serves as a garden façade to the palace. It is a masterpiece of Florentine Mannerist architecture, with bold rustication in three orders. Under the portico to the right is the entrance to the celebrated **Galleria di Palazzo Pitti** or **Galleria Palatina**, formed in the 17C by the Medici grand-dukes, and installed here in the 18C. The reception rooms on the piano nobile were decorated in the 17C by Pietro da Cortona for the Medici grand-dukes. They contain the masterpieces of the collection, including numerous famous works by Raphael and Titian. The arrangement of the pictures (most of them richly framed) still preserves to some extent the character of a private royal collection of the 17–18C, the aesthetic arrangement of the rooms being considered rather than the chronological placing of the paintings. This produces a remarkable effect of magnificence even though in some cases the pictures (all of which are well labelled) are difficult to see on the crowded walls.

Tickets for the Galleria Palatina (and a separate ticket for the Museo degli Argenti, which includes admission to the Galleria del Costume and the Museo delle Porcellane) are purchased off the courtyard, left of the stairs up to the gallery.—For the Galleria d'Arte Moderna tickets are purchased at the entrance on the second floor.
   Admission 9–14; fest. 9–13; closed Monday.

The Grand Staircase by *Ammannati* ascends to the entrance to the Galleria Palatina. Beyond three reception rooms (A, B, and I) is the

The courtyard by Ammannati of the Palazzo Pitti in Florence

490

PALAZZO PITTI
Florence
Galleria Palatina

SALA DI VENERE (1), with the earliest ceiling (1641–42) of the fine group executed for the following four rooms by *Pietro da Cortona* for Ferdinand II. The paintings here include: *Titian*, *Concert (a famous work, also attributed to *Giorgione*); *Pietro Aretino, a splendid portrait; and *Portrait of a lady ('la bella'); *Rubens*, Ulysses in the Phaecian Isle, and *Return from the hayfields; seascapes by *Salvator Rosa*. The *'Venus Italica' was sculpted by *Canova*, and presented by Napoleon in exchange for the Medici Venus which he had carried off to Paris.—SALA DI APOLLO (2). Portraits by *Van Dyck, Rubens*, and *Sustermans; Guido Reni*, Cleopatra; *Andrea del Sarto*, *Holy Family, and *Deposition; *Rosso Fiorentino*, Madonna enthroned; *Titian*, *Portrait of a Gentleman, once thought to be the Duke of Norfolk, and *Mary Magdalen.—SALA DI MARTE (3). Portraits by *Tintoretto* (Luigi Cornaro), *Van Dyck* (Cardinal Bentivoglio), *Paolo Veronese*, and *Titian* (*Cardinal Ippolito de'Medici); *Rubens*, *Consequences of War, a huge allegorical painting, and *'The Four Philosophers' (Rubens, his brother Filippo, Justus Lipsius, and Jan van Wouwer).— THE SALA DI GIOVE (4). *Venetian School*, *Three Ages of Man (also attributed to *Giorgione*); *Raphael*, *Portrait of a lady ('la Velata', one of the most beautiful of all his paintings); works by *Andrea del Sarto* (including *Young St John the Baptist) and *Fra' Bartolomeo* (*Deposition; restored in 1988).

SALA DI SATURNO (5). *Raphael*, *Madonna 'della Seggiola', a beautifully composed tondo, among the artist's most mature and most popular paintings; *Maddalena Doni, and her husband; Vision of Ezekiel; Madonna 'del Baldacchino'; Cardinal Tommaso Inghirami; *Madonna 'del Granduca', an early work showing the influence of Leonardo; *Perugino*, *Deposition; and works by *Ridolfo del Ghirlandaio, Annibale Carracci*, etc.—SALA DELL'ILIADE (6). Portraits by *Sustermans, Francesco Poubus the Younger, Ridolfo del Ghirlandaio*, and *Joos van Cleve; Andrea del Sarto*, two large paintings of the *Assumption; *Titian*, *Philip II of Spain, *Diego de Mendoza; *Raphael*, *Portrait of a woman expecting a child.

The other rooms of the Galleria Palatina house the smaller works in the collection.

The SALA DELLE ALLEGORIE (8) contains works by *Volterrano* and *Giovanni da San Giovanni*. The rooms beyond (9–15) include works by *Cigoli, Carlo Dolci, Empoli, Lorenzo Lippi, Cristofano Allori, Jacopo Ligozzi, Jacopo Vignali, Francesco Furini, Giovanni Bilivert, Francesco Curradi, Salvator Rosa*, etc.—In the GALLERIA DEL POCCETTI (17) are portraits by *Rubens, Pontormo, Peter Lely*, and *Niccolò Cassana*. The SALA DI PROMETEO (18) contains: *Baldassarre Peruzzi*, Dance of Apollo with the Muses; *Rubens*, The Three Graces (a small monochrome painting); *Filippo Lippi*, *Tondo of the Madonna and Child, one of his best works; *Guido Reni*, Young Bacchus; *Botticelli* (attributed), Portrait of a lady in profile; and works by *Pontormo, Francesco Botticini, Luca Signorelli, Marco Palmezzano*, etc.—Beyond a CORRIDOR (19) with small Flemish paintings is the SALA DELLA GIUSTIZIA (20) with fine portraits by *Titian* (*Portrait of a man, once thought to be Vincenzo Mosti) and *Tintoretto*. R 21 contains the Story of Joseph by *Andrea del Sarto*; and R 22 Dutch works.—The SALA DI ULISSE (23) contains fine portraits by *Moroni* and *Tintoretto*. Also, *Filippino Lippi*, *Death of Lucrezia; and *Raphael*, *Madonna dell'Impannata. Beyond the delightful 'Empire' BATHROOM (24) is the SALA DELL'EDUCAZIONE DI GIOVE (25) with Judith with the head of Holofernes by *Cristoforo Allori*, and the Sleeping Cupid, a late work by *Caravaggio*; also typical pious works by *Carlo Dolci*. The *SALA DELLA STUFA (26) is beautifully frescoed by *Pietro da Cortona* (the four Ages of the World) and *Matteo Rosselli*.

The other half of the piano nobile along the façade of the palace is occupied by the **Appartamenti Monumentali** (ex *Reali*; closed for restoration). This series of state apartments, most of them lavishly decorated in the 19C by the Dukes of

Lorraine, are notable particularly for their numerous 17C portraits of the Medici by *Sustermans*, and a fine group of 18C Gobelins tapestries.

On the floor above the Galleria Palatina is the **Galleria d'Arte Moderna** (adm. as for the Galleria Palatina). The collection is particularly representative of Tuscan art of the 19C, notably the 'Macchiaioli' school (*Giovanni Fattori, Silvestro Lega, Telemaco Signorini*, etc.). Many of the rooms on this floor were decorated in the 19C by the last Grand-Dukes Ferdinand III and Leopold II. In every room there is a detailed catalogue of the works displayed which cover the period from the mid-18C up to the end of the First World War. They are arranged chronologically and by schools. The collection of 20C works is particularly representative of the years between the two Wars.

The **Museo degli Argenti** (adm., see above), arranged in the summer apartments of the grand-dukes, is entered from the left side of the courtyard. The main room contains exuberant and colourful frescoes by *Giovanni di San Giovanni*.—In the Sala Buia is displayed the magnificent *Collection of vases in pietre dure which belonged to Lorenzo il Magnifico, most of which date from the Late Imperial Roman era.—The reception rooms are decorated with trompe l'oeil frescoes by *Angelo Michele Colonna* and *Agostino Mitelli*. The rooms towards the gardens were the living quarters of the grand-dukes. Here, and on the mezzanine floor, are displayed their eclectic collection of personal keepsakes, gifts presented by other ruling families, objets d'art made specially for them, and the *Jewellery collection of the electress Anna Maria.

In the Palazzina della Meridiana, which was begun in 1776 by *Gaspare Maria Paoletti*, is the **Galleria del Costume** (adm. as for the Palatina) which illustrates the history of costume from the 18C to the early 20C. On the upper floor the *Collezione Contini-Bonacossi** was arranged in 1974 (closed; to be moved to the Uffizi). It contains a fine collection of Italian, and some Spanish, paintings, and furniture of the 15–17C, majolica, etc., including works by *Sassetta, Defendente Ferrari, Giovanni Bellini, Paolo Veronese, Gian Lorenzo Bernini, Francesco Goya, El Greco, Tintoretto*, and *Andrea del Castagno*.

On the hillside behind Palazzo Pitti lie the magnificent *Boboli** **Gardens** (Pl.10, 14; open 9—sunset), laid out for Cosimo I by *Tribolo*, and perhaps also *Ammannati*, after 1550, and extended in the early 17C. The biggest public park in the centre of Florence, the gardens are beautifully maintained. They are always cool even on the hottest summer days, and are a delightful place to picnic. Many of the statues which decorate the walks are restored Roman works, and others date from the 16C and 17C. Some of them have been restored in situ, while others have been removed for restoration and will be replaced by copies. The restored statues will be exhibited in Le Pagliere, a stable block of 1867 near Porta Romana.

Near the entrance from Piazza Pitti is the *GROTTA GRANDE, by Buontalenti or Ammannati, with statues by *Baccio Bandinelli, Vincenzo de'Rossi*, and *Giambologna* (Venus emerging from her bath), and murals by *Bernardino Poccetti*.—The main path emerges on the terrace behind the palace (good view of the Duomo). The AMPHITHEATRE was designed by *Ammannati* in imitation of a Roman circus. The huge granite basin comes from the Baths of Caracalla and the obelisk of Rameses II was taken from Heliopolis by the Romans in 30 BC.—On the upper terraces are Roman statues, the Neptune Fountain, and, at the top of the garden, a colossal statue of Abundance begun by *Giambologna* and finished by *Tacca*. A flight of steps leads up to the delightful secluded GIARDINO DEL CAVALIERE (charming view). Here is the MUSEO DELLE PORCELLANE (adm., see above) with a collection of 18–19C Italian, German, and French porcelain from the Medici and Lorraine grand-ducal collections.—The magnificent long cypress avenue called the 'VIOTTOLONE' descends steeply through the most beautiful part of the gardens past arboured walks towards Porta Romana. At the bottom is the ISOLOTTO and HEMICYCLE with numerous statues.

E. The Galleria dell'Accademia, Santissima Annunziata, Museo di San Marco, Palazzo Medici-Riccardi, and San Lorenzo

At No. 60 Via Ricasoli is the entrance to the ***Galleria dell'Accademia** (Pl. 7; adm. 9–14; fest. 9–13; closed Monday), visited above all for its famous works by Michelangelo, but also containing an important collection of Florentine paintings.

The collection was formed in 1784 with a group of paintings given, for study purposes, to the Academy by Pietro Leopoldo I. Since 1873 some important sculptures by Michelangelo have been housed here, including the David.

In the first room of the PINACOTECA: works by *Fra' Bartolomeo* (*Madonna enthroned with Saints), *Francesco Granacci, Mariotto Albertinelli, Filippino Lippi* and *Perugino* (Descent from the Cross), etc. The GALLERIA contains **Sculptures by *Michelangelo*. The four Slaves or Prisoners (c 1521–23) were begun for the ill-fated tomb of Julius II. The St Matthew (1504–08), one of the twelve apostles commissioned from the sculptor by the Opera del Duomo, was the only one he ever began. These are all magnificent examples of Michelangelo's unfinished works, some of them barely blocked out, the famous 'non-finito', much discussed by scholars.—The Pietà from Santa Rosalia in Palestrina is an undocumented work, and is not now usually considered to be by Michelangelo's own hand.

To the right are three more rooms of the Pinacoteca: *Frontal of a 'cassone' or marriage-chest of the Adimari family showing a wedding scene in front of the Baptistery; works by *Mariotto di Cristofano, Botticelli* (two *Madonnas), *Alesso Baldovinetti* (*Trinity and Saints), *Lorenzo di Credi* (Adoration of the Child), *Raffaellino del Garbo, Cosimo Rosselli*, etc.

The Tribune was specially built in 1873 to exhibit the *David by Michelangelo (1501–04) when it was removed from Piazza della Signoria. It is perhaps the most famous single work of art of western civilisation, and has become all too familiar through endless reproductions, although it is not the work by which Michelangelo is best judged. It was commissioned by the city of Florence to stand outside Palazzo Vecchio where its huge scale fits its setting. The figure of David, uncharacteristic of Michelangelo's works, stands in a classical pose suited to the shallow block of marble, 4.10m high. The hero, a young colossus, is shown in the moment before his victory over Goliath. A celebration of the nude, the statue established Michelangelo as the foremost sculptor of his time at the age of 29.

To the left are three more rooms containing early Tuscan works of the 13–14C, (including a Pietà by *Giovanni da Milano).—In the huge room at the end (not always open), 19C works by Academicians, including plaster models by *Lorenzo Bartolini*.—On the first floor (not always open), Florentine paintings of the 14C and 15C.

At the crossing of Via Ricasoli with Via degli Alfani is the *Conservatorio Luigi Cherubini*.—At No. 78 Via Alfani is the OPIFICIO DELLE PIETRE DURE, founded in 1588 by the Grand-Duke Ferdinando I. The craft of working hard or semi-precious stones ('pietre dure') was perfected in Florence. Beautiful mosaics were made to decorate cabinets, table-tops, etc. some of which are exhibited in a small Museum here (open 9–14, Monday, Wednesday and Thursday, 14.30–17.30; closed fest.).—Nearby is the *Rotonda di Santa Maria degli Angeli* (now used by the university; no adm.), one of the first centralised buildings of the Renaissance begun by Brunelleschi in 1434 and left unfinished.—Via dei Servi is lined with a number of handsome 16C palaces, including Palazzo dei Pucci attributed to Ammannati. The church of *San Michele Visdomini* (or San Michelino) contains a *Holy Family by Pontormo.—The *Tabernacolo delle Cinque Lampade* encloses a fresco by Cosimo Rosselli.

Piazza Santissima Annunziata (Pl. 7), designed by *Brunelleschi*, is surrounded on three sides by porticoes. It is the most beautiful square in Florence. The equestrian statue of the Grand-Duke Ferdinando I is by *Giambologna*, and the two fountains (recently restored) by *Tacca*. The *Spedale degli Innocenti*, opened in 1445 as a foundling hospital, the first institution of its kind in Europe, is still operating as a school. *Brunelleschi* began work on the building in 1419, and the *COLONNADE* of nine arches is one of the first masterpieces of the Renaissance. It takes inspiration from classical antiquity as well as from local Romanesque buildings. In the spandrels are delightful *Medallions, perhaps the best known work of *Andrea della Robbia* (1487), each with a baby in swaddling-clothes against a bright blue ground.

The CONVENT may be visited to see the **Museo dello Spedale degli Innocenti** (adm. 9–13; closed Wednesday). Among *Brunelleschi*'s works are the Chiostro degli Uomini (with a lunette by *Andrea della Robbia*), and the oblong *Chiostro delle Donne, with 24 slender Ionic columns beneath a low loggia.—Stairs lead up to the Loggia, with detached frescoes by Florentine artists. In the Long Gallery are Florentine paintings, including the splendid *Adoration of the Magi by *Domenico Ghirlandaio*. Also here, *Madonna and Child, one of the most beautiful works by *Luca della Robbia*.

The church of the *Santissima Annunziata* (Pl. 7), was founded by the seven original Florentine members of the Servite Order in 1250 and rebuilt, along with the cloister, by *Michelozzo* and others in 1444–81.

The series of frescoes on the walls of the CHIOSTRINO DEI VOTI is particularly interesting since most of them were painted in the second decade of the 16C by the leading painters of the time: (right to left): *Rosso Fiorentino*, Assumption; *Pontormo*, Visitation; *Franciabigio*, Marriage of the Virgin; *Andrea del Sarto*, *Birth of the Virgin, Coming of the Magi.—The frescoes by *Alesso Baldovinetti* (*Nativity) and *Cosimo Rosselli* (Vocation and Investiture of San Filippo Benizzi) are earlier works. The last five frescoes are damaged works by *Andrea del Sarto*.
   In the heavily decorated and dark INTERIOR is a highly venerated shrine of the Madonna. The huge *Tabernacle was designed by *Michelozzo* and executed by *Pagno di Lapo Portigiani.*—On the S side, monument to Orlando de'Medici, by *Bernardo Rossellino*, and a Pietà by *Bandinelli* who is buried here. The fine organ is by *Domenico di Lorenzo di Lucca* (1521). The unusual circular TRIBUNE was begun by *Michelozzo* and completed in 1477 by *Leon Battista Alberti*. In the cupola is a fresco by *Volterrano*. The high altar dates from the 17C. Near the *Tomb of Bishop Angelo Marzi Medici signed by *Francesco da Sangallo* (1546) is the burial place of Andrea del Sarto. In the semicircular chapels which radiate from the Sanctuary are paintings by *Alessandro* and *Cristoforo Allori*, *Bronzino* (Resurrection), and a statue of St Roch by *Veit Stoss*. The E chapel is the burial place of *Giambologna*; it contains reliefs and a Crucifix by him, and statues by his pupils including *Francavilla*. The Madonna is attributed to *Bernardo Daddi.*—The SACRISTY, with a fine vault, was built by *Pagno di Lapo* from *Michelozzo*'s design.—On the N side, statue of the Baptist by *Michelozzo*; an Assumption by *Perugino*; and a Crucifixion by *Giovanni Stradano*. The Last Judgement by *Alessandro Allori* is derived from Michelangelo's fresco. The last two chapels contain a *Holy Trinity with St Jerome, and *St Julian and the Saviour, two frescoes by *Andrea del Castagno*.
   In the CHIOSTRO DEI MORTI, over a side door into the church, is the *Madonna del Sacco, one of *Andrea del Sarto*'s best works. The other lunettes contain 17C frescoes by *Andrea Mascagni*, *Bernardino Poccetti*, *Matteo Rosselli*, and *Ventura Salimbeni*. The CAPPELLA DI SAN LUCA has belonged to the Accademia delle Arti del Disegno since 1565. Here are buried Cellini, Pontormo,

Franciabigio, Montorsoli, Bartolini, and many other artists. It contains works by *Vasari, Pontormo, Alessandro Allori, Luca Giordano*, and *Montorsoli*.

At No. 4 Via Gino Capponi is the *Chiostro di San Pierino* with 16C frescoes (restored in 1989).

At No. 38 Via della Colonna is the ***Museo Archeologico**** (Pl. 7; adm. 9–14; fest. 9–13; closed Monday), with one of the most important collections of Etruscan antiquities in existence (it has been undergoing rearrangement for years, and parts of the museum are still closed). On the GROUND FLOOR is displayed the famous *François Vase, a krater made by Ergotimos and painted by Kleitias in Athens (signed; c 570 BC).—On the FIRST FLOOR is the EGYPTIAN MUSEUM, with statues, bas-reliefs, sarcophagi, etc., and a Hittite Chariot in wood and bone from a Theban tomb of the 14C BC.—The ETRUSCO-GRECO-ROMAN MUSEUM on the first and second floors has a large collection of urns, and bronzes. The sculpture includes the *Idolino, a remarkable bronze statue of a young athlete, probably a Roman copy of a Greek original by Polykleitos of c 420 BC; a *Horse's Head, probably from a Greek quadriga group of the Late Hellenistic period; the *Chimera from Arezzo, an Etruscan work of the 5C BC; and the *Arringatore, an Orator (Etruscan 4C or 3C BC).—On the SECOND FLOOR is the Prehistoric Collection, and a fine display of Greek vases, and Etruscan imitations.

PIAZZA SAN MARCO (Pl. 3) is one of the liveliest squares in the city. Here, beneath the Loggia dell'Ospedale di San Matteo, is the seat of the ACCADEMIA DI BELLE ARTI, an art school opened in 1784. Across Via Cesare Battisti are the administrative offices of the University of Florence, and on Via La Pira is the *Giardino dei Semplici*, a botanical garden laid out in 1545–46 by Tribolo for Cosimo I. The N side of the square is occupied by the Dominican church and convent of San Marco, which contains the ***Museo di San Marco** (or *'dell'Angelico'*; Pl. 3), famous for its works by the 'Blessed' Fra' Angelico who was a friar here. Admission 9–14; fest. 9–13; closed Monday.

Cosimo il Vecchio founded a public library here, the first of its kind in Europe. Antonino Pierozzo (1389–1459) and Girolamo Savonarola (1452–98) were famous priors of the convent.—The beautiful **Cloister of St Antonino** was built by *Michelozzo*. The lunettes with scenes from the life of St Antonino are by *Bernardino Poccetti*. In the corners are frescoes by *Fra' Angelico*. The **Pilgrims' Hospice**, also by *Michelozzo*, contains a superb *Collection of paintings by *Fra' Angelico*, many of them from Florentine churches (all well labelled), including the *Tabernacle of the Linaioli, with a marble frame designed by *Ghiberti*.—The **Great Refectory** displays 16C and 17C works (Fra' Bartolomeo, Giovanni Antonio Sogliani, etc.).—The **Chapter House** contains a large *Crucifixion and Saints by *Fra' Angelico* and assistants, and the **Small Refectory** a charming Last Supper by *Domenico Ghirlandaio* and his workshop.

FIRST FLOOR. The ***Dormitory** consists of 44 small monastic cells beneath a huge wood roof, each with their own vault and adorned with a fresco by *Fra' Angelico* or an assistant (recently beautifully restored). The *Annunciation, at the head of the stairs, is justly one of the most famous works of the master. Among the most beautiful frescoes are those in Cells 1, 3, 6, and 9, and the Madonna enthroned in the corridor. Savonarola's cell contains his portrait by *Fra' Bartolomeo*. The *LIBRARY, a light and delicate hall, is one of the most pleasing of all *Michelozzo's* works; it contains illuminated choirbooks and psalters.

The church of SAN MARCO (Pl. 3) contains a *Madonna and Saints by Fra' Bartolomeo; an 8C mosaic of the *Madonna in prayer; and the tomb slabs of Pico della Mirandola (1463–94) and his friend Politian (Angelo Ambrogini, 1454–94).

In Via Cavour (Pl. 7,3) is the Casino Mediceo, built by Buontalenti and now occupied by the law courts. This was the site of the Medici Garden where Cosimo il Vecchio and Lorenzo il Magnifico collected antique sculpture, and where Bertoldo held a school of art. At No. 69 is the **Chiostro dello Scalzo** (Pl. 3; open 9–14; fest. 9–13; closed Monday), with fine *Frescoes in monochrome by Andrea del Sarto and Franciabigio.

A short way W of Piazza San Marco is the former convent of **Sant'Apollonia** (Pl. 3; open 9–14; fest. 9–13; closed Monday) which contains a *Last Supper, the masterpiece of *Andrea del Castagno*, and other works by him.

Via Cavour leads S from Piazza San Marco to ***Palazzo Medici-Riccardi** (Pl. 7), now the seat of the Prefect. This town mansion was built for Cosimo il Vecchio by *Michelozzo* after 1444, and was the residence of the Medici until 1540 when Cosimo I moved into Palazzo Vecchio. Its rusticated façade served as a model for other famous Florentine palaces.—The COURTYARD is decorated with medallions ascribed to *Bertoldo*. A staircase leads up to the dark little *CHAPEL (closed in 1990, but usually open 9–12.30, 15–17; fest. 9–12; Wednesday closed) the only unaltered part of Michelozzo's work, with a beautiful ceiling and marble inlaid floor. The walls are entirely covered with decorative *Frescoes, the masterpiece of *Benozzo Gozzoli* of the Procession of the Magi to Bethlehem, which includes portraits of the Medici (shown with their emblem of the three ostrich feathers). The decorative cavalcade is shown in a charming landscape with hunting scenes.—The Gallery (lift) has a vault fresco by *Luca Giordano* (1683), and a Madonna and Child by Filippo Lippi.

Via de'Ginori, behind the palace, has a number of fine palaces, and the Biblioteca Riccardiana (1718).

The back of Palazzo Medici-Riccardi stands on the corner of PIAZZA SAN LORENZO (Pl. 7), filled with a busy street market (leather-goods, straw, clothing, etc.). The church of ***San Lorenzo** (Pl. 7) was intimately connected with the Medici after they commissioned *Brunelleschi* to rebuild it in 1425–46. It is the burial place of all the principal members of the family from Cosimo il Vecchio to Cosimo III.

Thought to be the earliest church in Florence, a basilica on this site was consecrated by St Ambrose of Milan in 393. The grandiose façade designed by Michelangelo was never built; the exterior remains in rough-hewn brick.—The grey cruciform interior, built with pietra serena, with pulvins above the Corinthian columns in pietra forte, is one of the earliest and most harmonious architectural works of the Renaissance. It was completed on *Brunelleschi*'s design by *Antonio Manetti* (1447–60) and *Pagno di Lapo Portigiani* (1463). In the right aisle, *Marriage of the Virgin by *Rosso Fiorentino*, and *Tabernacle by *Desiderio da Settignano*. The two bronze *Pulpits in the nave are the last works by *Donatello*, finished by his pupils Bertoldo and Bartolomeo Bellano. Beneath the dome a simple inscription with the Medici arms marks the grave of Cosimo il Vecchio 'Pater Patriae'.—Off the left transept is the *OLD SACRISTY (1420–29) by *Brunelleschi*, one of the earliest and purest monuments of the Renaissance, with a charming vault. The decorative details (beautifully restored in 1988–89) are by *Donatello* (the *Tondi in the pendentives and lunettes, the reliefs above the doors, and the doors themselves). In the centre is the sarcophagus of Giovanni di Bicci de'Medici and Piccarda Bueri, by *Buggiano*. Set into the wall is the magnificent porphyry and bronze sarcophagus of Giovanni and Piero de'Medici by *Verrocchio*.—In a chapel in the left transept is an *Annunciation by *Filippo Lippi*, and a 19C monument marking the burial place of Donatello.

From the 15C Cloister a staircase ascends to the ***Biblioteca Lauren-ziana** (Pl. 7; adm. 9–13 except Sunday, but often temporarily closed), begun by *Michelangelo* c 1524 to house the collection of MSS made by Cosimo il Vecchio and Lorenzo il Magnifico. The heavily deco-rated VESTIBULE, filled with an elaborate staircase was constructed by

Vasari and Ammannati on Michelangelo's design. The peaceful READING ROOM provides an unexpected contrast. The collection is famous above all for its Greek and Latin MSS. *Exhibitions are held every year.

The entrance to the **Medicee Chapels** (*Cappelle Medicee*) (Pl. 7; adm. 9–14; fest. 9–13; closed Monday) is from outside San Lorenzo, in Piazza Madonna degli Aldobrandini. From the crypt a staircase leads up to the *CHAPEL OF THE PRINCES (*Cappella dei Principi*), the opulent, if gloomy, mausoleum of the Medici grand-dukes begun by *Matteo Nigetti* (1604), and its minor details only completed in this century. It is a tour de force of craftsmanship in pietre dure.—A passage to the left leads to the so-called *NEW SACRISTY (*Sagrestia Nuova*), begun by *Michelangelo* and left unfinished when he left Florence in 1534. It is built in dark pietra serena and white marble in a severe and idiosyncratic style. Here are the famous **MEDICI TOMBS of Lorenzo, Duke of Urbino, and Giuliano, Duke of Nemours with statues of the Dukes, and allegorical figures of Dawn and Dusk, Night and Day, all superb works (cleaned in 1988) by *Michelangelo*. On the entrance wall is the Madonna and Child, also by Michelangelo, intended for the monument to Lorenzo il Magnifico and his brother Giuliano.

On the walls behind the altar architectural graffiti have recently been uncovered, attributed to *Michelangelo* and his pupils including *Tribolo*. Nearby is a little room (adm. by appointment at the ticket office, 9.30–12) where charcoal *Drawings of great interest were discovered on the walls in 1975, attributed by most scholars to *Michelangelo* himself.

The animated Via dell'Ariento behind San Lorenzo with numerous market stalls leads past the huge MERCATO CENTRALE (in a cast-iron market building by Giuseppe Mengoni, 1874), the biggest food market in Florence, to the busy Via Nazionale. In Via Faenza, just to the left, is the so-called **Cenacolo di Foligno** (Pl. 2; not always open) with a fresco of the *Last Supper by Perugino.

F. Santa Maria Novella, Ognissanti, and Santa Trínita

*Santa Maria Novella** (Pl. 6) is the most important Gothic church in Tuscany. The Dominicans were given the property in 1221 and building was begun in 1246 at the E end. The Dominican friars *Sisto* and *Ristoro* are thought to have been the architects of the impressive nave, begun in 1279. The church was completed under the direction of *Fra' Jacopo Talenti* in the mid-14C. The lower part of the beautiful marble *FAÇADE, in a typical Tuscan Romanesque style, is attributed to *Fra' Jacopo Talenti*. In 1456–70 *Leon Battista Alberti* was commissioned by Giovanni di Paolo Rucellai to complete the upper part of the façade. Its classical lines are in perfect harmony with the earlier work. To the right of the façade are the Gothic 'avelli' or family-vaults of Florentine nobles, which extend around the old cemetery.—The CAMPANILE, also attributed to *Fra' Jacopo Talenti*, was grafted onto an ancient watch tower.

INTERIOR (closed 11.30–15.30). The spacious nave has remarkably bold stone vaulting, its arches given prominence by bands of dark grey pietra serena. The stained glass in the rose window at the W end is thought to have been designed by *Andrea di Bonaiuto* (c 1365), and over the W door is a good fresco of the Nativity, thought to be an early work by *Botticelli.*—In the SOUTH AISLE are 16C altarpieces by *Girolamo Macchietti, Giovanni Battista Naldini, Jacopo del Meglio,* and *Jacopo Ligozzi.*—In the SOUTH TRANSEPT are Gothic tombs including that of Joseph, Patriarch of Constantinople (died in Florence in 1440), with a contemporary fresco of him. Steps lead up to the CAPPELLA RUCELLAI (light on left) which contains a marble *Statuette of the Madonna and Child signed by *Nino Pisano,* and the bronze tomb slab of Francesco Leonardo Dati, by *Ghiberti.* The walls have traces of 14C frescoes. The CAPPELLA DEI BARDI (being restored) has damaged frescoes in the lunettes attributed to *Cimabue,* and an altarpiece by *Vasari.* The CAPPELLA DI FILIPPO STROZZI has exuberant *Frescoes by *Filippino Lippi* with stories from the life of St Philip the Apostle and St John the Evangelist. Behind the altar, *Tomb of Filippo Strozzi, exquisitely carved by *Benedetto da Maiano.* Boccaccio in the 'Decameron' takes this chapel as the meeting-place of a group of young people during the Plague year of 1348.

On the MAIN ALTAR is a bronze Crucifix by *Giambologna.* In the SANCTUARY (light behind the altar) are delightful *Frescoes (being restored) commissioned by Giovanni Tornabuoni. They are the masterpiece of *Domenico Ghirlandaio;* he was assisted by his brother *Davide,* his brother-in-law, *Sebastiano Mainardi,* and his pupils (including perhaps the young Michelangelo). In the scenes from the life of St John the Baptist, and of the Virgin, many of the figures are portraits of the artist's contemporaries, and the whole cycle mirrors Florentine life of the late 15C. On the end wall are the two kneeling figures of the donors, Giovanni Tornabuoni and his wife Francesca Pitti.—NORTH TRANSEPT. The CAPPELLA GONDI with marble decoration by *Giuliano da Sangallo* contains the famous wood *Crucifix by *Brunelleschi* traditionally thought to have been carved to show Donatello how the Redeemer should be represented (see Santa Croce, Rte 42H). The CAPPELLA GADDI has paintings by *Alessandro Allori* and *Bronzino.* At the end of the transept the *CAPPELLA STROZZI is a remarkably well-preserved example of a Tuscan chapel of the mid-14C. The *Frescoes of the Last Judgement, Paradise, and Inferno are the most famous work of *Nardo di Cione* (c 1357). The fine *Altarpiece is by his brother, *Orcagna.*—The SACRISTY has a fine cross-vault by *Fra' Jacopo Talenti* and stained glass windows dating from 1386. The lavabo is by *Giovanni della Robbia,* and the *Crucifix (removed for restoration) is an early work by *Giotto.* The paintings are by *Jacopo Ligozzi, Giovanni Stradano, Pietro Dandini,* and *Vasari.*—The altarpieces in the NORTH AISLE are by *Alessandro Allori, Vasari,* and *Santi di Tito.* Also here is the famous *Fresco of the Trinity with the Virgin and St John the Evangelist and donors, a remarkable work by *Masaccio.* The pulpit was designed by *Brunelleschi.*

To the left of the church is the entrance to the *CLOISTERS (9–14; fest. 8–13; closed Friday). The Romanesque *CHIOSTRO VERDE has damaged *Frescoes by Paolo Uccello (c 1446) painted in terraverde and illustrating stories from Genesis: (in the East walk) the Creation of Adam, and of the Animals, and the Creation and Temptation of Eve, and the Flood and the *Recession of the Flood (with Noah's ark), and the Sacrifice and Drunkenness of Noah. The other frescoes in the cloisters also date from the first half of the 15C.

Off the cloister opens the *CAPPELLONE DEGLI SPAGNUOLI, or *Spanish Chapel.* It received its name in the 16C when it was assigned by Duchess Eleonora di Toledo to the Spanish members of her suite. It was originally the Chapter House built by Jacopo Talenti in the mid-14C with a splendid cross-vault. It is entirely covered with colourful *Frescoes by *Andrea di Bonaiuto* (*Andrea da Firenze*) dating from c 1365. They represent the Mission, Works, and Triumph of the Dominican Order (including the artist's vision of the completed Duomo), and the Triumph of Catholic doctrine personified in St Thomas Aquinas.—In the CHIOSTRINO DEI MORTI are frescoes dating from the mid-14C.—In the large REFECTORY with fine cross-vaulting a fresco by *Alessandro Allori* surrounds a good fresco attributed to a follower of *Agnolo Gaddi*. Here, and in the adjoining chapel are displayed church silver, charming reliquary busts by the Sienese school, vestments, etc.

PIAZZA SANTA MARIA NOVELLA, with its irregular shape, was created by the Dominicans at the end of the 13C. The two obelisks were set up in 1608 (resting on bronze tortoises by Giambologna) as turning posts in the course of the annual Palio dei Cocchi. Beneath the 15C *Loggia di San Paolo* is a beautiful *Lunette showing the Meeting of St Francis and St Dominic by Andrea della Robbia. In the house on the corner of Via della Scala Henry James wrote 'Roderick Hudson' in 1872.

The church of **Ognissanti** (Pl. 6), reached by Via de'Fossi and Borgo Ognissanti, was founded in 1256 by the Umiliati, a Benedictine Order skilled in manufacturing wool. The church was rebuilt in the 17C; the façade incorporates a terracotta attributed to *Benedetto Buglioni*.

INTERIOR. On the S side are two frescoes by *Domenico* and *Davide Ghirlandaio*; the Madonna della Misericordia protects the Vespucci whose family tombstone (1471) is in the pavement. Between the 3rd and 4th altars, on the N and S side are *St Jerome by *Domenico Ghirlandaio*, and *St Augustine's vision of St Jerome, by *Botticelli*, both painted c 1481. Elsewhere in the church are altarpieces by *Santi di Tito, Matteo Rosselli, Maso di San Friano*, and *Jacopo Ligozzi*. Botticelli (Filipepi) is buried in the S transept. The Sacristy has late-13C wall paintings, and works by *Taddeo* and *Agnolo Gaddi*.—From the CLOISTER is the entrance (open Monday, Tuesday, & Saturday 9–12) to the REFECTORY with a *Last Supper by *Domenico Ghirlandaio*.— In the piazza is Palazzo Lenzi (now the French Consulate) built c 1470, with restored graffiti.

Ponte Santa Trínita (described in Rte 42J) crosses the Arno at the beginning of **Via Tornabuoni** (Pl. 7), the most elegant street in Florence with fashionable shops. Here is *Palazzo Spini-Feroni* (1269; restored), one of the best preserved and largest private medieval palaces in the city. Opposite is the church of ***Santa Trínita** (Pl. 10), dating in its present Gothic form from the end of the 14C. The façade was added by Buontalenti in 1593.

In the fine INTERIOR the interior façade of the Romanesque building survives. SOUTH AISLE: 3rd chapel, altarpiece by *Neri di Bicci*, and detached fresco and sinopia by *Spinello Aretino*; the 4th chapel is entirely frescoed by *Lorenzo Monaco*, who also painted the beautiful *Altarpiece of the Annunciation; 5th chapel, part of a monument to St John Gualberto by *Benedetto da Rovezzano*.— Outside the choir chapels are remains of frescoes by *Giovanni del Ponte*.—The *SASSETTI CHAPEL contains frescoes of the life of St Francis by *Domenico Ghirlandaio*. They include views of Florence and portraits of the Medici and personages of the Renaissance city. The *Altarpiece of the Adoration of the Shepherds, also by *Ghirlandaio*, is flanked by the donors, Francesco Sassetti and his wife Nera Corsi. Their tombs are attributed to *Giuliano da Sangallo*. In the SANCTUARY is a triptych by *Mariotto di Nardo* and remains of vault frescoes by *Alesso Baldovinetti*. In the 2nd chapel left of the altar, *Tomb of Benozzo Federighi by *Luca della Robbia* (1454–57).—NORTH AISLE: 5th chapel, Mary

Magdalen, a wood statue (removed for restoration) by *Desiderio da Settignano* (finished by *Benedetto da Maiano*); 4th chapel, frescoes by *Neri di Bicci* and *Bicci di Lorenzo*; 2nd chapel, paintings by *Ridolfo del Ghirlandaio*.

In Piazza Santa Trìnita, with the Column of Justice, a granite monolith from the Baths of Caracalla in Rome, are the *Palazzo Buondelmonti*, with a façade attributed to Baccio d'Agnolo, and, perhaps, his best work, *Palazzo Bartolini Salimbeni*. Beyond several more handsome palaces rises the huge **Palazzo Strozzi* (Pl. 6; used for exhibitions), the last and grandest of the magnificent Renaissance palaces in Florence, built for Filippo Strozzi by Benedetto da Maiano in 1489 (and finished by Cronaca). Via della Vigna Nuova leads past the home from 1614 of Sir Robert Dudley, and the house where George Eliot stayed while gathering material for 'Romola', to **Palazzo Rucellai* (Pl. 6). This was designed for Giovanni Rucellai by Leon Battista Alberti and executed by Bernardo Rossellino (c 1446–51). In modernised rooms on the ground floor is the *Museo di Storia della Fotografia Fratelli Alinari*, illustrating the history of the firm of Alinari, famous in black-and-white photography. Photograph exhibitions are often held here.

Behind the palace the ex-church of *San Pancrazio*, has been converted into a gallery (open 10–18 except Tuesday) to display sculptures by Marino Marini (1901–80), left to the city by him. The fine classical porch is by Alberti.—At No. 18 Via della Spada is the entrance to the remarkable *Cappella di San Sepolcro* (usually closed) built in 1467 also by Alberti for Giovanni Rucellai. It contains a *Model in inlaid marble of the Sanctuary of the Holy Sepulchre.

At No. 19 Via Tornabuoni *Palazzo Larderel*, attributed to Giovanni Antonio Dosio, is a model of High Renaissance architecture. Opposite is SAN GAETANO, the best 17C church in Florence (by Matteo Nigetti, Gherardo, and Pier Francesco Silvani). **Palazzo Antinori* (Pl. 6), attributed to Giuliano da Maiano (1461–69), is one of the most beautiful smaller Renaissance palaces in Florence.—Nearby, on Via de'Cerretani is the Gothic Cistercian church of SANTA MARIA MAGGIORE. It contains frescoes by Mariotto di Nardo, a relief in painted wood of the *Madonna enthroned attributed to Coppo di Marcovaldo, and an effigy of Bruno Beccuti attributed to Tino da Camaino.

G. The Museo Nazionale del Bargello and the Badia Fiorentina

*Palazzo del Bargello (Pl. 7,11), a massive battlemented medieval fortified building in pietra forte, was erected in 1250 as the 'Palazzo del Popolo'. Building was continued in the 14C and it was well restored in the 19C. At first the seat of the 'Capitano del Popolo', it became the residence of the 'Podestà', the governing magistrate of the city, at the end of the 13C. From the 16C, as the police headquarters, it became known as the 'Bargello'. The palace now contains the ****Museo Nazionale del Bargello**, famous for its superb collection of Florentine Renaissance sculpture, including numerous works by Donatello and the Della Robbia family. 16C Florentine sculpture is well represented by Michelangelo, Cellini, and Giambologna, among others, and an exquisite collection of small Mannerist

bronzes. There is also a notable collection of decorative arts. Admission 9–14; fest. 9–13; closed Monday.

GROUND FLOOR. The fine hall (right) contains 16C sculptures by Michelangelo and his Florentine contemporaries. Works by *Michelangelo* include: *Bacchus drunk (an early work; c 1497); *Tondo of the Madonna and Child with the infant St John made for Bartolomeo Pitti; *Bust of Brutus (c 1539–40); and *Apollo (or David).—Other sculptors well represented here include *Jacopo Sansovino* (Bacchus), *Bartolomeo Ammannati*, *Bandinelli* (bust of Cosimo I, Adam and Eve), *De'Rossi* (*Dying Adonis), and *Cellini* (Narcissus, Apollo and Hyacinth, *Bronzes from the pedestal of his statue of Perseus, Bust of Cosimo I).—The Gothic *CORTILE displays more 16C sculptures.—A room off the courtyard displays 14C sculpture (*Arnolfo di Cambio*, *Tino da Camaino*).

FIRST FLOOR. The LOGGIA contains good works by *Giambologna*, including his famous bronze *Mercury.—The SALONE DEL CONSIGLIO GENERALE, a fine vaulted hall, displays superb sculptures by Donatello and his contemporaries. Works by *Donatello* include: *St George from Orsanmichele (in a reconstructed tabernacle), two statues of *David, one in bronze and one in marble, *Atys-Amorino, a bronze putto, the Marzocco (heraldic lion), a Bust of a Youth with a medallion at his neck, and *Bust of Niccolò da Uzzano (the last two both attributed to Donatello). Also here: *Desiderio da Settignano*, *Busts of a young woman and a boy; fine works by *Giovanni di Bertoldo*; *Michelozzo*, *Reliefs of the Madonna; *Luca della Robbia*, *Madonnas in enamelled terracotta, and two marble reliefs of St Peter; the two trial *Reliefs of the Sacrifice of Isaac by *Ghiberti* and *Brunelleschi* made for the competition for the second bronze doors of the Baptistery; and a *Reliquary Urn by *Ghiberti.—The other rooms on this floor (closed in 1990) contain a *Collection of decorative arts (seals, glass, enamels, ecclesiastical ornaments, jewellery, goldsmiths' work, *Ivories, and majolica).—The CAPPELLA DEL PODESTÀ contains restored frescoes attributed to the school of Giotto.

SECOND FLOOR. The first room contains a number of colourful enamelled terracottas by *Giovanni della Robbia* and cases of plaquettes.—The room to the left contains beautiful *Works by *Andrea della Robbia*. The next room displays sculptures by Verrocchio and a number of fine Renaissance portrait busts. Works by *Verrocchio* include his bronze *David, and a *Bust of a lady holding flowers. Also here are works by: *Antonio del Pollaiolo* (*Bust of a young cavalier, and *Portrait-bust of a man); *Mino da Fiesole* (marble *Portrait busts, and two Madonnas); *Benedetto da Maiano* (*Pietro Mellini); *Antonio Rossellino*; and *Francesco Laurana* (*Bust of Battista Sforza). The Medici collection of *Medals was reopened in 1990.—The SALONE DEL CAMINO contains a superb display of small Renaissance *Bronzes, by *Antonio del Pollaiolo* (*Hercules and Antaeus), *Cellini*, *Giambologna*, *Tacca*, *Tribolo*, *Bandinelli*, *L'Antico*, *Briosco*, *Caradosso*, *Leone Leoni*, etc. The fine *Chimneypiece is by *Benedetto da Rovezzano*. The Anatomical figure made in wax by *Lodovico Cigoli* was cast by *Giovanni Battista Foggini.—Also on this floor (closed in 1990) is a magnificent collection of *Arms and Armour (well labelled).

In Piazza San Firenze is *Palazzo Gondi* by Giuliano da Sangallo (c 1489), and the huge Baroque *San Firenze*, now occupied by the law courts. Opposite the Bargello, in Via del Proconsolo, is the **Badia Fiorentina** (Pl. 7,11), the church of a Benedictine abbey founded in 978 by Willa, the widow of Uberto, Margrave of Tuscany. The graceful, slender Campanile is Romanesque below (1307) and Gothic (after 1330) above.

The 17C interior contains a painting of the *Madonna appearing to St Bernard by *Filippino Lippi*; a sculpted altarpiece, the tomb of Bernardo Giugni, and (left transept), *Monument to Ugo, Margrave of Tuscany, all by *Mino da Fiesole*; and frescoes attributed to *Nardo di Cione.—The CHIOSTRO DEGLI ARANCI, by *Bernardo Rossellino* has an interesting fresco cycle with scenes from the life of St Benedict by an artist known as the *'Maestro del Chiostro degli Aranci'* (c 1430).

Via Dante Alighieri leads left from Via del Proconsolo to Piazza San Martino with the splendid 13C *Torre della Castagna*, and the little chapel of SAN MARTINO DEL VESCOVO decorated with charming frescoes by the workshop of Ghirlandaio (Francesco d'Antonio del Chierico?) illustrating the life of St Martin and works of charity.—The area is traditionally associated with the great Florentine poet Dante Alighieri, who was probably born on the street that now bears his name. The so-called *Casa di Dante* is in a group of houses restored in the 13C style in 1911. In the little church of *Santa Margherita de'Cerchi* Dante is supposed to have married Gemma Donati (it contains an altarpiece by Neri di Bicci).

At No. 10 Via del Proconsolo is the handsome *Palazzo Pazzi-Quaratesi* attributed to Giuliano da Maiano. Here begins *BORGO DEGLI ALBIZI, one of the most handsome streets in the city, lined with numerous fine palaces, including two (Nos 28 and 26) by Bartolomeo Ammannati. Across the borgo is *Palazzo Nonfinito*, begun in 1593 by Buontalenti. It now houses the MUSEO NAZIONALE DI ANTROPOLOGIA ED ETNOLOGIA (open Thursday, Friday, & Saturday, & the 3rd Sunday of the month, 9–12.30), founded in 1869 by Paolo Mantegazza, and probably the most important museum of its kind in Italy. The most interesting material comes from Africa, North Pakistan, South America, Mexico, Asia. The exhibits from the Pacific Ocean were probably acquired by Captain Cook on his last voyage.

At No. 24 Via dell'Oriuolo is the **Museo di Firenze com'era** (Pl. 7; adm. 9–14; fest. 9–13; closed Thursday), a topographical historical museum of the city. The maps, paintings, and prints displayed in several rooms of the old Convento delle Oblate illustrate the life of the city since the 15C.—Nearby is the hospital of SANTA MARIA NUOVA founded in 1286 by Folco Portinari with a portico by Buontalenti, and the church of Sant'Egidio, both with a number of interesting works of art. In Via Sant'Egidio is the *Museo Fiorentino di Preistoria*.

H.   Santa Croce and the Casa Buonarroti

PIAZZA SANTA CROCE (Pl. 11), an attractive and spacious square, is the centre of a distinctive district of the city. Some houses in the piazza have projecting upper stories resting on 'sporti'. *Palazzo dell'Antella*, built by Giulio Parigi, has a worn polychrome façade painted in 1619. *Palazzo Cocchi (Serristori)* at the end of the square has recently been attributed to Giuliano da Sangallo. *Santa Croce (Pl. 11,12), the Franciscan church of Florence was rebuilt c 1294 possibly by Arnolfo di Cambio. The neo-Gothic façade dates from 1853.

The huge wide INTERIOR (closed 12.30–15) has an open timber roof. The Gothic church was rearranged by Vasari in 1560. For five hundred years it has been the custom to bury or erect monuments to notable citizens of Florence in this church; it is the burial place of Ghiberti, Michelangelo, Machiavelli, and Galileo.—SOUTH AISLE. 1st pillar, *Madonna 'del Latte' a relief by Antonio Rossellino. The Tomb of Michelangelo was designed by Vasari. The neo-classical cenotaph to Dante (buried in Ravenna) is by Stefano Ricci. The *Pulpit is by Benedetto da Maiano. There follow monuments to Vittorio Alfieri (by Antonio Canova), and to Niccolò Machiavelli (by Innocenzo Spinazzi, 1787). The altarpieces in this aisle are by Vasari, Jacopo Coppi di Meglio, Alessandro del Barbiere (Flagellation of Christ), and Andrea del Minga (Agony in the Garden). By the side door is a *Tabernacle with a beautiful high relief of the Annunciation by Donatello. The *Tomb of Leonardo Bruni by Bernardo Rossellino (c 1446–47) is one of the most harmonious and influential sepulchral monuments of the Renaissance.—SOUTH TRANSEPT. The Castellani Chapel contains decorative *Frescoes by Agnolo Gaddi and assistants. The Baroncelli Chapel has *Frescoes by Taddeo Gaddi (father of Agnolo), a pupil of Giotto. The restored altarpiece of the Coronation of the Virgin is by

Giotto and his workshop. Also here is a 15C fresco of the Madonna by *Bastiano Mainardi*, and a 16C statue of the Madonna and Child by *Vincenzo Danti*.—The *SACRISTY has frescoes by *Taddeo Gaddi*, *Spinello Aretino* (attributed), and *Nicolò di Pietro Gerini* and, in the Rinuccini Chapel, *Frescoes by *Giovanni da Milano*, one of the most gifted followers of Giotto.—The MEDICI CHAPEL by *Michelozzo* contains an *Altarpiece by *Andrea della Robbia*.

The small rectangular vaulted CHAPELS AT THE EAST END are notable for their frescoes by *Giotto* and his school. The two chapels right of the Sanctuary were decorated by *Giotto*; the frescoes are damaged and in poor condition. The *PERUZZI CHAPEL contains scenes from the life of St John the Evangelist and of St John the Baptist painted in his maturity; the frescoes illustrating the story of St Francis in the *BARDI CHAPEL were probably painted earlier and some of them may have been executed by Giotto's pupils. The painting of St Francis on the altar dates from the 13C. The SANCTUARY is frescoed with the *Legend of the Cross by *Agnolo Gaddi* (c 1380), who also designed the fine stained glass lancet windows. The polyptych is by *Nicolò Gerini* and *Giovanni del Biondo*, and the Crucifix above by the '*Master of Figline*'. In the last two E chapels are frescoes of the Lives of St Lawrence and St Stephen by *Bernardo Daddi*, and colourful and well-preserved frescoes of the *Life of St Sylvester by *Maso di Banco*, perhaps the most original follower of Giotto, who also probably painted the Last Judgement in the Gothic tomb here.

NORTH TRANSEPT. The Niccolini Chapel designed by *Giovanni Antonio Dosio*, has frescoes by *Volterrano*, statues by *Francavilla*, and paintings by *Alessandro Allori*. The second Bardi Chapel contains the wooden *Crucifix by *Donatello*. The story told by Vasari of Brunelleschi's complaint that it was a mere 'peasant on the cross' is now thought to be apocryphal. In the Salviati Chapel is the *Tomb of Sofia Zamoyska Czartoryska (died 1837) with a Romantic effigy by *Lorenzo Bartolini*.—NORTH AISLE. By the side door, *Monument to Carlo Marsuppini (died 1453) by *Desiderio da Settignano*. The classical sarcophagus may be the work of *Verrocchio*. In the pavement between the 5th and 4th altar is the handsome tomb-slab with niello decoration of Lorenzo Ghiberti, and his son Vittorio. The Monument to Galileo Galilei (1564–1642) was set up by *Giovanni Battista Foggini* in 1737 when the great scientist was allowed Christian burial inside the church. In the nave is the tomb-slab of his ancestor and namesake, a well-known physician in 15C Florence. The altarpieces in this aisle are by *Giovanni Stradano*, *Santi di Tito* (Supper at Emmaus and Resurrection), and *Giovanni Battista Naldini*.

On the right of the church is the entrance to the conventual buildings and the **Museo dell'Opera di Santa Croce** (Pl. 11,12; adm. 10–12.30, 14.30–18.30; winter, 9–12.30, 15–17; closed Wednesday). In the first cloister (14C) is the charming **Cappella de' Pazzi**, one of the most famous works of *Brunelleschi* (1442–46).

The portico may have been designed by *Giuliano da Maiano*; the shallow cupola bears delightful enamelled terracotta decoration by *Luca della Robbia*, who also made the medallion with *St Andrew over the door. The beautiful calm interior is one of the masterpieces of the early Renaissance. The twelve *Roundels of the seated Apostles are by *Luca della Robbia*; the polychrome roundels of the Evangelists may have been designed by *Donatello*.—The *SECOND CLOISTER (being restored in 1990) is another beautiful work by *Brunelleschi*.

Off the First Cloister is the entrance to the MUSEO DELL'OPERA DI SANTA CROCE. In the fine Gothic REFECTORY is displayed *Cimabue*'s great Crucifix which has been restored after it was almost completely destroyed in the flood of

1966. The huge *Fresco on the end wall of the Last Supper below the Tree of the Cross is by *Taddeo Gaddi*. Also here are fragments of a large fresco by *Orcagna* of the Triumph of Death and Inferno detached from the nave of the church, and several other fine 14–15C frescoes (including one with a view of the Baptistery and Duomo). In a reconstructed tabernacle is *Donatello's* colossal gilded bronze *St Louis of Toulouse from Orsanmichele.—The other rooms contain more frescoes (14–17C), Della Robbian terracottas, interesting large sketches detached from walls of the Cappella dei Pazzi, and sculptures by *Tino da Camaino*.—Beneath the colonnade, just before the exit from the cloister, is a memorial to Florence Nightingale, named after the city where she was born.

To the right of Santa Croce is the huge BIBLIOTECA NAZIONALE (severely damaged in 1966).—At the other end of Piazza Santa Croce VIA DEI BENCI, with its old rusticated houses, runs towards the Arno. The polygonal 13C *Torre degli Alberti* has a 15C loggia below. *Palazzo Bardi alle Grazie* (No. 5) is an early Renaissance palace attributed to Brunelleschi; No. 1, *Palazzo Malenchini* was reconstructed on the site of a 14C palace of the Alberti where the great architect Leon Battista died in 1472.—Off the interesting old Via dei Neri a road (right) leads to the church of SAN REMIGIO, founded in the 11C. The fine Gothic interior (often closed) contains a *Madonna and Child by a follower of Cimabue known as the 'Master of San Remigio'.—Nearby is the interesting medieval Piazza Peruzzi, and Via dei Bentaccordi which takes its shape from the curve of the Roman amphitheatre (2–3C AD). The church of SAN SIMONE, founded in 1192-93, has a fine interior by Gherardo Silvani (1630), and an altarpiece of St Peter enthroned (1307); opposite is *Palazzo da Cintoia* one of the best preserved medieval palaces in the city.

From the N side of Santa Croce Via delle Pinzochere leads to Via Ghibellina, where, at No. 70 is the ***Casa Buonarroti** (Pl. 7,12; adm. 9.30–13.30; closed Tuesday). Three houses on this site were purchased by Michelangelo in 1508 who left the property to his only descendant, his nephew Leonardo.

The GROUND FLOOR is used for interesting exhibitions. Also displayed here are: a fine head of Michelangelo by *Daniele da Volterra*, a statue of Venus attributed to *Vincenzo Danti*, and part of the eclectic collection of Antiquities and Renaissance works made by Michelangelo's descendants, including a copy from *Titian* of a *Love scene (removed for restoration in 1989), Etruscan stelae, etc.—FIRST FLOOR. Two early works by *Michelangelo*: *Madonna of the Steps, a marble bas-relief, carved at the age of 15 or 16, and a *Battle relief, modelled on a Roman sarcophagus; wood model for the façade of San Lorenzo designed by Michelangelo (but never carried out), and a *Torso by him, a model in clay and wood for a river god. A selection of his *Drawings owned by the museum are shown in rotation.—The four rooms decorated in 1612 by Michelangelo Buonarroti the Younger in celebration of his great-uncle and his family, contain paintings by *Cristofano Allori, Giovanni Biliverti, Empoli, Giovanni da San Giovanni, Matteo Rosselli, Jacopo Vignali*, etc. Also here: portrait of Michelangelo attributed to *Giuliano Bugiardini*, a predella by *Giovanni di Francesco*, and Roman and Etruscan sculpture and small bronzes.—The *Crucifix in painted poplar wood was found in Santo Spirito in 1963 and is now generaly attributed to *Michelangelo*. The small bozzetti are by or attributed to the master, or copied from his works, and other are by *Tribolo*.

The church of **Sant'Ambrogio** (Pl. 8), to the N, was rebuilt in the late 13C. It contains a number of interesting frescoes including a *Madonna enthroned with Saints attributed to the school of *Orcagna*. In the chapel on the left of the high altar is an exquisite *Tabernacle by *Mino da Fiesole* (who is buried here), and a large *Fresco by *Cosimo Rosselli* of a procession with the miraculous chalice (preserved here) in front of the church. On the N side, *Angels and Saints by *Alesso Baldovinetti* surrounding a Nativity by his pupil *Graffione*. The church is the burial place of Cronaca (died 1508) and Verrocchio (died 1488).—Nearby is the produce market of *Sant'Ambrogio* and the '*Mercatino*', a 'junk' and 'antique' market in Piazza dei Ciompi, with Vasari's graceful *Loggia del Pesce* (removed from the Mercato Vecchio). Lorenzo Ghiberti lived here, and Cimabue lived in Borgo Allegri which was given this name, according to Vasari, after his painting of the Madonna left his studio in a joyous procession down the street.

To the N, near the SYNAGOGUE (1874–82; small museum) with a green dome, is the interesting church of **Santa Maria Maddalena dei Pazzi** (Pl. 8), on Borgo Pinti (No. 56). The *Cloister is by *Giuliano da Sangallo*, and in the Chapter House (open 17–19) is a beautiful and very well preserved *Fresco of the Crucifixion and Saints by *Perugino*, one of his masterpieces.

I.   The Arno

Ponte alla Carraia (Pl. 6,10), first constructed in 1218–20, was the second bridge to be built over the Arno. It was several times rebuilt and repaired, and reconstructed after it was blown up in 1944. At the N end Lungarno Vespucci, opened in the 19C, leads away from the centre of the city towards the park of the Cascine past two modern bridges.

The **Cascine** (Pl. 5) is a huge public park which skirts the Arno for 3·5km, traversed by an avenue open to cars. It was used as a ducal chase by the Medici grand-dukes, and festivals were held here. It was first opened regularly to the public c 1811. In these gardens the 'Ode to the West Wind' was 'conceived and chiefly written' by Shelley in 1819. It is now used as a recreation ground, and it contains various sports facilities. At the far end is a monument to the Maharajah of Kolhapur who died in Florence in 1870. From here the view is dominated by a modern suspension bridge (1978) over the Arno.

Lungarno Corsini leads past the huge *Palazzo Corsini* built between 1650 and c 1737. It contains the most important private art collection in Florence (adm. by appointment only at 11 Via Parione), with works attributed to Raphael, Giovanni Bellini, Signorelli, Pontormo, and Filippino Lippi.—Farther on is *Palazzo Masetti* (now the British Consulate) where the Countess of Albany, widow of Prince Charles Edward Stuart lived from 1793 to her death. ***Ponte a Santa Trínita** (Pl. 10) was first built in 1252. The present bridge is an exact replica of the bridge begun by Ammannati in 1567 and destroyed in 1944. The high flat arches which span the river are perfectly proportioned and the bridge provides a magnificent view of the city. The statue of Spring on the parapet is the best work of Pietro Francavilla (1593).— Lungarno Acciaioli continues to Ponte Vecchio (described in Rte 42D). The modern buildings on both banks of the river near the bridge replace the medieval houses which were blown up in 1944 in order to render Ponte Vecchio impassable.—Beyond the Uffizi opens Piazza dei Giudici with the medieval *Palazzo Castellani* which now contains the ***Museo di Storia della Scienza** (Pl. 11; adm. 10–13, 14–16; fest. 10–13; closed last Sunday of month), a beautifully displayed and well maintained collection of scientific instruments. It is in the process of rearrangement and only the first floor was open in 1990.

A large part of the collection was owned by the Medici grand-dukes. Excellent hand-lists are lent to visitors. FIRST FLOOR. ROOM I. Celestial globes, astrolabes, quadrants, solar clocks, and mathematical instruments.—RII. German instruments, and navigational instruments, including some invented by Sir Robert Dudley.—RIII. Scientifical instruments made for the Medici grand-dukes.—RIV. Precious collection of instruments which belonged to Galileo, including his compass, the lens he used in discovering the four largest moons of Jupiter (cracked by him before he presented it to Ferdinando II), and the 'Giovilabio'; models of his inventions.—RV. Astronomy, including Galileo's two wood telescopes.—RVI. Lenses and prisms.—RVII. Globes, including the armillary sphere made by Antonio Santucci in 1588.—RVIII. Microscopes.—RIX. Material relating to the Accademia del Cimento, an experimental academy founded by Cardinal Leopoldo in 1657 (including elaborate glass).—RX. Barometers, thermometers, rain gauges, etc.—RXI. Astronomy in the 18C and 19C (large telescopes).—The upper floors are to be reopened to display the rest of the collection which includes clocks, bicycles, anatomical models, instruments concerning fluids and gases, etc.

Farther on, at Ponte alle Grazie is Via dei Benci. Here at No. 6 *Palazzo Corsi*, attributed to Cronaca, contains the **Museo Horne** (Pl. 11; adm. 9–13; closed Sunday; winter, Monday, Wednesday & Saturday, 9–13). The interesting collection of 14–16C paintings, sculptures, and decorative arts (notable furniture and majolica) was presented to the nation, along with his house, by the English art historian Herbert Percy Horne (1864–1916). A handlist is lent to visitors.

FIRST FLOOR. Paintings by *Masaccio* (attributed), *Pietro Lorenzetti, Bernardo Daddi, Benozzo Gozzoli, Giotto* (*St Stephen), *Filippino Lippi, Beccafumi* (*Tondo of the Holy Family), and Renaissance sculptures.—SECOND FLOOR. 15C furniture, and paintings by the '*Master of the Horne Triptych*', *Neri di Bicci, Simone Martini* (attributed; removed for restoration 1989), etc.

Ponte alle Grazie (Pl. 11), first built in 1237, was replaced after 1944 by a modern bridge. At the S end is Piazza dei Mozzi, with the large *Palazzo Bardini* (No. 1), built by the famous antiquarian and collector Stefano Bardini in 1883 to house his huge collection of works of art bequeathed to the city in 1923 as the **Museo Bardini** (Pl. 11; adm. 9–14; fest. 9–13; closed Wednesday). His eclectic collection includes architectural fragments, sculpture, paintings, the decorative arts, furniture, ceramics, carpets, arms and armour, musical instruments, etc. Many of the rooms were built specially to contain the fine doorways, staircases, and ceilings from demolished buildings. The rooms are crowded with a miscellany of works.

GROUND FLOOR. Medieval and Renaissance architectural fragments; classical sculpture; medieval sculpture (statue of Charity attributed to *Tino da Camaino*); altarpiece attributed to *Andrea della Robbia*.—FIRST FLOOR. Armour; sculpture (two reliefs attributed to Donatello); paintings (St Michael by *Antonio Pollaiolo*); musical instruments, etc.

The Palazzi dei Mozzi built in the 13–14C are among the most noble private houses of medieval Florence. The severe façades in pietra forte have arches on the ground floor. The building was left to the State in 1965 together with a huge collection of decorative arts by Ugo, son of Stefano Bardini, and there are long-term plans to open it to the public. A huge park climbs the hillside behind.

*Via di San Niccolò, a narrow medieval street, leads left to the church of SAN NICCOLÒ SOPR'ARNO (Pl. 11), with several interesting 15C frescoes, including the *Madonna della Cintola (in the Sacristy) attributed to Alesso Baldovinetti, and St Ansano attributed to Francesco d'Antonio. The road continues past (right) the pretty 14C *Porta San Miniato* to the massive PORTA SAN NICCOLÒ with a high tower built c 1340.
  The winding *Via de'Bardi** leads right from Piazza dei Mozzi past a series of noble town houses to Ponte Vecchio.

J.   The Oltrarno

In the characteristic district on the S bank of the Arno known as the 'Oltrarno', the two most important churches are Santo Spirito and Santa Maria del Carmine, and around them focuses the life of this part of the city. The church of ***Santo Spirito** (Pl. 10) was rebuilt by *Brunelleschi* in 1444. Building was continued after his death by *Antonio Manetti* and others. The slender campanile is by *Baccio d'Agnolo* (1503), and the modest façade dates from the 18C.

The *INTERIOR, designed by *Brunelleschi*, was mostly executed after his death and modified in the late 15C. It is remarkable for its harmonious proportions, its solemn colour, and the perspective of the colonnades and vaulted aisles. The plan is a Latin cross with a dome over the crossing, and the columns with fine Corinthian capitals are carried round the transepts and E end forming an unbroken arcade with 38 chapels in semi-circular niches. The Baroque HIGH ALTAR by *Giovanni Caccini* disturbs the harmony of the architecture.—The interior façade was designed by *Salvi d'Andrea* (1483–87), and the stained glass oculus is from a cartoon by *Perugino*. SOUTH AISLE CHAPELS. 2nd chapel, Pietà, a free copy of Michelangelo's famous sculpture in St Peter's by *Nanni di Baccio Bigio*; 4th chapel, *Giovanni Stradano*, Christ expelling the money-changers from the Temple; 6th chapel, *Passignano*, Martyrdom of St Stephen.—SOUTH TRANSEPT CHAPELS. 10th, Madonna del Soccorso, a painting of the early 15C; 12th, *Filippino Lippi*, *Madonna and Child, with the young St John, Saints, and donors, one of his finest works (removed for restoration); 13th, *Felice Ficherelli*, Copy of Perugino's Vision of St Bernard, now in Munich; 14th, *Giovanni Camillo Sagrestani*, Marriage of the Virgin (1713), his best work.

CHAPELS AT THE EAST END. 15th, Madonna and Saints, a good painting in the style of *Lorenzo di Credi*; 16th, *Maso di Banco*, Polyptych (removed for restoration); 17th, *Aurelio Lomi*, Epiphany; 18th, 19th, *Alessandro Allori*, Martyred Saints, *Christ and the adulteress; 21st, 22nd, 15C Florentine paintings.—NORTH TRANSEPT CHAPELS. 23rd, '*Maestro di Santo Spirito*', Madonna enthroned between Saints; 24th, *St Monica and Augustinian nuns in black habits, traditionally attributed to *Botticini*, but possibly by *Verrocchio*; 25th, *Cosimo Rosselli*, Madonna enthroned between Saints; 26th, *Altarpiece by *Andrea Sansovino*; 27th, *Trinity with Saints, a good painting of the late 15C, attributed to the '*Maestro di Santo Spirito*' (removed for restoration); 28th, *Raffaellino dei Carli*, *Madonna enthroned with Saints.—A door beneath the organ in the N aisle leads into a grandiose *VESTIBULE built by *Cronaca* in 1491. The *SACRISTY, taking its inspiration from Brunelleschi, was designed by *Giuliano da Sangallo*.

To the left of the church, at No. 29, is the entrance to the REFECTORY (adm. 9–14; fest. 8–13; closed Monday), the only part of the 14C convent to survive. Above a fresco of the Last Supper (almost totally ruined) is a huge *Crucifixion, both of them painted c 1360–65 and attributed to *Andrea Orcagna* and his bottega. Here is displayed the **Fondazione Salvatore Romano**, an interesting collection of sculpture notable for its Romanesque works, two statuettes by *Tino da Camaino*, and sculptures attributed to *Jacopo della Quercia*, *Donatello*, and *Ammannati*.

PIAZZA SANTO SPIRITO is one of the most attractive small squares in the city, the scene of a little daily market. *Palazzo Guadagni* (No. 10) was probably built by Cronaca c 1505.—Via Sant'Agostino leads to Via de'Serragli, a long straight road with handsome 17–18C palaces. Via Santa Monica continues past a tabernacle by Lorenzo di Bicci into Piazza del Carmine. Here is the rough stone façade of the church of **Santa Maria del Carmine** (Pl. 10), famous for its frescoes by Masaccio in the Cappella Brancacci, which escaped destruction in a fire in 1771 which ruined the rest of the first church.

The huge wide INTERIOR was rebuilt in an undistinguished late Baroque style. At the end of the right transept is the small ****Brancacci Chapel** with frescoes illustrating the life of St Peter, commissioned by Felice Brancacci c 1424 from *Masolino* and *Masaccio*. Seriously damaged in the 18C and 19C they were beautifully restored in 1983–89, and many of the details formerly obscured by surface mould can now be seen. The chapel was finally reopened in 1990 after heated debate about how to redesign the altar wall where fragments of frescoes by Masaccio were discovered during restoration work behind the ungainly altar installed in 1780. The design of the whole fresco cycle may be due to Masolino, but his pupil Masaccio seems to have continued work on them alone in 1428. Later that year Masaccio himself broke off work abruptly on the frescoes and left for Rome, where by the end of the year, he had died at the early age of 27. The frescoes were at once recognised as a masterpiece and profoundly influenced Florentine art of the Renaissance. All the major artists of the 15C came here to study the frescoes which combine a perfect application of the new rules of perspective with a remarkable use of chiaroscuro. The cycle was only completed some 50 years later by *Filippino Lippi* (c 1480–85) who carefully integrated his style with that of Masaccio, possibly following an earlier design.—The frescoes are arranged in two registers.—UPPER ROW (right to left); *Masolino*, Temptation of Adam and Eve; *Masolino*, St Peter, accompanied by St John, brings Tabitha to life and heals a lame man (the figures on the extreme left may be by *Masaccio*); *Masaccio*, *St Peter baptising; *Masolino*, St Peter preaching; *Masaccio*, *The Tribute money, perhaps the painter's masterpiece; *Masaccio*, *Expulsion from Paradise, one of his most moving works.—LOWER ROW (right to left): *Filippino Lippi*, *Release of St Peter from prison; *Filippino Lippi*, Saints Peter and Paul before the proconsul, and Crucifixion of St Peter; *Masaccio*, Saints Peter and John distributing alms; *Masaccio*, *St Peter, followed by St John, healing the sick with his shadow; *Masaccio*, *St Peter enthroned with portraits of friars, his last work, and St Peter bringing to life the Emperor's nephew, finished by *Filippino; Filippino Lippi*, St Peter in prison visited by St Paul.—The altarpiece of the Madonna del Popolo is a Tuscan Byzantine work of the mid-13C attributed to *Coppo di Marcovaldo* or the 'Maestro del Carmine'.

The sumptuous 17C *Chapel of Sant'Andrea Corsini by *Gherardo Silvani* has a ceiling by *Luca Giordano* and marble reliefs by *Giovanni Battista Foggini*. The Gothic Sacristy has frescoes from the life of St Cecilia by the school of Bicci di Lorenzo. In the rooms off the Cloister are works by *Alessandro Allori, Starnina, Filippo Lippi* (*Rule of the Order), *Giovanni da Milano, Lippo Fiorentino*, and *Francesco Vanni*.

BORGO SAN FREDIANO (Pl. 10,9), at the N end of the piazza, gives its name to a characteristic district with numerous artisans' houses and workshops. The large church of *San Frediano in Cestello* with its main entrance on the Arno was rebuilt in the 17C by Antonio Maria Ferri with a fine dome. It contains paintings by Francesco Curradi, Jacopo del Sellaio, and Lorenzo Lippi. The fortified *Porta San Frediano* (Pl. 5,9) is the best preserved part of the last circle of walls built by the Commune in 1284–1333. The gate, built in 1324, perhaps by Andrea Pisano, has a high tower and huge wooden doors.

VIA DI SANTO SPIRITO (Pl. 10) runs parallel to the Arno in the other direction, past the 17C *Palazzo Rinuccini, Palazzo Manetti* with a 15C façade (the home of Sir Horace Mann in 1740–86 while serving as English envoy to the Tuscan court), and *Palazzo Frescobaldi*.—On Lungarno Guicciardini is *Palazzo Lanfredini* by Baccio d'Agnolo with bright (restored) graffiti decoration.—From the foot of

Ponte Santa Trìnita the handsome VIA MAGGIO leads away from the Arno. Its name (from 'Maggiore') is a reminder of its origin as the principal and widest street of the Oltrarno. *Palazzo Ricasoli* (No. 7) was built at the end of the 15C. *Palazzo di Bianca Cappello* (No. 26) with good graffiti decoration attributed to Bernardino Poccetti was built by the Grand-Duke Francesco I for Bianca Cappello. *Palazzo Ridolfi* (No. 13) dates from the late 16C, and *Palazzo Commenda di Firenze* (No. 42) first built in the late 14C was reconstructed in the 16C. Via Maggio ends in Piazza San Felice. No. 8 is the 15C *Casa Guidi*, where Robert and Elizabeth Barrett Browning rented a flat on the first floor and lived after their secret marriage in 1846 until Elizabeth's death in 1861. It is now owned by the Browning Institute and contains some mementoes of the two poets. SAN FELICE is a Gothic church with a Renaissance façade by Michelozzo. It contains a fresco fragment attributed to Nicolò Gerini, a large *Crucifix from the workshop of Giotto, a triptych by Neri di Bicci, and a triptych by a follower of Botticelli.

Via Romana continues SW to Porta Romana, a well-preserved gate built in 1327 on a design by Andrea Orcagna. No. 17, *Palazzo Torrigiani*, was built in 1775 as a natural history museum, known as 'La Specola'. Here in 1814 Sir Humphry Davy and Michael Faraday used Galileo's 'great burning glass' to explode the diamond. It now contains a Zoological Museum with a remarkable collection of anatomical models in wax, many of them by Clemente Susini (1775–1814).

In Piazza Pitti dominated by the huge Palazzo Pitti (see Rte 42D) the pretty row of houses facing the palace includes the home of Paolo dal Pozzo Toscanelli (1397–1482), the famous scientist and geographer. While staying at No. 21 in 1868 Dostoyevsky wrote 'The Idiot'. Via Guicciardini continues to Ponte Vecchio; on the left is the ancient BORGO SAN JACOPO with the *Torre Marsili di Borgo*, a fine towerhouse, and the church of *San Jacopo sopr'Arno* with an 11C portico transported here in the 16C from a demolished church.

K. Forte di Belvedere and San Miniato al Monte

San Miniato can be reached directly from the Station or Piazza del Duomo by Bus No. 13 (red), or on foot by the steps from Porta San Niccolò (Pl. 12). However, for those with time the following route on foot is highly recommended (and Bus 13 can be taken back from San Miniato).

Near Ponte Vecchio the narrow COSTA SAN GIORGIO (Pl. 11) winds up the hill towards Forte di Belvedere past the pretty Costa Scarpuccia (left). The church of SAN GIORGIO SULLA COSTA has a good Baroque interior by Giovanni Battista Foggini, altarpieces by Tommaso Redi, Jacopo Vignali, and Passignano, and a *Madonna, an early work by Giotto (restored, but not yet returned here). Beyond the house (No. 19) purchased by Galileo for his son Vincenzio the road reaches *Porta San Giorgio* with a fresco by Bicci di Lorenzo. Built in 1260 this is the oldest gate to have survived in the city. Here is the entrance to ***Forte di Belvedere** (Pl. 11), a huge fortress designed by Buontalenti for Ferdinando I in 1590. From the ramparts (adm. 9–20) there is a splendid *View in every direction. The fine interior is used for exhibitions.

***Via di San Leonardo** (Pl. 15), one of the most beautiful country roads on the outskirts of the city, leads to the church of SAN LEONARDO IN ARCETRI which contains a *Pulpit of the early 13C, and several 15C paintings.—Some 2km farther on, beyond Viale Galileo, the *Observatory* at Arcetri, and the 14C *Torre del Gallo* the road continues to the village of PIAN DE'GIULLARI. *Villa il Gioiello* (No. 42; being restored) was the house where the aged Galileo lived, practically as a prisoner, from 1631 until his death in 1642. Here he was visited by Thomas Hobbes, and possibly also Milton.

*VIA DI BELVEDERE (Pl. 15), a picturesque country lane, follows the straight line of the city walls (first built in 1258) from Forte di Belvedere to Porta San Miniato. From here Via del Monte alle Croci or Via di San Salvatore al Monte return uphill. Across the busy Viale Galileo, a monumental flight of steps leads up past a cemetery (1839) to *San Miniato al Monte (Pl. 16). The finest of all Tuscan Romanesque basilicas, with a famous façade, it is one of the most beautiful churches in Italy. Its position on a green hill above the city is incomparable.

Deacon Minias is thought to have been martyred c 250 during the persecutions of Emperor Decius and buried on this hillside. The church was built in 1013 by Bishop Hildebrand on the site of his tomb. The *FAÇADE, begun c 1090, is built of white and dark greenish marble in a beautiful geometrical design reminiscent of the Baptistery. The mosaic (restored) of Christ between the Virgin and St Minias dates from the 13C. The tympanum is crowned by an eagle, emblem of the 'Arte di Calimala' who looked after the fabric of the building. The fine *INTERIOR built in 1018–63, with a raised choir above a large hall crypt, is practically in its original state. In the centre of the pavement are seven superb marble intarsia *Panels (1207) with signs of the zodiac and animal motifs. At the end of the nave is the *CAPPELLA DEL CROCIFISSO, an exquisite tabernacle by *Michelozzo* (1448). The painted panels are by *Agnolo Gaddi*, and the enamelled terracotta roof and ceiling by *Luca della Robbia*.—In the aisles are a number of 13–15C frescoes. On the N wall is the *CHAPEL OF THE CARDINAL OF PORTUGAL, begun by *Antonio Manetti* in 1460. The exquisitely carved *Tomb is by *Antonio Rossellino*, and the ceiling with five *Medallions by *Luca della Robbia*. The altarpiece of Three Saints by Antonio and Piero del Pollaiolo is a copy of the original in the Uffizi. The *Annunciation is by *Alesso Baldovinetti*.

Before the CHOIR is a beautiful marble *Transenna dating from 1207, and *Pulpit. The low columns in the choir have huge antique capitals. The large apse mosaic, representing Christ between the Virgin and St Minias (1297), was first restored in 1491 by Alesso Baldovinetti.—The SACRISTY (S side) is entirely frescoed with scenes from the *Life of St Benedict, one of the best works of *Spinello Aretino* (restored in 1840).—The 11C CRYPT has slender columns with antique capitals. The original 11C altar contains the relics of St Minias. The frescoes are by *Taddeo Gaddi*.

The massive stone CAMPANILE was begun after 1523, but never finished. During the siege of Florence (1530) Michelangelo mounted two cannon here, and protected the bell-tower from hostile artillery by a screen of mattresses. The battlemented *Bishop's Palace* dates from 1295 (restored). There is a splendid view from the terrace in front of the church.

In a grove of cypresses on the side of the hill is the church of SAN SALVATORE AL MONTE, a building of gracious simplicity by Cronaca, called by Michelangelo his 'bella villanella' (his 'pretty country maid').—Steps lead down to PIAZZALE MICHELANGELO (Pl. 16), a celebrated viewpoint much visited by tourists. From the balustrade on the huge terrace is a remarkable panorama of the city. VIALE DEI COLLI (bus No. 13), a fine roadway 6km long, was laid out by Giuseppe Poggi in 1865–70. It is one of the best panoramic drives near Florence.

L. The Viali

The wide avenues (or 'viali') form a ring-road busy with traffic around the centre of the city N of the Arno. They were laid out in 1865–69 by Giuseppe Poggi after he had demolished the last circle of walls built in 1284–1333; he left some of the medieval gates as isolated monuments. Viale Filippo Strozzi skirts the huge FORTEZZA DA BASSO (Pl. 2; adm. only when exhibitions are in progress).

This massive fortress, on a grand scale (with its exterior wall still intact), was built for Alessandro de'Medici in 1534 by Antonio da Sangallo. It became a symbol of Medici tyranny, and Alessandro was assassinated here by his cousin Lorenzino in 1537. It is now used partly as conservation laboratories of the Opificio delle Pietre Dure, one of the two official schools of restoration in Italy, and partly as an international exhibition centre. Public gardens have been laid out on the glacis.
   From the Fortezza a bus (No. 4) runs NE to the *Museo Stibbert (adm. 9–13; closed Thursday), created in his home here by Frederick Stibbert (1838–1906). His eclectic collection has a remarkably bizarre atmosphere, with 57 rooms crammed with an extraordinary variety of objects, including a famous collection of Asiatic armour. The park is open daily (9–dusk; fest. 9–13).

Across Viale Strozzi is *Palazzo dei Congressi*, a modern international conference centre. At No. 14 is the *Istituto Geografico Militare*, the most important cartographical institute in Italy.—Viale Lavagnini continues towards Piazza della Libertà. In Via Leone X (left) is the delightful *Russian Church* built in 1904 by Russian architects. It is owned by the Russian Orthodox community of Florence and is open for services. In the arcaded PIAZZA DELLA LIBERTÀ is the medieval Porta San Gallo and a Triumphal arch erected in 1739.

Off the N side of the square begins VIA BOLOGNESE (Bus No. 25), the pretty old road to Bologna. Here is the *Horticultural Garden* with an elaborate greenhouse (1879; by Giacomo Roster), and, at No. 120 *Villa La Pietra* the residence of Sir Harold Acton, with a beautiful garden. It contains one of the most interesting private collections of works of art in Florence.

The Viali continue to PIAZZA DONATELLO, in the centre of which is the disused *English Cemetery* (Pl. 4) on a mound shaded by cypresses. Here are buried Elizabeth Barrett Browning, Isa Blagden, Arthur Hugh Clough, Walter Savage Landor, Frances Trollope, Theodore Parker of Lexington, Robert Davidsohn, and Gian Pietro Vieusseux.—From the next square, Piazza Beccaria, the ex-CONVENT OF SAN SALVI is reached (buses 6 and 20 from San Marco). In the refectory (entrance at No. 16 Via San Salvi; open 9–13.30; fest. 9–12.30; closed Monday) is the celebrated *CENACOLO DI SAN SALVI by Andrea del Sarto (c 1520–25), a masterpiece of Florentine fresco, remarkable for its colouring, and one of the most famous frescoes of the Last Supper in Italy. 16C altarpieces and other works by Andrea del Sarto are displayed in the conventual buildings.— Nearby is the sports ground of Campo di Marte with the *Stadio*

Comunale, a remarkable building (1932) by Pier Luigi Nervi (enlarged in 1989).

43   Environs of Florence

For a full description of the places described below, see 'Blue Guide Florence'.

A. Fiesole. Bus No. 7 (frequent service in 30 minutes from the Station, Duomo, and Piazza San Marco). Via di San Domenico ascends the hillside with a beautiful view of Fiesole and its villas to (6·5km) **San Domenico di Fiesole**, a little hamlet with several handsome private villas. The 15C church of SAN DOMENICO has a 17C portico and campanile (by Matteo Nigetti).

INTERIOR. 1st N chapel, *Fra' Angelico*, *Madonna with Angels and Saints (c 1430). The architectural background was added by *Lorenzo di Credi* in 1501, when the frame was redesigned (the Saints are by a follower of Lorenzo Monaco).—The other altarpieces are by the *School of Botticelli* (Crucifixion), *Lorenzo di Credi* (Baptism of Christ), *Giovanni Antonio Sogliani* (Epiphany), and *Jacopo da Empoli* (Annunciation).—In the Convent of San Domenico St Antoninus and Fra' Angelico were friars. In the little CHAPTER HOUSE is a *Crucifixion and Madonna and Child by *Fra' Angelico*.

Via della Badia descends (left) from San Domenico to the *__Badia Fiesolana__, in a beautiful position, the cathedral of Fiesole until 1028. It was rebuilt in the 15C under the direction of Cosimo il Vecchio. In the conventual buildings the *European University Institute* was established in 1976. The rough stone front incorporates the charming *FAÇADE of the smaller Romanesque church with inlaid marble decoration. The simple cruciform *INTERIOR is attributed to a close follower of Brunelleschi.

From San Domenico the ascent to Fiesole may be made either by the main road or (on foot) by the shorter and prettier old road (Via Vecchia Fiesolana, very narrow and steep); both are lined with fine villas and beautiful trees and provide splendid views of Florence.— 8km **Fiesole** (295m) is a little town in a magnificent position on a thickly wooded hill overlooking the valleys of the Arno and the Mugnone. It has always been a fashionable residential district with fine villas and gardens and stately cypress groves. An Etruscan city, its foundation preceded that of Florence by many centuries, and, with its own local government, it is still proudly independent of the larger city. It is crowded with Florentines and visitors in summer when its position makes it one of the coolest places in the neighbourhood of the city.

The bus terminates in Piazza Mino da Fiesole, the main square. The **Cathedral**, founded in 1028, was over-restored in the 19C. The tall battlemented bell-tower dates from 1213.

The bare stone INTERIOR has a raised choir above a hall crypt. The massive columns have fine capitals (some of them Roman). Above the W door is a statue of St Romulus in a garlanded niche by *Giovanni della Robbia*. In the CAPPELLA SALUTATI (right of the Choir) are frescoes by *Cosimo Rosselli*, and the *Tomb of Bishop Salutati with a fine portrait bust, and an *Altar-frontal, both superb works by *Mino da Fiesole*. Over the high altar is a large *Altarpiece by *Bicci di Lorenzo*.—The CRYPT (being restored in 1990) has interesting primitive capitals.

At the upper end of the piazza is the old *Palazzo Pretorio* next to the church of *Santa Maria Primerana* with a quaint porch. The equestrian monument (1906) in the square celebrates the meeting between Victor Emmanuel II and Garibaldi at Teano.—Between the 17C Seminary and Bishop's Palace Via San Francesco, a very steep paved lane, climbs up the hill past a terrace with a *View of Florence. The ancient church of *Sant'Alessandro* contains cipollino marble *Columns with Ionic capitals and bases from a Roman building. At the top of the hill (345m), on the site of the Etruscan and later Roman acropolis are the convent buildings of **San Francesco**.

The church contains altarpieces by Piero di Cosimo, the school of Cosimo Rosselli, and Raffaellino del Garbo. A small missionary MUSEUM contains Eastern objets d'art. The wooded hillside is a public park.

The piazza in Fiesole, an engraving by Antonio Terreni, published in 1801

From Piazza Mino the street behind the apse of the cathedral leads to the entrance to the ***Roman Theatre, Archaeological Excavations, and Museum** (adm. daily 9–19; winter 9–17). From the terrace there is a good comprehensive view of the excavations in a plantation of olive trees. The ROMAN THEATRE (1C BC) held 3000 spectators (some of the seats are intact, while others have been restored). To the right are the ROMAN BATHS, probably built in the 1C AD and enlarged by Hadrian. A small terrace provides a fine view of a long stretch of ETRUSCAN WALLS which enclosed the city. NW of the theatre is a ROMAN TEMPLE (1C BC), and, on a lower level, remains of an ETRUSCAN TEMPLE (3C BC).—The Museum, built in 1912, recently modernised, contains a topographical collection (well labelled) from Fiesole and its territory

('She-wolf' in bronze, Bronze Age material, Etruscan stelai, urns, architectural fragments from the Theatre and Temples, etc.). The Antiquarium contains the 'Stele Fiesolana' (5C BC). At No. 9 Via Portigiani is the fine Costantini Collection of Corinthian, Greek, and Etruscan vases, and new finds including frescoes of 1C BC–2C AD.

In Via Duprè is the small **Museo Bandini** (closed for restoration) with paintings by *Bernardo Daddi, Neri di Bicci, Taddeo Gaddi, Lorenzo Monaco, Bicci di Lorenzo, Jacopo del Sellaio,* and others; and Romanesque and Della Robbian sculptures.

There are many beautiful walks in the vicinity of Fiesole. From Piazza Mino *Via Santa Maria* and *Via Belvedere* climb up the hill with superb views to the wall along the E limit of the Etruscan city. Below are the beautiful woods of *Montececeri*.—*Via Vecchia Fiesolana* descends steeply from the piazza and passes the *Villa Medici* (no adm.) built by Michelozzo for Cosimo il Vecchio. A by-road leads to *Fontelucente* with a church built over a spring.—The pretty *Via Benedetto da Maiano* diverges from the main Florence road below Fiesole for the hamlet of *Maiano*.—From Piazza Mino the main street continues uphill through the town, and, beyond Borgunto, has lovely views of the wide Mugnone valley to the N. A by-road diverges right for Montebeni, Castel di Poggio, and the *Castello di Vincigliata* (restored in 1855 by John Temple Leader) through magnificent woods on a ridge with views of Florence. The road continues downhill for Settignano.

B. Settignano, Bus No. 10 from San Marco (frequent service in ½hr).—At the foot of the hill of Settignano in the village of **Ponte a Mensola**, Via Poggio Gherardo branches left from the main road past the *Villa di Poggio Gherardo*, traditionally thought to be the setting for the earliest episodes in Boccaccio's 'Decameron'. Nearby (right) is *SAN MARTINO A MENSOLA, a Benedictine church of the 9C, founded by St Andrew, thought to have been a Scotsman and archdeacon to the bishop of Fiesole, Donato, who was probably from Ireland.

In the graceful 15C INTERIOR is a Madonna enthroned with Saints attributed to *Cosimo Rosselli*, a *Triptych by *Taddeo Gaddi*, and, on the high altar, a triptych with the donor Amerigo Zati by a follower of Orcagna (1391), known as the '*Master of San Martino a Mensola*'. In the N aisle is an *Annunciation by a follower of Fra' Angelico, and a *Madonna and four Saints by *Neri di Bicci*. A tiny MUSEUM contains a wooden *Casket, decorated with paintings by the school of Agnolo Gaddi, which formerly contained the body of St Andrew and a reliquary bust of the Saint (late 14C).—Nearby is **Villa I Tatti** (entrance on Via Vincigliata), the home of Bernard Berenson (1865–1959), the art historian and collector, and left by him to Harvard University as a Center of Italian Renaissance Studies. It contains his library (open to post-doctorate scholars) and *Collection of Italian paintings (not open to the public, but shown to scholars with a letter of presentation by previous appointment). The Italianate garden was also created by Berenson.— The pretty by road continues up the hill through woods past the castles of Vincigliata (see above) and Poggio to (6km) Fiesole.—In Via Vincigliata at the bottom of the hill are two plaques recording the writers and artists who lived and worked in the neighbourhood. The Villa Boccaccio (rebuilt) was owned by the father of Giovanni Boccaccio who probably spent his youth here.

From Ponte a Mensola the road continues up to Settignano winding across the old road; both have fine views of the magnificent trees on the skyline of the surrounding hills.—7·5km **Settignano** (178m), a cheerful village, is known for its school of sculptors most famous of whom were Desiderio and the brothers Rossellino. In the church is a Madonna and Child with two angels attributed to the workshop of Andrea della Robbia. In the lower Piazza Desiderio there is a superb view of Florence. The famous garden of the **Villa Gamberaia** is open on request (fee).

C. The Medici villas of Careggi, La Petraia, and Castello. Sesto Fiorentino.

Bus No. 14C from the Station or Duomo to Careggi. At the top of the hill, beyond the main buildings of the large hospital of Careggi, is the VILLA MEDICEA DI

CAREGGI, now used as a nurses' home (no adm.). This was the literary and artistic centre of the Medicean court, the meeting place of the famous Platonic Academy which saw the birth of the humanist movement of the Renaissance. In the villa, Cosimo il Vecchio, Piero di Cosimo, and Lorenzo il Magnifico all died.

Bus No. 28 from the Station for La Petraia, Castello, and Sesto. From Piazza Dalmazia the bus continues to (5km) the locality known as Il Sodo, just beyond which (request-stop) a narrow road right leads up to VILLA DELLA PETRAIA (adm. 9–dusk except Monday). Once a castle of the Brunelleschi, the villa was rebuilt in 1575 for the Grand-Duke Ferdinando I de'Medici by Buontalenti. In 1864–70 it was a favourite residence of Victor Emmanuel II, and in 1919 it was presented to the State by Victor Emmanuel III. A pretty garden and moat precede the villa, which still preserves a tower of the old castle. On the upper terrace is a fountain by Tribolo with a bronze statue of *Venus by Giambologna (exhibited inside the villa since its restoration). A magnificent Park, with ancient cypresses, extends behind the villa to the E. The Villa (ring for adm.) contains decorative *Frescoes illustrating the history of the Medici family, by Volterrano and Cosimo Daddi (attributed). The rooms were furnished as state apartments in the 19C.

At the bottom of Via della Petraia, in front of the Baroque façade of Villa Corsini, Via di Castello leads shortly to VILLA DI CASTELLO (adm. to the gardens only, as for La Petraia), now the seat of the Accademia della Crusca, founded in 1582, for the study of the Italian language. The villa was acquired by Giovanni and Lorenzo di Pierfrancesco de'Medici, Lorenzo il Magnifico's younger cousins, around 1477. Here they hung Botticelli's famous 'Birth of Venus'. The typical Tuscan GARDEN, described by numerous travellers in the 16C and 17C, was laid out by Tribolo for Cosimo I c 1537. The *Fountain by Tribolo is crowned by bronze figures of Hercules and Antenaeus by Ammannati (removed for restoration). The gardens also contain a grotto, a colossus by Ammannati, and an Orangery.

The bus route ends at (9km) **Sesto Fiorentino**, a small town. Villa Corsi Salviati, where exhibitions are held, has an 18C garden. The MUSEO DELLE PORCELLANE DI DOCCIA (adm. Tuesday, Thursday & Saturday, 9.30–13, 15.30–18.30) contains a fine collection of porcelain made in the famous Doccia factory founded by Carlo Ginori in 1737. The firm, known as Richard-Ginori since 1896, continues to flourish.

D. The Certosa del Galluzzo and Impruneta. Bus No. 37 from the Station to the Certosa di Galluzzo. CAP bus from 13 Via Nazionale c every hour to Impruneta in 40 minutes.—Outside Porta Romana begins the long Viale del Poggio Imperiale, lined with handsome villas and their gardens, and bordered by a splendid avenue of trees. At the top is the huge villa of *Poggio Imperiale*, once the property of the grand-dukes of Florence (and now a school).—The Siena road continues to (5km) the *Certosa del Galluzzo on a picturesque hill.

Visitors are conducted by a monk (9–12, 15 or 15.30–17.30 or 18.30; Sunday 15–17.30; closed Monday). The monastery was founded in 1342 by Niccolò Acciaioli. In the CHURCH is the *Tomb-slab of Cardinal Agnolo II Acciaioli, now attributed to *Francesco da Sangallo*. The CHAPTER HOUSE and the *GREAT CLOISTER with tondi by the *Della Robbia* and the monks' cells are also of interest. In the PALAZZO DEGLI STUDI, a fine Gothic hall, are the five frescoed *Lunettes of the Passion cycle, by *Pontormo* detached from the cloister, painted while he was staying in the monastery in 1522, and Florentine paintings of the 14C and 15C.

A road continues via *Tavarnuzze* to (14km) **Impruneta** on a plateau. The clay in the soil has been used for centuries to produce terracotta for which the locality is famous. In the large central piazza where the fair of St Luke is celebrated in mid-October, is the COLLEGIATA, restored after severe bomb damage in 1944. Two chapels by Michelozzo contain beautiful *Decoration in enamelled terracotta by Luca della Robbia. The Treasury was reopened here in 1989: it contains church silver including a Cross attributed to Lorenzo Ghiberti, as well as a beautiful 15C bas-relief, and illuminated choirbooks.

Near Ponte a Ema is the little chapel of *Santa Caterina dell'Antella* frescoed by Spinello Aretino with the *Story of St Catherine (closed for restoration).

E. Monteoliveto and Bellosguardo. Badia a Settimo and Lastra a Signa. On the S bank of the Arno, near Ponte della Vittoria is the thickly wooded hill of MONTEOLIVETO with some beautiful private villas. Here the church of San Bartolomeo contains frescoes by Bernardino Poccetti and Sodoma (Last Supper; very damaged), and an altarpiece by Santi di Tito. The adjoining hill to the S is aptly called BELLOSGUARDO (Pl. 9), with superb views of Florence.

The Pisa road leads out of Florence passing near to the interesting churches of *San Quirico, San Martino alla Palma*, and *Santi Giuliano e Settimo*. The BADIA DI SAN SALVATORE A SETTIMO (13km) founded in the 10C, contains a tabernacle attributed to Giuliano da Sangallo and frescoes by Giovanni da San Giovanni.—13km LASTRA A SIGNA preserves its walls of 1380. The Pieve of *San Martino Gangalandi,* where Leon Battista Alberti was rector from 1432–72, contains frescoes by Bicci di Lorenzo, and a St John the Baptist by Bernardo Daddi (1346). There is a Diocesan Museum here.

F. Poggio a Caiano. Bus (COPIT) from Piazza Santa Maria Novella every ½ hour in c 40 minutes.—The unattractive road passes (6km) *Peretola* where the church contains a *Tabernacle by Luca della Robbia (1441), and (9km) *Brozzi* with frescoes by Domenico Ghirlandaio and pupils in the church of Sant'Andrea.—18km **Poggio a Caiano**. The *VILLA (open 9–13.30 except Monday) was rebuilt by Giuliano da Sangallo for Lorenzo il Magnifico, and it became his favourite country villa. The semicircular steps were added by Pasquale Poccianti in 1802–07. Inside is displayed the original polychrome enamelled terracotta *Frieze attributed to Andrea Sansovino, removed from the exterior. The *Salone has frescoes by Franciabigio, Andrea del Sarto, Alessandro Allori, and a *Lunette by Pontormo. The delightful garden and park are open 9–dusk (except Monday).

5km SW is *Carmignano* where the church has a remarkable *Visitation by Pontormo.—Also S of Poggio a Caiano is the Medici *Villa of Artimino* designed by Bernardo Buontalenti for Ferdinando I in a delightful position surrounded by superb Tuscan countryside. Etruscan excavations are in progress here. At *Comeana* is the Etruscan *Tumulus of Montefortini (adm. 9–13 except Monday), with an interesting funerary chamber (excavations of a second tomb are in progress).

44 Florence to Bologna

MOTORWAY, AI (part of the 'Autostrada del Sole', linking Milan with Rome and the South), 95km.—10km *Firenze Nord.*—13km *Prato-Calenzano.*—29km *Barberino.*—48km *Roncobilaccio.*—53km *Pian di Voglio.*—67·5km *Rioveggio.*—83km *Sasso Marconi.*—95km **Bologna**-Casalecchio (ring-road).

ROAD, N65, 105·5km.—24km *Novoli.*—44·5km **Passo della Futa.**—51·5km *La Casetta.*—57km *Passo della Raticosa.*—62·5km *Monghidoro.*—70·5km *Loiano.*—105·5km **Bologna**.

RAILWAY, 97km, express trains in 55–80 minutes, slow trains in 2 hours. This is part of the main railway route between N and S Italy, and is followed by through trains between the Channel Ports, Paris, and German and Austrian cities to Rome, Naples, etc. The line, opened in 1934, is a remarkable engineering feat, and penetrates c 30 tunnels, including the 'Galleria dell'Appennino', just over 18·5km long, between the stations of Vernio and San Simplon, which took ten years to complete. It is followed, beyond San Benedetto, by the *Piandisetta Tunnel* (3·25km), and after Vado comes the *Monte Adone Tunnel* (7km).

The quickest way to accomplish this mountainous route across the Apennines is usually by the **Motorway**, opened in 1960, which crosses the watershed by spectacular viaducts and tunnels. It is, however, used by much heavy traffic including numerous long-distance lorries (except on Sunday), and one lane is often partially closed for repairs. It is also subject to sudden snow storms up until Easter. In such conditions and when there is very heavy traffic queues some kilometres long can form causing considerable delays. There are 'SOS' points every kilometre along the route. If traffic comes to a standstill motorists are requested to turn off their engines in tunnels. There are long-term plans to double the motorway, and possibly keep one exclusively for the use of lorries.

The motorway is reached from Florence by following the green motorway signs N out of the city beyond the Fortezza da Basso. From the airport of Peretola (see Rte 45) the 'Autostrada del Mare' (A11, for Pisa) leads to the junction of 'Firenze Nord' where the Bologna motorway (A1) diverges. There are several service stations on the motorway and the exits are listed above. It follows the E slope of the Monti della Calvana, and beyond the watershed it joins the line of the Prato-Bologna road beyond Castiglione dei Pepoli. At Bologna it merges with the motorway ring-road with exits for all districts of Bologna.

The alternative route to Bologna, which is slower and very windy, is via the pass of **La Futa**, described below. For those with time this is the most pleasant route across the Apennines, because it is now virtually free of traffic. However it is not passable in snow, and there are no 'SOS' points.

Leaving Florence by Piazza della Libertà (Pl. 3) and Ponte Rosso, this route follows the old Roman Via Bolognese (N65). Beyond La Lastra the road climbs up to Trespiano, with a large cemetery. At Pian di San Bartolo Via della Docciola diverges left for the pretty Romanesque church of Cercina in lovely countryside N of Careggi (see Rte 43C).—The hilly main road continues and skirts the ruined walls of the huge *Parco di Villa Demidoff* (see 'Blue Guide Florence'), the entrance to which is at (12·5km) *Pratolino* (car park on the left of the main road). It is now owned by the Province, and the huge park is

open to the public in May–September (Friday, Saturday, & Sunday,
10–19). It contains Giambologna's colossal statue of *Appennino
(restored in 1988).—The beautiful but windy road descends steeply
into the Carza valley to (18km) *Vaglia*. On the right a by-road
(5km) leads to the convent of *Montesenario*, on a hill-top (817m).
Here seven Florentine merchants became hermits and established
the Servite Order of mendicant friars in 1233. The church and
convent are set in woods full of grottoes and cells, with good
views.—At (24·5km) *Novoli* the Bologna road forks left from the
Imola road (described in Rte 41).

San Piero a Sieve, on the Imola road, has a Della Robbia font in its church.
Outside the town, just after a bridge over the Sieve, a by-road (signposted)
leads, left, to *Bosco ai Frati*, a charming little Franciscan convent (four friars
live here) in pretty wooded country (locally famous for its mushrooms).
Visitors are conducted (closed 12–15). The church and convent were restored
on a design by Michelozzo. Off the cloister, a little Museum contains a
*Crucifix attributed to Donatello (repaired after earthquake damage). Another
Crucifix attributed to Desiderio da Settignano was stolen in 1969.
   A road diverges right from San Piero into the MUGELLO, the upper basin of
the Sieve and one of the most characteristic valleys of Tuscany. It is intensely
cultivated and is noted for its wine. The many little summer resorts have a
temperate summer climate.—Beyond the thriving market town of *Borgo San
Lorenzo* is *Vespignano* where the house in which Giotto (1266–1336) is
thought to have been born has been restored and opened to the public. It
contains photographs of his major works (ring for adm.; summer, Tuesday,
Thursday, Saturday, and Sunday, 15–19; winter, Saturday and Sunday,
15–19).—*Vicchio* was the birthplace of Fra' Angelico (1387–1455). The Museo
Civico (closed in 1990) has an interesting collection of works of art from
churches in the region. Beyond *Dicomano* (23km), with a restored Romanesque church, the road descends to Pontassieve (see Rte 50).

Just W of the Bologna road are the *Castello del Trebbio* (adm. by
previous appointment only), built by Michelozzo in 1461, and
Cafaggiolo, the delightful Medici country residence built for
Cosimo il Vecchio, also by Michelozzo (1451).—Beyond the racing
circuit of Barberino the road climbs to (44·5km) the Passo della Futa
(903m) on the main watershed of the Apennines. The strongest
German defences in the 'Gothic Line' were here, but the position
was turned by the capture of the Giogo Pass and Firenzuola.
Beyond the pass the road descends slightly to (46·5km) *Traversa*,
and passes beneath the rocky Sasso di Castro.—50·5km *Covigliaio*
(874m) is a little resort.—At (51·5km) *La Casetta* a steep road to
Firenzuola and Imola descends to the right, while this road climbs
to (56·5km) *Pietramala* (851m), a summer and winter holiday
resort.—Beyond (57·5km) the *Passo della Raticosa* (968m) begins
the descent into Emilia (old custom-house at the boundary).—
62·5km *Monghidoro* (841m) and (70·5km) *Loiano* are the best
known hill-resorts on the N side of the pass. On the left rise the
cliffs of Monte Adone, through which the railway tunnels to join
this route at (89km) *Pianoro* in the Savena valley.—At (99km) *Ponte
San Ruffillo* the Bolognese and their allies defeated Bernabò
Visconti in 1361.—105·5km **Bologna**, see Rte 40.

For other passes over the Apennines to Bologna from Prato and Pistoia, see
Rte 45.

45 Florence to Lucca and Pisa

MOTORWAY, A11, 97km. 10km *Firenze Nord.*—15km **Prato.**—
34·5km *Pistoia.*—46km *Montecatini.*—53·5km *Chiesina Uzzano.*—
57km *Altopascio.*—67km *Capannori.*—72km **Lucca.**—88km *Pisa
Nord*, where the Aurelia (NI) is joined for (97km) **Pisa**. From
Lucca an alternative (and shorter) route to Pisa follows the road
(N12r) via San Giuliano Terme (see below).

The ROAD (100km) offers little advantage over the motorway as
it is also busy with traffic and passes through built-up areas
most of the way. The old road to **Prato** passes through *Sesto
Fiorentino* (see Rte 43C). **Pistoia** can be reached either via Prato
(N 435) or (more directly) via *Poggio a Caiano* (N66, 35·5km),
described in Rte 43E.—Beyond Pistoia, N435 continues via
(51km) *Montecatini* and (59km) *Pescia* to (78km) **Lucca**. From
Lucca the most direct route to **Pisa** is by N12r which tunnels
through Monte Pisano and then descends to (94·5km) *San
Giuliano Terme* and enters (100km) Pisa beside the N stretch of
the city walls (near the Duomo and the Leaning Tower).

RAILWAY. The main line via Empoli to **Pisa** (81km in 55–95
minutes) goes on to Livorno. This is one of the earliest railways
in Italy, projected by Robert Stephenson in 1838–40. Through
carriages from Florence to Genoa and Turin run on this line.—
For **Prato** there is a train c every half hour (17km in c 20
minutes) going on to Bologna or Lucca and Viareggio.—The
Viareggio line serves **Pistoia** (34km in 30–45 minutes), and **Lucca**
(78km in 75–105 minutes) with stops at *Montecatini* and *Pescia.*

From Florence green 'autostrada' signs from the Fortezza da Basso
(Pl. 2) direct traffic N to the motorway, which starts at the small airport
of Peretola, 6km from the Fortezza. The motorway runs N past the
airport with good views right of the foothills of the Apennine chain,
with the large yellow Villa della Petraia (with a tower) conspicuous on
the side of the hill on the outskirts of the city. At 'Firenze-Nord' the
church of San Giovanni Battista by Giovanni Michelucci (1964) can be
seen (right) with its green cantilever roof near the motorway.

15km **PRATO** (143,200 inhab.) is a rapidly-expanding industrial
town, known as the 'Manchester of Tuscany', and long-famous for its
wool manufactures. It is one of the most important centres of the
textile industry in Europe. It preserves some beautiful monuments
within its old walls.

A.P.T. 51 Via Luigi Muzzi (N of the Duomo). *Information Office* in Via Cairoli
and Piazza Santa Maria delle Carceri.

Hotels. Most of the large hotels serve the industrial suburbs; the simpler hotels
within the walls are the most convenient for the visitor.

Railway Stations. *Centrale*, E of the town across the Bisenzio for all main line
trains; services on the Florence-Lucca line stop also at *Porta al Serraglio*, 200
metres N of the cathedral.—**Buses.** Frequent services (via the motorway) from
Florence (Railway Station) by *C.A.P.* (terminal in Piazza Duomo) and *Lazzi*
(terminal in Piazza San Francesco).—**Parking.** The centre is closed to traffic;
parking in Piazza Mercatale or Piazza dei Macelli.

Theatres. *Teatro Comunale Metastasio*, with a renowned theatre season
October–April. *Teatro Il Fabbricone*, Viale Galileo.—The traditional *Prato Fair* is
held in September.

History. Although probably already settled in the Etruscan period, the first
recorded mention of Prato is in the 9C. It became a free commune in the 12C and
after 1351 came under the influence of Florence. The manufacture of wool in the
city had reached European importance by the 13C, and it received further
impetus in the following century through the commercial activity of the famous
merchant Francesco di Marco Datini. Its textile factories continue to flourish, and

it has become the centre of the 'rag-trade' in Europe. As an industrial centre, its population is expanding faster than almost any other city in central Italy. It is to become the capital of a new province.

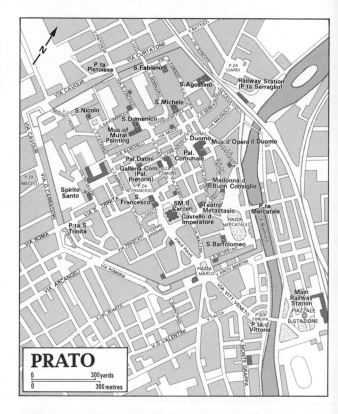

The approaches from the motorway and main station reach the walls of the old town at Piazza San Marco. Here has been set up a sculpture (1969–70) by Henry Moore. Viale Piave continues to the *CASTELLO DELL'IMPERATORE (restored). It was probably built in 1237–48 to protect Frederick II's route from Germany to Southern Italy, and is typical of the Hohenstaufen castles of the south. The empty interior (adm. 9–12, 15–18; fest. 9–12; closed Monday) is of little interest, except for the walkway (closed for restoration) around the ramparts, which provides a good view of the city and countryside. Concerts and plays are held here in summer. In the adjoining piazza stands the church of ***Santa Maria delle Carceri** (closed 12–16.30), a master-piece of the Early Renaissance. It is one of the most important works by *Giuliano da Sangallo*, begun in 1485 (the exterior was left in-complete in 1506).

The Greek-cross plan is derived from the architectural principles of Alberti and Brunelleschi. It was built where a miracle was performed in 1484 by the image of the Virgin painted on a prison wall (hence 'Carceri'). The exterior, in green and white marble, recalls the Romanesque buildings of Florence (the last side was completed in the 19C). In the domed centrally-planned INTERIOR pietra serena is used to emphasise the structural elements. The beautiful enamelled terracotta frieze and tondi of the Evangelists are by *Andrea della Robbia*. The stoup is by *Francesco da Sangallo*, and the stained glass windows date from the 15C.

In Via Cairoli, just behind the church, is the *Teatro Comunale Metastasio* (adm. on request at No. 61) with an elegant interior built in 1827–30 by Luigi Cambray Digny. It has a high theatrical reputation.

Farther on is the Romanesque church of *San Francesco*, with a handsome striped marble façade. At the foot of the altar steps is the tomb slab of Francesco di Marco Datini, the famous 'Merchant of Prato', by Nicolò Lamberti (1409). In the apse is a 15C wooden crucifix. On the N wall is the tomb of Gimignano Inghirami (died 1460), attributed to Bernardo Rossellino. From the charming 15C cloister (planted with olive trees) or from the Sacristy is the entrance to the Chapter House (or Cappella Migliorati) with good and well-preserved frescoes by Niccolò di Pietro Gerini (c 1395) of the Crucifixion, and Stories from the Life of St Anthony Abbot and St Matthew.—The church of *Spirito Santo* (open only for services; at other times ring at the Police Station; reached by Via Santa Trinita and, on the right, Via Silvestri), contains a *Presentation in the Temple by Fra Diamante, possibly to a design of Filippo Lippi; a coloured stucco tondo of the Madonna and Child from a design of Benedetto da Maiano, and a splendid *Annunciation of the school of Orcagna.

Via Rinaldesca leads out of Piazza San Francesco. On the corner of Via Ser Lapo Mezzei is the huge *Palazzo Datini*, with unusually large projecting eaves. Part of the decoration and some of the sinopie survive of the exterior mural paintings, attributed to Niccolò di Pietro Gerini and others, which illustrated the story of the life of Datini (1330–1410; see above). His papers and business documents (including over 140,000 letters), all of which were carefully preserved by him, provide a unique record of medieval life; they are housed in an archive in the palace. At the end of Via Ser Lapo Mazzei, Via Guasti leads right to the fine PIAZZA COMUNE with a statue (1896) of Datini and a fountain by Tacca (1659; original sculptures inside Palazzo Comunale, see below). Here stand the imposing Palazzo Pretorio and the arcaded Palazzo del Comune. The main stone façade of PALAZZO PRETORIO (being restored), with its Gothic windows and outside staircase, was added to a medieval core in the early 14C, and the battlements were completed in the 16C. The palace houses the *Galleria Comunale** (adm. 9–13, 15–19; closed Sunday).

FIRST FLOOR: frescoed tabernacle by *Filippino Lippi* (1498). A small adjacent room with cupboards and jars (removed for restoration) from the old pharmacy of the hospital, is used for lectures etc. Beyond is the 14C Salone, with a fine roof.—SECOND FLOOR. On the stairs is the alabaster model by Lorenzo Bartolini for the Demidoff monument in Florence. The MAIN HALL contains the most important *Works in the collection. *Bernardo Daddi*, Story of the Sacred Girdle, Madonna and Saints; *Fra Bartolomeo*, Madonna and Child (fresco fragment); *Giovanni di Milano*, Polyptych; *Pietro di Miniato*, Coronation of the Madonna; *Lorenzo Monaco* (workshop), Madonna enthroned with Saints; *Luca Signorelli* (attributed), Tondo of the Madonna and Child with Saints; *Filippino Lippi*, Madonna and Child with Saints; *Raffaellino del Garbo*, Tondo of the Madonna and Child with St John; *Andrea di Giusto*, Madonna and Child with Saints; *Filippo Lippi*, Madonna del Ceppo (with Francesco di Marco Datini), Nativity; *Francesco Botticini*, Madonna and Child with Saints; *Zanobi Strozzi*, Predella; *Ridolfo del Ghirlandaio*, Portrait of Baldo Magini; *Piero di Lorenzo Pratese*, Predella; *Andrea della Robbia*, St Anthony Abbot (lunette). The next two rooms contain later paintings, notably *Battistello* ('Noli me tangere'), and works by *Gaspare Vanvitelli*.

THIRD FLOOR (closed for repairs): later paintings, including works by *Gian Domenico Ferretti* (Annunciation), *Francesco Morandini* (Tobias and the Angel), *Giovanni Battista Naldini*, *Bilivert*, etc. Here, also is a fine collection of plaster-casts by *Lorenzo Bartolini* (1777–1850)

At the foot of the stairs of the *Palazzo Comunale* is the original Bacchus of Tacca's fountain (1665) from the piazza outside. Upstairs the Sala del Consiglio (shown on request, 8–14 except fest.) has a fine ceiling, two 15C frescoes, and a series of portraits (some by Alessandro Allori) of the Grand-Dukes of Tuscany, and of Cardinal Niccolò of Prato by Tommaso di Piero Trombetto.

Via Mazzoni goes on to the spacious PIAZZA DEL DUOMO. The *Duomo has a green and white striped marble façade by *Guidetto da Como*. In the 14C the transepts and apse were added, the design of which is attributed to *Giovanni Pisano*. The top of the fine campanile (early 13C) was added by *Niccolò di Cecco del Mercia* c 1356. At the SW corner projects the *PULPIT OF THE SACRED GIRDLE, designed by *Donatello* and *Michelozzo*, protected by a charming roof; the dancing putti by Donatello (1433–38) have been replaced by casts (the original panels are in the Museo dell'Opera del Duomo, see below). The Holy Girdle is displayed from the pulpit in a traditional ceremony on 1 May, Easter Day, 15 August, 8 September, and Christmas Day. Over the principal doorway is a *Madonna with Saints Stephen and Lawrence by *Andrea della Robbia* (1489).

The Romanesque INTERIOR (closed 12–16) has deep arcades decorated in stripes of marble carried on noble green marble columns. During restoration work of the whole building (begun in 1983) some of the works of art have been removed for safety to the Museo dell'Opera. Immediately to the left of the entrance is the *CHAPEL OF THE SACRED GIRDLE. The girdle was brought to Prato from the Holy Land in 1141. The good screen was begun by *Maso di Bartolomeo*, and continued by *Antonio di Ser Cola* and *Pasquino di Matteo*. It is entirely frescoed by *Agnolo Gaddi*, and on the altar is a statuette of the *Madonna and Child by *Giovanni Pisano* (1317).—The *PULPIT in the N aisle is by *Mino da Fiesole* and *Antonio Rossellino*.—In front of the high altar, on which is a bronze crucifix by *Ferdinando Tacca* (1653), is a bronze candelabrum by *Maso di Bartolomeo*, similar to that in the Duomo at Pistoia.—The CHOIR is decorated with celebrated *Frescoes by *Filippo Lippi* (helped by *Fra Diamante*). It is one of the most beautiful fresco cycles of the early Renaissance (1452–66), and the monumental figures repay close study (coin-operated light in chapel to the left). On the right wall: scenes from the Life of St John the Baptist; the Salome in the *Banquet of Herod is supposed to be a portrait of Lucrezia Buti, Lippi's mistress and later wife. On the left wall: scenes from the Life of St Stephen.—The first chapel on the right has fine 15C frescoes by a follower of *Paolo Uccello* and *Andrea di Giusto*. In the S transept are the Death of St Jerome, a painting by *Filippo Lippi* (1452; light in corner on the left; restored in 1987), and a tabernacle (1480) designed by *Giuliano da Maiano*, with a Madonna and Child and a Pietà in bas-relief by his brothers *Benedetto* and *Giovanni*.—In the first chapel to the left of the choir are early 15C frescoes, and in the 2nd chapel, the *Tomb of Filippo Inghirami (died 1480).

The **Museo dell'Opera del Duomo** (entered to the left of the cathedral façade; 9.30–12.30, 15–18.30; fest. 9.30–12.30; closed Tuesday) is beautifully arranged in rooms off the old cloister, part of which is a unique survival from the 12C, decorated in the marble Florentine style.

ROOM I displays 14C paintings, including a Madonna and Child, and two Evangelists and two Saints by *Giovanni Toscani*.—RII. Illuminated 15C anthem books, and two late 16C embroidered copes.—Off the cloister: Sculpted *Panels of dancing putti by *Donatello* from the Pulpit of the Sacred Girdle (outside the cathedral, see above), here displayed at eye level (but damaged by restoration); 'Maestro della Natività di Castello', Madonna and Child enthroned with Saints (from the church of Santi Giusto e Clemente at Faltugnano); *Fra' Diamante*, Annunciation; *Filippino Lippi*, *St Lucy; *Master of the early 15C* (attributed to Paolo Uccello), Jacopone da Todi (detached fresco); Reliquary for the sacred girdle, an exquisite work by *Maso di Bartolomeo* (1446). A treasury contains reliquaries, chalices, thuribles, reliquary busts, and a pax by *Danese Cattaneo.*—The last room contains a painted Crucifix by the school of Botticelli; *Michele Tosini*, Portrait of Lapo Spighi; *Carlo Dolci*, Guardian Angel.—From the cloister there is also access to the medieval arches beneath the transept of the Duomo with early-15C frescoes, the 14C altar of the Holy Girdle, a small antiquarium, and some remains of the earlier church.

From the Duomo the Largo Carducci leads into Via San Michele where the church of *San Michele* (or *Arciconfraternità di Misericordia*) has an altarpiece of the Assumption by Alessandro Allori (1603), and a Romanesque Crucifix.

At No. 30 Via del Seminario is the entrance to the church of *San Fabiano* (adm. on request at the Seminary) with fragments of a splendid pre-Romanesque pavement on the W wall, figured with animals, sirens, birds, etc. The other Romanesque details of the church are also notable (the façade can be seen from Via Giovanni di Gherardo which skirts the walls).

Via Convenevole da Prato leads NE to Via della Stufa, off which (left) opens a piazza with the church of *Sant'Agostino*, erected in 1271, but since considerably altered.

The interior contains 16–17C altarpieces, including, in the N aisle (2nd altar), a Madonna by Vasari (also attributed to Giovanni Battista Naldini) and (3rd altar) St Thomas of Villanova, by Lorenzo Lippi. A door in the N wall leads into the Cloister; from here are reached the Cappella di San Michele with a damaged frieze of saints (14C) and a Madonna and Child, by the School of Ghiberti, and the Chapter House with more 14C frescoes.

From San Michele, Via Convenevole leads back to the church of *San Domenico*, which has an arcaded flank; founded in 1283 it was finished by Giovanni Pisano before 1322. It contains a 17C organ, on which Domenico Zipoli (born in Prato in 1688 and died in Argentina in 1726) probably played, and a Baroque baldacchino. South Aisle. 2nd altar, Crucifix by Niccolò Gerini. North Aisle. 2nd altar, Madonna appearing to St Philip Neri, by Matteo Rosselli; 4th altar, Crucifix talking to St Thomas Aquinas, by Francesco Morandini; 5th altar, Annunciation, signed by Matteo Rosselli. In the adjoining convent is a MUSEUM OF MURAL PAINTING (entered from No. 8 in the piazza; open Sunday 9.30–12.30) housing detached frescoes from buildings in the town and surrounding area.

The works include: *Niccolò di Pietro Gerini*, Tabernacolo del Ceppo (with its sinopia); *Maestro delle Madonne* (?), Madonna and Child; *Antonio di Miniato*, Madonna enthroned with Saints (1411); sinopie of the Cappella dell'Assunta in the Duomo, attributed to Paolo Uccello; graffiti decoration from the Palazzo Vaj of courtly scenes (15C). Also objects from the church Treasury and a charming collection of ex votos.
Corso Savonarola leads to the church and convent of *San Niccolò*, with interesting 14C and 15C frescoes, and a della Robbian lavabo, attributed to Sante Buglioni.

From the SE corner of Piazza del Duomo, Via Garibaldi leads past the *Madonna del Buon Consiglio* (if closed ask at Santa Maria delle Carceri, see above) with a Della Robbian lunette (and other works by the Della Robbia in the interior) to the huge PIAZZA MERCATALE. Here the modern church of *San Bartolomeo* (the 14C church was destroyed in the last War) has a 15C marble tabernacle on the high altar with a painted Crucifix of the 14C Pistoian school above. The altarpieces include works by Santi di Tito (Presentation in the Temple), Leonardo

Mascagni (Holy Family), Livio Mehus (Rest on the Flight), and Empoli. In the crypt is a fine wood Crucifix of the 14C.

On the S outskirts of the town (in a Textile Institute at No. 9 Viale della Repubblica) the *Museo del Tessuto* was opened in 1975 (adm. 9–12; closed fest.). It contains a collection of textiles from the 5C AD to the present day (including examples of embroidery, tapestry, lace, velvet, and damask), a display of looms, etc.

Between the motorway exit ('Prato-est') and Viale della Repubblica is the *Centro per l'arte contemporanea Luigi Pecci*, designed by Italo Gamberini, and opened in 1988 (10–19 except Tuesday). The well illuminated huge galleries are used for contemporary art exhibitions. There is also an open-air theatre, auditorium, snack bar, etc.

FROM PRATO TO BOLOGNA, 100km. The road (N325) follows the main railway line across the Apennines, and for the last part also runs beside the motorway. It ascends the Bisenzio valley through (11km) the wide upland basin of *Vaiano*, with its 13C campanile. On a secondary road between Prato and Vaiano is *Figline* with the Romanesque Pieve di San Pietro (14–15C frescoes; and a small museum). In the hills to the right of Vaiano is *Savignano*, the birthplace of the painter Fra Bartolomeo della Porta (1475–1517) and of the sculptor Lorenzo Bartolini (1777–1850). Passing (right) the ruined 12–13C castle of *Cerbaia*, the road reaches (21km) *San Quirico di Vernio* (278m), a substantial village with another castle ruin. The watershed is crossed by an indefinite pass just before (31km) *Montepiano* (700m), a summer resort. Here the 11–12C Badia di Santa Maria contains 13–14C frescoes.—Emilia is entered near (40km) *Castiglione dei Pepoli* (691m), an ancient stronghold of the Pepoli of Bologna, whose castle is now the town hall.—Beyond (54km) *Lagaro* (391m) the road descends the scantily populated and steep-sided valley of the Setta in company with the motorway. The railway appears on the left, but beyond (69km) *Vado* it tunnels through the hills on the right.—Beyond the old railway this route joins the road from Pistoia at (78km) *Sasso Marconi*. From there to (100km) **Bologna**, see below.

The old road from Prato to Pistoia (19·5km) passes (7·5km) *Montemurlo*, where the medieval Guidi castle was the scene of the last attempt of the partisans of the Florentine Republic to overthrow the power of the Medici (1537).

The motorway continues from Prato past numerous nurseries to (35·5km) **PISTOIA**, a lively old Tuscan town (93,200 inhab.) with an unusual number of beautiful churches, whose character recalls its situation between Florence and Pisa. Many of them have good sculptures. It is an important horticultural centre, particularly noted for the cultivation of ornamental plants. There are extensive nurseries on the surrounding plain.

Tourist Office (E.P.T.), 110 Corso Gramsci (information office in Piazza Duomo).—*Post Office*, Via Roma.

Buses from Piazza San Francesco (COPIT) to *Abetone* and *Florence* (in 1 hour); and (Lazzi) from Via Gobetti for *Florence* (in 45 minutes), Pisa, Forte dei Marmi, La Spezia, Prato, Viareggio, Livorno, Lucca, Montecatini Terme, etc.

Parking. The centre is closed to traffic; parking at the ex-Officine Meccaniche Breda, off Via Pacinotti.

The *Giostra dell'Orso*, a medieval jousting tournament, is held on 25 July in Piazza del Duomo.

History. *Pistoria* is first mentioned as the scene of Catiline's defeat in 62 BC. It was a republic in the 12C but was seized by the Florentines in 1306 and in 1315 by Castruccio Castracani (died 1328), a military and political adventurer. From 1329 it existed under the protection of Florence, whose fortunes it shared, as the Medici arms on the walls testify. As an ironworking town in medieval times, it gave its name to the pistol (originally a dagger, afterwards a small firearm), and indirectly to the Spanish pistole, so called as smaller than the French crown. The Breda works here are famous for the production of railway carriages and buses; a new factory was built in 1973 on the outskirts of the town between the railway and the motorway (the huge old 'officine', off Via Pacinotti, have been abandoned and are at present used as a car park).—Guittone Sinibaldi, called

Cino da Pistoia (1270–1337), the friend of Dante, was born here; also Clement IX (Giulio Rospigliosi), Pope in 1667–69.

The approaches from Florence (or from the station) enter the town by the S gate; from here Via Vannucci and Via Cino lead to Piazza Gavinana. Corso Fedi, on the right before the piazza, leads to the church of **San Domenico** (late 13C, probably to the design of Fra Sisto and Fra Ristoro, with 14C alterations). Inside is the tomb of Filippo Lazzari (S wall, near the entrance), by *Bernardo* and *Antonio Rossellino*, and (beyond the 3rd S altar) the notable sculpted tomb effigy of Beato Lorenzo da Ripafratta (died 1457). In the S transept are the Rospigliosi tombs. The organ, by Rovani da Lucca, dates from 1617.

A door in the S aisle leads into the Cloister in which is buried, in an unknown spot, the body of Benozzo Gozzoli, who died here in 1497 during the plague. In several rooms of the Domenican convent off the cloister are interesting frescoes (many detached from the church) shown by a monk (ring at No. 1 Piazza San Domenico). The Chapter House has a damaged fresco of the Crucifixion by an unknown master of the mid-13C with its *Sinopia, thought to be the oldest known. The Refectory has more good frescoes from the church. A small museum contains other frescoes, mainly 16C, but including one with the portraits of Dante and Petrarch. Outside the entrance to the Library: Journey of the Magi,

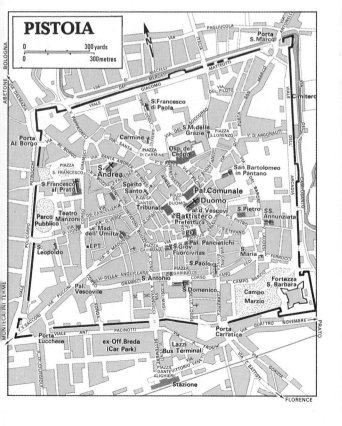

attributed to the school of Benozzo Gozzoli; St Jerome, attributed to Antonio del Pollaiolo; and *St Mary Magdalene (14C Sienese). To the S are remains of a 14C cloister with traces of vault paintings.

On the other side of Corso Fedi is a little garden with palm trees, an equestrian statue of Garibaldi (1904) and amusing lamp-posts. The CHAPEL OF SANT'ANTONIO ABATE (DEL TAU), restored in 1968, was closed in 1989. It is entirely covered with *Frescoes by 14–15C artists representing the story of Adam and Eve in the vaults, and, on the walls, various stories from the lives of the saints. They are the work of unknown masters, perhaps including Bonaccorso di Cino and Masolino di Panicale.—Farther on, on the left, is the church of San Paolo, with a fine façade of 1291–1302. Over the later door are a St Paul between two angels by Jacopo di Mazzeo, and (high up on the pinnacle) a figure of St James, attributed to Orcagna. Inside is a 14C wood Crucifix (left wall).

Via Cavour, leading E from Piazza Gavinana, passes the church of **San Giovanni Fuorcivitas** of the 12–14C. The handsome striped N side, with a blind arcade surmounted by two blind galleries, serves as a façade. The fine portal bears a relief of the Last Supper by Gruamonte (1162). In the dark interior the *Pulpit is by Fra Guglielmo da Pisa, a follower of Nicola Pisano (1270). Opposite is a white glazed terracotta *Visitation now attributed to Luca della Robbia. The *Stoup in the middle of the church is by Giovanni Pisano. On the wall to the left of the high altar is a polyptych by Taddeo Gaddi (restored). By the W end of the church, through the entrance to the Cinema Verdi (being restored), can be seen the charming cloisters.—Farther along Via Cavour, Via Roma leads left past (right) the Palazzo della Cassa di Risparmio (1905) and (left) the former Palazzo del Capitano del Popolo, on the corner of a street with interesting old shop fronts which leads to an old market square. Beyond is the spacious PIAZZA DEL DUOMO with its imposing buildings shown off to advantage now that cars are no longer allowed to park here.

The ***Duomo** has an arcaded Romanesque Pisan façade. The porch was added in 1311, and the high arch in the barrel vault is beautifully decorated by Andrea della Robbia, as is the *Lunette above the central door. The separate *CAMPANILE was originally a watch tower, and is supposed to have been adapted to its present use in the 14C by the addition of the three tiers of arches.

The INTERIOR (closed 12–16) retains traces of 13C and 14C frescoes. On the W wall are the tomb of St Atho, Bishop of Pistoia, with reliefs of the Sienese school (1337), and a *Font by Andrea Ferrucci da Fiesole, on a design of Benedetto da Maiano.—In the SOUTH AISLE: *Tomb of Cino da Pistoia, by a Sienese artist (1337), and a painted *Crucifix by Coppo di Marcovaldo (and his son, Salerno, 1275). CHAPEL OF ST JAMES (opened by the sacristan; fee): large silver *Altar of St James, started in 1287 and remodelled and added to during successive generations (and recently restored). It is a masterpiece of medieval goldsmiths' work. The statue of St James is by Gilio da Pisa (1349), the nine stories from the Life of St James, on the left flank, by Leonardo di Giovanni, and the two half figures on the left side by Brunelleschi. Andrea and Tallino di Jacopo d'Ognabene also worked on the altar. Behind the altar is a charming 15C Flemish tapestry. At the end of the aisle, in a Gothic niche, are 14C frescoes, and a triptych by the Sienese school (1424). The Chapel to the S of the high altar contains a good painting of Saints Baronto and Desiderio by Mattia Preti.—The CHOIR contains colossal statues of Saints James and Zeno by Vincenzo, a pupil of Giambologna (1603). To the right at the top of the sanctuary steps stands a bronze candelabrum by Maso di Bartolomeo (1440), similar to the one in the Duomo at Prato. At the entrance to the CHAPEL OF THE SACRAMENT (N of the choir) is a fresco fragment of the Madonna. Here, on the S wall, is a Madonna with Saints John the Baptist and Zeno by *Lorenzo di Credi*, on a design of Andrea del Verrocchio (usually covered), and a *Bust (N wall) of Archbishop Donato de'Medici, by *Antonio Rossellino*, or *Verrocchio*. In the N aisle, near the entrance, is the tomb of Cardinal Niccolò Forteguerri with two statues of Hope and Faith attributed to Verrocchio. The figure of Charity was added by *Lorenzetto* in 1515, and the bust and sarcophagus in 1753.—In the Crypt are remains of the former church, and fragments of the 13C pulpit dismantled in the 17C.

Opposite the Duomo is the octagonal ***Baptistery** (recently restored but still closed in 1990) started in 1338 by *Cellino di Nese* on a design of *Andrea Pisano*, and finished in 1359. The capitals and reliefs above the main entrance and the Madonna in the tympanum are particularly fine. On the right is a tiny Gothic pulpit of 1399. In the fine interior, decorating the font, are sculptured slabs of the 13C similar to those existing in several of the Pistoian churches, and possibly originally from the Duomo. **Palazzo dei Vescovi**, founded on this site at the end of the 11C and finished in the 12C (and enlarged in the 14C) was beautifully restored in 1982 by the bank which now owns it and uses part of it as offices. It contains an archaeological section, and the ***Museo della Cattedrale di San Zeno** (shown on a guided tour on Tuesday, Thursday, & Friday at 10, 11.30, and 15.30; entrance through the Tourist Information Office).

In the basement is displayed material found during excavations in the area of the palace, from the Roman period onwards, including two Etruscan cippi used in the foundations, and a hoard of medieval ceramics found in a well. The excavations themselves are shown and explained in detail.—MUSEO DELLA CATTEDRALE DI SAN ZENO. The first room contains a Roman cinerary urn (2C AD) with a carriage drawn by four horses, found during recent excavations in the Duomo. The 15C illuminated choirbooks are displayed in rotation. Also here are two *Reliquaries, one of 1379 by *Rombolus Salvei*, and one of 1444 by *Maestro Gualandi*; an octagonal ebony and ivory coffer by the *Bottega degli Embriachi* (late 15C); a chalice of 1384 signed by the local goldsmith *Andrea di Pietro Braccini*; a polychrome wood statue of an angel with the head of the Baptist, an interesting work thought to be by a French sculptor (c 1361).— Beyond are two 14C Sienese marble statuettes; the *Reliquary of San Zeno, made by the local goldsmith *Enrico Belandini* while in Aix-en-Provence in 1369; the Cross of St Atho (c 1280), and the Chalice of St Atho, attributed to *Andrea* and *Tallino d'Ognabene* (1286). The fresco of the Crucifixion is by *Giovanni di Bartolomeo Cristiani* (1387).—In the 12C Sacristy of San Jacopo, the 'sagrestia dei belli arredi', robbed by Vanni Fucci in 1293 and recorded by Dante ('Inferno', XXIV), is the *Reliquary of San Jacopo, by *Lorenzo Ghiberti* and his bottega (1407).—A spiral staircase leads up to a room with 17C vestments, and 18C church silver. Another room has been reconstructed to contain *Tempera murals by *Giovanni Boldini* (1868), with scenes of pastoral life and of the sea at Castiglioncello. They were detached from the Villa La Falconiera near Pistoia, where the Falconer family entertained Boldini and other Macchiaioli painters.—Beyond a room with two 16C carved panels by the local sculptor *Ventura Vitoni* (1442–1552) which survived the fire in 1641 which destroyed the choir in the Duomo, is more 17C church silver.—The 12C Cappella di San Nicolò, the Bishop's private chapel, contains 14C fresco fragments.—Steps lead up to the top of the façade of the cathedral (now closed in), above the present loggia. Another room has 17C reliquaries, including the Reliquary of St Bartholomew (1663).—The Sala Sinodali contains fragments of battle scenes, among the oldest medieval frescoes in Tuscany, and a triptych by *Giovanni di Bartolomeo Cristiani*.

On the W side of the piazza is **Palazzo Pretorio** (being restored), a Gothic building of 1367 and later, which has a good courtyard, with painted and sculptured armorial bearings of magistrates. On the E side is the **Palazzo del Comune**, a fine Italian Gothic building of 1294, with later additions. The **Museo Civico** was reopened here in 1982 (adm. 9–13, 15–19; fest. 9–12.30; closed Monday).

On the ground floor is a permanent exhibition of graphic works and sculpture by the native artist *Marino Marini* (1901–80). Stairs lead up to the Piano Nobile. SALA DEI DONIZELLI. 13C *Panel of St Francis, with stories from his life; 14C painting of Mourning over the Dead Christ; *'Master of 1310'* (attributed), Polyptych of the Madonna and Saints; 14C Tuscan statues; *Mariotto di Nardo*, Madonna enthroned with four angels; chalice by the local goldsmith *Andrea di Piero Braccini; Francesco di Valdambrino*, Angel; *Mariotto di Nardo* and *Rossello di Jacopo Franchi*, Annunciation and Saints; three paintings of the Madonna enthroned and Saints by *Lorenzo di Credi, Ridolfo del Ghirlandaio*, and *Gerino Gerini*; 15C marble relief of the Madonna and Child.—SALA DEI PRIORI. *Bernardino di Antonio Detti*, 'Madonna della Pergola'; *Agnolo di Polo*, Bust of the Redeemer; a 15C and a 16C statue of St Sebastian; *Fra' Paolino*, Annunciatory Angel and Virgin Annunciate.—Stairs lead up past the *Centro Michelucci*, with drawings and models of works by the local architect Giovanni Michelucci to three rooms on the top floor. The SALONE contains late-16C and 17C paintings, including works by *Gregorio Pagani, Matteo Rosselli, Il Cigoli, Empoli, Francesco Curradi, Carlo Saraceni* (Madonna and Child, attributed), *Giacinto Gimignani, Antonio Domenico Gabbiani, Lo Spagnoletto* (Portrait of Lanfredino Cellesi of Pistoia), *Giuseppe Gambarini*, and a contemporary copy of Carlo Maratta's portrait of Clement IX. The decorative arts displayed here include Venetian glass, and Italian majolica.—The PUCCINI COLLECTION includes: *Giovanni di Bartolomeo Cristiani*, Madonna enthroned with angel musicians; *'Frankfurt Master'*, Triptych; *Maso di San Friano* (bottega), Angels and the Madonna; *Giovanni Battista Naldini*, Holy Family; *Il Cigoli*, Marriage of St Catherine; *Mattia Preti*, Susannah and the Elders; *Pietro Dandini*, Portrait of the doctor Tommaso Puccini.—The last room contains 18C and 19C works by *Luigi Sabatelli, Anton Raphael Mengs* (Portrait of Cardinal Francesco Saverio de Zelada), and *Gilbert Stuart Newton*, and historical canvases by *Enrico Pollastrini*, and *Giuseppe Bezzuoli* (and Puccini portraits).

A few minutes' walk to the SE is the disused 12C church of *San Pietro*, with a characteristic façade; over the main portal is a relief of Christ giving the keys to St Peter, the Madonna, and the Apostles. To the N of San Pietro is the church of *San Bartolomeo in Pantano*, a 12C church, with a relief over the central door, possibly by *Gruamonte* (1167). In the fine basilican interior, with good capitals, the apse bears a fresco of Christ in majesty. On the walls, other fresco fragments have been exposed. The *Pulpit by *Guido da Como* (1250), still Romanesque in spirit, has been reassembled from fragments.

Behind the Palazzo Comunale Via Pacini (where, in Palazzo Rospigliosi, there are long-term plans to open a Museo Diocesano) leads N to the **Ospedale del Ceppo**, founded in 13–14C, and still in use. The façade is decorated with a colourful enamelled terracotta *Frieze (1514–25), excellently carved and very well preserved (cleaned in 1984). It depicts the seven works of mercy (six by *Santi Buglioni*, the seventh added by *Filippo di Lorenzo Paladini* in 1584–86), and the cardinal and theological virtues by *Giovanni della Robbia*. Beneath are medallions with the Annunciation, Visitation, and Assumption and the arms of the hospital, the city, and the Medici, also by *Giovanni della Robbia*. To the left of the hospital, above the door of the adjoining church, is a Coronation of the Virgin by *Benedetto Buglioni* (1510), the oldest work of the series.

To the E of the hospital, in Piazza San Lorenzo, is the church of *Santa Maria delle Grazie* or *del Letto* by Michelozzo, with a good presbytery. The high altar has a fine silver 17C tabernacle, and there is a 17C tomb on the S wall.

To the W of the hospital is the church of *Sant'Andrea*, with another good 12C façade. The relief, of the Journey and Adoration of the Magi, is by *Gruamonte* and his brother *Adeodato*, and is signed (1166). In the long narrow interior (similar to San Bartolomeo in Pantano) is a 14C font of the Pisan school, and a hexagonal *Pulpit

The Ospedale del Ceppo in Pistoia

with dramatic reliefs by *Giovanni Pisano* (c 1297), perhaps his masterpiece. In the apse is a statuette of St Andrew of the school of Giovanni Pisano (formerly on the façade), and in the right aisle, in a 15C tabernacle, a wood Crucifix by *Giovanni Pisano*. At the end of the left aisle, Madonna of Humility, by *Niccolò di Mariano* (15C Sienese).

At the end of Via Sant'Andrea is Piazza San Francesco, with the church of **San Francesco** (formerly known as *San Francesco al Prato*) begun in 1294, with a façade of 1717. The wide open roofed nave, with damaged remains of frescoes, ends in a wide vaulted transept with five E chapels. Behind the high altar (lights to right and left) are 14C frescoes showing strong Giottesque influence, possibly the work of a pupil, Puccio Capanna. The altarpiece of the Madonna and Saints, a polyptych of the 14C Sienese school, has been removed for restoration for many years. In the chapel to the left is a splendid fresco cycle of the *Allegory of the triumph of St Augustine, by the Sienese school. 14C frescoes also decorate the 2nd chapel to the right of the high altar. In the S transept are interesting remains of a huge frescoed Crucifix, attributed to the 'Master of 1310'. A door in this transept leads through the Sacristy to the *Chapter House* (not always open), both of which retain good late 14C frescoes, notably on the E wall of the latter, the Tree of Life with a Crucifixion. The 14C *Cloister* is beyond.

Via Bozzi and Via Montanara e Curtatone lead back towards the centre of town. To the left is the church of the SPIRITO SANTO, founded by the Jesuits in 1637, with a good Baroque interior by Tommaso Ramignani. It was beautifully restored in 1988. The two little organs are by Hermans, and the high altarpiece is by Pietro da Cortona (1668). To the right, Via della Madonna leads to the 15C basilican sanctuary of the *Madonna dell'Umiltà**, built by *Ventura Vitoni*, a pupil of Bramante. The dome was added by *Vasari* in 1561. The main portal is 17C. The octagonal centrally planned interior, preceded by a fine barrel vaulted vestibule (1495), is an interesting example of High Renaissance architecture. On the 1st altar on the right, *Lazzaro Baldi*, Rest on the Flight into Egypt; 2nd altar on the right, *Francesco Vanni*, Adoration of the Magi (removed); 3rd altar, *Il Poppi*, Assumption.— On the 1st altar left of the high altar, *Lodovico Buti* (on a design by Vasari), Annunciation; 2nd chapel on the left, *Passignano*, Adoration of the Shepherds. The marble high altar by *Pietro Tacca* (with two angels by *Leonardo Marcacci*) encloses a miraculous 14C fresco of the Madonna of Humility, attributed to *Bartolomeo Cristiani*, around which the sanctuary was built.

At 'La Verginina', 4km NW of Pistoia, is a small *Zoo*, on a pleasant hillside.

FROM PISTOIA TO ABETONE, 49km, bus in 1hr 45 minutes. The Bologna road diverges to the right while N66 climbs steeply to (10·5km) *Cireglio* (fine retrospective view of Pistoia). At (19·5km) *Pontepetri* is the junction with the road from Pracchia (see below). On a higher by-road (right) are the skiing resorts of *Maresca* and *Gavinana*. The Imperial defeat of the Florentine army at Gavinana in 1530, in which both commanders, Francesco Ferrucci and Philibert, Prince of Orange, were killed, sealed the fate of the Republic (the Museo Ferrucciano here commemorates the battle).—29km *San Marcello Pistoiese* (623m) is a pleasant summer resort.—Two kilometres beyond (30·5km) *Mammiano* this route joins N12 from Lucca.—37km *Cutigliano* (670m), to the right of the road, has a fine 14C Palazzo Pretorio. The winter sports facilities include a funicular which mounts to *Doganaccia* (1540m), another ski resort. A funicular continues to Croce Arcana (1730m).—Beyond (42km) *Pianosinatico* (948m) the road ascends through the splendid forest that still clothes the Tuscan slope of the mountains. *Rivoreto*, 3km N of Pianosinatico, has a local Ethnographical Museum.—50km The *Passo dell'Abetone* (1388m) takes its name from a huge fir-tree which has long disappeared. Round the road summit, still on the Tuscan side of the boundary with Emilia, has developed **Abetone**, one of the best-known ski resorts in the Apennines, specially favoured by Florentines. Numerous ski-lifts and chair-lifts ascend to the snow fields. It is also much visited in summer (swimming pools, tennis courts, etc.). Bus services run to Bologna, Florence, Pisa and Ferrara.—From Abetone to *Modena*, see Rte 39.

FROM PISTOIA TO BOLOGNA, 93·5km, N64. Railway, the 'Porrettana', 99km via Pracchia in 2hrs 15 minutes—3hrs, slow trains only, usually with a change at Porretta Terme; the mountain stretch between Pistoia and Porretta Terme, opened in 1863, is particularly fine. Until 1934 it was the main line across the Apennines.— Pistoia is left by Viale Dalmazia and this route soon diverges to the right from the Abetone road to ascend the Valle di Brana, with fine views downhill.—5km *La Cugna*.—At (14km) *La Collina* the road reaches the summit-level of the *Passo della Porretta* (or 'della Collina'; 932m) and enters Emilia. The descent leads into the deep valley of the Limentra.—34km **Porretta Terme** (360m), long known as *Bagni della Porretta*, is a popular little spa on the Reno, with warm springs of sulphurous and alkaline waters.

An alternative route from Pistoia (N632) follows the Abetone road (see above) as far as (19km) *Pontepetri*, and then descends the Reno valley to (23km) *Pracchia* (616m), a summer resort, fashionable between the Wars, at the mouth of a long railway tunnel (3km), to join the main road just before (36km) Porretta Terme.

The interesting cross-country road leading W through the Frignano hills from Porretta to Pievepelago passes (20km) *Lizzano in Belvedere* and (21·5km) *Vidiciatico* (810m), two pleasant little hill-resorts.—42·5km *Fanano* (640m), with an old church, lies beneath the oddly-named *Libro Aperto* (1937m).—48·5km *Sestola* (1020m), a winter and summer resort beneath *Monte Cimone* (2165m; ascended by cableway in two stages). Sestola is connected by bus with (70km) *Pievepelago*, on the Modena-Pistoia road (Rte 39).

At (37km) *Silla* the Pievepelago road (see above) bears to the left, and at (46·5km) *Riola* the E Limentra joins the Reno.—56km *Vergato*.—Just outside (68km) *Marzabotto*, in the park of Villa Aria (adm. 9–12, 15–sunset; closed Monday) are remains of an Etruscan city, thought to be *Misa* (6–4C BC). Excavations have revealed traces of houses, temples, and two necropoli. At the entrance is the Museo Etrusco Pompeo Aria.—At (76·5km) *Sasso Marconi*, near the junction of the Setta and the Reno, this route joins the road from Prato to Bologna, see above.—81km *Pontecchio Marconi*. Here is the mausoleum (by

Marcello Piacentini) of Guglielmo Marconi (1874–1937), whose first experiments in the transmission of signals by Hertzian waves were made at his father's Villa Griffone above the town. In the park is preserved a relic of the boat 'Elettra'from which, while at anchor in the port of Genoa in 1930, Marconi lit up the lights of Sydney.—86·5km *Casalecchio di Reno*, where the road turns right to cross the Reno, was the scene of a victory of the Visconti over the Bentivoglio in 1402, and of a battle in 1511 between the French under the Sieur de Chaumont and the army of Julius II, known as 'the day of the ass-drivers', because the victorious French knights returned driving asses laden with their booty.—93·5km Bologna (Rte 40) is entered by the Porta Saragozza.

Beyond Pistoia, and the huge Breda factory, the motorway, road and railway traverse the low pass between the Apennines and Monte

Detail of the Terme Tettuccio (1927) in Montecatini Terme

Pisano. The tall tower of the old fortress of *Serravalle Pistoiese* is conspicuous ahead. The motorway climbs and curves through the pass by a tunnel beside Serravalle and emerges above the wide plain of Lucca stretching towards the sea. On a hill with chestnut woods, but disfigured by quarries, stands the tower of *Monsummano Alto*, now abandoned and in ruins. This fortified medieval village stood at a strategic positon defending the pass between the plain of Lucca and the valley of Pistoia. The little spa of *Monsummano*, at the foot of the hill, with vapour baths was once visited by the wounded Garibaldi. Here was born Giuseppe Giusti (1809–50), the Tuscan poet.— The motorway descends to the plain and on a hill-top to the right Montecatini Alto comes into view on the approach to (46km) **Montecatini Terme** perhaps the best known of Italian spas (20,600 inhab.), with an international reputation, and numerous hotels.

First developed by the Austrian grand-dukes, Montecatini was one of the most famous spas in Europe by the beginning of this century. It is visited for digestive troubles, with warm saline waters used both internally and externally. The season runs from May–October. In a fine park are the eight spas used for drinking water and bathing. The *Terme Leopoldine* are in a neo-classical building of 1775, restored by Ugo Giovannozzi in 1927, who in the same year constructed the monumental *Tettuccio* nearby (restored in 1989). The Excelsior is an Art Nouveau building of 1915.

A funicular railway ascends from beyond the spa garden to **Montecatini Alto** (or *Montecatini Valdinevole*), an old hill town (290m; also reached by road in 5km), in a spectacular position, where Giuseppe Giusti lived. Above the piazza with several cafés, on a hill planted with cypresses and ilexes, is the Prepositurale of San Pietro (open only for services), with a small museum of vestments, reliquaries, and paintings. Here the men of Lucca were defeated in 1315 by Uguccione della Faggiola, leader of the Ghibellines of Pisa. Walks may be taken in the pleasant surroundings, especially in the Val di Nievole, to the N.

FROM MONTECATINI TO LUCCA VIA PESCIA AND COLLODI, 27km, N435.—3km *Borgo a Buggiano*. The huge Baroque Villa Bellavista here, built at the end of the 17C by Antonio Ferri, owned by the State, is in need of restoration. Above is *Buggiano Castello*, an ancient hill-town with a good Palazzo Pretorio and a church with Romanesque details.—8km **Pescia** a busy town (19,300 inhab.) is an important horticultural centre particularly noted for asparagus, carnations, lilies, and gladioli. The striking flower market (1951) has been superseded by an even larger one on the outskirts of the town. The *Duomo*, rebuilt in 1693, has a campanile of 1306 and remains of a 13C ambone. In a chapel in *Palazzo Vescovile* is an enamelled terracotta triptych of the Madonna and Child between Saints James and Blaise, a late work of Luca della Robbia. *Sant'Antonio* (1361) contains a 13C Deposition group in wood. In the 14C church of *San Francesco* is a *Painting of St Francis, with six stories from his life by Bonaventura Berlinghieri painted in 1235, nine years after the Saint's death, and considered to be one of the most faithful images of him. It was beautifully restored in 1982. The Cappella Cardini (1451) is by Buggiano. A slightly earlier work by the same artist is the church of the *Madonna di Pie di Piazza* (or Santi Pietro e Paolo). The *Museo Civico* (open 9–19 except Saturday afternoon and Sunday) has Tuscan paintings (14–16C). The handsome *Piazza Mazzini*, with the local tourist office, is the ancient centre of the civic life of the town (market on Saturday).—In the two valleys of the Pescia river are numerous paper mills.

12km Turning for **Collodi** (1km N) which gave Carlo Lorenzini (1826–90), who was born in Florence, the pen-name under which he wrote 'Le Avventure di Pinocchio', first published in 1881 and later translated into 63 languages. On the right is the entrance to *Villa Garzoni* (adm. daily 8–20), built in 1633–62, famous for its terraced gardens on a steep hillside, decorated with fountains and statues. They were first laid out in the 17C and embellished in 1786. From the hemicycle, beyond a sloping parterre, a double staircase leads to an upper terrace at the foot of a scenographic cascade, bordered by two water staircases. The gardens are now situated in disappointing surroundings and administered in a pretentious fashion. Paths lead up through ilex woods to the Villa itself, or 'Castello' (separate entrance ticket). It contains frescoed architectural perspectives attributed to Angelo Michele Colonna and 18C furniture. The old village of Collodi climbs up the hill behind the villa.—Across the river is the entrance to a

Illustration by Chiostri from 'Le Avventure di Pinocchio' by Collodi, published in 1901

childrens' park built in 1956 (in questionable taste) to commemorate Pinocchio (much visited by school excursions). There is a bronze monument to the puppet hero by Emilio Greco; a piazza with mosaics, and a garden with scuptured tableaux recalling episodes from the book.—*Castelvecchio*, 11km N, has a good Romanesque church. At *Altopascio*, 11km S, where Castruccio beat the Florentines in 1325, the Order of the Knights of Altopascio ('del Tau') ran a hospice for pilgrims in 1084; it has since been famous for its hoteliers. It is also well-known for its bread.

14km Turning for *San Gennaro* (2·5km right), where the Romanesque church has an ambone of 1162 by Maestro Filippo.—22km *Lunata*, with its tall Romanesque campanile, lies 2km S of *Lammari*, where the parish church contains a tabernacle, Matteo Civitali's last work.—27km **Lucca**.

Beyond Montecatini the motorway continues through the plain. —53km *Chiesina Uzzanese*. In the church of San Michele Arcangelo at *Ponte Buggianese*, 2km E, are frescoes of the Passion cycle by the Florentine painter Pietro Annigoni (died in 1988), including a striking Last Supper in the apse.—57km *Altopascio* (see above), with wide views of mountains on either side. Beyond the tiny airport at *Capannori*, the motorway crosses a 19C acqueduct which served Lucca.

72km **LUCCA**, seat of an archbishop and a provincial capital, remains a quiet and pleasant old town (91,000 inhab.) conserving its magnificent 16–17C ramparts intact; they enclose its still partly Roman street plan. It is especially rich in Romanesque architecture, and many medieval mansions line its narrow streets. Lucca produces large quantities of olive oil.

Tourist Office (E.P.T.), 2 Piazza Giudiccioni and 40 Via Vittorio Veneto (information office).—**Post Office**, Via Vallisneri.

Car Parking is not allowed inside the walls for longer than 1½hrs except with an hourly tariff. Space is usually available off the Viali which encircle the walls, and in car parks by the Baluardo di San Martino and the Baluardo di San Salvatore (see the Plan). **Buses** from Piazzale Verdi for *Abetone, Bagni di Lucca, Florence, Montecatini, Pistoia, Prato, Pisa, Livorno*, etc.; and for *Carrara, Viareggio*, etc.

An **Antique Market** is held in Piazza San Martino on the 3rd Saturday & Sunday of every month.

History. Stone implements recently discovered in the plain of Lucca show that it was inhabited some 50,000 years ago. The Roman colony of *Luca* was the scene in 56 BC of the meeting of Caesar, Pompey, and Crassus to form the First Triumvirate. The town is reputed to have been the first place in Tuscany to have accepted Christianity and its first bishop was Paulinus, a disciple of St Peter. In 552 the Goths here withstood a prolonged siege by Narses. In the Middle Ages it was an important city under the Lombard marquesses of Tuscany, and later waged constant war with Pisa, Florence and other cities. Under the rule of the adventurer, Castruccio Castracani, in 1316–28, Lucca achieved supremacy in Western Tuscany, but his death was followed by a period of subjection to Pisa (1343–69). Charles IV then gave the Lucchesi a charter of independence, and it maintained its autonomy, often under the suzerainty of noble families, until 1799. In 1805 Napoleon presented the city as a principality to his sister Elisa Baciocchi, and in 1815 it was given to Marie Louise de Bourbon as a duchy. A feature of the city are the Romanesque churches, greatly admired by Ruskin who spent much time here (at the Hotel Universo) studying the monuments. The sculptor Matteo Civitali (1435–1501) was born in Lucca, and nearly all his works remain in the town. Pompeo Batoni (1708–87), however, painted his fashionable portraits mainly in Rome. The city is the birthplace also of the musicians Luigi Boccherini (1743–1805) and Giacomo Puccini (1858–1924) whose forbears for four generations had been organists of San Martino, though he himself was only a chorister at San Michele.

The nearest entrance to the town from the Florence motorway and the Station is through Porta San Pietro at Piazza Risorgimento. Via Vittorio Veneto (with the tourist office) continues to PIAZZA NAPOLEONE (with a statue of Marie Louise, by Lorenzo Bartolini), planted with plane trees. Here is the former **Palazzo Ducale**, the old seat of the lords of Lucca, reconstructed by Ammannati in 1578, but many times remodelled (and now in need of restoration). It is used as Provincial government offices, and by the Prefecture. Behind the Prefecture is *San Romano* (usually closed), a huge Dominican church containing the tomb of St Romanus by Matteo Civitali (1490). Beyond the adjoining Piazza del Giglio is Piazza San Giovanni, in which rises *San Giovanni* (which has been closed for restoration for many years), a 12C church with a fine portal of 1187 in its rebuilt façade. Off the N side is the baptistery rebuilt late in the 14C when it was given its sculptured font; the Roman immersion font with tessellated marble surround was uncovered in 1885. Beyond is the attractive PIAZZA SAN MARTINO, and the adjoining Piazza Antelminelli, with the Duomo, Palazzo Micheletti by Ammannati (1556), with palm trees in its garden, a circular fountain, and the old 13C building of the Opera del Duomo (being restored, see below). The *Cathedral* (*San Martino*),

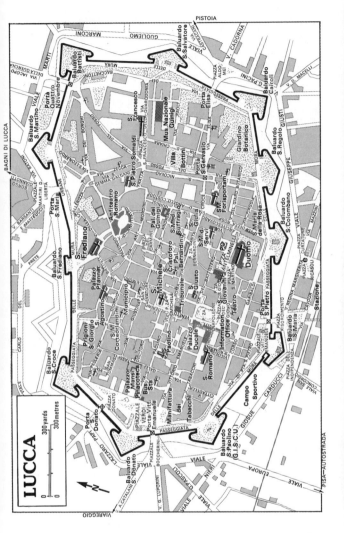

was consecrated in 1070 by Pope Alexander II, who had begun the rebuilding while bishop of Lucca.

EXTERIOR. The asymmetrical *FAÇADE is decorated with delightful sculptures in the Pisan-Lucchese Romanesque style. The statue of St Martin is a copy of the original 13C work, now inside the cathedral. The upper part, with three tiers of arcades, is signed by *Guidetto da Como* (1204). The columns are beautifully designed. The lower part of the embattled *CAMPANILE dates from 1060, the upper from 1261. The three wide Romanesque arches (the one on the right smaller to accommodate the campanile) lead in to the PORTICO, again beautifully decorated with sculptures, begun in 1233, and partly the work of *Guido Bigarelli da Como*, recently restored. On either side of the central door, bas reliefs with the story of St Martin, and the months of the year. Over the left doorway is a relief of the Deposition, and under it an Adoration of the Magi, perhaps early works by *Nicola Pisano*. Over the right doorway, in the architrave, is the meeting of St Martin with the Arians, and in the lunette, the Beheading of St Regolus. On the right pier of the portico is a symbolic Labyrinth (12C).—The sides of the building are also noteworthy, as well as the exterior of the *APSE, with its arcades and carved capitals, surrounded by a green lawn.

The tall *INTERIOR (closed 12–15 or 15.30) was rebuilt in the 14–15C in a Gothic style, with a delicate clerestory, and an attractive inlaid pavement designed by *Matteo Civitali*. On the entrance wall, *St Martin dividing his cloak (13C) was removed from the façade. The two stoups are by *Matteo Civitali* (1498). SOUTH AISLE. 1st altar, *Passignano*, Nativity; 2nd altar, *Federico Zuccari*, Adoration of the Magi; 3rd altar, *Tintoretto*, Last Supper (harshly restored); 4th altar, *Passignano*, Crucifixion. The pulpit is by *Matteo Civitali*. A door leads into the SACRISTY, with an altarpiece of the Madonna and Saints, with a good predella, by *Domenico Ghirlandaio*. Also here: a 14C Sienese triptych; Madonna enthroned, a 15C work attributed to the local artist *Michele Ciampanti*; an Annunciation by another local artist, *Leon Grazia*; and a detached fresco of the Trinity attributed to *Cosimo Rosselli*.—The 17C organ is the work of *Domenico Zanobi*. In the SOUTH TRANSEPT, *Tomb of Pietro da Noceto (1472), a beautiful Renaissance Humanist work, by *Matteo Civitali*, who also sculpted the tomb of Domenico Bertani (1479) here. The two angels flanking the tabernacle in the Chapel of the Holy Sacrament, and the altar of St Regulus (1484), right of the sanctuary, are also the work of Civitali. The modern bronze high altar was installed in 1987, and part of the marble screen by the school of Civitali moved to the side chapels, despite local protest. The stained glass in the apse is the work of *Pandolfo di Ugolino* of Pisa (1485), and the choir stalls by *Leonardo Marti* (1452).—NORTH TRANSEPT. Altar with figures of the Risen Christ and Saints Peter and Paul, by *Giambologna* (the predella with a view of Lucca is of slightly later date); *Statue of St John the Evangelist by *Jacopo della Quercia*, removed from the exterior of the cathedral in 1938. The celebrated *Tomb of Ilaria del Carretto Guinigi, with a serene effigy, is the masterpiece of *Jacopo della Quercia* (1405–06), and one of the most original works of the very early Renaissance. In the Cappella del Santuario, *Virgin and Child enthroned, with saints, by *Fra Bartolomeo* (1509).—In the middle of the N aisle is the octagonal marble *TEMPIETTO, also by *Civitali* (1484), built to house the famous *Volto Santo, a wooden likeness of Christ, supposed to have been begun by Nicodemus and miraculously completed. The favourite oath of William Rufus is said to have been 'Per Vultum de Lucca'; the effigy is usually assigned stylistically to the 11C. On the outside of the Tempietto is a statue of St Sebastian by *Civitali* (1484). NORTH AISLE. 5th altar, *Stefano Tofanelli*, Assumption; 4th altar, *Jacopo Ligozzi*, Visitation; 2nd altar, *Alessandro Allori*, Presentation of Maria in the Temple (restored in 1989).

The Opera del Duomo (No. 5 Piazza Antelminelli) is being restored to house the CATHEDRAL MUSEUM, which includes the rich treasury, with some fine examples of medieval silversmiths' work, notably the *Croce dei Pisani, an elaborate crucifix of 1424–39.

From Piazza San Giovanni a short road leads N across Via del Battistero to the 12C church of *San Giusto* (left), with a pretty façade and good portal. Farther on, across Via Santa Croce, in the pictures-que Via Fillunga, is the 13C church of *San Cristoforo* with a fine interior (now used for exhibitions). It is the burial place of Matteo Civitali (died 1501) and also serves as a War memorial (the walls are covered with the names of the Dead). Beyond are two old towers, one, with a bell, dating from the 13C. Via Roma ends on the left in the delightful PIAZZA SAN MICHELE, on the site of the Roman Forum and still the centre of the life of the city. On the left is *Palazzo Pretorio* (1492; enlarged 1588), in the portico of which is a statue of Civitali, the architect of the original building. ***San Michele in Foro** is a church

San Michele in Foro, Lucca

typical of the Pisan Romanesque style as developed in Lucca. Mentioned as early as 795, the present church was largely constructed in the 11C and 12C, though work continued until the 14C. The imposingly tall *Façade (recently restored) is richly decorated with coloured marbles, carved columns, and capitals. The upper part and lateral arcading date from the 14C when it was intended to raise the height of the nave (the project was abandoned because of lack of funds). On the tympanum is a huge statue of St Michael Archangel. The façade was often sketched by Ruskin. The Madonna on the SW corner by Civitali has been removed for years for restoration; when it returns it will be exhibited inside the church, and replaced here by a copy.

In the interior (closed 12.30–15) the vaulting which covers a traditional beamed roof, was carried out in the early 16C. In the apse hangs a Crucifix painted in the late-12C. In the S aisle is a white enamelled terracotta relief of the Madonna and Child now attributed to *Luca della Robbia*. In the S transept, *Saints Helena, Jerome, Sebastian, and Roch, by *Filippino Lippi*, and in the N transept, Madonna by *Raffaello da Montelupo* (1522), a relief that formed part of the tomb of Sylvester Giles, Bishop of Worcester, who died in Italy in 1521.

Opposite the W door Via di Poggio leads to Corte San Lorenzo, where, at No. 9, is the entrance to the *Birthplace of Giacomo Puccini*. The house (open 10–18; 10–16 in winter; closed Monday) contains interesting mementoes of the composer.

Via San Paolino continues Via Roma W to SAN PAOLINO, by Baccio da Montelupo and Bastiano Bertolani (1522–36). The interior has early-16C stained glass. South Aisle. 3rd altar, 15C polychrome wood statue of St Ansano, by *Francesco di Domenico Valdambrino*; 4th altar, *Pietro Testa* (Il Lucchese), St Theodore. The two small cantorie in the nave are by *Nicolao* and *Vincenzo Civitali*. In the S transept (right chapel) is the Burial of St Paulinus and three other Saints, an unusual 14C painting attributed to *Angelo Puccinelli*. In niches on either side of the presbytery, 14C wood statues. In the chapel to the left of the presbytery, Coronation of the Virgin, with a view of Lucca, an unusual 15C work. In the N aisle is a rare stone statuette of the Madonna and Child dating from the end of the 13C brought from Paris by merchants in the Middle Ages.

Nearby, in Via Galli Tassi, is the 17C *Palazzo Mansi*, with a **Museo and Pinacoteca Nazionale** (adm. 9–19; fest. 9–13; Monday 14–19).

The four rooms of the Pinacoteca were closed for restoration in 1989, but some of the paintings were temporarily exhibited in other rooms of the palace. On the GROUND FLOOR (also used for exhibitions) are displayed: *Jacopo Vignali*, Tobias and the angel; *Jacopo Ligozzi*, Madonna appearing to St Giacinto; *Morazzone*, Annunciation; *Domenichino*, Samson; *Van Dyck* (attributed), Holy Family and St Anne. —A fine staircase leads up to the loggia and (left) Sala da Pranzo. In the SALONE DA BALLO, with late-17C frescoes by *Gian Gioseffo dal Sole* are exhibited: *Rosa da Tivoli* and *Nicolò Cassana*, Battle scenes and landscapes; *Guido Reni*, Crucifixion and two Saints; *Rutilio Manetti*, Triumph of David; *Carlo Dolci*, St John the Baptist, St Anthony Abbot; *Ventura Salimbeni*, Portrait of a lady as St Catherine of Alexandria; good copy of a Madonna and Child with St Anne and the young St John, by *Andrea del Sarto*; *Ferdinando Bol*, Sacrifice of Isaac.—Three small drawing rooms are hung with 17C Flemish tapestries and the Bedroom has 18C hangings made in Lucca. Another room has Venetian paintings: small copy of *Tintoretto*'s St Mark freeing a slave; *Tintoretto*, Portrait of a man, Venetian senator; *Paolo Veronese*, St Peter the Hermit before the 'Consiglio Veneto', a painting in very poor condition.—The 'Camera dell'Alcova' was closed in 1989.

Other works which belong to the Pinacoteca which will be on view when it is reopened include: *Sustermans*, Medici portraits; *Bronzino*, Cosimo I (one of several versions of this well-known portrait), and Ferdinando de'Medici as a boy; *Federico Zuccari*, Self-portrait; *Pontormo*, *Portrait of a boy (once thought to be Alessandro de'Medici); *Bronzino*, Don Garzia de'Medici as a child; *Zacchia il Vecchio da Vezzano*, Self-portrait (?); *Federico Barocci* and *Alessandro Vitali*, Portrait of Federico Ubaldo della Rovere at the age of two. *Francesco Avanzi*, Madonna and Child (the only known work by this 16C Milanese artist); *Francesco Bassano*, Prayer in the Garden; *Domenico Beccafumi*, Scipio. Flemish works including two paintings by *Paul Brill*; an Annunciation (late 15C); *Michel Sweerts*, Portrait of a boy; and *Mabuse*, Madonna and Child.

Via Calderia leads N from Piazza San Michele to the church of *San Salvatore*, a 12C church with good sculpture by Biduino above its S

The font in San Frediano, Lucca

portal. Via del Moro, behind, is lined with medieval mansions. Via Cesare Battisti winds between 17–18C palazzi towards the tall campanile on the façade of *San Frediano* (1112–47). The much restored mosaic on the façade is possibly the work of Berlinghiero Berlinghieri (13C). The church replaced an earlier basilica and has its apse at the W end.

In the splendid basilican *INTERIOR the columns of the nave have handsome classical capitals. At the beginning of the S aisle is a magnificent *Font (probably dating from the mid-12C), in the form of a fountain covered by a small tempietto, sculpted with reliefs of the story of Moses, the Good Shepherd, and the Apostles. Behind the font is a lunette of the Annunciation by *Andrea della Robbia*. Nearby are two interesting frescoes detached from behind the organ on the W wall. In the corner is the *Virgin Annunciate, a polychrome wood statue by *Civitali* (coin-operated light). Above the entrance, organ attributed to *Domenico di Lorenzo*. Beneath it, two framed detached frescoes: *Amico Aspertini*, Madonna and Child with Saints, and a Visitation. Near the font is the 17C Chapel of Santa Zita (died 1278), with paintings of miracles of the Saint by *Francesco del Tintore*, and a 14C frescoed Crucifixion above the altar. Outside is a high relief of St Bartholomew by *Andrea della Robbia*. In the next chapel is a Deposition by *Pietro Paolini*. In the last right chapel, wood relief of the Assumption by *Matteo Civitali* (in a marble frame). On the left wall of the presbytery, huge marble monolith, probably from the Roman amphitheatre. In the Cappella Trenta (4th chapel in the N aisle) is an elaborately carved *Altarpiece by *Jacopo della Quercia* (1422; assisted by Giovanni da Imola) and two pavement tombs by the same artist; opposite is an Immaculate Conception and saints, by *Francesco Francia*. Outside the chapel is a statue of St Peter by *Vincenzo di Bartolomeo Civitali*. The 2nd N chapel contains beautiful early *Frescoes by *Amico Aspertini* (c 1508–09), suffering from humidity. They depict stories of San Frediano, St Augustine, and the bringing of the Volto Santo to Lucca, with interesting local details and classical ruins in the landscapes.

Just SW of the church is *Palazzo Pfanner* (temporarily closed in 1989) with an 18C garden and statues, and a delightful galleried staircase. On the first floor is a permanent exhibition of 18C and 19C local costumes. Nearby is the 14C church of *Sant'Agostino*, with a plain unfinished façade, and its small campanile resting on arches of a Roman theatre. Inside, a chapel with a little Baroque cupola, contains a venerated painting of the Madonna.—Farther SW, the church of *Santa Maria Corteorlandini*, built c 1187 but exuberantly altered in the 17C, retains part of its 12C structure on the S side. A precious collection of silk altar frontals made in Lucca belongs to the church.

The medieval houses of the Via dell'Anfiteatro, on the other side of Via Fillungo, follow the ellipse of the Roman *Amphitheatre*, whose arena forms a delightful *Piazza. From the NE corner a road winds towards *San Pietro Somaldi* a 12C church with a grey and white banded façade of 1248, though the relief above the centre door is by Guido da Como and assistants (1203). It contains a painting of St Anthony Abbot and four Saints attributed to Raffaellino del Garbo. Farther on, the 17C column known as the 'Madonna dello Stellario' stands at a crossroads by the pretty canal which runs along Via del Fosso. To the S is *Villa Bottini* (entrance on Via Elisa), built in 1566 with a fine garden (open 9–14). The villa has been restored; some rooms are frescoed by Ventura Salimbeni. It is now used for conferences and it contains a newspaper library. In July and August concerts are usually held in the garden.—Beyond the canal and the column (see above) rises the handsome marble façade with a rose window of *San Francesco*, a restored 13C church with memorials to Castracani (died 1328) and Boccherini (died 1805), and a detached *Fresco of the 15C Florentine school in the chapel to the right of the high altar. The lunette, of remarkably high quality, but very damaged, shows the Presentation of the Virgin in the temple and the Marriage of the Virgin. In the cloister is the tomb of Bonagiunta Tignosini (1274) with a ruined fresco by Deodato Orlandi.

Nearby is the unusual brick VILLA GUINIGI, a castellated suburban villa built in 1418. The austere building has been restored to house the **Museo Nazionale Guinigi** (open 9–14, fest. 9–13, closed Monday) which contains a fine collection of sculpture and paintings from Lucca and its province.

In the garden is a Roman mosaic (1–2C AD), and a group of carved lions from the walls.—GROUND FLOOR. ROOM I. Roman objects found in Lucca including a mosaic pavement (1C AD), and a Hellenistic relief of a funerary banquet.—RII. Four Ligurian tombs (reconstructed); Etruscan tomb with gold jewellery and an Attic krater (3C BC).—SOUTH PORTICO. Medieval architectural fragments and a tomb slab of a member of the Antelminelli family attributed to *Jacopo della Quercia*.—RIII. Fine examples of Lucchese sculpture (8–14C) including a transenna with a relief of Samson and the lion; fragment of a statue of St Martin (12–13C) from the Duomo; bas-reliefs from the church of San Jacopo in Altopascio; statuette of the Madonna and Child attributed to *Biduino* (late 13C).—RIV. Virgin annunciate, attributed to *Nino Pisano*; marble statues by various masters from a polyptych attributed to Priamo della Quercia (see below, RXII).—RV. Fine *Works by *Matteo Civitali*.—RVII. Weights and measures of Lucca (18–19C), and neo-classical reliefs from Palazzo Ducale by *Vincenzo Consani*.

Stairs lead up to the Pinacoteca. RX. Early painted Crucifixes. Inlaid stalls from the Duomo, and intarsia with views of Lucca by *Ambrogio* and *Nicolao Pucci* (1529) from the Cappella degli Anziani. The 15C panels from the Sacristy are by *Cristoforo Canozi da Lendinara*.—RXI. *Berlinghiero*, Painted Crucifix; '*Ugolino Lorenzetti*', *Madonna and Child, St John the Evangelist; *Luca di Tommè*, Madonna and Child from the church of San Michele a Granaiola (Bagni di Lucca).—RXII. *Maestro del Bimbo Vispo*, Saints; *Priamo della Quercia* (attributed), Polyptych; *Angelo Puccinelli*, Marriage of St Catherine; *Zanobi Machiavelli*, Madonna and Child with Saints; and other works by the Tuscan school.—RXIII. *Vecchietta* and *Neroccio*, reliefs in wood; Lucchese works by followers of Filippino Lippi.—RXIV. *Fra Bartolomeo*, *Madonna della Misericordia (1515), *God the Father with Saints Mary Magdalene and Catherine; works by *Amico Aspertini*.—RXV. *Il Riccio*, Nativity of the Virgin; *Giorgio Vasari*, Immaculate Conception and Saints.—RRXVI and XVII are being rearranged. They contain Church vestments, and paintings by *Giorgio Vasari*, and *Jacopo Ligozzi* (Baptism of Christ).—RXVIII. *Matteo Civitali*, Ecce Homo.— RXX. Three good works by *Pompeo Batoni*.

From Piazza San Francesco Via Fratta (see the Plan) leads towards Via Guinigi, dominated by two large brick Gothic palaces, the **Case dei Guinigi** (one facing the other; Nos 29, and Nos 20–22), both built in the 14C and remodelled in the 16C. The *Guinigi Tower*, on Via Sant'Andrea is open to the public (daily 9–19; winter 10–16).

The upper part is ascended by an iron staircase and on the top is a delightful little garden of six ilex trees. The view takes in the city and its tree-planted walls, and the hills beyond. To the S is the flank of the cathedral and the curious dome of San Giovanni; farther to the right is the campanile of San Michele, behind which can just be seen the rear of its tall façade (with an outside staircase). Nearer at hand is the high medieval bell-tower in Via Fillunga. To the N the tall campanile of San Frediano stands beside the conspicuous mosaic on its façade. Nearby the oval shape of the amphitheatre can be seen, and the campanile and white colonnaded façade of San Piero Somaldi; farther round is the white façade and rose window of San Francesco near the castellated roof of Villa Guinigi. To the E is visible the top of Santa Maria Forisportam with its campanile.

In Via Santa Croce, beyond and to the left, is *Santa Maria Forisportam**, another fine church with a marble façade in the 13C Pisan style, named from having been outside the city gates until 1260. The pleasant grey interior was altered in 1516 when the nave and transepts were raised. The handsome high altar, with a statue of the Assunta, fits well into the architecture. On the 4th S altar, St Lucy by *Guercino*, who also painted the much-darkened Assumption and

Saints in the N transept. Also here is a neo-classical monument to Antonio Mazzarosa, by *Vincenzo Consani*. The font at the W end was made from an early-Christian sarcophagus. In the Sacristy (off the S transept) is a Dormition and Assumption of the Virgin by *Angelo Puccinelli* (1386).

Farther E is the *Porta San Gervasio* (1260), the best of the gates remaining from the second enceinte. Across the 'fosso' in Via Elisa is the church of the *Santissima Trinità* (key from adjoining convent), which contains a sentimental Madonna della Tosse, by Matteo Civitali.

In the other direction Via Santa Croce crosses Piazza Bernardini, dominated by its 16C palazzo. To the N, in Piazza del Suffragio, is the *Oratorio di Santa Giulia* (13–14C; closed).—To the S of Santa Maria Forisportam is the charming little oratory of SANTA MARIA DELLA ROSA (also usually closed), built in 1309–33 in the Pisan Gothic style, inside which are some traces of the original Roman wall.

An interesting walk (c 4km) may be taken round the *Ramparts** (in the process of restoration; partly closed to traffic), among the oldest of their kind (1561–1645), built on the system afterwards developed by Vauban, and recalling the ramparts of Berwick-on-Tweed and Verona. Their tree-planted bastions, many of which are decorated with monuments, command good views. The severe *Porta Santa Maria* (1593) on the N side contrasts with the florid *Porta San Pietro*, by Alessandro Resta (1566), leading to the station. The *Baluardo di San Paolino* is aptly occupied by the Centro Internazionale per lo studio delle Cerchia Urbane (C.I.S.C.U.), with a photographic archive. Admission is granted by appointment (also to see the defensive tower). The most attractive walk is from here E above the *Botanical Gardens* (open October–April on weekdays, 9–12; May–September, daily except Monday 9.30–12.30, 16–19), and then N to the Baluardo di San Martino.

The environs of Lucca are noted for their fine villas and gardens built between the 16C and 19C, although only three of them are at present open to the public (many others are being studied and may be restored and opened to the public). In the foothills, NE of the city is the late-17C *Villa Reale* (at Marlia, 8km), now owned by the Pecci-Blunt. It was once the home of Elisa Baciocchi, and here Niccolò Paganini, Metternich and John Singer Sargent stayed. The house is not open to the public, but the 17C Orsetti *Garden, with notable statuary and a 'theatre', is shown every hour on the hour (or by request at the lodge) in July–September on Tuesday, Thursday, and Sunday, 10–12, 16–19. For the rest of the year it is shown daily except Monday, 9–12, 15–18.—At Segromigno (10km) is the 17C *Villa Mansi*, (adm. to the park daily, 10–12.50, 15–18; in summer the house is also open). Part of the garden altered by Juvarra in 1742 survives near the house, with a pescheria, the 'Bagno di Diana', and fine statues. The 'English' park was created in the 19C. The Villa has late-18C decorations, including frescoes of the Myth of Apollo in the Salone by Stefano Tofanelli.—At Camigliano, nearby, is the *Villa Torrigiani* (adm. April–October, 14.30–17, Saturday & Sunday 9.30–12, 14.30–18; winter, Saturday & Sunday only 9.30–12, 14.30–17) with a rococo façade and fine park. It contains contemporary furnishings, 17C and 18C paintings, and a collection of porcelain. From *Vinchiana* (11km N of Lucca on N12) a by-road winds up through beautiful scenery to (5km farther) *San Giorgio di Brancoli*, where the Romanesque church has an *Ambone and a font, both 12C, a St George of the Della Robbian school, and a 14C painted Crucifixion.—At Badia di Cantignana, 6km S of Lucca, was born Carlo Piaggia (1827–82), the African explorer who (with Romolo Gessi) first circumnavigated Lake Albert.

FROM LUCCA TO AULLA, 115km by road (bus to Barga in 80 minutes); railway (90km) in 2hrs (a magnificent line with fine scenery). This route traverses the GARFAGNANA, the beautiful valley of the Serchio, well-wooded (famous for its chestnuts) and richly cultivated, lying between the Apennines and the Apuan Alps. There are many marble quarries in the area. From (9km) *Ponte a Moriano* the more interesting road follows the W bank of the Serchio, past (18km) *Diecimo* (at the 10th Roman mile from Lucca) with its 13C Romanesque church, and (22km) *Borgo a Mozzano*, where the church contains expressive 16C sculpture and a wooden figure of St Bernardine by Matteo Civitali. The Ponte della Maddalena is a remarkable ancient footbridge. There are many Romanesque churches in the vicinity. A road crosses the stream for (29km) **Bagni di Lucca**

(150m), a little spa with warm sulphur and saline waters, somewhat off the main valley on N12. Noted for its waters since the 12C, it has had many famous visitors including Shelley, Byron, Browning (who advised Tennyson, Poet Laureate, to stay here in 1851), and Walter Savage Landor. Here was born Francis Marion Crawford (1854–1909), the novelist, and in the litte Protestant cemetery Ouida lies buried. The town, entered by Ponte a Serraglio, is unusually spread out. From the bridge a lower road leads left to the Casinò, founded in 1837 as the first licensed gaming house in Europe, while the upper road leads to the pretty little spa of Bagni Caldi. In the other direction, a road leads from the bridge to La Villa, typical of modern spa towns.

The road, keeping to the E bank, enters the country of the Castracani family, whose tombs and castle adorn the village of *Ghivizzano* (right). The village of *Coreglia Antelminelli*, also to the right of the main road, contains an interesting church and a museum of 18C–20C figurines, for which the locality is famous.—From (38km) *Fornaci* a road leads to the right for (42km) **Barga** (410m) above a new town, a pretty little hill-town with very narrow streets. At the entrance is the Bastion, with War memorials, where cars can be parked. Beyond the old Porta Reale, Via del Pretorio (right) leads to the steps which ascend to a grassy terrace in front of the Duomo. From here there is a *View which takes in the snow-capped Apuan Alps and the Apennines. The fine Romanesque *DUOMO (restored in 1920 after earthquake damage) has a fine white stone exterior, with a good façade and N door, an an embattled campanile. In the interior is a sculpted *Pulpit of the late-12C, and in the main apse is a huge figure of *St Christopher in polychrome wood (early-12C). In the chapel to the right of the high altar, terracotta altarpiece of the Madonna and Saints Sebastian and Roch (restored), and Della Robbian works. In the chapel to the left of the high altar, large painted Crucifix (15C) and a 15C painting of St Joseph with a view of Barga (in an elaborate frame). The rich Treasury is to be exhibited in the adjoining *Palazzo Pretorio*, which also houses a small Museum illustrating the prehistory of the Garfagnana.—From Porta Reale (see above) Via di Mezzo leads left through the old centre of the town. A well-known opera festival is held here in July and August.

A by-road leads along the Turrite to the *Grotta del Vento* (14km), above Fornovolasco, a huge cave extending for hundreds of metres below the Apuan Alps (guided tours every hour, April–October, 10–12, 15–18; in winter only on fest.).—45km *Castelvecchio Pascoli*. Nearby on the hill of Caprona is the house where the poet Giovanni Pascoli (1855–1912) lived from 1895 until his death. He is buried in a chapel here.—56km *Castelnuovo di Garfagnana* preserves some remains of its Rocca, or governor's palace, the residence of the poets Ariosto and Fulvio Testi when they were governors of the district. The *Comunità Montana della Garfagnana* has its information office here (Piazza delle Erbe); beautiful walks can be taken in the upper Garfagnana in the Apuan Alps and the Apennines (Parco dell'Orecchiella). Near the village, the Fortezza di Montalfonso (16C) is now owned by the Province of Lucca. On the road to Pievepelago and Modena (see Rte 39) c 7km N of Castelnuovo, is *Castiglione di Garfagnana*, with 14C walls, where the church of San Michele preserves a Madonna (1389), the only signed work of Giuliano di Simone of Lucca.—The picturesque road ascends to (82km) the *Foce dei Carpinelli* (842m), beyond which it enters the valley of the Aulella at (92km) *Casola*, and farther on leaves on the left a road to the little spa of *Equi*, 7km SE.—115km *Aulla*, see Rte 39.

The most direct road from Lucca to Pisa (22km) is the N12r which tunnels through Monte Pisano and emerges above the plain of Pisa (view). It then descends to *San Giuliano Terme*, a small spa. A bust and plaque mark the Casa Prinni where Shelley stayed in the summer of 1820. The road continues, lined with trees, to enter Pisa beside the N walls. The old road from Lucca to Pisa (N12), slightly longer, passes between the castle of *Nozzano*, a Luccan outpost, and the Pisan castle of Ripafratta, before joining the above route at San Giuliano Terme. The motorway from Lucca continues for another 16km towards the sea, and at 'Pisa Nord' the busy Aurelia is joined for (97km) **Pisa**.

46 Pisa

PISA (103,400 inhab.), standing on the Arno a few miles from its mouth, is famous among the cities of Italy for its sculpture and architecture. The cathedral, campanile, baptistery, and camposanto (despite irreparable damage to the last) make up a group unrivalled in beauty, a fitting reminder of the ancient greatness of the Pisan Republic.

A.P.T., 42 Lungarno Mediceo (*Information Offices* in Piazza del Duomo, and at the main railway station).

Airport, *Galileo Galilei* (San Giusto), 3km S for international services to London, Paris, and Frankfurt, etc., and internal flights to Rome, Milan, Cagliari, Catania, and Genoa. Direct train service from Florence via Pisa to the airport.

Railway Stations. *Centrale* for all services; *San Rossore*, nearer the cathedral, served by all trains on the Lucca line and a few slow trains on the Spezia line.

Hotels mostly near the main Station; some in the area round the Duomo.—**Post Office**, Piazza Vittorio Emanuele.

Town Buses (Nos 1 & 3) from the Station to Piazza Garibaldi and the Duomo, etc.—**Country Buses** from Piazza Sant'Antonio for *Marina di Pisa; Livorno; Casciano Terme; Pontedera; San Giuliano Terme*, etc.; and from Piazza Azeglio (SITA) for *Lucca* and *Florence*.

History. Pisa was a Roman colony from the 2C BC, and a naval and commercial port. In the Middle Ages it became a maritime republic, rivalling Genoa, Amalfi, and Venice. Constantly at war with the Saracens, Pisa captured from them Corsica, Sardinia, and the Balearic Isles (1050–1100), and at the same time combined war and trade in the East. In 1135, assisting Innocent II against Roger of Sicily, Pisa destroyed Amalfi; but subsequently joined the Ghibelline party, and remained proudly faithful to it, even though surrounded by Guelf republics. In 1284 Pisa was defeated by the Genoese in the naval battle of Meloria and lost her maritime supremacy; from then onwards the city had to submit to a succession of lordships, including those of the Gherardesca family (1316–41) and of Gian Galeazzo Visconti (1396–1405). The Florentines gained possession of Pisa in 1405, and after one or two vain efforts at rebellion it became a quiet refuge of scholars and artists, a university having been established there by the Gherardesca c 1330. When Charles VIII entered Italy in 1494 he was expected to restore her liberty to Pisa, but he broke his promise, and Florence took final possession of the city in 1509. In 1944 the town was bombarded by both German and Allied artillery; the Camposanto and the area near the station suffered worst, and further damage was caused when all the bridges were blown up.—The most illustrious native of Pisa is Galileo Galilei (1564–1642), physicist and astronomer. Pisa was visited by Landor in 1819–21, by Shelley in 1820–22, and by Byron in 1821, and here Browning brought his bride in 1846, before they settled in Florence. Titta Ruffo (1877–1953), the famous baritone, was born in Pisa.

In June the Festa di San Ranieri is celebrated with candle-light festivities on the Arno and the *Gioco del Ponte*, a sham fight between the people living on either side of the Arno. The combatants wear 16–17C costumes, and the day ends with a procession of both parties.

Art. The Romanesque architecture of Pisa, a remarkable development of the North Italian Romanesque style, had a far-reaching effect on the neighbouring cities, spreading as far afield as Prato and Arezzo, and also into Sardinia, and leaving its imprint on the Gothic buildings that appeared later in the city. Pisan sculpture at the same time was a potent influence in the advance from hieratic formalism, its greatest exponent being Nicola Pisano (c 1200–c 1280), probably a native of Apulia established at Pisa. In painting Pisa produced no great master, but Giunta Pisano (fl. 1202–55) is believed to be the earliest painter whose name is inscribed on any extant work.

Piazza del Duomo (or *Campo dei Miracoli*) lies well NW of the centre and is unusual in not providing the focus of city life as in other Italian cathedral towns. The bright marble monuments (the cathedral, the leaning tower, baptistery, and camposanto) are superbly set off by the spacious green lawns between them, and enclosed to the N by the crenellated city walls in an almost rural setting.

The Duomo, Baptistery and Museo delle Sinopie are closed from 12.45–15; the Camposanto, Campanile, and Museo dell'Opera del Duomo remain open throughout the day, 9–19 (17 in winter).

The Baptistery and the Duomo of Pisa

The ***Duomo**, begun by *Buscheto* in 1063 and continued by *Rainaldo*, is the most important example of the Pisan style and one of the most celebrated Romanesque buildings in Italy. It was restored in 1602–16 after a serious fire in 1595.

The building stands on a white marble pavement and is covered inside and out with black and white marble, toned on the exterior to a delicate grey and russet. The *Façade shows four tiers of columns with open galleries, with a row of seven tall arches below. In the left-hand arch is the tomb of Buscheto. The bronze doors were remodelled after the fire by various sculptors of the school of Giambologna. The W door is open in summer; otherwise the usual entrance is from the S transept, opposite the *Portale di San Ranieri*, with bronze *Doors by Bonanno da Pisa (1180; restored in 1989). Above is a lunette with a 15C Madonna and Child and two angels by Andrea di Francesco Guardi.

The cruciform INTERIOR is over 94·5m long and 32m wide (72m across the exceptionally deep transepts). The 68 pillars have 11C capitals in imitation of classical ones. The rich ceiling of the nave was remodelled after 1596. The walls of the aisles between the altars are covered with large 18C paintings. SOUTH AISLE. Three altarpieces by *Cristofano Allori*, *Francesco Vanni*, and *Andrea del Sarto* and *Giovanni Antonio Sogliani*. In the SOUTH TRANSEPT are more large 18C canvases, and an altarpiece (right) of the Madonna enthroned with Saints by *Perin del Vaga* and *Giovanni Antonio Sogliani*. To the right of the bronze doors, *Tomb of Emperor Henry VII (died 1313), by *Tino di Camaino* (it has been partly reassembled here; other statues are in the Museo dell'Opera del Duomo).

Beneath the dome (frescoed in the 17C) are remains of a Cosmatesque pavement; another fragment, discovered near the high altar in 1977, may date from the end of the 11C. On the triumphal arch is a large fresco of the Madonna and Child by the '*Maestro di San Torpè*'. The balustrade at the entrance to the CHOIR bears two bronze angels by *Giambologna* and assistants (1602). The stalls (15C) were reconstructed in 1616 from what survived of the fire. On the entrance piers, in rich frames, are a delightful *St Agnes, by *Andrea del Sarto*, and a Madonna, by *Sogliani*. The lectern and candelabra are by *Matteo Civitali*. On the walls beneath the Cantoria are paintings by *Del Sarto*: *Saints John, Peter, Margaret and Catherine. The crucifix on the high altar is by *Giambologna*; the angel on the column to the left is by *Stoldo Lorenzi* (1483). Round the APSE (adm. only with special permission): *Sodoma*, Descent from the Cross (1540) and Sacrifice of Abraham (1542); works by *Sogliani*, and *Beccafumi*. In the vault is a fine mosaic, *Our Lord in Glory, a 13C work completed by *Cimabue* in 1302. In the 1st chapel left of the high altar is a much venerated Madonna (13C).

The *Pulpit (light) beneath the cupola, by *Giovanni Pisano* (1302–11; perhaps with the assistance of *Tino da Camaino*), removed in 1599 after the fire, was reconstructed in 1926. The columns, on plain bases, resting on lions, or carved into figure sculpture, have statues of sibyls above the capitals, and florid architraves. Above, deeply carved relief panels representing scenes from the New Testament are separated by figures of prophets.—The bronze lamp hanging over the nave, supposed to have suggested to Galileo the principle of the pendulum, was in fact cast by Battista Lorenzi in 1587, six years after the discovery. The wooden throne and benches opposite the pulpit have good marquetry work.—The NORTH AISLE has altarpieces by *Ventura Salimbeni*, *Passignano*, and *Giovanni Battista Paggi*, and stained glass windows attributed to *Alesso Baldovinetti* (restored in 1947).

Outside the E end of the cathedral rises the ***Campanile**, the famous **Leaning Tower**. It is a superb work, circular in plan and having eight storeys of round arches, made up of a blind arcade, six open galleries, and a bell-chamber of smaller diameter. The tower is 54·5m high, and leans 4·5m out of the perpendicular. A spiral staircase (294 steps) leads to the top (splendid *View). It was closed to the public in 1990 for safety and conservation reasons.

Begun in 1173, the tower was only 10·5m high when a subsidence of the soil threw it out of the perpendicular. During the 13C the architect in charge appears to have been *Giovanni di Simone*, who endeavoured to rectify the inclination as the building proceeded. By 1301 the building had risen as far as the bellchamber, and *Tommaso di Andrea da Pontedera* (c 1350) completed the tower as it now stands. Galileo made use of it in his famous experiments on the velocity of falling bodies. The lean has been increasing by c 1mm a year, and a long and complicated operation is to be carried out on the subsoil in order to stabilise the structure.

The ***Baptistery**, W of the Duomo, is a noble circular building begun in 1152 by *Diotisalvi*. The Gothic decoration was added to the Romanesque building by *Nicola Pisano* (1270–84), and his son *Giovanni* (1297). The Gothic dome and cusped arches were added in the 14C by *Cellino di Nese*. There are four portals, of which the most elaborate, facing the Duomo, is embellished with foliated columns and a Madonna by *Giovanni Pisano* (copy; original in the Museo dell'Opera). In the middle of the impressive INTERIOR, with a two-storeyed ambulatory, stands a beautiful octagonal *Font of white marble, carved and inlaid in mosaic, by *Guido da Como* (1246). A statue of St John the Baptist by a local artist, Italo Griselli (1880–1958) stands in the centre. The *Pulpit, by Nicola Pisano, is signed and dated 1260. Resting on slender pillars bearing figures of the Virtues, it bears panels sculptured in bold relief (Nativity, Adoration of the Magi, Presentation, Crucifixion, Last Judgement).

The rectangular **Camposanto**, or cemetery, begun in 1278 by *Giovanni di Simone* and completed in the 15C, takes the form of an enclosed cloister lit by graceful traceried windows. The marble exterior wall has handsome blind arcading and a Gothic tabernacle over one door. It contains extremely important frescoes and classical sculptures. All of these, along with many funerary monuments, were severely damaged in the last War, and the condition of the frescoes has deteriorated even further in the last few decades (and some have been removed or covered by scaffolding).

It is traditionally said that Archbishop Lanfranchi (1108–78) brought shiploads of earth from the Holy Land to form a burial-ground here. **Frescoes**. The sinopie of the frescoes have been detached and removed to the Museo delle Sinopie (see below). The following description starts from the E corner of the SOUTH (entrance) WALL: *Benozzo Gozzoli*, Fall of Jericho; Childhood and Youth of Moses; Visit of Queen of Shebah to Solomon; Innocence of Joseph; Joseph at court of Pharaoh; Departure of Abraham and Lot for Palestine; Story of Agar and Abraham; Abraham and the worshippers of Baal; Abraham victorious. *Antonio Veneziano*, Return of St Ranieri (removed). *Andrea Buonaiuti*, St Rainieri in the Holy Land (removed), and his Conversion and Temptations (removed). *Spinello Aretino*, Scenes from the Life of St Ephysius (removed). (Right of the entrance door) *Taddeo Gaddi*, Job the alms-giver; with his guests; with his herds; the pact of Satan with God; the first misfortune of Job; his patience; and a landscape.— NORTH WALL: *Piero di Puccio*, Theological Cosmograph; The Story of Cain and Abel; Story of Adam, Building of the ark and the flood; (right of the door) *Benozzo Gozzoli*, Construction of the Tower of Babel.

The door gives access to two halls. To the left is the CAPPELLA AMMANNATI with *Frescoes of the Triumph of Death, Last Judgement, Stories of the Anchorites, etc. These have been variously attributed to Orcagna, Francesco Traini, Vitale da Bologna, Buffalmacco, etc. but are generally held to be by an unknown 14C master named from these frescoes '*The Master of the Triumph of Death*' (1360–80). A bust of Liszt (removed) recalls his inspiration from these frescoes which led to the creation of his 'Totentanz'. Also here, Crucifixion by the '*Maestro della Crocifissione di Camposanto*' (c 1380), and *Taddeo Gaddi*, Patience of Job.—The adjacent gallery (right) displays photographs of other frescoes formerly in the camposanto by Buffalmacco, Francesco di Traino, Benozzo di Lese, etc. In the centre, Greek *Vase (2–1C BC), with dancing nymphs and satyrs and Dionysiac scenes carved in low relief, a superb work which was studied by sculptors of the Renaissance.—At the E corner of the N wall (temporarily closed), *Gozzoli*, Wine harvest and drunkenness of Noah.

Monuments and Sculptures. The Roman sculpture and sarcophaghi in the Camposanto, most of which have either been destroyed or removed, made up one of the most important classical collections in Europe in the early

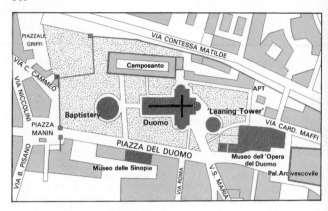

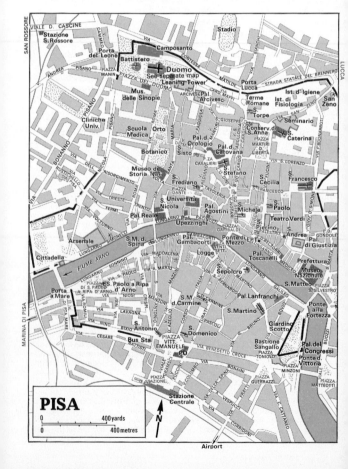

PISA

0 — 400 yards
0 — 400 metres

N

Airport

Renaissance. Of those that remain the most important are: SOUTH WALL (SE corner). Inscribed decrees ordaining honours for Gaius and Lucius Caesar, nephews of Augustus; Roman milestones; Sarcophagi with tritons and nereids; Sarcophagus with the Rape of Proserpine; on this and other sarcophagi (many of which were reused in the Middle Ages), Roman portrait-heads; Tomb of Andrea Berlinghieri (died 1826), oculist, by *Thorvaldsen*; Tomb of Francesco Algarotti (died 1764), physicist; Sarcophagus with the Good Shepherd.—WEST WALL. Harbour chains of the ancient port of Pisa, carried off by the Genoese in 1342; Sarcophagus formed of a bath-tub; Sarcophagus of the 1C.

NORTH WALL. Sarcophagus with a matron and a figure in a toga; Sarcophagus with victories and other figures.—CAPPELLA AULLA, Assumption, by *Giovanni della Robbia* (damaged).—Sarcophagus of a married couple; Sarcophagus with Thanatos and Hypnos; Sarcophagi, with Meleager and the Seasons; others, with a battle scene, and with the Good Shepherd; huge Sarcophagus with the Muses.—EAST WALL (temporarily closed off). Tomb of Filipo Decio (died 1535), by *Stagio Stagi*; Statue for the tomb of Count Mastiani, by *Lorenzo Bartolini* (1842); Tomb of the scientist Mossotti (died 1863), by *Giovanni Dupré*; fragment of a medieval mosaic.

On the S side of the lawn is the former OSPEDALE NUOVO DI MISERICORDIA (13–14C), where the ***Museo delle Sinopie del Camposanto Monumentale** (adm., see above) was opened in 1979.

A sinopia is the name given to the sketch for a fresco made on the rough wall (prepared with 'arriccio') in a red earth pigment (called 'sinopia' because it originally came from Sinope on the Black Sea). The sinopia was then gradually covered with 'grassello', another type of wet plaster, as work proceeded day by day on the fresco itself. By detaching a fresco from the wall it has been possible in many instances to recover the sinopia from the inner surface. The 14–15C frescoes of the Camposanto (see above) were severely damaged in the last War and had to be detached; the sinopie were then restored and are now displayed together here.

In the modern gallery stairs lead up to a platform from which may be viewed (right) three huge *Panels with Stories of the Anchorites, the Last Judgement and Hell, and the Triumph of Death, all generally attributed to the '*Master of the Triumph of Death*' (but thought by some scholars to be by *Buffalmacco*). On the far (end) wall, Crucifixion by *Francesco Traini* and Ascension, attributed to *Buffalmacco*. On the N wall, Theological Cosmograph by *Piero di Puccio*. On the last wall are smaller sinopie (very damaged) by *Spinello Aretino, Antonio Veneziano, Andrea Bonaiuti*, and *Taddeo Gaddi*. On the upper level are frescoes and sinopia fragments by *Buffalmacco* (Incredulity of St Thomas, Resurrection, etc.).—On the Ground Floor the sinopie are by *Piero di Puccio* and *Benozzo di Lese*.

The **Museo dell'Opera del Duomo** (adm., see above) was opened in 1986, using the latest methods of security and display, in the former Chapter House of the Cathedral behind the leaning tower. The collection includes works of art from the Duomo, Baptistery, and Camposanto. The fine building, with a double loggia, overlooking a little garden, has good views of the Leaning Tower. Handlists are supplied in each room.

ROOM 1. 12C sculpture from the Duomo, showing Islamic and French influences. The intricately carved transenna (probably an altar frontal) is attributed to *Rainaldo*. On the left wall are capitals and inlaid marble panels from the façade of the Duomo (their original positions are shown on a diagram). In front is a long transenna from the presbytery by the school of *Guglielmo*, carved on the back of a Roman panel with a frieze of dolphins. The striking polychrome wood Crucifix is attributed to a Burgundian artist. The splendid bronze *Griffon (11C) and the basin and capital (10C) are Islamic works brought from the East as war booty. The statue of St Michael is attributed to *Biduino*, and the seated statue of David playing the Cithern shows the influence of Provence sculptors. The small R. 2 contains 13C heads from the exterior of the Baptistery (their original positions are shown on a diagram) and fragments from the transenna.—R. 3 contains two 19C models of the Duomo in wood and alabaster.—R. 4, a pretty barrel vaulted room with wall paintings, displays the Gothic statues (very worn) from the summits of the triangular tympanums on the exterior of the Baptistery. They are by *Nicola* and *Giovanni Pisano*, and assistants. Facing them are busts of *Christ blessing, by *Nicola Pisano*, between the Madonna and St John the Evangelist, originally above the main entrance of the Baptistery facing the Duomo.—In the corridor and R. 5 are parts of the late-13C frieze with carved rectangles which ran round the base of the exterior of the Duomo. R. 5 displays sculptures by *Giovanni Pisano*, including a (headless) Madonna and kneeling figure representing Pisa, formerly part of an allegorical group with the Emperor Henry VII. The Madonnna and Child and Saints John the Evangelist and John the Baptist were removed from the main door of the Baptistery (two of the statues are removed for restoration). The half-length Madonna 'del Colloquio' is a beautiful composition.—R. 6 contains works by *Tino da Camaino*: fragments of the font from the Duomo; statues of the Annunciation and two deacons from the tomb of the Emperor Henry VII in the S transept of the Duomo; the tomb of St Ranieri; and the seated Henry VII between dignatories of the state.—R. 7. Funerary monuments of two archbishops by *Nino Pisano.*— R. 8. Funerary monument of Archbishop Pietro Ricci by the Florentine sculptor *Andrea di Francesco Guardi*; architectural fragments by *Matteo Civitali*, and the workshop of *Lorenzo* and *Stagio Stagi.*

The Cathedral treasury is displayed in RR. 9 & 10: 12C Cross, known as the 'Croce dei Pisani' in bronze and silver; two 12C Limoges enamelled caskets; Tuscan embroidered altar-frontal (1325); and a cope, also dating from the 14C. The *Cintola with five reliefs decorated with enamels and precious stones dates from the end of the 13C or beginning of the 14C. Also displayed here: 15C reliquary of St Clement, and an 11C ivory casket. The ivory statuette of the *Madonna and Child, is a superb work by *Giovanni Pisano* (1299–1300), originally over the main altar in the Duomo. The Crucifix is also by *Giovanni Pisano.* In the 17C chapel (R. 10) are displayed 17C reliquaries and the service of gilded church silver (French, 1616–17) given by Maria de' Medici to Archbishop Bonciani.

Stairs lead up to the FIRST FLOOR. R. 11. Paintings by a follower of *Benozzo Gozzoli* (Madonna and Child, four Saints, and patrons), and by *Battista Franco* and *Aurelio Lomi.* Marble angels by *Tribolo* and *Silvio Cosini.*—R. 12. 18C paintings by *Giuseppe* and *Francesco Melani* and *Giovanni Domenico Ferretti.*—R. 13 displays wood intarsia: allegories of Faith, Hope, and Charity by *Baccio* and *Piero Pontelli* (1475) are displayed opposite two works by *Cristoforo da Lendinara.* Also here are panels from choir-stalls by *Guido da Seravallino.* R. 14. Two liturgical parchment scrolls, known as 'Exultets' (12C and 13C), with illuminations. 14C illuminated choirbooks, and a 16C wooden lectern.—RR. 15–18. Church vestments (16–19C).—R. 19. Engravings and watercolours by *Carlo Lasinio* (1759–1838) responsible for the restoration of the Camposanto. The delightful copies in watercolour of the frescoes of the Camposanto provide a precious record of them before their almost total destruction in the War.—RR. 20–23 contains an archaeological collection displayed by Lasinio in the Camposanto in 1807: cinerary urns, sarcophaghi, busts, including one of Julius Caesar, Etruscan urns, and Egyptian antiquities. The exit from the museum is along the PORTICO on the ground floor where the colossal *Half-figures of Evangelists, prophets, and the Madonna and Child, by *Nicola* and *Giovanni Pisano* from the exterior of the Baptistery (1269–79) are displayed.

The dignified Via Santa Maria leads S from Piazza del Duomo towards the centre. On the left Via dei Mille passes (right) *San Sisto*, an 11C church beautifully restored, to reach the *PIAZZA DEI CAVA-LIERI, named from the Knights of St Stephen, an order founded by Cosimo I in 1561 in imitation of the Knights of Malta. *Santo Stefano dei Cavalieri* (usually closed), their church, was built to a design of Vasari (1565–69) with a façade by Giovànni de'Medici (1594–1606). It contains banners captured from the infidel and ornaments from the galleys of the knights. To the left is *Palazzo dei Cavalieri*, formerly *della Carovana*, modernised in 1562 by Vasari, with spectacular graffiti decoration. It is now the seat of the *Scuola Normale Superiore*, a university college of extremely high standing, founded by Napoleon in 1810, and modelled on the École Normale Supérieure in Paris. It incorporates a large medieval hall of the old Palazzo del

Popolo, now used as a lecture hall. Concerts are given here from December–May. Outside is a statue of Cosimo I by Francavilla (1596).

The *Palazzo dell'Orologio*, closing the N side of the square, occupies the site the old *Torre dei Gualandi* or *della Muda* (later the Torre della Fame), the 'mews' of the eagles that figure in the Pisan coat-of-arms. Here in 1288 Count Ugolino della Gherardesca, suspected of treachery at the battle of Meloria, and his sons and grandsons were starved to death ('Inferno', XXXII). The building is now used as a library by the Scuola Normale, and the tower can be seen from the entrance, incorporated in the structure.

Via Ulisse Dini leads down to Borgo Stretto, a pretty arcaded street closed to private traffic. Off the narrow old Via Notari (parallel to the right) a market is held in the charming arcaded Piazza delle Vettovaglie. In Borgo Stretto is the church of *San Michele in Borgo*, built in 990, with a 14C façade, by Fra Guglielmo Agnelli, typical of Pisan Gothic. It has good capitals in the interior. Both roads end in Piazza Garibaldi, a small but animated square opening on the Arno at the N end of *Ponte di Mezzo* (scene of the Gioco del Ponte in June, see above). From Borgo Stretto, opposite Via Ulisse Dini (see above) the narrow Via San Francesco leads to the church of *Santa Cecilia* (1103) with a façade and campanile decorated with majolica (now mostly disappeared). To the N across Piazza Martiri (planted with plane trees), stands the church of **Santa Caterina** (sometimes closed), built for the Dominicans in the 13C, with a façade in the Pisan Gothic style of 1330. The best of the early tombs in the impressive interior is that, on the left, of Archbishop Simone Saltarelli (died 1342), by *Nino Pisano*, by whom are also the Annunciation figures flanking the high altar. On the left wall, Apotheosis of St Thomas, by *Francesco Traini*.

To the NE (see the Plan) are vestiges of *Roman Baths*, uncovered in 1942. From Via Cardinale Maffi there is a dramatic view of the Leaning Tower.—In the other direction, Via San Zeno leads NE to (c 400m) the little Romanesque chapel of *San Zeno (usually closed) of ancient foundation, showing various architectural styles from the 5C, and incorporating Roman fragments in its façade. It has been deconsecrated and is now used for exhibitions, concerts, and conferences.

Via San Francesco (see above) continues E to the Gothic church of **San Francesco** which has a good campanile. Over the high altar, with a reredos by *Tommaso Pisano*, the vault is painted by *Taddeo Gaddi*. In the flanking chapels: (2nd right) polyptych attributed to Spinello Aretino; (1st left) St Francis, early 13C Pisan school, and frescoes (high up) by *Taddeo Gaddi*; (2nd left), more frescoes and sinopie. In the Sacristy, which has frescoes by *Taddeo di Bartolo*, are displayed interesting sinopie by *Taddeo Gaddi*.

On the S side of Via San Francesco is Piazza San Paolo, where the church of *San Paolo all'Orto* retains the lower part of a handsome 12C façade. Farther S is *San Pierino* (1072–1119; closed), which has a large crypt (seen from the outside). Via Palestro leads E to *Sant'Andrea*, another good 12C church (closed).

From San Pierino Via delle Belle Torri, with 12–13C houses, runs parallel with the river, then curves to join the Lungarno Mediceo. At the corner, on the river, is the 16C *Palazzo Toscanelli* (formerly Lanfranchi), occupied by Byron in 1821–22. Farther on is *Palazzo de'Medici*, built in the 13–14C and now restored as the *Prefettura*. Beyond, behind the church of *San Matteo* (11–13C, with fine 17C work), is the ex-convent of San Matteo (used as a prison in the 19C), and occupied since 1947 by the *Museo Nazionale di San Matteo (adm. 8.30–19.30; fest. 8.30–13.30; closed Monday).

The museum has recently been reopened after years of partial closure, although by no means all of the collection is yet on display. The rooms are un-numbered, and the works are poorly labelled. In the entrance hall, sarcophagus with the Good Shepherd (4C). Beyond the CLOISTER, with sculptural fragments, stairs lead up to the FIRST FLOOR. ROOM 1 (left). Early Tuscan painted Crucifixes (12–13C), including one signed by *Giunta Pisano*, and one (recently restored) signed by *Berlinghiero*; and early Pisan panel paintings including St Catherine with stories from her life (13C).—R. 2. Panels by *Deodato Orlandi* and the *'Maestro di San Torpè'* (early 14C); *Francesco Traini*, *Polyptych of St Dominic with stories from his life (signed), Madonna and Child with Saints; *Lippo Memmi*, Polyptych.—At the end of the room: *Simone Martini*, *Polyptych (signed, 1319–21); works by *Giovanni di Nicola*, and a wood statue of the Virgin Annunciate by *Agostino di Giovanni*.—R. 3 (right). 14C and 15C Pisan wood sculptures: works by *Francesco di Valdambrino*; *Madonna del Latte*, a half-length polychrome marble gilded statue from Santa Maria della Spina by *Andrea* and *Nino Pisano*; *Nino Pisano*, Christ in pietà, wooden high relief of the Madonna and Child, and marble statuette of the Madonna and Child (the last two from Santa Maria della Spina); *Andrea* and *Nino Pisano*, *Annunciatory angel, a wooden statue from San Matteo.—In the Long Gallery (4) overlooking the cloister are displayed Islamic and Pisan 12–14C ceramics, and some majolica tondi from Pisan church façades.—R. 5 (closed in 1990). Displayed on stands to the left: *Barnaba da Modena*, Madonna enthroned, Madonna and Child; *Antonio Veneziano*, Assunta, and processional standard with the Crucifixion and St Ranieri.—Works by *Jacopo di Michele*; polyptychs by *Martino di Bartolomeo*; *Taddeo di Bartolo*, Processional standard with the Crucifixion and St Donnino; Cross in rock crystal decorated with miniatures (Venetian, early 14C); *'Maestro di Barga'*, Processional standard (Crucifixion and St Ursula).—On the stands opposite: *Taddeo di Bartolo*, Madonna and Saints and two angels; *Spinello Aretino*, Coronation of the Virgin, fragment of a polyptych, six frescoed heads; *Agnolo Gaddi*, two fragments of a polyptych; works by *Luca di Tommè*, *Cecco di Pietro*, and *Francesco Neri da Volterra*.—In the short gallery (6) overlooking the cloister is a delightful display of polychrome wood statues (14C, Pisan), and reliquary busts, and a bust of the Redeemer in terracotta attributed to the circle of Verrocchio.—R. 7 (also closed) contains 15C works, including some by *Lorenzo di Bicci* and *Turino Vanni*.—R. 8. *Neri di Bicci*, Coronation of the Virgin; *Masaccio*, *St Paul; *Benozzo Gozzoli*, Madonna and Child with Saints (very ruined), Madonna and Child with St Anne (being restored), Crucifix and Saints and a donor; *Zanobi Machiavelli*, Madonna and Child with four Saints; *Michele di Matteo*, Coronation of the Virgin; *Fra Angelico* (attributed), *Christ blessing (tempera on canvas; very ruined); *Gentile da Fabriano*, Madonna of Humility; *'Maestro della Natività di Castello'*, Madonna and Child with angel musicians; *Neri di Bicci*, Coronation of the Virgin.—R. 9. Late-15C works, including some by *Giuliano Amidei*.—R. 10. 15C and 16C works including an interesting Resurrection of Lazarus, and Madonna and Child with Saints; Flemish polyptych; and St Catherine and stories from her life.—In the second long gallery (11; still being arranged) overlooking the cloister, is the splendid *Reliquary bust of St Rossore (or St Luxorious) in gilded bronze by *Donatello* (1424–27; originally in Santo Stefano dei Cavalieri).—In small rooms of the cloister (opened on request) are high reliefs from San Michele, and tournament armour of the 15C and 16C used in the Gioco del Ponte.

Many more rooms are to be opened to display the rest of the collection which includes: detached frescoes by *Davide Ghirlandaio*, and paintings by *Francesco Francia*, *Botticini*, *Rosso Fiorentino* (Rebecca and Eliezer at the well), and *Guido Reni* (*Sacred and Profane Love; a drawing and a painting). Later Italian schools are represented by *Giovanni Maria Crespi* and *Bernardo Strozzi*. Foreign works include: *Jan Brueghel*, Holy Family; *Lawrence*, George IV; *Henri met des Bles* (attributed), a small painting of the Crucifixion. The museum also possesses a remarkable collection of medals.

The *Ponte alla Fortezza* (reconstructed in 1958) crosses the Arno to the Lungarno Galilei and the ruined *Palazzo Scotto*. Here Shelley lived in 1820–22, the period of 'Epipsychidion', inspired by the Contessina Emilia Viviani, and of 'Adonais'. The old *Fortezza* is now a public garden.

At No. 19 in Via San Martino, to the W, is a Roman statue called the 'Chinsica', after a legendary heroine who saved Pisa from the Saracens. The church of *San Martino* preserves remains of the older building (1332) and inside, a relief of St Martin and the beggar, attributed to Andrea da Pontedera (replaced on exterior by a copy), and a 13C painted Crucifix.

On the Lungarno Galilei is *San Sepolcro*, an octagonal church of c 1150, built for the Templars by Diotisalvi (with a pyramidal roof). Beyond is Piazza XX Settembre, at the S end of the Ponte di Mezzo. Here is a market-hall of 1603–05, an open portico known as the *Logge di Banchi*.

To the S opens the Corso Italia, the main street of the city, leading to the church and convent of *San Domenico* (deconsecrated). To the right, near the church of *Sant'Antonio* (14C; mostly reconstructed), at No. 29 Via Mazzini, is the *Domus Mazziniana*, rebuilt on the foundations of the mansion in which Giuseppe Mazzini died in 1872; it houses a library and museum (adm. 8–14; Saturday 8–12; closed fest.).

The Lungarno Gambacorti leads on past (No. 1) the 14C *Palazzo Gambacorti*, now the Municipio, to the church of ***Santa Maria della Spina**, a gem of Pisan Gothic architecture, named from a thorn of the Saviour's crown, the gift of a Pisan merchant. It was restored after war damage. The interior is only open in summer (usually in the morning), but the Madonna and Child by *Nino* and *Andrea Pisano*, which was over the altar, has been removed to the Museo di San Matteo.—The Lungarno Sonnino leads on past the ex-Convent of San Benedetto with good terracotta decoration (restored) to the 11–12C church of ***San Paolo a Ripa d'Arno** which has a splendid façade and exterior, recalling that of the Duomo. The solemn bare interior has a handsome Roman sarcophagus, and a fine Romanesque capital (2nd on left). Behind the church is the curious Romanesque chapel of *Sant'Agata*, a tiny octagonal brick building (12C).

Beyond the 14C Porta a Mare, Ponte della Cittadella crosses the Arno to the Lungarno Simonelli and Lungarno Pacinotti, which lead back towards the centre. On the left, behind the *Palazzo Reale*, built on to an old tower-house, is the church of **San Nicola**, built c 1150 but much altered. In the 13C *Campanile is a remarkable spiral staircase on which Bramante (according to Vasari) modelled his Belvedere staircase in the Vatican.

INTERIOR. S side, 4th chapel, St Nicholas of Tolentino protecting Pisa (clearly depicted) from the plague, c 1400.—N side, 4th chapel, *Madonna, statue in polychrome wood, attributed to *Nino Pisano*. The Sacristy preserves a wood statue of the Madonna attributed to the school of Jacopo della Quercia, and a *Madonna and Child by *Francesco Traini*. A Crucifix attributed to Giovanni Pisano has been removed for restoration.

Farther along the quay are *Palazzo Upezzinghi* (13–16C) and *Palazzo Agostini* (early 15C), with terracotta decoration. Between them Via XXIX Maggio leads past the *University* (courtyard of 1550) to the church of *San Frediano* (11C), preserving good capitals in its altered interior and a 13C Crucifixion on panel. Straight ahead is Piazza dei Cavalieri, while to the left are the *University Museums* and the *Botanic Gardens* (adm. weekdays 8–12.30; good palms, bamboos, etc.) and, in Via Santa Maria, *Galileo's House* (adm. 9.30–12.30; closed festivals).

Marina di Pisa, 12km SW of Pisa, is reached by a long straight road (buses from Pisa) lined with plane trees which skirts the Arno (with boat building yards, fishing huts, etc.). The road passes close to (6km; left) the church of ***San Piero a Grado**, built on the site where St Peter is said to have landed on his journey from Antioch to Rome. In Roman times this was the site of the last ferry across the Arno. The present Romanesque basilica dates from the 11C. The pretty exterior has blind arcading and majolica tondi, and a central lateral door. The interior is unusual in having apses at both the E end and the W end (similar in plan to ancient Roman basilicas). The reused columns, with a variety of Roman capitals, came from an earlier structure, the foundations of which have been exposed at the W end. The ciborium marks the spot where St Peter is said to have preached. The interesting fresco cycle dates from the beginning of the 14C and is attributed to Deodato Orlandi. Above portraits of the popes from St Peter to John XVIII (1003) are scenes from the life of St Peter.—MARINA DI PISA, a pleasant old-fashioned bathing resort (with several art nouveau houses), at the mouth of the Arno, is backed by dense pinewoods, whose seeds are used for making confectionery.— Between the Arno and the Serchio lies the *Tenuta di San Rossore*, a summer estate of the President of the Republic, with bird and animal sanctuaries (wild boar, deer, etc.), donated to the State in 1988. This area, and the Tenuta di Tombolo to the S, and (beyond the Serchio) Migliarino and Massaciuccoli (see Rte 7) have been protected since 1979 as a *Parco Naturale*, although the trees are threatened with disease, the rivers are polluted, and the coastline is being eroded. Part of the Tenuta di San Rossore is open on Sunday & fest. (entrance from Viale delle Cascine). Other areas are nature reserves (information from the Consorzio per il Parco, 10 Via Cesare Battisti, Pisa).—On the beach of *Il Gombo*, N of the mouth of the Arno, Shelley's body was washed ashore in 1822 (see Rte 7). Allan Ramsay, the painter, was more fortunate and escaped with his life from a shipwreck here in 1736 on his first journey to Rome.—To the S of Marina di Pisa the modern resort of *Tirrenia* extends towards Livorno.

From Pisa to *Genoa*, see Rte 7; to *Florence* and *Lucca*, see Rte 45; to *San Miniato* (and for the Certosa di Pisa), see Rte 47C; to *Livorno* and *Grosseto*, see Rte 54.

47 Florence to Siena

A. Via the 'Superstrada del Palio' and San Gimignano

ROAD, 68km.—16km *San Casciano.*—40·5km *Poggibonsi* (for **San Gimignano**).—45km *Colle Val d'Elsa.*—53km *Monteriggioni.*— 68km **Siena**.

This is a fast four-lane highway (no toll, and no service stations), usually busy (speed limit), and not very well engineered. It is, however, the normal route between Florence and Siena, preferable to the parallel windy Via Cassia (N2) since it has exits at all the main places of interest.

BUSES. Frequent service (SITA) from Florence, near the main railway station and Porta Romana in 75 minutes via the 'superstrada' terminating at *Siena* in Piazza San Domenico. The service which follows the old road (Via Cassia) takes c 2 hours.—For *San Gimignano*, frequent service (SITA) via Poggibonsi in 1 hour 40 minutes.—For the RAILWAY from Florence to Siena, see Rte 47C.

From Florence the superstrada is reached via Via Senese which starts at Porta Romana (Pl. 13,14). Beyond the Certosa di Galluzzo (see Rte 43D) the superstrada begins near an exit from the 'Autostrada del Sole'. After a tunnel it passes close to the *U.S. Military Cemetery* where are buried 4403 American soldiers who died in service N of Rome in 1944–5.—16km *San Casciano.*

The village of **San Casciano in Val di Pesa** is situated high up on a hill. Inside the walls, in Via Roma, is the church of Santa Maria del Gesù (known as 'Il Suffraggio') where a *Museo d'Arte Sacra* was opened in 1989 (Saturday 16.30–19; Sunday 10–12.30, 16–19). In the church, on the high altar, Madonna and Child by Lippo di Benivieni, and 16C paintings. Behind the altar, 14C Sienese wood Crucifix. In a little room on the right, polychrome marble statue of the Madonna and Child of 1341. In the Nun's choir: 'Master of the Horne Triptych', Madonna and Child; church silver; unusual 12C sculptural fragment; Jacopo del Casentino, Madonna and Child; Triptych of 1398; Cenni di Francesco, Madonna and Child.—Beyond the crossroads by the clock tower, at the end of Via Marrocchesi, is the church of the *Misericordia* (or Santa Maria sul Prato) which contains some fine paintings including (over the high altar) Ugolino di Nerio, Madonna and Child and two Saints; Jacopo Vignali, Circumcision; Simone Martini (attributed), small Crucifix; Paolino da Pistoia, Madonna enthroned with four Saints; Francesco Furini, Ecstasy of St Charles Borromeo.—A pretty by-road leads N from San Casciano to the hamlet of *Sant'Andrea in Percussina*, with the 'Albergaccio' where Niccolò Machiavelli lived from 1513. The hostelry here succeeds the one frequented by the politician and writer.

23km *Tavarnelle.* Just outside the village (signposted off the Via Cassia), some 500 metres along a narrow road, is the Romanesque church of *San Pietro in Bossolo* in a lovely position with wide views. In the Canonry, beyond a little cloister, another Museo d'Arte Sacra was opened in 1989. The collection includes five paintings by Neri di Bicci, a Madonna and Child (c 1270–80) attributed to Meliore, a triptych by Ugolino di Nerio, Madonna and Child; Madonnas by Rossello di Jacopo Franchi and the 'Maestro di Marradi', and church silver.—A pretty by-road diverges left from the road for Sambuca to climb through beautiful open countryside with olive groves and woods to *Badia a Passignano* in a superb position surrounded by cypresses. The Badia was founded by San Giovanni Gualberto in 1049 who died here in 1073. It was fortified in the 15C. In 1987 the Vallombrosan Order returned to the monastery (shown on request at weekends). The interior was redesigned by Domenico Cresti, called 'Il Passignano' after his birthplace. He also carried out the frescoes in the presbytery. The statue of San Giovanni Gualberto is by Giovanni Battista Caccini (1580). In the refectory is a fresco of the Last Supper by Domenico Ghirlandaio.—40·5km **Poggibonsi** (116km), an unattractive commercial town of 25,400 inhabitants and important road centre, at the foot of its 15C castle. The 13C church of *San Lucchese*, c 2km S, restored after War damage, has frescoes by Bartolomeo di Fredi, and a Della Robbian altarpiece.

A pretty road (11km) leads W to **SAN GIMIGNANO** (324m), a charming small hill-town of 7670 inhabitants, which has perhaps preserved its medieval appearance more completely than any other town in Tuscany. It can, however, be uncomfortably crowded with tourists (mostly on day tours from Florence or Siena) in spring and summer. The town is famous for its numerous towers which make it conspicuous from a great distance and provide one of the most remarkable views in Italy. It is surrounded by rich agricultural land, famous for its wine (notably the white 'Vernaccia').

The town was long known as 'San Gimignano delle belle Torri' from the noble towers of its palazzi, most of which were constructed in the 12–13C; 13 still survive out of the 76 traditionally thought to have existed. Dante was sent here in 1299 as an ambassador of Florence to attach the smaller town to the Guelf League. The town suffered some war damage.—**Car Parks** outside the walls.

The entrance to the town is through *Porta San Giovanni* (1262), finest of the town gates. Via San Giovanni, with a good view of the tall tower of Palazzo del Popolo at the end, continues past the little Pisan-Romanesque façade of the church of *San Francesco* (the interior is now used as a wine cellar; adm. is freely granted to the little garden beyond on a terrace with a good view of the countryside and part of the town). Beyond *Palazzo Pratellesi* (14C), now the Biblioteca

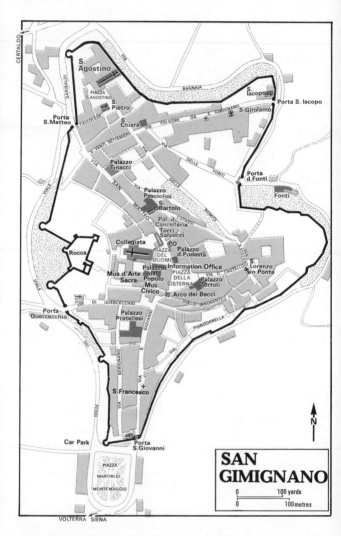

Comunale, is the *Arco dei Becci*, another ancient gate beside several
tall towers. Beyond it opens the charming *PIAZZA DELLA CISTERNA,
named from its well of 1237, with 13–14C buildings, notably *Palazzo
Tortoli* with its two-light windows. A few paces to the N is *PIAZZA
DEL DUOMO, another handsome medieval square with a number of
towers. The crenellated Palazzo del Popolo, with its tower and loggia,
stands to the left of the Collegiata at the top of a flight of steps.
Opposite the church is *Palazzo del Podestà* (1239, enlarged 1337),
with an unusual vaulted loggia surmounted by the *Torre della

Rognosa (51m) which was once appointed the maximum standard of height in order to diminish rivalry in tower-building.

The Romanesque *Collegiata* (closed 12.30–14.30 or, in summer, 15.30) was enlarged in 1466–68 by *Giuliano da Maiano*. The interior aisle walls are entirely covered with two cycles of *Frescoes (coin operated light in the nave), scarred by war but mainly well restored. The beautiful New Testament scenes in the S aisle, for long attributed to *Barna da Siena* (c 1381) and *Giovanni d'Asciano*, are now thought to have been executed in 1333–41 by a master working in the bottega of Simone Martini. The Old Testament scenes in the N aisle are signed and dated 1367 by *Bartolo di Fredi*. On the W wall, Last Judgement, by *Taddeo di Bartolo* (1393) above the Martyrdom of St Sebastian, by *Benozzo Gozzoli*. The two fine *Statues of the Virgin Annunciate and the Angel by *Jacopo della Quercia* (1421) were painted in 1426 by Martino di Bartolomeo. Over the high altar is a ciborium by *Benedetto da Maiano* (1475). The choir stalls, pulpit and lectern are by *Antonio da Colle*. The sacristan shows the *Cappella di Santa Fina*, off the S aisle (ticket includes the Museo Sacro and Museo Civico), a beautifully preserved Renaissance chapel. Built by *Giuliano da Maiano* (1468), with an altar by *Benedetto da Maiano*, it has *Frescoes by *Domenico Ghirlandaio* (helped by *Sebastiano Mainardi*), depicting the life of the saint.

An archway, surmounted by a statue of San Gimignano (1342), left of the church façade, leads into a courtyard where the Baptistery loggia has an Annunciation by *Domenico Ghirlandaio* or *Sebastiano Mainardi*, and a font of 1378. Here is the entrance to the small MUSEO D'ARTE SACRA and MUSEO ETRUSCO (April–October, every day 9.30–12.30, 15.30–18.30; winter 9.30–12.30, 14.30–17.30, closed Monday).

The little chapel on the ground floor contains tomb slabs, etc. On the floor above the room to the left contains a wood figure of Christ of the type of the 'Volto Santo' of Lucca, probably a Sienese work of the early 13C; 14C polychrome wood statues of the Virgin and the Annunciatory angel, formerly in the Duomo; *Benedetto da Maiano*, marble bust of Onofrio di Pietro; bust of the Redeemer by *Pietro Torrigiani*.—In the next room, *Bartolo di Fredi*, Madonna and Child; altar-cloth made in Florence in 1449; Crucifix attributed to *Benedetto da Maiano*. In the room on the right of the stairs are displayed 15C–18C church silver, and a statue of St Anthony Abbot attributed to *Francesco di Valdambrino*. The collection also includes some 14C illuminated choirbooks.—In the Loggia is displayed a small collection of Etruscan material found locally.

Behind the cathedral is the ruined *Rocca*, begun in 1353; the surviving tower commands a remarkable *View of the town and countryside.

Palazzo del Popolo (1288–1323) was restored after war damage. It still serves as town hall. The splendid tower, known as the Torre Grossa (54m), was begun in 1300. The fresco under the loggia, of the Madonna and Saints, is by a 14C master. A passageway leads into a pretty courtyard with fresco fragments (two by *Sodoma*) and a stairway mounts to the MUSEO CIVICO (adm. as for the Museo d'Arte Sacra, see above). The Sala del Consiglio, where Dante is supposed to have delivered his appeal, contains a large *Fresco of the Maestà by *Lippo Memmi* (signed and dated 1317). This superb work, showing the Madonna enthroned beneath a canopy surrounded by angels and saints, with the podestà Mino de' Tolomei kneeling in adoration, recalls the famous work by Simone Martini in the Palazzo Pubblico of Siena. The other walls are decorated with Sienese frescoes of hunting and tournament scenes.—A small adjoining room (closed) displays

pharmacy jars and a terracotta bust of Guido Marabottini (15C). The
chapel with a fresco of the Trinity by *Pier Francesco Fiorentino* has
been closed for restoration for many years.—Stairs lead up to the
PINACOTECA, with fine views over the town. In a small room off the
stair landing (left) are charming frescoes of domestic scenes by
Memmo di Filippuccio (early 14C). In the main hall: *Coppo di
Marcovaldo*, *Crucifix; *Guido da Siena*, Madonna and Child enthroned (very damaged); *Sebastiano Mainardi*, Madonna and Saints;
Benozzo Gozzoli, Madonna and Child with two Saints; *Filippino
Lippi*, two tondi of the Annunciation; *Pinturicchio*, Madonna in glory
with Saints Gregory and Benedict; *Domenico di Michelino*, Madonna
and Child with four Saints; *Benozzo Gozzoli*, Madonna and Child
with four Saints; *'Maestro delle Clarisse'*, Crucifix (c 1280–85).—In
the two side-rooms: *13C Sienese school*, Crucifix; *Memmo di Filippuccio*, Madonna and Child with Saints; *Bartolo di Fredi*, Female
heads; *Lorenzo di Niccolò Gerini*, Saints Fina and Gregory, two
angels, and stories from their lives.—*Lorenzo di Niccolò Gerini*, St
Bartholomew and stories from his life; *Taddeo di Bartolo*, *San
Gimignano and stories from his life; *Niccolò Tegliacci*, Madonna in
glory with Saints.—The TOWER may be climbed to see the splendid
view.

Beyond the twin *Torri dei Salvucci*, *VIA SAN MATTEO, the most
attractive street in the town, lined with medieval buildings, runs
towards *Porta San Matteo* (1262). It passes *Palazzo della Cancelleria*,
the Romanesque church of *San Bartolo*, and the 13C Pesciolini
tower-house, all grouped outside a double arch from an earlier circuit
of walls: farther on is *Palazzo Tinacci*. Just inside the gate, Via
Cellolese leads right for **Sant'Agostino** (1280–98), an aisleless church
with three apsidal chapels.

INTERIOR. To the right of the main door, in the Cappella di San Bartolo is a marble
reredos by *Benedetto da Maiano*, and frescoes by *Sebastiano Mainardi*. Right
wall: Madonna and Child with eight Saints by *Pier Francesco Fiorentino*, in the
lunette, Pietà by *Bartolo di Fredi*. In the right apse, Birth of the Virgin by
Vincenzo Tamagni (1523) and restored frescoes by *Bartolo di Fredi*. On the high
altar, Coronation of the Virgin by *Piero del Pollaiolo* (1483), and, in the choir,
charming *Frescoes (1465) illustrating the Life of St Augustine in 17 scenes by
Benozzo Gozzoli (coin-operated light).—On the left nave wall: frescoes by
Sebastiano Mainardi, *Lippo Memmi* (Madonna and Child; very ruined), and
Benozzo Gozzoli (St Sebastian with the faithful). The fine cloister dates from
1465.—The Romanesque church of *San Pietro* in the piazza is closed. It contains
frescoes by Memmo di Filippuccio.

The *Circonvallazione*, round the 13C walls (in need of restoration), provides
fine views and access to picturesque parts of the town. All the churches in the
town (and near it) are of interest for architecture or painting (or both), but nearly
all of them are kept locked. Especially noteworthy are *San Girolamo* and *San
Jacopo* (reached by Via XX Settembre), the former with works by Vincenzo
Tamagni (1522), the latter, a charming little Pisan-Romanesque building, with a
St James, by Pier Francesco Fiorentino. Outside the Porta alla Fonte, just to the S,
are the arcaded *Fonti*, a medieval public wellhouse.

The pretty Romanesque parish church (1237) at *Cellole*, 4km outside Porta San
Matteo, gave Puccini the setting for 'Suor Angelica'.

The Siena 'superstrada' continues from Poggibonsi (see above) past
(46km) the exit for **Colle Val d'Elsa** (see Rte 49). A by road (2km) leads
E to *Staggia* which preserves some 14C fortifications and a ruined
rocca of 1432. The parish church has a painting by Antonio del
Pollaiolo. 53km ***Monteriggioni**, a beautifully preserved tiny
medieval hamlet standing on a hillock. Its 13C *Walls, complete with
fourteen towers, provide a romantic view from below. It was once a
Sienese fortress (mentioned by Dante: 'Inferno', xxxi, 41-4).

The *Abbadia Isola*, c 3km W, has a church with a basilican interior (restored) with a good altarpiece by Sano di Pietro (1471). A fresco by Taddeo di Bartolo has been detached for restoration. A fine painting of the *Maestà from the church has recently been restored and attributed to the 'Maestro di Badia a Isola'.—On Monte Maggio, 8km S of Monteriggioni, in the little church of *San Lorenzo al Colle* (reached from the main road, N2) frescoes were discovered in 1986, including a Maestà attributed to the 'Maestro di Città di Castello'.

The superstrada continues towards Siena. It has recently been linked to the ring-road which by-passes the town to the W. Various exits lead in to (68km) **Siena** (see Rte 48).

B. Via the 'Chiantigiana'

ROAD, N222, 70km.—10km *Grassina.*—29km *Greve.*—49km *Castellina in Chianti.*—70km **Siena**.

This is a beautiful route, longer and slower than the 'superstrada', but with much less traffic, through the hilly Chianti region. The world famous 'Chianti Classico' red wine is produced from grapes grown in this limited geographical area (the 'Chianti' wines produced in other parts of Tuscany are not allowed to be called 'Classico'). There are numerous beautiful old farmhouses ('case coloniche') in this area, always splendidly sited, and often with towers (formerly dovecotes). Many of them were built in the 18C during the agricultural reforms carried out by the Grand-Duke Pietro Leopoldo. Some of them have been carefully restored in the last few decades, often by foreigners, and Chianti has become a fashionable place to live. Also in this area are many old Romanesque churches ('pieve') and feudal castles, too numerous to mention in the text. For those with time and their own transport, it is well worth deviating from the route described below to explore the magnificent surrounding countryside.

Florence is left across the Arno upstream by the new Ponte di Rovezzano, where green 'autostrada' signs for Rome should be followed. N222 passes beneath the motorway at San Piero a Ema, and ascends to (10km) *Grassina*. It continues to ascend through beautiful countryside past the golf-course of *Ugolino*. Just before *Strada* a by-road diverges right for **Impruneta** (7km; see Rte 43D). The 'Chiantigiana' continues to cross the Passo dei Pecorai (344m) into the Greve valley.—29km **Greve**, a centre of the wine trade, has a particularly attractive central market square with ample terraces above porticoes. It has a monument to Giovanni da Verrazzano (died 1528?), the explorer of the N American coast, who is commemorated also in New York. In Piazza Matteotti is a little puppet theatre which gives regular performances for children in summer. A by-road leads W to the charming little town of *Montefioralle* (1·5km), the birthplace of the Vespucci family. In the church of Santo Stefano is a 13C Madonna and Child attributed to the 'Maestro di Bagnano'. The unmade-up road continues to Badia di Passignano (see Rte 47A).— Beyond (32km) *Panzano*, a by-road left leads shortly to the *Pieve of San Leolino*, a Romanesque church with an altarpiece of the Madonna between Saints Peter and Paul, and stories from their lives, attributed to Meliore di Jacopo (mid-13C), and a triptych of the Madonna and Child with Saint Catherine of Alexandria, between Saints Peter and Paul, attributed to the 'Maestro di Panzano', both restored in 1988.

—39km A road for Radda in Chianti diverges left from the Chiantigiana.

The road ascends towards Radda in Chianti, leaving on the left a by-road for the *Castello di Volpaia* a tiny fortified hamlet (restored) in a splendid position, where an art exhibition is held in September.—**Radda in Chianti** (10km), in beautiful countryside. A road continues to the 11C *Badia di Coltibuono*, in fine woods, another centre of wine production. This road continues over the hills to descend to Montevarchi in the Arno valley, see Rte 50. An alternative route to Siena (N 408) may be reached from Radda or the Badia di Coltibuono. Off this road is *Gaiole*, a medieval village traversed by a stream, and the *Castello di Brolio* reconstructed in the 19C, and well-known for its wine.

49km *Castellina in Chianti* preserves its 15C castle and a town gate.—70km **Siena**, see Rte 48.

C. Via Empoli and Certaldo

ROAD, N67, 100km.—13km *Lastra a Signa.*—33km **Empoli**.—38km *Ponte a Elsa* (for **San Miniato**).—N429. 50km *Castelfiorentino.*—59km **Certaldo**.—72km **Poggibonsi**. From here to (100km) **Siena**, by the 'superstrada del Palio', see Rte 47A. This is not a direct route to Siena, but it takes in some interesting small towns on the way.

An alternative fast route to Empoli and San Miniato leaves Florence by the 'Firenze-Signa' exit of the 'Autostrada del Sole' and runs direct to (27km) *Empoli* and (30km) *San Miniato*. This is the 'superstrada' for Livorno, which is nearing completion, but is interrupted for a stretch near Pontedera.

RAILWAY, 97km via Empoli and Poggibonsi, recently improved, c hourly in c 1½hrs. A change is sometimes necessary at Empoli. A pretty line, but less convenient than the bus service to Siena as the station is outside the town.

The busy old road from Florence to Pisa (N 67) begins at Ponte della Vittoria (Pl. 5). From Florence to (13km) *Lastra a Signa*, see Rte 43E.—At (15km) *Ponte a Signa* an old bridge crosses the Arno to *Signa*, a village noted for straw-plait and terracotta. Road and river enter the *Gonfolina Gorge*, where the Arno cuts through Monte Albano.—25km *Montelupo Fiorentino*, at the meeting of the Pesa with the Arno, was fortified by the Florentines in opposition to the now demolished stronghold of *Capraia*, beyond the river; thus the wolf ('lupo') was to devour the goat ('capra'). The town has been famous for the production of ceramics since at least the 15C; examples of local manufacture are exhibited here in a museum opened in 1989 (Tuesday–Sunday, 14.30–19). Baccio d'Agnolo, the sculptor and architect, was born at Montelupo (1460). In the church of San Giovanni is a *Madonna enthroned with Saints Sebastian, Lorenzo, John the Baptist, and Roch by Botticelli and his workshop. On the right farther on, is the villa of *L'Ambrogiana* (1587), now an asylum, with angle towers.—30km *Pontorme* was the birthplace of Jacopo Carucci, called Pontormo (1494–1557), the painter. In the church of San Martino is a statue of the Madonna by Michele da Firenze. Also here are two Saints painted by Pontormo (and recently restored).

33km **Empoli**, is a pleasant small town (44,100 inhab.) of ancient origins, famous for its glassworks. Here in 1260 the Ghibelline party held their famous 'parliament' after their victory at Montaperti; the proposal to raze Florence to the ground was defeated by Farinata degli Uberti, who is honoured for his protest by Dante ('Inferno' X). Jacopo Chimenti, the painter, known as L'Empoli (1554–1640) was a native of the town.

In the central Piazza Farinata degli Uberti stands the COLLEGIATA (Sant'Andrea); the lower part of the façade (covered for restoration) dates from 1093, the upper part is a successful imitation carried out in the 18C by Ferdinando Ruggieri. Over the high altar is a triptych of the Madonna and Saints by Lorenzo di Bicci. Off the cloister behind the church (to the right) is the **Museo della Collegiata** to reopen in 1990. Many of the paintings have been restored. The arrangement will be changed. The works include: a lectern (1520) of English workmanship.—*Bicci di Lorenzo*, St Nicholas of Tolentino (with contemporary view of the city).—*Penitent Magdalene, polychrome wooden statue (1455); *Lorenzo Monaco*, *Madonna and Saints; *Lorenzo di Bicci*, Crucifixion; *Bicci di Lorenzo*, Madonna, *Tabernacle of St Sebastian, painted by *Francesco Botticini* with sculptures by *Antonio Rossellino*. —*Tabernacle of the Holy Sacrament, by *Francesco Botticini*, the left part finished by his son Raffaello; painted Madonnas by *Lippi* and *Nicolo di Pietro Gerini*; *Bernardo Rossellino*, *Annunciation, marble group; sculptured *Madonnas by *Mino da Fiesole* and *Tino di Camaino*.—*Masolino*, *Pietà, a superb fresco (damaged when detached from the Baptistery in 1946 and restored in 1987), and other pieces of fresco from Santo Stefano; *Gherardo Starnina*, frescoes; font of the School of Donatello.—Works by *Andrea della Robbia*.—In the church of **Santo Stefano** (usually called *Sant'Agostino*, and often closed) are *Frescoes by Masolino in the Cappella di Sant'Elena (detached in 1959 and restored in 1987). In the left transept is a Nativity by Passignano.

On the SW slope of Monte Albano, 11km N, in beautiful countryside, is the little village of **Vinci** (bus), dominated by the restored 13C castle of the Guidi. It is famous as the birthplace of Leonardo da Vinci (1452–1519). The *Castle* houses a *MUSEUM (open daily, 9.30–12, 14.30–18), beautifully rearranged in 1986. It contains numerous *Models of the machines invented by Leonardo, exhibited beside facsimiles of his drawings (well labelled, also in English). Next door is the *Biblioteca Leonardiana*, a library relating to Leonardo (open Tuesday–Friday, 15–19). The nearby church of *Santa Croce* preserves the font in which Leonardo was baptised. In the hamlet of *Anchiano*, higher up on the hill (also approached by an old path, c 2km long), amidst magnificent olive groves, is the house which is traditionally thought to be the actual birthplace. It was restored in 1952 as a humble memorial (open as for the Museum, but closed on Wednesday). In the lower town, preceded by a porch is the *Santissima Annunziata*, with an Annunciation (over the high altar) attributed to Fra Paolino da Pistoia.

Cerreto Guidi, 8km NW of Empoli, is a centre of wine production (Chianti Putto). The Villa Medici here has been restored and opened to the public (9–14; fest. 9–13; closed Monday). It is approached by a splendid double ramp built in brick to a design of Buontalenti. The early Medici grand-dukes used the palace which now contains portraits of the family, and decorations carried out in the early 20C. In the church next door (open only on Sunday) is a *Font by Giovanni della Robbia.

The Pisa road, outside the town, passes the church of *Santa Maria a Ripa*, with a St Lucy by Andrea della Robbia.—At (37·5km) *Osteria Bianca* the road and railway to Siena diverge on the left, while this road crosses the Elsa for (40km) *La Scala*, beneath **San Miniato** (22,800 inhab.), a pretty little town in a fine position. The Lombard town became the seat of the Imperial Vicariate in Tuscany. Here Countess Matilda was born in 1046. Only two towers now remain of the *Rocca* rebuilt by Frederick II; from the higher one Pier della Vigna killed himself ('Inferno', xiii). The second one now serves as the belfry of the Duomo. On the Prato del Duomo, with pretty trees, is the handsome 17C *Palazzo Vescovile* with a curved façade, the 12C *Palazzo dei Vicari dell'Imperatore* and the Romanesque brick façade of the *Duomo* (which contains 17C altarpieces and sculptures). To the left of the Duomo is the MUSEO DIOCESANO (10–12.30, 15.30–18 except Monday) into which works of art have been collected from churches in the region. Among these are: *Deodato Orlandi*, Crucifixion; remains of a frescoed Maestà by the 'Maestro degli Ordini'; *Neri di Bicci*, Madonna; *Filippo Lippi*, Crucifixion; attributed to *Verrocchio*, *Bust of Christ in terracotta; *Madonna of the girdle, attributed to the young *Andrea del Castagno; Jacopo di Michele*, *Panel painted on both sides (Flagellation, Crucifixion).—Steps lead down beneath Palazzo Vescovile to Piazza della Repubblica where the big *Seminario* has a fine façade (the painted decoration and the shops beneath have been restored). In Piazza del Popolo (reached by Via Conti) is the church of *San Domenico* which contains the tomb of Chellini (died 1461), a fine work now attributed to Pagno di Lapo Portigiani (on a model by Donatello), and frescoes and paintings by the Florentine school (including Masolino, Niccolò di Pietro Gerini, and the Maestro di San Miniato).

FROM SAN MINIATO TO PISA, 40km, N67. The Florence-Livorno 'superstrada', nearing completion (see above), follows close to this route. From San Miniato Basso N67 continues to (7km) *San Romano*, scene of the indecisive battle of 1432 between the Florentines and Sienese. There is a good collection of old pharmacy jars here.—18·5km **Pontedera** is a busy market town (26,500 inhab.) making motor-scooters. In the Caldana valley, 16km S (bus), is the little spa of **Casciana Terme** with warm anti-rheumatic waters used for both bathing and drinking.— *Vicopisano*, 8km NW of Pontedera, preserves many of its old *Fortifications, restored by Brunelleschi, and a plain early-Romanesque church (11C) with a 14C statue of the Baptist and a carved Deposition (12C, much repainted).
   At (23km) *Fornacette* the Livorno road (N67 bis) bears to the left.—25km *Cascina*, a centre of the furniture trade, beneath Monte Verruca (536m), a prominent peak of Monte Pisano, was the scene of a Florentine victory over the Pisans in 1364. The Oratorio di San Giovanni contains a cycle of frescoes by Martino di Bartolomeo (1398) and an altarpiece by Luca di Tommé (temporarily removed to Florence). *Santa Maria is a fine 12C parish church, almost unaltered.—At (28km) *San Benedetto*, the church contains a splendid English alabaster (14C).—31km *Navacchio*. To the right is the road to *Calci* (7km), at which are an 11C *Church and the *Certosa di Pisa* (adm. 9–19; winter 9–16; Sunday 9–12), a charming group of Baroque buildings, with three cloisters. In part of the monastery is a *Natural History Museum* (founded at Pisa University in the 16C; adm. by appointment weekdays 9–13).—40km **Pisa**, see Rte 46.

From Ponte a Elsa (see above) the Siena road (N429) leads S. —50km *Castelfiorentino*, a busy town (17,500 inhab.) largely rebuilt after war damage. The church of Santa Verdiana (18C) has interesting paintings, including a Madonna by Francesco Granacci. A Museo Diocescano is to be opened here, with a Madonna and Child variously attributed to Cimabue or Duccio. In the Cappella della Visitazione are frescoes by Benozzo Gozzoli and his workshop.

A pretty by-road leads E from Castelfiorentino to Florence through (12·5km) *Montespertoli* and (17·5km) *Montegufoni* where the medieval Acciaiuoli castle (with Baroque additions), purchased in 1909 by Sir George Sitwell, was the home of his three children, Edith, Osbert, and Sacheverell, until Sir Osbert's death in 1969. Many paintings from the Uffizi were stored here during the last War.—Beyond (21·5km) *Cerbaia* the road continues through a wooded valley and pine groves to the (34km) *Certosa di Galluzzo* (see Rte 43D) and (39km) *Florence*.

59km **Certaldo**, in the Elsa valley, is an old town (15,600 inhab.) noted for its associations with Boccaccio (1313–75). The author of the 'Decameron' was probably born in Paris, but his father was from Certaldo and the writer spent most of his life and died here. A house in the upper town, which is thought to have belonged to the family, was restored in the last century. Boccaccio was buried in the interesting church of *Santi Michele e Jacopo*, under an inscription written by himself. A later cenotaph (1503) was destroyed in 1783 in disapproval of his writings. A Diocescan Museum is to be opened in the Compagnia dei Bianchi building. The 15C *Palazzo Pretorio* has an attractive courtyard and frescoes by Pier Francesco Fiorentino.—A pretty by-road climbs S into the hills for San Gimignano (13km; see Rte 47A).—The main road continues to (72km) **Poggibonsi** and from there to (100km) **Siena**, see Rte 47A.

48 Siena

SIENA, with 65,600 inhabitants, capital of the Tuscan province of the same name, is second to Florence alone among the cities of Tuscany in its profusion of works of art, preserving its medieval character to a remarkable degree. It stands on a Y-shaped ridge (320m) and spreads into the adjacent valleys; the streets are consequently often steep, and to pass from one part of the city to another it is often necessary to cross a deep valley. For this reason, and also because its treasures are unusually scattered, several days are needed for an adequate visit.

Railway Station, below the city and c 1·5km N of it; bus to the centre in 7 minutes.—**Parking.** The centre has been entirely closed to traffic. Parking areas are clearly indicated at the entrances to the town; best near San Domenico (Pl. 10); also near the Stadium, the Fortezza, and La Lizza, except on market day (Wednesday) and on Sunday (when football matches are held). Other car parks at Fontebranda (Pl. 9,10) and at the Railway Station (N of Pl. 2). Permission to enter the centre of the city (for access to hotels and garages) can be obtained from the 'Vigili Urbani' (town police) at San Domenico or No. 7 Viale Tozzi.—**Buses** for various districts of the town from Piazza Gramsci (Pl. 6); for other towns (*Grosseto, Lucca, Arezzo, Florence*, etc.) from Piazza San Domenico (Pl. 6).

Hotels, mostly in N part of the town near Piazza Matteotti; others outside the walls.

Tourist Offices. **Azienda Autonoma**, 43 Via di Città (Pl. 10); *Information office*, 56 Piazza del Campo; *E.P.T.*, 92 Via dei Montanini (Pl. 6).— **Post Office** (Pl. 6), Piazza Giacomo Matteotti.

Theatres. *Dei Rinnovati*, Palazzo Pubblico, for opera.—Concerts in the *Accademia Musicale Chigiana*, 82 Via di Città, with international courses in July–September.—*English Church, St Peter's*, Via Garibaldi, occasional services.

Palio, see below.

History. Siena appears in history as *Sœna Julia*, a Roman colony founded by Augustus. Under Charlemagne the town had its own counts, and about 1125, it became a free republic, which soon entered into rivalry with Florence. The chief of the Lombard League, Pope Alexander III, being a Sienese, the town took his part against Barbarossa, who besieged it without success (1186); but afterwards, as head of the Tuscan Ghibellines, Siena helped the exiles from Florence and defeated that city at Montaperti (1260). When the Ghibellines were defeated by Charles of Anjou (1270), Siena established a Guelf oligarchy of the middle class ('popolo grosso') ruled by a Council of Nine. In 1348 the town was devastated by plague, and later it was engaged in struggles with Charles IV (1355–69); in 1399 it fell into the power of Gian Galeazzo Visconti, who was scheming to hem in Florence. After his death the city regained its liberty for a while, but Pandolfo Petrucci ('Il Magnifico') made himself autocrat in 1487. Another spell of liberty was marked by a victory over the Florentines and Clement VII (1526), but the Spaniards captured Siena in 1530, and Cosimo I de'Medici entrusted the final suppression of the Sienese to the bloodthirsty Marquis of Marignano, who took the city in 1555 after a disastrous siege of 18 months. Some 700 families, refusing to live beneath the Medicean yoke, migrated to Montalcino, where they maintained a republic until 1559 when that too was handed over to Florence by the treaty of Cateau Cambresis. From then on Siena shared the history of

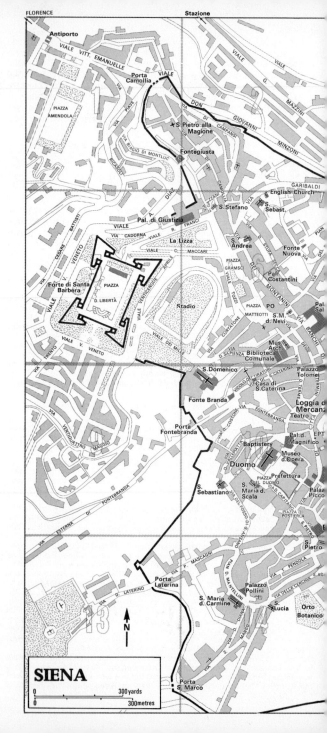

SIENA

0		300 yards
0		300 metres

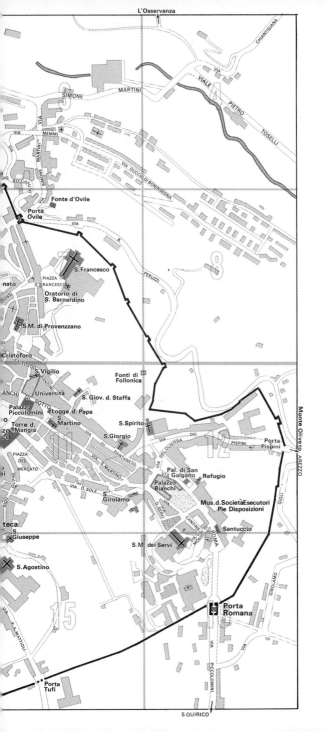

Florence and Tuscany. On 3 July 1944, French Expeditionary Forces entered Siena unopposed.—The famous natives of Siena (other than painters and sculptors, see below) include Pope Alexander III (died 1181), St Catherine (Caterina Benincasa; 1347–80), made a Doctor of the Church in 1970, Lelio Sozzini (1525–62) and his nephew Fausto (1539–64), the forerunners of positivism, and Senesino (Francesco Bernardi; 1680–1750), the castrato mezzosoprano, star of Handel opera in London.

Since the 13C the city has been divided into three *Terzi*: di Città, di San Martino, and di Camollia. (The three routes below keep only very roughly to their divisions.) Each Terzo is subdivided into wards, or *Contrade*—originally 59, but now reduced to 17. Each Contrada has a headquarters, a church, a baptismal font, a little museum, etc., and 10 are selected to compete in the famous **Corsa del Palio**, a horserace which takes place twice a year in the Campo: on 2 July (Visitation) and 16 August (the day after the Assumption). The Palio has survived as one of the most spectacular festivals in Italy, in which the whole city participates. Rivalry between the Contrade is strongly felt and provides an extraordinary atmosphere of excitement in the city throughout the summer. The events leading up to the Palio include several rehearsals of the race, and celebrations in each contrada including a banquet with the jockey the evening before the race. On the day of the Palio there is a rehearsal in the morning, the blessing of the horse and jockey in the church of each Contrada in the early afternoon, and a parade (at 17.30 in July and 16.50 in August) in Renaissance costume enlivened by 'sbandierata' (flag-throwing), and culminating in a triumphal chariot drawn by four white oxen. The race itself takes place at 19.30 in July & 19.00 in August (and consists of three laps of the Campo). The jockeys ('fantini') of the teams, which are named after the Contrade (Aquila, Pantera, Leocorno, Drago, etc.) carry distinctive colours and are dressed in modern livery. They race for the *Palio*, or banner, which goes to the winning Contrada, not to an individual. Celebrations by the winning Contrade continue for many weeks after the victory. The later, and more important, contest is believed to commemorate the victory of Montaperti; the earlier race was established in 1659. The race can be watched from the centre of the Campo (standing room only; extremely crowded and hot), or tickets purchased (expensive) for a place in the stands.

Art. Sienese ARCHITECTURE, representing a blend of the Gothic style with the Italian spirit, produced the fine Palazzo Comunale, the cathedral, and numerous palaces. The Renaissance was late in influencing Siena (chiefly through Bernardo Rossellino and Giuliano da Maiano). The architects Lorenzo Maitani (1275–1330), Francesco di Giorgio Martini (1439–1502), and Baldassare Peruzzi (1481–1537) were natives of the town.—SCULPTURE was represented by Tino di Camaino, Goro di Gregorio, and others of their school in the early 14C; later Jacopo della Quercia (1371–1438) gathered round him numerous pupils, and the school renewed its splendour (c 1450–1550) in Neroccio di Bartolomeo, Lorenzo di Pietro (Il Vecchietta), Giovanni di Stefano, Francesco Martini (see above), Giacomo Cozzarelli, Lorenzo di Mariano (Il Marrina), and Bartolomeo Neroni (Il Riccio).—In the art of woodcarving Siena held a distinguished place, thanks to Domenico di Niccolò (1363–1450) and Antonio Barili (1453–1516).

The justly famous Sienese school of PAINTING, which flourished from the second half of the 13C to the first half of the 14C, 'arte lieta fra lieto popolo', awoke in Guido da Siena; but it was in Duccio di Boninsegna (1260–1319), contemporary with Cimabue, that Sienese painting was emancipated from the spirit of the past. His celebrated 'Maestà' (now in the Museo dell'Opera del Duomo) was for a long period the inspiration of the school. The art was carried on by Simone Martini (1283–1344), the friend of Petrarch, and by Lippo Memmi (fl. 1317–47), and it reached maturity in Pietro and Ambrogio Lorenzetti (fl. 1306–50). Later came Taddeo di Bartolo, Domenico di Bartolo, Sano di Pietro, Matteo di Giovanni (the boldest painter of the school), Benvenuto di Giovanni, Lorenzo di Pietro (see above), Stefano di Giovanni (Sassetta), Francesco Martini (see above), Giovanni di Paolo, Bernardo Fungai, Giacomo Pacchiarotti, and Girolamo del Pacchia. At the beginning of the 16C Sodoma, influenced by the art of Leonardo da Vinci, introduced a new spirit among the artists already mentioned and their immediate successors (Fungai, Domenico Beccafumi, Brescianino). In the later 16C and early 17C artists active in the city included Francesco Vanni, Ventura Salimbeni, Rutilio Manetti, and Bernardino Mei. In the 19C the town produced the painter Cesare Maccari (1840–1919), and sculptor Giovanni Duprè (1817–82).

The WALLS OF SIENA survive almost entire (well seen from Via Girolamo Gigli, Via Peruzzi, etc., Pl. 16, 12, 8, & 7) but, of the original 38 gates, only eight are extant. These are, from the W, clockwise, *Porta Camollia, Porta Ovile, Porta Pispini, Porta Roma, Porta Tufi, Porta San Marco, Porta Laterina,* and *Porta Fontebranda.*

The three main streets of Siena, the Banchi di Sopra, the Banchi di Sotto, and the Via di Città, meet at the so-called *Croce del Travaglio* opposite the ***Loggia della Mercanzia** (Pl. 10; being restored), begun in 1417 from the plans of Sano di Matteo; the upper storey was added in the 17C. The five statues of saints (1456–63) are by *Antonio Federighi* and *Vecchietta,* the former of whom carved the marble bench (right) beneath the portico. In the Loggia formerly sat what was regarded as the most impartial commercial tribunal, to which even foreign States resorted.

A. The Campo and the Terzo di San Martino

Steep alleys lead down from Via di Città and Via Banchi di Sotto to the ****Campo** (Pl. 10,11), the main piazza of Siena. Paved in red brick and marble, it has the remarkable form of a fan or scallop-shell and slopes down to the Palazzo Pubblico on the flat SE side. Occupying the site of the Roman forum, it is the scene in summer of the famous Palio. It is enclosed by a picturesque medley of palaces (with restaurants, cafés, and shops); the only survivors of the original 14C buildings are the Palazzo Pubblico, and Palazzo Sansedoni, dating from 1339, at the NE end of the semicircle. The *Fonte Gaia* is a tame reproduction (1868; by Tito Sarrocchi) of the original fountain by Jacopo della Quercia (fragments of which are preserved in the Palazzo Pubblico, see below).

*Palazzo Pubblico (Pl. 11) was built in an austere but graceful Gothic style in 1297–1310, with a characteristic Sienese arcade at street level. The lower part is built of stone, the upper part of brick; the top storey of the wings was added in 1681. The central section has four stories, and the whole façade is crowned with battlements. The slim tall tower (102m high), known as the **Torre del Mangia*, was built by Muccio and Francesco di Rinaldo of Perugia in 1338–48 in ruddy brown brick. The beautiful stone cresting, possibly designed by Lippo Memmi, was constructed by Agostino di Giovanni. The tower may be climbed (see below). At its base is the *Cappella di Piazza* (1352–76), an open loggia with round arches, beautifully decorated. Most of the statues are by Mariano d'Agnolo Romanelli (1376–80). It was built to commemorate the deliverance of the city from the plague of 1348, and the chapel was heightened by Antonio Federighi in 1463–68.

The ground floor, decorated with frescoes by Bartolo di Fredi, Sano di Pietro, Vecchietta, Sodoma, and others, is used as municipal offices and is difficult of access, but the upper floor, with its superb frescoes of the Sienese school from Simone Martini and Ambrogio Lorenzetti to Sodoma, and the **Museo Civico** is open (daily 9–13.30; April–October 9–18.30; Sunday & fest. 9–13). The Torre del Mangia is also usually open at the same times.

The door beside the loggia leads into the *Cortile del Podestà* (14C). On the left is the entrance to the tower (see below), and on the right is the entrance to the Upper Floor. An iron staircase (1979) leads up to the First Floor. On the landing is a case of Sienese ceramics, mostly 17–18C. The first four rooms of the Museum were opened in 1985 to display paintings which form part of the MUSEO CIVICO

PALAZZO PUBBLICO
Upper Floor   Siena

(diagrams are provided in each room). ROOM 1. 16–18C non-Sienese and foreign schools, including works by *Felice Brusasorci*, *Johann Heinrich Schönfeld*, and *Il Bamboccio*.—R. 2 (right) and R. 3 contain 16–17C Sienese paintings including works by *Alessandro Casolani*, *Il Pomarancio*, *Ventura Salimbeni*, and frescoes and sinopie by *Sodoma* detached from the Cappella di Piazza.—R. 4. 17–18C Sienese paintings (*Domenico* and *Rutilio Manetti*) and a case of church silver.

The SALA DEL RISORGIMENTO was designed in 1878–90 and decorated under the direction of *Luigi Mussini* to illustrate the life of Victor Emmanuel II by Sienese painters including *Amos Cassioli* and *Cesare Maccari*. Here are 19C busts of famous Sienese, and sculptures by *Tito Sarrocchi* ('Flora') and *Giovanni Duprè* (reclining figure of a child).—A flight of stairs leads up to the spacious LOGGIA with a view of the covered market building and orchards beyond. It has a restored timber ceiling. Here are preserved remains (partly restored) of the very damaged Fonte Gaia, by *Jacopo della Quercia* (1408), removed from the Campo (see above).—Through a glass door may be seen the SALA DELLA SIGNORIA (being restored), the seat of the Consiglio Comunale. The 16C lunettes are decorated with frescoes illustrating events in Sienese history and the walls are hung with 19C paintings.—The SALA DI BALIA is entirely frescoed with *Scenes from the life of Pope Alexander III by *Spinello Aretino* and his son *Parri* (1407–08), including a splendid naval battle. The damaged entrance wall is being restored. Also here is an inlaid seat by *Barna di Turino*.—The ANTICAMERA DEL CONCISTORO contains some detached frescoes (one attributed to *Ambrogio Lorenzetti*), a 14C painted Crucifix, Madonna and Child attributed to *Matteo di Giovanni*, and wood statues attributed to *Jacopo della Quercia* and his workshop.—The SALA DEL CONCISTORO has a marble doorway by *Bernardo Rossellino* (1448). The *Vault is frescoed by *Beccafumi* (1529–35), illustrating heroic deeds of ancient Greece and Rome. Three large Gobelins tapestries represent the elements Earth, Air, and Fire; five other tapestries are 16C Florentine works. Above the door, Judgement of Solomon attributed to *Luca Giordano*.

In the VESTIBULE is a ruined fresco of the Madonna from the Loggia by *Ambrogio Lorenzetti*, and the gilded bronze she-wolf (part of the arms of Siena, evincing pride in her Roman origin) by *Giovanni di Turino* (c 1429), removed from the exterior of the palace. The ANTICAPPELLA is decorated with frescoes by *Taddeo di Bartolo* illustrating the Virtues and famous Roman and Greek heroes and divinities, and a colossal St Christopher. Two 15C intarsia panels and a case of goldsmiths' work (12–17C) are also displayed here.—The CAPPELLA, with a fine wrought-iron screen (1435–1445) on a design attributed to *Jacopo della Quercia*, is also frescoed by *Taddeo di Bartolo*, with scenes from the life of the Virgin (1407–08). The altarpiece is by *Sodoma*. The 15C chandelier and the carved *Stalls are by *Domenico di Niccolò* (1415–28).

The SALA DEL MAPPAMONDO was named after a circular map of the Sienese state painted for this room by Ambrogio Lorenzetti (see below). The Council met here before 1342. Here is the famouś *Maestà, the earliest work of *Simone Martini* (1315; partly repainted by him in 1321), a beautiful Madonna seated beneath a baldacchino borne by apostles and surrounded by angels and saints. It is covered for restoration in 1990. On the opposite wall is the famous fresco of *Guidoriccio da Fogliano, Captain of the Sienese army, setting out for the victorious siege of Montemassi, a delightful work (partly repainted, but recently cleaned), traditionally attributed to *Simone Martini* (1330). Since 1977 it has been the subject of a heated debate among art historians, some of whom suggest it may be a later 14C work, and therefore no longer attributable to Simone Martini. The fresco beneath, discovered in 1980, and thought to date from 1315–20, which represents the deliverance of a borgo (with a castle) to a representative of the Sienese Republic has been variously attributed to *Duccio di Boninsegna*, *Pietro Lorenzetti*, or *Memmo di Filippuccio*. The traces here of a circular composition are thought to mark the position of the lost fresco of the Sienese state which gave its name to the room (see above). On either side are *Saints Victor and Ansanus, by *Sodoma*.—On the long wall: Victory of the Sienese at Poggio Imperiale by *Giovanni di Cristofori Ghini* and *Francesco d'Andrea* (1480), and Victory at Val di Chiana, by *Lippo Vanni*, both predominantly in 'burnt sienna'. On the pilasters below (left to right): (in the angle) Blessed Bernardo Tolomei by *Sodoma* (1533); St Bernardine by *Sano di Pietro* (1450), and St Catherine of Siena by *Vecchietta* (1461).

The *SALA DELLA PACE was the room of the Nine, who ruled Siena after 1270. The remarkable allegorical *Frescoes (beautifully restored in 1983–88) by *Ambrogio Lorenzetti* (1338) are considered the most important cycle of secular paintings left from the Middle Ages. On the wall opposite the window is an Allegory of Wise Government: on the entrance wall are illustrated the effects of Good Government in the town and countryside. The city represents Siena. Opposite is an Allegory of Evil Government with its effect on the town and countryside (very damaged).—The SALA DEI PILASTRI contains 13–15C paintings including a *Maestà, a splendid huge painting by *Guido da Siena* (second half of the 13C, but dated 1221), a 13C Crucifix, part of a polyptych by *Martino di Bartolommeo*, a stained glass window with St Michael Archangel by *Ambrogio Lorenzetti*; *Niccolò di Ser Sozzo*, Annunciation; and some carved wooden painted and inlaid coffers.—The visit is back down the iron staircase.

The entrance to the tower, the *Torre del Mangia** is on the left-hand side of the Courtyard. Stairs lead up to the ticket office (adm., see above), and then out onto a little roof terrace at the foot of the tower. A stone staircase continues up past the mechanism of the clock. Higher up there is a view of the church of Santa Maria dei Servi, before the two bells are reached. Narrow wooden stairs continue right up to the top of the lantern with another bell. There is a splendid view: to the NW are the Campo and San Domenico with the tree-covered Fortezza; to the NE in the foreground the domed church of Santa Maria Provenzano and San Francesco, and a stretch of walls enclosing fields beyond. On the hill behind is the Osservanza. To the SE can be seen the church of Santa Maria dei Servi with its tall brick campanile, and orchards, and to the SW the church of Sant'Agostino and the Duomo, with the tall nave of the 'Duomo Nuovo'.

Siena and the Torre del Mangia

From the NE angle of the Campo Via Rinaldini leads to *Palazzo Piccolomini* (Pl. 11), a handsome building of the Florentine Renaissance, probably designed by Bernardo Rossellino and begun by Porrina in 1469. In the courtyard are good suspended capitals by Marrina (1509). The palazzo contains the ARCHIVIO DI STATO, one of the finest extant collections of archives. The exhibits (open weekdays 9–13; Saturday 9–12.30) include charters and other manuscripts, autographs, Boccaccio's will, and a unique series of book bindings, among them the *Tavolette di Biccherna*, the painted covers of the municipal account-books, some by the most famous artists of the 13–17C. The study room is open to students (except 15–30 August).

Opposite are the administrative offices of the *University*, founded in 1203. Behind are *San Vigilio* and the characteristic Via Sallustio Bandini, with 13C houses.

Via Banchi di Sotto leads right to the elegant *Logge del Papa* (being restored) built for Pius II by Antonio Federighi (1462), with decorations attributed to Francesco di Giorgio. Via di Pantaneto descends to the church of *San Giorgio* (Pl. 11), with an 18C façade and a campanile of 1260. Beyond the church Via dei Pispini leads left. In the piazza which opens on the left, the Renaissance church of *Santo Spirito* (Pl. 12) has a portal of 1519, the tympanum attributed to Baldassare Peruzzi, and a cupola by Giacomo Cozzarelli (1508). In the interior (S side) are paintings and frescoes by Sodoma and statues by Cozzarelli (1st chapel), and the Coronation of the Madonna by Beccafumi (3rd chapel). Beside the high altar, four Saints by Rutilio Manetti. North Side (3rd chapel), Crucifix by Sano di Pietro, and a Madonna enthroned by Andrea Vanni; 1st chapel, altarpiece attributed to Matteo Balducci.

Via dei Pispini ends at the *Porta Pispini* or *San Viene* (Pl. 12) above which are the remains of a fresco of the Nativity by Sodoma. To the left of the gate, at an angle of the city walls, is the only surviving bastion of the seven designed by Peruzzi in the 16C to strengthen the earlier defences.—The church of *Santa Eugenia*, outside the gate, has a gentle Madonna, by Matteo di Giovanni.

Vicolo del Sasso opposite Santo Spirito leads shortly to Via Roma. This leads past *Palazzo di San Galgano* (No. 47), built in the style of Giuliano da Maiano (1474; but altered), towards the *Porta Romana* (Pl. 16), an impressive double fortified gate, attributed to Agnolo di Ventura (1327). At No. 71 Via Roma are the premises of the *Società Esecutori di Pie Disposizioni* (Pl. 12), with their MUSEUM (adm. 9–12, except fest.; ring on the first floor). This society of executors of benevolent legacies is the successor to the medieval lay brotherhood of the Compagnia della Madonna, suppressed in 1785. The paintings include: a lunette showing St Catherine of Siena leading Pope Gregory XI back to Rome, by Girolamo di Benvenuto; a Crucifix by the school of Duccio; Madonna and Child by Sano di Pietro; Madonna and Child, Saints Peter and Paul, by Niccolò di ser Sozzo Tegliacci; and Holy Family by Sodoma. The custodian conducts visitors across the road to another museum opened in 1981, donated by the Bologna-Buonsignori families, which contains an eclectic collection of prehistoric material, Etruscan and Roman ceramics and glass, jewellery, Deruta majolica, Chinese porcelain, the Portrait of a Lady by Gino Severini, arms, etc.—Via Val di Montone (partly stepped) leads up to **Santa Maria dei Servi** (Pl. 16), a large church with a massive brick

campanile. From the top of the steps there is an unusual view of the
Duomo Nuovo, the campanile and Duomo, and Palazzo Pubblico.

The Renaissance INTERIOR, with nave and aisles, was planned by Peruzzi. SOUTH
AISLE. Beyond fragments of 14C frescoes, 2nd chapel, *Madonna del Bordone,
by *Coppo di Marcovaldo*, signed and dated 1261, partly repainted by a pupil of
Duccio; 5th chapel, *Massacre of the Innocents, by *Matteo di Giovanni* (1491).
SOUTH TRANSEPT, 14C Crucifix (Sienese school), and, above the Sacristy door,
Madonna and Child by Segna di Bonaventura; 2nd chapel right of high altar,
*Massacre of the Innocents, fresco by *Pietro Lorenzetti*; 2nd chapel left of high
altar, Stories from the Life of St John the Baptist, frescoed by *Pietro Lorenzetti*,
and an altarpiece of the Adoration of the Shepherds by *Taddeo di Bartolo*. In the
chapel in the N transept, Madonna del Manto by *Giovanni di Paolo* (1436). On
the wall here has been placed the *Madonna del Popolo by *Lippo Memmi*
(c 1317).

Via San Martino leads back to the Campo past the church of *San
Martino* (Pl. 11), with a façade by Giovanni Fontana (1613); it contains
altarpieces by Beccafumi (Nativity) and Guido Reni (Circumcision;
recently restored), and statues by Giovanni Antonio and Giuseppe
Mazzuoli.

B.   The Cathedral and the Terzo di Città

From the opposite side of the Campo VIA DI CITTÀ, bordered by
medieval mansions, winds upward to the S. To the left is the 14C
PALAZZO CHIGI-SARACINI (Pl. 10), housing the *Accademia Musicale
Chigiana* (concerts, see above). Exhibitions are held here periodically
of parts of the famous Chigi-Saracini *Collection of works of art.

The huge collection was formed at the end of the 18C by Galgano Saracini, and is
particularly important for its Sienese works, ranging from the 13–17C. Most of it
is now owned by the Monte dei Paschi bank (the Accademia Chigiana owns the
remaining part of it). Admission to scholars sometimes granted by previous
appointment at the head office of the Monte dei Paschi in Piazza Salimbeni (see
Rte 48/C). The paintings include: 'Maestro di Tressa' (early 13C), Madonna and
Child; *Margarito d'Arezzo*, Painted Cross; *Pisan follower of Francesco Traini*, St
Paul; works by *Mariotto di Nardo, Sano di Pietro*, and *Matteo di Giovanni*; a
tabernacle by the 'Maestro dell'Osservanza; a tondo by *Botticelli* and his
bottega; and fine works by *Sassetta*, including the *Adoration of the Magi. Later
masters represented include *Bernardino Mei*. There is also a collection of small
sculptures, drawings, archaeological material, etc.

To the right is *Palazzo Piccolomini delle Papesse* (No. 128), built by
Caterina Piccolomini, sister of Pius II, from the plans of Bernardo
Rossellino (1460–95); it is now occupied by a bank. Then comes
Palazzo Marsili of 1459. In Piazza di Postierla, a column (1487) with a
fine iron standard-holder is surmounted by a she-wolf. In Via del
Capitano (right) are the 16C *Palazzo Piccolomini Adami* (on the left, at
the corner) and the late 13C *Palazzo del Capitano* (No. 15). The street
ends in the handsome PIAZZA DEL DUOMO, the cathedral square, just
before which is (right) Piazza Jacopo della Quercia.
    The **Cathedral** (Pl. 10; open all day in summer; closed 13.15–
14.30 in winter), dedicated to the *Assumption*, is the earliest of the

great Tuscan Gothic churches, despite certain Romanesque elements. It was begun in 1196 and the main structure was complete by 1215.

Towards the close of the 13C the façade was begun on the plans of *Giovanni Pisano*, and in 1339 a scheme was adopted by which an immense nave was to be constructed S of the original church, which was to become a transept. *Lando di Pietro* and *Giovanni di Agostino* began this herculean task, but the plague of 1348 and the political misfortunes of the city compelled its abandonment. The original plan was resumed, leaving the huge unfinished nave to record the ambition of the Sienese. The existing dimensions are 89m long by 24m wide (52·5m across the transepts). The apse was completed in 1382. The upper part of the façade, in the style of the cathedral of Orvieto, was added by *Giovanni di Cecco* after 1376.

Restoration work, necessitated by the effects of time and weather, was completed in 1951. The famous inlaid pavement was strengthened and cleaned; other repairs were carried out to the façade, pinnacles, buttresses, cupola, and roof.

EXTERIOR. Marble steps, flanked by columns bearing the she-wolf of Siena (the originals by Giovanni Pisano and Urbano da Cortona are now in the Museo dell'Opera, see below), ascend to a plinth of white marble inlaid with black, on which the cathedral stands. The *FAÇADE in polychrome marble is remarkable for its magnificent statuary, mostly now replaced by copies (originals in the Museo dell'Opera del Duomo). The lower part, with three richly decorated portals of equal height and size, with triangular pediments, was designed by *Giovanni Pisano*, who, together with his pupils, was responsible for the sculptures of Prophets, Philosophers, and Patriarchs. The architrave of the main portal bears stories from the life of the Virgin, an early work by *Tino di Camaino*. The upper part of the façade, with a great rose window, was added in the second half of the 14C in a less harmonious design; in the three gables are bright 19C Venetian mosaics.—On the E side the *CAMPANILE (1313) rises from the transept (on the base of an earlier tower); its six storeys, banded in black and white, are pierced by windows whose openings increase in progression from single to sixfold.—The door into the S transept ('Porta del Perdono') bears a tondo of the Madonna and Child by *Donatello*. On the roof of the nave and S transept are copies of 14C statues of the Apostles (originals in the 'Cripta delle Statue') placed here in 1681 when they were removed from the interior and replaced there by statues by Giuseppe Mazzuoli (in turn removed in the 19C to the Brompton Oratory, London).

The dichromatic style of the exterior familiar to many Tuscan Romanesque churches is repeated with greater emphasis in the *INTERIOR. Here the elaborate use of bands of black and white marble on the walls and columns provides a magnificent effect. The round arches of the nave support pointed vaulting. Beneath the fine cornice in the nave, large stucco busts of popes were added in the 15C and 16C. The interior contains numerous important sculptural works.

*PAVEMENT. The floor of the whole church is ornamented with a remarkable series of 56 historical and other designs, of which the oldest (1369) are in simple 'graffiti' (black outlines on the white marble), while the others are inlaid with black, white, or (after 1547) colours. Some have been replaced by copies (the originals are in the Opera del Duomo). Those in the nave and aisles are usually uncovered, but the earliest parts are covered by a protective floor and are shown only from c 7–22 August. More than 40 artists, most of them Sienese, worked at this pavement; among them were *Domenico di Niccolò dei Cori* (Story of David, 1423: 2nd bay of nave, E of the

dome), *Pietro del Minella* (Death of Absalom, 1447: S transept),
Matteo di Giovanni (Massacre of the Innocents, 1481: N transept; and
Ten Sibyls, 1481–83: side aisles, with the help of *Neroccio di
Bartolomeo*, *Benvenuto di Giovanni* and others), *Pinturicchio* (Fortune, 1506: 4th bay of nave), *Antonio Federighi* (Erythaean sibyl: S
aisle), and *Beccafumi*, the most original and productive (1517–47; 35
pictures).

NAVE. The columns of the main W door are attributed to *Giovanni di
Stefano*; the reliefs of the pedestals are by *Urbano da Cortona*. The
glass of the rose window represents the Last Supper, on a cartoon by
Perin del Vaga (1549; by Pastorino de' Pastorini, a pupil of Guglielmo
de Marcillat). The two stoups near the first pillars are by *Antonio
Federighi* (1462). In the S aisle, statue of Pope Paul V (Camillo
Borghese) by *Signorini* (1605). The hexagon of the dome was
decorated at the end of the 15C with gilded statues of saints, by
Ventura di Giuliano Turapilli and *Bastiano di Francesco*, and figures
of patriarchs and prophets in chiaroscuro, by *Guidoccio Cozzarelli*
and *Benvenuto di Giovanni*. During restoration work in 1982, on the
dome sculptures were discovered on the capitals and brackets, and
attributed to *Nicola Pisano*. Farther E stands the octagonal *PULPIT, a
remarkable Gothic work by *Nicola Pisano* (1265–68), completed six
years after his famous pulpit in the Baptistery of Pisa. He was assisted
by his son *Giovanni*, and *Arnolfo di Cambio*.

Around the base of the central column are the figures of Philosophy and the
seven Liberal Arts, and at the top of the columns, the Christian Virtues,
Evangelists, and Prophets. The seven panels beautifully carved in high relief
symbolise the Redemption, with scenes from the life of Christ and two scenes of
the Last Judgement. They are divided by another series of carved figures,
including a beautiful Madonna and Child.—The elegant staircase was added in
1543 to a design of *Riccio*.

In the SOUTH AISLE, above the doorway to the campanile, is the tomb
of Bishop Tommaso Piccolomini by *Neroccio* (1484–85).—In the
SOUTH TRANSEPT are statues of Alexander III, by *Raggi* (1663), and of
Alexander VII, by *Ercole Ferrata* (1668). Here the Baroque CAPPELLA
CHIGI was built for Alexander VII in 1659–62 on a design by *Bernini* to
house the Madonna del Voto. The statues are by *Antonio Raggi* (St
Bernardine), *Ercole Ferrata* (St Catherine), and *Bernini* (St Jerome
and St Mary Magdalene). *Maratta* painted the Visitation (in very poor
condition), and the Flight into Egypt is a mosaic after a painting by the
same artist. The Madonna del Voto, a fragment of a larger painting, is
by a follower of *Guido da Siena*.

This venerated painting has been the traditional focus of entreaty of the Sienese
in time of crisis. On six occasions in their history the inhabitants have placed the
keys of their threatened city before it and prayed for deliverance. The first
occasion was before the battle of Montaperti; the latest on 18 June 1944, a
fortnight before the liberation of Siena.

CHOIR. The high altar is by *Peruzzi* (1506); the huge bronze *Ciborium by *Vecchietta* (1467–72). At the sides the uppermost angels
carrying candles are by *Giovanni di Stefano* (1488), the lower two by
Francesco di Giorgio Martini (1499). The cross and candelabra are to a
design of *Riccio* (1570). The eight candelabra in the form of angels on
brackets against the pillars of the presbytery are fine works by
Beccafumi (1548–50) and *Riccio*. The intarsia *Choir stalls are of
varying dates: 1362–97, by several artists under *Francesco del
Tonghio*; 1503, by *Giovanni da Verona*; and those by *Riccio* and his

school, 1567–70. The round window in the apse contains *Stained glass (1288) from cartoons by *Duccio*, probably the oldest existing stained glass of Italian manufacture.—To the left of the altar is the entrance to the SACRISTY and CHAPTER HOUSE (sometimes shown by the sacristan), the former with frescoes (1410–12) by *Nicola di Naldo, Gualtieri di Giovanni*, and *Benedetto di Bindo*. Beyond a vestibule with a fine bust of Alexander VII by Melchiorre Caffà, a follower of Bernini, is the Chapter House, with two interesting paintings showing San Bernardino in Siena, by *Sano di Pietro*, and a Madonna with Saints, attributed to *Giacomo Pacchiarotti*.

In the NORTH TRANSEPT is the *Tomb of Cardinal Riccardo Petroni (died 1314), by *Tino di Camaino*, the design of which was frequently copied throughout the 14C. In front is the bronze pavement *Tomb of Bishop Giovanni Pecci, signed by *Donatello* (1426). The statue of Pius II is by *Giuseppe Mazzuoli* (1698); that of Pius III, by *Pietro Balestra* (1706). The *CAPPELLA DI SAN GIOVANNI BATTISTA (light) is a graceful Renaissance structure by *Giovanni di Stefano* (1482). The elegant portal is by *Marrina* (and the classical bases to the columns by *Antonio Federighi*); the wrought-iron gate is the work of *Sallustio Barili*. In the interior are (restored) frescoes by *Pinturicchio* including three scenes from the life of St John the Baptist, and portraits of two kneeling figures (the one shown in the robes of the Order of St John is Alberto Aringhieri, the founder). The statue of St Ansanus is by *Giovanni di Stefano*; that of St Catherine is by *Neroccio*. The bronze statue of *St John the Baptist is one of *Donatello's* later works (1457) which recalls his St Mary Magdalene in Florence. The font is by *Antonio Federighi* (after 1484).

In the NORTH AISLE is the entrance to the *LIBRERIA PICCOLOMINI (open every day 10–13, 14.30–17; summer 9–19), one of the most delightful creations of the Renaissance, founded in 1495 by Cardinal Francesco Piccolomini (afterwards Pius III) to receive the library of his uncle Aeneas Silvius Piccolomini (Pius II). Its marble façade is by *Marrina* (1497); above the altar (right) was placed a relief of St John the Evangelist by *Vecchietta*. The large fresco above by *Pinturicchio* shows the coronation of Pius III.

The bright interior consists of a hall decorated with colourful and highly decorative *Frescoes by *Pinturicchio* and his pupils (1502–9) in an excellent state of preservation. They represent ten scenes from the life of Pius II (beginning to the right of the window): 1. Aeneas Silvius goes to the Council of Basle; 2. He presents himself as envoy to James II of Scotland; 3. He is crowned as poet by Frederick III (1442); 4. He is sent by the Emperor to Eugenius IV (1445); 5. As Bishop of Siena, he is present at the meeting in 1451 of the Emperor Frederick and his betrothed Eleonora of Portugal outside the Porta Camollia; 6. He is made Cardinal by Calixtus III (1456); 7. He becomes Pope (1458); 8. He proclaims a Crusade at Mantua (1459); 9. He canonises St Catherine of Siena (1460); 10. He arrives, dying, at Ancona (1464). The beautiful vault decoration is also by *Pinturicchio* and his pupils.—In the centre is the celebrated antique group of the *Three Graces, a Roman copy of an original by Praxiteles, acquired in Rome by Cardinal Francesco Piccolomini. It served as a model to Pinturicchio, Raphael, and Canova. Here are exhibited the *Choir Books of the cathedral and the Scala hospital, illuminated by *Liberale da Verona, Girolamo da Cremona, Sano di Pietro*, and others.

Farther W the great *Piccolomini Altar by *Andrea Bregno* (1485) has statuettes in the four lower niches of *St Peter, St Pius, St Gregory, and *St Paul, documented early works of *Michelangelo* (1501–4), who may also have worked on the figure of St Francis above, begun by *Pietro Torrigiani*. The Madonna and Child at the top is thought to be *Jacopo della Quercia's* earliest work (c 1397–1400). The painted Madonna

and Child over the altar (framed by marble reliefs) is attributed to
Paolo di Giovanni Fei (1381).—Near the W end, statue of Marcellus II,
by *Domenico Cafaggi* (1591).

In the piazza, opposite the cathedral, stands the *Ospedale di Santa
Maria della Scala* (Pl. 10) of ancient foundation. The façade is covered
for restoration and the hospital is in the process of being moved. There
are numerous ambitious projects to transform the huge edifice into a
museum. The Pilgrims' Hall has a fine series of frescoes by Domenico
di Bartolo (restored in 1987); in the adjoining *Church* (1252; enlarged
in 1466) are a bronze figure of Christ by Vecchietta (on the high altar),
an apse fresco by Sebastiano Conca, and an organ-case by Peruzzi.
Along the other side of the piazza is *Palazzo Reale*, by Buontalenti,
now the Prefettura. The unfinished nave of the 'Duomo Nuovo' (see
above) gives some idea of the size and beauty of the projected
building; its S aisle has been converted into the *Museo dell'Opera
del Duomo* (Pl. 10; adm. daily 9–13.30; mid-March–October,
9–19.30).

Ground Floor. SALA DELLE STATUE. Original *Statues and sculptural fragments
from the façade of the cathedral, by *Giovanni Pisano* and his school, constituting
one of the most important groups of Italian Gothic sculpture. In the centre,
bas-relief of the Madonna and Child with St Anthony Abbot and Cardinal
Antonio Casini, by *Jacopo della Quercia*. Works by *Urbano da Cortona* (St Peter,
St Bernardine in glory); (left wall) fragments of four symbolic animals sculpted
by *Giovanni Pisano*; (near the grille), two wolves nursing twins, from the
columns outside the Duomo (see above), one attributed to *Giovanni Pisano*, and
the other by *Urbano da Cortona*. In the floor, fragments of the original pavement
of the Duomo. At the end, altarpiece of the Baptism of Christ, by *Andrea del
Brescianino* (1524).—In a small room off the entrance hall, kneeling figure of St
John the Evangelist, by *Giacomo Cozzarelli* (being restored); and St John the
Baptist, statue in wood by *Francesco di Giorgio Martini* (1464).
    First Floor. SALA DI DUCCIO. **La Maestà, by *Duccio di Buoninsegna*
(1308–11), a celebrated work painted on both sides, now divided to show both
faces: Madonna and Child enthroned and the Story of the Passion. Until 1505 it
hung over the high altar in the Cathedral. Also *Birth of the Virgin, by *Pietro
Lorenzetti* and *Madonna and Child, an early work by *Duccio* (from the church of
Santa Cecilia in Crevole).—The other rooms contain illuminated MSS,
drawing projects related to the cathedral and Piazza del Campo, and a drawing
of the pavement of the Cathedral by *Giovanni Paciarelli* (1884); and gilded wood
statuettes of the Madonna and Child and four Saints, by *Jacopo della Quercia*
and his workshop (from the Church of San Martino).
    Second Floor. The SALA DEL TESORO contains croziers, reliquaries (including
the Reliquary of St Galgano from the end of the 13C); paxes, crucifixes (among
which *Christ on the Cross in wood by *Giovanni Pisano*), etc. Sculptural works
include three busts of Saints, by *Francesco di Valdambrino* in polychrome wood
(1409), and 12 statuettes of Saints by *Mazzuoli* (models for the marble statues
now in the Brompton Oratory, London).
    In a small room (grille usually locked) off the Treasury; works by *Beccafumi*,
three panels by *Sassetta*, and a detached fresco of the Pietà, by *Vecchietta*.—
SALA DELLA MADONNA DAGLI OCCHI GROSSI. In the centre, the *Madonna dagli
Occhi Grossi, by an unknown Sienese painter (c 1210–20). It adorned the high
altar before Duccio's Maestà. *Ambrogio Lorenzetti*, Four Saints; *Giovanni di
Paolo*, St Jerome; *Simone Martini*, *Blessed Agostino Novello and four Scenes of
his miracles (from the church of Sant'Agostino); *Gregorio di Cecco*, Polyptych;
Matteo di Giovanni, Madonna and Child; *Sano di Pietro*, Madonna and Child
with Saints; *Maestro della Città di Castello*, Madonna and Child.—SALA DEI
CONVERSARI. Works by *Matteo di Giovanni*; *Beccafumi*; *St Paul; *Il Pomerancio*,
Madonna and Child with Saints; altar frontals.—The SALA DEI PARATI contains
vestments and a marble statue of a child by *Giovanni Duprè*. From here is
reached the Scala del 'Falciatore', a stair which winds up to the façade of the
'new' cathedral (extensive views of the city and countryside).

Beyond a beautiful Gothic *Portal with sculptures attributed
to Giovanni d'Agostino, between the incomplete nave and the

cathedral, a steep flight of steps constructed in 1451 descends to the Baptistery. Half-way down is the entrance to the so-called 'CRIPTA DELLE STATUE' (usually open in summer at the same time as the Museum). Here may be seen part of the exterior wall of the Duomo before it was enlarged, and remains of the crypt with fresco fragments of the Madonna and Saints and scenes from the Passion by a follower of Guido da Siena (c 1270–80; the earliest known frescoes of the Sienese school). The statues of Apostles displayed here, formerly on the outside of the cathedral, are by followers of Giovanni Pisano.—At the bottom of the steps is the *__Baptistery__ (Pl. 10; beneath part of the cathedral) with a noble but unfinished façade by *Jacopo di Mino del Pellicciaio* (1382).

The INTERIOR (closed 13–15), finished c 1325 probably by *Camaino di Crescentino*, is frescoed in the upper part and vault by *Vecchietta* and his school (repainted in the 19C). The beautiful hexagonal *FONT is one of the most interesting sculptural works of the early Renaissance (1417–30). The gilded panels in relief illustrate the life of St John the Baptist: the Angel announcing the birth of the Baptist to Zacharias, by *Jacopo della Quercia*; Birth of the Baptist, and his preaching, by *Giovanni di Turino*; Baptism of Christ and St John in Prison, both by *Lorenzo Ghiberti*; *Herod's Feast, by *Donatello*. The six statues at the angles are by *Donatello* (Faith and Hope), *Giovanni di Turino* (Justice, Charity, and Prudence), and *Goro di Ser Neroccio* (Fortitude). The marble tabernacle was designed by *Jacopo della Quercia* who carved the five statues of Prophets in niches and the crowning statue of the Baptist. The six bronze angels are by *Donatello* and *Giovanni di Turino*.

Immediately E of the Baptistery is the *Palazzo del Magnifico*, built for Pandolfo Petrucci from the plans of Cozzarelli, who designed also the bronze ornaments of the façade (1504–8).

From the cathedral square Via del Capitano leads to Piazza di Postierla. Beyond this square extends Via San Pietro, on the left of which is the handsome 14C *__Palazzo Buonsignori__, restored in 1848. The palace houses the **__Pinacoteca__ (Pl. 10,11), the most important gallery for the study of the great Sienese masters, all of whom are well represented. The works by Sodoma are also important. The gallery is open daily except Monday, 8.30–19; fest. 8.30–13; the display is chronological. Many of the paintings have been restored; others are in the course of restoration.

SECOND FLOOR. ROOM I. *1. Altar frontal, partly in relief, representing Christ blessing between symbols of the Evangelists and six scenes from the Passion, the first securely dated work (1215) of the Sienese school; 597. Crucifix, also with six Passion scenes (first years of 13C); works of the *School of Guido da Siena*—RII. *Guido da Siena*, *16. Madonna and Child, dated 1262, 7. Reredos, Madonna and Saints; *Guido da Siena and assistants*, 9–13. Scenes from the Life of Christ; and other works of the school of Guido.—RIII. *28. *Duccio di Buoninsegna and assistants*, Polyptych of the Madonna and Saints; 39. *Ugolino di Nerio* (attributed), Dossal; *Niccolò di Segna*, 38. Four Saints, 46. Crucifix (1345); 47. *Duccio di Buoninsegna and assistants*, Polyptych, Madonna and Saints, a late work; 21. *Segna di Bonaventura*, Crucifix (from the church of San Giusto in Siena).—RIV. *20. *Duccio*, the 'Madonna dei Francescani', a tiny work of jewel-like luminosity, considered to be one of his masterpieces (c 1285; much ruined); 18. *School of Duccio* (attributed to the 'Maestro di Città di Castello'), Madonna and Child (from the church of San Pellegrino, Siena); 40. *Segna di Bonaventura*, Four Saints; works attributed to the *Maestro di Città di Castello*; *Ugolino di Nerio*, 36. Crucifix, 34. Crucifixion and St Francis. —RV. Minor painters of the 14C, including *Bartolo di Fredi* and *Luca di Tommè*.

RVI (temporarily closed). *Simone Martini*, Madonna and Child (from the Pieve of San Giovanni Battista in Lucignano d'Arbia); 595. *Lippo Memmi*, Madonna.—RVII. In the main room: 76. *Maestro d'Ovile*, Madonna and Child; 598. *Ambrogio Lorenzetti*, Crucifix (very damaged); *Paolo di Giovanni Fei*, 116. Birth of the Virgin and Saints, 300. Madonna and Child with Saints; *Maestro d'Ovile*, 61. Assumption, St Peter enthroned between Saints (from the church of San Bartolomeo a Sestano). In the side rooms: *Ambrogio Lorenzetti*, 77. Madonna and Child between Saints Mary Magdalene and Dorothy, 605. Madonna and Child; works by his school. 147. *Pietro Lorenzetti*, Crucifixion.— *Pietro Lorenzetti*, *Madonna enthroned (from the church of Sant'Ansano a Dofano, near Montaperti), 578–9. Saints Agnes and Catherine of Alexandria, two panels from a polyptych; *Ambrogio Lorenzetti*, 88. Annunciation, the last dated work by the artist (commissioned in 1344), 70–1. Two small landscapes (a city by the sea, and a castle on the edge of a lake), perhaps part of a larger decoration, 65. Madonna between Saints and Doctors of the church.—RVIII. *Pietro Lorenzetti*, 50. Madonna and Child with Saints.—The first arm of the corridor (RIX; being rearranged) displays works of the Sienese and Florentine schools, including 119–25. *Spinello Aretino*, Coronation and Dormition of the Virgin, parts of a polyptych (in restoration). To the right opens RX (temporarily closed), comprising the Chapel, with a good terracotta of St Mary Magdalen attributed to Giacomo Cozzarelli, and the Antechapel: *Paolo di Giovanni Fei*, 137. Triptych, Mystical marriage of St Catherine, 146. Diptych.—RXI (temporarily closed). *Taddeo di Bartolo*, 55. Crucifix, *128. Triptych, *131. Annunciation, Dormition, and Saints Cosmas and Damian (signed and dated 1409); 133. *Andrea di Bartolo* (attributed), Nativity and Resurrection.

Second arm of the corridor (also being rearranged): 60. *Bernardo Daddi*, Triptych, dated 1336; 157. *Lorenzo Monaco*, Madonna and Saints (in restoration); *164. *Domenico di Bartolo*, Seated Madonna with angel musicians (dated 1433); 171. *Michelino da Besozzo*, Marriage of St Catherine (the only signed work by this artist). From the chapel end opens RXII, devoted to *Giovanni di Paolo*: 173. St Nicholas of Bari and other saints (signed and dated 1453), *200. Crucifixion (signed and dated 1440).—RXIII. *Giovanni di Paolo*, 206. Madonna dell'Umiltà, 172. Last Judgement, *Sassetta*, 9. Presentation in the Temple, 95, 87. Prophets, 168–9. Saints, 167. Last Supper, 166. Temptation of St Anthony (all from an altarpiece painted in 1423–26).—RXIV. *Neroccio*, 295, 285, 281. Three paintings of the Madonna and Child with Saints; *Matteo di Giovanni*, *286. Madonna and Child with angels (signed and dated 1470); *Francesco di Giorgio Martini*, 288. Madonna and Child with an Angel, 277. Annunciation; 400. *Matteo di Giovanni*, Madonna and Child with Saints and angels; 437. *Francesco di Giorgio Martini*, Nativity and Saints; 280. *Matteo di Giovanni*, Madonna and Child; 282.*Neroccio*, Madonna and Child (signed and dated 1476); 432. *Matteo di Giovanni*, Maestà. In the centre, 278. *Neroccio*, Madonna and Child.—RXV. Late 15C works including (414b.) an Adoration of Shepherds by *Matteo di Giovanni*.

RRXVI–XVIII display works by *Sano di Pietro*: in RXVI notably (237. and 224.) Madonnas; in RXVII, 227. Assumption with St Thomas receiving the girdle (an early work), 255. Triptych, Madonna and Child amid saints with (above) Christ, and an Annunciation, and (below) scenes from the Life of St Blaise (signed and dated 1449); in RXVIII, 246. Polyptych, the first securely dated work by the artist (1444), *241. The Madonna appearing to Pope Calixtus III (1456). RXIX. *Vecchietta*, 210. Madonna and Child with Saints, (in the centre) *204. Painted cupboard for reliquaries (from Santa Maria della Scala) with Scenes from the Passion and lives of the Saints; 440. *Francesco di Giorgio Martini*, Coronation of the Virgin.

On the stairs down to the **First Floor**, are fresco fragments by *Domenico di Bartolo* from the Ospedale di Santa Maria della Scala. RXX. 309. *Girolamo da Cremona*, Annunciation; 581. *Benvenuto di Giovanni* (attributed), Noli me tangere.—RXXIII–RXXVI are temporarily closed. RXXIII. Umbrian and Umbrian-Sienese schools. 426. *Giacomo Pacchiarotti*, Visitation; 495. *Pinturicchio*, Holy Family with the young St John; *Girolamo Genga*, 333, 334. Ransom of prisoners, and Flight of Aeneas and Anchises from Troy (frescoes from Palazzo del Magnifico Pandolfo Petrucci).—LOGGIA (RXXIV). *Francesco Maffei*, Allegorical works from the Palazzo Reale; 633. *Giuseppe Bazzani* (18C), Deposition.—RXXV. *Rutilio Manetti*, 626. St Eligius among the plague-stricken, 625. Martyrdom of St Ansanus; 634. *Simondio Salimbeni* (attributed), St Bernardinus writing the Holy Name of Jesus.

RXXXVI (Belvedere; views of the city). 61. *Rutilio Manetti*, The Vestal demonstrates her innocence (from the Palazzo Reale).—RXXVII. Works of 16C Florentine artists.—RXXVIII. *Brescianino*, 650–2. Charity, Hope, Fortitude.—RXXIX. Works of 16C Sienese artists.—RXXX. 350. *Girolamo del Pacchia*, Madonna and Child; 512. *Sodoma*, Nativity.—RXXXI–XXXIV are closed. RXXXI contains: *352. *Sodoma*, Scourging of Christ (fresco from the cloister of San Francesco), a superb work from the period 1511–14.—RXXXII. 413. *Sodoma*, Deposition.—RXXXIII. 354. *Sodoma*, Judith; *Beccafumi*, 420. St Catherine receiving the Stigmata, 405. Birth of the Virgin; 307. *Francesco Vanni*, Self-portrait.—RRXXXIV–XXXVII are in the course of rearrangement. RXXXV is used for exhibitions. Here are displayed the splendid huge *Cartoons by *Beccafumi* for the pavement of the Duomo (restored). In RXXXVII, *Beccafumi*, *427. Descent into Hell, and St Michael and the Rebellion of the Angels.—In a room on the **Third Floor** the small paintings of the COLLEZIONE SPANNOCCHI, formed in the 17C, have been arranged. *Dürer*, St Jerome (a signed work); *Lorenzo Lotto*, *Nativity; *Francesco Furini*, Mary Magdalene; Flemish works; *Giovanni Battista Moroni*, Two portraits of gentlemen; *Bernardo Strozzi*, St Francis; *Paris Bordone*, *Annunciation, Holy Family; *Bartolommeo Montagna*, Madonna and the Redeemer (two fragments of a larger work); *Palma Giovane*, The Serpent of bronze (signed and dated 1598); *Padovanino*, Rape of Europa; *16C Flemish school*, Portrait of a jeweller; *Girolamo Mazzola Bedoli*, Portrait of a young man.

Next to the Pinacoteca is the church of *San Pietro alle Scale* (Pl. 14), rebuilt in the 18C, with a fine altarpiece, the *Flight into Egypt by Rutilio Manetti, and fragments of a polyptych by Ambrogio Lorenzetti. The road leads down to the *Arco di Sant'Agostino*, beyond which is the church of **Sant'Agostino** (Pl. 15), a church dating from 1258. From the terrace there is a good view of the town and countryside. The church has been closed since 1982, but is unlocked on request by a custodian (ring four times at No. 1 in the piazza).

The attractive bright INTERIOR was remodelled in 1749 by *Vanvitelli*. South Side. 1st altar, *Astolfo Petrazzi*, Communion of St Jerome; 2nd altar, *Perugino*, *Crucifixion. The *PICCOLOMINI CHAPEL has three beautiful Sienese works: an *Epiphany by *Sodoma*, a *Massacre of the Innocents, by *Matteo di Giovanni* (1482), and a lunette fresco of the *Madonna seated among Saints by *Ambrogio Lorenzetti*. The Pala of the Blessed Agostino Novello by Simone Martini, also painted for the chapel is now in the Museo dell'Opera del Duomo.—4th altar, *Ventura Salimbeni*, Calvary. In the S transept the Cappella Bichi has two splendid monochrome frescoes of the Birth of the Virgin and the Nativity, attributed to *Francesco di Giorgio Martini* (discovered in 1978). Above are two monochrome lunettes by *Signorelli*. The majolica pavement dates from 1488. In the adjacent chapel, 15C wood statue of the Madonna and Child (removed for restoration). The High Altar is by *Flaminio del Turco*. Beneath it is a reliquary of the Beato Agostino Novello. NORTH TRANSEPT. In the 1st chapel, a fresco with a view of Jerusalem has recently been discovered. 2nd chapel, fresco fragment by *Bartolomeo Neroni* (Il Riccio) of a sepulchral monument; and *Rutilio Manetti*, Temptations of St Anthony. The wooden statues in the transepts, one of which is attributed to *Jacopo della Quercia* have been removed for restoration. NORTH AISLE. 3rd altar, *Francesco Vanni*, Baptism of Constantine; (beyond the door), *Carlo Maratta*, Conception; *Giovanni Francesco Romanelli*, Adoration of the Shepherds.

In the Prato di Sant'Agostino is the entrance (No. 4) to the *Accademia dei Fisiocritici*, with geological, mineralogical, and zoological collections (open weekdays 9–13, 15–18). From Sant'Agostino Via Sant'Agata, continued by the picturesque Via Giovanni Duprè, descends to Piazza del Mercato (Pl. 11), from which the Palazzo Pubblico is seen from the rear.—To the SE of Sant'Agostino Via Pier Andrea Mattioli leads past the entrance (No. 4) to the *Orto Botanico* (Pl. 14), transferred here in 1856 (shown on guided tours, weekdays, 8–13, 15–17) to the *Porta Tufi* (Pl. 15).

From the Prato di Sant'Agostino Via della Cerchia leads SW towards the church of *Santa Maria del Carmine* (Pl. 14), probably rebuilt by Peruzzi. It contains (S side) a Nativity by Bartolomeo Neroni, a niche frescoed by Gualtieri di Giovanni with angels with musical instruments (the Madonna in the centre has been destroyed), and a splendid *St Michael by Beccafumi. At the extreme E end, the Madonna dei Mantellini (c 1240) is set into a painting of Saints by Francesco Vanni. On the North Side is an Ascension of Christ by Girolamo del Pacchia.—Opposite is *Palazzo Pollini* (1537), also by Peruzzi. Pian dei Mantellini, continued by Via del Fosso di Sant'Ansano, curves N past fields planted with olives and vines to *San Sebastiano* (Pl. 10; not always open), a small Renaissance church by Domenico Ponsi (1507) with good paintings and a reliquary of 1379 in its attractive interior. Via di Valle Piatta and (left) Via del Costone descend to the *Fonte Branda*, a spring mentioned as early as 1081 and covered over in 1248 with brick vaults by Giovanni di Stefano. The water is channelled from a large reservoir. This marks the entrance to the Terzo di Camollia. On the hill above San Domenico is conspicuous.

A pretty little lane leads uphill (right) from the spring and Vicolo dei Tiratori passes under the house of St Catherine (entrance in Costa Sant'Antonio). The rooms of the **Casa di Santa Caterina** (Pl. 10) were converted into small chapels in 1464. The house is open daily 7–12.30, 15.15–18.

Caterina Benincasa (1347–80), or Catherine of Siena, was the daughter of a dyer and took the veil at the age of eight. Her visions of the Redeemer, from whom she received the stigmata and, like her Alexandrian namesake, a marriage-ring, have been the subject of countless paintings. Her eloquence persuaded Gregory XI to return from Avignon to Rome, and her letters (preserved in the Biblioteca Comunale; see below) are models of style as well as of devotion. She died in Rome, was canonised in 1461, and in 1939 was proclaimed patron saint of Italy. She was made a Doctor of the Church in 1970, the first female Saint, with St Teresa of Avila, to be given this distinction.

The charming little LOGGIA was built perhaps by *Peruzzi* but altered by *Giovanni Battista Pelori* (1533). Adjoining it is a portico constructed in 1941. Here is (left) the ORATORIO DELLA CUCINA, the family kitchen, with the most interesting decorations. The altarpiece is by *Fungai*, and the frescoes by followers of Sodoma, and (W wall) paintings by *Riccio, Francesco Vanni, Salimbeni*, and others. Opposite is the ORATORIO DEL CROCIFISSO, on the site of the saint's orchard, with a Crucifixion (13C Pisan school), before which St Catherine received the stigmata at Pisa in 1375. Stairs lead down to the ORATORIO DELLA CAMERA, St Catherine's cell, and the ORATORIO DELLA CONTRADA DELL'OCA (or church of Santa Caterina in Fontebranda; usually closed, but sometimes open in the afternoon), which was the dyer's workshop. Here is a polychrome statue of the saint by *Neroccio*, a fresco of St Catherine receiving the stigmata by *Girolamo del Pacchia*, and five angels by *Sodoma*.

From the house San Domenico (described below) can be reached from Costa Sant'Antonio by taking Vicolo del Campaccio through the first archway on the left, a lane which climbs up above St Catherine's house to Via Camporegio.

Via di Santa Caterina runs W and E, below St Catherine's House. From the house Via delle Terme leads back to the Croce del Travaglio.

C. The Terzo di Camollia

Via Banchi di Sopra leads N from the Croce to Piazza Tolomei, where from the 11C the Sienese parliament used to assemble. The magistrates of the Republic officiated in the adjoining church of *San Cristoforo* (Pl. 7), a Romanesque church much rebuilt in the 18C, with a pretty cupola. It contains a good Madonna with Saints by Girolamo del Pacchia (1508), a panel of St George and the Dragon (15C Sienese school), and a 14C wooden Crucifix. Opposite stands *Palazzo Tolomei* (Pl. 10), one of the oldest Gothic palaces in Siena (now owned by a bank), begun c 1205 and restored some 50 years later. Via del Moro, flanking San Cristoforo, descends to Piazza Provenzano Salvani (from which a stretch of the city walls can be seen). Here is the church of *Santa Maria di Provenzano* (Pl. 7; 1594; closed), with a pretty exterior and a cupola. It contains a much venerated 15C terracotta relief of the Madonna. Via Provenzano Salvani continues to Via dei Rossi and (right) Piazza San Francesco (good view of the Osservanza), with the large Gothic church of **San Francesco** (Pl. 7), built in 1326–1475, all but destroyed in the fire of 1655, and afterwards used as a barracks for a long period. In 1885–92 it was restored; the façade is by Vittorio Mariani and Gaetano Ceccarelli (1894–1913).

The cold interior contains 14–15C fresco fragments in the nave, and (in the choir) portrait-busts of the father and mother of Pius II (Aeneas Silvius Piccolomini), sole relics of their tomb by *Francesco di Giorgio Martini*. The first and third chapels in the N transept contain frescoes by *Pietro* and *Ambrogio Lorenzetti* (c 1331). In the 1st chapel in the S transept is a painting of the Madonna and Child by *Andrea Vanni* (light on right). The Renaissance cloisters have been restored to house the Faculty of Political Science of the University.
    To the right of the church stands the **Oratorio di San Bernardino** (Pl. 7; 15C), on the spot where the saint preached (apply to the doorkeeper next door; but usually closed). The LOWER CHAPEL is painted with frescoes by various artists (17C), representing the saint's life; it contains also a Madonna and Saints by *Brescianino* and terracotta statues of Saints Catherine and Bernardine. In the vestibule on the first floor is a standard by *Francesco Vanni*, and a bas-relief signed by *Giovanni di Agostino* (1341).—The *UPPER CHAPEL*, beautifully decorated by *Ventura Turapilli* (after 1496), contains good frescoes, mainly by *Sodoma*, and others by *Beccafumi* and *Girolamo del Pacchia* (1518–32). Here, also is a *Madonna by *Sano di Pietro*.

To the N of San Francesco is the 14C *Porta Ovile*. Outside it is the picturesque *Fonte d'Ovile* (Pl. 7; 1262), while within the walls, in Via Pian d'Ovile, is the brick *Fonte Nuova* of 1293.
    From Via Vallerozzi the Via dell'Abbadia passes *San Donato*, a church with a 12C cupola. Via dei Rossi, arched at either end, returns to Via Banchi di Sopra, off which a turning (right) leads to Piazza Salimbeni (Pl. 6). Here are the Gothic *Palazzo Salimbeni* (centre), the *Palazzo Spannocchi* (right), begun by Giuliano da Maiano (1473) and completed in 1880 by Giuseppe Partini, and the *Palazzo Tantucci* (left), by Bartolomeo Neroni (1548). These palaces form the seat of the MONTE DEI PASCHI, a banking establishment founded in 1624, which owns an interesting collection of works of art (adm. only with special permission). The bank also owns most of the Chigi Saracini Collection (see Rte 48/B). Farther on, the little oratory of *Santa Maria delle Nevi* (Pl. 6; usually locked), an elegant Renaissance building (1471) attributed to Francesco di Giorgio Martini, contains an *Altarpiece (Our Lady of the Snows) by Matteo di Giovanni (1477).

Via della Sapienza descends SW from Piazza Salimbeni passing the **Biblioteca Comunale** (Pl. 6; open weekdays 9–20; Saturday 9–14). This library contains over 100,000 volumes and 5000 MSS, as well as illuminated missals, breviaries, and books of hours, St Catherine's letters, a 7C papyrus from Ravenna, drawings by Peruzzi and Beccafumi, a work by Dante with illuminations by Botticelli, and fine examples of bookbinding.—Adjoining the library is the *Museo Archeologico Etrusco* (9–14, fest. 9–13; but the museum is to be moved to Santa Maria della Scala), a collection of Etruscan and Roman antiquities including the Bargagli Etruscan collection from Sarteano. At the top of the hill of Camporegio stands the austere Gothic church of **San Domenico** (Pl. 10), begun in 1226, enlarged, damaged, and altered in successive centuries. The campanile dates from 1340. From the edge of the hill there is a view of the Duomo and Palazzo Pubblico above old houses on a hillside.

Internally it is built after the usual Dominican form, with a wide aisleless nave, transepts, and a shallow choir with side chapels. A chapel at the W end contains the only authentic portrait of St Catherine, by her contemporary and friend, *Andrea Vanni*; in this chapel she assumed the Dominican habit and several of her miracles occurred. On the S side opens the CAPPELLA DI SANTA CATERINA. On the entrance arch, Saints Luke and Jerome, by *Sodoma*. The tabernacle on the altar, by *Giovanni di Stefano* (1466) encloses a reliquary containing St Catherine's head. On the right and left of the altar are celebrated *Frescoes by *Sodoma* (1526), representing the saint in ecstasy and swooning. The pilasters have good grotesques. On the left wall, the saint interceding for the life of a young man brought to repentance, also by *Sodoma*; on the right wall, *Francesco Vanni*, the saint liberating a man possessed.—At the end of the S aisle is a *Nativity by *Francesco di Giorgio Martini*. Stairs lead down to the huge crypt (usually closed), begun in the 14C. Above the high altar is a fine *Tabernacle, with two angels, by *Benedetto da Maiano* (c 1475; difficult to appreciate because of the incongruous stained glass in the E windows). In the 1st and 3rd chapels right of the altar have been hung fragmentary remains of frescoes by *Andrea Vanni* and *Lippo Memmi*, detached from the cloister, and in the 1st chapel to the right is a triptych of the Madonna and Child with Saints Jerome and John the Baptist by *Matteo di Giovanni*. In the 2nd chapel left of the altar, incongruous 18C frescoes by *Giuseppe Nasini* surround St Barbara enthroned between angels and Saints Mary Magdalene and Catherine; opposite a Madonna and Child with four Saints by *Benvenuto di Giovanni*. On the last altar on the N side, *Sodoma*, Four Saints and God the Father (surrounding a 14C Madonna and Child).

From Piazza San Domenico Viale dei Mille leads above the *Stadium* on the floor of the valley, to the huge **Fortezza Medicea** (Pl. 5), or *Forte di Santa Barbara*, built for Cosimo I de'Medici by Baldassarre Lanci in 1560. The views from here over the city and the surrounding country are delightful, especially at sunset. In the vaults of the fortezza is the *Enoteca Italica*, a permanent exhibition of Italian wines (open 15–midnight). To the NE of the fortress extends the LIZZA (Pl. 5,6), a small but attractive public park, with a good statue of Garibaldi (by Raffaello Romanelli; 1896) flanked by two diverging avenues (a market is held in this area on Wednesdays). The *Palazzo di Giustizia* was built here in 1986. From here Via dei Gazzani, passing *Santo Stefano* (Pl. 6; closed), a little Romanesque church rebuilt in 1641 (with an altarpiece by Andrea Vanni and predella by Giovanni di Paolo), leads into Via di Camollia. Some distance along this street, on the left, the Vicolo Fontegiusta descends left to the elegant little Renaissance church of *Fontegiusta* (Pl. 2; 1482–84), with a good portal by Urbano da Cortona (1489). In the dark interior, on a centralised plan, is (W wall) a Visitation by Bartolomeo Neroni. On the right side, Coronation of the Virgin by Bernardino Fungai. At the high altar, sculpted tabernacle by Marrina, and frescoes by Girolamo di Benvenuto. On the left side, fresco of the Sibyl announcing to Augustus the Birth of Christ, signed by Baldassarre Peruzzi.—Via di Camollia continues past *San Pietro alla Magione* (Pl. 1; 11C) with a lovely simple interior and remains of 14C frescoes, to the *Porta Camollia* (1604), inscribed 'Cor magis tibi Sena pandit', to commemorate a visit of the Grand-Duke Ferdinand I. A few steps beyond is a column recalling the meeting on this spot of Frederick III and Eleanora of Portugal (7 March 1451; depicted in the frescoes in the Libreria

Piccolomini, see above). Beyond the column is the *Antiporto* (Pl. 1) or barbican (1675), in imitation of the Porta Romana. About 10 minutes farther on is the Renaissance *Palazzo dei Diavoli* or *dei Turchi*, by Antonio Federighi (1460). From either end of the Via Camollia roads descend to the Piazzale Francesco di Giorgio (Pl. 3) and the Viale Mazzini, leading to the railway station.

About 2·5km from the Porta Ovile (Pl. 7) by Via Simone Martini and the 16C *Madonnina Rossa* (beyond the railway crossing), are the convent and church of **L'Osservanza** (adm. 9–13, 16–19), founded in 1423 by St Bernardine with the object of restoring the observance of the original Franciscan rule, relaxed by papal dispensations. The convent was enlarged in 1485, and confiscated by the city in 1874. The church was well rebuilt in 1949 after severe war damage to the original design of *Francesco di Giorgio Martini* and *Giacomo Cozzarelli*.

INTERIOR. The stucco and terracotta roundels in the vaults and in the sanctuary are attributed to *Giacomo Cozzarelli*. On the W wall the two roundels with Saints surrounded by garlands of fruit are attributed to *Andrea della Robbia*. On either side of the entrance to the sanctuary, white glazed figures of the Annunciatory Angel and the Virgin in tabernacles, by *Andrea della Robbia*. LEFT SIDE, 1st altar, *Sano di Pietro*, Madonna and Child with four angels; 2nd altar, *Andrea della Robbia*, blue and white enamelled terracotta altarpiece of the Coronation of the Virgin. RIGHT SIDE, detached fresco of the Crucifixion by *Bartolomeo Neroni*; 3rd altar, *Sano di Pietro*, Madonna and Child with Saints. Beneath it is the *Reliquary of St Bernardine by *Francesco d'Antonio* (1454). On the right wall, St Elizabeth of Hungary by *Girolamo di Benvenuto*, and on the left wall, St Bernardine by *Pietro di Giovanni d'Ambrogio*. 4th altar, triptych attributed to the *Maestro dell'Osservanza'*. In the Sacristy, *Mourning over the dead Christ, a group of 7 polychrome terracotta figures by *Giacomo Cozzarelli* (beautifully restored in 1984). A small museum contains a Head of Christ by *Lando di Pietro* (1337).

About 8km from the Porta Ovile is the *Certosa di Pontignano*, owned by the University and used for conferences, etc., with three 14–15C cloisters.

From the Porta San Marco (Pl. 13) N73 (for Massa Marittima and Grosseto) passes near (3km; left) the battlemented *Villa di Monastero*, formerly the abbey of Sant'Eugenio (suppressed in 1810). About 0·5km farther on a by-road on the right leads to (5km from Siena) the 12C *Castello di Belcaro* (adm. weekdays 14–16, on application), enlarged in the 16C by Peruzzi. In the hills farther W are the hermitages of *Lecceto* (14C) and *San Leonardo al Lago* (12C).

FROM SIENA TO MONTE OLIVETO, 35km. By public transport the only way of reaching Monte Oliveto from Siena is now by train (the Chiusi line) to Asciano; but from the station it is 9km on foot to the convent.—The approach by car follows the Arezzo road for 6km then bears right through *Taverna d'Arbia*. The main road (see Rte 50) continues past the site of the battle of Montaperti (1260). The road traverses the mud-covered hills in which is quarried the ochre that yields the well-known pigments 'burnt sienna' and 'raw sienna'.—2km off to the right of (21km) *Pievina* is the former abbey church of *Rofeno*, now abandoned.—26km **Asciano**. The road enters the town through a gateway in the walls built by the Sienese in 1351. In the main street (left) is the *Museo Etrusco* (10–12.30 except Monday) in the ex-church of San Bernardino, where finds from the necropolis at Poggio Pinci, 5km E, are displayed. At the end of the street is the Romanesque *Collegiata*, approached by steps, and (on the left) the *Museo di Arte Sacra*. Among its pictures are a Nativity of the Virgin by the Maestro dell'Osservanza, a St Michael by Ambrogio Lorenzetti, a polyptych by Matteo di Giovanni, a Madonna by Barna, and works by Giovanni di Paolo and Taddeo di Bartolo. The Gothic church of San Francesco contains fresco fragments attributed to Giovanni da Asciano. In the private Casa Corboli are frescoes (in poor condition) attributed to Ambrogio Lorenzetti.—The narrow hilly road (with fine views) continues southwards through beautiful countryside dotted with fine old farmhouses and thin rows of cypresses, and soon the little village of Chiusure comes into view on a hill just beyond (35km) *Monte Oliveto Maggiore, on a promontory in a thick wood of cypresses. There is a car park outside the gate (and a bar and restaurant). Visitors are admitted daily 9.30–12.45, 15–17.30. This famous convent was founded for hermits by Giovanni Tolomei di Siena (1313), who assumed the religious name of Bernardo and was beatified. The new 'Olivetan' Order, under Benedictine rule, was confirmed by John XII in 1319. Pius II and Charles V sojourned here, the latter with 2000 followers; the monastery was suppressed by Napoleon in 1810, and after restoration was made a 'National Monument' in 1866. Some monks remain as caretakers and hospitality is available at the guest house. From the gateway beneath a great tower (1393) decorated with terracottas by the Della Robbia, a road (and path parallel to the left) wind down to the Monastery through an avenue of cypresses. The huge brick monastery buildings stand bedside the façade of the CHURCH (1400–17). The GREAT CLOISTER (1426–74) is famous for its 41 *Frescoes from the life of St Benedict, nine of which are by *Signorelli* (1497) and the remainder by *Sodoma* (1505–08); the cycle begins in the E walk. On the entrance into the vestibule of the church (left) is a small picture of Christ carrying the Cross by Sodoma. In the vestibule is a statue of the Madonna and Child by *Fra Giovanni da Verona*. Inside the church are fine *Choir-stalls by *Giovanni da Verona* (1503) and a lectern by *Raffaele da Brescia*. From the Middle Cloister is the entrance to the REFECTORY (fresco by Bartolomeo Neroni above the lavabo). The rest of the convent is not at present shown. It includes the LIBRARY, on the second floor, which had 16 of its 20 valuable codexes stolen in 1975 (it has notable carving by *Giovanni da Verona*), and the PHARMACY, with jars.—Beyond Monte Oliveto the pretty road (passing olive groves, many of which suffered in the great freeze of 1984) goes on to join N2 at (44km) *Buonconvento* (Rte 57).

From Siena to *Perugia*, see Rte 56.

49   Florence to Volterra

ROAD, 75km. ('Superstrada del Palio' and N68). From Florence via the Siena 'superstrada' to (45km) the exit for Colle Val d'Elsa, see Rte 47A. N68.—48km **Colle Val d'Elsa**.—75km **Volterra**.

BUS (SITA) from Florence to Volterra in c 2hrs.—Colle Val d'Elsa is connected by a bus service (15 minutes) with Poggibonsi on the Florence–Siena railway line, see Rte 47C.

From Florence to (45km) the exit for Colle Val d'Elsa, see Rte 47A. N68 continues to (48km) **Colle di Val d'Elsa** (223m; 14,800 inhab.), birthplace of the architect Arnolfo di Cambio (1232–1302). A car park has recently been opened below the walls, and an easy flight of steps leads to the upper town. The long main street of the upper town runs along the ridge of the hill to a bridge (views) across which the road passes through the fine *Palazzo Campana* (1539; by Giuliano di Baccio d'Agnolo) into the 'CASTELLO' or old town with many interesting medieval buildings.

The *Duomo* has a pulpit of 1465. In the right transept is the 'Cappella del Chiodo' with a carved tabernacle attributed to Mino da Fiesole, and a delicate bronze lectern, an unusual work by Pietro Tacca. The bronze Crucifix over the high altar is attributed to Giambologna. Nearby, at No. 27 Via Castello, the *Palazzo Vescovile* houses the MUSEO D'ARTE SACRA (closed for restoration in 1989). In a room with charming frescoes of hunting scenes attributed to Bartolo di Fredi or Taddeo di Bartolo are a triptych of the Sienese School (late 14C), a Madonna and Child by Luca di Tommè, church vestments, and a chalice of the 12C. The Museum also owns a painting of Christ at the Column by Il Riccio. Beyond, on the right, is the old *Palazzo dei Priori*. The MUSEO CIVICO here is closed and there are plans to move it to another building. The collection includes works by Rutilio Manetti, Sebastiano Conca, and the school of Mantegna (a Pietà, almost completely ruined). The road continues past more medieval houses including the tower house of Arnolfo di Cambio. In Piazza del Duomo, the ANTIQUARIUM (also closed in 1989) displays the Terrosi collection excavated from a necropolis at Casone, in use from the late Iron Age up to Imperial Roman times. The well-displayed objects include large black-varnished kraters known as 'Malacena' ware. Here also is a fresco of the Madonna and Child by Giacomo Pacchiarotti. In the lower town, the church of Sant'Agostino contains a wood Crucifix attributed to Marco Romano.

The fine Porta Nuova (probably designed by Giuliano da Sangallo) marks the entrance to the town from Volterra. N68 now runs along a pretty ridge of hills with wide views. Just outside the town a by-road diverges left for *Casole d'Elsa* (11km).

At the beginning of the road an unmade-up track (right) leads to the *Badia a Coneo*, a Sienese Romanesque building of 1125 in a pretty position (the custodian lives next door). The road continues into **Casole d'Elsa** where the *Collegiata* (painstakingly restored after war damage) has an interesting interior with two monuments by Gano da Siena, a damaged fresco of the Madonna enthroned (School of Duccio), and a terracotta frieze by Giovanni della Robbia surrounding reliefs by Cieco da Gambassi. In the adjoining *Canonica* (ring) the paintings include a Madonna and Child attributed to Duccio, a Madonna and Child with Saints (and a lunette of the Massacre of the Innocents) by Andrea di Niccolò, and works by Rutilio Manetti. A choir-book has beautiful illuminations by Lippo Vanni. In the *Palazzo del Comune* is a fresco recently restored and attributed to Giacomo Pacchiarotti.—At *Mensano*, 7km farther S, the Romanesque church has splendid large capitals.

The main road continues through magnificent countryside.—59km View of the towers of **San Gimignano**, 12·5km N (described in Rte 47A), reached from here along a pretty by-road with fine views.—The road begins to climb through the hills of the 'Volterrano' in a distinctive open landscape to (75km) **VOLTERRA** in a magnificent position on a precipitous hill (555m) with open views in every direction across a splendid yellow and grey landscape of rolling hills. It is an austere medieval walled town, the successor to an Etruscan city of much greater extent.

Railway Station at *Saline di Volterra*, 10km SW in the valley, branch line (some trains are substituted by buses) to Cecina, with through trains to Pisa.—Bus connection with trains from Piazza XX Settembre.

Parking outside the walls (Piazza Martiri della Libertà, Bastione Mediceo, etc.); difficult on market days (Saturday).

Tourist Office (Pro Loco), Via Turazza (at the side of Palazzo dei Priori).

Buses to Pisa, Florence, Massa Marittima, San Gimignano and Siena.

History. *Velathri* was the northernmost of the 12 cities of the Confederation of Etruria Propria and one of the most prominent. In the 3C BC it became the Roman *Volaterrae*. It supported the cause of Marius against Sulla and underwent a siege of two years before falling to the troops of the latter. It gained some importance under the Lombards and was for a time the residence of the Lombard kings. After bitter struggles, it was subdued by Florence in 1361. Its natives included the satirist Persius Flaccus (AD 34–62), St Linus, the reputed successor of St Peter in the papal chair, and the painter Daniele Ricciarelli da Volterra (1509–66). Almost all the buildings are of a kind of limestone, *panchina*, the matrix of alabaster, which is found here in abundance. There are still numerous alabaster workshops in the town which sell 'objets d'art'.

Piazza Martiri della Libertà forms the S entrance to the town. Via Marchesi leads left to *PIAZZA DEI PRIORI, bordered by mansions medieval or in the medieval style. To the NE is the *Palazzo Pretorio* with its *Torre del Porcellino*, while on the SW side are the *Bishop's Palace*, originally the town granary, and the austere **Palazzo dei Priori** (1208–54), now the town hall, the oldest building of its kind in Tuscany. The battlemented tower, with a fine view, has been closed for years. On the first floor the council chamber (adm. when not in use) has a 14C Florentine fresco (repainted). On the second floor is a detached fresco of Justice by Daniele da Volterra (Ricciarelli).

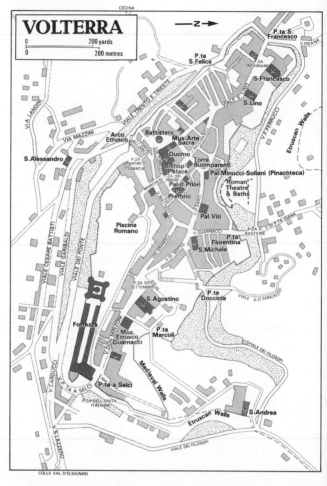

The **Duomo**, at the back (reached by Via Turazza left of Palazzo dei
Priori), is a 12–13C building altered internally in 1584 by Leonardo
Ricciarelli, and restored after damage in the Second World War. The
campanile dates from 1493. The nave and crossing have a 16C
coffered ceiling. Beneath the N arcade is a 13C pulpit considerably
restored, and, in the N aisle an Annunciation by *Albertinelli* (1497).
On the W wall (left of door) is a Romanesque altar placed beneath a
19C tomb. Above the high altar is a *Ciborium (1471) by *Mino da
Fiesole* who also sculpted the two angels on either side on twisted
columns (12C). On the altar, silver bust of St Octavian, by *Antonio
Pollaiolo*. The stalls in the apse date from 1404. In the transeptal
chapels are a 13C *Deposition group in polychrome wood, and the
tomb of St Octavian by *Raffaello Cioli* (1522; right-hand angel by

Andrea Ferrucci). In the Lady Chapel (entered from the W end of the N aisle) is a charming fresco of the Magi by *Benozzo Gozzoli* (in a niche behind a 15C group of the Nativity in terracotta; light on right).—The octagonal **Baptistery**, a fine building by *Giroldo di Jacopo* (1283), facing the cathedral, has a font (right of altar) sculpted by *Andrea Sansovino* (1502). The altar is surrounded by a fine sculptured arch by *Mino da Fiesole*.

The MUSEO DIOCESANO DI ARTE SACRA (closed), at No. 1 Via Roma, has good architectural fragments, a bust of St Linus by *Andrea della Robbia*, a gilded Crucifix by *Giambologna*, vestments, and 15C antiphonals.

From Via Marchesi (see above) Via Porta all'Arco descends to the **Arco Etrusco*, a gateway rebuilt in Roman times, with the remains of three colossal Etruscan heads. The little church of *Sant'Alessandro*, mainly 11–12C, is at the foot of the hill.

Just N of the main piazza (see above), in Via dei Sarti, *Palazzo Minucci-Soliani*, attributed to Antonio da Sangallo the Elder, was restored in 1982 to house the **Pinacoteca Comunale**, formerly displayed in Palazzo dei Priori. This is a delightful small collection of paintings, almost all of which are by Tuscan masters. The charming little palace has a pretty courtyard. Admission daily 9.30–13.

The collection is arranged chronologically. 13C Tuscan Crucifix, Romanesque capitals, and a case of ivories.—*Taddeo di Bartolo*, *Polyptych of Madonna and Saints (1411, from Palazzo dei Priori), Madonna and Child.—Works by *Cenni di Francesco*.—Two statues of the Annunciation by *Francesco di Valdambrino* and a triptych of the Madonna enthroned with four Saints by the Portuguese painter *Alvaro Pires* (c 1430, recently restored).—*Stefano d'Antonio di Vanni*, *Madonna and Child.—*Benvenuto di Giovanni*, Nativity (1470), predella with scenes from the life of the Virgin.—*Neri di Bicci*, Saints Sebastian, Bartholomew, and Nicholas of Bari (1478).—*Ghirlandaio*, Christ in glory with Saints and a donor; *Leonardo da Pistoia*, Madonna enthroned with Saints (1516).—*Signorelli*, *Annunciation (1491), a charming composition, Madonna enthroned with Saints; *Rosso Fiorentino*, *Deposition (1521), a beautifully composed painting (damaged by poor restorations in the past).—SECOND FLOOR. Large paintings by *Pietro Witte (Pier Candido)*.—The collection of small Flemish paintings, includes a ruined 16C Madonna and Child (a case of 17C and 18C silver is also to be displayed here).—The last room contains a Madonna enthroned by the local 17C painter *Baldassarre Franceschini (Volterrano)*. More rooms are to be opened, one of which will contain the collection of coins and medals from the Museo Guarnacci.

Opposite Palazzo Minucci-Soliani is the Renaissance *Palazzo Viti* with a collection of porcelain, alabaster, etc.

Via Ricciarelli, forming a picturesque corner (12–13C *Tower-houses) with Via Buonparenti, leads down from the main piazza past the house of Daniele da Volterra (No. 12) to the church of *San Lino* (1480–1513). It contains a 17C painting of the Birth of the Virgin by Cesare Dandini (recently restored). The church of *San Francesco*, has a separate chapel of 1315, completely frescoed in 1410 by Cenni di Francesco Cenni.

Outside the 14C *Porta San Francesco* an uninteresting narrow road continues past the ruins of *Santo Stefano* (12C) to (nearly 1km from the gate) the imposing church of *San Giusto*, its tall façade (1628) rising above a grassy slope flanked by cypresses. A few hundred metres beyond the road ends at the remains of the **Etruscan Walls*, which are well preserved at many points (but in need of restoration). They included pastures and springs within their circumference of c 9km–nearly three times that of the medieval walls. From here there is a view of the formidable precipice of the BALZE, where landslips have engulfed the greater part of the earliest necropolis of Volterra, and the remaining area is

The Arco Etrusco in Volterra

threatened by further falls. The ruined *Badia* is conspicuous; it is now abandoned but preserves its cloister.

Viale Francesco Ferrucci, outside the medieval walls, runs E past the *ROMAN THEATRE AND BATHS (closed for years while excavations continue), well seen from the road. Built at the end of the 1C BC, part of the cavea and scena remain. Inside the portico, which was added a century later, are remains of baths with various rooms, one with a mosaic pavement. From Porta Fiorentina Via Guarnacci leads in to the *Casa-Torre Toscano* otherwise reached from the centre by Via Buonparenti and Via Sarti (see above). The church of *San Michele*, opposite the tower-house, has a façade in the Pisan style and, inside a

Della Robbian Madonna.—At No. 15 Via Don Minzoni, to the SE, is the ***Museo Etrusco Guarnacci** (open daily 9.30–13, 15–18.30), founded by Monsignor Mario Guarnacci (1701–85).

The delightful building, with a garden, has appropriate decorations and some of the original show-cases survive. It contains more than 600 Etruscan cinerary urns, found locally, mostly of the 3C BC, in alabaster or terracotta; the terracotta urns are probably the oldest. On the lids are generally the recumbent figures of the dead, with the cup of life reversed; many are sculptured with fine reliefs, including mythological subjects from the Theban or Trojan cycles. In RXX is a carved terracotta tomb cover with a striking portrait of a husband and wife (early 1C BC). In RXXII is a famous bronze elongated votive figure (2C BC). Another group of rooms, opened in 1986, illustrate the daily life of the Etruscans with finds from the excavations in Vallebona.—In RXXVI are finds from tombs in the necropolis of Ripaie (9–7C BC). The Roman material includes fragments of Roman wall paintings, decorative sculptural fragments, and mosaics from the Roman baths, and two portrait heads of Augustus from the Roman theatre.—The Second Floor is used for exhibitions.

At the end of the street is the massive *Fortezza*, a castle begun by Walter de Brienne, Duke of Athens, in 1343, and completed by Lorenzo il Magnifico in 1472; it has always been used as a prison.

From the nearby *Porta a Selci* a road descends to (1km) the 15C church of *San Girolamo*, containing terracottas by Giovanni Della Robbia and an *Annunciation by Benvenuto di Giovanni (1466).

FROM VOLTERRA TO MASSA MARITTIMA, 66km, bus in 3hrs. The beautiful winding hill-road, with fine views, diverges from N68 at (9km) *Saline di Volterra*, see below.—23km *Pomarance*, an old walled town with palazzi of the Larderel and other local families, was the birthplace of two painters called Pomarancio, of whom Cristofano Roncalli (1552–1626) was the more famous.—33km *Larderello*, on a side road to the left, is noted for the production of boric acid, evaporated from natural vapour-jets (soffioni) which burst forth from the ground.—From the pass of *Aia dei Diavoli* (875m) the road descends to (66km) *Massa Marittima*, see Rte 54.

FROM VOLTERRA TO CECINA (N68), 42km; bus in 1¼ hrs; railway from Saline di Volterra in 35 minutes; most of the trains go on to Pisa.—The road descends from the hills of Volterra to (10km) *Saline di Volterra*, named from its salt deposits (which belong to the State). It is at the junction of roads to Pomarance and to Pontedera (43km N).—N68 descends the pretty valley of the river Cecina and crosses the new by-pass before reaching the old Via Aurelia 2km N of Cecina (see Rte 54).

50 Florence to Arezzo

MOTORWAY (Autostrada del Sole, AI), 63km (80km centre to centre).—6km *'Firenze Sud'*.—25km *Incisa.*—41km *Valdarno.*—63km **Arezzo**.

RAILWAY, 88km in just under 1hr; three 'Inter-City' trains a day in 50 minutes stop at Arezzo on the new 'direttissima' main line between Rome and Florence.

BUSES (CAT) in 2½hrs, via Figline Valdarno and Montevarchi (continuing to Sansepolcro and Città di Castello); also direct service (once a day) in 1½hrs via the motorway.

A secondary road to Arezzo (77km) leaves Florence by the S bank of the Arno and Bagno a Ripoli. It has splendid retrospective views of Florence and there are fine villas around (15km) San Donato in Collina. It then follows close to the motorway. At (26km) Incisa it joins N69 and runs through all the small towns of interest, described below.

From Florence the motorway is joined at 'Firenze Sud', reached by the new Ponte a Rovezzano over the Arno.—It passes under San Donato in Collina by a tunnel, and enters the Valdarno just N of (25km) *Incisa Val d'Arno*, so called from the deep chalky cutting made by the river. It was an important stage in the battle for Florence in 1944.—The motorway now follows the E bank to (41km) *Valdarno*.

San Giovanni Valdarno (134m; 19,700 inhab.), 3km N of the motorway exit, has lignite mines and blast furnaces. It was the birthplace of the painters Masaccio (Tommaso Guido or Tommaso di Ser Giovanni, 1401–c 1428) and Giovanni da San Giovanni (Giovanni Mannozzi, 1592–1636). In the centre of the two main squares is the 14C *Palazzo Pretorio*, a fine building with a tall tower surrounded by a portico, attributed to Arnolfo di Cambio (being restored in 1989). It has 'stemmi' by the Della Robbia workshop. In Piazza Masaccio is the unusual Basilica of *Santa Maria delle Grazie*, with a neo-classical façade of 1840. Beneath the portico is a polychrome terracotta of the Assumption by Giovanni della Robbia. Stairs ascend to the upper church (rebuilt after the War). Here in the Sagrestia Vecchia (usually open in the afternoon) is kept a beautiful painting of the *Annunciation, from the convent of Montecarlo, 2km S of the town, almost certainly thought to be the work of Fra Angelico since its restoration in 1984. The paintings in the church (all labelled) include works by Giovanni da San Giovanni, the 'Master of the Cassone Adimari', Paolo Schiavo, Mariotto di Cristofano, and Domenico di Michelino.—In the same piazza is the church of *San Lorenzo* with a good 14C triptych of the Coronation of the Virgin, and interesting 14C and 15C fresco fragments. The Pieve in Piazza Cavour has a wood sculpture of the Pietà.

8km N of San Giovanni is **Figline Valdarno**, a prosperous village with a Collegiata, mainly 16C in appearance, which preserves a Madonna and Child by the 'Maestro di Figline' (restored in 1985).—5km S of San Giovanni Valdarno is **Montevarchi**, an important market-town (22,700 inhab.). Next to the Collegiata is a little Museo d'Arte Sacra (adm. by appointment; ring at the door on the right of the church). Here is preserved a beautiful 'tempietto' with Della Robbian carvings (reconstructed in 1973), goldsmiths and silversmiths work including a Cross by Piero di Martino Spigliati, pupil of Cellini, wood sculpture, and illuminated choirbooks. At No. 36 Via Bracciolini is the Accademia Valdarnese del Poggio, founded in 1805 with a library and an important Paleontological Museum (open 9–12, 16–19; fest. 10–12; closed Monday), with rock, vegetable and animal fossils found in the Valdarno, including the 'canis etruscus' studied by Prof. F. Major of Glasgow. Georges Cuvier came here in 1810 to study the collection.—An interesting by-road leads E from Montevarchi via the little walled 'bastide' of *Terranuova Bracciolini* (surrounded by new buildings), founded in 1337, where Poggio Bracciolini was born in 1380, to the medieval village (also now surrounded by new buildings) of *Loro Ciufenna* (15km). *Gropina*, 2km S, reached through pine woods is a charming medieval hamlet built around a Romanesque *Pieve (open 8–12, 15–19 or ring at the priest's house in front of the side door). The bare interior built in pietra serena has delightful carved capitals and a primitive pulpit. Beneath the right aisle stairs lead down to remains of earlier buildings on this site (Roman and palaeochristian finds).

From Montevarchi Arezzo can be reached by the hilly old road (N69; 32km) which passes 6km S of *Laterina* where in 1973 were unearthed long and almost intact stretches of the Via Cassia Vetus. After crossing beneath the motorway and just before *Indicatore* station N 69 passes, on the S, *Arezzo British Military Cemetery*, with 1267 graves. The road now descends into the Valdichiana for Arezzo.

80km **AREZZO** pleasantly situated on a hillside (296m) about 5km S of the Arno, but now surrounded to the S by industrial suburbs. It is a lively agricultural provincial town (87,300 inhab.), with several notable churches and interesting museums. In the church of San Francesco is the famous fresco cycle painted by Piero della Francesca.

A.P.T. Information Office, Piazza Stazione.—**Post Office**, 34 Via Guido Monaco.—**Hotels** on Via Guido Monaco which leads from the station to San Francesco.

Buses from the Bus Station near the railway station to *Florence* (see above); also to *Sansepolcro* and *Città di Castello* via Anghiari (C.A.T.). Weekday services (once a day) to *Siena*, *Urbino* (Fano and Pesaro), *Gubbio*, *Castiglion Fiorentino* and *Cortona*; and to *Rimini* in summer.

The antiques fair in Piazza Grande, Arezzo

A popular **Antiques Fair** is held in Piazza Grande and the surrounding streets on the first weekend of every month.—A famous international choral festival (*Corso Polifonico Internazionale Guido d'Arezzo*) is held in the city in late August.

History. *Arretium*, one of the more important of the 12 cities of the Etruscan Confederation, was originally the enemy and later the faithful ally of Rome. It emerged as a free republic in the 10C. Generally supporting the Ghibelline party it was frequently at odds with Florence; it shared in the defeat at Campaldino in 1289 and submitted to Florence in 1384.—As a road junction the town had tactical importance in the Second World War when nearly every important building was harmed to some extent by bombing.

Ever since the Etruscan period Arezzo has produced notable artists and craftsmen, including the potters who produced the 'vasi aretini'. Among its eminent citizens were C. Cilnius Maecenas (died 8 BC), the friend of Augustus and the patron of Virgil and Horace; Guido d'Arezzo (c 995–1050), the inventor of the musical scale; Margaritone, the painter (1216–93); Petrarch, the poet (1304–74); Spinello Aretino, the painter (c 1350–1410); Aretino (1492–1566), the most outspoken writer of the late Renaissance, and Giorgio Vasari (1512–74), the architect, painter, and historian of art.

Arezzo is noted for its *Giostra del Saracino*, a tournament held annually in the Piazza Grande on the 1st Sunday in September in the late afternoon, with an origin going back to the 13C. Two competitors from each of the four quarters of the town, mounted and armed with lances, charge in turn across the piazza at a pivoting quintain called 'Buratto Re delle Indie' which holds the target in its left hand and in its right a whip, ending in three wooden balls. Points are awarded (from 1–5) for aim, with bonus points for a broken lance, and penalties if the horseman is struck by the wooden balls as the figure turns on its pivot. Each of the four ancient quarters of the town enters a team under a captain, with standard-bearers, foot-soldiers, bowmen, and a band, which plays the 'Saracino hymn'. The four quarters have their own colours: Porta Sant'Andrea, white and green; Porta Crucifera, red and green; Porta del Foro, yellow and crimson; Porta Santo Spirito, yellow and blue. The team (not the individual) scoring the most marks is declared the winner. Tickets for seats (in the shade) are available in advance; standing room only on the day.

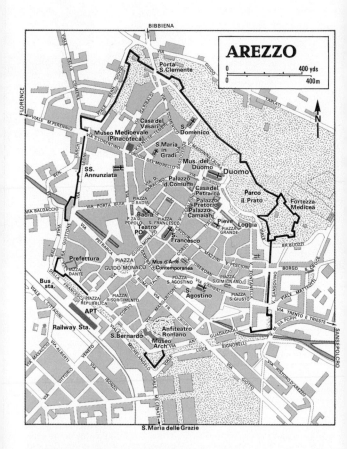

The pleasantest approach from the station is by Corso Italia, the main street of the medieval town. In the central PIAZZA SAN FRANCESCO is the church of **San Francesco** (open 8–12.30, 14–18.30; on Sunday visitors are asked to visit the church 10–11, 14.30–18.30), built by Fra Giovanni da Pistoia in 1322. The rose window in the façade wall (covered for restoration) has stained glass (removed for restoration) by *Guglielmo di Marcillat* (William of Marseille; 1520) showing St Francis and Honorius III. Among the numerous good frescoes by local artists on the nave walls (mostly fragments) are an Annunciation by *Spinello Aretino* (towards the E end of the right wall). Chapel to right of choir, damaged frescoes (restored) by *Spinello:* right, Deeds of St

Michael; left, Legend of St Giles. Triptych: Our Lady and St Thomas, by *Nicolò di Pietro Gerini*. In the choir hangs a painted *Crucifix attributed to the 'Master of San Francesco' (1250). On the walls of the choir is the **LEGEND OF THE TRUE CROSS (light; offering), by *Piero della Francesca* (c 1454–66), his masterpiece, and one of the greatest fresco cycles ever produced in Italian painting.

Lengthy studies and tests are being carried out as part of a restoration programme (1985–92) of the frescoes. The chronological order of the scenes, as they
illustrate the story is as follows: RIGHT WALL (lunette) Death of Adam; (middle
band) Queen of Sheba recognises the sacred wood, and she is received by
Solomon; (right of the window) the beam is buried by the order of Solomon, and
(lower panel) Constantine's Dream; (right wall, lower band) Constantine's
victory over Maxentius.—OPPOSITE WALL: (central panel left of window) Torture
of Judas; (middle band) Discovery and Proof of the Cross by St Helena; (lower
band) Victory of Heraclius over Chosroes; (lunette) Heraclius restores the Cross
to Jerusalem.—Also by Piero are the two figures of Prophets on the window wall,
and the Annunciation (thought by some scholars to be St Helena receiving the
news of her death, and thus connected to the main cycle).—On the triumphal
arch are frescoes of the Last Judgement (restored in 1987) by *Bicci di Lorenzo*,
who also painted the four Evangelists in the vault of the Choir.

In the chapel left of the high altar is an Annunciation attributed as an early
work to Luca Signorelli, or to Bartolomeo della Gatta and a detached ruined
fresco of the same subject; (N side of nave), monument by *Michele da Firenze*. In
the small chapel in the middle of the N side are frescoes (being restored) by
Lorentino di Arezzo (possibly on a cartoon by Piero della Francesca).—The lower
church (13–14C) has been restored and is open only for exhibitions.

Via Cavour (right) and Corso Italia (left) lead to the ***Pieve di Santa Maria** (closed 13–15), a 12C church replacing an earlier edifice sacked in 1111. It is one of the most beautiful Romanesque churches in Tuscany. The superbly conceived *FAÇADE has a deep central portal flanked by blind arcades which support three tiers of colon-nades, the intercolumnations of which diminish towards the top. The 68 diverse pillars include a human figure. The portal (covered for restoration) bears reliefs of 1216 and the months are illustrated in the intrados. The beautiful tall *INTERIOR has clustered pillars with good capitals and arches showing the transition to Gothic. In the raised presbytery is the *Polyptych by *Pietro Lorenzetti* commissioned by Bishop Guido in 1320. The crypt below has good capitals, and a reliquary bust of St Donato (1346) by a local goldsmith. In a chapel on the left side of the nave is a polychrome Madonna and Child of the 15C Florentine school. The arcaded apse and the original *Campanile* (1330), with its 40 double openings, are best seen from the steeply-sloping *PIAZZA GRANDE, behind the church (reached by Via di Seteria which skirts the interesting flank of the church opposite medieval shop-fronts). In the Piazza are held the annual tournament (see above) and a monthly antiques fair. Here stand the Gothic and Renaissance *Palazzo della Fraternità dei Laici*, with a sculpted lunette on the façade by Bernardo Rossellino, and the fine *Loggia*, built by Vasari in 1573. The Loggia continues NW back to Corso Italia in which is *Palazzo Camaiani* (16C), with a tower of 1351, now housing the Provincial Archives. Via dei Pileati continues uphill past the 14C *Palazzo Pretorio*, bearing on its façade the armorial bearings of many podestà; it is occupied by the Public Library. The road curves up hill to the left, and at No. 28 Via dell'Orto is the *Casa Petrarca* (adm. on request at the Accademia Petrarca, Via degli Alberghetti, 10–12, 15–16 or 16–17; closed Saturday afternoon and fest.), the supposed house of Petrarch reconstructed in 1948 as an academy and library for Petrarchian studies. Visitors are shown the library with MSS and an

Polyptych by Pietro Lorenzetti in the Pieve di Santa Maria, Arezzo

autograph letter of the poet (1370). A huge monument to Petrarch (by Alessandro Lazzerini, 1928) stands in the *Parco il Prato*, an attractive large park with trees and lawns, and pretty views of the Tuscan countryside. The 14–16C *Fortezza*, rebuilt by Antonio da Sangallo the Younger was dismantled in 1800.

The **Duomo** (closed 12–15.30) was begun in 1278 and continued until 1510, with a campanile added at the E end in 1859 and a façade completed in 1914. Fine travertine steps (1525–29) surround the exterior. The handsome S flank incorporates a good portal (1320–40), with worn reliefs, and terracotta statues of the Madonna and Child between St Donato and Gregory X, attributed to *Niccolò di Luca Spinelli*. The dark Gothic interior has a nave, tribune, and aisles, clustered columns, pointed arches, and beautiful stained glass *Windows by *Guglielmo di Marcillat* (1519–23), a French artist who lived in Arezzo. He also painted the first three vaults of the nave and the first of the N aisle (light at W end). In the S aisle near the entrance is the monument of Gregory X, who died at Arezzo in 1276. Farther along is a fragment of a fresco of the Madonna enthroned with Saints and the Resurrection of Christ by *Buffalmacco* (c 1330). Beyond is the canopied recess of the Tarlati Chapel by *Giovanni d'Agostino*, with a frescoed Crucifixion attributed to a local painter known as the *'Maestro del Vescovado'* (mid-14C) and a fine sarcophagus of the 4C.—The Gothic sculptured *High Altar, by many 14C artists including *Giovanni di Francesco* and *Betto di Giovanni*, encloses the body of St Donatus (martyred in 361), the patron saint of the city.—North Aisle. On the left of the Sacristy door is a beautiful fresco of *St Mary Magdalene, by *Piero della Francesca*. Next to it is the unusual *Tomb of Bishop Guido Tarlati, by *Agostino di Giovanni* and *Agnolo di Ventura*, with panels representing the warlike life of this zealous Ghibelline (died 1327). The cantoria is the first architectural work of *Vasari* (1535); the organ dates from 1534 (by Luca Boni da Cortona). Beneath it is a 13C wood statue of the Madonna and Child and 14C fresco fragments. Farther on is a fresco by *Luigi Ademollo* of the Aretines receiving the body of St Donato. The large LADY CHAPEL was added in 1796. On the right, *Andrea della Robbia*, Assumption. On the right wall, large painting of Judith (1804) by *Pietro Benvenuti*, much admired by Canova. In the chapel on the right of the main altar, *Andrea della Robbia*, Crucifix (right wall). The main altar was designed by *Giuseppe Valadier* (1823). In the chapel to the left of the main altar, statue of Bishop Marcacci by *Stefano Ricci* and on the left wall, a polychrome terracotta attributed to *Giovanni della Robbia*. On the wall near the entrance to the chapel, *Madonna and Child, by *Andrea della Robbia*.—At the W end of the nave opens the Baptistery. The three beautiful 'schiacciato' reliefs on the font are attributed to *Donatello* or his school.

It is necessary to return round the exterior of the E end of the Duomo to the Piazzetta dietro il Duomo to visit the **Museo del Duomo** (open Easter–September, weekdays 9–12; winter Thursday, Friday and Saturday only, 9–12). It contains a 12C wood Crucifix; a painting of the Annunciation by *Andrea di Nerio*; detached frescoes by *Spinello Aretino*; a Tabernacle with a terracotta relief of the Annunciation (1434) attributed to *Rossellino*; a fresco of St Jerome in the desert by *Bartolomeo della Gatta*; and the 'Pax of Siena', a 15C Flemish work.

On the cathedral steps stands a statue of Ferdinand I, by Francavilla after a design of Giambologna. It was erected by the Aretines in 1594 in gratitude for the grand-duke's agricultural reforms and land reclamation in the Valdichiana. Across Piazza della Libertà is the *Palazzo del Comune* of 1333. The old Via Sassoverde descends right from Via Ricasoli to **San Domenico** in a square of lime trees. The church, founded in 1275, has a Romanesque portal with a lunette frescoed by Angelo di Lorentino, and a Gothic campanile.

The bright Interior has a miscellany of fresco fragments of particularly high quality. On the W wall, *Parri di Spinello*, Crucifixion and Saints and (in the lunette) two scenes from the life of St Nicholas of Bari. On the S wall, in a Gothic canopied altar by *Giovanni di Francesco*, Christ with the Doctors in the temple by *Luca di Tommè*. Above, between the windows, Madonna and Child by the school of Duccio. In a pretty carved polychrome niche, St Peter Martyr by the *Della*

Robbian school. The large detached fresco of a triptych with St Catherine of Alexandria is by the school of Spinello. Above an 18C wall monument, fragment of a fresco by *Parri* with angel musicians. Beside the steps, damaged fresco of Christ blessing the faithful. In the chapel to the right of the main altar, a fine stone 14C statue of the Madonna and Child and a fresco of the *Annunciation by Spinello Aretino*. The *Crucifix in the main apse is by *Cimabue* (light). In the chapel to the left of the apse, *Giovanni d'Agnolo*, triptych with St Domenic, Archangel Michael, and St Paul. On the N wall of the church are frescoes by *Giovanni d'Agnolo*, *Parri di Spinello* (Marriage of St Catherine), and *Jacopo di Landino* (stories of St Christopher). Vasari records that the last fresco on this wall of St Vincent Ferrer is the only known work by his grandfather Lazzaro Vasari. On the W wall is a large frescoed composition by *Spinello Aretino*.

At No. 55 in Via XX Settembre is *Vasari's House* (1540–48; open 9–19; fest. 9–13; ring). It preserves its original painted decorations by Vasari and assistants (restored in the 19C). The ground floor is now a small museum with paintings by Vasari, Stradano, Maso di San Friano, Ligozzi, and Poppi. The family archives include letters of Michelangelo. The church of *Santa Maria in Gradi* (1592), farther on (left) has a good altarpiece by Andrea Della Robbia, and beneath are remains of an earlier church (probably 10C). At the corner of Via Garibaldi is the **Galleria e Museo Medioevale e Moderno**, housed in the 15C *Palazzo Bruni* (adm. every day 9–19, fest. 9–13).

Among fragments in the courtyard are capitals and columns from the Pieve.— Three rooms to the right (one closed for restoration) contain more medieval fragments, including two Madonnas (14C) from the old gates of the city.—**First Floor**. ROOM I. *Margaritone*, St Francis, Madonna, and Crucifix; *School of Guido da Siena*, Madonna; 'Maestro della Maddalena', Madonna and Child. Sculpture: *14C Sienese School*, Head of a Warrior; 13C portrait head; in cases, Romanesque Crosses and Crucifixes.—RII. 15C frescoes.—RIII. Frescoes by *Spinello Aretino* and his son *Parri Spinelli*, and an unusual painting of the Madonna della Misericordia by *Parri Spinelli*. Also displayed here are illuminated choirbooks.—RRIV and ·V. Early Renaissance. The chimneypiece is by *Simone Mosca*, and tournament armour is displayed in cases. Also here, *Bartolomeo della Gatta*, two paintings of St Roch, the smaller painting including a view of medieval Arezzo. On the opposite wall, *Lorentino di Arezzo*, Madonna and Saints.—RV contains frescoes, some attributed to *Signorelli*, and cases of small bronzes. The next five small rooms contain a magnificent *Collection of majolica from Faenza, Gubbio, Deruta, Castel Durante, and Urbino (13–18C), and terracottas by *Andrea della Robbia* and his followers.—In two small rooms has been arranged the MARIO SALMI BEQUEST which includes small works by *Il Poppi, Empoli, Agostino Ciampelli, Arcangiolo Salimbeni, Franciabigio, Francesco Granacci, Alessandro Magnasco, Ludovico Carracci*, and *Adriano Cecioni*. In the gallery is a painting by *Vasari*.—**Second Floor**. In the first room are small works by the Macchiaioli school and *Amos Cassioli*. The second room has works by *Gaspare Dughet, Salvator Rosa*, etc. In the last room are large works by *Vasari, Alessandro Allori* and others, and an excellent collection of glass.

On the opposite side of Via Garibaldi is the Renaissance church of the **Santissima Annunziata**, with an Annunciation by *Spinello Aretino* on the outside. The beautiful Renaissance grey and white *Interior is by *Bartolomeo della Gatta* (1491) and *Giuliano* and *Antonio da Sangallo the Elder* (c 1517).

The interesting plan includes a columned atrium and a dome over the crossing; the capitals of the columns and pilasters are superbly carved. The stained glass tondo in the atrium is by *Guglielmo di Marcillat*. There is a light on the right of the S aisle for the altarpieces. In the chapel to the right of the high altar, Madonna and St Francis by *Pietro da Cortona*, and a 16C terracotta Madonna and Child with Saints, and a relief of God the Father above. The 17C high altar incorporates Renaissance statues in silver and a venerated statue of the Madonna attributed to *Michele da Firenze*. The chapel on the left of the high altar has an Annunciation by *Matteo Rosselli* and a Nativity by *Niccolò Soggi* (1522; removed for restoration). On the 3rd N altar is a 14C Crucifix, and on the

1st altar, is a good painting of the Deposition painted by *Vasari* at the age of 18 on a cartoon by Rosso Fiorentino (recently restored).

On the left, farther on, is the **Badia** or abbey of SANTI FLORA E LUCILLA, rebuilt by *Vasari*, and containing on the W wall a delightful *Fresco of St Lawrence, by Bartolomeo della Gatta (1476). At the end of the left aisle is a ciborium exquisitely carved by *Benedetto da Maiano* (the bronze door was stolen in 1978). The high altar has good paintings by *Vasari*, including the Calling of the Apostles, intended for his own tomb. The Crucifixion at the end of the right aisle is by *Segna di Bonaventura* (1320). The former monastery preserves a fine 15C cloister.

Via Garibaldi continues SE, crossing the broad Via Guido Monaco to Piazza Sant'Agostino (scene of a daily market), with a 13C campanile. On Corso Italia is a local Museum of Contemporary art, containing works mostly dating from the 1960s. From here Via Margaritone leads to the *Convento di San Bernardo* whose rebuilt double loggie follow the curve of the *Roman Amphitheatre* (the well-kept ruins are entered from Via Crispi, 8–19.30). The charming rooms of the convent, overlooking the amphitheatre, now house the **Museo Archeologico Mecenate** (adm. 9–14; fest. 9–13; closed Monday). Other parts of the amphitheatre are visible in the museum rooms. Some of the display cases have been modernised and have excellent descriptions of the contents.

Ground Floor. ROOM 1. Archaic finds from Arezzo: architectural fragments and small bronzes.—R. 2. Hellenistic finds from Arezzo, including terracotta heads. R. 3 (right) finds from the Casentino (small bronzes, antefixes). RR. 4 & 5 contain finds from the Valdichiana, including a fine red-figure amphora (420–410 BC) and kraters and stamnoi of the 5C BC.—RR. 6 & 7 (right) have an excellent display of the famous 'terra sigillata' vases produced in Arezzo from 50 BC to 60–70 AD, in a shiny red glaze, usually decorated with exquisite bas-reliefs. Moulds and instruments are displayed as well as the production of individual workshops.—R. 8 continues the display with superb works from the Ateius pottery.—R. 9. Collection of grave-goods from the tomb of a young girl from Apulia (1C BC).—RR. 12–16 display Roman mosaics and bronzes, statues, sculpture, urns, a marble altar of the Augustan period, with the legend of Romulus and Remus, and the portrait of a woman of the Augustan period.
Upper Floor. To the left are three rooms of vases: a curious urn with a human head and arms from Chiusi (7C BC), good red-figure Greek vases (5C BC), bucchero ware, etc. The rooms to the left off the long corridor display: Roman glass and a *Portrait of a man moulded in gold (Aretine, 1C BC); small bronzes; and the Vincenzo Funghini (1828–96) collection (mostly 4–3C BC). The room to the right off the long corridor displays a Paleolithic and Neolithic collection from the territory of Arezzo. At the end of the corridor is another case of small bronzes.—Stairs lead back down to the entrance.

To the SE of the station (reached in 10 minutes by Viale Michelangelo and Via Mecenate) is the church of **Santa Maria delle Grazie** (1449), with a graceful *Loggia by *Benedetto da Maiano* and a handsome marble and terracotta altar by *Andrea Della Robbia*.

FROM AREZZO TO SIENA, c 64km. A new fast road from Arezzo by-passing Monte San Savino to connect with N326 for Siena is nearing completion. The old road (N73) is particularly pretty between Monte San Savino and the Ombrone. Monte San Savino is described in Rte 58.

FROM AREZZO TO SANSEPOLCRO, 38km. N73 climbs SE to (8km) the *Foce di Scopetone* (526m) and then descends nearly all the way, following the valley of the Cerfone beyond (12km) *Palazzo del Pero* (405m). At 25km this road leaves the Cerfone which descends (right), accompanied by N221 to *Monterchi* (3km), described in Rte 51. N221 continues to Città di Castello (Rte 52). At 29km a road leads left for Anghiari (see Rte 51). N3 crosses the Tiber short of (38km) Sansepolcro, described in Rte 51.
   From Arezzo to Cortona, see Rte 56.

51　Florence to Urbino

This is a cross-country route on minor roads, but it traverses
some beautiful countryside and takes in interesting small towns.

ROAD, 184km. N67 to (18km) *Pontassieve*.—N70. 34km *Passo
della Consuma*.—53km **Poppi**.—58km **Bibbiena**. N208.—80km
Chiusi La Verna (for La Verna, 4km).—97km *Pieve Santo
Stefano*. N3bis.—113km **Sansepolcro**. N73bis.—167km
Urbania.—184km **Urbino**.

A much faster route from Florence to Sansepolcro is via the
motorway to (73km) Arezzo, and then N73 to (112km)
Sansepolcro.

By public transport Urbino can be reached more directly from
the Adriatic coast (see Rte 60); bus in 40 minutes from Pesaro.

From Florence N67 and the railway ascend the N bank of the Arno to
(5km) **Rovezzano** past a new road and railway bridge and the remains
of an ancient (possibly Roman) bridge. Rovezzano was the home of the
sculptor Benedetto da Rovezzano (1474–1552; born near Pistoia). In
the church of *Sant'Andrea* is a delightful Madonna from the Della
Robbian workshop, and a 13C Madonna of the Florentine school.—
7·5km (right) The *Florence British Military Cemetery*, with 1551
graves. A by-road leads S to *Villamagna* where the Romanesque Pieve
di San Donnino contains a *Triptych by Mariotto di Nardo, altarpieces
by Davide del Ghirlandaio and Francesco Granacci, frescoes and
sinopie by the 'Maestro di Signa', and an interesting sacristy.—18km
Pontassieve, a centre of the wine trade (16,500 inhab.) stands at the
confluence of the Sieve and the Arno. N67 diverges left to ascend the
narrow Sieve valley for Rufina and the Mugello (see Rte 44), while the
old road to Arezzo (N69) keeps to the right, still ascending the winding
Arno in company with the railway, past *Sant'Ellero* with a castle and a
Vallombrosan convent (now a private villa; no adm.). The Casentino
road ascends to the left away from the Arezzo road, and in just over
1km, at another fork, the direct road again keeps to the left, omitting
Vallombrosa, described below.

The Vallombrosa road bears right and ascends through *Pelago* (3km) and *Tosi*
(7km).—**Vallombrosa** (12·5km; 958m) is a pleasant summer resort amid pine-
woods on the W slope of the Pratomagno hills. The famous Monastery was
founded by San Giovanni Gualberto in 1040, and was the first house of the
Vallombrosan Order. The monastery was suppressed in 1866, but re-instated in
1963. The church dates mainly from the 17C, and contains 16C stalls. Milton is
traditionally thought to have stayed at the guesthouse of the monastery in 1638
(tablet); the surrounding pine-woods are the 'Etrurian shades' of 'Paradise
Lost'.—Just under 2km from Vallombrosa is **Saltino** (995m) a summer resort in a
more open situation than Vallombrosa, with wide views. It is also visited by skiers,
and fine walks may be taken in the *Pratomagno*, to the SE, among summits 1463m
to 1524m high.

A road descends from Saltino to *Reggello* (11km). 1km outside the town (on the
Figline Valdarno road), is *Cascia*, birthplace in the 14C of the musicians Giovanni
and Donato da Cascia. Here is the Romanesque pieve of San Pietro, marked by its
tall bell-tower, probably founded by Countess Matilda and consecrated in 1073 (if
closed, ring at No. 1 in the piazza). At the end of the left aisle (light) is a beautiful
small *Triptych of the Madonna and Child with Saints Bartolomeo, Biagio,
Giovenale, and Antonio Abate, dated 1422 and the first known work by
Masaccio. It was rediscovered in 1961 in the nearby church of San Giovenale, restored in 1984, and installed here in 1988. The church also contains interesting
capitals, an ancient Crucifix in the apse, and an Annunciation on the left wall by
Mariotto di Cristofano, brother-in-law of Masaccio.

The road from Vallombrosa towards the Casentino traverses the forest of pine, beech, and oak, ascends the N side of a little valley, and joins the main road just before *Consuma*, see below.

28km *Borselli*. A few hundred metres along the Pomino road (left) is the Romanesque church of *Tosina*, which contains a beautiful triptych by Mariotto di Nardo (1389; restored in 1989).—34km *Consuma*, a summer and ski resort a few metres below the pass (1023m) connecting the Pratomagno with the main Apennine chain.—At 44km a road on the left diverges for *Pratovecchio* (5km) and *Stia* (6km; 441m) two large villages in the upper valley of the Arno.

This delightful wooded vale was the domain of the Guidi, the Ghibelline family with whom the exiled Dante sheltered. Their Castle of *Romena*, dating from the 11C, stands above Pratovecchio. The ruins may be visited (9–12, 15–19). Near it is the fine church of San Pietro (custodian lives next door) with an interesting primitive Romanesque apse (1152). The church of Stia, also Romanesque, contains works by Andrea della Robbia and his school. Just outside Stia is the Guidi castle of *Porciano*, with a massive square tower. Recently restored, it has a small museum of agricultural implements. A fine walk of 4hrs leads N from Stia to the Source of the Arno and from there to the summit of *Monte Falterona* (1654m). The adjacent summit of *Monte Falco*, 4m higher, is more easily reached from the *Passo la Calla* (1296m), on the road from Stia into the Romagna via the Bidente valley. On its slopes, visited by skiers, is the Rifugio La Burraia (1447m).

The main road descends into the Arno valley known as the **Casentino** at (51km) the plain of *Campaldino*, where a column marks the battlefield of 1289. Here Dante fought as a young man against the Ghibellines of Arezzo, who were defeated.—53km **Poppi**, the birthplace of Mino da Fiesole (1431–84), is a pretty little village whose splendid *Palazzo Pretorio, a 13C Guidi castle, dominates the valley. The delightful arcaded main street leads to the domed church of the Madonna del Morbo begun in 1657, which contains a Madonna and Child with the young St John by Pseudo Pier Francesco Fiorentino. The church of San Marco has altarpieces by Poppi and Jacopo Ligozzi. At the end of Via Cavour the church of San Fedele (1185–95) contains 16C and 17C altarpieces (Poppi, Passignano, Ligozzi, etc.), and a Madonna by the Maestro della Maddalena (being restored). There is a small zoo at Poppi.

About 15km NE is **Camaldoli** (816m), famous for the monastery of an order founded c 1012 by St Romuald for hermits living in entire isolation. The main buildings are largely of the 17–18C, but include the charming 16C *Pharmacy. Adjacent is the original Hospice with a cloister and little chapel. Farther up amid the fine forest of firs and pines is the *Eremo* (1104m), with a group of monastic cells and a Baroque church, on the site of the original hermitage. Hotels provide accommodation for the numerous summer visitors.

58km **Bibbiena**, the chief town (10,300 inhab.) of the Casentino, was the birthplace of Bernardo Dovizi, called Cardinal Bibbiena (1470–1520), the friend and patron of Raphael. The traditional carnival celebrations here date from the mid-14C. The early 16C *Palazzo Dovizi* stands opposite the church of *San Lorenzo* which contains fine Della Robbian terracottas. Just below the main piazza (with a view from the terrace of Poppi and La Verna) is the 12C church of *Santi Ippolito e Donato* (restored). It contains 14–15C fresco fragments in the nave, and, over the high altar, a triptych by Bicci di Lorenzo (1435). The Madonna and Child with angels, an interesting work by Arcangelo di Cola da Camerino, has been removed for restoration for many years. Arezzo (see Rte 50) lies 33km S of Bibbiena.

The winding road (N208) now leads E to (80km) *Chiusi della Verna*, amid pine-forests, above which stands the famous monastery of

La Verna in a remarkable position on a curiously shaped outcrop of rock (1129m) visible for many miles around. The site was given to St Francis in 1213 and here in 1224 he received the stigmata. It is still a Franciscan convent (c 30 friars) and a retreat. The sanctuary was embellished in 1433 by order of Eugenius IV when a number of altars were commissioned from Andrea della Robbia, who has here left his masterpieces of enamelled terracotta sculpture.

The *Basilica* (or *Chiesa Maggiore*; 1450–70) contains (1st S altar) a Madonna and Child enthroned between Saints, attributed to Andrea della Robbia, and beneath two pietra serena tabernacles in the nave are an *Annunciation, and *Adoration of the Child (c 1479), by Andrea. In the chapel to the left of the presbytery is an *Ascension, surrounded by cherubs and fruit, also by Andrea. At the entrance to the presbytery, the figures of St Anthony Abbot and St Francis are also probably by Andrea.—From the terrace in front of the church there is a fine view. The smaller church of *Santa Maria degli Angeli* (begun in 1216–18) contains an altarscreen with two altars attributed to Andrea or Giovanni della Robbia, and, beyond, in the earliest church, an altarpiece of the *Assumption of the Virgin, another fine work by Andrea, and Renaissance stalls. The *Museum* has been closed since its treasures were stolen in 1978.—A covered corridor leads past several sites which recall the life of St Francis here to the *Cappella della Stimmate* occupying the spot where the Saint received the Stigmata. It contains a *Crucifixion by Andrea (1480–81) in a delightful frame. The intarsia stalls date from 1531. Other holy spots are pointed out by the friars.—A path leads up to the summit of the rock (La Penna, 1283m).

The main road continues to (97km) *Pieve Santo Stefano*, which was systematically mined in the War, when the Collegiata was left standing almost alone amid ruins. It contains a Della Robbian figure of St Sebastian, a 15C polychrome Madonna, and a 14C wooden Crucifix. 12km SW of the town lies the isolated hamlet of *Caprese Michelangelo*, where Michelangelo, son of the podestà Leonardo Buonarroti, was born in 1475 in the little 14C town hall (now restored as a museum). He was christened in the 13C chapel of San Giovanni Battista.

From Pieve Santo Stefano the new fast N3bis (between Cesena and Perugia, see Rte 52) leads S to (113km) **Sansepolcro**, properly '*Borgo Sansepolcro*' (335m), a small town (15,500 inhab.) on an upland plain growing tobacco. It is famous as the birthplace of the painter Piero della Francesca (1416–92). Raffaellino del Colle (1490–1566) and Santi di Tito (1538–1603) were also natives. The art of the crossbow is still practised (contest in medieval costume on 2nd Sunday in September against Gubbio). Here in 1827 the Buitoni family began their pasta business. The *PINACOTECA (Museo Civico) is arranged in the *Palazzo Comunale* (adm. 10–13, 15–18; winter 10–13, 14–17).

ROOM 1. Church vestments and ecclesiastical objects belonging to Bishop Costaguti (18C). On the end wall, Last Supper by *Antonio* and *Remigio Cantagallina* (1604).—R. 2. The crown and vestments (mid-14C) used to adorn the Volto Santo in the cathedral (see below).—R. 3. Triptych by *Matteo di Giovanni* (removed from the Duomo); the central panel, with the Baptism of Christ, by Piero della Francesca, is now in the National Gallery of London.—R. 4. Tabernacle in terracotta of the Nativity, by the *School of Giovanni della Robbia*; *Luca Signorelli*, Standard painted on both sides (Crucifixion and Saints); *Gerino da Pistoia*, Saints Peter and Paul.—R. 5 contains the masterpieces of the gallery by *Piero della Francesca*: the *Resurrection, a fresco (justly one of his most famous works); Madonna of the Misericordia, polyptych commissioned by the local Confraternity of the Misericordia (1445–62); Bust of a Saint (St Julian ?), and St Louis of Toulouse (both frescoes).—R. 6. *Raffaelino del Colle*, Assumption (in a beautiful frame), St Leo, and Annunciation; *Pontormo*, Martyrdom of San Quintino.—R. 7. *Giovanni de'Vecchi*, Presentation of the Virgin in the Temple, and Birth of the Virgin; *Santi di Tito*, St Nicholas of Tolentino, Pope St Clement among the faithful, and Pietà.—R. 8. *Agostino Ciampelli*, Destruction of the idols; *Leandro Bassano*, Adoration of the Magi.—Stairs mount to rooms with 14C (detached) frescoes, and another flight of stairs lead up to a local archaeological collection.

Across Via Aggiunti, with (right) the 15C *House of Piero della Francesca*, is the church of *San Francesco* with an altar of 1304. The DUOMO, nearly opposite the side door of the Pinacoteca, with an 11C façade, has a Romanesque interior with Gothic elements (restored).

INTERIOR. On the W wall are two Della Robbian statues of Saints. South Aisle. *Riminese School* (1383), Fresco of the Madonna and Child with Saints Catherine of Alexandria and Thomas Becket; *Santi di Tito*, Incredulity of St Thomas (removed for restoration); *Bartolomeo della Gatta*, Fresco of the Crucifixion. The main altarpiece is a Polyptych of the Resurrection attributed to *Nicolò di Segna* (on loan from the Pinacoteca). In the N chapel a large wood Crucifix (the 'Volto Santo') which dates in part from the 10C has been restored. Outside the chapel is a Florentine terracotta statue of the Madonna and Child. North Aisle. Beyond a pretty Della Robbian tabernacle is a painting of the Ascension now attributed to *Gerino da Pistoia* on a cartoon by Perugino. The tomb of Simone Graziani is in the manner of Rossellino; *Raffaellino del Colle*, Resurrection of Christ.

Via XX Settembre, to the S, has some interesting palaces. The church of *San Lorenzo*, in Via Luca Pacioli (ring at the Convent next door before 17.00) contains a dark and crowded *Deposition by Rosso Fiorentino.

8km W of Sansepolcro, beyond the new fast by-pass (N3bis) and the Tiber, a straight road (8km) runs across the plain and up to **Anghiari** (429m), in a spectacular position, once *Castrum Angulare*. It was the scene in 1440 of a victory of the Florentines under Francesco Sforza over the Visconti of Milan, and in 1796 of a French defeat of the Austrians. Local artisans are particularly skilled in furniture making, and there is an institute here for the restoration of antique furniture. The road from Sansepolcro enters the town beside *Piazza Baldaccio*, the old market place (car park) of the borgo. Here is the unexpected Galleria Magi (1889) beyond which is a neo-classical theatre. On the other side of the piazza is the unspoilt walled medieval town. Sign-posts indicate the way to the fine Renaissance *Palazzo Taglieschi* (open 9–14, except Monday; Sunday 9–13) which contains a good local museum. In the basement are architectural fragments, and in the entrance hall an enamelled terracotta lunette by Benedetto and Santi Baglioni. On the upper floor: Andrea della Robbia, Nativity and Saints (from the church of the Badia); Tino da Camaino, Madonna; interesting wood statues include a polychrome Madonna and Child attributed to Jacopo della Quercia (the Child has been removed for restoration), and an Annunciation, also by him; and 17C paintings (including some by Matteo Rosselli).—The church of *Sant'Agostino* (closed during excavation work), nearby, contains a triptych by Matteo di Giovanni. The *Badia*, with an unusual interior, has a carved dossal attributed to Desiderio da Settignano. A road leads uphill to the *Palazzo Pubblico* with 'stemmi' on the façade. The church of *Santa Maria delle Grazie* contains a charming Last Supper and Christ washing the disciples' feet, both by Sogliani (in their original frames). Also here are a Della Robbian tabernacle and high altar.—The little church of *Santo Stefano* at the foot of the road to Sansepolcro, was built on a Greek-cross plan in the 7–8C.

FROM SANSEPOLCRO TO AREZZO, 38km N73. At (13km) *Le Ville*, a road to Città di Castello (N221) leads E passing beneath the quiet little village of **Monterchi**, on a fortified hill to the right of the road. The church of San Simone contains a little polychrome terracotta ciborium (damaged but with its original painted door), and a fragment of a 14C fresco found beneath the Madonna del Parto (see below), as well as interesting 15C bas-reliefs. Monterchi was the birthplace of the mother of Piero della Francesca, and, beyond the village (well signposted off the main road) a pine avenue leads left to the tiny chapel beside the cemetery which contains the famous *Madonna del Parto by Piero (open every day 10–12.30, 14.30–17). The fresco (c 1460) shows the pregnant Madonna revealed by two angels pulling back the curtain of a pavilion. The subject is unique in Italian painting. It is thought that Piero's mother may have been buried in the cemetery and the fresco was intended as a memorial to her. The fresco, formerly in the church of Momentana, partially demolished in 1785, was then included in a cemetery chapel. It was detached in 1910, and in 1956–69 the chapel was transformed to isolate it from the cemetery, and the fresco placed at a different height and in a different light than was originally intended by Piero. Studies are being carried out as a preliminary stage in a project to restore the fresco. N221 continues to Città di Castello (17km; Rte 52).

From Le Ville the Arezzo road continues through the beautiful wooded valley of the Cerfone, with vineyards on the hills, to (38km) Arezzo, see Rte 50.

Città di Castello, which is reached by a direct road 16km S of Sansepolcro, is described in Rte 52.

118km *San Giustino*, with the Bufalini castle (1492; transformed by Vasari). A by-road leads S to *Colle Plinio* (6km) where excavations begun in 1979 have revealed remains of the villa of Pliny the Younger (recognised as being his by the brick stamps found here in 1988). The winding mountainous road for Urbino (N73 bis) climbs NE to the *Bocca Trabaria* (1049m), the pass between Umbria and the Marches. From there it descends the Metauro valley to the little old town of (157km) *Sant'Angelo in Vado*, going on to (167km) *Urbania*, named after Urban VIII (1623–44). Under its previous name of Castel Durante it was noted for its majolica. The little town preserves some fine 15C buildings and a Museum and Art Gallery in the Palazzo Ducale (ring) where the Ducal Library has a large collection of engravings and drawings. From here Urbino may be reached either by the direct but hilly road (17km) via San Giovanni in Pozzuolo, or by continuing along the main road via (179km) *Fermignano*, birthplace of Bramante.—184km **Urbino**.

URBINO (485m; 16,200 inhab.) lies in a splendid position set deep amidst rolling hills. It is indelibly associated with the name of Federico da Montefeltro who built his famous palace here and made it one of the greatest centres of the Italian Renaissance. It is also the birthplace of Raphael. The fascinating old city is still contained within its mighty walls and its exceptional urban structure has been preserved. It attracts visitors from far and wide despite its isolated position which makes access difficult from central Italy. Its university dates from 1506.

Hotels near Piazza della Repubblica; others outside the walls (not convenient for those without a car).

Post Office, 24 Via Bramante.—**Tourist Office**, Piazza Duca Federico.

Car Parking, Piazza Mercatale (with underground park).

Buses to *Pesaro* in 40 minutes; to *Fano* via the motorway and Fossombrone; to *Ancona* in c 2¼hrs; to *Arezzo* in 2¾hrs; to *Rome* via Gualdo Tadino, Foligno and Terni in 5½hrs.

History. *Urvinum Metaurense* is said to have been founded by the Umbrian leader Metaurus Suassus, and as *Urbinum Hortense* it is mentioned by Pliny as a Roman municipium. The town rose into prominence in the late 12C, when it became subject to the house of Montefeltro. Count Oddantonio da Montefeltro was made the first Duke of Urbino in 1443, and he was succeeded in 1444 by his illegitimate half-brother Federico, who was not only a great soldier but a generous patron of art and an enlightened ruler. Under him Urbino became a famous centre of the Renaissance. He received the Order of the Garter from Edward IV of England, and a painting of him in the robes of the order, by Melozzo, is now at Windsor; his marriage with Battista Sforza is commemorated in the portraits by Piero della Francesca (1465) in the Uffizi (Florence). His invalid son Guidobaldo I, husband of Elisabetta Gonzaga, was treacherously expelled from his duchy by Cesare Borgia in 1497 but restored after an insurrection. Francesco Maria Della Rovere, nephew of Pope Julius II and of Guidobaldo, who succeeded to the duchy in 1508, proved himself also a brave soldier and a patron of art and learning. He received the Order of the Garter from Henry VII, an occasion commemorated by Raphael's painting of St George (1508), now in Leningrad. Francesco Maria II ceded his possessions to the Church in 1626, and as a consequence Urbino was robbed of many treasures.

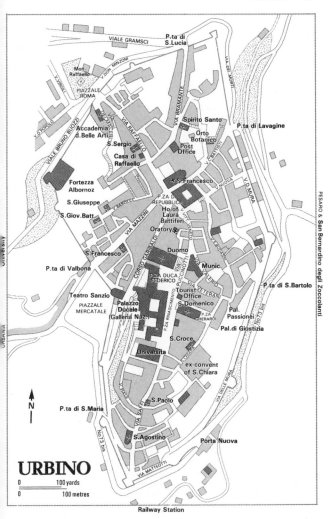

Giovanni Francesco Albani, a native of the city, became Pope Clement XI in 1700. James Stuart, the Old Pretender, was entertained in the palace in 1717–18 and 1722. In the Second World War the city walls were mined, but only those at the SW corner went off and the rest were rendered harmless by the British after they had entered the city on 29 August 1944. This deliverance was doubly fortunate since Urbino had been chosen as a safe repository for works of art from many places in Italy.

Raphael (Raffaello Sanzio or Santi: 1483–1520), was born at Urbino but, with one exception, no genuine work of his remains in his native city. The artistic movement began at Urbino in the early 15C, with the brothers Salimbeni, Ottaviano Nelli, Antonio da Ferrara, and Luca Della Robbia. Federico's court attracted a remarkable group of artists: Luciano Laurana, Francesco di Giorgio Martini, Alberti, Baccio Pontelli, Domenico Rosselli, Pisanello, Sperandio di

Bartolomeo, Piero della Francesca, Justus of Ghent, and the Urbinese masters Fra Carnevale and Giovanni Santi. Later came the Urbinese Timoteo Viti (1467–1524) and Donato Bramante (1444–1514), from Fermignano. In the 16C Federico Barocci was the chief painter of Urbino. The town was long celebrated for its majolica, the manufacture of which was introduced from Castel Durante (c 1477), and was later perfected by the Fontana family (1520–1605).—Among other natives of Urbino were Polydore Virgil (c 1470–1555), author of the *Historia Anglica* and the last collector of Peter's Pence in England, and Clement XI (born 1649).

The main approach to the town passes Via Matteotti (which diverges right along the bastions of the walls before reaching the Teatro Sanzio below Palazzo Ducale) and continues below the walls to Piazzale Mercatale where there is ample car parking (and a ramp or lift up to the Teatro Sanzio on Corso Garibaldi below the Palazzo Ducale).

Urbino is dominated by the delightful ****Palazzo Ducale** built by Federico da Montefeltro, Duke of Urbino, famous condottiere and man of learning. He employed *Luciano Laurana*, a Dalmatian architect to work on the palace from 1465 to 1472, and after him *Francesco di Giorgio Martini*. It is one of the most remarkable Renaissance buildings in Italy and the attribution of the various elements is still under discussion: it is known that Federico himself took an active part in its construction. In the second half of the 15C under Federico and his wife, Battista Sforza, Urbino was famous in Europe as a centre of learning, and artists such as Alberti and Piero della Francesca stayed with the Duke. Castiglione took the Court of Urbino under Federico's son Guidobaldo and his Duchess, Elisabetta Gonzaga, as a setting for his book, 'The Courtier'. Federico's library now forms an important part of the Vatican Library. The palace houses the **Galleria Nazionale delle Marche**, formed in 1912.

The second floor was added in 1536 by *Girolamo Genga* for Guidobaldo II della Rovere. In 1975 the three masterpieces from the gallery (Piero della Francesca's Flagellation and Madonna di Senigallia, and Raphael's Portrait of a Lady) were stolen; the news of their recovery in 1976 was greeted by the ringing of all the church bells in the city. The itinerary of the visit has recently been reversed and the collection rehung. In 1985 the service rooms in the basement were partially opened after restoration, and restoration work continues in several parts of the palace. A remarkably detailed study of the building is being carried out during restoration work, and it is now in excellent condition. In 1987 the Lapidary collection formed in the 17C and 18C, and archaeological material collected by Cardinal Stoppani in the 18C were arranged in the former salt warehouses. Also the Duke's Library was restored and reopened (and stone reliefs designed by Francesco di Giorgio removed from the façade in the 18C exhibited here). The palace is also the seat of the *Soprintendenza per i Beni artistici e storici delle Marche* and an Art School.

The **Opening Times** often vary, but at present they are as follows: Monday–Thursday 9–14, Friday and Saturday, 9–14, 15–19; fest. 9–13. Some parts of the palace are closed without warning when there is a lack of custodians. From January to late Spring the rooms of the palace are bitterly cold.

Exterior. The simple E façade on Piazza Rinascimento is the earliest part of the palace, probably begun before 1460 by the Florentine *Maso di Bartolomeo*. Built in brick it has an irregular design with double windows. The most impressive side of the palace overlooks the valley to the W where it drops sheer down the hillside. Here is the famous 'Torricini' façade attributed to *Laurana*: three tiers of graceful loggie are inserted between two very tall cilindrical towers ending in spires, giving a fairy-tale air to the palace. This can be seen from the ramp which descends between the Duomo and the palace from Piazza Duca Federico. It is particularly impressive when seen from a distance (Piazza Mercatale, Via Barocci, or the Fortezza Albornoz).

The Cortile d'Onore by Laurana in Palazzo Ducale, Urbino

The entrance is in Piazza Duca Federico where two wings of the palace have a rusticated lower façade with three fine doorways and above a carved cornice, four handsome windows with pilasters bearing the inscription 'FE DUX' ('Federico Duke'). This unfinished and damaged façade is also probably the work of *Laurana*. The *CORTILE D'ONORE by *Laurana* is one of the most beautiful Renaissance courtyards ever built. It is well proportioned, with superb composite capitals and very tall arcades (twice as high as they are wide). The inscription in handsome classical lettering is in celebration of Duke Federico. The courtyard is built of red brick and white travertine. The *SCALONE D'ONORE, also by *Laurana* leads up to the **First Floor**, past a statue of Duke Federico by *Girolamo Campagna* (1604). The monumental staircase with its broad shallow steps has beautiful carved details executed in creamy Dalmatian limestone which takes on a polish like that of marble. These are the work of *Ambrogio Barocci* and are typical of the exquisite sculptural decoration throughout the palace on the doors, windows, friezes, cornices, and vaults of many of the rooms which are painted white and otherwise bare of ornament. Many of the carved details include the inscriptions 'FC' ('Federico Conte') and 'FD' ('Federico Duca'): the latter can usually be dated after 1474, the year in which Federico became Duke.

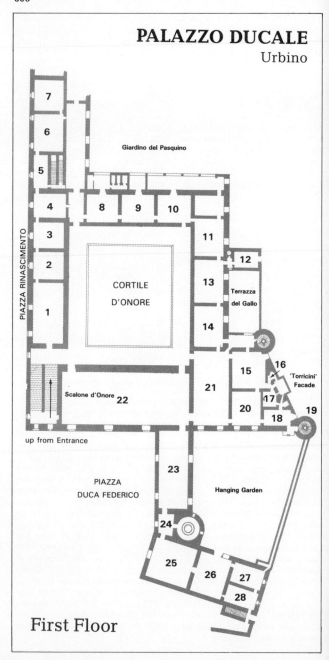

PALAZZO DUCALE
Urbino

Giardino del Pasquino

PIAZZA RINASCIMENTO

CORTILE D'ONORE

Terrazza del Gallo

'Torricini' Facade

Scalone d'Onore 22

up from Entrance

PIAZZA DUCA FEDERICO

Hanging Garden

First Floor

At the top of the stairs is the entrance to the APPARTAMENTO DELLA JOLE (Rooms 1–4), in one of the oldest parts of the palace, through a fine doorway attributed to *Giovanni da Fiesole (Il Greco)* with intarsia doors on a design by *Francesco di Giorgio Martini*. The SALA DELLA JOLE (Room 1) has a splendid *Fireplace, also attributed to *Giovanni da Fiesole*, with a classical frieze and two figures in high relief of Hercules and Jole. Here are displayed a fragment of the head of a Madonna by *Agostino di Duccio*, two portrait reliefs in profile of Guidobaldo da Montefeltro and Battista Sforza attributed to *Francesco di Giorgio Martini*, and a *Lunette with the Madonna and Child and Saints Dominic, Thomas Aquinas, Albertus Magnus, and Peter Martyr, by *Luca della Robbia* (1449) removed from above the portal of San Domenico (seen from the window), and beautifully restored. Here also is a relief of the Madonna and Child by *Giovanni da Fiesole*.

R. 2 (closed for restoration) is the only room in the palace where frescoes have been found: they are attributed to *Giovanni Boccati da Camerino* (1458–66).—R. 3 contains an unusual wooden 'alcove' used

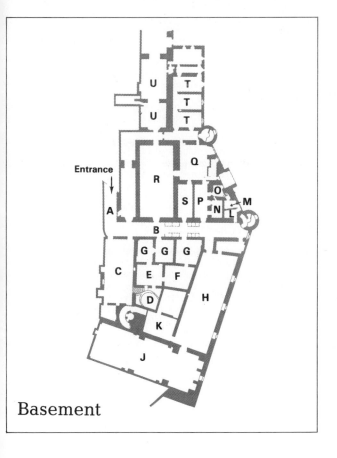

Basement

Lunette by Luca della Robbia from San Domenico (now in the Palazzo Ducale, Urbino)

as a bed by Federico. It is charmingly decorated by *Giovanni Angelo di Antonio da Camerino*. Here also is a 15C Cassone.—R. 4 contains works by *Nicola di Maestro Antonio, Girolamo di Giovanni,* and *Giovanni Boccati*.—R. 5. Paintings by *Andrea di Bartolo di Fredi* and *Marino Angeli*.—R. 6 contains works by *Antonio Alberti da Ferrara* (including a detached fresco of the Crucifixion) and a bas-relief of the Madonna and Child attributed to *Lorenzo Ghiberti*. The room beyond (7) is normally closed.

In the small room off R. 4 are displayed 14C detached frescoes from the abbey of San Biagio in Caprile (Fabriano). The following rooms (8–14) are known as the APPARTAMENTO DEGLI OSPITE. RR. 8 & 9. Good paintings by the Riminese school: *Giovanni Baronzio*, Polyptych signed and dated 1345; *Pietro da Rimini* (attributed), Crucifix; *Maestro del Crocifisso di Verrucchio*, Crucifix; Coronation of the Virgin by an unknown artist named after this painting.—R. 10. Painters from the Marches: *Allegretto Nuzi*, Madonna and Child enthroned; *Carlo da Camerino*, Annunciation.—R 11 contains 15C wood sculptures from the Marches and Abruzzi.—Off R 13 is the little *STANZA DEL RE D'INGHILTERRA (12) where James Stuart, the Old Pretender stayed as a guest of Pope Clement XI. The tiny oval vestibule has a window overlooking the Terrazza del Gallo added by *Francesco di Giorgio Martini*. The little room, with a view over the valley and a fireplace has a charming gilded stucco vault by the local 16C sculptor *Federico Brandani*, with symbols of the Montefeltro and Della Rovere. Here are exhibited a hoard of 14–16C gold coins found locally in 1970.—R 13. Paintings by *Carlo Crivelli, Giovanni Antonio da Pesaro, Pietro Alemanno, Lorenzo d'Alessandro* (Baptism of Christ).—R 14. Venetian paintings by *Giovanni Mansueti, Giovanni Bellini* (Madonna and Child with the young St John and St Anne), *Alvise Vivarini,* and *Marco Basaiti*.

Beyond R 21 (described below) is the APPARTAMENTO DEL DUCA (15–21). In the SALA DELLE UDIENZE (15) are two famous paintings by *Piero della Francesca*: the *Madonna di Senigallia, and the *Flagellation, almost certainly commissioned by Duke Federico. The latter is one of the masterpieces of Italian painting and one of the most discussed for its subject matter and remarkable perspective. The beautiful doorways and window here were probably made after 1474, and the fireplace, surmounted by the black eagle of the Montefeltro arms, is by *Francesco di Simone* and *Domenico Rosselli*.—The tiny CHAPEL (16) was decorated in the 16C for Guidobaldo II Delle Rovere by *Federico Brandani*.—The famous *STUDIOLO (17) is panelled with splendid *Intarsia work by *Baccio Pontelli* on designs by *Francesco di Giorgio*, *Botticelli*, and *Bramante*. This was Duke Federico's study and epitomises his Humanist virtues. The remarkable trompe l'oeil panelling imitates cupboards, some closed and some open to show his books and instruments of study, his armour, and musical instruments. There is also a portrait of the Duke, the Theological Virtues and a landscape. Above are *Portraits of illustrious men by *Pedro Berruguete* and *Justus of Ghent* (photographs replace the originals now in the Louvre). The blue and gold coffered ceiling incorporating the ducal emblem is attributed to *Benedetto da Maiano* (1476).—From the GUARDAROBA DEL DUCA (R 18), overlooking Francesco di Giorgio Martini's hanging garden, a door is open in summer onto the charming upper loggia in the 'Torricini' W façade (see above). Another door from R 18 (unlocked by the custodian) leads into one of the circular towers (19). The fine spiral staircase leads down to the lower loggia and two tiny private chapels of Duke Federico: the TEMPIETTO DELLE MUSE, attributed to *Bramante* (formerly containing paintings of the Muses by Giovanni Santi and Timoteo Viti, now in the Corsini Gallery, Florence); and the exquisite little *CAPPELLINA DEL PERDONO also attributed to *Bramante* with marble inlay, carved friezes, and cherubs' heads on the vault by *Ambrogio Barocci*.

The STANZA DA LETTO DEL DUCA (20) contains the famous *Portrait of Duke Federico with his son Guidobaldo by *Pedro Berruguete* (the Duke is shown in profile since he lost an eye in a tournament). Also here: *School of Verrocchio*, *Madonna and Child. The lovely fireplace, surmounted by the Montefeltro eagle, is by *Domenico Rosselli*. The beautiful doorways (the most elaborate one attributed to *Domenico Rosselli*) have intarsia panels with Hercules and Mars, perhaps designed by Botticelli, and architectural perspectives. The SALA DEGLI ANGELI (21) is named after the superb *Fireplace with reliefs of putti against a blue ground by *Domenico Rosselli*. Here are hung the *'Ideal City', a famous painting of the late 15C attributed to *Piero della Francesca, Laurana, Francesco di Giorgio Martini*, or *Donato Bramante*; *Justus of Ghent*, *Communion of the Apostles; *Paolo Uccello*, *Predella of the Profanation of the Host, an important work; and reliefs by *Domenico Rosselli* and *Tommaso Fiamberti*. The doorway (closed) which leads into the Salone d'Onore has splendid intarsia panels with Apollo and Minerva above two architectural perspectives.

The SALONE D'ONORE (22; known as the SALA DEL TRONO) is reached from the beautiful 'sopralogge' overlooking the Cortile d'Onore. This lovely room with a fine vault was built by *Laurana* as a ceremonial hall. The fireplaces ('FE DUX') were added later.

Guidobaldo I, Captain of the Republic of Venice, put up the Lion of St Mark. 17C Brussels tapestries adorn the walls.

The last group of rooms (23–28) are known as the APPARTAMENTO DELLA DUCHESSA. They were begun by *Laurana* and finished by *Francesco di Giorgio* in the old medieval castle on this site. The SALA DELLE VEGLIE (23) is named after the evening reunions held here by Elisabetta Gonzaga, wife of Guidobaldo, and described by Baldassarre Castiglione in 'The Courtier'. Here are exhibited paintings by *Giovanni Santi*, father of Raphael, and a processional standard by *Luca Signorelli*.—R 24 is a vestibule outside a circular ramp (no adm.) which leads down to the piazza. Here are works by *Timoteo Viti*.— The last rooms (25–28) were adapted by *Francesco di Giorgio* and have delightful ceilings. R 25 has a beautifully decorated ceiling, fireplaces, and doorway by *Francesco di Simone Ferrucci* and *Ambrogio Barocci*. Here is *Raphael*'s splendid *Portrait of a Lady (Maddalena Doni?, called 'La Muta'); also *Redeemer, formerly attributed to Melozzo da Forlì but now thought to be by *Bramantino*; and works by *Timoteo Viti*.—R 26 (STANZA DA LETTO DELLA DUCHESSA) has a window onto the hanging garden (being restored). Here are three 16C Flemish tapestries; a standard by *Titian*; and an Annunciation by *Vincenzo Pagani*.—R 27, the GUARDAROBA has a tiny inlaid door (kept closed) leading to the walkway above the hanging garden which connected this apartment with that of the Duke. Here are works by *Pellegrino Tibaldi* and *Federico Zuccari*.—R 28 has a stucco ceiling by *Federico Brandani* removed from Palazzo Corboli in Urbino, and reliefs by him.

The **Upper Floor** (not always open) contains 17C paintings. The first room (29) has decorations by the sculptor *Federico Brandani*. Here are exhibited good works by *Federico Barocci*, born in Urbino, including a Crucifixion, St Francis receiving the stigmata, the Immaculate Conception, the Assumption, and a bozzetto for the Entombment of Christ.—R 30 contains works by followers of Barocci including a small St Lawrence, and God the Father with angels, and works by *Alessandro Vitali*. R 31 contains a fireplace by *Brandani* removed from Palazzo Bonifazi in Urbino, and paintings by *Orazio Gentileschi* (Madonna and Child with St Francesca Romana), *Simone De Magistris* (Madonna and Child with Saints) and works by *Simone Cantarini*.—R 32. *Claudio Ridolfi*, Assumption; *Andrea Lilli*, St Roch; works by *Pomarancio*.—In the small R 33 is a collection of portraits by the school of Barocci, and *Barocci*'s own self-portrait.— Beyond R 32 is R 34 with a series of monochrome paintings of the Life of St Paul by *Claudio Ridolfi*.—In the following two large rooms restorations in 1972–81 revealed parts of the earlier 15C structure. In R 35 are exhibited drawings by *Federico Barocci* and a fine large cartoon of the Triumph of Bacchus and Ariadne by *Annibale Carracci*. Also here, polyptych by *Giovanni Antonio da Pesaro*. R 36 contains a fine collection of Italian ceramics.—In the long gallery (37) overlooking the Giardino del Pasquino the castellations which mark the original height of Federico's palace can be seen incorporated into the 16C wall. Here are exhibited monochrome paintings by *Claudio Ridolfi* and *Girolamo Cialdieri* made for the marriage of Duke Federico Ubaldo Della Rovere with Claudia de'Medici (1621).

The *Basement has recently been reopened to the public, and is still being restored. The service rooms here are of the greatest interest and complement a visit to the state rooms. A ramp (A) leads down from the Cortile d'Onore. The long corridor (left; B) gives access to the various service rooms: on the right the laundry, cisterns, etc., and the stables and tack rooms. To the left the kitchens, cellars, storerooms, and the Duke's bathroom. The first room (C) is the laundry and dyers room, with an ice-house (D) off it where provisions were stored. The ice was collected from the hanging garden above by means of a chute. Other rooms here were used for filtering water, collected from the roof into a huge cistern (E) for washing (F), and as storerooms (G). The long hall (H) was used for tack and for hay (a chute here enabled the stables to be cleaned easily), and beyond are the stables (J). There was also a bathroom for the stable boys (K). On the other side of the corridor are the little rooms designed as the Duke's bathroom (L–O), with a frigidarium and tepidarium (L), and a Caldarium (M), all of them at the foot of the spiral staircase from his studiolo. Adjoining is a woodstore (P) and the secondary kitchen (Q) and the huge main kitchen (R). Off these is a room which may have been the cook's room (S). Beyond are the pantries (T), and wine cellars (U).

From Piazza Duca Federico a flight of steps between the Palace and the Duomo lead down to a ramp which, hugging the wall of the Palace, descends to Corso Garibaldi. From here there is a splendid view of the W side of the palace, including the famous 'Torricini' façade. Behind the *Teatro Sanzio* (1845–53, by Vincenzo Ghinelli; recently restored) a spiral *Ramp (built by Francesco di Giorgio) or lifts descend to the huge *Mercatale* constructed by Francesco di Giorgio as a market place. It is now a car park (including underground garage) and a bus station. Below the walls beside the theatre can be seen a roofless and grass-grown stable block, also built by Francesco di Giorgio (the ramp originally served for leading the horses up from here to the Palazzo Ducale). The arcaded Corso Garibaldi, skirting the immense buttressed wall of the palace leads direct from here to Piazza della Repubblica (see below).

In Piazza Duca Federico, beside Palazzo Ducale, is the **Duomo** dating from 1477, but completely rebuilt by Giuseppe Valadier after the collapse of the cupola during an earthquake in 1789. The imposing façade is by *Camillo Morigia* (1802). It contains (S aisle), *Barocci*, Martyrdom of St Sebastian (damaged in 1980 when the head of a boy was cut out of the canvas); and St Cecilia and Mary Magdalene with Saints. The chapel to the right of the high altar, designed by *Carlo Maratti* (with an Assumption by him on the right wall) has a 14C fresco fragment over the altar. In the main apse is a huge work by *Cristoforo Unterberger*. In the pretty chapel left of the high altar (light on right): *Barocci*, *Last Supper; *Giovanni Battista Urbinelli da Urbino*, Epiphany. In the N aisle is a Visitation by *Antonio Viviani*.

The MUSEO ALBANI DEL DUOMO (open 9–12.30, 14.30–19; in winter on request) contains an interesting large collection of works from the sacristy and churches in the diocese, displayed in six rooms: frescoes from San Domenico, 17C Casteldurante ceramics; vestments, chalices, etc. (displayed in fine cupboards); bronze lectern of 12C Rhenish work; and paintings by *Agostino Masucci, Andrea da Bologna* (Madonna del Latte); *Battista Franco, Scipione Pulzone, Giorgio Picchi, Federico Barocci, Antonio Viviani, Alessandro Vitali, Raffaellino del Colle* (Madonna della Misericordia; formerly attributed to Gerolamo Genga). The room with 14–15C illuminated MSS is closed for restoration.—The custodian also shows four underground chapels in the crypt, where a marble statue of the Dead Christ by *Giovanni Bandini dell'Opera* has been placed.

Beside the Egyptian Obelisk brought here from Rome by Cardinal Albani in 1737 is the Romanesque and Gothic church of **San Domenico** (1365; closed for restoration) with a Renaissance portal by *Maso di Bartolomeo*, 1449–51.

Behind the church Roman remains have been found including part of the Roman Theatre (not visible). Nearby in Via Valerio is *Palazzo Passionei* in the style of Francesco di Giorgio. Via Santa Chiara leads past the *Oratorio di Santa Croce* to the ex *Convent of Santa Chiara*, probably by Francesco di Giorgio (now occupied by a school, but being restored). From here there is a good view of San Bernardino (see below) and the hills.
   At the upper end of Piazza Rinascimento Via Saffi continues past *Palazzo Bonaventura*, the first residence of the Montefeltro and now the seat of the University. Other buildings in this area have been unobtrusively adapted in recent years by Giancarlo De Carlo for use by the university faculties. Beyond the ancient little church of *San Paolo* (now used as a restoration centre) the street descends sharply to the church of *Sant'Agostino* (1292). Beyond can be

seen the bastions of the city walls (almost completely preserved) begun in 1507 to replace an earlier circumvallation of which traces survive.

From Piazza Duca Federico Via Puccinotti and Via Veneto descend past (right) the interesting Via Veterani and Via Valerio towards Piazza della Repubblica. On the left in Via Porta Maia is the house (No. 6) of Laura Battiferri wife of Ammannati and an Oratory with a Crucifixion by Federico Barocci. PIAZZA DELLA REPUBBLICA is the centre of the life of Urbino and always crowded. From here Corso Garibaldi leads to the Teatro Sanzio skirting the huge walls of the Palazzo Ducale (see above).—Via Mazzini descends straight past several 15–16C palaces and the church of *San Francesco di Paola* decorated by Antonio Viviani in 1614, to *Porta di Valbona* in the city walls. The gateway (a walkway is open across it) was erected in 1621 to celebrate the marriage of Federico Ubaldo della Rovere with Claudia de'Medici. The hillside to the NW of Via Mazzini has numerous pretty little medieval streets, many of them stepped, with houses on a much smaller scale than those on the opposite hill around Palazzo Ducale. Here in Via Barocci (No. 18) is the house where Federico Barocci was born and died, and the **Oratorio di San Giuseppe** (open 10–12, 15–17) with a *Nativity by *Federico Brandani*, a masterpiece of stucco. The little 14C **Oratorio di San Giovanni Battista** (adm. as for San Giuseppe), with a ship's keel roof, contains charming colourful *Frescoes by *Giacomo* and *Lorenzo Salimbeni* (1416) in the International Gothic style (recently restored).

From Piazza della Repubblica Via Raffaello climbs uphill past **San Francesco**, rebuilt in 1740, but retaining a 14C portico and campanile.

In the nave are two good 15C sarcophaghi: one with a worn effigy of 1478 and the other with a Pietà of 1416. The high altarpiece is a good painting by *Federico Barocci* (St Francis). In the chapel to the right, good carving by *Costantino Trappola* (1516–27) and in the chapel to the left, a 15C Pietà. In the left transept, *Giuseppe Passeri*, St Peter baptising two Saints.

Beyond a charming little market and Via Bramante (right) which leads to the *Orto Botanico*, is the **Casa di Raffaello** (adm. 9–13 except Monday; Tuesday, Wednesday, Friday, and Saturday also 15–19), a delightful 15C house owned by Raphael's father Giovanni Santi in which in 1483 the famous painter was born. The evocative rooms are well furnished. The paintings include an Annunciation by *Giovanni Santi*, a Madonna and Child with the young St John by *Giulio Romano*, and a predella by *Berto di Giovanni*, a fine copy of a work by Raphael in Santa Maria Nova in Fano. A fresco of the Madonna and Child (being restored) may possibly be an early work by *Raphael* himself. Since 1872 the house has been the seat of the Accademia di Raffaello.—Just beyond is the church of *San Sergio*, with a raised floor marking the site of a Roman piscina. Over the high altar is a fragment of a votive fresco of the Madonna del Latte, and in the nave a 15C fresco of the same subject by Ottaviano Nelli. Also here, Martyrdom of San Sergio, by Ridolfi.

At the top of Via Raffaello is *Piazzale Roma*, a little garden with a monument to Raphael by Luigi Belli (1897). From here Via dei Maceri leads past the Accademia di Belle Arti to the entrance of a park (9–13, 16–20) around the *Fortezza dell'Albornoz* (closed for restoration), on the westernmost bastion of the walls. There is a splendid view from here of the Palazzo Ducale.

On a hill opposite Urbino (signposted road; or a 20 minutes' walk) is **San Bernardino degli Zoccolanti** ('*Mausoleo dei Duchi*'; open 9–20) next to the Cemetery. This is attributed to Francesco di Giorgio Martini and has a particularly graceful exterior (to be restored). Here were buried Dukes Federico and Guidobaldo I. The view of Urbino is superb.

Outside the walls, on the Colle dei Capuccini to the N, are the interesting College buildings of the University, built on the hillside in 1966 by Giancarlo De Carlo.

Urbino is connected by road with *Fano* (45km) and *Pesaro* (36km) on the Adriatic coast, see Rte 60.

52 Ravenna to Perugia

ROAD, 200km, N3bis ('E7'), a new 'superstrada' almost completed, by-passing the main towns and running parallel to the old road (N71). Distances are approximate and will be considerably shorter when the road is completed.—31km Exit for *Cesena* (4km E).—115km *Pieve Santo Stefano.*—131km **Sansepolcro.**—146km *Città di Castello.*—164km *Umbertide* (**Gubbio**, 29km).—200km **Perugia**.

From Ravenna (Rte 38) Via Cesarea leads out of the town to the by-pass where the new 'superstrada' (N3bis) for Perugia begins, running due S through level fields and orchards parallel to the old road (N71). The new road passes over the A14 motorway and the main Milan-Rimini railway and crosses Via Emilia 4km W of (31km) *Cesena* (see Rte 41). It now ascends the valley of the Savio into the Apennines. At 43km this route joins the N71 as the 'superstrada' is still under construction from here to Bagno di Romagna.—56km *Mercato Saraceno.*—63km *Sarsina*, the birthplace of the comic playwright Plautus (254–184 BC), has an interesting museum containing tombs from a Roman cemetery of the Republican and early Empire period. Beyond the artificial lake of *Quarto*, at (83km) *San Piero in Bagno*, a road from Forlì comes in from the right.—87km *Bagno di Romagna* (491m) is a small thermal spa in a pleasant wooded vale. From here N71 continues over the Passo dei Mandrioli (1173m) to Bibbiena (33km) in the Tuscan Casentino (Rte 51). This route however, continues in the Savio valley where the old road rises to a summit-level of 853m at the *Valico di Montecoronaro*, the lowest crossing of the central Apennines, and the new road tunnels beneath to enter Tuscany, beside the infant Tiber, the course of which is now followed all the way to Todi.

The **Tiber**, in Italian *Tevere*, rises on Monte Fumaiolo (1348m) just to the E of the road, and flows for 418km to the sea. Among its more important tributaries are the Paglia, the Nera, and the Aniene. Flowing through Rome, where it is c 134m wide, it divides the city proper from Trastevere and the Vatican City. On leaving Rome it takes a turn to the SW to its mouth near Ostia. The Tiber, fed by numerous turbulent mountain streams and sensitive to rainfall, is liable to sudden flooding. Its swift waters are discoloured with yellow mud, even far from its source: hence the epithet *flavus* given to it by Roman poets.

115km *Pieve di Santo Stefano* (by pass; described in Rte 51). The 'superstrada' is still under construction from here to the N outskirts of Sansepolcro.—131km **Sansepolcro**, also described in Rte 51.

146km **CITTÀ DI CASTELLO** occupies the site of *Tifernum*, an Umbrian town (35,200 inhab.). In the Middle Ages it gave employment to many artists, among them Raphael, Signorelli, and the

Della Robbia. The Vitelli family held the lordship in the 15C. It now has
tobacco factories. There is an escalator from the car park to the centre
of the town. The *Palazzo del Governo*, with a 14C façade, and the
Palazzo Comunale were built by Angelo da Orvieto (1334–52). The
Torre Civica may be climbed (stairs only; 10–13, 15.30–17.30 except
Monday). The DUOMO, by Elia di Bartolomeo and his assistants
(1466–1529), retains parts of an earlier Romanesque building, with a
tall plain round tower. It has a finely carved side portal of the 14C and
an imposing interior. In a chapel off the right side is an altarpiece of the
Risen Christ in Glory by Rosso Fiorentino (restored). In the Treasury
(closed for restoration) is a silver *Altar-font presented by Celestine II
(1143), and the treasury of Canoscio (5–6C). To the SE of the cathedral
is the church of *San Domenico* with a good side portal and remains of
15C frescoes. In a chapel at the E end of the nave the two Renaissance
altars (1503) formerly held a Crucifixion by Raphael (now in the
National Gallery of London; replaced by a copy) and a St Sebastian by
Signorelli (now in the Pinacoteca, see below). Beyond the church, near
the town wall, is the *Palazzo Vitelli*, built by Antonio da Sangallo the
Younger (1531–32). The fine rooms of the palace are now occupied by
the PINACOTECA (adm. daily 10–13, 15–18; closed Monday in winter).

The garden *Façade has fine graffiti decoration by *Vasari*. The palace is
undergoing restoration and rearrangement. ROOM I. *Reliquary of St Andrew
(1420), with two statuettes in gilded bronze by *Lorenzo Ghiberti*.—RII. Paintings
of the Madonna and Child by *Luca Spinello Aretino, Antonio Vivarini* and
Giovanni d'Alamagna,Giorgio di Andrea di Bartolo, and *Neri di Bicci*. RIII. *Head
of Christ with symbols of the Passion (late 15C); *Signorelli* and his bottega,
*Martyrdom of St Sebastian; *School of Signorelli*, Standard of St John the Baptist;
Bottega of Domenico Ghirlandaio, Coronation of the Virgin.—RIV. Works by
Pomarancio.—RVI. *Standard with the Creation of Eve and the Crucifixion of
Saints Roch and Sebastian, a beautiful but very damaged work by *Raphael*.—
RRVII & VIII have 16C murals. RX, the Salone, is frescoed by *Cola dell'Amatrice*
(1537). The collection also includes: a Sienese marble relief of the 14C showing
the Baptism of Christ; *Maestro della Città di Castello*, *Maestà; *Antonio da
Ferrara*, Triptych; works by *Raffaellino del Colle, Santi di Tito*, and *Domenico
Puligo*, and fine *Della Robbian* works.
     In the church of *San Francesco* is the Vitelli chapel built by Vasari and
containing a Coronation of the Virgin by him, and fine intarsia stalls. On the E side
of the town, in another Palazzo Vitelli (Piazza Garibaldi), is the Tourist Office and
a small archaeological collection relating to the Tiber valley. Palazzo Albizzini
has a museum of paintings by the native artist Alberto Burri.—2km outside the
town, at *Garavelle* on the old Perugia road, an interesting local ethnographical
museum has been arranged in an old farmhouse.

164km **Umbertide** (13,400 inhab.), though heavily bombed in 1944, is
now a busy town with industrial outskirts. The conspicuous church of
Santa Maria della Reggia has a fine octagonal exterior by Bino Sozi
(16C). The crenellated towers (1385) of the *Rocca* survive. On the other
side of the railway is the pretty Piazza San Francesco with three
churches; the first one, *Santa Croce* (restored) has a Deposition by
Signorelli (temporarily removed to the Cappella dell'Ospedale).

A pretty road (28km) runs from Umbertide through typical Umbrian countryside
via Castel Rigone to Lake Trasimene and Passignano (see Rte 56).

On an attractive minor road to Gubbio, c 4km E, is the fine 16C castle of
Civitella Ranieri. The easier road (N219) to Gubbio (29km) leaves the
Perugia road 4km S of Umbertide and passes tobacco fields with their
drying houses (identified by their numerous chimneys).
     GUBBIO (529m), a town of 31,400 inhabitants, in an isolated position
on the lower slopes of Monte Ingino, has preserved to a large degree its

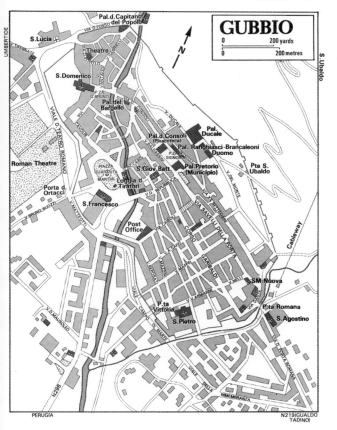

medieval character. Its main roads run parallel with each other following the contours of the steep hillside. Many of its handsome buildings are built of polished light grey stone quarried locally. The high green hillside which forms a background above the town, and the wide plain at its foot are special features of Gubbio, the outskirts of which have been disfigured in the last few decades by new buildings.

Post Office, Via Cairoli, *Azienda Autonoma di Turismo*, 6 Piazza Oderisi.— **Buses** from Piazza Quaranta Martiri to *Perugia*; to *Scheggia* and to *Fossato di Vico* (nearest railway station); to *Umbertide* and *Città di Castello*.

The town grew up beside the ruins of the Umbrian town of *Iguvium* or *Eugubium*, which had a celebrated temple of Jupiter. Gubbio was sacked by the Goths, but retained its independence until 1384, when it was surrendered to the Montefeltro of Urbino. The miniaturist Oderisio (died 1299?) is traditionally considered as the founder of Gubbio's school of painting, which included Guido Palmerucci, Ottaviano Nelli, and Sinibaldo Ibi. The town is famed for its majolica; the chief producer was Giorgio Andreoli da Intra, commonly called Mastro Giorgio, who discovered a peculiar ruby glaze, although hardly any examples of his work survive in the city itself.— The picturesque procession of the *Ceri*, which may have a pagan origin, is held yearly on 15 May, the feast day of St Ubaldo (died 1160), the town's patron saint and bishop who saved it from

Barbarossa in 1155. At this ceremony three wax figures of saints, on wooden 'candles', are carried through the streets at the double. On the last Sunday in May is held the 'palio dei balestrieri' (crossbowmen), a contest of medieval origin against the citizens of Sansepolcro. On Good Friday there is also a traditional procession.—Many of the old houses of Gubbio (as in other Umbrian towns) have the curious 'Porta del Morto' beside their principal doorway. This probably served to give access to the upper floors of the houses; it was formerly believed the small doorway was used when a coffin left the house. Many of the buildings were damaged by an earthquake in 1982 which left 1500 homeless.—Gubbio was the birthplace of Vittoria Accoromboni (1557), the model for Webster's heroine in 'The White Devil'.

The entrance to the town from Umbertide passes the extensive remains of a *Roman Theatre* (restored) of the 1C AD, where classical plays are usually performed in summer, with the remains of a Roman Mausoleum farther S. The town is entered by the Porta degli Ortacci which leads into the large Piazza Quaranta Martiri planted as a public garden, from which there is a good view of all the main monuments of the town climbing the hillside. On the right is the church of *San Francesco* with interesting frescoes in the chapels at the E end: right chapel, 14C frescoes (recently restored); main chapel, 13C frescoes; left chapel, complete cycle by Ottaviano Nelli of the life of the Madonna. The convent buildings are of interest, and include a small museum. The long *Loggia dei Tiratori* was used for drying wool and hides. The steep Via della Repubblica (off which is the little Romanesque 13C church of *San Giovanni*) leads up from the square to Via Savelli della Porta. From here cars continue up to the centre by Via Baldassini (left) and Via dei Consoli (right), while for those on foot steps mount directly to Via dei Consoli the main street of the city. To the left opens the impressive *PIAZZA DELLA SIGNORIA (closed to traffic), with a high balustrade overlooking the plain. Above the long neo-classical *Palazzo Ranghiasci-Brancaleoni*, with tall columns decorating its façade, can be seen the Duomo and Palazzo Ducale on the hillside. The splendid *Palazzo dei Consoli*, one of the most impressive medieval public buildings in Italy (1332–37) is now thought to be by Angelo da Orvieto, although it is also attributed to the local architect Gattapone. It towers over the city, and the SW side, which rests on massive vaulting, is nearly 100m high. It is approached by a delightful outside staircase. In the interior is the MUSEO E PINACOTECA (open 9–13, 15–17; summer 9–12.30, 15.30–18).

The huge barrel-vaulted hall contains sculptural fragments. In the former chapel, off the hall, with a fresco of the Madonna and Child with Saints by *Palmerucci* are the seven celebrated *Eugubian Tables*. These are bronze tables found in 1444 near the Roman theatre, bearing inscriptions in the Umbrian language, five in Etruscan, two in Latin characters. They record the rules of a college of priests, and date probably from 250–150 BC.—A very steep flight of stairs leads up to the Pinacoteca (which also contains some furniture). ROOM I is on the extreme left, and contains works by *Guido Palmerucci*, two 14C reliquaries, 13C Crosses, and a Byzantine diptych.—RII has 14C and 15C frescoes.—RIII. 16C doorway, and the Madonna of the Pomegranate attributed to *Pier Francesco Fiorentino* (still missing after its theft in 1979).—The MAIN HALL has a good brick vault, and the gonfalon of the Confraternity of the Madonna of the Misericordia, a fine work by *Sinibaldo Ibi*, and a symbolic fountain.—RV. Works by *Spagnoletto, Procaccini, Simon Vouet*, and the schools of Caravaggio and Leonardo. A door opens on to the Loggia with a splendid view.

Also in the Piazza is *Palazzo Pretorio* (or *dei Priori* or *Podestà*) now the town hall, built to a design of Gattapone, but left unfinished in 1350. In the neighbouring Via dei Consoli the most notable of many fine old houses is the *Palazzo del Bargello* built for the 13C governors. Near this palace is the 14C church of *San Domenico* and, in the medieval district to the N, is *Palazzo del Capitano del Popolo* and an 18C *Theatre*.

A narrow archway off the main piazza is signposted for pedestrians to the Duomo, also reached by Via Ducale, both of them steep climbs. The ***Palazzo Ducale** (used for exhibitions; adm. to the courtyard 8.30–13.30) was built for Federico da Montefeltro after 1470. It is now attributed to Francesco di Giorgio Martini, and has a fine courtyard similar to that at Urbino. From the hanging garden there is a magnificent view. Opposite is the 13C **Duomo** (open all day) with remarkable stone vaulting and fine works of art in its chapels. Right wall: 1st niche, *Antonio Gherardi*, Adoration of the Magi; 2nd, *Virgilio Nucci*, Madonna of the Consolation. In the presbytery is a fine carved episcopal throne by *Girolamo Maffei* (1557). Left wall: 10th niche, *Benedetto Nucci*, Sant'Ubaldo; 8th, *Sinibaldo Ibi*, Madonna enthroned with Saints; 6th, Nativity by the school of *Pinturicchio*; 4th, *Dono Doni*, Pietà.—The MUSEUM (reached from the right side; ring for the custodian) has been arranged in the Refectory of the old convent which has a fresco of the Crucifixion and Saints attributed to *Palmerucci* (restored). Here too is displayed the celebrated Flemish *Cope, designed by a disciple of Justus of Ghent and presented by Marcello Cervini (Pope Marcellus II; 1555), and some detached frescoes by *Giacomo di Benedetto di Bedi* (13C), from the crypt of the church of Santa Maria dei Laici; and a painting of the Madonna and Child by *Palmerucci*.—A pretty lane climbs the hillside, with orchards and olive groves, behind the Duomo, where the N flank can be seen.

Just inside the Porta Romana, at the SE end of the town, is the ex 14C church of *Santa Maria Nuova* (ring for the custodian at No. 64 Via Dante; 10–12, 16–19) containing the fresco of the *Madonna of the Belvedere, an outstanding work by Ottaviano Nelli (1403). Here too are displayed church vestments, and, on the W wall are frescoes by the school of Nelli. The large church of *San Pietro* is reached from here by Via Nelli and Via Armanni. Of ancient foundation, it has an 18C interior with paintings by Rutilio Manetti, Raffaellino del Colle, and a Baroque organ by Antonio and Giovanni Battista Maffei (1598). — Outside Porta Romana (see above) is *Sant'Agostino*, a 13C church with the triumphal arch and apse entirely frescoed by Ottaviano Nelli and his pupils (1420). On the 5th S altar, fresco of Sant'Ubaldo and two Saints, with scenes from the life of St Augustine, also by Nelli.

On the S outskirts of the town (on the Perugia road) is the church of the *Madonna del Prato* (1662; the plan is taken from San Carlino alle Quattro Fontane by Borromini in Rome), which is being restored.

A cable-car mounts in 6 minutes from the Porta Romana to *Sant'Ubaldo* (827m; a steep climb by a serpentine path from the cathedral) on Monte Ingino, with a superb panorama. In the church are kept the three 'Ceri' (see above).

Beyond Umbertide the main road leaves on the left a road to Gubbio (see above).—At (188km) *Bosco* N298, coming S from Gubbio, joins the main road from the left. 2km farther on a road crosses the Tiber for (200km) **Perugia**, described in Rte 56.

53 Siena to Grosseto

A. Via Paganico

ROAD, 70km, N223.—26km *Bagni di Petriolo.*—35km *Paganico.*—60km *Roselle.*—70km **Grosseto**.

RAILWAY, 128km. Slow trains only in 2¾hrs.

The main road to Grosseto leads S from the Siena by-pass and runs through attractive open countryside, with a distant view of the peak of Monte Amiata (left). It traverses rice fields before passing above (26km) *Bagni di Petriolo* (by-road, left), a little spa enclosed in 15C walls, recently modernised. The road negotiates spectacular viaducts and tunnels.—45km *Paganico*, where the town walls were built in 1292–93 by Lando di Pietro and the 14C church contains contemporary Sienese *Frescoes attributed to Bartolo di Fredi.—60km By-road (left, signposted) for the ruins of **Roselle**, one of the most important Etruscan cities in N Etruria. It became a bishopric in the Middle Ages and was pillaged in 935 by the Saracens; it was abandoned after 1138. The picturesque *Ruins on a beautiful hillside include the polygonal Etruscan walls, and a forum, roads, and other buildings constructed by the Romans. Nearby are a small amphitheatre and baths, also of the Roman period. Excavations are still in progress, and some medieval remains have also been found here.

70km **GROSSETO**, with 62,500 inhabitants, is the capital of the province of the same name, one of the nine in Tuscany. It is also the chief town of the *Maremma Toscana*, a district ravaged by malaria throughout the Middle Ages. Reclamation work, started on a considerable scale by the Lorraine grand-dukes of Tuscany, has gradually drained the marshes; and a modern 'bonifica' (land reclamation) on a large scale was undertaken after 1930, so that it is now in the centre of a rich agricultural zone. The town was subject to Siena and later to Florence.

Tourist Office, 20 Via Monterosa.

Buses to *Marina di Grosseto* in ½hr, going on less frequently to *Castiglione della Pescaia* in 1hr and to *Follonica* in 2hrs; to *Alberese* in ½hr; to *Scansano* in 1½ hrs and *Roccalbegna* in 2½hrs; to *Pitigliano* in 2½hrs; to *Rome* in 3½ hrs; to *Siena* in 3–3¼hrs (see below); to *Florence* in 4hrs; to *Arezzo* in 6hrs.—AIRPORT, with flights to Rome and Milan.

The old town is enclosed in a hexagonal *Rampart* of brick, built by the Medici in 1574–93; five of the bastions were laid out as public gardens by Grand-Duke Leopold II in 1835; the sixth retains something of its military appearance.

The **Duomo**, founded c 1190 and consecrated before 1250, is faced with red and white marble (1294); largely rebuilt in the 16C, it was indifferently restored in 1840–45. The campanile dates from 1402. On the S side of the church are Gothic windows and a sculptured portal. In the interior are a stoup of 1509; a font (1470) by *Antonio Ghini*; and the altar of the Madonna delle Grazie by the same artist, incorporating an Assumption by *Matteo di Giovanni*. San Francesco has a Crucifix attributed as an early work to Duccio di Buoninsegna, dating probably from a rededication of the church in 1289. The MUSEO

ARCHEOLOGICO E D'ARTE DELLA MAREMMA (adm. 9.30–13, 16.30–19 except Wednesday; fest. 9.30–13), opened in 1975, contains Etruscan and Roman antiquities from Roselle, Vetulonia, and sites in the Maremma, including a black bowl on which is scratched the Etruscan alphabet of 22 letters. On the top floor, the Museo Diocesano displays Sienese paintings of the 13–17C including a Last Judgement of the school of *Guido da Siena*, a Madonna by *Segna di Bonaventura*, and a Madonna of the Cherries, by *Sassetta*.

In the Etruscan period the plain between Grosseto and the sea was a shallow gulf, above which rose the islets of Vetulonia and Roselle. By the time of the Romans the gulf had become a salt lagoon called *Prelius*; by 1380 the lagoon had become a fresh-water lake, the *Lago di Castiglione*, which in turn gave place to malarial swamps, now drained and cultivated (see above). At Badiola a memorial stone has been set up to the Grand-Duke Leopold II. The attractive local seaside resorts are served by N322, which continues to Follonica (46km; see Rte 54).—13km *Marina di Grosseto*, borders a wide sandy beach backed by extensive pinewoods. *Principina a Mare* lies 2km S. Farther up the coast stands (24km) **Castiglione della Pescaia**, the most elegant resort of the Maremma, with a port for private boats, on the site of the Roman *Salebro*. It has a castle and old walls. Here is buried the author Italo Calvino (1923–1985) who lived nearby from 1972 until the end of his life.—The coast to the N has numerous exclusive holiday villas at *Rive del Sole* and *Roccamare*, set in shady woods, all of them with private beaches beyond low sand dunes.—The road now crosses inland at the rocky *Punta Ala* to (46km) Follonica (see Rte 54).

FROM GROSSETO TO ARCIDOSSO, 78km; bus to Scansano and Roccalbegna. At first the road follows the valley of the Ombrone. At (7km) *Istia* it bears E and then SE.—From (29km) *Scansano* (500m), roads run SE to Montemerano and Manciano, and S to Magliano and Orbetello (all described in Rte 54). This road turns NE.—58km *Roccalbegna* (522m) has a crumbling *Rocca* and a decayed Romanesque church, from which a fine painting by Ambrogio Lorenzetti has been removed to the canonry.—At (65km) *Triana* the road from Manciano (Rte 54) is joined.—78km *Arcidosso* (500m) is connected by bus with Pitigliano and with Radicofani. Monte Amiata (Rte 57) lies to the E but is better ascended from the other side.

B.   Via Roccastrada

ROAD, 92km, N73, N1. This route follows a secondary road, which is very windy, but it has fine views and passes close to the abbey of San Galgano.—14km *Rosia*.—30km **San Galgano** (2·5km right).—34km *Monticiano*.—59km *Roccastrada*.—77km This route joins the N1.—92km **Grosseto**.

Siena is left to the S and N73 is carried over the by-pass.—14km *Rosia*, with a Romanesque campanile, is 2km N of the abbey of *Torri*, with its fine 11C three-tiered cloister (open weekdays only).—A road on the right diverges at 20km for Colle Val d'Elsa (Rte 47A), and at 30km for Massa Marittima (Rte 54). On the left 2·5km towards Massa is the ruined church of *San Galgano* in an isolated position on a plain in beautiful farming country.

The abbey, once the chief Cistercian house in Tuscany, was built beneath the little hill-top mausoleum on Monte Siepi of St Galgano Guidotti (1148–81), canonised in 1185. The church is a remarkable French Cistercian Gothic building (1218–88). In the 14C and 15C the abbey was corruptly administrated, and in the 16C the abbot sold the leading of the roof which by 1786 had collapsed, and the buildings were subsequently abandoned. The entrance to the church is on the right of the ruined façade past the Chapter House and a fragment of the cloister. The roofless church with a grass-grown nave and a magnificent E end is one of the most romantic sites in Tuscany. The little rectangular detached cemetery chapel also dates from the 13C.—On Monte Siepi, the little hill above, is the round chapel of San Galgano (if closed, ask for the key at the farm next door). This was erected in 1182 over the tomb of St Galgano and on the site where he lived as a hermit (but it has been altered in later centuries). The unusual primitive *Dome is built of concentric rings of red brick and white travertine. The sword in the stone here commemorates St Galgano's renunciation of knightly pursuits in favour of a life of prayer before the Cross. A little 14C chapel has interesting frescoes and sinopie by Ambrogio Lorenzetti. There is a splendid view of the abbey from the hill.

34km *Monticiano*, a walled village where the 13C church of Sant' Agostino has frescoes in its chapter house by Bartolo di Fredi and others.—59km *Roccastrada* (477m) has a good town belfry. *Roccatederichi*, 13km NW, is a typical old Tuscan hill-village. The road now descends to the plain and at 77km joins the Via Aurelia (N1) for (92km) **Grosseto**, see above.

54 Pisa to Livorno, Grosseto, and Monte Argentario

ROAD, 193km, N1 (Via Aurelia) a busy road being realigned and made into dual carriageway in places (distances are approximate).—19·5km **Livorno**.—41km *Castiglioncello*.—55km *Cecina*—80km *San Vincenzo*.—106km *Follonica* (for **Massa Marittima**, 23km).—153km **Grosseto**.—193km *Orbetello Scalo* (for **Orbetello** and **Monte Argentario**).

RAILWAY. Slow trains to (186km) *Orbetello-Monte Argentario* in over 2 hours.—Fast trains to *Livorno*, 20km in 15 minutes; to *Cecina*, 54km in 40 minutes; and to *Grosseto*, 148km in 1½hrs. This important line is followed by international trains to Rome with through carriages from Turin, Genova, Paris, Marseille etc. The night trains have sleeping cars.

The Via Aurelia (N1) leads out of Pisa S of the Arno and runs beneath the A12 motorway to (11km) *Stagno* in the midst of the former marshes of the Arno, drained (c 1620) by Sir Robert Dudley, and now occupied by a huge oil refinery. Here N67bis diverges inland; it is now part of a 'superstrada' (nearing completion) from Livorno to Florence (see Rte 47C). Across the canal the Livorno by-pass begins.

19·5km **LIVORNO** (Tourist Office, 6 Piazza Cavour) is a flourishing seaport (174,700 inhab.) which, in the last decade, has become the biggest container port in the Mediterranean. It was called by the English *Leghorn*. Beyond the fortifications it preserves few old buildings, especially since the systematic destructions of 1943, but the town has been well reconstructed on open symmetrical lines. The spacious seaboard is particularly attractive and the town has a lively air, and good fish restaurants. It has a well-known street market where American goods are sold (Camp David, the U.S. army base is nearby).

Though a fortress was contested here between Pisan, Genoese, and Florentine overlords from the early Middle Ages, Livorno dates its rise from 1571, when the new port was begun by decree of Cosimo de'Medici. Ferdinand I (1587–1609) continued the work and employed Sir Robert Dudley, son of the Earl of Leicester, Elizabeth I's favourite, to construct the great mole (1607–21). Sir Robert, a marine engineer, built warships and administered the port for the Grand-Duke. Ferdinand by his proclamation of religious liberty made the town a refuge for persecuted Jews, Greeks who had fled from the Turks, converted Moors expelled from Spain and Portugal under Philip III, and Roman Catholics driven

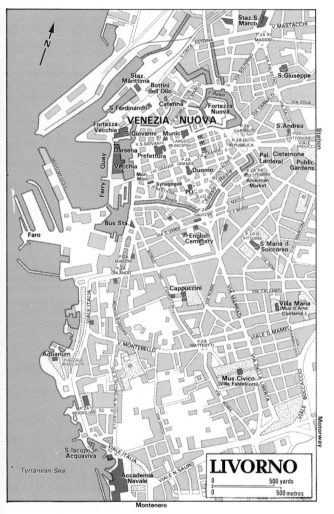

from England under the penal laws. They were joined by many Italians fleeing from the oppression of their own states, and by exiles from Marseilles and Provence. The policy of Ferdinand was pursued by his successors, and Livorno became a great port, now the third largest in Italy. As a neutral port it was able to supply numerous ships for the naval battles against Napoleon, and Lord Nelson came here in 1793. In 1749 Sir Joshua Reynolds landed here on his only visit to Italy, and Tobias Smollett, Byron, and Shelley all lived here (see below). Pietro Mascagni (1863–1945), composer of 'Cavalleria Rusticana', was born here, as was also Amedeo Modigliani (1884–1920), the artist. In 1984 two sculptures were dredged up from the Fosso Reale and acclaimed by numerous art critics to be lost masterpieces by Modigliani. These were soon proved to be fakes made by a group of young students, and the incident was recognised as one of the most successful hoaxes of recent years.

Nearly 5km off Livorno rises the reef of *Meloria*, where the maritime power of Pisa was crushed by the Genoese in 1284; hereabouts also in 1653 an English trading fleet was routed by the Dutch.

Car ferries connect Livorno with Sardinia, Corsica and Elba.

Beside the main harbour for the fishing fleet in the *Darsena Vecchia* (1591) are the famous 'Quattro Mori', the *Monument to Ferdinando I*, with his statue by Giovanni Bandini (1595) and four Moorish slaves in bronze by Pietro Tacca (1623–26; covered for restoration). On the fortified wall here (restored as part of a hotel) is a plaque set up in 1896 by John Temple Leader to Sir Robert Dudley (see above). In the harbour is the wall of the crumbling *Fortezza Vecchia*, built to the design of Antonio da Sangallo in 1521–34, embodying the so-called Matilda Tower (11C) and remains of the Pisan fort of 1377. Beside it a new bridge is under construction across the canal. The unattractive Via Grande leads to Piazza Grande with the *Duomo*, rebuilt in 1954–59. The Doric portico still owes something to the original design by Inigo Jones (1605). The interior contains ceiling paintings by Ligozzi, Passignano, and Empoli.

Behind the cathedral, Via Cairoli (closed to traffic) leads past the Post Office, at the back of which in Via del Tempio is the modern *Synagogue*, built in 1962 on a design by Di Castro, after the destruction of the old synagogue in the War. Via Cairoli ends in Piazza Cavour across two branches of the attractive Fosso Reale. Beyond, in Via Verdi (right) is the entrance (at No. 59) to the *Old British Cemetery* (for the key to the gate apply at the offices of the Misericordia, 9–12, 15–18.30; fest. 9–12). The monumental tombs, many of them dating from the 1660s, are surrounded by thick vegetation. Here Tobias Smollett (see below) was buried (probably in 1773). The cemetery was visited by Shelley, Longfellow, and Fenimore Cooper and was closed in 1840 when the new cemetery was opened in the N suburbs. The Anglican church outside, dating from 1840, is now used by the Misericordia as a chapel.—About 1km S in Piazza Matteotti is the entrance to the park (open 10–20) of the *Villa Fabbricotti* where the MUSEO CIVICO (adm. 10–13, except Monday & Thursday also 16–19) has a fine collection of works by the 'Macchiaioli' painters including Giovanni Fattori (1825–1908), a native of the town. In the park of Villa Maria (entered from 22 Via Redi) is a modern art gallery.

Piazza Grande is linked by Via Grande with the huge Piazza della Repubblica, overlooked by the moated *Fortezza Nuova* (1590). Via de Larderel runs towards the Railway Station past the huge *Palazzo Larderel* (1832–50), the *Cisternone*, a neoclassical water cistern by Pasquale Poccianti (1829–32), and a public garden. To the S in Piazza XX Settembre is the famous 'Mercatino' where American goods are sold. From Largo Municipio (see the Plan) Via San Giovanni (the old main street) passes the church of *San Giovanni* with a high altar by Ferdinando Tacca. On the right a road leads across a bridge to Via Borra with a few palaces (some being restored). Beyond the next pretty bridge is the octagonal church of *Santa Caterina* (being restored; it contains a Coronation of the Virgin by Vasari). This area, laid out in 1629–44, is known as 'Nuova Venezia' because of its numerous canals. From the bridge here there is a good view right of the wall of the Fortezza Nuova. Via San Marco traverses the interesting Via dei Floridi with houses built above the old bastions, to the ruined façade of the ex-theatre of San Marco where a worn plaque records the founding of the Italian Communist party here in 1921. The Scali del Rifugio skirts the canal past the ex-convent of Santa Caterina where Sandro Pertini (elected President of the Republic in 1978) was held as a political prisoner during the Fascist regime (plaque set up in 1977). To the right a roadway descends above an archway giving access to the canal. The *Bottini dell'Olio* here were built in 1705–31 on a design by Giovanni Battista Foggini as a warehouse (some 24,000 barrels of oil could be housed here). The fine vaulted hall has been restored and is now used for exhibitions. Amidst evident signs of bombing from the last War is the church of *San Ferdinando*, recently restored with a good interior, also by Foggini, and sculpture by Giovanni Baratta.

The pleasant VIALE ITALIA skirts the shore with a wide promenade passing gardens and elegant seaside houses, and 19C hotels and bathing establishments. On the Piazzale Mascagni, a pretty terrace built out into the sea, is the *Aquarium* (10–12, 16–19 or 14.30–17.30 in winter) and, farther on, the huge *Naval Academy*, founded in 1879, next to the 17C church of *San Jacopo in Acquaviva*, sited where St James the Great is supposed to have landed on his way to Spain; St Augustine also is said to have stayed here after his baptism. The Viale continues past Art Nouveau houses and the attractive suburbs of *Ardenza* (with a neo-classical crescent, built in 1840, overlooking the sea) and *Antignano*, built as bathing resorts.

A bus runs to **Montenero** (193m; also reached by funicular railway) where Tobias Smollett (born in 1721) lived for the last two years of his life and finished 'Humphrey Clinker'. Byron, who spent a holiday at the Casa Dupuy, may have sailed from here in his boat, the 'Bolivar', to visit Shelley at the Casa Magni (see Rte 7). While staying at the Villa Valsovona near here, in 1818 Shelley wrote his tragedy 'The Cenci'. The pilgrimage church of Montenero contains a miraculous picture of the Madonna, supposed to have sailed by itself in 1345 from the island of Negropont (Euboea) to the shore of Ardenza.

Beyond Livorno the Aurelia has been improved and made into dual-carriageway as far as the Cecina by-pass. Instead the old road hugs the shore, and, beyond the seaside suburbs of Ardenza and Antignano, passes (32km) *Quercianella*, another little seaside resort among pine woods.—41km **Castiglioncello**, an elegant resort on a promontory, has a small archaeological museum. At (43km) *Rosignano Solway* are the factories processsing the soda from the Saline di Volterra. The old town of Rosignano is 4km inland.—At (48km) *Vada* the railway from Pisa via Colle Salvetti joins the main line.—55km **Cecina** is the junction for Volterra (described in Rte 49), which lies 42km inland along N68. Here in 1985 the Etruscan-Roman museum in the Villa della 'Cinquantina' was reopened.—67km *San Guido*. A splendid *Avenue of cypresses, nearly 5km long, planted in 1801 by Camillo della Gherardesca, leads from the main road up to the village of *Bolgheri* where the poet Carducci spent his childhood (1838–49). The cypress avenue is the subject of a famous poem by him. Another road leads inland at 72km to the village of *Castagneto Carducci*, opposite a road for the resort of *Castagneto-Donoratico*.—80km *San Vincenzo* is a large seaside resort extended to the S by the Riva degli Etruschi, a vast bungalow colony. At San Vincenzo N1 runs inland (see below), while another road continues due S along the coast for Populonia (17km) and Piombino (22km).

12km S a by-road diverges right for the gulf of *Baratti*, a pretty bay with a little port. Here in the sea in 1968 was found a silver amphora (recently restored) decorated with 132 concave medallions with figures in bas-relief thought to be from Antioch and to date from the end of the 4C, possibly the work of a Syrian silversmith. The road passes the Necropolis of **Populonia** (San Cerbone) on the sea (groups are conducted every hour 9–12.30, 15.30–19; September–April, 9–dusk). Populonia (or *Pupluna*), possibly one of the cities of the Etruscan Confederation, had a continuous history from the Iron Age through the Roman

era. Iron ore from Elba was discharged and smelted in the port of Baratti and
Populonia was important for its iron works. It was sacked by Sulla, by Totila, and
by the Lombards. Several interesting large tumulus tombs (7C–5C BC) are
shown as well as one in the form of an aedicule. Another necropolis known as
'Porcareccia' in woods nearby and a 'factory' area where iron was worked in the
Etruscan era are shown only by special request. The road goes on over a hill to
the tiny little castellated village which preserves the name of Populonia—'seagirt' in Macaulay's lay—where the castle is well preserved. There is a small
Etruscan Antiquarium here (No. 21) and remains of the walls of 6–5C BC are
signposted. A Roman villa has also been identified in the vicinity.

The main road continues S to **Piombino** (22km), with 39,600 inhabitants,
situated at the S end of the Massoncello promontory, once an island. It is an old
seaport which has thrived in recent years and is now entirely dominated by large
and ugly metal works. It is the port for Elba (see Rte 55). Buses run from the
station to *Porto Vecchio* (for the Elba boats) in 10 minutes; to Volterra (2¾hrs);
and to Livorno (2¼hrs); and a branch railway runs to Campiglia (see above) in 20
minutes.

90km *Venturina* is at an important crossroads. *Campiglia Marittima*,
4·5km to the left, is a prosperous town commanding a wide view, on
the Colline Metallifere. Slag heaps and remains of furnaces survive in
the Val di Fucinaia. *Rocca San Silvestro*, c 5km N of Campiglia, is a
little medieval mining town abandoned in the 15C and exceptionally
well preserved (extensive excavations in progress). To the right of
Venturina is another road for Piombino (14km) via Campiglia
station.—The main road reaches the sea again just before (106km)
Fallonica, an unattractive industrial town (16,700 inhab.) situated on
the gulf of the same name. It has a popular sandy beach and
commands views of the island of Elba and of the promontory on which
Piombino is situated. From the little *Cala Martina*, to the S, Garibaldi
escaped by fishing boat in 1849.

A road diverges inland (left) for **Massa Marittima** (19km; 399m), in
beautiful countryside amidst woods of ilex, oak, and olives. It was the
birthplace of St Bernardine of Siena (1380–1444). This ancient mining
town (10,500 inhab.), once an independent republic, preserves its old
walls. There is a car park below the cathedral. In the delightful *Piazza
Garibaldi* (usually called Piazza del Duomo) the Duomo is magnificently positioned at an angle above an irregular flight of steps, with
the campanile closing the vista. Next to it is the Palazzo del Podestà
with the museum, and opposite, Palazzo Comunale. The *Duomo
(San Cerbone*; closed 12–15) has a splendid Romanesque exterior in
travertine with blind arcading. The upper part of the façade was
added in the Pisan Gothic style in 1287–1314. The story of its patron
saint is sculpted above the main doorway.

The **Interior** has remains of 15C frescoes and 14C stained glass in the rose
window. The splendid rectangular *Font with reliefs by *Giroldo di Jacopo da
Como* (1267) has a 15C tabernacle rising from its centre. Behind the high altar is
the *Arca di San Cerbone (died c 580) with scenes of his life sculpted by *Goro di
Gregorio* (1324), and on the wall is a painted Crucifix (restored) by *Segna di
Bonaventura*. Eleven statuettes by the school of *Giovanni Pisano*, at present in
the undercroft, may also be exhibited here. In the chapel to the left of the high
altar, *Madonna delle Grazie (1316; recently restored), and, behind it, Crucifixion and scenes of the Passion, inspired by the Maestà in Siena. This is thought to
be the work of *Duccio di Boninsegna*, or of a close follower. On the W wall are
interesting carved Lombard panels of the 11C with the Massacre of the
Innocents and the Apostles, from the old high altar.

Next to the Cathedral is *Palazzo del Podestà*, with the *Museo
Archeologico*, the *Pinacoteca*, and a *Garibaldi Museum* (10–12.30,
15.30–19 except Monday). The interesting archaeological material on
the ground floor dates from the Paleolithic to Roman era, all of it well

labelled, mostly from near the Lago dell'Accesa (see below). The interesting funerary stele carved in a stylized human form is reminiscent of the 'statue-stelae' of Luni. On the floor above is the Pinacoteca, with a *Maestà (Madonna with angels and Saints) by *Ambrogio Lorenzetti* (c 1330), and some ceramics. The Garibaldi museum is closed for restoration.

Opposite the *Palazzo Comunale*, a fine 13C building, Via Moncini rises to the upper 'new' town. The steps lead up beneath the remains of the fortress erected by the Sienese after their conquest of Massa in 1337. At the top the road passes a long flying arch joining the fortress to the *Torre del Candeliere*, the tower of an older castle (1228). It may be climbed (10.30–12.30, 15.30–18.30 except Monday). Behind it is Piazza Matteotti with a view down to Porta San Francesco and (at the end of Via Balilla) a view of the walls. In Palazzo delle Armi here is a small museum illustrating the history of mining in the area. Corso Diaz leads to *Sant'Agostino* (c 1300; paintings by Rutilio Manetti) with a fine cloister. In the S part of the town, off Via Corridoni, is a *Museum of Mines* (guided tours only, 9–13, 15–17; April–September 10–12.30, 15.30–19; closed Monday), in an old mine gallery. This shows how metals were extracted and illustrates the riches of the metalliferous hills in the vicinity (iron, copper and lead ores). Mining has taken place here since Etruscan times and was a flourishing industry in the Middle Ages, and again in the last century.

8km from the town a pretty road (signposted) leads through wooded country to the little *Lago del'Accesa* where Etruscan finds have been made.

The winding road from Massa Marittima to Siena (N73, 64km) traverses pretty farming country and crosses the metalliferous hills with interesting rock formations and a few abandoned mines. There are also thick woods of oak trees. It passes San Galgano (described in Rte 53).

Another road (N439) leads N from Massa to (68km) Volterra, via Larderello, described in Rte 49.

From Follonica (see above) the modern Via Aurelia (A1, being improved) turns inland and offers the fastest approach to Grosseto; the Roman road followed the line of the coastal by-road (N322) which continues S and provides an alternative route to Grosseto via Castiglione della Pescaia and Marina di Grosseto (described in Rte 53). Among the wooded hills to the right of the modern road are the iron mines that supply the furnaces of Follonica.—At 129·5km a by-road on the right leads in 5km to the hill-top village of *Vetulonia*, on the site of the city of **Vetulonia** or *Vetluna*, one of the most important members of the Etruscan Confederation. Here the Romans defeated the Gauls in 224 BC. The Romans are said to have borrowed from Vetulonia the insignia of their magistrates—the fasces, curule chair, and toga prætexta—and the use of the brazen trumpet in war. There survive remains of the citadel wall and of a street of houses. The small Antiquarium has been closed, but there are long-term plans to open a bigger museum here. The most remarkable tombs in the 8C necropolis, nearly 3km NE of the village, are the huge domed Tumulo della Pietrera, and the Tumulo del Diavolino (difficult to find, and reached by poor roads).

139km Junction of N73 for Siena (via Roccastrada, described in Rte 53). On a hill to the left stands *Montepescali*, the 'balcony of the Maremma'. The parish church has an altarpiece attributed to Matteo di Giovanni, and San Niccolò, higher up, has frescoes by a follower of Bartolo di Fredi.—153km **Grosseto**, see Rte 53. N1 continues S from Grosseto across the Ombrone, the classical Umbro, one of the chief rivers of Etruria.—159km *Rispescia*. Here a by-road leads towards the coast for **Alberese** (9km), at the N entrance to the **Parco Naturale della Maremma**, an area of some 70 sq. km designated a national park in 1975, which stretches S across the beautiful wooded and roadless **Monti dell'Uccellina** (417m) to Talamone.

There are two entrances (where tickets must be purchased) to the park, one at Alberese and one at the museum of Talamone on the S border. Part of the park is usually open 9–one hour before sunset, but on Wednesday, Saturday, and fest. more areas can be visited. From 15 June–30 September admission is only allowed at 7 and 16.00 on Wednesday, Saturday, and fest. Various itineraries are indicated along marked footpaths (most of them require a minimum of 3hrs), and for some of them transport is provided for part of the way. There is a museum illustrating the various aspects of the park at Talamone. The vegetation varies from pine woods to marshlands, and the typical Mediterranean 'macchia'. Animals which run wild here include deer, foxes, goats, cattle, wild cat, horses, and wild boar. The cattle and horses are herded by cowboys known as 'butteri'. Migratory birds and numerous aquatic species abound. The *Torre della Bella Marsilia* is the lonely remnant of the castle of Collecchio, home of the Marsili of Siena. In 1543 the castle was destroyed by the corsair Barbarossa and the entire household murdered except for the lovely Margherita, who was carried off to the harem of Sultan Suleiman the Magnificent, soon to become his legitimate sultana and the mother of Selim II. Farther N are the romantic ruins of the 12C abbey of *San Rabano*.

176km *Fonteblanda*. A road leads past Talamone station for **Talamone** (4km) on a little bay at the S boundary of the Parco Naturale della Maremma (see above). This was once an Etruscan city said to have been founded by the Argonaut Telamon c 1300 BC. Here the Romans routed the Gauls in 225 BC and here Marius landed on his return from Africa in 87 BC. Near the top of the hill are the scant remains of a large temple (enclosed; no adm.). Finds made during excavations here include the splendid pediment of the temple, now displayed in Orbetello, see below. Here also Garibaldi and the Thousand put in on their way to Sicily in 1860 to collect arms and ammunition and to land a party for a feint attack on the Papal States.—Beyond Fonteblanda the road crosses the Osa and then the Albenga.—184km *Albinia* with a bird sanctuary administered by the World Wildlife Fund. The road now skirts the extensive lagoon of Orbetello, with interesting bird life (although its waters are now threatened with pollution). In the middle of the lagoon, on a sandy isthmus, 4km from (143km) *Orbetello Scalo* (which has grown up round the station), is **Orbetello** (13,500 inhab.), an old-fashioned resort with palm trees on the waterfront. It was an Etruscan colony and a place of importance in the Middle Ages. It was fortified in 1557 by the Spaniards, who left also the unusual *Polveriera Guzman* (powder-works), which has recently been restored. The Museo Civico contains archaic sculpture in bronze and stone (6C BC), and the remarkable sculptured *Pediment of a huge Etruscan temple (2C BC) found at Talamone and restored in 1982. The *Cathedral*, rebuilt in 1600, preserves a lovely façade of 1376, and an early Romanesque marble altarpiece. On clear mornings there is a wonderful view across the lagoon to Monte Argentario. In 1933 Italo Balbo led a formation flight to Chicago from here.

Monte Argentario (635m), usually known simply as 'L'Argentario' is an almost circular peninsula joined to the mainland by three narrow strips (tomboli), the outer two, both pine-clad, defining the *Laguna di Orbetello*; the town of Orbetello occupies the central strip. It has beautiful vegetation with fine woods, threatened by forest fires in summer. Caravaggio met his end in the lagoon in 1609. **Porto Santo Stefano**, 10km from Orbetello, and the smaller **Porto Ercole**,

7km from Orbetello, are now famous as exclusive summer resorts with harbours for yachts and lively fish markets. Porto Ercole, a particularly sheltered port, has fortifications of the Spanish period (16C). A port for private boats recently constructed at Cala Galera nearby has eroded the coastline of the *Tombolo di Feniglia*, a beautiful sandy beach. Queen Giuliana, who abdicated from the Dutch throne in 1980, has a house here. The rocky bays on the S coast provide private beaches for the grand summer hotels. A road (unmade-up in places) encircles the mountain (26·5km), and another road (signposted for the 'Punto Telegrafo') leads up towards the summit. It passes the motherhouse of the Passionist Order, founded by St Paul of the Cross in 1720 in cypress woods. Eight monks now live here and the church, threatened by landslides, has had to be propped up. The road ends above ilex woods which shelter numerous wild flowers at a mast and military installations. The splendid view N embraces the Tombolo di Giannella.

From Santo Stefano boats, car ferries, and hydrofoils run frequently (in c 1hr) to the pretty **Isola del Giglio**, 17·5km W. It has an area of 21 sq. km, and has a little grey granite fortress-village (bus from the port), and vineyards. Pathways lead down to the sandy beach from the village. The island is crowded at weekends in summer, and new buildings are spoiling its natural beauty. In 1961 in the Bay of Campese a boat was discovered offshore some 50 metres below the surface, shipwrecked c 600 BC. Its cargo of Greek and Etruscan ceramics, including numerous aryballoi and Corinthian ware, wooden flutes, and a rare bronze Corinthian helmet has mostly been recovered, and in 1985 part of its keel, 3m long, was salvaged. Oxford University has been in charge of the project.

The island of *Giannutri*, to the SE, which has also been threatened with tourist 'development', has ruins of a Roman villa of the family of Domizi Enobardi.

FROM ORBETELLO TO PITIGLIANO, 62km. This pretty route follows the Via Aurelia N to (10·5km) *Albinia* (see above), turning right there on N74 up the beautiful wooded valley of the Albenga, through countryside typical of Tuscan Etruria.—
14km On the left a road leads to Scansano (29km; Rte 53) via *Magliano in Toscana* (11km), an ancient town with splendid walls. It has a 15C church, and, in another church outside the SE gate, is a Madonna by Neroccio. A road (signposted right just before the town) leads SE to the Romanesque ruin of *San Bruzio* near the extensive remains of an Etruscan necropolis (no adm. while excavations are in progress). Beyond Magliano the road continues to Scansano past *Pereta*, a charming small village preserved intact with a tall tower and two red stone churches.

N74 continues up the valley to *Marsiliana*, situated in beautiful woods of pine and cypress, with an Etruscan necropolis. It then climbs to (43km) *Manciano* (443m) an old Sienese fortress now surrounded by a small town. Here is the Museo di Preistoria e Protostoria della Valle del fiume Fiora (October–May, 9.30–12.30, 14.30–17.30; in summer 10–13, 16–19; closed Monday) opened in 1985, with Paleolithic, Neolithic, and Bronze Age finds from the Fiora river valley which flows from Monte Amiata to the sea.

From Manciano a by-road runs N to Arcidosso (51km; described in Rte 53), passing Montemerano and Saturnia. *Montemerano* (6km) is an old walled town whose church of San Giorgio has 15C frescoes. A Museum is to house the works of art from the church which include a fine pentaptych by Sano di Pietro (1458). *Saturnia* (13km) is a pretty town with impressive prehistoric walls and medieval ramparts. Below the town is a little spa where the 'terme' (37°) have therapeutic qualities (used since Roman times). There is an unenclosed waterfall nearby where anyone can enjoy the waters.

N74 continues from Manciano to (62km) **Pitigliano** (313m) of Etruscan foundation, in a magnificent position on a tufa outcrop above a gorge. This is a wine-producing town and was the seat of the Orsini and preserves their palace. About 8km N is the tiny village (recently restored) of *Sovana*, situated above the Celesina valley. In the Middle Ages it was a bishopric and was the birthplace of Gregory VII (Hildebrand). Here is an Etruscan necropolis (signposted; unenclosed), with the 'Tomba Ildebranda' (named after Gregory VII), a monumental tomb in the form of a temple (early 3C BC), and the 'Tomba della Sirena', an 'aedicule' tomb, and the 'Cavone', a remarkable Etruscan road cut through the tufa. The remains survive of the keep of the fortress of Gregory's family, the Aldobrandeschi. In the ancient piazza are the Romanesque church of Santa Maria with a splendid ciborium (?9C) and a fresco of the Madonna and Child with Saints dated 1508, the ruins of the church of San Mamiliano (with Roman masonry), and remains of several medieval palaces. The fine 11C Cathedral (open all day in summer; Saturday and Sunday only in winter) also survives.—**Sorano**, another interesting medieval borgo built into the tufa, lies 10km E of Sovana (also reached by road from Pitigliano). It is in a fine position, typical of the Maremma, and has a 15C castle and palace of the Orsini. The charming village, which was declared uninhabitable in 1929 because of landslides, has nearly all been restored except for the outskirts on the edge of a steep gorge.

Beyond the S limit of the lagoon of Orbetello (see above) lies the little resort of *Ansedonia*, reached from the Aurelia by a road at 146km. On a flat-topped hill (113m) here is the site of the city of *Cosa*, founded by the Romans in 273 BC, and later called Ansedonia.

Excavations continue, and some of the remains are on private land, but the excellent little Museum is open 9–14, fest. 9–13 except Monday. On top of the hill, in a beautiful position with fine views, surrounded by polygonal walls with 18 towers and three gates, are the forum, basilica, and remains of the Capitolium, a Roman temple with a triple cella (replacing an earlier Etruscan temple), dedicated to Jupiter, Juno, and Minerva. At the foot of the hill is the Torre Puccini, where Puccini composed part of 'Tosca'. This is the site of the port of Cosa, formerly on a lagoon connected to the Lago di Burano, now silted up. It was connected to the sea by the 'spacca della Regina', a natural cleft in the rock 260m long, which was later substituted by the so-called 'Tagliata Etrusca', a shorter channel cut through the rock (still clearly visible), designed also to prevent the silting up of the harbour. A project to construct a port for private boats threatens to damage these interesting remains.

On the other side of the Aurelia a by-road (signposted 'Villa Romana') leads inland past the ruins of a Roman villa ('delle Colonne') with an interesting perimeter wall with unusual cylindrical towers. The road continues for c 1km; the second road on the left (unmade-up) mounts a small hill (not signposted; keep left) to a house in pine trees, beside which a sign for the 'scavi archeologici' indicates the overgrown ruins of the Roman villa of *Settefinestre* in a romantic setting (on the hillside below, beside a fence). Excavations (some of them since covered over) in 1976–81 by student volunteers from Tuscany and London revealed remains of a large villa of the 1C BC (probably abandoned by the mid-2C AD), with farm buildings attached. Numerous rooms with geometric mosaic floors were identified, and part of its front wall (3·5–4·5m high), as well as wall-paintings of the 2nd and 4th Pompeian style. The farm (with wine and olive presses, and buildings thought to have been used as pigsties) appears to have been run by slaves whose modest quarters have also been found. The visible remains, now abandoned, include a high wall with buttresses and arches.

The Aurelia continues towards Rome, and, at 157km, is the turning for **Capalbio**, a charming little medieval village, 10km NE, in a beautiful position on a low hill above thick ilex woods in the centre of the Maremma game reserve (well seen from the main road). The walkway along the walls can be followed on two levels. It has recently become fashionable as a summer resort. 9km W, at Pescia Fiorentina, an old iron foundry survives, of great interest to industrial archaeologists (there are long-term plans to restore it).—On the other side of the Aurelia is Capalbio Station, and across the railway line by an old red farmhouse is the *Lago di Burano*, a lagoon 4km long, now a bird sanctuary administered by the World Wildlife Fund (adm. only with special permission).—The Aurelia now enters northern Lazio and crosses the Fiora just before (176km) *Montalto di Castro* and the turning for the Etruscan remains of *Vulci*, described in Rte 63. From here the Via Aurelia continues S to Tarquinia and Civitavecchia, see Rte 63.

55 The Island of Elba

ELBA, the Greek *Æthalia* and the Roman *Ilva*, an island 27km long and 18km across at its broadest, has been famous since ancient times for its iron ore (mentioned by Virgil) and more recently as Napoleon's place of exile in 1814–15. The inhabited part of the island has pretty hills covered with low vegetation known as the 'macchia', while other parts are barren and deserted. It produces good wines (Aleatico, Moscato, etc.) and vegetables. The climate is mild and sunny and the sea bathing good, and it is popular with holiday-makers (particularly from Germany) in summer. The English have been coming here since the 17C, and Joseph Conrad based his last unfinished novel 'Suspense' (begun in 1905) on Elba, although he never visited the island. **Map on Atlas page 15**.

Approaches. The port for Elba is *Piombino* (see Rte 54). Frequent car ferries (run by two companies) and hydrofoils (much more expensive) run to Portoferraio on the N coast in c 1hr (hydrofoil in half an hour). It is advisable to book in summer. Another boat and hydrofoil serves Porto Azzurro on the E coast (via Cavo and Rio Marino).—Other car ferries connect Portoferraio and Marciana Marina with *Livorno* (direct car ferry in c 3hrs).

By rail, the slower trains on the main line from Pisa and Livorno to Rome stop at *Campiglia Marittima*, where there are frequent services to *Piombino Marittima* for the ferry. In summer there is one return train a day from Florence direct to *Piombino Marittima* (the 'Freccia dell'Elba') in c 2 hours 15 minutes, in connection with the ferry.

The chief town and port is **Portoferraio** (10,600 inhab.), with the great 'Ilva' blast furnaces. It was founded in 1548 by the Medici Grand-Duke Cosimo I when the remarkable fortifications were begun by Giovanni Battista Bellucci and Giovanni Camerini. The modern seafront, where the ferries dock is unattractive; the old port, now used by private boats is at the end of the promontory. It was occupied by the British fleet in 1795–97. The fortified *Porta a Mare* (1637) leads into the old district, still the centre of the town, with a covered market. The *Museo Archeologico della Linguella*, in the ex-Magazzini di Sale, was opened here in 1988. It contains material from the 7C BC to the Roman era. A road (or steps) lead up from the main Piazza della Repubblica to the Medici *Forte Stella* (recently restored) which dominates the port and from which there is a good view. Napoleon's principal residence was the *Villetta dei Mulini*, overlooking the sea. The modest house (open 9–13.30; fest. 9–12.30; closed Monday) contains Napoleonic souvenirs. The principal defensive system is to the W around *Forte Falcone*; this can be visited descending to the *Porta a Terra* on the sea front.

The 'Comunità Montana dell'Elba e Capraia' (No. 11a Via Manzoni) publish a map of the numerous footpaths on the island.—**Buses** from near the ferry quay run to Procchio and Marciana, to Cavo via Porto Azzurro and Rio Marina, to Capolivieri via Porto Azzurro, and to Marina di Campo.

A road runs W from Portoferraio for Marciana. Beyond the junction with the road for Porto Azzurro (see below), is (2·5km) the fork left for the VILLA SAN MARTINO (adm. as above), in a pretty fertile valley, Napoleon's summer residence. The large one-storey neo-classical edifice was built in front of Napoleon's house by Prince Demidoff in 1851 as a memorial to him. It contains the Pinacoteca Foresiana (Tuscan works of the 16–19C). Napoleon's simple house above is reached by a path on the left. It is charmingly decorated with frescoes by Pietro Ravelli (1814).—The main road continues above the pretty little bay and sandy beach of (6km) *Biodola* (by-road right), with a small bungalow colony and camping site.—11·5km *Procchio*, a bathing resort. A road leads from here past the little airport to *Marino di Campo*, another attractive bathing resort (with a fishing fleet) on the S coast.—A winding road continues along the N coast from Procchio (access to the sea is limited).—19km **Marciana Marina**, a pretty little port with sardine fisheries, also a small bathing resort. The cylindrical tower on the mole was built by the Pisans in the 12C. There are long-term plans to expand the harbour. From here the road runs uphill to (21km) *Poggio* (330m), and (27km) *Marciana Alta* (cable-car to the summit of Monte Capanne, 1018m), with a small archaeological museum.—The road continues around the W shore of the island with finer views and wilder scenery via the pretty village of *Chiessi* amidst vineyards, to Marina di Campo (see above).

The main town in the E part of the island is **Porto Azzurro**, a fashionable resort overlooking a beautiful bay. With its great Spanish fort of 1602 (now a prison), it was formerly called *Porto Longone*. It is reached by a road (15·5km) from Portoferraio which passes *Terme di San Giovanni*, a small spa near remains of an Imperial Roman villa. A by-road right just before Porto Azzurro leads to *Capoliveri*, a little old miners' town in a charming position.—12km N of Porto Azzurro, reached by an inland road, is *Rio Marina*, interesting as the chief ore-port and centre of a mining area, with tall grim houses. A road continues along the E coast to (7·5km) *Cavo* at the northernmost point of the island.—Some of the most beautiful scenery on the island can be seen on the unmade-up road from *Bagnaia* (10km E of Portoferraio) to *Rio nell'Elba*.

To the N of Elba are the mountainous volcanic islets of **Capraia** and **Gorgona** (ferry service from Livorno). The prison on Capraia was closed in 1986; that on Gorgona is scheduled to close also. They are both beautiful wild islands, and Capraia has been acquired by the Fondo per l'Ambiente Italiano.

To the S of Elba are the low-lying islet of **Pianosa**, used as a state prison, and the romantic island of **Montecristo** (now deserted and declared a European nature reserve in 1988). It is formed of a granite mass covered with woods (10 sq. km), rising in the centre to Monte Fortezza (645m). Here are the ruins of the Benedictine monastery of San Salvatore and San Mamiliano devastated by the pirate Dragut in 1553. A legend that the monks had buried their treasure here before abandoning the island gave inspiration to Alexandre Dumas for his historical novel 'The Count of Montecristo'. The island was acquired by George Watson Taylor in 1852, who built a villa at Cala Maestra (the only port of the island), later used as a hunting lodge by Victor Emmanuel III.

56 Siena to Perugia and Assisi

ROAD, 127·5km. N326.—43km *Sinalunga*.—48km 'Val di Chiana'. N75bis (a 'superstrada').—61km Exit for **Cortona** (11km N).—73km *Tuoro* (for **Lake Trasimene**).—109km **Perugia**.—127·5km **Assisi**.

RAILWAY, 161km in c 3hrs; a very roundabout route with two changes at Chiusi and Torontola.

The road from Siena, at first combined with that to Arezzo, passes S of the battlefield of *Montaperti* (1260), and at (20·5km) the Ombrone bridge, leaves the old Arezzo road (N73) and turns SE.—27km *Rapolano Terme*, now by-passed, is a medieval town with spa waters and travertine quarries. The new 'superstrada' to Arezzo diverges left.—43km **Sinalunga** (364m) is also by-passed and is the junction of a branch railway to Arezzo. Here the Sienese defeated the English mercenaries of Nicolò da Montefeltro in 1363; here also Garibaldi was arrested in 1867 by Victor Emmanuel II, to prevent an ill-timed descent on Rome. There is a Descent from the Cross by Girolamo del Pacchia in the *Collegiata*, and paintings by Benvenuto di Giovanni, and Cozzarelli (Baptism of Christ) in *San Bernardino*, outside the town. The altarpiece by Sano di Pietro was stolen from here in 1971.—6km S is *Torrita di Siena*, with its nine 16C towers and interesting churches (usually locked). At (48km) '*Val di Chiana*' is the junction with the A1 motorway ('Autostrada del Sole' from Milan to Rome. This route now follows the 'superstrada' (N75bis) recently completed all the way to Perugia. At the next exit (51km) a by-road leads to the *Abbazia di Farneta*, an interesting Romanesque building with a fine crypt. In the priest's house (adm. on request) is a local paleonthological collection.—61km Exit for Cortona, which lies 11km N. There is a splendid view of the town on the hillside from the road which runs along the plain.

CORTONA (22,600 inhab.) is a delightful, peaceful little town, particularly well preserved, with olive groves and vineyards reaching up to its walls. It is built on a long hillside with narrow winding streets covering the steep slopes. One of the most ancient cities in Italy, it is interesting for its Etruscan remains and for its works of art, which include numerous paintings by Luca Signorelli who was born here. There are magnificent views over the wide agricultural plain which provides the main source of its economy.

Tourist Office, 70–72 Via Nazionale.—The centre of the town is closed to traffic for most of the day; **Car Parking** near San Domenico, Piazza Mercato, and Porta Colonia.—**Railway Stations**: *Cortona-Camucia*, 5km from the centre; *Terontola*, 11km from the centre, on the main line from Milan to Rome.—**Buses** run by LFI frequently to the two railway stations, and to Castelfiorentino and Arezzo.—An *Antiques Fair* is held in September.

History. Cortona, probably one of the 12 cities of the Etruscan Confederation, was already ancient when taken by the Etruscans. It is said to have been originally called *Corythus*, after its founder Corythus, reputed father of Dardanus, the mythical ancestor of the Trojans. Subjugated by Rome about 390 BC, it sank into insignificance. Its lands were wasted by Hannibal and its territory was three times distributed among Roman soldiers. Fra Angelico lived and worked here c 1408–18, but most of his paintings have been destroyed; and the city's artistic fame comes chiefly from Luca Signorelli (1441–1523), the great precursor of Michelangelo; another outstanding native painter (and architect) was Pietro Berrettini (1596–1669), called Pietro da Cortona. The medieval walls of the town incorporate portions of the Etruscan walls, dating from the 6C or 5C BC. Many of the old houses have the curious 'Porta del Morto'.

Half-way up to the town is the church of ***Santa Maria del Calcinaio**, a masterpiece of Renaissance architecture. It is one of the few works certainly by *Francesco di Giorgio Martini* (1485). It is built on a Latin cross plan with an octagonal cupola. Set into the hillside, its beautiful form can be fully appreciated as it is approached from above along a short road with a few ancient cypresses. The exterior is in very poor repair. It is unlocked by the custodian who lives at the house beyond a garden, to the right of the façade.

It was built on the site of a tannery (called a 'calcinaio' from the use of lime), on the wall of which a miraculous image of the Madonna appeared. The Arte dei Calzolai (guild of shoe-makers) commissioned the church to house the venerated Madonna from Francesco di Giorgio, on the advice of Signorelli. The beautiful light grey-and-white INTERIOR, with clean architectural lines, has a handsome high altar of 1519 by *Bernardino Covatti* which encloses the devotional image of the Madonna del Calcinaio. The stained glass in the rose window is by *Guglielmo di Marcillat*, and the two smaller windows are by his pupils. On the right side the 1st and 3rd altars have an Annunciation and Assumption by the local painter, Tommaso Barnabei, called *Papacello*. The

Madonna and Child with Saints by *Alessandro Allori*, in the right transept, has
been removed for restoration for years. Left side: 3rd altar, Madonna and Saints,
a good Florentine Mannerist painting by *Jacone*; 2nd and 1st altars, Immaculate
Conception, and Epiphany, both by *Papacello*.

The road continues up towards the centre (car parks signposted): to
the right, near the main entrance to the town is the early-15C church
of *San Domenico*, with a large *Ancona of the Coronation of the
Virgin, signed by Lorenzo di Niccolò Gerini (1402) on the high altar.
In the chapel to the right, Madonna and Saints, an early work by
Signorelli. The *Passeggiata* along the hillside behind the church
through public gardens has fine views: Via Santa Margherita leads up
from the gardens to the church of the same name (described below).
At the entrance to the town Piazza Garibaldi has a superb view of
Santa Maria del Calcinaio and Lake Trasimene.

Via Nazionale, popularly 'Rugapiana', the main and only level
street, leads to Piazza della Repubblica, the centre of the town. The
13C *Palazzo Comunale* was enlarged in the 16C and extends to
Piazza Signorelli, where the façade has a worn 'Marzocco' (the
Florentine lion) of 1508. Here is **Palazzo Casali** (or *Palazzo Pretorio*),
the handsome 13C mansion of the Casali who became governors of
the city. The Renaissance façade was added by Filippo Berrettini in
1613. The 13C flank, on Via Casali, has numerous coats-of-arms of the
governors of the city. It houses the **Museo dell'Accademia Etrusca**
(adm. 10–13, 16–19; winter 9–13, 15–17; closed Monday).

The palace is the seat of the *Accademia Etrusca*, a learned society founded in
1727 for historical and archaeological research. Famous throughout Europe in

the 18C, Montesquieu and Voltaire were both early members. The important *Library* has c 30,000 vols, and 620 codices.

The **Museum** is entered from the outside staircase in the courtyard. In the main hall (2) are cases of small bronzes, including two Etruscan statuettes of divinities (2C BC), numerous Etruscan figurines, and Tuscan 16C works; as well as 15C ivories and a palaeochristian glass chalice. In the centre is the famous Etruscan *CHANDELIER (late 5C BC), designed to be lit by 16 oil lamps. The under side has intricate allegorical carved decorations surrounding a gorgon's head. The paintings around the walls include: 13C Pisan Crucifix (very worn); tondi by *Francesco Signorelli* and *Pinturicchio*; works by *Pietro da Cortona, Ciro Ferri*, and *Cristofano Allori* (self-portrait with Ludovico Cigoli).—In a room (3), off the right end of the hall, is an interesting and representative Egyptian collection made by Monsignor Corbelli, Papal delegate in Egypt in 1891–96. It includes a rare wood model of a funerary boat (2060–1785 BC), statuettes, mummies, canopic vases, papyri, etc.—In the other room (4), off the hall, *Niccolò Gerini*, Four Saints; *Bicci di Lorenzo*, Triptych; 12–13C Tuscan mosaic of the Madonna in prayer.—The small rooms (5–7) to the right contains furniture, material relating to the military architect Francesco Laparelli (1521–70), born in Cortona, who designed La Valletta in Malta, fans, ivories, miniatures, swords, 18–19C livery, and the portrait of an old lady by *Bartolomeo Passarotti*.—Beyond the hall (8) with a good ceiling, is a room (9) with 18C globes, an elaborate porcelain 'tempietto' presented by Carlo Ginori to the Academia in 1756, and the famous encaustic painting of the 'Musa Polimnia', for long thought to be a Roman work of 1–2C AD, but now considered a fake of c 1740.—R. 10 (left) contains the Numismatic collection, including rare Etruscan coins, and medals by *Pisanello* and *Matteo de'Pasti*. The ceramics include Ginori, Delft, Deruta, and Gubbio ware.—R. 11. Roman and Etruscan bronzes and terracottas and votive statuettes.—R. 12 contains Etruscan cinerary urns, Bucchero ware, and Attic vases.—A door leads out onto a walkway above the courtyard back into the main hall. The last room, next to the ticket office, has a representative display of works by *Gino Severini* (1883–1966), born in Cortona.

The **Duomo**, to which Via Casali descends, was enlarged in the 16C to designs by Giuliano da Sangallo, incorporating earlier elements of the façade, but has been much modified. The Campanile (1566) is by Francesco Laparelli. There is a fine view of the countryside from outside the W door. In the pleasant interior, with a barrel vault, the main altar with four carved angels is a fine work by *Francesco Mazzuoli* (1664). Behind are a group of good paintings (right to left): *Cigoli*, Madonna and Saints; *School of Signorelli*, Crucifixion, Incredulity of St Thomas; *Alessandro Allori*, Madonna and Saints. At the end of the N aisle, carved ciborium by *Ciuccio di Nuccio*.—The **Museo Diocesano** (adm. 9–13, 15–18.30; winter 9–13, 15–17; closed Monday), opposite, incorporates the former church of the Gesù, and contains some beautiful paintings.

The room (2) to the right of the entrance has a Roman sarcophagus (end of 2C), with the battle of the Amazons and Centaurs, admired by Donatello and Brunelleschi. Fresco fragments here include the Way to Calvary by *Pietro Lorenzetti*. Beyond the stairs is the former church of the Gesù, with a fine wooden ceiling by *Michelangelo Leggi* (1536). Here are displayed: *Sassetta*, Madonna and Child with four Saints; *Pietro Lorenzetti*, large painted Crucifix; *Fra Angelico*, Madonna enthroned with Saints, with a fine predella (removed for restoration), *Annunciation (1428–30), one of his most beautiful works; Baptismal font by *Ciuccio di Nuccio*; *Bartolomeo della Gatta*, *Assumption of the Virgin.—In the room (4) behind the font, 'Maestro della Madonna di Lucignano' (School of Duccio), *Madonna and Child; *Pietro Lorenzetti*, Madonna enthroned with four angels, signed and dated 1320; *Giusto da Firenze*, Vagnucci reliquary, signed and dated 1458; 13C Aretine Master, St Margaret and stories from her life (very damaged); the Passerini church vestments of 1515. A case of church silver includes a chalice by *Michele di Tommaso da Siena* (late 14C).—In R. 5 (at the end of R. 1): *Luca Signorelli*: *Deposition, with a fine predella; *Communion of the Apostles, signed and dated 1512; and four works by his bottega.—R. 6. *Bottega of Signorelli*, Assumption.—At the bottom of the stairs leading to the Lower Church, *Pietro Lorenzetti*, painted Crucifix. The vault of the lower church was painted by *Giorgio Vasari*, and (lunettes) *Cristoforo Gherardi* (Il Doceno). The plain stalls are by *Vincenzo da Cortona* (1517), and the terracotta Deposition group is a 15C Florentine work.—Other rooms are still being arranged.

From Piazza Signorelli, beyond the 19C Teatro Signorelli, the pretty old Via Dardano leads uphill before descending to the simple *Porta Colonia* (which preserves its wooden doors), around which are the most considerable relics of the Etruscan walls, the huge blocks conspicuous below the Roman and medieval walls above, which stretch away up the hill towards the Fortezza Medicea, above the church of Santa Margherita, the top of which can just be seen in the woods (both described below). Outside the gate, in the beautiful countryside below the town, the fine centrally-planned church of *Santa Maria Nuovo* is well seen. It was built in 1550–54 by Cristofanello, and altered in 1600 when the cupola was finished. From the gate Via delle Mura del Duomo, a charming little lane with acacia trees, leads back along the top of the walls to the Duomo.

The stepped Via Santucci mounts through the Palazzo del Popolo in Piazza della Repubblica to the church of SAN FRANCESCO which preserves a portal of 1245. Inside are attractive wooden pews. The 17C marble tabernacle by Bernardino Radi on the high altar encloses a precious Byzantine ivory reliquary of the Holy Cross. On the 4th right altar, *Cigoli*, Miracle of St Anthony of Padua; in the chapel to the right of the main altar, Gothic tomb of Bishop Ubertini (1345). Behind the high altar is buried Brother Elias of Cortona, the disciple of St Francis. It is thought that Luca Signorelli was buried in the crypt below. Left side: 3rd altar, Annunciation, the last work (left unfinished) by *Pietro da Cortona*; 2nd altar, *Camillo Sagrestani*, Martyrdom of St Lucy. On the W wall are 14C fresco fragments attributed to *Buffalmacco*.

Via Berrettini, a very steep road, leads up from San Francesco through a delightful part of the town, with bright gardens and plants around the well kept houses. Beyond a large circular water cistern is the birthplace of Pietro da Cortona (No. 33; plaque). The road follows the high convent wall of Santa Chiara to end in the little triangular Piazza della Pescaia, beautifully planted with ilex trees. The road continues to ascend (keep left) towards the charming little Romanesque bellcote of *San Cristoforo*, one of the oldest churches in Cortona (entered to the left). It contains damaged detached frescoes by the 13C Umbrian school. Beside a large square water cistern a road (right) descends shortly to **San Niccolò**, a 15C church approached through a peaceful little walled garden with cypresses. It has a delightful wooden porch with Ionic capitals. The church is opened by the custodian who lives here (ring at the door on the left). Over the altar is a Standard painted on both sides by Luca Signorelli with a *Deposition (in excellent condition) and a Madonna and Child (shown by the custodian). On the N wall is a votive fresco of the Madonna and Saints by Signorelli or his school.

Via Santo Stefano continues uphill; on the left Via Porta Montanina leads to the edge of the hillside planted with pine trees beside the charming *Porta Montanina*, decorated with four arches, with its doors still intact. Here can be seen remains of the Etruscan walls, and of a second fortified gate. A fine stretch of walls leads steeply down the hillside beside orchards, and uphill to the Fortezza Medicea. Outside the gate there is a view of Santa Maria Nuova and the pretty countryside below the town.

From Via Santo Stefano, Via Santa Croce (signposted for Santa Margherita), a stepped lane with pretty gardens on either side, continues uphill. It traverses cypress woods before reaching the sanctuary of SANTA MARGHERITA, rebuilt in 1856–97 in the Romanesque-Gothic style, and preserving a single rose window of its predecessor. The *Sarcophagus of St Margaret of Laviano (1247–97) is probably by the native artists Angiolo and Francesco di Pietro (1362; also attributed to Giovanni Pisano). Below the church Via Santa Margherita descends to the public gardens (see above), past a Via Crucis in mosaic by Gino Severini. A road continues up to the **Fortezza Medicea**, built by Francesco Laparelli in 1549, and recently restored. At present the interesting interior is open only for exhibitions. It commands a magnificent view of Lake Trasimene, and part of the outer circle of walls built by the Etruscans can be seen from here.

From the road junction, known as the Cinque Vie, near Santa Maria del Calcinaio (see above), a road (signposted for Sodo) leads to the *Tanella di Pitagora* (ring for custodian), a vaulted Etruscan hypogeum (4C BC), nothing to do with Pythagoras (who lived at Crotone in Southern Italy). Farther down the hill are three chamber tombs of the 7C or 6C BC.—Two Etruscan tumulus tombs have been discovered in the plain: one, near the railway station, known as the 'Melone di Camucia', with a tumulus 200m round, and one in the locality of Sodo (near the Montecchio road), with an inscription.

Outside Porta Colonia (see above) the Città di Castello road leads NE to the wooded Mount Sant'Egidio (c 4km), with the picturesque *Convento delle Celle* (or 'dei Cappuccini'), founded by St Francis between 1211 and 1221.

Below the Public Gardens (see above) Via delle Contesse and Via del Palazzone (left) lead to *Villa Passerini*, known as 'Il Palazzone', built for Cardinal Silvio Passerini by Giovanni Battista Caporali (1521), and now used in the summer by the Scuola Normale di Pisa. The Salone has frescoes by Papacello and a chapel is frescoed by Signorelli and his pupils.

FROM CORTONA TO AREZZO, 33km, N71. A pretty by-road descends through beautiful countryside from Cortona, with a restrospective view of its monuments strung out along the skyline of the long sloping hillside. At the foot of the hill it joins N71.—9km A narrow road (signposted on the right) winds through charming countryside up a hill, on the top of which is the castle of **Montecchio Vesponi**. From the small car park a track leads shortly to the entrance (bell on left; open April–October only, 9–13). Its 13C walls are still intact. It was given in the 14C by the grateful Florentines to Sir John Hawkwood, the English-born condottiere.—The main road continues (good view back of the castle) to (12km) **Castiglion Fiorentino** dominated by the oddly-shaped Torre del Cassero. It is a walled agricultural market town on a hill.

From the Porta Fiorentina the Corso leads up past (left) the church of *San Francesco* (closed many years ago) to *Piazza Municipio* (car parking) with a pretty 16C loggia with some arcades open to provide a view of the valley (the Collegiata church is conspicuous on the side of the hill). Opposite is *Palazzo Comunale* (open in the mornings, except fest.). In a room here (unlocked on request; in need of repair) is the *Pinacoteca*. Here are displayed: Bartolomeo della Gatta, St Francis receiving the stigmata; 13C and 14C Crucifixes; Margaritone d'Arezzo, St Francis; Giovanni di Paolo, Madonna and Child, St Catherine; Taddeo Gaddi, Madonna and Child; silver gilt enamel reliquary bust of St Ursula, and a 12C French Cross.—On the hillside above, built into the rock, is the ancient church of the *Cassero* (recently restored; open in the afternoon), and on the top of the hill, the Torre del Cassero. From Piazza Municipio Via San Michele continues downhill to Piazza Verdi, and, by a pretty little Mannerist door, Vicolo dei Signori leads on down towards the piazza in front of the Collegiata, with a good view of the countryside. The neo-classical *Collegiata* contains: right side, 1st altar, a Della Robbian terracotta of St Anthony Abbot; (3rd altar), Bartolomeo della Gatta, Madonna enthroned with Saints (recently harshly restored); (altar in the right transept), Annunciation, another Della Robbian relief; (chapel to the right of main altar), Lorenzo di Credi, Adoration of the Child. In the left transept is a large *Maestà signed by Segna di Bonaventura.—The *Pieve* next to the church (half of which was demolished, and now deconsecrated) is entered from the right side of the Collegiata (unlocked on request). Near the 15C font is a Deposition by Signorelli and a Della Robbia Baptism of Christ.—Behind the Pieve is the *Gesù* with a portico. Via San Guiliano leads downhill to the Porta Romana, outside of which is the octagonal

Madonna della Consolazione. Nearby is the ex-church of *San Lazzaro*, now a small museum of frescoes (Crucifixion by the school of Giotto).

The road continues skirting the Valdichiana with low hills on the right, some of them planted with olives and vines, into (33km) **Arezzo**, see Rte 50.

N71 provides the most direct route from Cortona back to the Perugia 'superstrada', via *Torontola* station on the main line to Rome, where the Perugia branch diverges.—67km Exit for Castiglione del Lago on Lake Trasimene.

N71, the old main road from Arezzo to Orvieto and Rome, leads S from here, entering Umbria at the NW corner of Lake Trasimene (see below).—9km *Castiglione del Lago* (304m), with its castle (splendid view), has a fine situation on a promontory jutting into the lake. The church of the Maddalena has a Madonna and Saints by a follower of Perugino (Sinibaldo Ibi?).—The road turns SW to join (19km) the road from Siena and Montepulciano 1km E of *Chiusi* station (see Rte 58), with a view of the Valdichiana on the right.—26km **Città della Pieve** (6400 inhab.), standing on high ground (508m) 5km NE of its station, was the birthplace of Pietro Vannucci (1446–1523), called Il Perugino. The pretty main street, named after the painter, leads along the ridge to the Duomo past several interesting brick palaces. On the left is the *Oratorio di Santa Maria dei Bianchi* (adm. 10.30–12.30, 16.30–18.30; if closed a notice indicates where the custodian lives). This contains a fresco of the *Adoration of the Magi by Perugino (1504; restored in 1984) with Lake Trasimene in the background. The street ends at the *Duomo* which contains paintings also by Perugino (all labelled and provided with lights), including a Madonna and Saints and a Baptism of Christ, and works by Avanzino Nucci and Pomarancio, as well as a 16C wood Crucifix. The church of *Santa Maria dei Servi* (if closed apply to the custodian of Santa Maria dei Bianchi) contains a Deposition by Perugino, commissioned in 1517. The church of *San Pietro* contains St Anthony Abbot enthroned between Saints Marcellus and Paul the Hermit also by Perugino (to be restored).

The road, winding and undulating, passes the large villages of (33km) *Monteleone d'Orvieto* and (49km) *Ficulle*, then descends into the valley of the Paglia, crossing under the Autostrada del Sole to reach (73km) *Orvieto* Station (124m). **Orvieto**, see Rte 58. N71 continues SW, winding up to (90km) the *Poggio di Biagio* (590m), from where N74 diverges W via *Pitigliano* to reach the coast just N of Orbetello (see Rte 54). This road turns due S, passes into Lazio, and at (106km) *Montefiascone* joins the Via Cassia. From there via (122km) *Viterbo* to (203km) **Rome**, see Rte 57.

The road from Città della Pieve to Perugia (N220; 43km; bus in 1½hrs starting from Chiusi station) leaves on the left, at 15km, a road to *Panicale* (7km), a pretty little town, where the church of San Sebastiano contains frescoes by Perugino (recently restored). The best view of Lake Trasimene can be enjoyed from the old walls.—From (17km) *Tavernelle* is visited the imposing *Santuario della Madonna di Mongiovino*, by Rocco da Vicenza (1513), 2km N.—At (21km) *Fontignano* (1km left), with its castle, Perugino died of the plague in 1523. The little church of the Annunziata contains his (modern) tomb and a fresco by him.

Beyond the Castiglione del Lago exit, the 'superstrada' continues to Perugia, by-passing Tuoro and Passignano, both reached by the old road which runs close to Lake Trasimene with fine views of the islands.

The beautiful *Lago Trasimeno* or *Lake Trasimene*, has a circumference of nearly 45km; its depth, never more than 7m, is constantly diminishing because of the formation of peat, and there is some danger of it drying into a marsh. The shores are flat and reedy. The lake once abounded in fish (especially eels). There is good swimming at Tuoro (see below). It has three islands, the largest of which is the *Isola Polvese*. Near the N shore are the *Isola Maggiore* and the *Isola Minore*. At the SE end of the lake is a subterranean outlet built by the Romans and several times reopened. The scene of Hannibal's great victory over the Romans in 217 BC is by the N shore.

73km *Tuoro sul Trasimeno*. To the NW is the village of *Sanguineto*, whose name ('a name of blood from that day's sanguine rain') commemorates the momentous victory of Hannibal, in the plain below, over the consul Flaminius in 217 BC in which 15,000 Romans died. An interesting itinerary of the battlefield is signposted from Tuoro. For the boat services on the lake, see below. The old road continues to *Passignano sul Trasimeno* (5·5km), with an old fortified district on a promontory. It is an attractive little lakeside resort with aircraft construction works. A pier on the lake is the starting point for the regular boat services to (¼hr–½hr) the *Isola Maggiore* (some boats call on the way at Tuoro), with its picturesque hamlet and the church of San Michele containing paintings by Caporali; also two chapels commemorating a visit of St Francis in 1211. Other boats run to San Feliciano, on the E shore of the lake, and the *Isola Polvese*, now almost deserted.

Just beyond Passignano a by-road (left), with fine retrospective views of the lake climbs to (7·5km) *Castel Rigone*, a little resort, with a pretty Renaissance church (1494) and (28km) *Umbertide* (see Rte 52).—A beautiful road skirts the shore of Lake Trasimene through *Monte del Lago* which juts into the E side, and *San Feliciano*, and other little resorts. Near Monte Buono there are splendid views across fields and marshes down to the lake and Isola Polvese and the promontory of Castiglione del Lago (see above).

The new 'superstrada' leaves the lake to tunnel under the saddle of *Magione*, which preserves the Badia, a castle of the Knights of Malta, built by Fieravanti c 1420. The fast road continues to (109km) Perugia.

PERUGIA (129,900 inhab.), capital of the province of the same name (6357 sq. km), which comprises nearly the whole of Umbria, has a booming economy. Disorderly suburbs with ugly tower blocks (especially prominent on the approach from Florence and Siena) have sprawled onto the lower hills below the old town in the last ten years or so. The historical centre, however, preserves its character and numerous tortuous streets climb up and down the oddly-shaped hilly spurs of land (494m above sea level and some 300m above the Tiber) on which the town is built. It is perhaps the most difficult town in Italy in which to find ones bearings. It has numerous interesting monuments, including the Palazzo dei Priori on the delightful Corso, where the Pinacoteca has a magnificent display of Umbrian art. There are many interesting churches on the edges of the hills. The famous painter, Pietro Vannucci was called 'Perugino' from his long associations with the town, and numerous works by him survive here, notably in the Collegio del Cambio. Students from all over the world come to Perugia to attend the famous 'Università Italiana per Stranieri'.

Railway Stations. The main station is at *Fontivegge* (Pl.13), below the city to the SW, for Foligno (Rome) and Terontola (Florence); bus, see below.—*Perugia Sant'Anna* (Pl.11) and *Ponte San Giovanni* (6km ESE) are on the branch line to Sansepolcro and Terni.

Car Parking. The centre of the city (on the highest hills) is mostly closed to traffic: car parks are indicated on the approaches, but the most convenient one for visitors is in Piazza Partigiani (Pl. 11,15), signposted from Via Cacciatori degli Alpi or Via Baldassare Orsini. This huge new two-storeyed car park has an hourly tariff (special reduced tariff for overnight periods). From here escalators (open 6.30–24.30) mount to Piazza Italia (Pl. 11), in the centre of the city.

Tourist Offices. *Assessorato al Turismo della Regione dell'Umbria* (Pl. 7), 30 Corso Vannucci; *A.P.T.*, 21 Via Mazzini (*Information Office*, 94 Corso Vannucci; to be moved to Piazza Quattro Novembre).

Hotels on and near the Corso Vannucci.—**Post Office**, Piazza Matteotti. *Telephone Exchange*, Piazza della Repubblica, Via Mazzini.

Buses. Nos **11, 12**, and **36** from the main railway station at Fontivegge to Piazza Matteotti; No. **22**, San Marco—Via Fani—Porta San Costanzo—Montebello; etc.—**Country Buses** from Piazza Partigiani to *Rome* (once daily on weekdays);

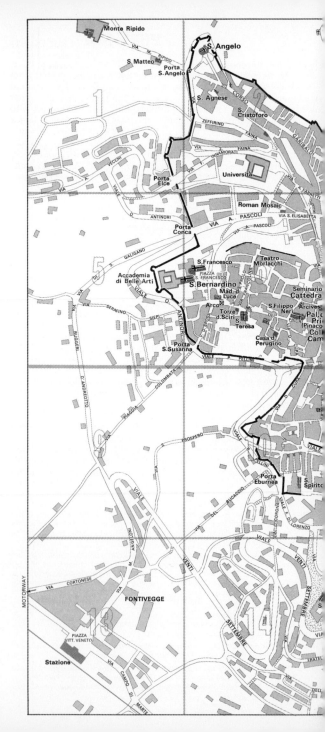

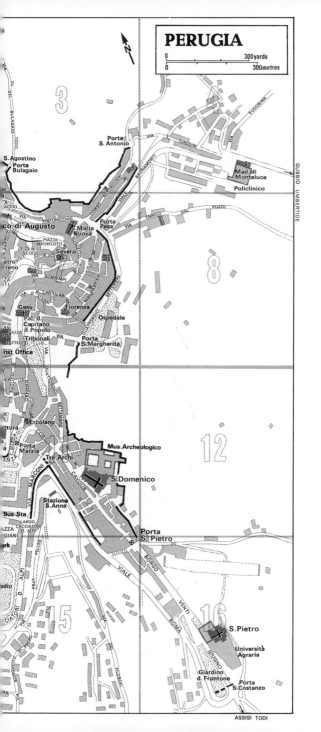

to *Assisi*; to *Florence*; to *Ponte San Giovanni*; to *Bettona*; via *Spello* to *Foligno*; via *Foligno* to *Spoleto* (more easily reached by train); to *Gualdo Tadino*; to *Gubbio*; and to *Todi*.

History. *Perusia* was one of the 12 cities of the Etruscan Confederation and it is to the Etruscans and not to the Umbrians that the city owes its ancient walls and gates. It submitted to the Romans under Q. Fabius in 310 BC. In the civil war between Octavian (Augustus) and Mark Antony, L. Antonius, brother of the triumvir, was besieged in Perusia in 41–40 BC. Famine compelled the city's surrender; but one of its citizens, Gaius Cestius, in panic set fire to his own house, and the flames spread, razing all Perusia to the ground. Augustus rebuilt the city and called it *Augusta Perusia*. It is said to have been besieged by Totila in 547, and saved by the wisdom of its bishop, St Herculanus. In 592 it became a Lombard duchy, and after the restoration of the Western Empire its history is one of obscure and intricate wars with neighbouring towns in which it generally took the Guelf side. The first despot was one of the Raspanti ('scratchers'; the nickname of the burghers), named Biondo Michelotti (1393), who murdered two of the noble family of the Baglioni, became leader of the Florentine army, and allied himself with Gian Galeazzo Visconti. The city passed to the latter family, and afterwards to Braccio Fortebraccio (1416–24), the famous 'condottiere' and a wise governor. Perugia was subsequently torn by strife between the rival families of Oddi and Baglioni; and when the latter prevailed they in turn quarrelled, until the day (14 August 1500) when all their leaders were massacred as the result of a conspiracy, with the exception of Gian Paolo, who revenged himself upon the murderers. Pope Paul III seized the town in 1535 and, when it rebelled against his salt tax, built a fortress known as the Rocca Paolina on the ruins of the old Baglioni mansions. From then onwards Perugia was ruled by a papal governor. In 1809 it was annexed to the French Empire, and it was called *Perouse* by the French; in 1815 it was restored to the Church. In 1859 the papal Swiss Guards occupied the city after an indiscriminate massacre, but a year later they were expelled, and a popular insurrection destroyed the Rocca Paolina, the badge of subjection.—The British 8th Army entered Perugia on 20 June 1944. The city is noted for its chocolate and pasta.

Art. Perugia was the chief centre of Umbrian painting, which flowered in calm through the storms of civic history. The Umbrian school was formed in the 12C, but it was only in the 15C that it became independent of Siena and Florence, producing such masters as Gentile da Fabriano, Ottaviano Nelli, Nicolò da Foligno (L'Alunno), Matteo da Gualdo, Bartolomeo Caporali, and Benedetto Bonfigli (c 1420–96), the first great Perugian painter. His immediate follower was Fiorenzo di Lorenzo (1445–1522), but the greatest Perugian painter was Pietro Vannucci (c 1445–1523), born at Città della Pieve, but called *Perugino*. Among his numerous disciples of the Umbrian school alone were Pinturicchio (Bernardino di Betto; 1454–1513), Andrea d'Assisi (L'Ingegno), Tiberio d'Assisi, Francesco Melanzio of Montefalco, Lo Spagna, Bernardino di Mariotto, Eusebio da San Giorgio, Domenico and Orazio Alfani, Giannicola di Paolo and Raphael.

The approach to Perugia from the W or from the main station is by Via Venti Settembre (Pl. 13, 9, 14), which winds uphill towards the old city. Off Largo Cacciatori degli Alpi (Pl. 11), with its monument to Garibaldi by Cesare Zocchi (1887), is PIAZZA PARTIGIANI (Pl. 10, 11) with its double-storeyed car park (signposted). From the car park the stadium is conspicuous beside the 13–14C church of *San Giuliana* (Pl. 14), with a graceful 14C campanile, and two cloisters (13C and 14C; now incorporated in a military hospital). A series of ESCALATORS (and some steps), opened in 1983, lead up from the car park to the centre of the city; beyond Via del Circo they traverse the huge vaulted **Rocca Paolina** (Pl. 11), built by Antonio Sangallo the Younger in 1540–43 at the command of Paul III, to which end a whole medieval quarter was vaulted over. Called a 'bellissima e inutilissima opera', it was partly destroyed in 1860. Near the top is the subterranean *VIA BAGLIONA, lined with remains of medieval dwellings. It leads right to emerge on Via Marzia beneath the splendid Etruscan *Porta Marzia*, re-erected in its present position by

Sangallo (closed 14–16). The escalators end beneath the portico of Palazzo della Provincia (1870; now the Prefettura), whose front bears the Perugian griffin in bronze, on PIAZZA ITALIA (Pl. 11), flanked by imposing buildings. Behind the Prefettura is the charming little terraced *Giardino Carducci* with a *View extending from Monte Amiata to the summits of the central Apennines, with Montefalco, Assisi, Spello, Foligno, Spoleto, and other centres.

The exceptionally wide and undulating *CORSO VANNUCCI (Pl. 11,7; totally closed to motor traffic), is at the centre of the old city, and it provides a magnificent setting for the 'passeggiata' at dusk when it is even more crowded than at other times. It is named in honour of Perugia's greatest painter. Near its N end is the ***Collegio del Cambio** (Pl. 6), the hall and chapel of the Bankers' Guild, by *Bartolomeo di Mattiolo* and *Lodovico di Antonibo* (1452–57). The hall is decorated with superb frescoes painted by *Perugino* and his pupils for the merchants, who paid 350 ducats for the work. The Collegio is open on weekdays 9–12.30, 14.30–17.30; winter 8–14; fest. 9–12.30; closed Monday.

INTERIOR. In the vestibule are walnut-wood carvings by *Giampietro Zuccari* (1615–21).—The ***Sala dell'Udienza del Cambio** is painted with frescoes by *Perugino* and his pupils (1499–1507). On the left wall are Prudence and Justice, with classical heroes; and Fortitude and Temperance, similarly attended. On the end wall, Transfiguration and Nativity. On the right wall are the Eternal Father, with Prophets and the Sibyls. This wall and the paintings of Fortitude (see above) are usually attributed to *Raphael*, then only 17 years old. On the ceiling are liberal arts and pagan divinities, by Perugino's assistants. On the middle pilaster of the left wall is a portrait of Perugino by himself. The splendid carved and inlaid furniture is by *Domenico del Tasso* and *Antonio da Mercatello* (1492, 1508). In the niche is a gilded statuette of Justice attributed to *Benedetto da Maiano*.—The good frescoes in the *Cappella di San Giovanni Battista* (restored in 1989) are mostly by Perugino's disciple, *Giannicola di Paolo*.

The same ticket gives access to the *Sala di Udienza del Collegio della Mercanzia*, on the ground floor of Palazzo dei Priori (see below), entered at No. 15 on the Corso. It contains early 15C wood-carving and intarsia work.

Adjacent is the ***Palazzo dei Priori** (Pl.6), now the *Palazzo Comunale*, a massive structure by *Giacomo di Servadio* and *Giovannello di Benvenuto* (1293–97), afterwards enlarged, and completed in 1443. Part of the façade is still covered for restoration, but the Portale Maggiore (late 14C) has been restored (for the older façade on Piazza 4 Novembre, see below). From the vaulted entrance court stairs (or a lift) lead up to the third floor with the ***Galleria Nazionale dell'Umbria**, the most important collection extant of Umbrian paintings. Some of the rooms are being restored. The gallery is open every day 9–13.30, 15–19; fest. 9–13.

The SALA MAGGIORE was the hall of the Consiglio Generale del Comune. It contains interesting 13–15C frescoes of the Central Italian schools. ROOMS I and II. Works of the late 13C. RI. 29. *Duccio di Buoninsegna*, Madonna and angels; 26. *Maestro di San Francesco*, Crucifix, with St Francis in adoration (dated 1272); 32. *Vigoroso da Siena*, Madonna and Saints (dated 1269).—RII. 894–6. *Arnolfo di Cambio*, Statuettes.—RIII. *Meo di Guido da Siena*, 1. Polyptych, 13. Madonna and Child with four Saints, 8. Madonna and Child:—RIV contains 14C Perugian and Sienese works, and a stained glass window (168.) by *Giovanni di Bonino* (removed).—RV. Sienese 14C and early 15C. *Taddeo di Bartolo*, 72. Annunciation, 64. St Peter, 62. Five saints, 66. Madonna and Saints (signed and dated 1403), 63. St Paul; *Bartolo di Fredi*, 58. Triptych with the Marriage of St Catherine, Saints, Annunciation, 88. Madonna with Saints and the prophet Elijah; *59. *Lippo Vanni*, Madonna and Child; 116. *Domenico di Bartolo*, Polyptych; 67. *Taddeo di Bartolo*, Pentecost.—RVI. 79. *Bicci di Lorenzo*, Marriage of St Catherine (with a fine predella); 84. *Pietro di Domenico da*

Montepulciano, Madonna between Saints Francis and Anthony Abbot; 129. *Gentile da Fabriano*, Madonna and Child (early work).—RRVII and VIII. Revival of Umbrian art in the mid-15C.—RVII. *91–108. *Fra Angelico*, Madonna with angels and Saints, part of a triptych; in the predella, Miracles and Death of St Nicholas; *111–14. *Piero della Francesca*, Madonna with angels and Saints, with a beautiful Annunciation above, and, in the predella, Miracles of St Anthony, St Francis, and St Elizabeth; 746. *Francesco di Giorgio Martini*, Scourging of Christ (bronze relief); 124. *Benozzo Gozzoli*, Madonna of Humility and Saints.—RVIII. *Giovanni Boccati*, 437. Pietà, 149. Madonna della Misericordia, 150–1. Madonna del Pergolato, 147. Madonna dell'Orchestra; 879. *Francesco di Gentile da Fabriano*, Madonna and Child and Annunciation, processional banner painted on both sides; 169. *L'Alunno*, Gonfalon of the Confraternità dell'Annunziata; 126–8 *Giovanni Francesco da Rimini*, Madonna and Saints.

RIX. *Benedetto Bonfigli*, 138. Annunciation and St Luke; 140–1. Adoration of the Magi; in the predella, Baptism of Christ, Crucifixion, Miracle of St Nicholas.—RX. Minor 15C works. *Nicolò del Priore*, 204. St Francis receiving the Stigmata, 193–5, 197, 199. Dead Christ and Saints; 339–40. Crucifixion; 109. *Antoniazzo Romano*, Madonna; *Perugian School*, 152. Dead Christ, 174. Madonna and Child (fresco); *Antoniazzo Romano*, 109. Madonna and Child, 1054. Ecce Homo; *Mariano di Antonio*, 117–22. Miracles of Saints Anthony, John the Baptist, and Bernardine; 115. Scenes from the Passion; 236. *Gerolamo da Cremona*, Madonna with angels.—RXI. Perugian 15C artists. *Fiorenzo di Lorenzo*, 230. Madonna with angels, Saints, and donors (probably his earliest work), 235. Painted niche, signed and dated 1487; *Bartolomeo Caporali*, 160–3. Angels with the symbols of the Passion, 221. Pietà (fresco), 166–70. Assumption; above, Eternal Father; 153–4. Angel, St John the Evangelist, St Mary Magdalene, 125. Madonna with angels.—RXII. *Fiorenzo di Lorenzo*, 231. St Sebastian, 208–19. Madonna and Saints, 178–9. Adoration of the shepherds; 181–2, 206. Triptych of the Madonna and Saints.—RXIII. *Fiorenzo di Lorenzo*, 177. Madonna with Saints Nicholas of Bari and Catherine (fresco); 435. St Sebastian (fresco); 856. *School of Andrea della Robbia*, St Francis; *Perugino*, 220. Pietà, 180. Adoration of the Magi (c 1475; removed for restoration); 1056. St Jerome (fresco); 796. *Benedetto Buglioni*, Madonna in adoration (terracotta).

Rooms XIV–XVIII were closed for restoration in 1990. RXIV. *164, 237, 222–9. *Benedetto Bonfigli, Pinturicchio, Perugino*, and others, Niche of St Bernardine of Siena (1465 and after); below, Gonfalon of St Bernardine (*Bonfigli*); on the side walls: *Miracles of the Saint (*Pinturicchio* and *Perugino*), with remarkable architectural details.— RXV. *Perugino*, 238, 243, 245, 247, 249–61. Adoration of the Shepherds, Baptism of Christ, Saints Jerome and Mary Magdalene, Angel, Eternal Father, in the predella, Adoration of the Magi, Presentation in the Temple, Marriage of Cana, Preaching of St John the Baptist, Saints, 270. Madonna della Confraternità della Consolazione, *279. Madonna and Child with four Saints (1500; predella in Berlin; in a beautiful frame), 278. Gonfalon of the Confraternità della Giustizia (much restored), 266–9. Transfiguration; in the predella, Annunciation, Nativity, Baptism of Christ; 280. Saints Francis, Jerome, John the Baptist, Sebastian, and Anthony of Padua, *248. Christ in the tomb (1494), 358. Lunette of Adoration of the Shepherds (fresco); *Pinturicchio*, *274. Madonna, Saints Augustine and Jerome; in the predella, St Augustine and the Child, and St Jerome in the desert; above, Annunciation, Christ in the tomb, the Holy Ghost; 276. Gonfalon of St Augustine.

RXVI (left). 983. *Piero di Cosimo*, Pietà—RXVII. *Bernardino di Mariotto*, 156. Madonna with St John and two Saints, 155. Marriage of St Catherine, 175. Madonna and Saints, 157. Coronation of the Virgin; 203. *School of Luca Signorelli*, Madonna with angels and Saints; in the predella, St Bernardine, Dream of Innocent III, etc.—RXVIII. Followers of Perugino. *Giannicola di Paolo*, 323. All Saints' Day, 324. Madonna and St John, 325. Crucifixion (fresco); 273. *Lo Spagna*, Blessed Colomba da Rieti; 271. *Giovanni Battista Caporali*, Madonna and Child enthroned with Saints; *Perugino*, *263,200. Coronation of the Virgin, Crucifixion, painted on both sides.—RXIX. Pupils of Perugino. *Eusebio da San Giorgio*, 287. Adoration of the Magi, 282. Madonna and Saints, 343. Madonna with Saints John the Baptist and Benedict; 347. Three Saints; *Sinibaldo Ibi*, 357. Madonna with four Saints, 1005. Standard of St Anthony Abbot; 356. *Sinibaldo Ibi* and *Berto di Giovanni*, Madonna with Saints Augustine and Sebastian; *Berto di Giovanni*, 294. Birth of the Virgin, 295. Presentation of the Virgin, 303. Marriage of the Virgin, 304. Assumption; these four from the predella of *Pinturicchio's* Coronation of the Virgin, now in the Vatican; 309. Coronation of the Virgin, 327–26. St John the Evangelist.

RXX has ceiling frescos by *Tommaso Bernabei*. The paintings are by 16C followers of Perugino and Raphael. 363. *Pompeo di Anselmo* and *Domenico Alfani*, Holy Family (after Raphael); *Domenico Alfani*, 364. Madonna with Saints Gregory and Nicholas of Bari, 288. Eternal Father (after a drawing by Raphael; originally placed over Raphael's Descent from the Cross, now in the Villa

Borghese in Rome), *354. Madonna with angels and Saints; 275. *Pompeo Cocchi,*
Crucifixion; 414. *Dono Doni,* Birth of the Virgin.—RXXI. Late Renaissance. 415.
Giovanni Battista Naldini, Presentation in the Temple; 816. Bas-relief of Christ
expelling the merchants from the Temple, by *Vincenzo Danti.*—RXXII. 733, 763.
14C croziers; *744. Silver-gilt chalice and paten from the church of San
Domenico, by *Cataluccio di Pietro da Todi;* *742. Reliquary of gilt metal; 762.
Gold reliquary of St Juliana; 868, 317–18. Silver voting chest, used for the
election of magistrates; 859. 17C ivory crucifix.—RXXIII, formerly the Prior's
Chapel, with a majolica pavement. *Bonfigli,* Frescoes of the lives of St Ercolano
and St Louis of Toulouse, patrons of Perugia (1454–96); stalls by *Gaspare di
Jacopo da Foligno* and *Paolino da Ascoli* (1452; removed); 720–1. Voting
chests.—RXXIV. 855. *Agostino di Duccio,* Madonna and Child and other
sculptural fragments.

From the Sala Maggiore the stair landing is reached and the entrance to
RRXXVI–XXXVII, which display 16–18C works. RXXVI, in a fine large hall of
the palace, contains works by late 16C painters including *Lattanzio Pagani,
Cristoforo Gherardi, Arrigo Fiammingo,* and *Francesco Baldelli;* (on easels):
1084. *Federico Barocci,* Madonna and Child with the young St John; 1083.
Orazio Gentileschi, Female Saint at the piano; 1073, 1074. *Valentin,* Noli me
tangere, Christ with the Samaritan woman.—RXXVII. 535. *Pietro da Cortona,*
Birth of the Virgin; *Sassoferrato,* 381. Virgin in prayer, 380. Head of the
Madonna.—A spiral staircase leads up to RXXVIII. 614. *Francesco Trevisani,*
Martyrdom of St Andrew; 606. *Benedetto Luti,* Christ in the House of the
Pharisee; 379. *Corrado Giaquinto,* Trinity.—RXXIX. *Giuseppe Maria Crespi* and
the local painters of the 18C.—RXXX. *Lodovico Mazzanti,* St Bernard Tolomei
curing the pestilence in Siena in 1348; works by *Sebastiano Conca* and
Francesco Appiani.—From RXXVIII, RXXXI is entered. Here is a historical
topographical display with 16C views of Perugia.—RXXXII contains wood
carvings and Perugian textiles.—RXXXIII. 18C topographical drawings by
Giovanni Battista Wicar. From here a staircase leads down to the exit.

On the SECOND FLOOR is the **Biblioteca Augusta** (weekdays 9–14, 17–19,
Saturday 9–12) with a good collection of MSS and incunabula.

On the FIRST FLOOR is the **Sala della Consulta** (closed for restoration in 1990),
with a handsome Renaissance doorway surmounted by a Madonna by *Pinturicchio.* For a long time it was known as the *Sala del Malconsiglio,* from the
'ill-advised' consent of the Perugians to spare the lives of the English soldiers of
Sir John Hawkwood, the famous condottiere known in Italy as Giovanni Acuto
(died 1394), by whom they were afterwards defeated in 1366.

The Corso rises to end at the delightful PIAZZA QUATTRO NOVEMBRE
(Pl. 6,7), on a slope, with the ***Fontana Maggiore**designed by *Fra
Bevignate* (1277–80), with bas-reliefs by *Nicola* and *Giovanni Pisano*
and three nymphs by Giovanni Pisano (formerly attributed to Arnolfo
di Cambio). The fountain is to be restored. Here is the other façade of
the Palazzo dei Priori (see above), with the bronze Perugian griffin
and the Guelf lion, bearing chains, carried off from the gates of Siena
by the Perugians after a victory at Torrita in 1358. The latest
suggestion about the figures is that the wings of the griffin were
added before 1281 to an Etruscan body and the new lion made. To the
right are three arches, probably from the church of San Severo,
destroyed to make room for the palace. A charming flight of steps
leads up to the entrance to the *SALA DEI NOTARI (open 9–13, 16–20;
winter 9–13, 15–19; fest. 9–12, 15–19; closed Monday), a remarkable
vaulted hall with frescoes of Old Testament scenes and fables by a
close follower of *Pietro Cavallini* (1297). On the other corner of the
Corso is the mutilated *Palazzo del Collegio dei Notari* (15C), with
good windows.

Along the upper side of the piazza is the flank of the **Cathedral**
(Pl. 6; *San Lorenzo;* closed 12.30–16 in summer, 12–15 in winter), a
Gothic building of the 15C, orientated towards the W with an unfinished façade on Piazza Danti. The S side overlooking the fountain
has Gothic windows and 14C marble geometrical decoration. Here is

an exterior pulpit built for St Bernardine in 1425, a doorway by Galeazzo Alessi (1568), and a bronze statue of Julius II, by Vincenzo Danti (1555, the year of the Pope's death). The elegant Loggia di Braccio Fortebraccio, of four arches on octagonal travertine columns, was built in 1423.

The dark INTERIOR, imposing rather than harmonious, with aisles equal in height to the nave, has columns painted in imitation of impossible marbles. Surrounded by a little altar on a pillar of the nave, the handsome Madonna delle Grazie is attributed to *Giannicola di Paolo*. Above the W door, in an elaborate frame, Madonna and Child with the patron saints of Perugia, by Giovanni Antonio Scaramuccia (1616).—The 1st chapel of the right aisle, beside the tomb of Bishop Baglioni (died 1451), attributed to *Urbano da Cortona*, is the CAPPELLA DI SAN BERNARDINO, closed by a fine wrought-iron screen (15C). It contains a magnificent *Descent from the Cross, one of the best works of *Barocci* (1569), and a stained-glass window of 1565 designed by *Henri de Malines*. The carved decoration of the Baptistery dates from 1477. The Cappella del Sacramento is an elaborate work attributed to Galeazzo Alessi.—In the CHOIR are a bishop's throne of 1520 and stalls (covered for restoration after they caught fire in 1985) of tarsia work by *Giuliano da Maiano* and *Domenico del Tasso* (1486–91).—In the left aisle are bas-reliefs (*Pietà and Eternal Father) by *Agostino di Duccio*; and (4th altar) a gonfalon painted by *Berto di Giovanni*. In the first chapel of the aisle, the CAPPELLA DEL SANTO ANELLO (partly covered for restoration) contains the supposed marriage ring of the Virgin Mary, piously stolen by the Perugians from Chiusi. It is kept in a chased and gilded reliquary (1498–1511) under 15 locks and is exhibited only once a year on 30 July. The stalls of the chapel were carved by *Giovanni Battista Bastone* (1520–29).

In the SACRISTY, on the right side of the choir, are frescoes of the Life of St Laurence by *Giovanni Antonio Pandolfi da Pesaro* (1578) and inlaid cupboards by *Mariotto da Gubbio* (1494–97).—The CANONICAL CLOISTERS have a collection of antique and medieval marbles.—The **Museo dell'Opera** (closed in 1990), founded in 1923, contains works of art from the cathedral. The paintings include a Madonna, with saints and a donor, by *Luca Signorelli* (1484; removed for restoration), the Redeemer and saints, by *Lodovico di Angelo* and works by *Meo di Guido*, *Bartolomeo Caporali*, *Andrea Vanni*, and others. There is also a valuable collection of illuminated MSS (breviaries, missals, graduals, and antiphonals), as well as gold and silver reliquaries and other vessels.

To the W of the piazza is the 13C *Palazzo del Vescovado*, several times rebuilt. Nearby is the bell-tower of the cathedral (1606–12), replacing an octagonal Gothic campanile pulled down in 1462. Behind is the little church of the *Maestà delle Volte* (1567–90), named after a fresco of the early 14C Perugian school.

From Piazza Danti Via del Sole leads up past (left) *Le Prome*, with a terrace with a characteristic view of the old town to the N on a hilly spur, to *Piazza Michelotti* (Pl. 7), the highest point of the city (494m), built on the site of the medieval castle, and now surrounded by fine 17C houses. From the piazza a passageway leads downhill; to the left a short undulating lane continues under an archway to emerge in the secluded Piazzetta Raffaello, in a quiet corner of the old town. Here is the church of **San Severo** (Pl. 7). According to tradition in the 11C Camaldulensian monks built here, on the site of a temple of the Sun, a convent and church dedicated to Severus, Bishop of Ravenna. Both were rebuilt in the 15C. In 1748–51 the church was given its present Baroque form. One chapel of the 15C church survives (entrance next door; open 9–12, 15.30–18.30; Sunday 8.30–12.30; closed Monday) with a celebrated *Fresco by *Raphael* (c 1505; his earliest work of the kind; restored in 1976), representing the Holy Trinity with Saints. Beneath, in 1512, *Perugino*, already in decline, painted six other Saints. The terracotta Madonna and Child dates from the early 16C.

From Piazza Danti (see above) the narrow old Via Ulisse Rocchi, formerly the Via Vecchia, so called to distinguish it from the parallel Via Nuova, now Via Bartolo, descends steeply N to the *Arco d'Augusto* (Pl. 7), a noble gateway in which three periods of civilisation are represented. The Etruscan lower part dates from the 3–2C BC; the upper part, with the inscription *Augusta Perusia*, was added after 40 BC; the graceful Renaissance loggia on one of the buttresses in the 16C. In the busy PIAZZA FORTEBRACCIO (Pl. 7) beyond the arch is the *Palazzo Gallenga Stuart* (Pl. 6; being restored). This 18C palace was given a new wing, in harmony with the old construction, in 1935–37, and is now the seat of the UNIVERSITÀ ITALIANA PER STRANIERI (Pl. 6).

This institution was founded in 1921 for the diffusion abroad of the Italian language, literature, and culture. In 1931 it received a gift of $100,000 from the American F. Thorne Rider, for its enlargement. It owns a library (30,000 volumes) of Italian, English, French, and German books. The University is open to students of all nationalities, many of whom attend language courses here.

At Piazza Fortebraccio begins the long **Corso Garibaldi** (Pl. 2), an old medieval street leading out of the town along a narrow spur towards the Porta Sant'Angelo. It has some fine old houses and a number of convents. A short way along on the right is the church of *Sant'Agostino* (Pl. 3), with its admirable choir-stalls sculptured and inlaid by Baccio d'Agnolo (1502–32), perhaps from Perugino's designs. In the 1st S chapel (by Francesco di Guido di Virio da Settignano) is a fresco of the Madonna by Giannicola di Paolo; the 1st N chapel has a Crucifixion and other fresco fragments by Pellino di Vannuccio (1387). The 2nd N chapel has a 16C fresco of the Madonna and two Saints. The adjoining 15C *Oratory* (usually closed) has an interior beautifully decorated in the 17C. Corso Garibaldi continues uphill. Just beyond an archway the charming church of *Sant'Angelo* (Pl. 2), can be seen on the right, at the end of Via del Tempio. It is preceded by a delightful lawn with cypresses, in a peaceful corner of the town. This round Romanesque building of 5C foundation, is said to stand on the site of a temple. Inside are 16 antique columns of miscellaneous provenance.—Steps lead down to the *Porta Sant'Angelo* (being restored), with a tower of a castle built by Fortebraccio, beside a good stretch of medieval walls. Outside the gate on a little hill can be seen the *Convent of Monte Ripido* (Pl. 1), founded in the 13C, with an 18C library. Near the gate is the 13C church of *San Matteo*.—In Via Garibaldi a lane opposite Via del Tempio (see above) leads to the convent of *Sant'Agnese* (Pl. 2; visitors ring, 9.30–11, 15.30–18). A sister shows a chapel with a fresco by Perugino of the Madonna and Saints Anthony Abbot and Anthony of Padua. Another delightful fresco by Eusebio di San Giorgio is not shown since it is in part of the convent which is a closed order.

From Piazza di Fortebraccio (see above) Via Pinturicchio leads past (No. 47) the *House of Pinturicchio*. Near the end of the street, also on the right, is the church of *Santa Maria Nuova* (Pl. 7), containing good stalls (1476) and a *Gonfalon by Benedetto Bonfigli (1472), in which the Saviour is darting arrows at the Perugians, with their towers in the background. Nearby is the *Porta Pesa*, so called from the weighing of produce brought in from the country. About 500m farther on is the *Madonna di Monteluce* (Pl. 4), with a rose window and a double portal (13C) in its façade, and containing a marble tabernacle by Francesco Ferrucci (1487). Adjoining is the *Policlinico* (Ospedali Riuniti di Perugia), whose buildings are spread over the E part of the Colle di Monteluce.

From Piazza di Fortebraccio steps lead down beside the University for Foreigners to Via Goldoni which leads into Via Sant'Elisabetta. Here, beyond the span of a narrow footbridge (once a 13C acqueduct), a modern building of the University (on the right) covers a monochrome *Roman Mosaic* (Pl. 6) of the 2C, with the story of Orpheus charming the wild beasts (closed Sunday). The main buildings of the University founded in 1307 are in Via Fabretti (Pl. 2) in a monastery of Olivetan monks, suppressed by Napoleon. From Via Sant'Elisabetta Via Pascoli (left) winds up to the SW past fields (with the new buildings of the University prominent across the hillside) to end beside a little 14C church with a charming bell-tower. Here is Piazza San Francesco surrounded by green lawns, with the recently restored façade (of unusual design) of the large 13C church of **San Francesco** (Pl. 6). The church was ruined by a landslide and, now inhabited by birds, it presents a strange sight. Next to it is the *Oratorio di San Bernardino* (Pl. 6), a building of 1457–61 with a lovely façade decorated with bas-reliefs by *Agostino di Duccio*, and rich in polychrome marbles. A 3C Christian sarcophagus forms the altar. A second Oratory, behind, has a fine wood ceiling of 1558. The adjoining convent is now the seat of the *Accademia di Belle Arti*, a 16C foundation. Here is the *Cappella della Concezione*, restored in 1928, with another gonfalon by Bonfigli, painted on the occasion of the plague of 1464.

To the SE, beyond the church of the *Madonna della Luce* (Pl.6), with a graceful Renaissance façade (1512–18) the pretty old Via dei Priori climbs back up to Corso Vannucci. Near the beginning of the street are the *Arco di San Luca* (the Gothicised Etruscan Porta Trasimena) and the medieval *Torre degli Sciri* (Pl. 6). Farther on, on the right Via della Cupa affords a fine view of the *Porta Libitana* in the Etruscan walls and leads into Via Deliziosa, in which No. 5 is the *House of Perugino* (Pl. 6).

Across Corso Vannucci Via Fani leads into PIAZZA MATTEOTTI (Pl.7), built in part on the foundations of Etruscan walls. Here are the *Tribunali*, installed in the old University buildings (1453–1515) and in the former *Palazzo del Capitano del Popolo* (1472–81), with a good portal. From Piazza Matteotti Via Baglioni runs S, parallel to Corso Vannucci, towards Piazza Italia. A steep stepped street curves down to cross Via Oberdan and emerge beyond an archway on the busy Viale Indipendenza. Here is the unusual tall church of *Sant'Ercolano* (1297–1326), preceded by a double staircase of 1607. Above Via Marzia skirts the Rocca Paolina and the Porta Marzia, both described above, with the escalators that connect Piazza Partigiani with Piazza Italia. From Sant'Ercolano Corso Cavour descends past (right) the neo-classical *Tre Archi* (1842) beside the smaller *Arco di Sant'Ercolano* in the Etruscan and Roman walls, to the church of **San Domenico** (Pl. 11), founded in 1305 and rebuilt by Carlo Maderno in 1632. It is the largest church in Perugia (length 122m).

The fourth chapel of the S aisle, a relic of the earlier church, has a beautiful terracotta frontal, with statues in carved niches in a carved arch, by *Agostino di Duccio* (1459); by the side door, terracotta monument with a reclining figure of Guglielmo Pontano (1555). In the 1st chapel to the right of the high altar, Gothic *Monument of Benedict XI (died 1304), with four frescoed Saints in the vault above. In the 2nd chapel to the right of the high altar, remains of 14C votive frescoes. In the choir are good carved stalls (1498) and an immense stained-glass window, measuring 22·5km by 10m, with scenes of the miracles of St James Major, dated 1411 and signed by Fra Bartolomeo di Pietro da Perugia and Mariotto di Nardo. In the 1st chapel to the left of the high altar, tomb (1429) with the effigy of Bishop Benedetto Guidalotti, and two reliefs of female Virtues, attributed to Urbano da Cortona. In the 2nd chapel to the left of the high altar, interesting remains of frescoes. In the Left Transept, organ of 1660. Left Aisle. 5th chapel, late-14C damaged Umbrian frescoes; 3rd chapel, gonfalon by Giannicola di Paolo (1494). Benedict's robes are preserved in the sacristy.

The convent of San Domenico now houses the *Archivio dello Stato* and the *Museo Archeologico Nazionale dell'Umbria*, open every day, 9–13.30, 15–18.30; fest. 9–13.

The MUSEO ETRUSCO-ROMANO, founded in 1790, was housed in the University from 1812 to 1936; in 1946 the contents were installed at San Domenico. The exhibits are displayed on the upper floor of the convent, with good views of the countryside. The large cloister is being restored; normally displayed here (but removed during restoration work) are: Etrusco-Roman inscriptions; sarcophagus with the myth of Meleager; three cippi set up in honour of Augustus when he authorised the rebuilding of Perugia; Etruscan urns and Roman bas-relief fragments; and a colossal head of Claudius from Carsulae. The entrance is at the upper level of the Large Cloister. A door on the right leads to the Small Cloister, in the N walk of which are Roman portrait heads. ROOM I (right). Here is a stele with the representation of two warriors (6C BC), and an archaic sphinx from Cetona.—RII contains a large sarcophagus with a victorious return from battle (removed for restoration), and a circular cippus with a fine bas-relief.—RRIII and IV contain bronze objects.—RRV and VI. Finds from the necropoli of Monteluce and Frontone. Beyond a gallery with Greek and Cypriot vases, RVII has Etruscan mirrors and jewellery. Outside, Cippus in travertine with the celebrated Inscription of Perugia of 151 words, one of the most important monuments of Etruscan epigraphy. RVIII has a terracotta urn with Medusa.—RRIX–XI have more local finds. Just outside RXI is a terracotta statuette of a divinity signed by the artist. RXII contains small bronzes from Colle Arsiccio.

The MUSEO PREISTORICO, beyond, is one of the most important of its kind. Of particular interest are the discoveries made in 1928–29 at the site of Belverde sul Monte Cetona. In the small cloister are models of cave dwellings of the Iron Age. In the following eight rooms, objects of flint and pottery illustrating the development in Central Italy of civilisation from the Palaeolithic to the Neolithic Age. The long room (with a good view) around which these rooms are grouped contains material from many other countries. In the Salone, reached by a staircase, are flint axes, daggers and other implements; objects in copper and bronze; discoveries from Belverde (Iron Age): vases, some with geometrical decoration, bone implements, bronze shields and discs, armlets, articles of household use and adornment, and a fine bronze sword.

Corso Cavour ends at *Porta San Pietro*, with a lovely outer façade by Agostino di Duccio and Polidoro di Stefano (1473). Borgo XX Giugno continues along a narrow ridge to the Benedictine church of *San Pietro dei Cassinensi* (Pl. 16), with its graceful 14C tower.

The name is derived from the monks of Monte Cassino. The church belongs to a convent (now part of the University) founded by the monk Pietro Vincioli at the end of the 10C, and several times remodelled. The entrance is by a 16C portal on the left of the convent courtyard. Two Romanesque arches with 15C frescoes have been revealed beside the door, which has a lunette of the Madonna with two angels by Giannicola di Paolo. The basilican INTERIOR, with ancient marble and granite columns, is almost entirely covered with paintings, many of which are particularly good. In the NAVE, with a rich ceiling, are 11 large canvases by *L'Aliense* (1592–94), a pupil of Tintoretto. In the S aisle are the Madonna with Saints Mary Magdalene and Sebastian, by *Eusebio da San Giorgio*, and St Benedict (3rd altar), by the same artist (1492–93); in the N aisle (just beyond the 1st altar) Pietà, by *Perugino*, (beyond the 3rd altar) an Adoration of the Magi (1508) by *Eusebio*, (in the Cappella Ranieri) *Christ on the Mount, by *Guido Reni*, and (in the Cappella Vibi) a carved altarpiece by *Mino da Fiesole* (1473), and frescoes by *Giovanni Battista Caporali*. At the end of the aisle, Pietà, by *Fiorenzo di Lorenzo* (1469).—The SACRISTY (opened on application) contains admirable intarsia work of 1472, small panels of four Saints by *Perugino* (1496; the fifth one is a copy), a Head of Christ, by *Dosso Dossi*, and a fragment of Deruta majolica pavement (1563). Illuminated choir-books are displayed in a room off the N aisle (W end).—In the *CHOIR are stone pulpits with reliefs by *Francesco di Guido*, thrones by *Benedetto da Montepulciano* (1555–56), and richly inlaid *Stalls by *Bernardo Antonibi, Stefano Zambelli* and others (1526–85).

A *Door at the end of the choir, inlaid by *Fra Damiano* (1536), a brother of Stefano, leads out onto a balcony from which there is a splendid view of Assisi, Spello, etc. The autograph of the poet Carducci (1871) is indicated.—The former convent is now occupied by the Faculty of Agriculture of the University.

From the *Giardino del frontone*, on the other side of the street, there is another fine view in the direction of Foligno. Outside the *Porta San Costanzo*, dating from

1587, is the church of *San Costanzo* (1143–1205), partly rebuilt and decorated by Leo XIII, who was Bishop of Perugia before his election to the Holy See in 1878.

About 5km from the Porta San Costanzo by the Foligno road, near Ponte San Giovanni (see below; pleasant short-cuts for walkers), is the ****Ipogeo dei Volumni** (adm. 9–14; closed Monday), discovered in 1840, one of the finest Etruscan tombs known. Dating from the second half of the 2C BC, it has the form of a Roman house with atrium, tablinum, and two wings. The walls are adorned with stucco and reliefs. The coffered ceiling has heads hewn out of the rock. In the central chamber nine travertine urns containing the ashes of the Volumnii family show Roman influence (note the urn of Aruns Volumnius); a tenth, in marble, belongs to the 1C AD. Above the hypogeum, in a modern building, are several urns found in the adjacent cemetery.—To the right beyond the main station, near the little church of San Manno (6km from Perugia), is the *Tomb of San Manno*, a spacious vault faced with travertine slabs and having an arched ceiling. The Etruscan inscription states that this tomb belonged to the Precu family.

A winding descent (which passes above the tunnel of the new Perugia by-pass) leaves on the right a road (N317) to Orvieto, passes the Ipogeo dei Volumni (see above), and from (116km) *Ponte San Giovanni* to (120km) *Collestrada* briefly coincides with N3 bis (Rte 59B), crossing the Tiber. 2km farther on N147 diverges left direct to (127·5km) *Assisi*, while the main road continues towards Spello, affording an alternative approach (1km longer) via Santa Maria degli Angeli (see below) and the railway station.

ASSISI (4,600 inhab.), on a commanding spur of Monte Subasio (360–505m), is a quiet little medieval town which has retained its beautiful rural setting with olive trees and cultivated fields reaching right up to its walls. St Francis of Assisi, one of the most fascinating characters in history, here founded his Order. In the great Basilica begun two years after his death, the story of his life provided inspiration to some of the greatest artists of his time including Giotto, Simone Martini, Cimabue, and Pietro Lorenzetti. As one of the most famous shrines in the world, Assisi is now given over to the reception of its thousands of Italian and foreign visitors, and the town is slowly becoming depopulated.

Railway Station, near Santa Maria degli Angeli, 5km SW of the town (bus in connection with trains).

Car Parking. Outside Porta San Pietro; Piazza Matteotti; near Porta del Sementone; and outside Porta Nuova.

Hotels near the basilica of San Francesco, and Piazza del Comune. Numerous convents and monasteries of every nationality also provide hospitality.

Post Office, Piazza del Comune.—*Tourist Office*, 12 Piazza del Comune.— **Swimming Pool** on Monte Subiaso.

Buses from Piazzale Porta San Pietro to *Rome*; from Piazza Santa Chiara to *Perugia* 2–4 times daily in 50 minutes; to *Foligno* in ¾hr; via Foligno, Tolentino, Macerata, and San Benedetto del Tronto to *Ascoli Piceno* in 5¾hrs; to *Gualdo Tadino* in 1¾hrs.—**Coach Excursions** (1 July–30 September) to *Gubbio* (3 times a week); to *Spoleto, Montefalco*, and *Bevagna* (once a week); and to *Todi* and *Orvieto* (twice a week).

Annual Festivals connected with St Francis, with processions and liturgical ceremonies are held in Easter Week, Ascension Day, Corpus Christi, 22 June, 1–2 August, 11 August, 12 August, 3–4 October, and at Christmas. A medieval pageant known as the 'Kalendimaggio' is held for three days around 1 May.

History. The Umbro-Etruscan and Roman town of *Asisium* was evangelised by St Rufinus, who was martyred here in 238. Later under the dominion of the Dukes of Spoleto, it became a republic in 1184 and was involved in numerous wars with neighbouring towns. Eventually it passed to the Church. Sextus Propertius (c 46 BC–c AD 14), the elegiac poet, was a native of Assisi, and his house has recently been identified beneath the church of Santa Maria Maggiore.

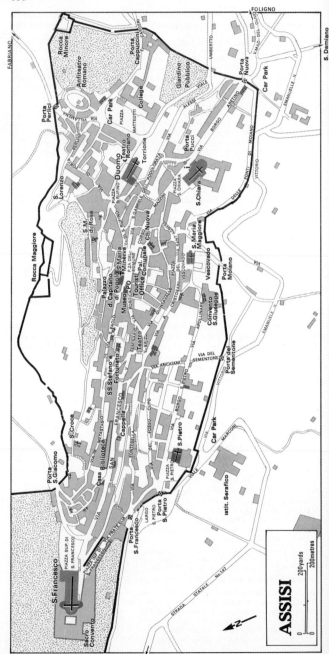

ASSISI

200 yards
200 metres

St Clare (Chiara), the daughter of a rich family, disciple of St Francis, and foundress of the Poor Clares, was born at Assisi in 1194, and died in her own convent in 1253.

St Francis of Assisi (1182–1226) was the son of a rich merchant, Pietro Bernardone, the husband of Pica (perhaps de Bourlemont, a Provencal). He was baptised as Giovanni, but his father, who at the time was trading in France, called him Francesco. At the age of 24, after a year's imprisonment at Perugia, followed by an illness, he changed his way of life. He gave all he had to the poor, looked after the sick, and led a humble, exemplary life. He extended his devotion to animals and birds. As he was praying in San Damiano he heard a Voice telling him to 'Rebuild my Church', and in the Chapel of the Porziuncola he heard the command 'Freely you have received, freely give'. He retreated with some followers to a stable in Rivotorto, and then settled in a hut around the Porziuncola. He and his companions also stayed on Monte Subasio in prayer and meditation. In May 1209 he obtained from Innocent III the verbal approval of his Order founded on a rule of poverty, chastity, and obedience. He preached his gospel in Italy, in Spain, in Morocco, in Egypt (1219) where the Sultan Melek-el-Kamel received him kindly, and in the Holy Land. In 1221 the Franciscan Rule was sanctioned by Honorius III, and three years later Francis himself retired to La Verna. On 14 September 1224 he had a vision of a seraph with six wings and found on his own body the stigmata or wounds of the Passion. He returned to Assisi and died at the Porziuncola on 3 October 1226. St Francis was canonised on 16 July 1228 and became a patron saint of Italy in 1939. The Franciscan Order has various divisions: the first, a religious order divided into four families (Friars Minor, Conventuals, Capuchins, and a Tertiary Religious Order); the second, the Poor Clares; and the third, a secular Order of tertiary lay brothers. In the 18C it consisted of more than 9000 houses with 150,000 members. Assisi has become increasingly famous as a centre of pilgrimage in this century: in 1982, the anniversary of the saint's birth, some 5 million pilgrims visited Assisi.

The main road provides a splendid view of the town built of pale pink and grey stone beneath its ruined castle, as it traverses the fields at its foot. The massive tiered vaulting and buttresses which support the convent and church of San Francesco are conspicuous on the N spur of the hill. Beyond the 13C *Porta San Francesco* Via Frate Elia leads steeply up to the colonnaded *Piazza Inferiore di San Francesco* laid out in the 15C and now used as a car park. The two-storeyed ****Basilica of San Francesco**, the principal monument to the memory of St Francis, contains a magnificent series of frescoes including Giotto's famous Life of the Saint.

At his death St Francis was interred in the church of San Giorgio, now included as a chapel in the basilica of Santa Chiara. A fund for a memorial church was started in April 1228, and its foundation stone was laid by Gregory IX the day following the canonisation ceremony. *Frate Elia*, close friend and follower of St Francis and Vicar-General of the Franciscans, took an active part in the construction of the church and it is thought may himself have been the architect; the work has also been attributed to *Filippo da Campello, Giovanni della Penna*, and *Lapo Lombardo*. The lower church was soon ready and on 25 May 1230 the remains were translated to it. The completed church was consecrated by Innocent IV in 1253. Early in the 14C the side chapels of the lower church were added. The campanile was completed in 1239.

The church is open all day in summer, but is closed 12–14 in November–March.—Lights (essential) in each chapel are operated by 100 lire coins.

In the piazza is the entrance to the lower church; a double flight of steps leads up to the lawn in front of the upper church (see below). Beside the graceful Renaissance doorway of the *Oratory of San Bernardino* (1488) is the fine Renaissance *Porch of 1487 (very ruined) designed by Francesco da Pietrasanta covering a Gothic *Portal (1) which leads into the **Lower Church**. The dark interior resembles a huge crypt with Gothic vaulting and low arches and stained glass windows. In the ENTRANCE TRANSEPT is a fresco (2) of the Madonna with Saints Francis, Anthony Abbot, and Rufinus, by *Ceccolo di Giovanni* of the school of Ottaviano Nelli (15C). Beyond on the right (3) is a Gothic tomb thought to be that of Philip I of Courtenay, Emperor of Constantinople (died 1283), probably a Sienese work. From the Cappella di Sant'Antonio (4) is the entrance (not always open) to a picturesque cloistered Cemetery (5; 14–15C). The Cappella di Santa Caterina (6) added in 1367 for Cardinal Albornoz by *Matteo Gattapone da Gubbio* is frescoed by *Andrea da Bologna*.

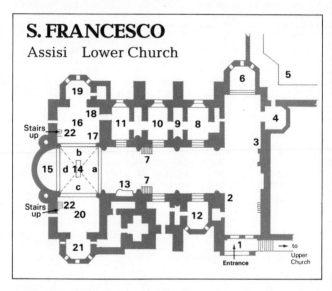

S. FRANCESCO
Assisi   Lower Church

NAVE. The floor slopes down towards the altar. Here are the oldest frescoes (1253) in the basilica damaged when the side chapels were opened. The Passion scenes (right wall) and Life of St Francis (left wall) and the geometric decoration of the rib vaulting are all attributed to an anonymous artist, known as the *'Maestro di San Francesco'* from these frescoes. On either side of the nave a staircase (7) descends to the CRYPT (opened in 1818 and remodelled in 1932), with the stone coffin of St Francis, rendered inaccessible in the 15C as a precaution against Perugian raids, and rediscovered in 1818. Round the tomb are grouped the sarcophagi of the saint's four faithful companions: Fra Leone, Fra Angelo, Fra Masseo, and Fra Ruffino.

SIDE CHAPELS. Right side (all three chapels have good 14C stained glass): 1st chapel (8), frescoes by *Dono Doni* (1575); in the passageway (9) 14C frescoes attributed to *Andrea da Bologna*; 2nd chapel (10) 17C frescoes by *Cesare Sermei da Orvieto*; 3rd chapel (11) *Life of St Mary Magdalene, traditionally attributed to *Giotto* and his school (c 1309).—The 1st chapel on the left side (12) contains the finest fresco cycle in the Lower Church, the *Story of St Martin by *Simone Martini* (c 1322–26) who also probably designed the stained glass. On the undersurface of the entrance arch are paired saints in niches, with St Martin receiving the donor Cardinal Gentile da Montefiore on the inner surface. On the left wall of the chapel from right to left: Dream of

St Martin, St Martin divides his cloak, St Ambrose's meditation, St Martin resuscitates a child, Obsequies of St Martin. On the right wall from left to right: Investiture of St Martin, St Martin renounces the sword, Mass of Albigensa, St Martin honoured by the Emperor, Death of St Martin.—Above the Cosmatesque Pulpit (13) in the nave, Coronation of the Virgin attributed to *Puccio Capanna* of Assisi, a pupil of Giotto.

Above the pretty HIGH ALTAR (14; the tomb of St Francis can be seen through a grille) the four vaults ('Quattro Vele') contain celebrated *Frescoes representing allegories of the three Virtues of St Francis, Poverty (a), Chastity (b), and Obedience (c), and his Triumph (d). Traditionally attributed to Giotto they are now ascribed to a pupil known as the *'Maestro delle Vele'* from these frescoes.—In the APSE (15) are beautifully carved Stalls by *Apollonio Petrocchi da Ripatransone* (1471).

RIGHT TRANSEPT (16). The vault and end wall are covered with frescoes of the Life of Christ and St Francis traditionally attributed to *Giotto* but now usually thought to be by an assistant. The *Madonna enthroned with four angels and St Francis is by *Cimabue*, one of the most famous representations of the Saint (on the first lower section of the vault). To the right (17), Tomb of five companions of St Francis with their portraits, and, to the left of the door (18), Madonna and Child with two King Saints (half-length) by *Simone Martini*. On the end wall are five Saints including one traditionally thought to be St Clare, also attributed to *Simone Martini*. The Cappella di San Nicola (19) at the end, is decorated with Giottesque frescoes of c 1330 illustrating the life of St Nicholas. Also here, tomb of Giovanni Orsini (died 1292) with a fresco of the Madonna and Child with St Nicholas of Bari and St Francis by a pupil of Giotto.

LEFT TRANSEPT (20). The vault and walls are covered with frescoes by *Pietro Lorenzetti* and assistants. Works by *Lorenzetti* himself include a large Crucifixion and (left wall) *Madonna and Child between Saints Francis and John the Evangelist, and (end wall) scenes from the Passion including a moving Descent from the Cross. In the chapel of San Giovanni Battista (21) there is a painting of the Madonna and Child with Saints Francis and John the Baptist by *Lorenzetti*, and fine late-13C stained glass.

Stairs (22) lead up from both transepts to a terrace outside the apse of the upper church overlooking the Cloister of Sixtus IV. Here a door leads into the SALA GOTICA where the ***Treasury** (9.30–12.30, 14–18; closed Monday) has been beautifully arranged (there are pretty views of the countrside from the windows).

Though several times despoiled it still contains precious treasures. In the entrance is the magnificent Flemish *Tapestry of St Francis, presented by Sixtus IV in 1479.—In the main hall, the first cases contain a 12C Processional Cross and a 13C painted Crucifix by a follower of Giunta Pisano; (on the wall) Umbrian Crucifix (c 1220–40). Cases 10–12: reliquary of St Andrew (c 1290), presented by Nicholas IV; panel painting of St Francis (1265–75); and a sinopia of the head of Christ from the Upper Church.—On a raised platform in the centre: silver gilt Reliquary presented by Queen Joanna of Burgundy in the 14C; Madonna and Child, a 13C ivory of French workmanship; and the illuminated Missal of St Louis of Toulouse (French, 1260–64).— On the left wall: sinopia of St Martin by *Simone Martini* from the Lower Church; tabernacle designed by *Galeazzo Alessi* and made by *Vincenzo Danti* (1570), and medieval ceramics found in Assisi in 1968. Case 17: silver gilt *Chalice of Nicholas IV (c 1290) by *Guccio di Mannaie*, with a portrait of the Pope in enamel. Cases 18–25 contain 14–16C reliquaries and Crosses, including a 14C Venetian Cross in rock-crystal with enamels. Case 26: Altar-frontal of Sixtus IV, perhaps designed by *Antonio del Pollaiolo* with figures of the Pope and St Francis (removed for restoration).—On the platform are displayed more reliquaries and Crosses of the 16–17C. At the end of the hall, 18C and 19C church silver, and, on the wall: *Tiberio di Assisi*, Crucifix and Saints; *Lo Spagna*, Madonna enthroned.

The room beyond was opened in 1986 to display the **Mason Perkins Collection** of paintings (some of them recently restored) left to the Convent by the art historian, collector, and dealer Friederick Mason Perkins (1874–1955), particularly interesting as an example of a private collection formed in Italy in the first half of this century. It includes works by *Mariotto di Nardo*; *Lorenzo Monaco* (Madonna of Humility); *Pier Francesco Fiorentino*; *Lorenzo di Nicolò*; *Ortolano* (St Sebastian); '*Maestro di San Martino alle Palme*' (portable triptych); *Segna di Bonaventura*; *Taddeo di Bartolo* (St Elizabeth of Hungary); *Pietro Lorenzetti* (Madonna and Child); and *Bartolomeo di Fredi*.

The immense **Convent** (now a missionary college; no adm.), is built on conspicuous arches. Here also is a papal apartment.—Giuseppe Tartini (1692–1770) may have composed his 'Devil's Trill' Sonata here (1715) while in hiding from the family of Elisabetta Premazone, whom he had secretly married in Padua.

Two more staircases continue up from the terrace to the transepts of the **Upper Church**. The tall light interior provides a strong contrast to the Lower Church. The good gothic portal and rose window in its façade overlook a green lawn. The architectural unity of this remarkable 13C Gothic building is enhanced by its contemporary frescoes and *Stained glass. The lower tier of *Frescoes in the NAVE are the famous scenes from the Life of St Francis, traditionally thought to be early works by *Giotto* and assistants (c 1290–95), but now no longer attributed to Giotto by some scholars. Giotto received commissions for other Franciscan fresco cycles in Rimini and Padua, both now lost, and in the Bardi Chapel of Santa Croce in Florence. A close study of the 28 frescoes (recently well restored) reveals that several different hands were at work here. The 2nd and 11th scenes have often been ascribed to Giotto himself.

The story begins on the right-hand wall nearest the right transept: 1. The young saint is honoured in the piazza of Assisi by a poor man who lays down his cloak before him; 2. St Francis gives his cloak to a poor man (with a panorama of Assisi in the background); 3. The saint dreams of a palace full of arms; 4. The saint in prayer in San Damiano hears a Voice exhorting him to 'Rebuild My Church'; 5. The saint renounces his worldly goods in front of his father and the Bishop of Assisi; 6. Innocent III dreams of the saint sustaining the Church; 7. Innocent III approves the saint's Order; 8. The saint appears to his companions in a Chariot of Fire; 9. Fra Leo dreams of the throne reserved for the saint in Paradise; 10. The expulsion of the Demons from Arezzo; 11. The saint before the Sultan offers to undergo the Ordeal by Fire; 12. The saint in Ecstasy; 13. The saint celebrates Christmas at Greccio.—WEST WALL: 14. The saint causes a fountain to spring up to quench a man's thirst; 15. The saint preaches to the birds.—LEFT-HAND WALL: 16. The Death of the Knight of Celano as foretold by the saint; 17. The saint preaches before Honorius III; 18. The saint appears to the friars at Arles; 19. The saint receives the Stigmata; 20. The death of the saint and his funeral; 21. The apparition of the saint to the Bishop of Assisi and Fra Augustine; 22. Girolamo of Assisi accepts the Truth of the Stigmata; 23. The Poor Clares mourn the dead saint at San Damiano; 24. Coronation of the saint; 25. The saint appears to Gregory IX in a dream; 26. The saint heals a man, mortally wounded from Ilerda; 27. The saint revives a devout woman; 28. The saint releases Pietro d'Alife from prison.

Above the fresco cycle by Giotto is another tier of 34 frescoes from Old and New Testament history (many of them sadly damaged), and, in the vaulting, the Evangelists and Doctors of the Church. These were all ascribed by Vasari to *Cimabue* but are now generally thought to be in part by pupils of *Cimabue* and in part by painters of the Roman school (*Jacopo Torriti* and *Filippo Rusuti*). The Isaac scenes are attributed as very early works to *Giotto*.

In the TRANSEPTS, CROSSING and APSE are very beautiful *Frescoes begun c 1277 by *Cimabue* and pupils. These are very damaged and have lost their colour and taken on the appearance of negatives, for reasons still not fully explained. In the LEFT TRANSEPT is a superb *Crucifixion and scenes from the Apocalypse. In the APSE, Life of the Virgin, and in the RIGHT TRANSEPT, Life of Saints Peter and Paul and another Crucifixion.

From the upper church of San Francesco Via San Francesco leads towards the centre of the town past many medieval houses (some of them restored) and some large 17C palaces by the local architect Giacomo Giorgetti. No. 14 is the 14C *Casa dei Maestri Comacini*. The *Oratorio dei Pellegrini* (No. 11) is a relic of a hospital of 1431 where pilgrims used to be lodged. It is covered with beautiful frescoes by Mezzastris and Matteo da Giovanni. The young saint to the left of the entrance is traditionally attributed as an early work to Perugino. At No. 3 is the small portico (1267) of the *Monte Frumentario*, beside which is a 16C fountain. An arch marks the beginning of the Via del Seminario, continued by Via Portica, which, after a steep climb, ends at the main square by the *Museo Civico* (adm. 9–12.30, 15 or 16–18 or 19; fest. 9–12.30; closed Monday). It occupies the crypt of the demolished church of San Nicola and has Etruscan funerary urns and Roman sculptural fragments. A long corridor gives access to extensive Roman remains, including walls and temple bases, thought to be part of the Forum.

In the beautifully-shaped PIAZZA DEL COMUNE are the *Palazzo del Capitano del Popolo* (13C; restored in this century) and the 13C *Torre Comunale*. The ***Temple of Minerva** dates from the time of Augustus. The perfectly-preserved pronaos consists of six Corinthian columns on plinths which support a low tympanum. The flight of travertine steps continues between the columns. This was particularly admired by Goethe when he visited Assisi in 1786, as it was the first Classical building he had ever seen. The cella was transformed in 1539 into the church of Santa Maria and given a Baroque interior by Giacomo Giorgetti in 1634. On the other side of the piazza is *Palazzo Comunale* or *dei Priori* (1337). It contains the *Pinacoteca Comunale* with a collection of Umbrian frescoes (adm. as for Museo Civico), and works by the school of Giotto, and by Tiberius d'Assisi and Ottaviano Nelli, and a standard painted by Nicolò L'Alunno. Just beyond, beneath an archway, a lane descends past a permanent exhibition of local handicrafts (open 10–12, 15-19) to the *Chiesa Nuova* (1615), built on the supposed site of the house which belonged to the parents of St Francis; an oratory of the 13C in an adjoining alley is indicated as the birthplace of the saint.

From the NE corner of the piazza Via San Rufino mounts to the charming quiet piazza with its wall fountain in front of the **Cathedral** *(San Rufino)*, dedicated to the missionary martyr of Assisi. It was rebuilt in 1140 by *Giovanni da Gubbio*. Its interesting old *Façade has rectangular facing between its doors with crude carvings. Above a gallery are three beautiful rose windows, the central one with good carved symbols of the Evangelists and telamones. It was heightened with a Gothic blind arch before the church was consecrated in 1253. The 11C campanile stands over a Roman cistern.

The interior was transformed by *Alessi* in 1571. At the beginning of the right aisle is the font at which St Francis and St Clare were baptised. The Emperor Frederick II may also have been baptised here

The Cathedral of Assisi

in 1197 (aged three). Beside the W door are statues of Saints Francis and Clare by *Giovanni Duprè* and his daughter *Amalia* (1881–88). At the beginning of the left aisle a little door gives access to a well-preserved Roman cistern with a barrel vault beneath the campanile. The handsome choir-stalls date from 1520. The small MUSEO CAPITOLARE is opened on request (10–12, 15–17). It contains architectural fragments from the 11C church, triptychs by *L'Alunno* (1470) and *Matteo da Gualdo*, and detached frescoes by *Puccio Capanna* from San Rufinuccio in Assisi. Visitors are also conducted on request (through a little door to the right of the façade) to the Crypt of the 11C church with a Roman sarcophagus. Parts of an even earlier building, as well as a Roman wall and channel for water (from the cistern) are also clearly visible here.—There is a fine view of the Rocca from the piazza.

The lane above the cathedral leads past the remains of a *Roman Theatre* to the *Giardino Pubblico*. Farther NE, beyond a group of 13C houses, are ruins of a *Roman Amphitheatre* and the *Porta Perlici* (1199). Dominating the town are two citadels, of which the *Rocca Maggiore* (adm. daily) was rebuilt by Cardinal Albornoz in 1367 (fine view).

From the cathedral a road descends to the red and white Gothic church of ***Santa Chiara** (open 6.30–12, 14–dusk), built in 1257–65. The great flying buttresses that span the road were added at the end of the 14C; the W front has a fine rose window. In the interior are frescoes of the school of Giotto. Off the right side are two chapels on the site of the former church of San Giorgio where St Francis was first buried and where he was canonised. The CHAPEL OF THE CRUCIFIX contains the painted *Crucifix (late 12C) that spoke to St Francis at San Damiano (see below), and relics of the saint. The adjoining CHAPEL OF THE SACRAMENT has late 14C frescoes of the Annunciation, the Nativity, the Adoration of the Magi, and St George, and a Madonna and Saints perhaps by *Puccio Capanna*. In the apse hangs a 13C Crucifix by the 'Maestro di Santa Chiara', and in the cross vault are well-preserved Giottesque *Frescoes. In the right transept is a painting of St Clare with eight stories from her life also attributed to the 'Maestro di Santa Chiara', and 14C frescoes with scenes from her life. The left transept has a Nativity by the 14C Umbrian school and a Madonna and Child painted at the end of the 13C. The frescoes high up on the walls here date from the end of the 13C. St Clare is buried in the richly decorated 19C Crypt.

Via Sant'Agnese returns towards Piazza Vescovado where the church of *Santa Maria Maggiore*, with a good wheel-window (1163), occupies the site of a Temple of Apollo and has an interesting crypt. The house of the Roman poet Sextus Propertius (see above; enquire at the Vescovado for the key), with interesting wall paintings, has been identified here. Via Bernardo da Quintavalle, higher up, retains its medieval character. Farther W is the Benedictine church of SAN PIETRO, first mentioned in 1029 but dating in its present form from 1268.—*Porta San Pietro* dates from the 13C.

The 13C convent of **San Damiano** below Porta Nuova can be reached on foot from the gate by a pretty lane in c 15 minutes (or by car; sign-posted from Viale Vittorio Emanuele). Here in 1205 St Francis renounced the world, and St Clare died. The little convent preserves the humility and simplicity of the Franciscan spirit. The vestibule of the Cloister is painted by Eusebio da San Giorgio (1507).

The **Eremo delle Carceri** (open 8–dusk), 4km E of Porta Cappuccini, is reached by another (signposted) road. This was the forest hermitage of St Francis, on the lower slopes of Monte Subasio. It is in a remarkably secluded and peaceful spot (790m) surrounded by thick woods of ilexes and oaks, with magnificent views. Here St Francis and his followers would come at times to live as hermits in caves, and later St Bernardine founded a convent here. A friar conducts visitors through the tiny convent to see the cave of St Francis with his bed hollowed out of the rock, and an ancient tree on which birds are

The Eremo delle Carceri, Assisi

supposed to have perched to receive his blessing.—A new road contiues up to the summit of the beautiful **Monte Subasio** (1289m; *View) which affords pasture for animals. This is a pleasant cool spot to picnic in summer.

The conspicuous church of **Santa Maria degli Angeli** (open 6–12.30, 14–dusk), on the plain below the town, can be reached by road (from Porta San Pietro) or by a path in c 40 minutes. It is now surrounded by an unattractive small suburb. Visited by thousands of pilgrims because of its associations with St Francis, it has all the usual characteristics of a famous holy shrine. It has an ugly monumental approach with flagstaffs and incongruous trees. It was designed in 1569 by *Galeazzo Alessi* and built by *Girolamo Martelli*, *Giacomo Giorgetti*, and others, and finished in 1679. It was rebuilt after an earthquake in 1832 by *Luigi Poletti* except for the fine cupola and apse which survive from the 16C church. The unattractive façade is by *Cesare Bazzani* (1928). The church was built on a place which belonged to the Benedictines known as the 'Porziuncola' where St Francis and his companions first came to live in simple huts and where, in a little chapel, he founded his Order. The church was built to cover this little 11C oratory (Cappella della Porziuncola), and other chapels used by St Francis. This was the meeting place of Saints Francis and Dominic, and here St Francis died.

The little CAPPELLA DELLA PORZIUNCOLA stands in the midst of the church beneath the cupola. It is a simple rustic hut built of stone with a fresco by *Overback* (1830) over the wide entrance, and a Calvary by *Andrea di Assisi* outside the pretty little apse. Inside a *Painting of the Life of St Francis, the only known work of *Ilario da Viterbo* (1393) fits the apse. The tiny CAPPELLA DEL TRANSITO concealed behind the entrance to the chancel (right) was built over the cell where St Francis died. It has frescoes by *Lo Spagna* and a statue of the Saint by *Andrea della Robbia*. Another fine work by *Andrea della Robbia* is the altarpiece in the Crypt (seen through windows in the chancel steps) which has been excavated beneath the high altar to reveal remains of the first Franciscan convent.

From the Sacristy there is access to a portico which leads past a garden of the thornless roses of St Francis which bloom yearly in May (and a bronze statue of the Saint, 1912) to the CAPPELLA DEL ROSETO (named from the roses), built by St Bonaventura over the cave of St Francis, and decorated with frescoes by *Tiberio d'Assisi*, a pupil of Perugino (1506). A corridor leads back to the church past an old pharmacy and the cloisters.—The MUSEO (open 9–12.30, 14.30–18.30) has a small collection of paintings including a *Portrait of St Francis, by an unknown master ('*Maestro di San Francesco*'; removed for restoration), a *Crucifix by *Giunta Pisano*, another portrait of the saint of the school of *Cimabue*, and a detached fresco of the Madonna enthroned attributed to *Mezzastris*. There is also a display of church vestments and a delightful missionary museum. The pulpit from which St Bernardine preached, in a room near the entrance to the museum, is shown on request.—A staircase leads up to the CONVENT OF ST BERNARDINE OF SIENA with cells, including that of St Bernardine.

From Assisi to Spoleto and Rome, see Rte 59A.

57 Siena to Viterbo and Rome

ROAD (VIA CASSIA: N2, a very beautiful and empty road, although spoilt now in parts by new stretches on stilts by-passing the little towns). 224km—43km *San Quirico d'Orcia*.—92km *Acquapendente*.—112km **Bolsena**.—127km *Montefiascone*.—143km **Viterbo**.—156km *Vetralla*.—174km *Sutri*.—224km **Rome**. Express bus (S.I.T.A.), twice weekly (Monday and Saturday) in 4¾ hrs.

RAILWAY, 254km in 3¼–4hrs; a change is usually necessary at *Chiusi*.

The Via Cassia leaves Siena by the Porta Romana.—27km *Buon-convento*, on the Ombrone, surrounded by pretty medieval walls, where the Emperor Henry VII died in 1313. In the attractive main street, paved in brick, the parish church has an altarpiece by Matteo di Giovanni and a beautiful polyptych, formerly attributed to Pacchiarotti, but now considered to be the work of Pietro di Francesco Orioli. Opposite is the Biblioteca Comunale with the Museo d'Arte Sacra della Val d'Arbia (Tuesday and Thursday, 10–12, Saturday 10–12, 16–18; Sunday 9–13) which has further notable Sienese paintings, including a triptych by Sano di Pietro and a Madonna by Luca di Tommè. The street continues past an Art Nuoveau house (1919) to the tiny Palazzo Pubblico with a typical tower.—A by-road leads from Buonconvento to the interesting convent of **Monte Oliveto Maggiore** (9km), described at the end of Rte 48.—At (37km) *Torrenieri* the road crosses the Asso and the local railway linking Siena with Grosseto.

Montalcino, 9km SW, is a beautifully situated little walled town (567m), surrounded by extensive olive groves (damaged in the winter of 1985). It is famed for its wine, the remarkably long-lived Brunello, considered by some experts to be Italy's finest. A theatre festival is held here in July. The last bulwark of Sienese independence, it is crowned by a *Rocca* of 1361 (adm. 9–13, 14–18 except Monday). In Piazza Cavour, the old pharmacy of the

Ospedale was frescoed by Vincenzo Tamagni of San Gimignano, a pupil of Sodoma. *Sant'Agostino* has a good rose window and interesting frescoes of the 14C Sienese school; the adjacent seminary houses the *Museo Diocesano* and the *Museo Civico* (adm. daily 10–12, 16–18, or 15–17 in winter). Here are displayed Sienese paintings (Sano di Pietro, Luca di Tommè, Bartolo di Fredi), an illuminated bible (12C), a painted Cross (12–13C), a Crucifixion by Sodoma, good polychrome wood statues, including two statues of the Annunciation (1369–70), one of them signed by 'Maestro Angelo', and archaeological remains (neolithic to medieval). In Piazza Garibaldi is the church of *Sant'Egidio* with a Crucifix recently attributed to Francesco di Valdambrino. In Piazza del Popolo is the oddly sited *Palazzo Comunale* with a very tall tower.— The splendid Benedictine abbey *Church of **Sant'Antimo** (open Sunday 9–12, 14–17; other days ask for custodian in the village of Castelnuovo dell'Abate), 8km S, lies in a remarkable position enclosed within low hills. It dates mainly from 1118 and preserves two doorways and a crypt of its 9C predecessor, supposedly founded by Charlemagne. The interior (entered at present by a sculptured doorway in the S side) is remarkable for its luminous effect, caused by the church having (in part) been built of alabaster. It has fine capitals and pretty apse chapels. The bell-tower, off the N aisle, has an ingenious dome. In the Sacristy (S aisle) is a primitive vault and monochrome frescoes. The Crypt has been closed for restoration. In the S aisle a spiral stair leads up to the Matroneum, fitted up with rooms (15C fireplace, wall-paintings, etc.) from which there is a good view of the church. A Romanesque wooden Crucifixion and Madonna have been removed from here to the church in Castelnuovo dell'Abate. The ruined Refectory and Chapter House now serve as barns.

From Torrenieri (see above) another by-road leads N to *San Giovanni d'Asso* (8km) with a castle with Gothic windows, and the church of San Giovanni Battista (triptych of the Sienese school). Below, in a group of cypresses, is the church of San Pietro in Villore (11–12C) with an ancient crypt. 1km NW is the church of Tribbio with a Madonna and Saints by Riccio (1550).

The landscape becomes prettier, although the road has been raised on stilts and so has spoilt the approach to (43km) **San Quirico d'Orcia** (409m), a little medieval town, with well preserved walls. The interesting 'Canta Maggio' takes place here on the last night of April. The splendid Romanesque *Collegiata* has a particularly pretty exterior. The beautiful S portal (covered for restoration), in the manner of Giovanni Pisano, with lions and caryatids, was damaged by shell-fire, as was the Gothic transeptal doorway (1298), but the W door (c 1080) was unharmed. Inside are a triptych by Sano di Pietro and good stalls of 1502 by Antonio Barili (removed for restoration). Next to the church is the crumbling *Palazzo Chigi* (also damaged in the War), built for Cardinal Flavio Chigi in 1679. In the church of *San Francesco* is a Della Robbian Madonna and statues of the Annunciation attributed to Francesco di Valdambrino. Near one of the gates are the *Horti Leonini* (open daily), lovely Italianate gardens laid out by Diomede Leoni in the 16C, with box hedges and ilex trees. The statue of Cosimo III 'Duke of Etruria' is by Giuseppe Mazzuoli (1688).

FROM SAN QUIRICO D'ORCIA TO CITTÀ DELLA PIEVE, N146, an important link road (54km), well served by buses, between the two main Tuscan roads. It traverses spectacular countryside with rolling hills and wide views, with Monte Amiata prominent to the SW beyond the fertile Val d'Orcia.—Just before Pienza a rough by-road leads left via *Sant'Anna in Camprena* (4km), a monastery in oak woods with good frescoes by Sodoma in the Refectory, to *Castelmuzio* (with a parish museum of Sienese paintings) and the medieval village of *Montisi* (10km) with an interesting church (Crucifix attributed to Ugolino di Nerio, and an altarpiece by

Neroccio, signed and dated 1496).—9km **Pienza* (491m) is a charming compact little town, the birthplace in 1405 of Aeneas Silvius Piccolomini, afterwards Pius II, who changed its name from *Corsignano* by papal bull (1462) after appointing Bernardo Rossellino to design the monumental main square with its splendid buildings. These were all built between 1459 and 1462 and **PIAZZA PIO II* is a remarkable example of Renaissance town planning. The influence of Leon Battista Alberti, Rossellino's master, is clearly to be seen here. The pavement is also very handsome. The **Duomo* (closed 13–15) has an interesting classical façade in Istrian stone, with a central oculus beneath the papal arms of Pius II surrounded by a garland of fruit.

The unusually tall and short INTERIOR, with clustered columns and five light Gothic windows at the E end recalls Northern European models. The fine series of altarpieces were painted for the church in 1461–63. South Aisle: *Giovanni di Paolo*, Madonna and Child with four Saints (and a Pietà in the lunette); 1st apse chapel: *Matteo di Giovanni*, Madonna and Child with four Saints (and the Flagellation in the lunette); 2nd apse chapel: marble tabernacle attributed to *Rossellino*; East chapel: four stalls of 1462; 4th apse chapel: *Vecchietta*, Triptych of the Assumption and four Saints (and an Ecce Homo above). In the Baptistery below is a font by *Rossellino*. The whole church has had to be shored up at the E end and the structure is still unstable.

Beside the well in the piazza, also by Rossellino, is *Palazzo Piccolomini*, begun by Pius II and finished by Pius III, his nephew. It is considered Rossellino's masterpiece, and shows the influence of Alberti's Palazzo Rucellai in Florence. From the courtyard stairs mount to the first floor (open 10–12.30, 15–dusk, except Monday; ring). Inhabited by the Piccolomini up until 1962 the old-fashioned and faded decorations survive. It contains 15–17C furniture, a Sala di Musica, and a large Sala degli Armi. There is access to the loggia on the delightful garden façade, which has a wonderful view beyond the hanging garden over the Val d'Orcia to Monte Amiata, and (on the left) Radiocofani and (on the right) San Quirico and Montalcino.—In the piazza opposite is *Palazzo Vescovile* which contains a Rest on the Flight into Egypt attributed to Fra Bartolomeo. The *Museo della Cattedrale* is to be transferred here; it is at present arranged on the top floor of the *Palazzo dei Canonici* next to the Duomo, and is open 10–13, 14–16 or 15–17 (closed Tuesday).

The contents include: 16C Flemish tapestries; 15C illuminated antiphonals, including one by *Sano di Pietro*; *School of Bartolomeo di Fredi*, Portable triptych with numerous small panels; *Bartolomeo di Fredi*, Madonna of the Misericordia, signed and dated 1364 (restored in 1979); *Ugolino di Nerio*, Polyptych; *Cope of Pius II, embroidered in opus anglicanum (first half of the 14C); a portable triptych attributed to *Sassetta*, *Sano di Pietro*, or the *'Maestro dell'Osservanza'*; a 15C Brussels tapestry; and a small local Etruscan archaeological collection.

Behind the Museum a delightful raised walkway beside cypresses surmounts the walls. On the other side of the Duomo steps lead down to a continuation of this walk past the garden wall of Palazzo Piccolomini.

On the side of the piazza opposite the Duomo is *Palazzo Comunale* with a portico and clock tower. Just out of the square, facing Palazzo Piccolomini, is *Palazzo Ammannati*, built by Cardinal Ammannati of Pavia (with an interesting third floor), next to the smaller *Palazzi dei Cardinali* on the Corso Rossellino. On the other side of the Corso, beside Palazzo Piccolomini, is *San Francesco* (often closed), an early Gothic church with a Crucifix attributed to Segna di Bonaventura (1315–19), a Madonna of the Misericordia attributed to Luca Signorelli, and apse frescoes of the late-14C.

To the S of the town the charming *Pieve di San Vito* is a relic of the earlier town of Corsignano. Founded in the 7C, it has an ancient round campanile. The present church dates from the 12C.—The sheep's cheese ('pecorino') of Pienza is famous.

A pretty road leads S from Pienza and then left to Monticchiello (6km; see below); from this road there is the best view of the remarkable garden façade of Palazzo Piccolomini with its triple row of loggie and the great apse of the Duomo. The first signposted road to Montichiello is unmade-up.

22km **Montepulciano** (14,300 inhab.) is a dignified and interesting town on a hilltop (left; 665m) commanding the SE part of Tuscany and Umbria. It was the birthplace of and gave its late-Latin name to Politian (Angelo Ambrogini, 1454–94), the tutor of Lorenzo de'Medici. Another distinguished native was Cardinal Bellarmine (Roberto Bellarmino, 1542–1621), the scourge of Galileo and of British Protestants in James I's day. The town is noted for its wines. The new one-way system of streets make it particularly difficult to find ones bearings. Outside the *Porta al Prato* stands the 14C church of *Sant'Agnese*. Inside the gate Via Sangallo leads up to Via di Gracciano. Immediately to the left in Via Sangallo is *Palazzo Tarugi* (No. 82) by Vignola, and, opposite, the handsome *Palazzo Avignonesi* (No. 91), attributed to the same artist. A little farther on to the right is *Palazzo Bucelli* (No. 73) with Etruscan urns, reliefs, and inscriptions embedded in the lower part of its façade.

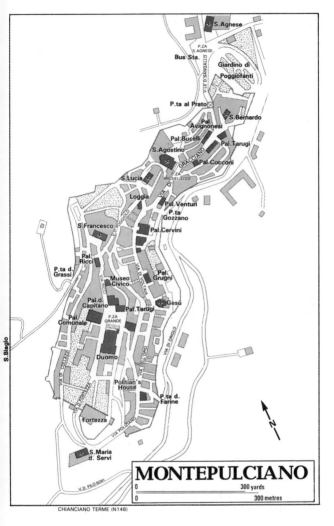

CHIANCIANO TERME (N146)

The church of *Sant'Agostino*, farther on (right) has a good Istrian stone *Façade by Michelozzo, who also carved the terracotta high relief over the door. Inside is a Crucifixion by Lorenzo di Credi (3rd N altar) and St Bernardine of Siena by Giovanni di Paolo (2nd S altar). Opposite the church is an old tower house with a quaint statue on top. Via di Gracciano continues to climb steeply to reach the arcaded market; here it joins Via di Voltaia nel Corso which continues left. On the left are the huge *Palazzo Cervini*, begun for Marcellus II before his pontificate, perhaps by Antonio Sangallo the Elder; then (No. 55) *Palazzo Grugni*, with a balconied portal by

Vignola; and the church of the *Gesù*, with a Baroque interior by
Andrea del Pozzo. In Via Poliziano, reached by continuing along
Via dell'Opio, are the 14C house where Politian was born (No. 5;
plaque), and, outside the town wall, the church of *Santa Maria*
(13C; but with a Baroque interior), containing a small panel of the
Madonna and Child (end of N aisle; inserted into a larger painting)
attributed to the school of Duccio, and commanding a good view.
The road now skirts the rebuilt *Fortezza* and re-enters the walls by
Via della Fortezza to reach the *Piazza Grande with a pretty
fountain. Here stands the DUOMO (1592–1630; closed 12.15–15 or
16).

Inside is a splendid *Triptych at the high altar, by *Taddeo di Bartolo*. The
fragments of the tomb of Bartolomeo Aragazzi, secretary to Pope Martin V,
by *Michelozzo* (1427–36), include the statue of the defunct (right of W door),
two bas-reliefs on the first two nave pillars, two *Statues on either side of the
high altar, a statue in a niche on the right of the high altar, and a frieze of
putti and festoons on the high altar. In 1st chapel in N aisle, a Della Robbia
tabernacle surrounds a bas-relief of the Madonna attributed to *Benedetto da
Maiano*, which is flanked by two early statues of prophets, attributed to *Tino
da Camaino*. The font is by *Giovanni di Agostino*. In the N aisle (on a pillar)
is a small Madonna by *Sano di Pietro*.

In the same square are two mansions by Antonio da Sangallo the
Elder and (on the W side) the 14C *Palazzo Comunale* (from the
tower of which there is a view). In the characteristic Via Ricci
(Renaissance mansions) is the Gothic *Museo Civico* (adm. 10.30–
12.30, 16.30–19.30; closed on Monday and in winter) with a small
gallery of paintings of the Tuscan and Umbrian schools, and an
Etruscan collection. Via del Poggi leads to the church of *Santa
Lucia* with a *Madonna by Signorelli in an inconspicuous little
chapel to the right (locked; light switch behind grille operated by a
rod). A road descends the hill outside the walls to the church of the
*MADONNA DI SAN BIAGIO (open all day), approached by a noble
cypress avenue. Built on a Greek-cross plan, with a dome, this is
one of the most important church buildings of the Renaissance. It
was built in 1518–45 by Antonio da Sangallo the Elder, and has a
remarkably well proportioned design, with one detached campanile (the other was left unfinished). The interior is also very
beautiful with sculptural decoration carved in high relief in the
yellow sandstone, and a little balcony above the apse at the E end.
The Canons' House nearby is also by Sangallo.

Montepulciano railway station, on the Siena-Chiusi line, is in the Val di
Chiana, 10km E of the town.

A by-road leads SW from Montepulciano to the lovely little medieval village of *Monticchiello* with a 13C Castle and walls. The 13C
church has a Gothic doorway and a number of 14C Sienese
frescoes. The Madonna and Child by Pietro Lorenzetti is at present
kept in the Pinacoteca in Siena. In the adjacent Piazza San Martino
a remarkable local open-air theatre season is held in July.
   The road continues SE to the pleasant village of (29km) *Chianciano Vecchia* (closed to traffic). In the small piazza is the Palazzo
del Podestà and Palazzo dell'Arcipretura with a Sala d'Arte Antica
(ring on the first floor; 10–12, 16–18; fest. 10–12), where the small
collection is well labelled. The large *Crucifix is attributed to the
'Maestro di San Polo in Rosso' (school of Duccio), and the Ancona
(formerly on the high altar of the church) attributed to the

'Maestro di Chianciano' (early 14C). The Collegiata, beyond, has a detached fresco of the Assunta.—The old village is now adjoined by **Chianciano Terme** (455m), a famous spa with warm saline and chalybeate waters, rebuilt in the 1950s. Numerous hotels cater for visitors. The place was known to the Romans as *Fontes Clusinae*. The *Acqua Santa* waters are taken internally for liver complaints; the *Sillene* spring is used for baths.—The road goes on over the Autostrada del Sole and, beyond (42km) **Chiusi** (Rte 58), passes the railway station of *Chiusi-Chianciano Terme* before joining N71.—54km *Città della Pieve*, see Rte 56.

From San Quirico an unmade-up road leads up through beautiful countryside to the tiny hamlet of *Vignone* (3km; keep left), now almost totally abandoned. It has a truncated medieval tower, and the little street runs past the 15C Palazzo Amerighi (now Chigi) to the Romanesque church on the edge of the hill. The other fork of the road ends at the restored castle of Ripa d'Orcia in cypress trees.

Beyond San Quirico d'Orcia (see above) the Via Cassia passes just below (48km) *Bagno Vignoni (right), a tiny medieval thermal station with two hotels on a small plateau (threatened with 'development'). The warm waters, known since Roman times, bubble up into a large 'piscina' constructed by the Medici in the charming piazza. The road crosses the Orcia, which farther on is well seen (left) from a sharp rise. A road (right) leads up to *Castiglione d'Orcia* (3km) another beautifully situated little village, the birthplace of the painter and sculptor Il Vecchietta (c 1412–80), after whom the charming piazza is named. In the pieve of Santi Stefano e Degna is a Madonna and Child by Pietro Lorenzetti (restored in 1979), and in the church of Santa Maria Maddalena the paintings of the Madonna are attributed to Simone Martini and Il Vecchietta. Nearby is *Rocca d'Orcia*, a medieval borgo.—At 63km the main road now keeps right, traversing the watershed between the Orcia and the Paglia by a long tunnel, while the old road rises steeply via *Le Conie* to *Radicofani* (783m; 10km), strikingly placed on a basaltic hill. It preserves some remains of a castle built by the English Pope Hadrian IV, in which Ghino di Tacco imprisoned the Abbot of Cluny, as related in the 'Decameron'. The church of San Pietro has Della Robbian work, and the Rocca is being restored. The Palazzo La Posta was used as a hotel by Montaigne, Chateaubriand, and Dickens.

From Le Conie (see above) a road runs W to the summer resorts and winter sporting centres on the slopes of Monte Amiata, passing above the Via Cassia in its tunnel. —20km **Abbadia San Salvatore** (812m), an ancient little hill-town, takes name from a once powerful Cistercian abbey. It has now been developed as a summer and winter resort. The Romanesque *CHURCH, founded in 743, was rebuilt in 1036 and restored in 16C. It has a 12C Crucifix, frescoes by Giuseppe Nasini, and a huge crypt (8C) with good capitals. The medieval district of the town is of exceptional interest. To the W rises **Monte Amiata** (1738m), the highest point in Southern Tuscany, noted for its rich mercury (cinnabar) deposits. The ascent of this extinct tree-clad volcano (wide view) can now be made by a steep road (13km); there are refuges for climbers, cableways, and ski-lifts.—24km *Piancastagnaio*, amid chestnut groves, has the impressive Palazzo Bourbon del Monte.—36km *Santa Fiora* (687m) has terracottas by Andrea Della Robbia in its parish church.—A road goes on via (43km) *Arcidosso* (Rte 53) to (47km) *Castel del Piano* (632m), another hill resort, from which Monte Amiata may be approached via the Piano di Macinaie (winter sports).

72km The old and new roads rejoin in the valley of the Paglia which is now followed and, at 89km, crossed by the Ponte Grego-riano. A sharp rise brings the road to (92km; by-pass under construction) **Acquapendente** (423m), an attractive little resort (6000 inhab.), named after its cascades. The 18C *Cathedral* covers an early Romanesque crypt and contains two reliefs by the school of Agostino di Duccio. Hieronymus Fabricius (1533–1619), the master of William Harvey at Padua, was a native of the place.— From (100km) *San Lorenzo Nuovo*, situated in the Monti Volsini at the crossing of the road from Orvieto to Pitigliano, N2 descends to follow the N shore of Lake Bolsena.

112km **Bolsena** (315m; 3900 inhab.), on the lake shore, was founded by refugees from Volsinii Veteres (Orvieto) in 265 BC, and preserves a pretty medieval district.

The town is famous for the miracle of 1263, when a Bohemian priest was convinced of the Real Presence by the dropping of blood from the Host on the altar linen. It was in commemoration of this miracle that Urban IV (1261–64) instituted the feast day of Corpus Domini and ordered the building of the cathedral at Orvieto. The reliquary containing the linen cloth of the miracle is kept in the Cappella del Corporale at Orvieto.

The 11C church of *Santa Cristina* has an elegant Renaissance façade (1492–94) attributed to Francesco and Benedetto Buglioni (with an enamelled terracotta attributed to the latter). On the right is the 15C Oratorio di San Leonardo (which contains Roman sculptures and material found in the catacombs) with another lunette attributed to Benedetto. On the left is the domed Cappella del Miracolo with a neo-classical façade.

INTERIOR. In a chapel in the right aisle is a well-preserved *Polyptych by *Sano di Pietro*, and interesting 15C frescoes attributed to the school of *Pastura*. In the chapel to right of the main altar, bust of a female Saint attributed to *Benedetto Buglioni* and 14–16C frescoes.—A fine Romanesque door in the N aisle (unlocked by the custodian) leads into the CAPPELLA DEL MIRACOLO where are preserved the altar stones marked with Christ's blood and an altarpiece of the miracle by *Francesco Trevisani* (removed for restoration). Another door leads into the GROTTA DI SANTA CRISTINA with a finely carved enamelled terracotta altarpiece by *Giovanni della Robbia*, and a 9C ciborium with four pink marble Corinthian columns where the miracle took place.—In an adjacent chapel is an effigy of St Cristina in terracotta attributed to *Benedetto Buglioni*. From here can be seen the CATACOMBS built into an Etruscan cave and a burial place of the Lombard period.

At the other end of the town (on the Orvieto road) is the *Castle (13–14C) which dominates the pretty medieval district and has picturesque houses clustered around its walls. It contains the Museo Civico, an archaeological museum still in the process of arrangement, illustrating the history of Volsinii and its territory. A prehistoric and Etruscan section illustrates lake dwellings, and a Roman section contains ceramics from Poggio Moscini and archi-tectural fragments, and the terracotta 'Panther throne' (2C BC; recently restored). Above the castle, on the Orvieto road (left) are the excavations of the Etruscan *Volsinii Novi* (adm. 8–13, except Monday) including walls. The city was built in terraces on the hillside with magnificent views of the lake. Remains of the Roman amphitheatre, baths, and basilica, and funerary monuments of the 1C AD have also been found.

Several roads (one with a fine avenue of plane trees) lead down to the lakeside where the trattorie serve fish from the lake.

The beautiful **Lago di Bolsena** is the classical *Volsiniensis Lacus*, named after the inhabitants of Volsinii Veteres. The northernmost and the largest of the three volcanic lakes in northern Lazio, it occupies a large crater in the Monti Volsini, 13·5km long from N to S and 12km across, with a circumference of 45km and a maximum depth of 146m. In it are two beautiful small islands. The *Isola Bisentina* (owned by the Principi del Drago of Bolsena; adm. sometimes granted) has two buildings attributed to Antonio da Sangallo the Younger: the Palazzo Farnese and the church of Santi Giacomo e Cristoforo, with a cupola by Vignola. Some of the Calvary chapels that ascend the hill contain remains of frescoes by a follower of Benozzo Gozzoli. On the *Isola Martana* Amalaswintha, Queen of the Ostrogoths, was strangled in 532 by her cousin Theodahad, whom she had chosen to share her throne. The lake abounds in eels and other fish. Dante ('Purgatorio', xxiv) mentions Pope Martin IV, who is believed to have died of a surfeit of eels. A road (60km) encircles the lake, serving the villages of Marta, Capodimonte, and Valentano on the S and W shores.

A hilly road, climbing 229m in 7km, runs ENE out of Bolsena through lovely wooded country, joining N71 just S of (9km) *Poggio di Biagio* (Rte 56). The spectacular road continues with magnificent *Views of (22km) Orvieto*.

The road continues round the E shore.—119km On the right, between the road and the lake, is *Bolsena British Military Cemetery*, with 600 graves of those who fell in action in June 1944 between Lake Bolsena and Orvieto. The woods near the cemetery later became the Advanced Headquarters of the Allied Armies in Italy. The road climbs with fine views back of the lake and its islands and wooded shore.

127km **Montefiascone** (11,800 inhab.) stands on a hill (560m) at the SE edge of Lake Bolsena, of which it commands a magnificent view. The town was perhaps originally Etruscan; it later became a Roman municipium. As a medieval commune it was involved in the struggles between the papacy and the empire. On the outskirts of the town (on the Orvieto road) is the interesting Romanesque church of *San Flaviano* (closed for extensive restoration) on two levels. The façade (1262) has a Gothic portal and an unusual 16C balconied loggia above. The lower church has splendid capitals and substantial remains of frescoes (14C). To the right of the main entrance is the famous tomb slab of Bishop Fugger of Augsburg, with its strange epitaph: 'Est, est, est pr(opter) nim(ium) est hic Jo(annes) de Foucris do(minus) meus mortuus est' ('Est, est, est' on account of too much 'Est' here my lord Bishop Fugger died.)

The story is that the prelate used to send his servant in advance to mark with the word 'est' ('here it is') the inns where good wine was to be found; at Montefiascone the servant found such exquisite wine that he wrote 'est, est, est', with the result that his master overdrank and died. The wine of the district is called 'Est, est, est' to this day.

In the centre of the town is the *Duomo*, attributed to Sanmicheli (1519), but continued and the conspicuous dome added during the 17C by Carlo Fontana. James Stuart and Clementina Sobieska were married here in 1719 before taking up residence in Rome. Farther on (right) is the small Romanesque church of *Sant'Andrea*, with interesting capitals. At the top of the town the ruins of the *Rocca Papale* command a good view of the lake.

This route joins N71, coming from Orvieto (Rte 58), then descends a steep hill to (129km) *Montefiascone Station*, and follows the railway.

143km **VITERBO** (325m), once a rival of Rome as the residence of the popes, is a town (54,400 inhab.) of great interest, which preserves its old walls as well as numerous medieval buildings. The lion, the

ancient symbol of the town, recurs frequently as a sculptural motif.
The town is justly famous for its many beautiful fountains.

Car Parks in Piazza della Rocca and Piazza dei Caduti.

Railway Stations. *Porta Fiorentina*, at the N end of the town, for Orte, and for
Rome via Capranica-Sutri; *Porta Romana*, an intermediate stop on the latter
line; *Nord*, adjoining Porta Fiorentina, for Rome via Civita Castellana.

Post Office, Via Ascenzi.—TOURIST OFFICE, 16 Piazza dei Caduti.

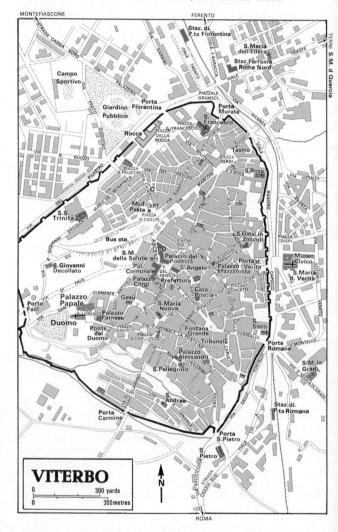

Buses from Viale Trento to *Vetralla, Capranica, Sutri, La Storta,* and *Rome.*—Also to *La Quercia, Bagnaia, Orte,* and *Terni,* via Tuscania to *Cellere,* to *Montalto di Castro,* and to *Valentano;* via Montefiascone to *Capodimonte, Valentano, Farnese,* and to *Pitigliano;* also to *Manciano;* via Montefiascone to *Bolsena, Acquapendente,* and *Proceno;* via Montefiascone and via Bagnoregio to *Orvieto;* via Vetralla to *Tarquinia* and *Civitavecchia;* via Bolsena and Acquapendente to *Siena,* and *Florence.*

History. Viterbo, a minor castle in the 8C, was for centuries in dispute between the papacy and the empire. For a short time, in 1095, it was a free commune; in 1145 it gave refuge to Eugenius III (1145–53); in 1157 it was raised to the dignity of a city; and in 1243 the Emperor Frederick II unsuccessfully besieged it. In 1257 Alexander IV chose the city as his residence. Five popes were elected at Viterbo, Martin IV (1281–85) being the last, and four died here. During this short period Viterbo grew in importance at the expense of Rome. The struggle between the two cities lasted some three centuries. After the removal in 1309 of the popes to Avignon, Viterbo was disputed between various factions, then became subject to the tyranny of the Di Vico family, and ultimately declined. In the Second World War Viterbo suffered heavy damage from bombardment.

Via Cassia runs past the *Giardino Pubblico* to *Porta Fiorentina.* Inside the gate opens PIAZZA DELLA ROCCA, with a fountain by Raffaele da Montelupo, altered by Vignola. It is dominated by the *Rocca,* or castle of Cardinal Albornoz (1354), many times altered and enlarged. It now houses an *Archaeological Museum* (9–14 except Monday), and is used for exhibitions. So far two rooms are open with Etruscan material from the excavations at Acquarossa (see below). Nine colossal statues (1C AD) of the Muses and Pothos from an original by Skopas have been moved here since their restoration, but are not yet on display. They were found in 1902 in the Roman theatre of Ferento, where they formerly decorated niches in the scena.—Via Cairoli leads to the busy Piazza dei Caduti, in the centre of which stands the small octagonal oratory of *Santa Maria della Peste* (1494). On the left is the deconsecrated Renaissance church of *San Giovanni Battista* (1515). Via Ascenzi mounts past *Santa Maria della Salute,* a small 14C church built on a centralised plan with a fine sculpted *Portal,* then threads an archway into PIAZZA DEL PLEBISCITO, the centre of the town, and the junction of numerous busy roads. On its W side is the *Palazzo Comunale,* begun in 1460, with a picturesque open courtyard containing a fountain and Etruscan fragments. On the first floor (entered from No. 1 Via Ascenzi; shown on request) are rooms with 15–17C frescoes and a Baroque chapel. On the N side of the piazza stands the *Palazzo del Podestà* of 1247, with a slender tower of 1487. To the E is the Romanesque church of *Sant'Angelo,* much altered in the 18C.

Embedded in the façade is a Roman sarcophagus said to contain the body of Galiana, a girl whose beauty caused a war between Viterbo and Rome in the Middle Ages, and whose purity was such that, when she drank, the wine was said to be seen passing down her throat.

Off Via San Lorenzo, which runs S from Piazza del Plebiscito, stands (right) the rambling *Palazzo Chigi,* a fine Renaissance building of the 15C, and, to the S, in an attractive old market square, the *Gesù* dating from the 11C (formerly the church of San Silvestro; being extensively restored). In this church, in March 1271, Prince Henry of Cornwall, nephew of Henry III of England and son of Richard Plantagenet, King of the Romans, was murdered at the altar by Simon and Guy de Montfort in revenge for the death of their father Simon at the battle of Evesham in 1265 (see Dante 'Inferno' Canto xii, 118–20). At the end of the street is the shaded Piazza della Morte, with a fountain and three bays of a 12C colonnade. To the W (right) is the old *Ponte del Duomo*, with visible remains of its Etruscan origins. Beyond the bridge, hospital administration offices occupy the restored 15C *Palazzo Farnese*, the supposed birthplace of Paul III (Alessandro Farnese). The secluded *PIAZZA SAN LORENZO is a charming survival of the Middle Ages, on the site of the ancient acropolis. On the S side is the *Casa di Valentino della Pagnotta* (late 13C; reconstructed after war damage). On the N side rises the ***Palazzo Papale** (c 1266), used as the episcopal palace since the 15C, with an elegant Gothic loggia.

The large and sombre hall (usually open; otherwise ring for the key) at the top of the steps, witnessed the elections of Popes Gregory X (1271), John XXI (1276), and Martin IV (1281). Intrigues protracted the first of these elections for two years, and Raniero Gatti, captain of the people of Viterbo, forced a decision—on the advice of St Bonaventura—by shutting the electors in the palace, then removing the roof of the hall, and finally reducing the food supply. The holes made in the floor for the cardinals' tent-pegs are still visible. It was Gregory X who made the rules under which conclaves are held to this day.—John XXI died of injuries when the ceiling of the new wing collapsed on his head in 1277.—In two rooms beyond the hall, the *Museo Diocesano* has recently been arranged. It contains 16C paintings, and various sculptures, etc.

On the W side of the square is the Romanesque **Cathedral** of *San Lorenzo*, built in 1192, with a façade erected after 1560. The fine campanile dates from late in the 14C. The nave arcades have good capitals. On the interior W wall is a tomb figure of John XXI; the panel showing Christ blessing, in the left aisle, is by Gerolamo da Cremona. To the left of the high altar a panel representing the Madonna della Carbonara is a good 12C work. The floor retains some 12C mosaic. The font in the right aisle has a basin by Francesco da Ancona (1470). From the sacristy (if closed, apply at the Curia Vescovile in Palazzo Papale) is the entrance to the Chapter House library with the 'Pantheon' of Gottofredo Tignosi, which has 14C miniatures of great interest.

In a small square off Via Cardinale La Fontaine (which runs parallel to Via San Pellegrino, see below) stands the church of **Santa Maria Nuova**, one of the finest in the city. It dates from the 12C, and was restored after war damage. The central portal is surmounted by a head of Jupiter, and on the left angle of the façade is a tiny outdoor pulpit from which St Thomas Aquinas preached. The most notable features of the basilican interior are the excellent capitals and a fine *Triptych of Christ with saints, a panel of the 13C. The minute cloister probably dates from the Lombard period.

The medieval *District traversed by Via San Pellegrino, to the E of Piazza della Morte, provides an almost unspoiled picture of 13C Italy. In PIAZZA SAN PELLEGRINO are the church of *San Pellegrino* and *Palazzo degli Alessandri*, a severe 13C building. Via San Pietro continues SE to Porta San Pietro, outside which Via delle Fortezze skirts the fine city walls. Inside the walls (see the Plan) is the 12C church of *Sant'Andrea* (restored) with interesting frescoes. The *Porta Romana*, a busy entrance to the city, was rebuilt in 1653. Just beyond it rises the massive campanile, in part 9C Romanesque, of the church of **San Sisto** (restored). Its fine basilican interior has a splendid raised choir with massive pillars. It contains a high altar composed of 4–5C architectural fragments, to the right of which is a painting by Neri di Bicci (removed for restoration). The last column in the N aisle is interesting.

Outside Porta Romana Via Romana leads shortly to the prison (there are plans to transfer it to a new building under construction), in the grounds of which (adm. at present only with special permission) stand the remains of the church of *Santa Maria in Gradi*, destroyed in the war, with the exception of its façade, but still retaining its splendid 13C cloister, built in Gothic style by Roman marble workers. A second Renaissance cloister has at its centre a fountain of 1480.

Inside the walls Via Garibaldi runs to Piazza della Fontana Grande where the fountain, the finest and oldest in the city, was begun in 1206 by Bertoldo and Pietro di Giovanni, finished in 1279, and restored by Benedetto da Perugia in 1424. To the right of Via Cavour (which leads directly to the centre) is the narrow Via Saffi, in which stands the *Casa Poscia*, a picturesque 14C house. Via della Pace and its continuation lead NE to the *Porta della Verità*. Just outside this gate is **Santa Maria della Verità**, a 12C church altered and decorated at later dates. On the W wall is a damaged detached fresco of the Annunciation (copy of a fresco by Melozzo da Forlì in the Pantheon in Rome) and Saints, attributed to Lorenzo da Viterbo. The Cappella Mazzatosta is decorated with *Frescoes by *Lorenzo da Viterbo* (1469; restored). The convent on the N side now houses the **Museo Civico** (8.30–14.30; October–April 9–16; fest. 9–13). Rooms leading off the NE corner of the splendid *Cloister* (of which three walks date from the 13C and the fourth from the 14C) contain Etruscan antiquities.

ROOM I. Cases of finds from Bisenzio (end of 7C BC), pottery, small bronzes, etc.; vases, including Bucchero ware; terracotta votive statues from Bomarzo; finds from Norcia and Ferento.—ROOM II. Terracotta tombs; case of bronze ware and gold jewellery.—FIRST FLOOR. The first rooms contain a marble sphinx by *Pasquale Romano* (signed and dated 1268) and a lion, both from Santa Maria in Gradi; St Bernard, by *Sano di Pietro*; an unglazed terracotta bust of Giovanni Battista Almadiani by *Andrea Della Robbia* (and a glazed lunette by his school); also a fine bronze ewer in the shape of a lion, an early 13C Sassanian work. In the main room the paintings include: *Antoniazzo Romano*, Madonna and Child, part of a larger work; a 13C Madonna and Child of the Byzantine school; and works by *Giovanni Francesco Romanelli*. There is also a Pinacoteca of works by local 15–16C artists. The most important pieces, however, have been in restoration in Rome for many years: the superb *Pietà by *Sebastiano del Piombo*, on the back of which are studies from his hand, and a Flagellation attributed to him; and the Incredulity of St Thomas, an early work of *Salvator Rosa*.

Viale Raniero Capocci follows the best preserved sector of the medieval *Walls*, here battlemented and strengthened by towers. Via Mazzini, on the right inside Porta della Verità, leads N to *San Giovanni in Zoccoli*, a much restored 11C church with a rose window and handsome interior with an unusual variety of capitals. It contains a primitive episcopal throne and a polyptych by Balletta (1441). The confined Via della Marrocca and Via dell'Orologio Vecchio descend to Piazza delle Erbe (fountain of 1621) at the S end of the long CORSO D'ITALIA, venue of the evening *passeggiata*.

From the N end of the Corso the Via di Santa Rosa leads to the right (E) to the church of *Santa Rosa* (1850), in which is preserved the body of St Rosa (died 1252), who appeased the strife of the city and inspired it to resist Frederick II. The festival of her translation (3 September) is celebrated by a grand procession (traditional since 1663), when a great 'macchina' is carried through the streets by some 80 men. Its design is changed every five years (earlier designs displayed in the Museo Civico).

At the N end of the town stands *San Francesco*, a Gothic church of 1237, restored after war damage. A 15C pulpit built into the façade records the preaching in 1426 of St Bernardine of Siena. Inside are the tombs of Adrian V (died 1276), attributed to Arnolfo di Cambio, and of Clement IV (died 1268) by Pietro di Oderisio.

ENVIRONS. The church of Santa Maria della Quercia and the Villa Lante at Bagnaia are both easily reached by bus (No. 6) which departs from Piazza Caduti every 20 minutes.—Crossing the railway from the Porta Fiorentina, the straight Viale Trieste runs to (3km) *La Quercia*, where the church of *Santa Maria della Quercia* (closed 12–16), built in 1470–1525, is one of the finest buildings of the Renaissance. The simple façade is by *Carlo di Mariotto* and *Domenico di Jacopo da Firenzuola* (1509) and the graceful main portal by *Giovanni di Bernardino da Viterbo*. The terracotta lunettes above the three doors are by *Andrea della Robbia*. The massive campanile is the work of *Ambrogio da Milano*.

*INTERIOR. The ceiling is by Giovanni di Pietro to a design of Antonio da Sangallo (1518–25). The splendid *Tabernacle, by *Andrea Bregno* (1490), behind the high altar, encloses a tile with a miraculous image of the Madonna. In the apse are fine inlaid stalls (1514) and an altarpiece by *Fra Bartolomeo*, *Mariotto Albertinelli*, and *Fra Paolino da Pistoia*. In the S aisle is a Madonna and Child with St Anthony Abbot, by *Monaldo da Viterbo* (1519). A door in the N aisle leads to a small museum with a collection of ex votos (15–18C). From the right of the high altar a door leads to a cloister in two orders: the lower by *Daniele da Viterbo* (1487) was inspired by that of Santa Maria in Gradi, the upper part was added in the 16C. The other conventual buildings, including a second (17C) cloister, and the refectory, constructed by Giovanni Battista di Giuliano da Cortona (1519–39) to a design of Antonio da Sangallo the Younger, are now closed.

Bagni di Viterbo, 4km W of the town, has spa baths. Nearby is the *Bullicame*, a hot sulphur pool mentioned by Dante ('Inferno', XIV, 79). About 5km farther SW (8km from Porta Faul in Viterbo) is the 15C ruin of *Castel d'Asso*, which preserves the name of *Castellum Axia*, an Etruscan town. Below the castle are some scanty remains of the town and an extensive necropolis, with the two-storeyed Orioli tomb, and the Tomba Grande, which contained 40 sarcophagi.

FROM VITERBO TO CIVITA CASTELLANA, by-roads, 49km. Beyond La Quercia (see above) N204 continues to (5km) **Bagnaia** where the Piazza Castello is overlooked by a fine round crenellated tower and has a fountain designed by Vignola. From the piazza several roads mount to **Villa Lante**, famous for its formal *Gardens (guided tours every half hour every day, 9–dusk), perhaps the most beautiful and best preserved in Italy. They were created by Cardinal Giovanni Francesco Gambara after 1566 who almost certainly employed Vignola to lay them out around his little summer residence (at present closed for restoration; with frescoes by Antonio Tempesta, Raffaellino da Reggio, and Giovanni Battista Lombardelli). Work on the gardens was continued by Cardinal Alessandro Montalto who also constructed the second little pavilion (adm. sometimes granted on request in the mornings). The delightful gardens, greatly admired by Montaigne and John Evelyn, planted with plane trees and box hedges are designed around numerous fountains, including one on the water parterre with four moors holding up the Montalto arms. The villa was the property of the Lante family from 1656 until 1973 when it was bought by the Italian State.—17km *Soriano nel Cimino* (510m), a small resort, overlooked by a 13C castle of the Orsini (the prison here is to be removed). The imposing Palazzo Chigi (now used for exhibitions), by Vignola (1562), has a fantastic fountain.

The ascent of the extinct volcano *Monte Cimino* (1053m) may be made by road (8km) from Soriano. Some 45m below the summit is the curious *Sasso Menicante*, a trachyte block 8·5m long which, ejected by the volcano, has been caught by a projecting crag and become a rocking stone.

At the interesting town (27km) of *Vignanello* the moated Castello Ruspoli is well preserved; *Vallerano*, nearby, has a fine church of 1609.—Beyond (37km) *Fabrica di Roma* the road descends past Falerii Novi to (49km) *Civita Castellana*, both described in Rte 59.

Bomarzo 19km NE of Viterbo, off the N204 (see above) shows remains of its Etruscan origins. It is dominated by Palazzo Orsini (1523–83), now the town hall, with frescoes in the Salone by Anton Angelo Bonifazi, pupil of Pietro da Cortona. It is famed for its *PARCO DEI MOSTRI (adm. daily, 9–dusk) in the valley, created by Vicino Orsini in the mid-16C. This was a wood populated by numerous bizarre figures and exotic animals, some of them carved from the rocky outcrops. The gigantic fantastic creatures, lop-sided buildings, etc. were once one of the strangest sights in Italy, before alterations robbed the park of its original character. Near the entrance is an exquisite little formal temple attributed to Vignola.—*San Martino al Cimino*, 6km S of Viterbo, has a splendid 13C Cistercian abbey church.

FROM VITERBO TO ORVIETO, 48km (bus to Bagnoregio). At 7km a by-road (signposted) leads right to *Acquarossa* where excavations still in progress have revealed remains of an Etruscan city including interesting houses of 7–6C BC.—8km By road right (signposted) for the ruins of **Ferentium** (*Ferento*; 2km; adm. 8–14, March–8–20 September). Originally Etruscan, this was a flourishing town in Roman times and the birthplace of the Emperor Otho (AD 32), but it was destroyed by Viterbo in 1172 for heretically representing Christ on the Cross with open eyes. The most interesting ruins are those of a theatre (now restored and used in summer), and recent excavations have revealed remains of the baths and other buildings. The church of San Bonifacio lower down the hillside, dates from the 9–10C.—27km *Bagnoregio*, once Balneum Regis, was the birthplace of St Bonaventura (1221–74), the 'doctor seraphicus'. The picturesque medieval *Civita*, 2km E on a tufa rock is being undermined by erosion and is now almost deserted. Here the old cathedral of Bagnoregio (the Mannerist interior spoilt by successive restorations) has an interesting treasury and a fine Crucifix of the school of Donatello.—48km *Orvieto*, see Rte 58.

From Viterbo via Tuscania to Tarquinia, see Rte 63.

The VIA CIMINA provides an alternative continuation towards Rome, hilly but most attractive and 5·5km shorter, across the MONTI CIMINI, rejoining N2 at Gabelletta (see below). The road climbs continuously for 10km to the edge of the crater of *Monte Venere* whose cone (838m) rises above the *Lago di Vico*. This, the ancient *Lacus Ciminus*, is a crater-lake 17·5km round with a surface at 507m; it is now a protected area. The road follows the rim, passing above (15km) **Caprarola** (3·5km; left). The town (510m; 4600 inhab.) is dominated by the *Villa Farnese* (adm. daily 9–dusk; the garden, recently reopened to the public, is closed on fest.). It is one of the most magnificent palaces in Italy, surrounded by superb gardens in a splendid position. They were designed by Vignola (1559–75) for Cardinal Alessandro Farnese. The Mannerist palace was built on the foundations of a pentagonal fortress begun c 1515 by Antonio da Sangallo the Younger, around a beautiful circular courtyard. A magnificent staircase mounts to the piano nobile with apartments richly decorated with stuccoes and frescoes by the Zuccari and Tempesta. The figure of St James the Greater by Federico Zuccari, in the chapel, is supposed to be a portrait of Vignola. The beautiful *Gardens, with terraces and fountains are surrounded by woods, and contain the Casinò by Giacomo del Duca. To the SW of the palace stands the early 17C church of *Santa Teresa*, by Girolamo Rainaldi.—21km **Ronciglione** (441m; 6000 inhab.), once perhaps an Etruscan settlement, became a duchy of the Farnese family. A picturesque medieval district survives near the castle remains. In the Piazza del Duomo stands a 16C fountain decorated with unicorns' heads. The churches of *Sant'Andrea* and *Santa Maria della Provvidenza* have good campanili, respectively 15C (by Galasto da Como) and 13–14C. By-roads (and a pretty branch railway) descend to Capranica and to Sutri (see below), while the Via Cimina runs SE to join N311 from Civita Castellana (see Rte 59) at 33km and N2 (see below).

From Viterbo the main road runs S over open uplands.—156km **Vetralla** (300m; 9300 inhab.) contains a Vignolesque Palazzo Comunale, and an 18C cathedral. On the main road is the Romanesque church of *San Francesco*, with good capitals, a restored Cosmatesque pavement, an interesting crypt, the sepulchral monument of Briobris by Paolo Romano (early 15C), and restored 15C frescoes. The church of *Santa Maria Furcassi*, 3km NE, preserves the name of the ancient *Forum Cassii*.

N1 bis (parallel to a new 'superstrada' under construction between Orte and Tarquinia) crosses the hills westwards to (30km) *Tarquinia*; a minor road runs N to (21km) *Tuscania* (see Rte 63). A good by-road diverges left from N1 bis (signposted) through fertile farming country with numerous eucalyptus trees to (6km) the unenclosed site of the Etruscan necropolis of **Norchia** (a rough track continues for 500m from the end of the made-up road to the edge of the ravine). In this romantic isolated spot there is a view across the valley of two ruined medieval buildings (a castle wall and the apse of San Pietro). Steep paths lead down the side of the cliff face; the path on the left soon emerges beside *Rock-cut tombs of the 4–2C BC, some with the appearance of temples with figured pediments (a torch is necessary to see the interiors).

To the S of Vetralla (reached via Cura, see below; bus to Blera) lie areas where, since 1956, the Swedish Institute in Rome has been investigating Etruscan remains in an attempt to discover the origins of the Etruscan people.—12km *Blera* is the *Phleva* of the Etruscans. The remains of the ancient town include a large necropolis, two bridges, and a sarcophagus (in the church of Santa Maria). 4km NW is the Grotta Porcina, a conical tomb 28m in diameter dating from the early 6C BC.—About 11km S, reached by a minor road, is *Civitella Cesi*, c 3km W of which is the ancient citadel of *San Giovenale*, crowned by the ruins of a medieval castle. Here the Swedes have excavated the oldest Etruscan houses known, and abutments of bridges dating from the 6C BC.—18km *Barbarano Romano*, a picturesque hill-village, is built near the site of an Etruscan township; here in 1963 was unearthed an obelisk, a form of monument not previously associated with the Etruscans. In the 18C town hall is a small archaeological museum. In the locality known as San Giuliano, 2km NE, recent excavations have brought to light an interesting necropolis (6–5C BC).

The Via Cassia passes the Blera turning (see above) at (159km) *Cura*, just short of Vetralla Station.—At (164km) *Quercie d'Orlando* the Via Claudia (N493) starts its winding course W of Lake Bracciano to Rome (77km; see 'Blue Guide Rome').—On the way in to (169km) **Capranica** (373m; 3700 inhab.) the road passes the church of the *Madonna del Piano*, with frescoes attributed to Francesco Cozza or Antonio Carracci. The church of *San Francesco* contains a tomb of two Counts Anguillara. The *Ospedale* has a fine Romanesque portal.—174km **Sutri** (291m) is the ancient *Sutrium*, called the 'Gate of Etruria', which was captured by Camillus in 389 BC. Its cession by the Lombard king Liutprand to Pope Gregory II in 730 marks the beginning of papal temporal power. The rival Popes Gregory VI and Sylvester III were deposed for simony by a synod held here in 1046. Sutri claims to be the birthplace of Pontius Pilate. The *Duomo*, though greatly altered, retains its campanile of 1207. The 18C interior contains remains of Cosmatesque pavement. Above the 2nd altar (left) is an early 13C panel in the Byzantine style of Christ blessing (removed for restoration). The crypt dates from the Lombard period. The *Municipio* contains a collection of Etruscan antiquities. Besides considerable remains of the walls, and of a so-called Palace of Charlemagne, there are several Etruscan tombs, one of which, converted into the church of the *Madonna del Parto*, surrounded by a charming garden, retains fragmentary frescoes. On the main road (signposted) is an *Amphitheatre carved out of the tufa rock (open 8.30–13.30 except Monday; otherwise ask for the key at the Municipio).—*Bassano Romano*, where the Palazzo Odescalchi has rooms frescoed by Domenichino and Francesco Albani (adm. only by special permission), is 5km SW.

At (183km) *Gabelletta*, by the tiny *Lago Monterosi*, the Via Cimina (see above) comes in on the left. The Via Cassia by-passes *Monterosi* (276m; right), then at (189km) *Sette Vene* leaves on the right a road for Lake Bracciano. It now becomes a fast 'superstrada' all the way to (216km) the 'Grande Raccordo Annulare' (ring road) around Rome; alternatively, at 202km the old Cassia (described in 'Blue Guide Rome') can be followed due S undulating across the Monti Sabatini past (207km) *Madonna di Bracciano*, just W of the Etruscan site of *Veio* into (224km) **Rome** (see 'Blue Guide Rome').

58 Arezzo to Orvieto and Rome

AUTOSTRADA DEL SOLE (A1), 218km.—24km *Monte San Savino.*— 62km **Chiusi**.—102km **Orvieto**.—143km *Orte*.—218km **Rome**.
N327 and N326 follow roughly the same course to Chiusi (66km), serving the villages on the W side of the Val di Chiana. For an alternative route (N71), see Rte 56.

RAILWAY from Arezzo to *Rome*, 228km, part of the new main line between Florence and Rome recently completed. Four 'Intercity' express trains a day in 1½hrs; otherwise slower trains, most of them stopping at *Chiusi* and *Orvieto* in 2–2½hrs.

Leaving Arezzo by the Porta San Lorentino this route joins the Autostrada in just under 11km and turns S in the foothills W of the Val di Chiana.—24km **Monte San Savino** (330m), 3km to the W, was the birthplace of the sculptor Andrea Contucci, called Sansovino (1460–1529), who is the probable architect of the attractive *Loggia del Mercato*. The *Palazzo Comunale* was designed by Antonio Sangallo the Elder. The church of *Santa Chiara* contains sculptural works by Sansovino and others; *Sant'Agostino*, rebuilt in the 16C, perhaps by Sansovino, contains an altarpiece by Vasari and 14–15C frescoes. The *Rocca del Cassero* was built in 1383 and was restored in 1989.

A hilly minor road runs S to (8km) *Lucignano*, a little fortress town, where the Museo Civico has paintings by Luca di Tommè, Ugolino di Nerio, and Luca Signorelli, and a reliquary by Ugolino di Vieri (1350; most of which has been recovered since its theft). In the Collegiata is a 14C wooden statue of the Madonna by Mariano di Angelo Romanelli.—16km *Sinalunga* (see Rte 56).

This route passes beneath the Siena-Perugia 'superstrada' just short of (38km) the exit named after the VALDICHIANA, the once unhealthy plain lying between the upper basins of the Arno and Tiber. In prehistoric times this valley was the bed of the Arno, which flowed not into the Tyrrhenian Sea but into the Tiber. The marshes left behind when it took its new direction were first drained by the efforts of Cosimo de'Medici; and draining and irrigation operations have gone on almost continuously since. The waters of the valley are carried off N to the Arno by the *Canale Maestro della Chiana* (begun in 1551), and S to the Tiber by the much smaller *Chianetta*.

At *Foiano della Chiana*, 5km NE, the churches have attractive Della Robbian groups. In the Collegiata, with a Madonna della Cintola by Andrea della Robbia, the altarpiece attributed to Luca Signorelli (1523) was stolen in 1978.

The autostrada commands views (left) across the Canale Maestro and of the Lago di Montepulciano and Lago di Chiusi, now only marshy pools.—62km The exit for Chiusi joins N146 coming from Chianciano Terme (Rte 57), 4km W of the town. **Chiusi**, a little town of 8700 inhabitants, stands on a hill to the left of the road.

Chiusi is supposed to have been founded by the Umbrian Cambertes; hence its Etruscan name of *Camars*. One of the 12 cities of the Etruscan Confederation it reached its greatest splendour about the 7C or 6C BC. Lars Porsena, the *Lucumo* or king, attacked Rome in 508 BC. (see Macaulay's 'Horatius'), but the town became subject to Rome after 295 BC and took the Roman name of *Clusium*. The neighbourhood of the unhealthy marshes of the Valdichiana brought about the decline of Chiusi, but the drainage works begun by Cosimo de'Medici restored some degree of prosperity. Under the streets runs a labyrinth of Etruscan galleries, and a vast Etruscan necropolis surrounds the town.

The Romanesque *Duomo* was heavily restored in 1887–94. The fine columns and capitals in the interior come from various local Roman edifices. The paintings, imitating antique mosaics are by Arturo Viligiardi (1887). Off the left aisle is an Adoration of the Child by Bernardino Fungai. A tall fortified tower was transformed into the Campanile in 1585. It covers a huge cistern of 1C BC (for adm. apply at the Museum).

Under the portico to the right of the façade is the **Museo della Cattedrale**, reopened in 1984 and well arranged and labelled (open 9.30–12.45; June–Oct and fest. also 15–18 or 16.30–19.30). The first room contains finds from the local catacombs and Roman fragments from the Duomo, as well as Lombard and late Medieval material. In the garden excavations are in progress of an Etruscan building. At the top of the stairs: *Girolamo da Benvenuto*, Madonna and Child with Saints (very ruined; recently restored); church silver and vestments; 15C ivories by the *Bottega degli Embriachi*. Stairs continue up to a long passage above the portico with a fine display of antiphonals dating from the second half of the 15C, illuminated by *Liberale da Verona*, *Sano di Pietro*, *Lorenzo Rosselli di Bindo*, and others.

Tickets can be purchased here for admission to the *Catacombs of San Mustiola*, in use from the 3C to the 5C beneath a farm house. The *Catacombs of Santa Caterina*, near the Station, can also usually be seen by appointment.

The church of *San Francesco* dates from the 14C, and the ruined *Fortezza* perhaps from the 12C. The ***Museo Nazionale Etrusco** (adm. 9–14; fest. 9–13; closed Monday) was founded in 1870 and opened in this fitting neo-classical building in 1901. It is undergoing rearrangement and a lower floor is to be opened eventually.

In the first room (A) are displayed prehistoric and Villanovian material, and canopic vases of the 7C–6C BC.—In a small room, Archaic sculptures.—Room B contains Bucchero ware and black-figure Attic vases. In the outer corridors, Etruscan vases and sarcophaghi and cinerary urns (4C–2C BC) in alabaster and terracotta, including the sarcophagus depicting the deceased Lars Sentinates.

From Via della Violella can be seen part of the Etruscan walls of the city, recently discovered.

The ETRUSCAN *TOMBS in the neighbourhood have all been closed for conservation reasons, except for the Tomba della Pellegrina, which is usually open (ask at the Museum). There are long-term plans to reopen the others. They are approached by pretty country lanes, most of which can be negotiated by car. Just outside the town, on the road to Chianciano Terme, Via delle Tombe Etrusche diverges right for (3km) the *Tomba della Pellegrina*, with several urns and sarcophagi (for adm. ask at the Museum). The *Tomba della Scimmia* ('of the Ape'), has important wall-paintings, and the *Tomba del Leone* has recently been restored. The *Tomba del Granduca*, has eight cinerary urns remaining on their stone benches.—Another itinerary leaves the city beyond the Cimitero Nuovo, and includes the *Tomba Casuccini* (or del Colle), with a fine doorway (now visible through a glass door) and wall-paintings of sports and games, and the *Tomba delle Tassinaie*. —The *Poggio Gaiella*, a tufa hill 4km N, has three storeys of passages and galleries; according to tradition, it is the mausoleum of Lars Porsena.

BUSES run from Chiusi station to the town in 5 minutes, going on to *Chianciano Terme* (½hr) and *Montepulciano* (1hr); to *Perugia* in 1¾hrs; to *Siena* in 3hrs; and to *Radicofani* in 1hr, going on to Santa Fiora.—The Radicofani bus passes (12km) *Sarteano*, where there are Madonnas by Giacomo di Mino in the churches of San Francesco and San Martino. A small Antinquarium has been opened in Piazza Vittorio Emanuele. *Cetona*, 6km S of Sarteano, is a small medieval borgo which, in the last few decades, has become a fashionable place to have a country house. It has an old castle and prehistoric caves.

Beyond Chiusi the autostrada and the railway follow the same course, crossing into the muddy Paglia valley.—The exit for *Orvieto* is at 102km beyond the crossing of N71 (Rte 56), which is soon joined at *Orvieto Scalo* (railway station). The town is approached by a long winding ascent (5·5km).

ORVIETO (23,600 inhab.) built on a precipitous tufa crag (315m) dominating the valley is famous for its splendid position (it is especially well seen from the Bolsena road to the SW). Landslips here in recent years have caused much alarm and funds have been designated by the State and work has been in progress since 1980 to consolidate the rock on which the town is built. It is a city of great antiquity, preserving its medieval aspect and renowned for the beauty of its cathedral, which, at the highest point of the town, stands out on the skyline. New building has taken place around the station (*Orvieto Scalo*) leaving the old town and the cultivated fields beneath its rock remarkably unchanged. It is the centre of a famed wine-growing area and has notable Etruscan remains. Local crafts include lace and pottery.

Bus from the Railway Station to the upper town every 20 minutes. The **Funicular**, from the station, opened in 1888 and operated by water, has been out of operation since 1970. Work is under way to reactivate it using electricity.

Hotels in the old town (near Corso Cavour and the Duomo) and (in a less pleasant position) in Orvieto Scalo, near the station.

Post Office, off Corso Cavour.—**A.P.T. Tourist Information Office** Piazza Duomo.—**Buses** from Piazza San Domenico and Via Loggia dei Mercanti to *Bolsena*; to *Perugia*; to *Acquapendente*; to *Viterbo*, via *Bagnoregio* or via *Montefiascone*; to *Rome*; to *Pitigliano*; to *Todi*, etc.

History. The rock of Orvieto was already occupied in the Iron Age, and an important Etruscan city grew up here in the 7C BC, usually identified as *Volsinii Veteres*, one of the chief cities of the Etruscan Confederation. The town was destroyed in 265 BC by the Romans, and the inhabitants resettled at a spot on the NE side of Lake Bolsena which developed into the town of Bolsena (Volsinii Novi). In the Middle Ages the Commune of *Urbs Vetus* (from which the modern name is derived) was important, and it became especially powerful in the 13C. Gregory X here received Edward I of England on his return from the Crusades. The rivalries between the Guelf Monaldeschi and the Ghibelline Filippeschi dominated events in the town during the 14C, and later Alexander VI and Clement VII were to take refuge here from revolts in Rome.—Angelo da Orvieto (14C), Ascanio Vittozzi (died 1615), and Ippolito Scalzo (c 1532–1617), the architects, were born here. There are now several military barracks in the town.

The main road reaches the town at Piazzale Cahen. Here also is the upper terminus of the funicular (being renovated). Conspicuous on the left is the *Fortezza* (1364), the grounds of which are now a public garden with fine views of the valley.

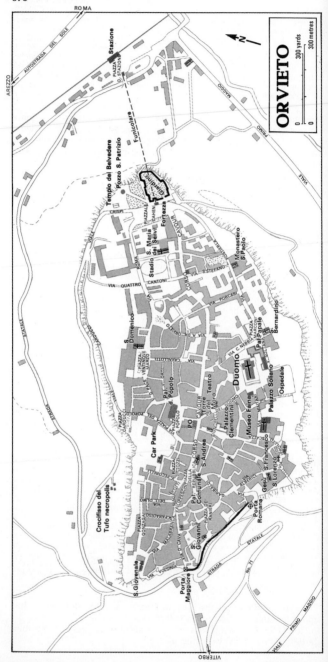

A short distance to the N of the Fortezza is the interesting *Pozzo di San Patrizio* (open daily 8 or 9–18 or 19), built by Antonio da Sangallo (1527–37) to provide an emergency water supply in the event of a siege by order of Clement VII, who fled to Orvieto after the sack of Rome. The well, surmounted by a low tower, is 63m deep, and is encircled by two spiral staircases each of 248 wide steps and lit by 72 windows. The descent is difficult. It is called 'St Patrick's Well' because it is supposed to be similar to St Patrick's cavern in Ireland. A few metres to the W are the ruins of an Etruscan temple, known as the *Tempio del Belvedere*.

From the piazza, Corso Cavour (open to access traffic only) runs through the town from E to W. At the *Torre del Moro* (12C), Via del Duomo on the left leads to the quiet *PIAZZA DEL DUOMO, with a quaint row of small houses lining its N side. At the entrance to the square is a clock tower called *Torre del Maurizio*, surmounted by a bronze figure known as 'Maurizio' (1351) which strikes the hours.

The **Duomo** is one of the most striking buildings of its period in the country. It dominates the view of the city for miles around. Its construction was ordered by Urban IV to commemorate the miracle of Bolsena (1263; see Rte 57). The first stone was laid on 13 November 1290, when it was blessed by Nicholas IV. The church was begun to a Romanesque plan, but continued in the newly arrived Gothic style by *Lorenzo Maitani*, who took over in 1310. He was followed by his son *Vitale; Andrea Pisano* (1331–45); *Nino Pisano* (1349); *Andrea di Cecco da Siena* (1356–59); and *Andrea Orcagna* (1359). *Michele Sanmicheli* became master in 1509–25, and the façade was not completed until the early years of the 17C. The church stands on a plinth of seven steps, alternately red and white. The two beautiful flanks built in horizontal bands of white travertine and grey basalt are decorated with the exteriors of the tall semi-circular side chapels and handsome Gothic windows. On the N side are the Porta di Canonica, with a fresco by *Andrea di Giovanni*, and the Porta del Corporale (three statues by *Andrea Pisano* have been removed from the lunette for restoration). On the S side is the Porta di Postierla, probably the oldest doorway.

The huge *FAÇADE, designed and begun by *Lorenzo Maitani*, which covers the W end, is one of the finest Italian Gothic works and has been compared in design to a painted triptych in an elaborate frame. In fact it is chiefly remarkable for its sculptural details rather than for its harsh polychrome mosaics, mostly remade in the 17–19C. Four elegant spires with high crocketed turrets divide the façade vertically: on the pilasters at their bases are superb marble *Bas-reliefs (c 1320–30) ascribed to *Maitani*, his son *Vitale*, and *Nicolò* and *Meo Nuti*. They depict the story of the Creation to the time of Tubal Cain, the stories of Abraham and David, scenes from the Life of Christ, the Last Judgement, Hell, and Paradise. Above them are bronze symbols of the Evangelists also by *Maitani*. The Madonna by *Andrea Pisano* and bronze angels by *Maitani* formerly in the lunette above the main door have been removed and may be replaced here by copies: they will be exhibited in a museum in the city after their restoration. The bronze doors are by *Emilio Greco* (1964–70). The great rose window is *Orcagna*'s work.

In the uncluttered *INTERIOR (closed 13–14.30) the fine architectural lines can be appreciated to the full. The walls are lined with horizontal bands of white and grey. The columns of the nave, with fine capitals, carry round arches, over which a graceful triforium, with a clerestory above it, runs all round the church, except in the transepts. The semi-circular side chapels are particularly graceful (and many of them have interesting fresco fragments of the 14–15C). The lower panels of the stained glass windows are made of alabaster.—In the NAVE are a stoup by *Antonio Federighi* (1485) and a font of 1390–1407; near the latter is a fresco of the *Madonna by *Gentile da Fabriano* (1425; restored in 1987). In the N aisle are three attractive 16C stoups. In the N transept (against the nave pillar) is a Pietà by *Ippolito Scalza* (1579) and a sculptured altarpiece by *Simone Mosca* and *Raffaelo da Montelupo*. Here is the CAPPELLA DEL CORPORALE. On the walls are restored frescoes by *Ugolino di Prete Ilario* (1357–64) and, on the right, a huge panel of the *Madonna dei Raccomandati by *Lippo Memmi* (1320).

Over the altar incorporated in a large tabernacle, designed by *Nicolò da Siena* (1358) and continued by *Orcagna*, is the *Reliquary of the Corporal, a superb work in silver-gilt with translucent enamels, by the Sienese *Ugolino di Vieri* (1337). This contains the corporal (linen cloth) of the miracle of Bolsena, and is revealed only on religious festivals. The corporal is taken in procession on Corpus Domini, but since 1979 it has been exposed in a substitute reliquary for this occasion.

The CHOIR is decorated with frescoes by *Ugolino* and his assistants; the carved and inlaid stalls are the work of *Giovanni Ammannati* and other Sienese artists (1331–41; being restored). The restored stained glass of the great E window is by *Giovanni di Bonino* (1325–34).— The SOUTH TRANSEPT contains the Altare dei Magi (begun 1514), a good early work of *Sanmicheli*, with bas-reliefs by *Raffaello* and *Francesco da Montelupo*. At the end is the ***Cappella della Madonna di San Brizio**, or *Cappella Nuova*, containing the *Frescoes by *Fra Angelico* and *Signorelli* which are the chief treasures of Orvieto. They are suffering from humidity and restoration work is under way.

In 1447 *Fra Angelico*, with the help of *Benozzo Gozzoli*, began the decoration of the chapel: he had completed just two sections of the vault over the altar (the Saviour in Glory and the Prophets) before he was recalled to Rome. At the end of the century *Luca Signorelli* was commissioned to complete the frescoes (1499–1504) and he produced one of the most remarkable fresco cycles of the Italian Renaissance, with beautiful nude figure studies. On the Left Wall (near the entrance) is the Sermon of Antichrist, with Fra Angelico and Signorelli as two solemn bystanders, and the figure of Dante as one of the crowd; on the Entrance Wall, the Day of Judgement; on the Right Wall the Resurrection of the Body, and the Casting out of the Wicked; and on the Altar Wall, Angels drive the sinners into Hell and guide the elect to Paradise; on the adjacent half of the Left Wall, the Blessed entering Heaven. The exquisite decoration on the lower part of the walls is also by *Signorelli* and includes medallion portraits of Homer, Dante, Virgil, Ovid, Horace, Lucan, and Empedocles, and scenes from classical myth and from Dante's 'Divine Comedy'. The Pietà in the recess on the right is also the work of Signorelli. On the Baroque altar is a local 14C painting called the 'Madonna di San Brizio'.—The Crypt, with traces of frescoes and part of the substructure of the Duomo, can be seen outside the East End (reached along the N flank).

Opposite the façade of the cathedral is **Palazzo Faina** (covered for restoration). Part of the archaeological collection of the **Museo Civico** is displayed on the Ground Floor, including a tomb with bas reliefs (4C BC), finds from the Belvedere Temple (5C BC), the so-called

'Venus of Cannicella', an Etruscan copy of an Archaic Greek original, and the colossal stone head of a warrior.—The **Museo Claudio Faina** is provisionally arranged in four rooms on the piano nobile while the top floor is being restored. It includes an extensive collection of Greek vases of all types found in Etruscan tombs.

Via Maitani leads W to the church of *San Francesco*, built in the mid-13C. Here, in the presence of Edward I of England, took place the funeral of Prince Henry of Cornwall, murdered at Viterbo in March 1271; here also Boniface VIII canonised St Louis of France.

To the left farther on, in Via Ippolito Scalza, is the 14C church of *San Lorenzo de Arari*, with a lovely interior, which takes its name from an Etruscan altar beneath the altar-table. Above it is a pretty 12C ciborium. The curious frescoes include four stories from the Life of St Lawrence (1330; restored).

In **Palazzo Soliano** (or dei Papi), immediately S of the cathedral, begun in 1264 by Urban IV, and continued in 1296–1304, is installed the *MUSEO DELL'OPERA (closed for restoration in 1990; entrance at the top of the external stairs). In one huge hall is a miscellany of works of art (mostly from the cathedral). The contents include: *Statues of the Madonna in marble by *Andrea Pisano* and his school, by *Nino Pisano* (1349), and (in wood), by *Giovanni Pisano*. The Madonna and angels by Pisano and Maitani from the central door of the Duomo may be exhibited here after their restoration. Among unfinished works by *Arnolfo di Cambio* are two damaged angels. The wooden statue of Christ blessing is attributed to an assistant of Maitani (1330). The paintings include parts of a fine polyptych by *Simone Martini*; a self-portrait and other works by *Signorelli*, and a Madonna by *Coppo di Marcovaldo* (1268). Outstanding among the metal work is the Reliquary of the Head of San Savino, by *Ugolino di Vieri*; and the collection of vestments is notable. Displayed are two sketches for the façade of the cathedral: as built with three gables (by Maitani), and with only one gable, now thought to be by Arnolfo di Cambio.—The colossal figures of the Apostles (16–18C) which formerly lined the nave of the cathedral, and two *Statues of the Annunciation by *Francesco Mocchi* formerly on either side of the high altar, are stored in a room below not usually open. There are plans to return these to the Duomo, and exhibit here the works of Emilio Greco left to the city in 1980.

At the end of the piazza is ***Palazzo Papale**, in golden tufa, with three large arches, a fine 13C building, recently restored. The huge ground-floor rooms are to house the *Museo Nazionale Archaeologico*, part of which has already been arranged. Local Etruscan material includes finds from the Crocifisso del Tufo and Cannicella necropoli (6C BC); Greek red and black figure vases; painted tombs of Settecamini; and finds from a 4C BC necropolis. Other material is to be transferred here.

Corso Cavour (see above) leads W to the church of *Sant'Andrea* (entered from the portico on the N side, under which flowers are sold), a 12C building with remains of 14C and 15C frescoes, and a fine twelve-sided campanile. Here in 1216 Innocent III proclaimed the Fourth Crusade and in 1281 Martin IV was crowned in the presence of Charles of Anjou. The sacristan (who lives at No. 17 Via Cipriano Manente, through the archway to the S of the church) will admit to the excavations beneath the church. Here a

6C pavement from the primitive basilica overlies Etruscan and Roman remains. Here, also, are pieces of relief sculpture (8–9C ?) from a choir screen, embedded on the reverse side with Cosmatesque mosaic work (other pieces have been fashioned into a pulpit in the upper church). The Corso ends in PIAZZA DELLA REPUBBLICA, the centre of the life of Orvieto. Here is *Palazzo Comunale*, built in 1216, with a façade of c 1580 by Ippolito Scalzo, the local architect, and a neo-classical palace by Virginio Vespignani. Via Loggia dei Mercanti, which leads from here to Piazza de'Ranieri, is one of the most characteristic streets of the old city. From here it is a short way to *San Giovanni*, with views of the valley and sheer rock face on which the town is built (being shored up). Across Via della Cava (see the Plan) old roads lead up to *San Giovenale*, in a beautiful position on the edge of the rock with orchards below. The church (being restored) dates possibly from 1004 and it contains interesting frescoes by local artists (13–16C). Pleasant walks may be taken in this old part of the town.

Palazzo del Popolo, in Piazza del Popolo, a fine building in tufa, was begun in 1157 and later altered. It is being restored as a conference centre. A market is held in the surrounding piazze on Thursdays and Saturdays. To the NE, in a less attractive part of the town, is **San Domenico**, the first church dedicated to St Dominic, built in 1233–64. In its former convent St Thomas Aquinas taught theology. The church, of which only the transept remains, has a pretty exterior. In the interior are the *Tomb of Cardinal de Braye (died 1281), by *Arnolfo di Cambio*, and the Cappella Petrucci (below the main church, entered from a door in the S wall unlocked by the sacristan), an interesting architectural work by *Sanmicheli*. It also has various mementoes to St Thomas Aquinas.

Just off the road to the station (1·5km from Piazzale Cahen) is the Etruscan Necropolis of *'Crocifisso del Tufo'* (adm. daily) of the 4C BC, with small but well-preserved chamber tombs.—The Premonstratensian abbey of *Santi Severo e Martirio*, dating from the 12C, lies SW of the city (2·5km by road or 20 minutes by footpath from the Porta Romana). The most interesting of the ruined buildings are the abbot's house, the former refectory (now the Chiesa del Crocifisso), and the original church with its twelve-sided campanile. About 1km farther on, at *Settecamini*, is another 4C Etruscan burial-ground.

FROM ORVIETO TO TODI, 43km, N448. This route follows close to the autostrada and then at 12km turns left to skirt the *Lago di Corbara* and the Tiber. An alternative longer route (48km) diverges right beyond Orvieto station and the Paglia bridge on N79bis, which climbs, at first steeply, to a height of 367m, and then descends into the Tiber valley. The views are superb; the Tiber is crossed at (43km) the old walled village of *Pontecuti*.—48km *Todi*, see Rte 59.

About 5km beyond Orvieto this route joins the lower valley of the Tiber, the most famous though not the longest of the rivers of Italy (see Rte 52).—131km *Attigliano* (for *Bomarzo*, 5km W, see Rte 57). At *Lugnano in Teverina* (419m), 10km NE, the charming church, dating from the late 12C but altered in the 15C, contains a triptych by L'Alunno.—143km **Orte**, occupying the site of Etrusco-Roman *Horta* on the right bank of the Tiber, has a *Museo d'Arte Sacra* (key at No. 6 Piazza Colonna) occupying the former Romanesque church of San Silvestro (good campanile). The collection includes a Madonna in mosaic (8C, restored) from the old basilica of St Peter's in Rome; a Madonna by Taddeo di Bartolo; a 13C panel of St Francis; four 15C panels depicting the life of Sant'Egidio; and a reliquary Cross by Vannuccio di Viva da Siena (1352).—The autostrada passes over the

Nera near its confluence with the Tiber, crosses the main river twice, and at (153km) *Magliano Sabina*, with good views W towards the Monti Cimini, passes beneath the Via Flaminia (Rte 59).

At 186km (Exit 'Roma Nord') a slip road joins the Via Tiberina on the right bank of the Tiber, near the excavations of Lucus Feroniae (described in 'Blue Guide Rome'), for (218km) **Rome**. The autostrada continues and crosses the river for the last time.—At (204km) *Settebagni* another slip road joins the Via Salaria on the left bank, providing the most direct approach to the centre of (220km) **Rome**, while the autostrada joins the ring road 4km farther on.

59 Perugia to Rome

A. Via Spoleto

ROAD, N75, N3, 193km.—13km Turning for **Assisi** (described in Rte 56).—29·5km *Spello*.—37km *Foligno*. N3.—46km *Trevi*.—65km **Spoleto**.—92km **Terni**.—106km **Narni**.—140km *Civita Castellana*.—193km **Rome**.

A faster route to Rome leaves this road just before Terni and follows the 'superstrada' (N204) which by-passes Narni and joins the Autostrada del Sole at Orte (see Rte 58).

RAILWAY, 195km via Foligno, where a change is necessary. To *Foligno*, 29km in c 40 minutes. From Foligno (on the Ancona line), slow trains via *Trevi, Spoleto, Terni, Narni*, and *Orte* in c 2hrs; or 'Inter-city' trains in 1hr 40 minutes stopping at Spoleto and Terni only. The line between Spoleto and Orte is particularly spectacular.

From Perugia to (13km) the turning for **Assisi**, see Rte 56.—The 'superstrada' (N75) continues to (29·5km) **Spello**, the Roman *Hispellum*, an ancient little fortified town (6800 inhab.), charmingly situated on a hillside (314m), with some interesting Roman remains. The main entrance to the town is through the *Porta Consolare* with three Republican statues on its impressive façade. The steep and winding Via Consolare and Via Cavour (one-way up) climb to the centre of the town, passing (left) the *Cappella Tega* with 15C frescoes, attributed to L'Alunno. In the first piazza is the church of SANTA MARIA MAGGIORE (12–13C) with a fine portal reworked in 1644 using a Romanesque frieze. At the base of the Romanesque campanile are two Roman columns.

INTERIOR (closed 12–15). The two stoups are made from Roman fragments. Off the left side of the nave the Cappella Baglioni (light on left) is entirely decorated with *Frescoes by *Pinturicchio*, the Nativity, Annunciation (with a self-portrait nearby), the Dispute in the Temple, and four Sibyls in the vault above. Signed and dated 1501, they have been beautifully restored. The floor is made of Deruta majolica (1566). The high altar is covered by a fine baldacchino carved by *Rocco da Vicenza* (1515). On the two pilasters flanking the apse are two very late works by *Perugino*. The choir-stalls date from 1512–20. In the left transept, the Chapel of the Sacrament has a lavabo (on the wall to left of altar) with an angel frescoed by *Pinturicchio*, and (behind a door near the lavabo) another little chapel has a fine Madonna and Child also by *Pinturicchio*. In the Chapel of the Crucifix, off the right transept, are two detached frescoes by the school of Pinturicchio. From here there is access to a small MUSEUM (unlocked by the sacristan) with a precious enamelled cross (1398). A Madonna and Child by Pinturicchio stolen from here some years ago has still not been refound.

Farther up is the church of SANT'ANDREA. Inside, on the right wall, is a fresco fragment of the Madonna (14C), and, in the right arm of the crossing, a large altarpiece of the *Madonna and Child with Saints (light on the door to the right) by Pinturicchio and Eusebio da San Giorgio, and a tondo of the Redeemer also by them (restored in 1979). A large *Crucifix attributed to an Umbrian master of the late-13C (a follower of Giotto, perhaps the 'Maestro del Farneto') hangs over the pretty high altar with 14C columns. At the beginning of the nave (left) is a chapel with local 15C frescoes (recently uncovered).

From the piazza, Via Torri di Properzio descends steeply to the Roman *PORTA VENERE, of the Augustan age, the best preserved of the three gateways in the Roman walls. The two handsome pink 12-sided towers may date from the 12C.

A short way beyond Sant'Andrea opens the unattractive Piazza della Repubblica (car parking). A small Museum may by opened in the *Palazzo Comunale* here. Still higher is the Romanesque church of *San Lorenzo*, with an 18C chapel (of the Sacrament), a 17C carved wood pulpit, and a 15C tabernacle. The Via della Torre Belvedere (one-way downhill; another road is indicated for cars) leads up past the Romanesque church of *San Martino* to the top of the hill where a single Roman arch marks the site of the ancient acropolis, and a belvedere, near the remains of a 14C Rocca, provides a fine view (the Roman amphitheatre is well seen beyond the main road next to the modern sports stadium).

The road below the town passes the ruined *Roman Amphitheatre*, the Porta Urbica, the *Chiesa Tonda* (1517–39), an attractive work of the Renaissance, and *San Claudio*, a charming little 12C church.

Beyond Spello the 'superstrada' joins N3 from Nocera Umbra (see Rte 61A) and continues S to by-pass (37km) **Foligno** (234m), an industrial town of 50,000 inhabitants, on the River Topino, and the seat of a bishop. It has numerous interesting palaces and a number of churches with good 18C interiors.

It was the *Fulginia* of the Romans and absorbed the population of *Forum Flaminii*, another Roman town 3·5km E. Long a free town, latterly under the rule of the Trinci family, it passed to the States of the Church in 1439. Here was born St Angela of Foligno (1248–1309), a noble lady who became a Franciscan tertiary. Its school of painting was largely indebted to Nicolò da Foligno, or Nicolò di Liberatore, called L'Alunno (c 1430–1502). Printing was introduced at Foligno in 1470, only six years after the first book printed in Italy had appeared at Subiaco. Serious damage was done to the town by bombing in 1943–44. Raphael's Madonna di Foligno is now in the Vatican.

The *Palazzo Comunale*, in the spacious Piazza della Repubblica, has a neo-classical façade by Antonio Molari, and it retains a 14C tower. In the same square are the Renaissance *Palazzo Orfini* (with traces of external painted decoration) and *Palazzo Trinci* (1395–1407), with a restored brick courtyard and a Gothic stair. The chapel and hall contain paintings by Ottaviano Nelli. The *Pinacoteca* here (closed in 1990; for information ring at the Biblioteca Comunale) is undergoing much needed restoration. The Sala delle Arti Liberali e dei Pianeti and the Sala dei Giganti contain interesting faded mural *Paintings of the 15C. Here also are exhibited paintings by the native artist Pierantonio Mezzastris, detached frescoes by Bartolomeo di Tommaso, and a fresco of the Annunciatory Angel from the disused church of San Domenico attributed to Benozzo Gozzoli.—The much modernised Romanesque *Duomo* (1133–1201) has a magnificent N façade with a beautiful portal, and a huge ornate 18C interior by Luigi Vanvitelli, reminiscent of St Peter's. In the Sacristy two busts of Bartolomeo and Diana Roscioli have recently been identified as works by Gian Lorenzo Bernini. The silver reliquary of San Feliciano was stolen from the church in 1982, but was later recovered. Adjoining Palazzo Trinci is the graceful *Palazzo Deli* or *Nuti* (16C; beautifully restored in 1989), with a fine portal and incorporating a medieval tower.—*Santa Maria Infraportas* is a Romanesque basilica with an interesting exterior and ancient bell tower, with Byzantine and other frescoes. The church of *San Nicolò*, in this part of the town, has two paintings by L'Alunno. The *Nunziatella*, a chapel in the street of the same name (usually closed) contains a fresco by Perugino.

Via Gramsci has a number of fine palaces including *Palazzo Alleori Ubaldi* with a neo-classical façade and contemporary painted decorations inside by Marcello Leopardi. Since 1986 it has been restored as a cultural centre (adm. on request). In Via Cesare Agostini is *Palazzo Pandolfi Elmi*, still owned by the family and beautifully maintained.—On a canal in Via delle Conce near the 17C Palazzo Barnabò are the old porticoed tanneries (where the 'Quintana' is celebrated in September). In this area, near remains of a Roman bridge, is the church of *Santa Margherita* with a rococo interior.—Other churches of interest include: *San Domenico* (deconsecrated and being restored as an auditorium) where medieval frescoes have recently been uncovered, which is next to the 17–18C Oratorio del Crocifisso, and, in the S part of the town, *San Francesco*, with early frescoes, next to the church of the Gonfalone (1735).

BUSES to *Montefalco*; to *Bevagna* and *Todi*; to *Perugia* direct and via *Assisi*; via Tolentino, Macerata, and San Benedetto del Tronto to *Ascoli Piceno*; to *Rome*.

About 5km E of Foligno, on the slopes of Monte Serrone, is the **Abbadia di Sassovivo**, with a beautiful cloister of round arches by a Roman artist (1229).— About 9km W is **Bevagna**, a charming ancient little walled town (4700 inhab.). Near *Porta Foligno* are remains of Roman buildings. The Corso leads through the town to the main square passing Via Crescimbeni which leads up to Piazza Garibaldi. Here are remains of a Roman temple (later converted into a church) and, in Via Porta Guelfa, a *Roman Mosaic* (2C AD; closed for restoration in 1990) with marine figures. At No. 72 in the Corso is the Municipio with the *Pinacoteca* (9–13, 15.30–18 except Sunday and Monday, and Saturday afternoons). On the stairs the local Archaeological Museum is arranged, including Roman material. The paintings (many of them in poor condition) include an Adoration of the Magi by Corrado Giaquinto. Beyond is *Piazza Silvestri*, centre of the medieval city, and one of the finest piazze in Umbria. Here is the 13C *Palazzo dei Consoli* with Gothic two-light windows (inside is a theatre of 1886, being restored), with an outside stair. Beside it is the church of *San Silvestro* (1195) with an unfinished façade and a good Romanesque interior with a raised chancel. Opposite is the church of *San Michele Archangelo* with a good portal, 14C campanile, and an interior similar to that of San Silvestro. In Largo Gramsci (car parking) the apse of San Silvestro can be well seen next to the theatre.

12km SW is **Montefalco** (427m), named from its panoramic position the 'Ringhiera dell'Umbria'. It is surrounded by extensive olive groves, and its water tower is conspicuous for miles around. It has numerous interesting frescoes in its churches. The road enters the town through the Porta Sant'Agostino with a fresco of the Madonna and Saints (14C?) on the inside façade. Via Umberti ascends past *Sant'Agostino*, with numerous frescoes, and a Madonna and Saints by Giovanni Battista Caporali (1522), to the charming circular Piazza della Repubblica (car parking) with the *Palazzo Comunale* (the tower can be climbed on request; *View). Just out of the square (downhill along Via Ringhiera Umbra) is the 14C church of *San Francesco* (adm. 10–12, 16.30–18.30; closed Thursday) which serves as a Museum (restoration work in progress). Here are paintings by Francesco Melanzio, a native artist, Melozzo da Forlì, Antoniazzo Romano, Pier Antonio Mezzastris, and Benozzo Gozzoli (a fresco cycle in the apse of the *Life of St Francis). In the convent church of *Santa Chiara*, on the Spoleto road, the

Cappella Santa Croce has 14C Umbrian frescoes. *Santa Illuminata* has three large semi-circular chapels on either side of the nave decorated with more early-16C frescoes by Francesco Melanzio and Bernardino Mezzastris. *San Fortunato* (open all day), outside the Porta Spoleto, is in a beautiful position surrounded by ancient ilex trees. In the chapel off the cloister are frescoes (restored 1982) by Tiberio d'Assisi with a charming vault. In the lunette of the door of the church, Madonna and Saints frescoed by Benozzo Gozzoli, and inside on the right, St Fortunato enthroned, also by Gozzoli. In the little chapel off the left side of the nave, is the sarcophagus of St Severus with three frescoed tondi by Gozzoli (very worn).

Gualdo Cattaneo, 13km W of Montefalco, is a tiny medieval town in a beautiful position.

N3 continues S from Foligno past (47km) **Trevi** (6500 inhab.), conspicuous on a hill (424m) covered with olive groves, 4km E of its station. Half-way up is the church of the *Madonna delle Lacrime* (if closed, ring at convent) dating from 1487, with a good sculptured portal, and containing an *Adoration of the Magi, by Perugino (right wall). In the left transept is a frescoed tabernacle in by Lo Spagna. Behind the high altar a detached fresco of the Crucifixion by an Umbrian master of the mid-14C has been placed. In the small picture gallery in the 15C *Municipio* are examples of Lo Spagna and Pinturicchio. *Sant'Emiliano* (12C, restored) has a triple altarpiece by Rocco di Tommaso (1522). The church of *San Martino* (14C), NE of the town, has a detached chapel with further work by Lo Spagna.

In the scattered commune of (54km) *Campello sul Clitunno* are (left of the road) the ruins of the little 8C church of Cipriano and Giustina. The *Tempietto di Clitunno* (ring for custodian) was re-made from antique fragments in the 4C or 5C above a pagan temple which covered another spring (now dry), mentioned by the younger Pliny. The charming little interior has primitive frescoes of Saints Peter and Paul and God the Father (7–8C).—The road continues to (1km farther on) a green oasis on the right of the road which marks the *Fonti del Clitunno*, where the river gushes forth in a sudden flow. This is the classical *Clitumnus*, famed for the white oxen bred on its banks. Its crystal-clear waters have been praised by Byron and Carducci.

65km **SPOLETO** (317m; 36,100 inhab.) is an interesting old town on the Via Flaminia, with some fine Roman and medieval monuments. It lies in a beautiful landscape of high and thickly wooded hills, but the plain to the N has been spoilt by untidy suburbs. It has become famous for its music and drama festival held here since 1958 in June and July.

Hotels near Piazza della Libertà and Piazza della Vittoria.

Post Office, Viale Matteotti.—*Tourist Office*, Piazza della Libertà.

Theatres. *Teatro Nuovo*, Via Vaita Sant'Andrea; *Teatro Caio Melisso*, Piazza Duomo.—The FESTIVAL OF TWO WORLDS (June and July) is held in these two theatres, the Roman theatre, and the ex-church and cloister of San Nicolò. Open-air concerts are given in Piazza Duomo.

Buses from the station ('Circolare B') every 10 minutes through the town. Country Buses to *Rome*; to *Urbino*; and to *Florence*, via *Perugia* and *Siena*.

Parking. Long-term car parks in Viale Giacomo Matteotti and Piazza Campello. Nearly all the roads within the walls are one-way.

The Umbrian *Spoletium* was colonised by the Romans in 242 BC, and survived an attack by Hannibal in 217. It suffered severely in the conflict between Marius and Sulla. In 576 Spoleto became the seat of a Lombard (and later Frankish) duchy which ruled over a large area of Umbria and the Marches during the Middle Ages. In 1354 it was incorporated in the States of the Church. It was the birthplace of the painter Lo Spagna (died 1528).

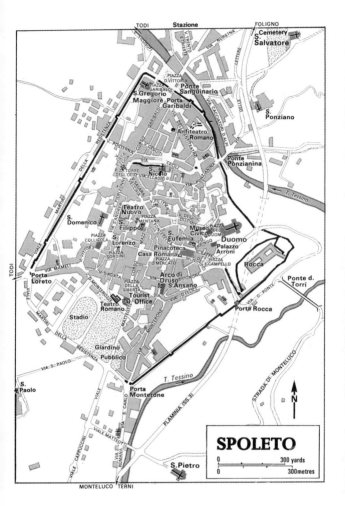

In Piazza della Libertà there is a good view of the **Roman Theatre** (adm. 9.30–13). It has been heavily restored (and was, until recently, covered by other buildings), but retains a remarkable barrel-vaulted passageway beneath the cavea. Behind the scena the apse and conventual buildings of *Sant'Agata* are conspicuous (the little church has become a restoration centre).—The steep Via Brignone leads uphill to the church of *Sant'Ansano* which contains a fresco fragment of the Madonna and Child by Lo Spagna. Remains of a Roman temple (1C AD) have been exposed around the altar. Steps lead down (lights on left) to the *Cappella di Sant'Isacco* (the crypt) with primitive (11–12C) frescoes (detached and restored). The foundations of the cella of the Roman temple and Roman shops (for adm. ring at the Convent) abut the *Arco di Drusa* (AD 23) under which the road now passes into *Piazza del Mercato*, on the site of the Roman Forum. The wall fountain by Costantino Fiaschetti (1746) incorporates a monument to Urban VII by Carlo Maderno (1626; restored).

Via del Municipio leads up to *Palazzo Comunale* begun in the 13C, but transformed in the 18C (and with a left wing of 1913). It faces a pretty row of old houses (being restored) including the remains of a Roman building. Here is the PINACOTECA (shown by a custodian, 9–12, 15–18 except Tuesday).

The collection (not labelled) in the three main rooms includes: (ROOM 1) *Guercino*, Mary Magdalene; (R. 2, with a view of the Duomo), detached frescoes by *Lo Spagna* including a Madonna and Child with Saints; *Reliquary Cross with miniature paintings (1200), two 13C painted Crucifixes; (R. 3) detached frescoes and a Madonna by *Antonello de Saliba*; 14–15C paintings including a triptych by *Nicolò d'Alunno*.—Beneath the palace there is a *Roman House*, supposed to have belonged to Vespasia Polla, the mother of Vespasian, with mosaic floors, an impluvium, etc.

Uphill to the east is Piazza Campello with a colossal mask serving as a wall fountain. Here is the entrance gate to the huge ***Rocca Albornoz** which ceased to be used as a prison in 1982, and which is being extensively restored. It is used for exhibitions. It was erected in 1359–64 by Gattapone for Cardinal Albornoz and still dominates the town. Groups are conducted (: every half hour (8.30–13.30, 14.30–17, except Monday; fest. 8.30–12.30). A long climb leads up the hill to the main building with the Cortile d'Onore. Here is a well by Bernardo Rossellino, added when Nicholas V enlarged the castle. A number of frescoes have been uncovered, and when restoration work is completed there are plans to open a historical museum here relating to the medieval Duchy of Spoleto. Interesting remains of the 7C church of *Sant' Elia* have recently been excavated on the hillside. The delightful view to the S takes in the Ponte delle Torri, the unspoilt valley of the Flaminia, and the walls which descend the hillside enclosing old houses with their orchards. To the N, instead, the view extends over new buildings on the plain towards Assisi.—To the S is the Porta della Rocca and outside the gate are further remains of the old wall and the remarkable ***Ponte delle Torri**, a bridge and aqueduct also probably by Gattapone, but possibly on Roman foundations. It spans a deep ravine amidst ilex groves, and is 230m long and 80m high; it is one of the most remarkable sights in Italy (and was greatly admired by Goethe in 1786). A path on the far side leads across to the Monteluco road (see below).

Via Saffi leads back towards the centre of the town past the stepped Via dell'Arringo (opened in the 13C) from the top of which is a remarkable *View of the cathedral and the green hillside behind it. The steps descends past the pretty apse of Sant'Eufemia (see below) and the Renaissance *Palazzo Arroni* (right) to the ***Duomo** (closed 13–15), consecrated by Innocent III in 1198, and later much altered. The façade is preceded by an elegant Renaissance portico (1491), by *Ambrogio Barocci* and *Pippo Fiorentino*, incorporating two pulpits. Above are eight rose windows, and a mosaic signed *Solsternus* (1207), while the main portal is a fine 12C Romanesque work. The companile (12C, with additions of 1416 and 1518) incorporates Roman fragments.

The INTERIOR was modernised in 1634–44 for Urban VIII, whose bust, by *Bernini*, surmounts the central door. In the 1st chapel in the S aisle (unlocked by the custodian) are frescoes by *Pinturicchio* (Madonna and Child with two Saints, and the Eternal Father). In the S transept are a Madonna and Saints by *Annibale Carracci*, the tomb of Giovanni Francesco Orsini by *Ambrogio Barocci* and the *Tomb of Fra Filippo Lippi, erected by Florentine artists at the order of Lorenzo de'Medici, with an inscription by Politian. The apse is painted with *Frescoes (damaged) by *Filippo Lippi* (1468–69; light, fee), finished after his death by *Fra Diamante*. The Cappella delle Reliquie (last chapel in N aisle) has painted stalls of 1548–54, a Crucifixion by *Sozio* (1187), and a Madonna and Child sculpted in wood (14C).

In Piazza del Duomo (where concerts are held during the Festival), the 14C *Palazzo della Signoria* contains the *Museo Civico* (ring for the custodian at the theatre). Here is a good collection of sculpture from the 4C to the 14C; also an inscription of the 3C BC forbidding the cutting of timber in a sacred grove. Above the museum is the *Chamber Theatre* (Caio Melisso), built by Giovanni Montiroli (1877) and restored for the Festival. The arcades seen from below the left side of the piazza belong to Palazzo della Signoria.

In Via Saffi, at the top of Via dell'Arringo (right) is *Palazzo Arcivescovile*, with a small Diocescan Museum, and a fresco by the 'Maestro di Fossa' (recently restored). In the courtyard is the 12C church of *Sant'Eufemia**. The beautiful plain Romanesque interior (usually unlocked) has a matroneum, interesting capitals, and some 15C frescoes on the columns. The 15C triptych, behind the 13C Cosmatesque altar, has been removed for many years.

Via Saffi and Via Fontesecca continue downhill. In Piazza Mentana the church of *San Filippo*, begun in 1640, contains a bust of St Philip Neri in the Sacristy by Alessandro Algardi, and a Holy Family by Sebastiano Conca. Farther downhill is the *Teatro Nuovo* (by Ireneo Aleandri, 1864). Nearby is the 18C *Palazzo Collicola* and the tiny 12C church of *San Lorenzo*. The 13C church of **San Domenico** has a banded exterior. Inside are fragments of votive frescoes in the nave, and (1st S altar) the Triumph of St Thomas Aquinas (detached and restored) dating from the early 15C. To the right of the presbytery a barrel-vaulted chapel is entirely covered with frescoes by a 15C artist. In the right transept is a Madonna and Child with four Saints by Giovanni Lanfranco, and on the E wall of the church (below the windows) are more frescoes. From the chapel to the left of the high altar, decorated by Liborio Coccetti, steps (light on left) descend to a crypt with further remains of frescoes. On the S wall of the nave is an Umbrian painting of St Peter Martyr.

Via Pierleone Leoni leads down to Piazza Torre dell'Olio which takes its name from the tall thin tower beyond *Porta Fuga* (12C?) or *di Annibale*, beneath which Via Porta Fuga descends to join Corso Garibaldi. The busy Via Cecili skirts the best section of WALLS—of all periods from the 6C or 4C BC to the 15C—interrupted by the 14C apse of *San Nicolò*. The church, together with the ex-convent, have been restored as a cultural and congress centre. The *Galleria Comunale d'Arte Moderna* is also provisionally housed here. The Cloister may be visited (10–13, 15–18 except Tuesday). The ruins of the *Amphitheatre*, farther on, are within the ex-conventual barracks and difficult of access.

The church of San Pietro, Spoleto

Via Garibaldi and Via dell'Anfiteatro meet at the unattractive Piazza Garibaldi where the church of SAN GREGORIO was well restored in 1949. In the good Romanesque interior is a tabernacle attributed to Benedetto da Rovezzano (chapel to the left). Outside Porta Garibaldi (rebuilt since the War) are remains (below ground level) of the *Ponte Sanguinario*, a Roman bridge, abandoned when the river was diverted in the 14C and rediscovered in 1817 when the existing bridge was built. From *Piazza della Vittoria*, a busy road junction, Viale Trento e Trieste lead to the *Station*, outside of which is a huge iron sculpture by Alexander Calder (1962).

From Piazza della Vittoria the remarkable church of San Salvatore is reached. A road (signposted to the Cemetery; not a pretty walk) leads beneath the Flaminia superstrada to the Cemetery church of *San Salvatore (or *Il Crocifisso*), a palaeochristian church of the late 4C or early 5C of the greatest interest for its numerous classical elements. The damaged façade has fine portals and three unusual windows showing Oriental influence. The interior (being restored) has Corinthian columns and a Roman architrave. Remarkable acanthus leaf capitals at the four corners of the presbytery stand out above the classical cornice.

A side road off Via di San Salvatore leads to the 12C church of *San Ponziano* (shown by a custodian, 8–12, 15–18), dedicated to the patron saint of Spoleto. It has a fine façade. The interior was remodelled by Giuseppe Valadier in 1788. The crypt has two conical pillars serving as columns thought to be metae from a Roman circus, 14C and 15C fresco fragments, and a palaeochristian sarcophagus.

At the S end of the town is the ancient church of **San Pietro** (reached on foot from Piazza del Mercato by the steep old Via Monterone, Via San Carlo, and then left across the Flaminia 'superstrada'; or, by a pretty walk across Ponte della Torre by the Strada di Monteluco). The church, reconstructed in the 13C, has a Lombard *Façade with a magnificent variety of reliefs. The interior has been closed for many years.

A road (8km) ascends from San Pietro to Monteluco via the 12C church of *San Giuliano*, incorporating fragments of a 6C predecessor. The road climbs through the ilex woods of **Monteluco** (804m), occupied from the 7C by anchorites, to the convent of *San Francesco* (belvedere). The slopes are now a summer resort.

On the W side of the town, beyond Porta Loreto, a straight road lined with a long portico leads to the church of the *Madonna di Loreto*, begun in 1572 by Annibale Lippi on a Greek-cross plan with three paintings by Giovanni Baglione (1609). Also on this side of the town is the church of *San Paolo inter vineas*, mentioned by St Gregory the Great. It was reconstructed in the 10C and again in the 12C and 13C. It contains an early 13C altar and frescoes.

The main road follows the wooded glen of the Tescino between Monte Fionchi (1337m) on the left and Monte Acetella (1016m) on the right, and crosses the Passo della Somma (646m). It descends and leaves on the right the by-pass and 'superstrada' link (N204) for the Todi road (N3bis, see Rte 59B) and the Autostrada del Sole at Orte (see above).

92km **TERNI** (130m), a thriving industrial town (106,900 inhab.) making plastics and machinery, is capital of the province of the same name. It faces the broad plain of the Nera river, while hills rise to the N. Badly damaged in the Second World War, it was reconstructed with pleasant residential suburbs, under the guidance of the architect Mario Ridolfi (1904–1984), who lived here at the end of his life. It was shaken by an earthquake in 1979.

Post Office, Piazza Solferino.—*A.P.T. Tourist Office*, Viale Cesare Battisti.— **Buses** to *Marmore*, *Piediluco* and *La Luce*; to *Sangemini*; via Amelia to *Orvieto*; to *Rieti*; to *Perugia*; (from the Railway Station) via Narni to *Rome*; from the Bus Station via Visso to *Tolentino*; to *Spoleto*.

Terni occupies the site of *Interamna Nahars*, so called because it was built between the two streams (inter amnes) Nar and Serra. It is not now considered to be the birthplace of Tacitus the historian, but it is probably that of his fellow-clansman Claudius Tacitus, who was Emperor for six months in 275–276. The Emperor Gallus was murdered here in 253. The medieval history is insignificant, but in 1798 the French, under General Lemoine, won a victory here over the Neapolitans.

A new bridge over the Nera and the modern Corso del Popolo lead to the central Piazza della Repubblica, from which Corso Tacito continues N to the station. From the square Via Cavour runs W past the 16C *Palazzo Mazzancolli*, beyond which, on the right, at No. 55 Via Frattini, is *Palazzo Fabrizi*, which since 1987 has housed the *Pinacoteca* (10–13, 16–19, except Monday) with a Marriage of St Catherine, by Benozzo Gozzoli, a Crucifixion, with Saints Francis and Bernardine, by L'Alunno, and a triptych of the Madonna and Saints dated 1485, by the 'Master of the Gardener Annunciation' (recently identified as Pier Matteo da Amelia). The 19C and 20C section includes works by Carlo Carrà and Gino Severini. The archaeological collection, which includes material from the Iron Age found in the area, is not at present on view (but see Palazzo Carrara, below). Via Undici Febbraio turns left out of Via Cavour, and, in a lane (right) is the 12C church of *Sant'Alò* (being restored). Farther on is the *Duomo*, practically rebuilt in 1653, which retains two early doorways, one Romanesque, the other 14C. Adjacent are the ruins of a Roman *Amphitheatre* dating from AD 32. From here Via del Vescovado joins Via Roma, the old main street, which leads left towards the centre. By a medieval tower a turning right crosses the Corso to *San Salvatore*, a church consisting of a 5C rotunda on earlier Roman foundations, and a 12C nave. At the end of Corso del Popolo is the *Palazzo Spada*, the last work of Antonio da Sangallo the Younger (who died here in 1546).

Corso Vecchio continues the old main street through the old district to the NE. In a little square (right) rises the restored church of *San Pietro* (14C), and in a road to the right is Palazzo Manassei which used to house the Pinacoteca (see above). On the far side of the church, in *Palazzo Carrara* some of the archaeological collections of the Museo Civico are kept. *San Lorenzo* and *San Cristoforo*, two 13C churches, are farther NE, while on the W side of Corso Tacito is *San Francesco* (1265, enlarged 1437), with a charming campanile by Angelo da Orvieto (1345). In the Paradisi chapel are *Frescoes by Bartolomeo di Tommaso da Foligno (c 1447), restored in 1987, inspired by Dante's 'Divina Commedia'.

The *Cascata delle Marmore, 6km ESE, are reached either by the Rieti road (Via Garibaldi) or the Ferentillo road (Piazza Dante). A bus runs from Piazza Dante along the Valnerina road in 10 minutes. These falls (165m) have been diverted entirely for industrial purposes, but are released to their original channels on Sundays and holidays. In great measure they are the work of man, for Curius Dentatus, conqueror of the Sabines (271 BC), was the first to cut a channel by which the river Velinus (Velino) was thrown over a precipice into the River Nar, to prevent floods in the plain of Reate (Rieti). Another channel was cut in 1400 and a third (draining the plain of Rieti without flooding Terni) in 1785. In recent years landslips have threatened the stability of the travertine rock. A path leads to the best viewpoint, and it continues to the station of Marmore, on the railway to Rieti.

The abbey of *San Pietro in Valle* is reached by keeping along the lower Marmore road, past (19km) *Ferentillo*, to (23km) *Macenano*. Just beyond this hamlet a side turning (left) leads in c 1·5km to the abbey. The domed church (key at Ferentillo, or ask at the Tourist Office in Terni), founded in the 8C, preserves its triapsidal plan and contains remarkable though damaged mural paintings of scriptural scenes (c 1190). The charming two-tiered cloister and the campanile are of 12C workmanship.—Continuation N, see below.

The Rieti road (N79) continues, skirting the irregular *Lago di Piediluco*, and farther on descends between two smaller lakes, *Lago di Ripa Sottile* (right) and *Lago Lungo* (left), into the Plain of Rieti.—40km *Rieti*, see Rte 64.

FROM TERNI TO VISSO, 72km (N209), following the Nera valley. To (23km) *Macenano*, see above.—At (41km) *Piedipaterno*, a by-road from Spoleto comes in on the left.—52km *Triponzo* at the confluence of the Nera and the Corno (see below).—72km **Visso**, a bleak little town (606m) is a centre for climbing in the Monti Sibillini, to the E. The Gothic church of *Santa Maria*, with a cross by Nicolò da Guardiagrele, and several 15–16C palazzi surround the central square.

From Triponzo N396 follows the Corno to (11km) *Serravalle*, junction for **Cascia** (12km S on N320), the home and death-place of St Rita, the 'saint of impossibilities', who was born in 1381 at *Roccaporena*, 5·5km W. Her sanctuary-church was built in 1937–42. The town was heavily damaged by earthquake in 1979.—18km **Norcia** (5400 inhab.), the *frigida Nursia* of Virgil, an old town which has suffered much from earthquakes (last in 1979), was the birthplace of St Benedict (480–543) and of his twin sister St Scholastica. The castle was erected in 1554 by Vignola for Pope Julius III. It houses a Museum (closed since

1979) with Umbrian paintings and sculptures. The church of *San Benedetto* has a good 14C façade and remains of a late-Roman house in its crypt. Several other churches have good Gothic portals. The *Palazzo Comunale* dates in part from the 13C, while in the Via Umberto is the curious little building called the *Tempietto* (mid-14C).—The road goes on to Tufo, on the Via Salaria (see Rte 64).

106km **Narni** is an old hill town (244m) with 20,600 inhabitants, preserving many medieval streets and buildings. Originally called *Nequinum*, it changed its name to *Narnia* (after the river) when it became a Roman colony in 299 BC. It was the birthplace of the Emperor Nerva (AD 32), of John XIII (pope 965–972), and of Erasmo da Narni, called Gattamelata, the condottiere (died 1443). Virgil, followed by Macaulay ('the pale waves of Nar'), refers to the whitish turbidity of the stream washing the foot of the hill, due to its content of sulphur and lime. On the first Sunday in May a medieval tournament, the 'Corso all'anello', is held here. The *Duomo*, founded in the 12C, has an outer S aisle added in the 15C, with a wooden statue of St Anthony Abbot by Vecchietta (1475). At the E end of the nave are two white marble pulpits (1490), and in the N aisle, is a curious marble screen with very ancient reliefs and Cosmatesque decoration, and a fresco of the Madonna of the school of Foligno. Throughout the church are good 15C monuments. The *Palazzo Comunale* (open Monday–Friday 8–19) is adorned with 13–14C sculptures and contains a painting by Domenico Ghirlandaio. The *Loggia dei Priori*, opposite, is attributed to Gattapone. *Santa Maria in Pensole* (1175) has an elegant Romanesque portico. Beyond is Via Mazzini, a characteristic medieval street. In the ex-church of San Domenico is an interesting *Museum* of works of art from other buildings, including an Annunciation by Benozzo Gozzoli. *San Francesco* (14C) on the W flank of the town, and *Sant'Agostino* (15C), on the E, are interesting churches, and the square-towered castle (c 1370) on the hilltop to the S commands a good view.

The road descending towards the station (3km; in *Narni Scalo*) crosses the Nera (Nar) near the fine ruined *PONTE D'AUGUSTO which carried the Via Flaminia across the river. To the left is a good view of the 12C Benedictine abbey of San Cassiano, recently restored (open on Sundays). From here, passing the *Madonna del Ponte* (rebuilt, after having been blown up along with the medieval road bridge in 1944), the road ascends to (12km) **Amelia**, a hilltop town with fine views. This was the ancient *Ameria*, said by Pliny to have been founded three centuries before Rome. A remarkable bronze head of a statue of Germanicus, father of Caligula, was found here in 1963. It was exhibited in Palazzo Patrignani in 1988 after its restoration. Alessandro Geraldini (1455–1525) was born here: he helped obtain the approval at the court of Spain for Columbus' expedition, and later travelled as bishop to Santo Domingo. The town preserves splendid remains of polygonal (Pelasgic) walls, c 8m high and 3·5m thick, dating from the 5C BC. The twelve-sided campanile of the *Duomo* dates from 1050. In the churches of *Santi Filippo e Giacomo* and *Sant'Agostino* are traces of antique material. Beneath the *Municipio* is a Roman piscina; the *Palazzo Farrattini* contains Roman mosaics. The charming 18C theatre is being restored.

BUSES run from Amelia to *Terni*, *Orte*, and to *Orvieto*; and from Narni to *Rome*, to *Cascia*, and to *Terni*.

From Narni N3 and the newer road (N3bis) ascend the Nera valley and join up at (114km) *Ponte Sanguinaro*. Just beyond (122km) *Otricoli* the road passes (right) the site of its Umbrian predecessor, *OCRICULUM, between the road and the Tiber. The romantic overgrown ruins survive of the theatre, baths, and amphitheatre. Excavations here in 1776–84 by order of Pius VI resulted in numerous finds, now in the Vatican. The site, of the greatest interest, is now semi-abandoned, and in need of protection, although excavations continue. On a steep descent the road enters Lazio. The road crosses the Autostrada del Sole and the Tiber just below the village of *Magliano Sabina*.—133km *Civita Castellana-Magliano* station (on the Orte line).

140km **Civita Castellana** (148m) stands on a tufa hill surrounded by picturesque and precipitous ravines spanned by lofty bridges. The town (14,500 inhab.) is on the site of the ancient *Falerii*, originally named *Halesus* after its founder, a chief of the Auruncans and Oscans. Falerii was one of the Etruscan lordships and the capital of the Falisci, a tribe belonging to the Etruscan Confederation but otherwise distinct and speaking its own language.

The town was taken by Camillus in 394 BC; in 241 BC the Romans destroyed it and built *Falerii Novi*, 6km W. The new town prospered, but in the 8C and 9C the population returned to the ancient site, which acquired its present name.

The *Duomo* has a magnificent *Portico and West door by the Cosmati family (1210), of unique design and particularly delicate work-manship, considered the masterpiece of this Roman family of marble sculptors. Beneath the portico are interesting architectural fragments, including Roman and medieval pieces, and a rare 8C relief showing a wild-boar hunt. In the 18C interior is an extensive and well-preserved Cosmatesque pavement. The modern pulpit and altar incorporate paleochristian fragments. The interesting Crypt has good antique columns and capitals. In the Sacristy are preserved two *Plutei from the Cosmatesque choir-screen (1237). A Museo Diocesano is being arranged at No. 4 in the piazza.

Nearby in Via Roma is the entrance to the *Rocca, a remarkable pentagonal fortress with two fine courtyards begun by Alexander VI and completed for Julius II by Antonio Sangallo the Elder. Used until recently as a prison, it has now been well restored.

Cells open off the courtyard which has some frescoes in the vault attributed to Zuccari. The *Museo Nazionale Falisco* (adm. 9–13 except Monday) has been beautifully arranged here. The collection includes vases, bronzes, etc. from Civita Castellana, Narce, and Corchiano. In the vestibule are architectural terracottas from Etruscan temples in the area.

Of **Falerii Vetres**, 1km W on the road to Fabrica di Roma (Rte 57), the most interesting relics are an aqueduct, a ruined Temple of Mercury, and the nucleus of the necropolis, in which the tombs, cut in the tufa, take the form of an antechamber with a vertical shaft (apparently for the escape of the gases of decomposition) and a sepulchral chamber. Beyond the medieval bridge over the Fosso Maggiore are the ruins of the so-called Temple of Juno Curitis, with a triple cella. The same road leads on to (6km) the romantic site of **Falerii Novi**, its remarkable *Walls marked by a line of vegetation conspicuous in the open countryside. Triangular in plan and c 2100m round, they retain 50 of the original 80 towers and two of the nine gates. No other ruins give so complete an idea of a Roman walled town. The Porta di Giove gives access to a pine avenue which ends at the old abbey, now a farmhouse, with fine windows and ancient masonry. Here is the large roofless church of *Santa Maria di Falleri* built in the 12C (opened in the morning by a custodian), and the area of the forum and theatre may be recognised. The view embraces the line of walls and Monte Soratte in the distance. A track follows the walls from the gate; the Porta del Bove ('Ox Gate') is also well preserved.

Nepi, 13km SW (bus in 20 minutes), is another ancient place known for its mineral water. At the entrance to the town an 18C aqueduct stands beside the huge ruined Rocca and the medieval walls on Etruscan foundations. In the main square is the town hall begun by Antonio da Sangallo and completed in the Baroque period. The Duomo, nearby, has an ancient crypt.—3km E of Nepi is *Castel Sant'Elia*. The approach road passes the Franciscan convent of Santa Croce in Sassonia; at the other end of the town a road descends (left) to the cemetery with its old cypresses beside the *Basilica of Sant'Elia, an 11C

Benedictine foundation on the site of an ancient temple, in a splendid position below a tufa cliff in a wooded valley. The simple façade incorporates ancient sculptural fragments. The interior (if closed, the entrance is through the crypt from the cemetery) has Roman columns and capitals and fragments of a Cosmatesque pavement, as well as a pergamum made up from ancient fragments, and a pretty ciborium. The interesting primitive *Frescoes at the E end are signed by the brothers Giovanni and Stefano (late 11C or early 12C). The bright colours and delightful costumes show Byzantine influence.

Via Flaminia continues, with a good view of Monte Soratte on the left to (151km) *Sant'Oreste* station; from here to (193km) **Rome**, see 'Blue Guide Rome'.

B.   Via Todi

ROAD, 172km, N3bis.—19km **Deruta**.—44·5km **Todi**.—62km *Acquasparta*.—76km Junction with Terni by-pass. From here to (172km) Rome, see Rte 59A.

RAILWAY to *Terni*, slow trains only, 79km in 2½hrs, stopping at Deruta, Marsciano, Todi (Ponte Rio), Acquasparta, etc. From Terni to Rome, see Rte 59A.

From Perugia, the motorway by-pass links with the 'superstrada' (N3bis), or the old road runs due S to join the 'superstrada' at (10km) *Osteria dei Cipressi*. A by-road leads left for Torgiano (4·5km) and Bettona (11km).

At *Torgiano*, situated between the Tiber and Chiascio rivers, a private *Wine Museum was opened in 1974. The exhibits are excellently displayed and labelled in the cool cellars of Palazzo Baglioni, also used for exhibitions (open every day; ring). The particularly interesting collection illustrates the history of wine, with archaeological material (Roman amphorae, an Attic kylix from Vulci, etc.); a section illustrating wine making, with agricultural tools, wine presses, etc; and Italian majolica (including Deruta, Gubbio, and Faenza ware).—The road continues through thick olive groves to **Bettona** (11km), the ancient Vettona, which has a fine view from its little hill (355m). On the approach the road passes the remarkable golden-coloured Etruscan walls. In the simple little piazza with a fountain is Palazzo del Podestà (enquire at the police station) with a small collection of Umbrian paintings. This has been closed after the theft in 1987 of two paintings by Perugino and a predella by Dono Doni. A Madonna and six Saints, and a Nativity (from the church of San Crispolto), both by Doni are kept here. Below the fountain is the church of San Crispolto (the first bishop of Bettona) with a pyramidal campanile. To the right of the church is the restored cloister, and (beyond glass doors) a pretty covered passageway (restored) leads out on to the hillside with a view of the town and its walls. The contents of the other church in the piazza, Santa Maria Maggiore, have been removed for safekeeping.

The main road continues to (16km) *Ponte Nuovo* (where another by-road leads left for Bettona).—19km **Deruta** (218m), famed for its majolica, which is still made in great quantity in modern factories in the new town below.

In the old town the Palazzo Comunale houses a PINACOTECA and collection of majolica (open every day, 10–13, 15.30–18.30). In the first room, works by *Baciccia, l'Alunno* (Madonna and Child, 1453), and a detached *Fresco (c 1478; in very poor condition) from the church of San Francesco by *Fiorenzo di Lorenzo*. It includes a view of Deruta with Saints Roch and Romano (the head is attributed to Perugino). A gonfalon by *L'Alunno* is being restored.—2nd room: portraits by *Antonio Amorosi* (1660–1736) and two small works by *Francesco Trevisani*.— Beyond is a room of Deruta majolica from the 14C and 15C onwards; three other rooms on the upper floor display 19C and 20C majolica. Opposite the Museum is the church of *San Francesco* with 14C and 15C frescoes.

A by-road from Deruta leads across the Tiber and the railway for *Marsciano* (13km) with remains of a feudal castle. *Cerqueto* lies 7km N of Marsciano on a charming secondary road (N317) from Perugia which follows the ridge of hills through beautiful countryside. The parish church contains a fresco fragment of St Sebastian, the earliest dated work of Perugino (1478).

44·5km *TODI (410m), with 17,300 inhabitants, is a beautiful old Umbrian town in a delightful isolated position. It is now by-passed well to the E, and stands on a hill just W of the old road. The ancient Umbrian city of *Tuder*, it preserves many interesting buildings and old streets. The terrain is subject to landslips and work is being carried out to shore up the hill.

A.P.T. Tourist Information Office, 19 Via Mazzini.—*Railway Station*, Ponte Rio, 2km SE of the Porta Romana (bus in connection with trains). The other station at Ponte Naia is less convenient.—BUSES to *Rome* via Massa Martana (daily except Sunday).—An *Antiques Fair* is held here in Spring.

Todi was the birthplace of Jacopo de'Benedetti (c 1250–1306), called Jacopone da Todi, poet and mystic, the reputed author of the 'Stabat Mater'. The local carpenters produce good inlay work.

The prettiest approach (unsignposted) from Perugia is by the country road which leads right up to the double *Porta Perugina*, with its two round towers, in the 13C walls. The central *Piazza del Popolo, or Piazza Vittorio Emanuele, redolent of past ages, is bordered by well proportioned Gothic and Renaissance buildings. Here stands the battlemented *Palazzo dei Priori* (1293–1337, with 16C additions). PALAZZO COMUNALE occupies the Gothic *Palazzo del Popolo* (1213, with later alterations), also battlemented, and *Palazzo del Capitano* (1290), which is preceded by a monumental flight of steps. The last contains a picture gallery (closed many years ago for restoration) with a large polyptych by Lo Spagna, a Crucifix in bronze attributed to Giambologna, frescoes, terracottas, and Etruscan bronzes. The **Duomo** (closed 12–15) has a 13C façade with a good portal and rose window, and is also approached by an imposing flight of steps.

The lovely interior, with good Gothic capitals, has a raised presbytery and semi-dome in the apse. On the W wall, Last Judgement, a 16C fresco by *Ferrau da Faenza*. In the pretty Gothic arcade, with 19C local stained glass, on the right side of the nave, are a 14C altarpiece of the Madonna and Child (partly in relief), a 15C font, remains of a fresco of the Trinity by *Lo Spagna* (1525), and an altarpiece by *Giannicola di Paolo*. On either side of the presbytery, Saints Peter and Paul, small paintings by *Lo Spagna*. A Crucifix of the late 13C hangs in the apse which has inlaid stalls of 1530. On the left side of the nave are statues of the school of *Giovanni Pisano*. The 12C crypt has a small lapidary museum.

Via Mazzini leads out of the S end of the piazza past the handsome façade of the *Teatro Comunale* (enlarged in 1872 by Carlo Gatteschi; being restored) to **San Fortunato** (1292; closed 12.30–15.30) in a raised position above a garden laid out with box hedges. The fine portal has statues of the Annunciation in the style of Jacopo della Quercia.

The exceptionally light Interior has Gothic clustered pilasters and a polygonal apse. The grey stone brackets have been installed to counteract the outward lean of the pilasters. On the right wall of the 4th S chapel is a *Madonna and Child with two angels, a fresco fragment by *Masolino* (restored in 1987). In the 6th S chapel, very ruined 14C frescoes of the life of St Francis. At the end of the S aisle (closed for restoration) are fresco fragments by *Nicolò Vannucci da Todi*. In the crypt is the tomb of Fra Jacopone. The large cloister dates from the late 14C.

To the right of the church a lane leads up to the top of the hill and the ruined *Citadel* surrounded by a delightful large public garden; while on the left of the church Via San Fortunato leads down to an archway (right) on Via Lorenzo Leoni, and out to the side of the hill just above the ruined *Porta Libera*, a gate in the inner Etruscan or Roman walls. The dome of Santa Maria della Consolazione (see below) can just be seen from here. Crumbling steps lead on down through orchards to the old borgo and another gate, the Porta Aurea (lovely view). Nearby is the Romanesque church of *Santa Maria in Camuccia*, with a 12C wood statue of the Madonna and Child. Farther downhill can be seen the *Porta Amerina*. The charming old stepped Via San Fortunato (see above) continues down through a medieval district to *Porta Marzia*, a medieval arch constructed with Roman material.

Adjoining Piazza del Popolo is *Piazza Garibaldi* with a monument and Palazzo Atti (1552). There is a superb view of the countryside beyond a tall cypress and small garden; below can be seen the centrally-planned church of the Crocifisso. Corso Cavour descends towards Porta Marzia (see above); on the left the stepped Via del Mercato Vecchio leads down through an archway to Piazza Mercato Vecchio with four remarkable tall *Niches with semi-domes from a Roman building. Below the piazza is the Romanesque church of *Sant'Illario* (San Carlo).

Via del Duomo skirts the charming flank of the Duomo past the campanile, and an outside stair and the beautiful exterior of the apse. In Via del Seminario is *Palazzo del Vignola* (restored after a tragic fire in 1982), named after its architect, which ingeniously fits its corner site. Via Santa Prassede descends past an old arch and fragments of the earliest walls built into the houses (right; plaque). Via delle Mura Antiche, a lane beneath a low arch, leads right to emerge beside the walls. Via Santa Prassede, a peaceful old street, continues right (at the end of Via della Maleretta a stretch of medieval walls may be seen) and descends steeply past the 14C church of Santa Prassede through Porta Santa Prassede. Beyond the monastery of San Francesco (with its arch over the street) Via Borgo Nuovo continues out of the town and into the countryside through Porta Perugina (see above).—Another fine stretch of walls and medieval houses can be seen in the area to the W of Piazza del Popolo.

Outside the walls to the SW, on a busy road, is ***Santa Maria della Consolazione**** (1508–1607), a domed church on a Greek cross plan designed by Cola da Caprarola and completed by Ambrogio Barocci and Francesco da Vita. The exterior is a masterpiece of the Renaissance, showing the influence of Bramante.

13km E of Todi is the little fortified town of *Massa Martana*. There are a number of interesting ancient churches nearby, including Santa Maria in Pantano, Sant'Illuminato, and the 12C abbey church of Santi Fidenzio e Terenzio.—From Todi to Orvieto, see Rte 58.

The Todi by-pass (2km shorter) crosses in a tunnel beneath the old road, which it rejoins just short of San Faustino station.—62km *Acquasparta* (322m), visited for its mineral waters, has medieval ramparts and a fine 16C mansion. A by-road leads via Avigliano Umbro to *Toscolano* (25km) where in the church a fresco of the Madonna and Child was restored in 1987 and attributed to Pier Matteo d'Amelia (1481–83).—68km Turning for the remains of Roman CARSULAE, never rebuilt since its destruction by the Goths. The site, in lovely country, is unenclosed. It was an important Roman station on the Via Flaminia which has been uncovered, together with two temples, an amphitheatre and a theatre. The limit of the town is marked, just over the hilltop, by the Arch of St Damian, near which is a large circular sepulchre. The little church of St Damian was made from Roman materials. The unmade-up road continues to *San Gemini*

Fonte, another spa, from which the main road may be rejoined just N of (70km) *San Gemini* (331m), an old place with interesting architectural details.—76km This route joins the Terni by-pass near its W end; from here to (172km) **Rome**, see Rte 59A.

VI THE MARCHES AND NORTHERN LAZIO

The **Marches** (*Le Marche*) occupy the E slopes of the Apennines between the rivers Tavullo on the N and Tronto on the S. They are divided into the provinces of Ancona, Ascoli Piceno, Macerata, and Pesaro e Urbino and have a total area of 9,693,000 sq. km, and a population of 1,359,000.

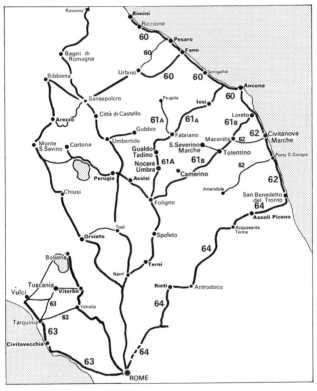

The Piceni, the earliest known natives, were for many years a thorn in the flesh of Rome, but their district, when subdued, became one of the chief granaries of the empire and was named *Picenum Anno-narium* (annona, the year's agricultural produce, especially grain). Later the district was called *Pentapolis Annonaria* (with part of Romagna, a sub-district of Emilia) and *Pentapolis Picena*. The present name comes from the 11C division of the region into the Marca Anconitana, the Marca Camerinese, and the Marca Fermana. Always, since the 8C, more or less under the jurisdiction of the Pope, the Marches were united to the Church in 1354 by Cardinal Egidio Albornoz, who offered the inducement of a special constitution. They remained papal territory (except for a brief period after the French Revolution) until the capture of Ancona in 1860 by the Piedmontese army. The region is given up almost entirely to agriculture.

Lazio (*Latium*), consists of five provinces: Frosinone, Latina, Rome, Rieti, and Viterbo, of which only the last two are included in this volume. These are, in addition, the least characteristic, sharing their common features rather with Umbria.

60 Rimini to Ancona

ROAD, 97km N16, VIA ADRIATICA.—35km **Pesaro**.—47km *Fano*.—70km *Senigallia*.—97km **Ancona**. The road is badly ribbon-developed and overcrowded.

AUTOSTRADA (A14), a little shorter, roughly parallel but farther inland.

RAILWAY, 92km in 1–1½ hours, closely following the road, with frequent trains.

The **Adriatic Riviera**, an endless succession of resorts as far as Ancona, was developed in the 1950s with innumerable hotels, liberally supplied with popular entertainments and sports and many small yacht harbours. The sea has been declared polluted along much of this coast. The hinterland (Urbino excepted) provides little of the first interest. The whole coast suffers from the proximity of the busy railway.

From *Rimini* N16 runs SE, by-passing (10km) *Riccione* and (18km) *Cattolica*, described with Rimini in Rte 41. It crosses the tiny Tavollo which, emptying into the sea at Cattolica, here marks the boundary between Romagna and the Marches. The hills now reach the sea. The walled town of *Gradara*, long visible on its hill (142m) to the right, has a fine 14C castle (15–19.30; winter 9–13.30; fest. 9–12.30; closed Monday), the supposed scene of the tragedy of Francesca da Rimini. About 2km E is *Gradara British Military Cemetery*, with 1192 graves.

To seaward lies *Gabicce Mare*, but for the Tavollo an extension of Cattolica, from where a winding panoramic road follows the cliffs through the ancient village of *Gabicce Monte*, affording splendid sea views all the way to (28km) *Pesaro*.

35km **PESARO** occupies the site of the Roman *Pisaurum*, at the mouth of the Pisaurus, now the Foglia. Formerly one of the cities of the Maritime Pentapolis, it is the pleasant seaside capital (84,700 inhab.) of the province of Pesaro e Urbino, one of the four comprising the Marches. The N district, along the sea, was laid out as a resort at the beginning of this century. It is a good centre from which to visit Urbino.

Hotels on the sea front.—**Post Office**, Piazza del Popolo.—**Tourist Office**, 4 Via Mazzolari.—**Buses** from the station forecourt to *Urbino*, in 40 minutes; to *Rimini* in 1hr; via Urbino, Foligno, Spoleto and Terni to *Rome* in 8hrs; to *Ancona* in 1½ hrs; via Fano to *Cagli* in 1½hrs; via Fano, Fossombrone, and Urbania to *Lamoli* in 2½hrs.

History. Pesaro was the seat of a lordship of the Malatesta and the Sforza, and, after 1512, of the Della Rovere; and it is the birthplace of the composer Gioacchino Rossini (1792–1868). The manufacture of majolica here, an industry which still survives, reached its artistic zenith between the late 15C and early 17C. During the Second World War its position at the Adriatic end of the Gothic Line meant that it was bombed and shelled by the Allies and mined by the Germans.

The **Gothic Line**, never completed by the Germans, but still a formidable obstacle to the Allied advance in the autumn of 1944, ran across Northern Italy from La Spezia, and passed near Carrara, to the N of Pistoia, across the Futa Pass, and by the line of the River Foglia to Pesaro. The assault on the line was begun by the crossing of the Metauro on 22 August 1944, and Rimini was captured on 21 September. There followed the fierce 'Battle of the Rivers'.

The *Cathedral*, in Via Rossini, has an early 14C façade, incomplete and retaining earlier details. This street runs past *Rossini's House*, being restored. The museum is being renovated, and includes the composer's spinet. Opposite, Via Mazzolari leads to *Palazzo Toschi-Mosca* which houses the **Musei Civici** (adm. 9.30–12.30, 16–19; winter 8.30–13.30; fest. 9.30–12.30; closed Monday), a choice and well-arranged collection of paintings and majolica.

At the top of the stairs: Triumph of Caesar in majolica by *Ferruccio Mengaroni* (1865–1925).—ROOM 2 is dominated by the famous 'Pala di Pesaro', a splendid altarpiece of the *Coronation of the Virgin, in a beautiful frame, painted by *Giovanni Bellini* for the church of San Francesco c 1474 (restored in 1988). It had a fundamental influence on the Venetian school of painting. The Crucifixion is an early work also by *Giovanni Bellini*. Also here: *Johannes Sagitanus*, St Bernardine, Louis of Toulouse, and Catherine; *Marco Zoppo*, Tondo of the head of the Baptist, Christ between angels; *Jacobello del Fiore*, Polyptych of the Blessed Michelina. A number of rooms of the pinacoteca are at present closed;they contain: *Domenico Beccafumi*, Holy Family; *Giovanni Bellini*, God the Father; *Simone Cantarini*, St Joseph; *Guido Reni*, Fall of the Giants; *Elisabetta Sirani*, Madonna and St John; and works by the local artist *Gian Andrea Lazzarini*.—R. 6. *Mariotto di Nardo*, Triptych; *Niccolò di Pietro*, Four Saints.—The splendid *Collection of majolica, much of it acquired in 1857 from Domenico Mazza, begins in R. 7. Here are displayed works from Urbino (16C), Castelli d'Abruzzo (17–18C), and Pesaro (18C).—R. 8. Bas-relief portraits in profile of Federico da Montefeltro, attributed to *Paolo da Ragusa* (15C), and of Battista Sforza by *Francesco Laurana*. The 16C 'Metaurensi' majolica illustrated with historical scenes comes from Casteldurante and Urbino.—R. 9 (left) has a wonderfully lustrous collection by *Giorgio Andreoli ('Mastro Giorgio')* of Gubbio.—R. 10. 16C ware from Deruta, Faenza, and Casteldurante. Marble bust of Napoleon by *Canova*; a bas-relief of the Madonna and Child by the 15C Tuscan school;and the bust of a prelate attributed to *Gian Cristoforo Romano*.—RR. 11 & 12. 16C majolica from Urbino, and the head of a warrior by *Andrea della Robbia*.

In Piazza del Popolo, with a fountain by Lorenzo Ottoni (1685), is the *Palazzo Ducale* (1450–1510), begun by Alessandro Sforza, with an imposing portico. At the W corner the Gothic façade (1395) of the demolished church of *San Domenico* forms the side wall of the Post Office. Its cloister is a vegetable market. Another excellent portal (1376–73) is that of the *Madonna della Grazia* (formerly *San Francesco*), off the SE side of the square. In the interior are 14–15C fresco fragments on the W wall and a very unusual high altar. *Sant'Agostino* (1413), in the Corso Undici Settembre, in the opposite direction, has a more richly decorated portal, and contemporary inlaid stalls. Across the Corso, in Via Petrucci, is the *Nome di Dio* (open 10–12), a little church with a fine interior decorated in 1634. In Piazza Olivieri is the *Conservatorio Rossini*, founded by a bequest from the composer. Inside are a striking portrait of Rossini by Gustave Doré, and the manuscripts of several of his operas (apply to custodian). Mascagni was director here from 1895 to 1905. Behind in Via Mazza, the Palazzo Almerici is the seat of the *Museo Oliveriano* (adm. on request) with Etruscan monuments, inscriptions, and bronzes; and a collection of antique coins. The *Rocca Costanza*, overlooking the seaside district, is a regularly planned fort by Luciano Laurana (1474–1505; used as a prison).

On the hill of San Bartolo (on the road to Cattolica 2km NW of Pesaro) are the two villas (*Villa Caprile* and *Villa Vittoria*) where Princess Caroline of Wales lived in 1817–19, in each for a little over a year. Villa Caprile has a fine garden. Here also is the '*Imperiale*' a villa of Alessandro Sforza (1469–72), enlarged by Genga for the Della Rovere (open in summer; apply at Tourist Office).

FROM PESARO TO URBINO, N423, 36km (bus in 40 minutes). This route at first follows the N16 in the direction of Rimini, but at (3·5km) *Santa Maria* it branches left and ascends the valley of the Foglia.—Before (15km) *Montecchio*, on the right of the road, is *Montecchio British Military Cemetery*, with 592 graves. Beyond the village, which was all but destroyed in 1944, the road bears left across the river and ascends. After (31km) *Trasanni* (172m) the rise becomes acute.—36km **Urbino**, see Rte 51.

47km **Fano** (47,800 inhab.) is the ancient *Fanum Fortunae*, named after its celebrated Temple of Fortune, and lies at the NE end of the Via Flaminia (N3; see below). It has good beaches; to the W is the sandy Lido, while a pebbly beach extends to the E. The hotel district lies N of the Canale del Porto; the old town, which was mined in 1944, to the S.

The main road (by-passed by the Circonvallazione) continues directly into the town as the Corso Matteotti. Beyond its crossing with Via Arco d'Augusto, in Piazza Venti Settembre are the *Palazzo della Ragione* (1299), which has contained a theatre since the 16C; the present one was built by Luigi Poletti in 1863 (being restored). Next to it is the *Corte Malatestiana*, part Gothic from the time of Pandolfo III (1413–21) but enlarged in 1544, with a fine courtyard (used as an outdoor theatre in summer) and loggia, attributed to Jacopo Sansovino. Here is housed the MUSEO CIVICO MALATESTIANO (adm. 8.30–12.30 except Monday; summer also 17–19). In a room off the stairs is the numismatic collection with the Malatestian medals (1446) attributed to *Matteo de'Preti*, and Roman coins from the Fano mint. The paintings and prints of stage designs are by the local artist *Giacomo Torelli* (1608–78). Off the loggia the great hall has a well displayed and labelled collection of paintings by local artists of the 17C and 18C, including *Pompeo Morganti, Francesco Mancini,* and *Sebastiano Ceccarini* (1702–82). Other fine works include: *Guercino,* Guardian Angel; *Guido Reni,* Annunciation; *Domenichino,* David; *Mattia Preti,* St Nicholas; *Giovanni Santi,* Madonna and Saints. A fine polyptych by *Giambono* is to be displayed with some detached frescoes in a small room, and another room is to be opened to display more 18C local works.—On the ground floor the archaeological collection is displayed. Beneath the loggia is a large monochrome mosaic, and in five little rooms here is a good Roman collection (mosaics, architectural fragments, sculptures, bronzes, etc.), as well as a model of the arch of Augustus.

Via de'Pili leads to *Santa Maria Nuova* with a porch of 1543 and a fine marble portal of 1498 by Bernardino di Pietro da Carona. On the right side, Visitation, by *Giovanni Santi,* and Annunciation by *Perugino*; on the left side, Madonna enthroned with a *Pietà above by *Perugino*. The predella with scenes from the life of the Madonna has been attributed as an early work to *Raphael*.

From the E corner of Piazza Venti Settembre may be reached the portico of *San Francesco* (church demolished in 1931) with the tombs of Pandolfo III Malatesta (died 1427) and of his wife, Paola Bianca (died 1398).

In Via Arco d'Augusto, to the right is *San Domenico* (used for exhibitions), decorated with frescoes attributed to Ottaviano Nelli, while to the left is the *Duomo* with a restored Romanesque façade. In the elaborate Nolfi chapel in the S aisle are frescoes by Domenichino (in poor condition after numerous restorations). In the chapel to the right of the apse, Lodovico Carracci, Madonna in glory. The Romanesque square stone pulpit resting on four lions, and with large reliefs of the Life of the Virgin, is by Maestro Rainiero, the architect. At the end of the street are the *Logge di San Michele*, a pawnshop of the 15C, constructed partly with material from the neighbouring *Arco di Augusto*, a Roman triumphal arch erected in the year 2 AD (the upper storey was destroyed in 1463). Beyond the arch is the disused church of *San Michele*, with a rich portal by Bernardo da Carona (1504–13), which also acquired material from the arch (a relief of which is on the exterior). A fragment of Roman road is visible near by.—Viale della Rimembranza, to the NW, skirts a fine section of the Augustan *Walls*.

The *Rocca Malatestiana* (1452) occupies the N corner; the wall adjoining the railway is medieval with an extension beyond Piazza Rosselli by Antonio and Luca da Sangallo.

FROM FANO TO FOSSOMBRONE AND URBINO, 48km (bus). The Via Flaminia (or the parallel motorway, N3) follows the valley of the Metauro (see below), scene of bitter fighting in the assaults on the Gothic Line in August 1944.—At (13km) Calcinelli a by-road leads N to *Cartoceto* (4km) where fragments were unearthed in 1944 of gilded bronze statues of the Roman period. After their restoration and exhibition here in 1989, they have been 'held' by the local custodians in an attempt to prevent their return to the Museo Archeologico in Ancona, see below.

25km **Fossombrone**, an unusual little town of 10,200 inhab. at the foot of a hill, has a long arcaded main street with a number of rusticated palaces including *Palazzo Cattabeni*, *Palazzo Comunale*, and the *Palazzo Vescovile*. In the *Duomo* is a fresco fragment of the Madonna (1st left chapel) and, in the inner sacristy (unlocked by the sacristan), is a carved dossal by Domenico Rosselli (1480). From the little piazza here an archway and steps lead steeply up the hillside to the round 18C church of the *Madonna del Popolo* and the pretty *Corte Alta*, a Gothic building altered in 1464–70 for Federico da Montefeltro probably by Laurana, Francesco di Giorgio Martini, and Girolamo Genga. It houses the *Museo Civico Vernarecci* (for adm. apply at the Biblioteca Passionei, 2 Via Torricelli), with an archaeological section. Steps go on up to the *Rocca Malatestiana* (13–15C). Other palaces of interest lower down the hillside include the *Corte Rossa* and *Corte Bassa*.—Outside the town, on the Urbino road, is the 16C *Palazzo Pergamino* (for adm. apply at the Biblioteca Passionei) which contains the *Cesarini Collection* of good modern and contemporary Italian paintings, and a section of the *Pinacoteca Comunale* including engravings.

Scanty ruins of *Forum Sempronii*, the Roman predecessor of Fossombrone, may be seen at San Martino, 3km downstream; but the Roman *Ponte di Diocleziano* (at San Lazzaro), 2km upstream, and *Ponte di Traiano* (just S of Calmazzo) were blown up in the war.— At (30km) *Calmazzo* N73bis continues (right) for (48km) **Urbino** (see Rte 51), while N3 continues S through the *Gola del Furlo* ('forulus'), the narrow ravine of the Candigliano. The road threads a tunnel cut by Vespasian in AD 76 to replace an earlier one (still visible) of 220 BC.—At (42km) *Acqualagna* (famous for truffles) a road runs W to Città di Castello (see Rte 52).—50km *Cagli*, with a Renaissance Palazzo Comunale, preserves good Gothic work (14–15C) in three of its churches. The road goes on to (71km) *Scheggia*, and to (84km) *Gubbio*, see Rte 52.

Beyond Fano the road crosses the Metauro, the ancient *Metaurus*, where the Consuls Claudius Nero and M Livius Salinator defeated and killed Hasdrubal in 207 BC. Here in August 1944 began the assault on the Gothic line (see above).—61km *Marotta*, a bathing resort. *Mondavio*, 20km SW up the Cesano valley, has an imposing fortress begun in 1482 by Francesco di Giorgio Martini (adm. 8–12, 14–20; museum with historical tableaux).

70km **Senigallia**, with 38,000 inhabitants, is an unusual town of ancient foundation with several interesting buildings. Numerous hotels and a pier were built at the mouth of the river Misa on the other side of the railway when it became well known for its bathing beaches in the 19C. Since the 1960s it has become the most popular seaside resort in the Marches.

The town of *Sena Gallica* was founded by the Senonian Gauls and colonised by the Romans in 289 BC. Devastated in the wars between the Guelfs and the Ghibellines, Senigallia attracted the attention of Dante as a typical ruined city. Its famous fair, however, founded in the 13C, survived until the close of the 19C. It was the birthplace in 1792 of Pius IX. The huge La Fenice theatre built in 1838 by Vincenzo Ghinelli was famous for its opera productions up until 1930.

The arcaded *Via Portici Ercolani*, along the river, designed in the 18C by Alessandro Rossi, is the most attractive street. It ends at the *Foro Annonario*, a fine neo-classical marketplace in the shape of a huge horseshoe built by the local architect Pietro Ghinelli in 1837. Behind it is the well preserved *ROCCA ROVERESCA (adm. 9–12, 15–18; summer 17–22;fest. 9–13;Monday closed), built in 1480 for Giovanni Della Rovere, nephew of Sixtus IV and son-in-law of Federico of Montefeltro, by Baccio Pontelli (possibly with the help of Laurana). Traces of earlier fortifications here survive including a Roman tower. The beautifully carved portals, windows, and capitals, and a small spiral staircase all recall Palazzo Ducale in Urbino. The wide terraces above the fortifications with four massive round towers, and the dungeons, can also be visited.

In Piazza del Duca is the *Palazzetto Baviera* with palm trees in its courtyard and six superb *Ceilings decorated in stucco in 1560 by Federico Brandani (adm. 10–12, 16–18).—In the central Piazza Roma is the *Municipio* (1611, by Muzio Oddi) and a statue of Neptune, throught to be a Roman work. The *Museo Pio IX* (open 16–19 except Sunday) is housed nearby in *Palazzo Mastai*. It contains mementoes of the Pope and a small pinacoteca. The church of *La Croce* has a fine altarpiece of the Deposition by Barocci. The *Duomo* in the handsome Piazza Garibaldi dates from 1787.—The church of *Santa Maria delle Grazie*, 3km W of the town, probably designed by Baccio Pontelli contains a Madonna enthroned with Saints by Perugino. In the convent, with two fine cloisters, is a *Museum* (9–12, summer also 16–19.30) illustrating the history of agriculture in the Marches (good 19C section).

Ostra, 15km S, and *Corinaldo*, 22km SW (reached by turnings off the road to Arcevia), have their 15C fortifications, and the latter has an interesting urban structure.

At (84km) *Rocca Priora* the road crosses the Esino near its mouth; here N76 from Jesi and Fabriano (Rte 61) joins N16.—At (86km) *Falconara Marittima*, much disfigured by an oil refinery, the railway to Foligno and Rome diverges inland.—90km *Palombina*.

97km **ANCONA**, capital of the province of the same name and chief town of the Marches, is splendidly situated in an amphitheatre above the Adriatic and is the only considerable seaport on the E coast of Italy between Venice and Bari. The town is divided between the 19C district with its long broad Viali and spacious squares which extend eastwards to fill the plateau behind the headland, and the more interesting old town on Monte Guasco which overlooks the port. An earthquake in 1972 rendered over half the houses in the historical centre uninhabitable; many of them are still being restored. As a result, the old town is sparsely populated and has a desolate air. The population moved out to new suburbs in the South which have

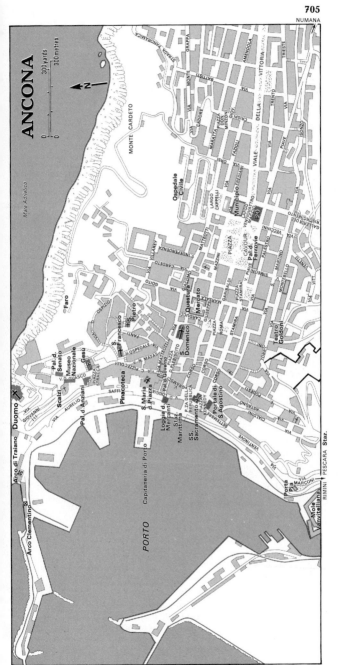

ANCONA

300 yards
300 metres

Mare Adriatico

MONTE CARDETO

Faro

Ospedale Civile

Pal. d. Senato
Museo Nazionale
Gesù
S. Pietro
S. Francesco
Scalzi
Duomo
Arco di Traiano
Arco Clementino

Pal. d. Anziani
Pinacoteca
S. Maria d. Piazza
Loggia d. Mercanti
Marittima
SS. Sacramento
Portale di Corso
S. Agostino
S. Domenico
Questura
Mercato
Municipio Eridiani
Pal. d. Ferrovie
PIAZZA CAVOUR

PORTO

Capitaneria di Porto

Porta Pia
Mole Vanvitelliana

RIMINI PESCARA Staz.

Teatro Goldoni

changed the aspect of the city. The population of the commune is 109,700.

Railway Stations. *Centrale*, nearly 2km S of the town; *Marittima* is now used only by a few slow trains serving Foligno or Rimini.

Hotels are scattered in the modern district.

Post Office, Piazza Ventiquattro Maggio.—**Tourist Office**, Via Marini (Information Office in the Railway Station).—**A.P.T.**, Via Revel.—*C.I.T.*, 117 Corso Garibaldi (with railway and ferry ticket office).

Buses from the station to Piazza della Repubblica, Piazza Cavour, and Piazza Quattro Novembre; from Piazza Cavour to Piazza Bassi; from Via Castelfidardo (near Piazza Cavour) to *Torrette, Palombina,* and *Falconara,* and *Chiaravalle.*—LOCAL BUSES to *Le Grazie, Valle Miano, Paterno,* via Sappanico to *Gallignano* and *Montesicuro,* to *Aspio, Varano,* and *Castelferretti.*—**Country Buses** to *San Benedetto del Tronto* and *Ascoli Piceno;* to *Montacuto;* via Castelfidardo to *Recanati* and to *Loreto;* to *Pescara;* via Senigallia to *Mondolfo,* to *Pergola,* and to *Sassoferrato;* via Falconara to *Jesi* and *Cupramontana;* via Jesi to *Fabriano;* via Porto Civitanova and via Osimo to *Macerata.*

Ferries to Yugoslavia (Zadar, Polo, Split, Dubrovnik), Greece (Pireaus), and Turkey. In summer, cruises, starting in Trieste via Venice and Ancona to Yugoslavia.

History. Ancona is said to have been founded c 400 BC by Syracusan exiles fleeing from the tyranny of Dionysius. Its name, meaning 'an elbow', refers to the curved promontory forming its harbour. It was a flourishing port under the Roman emperors, and was favoured by Trajan. It was one of the cities of the *Maritime Pentapolis,* the others being Fano, Pesaro, and Sinigaglia, and the Emilian city of Rimini; and later it belonged to the exarchs of Ravenna and the States of the Church; Barbarossa twice besieged it without success. Ancona became a free city in 1177 and, although for a time under the rule of the Malatesta and Albornoz families, it enjoyed its privileges until 1532, when Gonzaga occupied it with papal troops under the pretence of garrisoning it against the Turks. In 1799 it withstood a siege of Russians, Austrians, and Turks; in 1860, after another siege, lasting 11 days, it was united to Italy. On 25 May 1915, during the First World War, the port was bombarded by the Austrian fleet. In the Second World War it was occupied in September 1943 by the Germans; between October 1943, and its capture by the Polish Corps in July 1944, it underwent a series of bombardments. The populous ancient district of the Porto was destroyed. The city and port have recovered steadily, despite setbacks by floods in 1959, an earthquake in 1972, and a landslide which rendered 3600 people homeless in 1982.

The main approach from the W follows the sea front and passes the Central Station. The long Via Marconi continues straight on passing the pentagonal *Lazzaretto,* in the harbour, by Vanvitelli, now used as a mooring for the fishing fleet and private boats. Beyond the 18C *Porta Pia* Via Ventinove Settembre continues to Piazza Kennedy. Here is the splendid *Portale di Sant'Agostino* (1460–93), begun by Giorgio Orsini (Juraj Dalmatinac) for the former church of that saint. The adjacent Piazza della Repubblica, the business centre, opens on to the harbour. Here is the *Teatro Comunale delle Muse* (1826; being restored).

The modern Corso Garibaldi leads E through Piazza Roma, on the left side of which is the *Fontana del Calamo* (1560), to the spacious PIAZZA CAVOUR, the modern administrative centre. In it is a statue of Cavour (1810–61). Adjoining is Piazza Ventiquattro Maggio, with the Town Hall and Post Office. From here the broad Viale della Vittoria leads (in over a kilometre) to the *Monumento ai Caduti* (1928), an imposing white circular structure overlooking the sea.

From Piazza della Repubblica Via Gramsci leads up to the long, narrow Piazza del Plebiscito, commonly 'del Papa' from its statue of Clement XII. It rises picturesquely to the 18C church of *San Domenico,* reopened since the earthquake. It contains, in the apse, a dark Crucifixion by Titian (1558), and an Annunciation by Guercino. Nearby, across Via Matteotti, is an archway (with two lions) signed and dated 1221. At the lower end of the piazza is Palazzo del Governo, rebuilt in the 15C by Francesco di Giorgio. From its courtyard Via Pizzecolli climbs up the hill past (No. 17) *Palazzo Bosdari*, the seat of the small PINACOTECA COMUNALE FRANCESCO PODESTI and GALLERIA DELL'ARTE MODERNA (adm. 10–19 except Monday; fest. 9–13). The palace has a good courtyard and fine ceilings.

First Floor. ROOM 1. *Carlo Crivelli*, *Madonna and Child, an exquisite tiny work; sculptured heads by the Tuscan school; *Arcangelo di Cola da Camerino*, Madonna dell'Umiltà.—*Carlo da Camerino*, Dormition of the Virgin, and Coronation of the Virgin (fresco fragment).—*Neri di Bicci*, Madonna and Child in relief (an unusual work); *Carlo da Camerino*, Circumcision.—In the hall are two reliefs by *Margaritone d'Arezzo*.—R. 2. *Titian*, *Madonna and Child with two Saints and a donor, with the Venetian lagoon in the background (the 'Pala Gozzi'). This is his first signed and dated work (1520), and was restored in 1988. *Andrea del Sarto* (and pupils), Madonna and Child with the young St John; *Carlo Maratta*, Madonna and three Saints, Joseph and the wife of Potiphar.—R. 3. *Sebastiano del Piombo*, Portrait of Francesco Arsilli.—R. 4. Works by *Andrea Lilli* (1555–1610).—On the **Third Floor** are 18C works including paintings by *Francesco Podesti*. A spiral staircase gives access to the top of the palace with a dramatic view over the old deserted houses of the city to the port beyond.—**Ground Floor** (beyond the ticket office). *Guercino*, Immaculate Conception; *Lorenzo Lotto*, Madonna and Child with Saints.—The GALLERIA DELL'ARTE MODERNA is being arranged in the basement. It includes paintings by *Carlo Levi*, *Luigi Bartolini*, etc.

The church of *San Francesco delle Scale* has a rich Gothic portal by Giorgio Orsini. Above the high altar is an Assumption by Lorenzo Lotto (1550), and over the 1st altar on the right is a Baptism of Christ by Pellegrino Tibaldi. The ruined Renaissance portal to the right of the façade is all that remains of the convent destroyed in the last War. Farther on are the *Gesù* with a scenographic façade by Vanvitelli (1743; deconsecrated, and now used for exhibitions) and *Palazzo Anziani,* incorporating 13C fragments. Here is housed the Faculty of Economics and Commerce of the University of Urbino. The Gothic arches beneath the piazza, with piles of stone projectiles, are interesting.

The *Palazzo Ferretti*, higher up the street, is occupied by the ***Museo Nazionale delle Marche**, arranged on three floors. This was closed from 1972 until 1988 when it was partially reopened (daily 9–13.30; fest. 15–19.30); the arrangement may be changed when renovation is completed.

GROUND FLOOR. Mosaics (1–4C AD), Roman funerary reliefs; Hellenistic female statue from Fermo.—On the SECOND FLOOR and the floor below is an exceptionally interesting collection of antiquities, illustrating the civilisation of Picenum from prehistoric times to its penetration by the Greeks, the Gauls, and the Romans. In R. 8 are bronzes, grave goods, and cinerary urns showing early Greek influence on the district; also armour in the Etruscan style.—R. 12. Celebrated *Dinos of Amandola, a masterpiece of Ionic art.—FIRST FLOOR. R. 13. Large Vase decorated with figures of divinities (early 5C BC).—R. 14. Bronzes; massive Vase from Numana.—R16. Greek art, including a bronze Vase decorated with mermen, fish, and snakes.—RR. 18, 19, 21, and 22. Rich collection of jewellery in the Etruscan style. In R. 21 the bronze Dish with figures of warriors shaped to make handles is noteworthy.—R. 23. Handsome Vase from Numana, slender and with a stem, decorated with the head of a god.—Material from recent excavations at Recanati and San Severino is also exhibited here.—On the ground floor are to be exhibited fragments of a gilded bronze group of two equestrian and two female statues of the Giulia family, found at Cartoceto di Pergola (see above) in 1946. Part of a monument probably erected in AD 23–28, they are thought to represent Livia, mother of Tiberius, Nero Caesar, Agrippina, and Drusus III. They were restored and reconstructed in 1975–88.

To the left of the pretty 13C *Palazzo del Senato* the remains of a
Roman amphitheatre have been located. Standing at the top of Monte
Guasco and approached by narrow streets or stairs, and commanding
a magnificent view of the port, is the ***Duomo**, dedicated to St
Cyriacus, Bishop of Ancona and a martyr under Julian in 362. This
stately church sustained heavy damage in both World Wars, losing its
roof in the Second, and after restoration work was completed, it again
had to be repaired after the 1972 earthquake. It is a Romanesque and
Byzantine building, begun in the 11C, with a handsome façade and
huge porch, both added perhaps by Margaritone d'Arezzo (c 1270).
The campanile dates from before 1314. The colour of the exterior is
particularly beautiful.

The INTERIOR is designed on a Greek-cross plan. The 12-sided cupola of the 12C,
one of the earliest in Italy, is sustained by four angels in bas-relief in the
pendentives. The four arms are covered with a ship's keel roof. The unusual
transennae, decorated with *Bas-reliefs in marble on sandstone, probably date
from the 12C. Some of the columns may have belonged to a Temple of Venus,
mentioned by Juvenal as occupying this site, the remains of which have been
identified below foundations of a 6C church in the *Crypt*. In the chancel (N side)
is the tomb of Cardinal Ginelli, by *Giovanni da Traù* (1509). The *Museum*
(closed) contains fragments of 13C reliefs and the fine sarcophagus of Flavius
Gorgonius, praetor of Ancona (4C).—In the neighbouring bishop's palace Pope
Pius II died in 1464 while trying without success to start a new crusade.

From the Piazza outside is a fine view of the harbour and docks and
the splendid *Arco di Traiano*, on the old N mole of the harbour, a
triumphal arch, erected by Apollodorus (AD 115) in honour of Trajan,
who had developed the port. Close by is the *Arco Clementino*, by
Vanvitelli (18C).

At the bottom of the hill near Palazzo del Governo (see the Plan) is
the church of *Santa Maria della Piazza*, which also had to be restored
after 1972. It has a Romanesque façade (1210) with miniature blind
arcading, decorated with sculptures by 'Master Philippus'. Important
remains of mosaics from two earlier churches (5–8C), discovered
beneath the present building, may be seen on application to the
sacristan.—The *Loggia dei Mercanti*, in the street of the same name,
has a rich façade by Giorgio Orsini (1454–59), most of which has
survived (restored).

About 3km S of Ancona, to the E of N16, on the road to Verano, is *Ancona British
Military Cemetery*, with 1029 graves.
　　The hilly coast road to Porto Recanati (32km) is interesting, and it traverses the
'Riviera del Conero' with bathing beaches. At 11km a road diverges left for *Santa
Maria di Portonovo*, 2km E beside the sea, an unaltered example of a small
church of 1034–48.—The road leads round the inland side of *Monte Conero*
(572m; view), on the seaward slopes of which is the former *Abbey of San Pietro*
(Camaldulensian), with 11C and 16C buildings, reached by a side road
diverging at 18km.—20km *Sirolo*, a little resort with a pine wood.—22km
Numana, reached in summer by boat trips from Ancona, has two beaches and
the Santuario del Crocifisso, containing a venerated Byzantine Crucifixion (13C
or 14C).—32km *Porto Recanati*, see Rte 62.
　　From Ancona to *Foligno* see Rte 61; from Ancona to San Benedetto del Tronto,
see Rte 62.

61 Ancona to Foligno

A. Via Fabriano

ROAD, 131km. N76, being improved and made into dual
carriageway in places (distances are therefore approximate).—
29·5km **Jesi**.—73km **Fabriano**.—87·5km Junction with N3.—95km
Gualdo Tadino.—109km *Nocera Umbra*.—131km **Foligno**.

RAILWAY, 131km, in 1hr 40 minutes–2hrs 15 minutes, following
close to the road; the slow trains stop at all the places of
interest. This is part of the main line from Ancona to Orte and
Rome.

From Ancona the coast road to Rimini leads out of the town and at
(4km) *Torrette* the main road turns inland through several tunnels and
becomes dual cariageway before its junction with (14km) the A14
motorway at 'Ancona Nord'. A by-road leads across the Esino to
Chiaravalle (3·5km), a modern-looking town which grew up around a
late-12C Cistercian abbey (the plain brick church of which survives).
It was the birthplace of Maria Montessori (1870–1952), the educa-
tionalist. *Monte San Vito* and *Morro d'Alba*, 5km and 10km W,
preserve important remains of medieval castles. The new 'superstrada' continues along the Esino valley to the exit for (29·5km) **Jesi**,
a pleasant town (40,100 inhab.) on the Esino, the Roman Aesis.
   The splendid *Walls* date mostly from the 14C (strengthened by
Baccio Pontelli in 1488): they are well seen from the approach road,
Via Garibaldi. Via del Fortino leads into *Piazza Federico II* on the site
of the Roman Forum. Here in 1194 Constance, the last Hauteville,
ordered a tent to be set up and gave birth (at the age of 40) to the
future Emperor Frederick II. This 'public' birth established her son as
legitimate heir to the Empire. The *Duomo* stands next to the Baroque
Palazzo Balleani with four caryatids. The road descends past the
Renaissance *Palazzo della Signoria* by Francesco di Giorgio Martini
(1486–98). The handsome main façade, with the huge coat-of-arms of
the city, faces Piazza Angelo Colocci. From the fine courtyard is the
entrance to the *Library* and *Museo Civico* (open weekdays 9–12,
15–18; Saturday 9–12; 1st and 3rd Sunday, 10–12). The museum
contains Roman material, 15C sculpture, 18C majolica, etc.—Via
Pergolesi continues to an archway (the old city gate) beside the town
hall which leads into Piazza della Repubblica with the *Teatro
Pergolesi* (being restored), crowned with two huge eagles, opened in
1798 and named after the composer Giovanni Battista Pergolesi
(1710–36) who was born in Jesi.—In Via XV Settembre *Palazzo
Pianetti-Tesei*, a splendid rococo building of c 1730, now houses the
Pinacoteca Civica (open 9.30–12.30, 16–19; fest. 10–13; Monday
closed). It has a charming Italianate garden with statuary. The long
*Gallery on the first floor is decorated with stuccoes and frescoes in
pastel shades. The other rooms have scenes from the Aeneid. The
collection includes works by Pietro Paolo Agabiti da Sassoferrato
(1470–1540), and *Christ in Pietà with two angels, a 15C work by
Nicola di Maestro Antonio da Ancona, but is chiefly remarkable for its
five superb colourful *Paintings by Lorenzo Lotto: Visitation (with an
Annunciation in the lunette); Madonna enthroned with Saints; St

Lucy altarpiece; Deposition; and the Annunciation.—Via XV Settembre ends in Piazza Pergolesi with the churches of *San Nicolò* (12–13C) and *Santa Maria delle Grazie*, with a venerated 15C fresco fo the Madonna of the Misericordia.—The church of *San Marco*, outside the walls, has interesting frescoes by the Riminese school.

To the S (24km) is *Cingoli*, an ancient little town famed for its splendid views. It has an archaeological museum, and a Madonna and Saints (1539) by Lorenzo Lotto (in San Nicolò). The church of San Esuperanzio has an interesting interior, and a late Flagellation by Sebastiano del Piombo.

48km *Gli Angeli*. At *Maiolati*, in the hills 8km E, Gaspare Spontini (1774–1851), the composer, was born and died.—Beyond (52km) *Serra San Quirico* exit, N76 traverses the Gola della Rossa, a gorge in the red limestone.—56km Turning right for the *GROTTE DI FRASASSI at the end of the *Gola di Frasassi*, a limestone gorge 2km long. Beside a small thermal bath and the interesting 11C church of *San Vittore delle Chiuse*, with a Byzantine plan, is the large car park and ticket office of the remarkable caves of Frasassi which include the Grotta Grande del Vento discovered in 1971. They have become a well-known local tourist attraction in recent years. Tours, which take c 1hr, are conducted daily c every hour on the hour (more frequently in summer). The caves, with stalictites and staligmites, are unusually extensive and are still in the process of exploration.—This road goes on to *Genga* (9km), a little town with a triptych by Antonio da Fabriano in its parish church, and to Sassoferrato (14km; see below).—The main road threads three tunnels and at 64km turns sharp right below *Albacina*. In the hills c 9km E (reached from Poggio San Romualdo) is the abbey of *Val di Castro*, where St Romuald died in 1027. The crypt and chapter-house (11–12C) are the most striking parts of the surviving buildings.

N256 continues S via *Cerreto d'Esi*, an ancient walled village, to (10km) **Matelica** (357m), a small town (8100 inhab.) whose troubled history is that of its struggle against Camerino. In the church of *San Francesco* are paintings by Marco Palmezzano and Francesco da Fabriano. The *Palazzo Piersanti* has a picture gallery (for adm. apply at the tourist office in the piazza). In the main piazza, with a fountain of 1619, the medieval Palazzo Pretorio stands next to an elegant 16C loggia. The Cathedral has a bizarre 'Victorian' façade.—The road goes on via (18km) *Castelraimondo* to Camerino (see Rte 61B).

The main road (being improved to by-pass Fabriano) continues to (73km) **Fabriano** (325m), a considerable town (27,200 inhab.) noted since the 13C or 14C for its paper mills (the modern mill on the Rome road may be visited). The unusual main *PIAZZA (information office), with a fountain of 1351, is closed to traffic. It is bounded on one side by the long 17C *Loggiato San Francesco*, of 19 arches, and the *Palazzo Comunale*, and on the other by the *Palazzo Vescovile* and Clock Tower, and closed at the end by the severe *Palazzo del Podestà* (1255). The *Pinacoteca* (closed since 1979) is to be moved to the ex convent of San Domenico (see below). It contains paintings of the local school, whose most conspicuous members were Allegretto Nuzi (died 1374) and his follower Gentile da Fabriano (1370–1427); also good Flemish tapestries.—In another charming square with a fountain and the portico of the Ospedale di Santa Maria del Buon Gesù, just above the main piazza, is the *Duomo* which preserved its 14C apse and cloister through a rebuilding in 1617. It contains works by Nuzi and Orazio Gentileschi. Via Baldo leads from behind the Duomo to the 14–15C church of *San Domenico* (also called Santa Lucia) which contains a

Madonna by Francescuccio di Cecco Ghissi (1359), and frescoes by the school of Allegretto Nuzi. The former convent is being restored and a Paper Museum was opened here in 1985. There are long-term plans to rehouse the Pinacoteca here also (see above).—To the N of the main piazza is the church of *San Biagio e Romualdo* with stuccoes, 17C stalls, and an organ by Callido, and a 16C cloister. Farther N is *Sant'Agostino* with local 14C frescoes.

FROM FABRIANO TO PERGOLA, 36km, bus or railway in 40 minutes. The route runs through a fertile and well-wooded valley. 18km **Sassoferrato**, with 7400 inhabitants, is the birthplace of Giovanni Battista Salvi (1605–85), called Sassoferrato, whose Madonnas are to be seen in numerous Italian churches. The Museo Civico in the Town Hall contains finds from *Sentinum*, where the Romans defeated the Samnites and Gauls in 295 BC (ruins SW of town). Spoils from the site were used in the construction of *Santa Croce* (1km E), a 12C church with frescoes and an altarpiece of 1471.—Just before (31km) *Bellisio*, with sulphur mines, a by-road leads W to the *Eremo di Fonte Avellana* (11·5km), founded in 980 with a 12C cloister. Dante is supposed to have stayed here c 1310.—36km *Pergola*, which has several interesting churches.

About 13km NE of Sassoferrato is *Arcevia*, which preserves its medieval fortifications, and where the church of San Medardo contains two good paintings by Signorelli, and a dossal by Giovanni della Robbia.

The road continues from Fabriano and passes in a tunnel beneath a ridge marking the boundary of the Marches with Umbria. At (87·5km) this route joins N3 (from the Adriatic coast at Fano; see Rte 60), which is now followed S.—95km *Gualdo Tadino*, 2km E of its station and considerably above it (536m), stands near the site of the ancient *Tadinum*, where Narses routed the Goths and killed Totila in 552. It is the birthplace of Matteo di Pietro or da Gualdo (active 1462–98), some of whose works may be seen in the ex church of San Francesco (being restored) which now houses the Pinacoteca (for adm. apply to the Vigili Urbani in the piazza). Here, too, is a good altarpiece by L'Alunno (1471). In the main square is the Duomo with a pretty rose window and W door.—After (101km) *Gaifana*, on the plateau of the same name, the road undulates sharply and the railway reaches its highest point (483m).—109km **Nocera Umbra** is a pretty little spa (547m), with 6300 inhabitants, 3km NE of its station (396m). The waters of the *Sorgente Angelica* are bottled and sent all over Italy. Nocera is the *Nuceria Camellaria* of Pliny, and was a lordship of the Trinci family. The former Gothic church of *San Francesco* houses a good collection of paintings, including a 13C Crucifix and a Nativity and Saints, by L'Alunno. At the top of the hill stands the Duomo (rebuilt in 1448) beside a tower of the Rocca (view of the Topino valley from the terrace).—The road and railway descend the valley of the Topino and join N75 from Perugia and Assisi (Rte 56) on the by-pass (129km) for (131km) **Foligno**, see Rte 59A.

B. Via Macerata

ROAD, 146km. From Ancona to (28km) *Loreto*, see Rte 62. N77.—35km *Recanati*.—56km **Macerata**.—74km **Tolentino** (turning for **San Severino Marche**, 11km).—94km Turning for **Camerino**.—146km **Foligno**.

An alternative faster route from 'Ancona Sud' to Macerata and Tolentino is by the motorway (A14) to (32km) Civitanova Marche and then by the motorway spur along the Chienti valley to (60km) the exit for Macerata (7km N) and (74km) Tolentino (3km).

An alternative route (little difference in distance) for San
Severino Marche and Camerino leaves the coast at Porto
Recanati and runs via N571, N361, and N256 to rejoin this route
at Muccia.

RAILWAY. Branch line via Civitanova Marche to Macerata,
Tolentino, San Severino Marche and Fabriano, 96km in c 2hrs.

From Ancona to (28km) **Loreto**, see Rte 62. N77 continues to (35km)
Recanati (293m), an attractive little town (17,800 inhab.) in a commanding position between the Potenza and the Musone. It was the
birthplace of the poet Giacomo Leopardi (1798–1837), mementoes of
whom may be seen in *Palazzo Leopardi* (adm. in summer 9–12, 16–19;
15–18 in winter), and of Beniamino Gigli (1890–1957), the tenor,
whose tomb recalls the last act of *Aida*. The *Palazzo Comunale* (9–12,
16–18; festivals 10–12) contains a little Gigli museum, and a fine
collection (which may be moved, see below) of paintings by Lorenzo
Lotto, including an *Annunciation (a very unusual composition, and
in very good condition) and *Polyptych signed and dated 1508, his
early masterpiece. The massive 13C *Torre del Borgo*, opposite, bears
a bronze relief (1634) by Pier Paolo Iacometti. The church of *San
Domenico* has a marble portal of 1481 attributed to Giuliano da
Maiano and a Lotto fresco. The *Museo Diocesano* (apply to sacristan
of Duomo) contains a picture gallery. In the park of the *Villa Colloredo
Mels* is a natural history museum and a small zoo. The Musei Civici
may be moved here from Palazzo Comunale when the Villa has been
restored.—44km Junction with the road (N571) from the coast near
Porto Recanati.—This route follows the Potenza valley to (52km) the
extensive ruins (including a large theatre) of *Helvia Ricina*, a town of
dubious origin destroyed in the 5C. N361 continues via the ancient
hilltown of *Treia* (4km right) to San Severino Marche (24km; see
below). The main road crosses the river and climbs steeply up to
(56km) **MACERATA** (315m), which stands 51·5m above its station. It
is an attractive modern town of 43,500 inhabitants situated on the
crest of the hills between the Potenza and the Chienti; the views are
charming. First mentioned in 1022, it came under the rule of the
Church in 1445 and acquired a university in 1543. Macerata was the
birthplace of Pier Paolo Floriana (1585–1638), the military engineer,
who gave his name to Floriana in Malta.

Tourist Office, 12 Piazza Libertà.—*Post Office*, Via Gramsci.—**Buses** via Osimo
and via Civitanova Marche to *Ancona* in 1½–2hrs; via Porto Civitanova and
Grottammare to *Ascoli Piceno* in 2¾hrs; via Tolentino, Foligno, and Assisi to
Perugia in 3¼ hrs; via Tolentino to *Camerino* in 1¾hrs; to *Fermo* in 2hrs; to
Rome in 5½hrs.

Broad avenues encircle the old town; Viale Puccinotti on the SW,
between the 14C *Walls* and the *Giardini Diaz*, provides fine views to
the distant Monti Sibillini. The centre of the town (closed to through
traffic) is the Piazza della Libertà. At the upper end stand *Palazzo del
Comune*, with antiquities from Helvia Ricina (see above) in its
courtyard, and the graceful *Loggia dei Mercanti* attributed to Cassiano da Fabriano (1504–5). The long *Palazzo del Governo*, with a
portal of 1509 and some medieval portions, faces the *Teatro Comunale* (1767 on a design by Antonio Bibiena) and a 17C clock tower. At
the lower end of the square, beside an archway which gives access to
the 19C buildings of the University, is the bare brick façade of *San
Paolo*, with a good Baroque interior (1623–55). In the apse are frescoes
by Pier Simone Fanelli and large chiaroscuro figures by the local

painter Francesco Boniforti. The Holy Trinity in the right transept is signed and dated 1742 by Sebastiano Conca.

The steep Via Don Minzoni leads downhill past (left) the portico of the *ex-Foro Annonario* (1841; now part of the university) and (right) *Palazzo Compagnoni Marefoschi*, where on Good Friday 1772 Charles Edward Stuart married Princess Louise of Stolberg. He signed himself in the chapel register 'Charles III of Great Britain, France, and Ireland'. His mother, Clementina Sobieska (1702–35), had been born in the same palace. Beyond (left) *Palazzo Buonaccorsi*, by Giovanni Battista Contini (1705; now the Accademia) the road ends in front of the *Duomo* by Cosimo Morelli (1771–90). It contains paintings by Andrea Boscoli, and Cristoforo Unterberger, and (in the sacristy) a triptych by Allegretto Nuzi (1369). Beside an incongruous modern building is the *Madonna della Misericordia* with an elegant façade of 1735. The decorations in the graceful dark interior by Luigi Vanvitelli (1735–41) are difficult to see; they include vault frescoes and painted ovals by Francesco Mancini, two large canvases (in the presbytery) by Sebastiano Conca, and a highly venerated 15C Madonna to whom the sanctuary is dedicated.—In the SE corner of the town stands the huge *Sferisterio*, a remarkable neo-classical arena (90 × 36m) designed by Ireneo Aleandri (1820–29) where concerts are held in summer (for adm. at other times apply at the Tourist Office). Beyond lies the modern district with the station, c 1km E of which is the church of *Santa Maria delle Vergini*, by Galasso Alghisi (1550–65).

Steps descend S from the central piazza to *Santa Maria della Porta*, with an unusual Gothic doorway. Via Santa Maria leads W to the Baroque church of *San Filippo Neri* with an elaborate eliptical interior by Giovanni Battista Contini (1705–30) and a high altarpiece by Francesco Mancini. Opposite stands the 17C church of *San Giovanni* with paintings by Lanfranco, Vincenzo Pagani, and Cola dell'Amatrice (attributed). The ex-Jesuit college next door houses the library and various museums (adm. 9–13; festivals 9–12; closed Monday). Beyond a small archaeological display, is the PINACOTECA. The works include: *Carlo Maratta*, a small self-portrait; *Carlo Crivelli*, Madonna and Child dated 1470; *Giacomo da Recanati*, Madonna and Child with angels and Saints (1415); *Sassoferrato*, Head of the Madonna; *Baciccia*, Head of an apostle; *Federico Zuccari*, Deposition.—The CARRIAGE MUSEUM below has a delightful collection in excellent condition.—In Corso Matteotti, leading W from the centre, *Palazzo Mozzi* has diamond-pointed rustication. In *Palazzo Torri*, in Via Garibaldi, farther W, Napoleon stayed in 1797 and Murat in 1815.

From Macerata to Civitanova Marche, see Rte 62. At *Corridonia* (known as Mont'Olmo until 1851, and as Pausula in 1851–1931), nearly 5km S of Pie' di Ripa, the Pinacoteca next to the Collegiata contains a fine triptych by Lorenzo d'Alessandro (1481), and Madonnas by Andrea da Bologna (1372) and by Carlo Crivelli.

The road descends to (62km) *Sforzacosta* on the Chienti and joins the railway to Fabriano at *Urbisaglia* station. Below the town of Urbisaglia, 8km SW, are some remains of Roman *Urbs Salvia*, including an amphitheatre (2C AD); the road to it (N78) passes the Cistercian abbey church of *Fiastra*, a well-restored 12C building in brick, with a cloister of some 200 years later.—The motorway spur from Civitanova Marche now follows close to N77 which is being improved as far as Muccia, see below. At 68km the 14C castle of *La Rancia* is conspicuous on the left.—74km **Tolentino** (228m) gave its name to the treaty of 1797 whereby Pius VI ceded the Romagna and Avignon to Napoleon, together with many works of art. It is now a manufacturing town (16,700 inhab.) surrounded by ugly modern buildings. A pretty 13C fortified bridge leads across the Chienti to the old walled town. The BASILICA OF SAN NICOLA (closed 12–15) is dedicated to St Nicholas of Tolentino (1245–1305) born at Sant'Angelo in Pontano, 30km SE, and is a popular pilgrimage shrine.

It has a magnificent portal (1432–35) by *Nanni di Bartolo*.—In the Interior is a notable ceiling of 1628, and altarpieces by *Guercino* and *Giuseppe Lucatelli*, and a relief of the Madonna and Child attributed to *Antonio Rossellino*. On the right of the apse is an elaborate reliquary chapel finished in the 19C. The large square vaulted *CAPPELLONE DI SAN NICOLA is entirely covered with well-preserved *Frescoes on a dark blue-green ground (lights) remarkable for their composition and figure studies. They are attributed to the 'Maestro di Tolentino' of the Riminese school, and were carried out probably between 1330 and 1348. They illustrate the life of St Nicholas, whose Renaissance cenotaph and statue are also here (his tomb is in the crypt).—The charming 13–14C CLOISTER is planted with wisteria.—Attached to the basilica are four museums: the Museo Civico, with a small archaeological collection including neolithic finds; a charming collection of ex votos (15–19C); a ceramics museum (Faenza, Deruta, Casteldurante, etc.), and a Museo dell'Opera with church furniture, vestments, etc.

The rebuilt Duomo contains a large 4C sarcophagus. In the central Piazza della Libertà is the Renaissance Palazzo Parisani (with the tourist office), the ground floor of which is attributed to Antonio da Sangallo the Younger. An unusual clock tower stands next to the 13C brick apse of San Francesco. Near the piazza, in Via della Pace, is the Museo Internazionale della Caricatura, with cartoons, caricatures, etc., and a Napoleonic Museum (for adm. apply at the tourist office, 9–12.30, 16–18.30).—The Terme di Santa Lucia, 3km NW, are locally famed for their mineral waters.

A hilly by-road leads NW to **San Severino Marche** (11km), with 13,100 inhabitants. This was the ancient Septempeda (recently identified by excavations 2km E of the town at the locality of La Pieve), sacked by Totila. It is the birthplace of the anatomist Bartolomeo Eustachi (c 1500–74), after whom the Eustachian tube is named, and of the painters Lorenzo Salimbeni (c 1374–1420) and Lorenzo d'Alessandro (later 15C).

Signposts indicate the way to the MUSEO ARCHEOLOGICO and PINACOTECA (adm. 9–13.30; July–September also 16.30–18.30; closed Monday). On the ground floor is displayed prehistoric material and Roman sculptures. Upstairs is the well-arranged Pinacoteca. ROOM 1. Allegretto Nuzi, *Madonna dell'Umiltà; wood *Christ from a Deposition group by a local master of the late 13C; Paolo Veneziano (attributed), Polyptych (incomplete).—RII. Detached fresco fragments from the destroyed 14C church of San Francesco.—RIII contains detached *Frescoes by the Salimbeni including a Madonna dell'Umiltà, and a triptych with the Marriage of St Catherine by Lorenzo Salimbeni.—RIV Bernardino di Mariotto, Dead Christ; Vittorio Crivelli, Polyptych in a Gothic frame.—RV. Fra Coda da Rimini (attributed), Pietà; Nicolò L'Alunno, Polyptych; Pintoricchio, *Madonna della Pace; Bernardino di Mariotto, Madonna del Soccorso (1509; temporarily removed). The last room contains the remains of the fine inlaid wood stalls by Domenico Indivini and his school (1483–1513) from the Duomo Vecchio.—Nearby is the ancient church of San Lorenzo.—On a second hill above the town is the CASTELLO, the medieval city now virtually uninhabited. Here, beside a 14C tower is the Duomo Vecchio (11C and 14C) with frescoes by the Salimbeni and a 15C cloister.

77km Le Grazie, the 'lido' of Tolentino. The road now skirts the Lago di Borgiano and passes close to (94km) the Rocca di Varano (see below). A by-road diverges right for **Camerino** (9km), a cathedral and university town (8500 inhab.) of Umbrian origin in a splendid position in the midst of hilly countryside. At the entrance to the town is the huge church of San Venanzio with an incomplete 19C portico and a Gothic portal. Nearby is the ex-16C church of the Annunziata, attributed to Rocco da Vicenza.—In the central piazza (with the tourist office) is a statue of Sixtus V by Tiburzio Vergelli (1586). Next to the Duomo which contains interesting sculptures, is the Palazzo Arcivescovile, probably designed by Vignola, with the MUSEO DIOCESANO which houses works from churches in the territory.

ROOM I contains detached 14C frescoes by a local painter from the church of Santa Maria at Colle d'Altino, including a Crucifixion, and the *Madonna appearing to St Philip Neri by Gian Battista Tiepolo, discovered in the church of San Filippo in 1960.—RII. Girolamo di Giovanni, *Triptych dated 1453, from the Duomo (recently restored); Luca Signorelli and Bartolomeo della Gatta, *Annunciation and the Martyrdom of St Sebastian, temporarily stored here from the church of the Crocifisso in Pioraco.—RIII. *Daniele da Volterra* (attributed), Deposition, and local 13–14C wood statues.—The last two rooms contain church furniture and vestments.

The old *Palazzo Ducale* in the square is now the seat of the *University*, founded in 1727 as the successor to the 14C Studio Camerinese. The fine 15C cloister has been restored. From the balcony above the massive walls beyond the second portico there is a magnificent view. At the foot of the walls is the *Botanical Garden* founded in 1828 (for adm. apply at the Botanical Institute, 9–12, 15–18 except Saturday and fest.).

The PINACOTECA AND MUSEO CIVICO are housed in the ex-13C church of *San Francesco* (adm. daily 9–13, 17–20; in winter apply at the Tourist Office). The attractive plain interior has a clerestory and an open wood roof, a Gothic fan vault in the apse, and 14C frescoes.

Here is displayed Roman material including a fine polychrome Roman mosaic pavement (2C AD), with a geometric design and floral motif, found in 1975 in the centre of the city, and a collection of coins, and some prehistoric finds. The fine frescoes and paintings by the local painter *Girolamo di Giovanni* (active 1449–73) include an *Annunciation, a Madonna della Misericordia, and a *Madonna and Child with Angels and Saints. A frescoed chapel from the church of Patullo, with scenes from the Passion by a follower of Girolamo di Giovanni and Boccati (1477), has been reconstructed here. There are also works by the local artists *Arcangelo di Cola* and *Venanzio da Camerino*.

Camerino from c 1260 to 1539 was a fief of the Varano family, whose *Castle* survives at the top of the town as a picturesque ruin.

103·5km *Muccia* stands at the junction of another road to Camerino. The road now ascends the Chienti in a deep enclosed valley to the watershed where the river rises. There is a small cultivated plain on the borders of the Marches and Umbria just before (120km) *Colfiorito*. The pretty villages are built of the light local stone. To the N *Monte Pennino* (1571m) is seen behind Monte Acuto, while to the left of the road rises *Monte Profoglio* (1322m). Beyond the *Valico Colfiorito* (821m) for 16km the road winds downwards through the wooded river valley, in places steeply, with splendid views on the left.—146km **Foligno**, see Rte 59A.

62 Ancona to San Benedetto del Tronto

ROAD, N16, 89km.—28km **Loreto**.—46km **Civitanova Marche**.—62km *Porto San Giorgio*.—85km **Grottammare**.—89km **San Benedetto del Tronto**. Beyond Porto Recanati (31km) the road skirts the sea.

AUTOSTRADA (A14), a little shorter, roughly parallel, but further inland.

RAILWAY, along the coast, 85km in 45 minutes–1hr 15 minutes. This is part of the main line to Pescara, Foggia and Brindisi.

This route gives access to regions remarkable for their historic memories, their magnificent castles, and their austere medieval churches. Many small resorts lie on the coast, with a gently sloping sandy shore, and even some of the most attractive spots are less crowded.

Beyond Ancona the main road runs inland at first, ascending the hills behind the city to enter the valley of the Aspio. About 2km E of (12km) *Aspio Terme*, which has mineral springs, is the market town of *Camerano*, birthplace of the painter Carlo Maratta (1625–1713).—17km *Osimo-Castelfidardo* station.

About 5km W is **Osimo** (265m), the ancient *Auximium*, the metropolis of Picenum in the 5C, and now a rapidly expanding town. The 13C *Duomo* (restored) has a fine exterior and an interesting crypt; the magnificent bronze font in the adjoining baptistery is by the Iacometti (1627). In the church of *San Francesco* (now San Giuseppe da Copertino) is a Madonna and Saints by Antonio Solario (1503). In the *Palazzo Comunale* are 12 headless Roman statues and a polyptych (Coronation of the Virgin) by the Vivarini. The Baroque church of *San Marco* has a Madonna by Guercino. The *Collegio Campana*, founded 1718, had as pupils Leo XII, Pius VIII, and Aurelio Saffi. Below the walls is the *Fonte Magno*, a Roman nymphaeum of the 1C BC.—BUSES from the town to *Ancona* via Aspio in ½hr; to *Macerata* in 1hr. The Macerata road, commanding splendid views, passes the conspicuous castle of Montefiore and (21km) *Montecassiano*, a fortified hill-town preserving a town hall and a church (San Marco) by Antonio Lombardo (1467).

The road passes (24km) the battlefield of *Castelfidardo* (ossuary) where General Cialdini defeated the papal troops in 1860. The town, 6km W which gave name to the victory, manufactures piano-accordions.

28km **LORETO** a little town of 9600 inhabitants, stands on a hill (127m) to the right of the road. Since the 15C it has been one of the most famous pilgrimage resorts in the world, and, with all the usual characteristics of holy shrines, it is entirely given over to the reception of pilgrims.

According to legend the house of the Virgin (Casa di Maria or Santa Casa) was transported by angels from Nazareth in Palestine to the hill of Trsat near Rijeka, in 1291, and again, by the same agency, across the Adriatic to the laurel woods which gave name to Loreto, on 10 December 1294. Here a church was built over it, which developed into the present sumptuous structure.—Richard Crashaw (?1613–49) was canon at Loreto and died there.

Station, 2·5km SW of the town on the main Ancona-Foggia line. A bus connects with some trains to outside Porta Romana; otherwise an easy walk leads up steps past the Polish Military cemetery and Via Crucis in c 20 minutes to the town.

The town is surrounded by 16C walls, with curiously shaped battle-ments; the tall tower of the *Town Hall* is also battlemented. In the centre is the elegant *PIAZZA DELLA MADONNA, with a fountain by Carlo Maderna (restored). The piazza is closed on two sides by the arcades and loggie of the Palazzo Apostolico; on the third side is the ***Santuario della Santa Casa** (open all day 6–20), begun in 1468 at the instance of Paul II, continued by Giuliano da Maiano, fortified by Baccio Pontelli, completed by Giuliano da Sangallo, Francesco Martini, Bramante, Andrea Sansovino, and Antonio da Sangallo the Younger.

The beautiful façade (1570–87) was built by Sixtus V, whose statue, with fine bas-reliefs by Tiburzio Vergelli and Antonio Calcagni (c 1589), stands on the steps. To the left is an original campanile by Vanvitelli (1751–54); the great bell cast by Bernardo da Rimini in 1516, weighs 22,000 Roman lb. The three magnificent bronze doors of the church bear *Scenes from the Old and New Testaments by various artists (1590–1610). The bronze statue of the Madonna and Child is by Girolamo Lombardo (and pupils), 1583.

In the mystic INTERIOR (95m long) is a *Font by Tiburzio Vergelli (1600–07). The other side chapels contain copies of works by Guido Reni, Domenichino, Maratta, and others. At the end of the right aisle is the *Sagrestia di San Marco*, with a cupola adorned with *Frescoes by Melozzo da Forlì and his assistants. In the right transept are chapels with frescoes by Carlo Donati (1936–38) and Modesto Faustini (1886–90), beyond which is the *Sagrestia di San Giovanni* (light behind door on right) with cupboards attributed to Domenico Indivini da San Severino, a beautiful lavabo by Benedetto da Maiano (1484–87), a majolica pavement, and a cupola with frescoes by Luca Signorelli and his assistants (c 1479). The roofs of the sacristies have been restored since 1944. The APSE frescoes are by Lodovico Seitz (1892–1908); on the right is the tomb of Cardinal

Nicolò Caetani, by Francesco da Volterra, with a figure designed by Giovanni
Battista Della Porta.—Off the left transept, which has frescoes of 1912, are the
Sagrestia di San Matteo and Sagrestia di San Luca, with good terracotta
lunettes of the Evangelists, of the Della Robbia school.—The frescoes in the
DOME, by Cesare Maccari (1892–1908), portray the various symbols of the
Litany of Loreto; they were partly destroyed when a bomb exploded in the
drum. Beneath the dome stands the *Santa Casa (closed 13–14.30), concealed
by a beautiful marble screen, designed by Bramante, with *Bas-reliefs and
*Statues by Sansovino, Raffaello da Montelupo, Francesco da Sangallo, Giro-
lamo and Aurelio Lombardo, Giovanni Battista and Tommaso Della Porta,
Nicolò Tribolo, Domenico de Amis, and Baccio Bandinelli. The interior of the
Santa Casa consists of a rectangular chamber with rough walls (traces of Gothic
frescoes), divided into two parts by a magnificent bejewelled altar surmounted
by a cedar wood image of the Madonna and Child. The altar and statue are
restorations after a fire in 1921. From the left transept a corridor gives access to
the Treasury (closed 13–16), plundered in 1797, with frescoes by Pomarancio.

The PALAZZO APOSTOLICO was begun in 1510 by Bramante; it was
continued in 1750, but the third side was never completed. The
MUSEO and PINACOTECA inside is open 9–13, 15–18; fest. 9–13;
winter 9–13; closed Friday. One room has eight paintings by Lorenzo
Lotto, who returned here in 1552 and died in Loreto in 1556 or 1557.
These include the Presentation of Christ in the Temple, a very
unusual work and probably his last. In the Papal bedroom is a dark
Nativity, attributed to Annibale Carracci. There are some fine 17C
Brussels tapestries and a splendid collection of majolica from Urbino
from the workshop of Orazio Fontana and Patanazzi.

An archway leads through the palace to a terráce overlooking the plain with a
statue of Pope John XXIII, by Alessandro Monteleone (1964).
    BUSES run from Loreto to Ancona in 1hr; via Recanati to Macerata in 1hr; via
Appignano to Tolentino in 1¾hrs.

The road now descends to the coast. On the left appears the steep
cliffs of the seaward side of Monte Conero.—31km Porto Recanati is
a seaside resort. Santa Maria di Potenza, an 11C abbey, lies 3km S,
just inland of Macerata Mare. Recanati, 11km inland, see Rte
61B.—Road and railway now run close to the sea with the autostrada
just inland.—40km Porto Potenza Picena; the old walled village lies
8km inland (bus, going on to Macerata). Fontespina is the N
extension of (46km) Civitanova Marche, a seaside resort, the
starting-point of the road and branch-railway to Macerata and
Fabriano. A Polar Museum (at present closed) in the Palazzo
Comunale contains material collected on expeditions made between
1959 and 1969 by Silvio Zavatti. A bus runs inland to Civitanova Alta
(5km; 157m), birthplace of the poet Annibal Caro (1507–66). In the
little town is the 16C Palazzo Cesarini.

FROM CIVITANOVA MARCHE TO MACERATA, 27km; railway in 35 minutes. The
road ascends the broad valley of the Chienti, passing near the huge Romanesque church (7km; left) of *Santa Maria a Pie' di Chienti, begun in the 9C and
recently beautifully restored. The interesting bare *Interior (ask for the key at
the adjoining house) has a vaulted ambulatory at the E end, a tall matroneum,
and an open timber roof. Stairs in the outer aisles lead to the upper level. In the
apse is a huge fresco of Christ blessing and scenes of the Nativity, Adoration of
the Magi, and Presentation in the Temple, attributed to the 'Maestro di Offida'
(late 14C). The Madonna and Child in the niche and other frescoes are
attributed to the same hand.—17km (right) San Claudio al Chienti, approached
by a fine avenue of cypresses, is another interesting Romanesque church. The
unusual exterior is flanked by two round towers of the Ravenna type. The tiny
interior, on two levels, has a remarkable square Byzantine plan with semicircu-

lar apses and brick vaulting.—At the crossroads of (21km) *Pie' di Ripa* this route turns right.—27km *Macerata*, see Rte 61B.

The road crosses the Chienti and, beyond (52km) *Porto Sant'Elpidio*, the Tenna. *Sant'Elpidio a Mare*, 9km inland, is worth a visit for the works by Vittorio Crivelli in its town hall.—*Casabianca* and *Lido di Fermo* are growing resorts.—159km **Porto San Giorgio** is an unsophisticated resort with numerous small hotels and a 13C castle, connected by bus with Fermo, Macerata, Ascoli Piceno, etc.

FROM PORTO SAN GIORGIO TO AMANDOLA, 55km; frequent bus service to Fermo in ½hr; bus via Fermo and Amandola in 1hr.—7km **Fermo** (319m) is a thriving traffic-ridden hill-top town (34,000 inhab.). It was the *Firmum* of Picenum, was a provincial capital in the 10C and afterwards a Guelf commune at war with Ascoli. It was later subject to the Euffreducci and from 1549 to the Church.

The *Girfalco*, or esplanade, on the top of the hill, commands a magnificent *View of the Monti Sibillini and the Gran Sasso. Here is the *Duomo* (open Sunday; other days, 16–20, or ring for the sacristan). It was rebuilt by Cosimo Morelli in 1789, but retains an imposing 13–14C façade, and, inside, considerable remains of a 5C mosaic pavement. It contains a funerary monument by Tura da Imola (1366), a Greek Byzantine Icon of the Madonna, and (in the sacristy) the *Chasuble of St Thomas Becket (presented to a bishop of Fermo), made from a Moorish silk embroidery woven at Almeria in 1116.—In the arcaded Piazza del Popolo are the 16C *Palazzo degli Studi*, the seat of a university suppressed in 1826 and now the Biblioteca Comunale, and *Palazzo dei Priori* with a 15–16C exterior and a statue over the door of Sixtus V by Accursio Baldi (1590). It houses the PINACOTECA CIVICA (adm. 10.30–12, 17–19). ROOM I. *Painter of the 15C Marches school*, *Madonna and Child enthroned with angels; *Andrea da Bologna*, Polyptych (signed and dated 1369) in a contemporary frame; *Jacobello del Fiore*, *Scenes from the life of St Lucy; *Francesco Ghissi*, Madonna dell'Umiltà; *Jacopo da Bonomo*, Panels from a polyptych.—RII. *Rubens*, *Nativity, painted in Rome in 1608, and the most precious work in the collection; *Giovanni Lanfranco*, Pentecost.—RIII contains a 15C Flemish tapestry of the *Annunciation on a design by *Giusto di Gand*.—Near the Palazzo Apostolico, in the piazza, is a local *Antiquarium* in a Roman warehouse of the Augustan period (open on weekdays). Nearby are the *Teatro dell'Aquila* (1780, by Cosimo Morelli) and the church of *San Domenico* (1233), with Gothic stalls, and, beneath the former convent, the *Piscina Epuratoria*, dating from AD 41–60.—At the entrance to the town, close to the Barriera Marina (with a view of the Duomo on the skyline above), is *San Francesco* (1240) with a fine exterior and containing the Euffreducci monument (1527). Towards the Porta Santa Lucia are the churches of *San Zenone* with a Romanesque portal (1186) and a campanile of 1222, and *Sant'Agostino*, partly Romanesque with early frescoes. Next door is the *Oratory of Santa Monica* with an interesting fresco cycle of the early 15C.

The road descends into the wide and fertile valley of the Tenna.—At (30km) *Piane di Falerone*, near the river, are the picturesque ruins of the theatre of the ancient *Faleria*. To the N beyond (4km) the village of *Falerone*, is (13km) *Massa Fermana*, a walled village with a 14C town-gate, and, in the (recent) parish church a *Polyptych by Carlo Crivelli, representing the Madonna, between Saints John the Baptist, Lawrence, Sylvester, and Francis (signed and dated 1468; in restoration), and a painting by Vittorio Crivelli on the same subject, but with St Rufinus taking the place of St John. In the Pinacoteca is a Nativity by Vincenzo Pagani.—55km **Amandola** (550m) was founded in 1248. The church of *Sant'Agostino* has a fine portal by Marino Cedrini of Venice and a graceful campanile (both dating from 1468). *San Francesco* has a portal of 1423 and good frescoes. The town (4400 inhab.), within its ancient walls, lies on N78 at the foot of the MONTI SIBILLINI, the watershed between the Adriatic and Tyrrhenian Seas. There are long term plans to protect this beautiful area of wooded mountains as a National Park. The chain, 19km long, extends from *Monte Rotondo* (1829m) on the N to *Monte Vettore* (2449m) on the S, and includes many peaks over 1830m.— BUSES run from Amandola to Ascoli Piceno in 1½hrs.

Sarnano, 12km NW of Amandola, is a spa and summer resort, with isolated hotels below the peaks to the W. The Sasso Tetto (1287m) has winter sports facilities.

Along this prolific coast, fishing boats ('paranze') may be seen in couples, with a net suspended between them. These craft, with their tall, parti-coloured sails on the blue sea, are a favourite subject with artists.—The road crosses the Aso before (72km) *Pedaso*; a road ascends the valley for Amandola.—81km *Cupramarittima* preserves the name of the goddess Cupra (see below); it is adjoined by a modern resort.—85km **Grottammare**, with a fine sandy beach, was the birthplace in 1521 of Pope Sixtus V. About 1km S is a ruined temple of Cupra, an Etruscan Sabine goddess perhaps of oriental origin.

About 13km W (bus) is **Ripatransone** (494m), a little town (5300 inhab.) with a notably wide *Panorama*. Inhabited perhaps by the same Umbrians that populated Cupra, this town waged continual warfare against Fermo. The walls and gates of the ancient 'urbs' are still extant. The *Duomo*, by Gaspare Guerra (1597), contains a San Carlo attributed to Guercino and wood carvings. In the *Palazzo Comunale*, is an archaeological museum containing antiquities from Umbrian tombs, including fibulae, helmets, and armlets. The *Palazzo del Podestà* dates from 1304. A road descends to the right, passing many 15–18C houses, to the church of *San Filippo*, with its fine interior (1680–1722) by Lucio Bonomi. The Palazzo Bonomi-Gera now houses the *Pinacoteca* (panel paintings by Vincenzo Pagani and Vittorio Crivelli; ceramics, including fragments of an altar by Mattia Della Robbia, etc.).—About 20km farther W is *Montalto Marche*, the ancestral home of Sixtus V (see above) and the birthplace of the architect Giuseppe Sacconi (1853–1905). Sixtus V founded the beautiful cathedral (1586).

Other buses run from Grottammare to *Ascoli* in 1¼hrs; to *Ancona* in 2hrs; to *Macerata*, etc.

89km **San Benedetto del Tronto** is an important fishing centre and a pleasant bathing resort, with 42,000 inhabitants. The Promenade is superbly planted with palms and oleanders. From San Benedetto del Tronto to Rome, see Rte 64. For the area further S, see 'Blue Guide Southern Italy'.

63 Rome to Civitavecchia and Tarquinia

ROAD, N1 (VIA AURELIA), 92km. From Rome to (41km) *Cerveteri*, see 'Blue Guide Rome'.—72km **Civitavecchia**.—92km **Tarquinia**.

AUTOSTRADA, A12, 86km, branching from the Fiumicino autostrada and ending 10km S of Tarquinia, roughly parallel to the road.

RAILWAY, 101km in c 1hr 10 minutes, part of the main line to Pisa, Genoa, and Turin. Only the slow trains stop at Tarquinia.

From Rome to (41km) *Cerveteri*, see 'Blue Guide Rome'. Beyond the turning for Cerveteri the Via Aurelia approaches the sea, crossing the railway. On the right the conical peaks of the Tolfa rise to 430m.—53km **Santa Severa**, a seaside resort, occupies the site of *Pyrgi*, a Pelasgic town, once the chief port of Caere (Cerveteri).

Pyrgi was famous in antiquity for its Temple of Juno Lucina, sacked by the elder Dionysius of Syracuse in 384 BC. In the locality are the ruins of a villa said to have been that of Nero's father Domitius Ahenobarbus (consul AD 32). The concentric *Castle*, founded in the 12C and largely rebuilt in the 16C. Approached through 18C walls, it encloses a little village inhabited in summer by holiday-makers. Between its second and third wards is the 16C church of the Assunta, and by the outer ward of the 14C is a little chapel with restored 15C frescoes. On the seaward side of the Castle, and connected with it by a wooden bridge, is an imposing cylindrical tower built over the foundations of a Norman fort. Here remains of the polygonal wall of the Roman castrum are visible; the port is now under water. In 1957–64 excavations S of the castle (approached by a road right, outside the castle walls) revealed the foundations of two Etruscan temples. The larger (Temple A), of the end of the Archaic period, has a large colonnaded pronaos and three cellae; the second (Temple B), smaller, with a single elongated cella, is older (c 500 BC). Associated painted terracotta reliefs of a Gigantomachia (showing marked Greek influence) have been found; most important, in a sacred area between the temples, were discovered three folded *Sheets of gold leaf, with inscriptions in Phoenician and Etruscan recording the dedication to Astarte (Uni) by Thefarie Velianus, tyrant of Cære (now in the Museo Nazionale di Villa Giulia in Rome). A hoard of Athenian 'owls' and Syracusan coins may have belonged to the sanctuary treasury looted by Dionysius. An *Antiquarium* houses finds from the site including part of the sculptural decoration from the temples.

The road next passes the *Grottini*, a seaside colony for children, founded by Pius X.—62km **Santa Marinella** is another attractive seaside resort. It occupies the site of the Roman station of *Ad Punicum* at the end of Cape Linaro. On a promontory E of the town in 1966 was unearthed a lead plaque bearing one of the longest known Etruscan inscriptions. This came from a sanctuary (6C BC) of Minerva. Here also is a 15C *Castle* of the Odescalchi. On the right the summits of the Tolfa range are still visible; prominent, as the road passes the 'Boys' Town' (Repubblica dei Ragazzi) founded in 1945, is Monte Paradiso (327m).

72km **Civitavecchia**, a town of 44,100 inhab., is the modern port of Rome and a base of sea communication with Sardinia. It has been largely rebuilt since the war, and is visited for its renowned fish restaurants.

Railway Stations. *Marittima*, on the dockside (with trains to Rome for those arriving by sea). Trains to the North pass through the main railway station only.

Buses to *Rome*; also to *Tolfa*; via Tarquinia to *Montalto di Castro, Canino*, and *Cellere*; to *Tuscania*; to *Monte Romano, Vetralla*, and *Viterbo*; to *Santa Marinella*, and *Santa Severa*.

Car Ferries of the Tirrenia line and Ferrovia dello Stato daily to Sardinia (most of them overnight, with sleeping berths; to *Olbia, Cagliari* and *Porto Torres*, and *Golfo Aranci*). It is essential to book well in advance in summer.

History. After the silting up of Ostia and to supplement his new harbour at Porto, Trajan instructed the architect Apollodorus c 106 to build a new port here, called Centum Cellæ. Among its buildings was a splendid imperial villa, described by the younger Pliny (see below). In 828 the port was destroyed by the Saracens and the inhabitants fled inland. In 855 Pope Leo IV established for them the village of Leopoli or Centocelle, which still exists, 14·5km N of the port. Soon the population returned to their original home, which they now called *Civitas Vetula*, italianised into *Civitavecchia*. From then on until modern times the city was included in the Papal States. Under the Renaissance popes Civitavecchia became one of the most important of the Mediterranean seaports. Gregory XII kept the pontifical fleet here; Sixtus V built the lighthouse; and Alexander VII commissioned Bernini to build the dock basin (both of them destroyed in the War). Stendhal was consul here (after 1831), and wrote 'The Life of Henri Brulard'—in fact an autobiography.

The **Forte Michelangelo** (no adm.), on the harbour, begun by Bramante in 1508 and continued by Antonio da Sangallo the Younger, was completed by Michelangelo. The central basin of Trajan's harbour and the docks are still of interest. The *Museo Archeologico Nazionale* (open 9–14 except Monday), in Largo Plebiscito, contains a good collection of local archaeological finds.

Frescoes in the *Franciscan Church*, by the Japanese artist Hasegawa (1950–54) commemorate the Franciscan missionaries to Japan, who sailed from Civitavecchia and were martyred with many converts at Nagasaki in 1597.

About 4·5km E, beyond the autostrada entrance, are the ruins of the so-called *Terme Taurine*, now identified as part of the large imperial villa mentioned by the younger Pliny, and used by Trajan, Marcus Aurelius, and Commodus. The baths were fed by the warm sulphur-impregnated waters, which are still effective in the treatment of rheumatism.

From Civitavecchia a hilly road winds inland to (22km) *Tolfa*, built on the ruins of an Etruscan town (finds are displayed in the small Museo Civico, open 9–14 except Monday). Farther on, but just off the road (S), are (36km) the ferruginous *Bagni di Stigliano*.—45km *Manziana* is on the Rome-Viterbo railway (via Capranica-Sutri).

Beyond Civitavecchia the road bears inland, with the railway now to seaward.—85km The road crosses the Mignone, flowing down from the volcanic Tolfa range. At the mouth of the stream is *Torre Bertolda*, or *Sant'Agostino*, supposed to be the spot where St Augustine found the child pouring the water of the sea into a hole in the sand, which he saw as the image of a finite conception of infinity.—2km farther, N1 bis diverges right via (14km) *Monte Romano* for (30km) *Vetralla* and (43km) *Viterbo* (Rte 57).

92km **TARQUINIA** stands on a hill (145m) E of the Via Aurelia, 3km from its railway station, and 5km from the sea. The town (12,300 inhab.), called *Corneto* until 1922, is close to the Etruscan *Tarxuna* or *Tarxna* which was built on another hill to the E. It is a pleasant town and its numerous towers give it a characteristic air. The ancient city and its great necropolis have yielded some of the most important Etruscan antiquities yet discovered.

History. *Tarxuna* (or *Tarxna*), cradle of the 'great house of Tarquin', was one of the 12 Etruscan cities and probably the head of the Etruscan Confederation. It is said to have been founded by Tarchon, son or brother of the Lydian prince Tyrrhenus, who is made by Virgil to help Aeneas against Turnus. According to legend here settled Demaratus of Corinth (c 700 BC) whose son, Lucius Tarquinius Priscus, became the fifth king of Rome. After the 3C BC it became a

Railway Station

Roman colony and municipium and its power declined. In 181 the Romany colony of Gavisca was founded on the coast. After invasions by the Lombards and Saracens, in the 7C it was deserted and the inhabitants founded *Corneto* on the opposite hill. In 1489 the first recorded archaeological 'dig' in modern times took place here.

At the entrance to the town (Piazza Cavour), with the Tourist Office, and an information office of the Comune (organised tours of the city) stands the Gothic-Renaissance *Palazzo Vitelleschi* (1436–39), with a fine courtyard, built by Cardinal Giovanni Vitelleschi. It contains the *Museo Nazionale Tarquiniese (adm. 9–14; summer usually 9–19; always closed Monday). The second floor has been closed for restoration for many years.

In the courtyard are a collection of sarcophagi and sculptured reliefs. Two rooms off the courtyard were reopened in 1988 to display some important Etruscan sarcophaghi, including the *Sarcophagus of Laris Palenas, who holds a scroll on which is an Etruscan inscription, the sarcophagus of the so-called Magnate, which retains much of its original polychrome work, and the sarcophagus of the *Obesus, surmounted by a splendid figure of the defunct.

FIRST FLOOR. Room at the top of the stairs (left): beautifully displayed polychrome *Group of two winged horses (4–3C) found on the Acropolis.—In rooms off the LOGGIA are displayed vases in chronological order. ROOM I (at the far end). Villanovan material (9–8C BC) from the necropolis of Monterozzi, including a cinerary urn in the shape of a hut, and an incense burner in the form of a carriage with a deer's head.—RII. Material from the tomb of Boccoris (7C BC) including a glass Egyptian vase.—RIII. Objects imported from Egypt and the East; series of small bronze griffins' heads (7C BC).—RIV contains Corinthian ware, bucchero vases, some with decoration in relief (6C BC), and black-figured amphorae.—RV. Fine black-figure vases of the 6C BC by various artists identified by their individual styles.—RVI. Red-figure Attic kylixes and kraters (500–480 BC) and two oinochoe by the Berlin painter.—The beautiful GREAT HALL contains the most precious red-figure Attic vases: *Stamnos by the Berlin painter (480–470 BC); *Amphora signed by Phintias (510–500 BC) with Apollo and Heracles fighting for the tripod and Dionysus amid satyrs and maenads; *Kylix attributed to Oltos and Euxitheos, with a meeting of the gods, and Dionysos in a quadriga between satyrs and maenads; a very well-preserved *Rhyton shaped like a woman's head by Charinos (510–500 BC); a kylix by Douris (500–490 BC), and a krater by the Kleophrades painter (500–490 BC).—In two connecting rooms off the great hall: votive terracottas from the Ara della Regina (3–2 BC), anatomical ex votos; red-figure vases (end of the 4C BC) including three askoi in the form of birds.—Roman glass and coins; Etruscan jewellery and bronze mirrors, candlesticks, utensils, ceramics with relief decoration, black-varnished ceramics, etc.

SECOND FLOOR (closed for many years). At the N end of the loggia (right) is the tomb of Aurelio Mezzopane (1500), and a short series of rooms containing sculptured remains, and a small collection of paintings, including portraits of Count Nicolò Soderini and Pius VII by Batoni and Camuccini. The second room constitutes the CAPPELLA GENTILIZIA and the third contains a fine painted ceiling, and the remains of 15C *Frescoes. In the large SALONE D'ARMI stand five tombs, the frescoes (restored) having been removed from their original sites and re-erected to their original shape, including the *Tomba del Triclinio, most famous of all Tarquinian tombs.—For the Etruscan Necropolis, c 1·5km from the Museum, see below.

Via Mazzini leads to the *Duomo*, interesting for its good frescoes in the sanctuary (1508) by Antonio da Viterbo (Pastura), showing the influence of Signorelli. Via di Porta Castello continues through a fine double gateway in the walls. From here there is a splendid view of the tallest and best preserved tower in the city standing beside the Romanesque church of *SANTA MARIA DI CASTELLO, with the Porta Castello beside them which leads out into the open country. The church was begun in 1121 and consecrated in 1208. The façade contains Cosmatesque work (very ruined) signed by Pietro di Ranuccio (1143). From the terrace beside the pretty apse there is a good view of the valley. The fine interior (unlocked by the custodian who lives in the house with steps beside the tower) has an interesting plan with a rose window and pretty dome in the nave. It contains remains of a Cosmatesque pergamum by Giovanni di Guittone (1208; some of the sculptures were stolen in 1969), two plutei and a ciborium by Giovanni and Guittone, sons of Nicolò Ranucci (1168), a font for total immersion, and parts of the Cosmatesque pavement.

From Via di Porta Castello signs indicate the way to the medieval district and *San Martino*, a small Romanesque church, with an interesting exterior, beside a tower. Nearby is *Santissima Annunziata* (closed) with a good rose window and portal. From here a short road leads to the tiny disused church of *San Salvatore* and the abandoned church of *San Giacomo* on a promontory on the edge of the cliff. From here there is a view of the valley, and of Santa Maria di Castello and the towers of the old city. Downhill, in the centre of the town, is the 13C church of *San Pancrazio* (disused; for adm. enquire at the Tourist Office) with an interesting exterior, a rose window, and a campanile, near the *Palazzo dei Priori* with a fine arch and four towers. Nearby, in the large Piazza Matteotti with an 18C fountain, is the *Municipio*, with Romanesque material incorporated into the fabric of the building behind. Via Porta Tarquinia leads to the 13C church and convent of *San Francesco*.

Near Piazza Cavour (by the Museum, see above) is the church of *San Giovanni* which has a good early-Gothic N aisle and apse with a fan vault. In Via di Valverde below the piazza is the Romanesque church of *Santa Maria di Valverde*, with a Byzantine Madonna.

The road leads on from San Francesco, through the Porta Tarquinia, along Via Ripagretta to the vast ***Necropolis of Tarquinia** (known as 'Monterozzi'; open at the same times as the Museum, see above). The tombs are of immense interest and value for their painted interiors.

The paintings range from the first half of the 6C to the 2C BC. The various phases are all represented: the Ionic influence of the 6C, the Attic influence of the 5C and, after a static period, the revival of the 4C, with the subsequent slow decadence. Unfortunately the opening of the tombs has, in many instances, hastened their deterioration; in one tomb, opened in 1823, the excavators found a warrior stretched on a bier who crumbled away on the admission of fresh air. So far 5735 tombs have been found, of which 62 are painted. In 1986 an important painted tomb was discovered, known as the *Tomba dei Demoni Blu*. Weather, neglect, and misuse have all contributed to their general ruin. The tombs are now protected with modern huts and kept locked. Many of them are closed for reasons of conservation, and some of them are closed for restoration.

In 1990 only the following tombs were open: on Tuesday, Thursday, and Saturday: the Tomba dei Giocolieri, Tomb No. 1701, the Tomba Cardarelli, and Tomb No. 5513; on Wednesday, Friday, and Sunday: the Tomba del Padiglione della Caccia, the Tomba delle Lionesse, the Tomba della Caccia e Pesca, and the Tomba del Fiore di Loto.

The *Tomba dei Giocolieri* (end of 6C, early 5C) has the standing figure of the defunct, an old man and boy, and the portrait of a dancing girl; the *Tomba Cardarelli* (end of 6C) has four groups of figures, probably depicted just after the funerary banquet; the *Tomba del Padiglione della Caccia* (early 4C) has painted hangings with hunting trophies, and a colourful frieze and ceiling; the *Tomba delle Leonesse* (6C) has lionesses or panthers, dolphins in the sea, and banqueting scenes; the *Tomba della Caccia e Pesca* (mid 6C), is a large tomb with two rooms with scenes of the chase and fishing; the *Tomba del Fiore di Loto* (mid 6C) has colourful paintings including a lotus flower.

Other notable tombs (none of them open in 1990) in the necropolis, some of them near the modern cemetery, and others further from the town gate, include: the Tomb of the *Pulzella* (Young Girl, mid 5C), with a banqueting scene (damaged in the War); the *Leopardi* (5C) with more banqueting scenes and musicians; the *Baccanti* (end of 6C) with a Bacchic scene; the *Tifone* (2C), of great size, with a central column, preceded by an altar on which is a painted figure of a demon; the *Scudi* (3C) with painted shields and banqueting scenes; the *Cardinale* (probably late 2C), restored in 1799 by Cardinal Garampi, the largest of all with four columns supporting a coffered ceiling; the *Orco (Ogre; first half of the 4C), with scenes of the inferno and the beautiful portrait head of a girl of the Velcha family.—The Tomb of the *Barone (end of 6C), with figures of men and women standing and of youths on horseback; the *due Bighe* (chariots; 5C); the *Auguri or augurs (mid 6C) with a cruel scene of a blindfold man tortured by the attacks of a fierce dog; *Tori (1st half of the 6C), in good preservation, with a painting of Achilles lying in wait for Troilus.

The necropolis road reaches in 4km the junction with the Monte Romano road (see above), where the turning on the left passes long stretches of aqueduct (first built by the Romans, adapted in the medieval period, and still in use). After a further 3km a rough road (yellow signpost) diverges left for the ETRUSCAN ACROPOLIS on the hill called Pian di Civita (locally famous for its mushrooms). After 1·5km another road (signposted) branches left for 600m. Here a sign indicates a path (left) which leads up in 100m to the so-called *Ara della Regina*, the impressive basement of a large temple or sacred area (77 × 35m). Here were found the Winged Horses, now in the museum. Skirting the hill are tracts of the old town walls with several gates, and the views are particularly fine. Excavations still in progress have revealed remains of Etruscan and Roman buildings.

Lido di Tarquinia, 6km SW of Tarquinia, has a long sandy beach. To the S are remains of Porto Celmentino, the port of the Roman *Gravisca*, destroyed in 1449 (excavations were begun in 1969). The extensive salt-flats nearby have been declared a bird sanctuary.

FROM TARQUINIA TO TUSCANIA, 24km. A secondary road runs NE from Tarquinia across the low hills. For several kilometres before Tuscania it is lined with fine cypresses. **Tuscania**, known until 1911 as *Toscanella*, is an attractively situated little town, retaining its old walls. The medieval buildings have been carefully restored since they were damaged in an earthquake in 1971 which left 30 dead. Within the walls the *Duomo* contains a polyptych by Andrea di Bartolo, St Bernard with angels by Sano di Pietro, and statues from a lost 15C altarpiece (all of these were removed to Palazzo Vescovile after the earthquake). In the Largo della Pace a ruined chapel (ask locally for the key) contains extensive 15C frescoes. In Via XX Settembre is the interesting church of *Santa Maria della Rosa*, Romanesque and Gothic. Just outside Porta San Marco the 15C church of *Santa Maria del Riposo* has a richly decorated portal and an attractive cloister. The *Museo Nazionale Archaeologico* has been opened in the convent here (adm. 9–13.30, 14.40–17, or 16–19 in summer; closed Monday). Four rooms have so far been opened to display interesting material from local necropoli. About 1·5km from the Museum is the Etruscan *Tomba della Regina*, with an intricate plan (shown by a custodian; enquire at the museum). —On a hill to the E of the town stands *SAN PIETRO (opened by a custodian), one of the most important churches of its date in Italy. It stands beside two medieval towers, the ruined remains of the Bishop's palace, and excavations of Etruscan, Roman, and medieval buildings. The apse retains externally its 8C appearance, as does much of the interior, though the building was altered in the 12C and given its splendid Cosmatesque *Façade (in which is embedded an Etruscan figure) in the 13C. The apse frescoes date from the 12C, the ciborium from 1093, and the altar screen and ambone are composed of 7–8C sculpted panels. There are substantial remains of a fine Cosmatesque pavement. The fine crypt has 20 columns of classical date, and a 14C fresco of local saints.—Lower down is the church of *SANTA MARIA MAGGIORE, another fine church begun in the 8C, built on the ruins of a Roman temple, but restyled and reconsecrated in 1207. A Romanesque tower stands in front of the good façade similar to that of San Pietro with a fine central portal. The interior (opened by a custodian, 8–12, 14–17 or 19) contains a fine Gothic ciborium with vault frescoes of the four evangelists, and interesting fresco fragments (13C and 14C) in the apse (Last Judgement) and aisles. The pulpit is composed of early and late Romanesque panels. The octagonal font was designed for total immersion.— Viterbo, see Rte 57, lies 24km E.

FROM TARQUINIA TO VULCI, 28km. The Via Aurelia (now dual carriageway) continues N to (17km) *Montalto di Castro* where the construction (halted in 1988) of a nuclear power station (the second largest in Italy; visitors centre open to the public) has caused much controversy in recent years. The medieval castle of Montalto belonged to the Guglielmi. A pretty by-road (signposted) diverges right from the Aurelia just beyond the river Fiora. It traverses fertile open country with 'hedges' of olive trees and vineyards to (28km) *Ponte dell'Abbadia*, one of the most remarkable ancient survivals in Italy. The foundations of this steeply hump-backed bridge which spans the ravine of the river Fiora are probably Roman, built with Etruscan material. The splendid central arch is 30m high. The medieval footpath across the bridge survives. **Vulci**, one of the most important cities of the Etruscans, was situated on the W side of the river; scanty remains of a temple, houses, etc. have been found (guided tours from the Casale dell'Osteria; c 2km from the Museum). Beside the bridge is the so-called **Abbadia**, a picturesque moated medieval castle, built of dark stone, restored to house an archaeological MUSEUM (open 9–13, 16–19; winter, 10–16; closed Monday).

The room on the ground floor contains two cases of proto-Villanovian ware from Ischia di Castro (10C BC), and material of the Rinaldone culture. The exhibits from Vulci include an urn in the form of a hut (9C BC), and sculpture from the necropolis.—FIRST FLOOR. RI. Finds from the necropolis (8C and 7C BC); bucchero ware (6C); an Attic red-figure kylix (510–500 BC); an Attic black-figure amphora with the birth of Athena (540–530 BC); and interesting material from the Panatenaica tomb. RII contains finds from the city including Roman terracotta heads from the N gate; and Etruscan and Roman small bronzes.—RRIII and IV. Material from the necropolis, including a fine black-figure amphora and vases (500 BC), and bucchero ware.

The immense NECROPOLIS of Vulci (at present closed to the public; enquire at the Museum) extends for many kilometres on the E side of the river and has yielded innumerable vases, bronzes, and other antiquities now scattered in museums all over the world. The necropolis is dominated by the *Cuccumella*, a gigantic hypogeum surrounded by a wall and containing a maze of passages, walls, and staircases. The smaller 'Tumulo della Cuccumelletta' was partially restored in 1985.

FROM MONTALTO TO VALENTANO (N312), 35km. The lonely road runs NE with arches of an aqueduct on the left, and, after 8km, leaves on the left a road to the ruins of Vulci (see above).—20km *Canino*, with an interesting Collegiata.—From (35km) *Valentano*, with a Farnese castle, a road on the right, skirting the S shore of the Lago di Bolsena, leads to Viterbo (see Rte 57). The left branch keeps above the W side of the lake for Acquapendente (Rte 57).

For the continuation of the Via Aurelia N of Tarquinia to Monte Argentario, Grosseto, Livorno, and Pisa, see Rte 54.

64 San Benedetto del Tronto to Rome

ROAD, 228km, N16, then N4 (VIA SALARIA), being improved in places. An autostrada spur from the Adriatic motorway (A14) runs parallel to N4 S of the river Tronto as far as Ascoli Piceno.—32km **Ascoli Piceno**.—52km *Acquasanta Terme*.—123km *Antrodoco*.—137km *Cittaducale*.—147km **Rieti**.—228km **Rome**.

BUSES from San Benedetto to Ascoli Piceno (c every 30 minutes) in 50 minutes; from Ascoli to Rome, twice daily, in 4½hrs; more frequently from Rieti to Rome in 2–3½hrs.

N16 leads S and at (4km) *Porto d'Ascoli* Via Salaria (N4) turns right. This ancient and scenically attractive highway follows the railway to Ascoli and the river Tronto on the left.—20km *Offida Station*. A bus follows a by-road N to *Offida* (11km; 293m), a small town with an aracaded Municipio (15C; with an archaeological museum); the 14C brick church of Santa Maria della Rocca has contemporary frescoes in its large crypt. Lace-making is a traditional local craft.

32km **ASCOLI PICENO** (154m; 55,200 inhab.) is the capital of its province, one of four making up the region of the Marches. Surrounded by hills, at the confluence of the Tronto and the Castellano, it is a town of medieval aspect built largely of travertine.

Tourist Office, Corso Mazzini.—**Post Office**, Via Crispi.—**Buses** to Rome (see above); to *San Benedetto del Tronto*; also to *Ancona*; to *Teramo*; via San Benedetto del Tronto, Macerata, Tolentino, Foligno and Assisi, to *Perugia*; to *Acquasanta Terme*; and to *Valle Castellana*.—**Railway** to *San Benedetto del Tronto*, 33km in c 40 minutes.—**Festivals**. Carnival with dancing in the streets on Shrove Tuesday; *Quintana* (first Sunday in August), costume procession and jousting.

History. *Asculum Picenum*, a Sabine town, at first allied with Rome but afterwards at the head of the Italic League against her, was destroyed in 89 BC by Pompeius Strabo, father of Pompey the Great. An independent commune in 1185, it was taken in 1242 by Frederick II, and in 1504 it put itself under the protection of the Holy See. In 1944 the retreating Germans blew up all the bridges.—About 1486 Carlo Crivelli initiated here an artistic movement which culminated with Nicolò Filostesio, generally known as Cola dell'Amatrice, later a follower of Signorelli. Pietro Vannini here brought the goldsmith's art to great perfection, while the art of wood-carving also was cultivated. Ascoli was the birthplace of Girolamo Masci (Pope Nicholas IV; c 1230–92, born at Lisciano, 5km S) and of the poet Francesco Stabili, called Cecco d'Ascoli, burned as an astrologer at Florence in 1327.

From the restored Ponte Maggiore (1373) over the Castellano there is a view of the *Fortezza Malatesta*, enlarged by Sangallo the Younger. On the left, behind the Giardino Pubblico, is the little church of *San Vittore* (10–16C), from which most of the 14C frescoes have been detached and are now on display at the Museo Diocesano (see below). Corso Vittorio Emanuele ends between the Baptistery and the Duomo at the handsome PIAZZA DELL'ARRINGO, now sadly disturbed by through traffic. The octagonal 12C *Baptistery (for admission, apply at the Curia) is absurdly isolated between two busy roads. The **Duomo** (*Sant'Emidio*), a 12C building reconstructed in 1482, has a magnificent unfinished façade of 1532–39, by Cola dell'Amatrice.

The INTERIOR contains frescoes by *Cesare Mariani* (1884–94). In a chapel on the S side is a beautiful *Polyptych by *Carlo Crivelli* (1473), in excellent conditon, and justly considered his masterpiece. It is set in a rich Gothic frame above a 14C silver altar frontal, and a painted wood ciborium (1573), thought to have been designed by *Giorgio Vasari*. The Gothic choir-stalls are by *Paolino d'Ascoli* and *Francesco di Giovanni*. The crypt (restored) dates from the 12C.—In the Palazzo

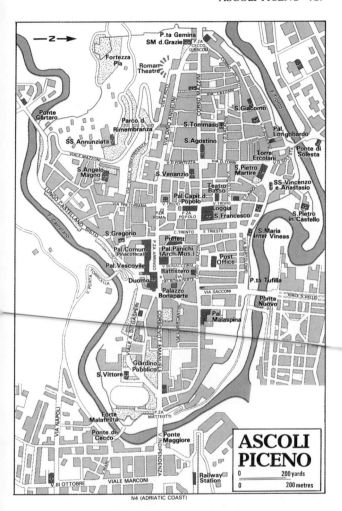

ASCOLI PICENO

| | 200 yards |
| 0 | 200 metres |

N4 (ADRIATIC COAST)

Vescovile is the MUSEO DIOCESANO (for adm. apply at the Curia). It contains sculptures, and paintings by *Pietro Alemanno, Cola dell'Amatrice*, etc.—In Via dei Bonaparte, opposite the side portal of the Duomo, is the *Palazzetto Bonaparte* (1507), beautifully decorated. The church of San Gregorio, behind Palazzo Comunale, incorporates a Roman Corinthian prostyle Temple of Vesta.

The huge **Palazzo Comunale** has a Baroque façade by Giuseppe Giosafatti (1683), and the two fine 13C Sale dell'Arringo, on the ground floor. The PINACOTECA (adm. 10–13, 16.30–18.30; winter 9–13; fest. 10–12) on the first floor contains a well labelled collection of paintings including works by *Bernardo Bellotto, Elisabeth Vigée Le Brun, Cola dell'Amatrice, Antony Van Dyck* (attributed), *Guercino,*

Pietro Alemanno, Carlo Crivelli, Andrea da Bologna, Titian (St Francis receiving the Stigmata), Carlo Maratta (portraits), Francesco Guardi, Annibale Carracci, Sassoferrato, Alessandro Magnasco, Luca Giordano, and Guido Reni. The extensive 19C and 20C collection includes works by Giulio Cantalamessa, Ettore Ximenes, Domenico Morelli, and Filippo Palizzi. Also displayed here is a famous *Cope, a very early example of opus anglicanum, given by Nicholas IV to the Duomo in 1288.

Palazzo Panichi, opposite, has recently been well restored to house the MUSEO ARCHEOLOGICO (adm. 9–17.30; fest. 9–13; closed Monday). On the ground floor are marble Roman portrait heads (including two good examples from the Flavian and Hadrianic periods); a plan of Roman Ascoli; a fine mosaic pavement found in the town; and other sculptural fragments including tomb frontals.—On the first floor is paleolithic material; elaborate bronze fibulae (9–8C BC); the inscribed cippus of Castignano (mid 6C BC); finds from recent excavations; and a small collection of Roman glass. The upper floor is awaiting arrangement.

Via XX Settembre and Via Trieste lead towards the *PIAZZA DEL POPOLO, the centre of the city, and now closed to traffic. It is a delightful secluded square with a bright travertine pavement. At the far end is the superb Gothic perpendicular flank and tower of San Francesco (see below). a long low arcaded building with crenellations (probably designed by Bernardo di Pietro da Carona, 1507–09) faces the 13C Palazzo del Popolo (modified in the 16C), with a portal by Cola dell'Amatrice surmounted by a monument to Paul III (1548). The palace is being restored for use as a cultural centre. Beside it is an Art Nouveau café. The church of *San Francesco, begun in 1258 and completed except for the roof in 1461, has beautiful portals (the W door has been cleaned) and a picturesque apse with seven chapels. The gothic interior has fine vaulting.—Via del Trivio leads past the main façade and the Great Cloister (1563–1623), now used as a friut and vegetable market (the 14C Small Clositer has been incorporated in a modern building). The Teatro Ventidio Basso (designed by Ireneo Aleandri, 1840–46), with a neo-classical façade and a fine interior, is to be reopened after restoration.—Via Cairoli continues N to the large Gothic church of San Pietro Martire (14C) which stands opposite Santi Vicenzo ed Anastasio (11C; enlarged in the 14C), with an unusual façade of 1389 decorated with quadrangles in relief (formerly frescoed), a fine doorway, and an ancient campanile. Behind San Pietro the pretty Via dei Solestà leads to *Ponte dei Solestà, a Roman single-arched bridge dating from the early years of the Empire and still in use. Beyond the old cobbled streets behind the bridge is the characteristic Via Soderini with the Palazzetto Longobardo and the fine tall Torre Ercolani (11–12C). Nearby is the church of San Giacomo, restored in the 15C, and the Roman Porta Gemina, with parts of the original Roman walls.

Corso Mazzini leads back towards the centre from Porta Gemina past the church of Sant'Agostino, rebuilt in 1485. It contains a St Francis Xavier, by Baciccia. Opposite are two imposing towers. Via della Fortezza (right) mounts the Colle dell'Annunziata (view), in which are large caves, probably substructures of the Roman citadel. On the E side of the hill is the church of Sant'Angelo Magno (1292), while to the W are remains of a Roman Theatre. The road continues through the Parco della Rimembranza to the ex-convent of the Annunziata. Steps mount to the Fortezza Pia, constructed by Pius IV in

1564.—In the NE district of the town, among many good 16–17C mansions, the *Palazzo Malaspina* is a bold and original 16C construction, perhaps by Cola. It houses a gallery of modern graphic art and ceramics.

At (39km) *Taverna Piccinini* (209m), N78 branches right for Amandola (35km; Rte 62) and Macerata (85km: Rte 61B).—52km *Acquasanta Terme* (392m), the Roman *Vicus ad Aquas*, has thermal sulphur springs, which cured Munatius Plancus of rheumatism. The ascent becomes steeper as the river is hemmed in by stratified rocks.—65km *Arquata del Tronto* (719m) has a castle built by Joan II of Naples. The road continues to climb the Tronto valley between the Monti Sibillini on the right and the Monti della Laga on the left (Pizzo di Sevo, 2419m). There is a long-term project to make this area into a National Park.—At (71km) *Bivio di Tufo* a difficult mountain road (a new road, with a long tunnel, is under construction) leads W over the *Forca Canapine* (1541m) to Norcia (35km; Rte 59A). The main road passes from the Marches into Lazio.—At (84km) *Ponte della Scandarella* the road divides. The left branch follows the Tronto to Amatrice (4km), then descends to L'Aquila (see 'Blue Guide Southern Italy'). This road climbs steeply above the artificial *Lago dello Scandarello* through *Torrita* to (93km) a summit level of 1043m (good retrospective views). Here is the source of the Velino which the road descends.—109km *Posta* (721m).

Mountain roads go off right to *Leonessa* (19km), a remote little place with a notable town-gate and two good Gothic churches; the left-hand road leads to *Montereale* (20km), on the road from L'Aquila to Amatrice (see above).

Via Salaria threads the *Gole del Velino*, narrow winding ravines between the Terminillo (2216m; see below), on the right, and Monte Giano (1820m) on the left.—123km **Antrodoco** (525m), the ancient *Interocrea*, at the junction of three gorges, is overlooked by a castle of the Vitelli, in a spur of Monte Terminillo. The church of the *Assunta* contains a fine processional cross, perhaps by Nicolò da Guardiagrele. Near the exit towards Rieti is the little Romanesque church of *Santa Maria*. Antrodoco is the starting-point of N17, here known as the *Via Sabina*, which runs across the Apennines through L'Aquila to Foggia (see 'Blue Guide Southern Italy').

The road runs SW with the Sulmona-Terni railway.—131km *Terme di Cotilia* uses the sulphur springs of *Cutilia*, where Vespasian died in AD 79. Across the railway rise a series of springs which unite to form the *Peschiera*, the second most copious source in Italy (15,456 litres per second).—137km **Cittaducale** (481m) is a medieval fortress on a regular plan, founded in 1309 and named after Robert the Wise, Duke of Calabria, afterwards King of Naples.

147km **RIETI** (405m), a provincial capital with 39,100 inhabitants, was the ancient *Reate*, chief town of the Sabines. It was the birthplace of the historian Terentius Varro (116–27 BC) and the cradle of the imperial Gens Flavia. It has many associations with St Francis of Assisi. The 13C walls and the medieval palaces impart an old-world look to the town.

Tourist Office, 87 *Via Cintia* (information office, Piazza Vittorio Emanuele II).—**Post Office**, Via Garibaldi.—**Bus Station**, Piazza Cavour. Services to *Rome* and to *Ascoli Piceno*; also to *Terminillo*; to *Avezzano*; to *L'Aquila* and *Pescara*; and to *Terni*.

The *North Wall* of the city stands almost complete except for the breach made by the Piazza Mazzini opposite the railway station. In the square stands *Sant'Agostino*, a 13C church. To the SW beyond

two more squares, lies Piazza Vittorio Emanuele, site of the ancient
forum, where the **Palazzo Comunale** hosues a small MUSEO CIVICO
(10–13). This displays an archaeological collection; classical and
medieval sculpture; and paintings including: *Antoniazzo Romano*,
Madonna with Saints Francis and Anthony of Padua (1464); *Luca di
Tommè*, Polyptych (1370), signed and dated; *Zanino di Pietro*,
Triptych (early 15C Venetian school); *Pirro Ligorio* (?), Banner with
the Ascension and the Assumption (1546). In the neighbouring
Piazza Battisti (view) is the **Cathedral**, a Romanesque edifice, largely
rebuilt but retaining a crypt of 1109–57. The 4th N chapel contains a
St Barbara designed by Bernini (1657). Here on Whit Sunday 1289
Pope Nicholas IV crowned Charles II of Naples with the empty title
of King of Sicily, thus beginning the confusion of the two Sicilies.
The Baptistery contains the Museo del Tesoro del Duomo. The
Palazzo Vescovile, restored in 1928–31, preserves its fine loggia of
1283–88. Inside, a plaque records the marriage in Rieti (1185)
between the Emperor Henry VI and Constance of Altavilla; in 1234
their son, Frederick II, was received here by Pope Gregory IX, then
in need of aid against the rebellious citizens of Rome.

From the centre Via Roma, passing the church of *San Pietro* (13C doorway),
and crossing the Velino river, leads to (5 minutes) the *Fonte Cottorella*, a little
mineral spring.—From the Porta Romana a road (6km) ascends SW to the
Convento di Fonte Colombo, in an ilex grove, where St Francis dictated the
rules of his Order in 1223. The *Convento La Foresta*, W of the town, marks the
site of another sojourn of the saint (1225).—To the N extends the beautiful
PLAIN OF RIETI, surrounded by mountains and watered by the Velino; its
scenery has been compared with that of the Vale of Tempe in Thessaly. It was
drained by Curius Dentatus (see Rte 59A). On the W side of the plain, 15km
NW of Rieti, is the *Santuario di Greccio* (638m), where St Francis celebrated
Christmas in 1223. The present convent, halfway up the hill above the station
(on the Terni line), though altered, still preserves an air of Franciscan
simplicity. The cave where St Francis slept is shown. The view of the plain is
superb. A by road leads S to *Greccio*.

FROM RIETI TO TERMINILLO, 21km; bus, see above. This mountain road diverges
to the left from N4 a little E of Rieti.—6km *Vazia* (579m).—Beyond (8km)
Lisciano (604m) the road winds up in sharp curves.—21km **Terminillo** (1575–
1675m) is a summer and winter sports resort, with numerous hotels, open in the
season only. From Terminillo the ascent may be made of **Monte Terminillo**
(2216m; guide available). The summit is reached (c 4hrs) via the *Rifugio del
Terminilletto* (2205m). A funicular railway is in operation all the year round.—
The descent may be made to Cittaducale (see below).—From Rieti to Terni, see
Rte 59A.

Beyond Rieti Via Salaria turns due S, ascending into the Sabine
Hills. A new road (N4 dir) continues more directly to join the
Autostrada del Sole at the Roma Nord Station. At 156km the old road
(high in the hills to the E) provides the best access to *Roccasinibalda*
(17km), where the stately Sforza castle was designed by Baldassarre
Peruzzi (1536), and covered with Michelangelesque frescoes. Also
off the old road, beyond *Torricella in Sabina*, is *Monteleone Sabino*,
anciently *Trebula Mutusca*, birthplace of Mummius, the Roman
general, who sacked Corinth in 146 BC. Its little Romanesque church
of Santa Vittoria (12C; 2km SE) has relics of a much earlier
building.—172km By-road (right) for Fara in Sabina (12km).

Fara in Sabina, a large village with a 16C church, commands a wide view. The
abbey of *Farfa*, 3·5km NW, was founded c 420 by St Lawrence 'the illuminator'
(he restored the sight of many blind persons). The church, rebuilt on new lines
by St Thomas of Maurienne in 672, was destroyed after 841 by Barbary pirates,
who made the abbey their trading centre. In 1567 (the date of the present

church) the Benedictines reoccupied it; and they now manage a school here. Mosaic pavements of both the 7C and the 5C have been preserved in the church.

To the left the Barberini castle of *Nerola* is seen on its hill long before the picturesque old road reaches (184km) its approach road.—At (193km) *Passo Corese*, the old road joins the old Florence-Rome railway on the left bank of the Tiber, while the new road joins the A1 motorway.—204km *Monterotondo Scalo*, and from there to (228km) **Rome**, see 'Blue Guide Rome'.

INDEX OF THE PRINCIPAL ITALIAN ARTISTS

whose works are referred to in the text, with their birthplaces or the schools to which they belonged.—Abbreviations: A. = architect, engr. = engraver, G. = goldsmith, illum. = illuminator, min. = miniaturist, mos. = mosaicist, P. = painter, S. = sculptor, stuc. = stuccoist, W. = woodworker.

ABBREVIATIONS OF CHRISTIAN NAMES

INDEX

Topographical names are printed in **bold** type, names of eminent persons in *italics*, other entries (including the sub-indexes of large towns) in roman type. The building activities of popes and emperors have generally been ignored.

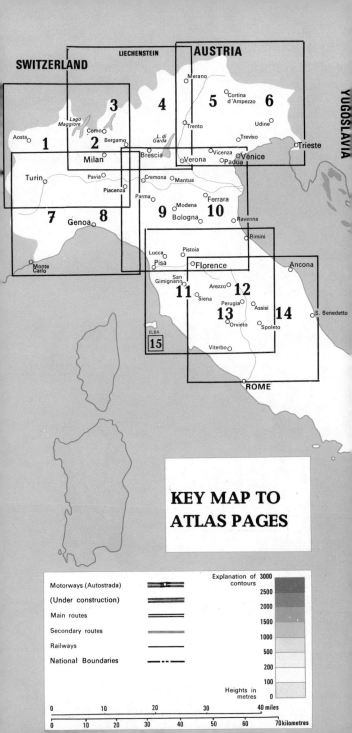

KEY MAP TO ATLAS PAGES

SWITZERLAND

LIECHENSTEIN

AUSTRIA

YUGOSLAVIA

Aosta **1**

Lago Maggiore

Como **3**

Bergamo

Milan **2**

Brescia

4

L. di Garda

Merano

Trento

5

Cortina d'Ampezzo

Udine

6

Treviso

Vicenza

Verona

Padua

Venice

Trieste

Turin

Pavia

Piacenza

7

Genoa **8**

Monte Carlo

Cremona

Mantua

Parma

9

Modena

Bologna

Ferrara

10

Ravenna

Rimini

Lucca

Pisa

Pistoia

Florence

San Gimignano

11

Siena

Arezzo

12

Perugia

13

Orvieto

Assisi

Spoleto

14

Ancona

S. Benedetto

ELBA **15**

Viterbo

ROME

Motorways (Autostrada)	
(Under construction)	
Main routes	
Secondary routes	
Railways	
National Boundaries	

Explanation of contours

3000
2500
2000
1500
1000
500
200
100
0

Heights in metres

| 0 | 10 | 20 | 30 | 40 miles |
| 0 | 10 | 20 | 30 | 40 | 50 | 60 | 70 kilometres |

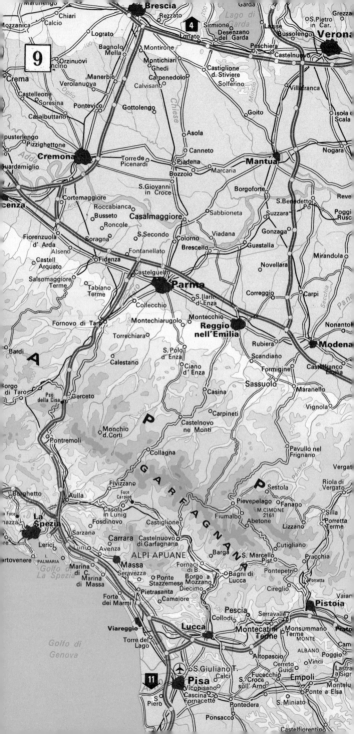

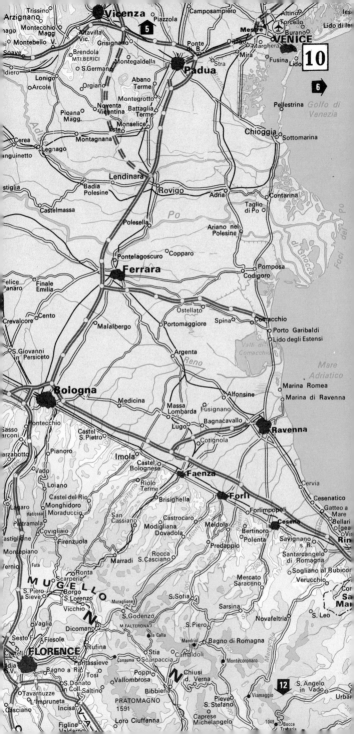

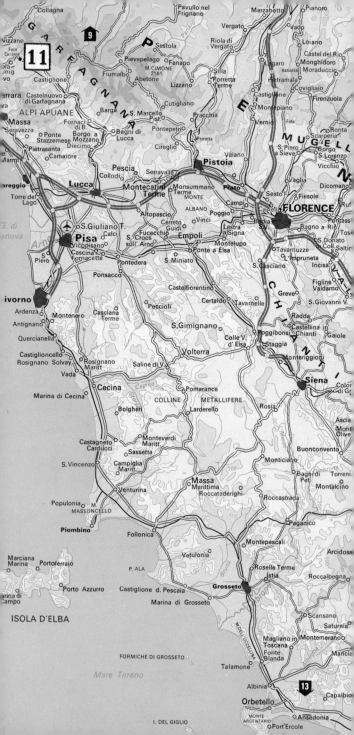

15

ELBA

0 1 2 3 miles
0 1 2 3 4 5 kms

C. DELLA VITA

I. PALMAIOLA

Cavo

Rio Marina

P. DELLE CANNELLE

Porto-Azzurro

Capoliveri

Ottone

le Grotte

Portoferraio

Carpani

Golfo
Stella

S. Martino

G. di
Lacona

Viticcio

C. D'ENFOLA

Biodola

G. d. Biodola

Procchio

G. di Procchio

Pila

Marina di
Campo

G. di Campo

C. PORO

Marciana Marina

Poggio

S. Piero

Cavoli

C. S. ANDREA

Zanca

Marciana

M. CAPANNE
1018

Fetovaia

Mortigliano

P. NERA

Chiessi

Pomonte